lonely planet

Indonesia

Peter Turner
Brendan Delahunty
Paul Greenway
James Lyon
Chris Taylor
David Willett

Indonesia

5th edition

Published by
Lonely Planet Publications
Head Office: PO Box 617, Hawthorn, Vic 3122, Australia
Branches: 155 Filbert St, Suite 251, Oakland, CA 94607, USA
             10 Barley Mow Passage, Chiswick, London W4 4PH, UK
             71 bis rue du Cardinal Lemoine, 75005 Paris, France

Printed by
SNP Printing Pte Ltd, Singapore

Photographs by

Gregory Adams	Glenn Beanland	Simon Bracken	Sara-Jane Cleland
Dushan Cooray	Brendan Delahunty	Greg Elms	Paul Greenway
Richard I'Anson	James Lyon	Peter Morris	Jane Rawson
Simon Rowe	Martin Tullemans	Peter Turner	Phil Weymouth
Tony Wheeler	Tamsin Wilson		

Front cover: Javanese wayang kulit puppet, David Moore, © Wildlight Photo Agency.

First Published
1986

This Edition
August 1997

Although the authors and publisher have tried to make the information as accurate as possible, they accept no responsibility for any loss, injury or inconvenience sustained by any person using this book.

National Library of Australia Cataloguing in Publication Data

    Indonesia

    5th ed.
    Includes index.
    ISBN 0 86442 454 X.

    1. Indonesia – Guidebooks. I. Turner, Peter. (Series :
    Lonely Planet travel survival kit).

    915.980439

text & maps © Lonely Planet 1997
photos © photographers as indicated 1997
climate charts of Pulau Ambon & Danau Toba compiled from information supplied by Patrick J Tyson © Patrick J Tyson, 1997

Peter Turner

Peter was born in Melbourne and studied Asian studies, politics and English before setting off on the Asian trail. His long-held interest in South-East Asia has seen him make numerous trips to the region. He has worked on Lonely Planet's *Singapore city guide*, *Jakarta city guide*, *Java*, *New Zealand*, *Malaysia, Singapore & Brunei* and *South-East Asia*.

Brendan Delahunty

Despite years in journalism, peppered with varied stints as an editor, outreach educator, farmer and teacher of Indonesian to pre-school toddlers, the prospect of unemployment brought Brendan into the Lonely Planet fold in 1994. With Lonely Planet's support, he established an alliance between far-sighted HIV/AIDS educators in Ujung Pandang, Sulawesi, and Australia, and goes 'home' to Sulawesi as often as possible. Brendan, now working as a legal researcher in Sydney, revised the Sulawesi chapter of this edition.

Paul Greenway

Paul updated the Maluku and Irian Jaya chapters. During his research, he managed to avoid serious rioting in Jayapura and Timika by a few days, but was not so lucky during an earthquake in Biak. Based in Adelaide, South Australia, Paul contributed to the previous edition of *Indonesia*, co-wrote *Indian Himalaya*, and updated *Mongolia* and *Madagascar*. During the rare times he is not travelling, or writing, reading or dreaming about it, Paul relaxes to tuneless heavy rock, follows useless Australian Rules football teams and will go to any lengths to avoid settling down.

James Lyon

James is a sceptic by nature and a social scientist by training. He worked for five years as an editor at Lonely Planet's Melbourne office, then jumped the fence to become a researcher and writer. He has travelled on Bali both by himself and also with his wife, Pauline, and their two young children. A keen gardener, he finds the flowers and landscapes of Bali a special delight.

Chris Taylor

Chris grew up in England and Australia. After completing a degree in English literature and Chinese, he joined the Lonely Planet team to head the phrasebook series. These days, he's based in Taiwan and works as a freelance travel writer. His work has appeared in newspapers and magazines worldwide. He is author of Lonely Planet guides to *Tibet*, *Cambodia* and *Tokyo*, and co-author of *China*, *Japan* and *Malaysia, Singapore & Brunei*.

David Willett

David updated the Sumatra chapter. He is a freelance journalist based on the mid-north coast of New South Wales, Australia. He grew up in Hampshire, England, and wound up in Australia in 1980 after stints working on newspapers in Iran and Bahrain. He spent two years working as a a sub-editor on the Melbourne *Sun* before opting to live somewhere warmer. Between jobs, he has travelled extensively in Europe, the Middle East and Asia. He lives with his partner, Rowan, and their seven year old son, Tom. David updated the Tunisia sections in Lonely Planet's guides to *North Africa* and *Mediterranean Europe*.

From the Authors

From Brendan Delahunty Jeff le Chef, take a bow for your ever-patient nurture and support. Wild applause for the hospitality of Gaya Celebes, especially Akbar, Ardhi and Babe, whose efforts kept me on the road. Three cheers for Catherine, Gerri, Vendela and the rest of the crew in Toraja; Sam Aldridge in Palopo; and Sidharta in Manado. Thanks too for the wise counsel of Karel and Rudi in Tentena; Pak Burhanuddin of Kendari and Gorontalo's Pak Alex Velberg; and to the kind folk who fed and entertained me when Lebaran celebrations left me hopelessly stranded. Lastly, a fond farewell to Alan 'Bruce' Lewis, whose life revealed much that is good about Indonesia, and whose sudden death highlighted some of the perils.

From Paul Greenway Paul would like to thank the following people, whose assistance and/or friendship enhanced his travel and research: Martin Kuhn in Seram (bad luck about Manusela) and Ambon islands; Jack Matuahitimahu and the great staff at the tourist office in Masohi, Seram; Eric Erler, who had some strange attraction to Pulau Halmahera, and to all his 'friends' at that hotel in Tobelo; Anne-Marie van Dam, who I met during my last trip and was so pleased to see her name acknowledged in the last edition that she wrote to me about her trip to Irian Jaya, so I will mention her name again; and to Ian and Penny Gibbs, who I stumbled across while drinking in a dingy bar in Darwin.

At Lonely Planet, thanks to my senior editor, Greg Alford, for sending me back to that wonderful part of Indonesia; and to Kristin Odijk. Lastly, thanks to all the unknown Indonesians who helped me along the way with some information, or at least with a smile.

From James Lyon Thanks to Hanafi in Kuta; Sarah in Singarajah; Richard and Tini at Lovina; Raka in Ubud; Hadji Radiah on Lombok; Yarnt, Earnst and Simon on the Gili Islands; and to the staff of the tourist offices in Kuta, Ubud, Singarajah and Mataram. At home, thanks to Peter Young at Ansett Australia, the designers and editors at Lonely Planet, and as always to Pauline.

From Chris Taylor Many thanks to Johan of Borneo Homestay in Banjarmasin, without whom much would have been impossible.

From David Willett My thanks go to Peter Pangaribuan and his staff at the Indonesian Tourist office in Sydney for their enthusiastic assistance, and also to the staff at regional offices throughout Sumatra who went out of their way to help. They include Sukri, Ynati and Yaman Aziz in Lampung; Ferry, Dudung and Lynette in Pandang; Amir, Suki and Agus in Palembang; Atin in Pekanbaru; Pak Sembiring and Pak Sibagarian in Medan; and Suleiman in Bandar Aceh. Special thanks go to my family, Rowan and Tom, for putting up with my frequent absences – and for allowing me to monopolise the computer when at home.

This Edition

Peter Turner, the coordinating author for this edition, updated the introductory chapters and the Java and Nusa Tenggara chapters. James Lyon updated the Bali chapter and the Lombok section of Nusa Tenggara, Brendan Delahunty did the Sulawesi chapter, Paul Greenway did the Maluku and Irian Jaya chapters, Chris Taylor updated the Kalimantan chapter and David Willett the Sumatra chapter.

This Book

The monumental task of compiling the 1st edition was the collective work of Alan Samalgaski, who roamed the far reaches of the archipelago, Ginny Bruce, who covered Java, and Mary Covernton, who did Sumatra and Bali. For the 2nd edition, Alan went to Sumatra and Sulawesi, Tony Wheeler explored Bali and Lombok as well as covering Sumatra, John Noble and Susan Forsyth island-hopped through Nusa Tenggara and Maluku, and Joe Cummings went to Java and Kalimantan. For the 3rd edition, Robert Storey oversaw the project and researched Nusa Tenggara, Maluku and Sulawesi. Dan Spitzer updated Java and Kalimantan, Richard Nebesky went to Sumatra, and Bali was covered by Tony Wheeler along with James Lyon, who also explored Lombok. For the 4th edition, Peter Turner was the coordinating author and researched Java. James Lyon covered Bali and Lombok, Brendan Delahunty explored Kalimantan and Sulawesi, Paul Greenway went to Maluku and Irian Jaya, Chris MacAsey looked after Nusa Tenggara and David Willett updated Sumatra.

From the Publisher

This 5th edition of *Indonesia* was edited and proofed at Lonely Planet's Melbourne office by Kristin Odijk and Michelle Coxall. Kristin, Michelle, Peter Cruttenden and Anne Mulvaney assisted with the proofreading and Sharon Benson with the indexing. Sally Gerdan, Glenn Beanland and Janet Watson coordinated the mapping and were assisted by Verity Campbell, Anna Judd, Margaret Jung and Paul Piaia. The cover was designed by Simon Bracken. The illustrations were drawn by Sally, Joanne Ridgeway and Tass Wilson. Design and layout was done by Glenn and Verity. Glenn was responsible for the design and layout of the Arts & Crafts colour section and the Surfing in Indonesia section.

Many thanks to Andrew Tudor who wrote the Surfing in Indonesia section.

Warning & Request

Things change – prices go up, schedules change, good places go bad and bad places go bankrupt – nothing stays the same. So, if you find things better or worse, recently opened or long since closed, please tell us and help make the next edition even more accurate and useful.

We value all of the feedback we receive from travellers. Julie Young coordinates a small team who read and acknowledge every letter, postcard and email, and ensure that every morsel of information finds its way to the appropriate authors, editors and publishers.

Everyone who writes to us will find their name in the next edition of the appropriate guide and will also receive a free subscription to our quarterly newsletter, *Planet Talk*. The very best contributions will be rewarded with a free Lonely Planet guide.

Excerpts from your correspondence may appear in updates (which we add to the end pages of reprints); new editions of this guide; in our newsletter, *Planet Talk*; or in the Postcards section of our Web site – so please let us know if you don't want your letter published or your name acknowledged.

Thanks

Many thanks to the travellers who used the last edition and wrote to us with helpful hints, useful advice and interesting anecdotes. Your names appear on page 1038.

Contents

Map Legend

BOUNDARIES

————·—·—·—·—·—·—·— ....International Boundary
——————·——·——·—— ....Regional Boundary
———————————————— ....Equator
————————————————— ....Marine Park

ROUTES

———————————————— ....Freeway
———————————————— ....Highway
———————————————— ....Major Road
— — — — — — — — .... Unsealed Road or Track
———————————————— ....City Road
———————————————— ....City Street
+—+—+—+—+—+—+—+— ....Railway
— — — — — — — — ....Walking Track
•••••••••••••••••••• ....Walking Tour
— — — — — — — — ....Ferry Route
—+—+—+—+—+—+—+— ....Cable Car or Chairlift

AREA FEATURES

....Parks
....................................Built-Up Area
..............................Pedestrian Mall
...................................Market
+ + + + + + ...Christian Cemetery
× × × × × ×   ....Non-Christian Cemetery
....................................Reef
....................................Beach
....................................Forest

HYDROGRAPHIC FEATURES

............................Coastline
...........................River, Creek
.... Intermittent River or Creek
.... Rapids, Waterfalls
.... Lake, Intermittent Lake
...............................Swamp

SYMBOLS

✪ CAPITAL		......................National Capital
◉ Capital		..................Regional Capital
⬤ CITY		.... Major City
● City		..........................City
● Town		......................................Town
• Village		......................................Village
▪	▼	.........Place to Stay, Place to Eat
⚲	♊	.... Cafe, Pub or Bar
✉	☎	..............Post Office, Telephone
❶	❽	..........Tourist Information, Bank
◓	🅿	.....................Transport, Parking
🏛	⌂	..............Museum, Youth Hostel
⚐	⚑	... Golf Course, Camping Ground
⛪	✚	......................Church, Cathedral
☾	卍	......................Mosque, Temple
卍	卐	Buddhist Temple, Hindu Temple
✿	⛩	.... Meru Temple, Stupa

◔	▣	............Embassy, Petrol Station
✈	✟	.........................Airport, Airfield
▭	✾	...........Swimming Pool, Gardens
❖	🐘	...............Shopping Centre, Zoo
✛	★	.... Hospital, Police Station
←	A25	One Way Street, Route Number
🏛	⚱	..........Stately Home, Monument
☗	▣	..............................Fort, Tomb
⌒	⌂	.... Cave, Hut or Chalet
▲	✳	.... Mountain or Hill, Lookout
🗼	⚓	.... Lighthouse, Shipwreck
)(	◎	.........................Pass, Spring
⚐	⚐	....................Beach, Surf Beach
	∴	...... Archaeological Site or Ruins
		.........................Fort or City Wall
⟿ ⟹	⟸	....Cliff or Escarpment, Tunnel
+—+—+—+—+—		.........Railway Station

Note: not all symbols displayed above appear in this book

Introduction

Like a string of jewels in a coral sea, the 13,000 plus islands of the Indonesian archipelago stretch almost 5000 km from the Asian mainland into the Pacific Ocean. And like jewels the islands have long represented wealth. A thousand years ago the Chinese sailed as far as Timor to load up cargoes of sandalwood and beeswax; by the 16th century the spice islands of the Moluccas (Maluku) were luring European navigators in search of cloves, nutmeg and mace, once so rare and expensive that bloody wars were fought for control of their production and trade. The Dutch ruled for almost 350 years, drawing their fortunes from the islands whose rich volcanic soil could produce two crops of rice a year, as well as commercially valuable crops like coffee, sugar, tobacco and teak.

Endowed with a phenomenal array of natural resources and strange cultures, Indonesia became a magnet for every shade of entrepreneur from the west – a stamping ground for proselytising missionaries, unscru-

pulous traders, wayward adventurers, inspired artists. It has been overrun by Dutch and Japanese armies; surveyed, drilled, dug up and shipped off by foreign mining companies; littered with the 'transmigrants' of Java and Bali; and poked and prodded by ethnologists, linguists and anthropologists turning fading cultures into PhD theses.

Now there is a new breed of visitor – the modern-day tourist. After the 1991 'Visit Indonesia Year', the government decided to promote the 'Visit Indonesia Decade' to encourage even larger numbers of visitors by the year 2000. Places like Bali, Lombok, Torajaland on Sulawesi, and the Hindu-Buddhist monuments of Borobudur and Prambanan in Central Java attract huge numbers of visitors. On the other hand, much of the country remains barely touched by mass tourism, despite great improvements in communications and transport connections. Indonesia has thousands of islands with a myriad of different cultures, offering adventure that is hard to find in the modern world.

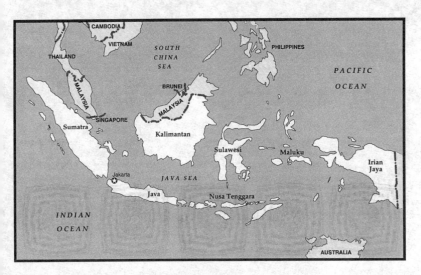

Indonesia possesses some of the most remarkable sights in South-East Asia and there are things about this country you will never forget: the flaming red and orange sunsets over the mouth of the Sungai (river) Kapuas in Kalimantan; standing on the summit of Keli Mutu in Flores and gazing at the coloured lakes that fill its volcanic craters; the lumbering leather-skinned dragons of Komodo Island; the funeral ceremonies of the Torajas in the highlands of Central Sulawesi; the Dani tribesmen of Irian Jaya wearing little else but feathers and penis gourds; the wooden *wayang golek* puppets manipulated into life by the puppet-masters of Yogyakarta; and the brilliant coral reefs off Manado on the north coast of Sulawesi.

You can lie on your back on Kuta Beach on Bali and soak up the ultraviolet rays, paddle a canoe down the rivers of Kalimantan, surf at Nias off the coast of Sumatra, trek in the high country of Irian Jaya, catch giant butterflies in Sulawesi, eat your way through a kaleidoscope of fruit from one end of the archipelago to the other, stare down the craters of live volcanoes, learn the art of batik in Yogyakarta or kite-making from any Indonesian kid – almost anything you want, Indonesia has got!

Facts about the Country

HISTORY

Prehistory

The Indonesian archipelago was first inhabited by *Pithecanthropus erectus*, or Java Man, one of the earliest human ancestors that migrated via land bridges to Java at least one million years ago. Java Man became extinct or mingled with later migrations, for the people of Indonesia today are of Malay origin, closely related to the peoples of Malaysia and the Philippines, and are descendants of much later migrations from South-East Asia that began around 4000 BC.

The Dongson culture, which originated in Vietnam and southern China about 3000 years ago, spread to Indonesia, bringing with it techniques of irrigated rice growing, ritual buffalo sacrifice, bronze casting, the custom of erecting large monumental stones (megaliths) and some of the peculiar *ikat* weaving methods found in pockets of Indonesia today. Some of these practices have survived only in isolated areas which were little touched by later arrivals and cultural currents – such as the Batak areas of Sumatra, Tanatoraja in Sulawesi, parts of Kalimantan and several islands of Nusa Tenggara.

From the 7th century BC there were well-developed and organised societies in the Indonesian archipelago. The inhabitants knew how to irrigate rice fields, domesticate animals, use copper and bronze, and had some knowledge of sea navigation. There were villages – often permanent ones – where life was linked to the production of rice, the staple crop.

These early Indonesians were animists, believing that all animate and inanimate objects have their own particular life force, *semangat*, or soul. The spirits of the dead had to be honoured because their semangat could still help the living; there was a belief in the afterlife, and weapons and utensils would be left in tombs for use in the next world. Supernatural forces were held responsible for natural events, and evil spirits had to be placated by offerings, rites and ceremonies.

Villages, at least on Java, developed into embryonic towns and, by the 1st century AD, small kingdoms (little more than collections of villages subservient to petty chieftains) evolved with their own ethnic and tribal religions. The climate of Java, with its hot, even temperature, plentiful rainfall and volcanic soil, was ideal for the wet-field method of rice cultivation, known as *sawah* cultivation. The well-organised society it required may explain why the people of Java developed a more sophisticated civilisation than those of the other islands. The dry-field, or *ladang*, method of rice cultivation is a much simpler form of agriculture and requires no elaborate social structure.

The social and religious duties of the rice-growing communities were gradually refined to form the basis of *adat*, or customary law. This traditional law was to persist through waves of imported religious beliefs – Hinduism, Buddhism, Islam and Christianity – and still remains a force in Indonesia today.

Coming of Hinduism & Buddhism

The oldest works of Hindu art in Indonesia, statues from the 3rd century AD, come from Sulawesi and Sumatra. The earliest Hindu inscriptions, in Sanskrit, have been found in West Java and eastern Kalimantan, and date from the early 5th century AD.

How Hinduism and Buddhism came to Indonesia remains a topic of speculation. One likely theory holds that the developing courts invited Brahman priests from India to advise on spirituality and ritual, thereby providing occult powers and a mythological sanction for the new Indonesian rulers. In the Hindu period the kings were seen as incarnations of Vishnu. Another factor was undoubtedly trade. Traders from South India, the conduit for Hinduism, established early contact and Indonesia's main link to the outside world. Indonesia's strategic position on the sea lanes between India and China meant that trade between the two main Asian civilisations was firmly established in Indonesia by the 1st century AD. Though Indonesia had its own products to trade, such as spices, gold and benzoin (an aromatic gum valued especially by the Chinese), it owed its growing importance to its position at the crossroads of trade.

Early Kingdoms

The Sumatran Hindu-Buddhist kingdom of Sriwijaya rose in the 7th century AD and maintained a substantial international trade – run by Tamils and Chinese. It was the first major Indonesian commercial seapower, able to control much of the trade in South-East Asia by virtue of its control of the Straits of Melaka between Sumatra and the Malay peninsula.

Merchants from Arabia, Persia and India brought goods to the coastal cities in exchange for goods from China and for local products, such as spices from the spice islands of Maluku (the Moluccas) in the eastern archipelago.

Meanwhile, the Buddhist Sailendra and the Hindu Mataram dynasties flourished on the plains of Central Java between the 8th and 10th centuries. While Sriwijaya's trade brought it wealth, these land-based states had far greater human labour at their disposal and left magnificent remains, particularly the vast Buddhist monument of Borobudur and the huge Hindu temple complex of Prambanan.

Thus two types of states evolved in Indonesia. The first, typified by Sriwijaya, were the mainly Sumatran coastal states – commercially oriented, their wealth derived from international trade and their cities highly cosmopolitan. In contrast, the inland kingdoms of Java, separated from the sea by volcanoes (like the kingdom of Mataram in the Solo River region), were agrarian cultures, bureaucratic and conservative, with a marked capacity to absorb and transform the Indian influences.

By the end of the 10th century the monuments of Borobudur and Prambanan were abandoned and Mataram mysteriously declined. The centre of power shifted from Central to East Java, where a series of kingdoms held sway until the rise of the Majapahit kingdom. This is the period when Hinduism and Buddhism were syncretised, and when Javanese culture began to come into its own, finally spreading its influence to Bali. By the 12th century Sriwijaya's power had declined and the empire broke up into smaller kingdoms.

Hindu Majapahit Kingdom

One of the greatest Indonesian states and the last great Hindu kingdom was Majapahit. Founded in East Java in 1294, Majapahit grew to prominence during the reign of Hayam Wuruk, though its territorial expansion can be credited to its brilliant military commander, Gajah Mada. Gajah Mada put down an anti-royalist revolt in the 1320s, and then brought parts of Java and other areas under control. Majapahit went on to claim control over much of the archipelago,

Gajah Mada, Majapahit's strongman prime minister, was a brilliant military commander who rose to prominence during Jayanegara's reign. Gajah Mada assumed virtual leadership from 1336, when Hayam Wuruk became king but was too young to rule. After Gajah Mada's death in 1364, the Majapahit kingdom declined.

GREGORY ADAMS

BRENDAN DELAHUNTY

GLENN BEANLAND

GREGORY ADAMS

BRENDAN DELAHUNTY

Top Left: Roadside seller in Tampaksiring, Bali.
Top Right: Diamond miner, Cempaka, Kalimantan.
Bottom Left: Harvest worker after threshing rice, Tampaksiring, East Bali.
Middle Right: Kampung children near Jalan Jaksa, Jakarta, Java.
Bottom Right: Mancong dancers, East Kalimantan.

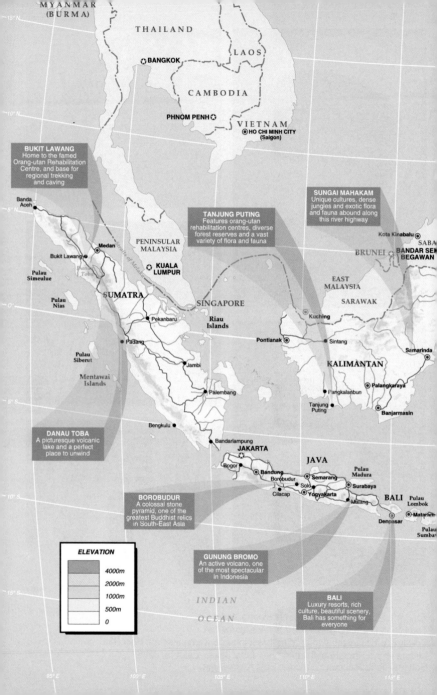

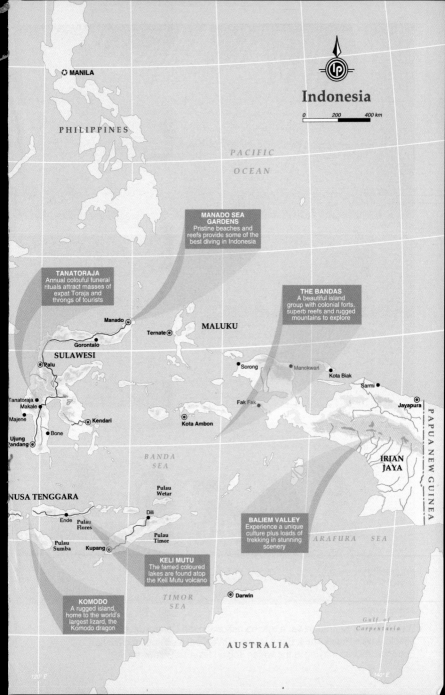

Top: A view of Karimunjawa, a marine national park, Central Java.
Middle: Idyllic Pulau Antuk Barat is one of West Java's Thousand Islands.
Bottom: Children playing in the water, Togian Islands, Sulawesi.

extracting trading rights and suzerainty from smaller kingdoms.

Hayam Wuruk's reign is usually referred to as an Indonesian golden age, comparable with the Tang dynasty of China. One account, by the court poet Prapanca, credits the Majapahits with control over much of the coastal regions of Sumatra, Borneo, Sulawesi, Maluku, Sumbawa and Lombok, and also states that the island of Timor sent tribute. The kingdom is said to have maintained regular relations with China, Vietnam, Cambodia, Annam and Siam. However, after Hayam Wuruk's death in 1389 (25 years after the death of Gajah Mada), the kingdom rapidly declined, and the coastal dependencies in northern Java were in revolt.

Penetration of Islam
Islam first took hold in north Sumatra, where traders from Gujarat (a western state in India) stopped en route to Maluku and China. Settlements of Arab traders were established in the latter part of the 7th century, and in 1292 Marco Polo noted that the inhabitants of the town of Perlak (present-day Aceh) on Sumatra's northern tip had been converted to Islam.

The first Muslim inscriptions on Java date back to the 11th century, and there may even have been Muslims in the Majapahit court at the zenith of its power in the mid-14th century. But it was not until the 15th and 16th centuries that Indonesian rulers turned to Islam and it became a state religion. It was then superimposed on the mixture of Hinduism and indigenous animist beliefs to produce the peculiar hybrid religion which predominates in much of Indonesia, especially Java, today.

By the time of Majapahit's final collapse at the beginning of the 16th century, many of its old satellite kingdoms had declared themselves independent Muslim states. Much of their wealth was based on their position as transhipment points for the growing spice trade with India and China. Islam spread across the archipelago from west to east and followed the trade routes. It was, at least initially, a peaceful transformation, but once

established it was carried further by the sword.

While pockets of the Indonesian population are fundamentalist Muslims, such as the Acehnese in northern Sumatra, the success of Islam was due to its ability to adapt to local customs. The form of Islam followed in much of Indonesia today is not the austere form of the Middle East, but has more in common with Sufism, the mystical variant of Islam.

Rise of Melaka & Makassar
By the 15th century the centre of power in the archipelago had moved to the Malay peninsula, where the trading kingdom of Melaka (also spelt Malacca) was reaching the height of its power. The rise of Melaka, and of trading cities along the north coast of Java, coincided with the spread of Islam through the archipelago – the Melaka kingdom accepted Islam in the 15th century. The Melaka kingdom controlled the trading lanes of the Melaka Straits, and gathered the ports of northern Java within its commercial orbit. By the 16th century it was the principal port of the region.

By the end of the 16th century a sea power had risen in the Indonesian archipelago – the twin principalities of Makassar and Gowa in south-western Sulawesi. These regions had been settled by Malay traders who also sailed to Maluku and beyond. In 1607 when Torres sailed through the strait which now bears his name, he met Makassar Muslims in western New Guinea. Other Makassar fleets visited the northern Australian coast for several hundred years, introducing the Aborigines to metal tools, pottery and tobacco.

Arrival of the Portuguese
When the first Europeans arrived in the Indonesian archipelago they found a varying collection of principalities and kingdoms. These kingdoms were occasionally at war with each other, but were also linked by the substantial inter-island and international trade, over which successive powerful kingdoms – Sriwijaya, Majapahit and Melaka –

had been able to exert control by virtue of their position or sea power.

Marco Polo and a few early missionary-travellers aside, the first Europeans to visit Indonesia were the Portuguese. Vasco de Gama had led the first European ships around the Cape of Good Hope to Asia in 1498; by 1510 the Portuguese had captured Goa on the west coast of India and then pushed on to South-East Asia. They came seeking the domination of the valuable spice trade in Maluku – the Moluccas. Under Alfonso d'Albuquerque they captured Melaka in 1511, and the following year arrived in Maluku.

Portuguese control of trade in Indonesia was based on their fortified bases, such as Melaka, and on their superior firepower at sea. This allowed them to exercise a precarious control of the strategic trading ports that stretched from Maluku to Melaka, Macau, Goa, Mozambique and Angola.

Soon other European nations sent ships to the region in search of wealth – notably the Spanish, then the Dutch and English. By the time these new forces appeared on the horizon, the Portuguese had suffered a military defeat at Ternate and, though they had taken Melaka, they couldn't force traders to trade there. Islamic Banten became the main port in the region, attracting Muslim merchants such as Arabs, Persians and Gujaratis away from Melaka. Of the newcomers, it was the Dutch who would eventually lay the foundations of the Indonesian state we know today.

Coming of the Dutch

A disastrous expedition of four Dutch ships, led by Cornelius de Houtman in 1596, lost half its crew, killed a Javanese prince and lost a ship in the process. Nevertheless, it returned to Holland with boat loads of spices that made a profit for the expedition's backers, and soon others followed.

Recognising the potential of the East Indies trade, the Dutch government amalgamated the competing merchant companies into the United East India Company or Vereenigde Oost-Indische Compagnie (VOC).

Portuguese travellers in Banten, 1596

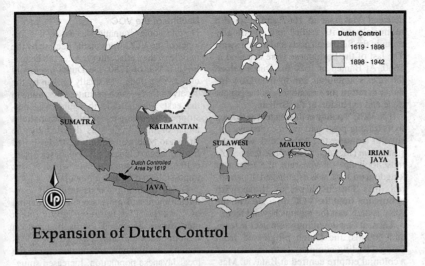

Expansion of Dutch Control

This government monopoly soon became the main competitor to secure the spice trade.

The intention was to create a force to bring military pressure to bear on the Portuguese and the Spanish. Dutch trading ships were replaced by heavily armed fleets with instructions to attack Portuguese bases. By 1605 the Dutch had defeated the Portuguese at Tidore and Ambon, and occupied the territory themselves.

The Dutch then looked for a base closer to the important shipping lanes of the Melaka and Sunda straits. The ruler of Jayakarta (present-day Jakarta) in West Java granted permission for the Dutch to build a warehouse in 1610, and he also granted the English trading rights. The Dutch warehouse became a fort, and as relations between the Dutch and the English came to the boil, skirmishes resulted in a siege of the fort by the English and the Jayakartans. The Dutch retaliated, razing the town in 1619. They renamed their new headquarters 'Batavia'.

Foundation of a Dutch Empire

The founder of the Dutch Empire in the Dutch East Indies was Jan Pieterszoon Coen,

an imaginative but ruthless man. Among his 'achievements' was the near-total extermination of the indigenous population of the Banda Islands in Maluku. Coen developed a grandiose plan to make his capital on Java the centre of the intra-Asian trade from Japan to Persia, and to develop the spice plantations using Burmese, Madagascan and Chinese labourers.

While the more grandiose plans were rejected, he was instrumental in realising Dutch plans to monopolise the spice trade. An alliance with Ternate in 1607 gave the Dutch control over the source of cloves, and their occupation of Banda from 1609-21 gave them control of the nutmeg trade.

The capture of Melaka from the Portuguese in 1641 completed the Dutch mastery of the seas in the region. The spice trade monopoly was supplemented by the important China trade, for South-East Asia was the great trading bazaar of the east where India and China traded halfway.

Batavia lived in constant fear of attack in its early years, but by the mid-16th century it was an important centre of trade after successfully repelling attacks from the Mataram Empire of Central Java. The Dutch defeated Makassar in 1667 and secured a monopoly of its trade, and eventually brought the Sumatran ports under their sway. The last of the Portuguese were expelled in 1660. At Banten in 1680 the Dutch helped the ruler's ambitious son to overthrow his father in return for a monopoly of the pepper trade and expulsion of the British.

The VOC's policy at this stage was to keep to its trading posts and avoid expensive territorial conquests. An accord with the *susuhunan* (literally, he to whose feet people must look up) of Mataram, the dominant kingdom on Java, was established. It permitted only Dutch ships, or those with permission from the VOC, to trade with the spice islands and the regions beyond them.

Then, at first unwillingly, but later in leaps and bounds, the Dutch progressed from being a trading company to the masters of a colonial empire centred at Batavia. Mataram declined after the death of its greatest leader, Sultan Agung (1613-46). Warring principalities and court intrigues allowed the Dutch to successfully follow a 'divide and rule' strategy.

Java was beset by wars from the end of the 17th century as Mataram fragmented. The VOC were only too willing to lend military support to contenders to the throne, in return for compensation and land concessions. The death knell for Mataram followed the Third Javanese War of Succession (1746-57), when Prince Mangkubumi and Mas Said contested the throne of the susuhunan, Pakubuwono II, largely because of his concessions and capitulation to Dutch demands.

In 1755 the Dutch split the Mataram kingdom into two – Yogyakarta and Surakarta (Solo). These new states and the other smaller states on Java were only nominally sovereign; in reality they were dominated by the VOC. Fighting amongst the princes was halted, and peace was brought to East Java by the forced cessation of invasions and raids from Bali.

Thus Java was finally united under a foreign trading company with an army that totalled only 1000 Europeans and 2000 Asians.

Decline of the VOC

Despite some dramatic successes, the fortunes of the VOC were on the decline by the middle of the 18th century. After the Dutch-English War of 1780, the Dutch monopoly of the spice trade was finally broken by the Treaty of Paris which permitted free trade in the east. Dutch trade in China was outstripped by European rivals, and in India much of their trade was diverted by the British to Madras. In addition, trade shifted from spices to Chinese silk, Japanese copper, coffee, tea and sugar – over which it was impossible to establish a monopoly.

Dutch trading interests gradually contracted more and more around their capital of Batavia. The Batavian government increasingly depended for its finances on customs dues and tolls charged for goods coming into Batavia, and on taxes from the local Javanese population. Increased smuggling and the illicit private trade carried on by company employees helped to reduce profits. The mounting expense of wars within Java and of administering the additional territory acquired after each new treaty also played a part in the decline.

The VOC turned to the Dutch government at home for support, and the subsequent investigation of VOC affairs revealed corruption, bankruptcy and mismanagement. In 1799 the VOC was formally wound up, its territorial possessions became the property of the Dutch government and the trading empire was gradually transformed into a colonial empire.

British Occupation & the Java War

In 1811, during the Napoleonic Wars when France occupied Holland, the British occupied several Dutch East Indies posts, including Java. Control was restored to the Dutch in 1816, and a treaty was signed in 1824 under which the British exchanged their Indonesian settlements (such as Bengkulu in Sumatra) for Dutch holdings in India and the Malay peninsula. While the two European powers may have settled their differences to their own satisfaction, the Indonesians were of another mind. There were a number of wars or disturbances in various parts of the archipelago during the early 19th century, but the most prolonged struggles were the Paderi War in Sumatra (1821-38) and the famous Java War (1825-30) led by Prince Diponegoro. In one sense the Java War was yet another war of succession, but both wars are notable because Islam became the symbol of opposition to the Dutch.

In 1814 Diponegoro, the eldest son of the Sultan of Yogya, had been passed over for the succession to the throne in favour of a younger claimant who had the support of the British. Having bided his time, Diponegoro eventually vanished from court and in 1825 launched a guerrilla war against the Dutch. The courts of Yogya and Solo largely remained loyal to the Dutch but many of the Javanese aristocracy supported the rebellion. Diponegoro had received mystical signs that convinced him that he was the divinely

Prince Diponegoro, of the Yogyakarta royal house, was the charismatic leader of a bloody guerrilla war against the Dutch from 1825 to 1830. Diponegoro was treacherously lured to discuss peace terms with the Dutch at Magellan, and then arrested. He was exiled to Sulawesi, where he died in 1856.

appointed future king of Java. News spread among the people that he was the long-prophesied Ratu Adil, the prince who would free them from colonial oppression.

The rebellion finally ended in 1830 when the Dutch tricked Diponegoro into peace negotiations, arrested him and exiled him to Sulawesi. The five year war had cost the lives of 8000 European and 7000 Indonesian soldiers of the Dutch army. At least 200,000 Javanese died, most from famine and disease, and the population of Yogyakarta was halved.

Dutch Exploitation of Indonesia

For 350 years, from the time the first Dutch ships arrived in 1596 to the declaration of independence in 1945, Dutch rule was always tenuous. Throughout the 17th century the VOC, with its superior arms and Buginese and Ambonese mercenaries, fought everywhere in the islands. Despite Dutch domination of Java, many areas of the archipelago – including Aceh, Bali, Lombok and Borneo – remained independent.

Fighting continued to flare up in Sumatra and Java, and between 1846 and 1849 expeditions were sent to Bali in the first attempts to subjugate the island. In south-eastern Borneo, the violent Banjarmasin War saw the Dutch defeat the reigning sultan. The longest and most devastating war was in Aceh, which lasted 35 years from the Dutch invasion in 1873 until the Aceh guerrilla leaders eventually surrendered in 1908.

Even into the 20th century Dutch control outside Java was still incomplete. Large-scale Indonesian piracy continued right up until the middle of the 19th century, and the Dutch fought a war in Sulawesi against the Buginese. Dutch troops occupied south-western Sulawesi between 1900 and 1910, and Bali in 1906. The 'bird's head' of West Irian did not come under Dutch administration until 1919-20.

The determined exploitation of Indonesian resources by the Dutch really only began in 1830. The cost of the Java and Paderi wars meant that, despite increased returns from the Dutch system of land tax, Dutch finances were severely strained. When the Dutch lost Belgium in 1830, the home country itself faced bankruptcy and any government investment in the Indies *had* to make quick returns. From here on Dutch economic policy in Indonesia falls into three overlapping periods: the period of the so-called 'Culture System'; the Liberal Period; and the Ethical Period.

Throughout all three periods, the exploitation of Indonesia's wealth contributed to the industrialisation of the Netherlands. Large areas of Java became plantations whose products, cultivated by Javanese peasants and collected by Chinese intermediaries, were sold on the overseas markets by European merchants. Before WWII, Indonesia supplied most of the world's quinine and pepper, over a third of its rubber, a quarter of its coconut products, and almost a fifth of its tea, sugar, coffee and oil. Indonesia made the Netherlands one of the major colonial powers.

Culture System A new governor-general, Johannes Van den Bosch, fresh from experiences of the slave labour of the West Indies, was appointed in 1830 to make the East Indies pay their way. He succeeded by introducing a new agricultural policy called the Cultuurstelsel, or Culture System. It was a system of government-controlled agriculture or, as Indonesian historians refer to it, the Tanam Paksa (Compulsory Planting).

Instead of land taxes, peasants had to either cultivate government-owned crops on 20% of their land or work in the government plantations for nearly 60 days of the year. Much of Java became a Dutch plantation, generating great wealth in Holland. For the Javanese peasantry, this forced-labour system brought hardship and resentment. Forced to grow crops such as indigo and sugar instead of rice, famine and epidemics swept Java in the 1840s, first at Cirebon in 1843 and then Central Java.

The Culture System was a boon to the Dutch and the Javanese aristocracy. The profits made Java a self-sufficient colony and saved Holland from bankruptcy.

Liberal Period Public opinion in Holland began to decry the treatment and suffering of Indonesians under the colonial government. The so-called Liberal Policy was introduced by liberals in the Dutch parliament, trying to reform and eliminate the excesses of the Culture System.

Agrarian reform in 1870 freed producers from the compulsion to provide export crops but opened the Indies to private enterprise, which developed large plantations. As the population increased dramatically, especially on Java, less land was available for rice production, bringing further hardship. Dutch profits grew dramatically in the latter part of the 19th century.

Sugar production doubled in 1870-85, new crops like tea and cinchona flourished, and rubber was introduced. At the same time, oil produced in south Sumatra and Kalimantan became a valuable export – a response to the new industrial demands of the European market.

The exploitation of Indonesian resources was no longer limited to Java but had filtered through to the outer islands. As Dutch commercial interests expanded, so did the need to protect them. More and more territory was taken under direct control of the Dutch government, and most of the outer islands came under firm Dutch sovereignty.

Ethical Period The 20th century heralded a new approach to colonial government as the Ethical Policy was introduced in 1901. Under this policy it became the Dutch government's duty to further the welfare of the Indonesian people in health, education and other social programmes.

New policies were to be implemented, foremost among them irrigation, transmigration from heavily populated Java to lightly populated islands and education. There were also plans for improved communications, agriculture, flood control, drainage, health programmes, industrialisation and the protection of native industry. Other policies aimed for the decentralisation of authority with greater autonomy for the Indonesian government, as well as greater power to local government units within the archipelago.

The humanitarian policies were laudable but ultimately inadequate. Increases in public health expenditure were simply not enough. While education possibilities for Indonesians increased, the vast majority of Indonesians were illiterate. Though primary schools were established and education was open to all, by 1930 only 8% of school age children received an education. Industrialisation was never seriously implemented, and Indonesia remained an agricultural colony.

Indonesian Nationalism

Though the Ethical Period failed to deliver widespread educational opportunities, it did provide Dutch education for the children of the Indonesian elite, largely to supply clerical labour for the growing bureaucracy. Western education brought with it western political ideas of freedom and democracy, but the first seeds of Indonesian nationalism were sown by the Islamic movements.

Sarekat Islam was an early, pre-modern nationalist movement, inspired more by Islamic and Javanese mysticism than by notions of independent self-rule. It rallied Indonesians under the traditional banner of Islam, in opposition to Dutch influence, but had no national agenda and was often more anti-Chinese than anti-colonial.

The Indonesian Communist Party (PKI) on the other hand was a fully fledged, pro-independence party inspired by European politics. It was formed in 1920 and found support among workers in the industrial cities. The PKI presumptuously decided to start the revolution in Indonesia in 1926 with isolated insurrections across Java. The panicked and outraged Dutch government arrested and exiled thousands of Communists, effectively putting them out of action for the rest of the Dutch occupation.

Despite Dutch repression of nationalist organisations and the arrest of its leaders, the nationalist movement was finding a unified voice. In an historic announcement, the All Indonesia Youth Congress proclaimed its Youth Pledge in 1928, adopting the notions of the one fatherland (Indonesia), one united country and one language (Bahasa Indonesia). In Bandung in 1929 Soekarno founded the Partai Nasional Indonesia (PNI), the most significant nationalist organisation. It was the first, all-Indonesia secular party devoted primarily to independence and not ideology.

Soekarno was educated in East Java and went on to receive a European education before studying at the Bandung Institute of Technology, where he was active in the Bandung Study Club. Bandung was a hotbed of political intellectualism, where the PKI and radical Muslim thought flowered. Soekarno was widely influenced by Javanese, western, Muslim and socialist ideals, and blended these various influences towards a national ideology.

Soekarno was soon arrested and a virtual ban placed on the PNI. Nationalist sentiment remained high in the 1930s, but with many nationalist leaders in jail or exiled, the hope of independence seemed a long way off. Even when Germany invaded the Netherlands in May 1940, the colonial government in exile was determined to continue its rule in the East Indies.

All was to change when the Japanese attacked Pearl Harbour and then stormed down through South-East Asia. After the fall of Singapore, many Europeans fled to Australia, and the colonial government abandoned Batavia, surrendering to the Japanese on 8 March 1942.

Japanese Occupation

The Japanese imperial army marched into Batavia on 5 March 1942, carrying the red-and-white Indonesian flag along side that of the rising sun. The city's name was changed to Jakarta, Europeans were arrested and all signs of the former Dutch masters eliminated.

Though greeted initially as liberators, public opinion turned against the Japanese as the war wore on and Indonesians were expected to endure more hardship for the war effort. The Japanese were keen to impress their superiority on the Indonesian population and soon developed a reputation as cruel masters.

Undoubtedly though, the Japanese gave Indonesians more responsibility and participation in government. The very top administrative positions were held by Japanese, but Indonesians from the top down ruled themselves for the first time. The Japanese also gave prominence to nationalist leaders, such as Soekarno and Mohammed Hatta, and trained youth militia to defend the country. Apart from giving Indonesia a military psyche that has endured in Indonesian politics, these militia gave rise to the *pemuda* (youth) of the independence movement who would later form the independence army.

Independence Struggle

As the war ended, the nationalist leadership of Soekarno and Hatta was in effect kidnapped and pressured by radical youth groups to immediately declare Indonesia's independence before the Dutch could return. On 17 August 1945, with tacit Japanese backing, Soekarno proclaimed the independence of the Republic of Indonesia from his Jakarta home.

Indonesians throughout the archipelago rejoiced, but the Netherlands refused to accept the proclamation and still claimed sovereignty over Indonesia. British troops entered Java in October 1945 to accept the surrender of the Japanese. Under British auspices, Dutch troops gradually returned to Indonesia and it became obvious that independence would have to be fought for.

Clashes broke out with the new Republican army, and came to a head in the bloody Battle for Surabaya. As Europeans and Dutch internees returned to the city,

---

Street Names & Indonesian Heroes

In every city, town and *kampung* in Indonesia, streets (as well as airports, parks and so on) are named after Indonesian heroes who, invariably, helped fight the Dutch during the colonial period or after independence was declared by Indonesia in 1945. Some of the more well known are:

Cokroaminoto, HOS (1883-1934) was from East Java and helped establish the Islamic Federation, also known as the PSII.

Diponegoro, Pangeran (1785-1855) was a prince from Yogyakarta. He was a leader in the Java War of 1825-30 against the Dutch, during which he was captured, and later exiled to Ujung Pandang where he died.

Gajah Mada was prime minister and a brilliant military commander in the Javanese Majapahit kingdom in the 14th century. He helped defeat rebels who fought King Jayanegara (but Gajah Mada later arranged the king's murder because he took Gajah Mada's wife!).

Hasanuddin, Sultan (1631-70), born in South Sulawesi, helped with the resistance against the Vereenigde Oost-Indische Compagnie (VOC).

Hatta, Mohammed (1902-80) was a Sumatran who was arrested in 1927 for promoting resistance against the Dutch. He was sent to the notorious prison, Boven Digul, and then Banda, but later released by the Japanese. On 17 August 1945 he declared Indonesian independence with Soekarno, and served as vice-president and/or prime minister from 1945-56.

Imam Bonjol (1772-1864) was an important Islamic leader, and a leader of the resistance against the Dutch in the Paderi War of 1821-38. He was captured by the Dutch, sent to Ambon and then Manado.

Kartini, Raden Ajeng (1879-1905) was a Javanese writer and activist, who became famous for her promotion of education and women's rights, especially through her letters which were discovered after her death during childbirth.

Monginsidi, Wolter (1925-49) was captured and shot at only 24 years of age by the Dutch during the resistance.

skirmishes developed with armed youth militia. The situation deteriorated when British Indian troops landed in the city. When General Mallaby, leader of the British forces, was killed by a bomb, the British launched a bloody retribution. On 10 November (now celebrated as 'Heroes Day') the British began to take the city under cover of air attacks. Thousands of Indonesians died as the population fled to the countryside, but though poorly armed, the numerous Republican forces fought a pitched battle for three weeks. The brutal retaliation of the British and the spirited defence of Surabaya by the Republicans galvanised Indonesian support and helped turn world opinion.

The Dutch dream of easy reoccupation was shattered, while the British were keen to extricate themselves from military action and broker a peace agreement. The last British troops left at the end of November 1946, by which time 55,000 Dutch troops had landed on Java. In Bogor (Java) and on Balikpapan (Kalimantan), Indonesian republican officials were imprisoned. Bombing raids on Palembang and Medan in Sumatra prepared the way for the Dutch occupation of these cities. In southern Sulawesi, a Captain Westerling was accused of pacifying the region by murdering 40,000 Indonesians in a few weeks. Elsewhere, the Dutch were attempting to form puppet states among the more amenable ethnic groups.

In Jakarta the republican government, with Soekarno as president and Hatta as vice-president, tried to maintain calm. On the other hand, youth groups advocating armed

---

Sisingamangaraja (1849-1907) was the last of a long line of Batak kings, first dating from the 16th century. His ancestors were spiritual leaders, and he became a leader of, and then was killed by, the resistance against the Dutch.

Subroto, Gatot (1907-62) fought for Indonesian independence in the 1940s, and helped quell Communist rebels in 1948. He became Military Governor of Surakarta, then a general and later a member of Soeharto's early cabinet.

Sudarso, Yos (1925-62) was a senior naval officer who died when his ship, the *Macan Tutul*, was sunk by the Dutch during the liberation of Irian Jaya.

Sudirman (1916-50) was a leader of the resistance against the Dutch during 1945-50. After independence, he was appointed General and Commander-in-Chief of the Indonesian Republic.

Supratman, WR (1903-38) composed the Indonesian national anthem, *Indonesia Raya*, which was first performed by Supratman at the 2nd Indonesian Youth Congress in 1928.

Syahrir, Sutan (1909-66), also referred to as Sjahrir, was a leading nationalist leader on Java in the 1930s, but was opposed to Soekarno. Syahrir was arrested by the Dutch, exiled to Boven Digul, and later denounced the Japanese Occupation. He served as prime minister from 1945-47, and was instrumental in obtaining former Dutch territories for the new Indonesia.

Thamrin, Mohammed (1894-1941) was a nationalist leader and politician in the 1920s and 1930s. He was arrested by the Dutch in 1941, after cooperating with the Japanese, and died soon after.

Yamin, Mohammed (1903-62) was a Sumatran writer, poet, lawyer and politician; he helped to form the Youth Pledge in 1928. He was arrested in 1946 by the Dutch, then became a cabinet minister and later the instigator of 'Guided Democracy'.

Yani, Ahmad (1922-65) was responsible for suppressing Sumatran rebels in 1958. He was commander of the 'liberation' of Irian Jaya three years later, and became Army Chief of Staff in 1962. He was one of the generals killed in the ill-fated coup of September 1965. ■

struggle saw the old leadership as prevaricating and betraying the revolution.

Outbreaks occurred across the country, and Soekarno and Hatta were outmanoeuvered in the Republican government. Sultan Syahrir became prime minister, and as the Dutch assumed control in Jakarta, the Republicans moved their capital to Yogyakarta. Sultan Hamengkubuwono IX, who was to become Yogya's most revered and able sultan, played a leading role in the revolution. In Surakarta, on the other hand, Pakubuwono XII was ineffectual, to the detriment of Surakarta come independence.

The battle for independence wavered between warfare and diplomacy. Under the Linggarjati Agreement of November 1946, the Dutch recognised the Republican government and both sides agreed to work towards an Indonesian federation under a Dutch commonwealth. The agreement was soon swept aside as the war escalated. The Dutch mounted a large offensive in July 1947, causing the United Nations (UN) to step in.

During these uncertain times, the main forces in Indonesian politics regrouped. The PKI and Soekarno's old party, the PNI, reformed, while the main Islamic parties were Masyumi and Nahdatul Ulama.

The army also emerged as a force, though it was split by many factions. The Republicans were far from united, and on Java, civil war threatened to erupt when the PKI staged a rebellion in Surakarta and then Madiun. In a tense threat to the revolution, Soekarno galvanised opposition to the Communists, who were defeated by army forces.

In February 1948 the Dutch launched another full scale attack on the Republicans, breaking the UN agreement and turning world opinion. Under pressure from the USA, which threatened to withdraw its postwar aid to the Netherlands, and a growing realisation at home that this was an unwinnable war, the Dutch negotiated for independence. On 27 December 1949 the Indonesian flag was raised at Jakarta's Istana Merdeka (Freedom Palace) as power was officially handed over.

Economic Depression & Disunity

The threat of external attacks from the Dutch helped keep the nationalists united in the first years after the proclamation of independence. With the Dutch gone, the divisions in Indonesian society began to appear. Soekarno had tried to hammer out the principles of Indonesian unity in his Pancasila speech of 1945 and while these, as he said, may have been 'the highest common factor and the lowest common multiple of Indonesian thought', the divisive elements in Indonesian society could not be swept away by a single speech. Regional differences in customs (adat), morals, tradition, religion, the impact of Christianity and Marxism, and fears of political domination by the Javanese all contributed to disunity.

Separatist movements battled the new republic. They included the militant Darul Islam (Islamic Domain), which proclaimed an Islamic State of Indonesia and waged guerrilla warfare in West Java against the new Indonesian republic from 1949 to 1962. In Maluku, the former Ambonese members of the Royal Dutch Indies Army tried to establish an independent republic, and there were revolts in Minahasa (the northern limb of Sulawesi) and on Sumatra.

Against this background lay divisions in the leadership elite, and the sorry state of the new republic's economy. When the Republic of Indonesia came into being, the economy was in tatters after almost 10 years of Japanese occupation and war with the Dutch. The population was increasing, and the new government was unable to boost production of food and other necessities to keep pace. Most of the population was illiterate, and there was a dearth of skilled workers and management. Inflation was chronic, smuggling cost the central government badly needed foreign currency, and many of the plantations had been destroyed during the war.

Political parties proliferated and deals between parties for a share of cabinet seats resulted in a rapid turnover of coalition governments. There were 17 cabinets for the period 1945 to 1958. The frequently postponed elections were finally held in 1955 and the PNI – regarded as Soekarno's party – topped the poll. There was also a dramatic increase in support for the PKI but no party managed more than a quarter of the votes and shortlived coalitions continued.

Soekarno Takes Over – Guided Democracy

By 1956 President Soekarno was openly criticising parliamentary democracy, stating that it was 'based upon inherent conflict' which ran counter to the Indonesian concept of harmony as the natural state of human relationships.

Soekarno sought a system based on the traditional village system of discussion and consensus under the guidance of the village elders. He proposed a threefold division – nationalism (*nasionalisme*), religion (*agaman*) and Communism (*komunisme*) – to be

Achmed Soekarno, founder of the Indonesian Nationalist Party (PNI), first President of the Republic of Indonesia and father of 'guided democracy' – the system which replaced the Westminster model with a parliament appointed by the president and a Supreme Advisory Council as the chief policy-making body.

blended into a cooperative '*Nas-A-Kom*' government, thereby appeasing the three main factions of Indonesian political life – the army, Islamic groups and the Communists.

In February 1957, with support from the military, Soekarno then proclaimed 'guided democracy' and proposed a cabinet representing all the political parties of importance (including the PKI). Western-style democracy was finished in Indonesia (and has never returned), though the parties were not abolished.

Sumatra & Sulawesi Rebellions

Clashes broke out in Sumatra and Sulawesi in 1958 as a reaction against Soekarno's usurpation of power, the growing influence of the PKI, and the corruption, inefficiency and mismanagement of the central government. There were also rebellions against Java, whose leaders and interests dominated Indonesia, despite the fact that the other islands provided most of the country's export income.

The rebellions were effectively smashed by mid-1958, though guerrilla activity continued for three years. Rebel leaders were granted amnesty, but the two political parties which they had been connected with were banned and some of the early nationalist leaders were discredited. Syahrir and others were arrested in 1962.

Soekarno was now able to exercise enormous personal influence and set about reorganising the political system in order to give himself *real* power. In 1960 the elected parliament was dissolved, and replaced by a parliament appointed by and subject to the will of the president. The Supreme Advisory Council, another non-elected body, became the chief policy-making body and the National Front was set up in September 1960 to 'mobilise the revolutionary forces of the people'. The Front was presided over by the president and became a useful adjunct to the government in organising 'demonstrations' – such as sacking embassies during the period of 'Confrontation' with Malaysia.

Soekarno – Revolution & Nationalism

With his assumption of power, Soekarno set Indonesia on a course of stormy nationalism. During the early 1960s he created a strange language of capital letters: the world was divided between the New Emerging Forces (NEFOS) and the Old Established Forces (OLDEFOS), in which westerners were the Neo-Colonial Imperialists (NEKOLIM).

His speeches were those of a romantic revolutionary. They held his people spellbound, uniting them against a common external threat. *Konfrontasi* became the buzz word as Indonesia confronted Malaysia (and their imperialist backers, the UK), the USA and indeed the whole western world.

With traditional Indonesian deference Soekarno was called *bapak*, or father, but he was more popularly referred to as *bung*, the daring 'older brother', a man of the people who carried the dreams and aspirations of his nation and dared to take on the west.

Soekarno is best remembered for his flamboyance and his contradictions. Abstinence, monogamy and temperance were conspicuously undervalued by Soekarno. He was a noted womaniser, claimed to be a pious Muslim and also a Marxist, yet he was also very much a mystic in the Javanese tradition. His contradictions were those of his nation, which he somehow held together through the force of his oratory and personality.

Economic Deterioration

What Soekarno could not do was create a viable economic system that would lift Indonesia out of its poverty. Soekarno's corrosive vanity burnt money on a spate of status symbols meant to symbolise the new Indonesian identity. They included the Merdeka (Freedom) Monument, the biggest mosque in the world, and a vast sports stadium built with Russian money. Unable to advance beyond revolution to the next stage of rebuilding, Soekarno's monuments became substitutes for real development.

Richard Nixon, who became the US president in 1968, visited Indonesia in 1953 and presented this image of Indonesia under Soekarno:

In no other country we visited was the conspicuous luxury of the ruler in such striking contrast to the poverty and misery of his people. Jakarta was a collection of sweltering huts and hovels. An open sewer ran through the heart of the city, but Soekarno's palace was painted a spotless white and set in the middle of hundreds of acres of exotic gardens. One night we ate off gold plate to the light of a thousand torches while musicians played on the shore of a lake covered with white lotus blossoms and candles floating on small rafts.

A more aggressive stance on foreign affairs also became a characteristic of Soekarno's increased authority. Soekarno believed that Asia had been humiliated by the west and had still not evened the score. He sought recognition of a new state that was once a 'nation of coolies and a coolie amongst nations'. Indonesia was also surrounded and, from Soekarno's view, threatened by the remnants of western imperialism: the British and their new client state of Malaysia; the hated Dutch who continued to occupy West Irian; and the Americans and their military bases in the Philippines.

Under Soekarno, Indonesia turned its attention towards attaining those territories it had claimed in August 1945. First on the agenda was West Irian, still under Dutch rule. An arms agreement with the Soviet Union in 1960 enabled the Indonesians to begin a diplomatic as well as military confrontation with the Dutch over West Irian. It was pressure from the USA on the Dutch that finally led to the Indonesian takeover in 1963.

The same year Indonesia embarked on Confrontation with the new nation of Malaysia. The northern states in Borneo, which bordered on Indonesian Kalimantan, wavered in their desire to join Malaysia. Indonesia wanted to bring the region into its sphere of influence and supported an attempted revolution in Brunei. Soekarno railed against British imperialism and revived the glories of Indonesia's revolution. The army increased its budget and mounted offensives along the Kalimantan-Malaysia border, and the PKI demonstrated in the streets in Jakarta. The west became increasingly alarmed at Indonesian foreign policy, but the main forces in Indonesia were happy.

Confrontation took the spotlight, but Indonesia's main concerns were economic. Foreign aid dried up after the USA withdrew its aid because of Confrontation. The cash-strapped government abolished subsidies in several areas of the public sector, leading to massive increases in public transport, electricity, water and postal charges. Economic plans had failed miserably and inflation was running at 500%.

Soekarno, the Army & the Communists

Though Soekarno often talked as if he held absolute power, his position depended on maintaining a balance between the different political powers in Indonesia, primarily the army and the PKI. Soekarno is often described as the great *dalang*, or puppet master, who balanced the forces of the left and right just as competing forces are balanced in the Javanese shadow puppet shows.

Confrontation had alienated western nations, and Indonesia came to depend more and more on support from the Soviet Union, then increasingly from Communist China. Meanwhile, tensions grew between the Indonesian Army and their mortal enemy, the PKI.

The PKI was the third-largest Communist Party in the world, outside the Soviet Union and China. By 1965 it claimed to have three million members; affiliate organisations of the PKI claimed membership of 20 million. Except for the inner cabinet, it penetrated the government apparatus extensively.

After the successes of the PKI in the 1955 election, Soekarno realised that he had to give it prominence in his guided democracy government. Increasingly the PKI gained influence ahead of the army, which had been the main power base of Indonesian politics since independence.

Guided democracy under Soekarno was marked by an attempt to give the peasants better social conditions, but attempts to give tenant farmers a fairer share of their rice crops and to redistribute land led to more confusion. The PKI often pushed for reforms behind the government's back and encouraged peasants to seize land without waiting for decisions from land-reform committees. In 1964 these tactics led to violent clashes in Central and East Java and Bali.

The pressure increased in 1965 with growing tension between the PKI and the army. In a visit to Jakarta in April 1965 Zhou Enlai (the then Premier of China) proposed a 'fifth force' – an armed people's militia independent of the four branches of the armed forces (the army, navy, air force and police). Soekarno supported this proposal to arm the Communists, the army opposed it, and the rumours of an army takeover became common in Jakarta.

Slaughter of the Communists

On the night of 30 September 1965 six of Indonesia's top generals were taken from their Jakarta homes and executed in an attempted coup. Led by Colonel Untung of the palace guard and backed by elements of the armed forces, they took up positions around the presidential palace and seized the national radio station. They claimed that they had acted against a plot organised by the generals to overthrow the president.

This bumbling exercise appears to have had little or no coordination with revolt in the rest of Java, let alone the rest of the archipelago. Within a few hours of the coup, General Soeharto, head of the army's Strategic Reserve, was able to mobilise army forces to take counteraction. By the evening of 1 October, the coup had clearly failed.

Exactly who had organised the coup and what it had set out to achieve remains shrouded in mystery. The Indonesian army asserted that the PKI plotted the coup and used discontented army officers to carry it out. Other theories are that it was primarily an internal army affair, led by younger officers against the older leadership. And then there are those who believe that Soekarno himself was behind the coup – and yet another story that Soeharto was in the confidence of the conspirators.

Certainly, civilians from the PKI's People's Youth organisation accompanied the army battalions that seized the generals, but whatever the PKI's real role in the coup, the effect on its fortunes was devastating.

Soeharto orchestrated a counter coup, and an anti-Communism purge swept Indonesia. Hundreds of thousands of Communists and their sympathisers were slaughtered or imprisoned, primarily on Java and Bali. The party and its affiliates were banned, and its leaders were killed, imprisoned or went into hiding. Estimates of the death toll vary widely. Adam Malik, the future Foreign Minister under Soeharto, said that a 'fair figure' was 160,000. Independent commentators quote 500,000.

Following the army's lead, anti-Communist civilians went on the rampage. On Java, where long-simmering tensions between pro-Muslim and pro-Communist factions erupted in the villages, both sides believed that their opponents had drawn up death lists to be carried out when they achieved power. The anti-Communists, with encouragement from the government, got the chance to execute their list. On top of this uncontrolled slaughter, perhaps 250,000 people were arrested and sent to prison camps for allegedly being involved in some way with the coup.

Soekarno's Fall & Soeharto's Rise

Soeharto took over leadership of the armed forces and set about manoeuvring Soekarno from power. Soekarno continued as president, maintaining that he was still in charge. Meanwhile the army-orchestrated campaign of killings in the countryside was accompanied by violent demonstrations in Jakarta between Soekarnoists and anti-Soekarnoists.

Despite the chaos, Soekarno still had supporters in all the armed forces and it seemed unlikely that he would topple. Then on 11 March 1966, after troops loyal to Soeharto surrounded the Presidential Palace, Soekarno signed the 11 March Order giving Soeharto the power to restore order. While always deferring to the name of Soekarno and talking as if he was acting on Soekarno's behalf, Soeharto rapidly consolidated his

power. The PKI was officially banned. Pro-Soekarno soldiers and officers and a number of cabinet ministers were arrested. A new six man inner cabinet, including Soeharto and two of his nominees, Adam Malik and Sultan Hamengkubuwono of Yogyakarta, was formed.

Soeharto then launched a campaign of intimidation to blunt any grassroots opposition to his power. Thousands of public servants were dismissed as PKI sympathisers, putting thousands more in fear of losing their jobs.

By 1967 Soeharto was firmly enough entrenched to finally cut Soekarno adrift. The People's Consultative Congress, after the arrest of many of its members and the infusion of Soeharto appointees, relieved Soekarno of all power and elected Soeharto acting president. On 27 March 1968 it 'elected' Soeharto president.

The New Order

Under Soeharto's 'New Order' government, Indonesia looked to the west in foreign policy, and western-educated economists set about balancing budgets, controlling inflation and attracting foreign investment.

In 1971 general elections were held to give a veneer of democracy to the new regime. Soeharto used the almost defunct Golkar Party as the spearhead of the army's election campaign. Having appointed his election squad, the old parties were then crippled by being banned, by the disqualification of candidates and by disenfranchising voters. Predictably, Golkar swept to power and the PNI was shattered. The new People's Consultative Congress also included 207 Soeharto appointments and 276 armed forces officers.

Soeharto then enforced the merger of other political parties. The four Muslim parties were merged into the Development Union Party (PPP) and the other parties into the Indonesian Democratic Party (PDI).

With the elimination of the Communists and a more repressive government, political stability has returned to Indonesia and the divisions in society are less prominent. A determined effort to promote national rather than regional identity has largely been successful, but the army's brutal reaction to dissent continues to tarnish Indonesia's international image. Indonesia's invasion of East Timor in 1975 and the continuing struggle with Irian Jaya's guerrillas, who have never accepted the Indonesian takeover of the province, will always hang over the government.

Soeharto's main legacy has been stability – political and economic. Corruption is ever present, disparity of wealth is increasing and real democracy is still a long way off, but the lot of the majority of Indonesians has improved considerably over the last 30 years.

The main political question now facing Indonesia is what will happen in the era after Soeharto. The death of the president's wife in 1996 more than ever made Indonesians consider the mortality of their aging leader. Though he has hinted that he will retire in 1998 at the end of his current five year term, many have called for him to continue rather than face the uncertainty of a post-Soeharto Indonesia.

At the same time Indonesia is rapidly changing. Though still poor, the country is undergoing an economic boom, and along with greater education are calls for greater freedom. Talk of a more open, freer society is common in Jakarta these days, but progress to democratisation is painfully slow. Growing press liberalisation in the 1990s suffered a set back in 1994 when three magazines were closed for criticising government minister Habibi, Soeharto's confidante in cabinet.

However, the political opposition, particularly the Partai Demokrasi Indonesia (PDI), grows in stature and popularity. So much so that in 1996 the government helped engineer a split in the PDI, resulting in its popular leader Megawati Soekarnoputri, Soekarno's granddaughter, being dumped. PDI supporters took to the streets and Jakarta was rocked by its worst riots in 30 years. The government received a strong warning that the nascent democracy movement is growing and cannot be ignored.

GEOGRAPHY

The Republic of Indonesia is the world's most expansive archipelago, stretching almost 5000 km from Sabang off the northern tip of Sumatra, to a little beyond Merauke in south-eastern Irian Jaya. It stretches north and south of the equator for a total of 1770 km, from the border with Sabah to the small island of Roti off the southern tip of Timor.

Officially, the archipelago contains 13,677 islands – from specks of rock to huge islands like Sumatra and Borneo – 6000 of which are inhabited. The five main islands are Sumatra, Java, Kalimantan (Indonesian Borneo), Sulawesi and Irian Jaya (the western part of New Guinea). Most of the country is water; the Indonesians refer to their homeland as *Tanah Air Kita* (literally, Our Earth and Water). While the total land and sea area of Indonesia is about 2½ times greater than the land area of Australia, Indonesia's total land area is only 1,900,000 sq km, or a little larger than Queensland.

Most of these islands are mountainous; in Irian Jaya there are peaks so high they're snowcapped year-round. North-central Kalimantan and much of central Sulawesi are also mountainous, but in most other parts of Indonesia volcanoes dominate the skyline. Running like a backbone down the western coast of Sumatra is a line of extinct and active volcanoes which continues through Java, Bali and Nusa Tenggara, and then loops around through the Banda Islands of Maluku to north-eastern Sulawesi. Some of these have erupted, with devastating effects – the massive blowout of Krakatau in 1883 produced a tidal wave killing 36,000 people, and the 1963 eruption of Gunung Agung on Bali wasted large areas of the island. To many Balinese the eruption of this sacred mountain was a sign of the wrath of the gods, and in East Java the Tenggerese people still offer a propitiatory sacrifice to the smoking Bromo crater which dominates the local landscape. However, it is the ash from these volcanoes that has provided Indonesia with some of the finest, richest and most fertile stretches of land on the planet.

Volcanoes

Indonesia is a virtual chain of volcanic islands. Some have caused extraordinary destruction, yet they are often the lifeblood of the local people who cling to the volcanoes because they produce such fertile soil and their height produces rain. The word for volcano in Bahasa Indonesia is *gunung api*, which literally means, appropriately, 'fire mountain'. Most can be climbed relatively easily and, naturally, offer uniquely spectacular views, particularly at sunrise; sometimes craters and temples can be seen. Many volcanoes are still active, smoking and rumbling constantly.

The most famous is probably Krakatau between Sumatra and Java. In August 1883 it exploded killing more than 36,000 people and destroying most of the island. The noise was reported several thousand km away in Indonesia and Australia. Its ash spread as far, and tidal waves were felt as far away as England. In early 1997, it showed ominous signs of activity again.

The highest mountain in Indonesia, outside of Irian Jaya, is Gunung Kerinci (3805m), which is along the western coast of Sumatra. Around the beautiful area of Padang and Bukittinggi (which means 'high mountain') are the active Gunung Merapi (2891m; last erupted in 1979) and Singgalang volcanoes. Stunning Danau Toba is a crater lake 800m above sea level, but the area is inactive: the last eruption was maybe 75,000 years ago.

On Java, Gunung Bromo is quite magnificent and still active. Nearly 2400m high, it is well cultivated and the site of an annual festival by the local Tenggerese people who throw offerings into the crater to pacify the gods. Gunung Semeru, 3676m high, is regarded by all Hindus as the 'father mountain'; further east are the joint Gunung Merapi (2911m; last erupted in 1994) and Gunung Raung (3332m), where coffee is planted. There are several other volcanic peaks over 3000m on Java.

The beautiful turquoise lake that fills the crater of Gunung Ijen is a popular destination for travellers in East Java. The walk around the crater's edge provides stunning views of the area.

PETER TURNER

In 1963 Gunung Agung, on Bali, erupted with immense destruction, which was interpreted by the Balinese as a sign of anger from the gods. Revered as the 'mother mountain', about 1000m up the 3142m slope of Agung is Pura Besakih, regarded as Bali's most important temple. Nearby, Gunung Batur (1717m) erupted in 1917, killing thousands and destroying untold number of homes and temples. It erupted again in 1963 and 1974.

Near Banda, on Maluku, jutting out of the sea spectacularly, is the unimaginatively named Gunung Api. It remains a constant threat to the nearby islands and villages perched around the volcano. The first eruption caused massive destruction in 1778 but less damage (because of warnings) during eruptions in 1901 and 1988. In northern Maluku, villages hug the ever-smoking Gunung Api Gamalama (1721m) on Ternate Island, which erupted in 1980, 1983 and October 1994.

The 2820m high Gunung Tambora on the island of Sumbawa, Nusa Tenggara, erupted in 1815, killing at least 10,000 people; many more – up to two-thirds of the island's population – died from resulting starvation or disease. On Flores, one of the great sights in Indonesia is the three coloured lakes at the top of the omnipotent Keli Mutu (1600m) volcano. Sulawesi has several more volcanoes in the south, not far from Ujung Pandang, and more active ones in the far northern parts and islands around Manado.

The interior of Gunung Bromo's crater features 350m-high walls which tower over the active volcano's smoking vent. Gunung Bromo is one of three peaks contained within the 10km-wide crater of the Tengger Massif in East Java.

PETER TURNER

Unlike its large sunburnt neighbour to the south, Indonesia is a country of plentiful rainfall, particularly in west Sumatra, northwest Kalimantan, West Java and Irian Jaya. A few areas of Sulawesi and some of the islands closer to Australia – notably Sumba and Timor – are considerably drier, but they're exceptions. The high rainfall and the tropical heat make for a very humid climate – but also for a very even one. The highlands of Java and Irian Jaya can get very cold indeed, but on the whole most of Indonesia is warm and humid year-round.

Because of this high rainfall and year-round humidity, nearly two-thirds of Indonesia is covered in tropical rainforest – most of it on Sumatra, Kalimantan, Sulawesi and Irian Jaya. Most of the forests of Java disappeared centuries ago as land was cleared for agriculture. Today the rest of Indonesia's rainforest, which is second only to Brazil's in area, is disappearing at an alarming rate as local and foreign timber companies plunder the forests. Other contributing factors are the clearing of forest for agriculture, transmigration settlements and mining.

In 1983 Indonesia was the scene of probably the greatest forest fire ever recorded, when 30,000 sq km of rainforest were destroyed in the 'Great Fire of Kalimantan', which lasted nine months. The government blamed shifting 'slash-and-burn' cultivators for this, but outside experts say the fire was triggered by the waste wood and debris left by loggers, setting off peat and coal fires beneath the ground which burned for months. The fire was followed in 1991 and 1994 by more huge fires both in Sumatra and Kalimantan.

Along the east coast of Sumatra, the south coast of Kalimantan, Irian Jaya and much of the northern coast of Java, there is swampy, low-lying land often covered in mangroves. In many areas the over-clearing of natural growth has led to a continual erosion as topsoil is washed down the rivers by heavy rains, simultaneously wreaking havoc with the Indonesian roads.

The tropical vegetation, the mountainous terrain and the break up of the country into numerous islands have always made communication difficult between islands and between different parts of each island. But it is these factors which have had a marked effect on its history and culture, and also explain some of the peculiarities of the country and its people.

Firstly, Indonesia straddles the equator between the Indian Ocean to the west and the Pacific Ocean to the east. To the north are China and Japan, to the north-west India and beyond that Arabia. Because of this central position, the Indonesian islands – particularly Sumatra and Java – and the Malay peninsula have long formed a stopover and staging ground on the sea routes between India and China, a convenient midway point where merchants of the civilised world met and exchanged goods.

Secondly, the regular and even climate (there are some exceptions – in some of the islands east of Java and Bali the seasonal differences are pronounced, and even within Java some districts have a sufficiently marked dry season to suffer drought at times) means that a rhythm of life for many Indonesian farmers is based less on the annual fluctuations of the seasons than on the growth pattern of their crops. In areas with heavy rainfall and terraced rice-field cultivation, there is no set planting season or harvest season but a continuous flow of activity, where at any one time one hillside may demonstrate the whole cycle of rice cultivation, from ploughing to harvesting.

Java is the hub of Indonesia and its most heavily populated island. The capital of Indonesia, Jakarta, is located on the island's north-western coast. While the Javanese are the dominant group in Indonesian politics and the military, their control over the other islands is a tenuous one for the reasons already mentioned. The diversity of the archipelago's inhabitants and the break-up of the country into numerous islands helps to fuel separatism; since the formation of the republic in 1949 the central administration in Jakarta has fought wars against separatists in West Java, Sumatra, Minahasa in northern Sulawesi, West Irian and Maluku.

Indonesia shares borders with Malaysia and Papua New Guinea. Relations with Malaysia were unhappy during the Soekarno era and the period of Confrontation, but since then they have very much improved. Trouble with Papua New Guinea results from continuing problems with the Free West Papua (OPM) guerrillas who refuse to recognise Indonesian sovereignty over West Irian and take refuge in Papua New Guinea. East Timor remained a colony of Portugal up until independence but was invaded by Indonesia in 1975.

CLIMATE

Straddling the equator, Indonesia tends to have a fairly even climate year-round. There are no seasons comparable with the four that westerners are familiar with, and you do not get the extremes of winter and summer as you do in Europe or some parts of Asia, such as China and northern India.

Indonesians distinguish between a wet season and a dry season. In most parts of Indonesia the wet season falls between October and April, and the dry season between May and September. In some parts you don't really notice the difference – the dry season just seems to be slightly hotter and not quite so wet as the wet season; moreover the rain comes in sudden tropical downpours. In other parts – like Maluku – you really do notice the additional water; it rains almost nonstop and travelling during this period becomes more than difficult.

The Indonesians may tell you it gets cold in their country – you'll often see them running around in long-sleeved shirts and even winter coats in the stifling heat! In fact it's invariably hot and generally humid during the day and warm during the night. Once you get up into the hills and mountains the temperature drops dramatically – in the evenings and during the night it can be amazingly cold! Camp out at night atop Gunung Rinjani on Lombok without a sleeping bag, and you'll be as stiff as those wood carvings they sell on Bali. Sleeping out at night on the deck of a small boat or ship can also be bitterly cold, no matter how oppressive the

heat may be during the day. You don't exactly need Antarctic survival gear, but bring jeans and some warm clothes. There is a 'cold season' if you want to call it that, mainly July and August, but you're only likely to notice it in the 'deep south' (about 10° south of the equator) and, again, mostly in the highlands.

At the other end of the thermometer, an hour's walk along Kuta Beach on Bali in the middle of the day will roast you a nice bright red – bring a hat, sunglasses and some sunscreen (UV) lotion.

See the climate charts of Pulau Ambon, Denpasar, Balikpapan, Dili, Jakarta and Danau (Lake) Toba in this section.

Java

Across the island the temperature throughout the year averages 22°C to 29°C (72°F to 84°F) and humidity averages a high 75%, but the north coastal plains are usually hotter, up to 34°C (94°F) during the day in the dry season, and more oppressively humid than anywhere else. Generally the south coast is a bit cooler than the north coast, and the mountainous regions inland are very much cooler.

The wet season is from October to the end of April, so the best time to visit the island is during the dry season from May to September. The rain comes as a tropical downpour, falling most afternoons during the wet season and intermittently at other times of the year. The heaviest rains are usually around January-February. Regional variations occur – West Java is wetter than East Java, and the mountain regions receive a lot more rainfall. The highlands of West Java average over 4000 mm (156 inches) of rain a year, while the north-east coastal tip of East Java has a rainfall of only 900 mm (35 inches).

Bali

Here it is much like Java: the dry season is between April and September. The coolest months of the year are generally May, June

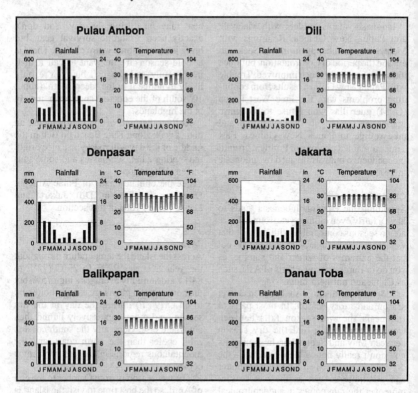

and July, with the average temperature around 28˚C (82˚F). The rainy season is between October and March but the tropical showers alternate with clear skies and sunshine; the hottest months of the year are generally February and March, with the average temperature around 30˚C (86˚F).

Overall, the best time to visit the island is in the dry and cooler months between May and August, with cool evenings and fresh breezes coming in off the sea.

Sumatra

The climate here resembles that of Java and is hot and extremely humid. The equator cuts this island into two roughly equal halves and, since the winds of northern Sumatra differ from those of the rest of the archipelago, so

does the timing of the seasons – though temperatures remain pretty constant year-round. North of the equator the heaviest rainfall is between October and April, and the dry season is from May to September. South of the equator the heaviest rainfall is from December to February, though it will have started raining in September. Heavy rains can make bad roads impassable.

Nusa Tenggara

In the islands east of Bali the seasonal differences are more pronounced. The driest months are August and September, and the wettest months are from November to February. However, the duration of the seasons varies from island to island. The seasons on Lombok are more like those on Bali, with a dry season from April to September and a wet season from October to March. Much the same applies to Sumbawa and Flores. The duration of the dry season increases the closer you get to Australia – the rusty landscapes of Sumba and Timor are a sharp contrast to well-vegetated Flores. At 11° south latitude, Timor is also the only island in Indonesia far enough from the equator to get typhoons (cyclones), but these are rare. Nearby northern Australia is not so lucky.

Sulawesi

The wettest months here tend to be from around November-December to March-April, but in central and northern Sulawesi the rainfall seems to be a bit more evenly spread throughout the year. In the mountainous regions of central Sulawesi, even in the dry season it may rain by late afternoon – likewise in the northern peninsula. The south-eastern peninsula is the driest part of the island.

Temperatures drop quite considerably going from the lowlands to the mountains. Average temperatures along the coast range from around 26°C to 30°C (79°F to 86°F), but in the mountains the average temperature drops by 5°C.

Except in south-western Sulawesi and the Minahasa region of the north (or in odd places where foreign mining companies operate), the wet season turns the mostly unsurfaced roads into excruciatingly frustrating vehicle-bogging mud. It makes travel by road in some parts of the island either impossible or tedious at these times. There's some improvement being made to the roads so check out the current situation when you get there – be prepared to fly, skirt the coast on ships or even do some walking.

Kalimantan

It's permanently hot and damp; the wettest period is from October to March and the driest period is from July to September. Although the sun predominates between April and September be prepared for heavy tropical downpours during this period.

Maluku

Maluku is the main exception to the climate rule in Indonesia. While the wet season everywhere else is from October to April, in central Maluku the wet season is from April through to July and may even carry on to the end of August. Travelling in Maluku during the wet is more difficult; the sea is rougher, inter-island connections are fewer and heavy rainfall can interrupt travel plans. The best time to visit is from September to March.

Maluku does have regional variations. Northern and central Maluku does not have an exclusive dry season and rainfall occurs throughout the year, and it is much drier in the south. Aru in far south-eastern Maluku has its wet season from September to April.

Irian Jaya

Irian Jaya is hot and humid in the northern coastal regions. In the highlands it's warm by day but can get very cold by night – and the higher you go the colder it gets! August and September in the highlands will be gloomy and misty. In the northern part of Irian Jaya, May to October is the drier season and May is the hottest month. Southern Irian Jaya has a much more well-defined dry season than the northern part of the island, and Merauke has a more distinct dry season from April to October.

ECOLOGY & ENVIRONMENT

Indonesia has a rapidly industrialising economy, a large and growing population putting a strain on resources, and is poor. All these point to ecological degradation in a country that does not have the resources to give environmental issues high priority. Nevertheless, there are environmental protection programmes in place in Indonesia, but typically they are poorly funded and enforcement is difficult or ignored.

Despite widespread logging, and development encroaching on the jungle, Indonesia still has large forest reserves representing 10% of the world's remaining tropical rainforest. The government policy of selective logging and reafforestation is all but ignored, and the forests are disappearing at anywhere up to one million hectares per year. The government has plans to control log exports to keep logging at a sustainable level by the year 2000, but it remains to be seen if this will be effectively implemented.

As the economy booms, industrial pollution is multiplying, mostly in the cities of Java. The use and search for more power has environmental impacts, and Indonesia is looking at nuclear power to solve its energy problems. The increasing wealth of the middle classes has seen the number of new motor vehicles increase dramatically, and along with it vehicle emissions.

As Indonesia becomes more urbanised – over 30% of Indonesians now live in cities compared to 15% in 1970 – more strains are put on the urban environment. Waste removal services have difficulty coping with the garbage, household and industrial, but the worst threat to living standards is the lack of decent sewerage. Very few cities have a sewerage system and rely on septic tanks or disposal of effluent through the canals and river systems. This in turn is a major source of pollution to water resources. Most Indonesians are simply not supplied with safe drinking water, and all water has to be boiled.

FLORA & FAUNA

Indonesia has one of the world's richest natural environments, harbouring an incredible diversity of plant and animal species. Lying across such a large area, Indonesia includes regions of separate natural history and unique ecosystems.

The British naturalist Alfred Wallace in his classic study *The Malay Archipelago* first classified the Indonesian islands into two zones – a western, Asian ecological zone and an eastern, Australian zone. The 'Wallace Line' dividing these two zones ran at the edge of the Sunda shelf between Kalimantan and Sulawesi, and south through the straits between Bali and Lombok. West of this line, Indonesian flora and fauna shows great similarities to that of the rest of Asia, while to the east the islands gradually become drier and the flora and fauna more like Australia. Later scientists have further expanded on

this classification to show distinct breaks between the ecologies of Sulawesi and Maluku, and further between Maluku and Irian Jaya.

Greater Sunda Islands
(Sumatra, Java, Kalimantan & Bali)

The western part of the country comprising Sumatra, Java, Kalimantan and Bali, lying on the Sunda shelf and known as the Greater Sunda Islands, was once linked to the Asian mainland. As a result some large Asian land animals, including elephants, tigers, rhinoceros and leopards, still survive, and the dense rainforests and abundant flora of Asia are in evidence.

Perhaps the most famous animal is the orang-utan ('man of the forest' in Indonesian), the long-haired red apes found only on Sumatra and Kalimantan. The Orang-utan Rehabilitation Centre in North Sumatra provides easy access to see orang-utans in their natural setting, as does the centre at the Tanjung Puting National Park on Kalimantan. Kalimantan is also home to the proboscis monkey, identified by its pendulous, almost

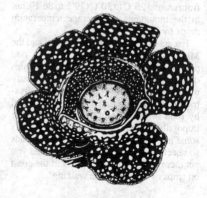

The rafflesia is the world's largest flower and the largest of the species is Sumatra's *Rafflesia arnoldii*. For much of its life the rafflesia lies hidden in the base of jungle vines until the hard bud bursts through the host plant and rapidly develops its huge cauldron flower. Pollinated by flies, it is a carrion plant, preying on insects.

comical nose. Various species of the graceful gibbon also exist throughout the Greater Sundas, as do other common varieties of primate.

Elephants are not numerous, but they still exist in the wild on Sumatra and can be seen at the Way Kambas Reserve in Sumatra's Lampung Province. Kalimantan also has a few wild elephants in the north-east, but they are very rare and probably introduced.

The magnificent tiger once roamed freely throughout Asia, and existed in large numbers on Sumatra, Java and Bali. A few places on Java and Bali claim to be the last refuge of the tiger on those islands, but tigers in Indonesia are now known only to exist on Sumatra. Leopards (the black leopard or panther is more common in South-East Asia) are also rare but exist on Sumatra and in Java's Ujung Kulon National Park. This park is also home to the rare, almost extinct one horned Javan rhinoceros. Rhinos have not fared well in Indonesia and the two horned variety, found on Sumatra, is also on the endangered species list.

Of all Indonesia's flora, the most spectacular is the rafflesia, the world's largest flower growing up to one metre in diameter. This parasitic plant is found primarily on Sumatra, but smaller versions are found on Kalimantan and Java.

The rainforests are also disappearing at an alarming rate. The mighty dipterocarp forests of Kalimantan are being logged ferociously, prized as they are for their durable tropical hardwoods, such as ironwood. Sumatran forests are also being logged and cleared as the jungle is pushed back for new settlements; however, both Sumatra and Kalimantan present some of the best opportunities in Indonesia to explore rainforest environments. The landscapes of crowded and heavily cultivated Java and Bali are dominated by wet-rice cultivation, but natural forest remains in national parks and in some remote mountain regions.

Irian Jaya & Aru Islands

Irian Jaya and the Aru Islands were once part of the Australian land mass and lie on the Sahul shelf. The collision between the Australian and Pacific plates resulted in a massive mountain range running along the middle of Irian Jaya, isolating a number of unique environments, but the fauna throughout is closely related to Australia. Irian Jaya is the only part of Indonesia to have kangaroos, marsupial mice, bandicoots and ring-tailed possums, all marsupials found in Australia. Aussie reptiles include crocodiles and frilled lizards. While the south is much drier, the mountain regions and the north are covered with dense rainforest and the flora includes Asiatic and endemic species. Irian Jaya has over 600 species of birds, the most well known being the cassowary and bird of paradise species.

The isolated Aru Islands, though administratively part of Maluku, share a common evolution with and are more closely related to Irian Jaya.

Sulawesi, Nusa Tenggara & Maluku

Lying between the two shelves, the islands of Sulawesi, Nusa Tenggara (also known as the Lesser Sunda Islands) and Maluku have long been isolated from the Continental land masses, and have developed unique flora and fauna.

Endemic to Sulawesi is the anoa, or dwarf buffalo, a wallowing animal which looks like a cross between a deer and a cow, standing only about 80 cm high. The babirusa (deer pig) has great curving tusks that come out the side of the mouth and through the top of the snout. The bulbous beaked hornbills are some of Indonesia's most spectacular birds and are often considered sacred. They are found throughout most of the Greater Sundas as well as Sulawesi, but the enggang Sulawesi, or Buton hornbill, with its brightly coloured beak and neck, is one of the most spectacular of the species.

Sulawesi is noted for its ebony, and teak is another export wood.

Maluku shows similarities with Sulawesi, but with fewer species of flora and fauna. The babirusa and smaller mammals are found, as are some primates, but it seems most of the migratory waves passed Maluku by. It is noted for its butterflies (Pulau Seram has reported some enormous species) and bird life, particularly the nuri raja, or Amboina king parrot (a large, magnificently coloured parrot).

The Wallace Line separates Lombok, the westernmost island of Nusa Tenggara, from Bali. From East Lombok eastwards, the flora and fauna of Nusa Tenggara reflect the more arid conditions of these islands. The large Asian mammals are nonexistent on Lombok, and in Nusa Tenggara mammal species in general are smaller and less diverse. Asian bird species diminish further east and Australian birds are found on the eastern islands. Nusa Tenggara has one astonishing and famous animal, the Komodo dragon, the world's largest lizard, found only on the island of Komodo and a few neighbouring islands.

East Timor is noted for its displays of sandalwood, the scented wood used in woodcarving and the manufacture of the perfumed oil.

National Parks

Although environmentalists have blasted Indonesia's government for its logging and transmigration development schemes, it's only fair to mention that the past decade has seen a rapid increase in the number of national parks, nature reserves and historical sites. While it's true that loggers, farmers and hunters have even violated national parks, there has been a sincere effort to enforce the rules – no easy task in a country with so much sparsely inhabited jungle.

The Indonesian national park service, Perlindungan Hutan dan Pelestarian Alam (PHPA), maintains information offices at various points around the country, including posts in the national parks and some reserves.

Sumatra Sumatra has some excellent national parks, Gunung Leuser being the most accessible and rewarding. Covering almost 10,000 sq km, this park contains the Orangutan Rehabilitation Centre at Bukit Lawang on its eastern flank, and from there and Berastagi it is easy to arrange treks into the park.

The Bukit Barisan Selatan National Park in southern Sumatra is difficult to reach, but contains varied flora from coastal to rainforest and large mammal species, including tigers, elephants and tapirs. Way Kambas National Park in Lampung Province is noted for its elephants, which are protected in the park but also exploited in an elephant training show. Lembah Anai Nature Reserve between Bukittinggi and Padang is known for its rafflesia.

Komodo Dragon *(Varanus komodoensisi)* – the world's largest lizard grows up to three metres long and weighs over 140 kg. It is only found on the islands of Komodo, Rinca and Padar near Flores in Nusa Tenggara. Known locally as the 'ora', the komodo uses its powerful tail to stun victims and its split yellow tongue is an olfactory organ, used to sniff out prey. These days the komodo's favourite meal is goat, but humans have also ended up on the komodo menu.

Java The pick of Java's national parks is Ujung Kulon on the south-west tip of the island. Though not easy to reach, it has superb coastal scenery, lush rainforest and coral reefs, and is home to the almost extinct Javan rhinoceros and leopards.

In complete contrast, Baluran National Park, on the dry north-eastern tip of Java, is one of the most easily visited parks in Indonesia, with grasslands reminiscent of Africa or Australia. This drive-in park is noted for its buffaloes, benteng, deer and bird life.

Bromo-Tengger-Semeru National Park is justly famous for its spectacular volcanic craters and Mt Bromo is one of Java's main attractions. For mountain climbers, the park also contains Java's highest peak, Mt Semeru.

Pangandaran National Park, being on the doorstep of a popular beach resort, receives many visitors. Wildlife includes benteng, deer and Javan gibbons and this coastal headland park has good jungle walks. In the mountains south of Jakarta, Gunung Gede-Pangrango National Park is another for volcano climbing through submontane forest. One of Java's most spectacular walks is to the active crater lake of Kawah Ijen in the plateau reserve near Banyuwangi in East Java. East Java also has some fine coastal parks, Alas Purwo and Meru Betiri, but access is very difficult. Pulau Dua, off the north coast near Banten, is a major sanctuary for coastal sea birds.

Bali Bali Barat National Park takes up a significant chunk of the western part of the island. Most of the park is savanna, with coastal mangroves and more tropical vegetation in the southern highlands. Over 200 species of plant inhabit the various environments, and animals include monkeys, deer, muncaks, squirrels, wild pigs, buffaloes, iguanas, pythons and green snakes. The bird life is prolific, with many of Bali's 300 species represented.

Nusa Tenggara Gunung Rinjani, at 3726m, is the highest mountain in Indonesia outside Irian Jaya, and dominates the island of Lombok. It is a very popular three to five day trek to the top, and the huge crater contains a large green crescent-shaped lake, Segara Anak, six km across at its widest point. Some 40,000 hectares of Rinjani's slopes are protected forest.

Two-thirds of Pulau Moyo, off the coast just north of Sumbawa Besar, is a nature reserve with savanna and some forest. Good coral reefs are at the southern end of the island.

The mostly dry, savanna Komodo National Park encompasses much of Komodo and the Rinca islands, and is home to Indonesia's most famous beastie, the Komodo dragon. The islands also have coral reefs.

In Flores, the three coloured lakes of Keli Mutu, one of Indonesia's most impressive sights, is a protected reserve managed by the PHPA.

Kalimantan Tanjung Puting is Kalimantan's national park, famous for its Camp Leakey urang-utan rehabilitation centre. Encompassing 3050 sq km of tropical rainforest, mangrove forest and wetlands, it is home to a vast variety of fauna, including crocodiles, hornbills, wild pigs, bear cats, crab-eating macaques, orang-utans, proboscis monkeys, gibbons, pythons, dolphins, mudskippers (a kind of fish that can walk and breathe on land!) and the dragon fish (a rare and valuable aquarium fish).

Kutai National Park in East Kalimantan is a strange mixture of national park and logging zone. The hardwood forests contain orang-utans, gibbons and leaf monkeys, but this park is difficult to reach and facilities are minimal. Tangkiling National Park is another nature reserve, 35 km north of Palangkaraya.

Sulawesi Lore Lindu in Central Sulawesi is a remote but untouched national park, rich in exotic plants and animal life. It is also home to several indigenous tribes, has ancient megalithic relics and great trekking, as well as a couple of mountains for peak bagging.

Sulawesi's other major park is Dumoga-Bone National Park in North Sulawesi, a watershed area with intact forest, but it is less interesting than Lore Lindu. Sulawesi has some good reserves. Tangkoko Reserve, 30 km from Bitung, is home to black apes, anoas, babirusas and maleo birds (the maleo looks like a huge hen and lays eggs five times the size of a hen's). The reserve also includes the coastline and coral gardens offshore. The Morowali Reserve in Central Sulawesi is good for treks that can be organised out of Kolondale. Wildlife includes maleo birds.

Sulawesi's most famous natural attractions are its coral reefs, and the government is developing conservation zones in some areas. The easily accessible, fabulous reefs of Pulau Bunaken are famous, and the Togian Islands also have some fine reefs for snorkelling and diving.

Maluku Manusela National Park, forming a large chunk of Seram's centre, comprises remote mountain regions, and sandy beaches and coral off the north coast. Access is not easy and facilities are limited, but it is possible to organise treks within the park.

The coral reefs of the beautiful Banda Islands are protected and the islands have been declared a marine reserve.

Irian Jaya With some effort you can visit two national reserves on Pulau Biak, the Lorentz Nature Reserve near Agats, the Wasur National Park near Merauke, the Wondiwoi Mountain Reserve and a marine reserve in the Cenderawasih Bay, and a reserve which covers most of the island of Pulau Yos Sudarso off the coast of Merauke.

The Baliem Valley is the main area for trekking in Irian Jaya.

GOVERNMENT & POLITICS

The ruling party is Golkar, which officially is not a political party but is designed to be an all-things-to-all-people 'group' representing wide interests inside and outside of government. One of the major interests that it represents is the army.

The opposition, what there is of it, is a two

party system resulting from the forced amalgamation of opposition parties in the 1970s to form the Partai Persatuan Pembangunan (PPP), representing Islamic groups, and Partai Demokrasi Indonesia (PDI), Soekarno's old party which became an amalgam of nationalists, Christians and 'the rest'.

Opposition parties must accept the national ideology of Pancasila (see the boxed aside in this section). The government has the power to decide the opposition parties' policies, leaders and election candidates. The opposition is not allowed to destabilise the government by criticising it, the media is tightly controlled and Golkar, as the government party, has enormous resources to put into its election campaigns. Not surprisingly, the government wins elections by handsome majorities, typically capturing around 70% of the vote.

Elections are held every five years to elect 425 of the 500 members of the House of Representatives. The other 75 members are appointed by the armed forces. This is the real house of government, proposing and passing government legislation. It is divided into permanent committees which carry out the day-to-day business of government.

The highest political institution is the People's Consultative Congress (MPR), which is composed of all the members of the House of Representatives along with 500 appointees representing various groups and regions – the armed forces and Golkar are again well represented. In theory, the congress is the supreme ruling body, but it seldom meets and the main function of this stacked house is to elect the president, ratify changes to the constitution and make sure the army has the numbers to force its will if need be. The congress also elects the vice-president and in 1993, General Try Sutrisno, the army's preferred candidate, was given the nod as the successor to the top job after Soeharto.

Executive power rests with the president, who is head of state and holds office for a period of five years. The president appoints cabinet ministers, and this inner sanctum is the core of government power in Indonesia.

Regional Government

Though national policy, international wranglings and the multimillion dollar deals are the preserve of the central government, for most Indonesians Jakarta is far removed and real government is at the district or village level.

Politically, Indonesia is divided into 27 provinces, including the three special territories of Aceh, Jakarta and Yogyakarta. Java has five provinces: Jakarta, West Java, Central Java, Yogyakarta and East Java. Sumatra has eight: Aceh, North Sumatra, West Sumatra, Riau, Jambi, Bengkulu, South Sumatra and Lampung. Kalimantan has West, Central, South and East provinces. Sulawesi has North, Central, South and South-Eastern provinces. Other provinces are: Bali, West Nusa Tenggara (Lombok and Sumbawa), East Nusa Tenggara (Sumba, West Timor, Flores and the Solor and Alor archipelagos), East Timor, Maluku and Irian Jaya.

Each province has its own political legislature, headed by a governor, with extensive powers to administer the province. The 27 provinces are further broken down into 241 *kabupaten* (districts) headed by a *bupati* (district head) and 56 *kotamadya* (municipalities) headed by a *walikota* (mayor). The districts are further broken down into 3625 *kecamatan* (subdistricts), each headed by a *camat* (subdistrict head). Kecamatan are further broken down into *kelurahan*, or village groupings.

Each level of government has its own bureaucracy, often with overlapping functions. For example, in one city you may find

---

Pancasila

Since it was first expounded by Soekarno in 1945 the Pancasila (Five Principles) have remained the philosophical backbone of the Indonesian state. It was meant by Soekarno to provide a broad philosophical base on which a united Indonesian state could be formed. All over Indonesia you'll see the Indonesian coat of arms with its symbolic incorporation of the Pancasila, hung on the walls of government offices and the homes of village heads, on the covers of student textbooks or immortalised on great stone tablets. These principles are:

1. *Faith in God* – symbolised by the star. This is perhaps the most important and contentious principle. As interpreted by Soekarno and the Javanese syncretists who have ruled Indonesia since independence, this can mean any god – Allah, Vishnu, Buddha, Christ etc. For many Muslims, it means belief in the only true God, Allah, but the government goes to great lengths to suppress both Islamic extremism and calls for an Islamic state in multi-ethnic and multireligious Indonesia.

2. *Humanity* – symbolised by the chain. This represents the unbroken unity of humankind, and Indonesia takes its place among this family of nations.

3. *Nationalism* – symbolised by the head of the buffalo. All ethnic groups in Indonesia must unite.

4. *Representative government* – symbolised by the banyan tree. As distinct from the western brand of parliamentary democracy, Soekarno envisaged a form of Indonesian democracy based on the village system of deliberation *(permusyawaratan)* among representatives to achieve consensus *(mufakat)*. The western system of 'majority rules' is considered a means by which 51% oppress the other 49%.

5. *Social justice* – symbolised by sprays of rice and cotton. A just and prosperous society gives adequate supplies of food and clothing for all – these are the basic requirements of social justice. ■

three or more separate tourist offices – a provincial government tourist office, a district tourist office, a city tourist office and regional representatives of the central government. Between them they may employ dozens if not hundreds of people, and still not be able to produce a decent map or intelligible brochure. Government is Indonesia's major employer, and it's a major frustration if you have to deal with it.

But despite this extended hierarchy of government, often the most relevant level of government is at village level. In the *desa* or *kampung*, the day-to-day running of the village, neighbourhood disputes and local affairs are handled as they always have been. The village elects a *lurah* or *kepala desa* (village chief), though often the position of kepala desa is virtually hereditary, falling in the same family and passed from father to son, even extending back to some long since defunct Hindu principality when the kepala desa was *rajah* (king). The kepala desa is the government representative at the most basic level, and the person to see if you wander into a village and need to spend the night or resolve a problem.

The village is the main social unit, providing welfare, support and guidance. If a fire destroys a house or a village needs a new well, then everyone pitches in. This grassroot system of mutual help and discussion is usually presided over by a traditional council of elders, but there are also village organisations or government representatives to carry out government policies and campaigns on economic development, population control, health etc. One of the main community organisations is the *rukun tetangga*, which organises neighbourhood security (every village and kampung has a security post – *pos kamling*), and the registration of families and new arrivals.

Armed Forces

Though Soeharto prefers a civilian image, and the present cabinet contains few military men, political power ultimately lies with the army. Military personnel, both former and present, are widely represented in government and in business, and, though the government rules with a degree of independence not always to the military's liking, when push comes to shove the military dominates.

The military influence in Indonesian culture is instantly noticeable. Paramilitary uniforms abound, from government employees to parking attendants, and Indonesians love to march – school children drill even on their days off. Since the military-backed government came to power in 1965, the glorification of the military has increased but it existed long before Soeharto came to power.

The Indonesian military psyche developed during WWII when the Japanese organised village militia to defend Indonesia in the event of reoccupation. When the Dutch returned, independence was gained only after a bloody battle of village armies united under the banner of the new republic. Indonesian freedom fighters became heroes, and their leaders' names adorn Indonesian streets, their exploits are endlessly retold in schools and their homes have become museums. Indonesia's history has become a military one, and even the most obscure leaders of ancient, easily crushed peasant rebellions have become national heroes. The military has been a part of the political process since independence, and it hardly regards itself as having usurped power that somehow 'rightfully' belongs to civilians.

Under Soekarno's guided democracy the military's powers and aspirations intensified. In 1958 General Nasution, chief of staff of the army, expounded the doctrine of *dwifungsi* (dual function) to justify the army's expanded role in Soekarno's government after the establishment of martial law. This stated that the army not only played a security role and was responsible to the government, but it also had to play an independent social and political role as 'one of the many forces in society'.

At this time the army developed a national defence policy based on the army, since the navy and air force would never be strong

President Soeharto

Soeharto was born in 1921 and spent his childhood amongst peasants in small villages in Central Java and on Solo, his father ensuring that he got a primary and middle school education. The time he spent from the age of 15 living in the house of a *dukun* (faith healer) appears to have imbued him with a sense of traditional Javanese mysticism which has lasted to this day. He joined the Royal Dutch Indies Army in 1940 and quickly became a sergeant. He served with the Japanese during the occupation and became an officer in the Japanese-sponsored Volunteer Army of Defenders of the Motherland. He led attacks against the Dutch during the independence struggle after WWII and rose rapidly through the ranks.

In 1962 he was promoted to major-general by Soekarno and was put in charge of the forces which were set up to take West Irian from the Dutch. In 1961 he became commander of the army's Strategic Reserve (later to be known as KOSTRAD). This was an important posting because the reserve, set up by the chief of staff of the army, General Nasution, was a well-equipped, highly mobile fighting force directly at the disposal of the top generals, thus avoiding any argument or even outright opposition from regional commanders.

Just why Soeharto took the role of overthrowing Soekarno is unclear – perhaps it was personal ambition, a reaction to the attempted coup, unease at the growing strength of the PKI, a reaction to the deterioration of the economy under Soekarno or a mixture of all four. Certainly Soeharto cut through his opponents with exceptional determination.

Soeharto has shown himself to be remarkably resilient. His rule is certainly not unopposed but he has continually sought to reaffirm his authority and has successfully met any challenges. In recent years, the main threat to his position has come from the army, and Soeharto is keen to promote greater civilian power in government at the expense of the military. An interesting trend is that Soeharto has been sounding more and more Islamic, and made his first-ever pilgrimage to Mecca in 1991. Despite extolling secularism and suppressing Islamic fundamentalism throughout his career (as is the army line), he has been seen to court the Muslim lobby to counterfoil the military.

Exactly who will succeed Soeharto and what tack Indonesia will take after him are the burning political questions. One thing is certain – Soeharto, and his relatives, have become very rich since he came to power. In Soeharto's 1989 autobiography, the president stated that his family's financial dealings were simply 'social work'. Being president of Indonesia is like riding a tiger – as the succession problem looms, unless Soeharto dies in the saddle, his real problem is to make sure he doesn't get eaten when he steps down.

As the 1998 elections loom, speculation as to whether Soeharto will retire continues. Though he has hinted at retirement, the wily Soeharto is keeping the nation guessing. ∎

enough to block an invasion, and only the army could continue, in the last resort, an indefinite guerrilla struggle. To be successful in such a war the army would have to be accepted and supported by the people, and so the army would need to establish contacts with the people at a local level to build up and sustain their goodwill. Thus developed the idea and the subsequent implementation of 'Territorial Management', a parallel administration down to village level where resident army personnel could supervise and prod the civil authorities.

After the 1965 coup the army became not just one of many, but the dominant force in society. Today the military still plays its dwifungsi role, with a civilianised government leading the country, but the military is the major behind-the-scenes player. However, as Indonesia slowly becomes more open politically, the government becomes more noticeably civilian and a nouveau riche and powerful middle class develops, the question being asked is: 'In these stable times, who needs the military?'. 'The people' is the military's answer, and it shows no signs of relinquishing its power. If anything, the military has indicated that it wants to play a stronger role in post-Soeharto Indonesia.

ECONOMY

Indonesia is part of the world's fastest developing economic region, and the Indonesian economy is bounding along with an annual growth rate of over 6%, a rate it has averaged for over 20 years. Jakarta is the centre for this economic boom and the signs of wealth are stamped all over the city – towering new office developments, freeways, multistorey shopping centres, thousands of imported luxury cars and horrendous traffic jams.

Away from the glossy business centre, Jakarta also has the worst slums in the country, and most of the city is without sewerage and a decent water supply – and therein lies the dilemma of Indonesia's economy. The economy is booming, but with its huge population and the strain on resources, Indonesia is still one of the poorest countries in South-East Asia. Furthermore, while the statistics show that life for the average Indonesian is getting better each year, the disparity between rich and poor grows even faster. Indonesia's middle class, earning over US$30,000 per year, is estimated to be over 20 million people, but many workers – those lucky enough to have a job – earn less than US$2 per day and the average per capita income is still only US$650.

The mainstay and saviour of the Indonesian economy for many years has been oil and gas. During the 1970s and early 1980s, the majority of export earnings came from oil, but the mid-1980s slump in oil prices saw a concerted effort to increase non-oil exports, particularly manufacturing. Oil and gas exports still account for over US$10 billion annually, about one-third of all exports. Other major exports are timber and wood products (Indonesia is the world's biggest supplier of plywood), tin, coal, copper and bauxite, and substantial cash crops like rubber, coffee, copra and fishing. Helped by increased foreign investment, Indonesia has a rapidly developing light industrial base and is now a major producer of textiles and clothing, and is a growing exporter of footwear, chemicals, fertilisers, cement and glassware. Tourism is also a growth industry, with Indonesia looking to increase the three million plus visitors to five million within the next few years.

New Order Economy

During the Soeharto era, the Indonesian economy has largely been governed by an alliance between army leaders and western-educated economists. Rigorous economic measures were taken in the first years of the regime designed to get Indonesia back on its feet after the economic mismanagement of the Soekarno years. Sufficiently large cuts were made in government expenditure to balance the budget; the plunge of the rupiah was halted; rice prices were kept temporarily in check by establishing a reserve which reduced speculation; inflation was dramatically reduced; and there was some success in stabilising the price of other basic commodities.

Under Soeharto's rule the Planning Body for National Development (Bappenas) has implemented a series of five year development plans, called Repelita, designed to rehabilitate and improve the economy.

Riding on the back of oil exports, Indonesian business grew up behind a protective wall of barriers. Import and export monopolies were granted to favoured clients, tariffs kept out imports, restrictions were placed on foreign ownership, and the government had monopoly control over key industries like banking, oil refining, airlines, telecommunications etc. These measures were supposedly designed to protect the economy.

Instead, these rules gave birth to a bungling and corrupt bureaucracy. Protected industries like banks were so inefficient they could charge usurious interest rates. Keeping out foreign investment meant Indonesia had to instead seek foreign loans to develop its own industries, resulting in a build-up of debt. High import taxes and government-sanctioned import monopolies meant Indonesian companies found the cost of foreign-made components so high that they couldn't develop export industries. Export monopolies meant that coffee farmers, for example, could look forward to low prices while the exporter got rich.

From the late 1980s onwards there has been a change in attitudes, and deregulation is the word. The banking industry was thrown open to foreign joint ventures, helping to spur investment. Import monopolies have been mostly eliminated, resulting in lower prices to consumers and export-oriented manufacturers. Rules on stock trading were liberalised in 1989, and 100% foreign ownership is now allowed in some industries. As a result, foreign money has started pouring in, much of it to Jakarta, Java and the island of Batam, a free-trade zone 20 km south of Singapore. The government still controls many enterprises, but privatisation is gaining speed.

All this has spurred economic growth in the past few years. The negative side of the coin is that privatisation and deregulation are a boon for middle-class investors with the capital to invest (especially if they have good government contacts), but the flow on to Indonesia's have-nots is painfully slow, if it reaches them at all. Indonesia's brave new economic world also has plenty of stories of corruption and incompetence. Banks have gone bust amid embezzlement and graft scandals, and while positive long-term investment is helping the country, non-productive speculation appealing to get-rich-quick merchants is also in evidence.

However, Indonesia's approach to freeing up the economy has been relatively cautious. Many tariffs remain and the government maintains some controls on foreign invest-ment and borrowing. Despite a large foreign debt, high interest rates, an everpresent inflation rate of around 10% and the obvious problems confronting a developing country, Indonesia's long-term economic future is destined to be one of continuing improvement.

Poverty & Prospects for the Future

Government-sponsored programmes enabled Indonesia's rice production to become self-sufficient by 1982, and thus reduce risky dependency on food imports. While this was a significant step forward, attempts to alleviate poverty have met with a mixed bag of successes and failures.

To help assure access to essential goods, both the Soekarno and the Soeharto governments operated a nationwide system of subsidies and price controls for necessities, including rice, wheat, sugar, cooking kerosene and gasoline. Increasing financial stringency in recent years has forced cutbacks on subsidies, plus the recognition that low prices hurt production. The free market is being given a freer hand, but the adjustments will be painful.

Health care has received high priority with considerable expansion in the number of health centres, and a noticeable drop in the infant mortality rate. Education also has a high priority and nearly all children have access to primary schooling. However, many drop out early, there is a shortage of qualified teachers and, in rural areas, the quality of education doesn't ensure that the majority of children will leave school literate.

The establishment of new industries and increased employment opportunities has occurred mostly in the cities, but Indonesia's population is still overwhelmingly rural, with a large proportion working on small farms. The average Indonesian farm labourer gets by on very little. Unemployed rural residents tend to migrate to the cities in search of the elusive pot of gold, but with poor education and skills they often wind up as squatters in the slums of Jakarta and other cities.

The lack of protective legislation and free unions or other organisations to defend workers has seen Indonesia's labour record come increasingly under attack, particularly from the USA. The government is keen to show that it is making progress, but resistance is still confined to sporadic outbursts of violence by disenfranchised workers and villagers, often with tragic consequences.

As elsewhere in developing countries, the rich get richer and the poor get children. Although initially a burden, children are regarded as an economic asset because they provide a form of social security for the parents, and birth rates are highest among the poor. The unfortunate result is that the fastest growing segment of the population is the least educated and least likely to succeed economically.

Although Indonesia is better off than it was 20 years ago, the fruits of this economic growth are very unevenly distributed. Yet somehow even the poorest of Indonesians show a remarkable resilience and capacity to survive. They sell food, clothing, plastic shoes, sit on the side of the street all day flogging off a few combs or a couple of bunches of bananas, or jump on crowded buses to hawk ice blocks, pineapple chunks or single cigarettes. They sift through garbage, recycle the tobacco from cigarette ends, pedal *becaks* (three wheeled bicycle-rickshaws), shine shoes, mind parked cars or scratch some of the money from the tourist industry as touts. And if they come home with nothing then their family or neighbours will help them to survive another day.

Rice Production

Although Indonesia produces a range of agricultural products, including exotic introductions from Latin America thanks to the early Spanish and Portuguese settlers, the staple produce remains rice.

With the exception of Bali and most of Java, plus a few much smaller patches across the archipelago, the soil is just as poor in Indonesia as it is elsewhere in the tropics. In sparsely populated areas of Sumatra, Kalimantan, Sulawesi and West Java, where the peasants moved from one place to another, a form of shifting cultivation *(ladang)* developed. In ladang cultivation, the jungle is burned off to speed up the normal process of decomposition and enrich the soil in preparation for planting, but the soil quickly loses its fertility. When the top cover of forest is removed, the intense heat and heavy rain soon leach the soil of its nutrients. As a result, settled agriculture is impossible without the continuous addition of soil nutrients.

On the other hand, the rich volcanic soils of most of Java, Bali and western Lombok have allowed wet rice, or *sawah*, cultivation in flooded rice fields. Rice cultivation in terraced sawah fields has been known for over 2000 years, the system being continually refined and developed, and is widely seen as a contributing factor to the development of the prolific civilisations on Java and later on Bali. The development of the fields, particularly in the highland areas where extensive terracing took place, required great organisation, either at a co-operative village level or through the suppression of a peasant work force.

The wonder of this method of agriculture is that sawah fields can keep producing two or even three crops a year, year after year, with little or no drop in soil fertility. The profundity of sawah fields cannot be attributed to soil fertility alone, however, for this astonishing ecosystem depends on the water to provide nutrients and the bacteria produced in the water which also aids the extraction of nitrogen. Other nutrients are provided by the remains of the previous crop, the addition of extra organic material and the aeration of the soil through water movement in the field.

After each harvesting of rice, the stubble from the crop is ploughed back into the field, traditionally using bullocks. Small carpets of the best rice seed are planted and, when ready, seedlings are prized apart and laboriously transplanted in even rows in an inundated field flooded to a few cm. The level of the water is crucial in the life cycle of the rice plant – the water is increased in depth as the plant grows and then slowly drained as harvest approaches, until the field is dry at harvest time. The field may also be drained during the growing period to weed the field or aerate the soil.

From 1968 the government has introduced schemes to improve productivity, such as the introduction of high-yield varieties of rice; however, the basic method of sawah farming has remained unchanged for generations. ∎

POPULATION & PEOPLE

Indonesia announced with great fanfare in 1997 that its population had reached 200 million. It is the world's fourth most populous nation after China, India and the USA. Java alone has almost 115 million people.

Indonesia's population is growing at a rate of about 1.7% per year. If it continues at that rate it will have 210 million people by the turn of the century and almost 400 million by 2035. Overpopulation, however, is largely a Javanese and, to some extent, a Balinese problem. Java's population was estimated as six million in 1825, 9.5 million in 1850, 18 million in 1875, 28 million in 1900, 36 million in 1925, 63 million in 1961 and 108 million in 1990.

Java and the island of Madura off Java's north coast have a total area of 130,000 sq km or about 1½ times the area of the UK. Java's population density is more than 800 people per sq km, more than twice that of either England or the Netherlands (the two most densely populated countries in Europe) and more than twice that of Japan. Population in Indonesia is very unevenly distributed, as can be seen from the last census (1990) figures. The following table reflects the percentages of total area and population:

Island(s)	Area (%)	Population (%)
Java	6.89	59.90
Sumatra	24.67	20.33
Sulawesi	9.85	6.98
Bali & Nusa Tenggara	4.61	5.67
Kalimantan	28.11	5.08
Maluku	3.88	1.03
Irian Jaya	21.99	0.92

Population Control

Each year two million people are added to the Indonesian population, most of them on Java. However, Indonesia's birth control programme is making inroads into population growth.

After taking power, Soeharto reversed Soekarno's policies of continued population expansion to provide a work force to develop the outer islands. He set up a National Family Planning Co-ordinating Board which greatly expanded the network of private clinics providing free contraceptive services. Efforts were concentrated on Bali and Java at first, and noticeable drops in the birth rate were reported. It was also reported that over 80% of the people who took part in the scheme were the wives of peasants, fisherpeople and labourers – the poorer end of the scale who normally have the most children. However, birth-control campaigns have been heeded more by better educated, urban families, and have been less successful in highly traditional and strongly Muslim areas. In poorer, isolated rural areas large families are still common.

The campaign has been most successful on Java, where many families are now firm believers in the slogan 'dua anak cukup' ('two children is enough'). As well as public awareness campaigns, coordinators are appointed at village level to advise on contraception, monitor birth rates and counsel, if not admonish, families that exceed two children.

Transmigration

As well as reducing the birth rate, attempts are also being made to take the pressure off heavily populated areas, particularly Java and Bali, by moving people out to less populated areas like Sumatra, Kalimantan, Irian Jaya and Maluku. These transmigrasi programmes started with Dutch efforts to relieve population pressure on Java in 1905. The Soeharto government's first Five Year Plan moved 182,000 people out of Java, Bali and Lombok – below target by only 8000. The second Five Year Plan aimed to move over a million people in the five years from 1974, but by 1976 the target figure had to be reduced by half. The third, fourth and fifth Five Year Plans ambitiously aimed at shifting 500,000, 750,000 and 550,000 families respectively – more than seven million people.

So far, however, the transmigrasi programmes seem to have had little effect on the population burden of Java. The main problem is that insufficient numbers of people can physically be moved to offset the growth in population. Furthermore, transmigration settlements have developed a poor reputation – one of the underlying faults has been the tendency to attempt wet-rice cultivation in unsuitable areas. Settlers have frequently ended up as subsistence farmers no better off than they were back on Java, if not because of poor soil and water then because of inadequate support services and isolation from markets.

In addition, most government-sponsored transmigrants are not experienced farmers; two-thirds of transmigrants are landless peasants, the poorest of the countryside, and another 10% are homeless city dwellers. Up until 1973 the urban poor of Jakarta were often virtually press-ganged into moving out of Java – they turned out to be the least successful transmigrants, often returning to the towns they came from. The most successful transmigrants are often those who move 'spontaneously' – because they emigrate on their own initiative to the outer islands and because they can choose where to live. Transmigration is a voluntary programme, but as officials strain to meet new targets there is increasing pressure on people to sign up.

Transmigration takes its toll on the natural environment through destruction of rainforest, loss of topsoil and degradation of water supplies. Tension, even conflict, with the indigenous people in some settled areas is not uncommon.

People

The rugged, mountainous terrain and the fact that the country is made up of many islands has separated groups of people from each other, resulting in an extraordinary differentiation of language and culture across the archipelago. Indonesians are divided – according to one classification – into approximately 300 ethnic groups which speak some 365 languages and dialects.

Indonesia's national motto is 'Bhinneka Tunggal Ika', an old Javanese phrase meaning 'They are many; they are one', which usually gets translated as 'Unity in diversity'. The peoples of the archipelago were not 'Indonesian' until 1949, when a line was drawn on the map enclosing a group of islands which housed a remarkably varied collection of people.

Most Indonesians are of Malay stock, descended from peoples who originated in China and Indochina, and spread into Indonesia over several thousand years. The other major grouping is the darker skinned, fuzzy-haired Melanesians who inhabit much of easternmost Indonesia.

Despite the Malay predominance, the culture and customs of the various islands are often quite different. There are different languages and dialects, different religions and differences in adat (the unwritten village law which regulates the behaviour of everyone in every village in Indonesia). The Indonesian terrain is partly responsible for the incredible diversity; mountains and jungles cut off tribes and groups on certain islands from the outside world – like the Kubu tribe of south Sumatra, thought to be descendants of the original settlers from Sri Lanka. They were barely known to outsiders until guerrillas fighting against the Dutch came into contact with them. Other isolated groups have included the Papuan Dani people of the Balim Valley in Irian Jaya, and the Dayaks – the collective name given to the people who inhabit the interior of Borneo. There are also the Badui of West Java, who withdrew to the highlands as the Islamic religion spread through the island and have had little contact with outsiders. Other distinctive groups, like the Balinese and Javanese, have had considerable contact with the outside world but nevertheless have managed to maintain their traditional cultures intact.

Of all the ethnic minorities in Indonesia, few have had a larger impact on the country than the Chinese, or 'overseas Chinese' as they are commonly known. Although comprising less than 3% of the population, the Chinese are the major force in the economy, operating everything from small shops, hotels and restaurants, to major banks and industries. The Chinese are by far the wealthiest ethnic group in the country, and there is much anti-Chinese resentment in Indonesia that sometimes threatens to boil over into a pogrom along the lines of the slaughter following the 1965 coup attempt, when many of the victims were Chinese.

Despite the diversity of peoples, cultures, languages and religions, and the inevitable conflicts that arise because of this diversity, Indonesia is surprisingly unified. When the republic was proclaimed, Indonesia was a group of hundreds of different societies, united through their subjection to Dutch colonialism, a tenuous reason upon which to build a nation. But Indonesia has done just that, through mass culture and prolonged campaigns, all conveyed through its national language, Bahasa Indonesia. Regional conflicts and loyalties remain, but the overwhelming majority of Indonesians now identify themselves proudly with their nation, flag and language.

EDUCATION

In Indonesia, education begins with six years of primary school (Sekolah Dasar or SD), then three years of junior high school (Sekolah Menengah Pertama or SMP) and three years of senior high school (Sekolah Menengah Atas or SMA), leading on to university. While school enrolments have risen to 90% for the seven to 12 year old age group, less than half will make it to secondary school and less than half again will graduate. Schooling is not free in Indonesia, not even at the primary level, though government schools charge only about 1200 rp per month. Unfortunately, many families cannot afford even this and send the children out to work rather than to school. The literacy rate is around 77%.

There are plenty of private schools, many operated by mosques and churches. Private schools generally have higher standards, and this is where the upper crust educate their children. Of course, private schools are more expensive.

Going to university is expensive and only a few can afford it. Higher education is concentrated on Java. No 1 and biggest in Indonesia is Universitas Indonesia (UI) in Jakarta, a government-run university. Yogya is Indonesia's main educational centre,

famous for its Universitas Gajah Mada. Bandung has the major high-tech school, Institut Teknologi Bandung (ITB). Lesser universities are located in the outlying provinces, such as Sulawesi's Universitas Hasanuddin (UNHAS) in Ujung Pandang.

ARTS

Indonesia has an astonishing array of cultures and all express themselves in different ways. The most readily identifiable arts are from Java and Bali. No travel documentary on Indonesia is complete without scenes of a *wayang kulit* (shadow puppet) performance or a Balinese dance, all performed to the haunting gongs and drums of the *gamelan* orchestra. Yet Java and Bali are only a small part of a vast archipelago, and Indonesia has an astonishing diversity of dance, music and especially crafts (see the colour Arts & Crafts section following this chapter).

Theatre

Javanese *wayang* (puppet) plays have their origins in the Hindu epics, the *Ramayana* and the *Mahabharata*. There are different forms of wayang: wayang kulit are the leather shadow puppets, *wayang golek* are the wooden puppets. A detailed discussion about wayang theatre can be found in the Java chapter.

Dance

If you spend much time in Jakarta or Bali's Kuta Beach, you could be forgiven if you thought that disco was Indonesia's traditional folk dance. But if you get out past the skyscrapers and tourist traps, you'll soon find that Indonesia has a rich heritage of traditional dance styles.

There are wayang dance dramas on Java. Yogyakarta has dance academies as well as its Ramayana Ballet, Java's most spectacular dance drama. Solo competes with Yogyakarta with its many academies of dance. Wonosobo (Central Java) has its Lengger dance, in which men dress as women. Jaipongan is a modern dance found in West

Java, with some erotic elements reminiscent of Brazil's Lambada.

Central Kalimantan has the Manasai, a friendly dance in which tourists are welcome to participate. Kalimantan also has the Mandau dance, performed with knives and shields.

Some of the most colourful performances of all, including the Barong, Kecak, Topeng, Legong and Baris dances, are found on Bali. For more information on these and other dances see the Bali chapter.

Music

Indonesia produces a lot of indigenous pop music, most of which does not suit western tastes. One thing you can be certain of is that Indonesians like their music *loud*.

Traditional gamelan orchestras are found primarily on Java and Bali. The orchestras are composed mainly of percussion instruments, including drums, gongs and shake-drums *(angklung)*, along with flutes and xylophones. See the Java chapter for more details.

Dangdut music is a very popular Indonesian modern music, characterised by wailing vocals and a strong beat. Though often attributed to Islamic Arabic influences, its roots lie in Indian pop music popularised by Hindi films. This is the music of Jakarta's kampungs, and is sometimes strongly Islamic in content. Seen as somewhat low class, it was popularised by performers such as Rhoma Irama back in the early 1980s and its popularity continues to grow and has spread across the nation.

Western rock music – both modern and vintage stuff from the 1960s – is also popular. Michael Jackson and the Rolling Stones have given concerts to packed audiences at the Senayan football stadium in south Jakarta.

One of Indonesia's rock idols is Iwan Fals and his band Kantata Takwa. Fals has a strong anti-establishment and anti-government bent; his songs have gotten him arrested several times. However, he always seems to get released fairly quickly, probably because his father is a general in the Indonesian army.

SOCIETY & CONDUCT

Indonesia is not one but hundreds of different societies and cultures. However, mass education, mass media and a policy of government-orchestrated nationalism have created a very definite Indonesian national culture, using Bahasa Indonesia as its medium.

Though Indonesia is predominantly Islamic, in many places Islam is infused with traditional customs and Hindu-Buddhism, making it barely recognisable from the more orthodox Middle East variety. In terms of area, rather than population, most of Indonesia is in fact Christian or animist. Just to leaven the mix, Bali has its own unique brand of Hinduism.

The relatively small but dominant island of Java is increasingly modern, but even here thousand-year-old traditions remain alive, as they do in the rest of the archipelago. While Java receives the lion's share of the country's new investment boom, and Bali is one of the richest provinces due to tourism receipts, parts of the outer islands have barely emerged from the Neolithic age. This rift is a great source of resentment, particularly in the eastern islands, where development is slow and Java's neglect, except as a distant ruler, is most noticed.

Indonesia is rent with opposing forces – orthodox Muslim versus syncretist Muslim, Muslim versus Christian versus Hindu, country versus city, modern versus traditional, rich versus poor, 'inner' (ie Java) versus 'outer'. Somehow the country still manages to hang together and, with notable exceptions like Irian Jaya and East Timor, the bonds grow stronger and an Indonesian as opposed to regional identity is growing.

Despite the changes and modernisation, Indonesia remains one of the most traditional countries in South-East Asia. Traditional values of the family and religion are maintained. The head of the family is accorded great respect, and children always acquiesce to their parents and elders. Beyond the extended family, the main social unit is the village. The concerns of the individual are of less importance than they are in western

Dari Mana?

Dari Mana? Where do you come from?
You will be asked this question frequently, in Indonesian or English, along with many others like *Sudah kawin?* (Are you married?) and *Mau kemana?* (Where are you going?). Visitors can find these questions intrusive, irritating and even infuriating, but Indonesians regard them as polite conversation.

An Indonesian approaching a friend might ask, in their local language, 'What are you doing?', even if it's perfectly obvious. Similarly, someone obviously going to the market might be asked 'Where are you going?', simply as a form of greeting. Indonesians are a curious and very friendly people, and seemingly inane questions are used as small talk and to express positive feelings for others. Indonesians will ask foreign visitors such questions in English (it may be their only English!), and you should not get annoyed – a smile and a 'hello', or a greeting in Indonesian, is generally a polite and adequate response. If the questions continue, which is likely, you will need to take a different approach, as one new arrival in Indonesia found out...

She was introduced to a young man, who immediately began asking her all manner of personal questions – 'Where did she come from?', 'Was she married?', 'Where was she staying?', 'Did she like Indonesia?', 'What were her plans?'. Anxious to be friendly and polite, she tried to answer every question, while becoming increasingly dubious about his motives. But he never seemed to be satisfied with her responses, because as soon as she answered one question, he would ask her another, and he seemed to become more morose with each exchange. Finally, and with a note of utter despondency in his voice, the young man announced, 'I have five children!'.

The message is that you don't really have to answer every question, but you should ask some questions yourself to show a polite interest in the other person. If the questioning becomes too nosey, try responding with an equally nosey question and you might be surprised at the warmth of the response. When you've had enough chatter, you can answer the question 'Where are you going?', even if it wasn't asked. ■

society, and western notions of individualism are seen as odd or selfish.

'Keeping face' is important to Indonesians and they are generally extremely courteous – criticisms are not spoken directly and they will usually agree with what you say rather than offend. They will also prefer to say something rather than appear as if they don't know the answer. They mean well but when you ask how to get somewhere, you may often find yourself being sent off in the wrong direction!

Avoiding Offence

Indonesians make allowances for western ways, especially in the main tourist areas, but there are a few things to bear in mind when dealing with people.

Never hand over or receive things with the left hand. It will cause offence – the left hand is used to wash after going to the toilet and is considered unclean. To show great respect to a high-ranking or elderly person, hand something to them using both hands.

Talking to someone with your hands on your hips is impolite and is considered a sign of contempt, anger or aggression.

Asians resent being touched on the head – the head is regarded as the seat of the soul and is therefore sacred. In Javanese culture, traditionally a lesser person should not have their head above that of a senior person, so you may sometimes see Javanese duck their heads when greeting someone, or walk past with dropped shoulders as a mark of respect.

The correct way to beckon to someone is with the hand extended and a downward waving motion of all the fingers (except the thumb). It looks almost like waving goodbye. The western method of beckoning with the index finger crooked upward won't be understood and is considered rude. It is fine to point at something or to indicate direction, but rude to point at someone – gesture with the whole hand.

Hand shaking is customary for both men and women on introduction and greeting. It is customary to shake hands with everyone in the room when arriving or leaving.

Hospitality is highly regarded, and when food or drink is placed in front of you, wait until asked to begin by your host, who will usually say *'silahkan'* or 'please'. It is impolite to refuse a drink, but not necessary to drink it all.

While places of worship are open to all, permission should be requested to enter, particularly when ceremonies or prayer are in progress, and you should ensure that you're decently dressed. Always remove footwear before entering a mosque. When entering someone's house, it is polite to remove your shoes, but this is often disregarded.

Indonesians will accept any lack of clothing on the part of poor people who cannot afford them; but for westerners, thongs, bathing costumes, shorts or strapless tops are considered impolite, except perhaps around places like Kuta. Elsewhere you should look respectable and revealing dress is not appropriate. Women are better off dressing modestly – revealing tops are just asking for trouble. For men, shorts are considered low class and only worn by boys.

RELIGION

The early Indonesians were animists, and practised ancestor and spirit worship. The social and religious duties of the early agricultural communities that developed in the archipelago were gradually refined to form a code of behaviour which became the basis of adat, or customary law. When Hindu-Buddhism spread into the archipelago it was overlaid on this already well-developed spiritual culture.

Although Islam was to become the predominant religion of the archipelago, it was really only a nominal victory. What we see in ostensibly Islamic Indonesia today is actually Islam rooted in Hindu-Buddhism, adat and animism. Old beliefs persist and on Java, for example, there are literally hundreds of holy places where spiritual energy is said to be concentrated. Meditators and pilgrims flock to these areas and to the graves of saints, despite the proscription of saint worship by Islam.

As for Christianity, despite the lengthy colonial era, the missionaries have only been successful in converting pockets of the Indonesian population – the Bataks of Sumatra, the Minahasans and Toraja of Sulawesi, some of the Dayaks of Kalimantan, the Florinese, Ambonese and some of the West Irianese. Christian beliefs are also usually bound up with traditional religious beliefs and customs.

There are still a few pockets where animism survives virtually intact, such as in west Sumba and some parts of Irian Jaya.

Hinduism

Outside India, Hindus predominate only in Nepal and Bali. Hinduism is one of the oldest extant religions, with roots extending back beyond 1000 BC, in the civilisation which grew up along the Indus River Valley in what is now modern-day Pakistan.

The Hindus believe that underlying a person's body, personality, mind and memories there is something else – it never dies, is never exhausted, it is without limit of awareness and bliss. What confuses westerners is the vast pantheon of gods found in Hinduism – you can look upon these different gods as representations of the many attributes of an omnipresent god. The symbols and images of Hinduism are meant to introduce the worshipper to what they *represent* – the images should not be mistaken with idolatry, and the multiplicity of them with polytheism. The three main physical representations of the one omnipresent god are Brahma the creator, Vishnu the preserver and Shiva the destroyer.

Central to Hinduism is the belief that we will all go through a series of rebirths or reincarnations. Eventual freedom from this cycle depends on your karma – bad actions during your present life result in bad karma and this results in a lower reincarnation. Conversely, if your deeds and actions have been good you will be reincarnated on a higher level and you'll be a step closer to eventual freedom from rebirth.

Hinduism specifies four main castes: the

highest is the Brahmin priest caste; next is the Kshatriyas, who are soldiers and governors; the Vaisyas are tradespeople and farmers; and lowest are the Sudras, who are menial workers and craftspeople. You cannot change your caste – you're born into it and are stuck with it for the rest of that lifetime.

Centuries ago Hinduism pervaded Java and spread to Bali. Today, Hinduism on Bali bears only a vague resemblance to the form practised on the Indian sub-continent. In Indonesia, Hinduism survives in a much more tangible form in the remains of great temples like Prambanan near Yogyakarta and those on the Dieng Plateau, and in stories and legends still told in dance and the wayang puppet performances of both Bali and Java.

These stories are drawn from a number of ancient Hindu texts, including the *Bhagavad Gita*, a poem credited to the philosopher-soldier Krishna in which he explains the duties of a warrior to Prince Arjuna. The *Bhagavad Gita* is contained in the *Mahabharata*, which tells of a great battle said to

Ganesh, the Hindu god of prophecy and son of Shiva (the destroyer) and Parvati.

have taken place in northern India. The *Ramayana* is another story; it tells of Prince Rama's expedition to rescue his wife, Sita, who had been carried away by the demon-prince Rawana. In this epic Rama is aided by the monkey-god Hanuman and by an army of monkeys. Rama is regarded as the personification of the ideal human and as an incarnation of the god Vishnu. Vishnu has visited the earth a number of times, the seventh time as Rama and the eighth time as Krishna.

The gods are also depicted in statues and reliefs in the ancient Hindu temples of Java. Often they can be identified by the 'vehicle' upon which they ride; Vishnu's vehicle is Garuda, the half-man half-eagle after whom Indonesia's international airline is named. Of all the Hindu gods, Shiva the destroyer is probably the most powerful and the most worshipped, but out of destruction comes creation and so the creative role of Shiva is frequently represented as the *lingam* – a phallic symbol. Shiva's consort is Parvati, by whom he had two children, one of whom is Ganesh, the elephant-headed god. Coming back from a long trip, Shiva discovered Parvati in her room with a young man and, not pausing to think that their son might have grown up during his absence, lopped his head off! He was then forced by Parvati to bring his son back to life but could only do so by giving him the head of the first living thing he saw – which happened to be an elephant. Ganesh's vehicle is the rat.

Buddhism
Buddhism was founded in India around the 6th century BC by Siddhartha Gautama. He was a prince brought up in luxury, but in his 20s despaired of ever finding fulfilment on the physical level since the body was inescapably involved with disease, decrepitude and death. At around the age of 30, he made his break from the material world and plunged off in search of 'enlightenment'. After various unsuccessful stratagems, one evening he sat beneath a banyan tree in deep meditation and achieved enlightenment.

Buddha founded an order of monks and for the next 45 years preached his ideas until his death around 480 BC. To his followers he was known as Sakyamuni. Gautama Buddha is not the only Buddha, but rather the fourth, and neither is he expected to be the last one.

Buddha taught that all life is suffering and that happiness can only be achieved by overcoming this suffering through following the 'eight-fold path' to *nirvana*, a condition beyond the limits of the mind, where one is no longer oppressed by earthly desires. Strictly speaking, Buddhism is more of a philosophy and a code of morality than a religion, because it is not centred on a god. Buddhism appears to retain some of the Hindu concepts, such as the idea of reincarnation and karma.

Hinduism & Buddhism in Indonesia

It remains one of the puzzles of Indonesian history how the ancient kingdoms of the archipelago were penetrated by Hinduism and Buddhism. The evidence of Hindu-Buddhist influence is clear enough in different parts of Indonesia, where there are Sanskrit inscriptions dating back to the 5th century AD, and many Hindu and Buddhist shrines and statues have been found in the archipelago. Disentangling the two is difficult, because there is usually a blending of Hindu and Buddhist teachings with older religious beliefs. It's been suggested, for instance, that the wayang puppet shows of Java have their roots in primitive Javanese ancestor worship, though the wayang stories that have been passed on are closely linked with later Hindu mythology or with Islam.

The elements of Indian religion and culture which had the greatest influence in Indonesia were those to do with courts and government: the Indian concept of the godking; the use of Sanskrit as the language of religion and courtly literature; and the introduction of Indian mythology. Even the events and people recorded in epics like the *Ramayana* and *Mahabharata* have all been shifted out of India to Java. Various Hindu and Buddhist monuments were built on Java, of which the Buddhist stupa of Borobudur and the Hindu temple complex at Prambanan are the most impressive. The Sumatran-based Sriwijaya kingdom, which arose in the 7th century, was the centre of Buddhism in Indonesia.

Bali's establishment as a Hindu enclave dates from the time when the Javanese Hindu kingdom of Majapahit, in the face of Islam, virtually evacuated Java to the neighbouring island – taking with them their art, literature and music, as well as their religion and rituals. It's a mistake, however, to think that this was purely an exotic seed planted on virgin soil. The Balinese probably already had strong religious beliefs and an active cultural life, and the new influences were simply overlaid on the existing practices – hence the peculiar Balinese variant of Hinduism.

The Balinese worship the Hindu trinity of Brahma the creator, Shiva the destroyer and Vishnu the preserver, but they also have a supreme god, Sanghyang Widi. On Bali, unlike in India, the threesome is always alluded to, never seen – a vacant shrine or an empty throne says it all. Secondary Hindu gods, such as Ganesh, may occasionally appear, but there are many other purely Balinese gods, spirits and entities. Other aspects of Balinese Hinduism separate it from Indian Hinduism – like the widow-witch Rangda. She bears a close resemblance to Durga, the terrible side of Shiva's wife Parvati, but the Balinese Barong and Rangda dance (in which she appears) certainly isn't part of Indian Hinduism.

Islam

Islam is the most recent and widespread of the Asian religions. The founder of Islam was the Arab prophet Muhammed but he merely transmitted the word of God to his people. To call the religion 'Muhammedanism' is wrong, since it implies that the religion centres around Muhammed and not around God. The proper name of the religion is Islam, derived from the word *salam* which means primarily 'peace', but in a secondary sense 'surrender'. The full connotation is something like 'the peace which comes by surrendering to God'. A person who follows Islam is a Muslim.

The prophet was born around 570 AD and came to be called Muhammed, which means 'highly praised'. His descent is traditionally traced back to Abraham. There have been other true prophets before Muhammed – among them Moses, Abraham and Jesus – but Muhammed is regarded as the culmination of them, as there will be no more prophets.

Muhammed taught that there is one all-powerful, all-pervading God, Allah. 'There is no God but Allah' is the fundamental tenet of the Islamic religion. The initial reaction to Muhammed's message was one of hostility; the uncompromising monotheism conflicted with the pantheism and idolatry of the Arabs. Apart from that, Muhammed's moral teachings conflicted with what he believed was a corrupt and decadent social order, and in a society afflicted with class divisions Muhammed preached a universal humanity in which all people are equal in the eyes of God. Muhammed and his followers were forced to flee from Mecca to Medina in 622 AD, and there Muhammed built up a political base and army which eventually defeated Mecca, although Muhammed died two years later in 632 AD.

Muhammed's teachings are collected in the Koran (or Qur'an), the holy book of Islam, compiled after Muhammed's death. Much of the Koran is devoted to codes of behaviour, and much emphasis is placed on God's mercy to humankind. Muhammed's teachings are heavily influenced by two other religions, Judaism and Christianity, and there are some extraordinary similarities, including belief in heaven, hell and a judgement day, and a creation theory almost identical to the Garden of Eden, as well as myths such as Noah's Ark and Aaron's Rod.

Islam hangs on four pegs: God; creation; humankind; and the day of judgement. Everything in Islam centres on the fact of

God or Allah, but the distinctive feature of Islam is the appreciation of the value of the individual. In Hinduism and Buddhism, the individual is just a fleeting expression with no permanence or value, but the Islamic religion teaches that individuality, as expressed in the human soul, is eternal, because once created the soul lives forever. For the Muslim, life on earth is just a forerunner to an eternal future in heaven or hell as appropriate.

Islam is a faith that demands unconditional surrender to the wisdom of Allah. It involves total commitment to a way of life, philosophy and law. Theoretically it is a democratic faith in which devotion is the responsibility of the individual, unrestricted by hierarchy and petty social prerequisites, and concerned with encouraging initiative and independence in the believer. Nor, in theory, is it bound to a particular locale – the faithful can worship in a rice field at home, in a mosque or on a mountain. It is also a fatalistic faith in that everything is rationalised as the will of Allah.

It is a moralistic religion and has its own set of rituals and laws, such as worshipping five times a day, recitation of the Koran, almsgiving and fasting annually during the month of Ramadan. Making the pilgrimage to Mecca is the foremost ambition of every devout Muslim – those who have done this, called *haji* if they are men or *haja* if women, are deeply respected. Other Muslim customs include scrupulous attention to cleanliness, including ritualistic washing of hands and face. The pig is considered unclean and is not kept or eaten by strict Muslims.

Islam also called on its followers to spread the word – by the sword, if necessary. In succeeding centuries Islam was to expand over three continents. By the time a century had passed the Arab Muslims had built a huge empire which stretched all the way from Persia to Spain. The Arabs, who first propagated the faith, developed a reputation as ruthless opponents but reasonable masters, so people often found it advisable to surrender to them.

At an early stage Islam suffered a split that

The Mosque

A mosque is an enclosure for prayer. The word *mesjid* means 'to prostrate oneself in prayer'. Mosques can be differentiated according to function: the *jami mesjid* is used for the Friday prayer meetings; the *musalla* is one that is used for prayer meetings but not for those on Friday; the 'memorial mosque' is for the commemoration of victorious events in Islamic history; and a *mashad* is found in a tomb compound. There are also prayer houses which are used by only one person at a time, not for collective worship – you'll often find that larger hotels and airport terminals in Indonesia have a room set aside for this purpose.

The oldest mosques in Indonesia – in Cirebon, Demak and Palembang, for example – have rooms with two, three or five storeys. It is thought that these multistoreyed roofs were based on Hindu *meru* (shrines) that you see on Bali. Today's mosques are often built with a high dome over an enclosed prayer hall. Inside these are five main features. The *mihrab* is a niche in a wall marking the direction to Mecca. The *mimbar* is a raised pulpit, often canopied, with a staircase. There is also a stand to hold the Koran, a screen to provide privacy for important persons praying, and a fountain, pool or water jug for ablutions. Outside the building there is often a *menara* – a minaret, or tower, from which the *muezzin* summons the community to prayer.

The dome of Jakarta's huge Istiqlal Mosque is classically Middle-Eastern in style and typical of modern Indonesian mosques.

GLENN BEANLAND

Apart from these few items the interior of the mosque is empty. There are no seats and no decorations – if there is any ornamentation at all it will be quotations of verses from the Koran. The congregation sits on the floor.

Friday afternoons are officially decreed for believers to worship, and all government offices and many businesses are closed as a result. All over Indonesia you'll hear the call to prayer from the mosques, but the muezzin of Indonesia are now a dying breed – the wailing will usually be performed by a cassette tape.

PETER TURNER

SARA-JANE CLELAND

Above: The 16th-century Mesjid Agung mosque at Banten in Western Java has a five-tiered meru (holy mountain) roof, also found in Hindu temples.

Left: While the traditional Sumbanese religion is based on the animist beliefs of marapu, Islam and Christianity are making steady inroads into the cultural life of the Sumbanese. Mosques and churches are now common sights across the island.

remains to this day. The third caliph, successor to Muhammed, was murdered and followed by Ali, the prophet's son-in-law, in 656 AD. Ali was assassinated in 661 by the governor of Syria, who set himself up as caliph in preference to the descendants of Ali. Most Muslims today are Sunnites, followers of the succession from the caliph, while the others are Shias or Shi'ites, who follow the descendants of Ali.

Islam only travelled west for 100 years before being pushed back at Poitiers in France in 732, but it continued east for centuries. It regenerated the Persian Empire which was then declining from its protracted struggles with Byzantium. In 711, the same year in which the Arabs landed in Spain, they sent dhows up the Indus River into India. This was more a raid than a full-scale invasion, but in the 11th century all of north India fell into Muslim hands. From India the faith was carried into South-East Asia by Arab and Indian traders.

Islam in Indonesia

Indonesia first came in contact with Islam through Muslim traders, primarily from India, who introduced a less orthodox form of Islam than that of Arabia. The state of Perlak in Aceh adopted Islam near the end of the 13th century, then the ruler of Melaka accepted the faith in the early part of the 15th century. Melaka became the centre of South-East Asian trade, and a centre of Islamic study, and trading ships carried the new religion to Java, from where it spread to the spice islands of eastern Indonesia via Makassar (now Ujung Pandang) on Sulawesi. Islam caught hold on Java in the 16th and 17th centuries. At about the same time, Aceh developed as a major Islamic power and the religion took root in west and south Sumatra, and on Kalimantan and Sulawesi.

By the 15th and 16th centuries centres for the teaching of Islam along the northern coast of Java may have played an important role in disseminating the new religion, along with previously established centres of Hinduism, which adopted elements of Islam. Javanese tradition holds that the first propagators of Islam on Java were nine holy men, the *wali songo*, who possessed a deep knowledge of Islamic teaching as well as exceptional supernatural powers. Another theory holds that Islam was adopted by the rulers of the coastal trading ports, who broke with the dominant Hindu kingdoms of the interior that claimed suzerainty over the north. The common people followed suit in much the same way as Europeans adopted the religions of their kings.

Whatever the reasons for the spread of Islam, today it is the professed religion of 90% of Indonesians, and its traditions and rituals affect all aspects of their daily life. Like Hinduism and Buddhism before it, Islam also had to come to terms with older existing traditions and customs.

Indonesian Islam is rather different from the austere form found in the Middle East; customs in Indonesia often differ from those of other Muslim countries. Respect for the dead throughout most of Indonesia is not expressed by wearing veils but in donning traditional dress. Muslim women in Indonesia are allowed more freedom and shown more respect than their counterparts in other Muslim countries. They do not have to wear facial veils, nor are they segregated or considered to be second class citizens. Muslim men in Indonesia are only allowed to marry two women and even then must have the consent of their first wife – Muslims in other parts of the world can have as many as four wives. Throughout Indonesia it is the women who initiate divorce proceedings. The Minangkabau society of Sumatra, for example, is a strongly Muslim group but their adat laws allow matriarchal rule, which conflicts strongly with the assumption of male supremacy inherent in Islam.

Like other Muslims, Indonesian Muslims practise circumcision. The laws of Islam require that all boys be circumcised, and in Indonesia this is usually done somewhere between the ages of six and 11.

One of the most important Islamic festivals is Ramadan, a month of fasting prescribed by Islamic law, which falls in the ninth month of the Muslim calendar. It's often preceded by a cleansing ceremony, Padusan, to prepare for the coming fast. Traditionally, during Ramadan people get up at 4 am to eat and then fast until sunset. Many Muslims visit family graves and royal cemeteries, recite extracts from the Koran, sprinkle the graves with holy water and strew them with flowers. Special prayers are said at mosques and at home. The first day of the 10th month of the Muslim calendar is the end of Ramadan. Mass prayers are held in the early morning, followed by two days of feasting. Extracts from the Koran are read and religious processions take place; gifts are exchanged and pardon is asked for past wrongdoings during this time of mutual forgiveness.

Islam not only influences routine daily living but also Indonesian politics. It was with the Diponegoro revolt in the 19th century that Islam first became a rallying point in Indonesia. In the early part of the 20th century Sarekat Islam became the first mass political party. Its philosophy was derived from Islam and its support was derived from the Muslim population. In post-independence Indonesia it was an Islamic organisation, the Darul Islam, which launched a separatist movement in West Java. Despite the Islamic background of the country and the predominance of Muslims in the government, the Indonesian government has not followed the trend towards a more fundamentalist Islamic state.

LANGUAGE
The 300 plus languages spoken throughout Indonesia, except those of North Halmahera and most of Irian Jaya, belong to the Malay-Polynesian group. Within this group are many different regional languages and dialects. Sulawesi has at least six distinct language groups and the tiny island of Alor in Nusa Tenggara has no fewer than seven. The languages of the Kalimantan interior form their own distinct sub-family. Sumatra is no less diverse, and languages range from Acehnese in the north to Batak around Danau Toba, and in southern Sumatra the main language is Bahasa Melayu (Malay Language) from which Bahasa Indonesia is derived.

Java has three main languages: Sundanese, spoken in West Java; Javanese, spoken in Central and East Java; and Madurese, spoken on the island of Madura (off the north coast of Java) and parts of East Java. The Balinese have their own language.

Bahasa Indonesia
Today, the national language of Indonesia is Bahasa Indonesia, which is almost identical to Malay. Most Indonesians speak Bahasa Indonesia as well as their own regional language.

A few essentials are listed in this section. You'll find a more comprehensive overview in Lonely Planet's *Indonesian phrasebook*. It is set out with a view to helping you communicate easily, rather than just listing endless phrases.

An English/Indonesian and Indonesian/English dictionary is also very useful. They're sold quite cheaply in Indonesia, and you can also get bilingual dictionaries in French, German, Dutch and Japanese.

Pronunciation
a	like the 'a' in 'father'
e	like the 'e' in 'bet' when unstressed; when stressed it is more like the 'a' in 'may'.
i	like the 'ee' sound in 'meet'
o	like the 'oa' in 'boat'
u	like the 'u' in 'flute'
ai	like the 'i' in 'line'
au	like a drawn out 'ow' as in 'cow'
ua	at the start of a word, like a 'w' – such as *uang* (money), pronounced 'wong'

The pronunciation of consonants is very straightforward. Most sound like English consonants except:

c	like the 'ch' in 'chair'
g	like the 'g' in 'garden'
ng	like the 'ng' in 'singer'
ngg	like the 'ng' in 'anger'

j	like the 'j' in 'join'
r	like Spanish trilled 'r'
h	like English 'h', but a bit stronger; almost silent at the end of a word
k	like the English 'k', except at the end of the word, when you stop just short of actually saying the 'k', eg, *tidak* sounds like 'tee-dah'
ny	like the 'ny' in 'canyon'

Basics

Yes.	*Ya.*
No/Not.	*Tidak.*
Thank you (very much).	*Terima kasih (banyak).*
You're welcome.	*Kembali.*
Please. (asking for help)	*Tolong.*
Please open the door.	*Tolong buka pinta.*
Please. (giving permission)	*Silakan.*
Please come in.	*Silakan masuk.*
Welcome.	*Selamat datang.*
Sorry.	*Ma'af.*
Excuse me.	*Permisi.*

Greetings

Good morning. (until 11 am)	*Selamat pagi.*
Good day. (11 am to 3 pm)	*Selamat siang.*
Good afternoon. (3 to 7 pm)	*Selamat sore.*
Good night.	*Selamat malam.*
Goodbye. (said by the person leaving)	*Selamat tinggal.*
Goodbye. (said by the person staying)	*Selamat jalan.*

Small Talk

How are you?	*Apa kabar?*
I'm fine.	*Kabar baik.*
What is your name?	*Siapa nama anda?*
My name is ...	*Nama saya ...*
I am from ...	*Saya dari ...*
Are you married?	*Sudah kawin?*
I am not married yet.	*Saya belum kawin.*
I am married.	*Saya sudah kawin.*

Language Difficulties

Do you speak English?	
Bisa berbicara bahasa Inggris?	
I (don't) understand.	
Saya (tidak) mengerti.	
Please write that word down.	
Tolong tuliskan kata itu untuk saya.	

Getting Around

I want to go to ...	*Saya mau pergi ke ...*
Where is ...?	*Di mana ada ...?*
Which way?	*Ke mana?*
How many km?	*Berapa kilometer?*

What time does the ...	*Jam berapa ...*
leave/arrive?	*berangkat?*
bus	*bis*
train	*kereta api*
ship	*kapal*
aeroplane	*kapal terbang*
motorcycle	*sepeda motor*

Stop here.	*Berhenti disini.*
Straight on.	*Jalan terus.*
Turn right.	*Belok kanan.*
Turn left.	*Belok kiri.*
Please slow down.	*Pelan-pelan saya.*

station	*stasiun*
ticket	*karcis/tiket*
first class	*kelas satu*
economy class	*kelas ekonomi*

Accommodation

Is there a room available?	
Ada kamar yang kosong?	
What's the daily rate?	
Berapa tarip hariannya?	
Can I see the room?	
Boleh saya lihat kamarnya?	
I want to pay now.	
Saya mau bayar sekarang.	

hotel	*hotel*
price list	*daftar harga*
bed	*ranjang/tempat tidur*
room	*kamar*
quiet room	*kamar tenang*
bathroom	*kamar mandi*

with private bath	*kamar mandi didalam*
with shared bath	*kamar mandi diluar*
air-con	*ac ('ah-say')*

Around Town

bank	*bank*
market	*pasar*
police station	*kantor polisi*
post office	*kantor pos*
postage stamp	*perangko*
telephone	*telepon*
telephone number	*nombor telepon*
toilet	*kamar kecil/WC* ('way say')
town square	*alun-alun*

What time does it open/close?
  Jam berapa buka/tutup?
What is the exchange rate?
  Berapa kursnya?

Shopping

How much is it?	*Berapa harga?*
Can you lower the price?	*Boleh kurang?*
film	*filem*
cigarettes	*rokok*
matches	*korek api*
mosquito coil	*obat nyamuk*
mosquito net	*kelambu*
soap	*sabun*
towel	*handuk*
toilet paper	*kertas WC*

Numbers

1	*satu*		6	*enam*
2	*dua*		7	*tujuh*
3	*tiga*		8	*delapan*
4	*empat*		9	*sembilan*
5	*lima*		10	*sepuluh*

After the numbers one to 10, the 'teens' are *belas*, the 'tens' are *puluh*, the 'hundreds' are *ratus* and the 'thousands' *ribu*. Thus:

11	*sebelas*
12	*duabelas*
13	*tigabelas*

20	*duapuluh*
21	*duapuluh satu*
25	*duapuluh lima*
30	*tigapuluh*
90	*sembilanpuluh*
99	*sembilanpuluh sembilan*
100	*seratus*
200	*duaratus*
250	*duaratus limapuluh*
254	*duaratus limapuluh empat*
888	*delapanratus delapanpuluh delapan*
1000	*seribu*
1050	*seribu limapuluh*

A half is *setengah*, which is pronounced 'stengah', so half a kilo is 'stengah kilo'. 'Approximately' is *kira-kira*.

Time

What is the time?	*Jam berapa?*
7 o'clock	*jam tujuh*
5 o'clock	*jam lima*
How many hours?	*Berapa jam?*
five hours	*lima jam*
When?	*Kapan?*
tomorrow/yesterday	*besok/kemarin*
rubber time	*jam karet*
hour	*jam*
week	*minggu*
month	*bulan*
year	*tahun*

Days of the Week

Monday	*Hari Senin*
Tuesday	*Hari Selasa*
Wednesday	*Hari Rabu*
Thursday	*Hari Kamis*
Friday	*Hari Jumat*
Saturday	*Hari Sabtu*
Sunday	*Hari Minggu*

Health & Emergencies

I'm sick.	*Saya sakit.*
doctor	*dokter*
hospital	*rumah sakit*
chemist/pharmacy	*apotik*
Call the police.	*Panggil polisi.*
Help!	*Tolong!*
Thief!	*Pencuri!*
Fire!	*Kebakaran!*

Indonesian Arts & Crafts

Indonesia's arts & crafts reflect the regional histories, religions and influences of the archipelago's mind-boggling array of ethnic groups. Indonesian arts & crafts can be classified into three major groupings, which roughly parallel the three cultural streams within Indonesia – a loose generalisation, but a useful one.

The first is that of 'outer' Indonesia, the islands of Sumatra, Kalimantan, Sulawesi, Nusa Tenggara, Maluku and Irian Jaya, which have strong animist traditions. Carvings, weavings, pottery etc have developed from a tribal art in which art objects are part of worship. For example, the ancestor statues from Nias in Sumatra are representational art adorning everyday objects, imbuing them with the power of the spirits.

The second stream is that of 'inner' Indonesia, the islands of Java and Bali that have come under the greatest influence from Hindu-Buddhist tradition. The techniques and styles that built Borobudur and the Indian epics such as the *Mahabharata*, that form the basis for wayang theatre, are still a major influence on arts & crafts.

The third influence is that of Islam, which not so much introduced its own art tradition, but modified existing traditions. Its more rigid style and its ban on human and animal representation restricted art, yet, because of it, the existing artistic traditions became more stylised and refined.

These days the religious influence or magic associated with many art objects is disappearing. For example, the *sahan*, the Batak medicine holder of buffalo horn with a wooden carved stopper, or the *tunggal*, the medicine man's wand, line Danau (Lake) Toba craft shops. These copies of the increasingly rare real thing have no significance to the maker apart from its sale value.

But while one can lament at the passing of traditional meaning and methods, it would be wrong to assume that the tourist trade is destroying traditional crafts. The sophistication and innovation of the craft 'industry' is growing. For example, Batak carvers now produce large sahan that are much bigger and more intricately carved than the original. While they lack spiritual meaning, they are fine pieces of craftwork and show increasing sophistication. The designs have changed to suit the market – small, simple sahan just don't sell and, anyway, the spiritual meaning of an original sahan has no relevance for most buyers.

Title Page: Intricate tulis batik from Cirebon, West Java (photograph by Peter Turner).

Right: A stone axe from Baliem valley, Irian Jaya (photograph by Glenn Beanland).

Of course, many of the trinkets turned out for the tourist trade are of poor quality and there is an increasing cross-fertilisation of craft styles. The 'primitif' Asmat or Kalimantan statues, so in vogue in Balinese art shops, may well have been carved just up the road in Peliatan. On the other hand, Javanese woodcarvers are turning out magnificent traditional panels and innovative furniture commissioned by large hotels, and Balinese jewellers influenced by western designs are producing new work of stunning quality.

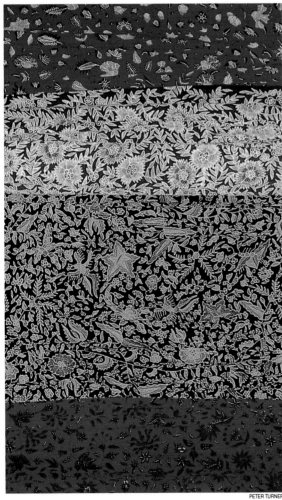

PETER TURNER

Cirebon in West Java has long been a notable centre for the production of batik. This colourful piece is an example of tulis *batik.*

Woodcarving

Woodcarving is the most enduring and widespread medium for artistic expression in Indonesia. Each culture has its own style, and the diversity and sophistication of Indonesia's woodcarvers is remarkable.

In Indonesia a house not only protects its inhabitants from the elements, but repels unwanted spirits. Examples include the horned *singa* (lion) heads that protect Batak houses, the water buffalo representations on Toraja houses signifying prosperity, or the serpents and magical dog carvings on Dayak houses in Kalimantan.

Woodcarvings and statues are an important expression of the spirits in the outer islands. Statues of the ancestors are an integral part of spiritual life on Nias and Sumba. The Toraja's famed funerals are important events for the artist also; a realistic statue is carved of the dead and the coffin is adorned with animal heads. In Ngaju and Dusun villages in Kalimantan, giant carved ancestor totems *(temadu)* depict the dead.

Perhaps the most famous and mythologised of Indonesia's woodcarvers are the Asmat of south-west Irian Jaya. Shields, canoes, spears, drums and everyday objects are carved, but the most distinctive and easily recognisable Asmat woodcarvings are the ancestor poles *(mbis)*. These poles show the dead one above the other, and the open carved 'wing' at the top of the pole is a phallic symbol expressing fertility and power. The poles are also an expression of revenge and were traditionally carved to accompany a feast following a head-hunting raid.

Woodcarving also has a decorative, as well as spiritual, function and everyday objects from the outer islands are often intricately carved. Some of the most common objects are the baby carriers and ironwood stools from Kalimantan, lacquered bowls from South Sumatra, carved bamboo containers from Sulawesi, and even doors from Timor and horse effigies from Sumba.

The islands of Bali and Java also have strong woodcarving traditions. Balinese woodcarving is the most ornamental and intricate in Indonesia. Carved statues, temple doors and relief panels are decorated with swirls of the gods and demons of Balinese cosmology. While religion still plays an important part in traditional Balinese woodcarving, nowhere in Indonesia has western art and souvenir demand made so much impact. Western influence saw a revolution in woodcarving akin to that in Balinese painting. Many years ago Balinese woodcarvers began producing simpler, elongated statues of purely ornamental design with a natural rather than a brightly painted finish. Nowadays Bali also turns out art copies from all over the archipelago, producing its own interpretations of Asmat totems or Kalimantan fertility statues, as well as unique modern statues.

Box: Batak coconut container used to carry spices, with carved totem stopper showing rider and animals (photograph by Glenn Beanland).

Above: Asmat shields from south-west Irian Jaya (photograph by Glenn Beanland).

Right: Carved Asmat wooden bowl from Irian Jaya.

GLENN BEANLAND

TAMSIN WILSON

Above: Asmat fertility statue from Irian Jaya (photograph by Glenn Beanland).

Left: Elaborately carved wooden wall frieze from Bali.

The centre for woodcarving on Java is Jepara on the north coast of Central Java. The intricate style is obviously of the same tradition as the Balinese, but Muslim and other influences have seen human representation replaced by heavily carved and stylised leaves, flowers and birds. Furniture is the main business in Jepara, with cupboards, sideboards, beds, chairs etc all heavily carved. Other centres on Java are Kudus, which produces mostly intricate panels seen in traditional houses, and Madura.

The most favoured wood in Indonesia is teak *(jati)*, though this is an increasingly expensive commodity. Teak is one of the best woods because it is easily carved and less susceptible to warping, splitting, insects and rot. Sandalwood, which is grown in East Timor, is also occasionally seen in Balinese carvings. Mahogany is also used, though not common, while ebony imported from Sulawesi and Kalimantan is used on Bali. This very heavy wood is also very expensive. Jackfruit is a common wood and cheap, though it tends to warp and split. Above all, local carvers use woods at hand so, for example, heavy ironwood and meranti are used in Kalimantan woodcarving and *belalu*, a quick growing light wood, is used on Bali.

Carved Masks

Masks are also a specialised form of woodcarving. Though they exist throughout the archipelago and may be used in funerary rites and the like, the most readily identifiable form of mask is the *topeng* used in the wayang topeng dances of Java and Bali. The introduction of wayang topeng is attributed to Sunan Kalijaga, an Islamic saint of the 16th century, but the dances are of the Hindu-Buddhist tradition. Dancers perform tales from the Indian epics such as the *Mahabharata* or distinctly local tales and the masks are used to represent the characters. Masks vary from the stylised but plain masks of Central and West Java to the heavily carved masks of East Java. Balinese topeng masks are less stylised and more naturalistic – the Balinese save their love of colour and detail for the masks of the Barong dance, which is more strongly pre-Hindu in influence.

Top: Balinese topeng *mask depicting a more* kasar *(unrefined) character. The teeth are made from gleaming mother-of-pearl shells (photograph by Glenn Beanland).*

Middle: Topeng *masks from Java are more stylised, as seen in this intricately carved* topeng *kartolo mask from Lumajang, East Java (photograph by Peter Turner).*

Right: A mask used in traditional Balinese dances, showing the long curved teeth which identify the evil characters.

GREGORY ADAMS

Textiles

Indonesian textiles come in a dazzling variety of fabrics, materials, techniques, colours and motifs. Basically there are three major textile groupings.

The first is *ikat*, a form of tie-dyeing patterns onto the threads before weaving them together; this technique is associated with the proto-Malay people of the archipelago such as the various ethnic groups of Nusa Tenggara (see the Nusa Tenggara chapter for more on ikat). The second is *songket*, where gold or silver threads are woven into silk cloth. This is strongest where Islam has made the most impact, such as Aceh on Sumatra and among the Malays of coastal Kalimantan. The third group is *batik*, the alternate waxing and dyeing technique most clearly associated with those parts of central Java where the great Javanese kingdoms were established. It was also taken up on Bali, Madura and in Jambi on Sumatra, all of which have been subject to considerable Javanese influence.

Ikat

The Indonesian word ikat, which means to tie or bind, is used as the name for intricately patterned cloth whose threads are tie-dyed by a very painstaking and skilful process *before* they are woven together.

Ikat cloth is made in many scattered regions of the archipelago, from Sumatra to Maluku, but it's in Nusa Tenggara that this ancient art form thrives most strongly. Ikat garments are still in daily use in many areas, and there's an incredible diversity of colours and patterns. The spectacular ikat of Sumba and the intricate patterned work of Flores are the best known, but Timor and Lombok and small islands like Roti, Sawu, Ndao and Lembata all have their own varied and high-quality traditions, as do Sulawesi, Kalimantan and Sumatra. On Bali the rare double ikat method, in which both warp and waft threads are pre-dyed, is used in the weavings of Gringseng.

Making Ikat Ikat cloth is nearly always made of cotton, still often hand spun, though factory-made threads have come into use. Dyes are traditionally handmade from local plants and minerals, and these give ikat its characteristically earthy brown, red, yellow and orange tones, as well as the blue of indigo.

GLENN BEANLAND

Box: The skull tree motif is featured extensively in Sumbanese weavings. Sumbanese head-hunters would display the heads of their enemies on trees (photograph by Glenn Beanland).

Left: Sumba weaving displaying lion figures.

Ikat comes in a variety of shapes and sizes, including *selendang* (shawls); sarongs; two metre long tubes which can be used as a cloak or rolled down to the waist to resemble a sarong; *selimut* (blankets); and four metre long pieces (known as *kapita* in Flores) used as winding cloths for burial of the dead.

Some aspects of ikat production are changing with the use of manufactured dyes and thread. A description of the traditional method follows.

All the work belongs to the women – they produce the dyes and plant, harvest, spin, dye and weave the cotton. Spinning is done with a spindle or sometimes a simple spinning wheel. The thread is strengthened by immersion in stiffening baths of grated cassava, finely stamped rice or a meal made of roasted maize, and then threaded onto a winder. The product is usually thicker and rougher than machine-spun cotton.

Traditional dyes are made from natural sources. The most complex processes are those concerned with the bright rust colour, known on Sumba as *kombu*, which is produced from the bark and roots of the kombu tree. Blue dyes come from the indigo plant, and purple or brown can be produced by dyeing the cloth deep blue and then overdyeing it with kombu.

Each time the threads are dipped in dye, the sections that are not due to receive colour are bound together ('ikatted') beforehand with dye-resistant fibre. A separate tying-and-dyeing process is carried out for each colour that will appear in the finished cloth – and the sequence of dyeing has to consider the effect of over-dyeing. This tying-and-dyeing stage is what makes ikat and it requires great skill, since the dyer has to work out – *before* the threads are woven into cloth – exactly which parts of the thread are to receive each colour in order to give the usually complicated pattern of the final cloth. After dyeing, the cloth is woven on a simple hand loom.

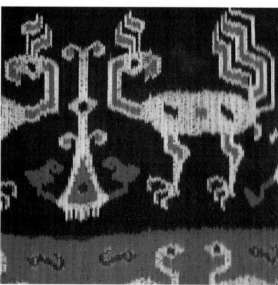

Right: Detail from a Sumbanese blanket showing animal motifs.

GLENN BEANLAND

There is a defined schedule of work for the traditional production of ikat. On Sumba the thread is spun between July and October, and the patterns bound between September and December. After the rain ends in April, the blue and kombu dyeing is carried out. In August the weaving starts – more than a year after work on the thread began.

Origins & Meaning of Ikat The ikat technique probably came to Indonesia over 2000 years ago with the migrants bringing the Dongson culture from southern China and Vietnam. It has survived in more isolated areas that were bypassed by later cultural influences.

Ikat styles vary according to the village and sex of the wearer, and some types of cloth are reserved for special purposes. In parts of Nusa Tenggara high-quality ikat is part of the 'dowry' that a bride's family must give to the bridegroom's family. On Sumba, less than 90 years ago only members of the highest clans could make and wear ikat textiles. Certain motifs were traditionally reserved for noble families (as on Sumba and Roti) or members of a particular tribe or clan (Sawu or among the Atoni of Timor).

In the 20th century traditional motifs have become mixed up with some of European origin, and ikat's function in indicating its wearer's role or rank has declined.

Motifs & Patterns An incredible range of designs is found on ikat. Some experts believe that motifs found on Sumba, such as face-on people, animals and birds, stem from an artistic tradition even older than Dongson. The main Dongson influence was in geometric motifs like diamond and key shapes (which often go together), meanders and spirals.

A particularly strong influence was cloth known as *patola* from Gujurat in India. In the 16th and 17th centuries these became highly prized in Indonesia and one characteristic motif was copied by local ikat weavers. It's still a favourite today – a hexagon framing a sort of four pronged star. On the best patola and geometric ikat, repeated small patterns combine to form larger patterns and the longer you look at it the more patterns you see – rather like a mandala.

Judging Ikat Not so easy! Books on the subject aren't much use when you're confronted with a market trader telling you that yes, this cloth is definitely hand spun and yes, of course the dyes are natural. Taking a look at the process is informative: you can see women weaving in many places, and at the right time of year you may see dye-making, thread-spinning or tie-dyeing. Cloths made in villages will nearly always be hand spun and hand woven. Here are some tips on distinguishing the traditional product:

Thread Hand spun cotton has a less perfect 'twist' to it than factory cloth.
Weave Hand woven cloth, whether made from hand spun or factory thread, feels rougher and, when new, stiffer than machine-woven cloth. It will probably have imperfections (perhaps minor) in the weave.
Dyes Until you've seen enough ikat to get a feel for whether colours are natural or chemical, you often have to rely on your instincts as to whether they are 'earthy' enough. Some cloths contain both natural and artificial dyes.
Dyeing Method The patterns on cloths which have been individually tie-dyed by the authentic method will rarely be perfectly defined, but they're unlikely to have the detached specks of colour that often appear on mass-dyed cloth.
Age No matter what anybody tells you, there are very few antique cloths around. Most of what you'll be offered for sale will be new or newly second-hand. There are several processes to make cloth *look* old.

GLENN BEANLAND

Above: The use of gold thread in weavings, known as songket, has long been prized in Indonesia. Real gold thread is traditionally used but look-alike thread is common.

Songket

Songket is silk cloth with gold or silver threads woven into it, although these days imitation silver or gold is often used. Songket is most commonly found in West Sumatra, but can be seen in parts of Kalimantan and Bali. Gold thread is also used in embroidery in the more Islamic areas of Indonesia.

Right: Gold embroidery is used in this Minangkabau wedding scarf from Bukittinggi, West Sumatra.

GLENN BEANLAND

Batik

The technique of applying wax or some other type of dye-resistant substance (like rice paste) to cloth to produce a design is found in many parts of the world. The Javanese were making batik cloth at least as early as the 12th century, but its origins are hard to trace. Some think the skills were brought to Java from India, others that the Javanese developed the technique themselves. The word 'batik' is an old Javanese word meaning 'to dot'.

The development of batik in Indonesia is usually associated with the flowering of the creative arts around the royal courts – it's likely that the use of certain motifs was the preserve of the aristocracy. The rise of Islam on Java probably contributed to the stylisation of batik patterns and the absence of representations of living things from most designs. More recently batik has grown from an art mainly associated with the royal courts into an important industry with a number of noted production centres.

In the older method of making batik the wax is applied hot to the smooth cloth with the *canting*, a pen-like instrument with a small reservoir of liquid wax. The design is first traced out onto the prepared cloth and the patterns drawn in wax on the white cloth, or on a cloth previously dyed to the lightest colour required in the finished product. The wax-covered areas resist colour change when immersed in a dye bath. The waxing and dyeing are continued with increasingly dark shades until the final colours are achieved. Wax is added to protect previously dyed areas or scraped off to expose new areas to the dye. Finally, all the wax is scraped off and the cloth boiled to remove all traces of the wax. The wax mixture usually includes beeswax, paraffin, resins and fats mixed in varying proportions. This type of batik is called *batik tulis* or 'written batik', because the patterns are drawn onto the cloth in freehand style.

PETER TURNER

Left: A selection of batik featuring traditional colours and designs from Yogyakarta and Solo.

PETER TURNER

PETER TURNER

Top: Hand-worked or tulis *batik involves drawing the designs in wax with the use of a copper pen (canting).*

Middle: In cap *batik, copper stamps (cap) are made with the desired design, dipped in wax and then pressed on to the fabric.*

Bottom: Modern cap *batik sarongs, produced mainly in Solo.*

PHIL WEYMOUTH

From the mid-19th century production was speeded up by applying the wax with a metal stamp called a *cap*. The cap technique can usually be identified by the repetition of identical patterns, whereas in the freer composition using the canting even repeated geometric motifs vary slightly. Some batik combines the cap technique with canting work for the fine details. It's worth noting that batik cap is true batik; don't confuse it with screen-printed cloth which completely bypasses the waxing process and is often passed off as batik.

Java is the home of Indonesian batik and each district produces its own style. The court cities of Yogyakarta and Solo in Central Java are major batik centres. Traditional court designs are dominated by brown, yellow and indigo blue. These days both cities produce a wide range of modern as well as traditional batiks. Solo is a major textile centre and many of the large batik houses are based there.

Batiks from the north coast of Java have always been more colourful and innovative in design. As the trading region of Java, the north coast came in contact with many influences and these are reflected in its batik. Pekalongan is the other major batik centre on the north coast, and traditional floral designs are brightly coloured and show a Chinese influence. Many modern designs and bird motifs are now employed and some of Indonesia's most interesting batik comes from Pekalongan. Cirebon also produces very fine traditional tulis work that is colourful.

GLENN BEANLAND

Left: Pekalongan batik, noted for its intricate design, use of bright colours and floral motifs.

Pottery

Indonesia's position on the trade routes saw the import of large amounts of ceramics from China. Indonesia is a fertile hunting ground for antique Chinese ceramics, which date back as far as the Han dynasty. The best examples of truly indigenous ceramics are the terracottas from the Majapahit Empire of East Java.

Indonesian pottery is usually unglazed and hand worked, although the wheel is also used. It may be painted, but is often left natural. Potters around Mojokerto, close to the original Majapahit capital, still produce terracottas, but the best-known pottery centre on Java is just outside Yogyakarta at Kasongan, where intricate, large figurines and pots are produced.

In the Singkiwang area of West Kalimantan, the descendants of Chinese potters produce a unique style of utilitarian pottery.

Lombok pottery is very fashionable and has an earthy 'primitive' look with subtle colourings. Balinese ceramics show a stronger western influence and are more inclined to use glazing.

Box: Detail of a bowl from Lombok, noted for its 'primitive' appearance (photograph by Glenn Beanland).

Right: Lombok pots have become quite widely known and are produced without a wheel. The clay is formed by hand then whacking the outside with a wooden paddle while the inside is supported by a smooth, round stone.

JAMES LYON

GLENN BEANLAND

PETER TURNER

Above: Antique Chinese ceramics are very common throughout Indonesia.

Left: A potter in Kasongan, Central Java.

Painting

Painting is widespread in Indonesia as an accompaniment to other art forms. For example, woodcarvings, masks and pottery are often painted, as are religious items, such as calendars or religious designs painted on houses (eg the tree of life paintings in Dayak longhouses). An individual painting on canvas that is an art form in itself is a modern western concept.

Temple and other painting exists on Java, but after the conversion to Islam, Bali became the centre for painting in Indonesia. The traditional wayang narratives were moral tales or told of the exploits of the gods. They were mostly wall paintings or decorative hangings for temples and palaces.

Balinese painting was turned around in the 1930s by western artists such as Walter Spies and Rudolf Bonnet who came to live and work on Bali. They encouraged painting as an art form and Balinese artists started to depict scenes from everyday life rather than religious narratives. Balinese paintings were still packed with detail, but rice harvesting or market scenes replaced the cartoon-like narratives of the Hindu epics like the *Ramayana*. Further transformations occurred with the naive 'young artists' style that developed in the 1950s, and Balinese painting continues to evolve with many noted modern artists producing innovative work.

Of course, Indonesia has many exponents of western-style painting using the same media as artists all over the world, but expressing Indonesian themes and incorporating traditional Indonesian styles. The Javanese painter Raden Saleh is credited with being one of the first modern Indonesian artists in the 19th century. Present-day artists cover all painting styles. Of particular note are the batik painters that sprung up in Yogyakarta in the 1960s. Using batik techniques they depicted traditional and modern themes and inspired a whole craft tourist industry. Like much of the painting on Bali, batik painting can be very imitative and of poor quality, but some is original.

Box: Rural scene by I Dab Alit, Ubud, Bali (photograph by Glenn Beanland).

Right: Painter at work in Ubud, Bali.

PHIL WEYMOUTH

TONY WHEELER

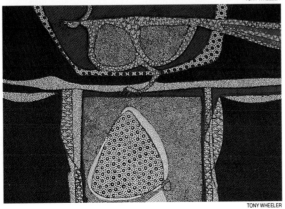

TONY WHEELER

Above: A Balinese temple festival scene showing Barong dance, by AA Rai.

Left: Batik painting from Yogyakarta, Java.

Basketwork & Beadwork

Some of the finest basketwork in Indonesia comes from Lombok. The spiral woven rattan work is very fine and large baskets are woven using this method, while smaller receptacles topped with wooden carvings are also popular.

On Java, Tasikmalaya is a major cane-weaving centre, often adapting baskets and vessels to modern uses with the introduction of zips and plastic lining. The Minangkabau, centred around Bukittinggi, also produce interesting palm leaf bags and purses, while the lontar palm is used extensively in weaving on Timor, Roti and other outer eastern islands.

The Dayak of Kalimantan produce some superb woven baskets and string bags, and they also produce some fine beadwork which can be seen on their baby carriers.

Some of the most colourful and attractive beadwork is produced by the Toraja of Sulawesi, and beadwork can be found throughout Nusa Tenggara from Lombok to Timor.

Small, highly prized cowrie shells are used like beads and are found on Dayak and Lombok artefacts, though the best application of these shells is in the Sumbanese tapestries intricately beaded with shells.

Box: Balinese dried palm leaf boxes decorated with small shells (photograph by James Lyon).

Right: Bone and cowrie shell necklace, fibre purse and dog teeth choker from Irian Jaya.

GLENN BEANLAND

GLENN BEANLAND

JAMES LYON

Above Left: Detail of a Kenyah Dayak basket from Kalimantan.

Left: Lombok is noted for its fine spiral woven rattan basketwork and caneware.

Puppets

The most famous puppets of Indonesia are the carved leather *wayang kulit* puppets. The intricate lace figures are cut from buffalo hide with a sharp, chisel-like stylus and then painted. They are produced on Bali and Java, particularly Central Java. The leaf-shaped *kayon* representing the 'tree' or 'mountain of life' is used to end scenes in the wayang and is also made of leather.

Wayang golek are the three dimensional wooden puppets found in Central Java, but are most popular among the Sundanese of West Java. The *wayang klitik* puppets are a rarer flat wooden puppet of East Java.

Box: Detail of a wayang golek *puppet depicting a Javanese nobleman (photograph by Glenn Beanland).*

Right: Wayang klitik *puppets are carved and painted two dimensional wooden puppets, most popular in East Java (photograph by Glenn Beanland).*

GLENN BEANLAND

GLENN BEANLAND

Above & Left: One of the many forms of wayang; the three dimensional wayang golek *puppets are most popular in West Java. Shown here are puppets for sale at the Jalan Surabaya Antique Market in Jakarta.*

Metalwork

The Bronze age in Indonesia began with the metal-working introduced from the Dongson culture in present-day Vietnam. Bronze work peaked with the Hindu-Buddhist empires of Java and brasswork is now more common, but in the eastern islands the ancient hourglass-shaped bronze drums are still produced.

Brassware was mostly of Indian and Islamic influence, and fine brass vessels and ornaments are produced in Indonesia. Some of the best workmanship is that of the Minangkabau in Sumatra, but brassware is also produced in Java, South Kalimantan and Sulawesi.

The most important ironwork objects are knives. As well as the famous kris, the *parang* of Kalimantan are sacred weapons used in everything from hacking through the jungle to head-hunting. Scabbards for ceremonial parang are intricately decorated with beads, shells and feathers.

Kris

Some think the Javanese kris – from the word *iris*, to cut – is derived from the bronze daggers produced by the Dongson culture around the 1st century AD. Bas-reliefs of a kris appear in the 14th century Panataran temple-complex in East Java, and the carrying of the kris as a custom on Java was noted in 15th century Chinese records. The kris is still an integral part of men's formal dress on ceremonial and festive occasions. A dalang will wear his kris while giving a wayang performance, and the kris is still part of the uniform of the guards at the palace in Yogyakarta.

The kris is no ordinary knife. It is said to be endowed with supernatural powers; adat law requires that every father furnish his son with a kris upon his reaching manhood, preferably an heirloom kris enabling his son to draw on the powers of his ancestors stored in the sacred weapon. Distinctive features and the number of curves in the blade, and the damascene, are read to indicate good or bad fortune for its owner. Damascening is a technique whereby another metal is hammered onto the blade of the kris to produce a design. The number of curves in the blade also has symbolic meaning: five curves symbolise the five Pandava brothers of the *Mahabharata* epic; three stand for fire, ardour or passion. Although the blade is the most important part of the kris, the hilt and scabbard are also beautifully decorated.

Box: Silver earring from Timor, used by the Tetum people as a wedding ornament (photograph by Glenn Beanland).

Right: Minangkabau betel container from West Sumatra (left), and etched brass bowl from Madura.

GLENN BEANLAND

Before the arrival of Islam, Hindu-inspired images were often used to decorate the wooden hilts – the mythological Garuda was a popular figure. After the spread of Islam such motifs were discouraged, but were often preserved in stylised forms. In any case, the origins and symbolism of the kris lay too deep in Javanese mysticism to be eradicated by the laws of Islam.

Though the kris is mostly associated with Java and Bali, it is also found in Sumatra, Kalimantan and Sulawesi. Kris from the outer islands are larger and less ornate than those on Java and Bali.

TAMSIN WILSON

Above: The wavy bladed kris is said to have spiritual power and will rattle in its scabbard to warn the owner of impending danger. The hilt often incorporates carved raksasa (demon) figures to ward off evil spirits and the blade is beaten, rolled and etched, and may include inlaid jewels.

Left: Silver coffee set from Kota Gede, Yogyakarta (photograph by Peter Turner).

Jewellery

Gold and silver work have long been practised in Indonesia. Some of the best gold jewellery comes from Aceh in the very north of Sumatra where fine filigree work is produced, and chunky bracelets and earrings are produced in the Batak lands. Gold jewellery can be found all over Indonesia and, while some interesting traditional work can be found throughout the islands, the ubiquitous *toko mas* (gold shop) found in every Indonesian city is mostly an investment house selling gold jewellery by weight, while design and workmanship take a back seat.

The best-known jewellery is the silver jewellery of both Bali and the ancient city of Kota Gede within the city boundaries of Yogyakarta. Balinese work is nearly always hand constructed and rarely involves casting techniques. Balinese jewellery is very innovative, employing traditional designs but, more often than not, adapting designs or copying from other jewellery presented by western buyers. The range is stunning and Bali is a major producer of export fashion jewellery. The traditional centre for Balinese jewellery is Cleek.

Kota Gede in Yogyakarta is another major silver centre famous for its fine filigree work. Silverware tends to be more traditional, but is also starting to branch out and adapt new designs. As well as jewellery, Kota Gede produces a wide range of silver tableware.

Above: Modern Balinese bracelet (photograph by Tamsin Wilson).

Right: Heavy silver rings and bracelets adorning a young girl at a temple in Manggis, East Bali.

GREGORY ADAMS

Facts for the Visitor

PLANNING

When to Go

Though travel in the wet season is possible in most parts of Indonesia, it can be a deterrent to some activities and travel on mud-clogged roads in less developed areas is difficult. In general, the best time to visit Indonesia is in the dry season between May and October (see Climate in the previous Facts about the Country chapter for more details).

Bali is Australia's favourite Asian get-away and everyone is duty-bound to make the pilgrimage eventually. The Christmas holiday period until the end of January brings a wave of migratory Australians, as do the shorter school breaks during the year. An even bigger tourist wave during the European summer holidays bring crowds of Germans, Dutch, French etc in July and August to Bali, Java, Sumatra and Sulawesi, the big European destinations. The main Indonesian holiday periods are the end of Ramadan, when some resorts are packed to overflowing and prices skyrocket, Christmas and the end of the school year from mid-June to mid-July when graduating high school students take off by the bus-load to tourist attractions, mainly on Java and Bali.

So that leaves May/June and September/October as the pick of the months to visit Indonesia, though even during the peak tourist months you can always find a place away from the crowds and travel in the wet season is not usually a major problem.

What Kind of Trip?

Indonesia has beaches, volcanoes, ancient cultures, magnificent wilderness, vibrant cities, archaeological ruins – the problem is which to visit in a limited time.

It is impossible to see all of Indonesia in the 60 days allowed by a tourist pass, if not a lifetime. Most visitors to Indonesia have one month or less to travel the vast archipelago, and it pays to choose only one, two or a maximum of three regions to explore.

The most visited islands tend to be Bali, Java and Sumatra, and it is possible to see the main highlights of these three islands in one month, but that doesn't leave much time for relaxation. Sulawesi is a growing tourist destination, and can be comfortably combined with a trip to another region. More visitors are heading out through Nusa Tenggara, but Maluku, Irian Jaya and Kalimantan are still unexplored territory for the vast majority of visitors to Indonesia. The outer islands are not so inaccessible these days, though travel costs are higher because flying becomes essential unless you have huge amounts of time.

If you are prepared to fly extensively you can easily visit a funeral in Torajaland on Sulawesi, lie on the beach on Bali, hear a *gamelan* orchestra at the *kraton* (walled city palace) in Yogya, see the orang-utans on Sumatra and climb up to the coloured lakes of Keli Mutu on Flores – all in one month (we met one Dutchman who did just that, and much more!). For this sort of trip you need stamina and a great deal of luck, especially if travelling to the outer islands where transport is limited and subject to cancellation, and bookings often go astray.

Always allow yourself some extra time. Travel can sometimes be hard and you may need extra time to recuperate, or you may find yourself sidetracked to some wonderful place that you never knew existed. Remember that schedules in Indonesia are flexible, and you may be forced to bend yours.

Maps

Locally produced maps are often surprisingly inaccurate. The Nelles Verlag map series covers Indonesia in a number of separate sheets, and they're usually quite good. Periplus also produces excellent maps of most of the archipelago and includes maps of the major cities. Both series are available in Indonesia and overseas.

The Directorate General of Tourism publishes a useful give-away information booklet, the *Indonesia Tourist Map*, which includes maps of Java, Bali, Sumatra and Sulawesi, and a good overall map of Indonesia. Maps of major Javanese, Sumatran and Balinese cities are easy enough to come by – ask at the tourist offices or try bookshops, airports and major hotels.

On the other islands the odd good map may pop up but quite often you'll be lucky to come across anything at all, or else only fairly simple maps. Hotels often have a good, detailed map of the town or city hanging on the wall of their foyer. The local police station should have a good map and will often allow foreigners to photocopy it.

What to Bring

Bring as little as possible. It is better to buy something you've left behind than to have to throw things away because you've got too much to carry. Except in the very remote areas, you can buy almost anything you can get at home.

Before deciding what to bring, decide what you're going to carry it in. For budget travellers the backpack is still the best single piece of luggage. Make sure that it can be locked. A small day pack is also very useful. Whatever you bring, try and make it small; in some parts of Indonesia *bemos* are packed to the hilt with passengers and there's next to no space left over to stow baggage.

Temperatures are uniformly tropical year-round in Indonesia, so short-sleeved shirts and T-shirts are the order of the day. Bring at least one long-sleeved shirt for the cool evenings. A few places in Indonesia get bloody cold at night, for example, the Baliem Valley on Irian Jaya, Kintamani on Bali and the Dieng Plateau on Java. You don't need Antarctic survival gear, but long jeans, shoes and possibly a jacket are necessary. Clothing is quite cheap in Indonesia and you can always buy more, though it can be hard to find clothes and shoes in sizes to fit western frames.

Modesty prevails. If you must wear shorts, they should be the loose-fitting type which come down almost to the knees, but shorts are considered very low class in Indonesia and only for the beach. Higher dress standards apply particularly whenever you're visiting a government office; have something suitable for more formal occasions.

Dark-coloured clothes hide the dirt better. Artificial fibres like rayon and nylon are too hot and sticky in this climate; drip-dry cotton or silk are best. You need clothes which will dry fairly quickly in the humidity – thicker jeans are a problem in this regard. You'll need some heavy clothing if you travel by motorcycle.

A hat and sunglasses are essential, and don't forget sunscreen (UV) lotion. A water bottle is a good idea but you can easily buy water in plastic throwaway bottles.

A sarong is an all-purpose Indonesian marvel. Besides wearing it, a sarong can serve as an impromptu blanket during cold evenings; or you can lie on it on a white sand beach; wrap it around your head to counter the pounding sun; use it as a top sheet or, alternatively, as a barrier between yourself and an unhealthy-looking mattress in an unhealthy-looking hotel; pin it up over the window of your hotel room to block the outside lights that burn fiercely all night long; and even use it as a towel – if it is still clean enough.

A sleeping bag is really only useful if you intend doing a lot of high-altitude camping.

Toiletries like soap, shampoo, conditioner, toothpaste and toilet paper are all readily available in Indonesia. Dental floss and shaving cream are hard to find, however, and tampons can be found only with some difficulty.

Stock up on passport or visa photos – these are readily obtained at photographic shops in Indonesia but you can never find these shops when you need them. A couple of places in Indonesia require permits to visit (like the interior of Irian Jaya) and photos are needed.

The following is a checklist of things you might consider packing, but don't feel obligated to bring everything on this list:

Namecards, Swiss army knife, electric immersion coil (for making hot water), cup, padlock, camera and accessories, sunglasses, alarm clock, leakproof water bottle, flashlight with batteries, compass, long pants, short pants, long shirt, T-shirt, nylon jacket, sweater, raincover for backpack, rainsuit or poncho, sewing kit, spoon, sunhat, toilet paper, tampons, thongs, nail clipper, tweezers, mosquito repellent and any special medications you use, plus a copy of the prescription.

A final thought: airlines do lose bags from time to time – you've got a much better chance of not losing your bag if it is tagged with your name and address *inside* as well as outside. Other tags can always fall off or be removed.

TOURIST OFFICES
Local Tourist Offices
The Indonesian national tourist organisation, the Directorate General of Tourism, maintains offices called Kantor Deparpostal in each province, which produce some literature but are generally not the places get specific queries answered. The head office of the Directorate General of Tourism (☎ 3838412) is at Jl Merdeka Barat 16-19, Jakarta.

Each provincial government has a tourist office called Departemen Pariwisata Daerah (DIPARDA), usually in the capital or major cities. In addition many *kabupaten* (districts) have their own tourist departments, and city governments may have their own tourist offices. The sign on the building is usually written only in Indonesian. Look for *dinas pariwisata* (tourist office).

The usefulness of the tourist offices varies greatly from place to place. Tourist offices in places that attract lots of tourists, like Bali or Yogya, provide good maps and information, while offices in the less-visited areas may have nothing at all – they'll always try to help, but it's pretty hopeless if they don't speak English and you don't speak Indonesian. Literature, if it is available, may not be displayed so ask to see what they've got.

For more details of local offices read the Information sections listed under the main cities in this book.

Tourist Offices Abroad
Indonesian Tourist Promotion Offices (ITPO) abroad can supply brochures and information about Indonesia. Useful publications are the *Travel Planner*, *Tourist Map of Indonesia* and the *Calendar of Events* for the whole country. ITPO offices are listed below. Garuda Airlines offices overseas are also worth trying for information.

Australia
  Level 10, 5 Elizabeth St, Sydney, NSW 2000
  (☎ (02) 9233 3630)
Germany
  Wiessenhuttenstrasse 17 D.6000, Frankfurt am
  Main 1 (☎ (069) 233677)
Japan
  2nd floor, Sankaido bldg, 1-9-13 Akasaka,
  Minatoku, Tokyo 107 (☎ (03) 3585 3588)
Singapore
  10 Collyer Quay, Ocean bldg, Singapore 0104
  (☎ 534 2837)
Taiwan
  5th floor, 66 Sung Chiang Rd, Taipei
  (☎ (02) 537 7620)
UK
  3-4 Hanover St, London W1R 9HH
  (☎ (0171) 493 0030)
USA
  3457 Wilshire Blvd, Los Angeles, CA 90010
  (☎ (213) 387 2078)

VISAS & DOCUMENTS
For many nationalities, a visa is not necessary for entry and a stay of up to 60 days. This includes: Argentina, Australia, Austria, Belgium, Brazil, Brunei, Canada, Chile, Denmark, Egypt, Finland, France, Germany, Greece, Iceland, Ireland, Italy, Japan, Kuwait, Liechtenstein, Luxembourg, Malaysia, Malta, Mexico, Morocco, Netherlands, New Zealand, Norway, Philippines, Saudi Arabia, Singapore, South Korea, Spain, Sweden, Switzerland, Taiwan, Thailand, Turkey, United Arab Emirates UK, USA and Venezuela.

If you're from one of these countries, a 60 day tourist pass (which is a stamp in your passport) is issued on arrival, as long as you enter and exit through recognised entry ports. Officially (but not always in practice) you must have a ticket out of the country when you arrive. Officially (and almost certainly) you cannot extend your visa beyond 60 days. If you're really intending to explore Indonesia in some depth, then 60 days is inadequate and you will have to exit the country and re-enter.

For citizen of countries not on the visa free list, a visitor visa can be obtained from any Indonesian embassy or consulate.

Recognised Entry/Exit Points

The Indonesian government's list of recognised 'no visa' entry and exit points are the airports of Ambon, Bali, Balikpapan, Bandung, Batam, Biak, Jakarta, Manado, Mataram, Medan, Padang, Pekanbaru, Pontianak and Surabaya, and the seaports of Ambon, Batam, Belawan, Benoa, Dumai, Jakarta, Manado, Padangbai, Semarang, Surabaya and Tanjung Pinang. The only 'no visa' land crossing is at Entikong in West Kalimantan, between Pontianak and Kuching. The official list is rarely updated and does change, so if you're planning an odd entry or exit find out the latest story. Entering by air on a regular flight is usually not a problem, and the airline will often be better informed than an Indonesian embassy. Entering or leaving Indonesia overland or by unusual sea routes usually requires a visa.

If you plan to arrive or leave through an unrecognised 'gateway', for example, to Jayapura from Papua New Guinea, then you have to get an Indonesian visitor visa (as opposed to a tourist pass) before arriving. A visitor visa is also required to *leave* Indonesia through a non-designated port, even if you entered through a designated one.

Visitor visas are only valid for one month, not 60 days as for visa-free entry, and can only be extended for two weeks. Indonesian embassies are usually not keen on issuing visitor visas.

Visa Extensions

Tourist passes are not extendable beyond 60 days. You may get a few extra days in special circumstances, like missed flight connections or illness, but don't count on it. Whatever you do, do not simply show up at the airport with an expired visa or tourist pass

and expect to be able to board your flight. You may be sent back to the local immigration office to clear up the matter. Overstaying attracts very steep fines, up to 500,000 rp per day, or a stint in jail if you can't pay.

If you arrived in Indonesia on a one month visitor visa, it is usually extendable only for two weeks. An extension costs around 50,000 rp and is obtained through any immigration office.

Study & Work Visas

Temporary stay visas for work or study purposes can be arranged if you have a sponsor, such as an educational institution or employer, in Indonesia. They are valid up to one year. Work visas are an almighty hassle to get and should be arranged by your employer. The Indonesian embassy in Singapore is the busiest and most troublesome for issuing working visas – foreign companies usually hire agents who know the ropes.

Onward Ticket

The best answer to the 'ticket out' requirement is to buy a return ticket to Indonesia, or include Indonesia as a leg on a through ticket. The main problem is for people with open-ended travel plans, for whom an onward ticket may not be an attractive option. Medan-Penang and Singapore-Jakarta tickets are cheap, popular options for satisfying the requirement.

However, the 'ticket out' requirement is less strictly enforced these days, and evidence of sufficient funds is sometimes acceptable in lieu. US$1000 is the magic number. If you fly to Kupang (on Timor) from Darwin, or take the ferry to Batam from Singapore, it's unlikely that any great fuss will be made. In Kupang, they may ask to see a wad of travellers cheques, but Batam is a breeze. Expect to flash your cash if arriving in Medan (Sumatra) on the ferry from Penang (Malaysia). On Bali they may still ask to see a ticket, but most Bali visitors are on short-stay package trips so you're unlikely to be troubled. Jakarta can be a hassle. Some visitors have been forced to buy an onward ticket on the spot.

The main problem is likely to be with airlines overseas, who may strictly enforce official requirements and not let you on flights to Indonesia without an onward ticket.

Documents

Check your passport expiry date. Indonesia requires that your passport has six months of life left in it on your date of arrival.

Keep a separate record of passport number and issue date, and a photocopy of your old passport or birth certificate. While you're compiling that info add the serial numbers of your travellers cheques, details of health insurance and US$200 or so as emergency cash – and keep all that material totally separate from your passport, cheques and other cash.

If you plan to drive in Indonesia get an International Driving Permit from your local automobile association.

A Hostelling International (HI) card is of very limited use in Indonesia, but there are a few hostels which will recognise it and give a slight discount.

The International Student Identity Card (ISIC) can perform all sorts of miracles, such as getting you a discount on domestic flights, though maximum age limits (usually 26) often apply. A student card will also get you discounts at a few museums and other attractions.

Remember that a student is a very respectable thing to be, and if your passport has a blank space for occupation you are much better off having 'student' printed there than something nasty like 'journalist' or 'photographer'.

EMBASSIES
Indonesian Embassies Abroad

Australia
  Embassy: 8 Darwin Ave, Yarralumla, ACT 2600 (☎ (06) 273 3222)
  Consulates: Adelaide, Darwin, Melbourne, Perth and Sydney
Belgium
  Ave de Turvueren 294, 1150 Brussels, Belgium (☎ (02) 771 1776)

Canada
  Embassy: 287 Maclaren St, Ottawa, Ontario K2P OL9 (☎ (613) 236 7403-5)
  Consulates: Vancouver and Toronto
Denmark
  Orehoj Alle 1, 2900 Hellerup, Copenhagen (☎ (45) 624422)
France
  Embassy: 47-49 Rue Cortambert 75116, Paris (☎ 01.45.03.07.60)
  Consulate in Marseille
Germany
  Embassy: 2 Bernakasteler Strasse, 53175 Bonn (☎ (0228) 382990)
  Consulates: Berlin, Bremen, Dusseldorf, Hamburg, Hannover, Kiel, Munich and Stuttgart
Hong Kong
  Consulate-General, 127-129 Leighton Rd, Causeway Bay (☎ 890 4421)
India
  50-A Chanakyapuri, New Delhi (☎ (011) 602348)
Italy
  53 Via Campania, Rome 00187 (☎ (06) 482 5951)
Japan
  5-9-2 Nighashi Qotanda, Shinagawa-ku, Tokyo (☎ (03) 3441 4201)
Malaysia
  Embassy: 233 Jl Tun Razak, Kuala Lumpur (☎ (03) 984 2011)
  Consulates: 467 Jl Burma, Penang (☎ (04) 282 4686); 5A Pisang Rd, Kuching, Sarawak (☎ (082) 241734); Jl Kemajuan, Karamunsing, Kota Kinabalu, Sabah (☎ (088) 219110); Jl Apas, Tawau, Sabah (☎ (089) 772052)
Netherlands
  8 Tobias Asserlaan, 2517 KC Den Haag (☎ (070) 310 8100)
New Zealand
  70 Glen Rd, Kelburn, Wellington (☎ (04) 475 8697)
Norway
  Inkonitogata 8, 0258 Oslo 2 (☎ 244 1121)
Papua New Guinea
  1+2/410, Kiroki St, Sir John Guise Drive, Waigani, Port Moresby (☎ (675) 253116)
Philippines
  Embassy: 185 Salcedo St, Legaspi Village, Makati, Manila (☎ (02) 285 5061 to 67)
  Consulate in Davao
Singapore
  7 Chatsworth Rd (☎ 737 7422)
Spain
  65 Calle de Agastia, Madrid (☎ (91) 4130294)
Sweden
  Singelbagken 12, 11521 Stockholm (☎ (08) 663 5470)

Switzerland
    51 Elfenauweg, 3006 Bern (☎ (031) 352 0983)
Thailand
    600-602 Petchburi Rd, Bangkok
    (☎ (002) 252 3135)
UK
    38 Grosvenor Square, London W1X 9AD
    (☎ (0171) 499 7661)
USA
    Embassy: 2020 Massachussetts Ave NW, Wash-
    ington DC 20036 (☎ (202) 775 5200)
    Consulates: Chicago, Honolulu, Houston, Los
    Angeles, New York and San Francisco
Zimbabwe
    3 Duthie Ave, Belgravia, Harare
    (☎ (263) 732561)

Foreign Embassies in Indonesia

Countries with diplomatic relations with
Indonesia have their embassies in Jakarta,
the capital. Australia, Denmark, Finland,
France, Germany, Italy, Japan, Netherlands,
Norway, Sweden, Switzerland and the USA
have consular representatives on Bali – see
the Bali chapter for details. A number of
countries also have consulates in Medan on
Sumatra and Surabaya on Java. Some of the
more useful foreign embassies in Jakarta
include:

Australia
    Jl Rasuna Said, Kav 15-16 (☎ 5227111)
Austria
    Jl Diponegoro 44 (☎ 338090)
Belgium
    Wisma BCA, Jl Jenderal Sudirman, Kav 22-23
    (☎ 5710510)
Brunei
    8th floor, Wisma BCA, Jl Jenderal Sudirman Kav
    22-23 (☎ 5712180)
Canada
    5th floor, Wisma Metropolitan I, Jl Jenderal
    Sudirman, Kav 29 (☎ 5250790)
Denmark
    4th floor, Bina Mulia bldg, Jl Rasuna Said, Kav
    10 (☎ 5204350)
Finland
    10th floor, Bina Mulia bldg, Jl Rasuna Said, Kav
    10 (☎ 5207408)
France
    Jl Thamrin 20 (☎ 3142807)
Germany
    Jl Raden Saleh 54-56 (☎ 3849547)
India
    Jl Rasuna Said, Kav S-1, Kuningan (☎ 5204150)

Italy
    Jl Diponegoro 45 (☎ 337445)
Japan
    Jl Thamrin 24 (☎ 324308)
Malaysia
    Jl Rasuna Said, Kav X-6 No 1 (☎ 5224947)
Myanmar (Burma)
    Jl H Agus Salim 109 (☎ 3140440)
Netherlands
    Jl Rasuna Said, Kav S-3, Kuningan (☎ 511515)
New Zealand
    Jl Diponegoro 41 (☎ 330680)
Norway
    4th floor, Bina Mulia bldg, Jl Rasuna Said, Kav
    10 (☎ 5251990)
Pakistan
    Jl Teuku Umar 50 (☎ 3144009)
Papua New Guinea
    6th floor, Panin Bank Centre, Jl Jenderal Sudir-
    man No 1 (☎ 7251218)
Philippines
    Jl Imam Bonjol 6-8 (☎ 3100334)
Russia
    Jl Thamrin 13 (☎ 3141477)
Singapore
    Jl Rasuna Said, Block X, Kav 2, No 4
    (☎ 5201491)
Spain
    Jl Agus Salim 61 (☎ 3142355)
Sri Lanka
    Jl Diponegoro 70 (☎ 3161886)
Sweden
    Bina Mulia bldg, Jl Rasuna Said, Kav 10
    (☎ 5201551)
Switzerland
    Jl Rasuna Said, B-1, Kav X-3 (☎ 5525107)
Thailand
    Jl Imam Bonjol 74 (☎ 3904055)
UK
    Jl Thamrin 75 (☎ 330904)
USA
    Jl Merdeka Selatan 5 (☎ 360360)
Vietnam
    Jl Teuku Umar 25 (☎ 3100357)

CUSTOMS

Customs allow you to bring in a maximum
of two litres of alcoholic beverages, 200
cigarettes or 50 cigars or 100g of tobacco, and
a 'reasonable' amount of perfume per adult.

Bringing narcotics, arms and ammunition,
TV sets, radio receivers, pornography, fresh
fruit, printed matter in Chinese characters
and Chinese medicines into the country is
prohibited. The rules state that 'film, pre-
recorded video tape, video laser disc, records,

records, computer software must be screened by the Censor Board', presumably to control pornography.

Photographic equipment, computers, typewriters and tape recorders must be declared to customs on entry and re-exported. Customs officials rarely worry about how much gear tourists bring into the country – at least if you have a western face. Personal effects are not a problem. There is no restriction on the import or export of foreign currency, but import or export of rupiah is limited to 50,000 rp.

MONEY
Costs

Indonesian costs are variable, depending on where you go. If you follow the well-beaten tourist track through Bali, Java and Sumatra, you may well find Indonesia one of the cheapest places in South-East Asia. Travellers centres like Danau Toba, Yogyakarta and Bali are superb value for accommodation and food. Elsewhere transport costs rise, budget accommodation can be limited and prices are higher because competition is less. Sulawesi and Nusa Tenggara are cheap enough, but accommodation on Maluku and Irian Jaya can be two to three times higher, and transport costs on Kalimantan are high.

Transport expenses also increase once you get into the outer provinces. On Bali, Java, Sumatra and Nusa Tenggara there's very little need to take to the air, while in the interior of Irian Jaya you have no choice but to fly. In more remote regions like Maluku, you really can't rely on ships – there may be only one ship every week or two between any two islands. If you're not prepared to fly you'll spend a good deal of your 60 day tourist pass just waiting around in port towns.

If you confine yourself to Sumatra, Java, Bali and Nusa Tenggara, rock-bottom budget travel works out to around US$10 to US$15 per day. Count on more like US$50 a day if you need such luxuries as air-conditioning and tour guides, or want to buy souvenirs.

Carrying Money

Preferably your money should be in relatively safe travellers cheques issued by a major bank. Also bring at least a few hundred US dollars in cash – there are a few odd towns where banks do not accept travellers cheques.

US dollars are the most widely accepted foreign currency. If you intend travelling extensively around Indonesia then bring US dollars – either in cash or travellers cheques from a major company such as American Express (Amex; the most widely accepted), Citicorp or Bank of America – or you'll be sorry. In big cities like Jakarta and in major tourist areas such as Bali, it's also easy to change Australian dollars and major European currencies, such as Deutschmarks, Netherlands guilders, pounds sterling, French or Swiss francs. Slightly more obscure currencies such as Canadian dollars can be difficult to change outside of the main tourist areas. If you bring other than US dollars, be prepared to put in more legwork – first to find a bank that will accept them and secondly to find one that gives a good rate.

Credit Cards & ATMs

If you have a credit card, don't leave home without it. If you are travelling on a low budget, credit cards are of limited use for day-to-day travel expenses in Indonesia as only expensive hotels, restaurants and shops accept them, but they are very useful for major purchases like airline tickets (though smaller offices in the back blocks may not accept them).

Another major advantage is that you can draw cash over the counter at many banks. You can always find a bank that will accept Visa or MasterCard in the major centres on Java and Bali, and in the big regional cities like Medan or Ujung Pandang, but it is difficult outside major cities and impossible in remote areas. Amex cards are less widely accepted; cash can be obtained at Amex agents, usually PT Pacto, in the major cities.

Though credit cards can be a viable way to carry money, especially if your account is always in the black to avoid interest charges, cash or travellers cheques are a far more convenient and reliable option in Indonesia.

Indonesian banks don't usually charge transaction fees for cash advances on credit cards, but always ask first. Also check with your home bank to make sure they don't charge transaction fees.

Credit card cash advances through ATMs are possible, but limited. On Bali and Java, Bank Bali and Lippobank offer cash advances through ATMs for MasterCard only. Bank Internasional Indonesia in Jakarta offers Visa and MasterCard withdrawals though its ATMs.

Giro

Dutch travellers with a Dutch post office account can conveniently obtain cash from Indonesian post offices. These *giro-betaalkaarten* are useful in the many Indonesian towns where there is no bank.

Currency

The unit of currency in Indonesia is the rupiah (rp). Coins of 25, 50, 100 and 500 rp are in circulation, both the old silver-coloured coins and the new bronze-coloured coins. The 25 rp coin has almost vanished. Notes come in 100, 500, 1000, 5000, 10,000, 20,000 and 50,000 rp denominations.

There is no restriction on the import or export of foreign currencies in cash, travellers cheques or any other form, but you're not allowed to take in or out more than 50,000 rp.

Currency Exchange

Australia	A$1	=	1879 rp
France	FF1	=	426 rp
Germany	DM1	=	1434 rp
Japan	¥100	=	1943 rp
Malaysia	M$1	=	908 rp
Netherlands	G1	=	1273 rp
Singapore	S$1	=	1666 rp
Switzerland	SFr1	=	1660 rp
UK	UK£1	=	3939 rp
USA	US$1	=	2400 rp

The rupiah has a floating rate, and in recent years it has tended to fall by about 4% a year against the US dollar.

Changing Money

Rates vary from bank to bank, and from town to town, so it pays to shop around. The rate for US dollars rarely varies by more than 10% but other currencies vary more. Banks sometimes give a slightly better rate for travellers cheques but overall you usually get a slightly better rate on cash. Banks may charge a transaction fee (ask first), and a 1000 rp 'stamp duty' (tax) is sometimes payable but most banks absorb this fee.

Indonesian banks are becoming much more competitive and generally don't view foreign exchange as some sort of crime, as they once did. Many banks handle foreign exchange. Bank Central Asia (BCA), Bank Duta and Bank Ekspor Impor are usually efficient for foreign exchange.

The best rates of exchange are found in Jakarta and on Bali. Touristy places have lots of moneychangers as well as banks, but banks usually have better exchange rates, except on Bali where moneychangers offer some of the best rates in Indonesia.

If you are travelling away from the major cities and tourist areas, change enough money to tide you over until you reach another major centre. For really remote places, carry stacks of rupiah because there won't be anywhere to change foreign cash or travellers cheques. Places where you can change cash and travellers cheques are noted in the relevant sections.

There are other problems to consider; it's often difficult to change big notes – breaking even a 10,000 rp note in a *warung* (food stall) can be a major hassle out in the villages.

Tipping

Tipping is not a normal practice in Indonesia but is often expected for special service. Someone who carries your bag, guides you around a tourist attraction etc will naturally expect a tip. Jakarta taxi drivers expect (demand?) a tip – the fare is usually rounded up to the next 500 rp. Hotel porters expect a few hundred rupiah per bag.

Bargaining

Many everyday purchases in Indonesia

require bargaining. This applies particularly to handcrafts, clothes and artwork but can also apply to almost anything you buy in a shop. Restaurant meals, transport and, often, accommodation are generally fixed price – restaurants usually display their menus and prices posted up on the wall and hotels usually have a price list. Sometimes when supply exceeds demand hotels may be willing to bend their prices rather than see you go next door. Though transport prices are fixed, bemos throughout Indonesia have a well-earned reputation for charging westerners whatever they're willing to pay – or even more than they're willing to pay!

Your first step should be to establish a starting price. It's usually easiest to ask them their price rather than make an initial offer, unless you know very clearly what you're willing to pay. As a rule of thumb your starting price could be anything from a third to two-thirds of the asking price – assuming that the asking price is not completely crazy. Then with offer and counter-offer you move closer to an acceptable price. Don't show too much interest when bargaining, and if you can't get an acceptable price walk away. You will often be called back and offered a lower price.

A few rules apply to good bargaining. First of all it's not a question of life or death, where every rupiah you chisel away makes a difference. Don't pass up something you really want that's expensive or unobtainable at home because the seller won't come down a few hundred rupiah more – it is nothing compared with the hundreds of dollars you spent on the airfare! Secondly, when your offer is accepted you have to buy it – don't then decide you don't want it after all. Thirdly, while bargaining may seem to have a competitive element in it, it's a mean victory knocking a poor *becak* driver down from 500 to 400 rp for a ride.

Bargaining is sometimes fun – and often not. A lot depends on whether you and the vendor are smiling or yelling at each other. Sometimes it seems as if people don't want your money if they can't overcharge you. Sometimes they will ask ludicrous prices and

will get very upset if you offer a ridiculously low price back, even if you mean it as a joke. This also works in the other direction; there is a nauseating category of westerner on the Asian trail who will launch into lengthy bitch sessions about being overcharged five cents for an orange.

Ask Indonesian friends or hotel staff for information about correct prices. If you don't know what the right price for transport is you might try asking another passenger what the regular price *(harga biasa)* is. Then you offer the correct fare. There's not much point doing this when you're buying something in a shop or at a market – onlookers naturally side with their own people.

Don't get hassled by bargaining and don't go around feeling that you're being ripped off all the time – too many people do. It is very easy to become obsessed with getting the 'local' price. Even locals don't always get the local price – Indonesian visitors to Bali will be overcharged on the bemos just like westerners. In Indonesia, if you are rich it is expected that you pay more, and *all* westerners are rich when compared to the grinding poverty of most Indonesians. Above all, keep things in perspective. The 500 rp you may overpay for a becak ride wouldn't buy a newspaper at home, but it is a meal for a poor becak driver.

POST & COMMUNICATIONS

Airmail for postcards is 600 rp to most foreign destinations. Aerograms and airmail letters up to 20g cost 1200 rp to Australia, 1600 rp to Europe and the USA. Parcel rates are quite expensive, but postal agencies offer good wrapping and sealing facilities, and have stands outside most post offices.

Sending Mail

The postal service is fairly reliable, but slow. Letters and small packets bound for overseas or domestic delivery may be registered for an extra fee at any post office branch. There are also two forms of express service available for mail within Indonesia: *kilat* for regular airmail and *kilat khusus* for airmail express.

Overseas parcels can be posted, insured and registered *(tercatat)* from a main post office, but staff may want to have a look at the contents first so there's not much point in sealing it up before you get there. If you're going to Singapore you'll find it considerably cheaper to post overseas packages and parcels from there than from Indonesia.

Post offices are usually open Monday to Friday from 8 am to 3 pm. In the larger cities, the main post offices are often open extended hours for basic postal services – until 8 pm during the week, and on Saturday and Sunday from 8 am to noon or later. Go during normal hours for poste restante. *Warpostels* and *warparpostels* are private post and telephone agencies that are open extended hours and provide an efficient postal service for slightly higher rates.

Receiving Mail

The postal service in Indonesia is generally pretty good and the poste restantes at Indonesian post offices *(kantor pos)* are reasonably efficient. Expected mail always seems to arrive – eventually. For poste restante, have your letters addressed to you with your surname in capitals and underlined, the poste restante, Kantor Pos and city in question. 'Lost' letters may have been misfiled under Christian names so always check under both your names.

Telephone

Telkom, the government-run telecommunications company, has offices *(kantor Telkom)* in most cities and towns. They are invariably open 24 hours, and often offer fax service as well as telephone and telex. These are the cheapest places to make international and long-distance *(inter-lokal)* phone calls, and the place to make collect calls.

Telecommunications agencies, either Telkom or privately run, are called *wartel*, warpostal or warparpostel and offer the same services. They may be marginally more expensive but are often more convenient. They are usually open from around 7 am until midnight, but sometimes 24 hours. As a rule, wartels don't offer a collect-call service – in the rare cases that they do, a first minute charge may apply.

Domestic calls are charged according to a system of zones. For example, if you're ringing from Biak on Irian Jaya, Zones I, II and III include the local area around Biak plus Nabire and Manok; Zone IV is the rest of Irian Jaya plus Ambon and Ternate; and Zone V is Bali, Java, Sumatra, Sulawesi, Nusa Tenggara and Kalimantan. The rates per minute are: Zone I, 900 rp; Zone II, 1000 rp; Zone III, 1200 rp; Zone IV, 1500 rp; and Zone V, 2000 rp. There is a 50% discount on calls placed between 9 pm and 6 am.

Public Phones Public coin phones are coloured blue and take 50 and 100 rp coins. When the phone begins to beep, feed in more coins or you'll be cut off. Card phones *(telepon kartu)* are also common. You can buy Telkom telephone cards *(kartu telepon)* with a face value of 60, 100, 140, 280, 400 or 680 units. They are sold at many wartels, bookshops, moneychangers etc. The standard cost is 82.5 rp per unit, so a 60 unit card is 4950 rp, a 100 unit card is 8250 rp and so on, but some places charge a lot more than the standard rate for the cards.

Direct Dial International calls can rarely be made from public phones, coin or card, though some card phones at big hotels and outside Telkom offices support this facility.

There are also some Home Country Direct phones, where one button gets you through to your home country operator and you reverse the charges. These telephones are found at some Telkom offices, airports, luxury hotels etc.

International Calls For International Direct Dialling (IDD) – dial ☎ 001 or ☎ 008, the country code, area code (minus the initial zero if it has one) and the number you want to reach. Two companies provide international connections – ☎ 001 is for Indosat and ☎ 008 is for Satelindo. Public phones rarely support this facility and you'll have to go to

Indonesian Telephone Codes

Ambon	0911	Jakarta	021	Nabire	0964	Singaraja	0362
Ampenan	0370	Jambi	0741	Nusa Dua	0361	Singkawang	0562
		Jayapura	0967			Soe	0392
Bacan Islands	0927	Jember	0311	Padang	0751	Solo	0271
Bajawa	0384			Padangbai	0363	Sorong	0951
Balikpapan	0542	Kendari	0401	Padangpanjang	0758	Sulu Islands	0929
Banda Aceh	0651	Kai Islands	0916	Pagaralam	0730	Sumbawa Besar	0371
Bandaneira	0910	Kaimana	0957	Palangkaraya	0514	Sungaipenuh	0748
Bandar Lampung	0721	Kalianda	0727	Palembang	0711	Surabaya	031
Bandung	022	Kerinci	0748	Palu	0451		
Bangka	0717	Kudus	0291	Pangandaran	0265	Takengon	0643
Banjarmasin	0511	Kupang	0391	Pangkalpinang	0717	Tanimbar	
Batam	0778	Kuta Beach		Pangkalanbun	0532	Islands	0918
Bengkulu	0736	(Bali)	0361	Parapat	0625	Tanjung Karang	0271
Berastagi	0628	Kutacane	0629	Pare-Pare	0421	Tanjung Pinang	0771
Biak	0961			Pekalongan	0285	Tapaktuan	0656
Bima	0374	Labuanbajo	0385	Pekanbaru	0761	Tarakan	0551
Bitung	0438	Labuha	0927	Pelabuhan Ratu	0266	Ternate	0921
Bogor	0251	Lagundri	0630	Pontianak	0561	Tidore	0920
Bukittinggi	0752	Lahat	0731	Poso	0452	Tobelo	0924
Buru	0913	Lombok	0370	Prapat	0625	Timika	0979
		Lovina Beach	0362	Probolinggo	0335		
Cilacap	0282					Ubud	0361
Cirebon	0231	Malang	0341	Rantepao	0423	Ujung Pandang	0411
Curup	0732	Manado	0431	Ruteng	0384		
		Maninjau	0752			Wahai	0914
Denpasar	0361	Manokwari	0962	Sabang	0652	Waikabubak	0387
Dili	0391	Masohi	0914	Samarinda	0541	Wamena	0969
Dumai	0765	Mataram	0370	Samosir	0625	Wiangapu	0386
		Maumere	0382	Sanur	0361	Wonosobo	0286
Fak Fak	0956	Meulaboh	0655	Sapura	0911		
		Minahasa	0436	Semarang	024	Yapen	0963
Garut	0262	Medan	061	Senggigi	0370	Yogyakarta	0274
Gorontalo	0435	Merauke	0971	Sentani	0967		
Gunung Sitoli	0639			Sibolga	0631		

a Telkom office or wartel. Many of the more expensive hotels allow IDD calls, but add a hefty surcharge.

Sample costs for a one minute international call from a Telkom wartel are 5000 rp to Australia, New Zealand and the USA, 5800 rp to Canada and the UK, and 6800 rp to Europe, including the 10% tax which applies to all calls. Person-to-person calls cost more.

Collect international calls can be made through the operator, from Telkom offices, or from Home Country Direct phones (see the previous Public Phones section). The Home Country Direct facility can also be used from any private phone where exchanges support the service by dialling ☎ 00 801 and the country code.

Useful Numbers Some useful numbers include:

Indonesia country code	☎ 62
Directory assistance, local	☎ 108
Directory assistance, long-distance	☎ 106
Directory assistance, international	☎ 102
Operator assisted domestic calls	☎ 100
Operator assisted international calls	☎ 101
International Direct Dial	☎ 001 or ☎ 008 + country code
Police	☎ 110
Fire Brigade	☎ 113
Ambulance	☎ 118

Fax, Telex & Telegraph

You can send messages by fax, telex and telegraph from the government-run telecommunications office in most cities and many mid-sized towns, or from wartels. Faxes from a Telkom office cost 4800 to 6100 rp per page for ASEAN countries; 8100 rp to Australia, New Zealand, Japan and the USA; 9800 rp per page to Canada and most of Europe; and 11,200 rp per page to Africa and South America.

BOOKS

Indonesia is not a straightforward country. Its history, economics, politics and culture – and their bizarre interactions – are wide open to interpretation, and different writers come up with astoundingly different interpretations of events. If you want to read about Java or Bali you'll be suffocated beneath the literature, but trying to find out anything about the other islands is like putting together bits and pieces of a jigsaw.

Lonely Planet

Lonely Planet's *Bali & Lombok* and *Java* are more detailed guides for exploring those islands in depth. Lonely Planet's *Jakarta city guide* covers the capital with insider information and detailed colour maps. Lonely Planet also produces the *Indonesia phrasebook* and the *Indonesian audio pack*.

Guidebooks

Bill Dalton's *Indonesia Handbook* is a classic guidebook, and, though sometimes dated, it will always be an inspiring read. Periplus Editions produces a number of beautifully illustrated, detailed books about Indonesia, including regional guides, and more specialised guides, such as *Underwater Indonesia* diving guide and *Surfing Indonesia*.

Another guide called *Surfing Indonesia* is published by Fielding Worldwide. It's comprehensive and presents a 'surfari' that will have surfers drooling. Order a copy from its US publisher.

Indo Surf & Lingo by Peter Neely is an informative book for finding good waves on Bali and the rest of Indonesia. Buy it in Kuta surf shops or order from the publisher at PO Box 950, Noosa Heads 4567, Queensland, Australia (fax (074) 475937).

Travel

If you think travel through the outer islands of Indonesia is time-consuming now, then just read Helen and Frank Schreider's *Drums of Tonkin* (published 1965) – they overcame the lack of transport by island hopping all the way from Java to Timor in a tiny amphibious jeep, defying landslides, oncoming monsoons, hostile (or just over-enthused?) indigenous inhabitants and the strange propensity Jakarta soldiers once had to shoot at vehicles making illegal turns.

While the Schreiders took only their pet dog with them, zoologist-TV personality David Attenborough left the UK with practically nothing and returned from the archipelago with an orang-utan, a couple of pythons, civets, parrots and assorted other birds and reptiles. The whole saga of the enterprise, eventually to be dignified by the title 'expedition', is recounted in his book *Zoo Quest for a Dragon*, published in 1957.

The Malay Archipelago by Alfred Russel Wallace is an 1869 classic of this famous naturalist's wanderings throughout the Indonesian islands.

Gavin Young's *In Search of Conrad* is an interesting account of this British author's retracing of Conrad's journeys by boat around Sumatra, Java, Kalimantan, Bali and Sulawesi.

Our Hotel in Bali by Louise Koke is a fascinating account of Louise and Robert Koke's running of the original Kuta Beach Hotel in the mid-30s up until WWII. It's a long way from the prewar Kuta to the Kuta of today.

History

An excellent general history is *A History of Modern Indonesia* (1981) by MC Ricklefs. It covers Indonesian history from the rise of Islam, circa 1300, to the present. It mainly covers Java, but ties in what was happening in the other islands. For an introduction to all the major empires, movements and currents in Javanese history, this book is a must.

Of the many general histories on Indonesia, a readable, popular history is *Indonesia: Land Under the Rainbow* (1990) by the noted Indonesian writer, Mochtar Lubis. This book is interesting for its view of the country through modern Indonesian eyes.

Indonesian Trade and Society by JC van Leur is a classic academic study of Indonesian social and economic history, looking at the early influences that shaped the history of the archipelago.

For the serious student of Indonesian history, Thomas Stamford Raffles' *The History of Java*, published in 1817, is a classic work covering all aspects of Javanese history and society. It is available in two hefty and very expensive volumes with numerous illustrations.

People & Society

A compilation of some of the intriguing religious, social and mystical customs of the diverse peoples of Indonesia is Lee Khoon Choy's *Indonesia: Between Myth & Reality*. It's a journalistic travelogue, derived from the author's short spells in the country as a journalist and politician and his stay as Singapore's ambassador to Indonesia from 1970 to 1975.

Indonesia in Focus, edited by Peter Homan, Reimar Schefol, Vincent Dekker and Nico de Jonge, is a Dutch publication with numerous glossy photos and well-illustrated articles exploring Indonesia's rich ethnic diversity. Various books explore regional cultures in detail. *The Religion of Java* by Clifford Geertz is not only a classic book on Javanese religion, culture and values, but revolutionised the study of social anthropology.

Robin Hanbury-Tenison's *A Pattern of Peoples* was based on his trip to Indonesia in 1973, visiting minority groups like the Danis of Irian Jaya and the Torajas of Sulawesi. It comments on the effects that tourism and other developments have had on what were, until recently, isolated peoples.

For a good general introduction to Indonesian culture, customs, language and food, designed for the expat or the traveller, *Culture Shock: Indonesia* by Cathie Draine and Barbara Hall is part of the well-known series. Another excellent general guide to living in Indonesia is *Introducing Indonesia: A guide to Expatriate Living* by the American Women's Association of Indonesia.

Fiction

Pramoedya Ananta Toer, a Javanese author, is Indonesia's most well-known novelist who has spent over 14 years in jail under the New Order government because of his political affiliations and criticism of the government. His most famous quartet of historical realist novels set in the colonial era includes *This Earth of Mankind*, *Child of All Nations*, *Footsteps* and *House of Glass*. They chart the life of Minke, a Javanese intellectual who has to reconcile his Javanese beliefs with the colonial world around him.

Mochtar Lubis is another well-known Indonesian writer. His most famous novel on Jakarta, *Twilight in Djakarta*, is a scathing attack on corruption and the plight of the poor in Jakarta in the 1950s. The book was banned and the author was jailed for this book. Much has changed, but the problems still remain.

Christopher Koch's *The Year of Living Dangerously* is an evocative reconstruction of life in Jakarta during the final chaotic months of the Soekarno period, and a sympathetic portrayal of the Indonesians and their culture and society. The movie by Australian director Peter Weir packs a feel for the place that few other movies could ever hope to achieve.

Much of Joseph Conrad's *Victory* is set in Surabaya, in a hotel very reminiscent of the Hotel Majapahit (see the Surabaya section in the Java chapter). Though not particularly evocative of Indonesia, it gives a wonderful account of the sea traders of the time.

Max Havelaar by Multatuli (the pseudonym of Douwes Dekker) is a classic Dutch novel first published in 1860. Written by a Dutch official based in West Java, it focuses on the inhumane treatment of the Javanese under the Dutch Culture System. The ensuing public outcry in the Netherlands helped to change government policy.

General

Two good illustrated books on Indonesian wildlife are *The Wildlife of Indonesia* by Kathy MacKinnon and *Wild Indonesia* by Tony and Jane Whitten.

Claire Holt's *Art in Indonesia: Continuities and Change* is an excellent introduction to the arts of Indonesia, focussing on traditional dance, *wayang* and literature. For an overall guide to Indonesian crafts, *Arts and Crafts of Indonesia* by Anne Richter is detailed and beautifully illustrated.

Language

Bookshops in Indonesia stock plenty of cheap Bahasa Indonesia/English text books and dictionaries, but most are of poor quality.

A good introduction to Bahasa Indonesia is Lonely Planet's *Indonesia Phrasebook* by Paul Wood or the *Indonesian audio pack*. They are structured to provide a good working knowledge of basic Indonesian with emphasis on the day-to-day vocabulary needed to travel around the country. John Barker's *Practical Indonesian* is another phrasebook emphasising travel vocabulary.

For serious students, *Bahasa Indonesia: Langkah Baru – a New Approach*, Book I, by Yohanni Johns, is a standard text used in schools and universities around the world. Though not really designed for self study, if you master this one you will have a substantial vocabulary and a solid grounding in Indonesian grammar. It can be bought in Indonesia and overseas.

Cheap pocket dictionaries abound in Indonesian bookshops but are riddled with errors and omissions. The only really decent dictionaries are *An Indonesian-English Dictionary* and its companion volume *An English-Indonesian Dictionary* by John Echols and Hassan Shadily. Nothing else matches these comprehensive, scholarly dictionaries but they are expensive (especially outside Indonesia) and far too weighty to lug around. *Kamus Lengkap* by S Wojowasito

and Tito Wasito is a complete Indonesian-English/English-Indonesian dictionary in one volume. Despite a number of odd and inaccurate translations, it is about the best comprehensive dictionary in a manageable (though still large) size for travelling. It is cheap in Indonesia.

One of the better pocket dictionaries is the small *MIP Concise Indonesian Dictionary*, but it is not available in Indonesia.

Bookshops

Books in English, usually only cheap novels, can be found in bookshops in the main cities, airports and in some of the large hotels. Good bookshops are hard to find, impossible in the outer islands and smaller cities. Bring your own books as they're expensive and the supply and range are extremely limited. Jakarta has the best bookshops in the country. Well-touristed places like Ubud and Yogya have second-hand bookshops, and these are the best bet for books in other languages, such as Dutch, French, German etc.

NEWSPAPERS & MAGAZINES

The news media is expected to – and does – practise self-censorship. 'Politeness' is the key word, and in typically indirect Indonesian style, stories of corruption, wastage of funds and government ineptitude are frequently run, but care is always taken not to point the finger too closely. Most importantly, criticism of Soeharto and his immediate family is not tolerated.

Whenever you buy newspapers and magazines in Indonesia, take a close look at the date. It is not uncommon for vendors to try to sell old news from two or three weeks ago.

Local

The English-language press is limited mostly to the *Jakarta Post*, published daily and available around the country, though difficult to get outside Jakarta and the major tourist areas. While subject to the same 'self-censorship' as other Indonesian publications, it manages to tell you quite a lot about Indonesia – and the rest of the world – in a roundabout way.

The other main English-language newspaper is the *Indonesian Observer*, but its coverage and independence are a long way behind that of the *Jakarta Post*.

Of course, Indonesian-language newspapers are on sale throughout the country. Two of the leading newspapers are the Jakarta daily *Sinar Harapan* and the Catholic newspaper *Kompas*. *Suara Karya* is the mouthpiece of Golkar, the government political party.

Foreign

The *International Herald-Tribune*, *Asian Wall Street Journal* and major Asian dailies are sold in Indonesia. Western magazines like *Time*, *Newsweek*, *The Economist* and the excellent Hong Kong-published *Far Eastern Economic Review* are available in Indonesia.

For information on what's happening in Indonesia today (including Indonesian politics, history and culture) take out a subscription to *Inside Indonesia*, published in Australia at PO Box 190, Northcote, Victoria 3070, Australia. Excellent articles cover everything from power plays within the army, to the environment, and it discusses issues not raised in the Indonesian media and rarely covered overseas.

RADIO & TV

Radio Republik Indonesia (RRI) is the national radio station, which broadcasts 24 hours in Indonesian from every provincial capital. Indonesia also has plenty of privately run stations.

Thanks to satellite broadcasting, TV can be received everywhere in Indonesia. You'll see plenty of satellite dish antennas around the country, aimed almost straight up, as broadcast satellites are put in geostationary orbit – they travel around the equator at the same speed the earth rotates at. You'll also see plenty of Indonesians in geostationary orbit around the TV set of any hotel – they are among the world's foremost TV addicts.

Televisi Republik Indonesia (TVRI) is the government-owned Indonesian-language TV station, which is broadcast in every province. It broadcasts on two channels, but the second channel is not available in more remote areas.

Private stations are Rajawali Citra Televisi Indonesia (RCTI), Andalas Telvisi (AN-TV), Indosair, Surya Citra Televisi (SCTV) and Televisi Pendidikan Indonesia (TPI), a government-owned educational station. Many of these stations have programmes and movies in English with Indonesian subtitles, though the government has announced that all foreign programming must now be dubbed into Indonesian.

Satellite dishes also pick up uncensored overseas stations transmitting in the region, which has worried some government sources and Islamic groups complaining about moral corruption. Other neighbouring governments, such as Singapore, have simply banned satellite receivers and are pursuing cable TV, a much more controllable medium.

Overseas TV can be seen at the large tourist hotels, and while many smaller hotels have satellite dishes, they are not usually interested in tuning them in to programmes in a foreign language they cannot understand. CNN, BBC, Television Australia, Malaysian TV and French TV can all be received.

PHOTOGRAPHY & VIDEO

Indonesia is an incredibly photogenic country and you can easily whip through large quantities of film. Colour print film is preferred to anything else, so slide film and B&W film are not as readily available. Nevertheless, in Jakarta, Bali and the major cities you can usually find most types of film, even Polaroid film, movie film and video tape. Fuji is by far the most widely available brand, for prints and slides, while Kodachrome is rarely seen and has to be sent overseas for developing. Film is cheap.

Developing and printing is quite good, and much cheaper than in the west. You can get Ektachrome and Fujichrome slide film developed in two or three days, and colour print film can be done the same day through photographic shops in major Indonesian towns all across the archipelago. Many of these shops have machines which churn out prints in 45 minutes, and the quality is usually good.

In the small towns and particularly in the outer islands or where few tourists go, many types of film aren't available at all. Turnover of stock is often slow, so it's best to check the expiry date of the film. Film manufacturers warn that films should be developed as quickly as possible once exposed – although in practice they seem to last for months without deterioration, even in Asia's summer heat.

Camera batteries and other accessories are readily available from photographic shops in major cities.

Technical Problems

Shoot early or late as from 10 am to 1 or 2 pm the sun is uncomfortably hot and high overhead, and you're likely to get a bluish washed-out look to your pictures. A polarising filter helps reduce glare and darkens an otherwise washed-out sunlit sky. A lens hood will reduce your problems with reflections and direct sunlight on the lens. Beware of the sharp differences between sun and shade – if you can't get reasonably balanced overall light you may have to opt for exposing only one area or the other correctly. Or use a fill-in flash.

Those lush, green rice fields come up best if backlit by the sun. For those sunset shots at Kuta, Kalibukbuk or Pontianak set your exposure on the sky without the sun making an appearance – then shoot at the sun. Photography from fast-moving trains and buses doesn't work well unless you use a fast shutter speed. Dust can be a problem – hazy days will make it difficult to get sharp shots.

People Photos

You get a fantastic run for your money in Indonesia – not only are there 200 million or so portraits to choose from but the variation in ethnic types is phenomenal.

Few people expect payment for their photos, the Baliem Valley on Irian Jaya being an odd exception. What Indonesians *will* go

for is a copy of the photo – if you hang around Indonesia long enough you'll wind up with a pocketful of bits of paper with addresses of people to send their photos to.

There are three basic approaches to photographing people: one is to be polite, ask permission and pose the shot; another is the no-holds-barred and upset everyone approach; and the other is surreptitious, standing half a km away with a metre-long telescopic lens. Some Indonesians will shy away from having their photo taken and duck for cover; some are shy but only too pleased to be photographed; some are proud and ham it up for the camera; and others won't get out of the way of the bloody lens when you want them too!

Whatever you do, photograph with discretion and manners. Hardly surprisingly, many people don't like having a camera lens shoved down their throats – it's always polite to ask first and if they say no then don't take the photo. A gesture, a smile and a nod are all that is usually necessary. In some places you may come up against religious barriers to taking photographs – such as trying to photograph Muslim women in the more devoutly Islamic parts of the archipelago. The taboo might also apply to the minority groups. Don't take photographs at public bathing places – intruding with your camera is no different to sneaking up to someone's bathroom window and pointing your camera through. Remember, wherever you are in Indonesia, the people are *not* exotic birds of paradise and the village priest is *not* a photographic model. And finally, don't be surprised if Indonesian people turn the tables on you – they have become fond of sneaking up on westerners and shooting a few exotic photos to show their friends!

Prohibited Subjects

Be careful of what you photograph in Indonesia – they're touchy about places of military importance and this can include airports, bridges, railway terminals and stations, seaports and any military installations or bases. Ask if in doubt.

Video

Properly used, a video camera can give a fascinating record of your holiday. As well as videoing the obvious things – sunsets, spectacular views – remember to record some of the ordinary everyday details of life in Indonesia.

Video cameras these days have amazingly sensitive microphones, and you might be surprised how much sound will be picked up. This can also be a problem if there is lots of ambient noise – filming by the side of a busy road might seem OK when you do it, but viewing it back home might simply give you a deafening cacophony of traffic noise. One good rule to follow for beginners is to try to film in long takes, and don't move the camera around too much. Otherwise, your video could well make your viewers seasick! If your camera has a stabiliser, you can use it to obtain good footage while travelling on various means of transport, even on bumpy roads.

Make sure you keep the batteries charged, and have the necessary charger, plugs and transformer suitable for Indonesia. It is possible to obtain video cartridges easily in Jakarta and Denpasar and the main tourist areas, but make sure you buy the correct format. It is usually worth buying at least a few cartridges duty free to start off your trip.

Finally, remember to follow the same rules regarding people's sensitivities as for a photograph – having a video camera shoved in their face is probably even more annoying and offensive for locals than a still camera. Always ask permission first.

TIME

There are three time zones in Indonesia. Sumatra, Java, and West and Central Kalimantan are on Western Indonesian Time, which is seven hours ahead of GMT. Bali, Nusa Tenggara, South and East Kalimantan and Sulawesi are on Central Indonesian Time, which is eight hours ahead of GMT. Irian Jaya and Maluku are on Eastern Indonesian Time, which is nine hours ahead of GMT. In a country straddling the equator, there is of course no daylight-saving time.

Allowing for variations due to daylight saving, when it is noon in Jakarta it is 9 pm the previous day in San Francisco or Los Angeles, midnight in New York, 5 am in London, 1 pm in Singapore and Ujung Pandang, 2 pm in Jayapura and 3 pm in Melbourne or Sydney.

Strung out along the equator, Indonesian days and nights are approximately equal in length, and sunrises and sunsets occur very rapidly with almost no twilight. Sunrise is around 5.30 to 6 am and sunset is around 5.30 to 6 pm, varying slightly depending on distance from the equator.

ELECTRICITY

Electricity is almost always 220V, 50 cycles AC, but a few rare places are still wired for 110V – so check first before you plug in a foreign electrical appliance. Sockets are designed to accommodate two round prongs of the European variety. Recessed sockets are designed to take earth (ground) facilities, but wiring in many hotels and most appliances aren't earthed, so take care. Electricity is usually reliable in cities, but occasional blackouts occur in rural areas. It's wise to keep a flashlight or candles handy for such occasions. Safe adaptors for foreign plugs are hard to find, so bring your own.

Electricity is expensive (for most Indonesians), so cheaper hotels have light bulbs of such low wattage that you can almost see the electricity crawling laboriously around the filaments. If you can't get by with just 25 watts then it might be worth carrying a more powerful light bulb with you.

Street lighting can also be a problem – sometimes there's very little, sometimes none at all. Walking down dark, potholed streets in some Indonesian cities is like walking through a minefield. Falling into a sewage canal is a real drag, so be sure you bring a flashlight.

WEIGHTS & MEASURES

Indonesia has fully adopted the international metric system.

LAUNDRY

Virtually every hotel – from the smallest to the largest – has a laundry service, and in most places this is very inexpensive. About the only thing you need be concerned about is the weather – clothes are dried on the line, so a hot, sunny day is essential. Give staff your laundry in the morning – they like to wash clothes before 9 am so it has sufficient time to dry before sunset.

HEALTH

Being a tropical country with a low level of sanitation and a high level of ignorance, Indonesia is a fairly easy place to get ill. The climate provides a good breeding ground for malarial mosquitos, but the biggest hazards come from contaminated food and water. You should not worry excessively about all this. With some basic precautions and adequate information few travellers experience more than upset stomachs.

In most cases you can buy virtually any medicine across the counter in Indonesia without a prescription. If you need some special medication, take it with you. However, you shouldn't have any trouble finding common western medicines in Indonesia, at least in big cities like Jakarta and Denpasar where there are lots of well-stocked pharmacies *(apotik)*. In rural areas pharmacies are scarce, but grocery shops will gladly sell you all sorts of dangerous drugs, which are often long beyond their expiry dates (check them). Many of the big tourist hotels also have drugstores.

In each apotik there is an English-language copy of the Indonesian Index of Medical Specialities (IIMS), a guide to pharmaceutical preparations available to doctors in Indonesia. It lists drugs by brand name, generic name, manufacturer's name and therapeutic action. Drugs may not be of the same strength as in other countries or may have deteriorated due to age or poor storage conditions.

As for medical treatment, Catholic or missionary hospitals or clinics are often pretty good, and in remote areas may be your only hope other than prayer beads and chanting. Missionary hospitals frequently have English-speaking staff. Back in the developed world, you can often locate a competent doctor *(dokter)*, dentist *(dokter gigi)* and hospital *(rumah sakit)* by asking at hotels or offices of foreign companies in places where large expatriate communities work. In the towns and cities there seems to be a fair supply of doctors and dentists to choose from. In the outback of places like Irian Jaya there are clinics set up by the missionaries. There are also public hospitals in the cities and towns.

Hospitals are open during the day, but private clinics operate mostly in the evening from 6 pm. It's first come, first served, so go early and be prepared to wait. Medical costs are generally very cheap, but drugs are expensive.

Jakarta has the best medical facilities in the country. In south Jakarta, most expatriates use Pondok Indah (☎ 7500157), Jl Metro Duta Kav UE, a perfectly modern hospital that rivals the best hospitals in the west, although it charges modern prices. Better known hospitals in central Jakarta (near Jl Jaksa) include the Rumah Sakit Cipto Mangunkusumo (☎ 330808), Jl Diponegoro 71, a government public hospital which is reasonably priced but very crowded. It has the best emergency care in Jakarta. St Carolus Hospital (☎ 3904441), Jl Salemba Raya 41, is a private Catholic hospital charging mid-range prices.

Another popular medical centre is Medical Scheme (☎ 5255367, 5201034) in the Setiabudi building, Jl H Rasuna Said, Kuningan. It's a private practice but it deals with all emergencies, and vaccinations are given to non-members for a small fee. Doctors speak English and Dutch.

For serious illnesses, Singapore has the best medical facilities in South-East Asia and is only a short flight away. Alternatively, Darwin is close for eastern Indonesia.

Travel Health Guides

There are a number of books on travel health:

Staying Healthy in Asia, Africa & Latin America, Moon Publications. Probably the best all-round guide to carry, as it's compact but very detailed and well organised.

Travellers' Health, Dr Richard Dawood, Oxford University Press. Comprehensive, easy to read, authoritative and also highly recommended, although it's rather large to lug around.

Where There is No Doctor, David Werner, Hesperian Foundation. A very detailed guide intended for someone, like a Peace Corps worker, going to work in an undeveloped country, rather than for the average traveller.

Predeparture Preparations

Health Insurance A travel insurance policy to cover theft, loss and medical problems is a wise idea. There are a wide variety of policies and your travel agent will have recommendations. Some policies offer lower and higher medical expenses options, and a mid-range one is usually recommended for Asia where medical costs are not so high. Check the small print:

- Some policies specifically exclude 'dangerous activities' which can include scuba diving, and even trekking and motorcycling (no doubt because of the legendary accident rate of tourists on Bali). A motorcycle licence acquired on Bali may not be valid under your policy. If such activities are on your agenda, you don't want that sort of policy.
- You may prefer a policy which pays doctors or hospitals direct rather than you having to pay on the spot and claim later. If you have to claim later make sure you keep all documentation. Some policies ask you to call back (reverse charges) to a centre in your home country where an immediate assessment of your problem is made.
- Check if the policy covers ambulances or an emergency flight home. If you have to stretch out you will need two seats and somebody has to pay for them!

Medical Kit A small, straightforward medical kit is a wise thing to carry. A possible kit list includes:

- Aspirin or Panadol – for pain or fever.
- Antihistamine (such as Benadryl) – useful as a decongestant for colds and allergies, to ease the itch from insect bites or stings, and to help prevent motion sickness. There are several antihistamines on the market, all with different pros and cons (eg a tendency to cause drowsiness), so it's worth discussing your requirements with a pharmacist or

doctor. Antihistamines may cause sedation and interact with alcohol, so care should be taken when using them.
- Antibiotics – useful if you're travelling well off the beaten track, but they must be prescribed and you should carry the prescription with you. Some individuals are allergic to commonly prescribed antibiotics such as penicillin or sulpha drugs. It would be sensible to always carry this information when travelling.
- Kaolin preparation (Pepto-Bismol), Imodium or Lomotil – for stomach upsets.
- Rehydration mixture – for treatment of severe diarrhoea. This is particularly important if travelling with children, but is recommended for everyone.
- Antiseptic such as Betadine, which comes as impregnated swabs or ointment, and an antibiotic powder or similar 'dry' spray – for cuts and grazes.
- Calamine lotion – to ease irritation from bites or stings.
- Bandages and Band-aids – for minor injuries.
- Scissors, tweezers and a thermometer (note that mercury thermometers are prohibited by airlines).
- Insect repellent, sunscreen, suntan lotion, chapstick and water purification tablets.
- A couple of syringes, in case you need injections. Indonesian medical workers are not always scrupulous about using new equipment. Ask your doctor for a note explaining why they have been prescribed.

Health Preparations Make sure you're healthy before you start travelling. If you are embarking on a long trip make sure your teeth are OK; there are lots of places where a visit to the dentist would be the last thing you'd want.

If you wear glasses take a spare pair and your prescription. Losing your glasses can be a real problem, although in many places you can get new spectacles made up quickly, cheaply and competently.

If you require a particular medication take an adequate supply, as it may not be available locally. Take the prescription or, better still, part of the packaging showing the generic rather than the brand name (which may not be locally available), as it will make getting replacements easier. It's also wise to have a legible prescription or a letter from your doctor to show that you legally use the medication – it's surprising how often over-the-counter drugs from one place are illegal without a prescription or even banned in another.

Immunisations Indonesia requires no vaccinations to enter the country, apart from yellow fever if you are arriving from a yellow fever infected area within six days. While not compulsory, other vaccinations are highly recommended. Record vaccinations on an International Health Certificate, which is available from your physician or government health department. While you may not ever be required to show it, a record of your vaccinations is useful for future travels, getting boosters etc.

Plan ahead for getting your vaccinations: some require an initial shot followed by a booster, while some vaccinations should not be given together. It is recommended you seek medical advice at least six weeks prior to travel.

Most travellers from western countries will have been immunised against various diseases during childhood but your doctor may still recommend booster shots against measles or polio, diseases still prevalent in many developing countries. The period of protection offered by vaccinations differs widely and some are contraindicated if you are pregnant.

Recommended vaccinations for Indonesia include:

Tetanus & Diptheria Boosters are necessary every 10 years.

Typhoid Available either as an injection or oral capsules. You may get some side effects such as pain at the injection site, fever, headache and a general unwell feeling. A new single-dose injectable vaccine, which appears to have few side effects, is now available but is more expensive. Side effects are unusual with the oral form but occasionally an individual will have stomach cramps.

Hepatitis A The most common travel-acquired illness which can be prevented by vaccination. A new vaccine, Havrix, provides long-term immunity (possibly more than 10 years) after an initial course of two injections and a booster at one year. The second injection should be administered at least three weeks prior to departure.

The other alternative is the less-effective gammaglobulin, which is not a vaccination but a ready-made antibody which has proven very successful in reducing the chances of hepatitis infection. Because it may interfere with the development of immunity, it should not be given until at least 10 days after administration of the last vaccine needed; it should also be given as close as possible to departure because its effectiveness tapers off gradually between three and six months.

Long stayers, those working or living in the country for three months or more, may consider vaccination against Hepatitis B, TB or others as felt appropriate on discussion with a doctor. See under Malaria later in this section for a discussion of malarial prophylactics.

Basic Rules

Food & Water Much of the water that comes out of the tap in Indonesia is little better than sewage water. Depending on how dirty it is and how sensitive you are, it might not even be safe to brush your teeth with tap water; use bottled or boiled water instead.

Bottled water is widely available in Indonesia. It's expensive at restaurants and hotels, but is reasonably priced in grocery shops or supermarkets. You can boil your own water if you carry an electric immersion coil and a large metal cup (plastic will melt), both of which are available in department stores and supermarkets in Indonesia. For emergency use, water purification tablets will help. Water is more effectively sterilised by iodine than by chlorine tablets, because iodine kills giardia and amoebic cysts. However, iodine is not safe for prolonged use, and also tastes horrible. Bringing water to a boil is sufficient to kill bacteria, though at high altitudes five minutes boiling may be required.

It's a good idea to carry a water bottle with you. You are dehydrating if you find you are urinating infrequently or if your urine turns a deep yellow or orange; you may also find yourself getting headaches. Dehydration is a real problem if you go hiking in Indonesia. Fruit juices, soft drinks, tea and coffee will not quench your thirst – when it's really hot, you need water – *clean* water.

When it comes to food, use your best judgement. Have a good look at that restaurant or warung – if it looks dirty, think twice. Street food generally runs a higher risk, but may be better than restaurants if it is cooked on the spot before your eyes. To be absolutely safe, everything should be thoroughly cooked – you can get dysentery from salads and unpeeled fruit. Fish, meat and dairy products are generally OK provided they are fresh – if they spoil, you could become violently ill. Fish can also be a problem if they lived in contaminated water, and shellfish is a much higher risk. Fish from the 'black rivers' of Indonesia are the fastest ticket to the hepatitis clinic.

Other Precautions Sunglasses will protect your eyes from the scorching Indonesian sun. Amber and grey are said to be the two most effective colours for filtering out harmful ultraviolet rays.

Sunburn is also a problem. Bring sunscreen (UV) lotion and something to cover your head. You can also buy sunscreen in better Indonesian pharmacies – two popular brands are Pabanox and Parasol.

Take good care of all cuts and scratches. In this climate they take longer to heal and can easily get infected. Treat any cut with care; wash it out with sterilised water, preferably with an antiseptic (Betadine), keep it dry and keep an eye on it – they can turn into tropical ulcers! It would be worth bringing an antibiotic cream with you, or you can buy one in Indonesia ('NB' ointment). Cuts on your feet and ankles are particularly troublesome – a new pair of sandals can quickly give you a nasty abrasion which can be difficult to heal. For the same reason, try not to scratch mosquito bites.

The climate may be tropical, but you *can* catch a cold in Indonesia. One of the easiest ways is leaving a fan on at night when you go to sleep, and air conditioners are even worse. You can also freeze your hide by sleeping out on the decks of ships at night, or going up to mountainous areas without warm clothes.

Medical Problems & Treatment
Diarrhoea A change of water, food or climate can all cause the runs; diarrhoea caused by contaminated food or water is more serious. Despite all your precautions you may still get a mild bout of travellers' diarrhoea but a few rushed toilet trips with no other symptoms is not indicative of a serious problem. Moderate diarrhoea, involving half-a-dozen loose movements in a day, is more of a nuisance. Dehydration is the main danger with any diarrhoea, particularly for children where dehydration can occur quite quickly. Fluid replacement remains the mainstay of management. Weak black tea with a little sugar, soda water or soft drinks allowed to go flat and diluted 50% with water are all good. With severe diarrhoea a rehydrating solution is necessary to replace minerals and salts. Commercially available oral rehydration salts (ORS) are very useful; add the contents of one sachet to a litre of boiled or bottled water. In an emergency you can make up a solution of eight teaspoons of sugar to a litre of boiled water and provide salted cracker biscuits at the same time. You should stick to a bland diet as you recover.

Lomotil or Imodium can be used to bring relief from the symptoms, although they do not actually cure the problem. Only use these drugs if absolutely necessary – eg if you *must* travel. For children under 12 years Lomotil and Imodium are not recommended. Under all circumstances fluid replacement is the most important thing to remember. Do not use these drugs if the person has a high fever or is severely dehydrated.

In certain situations antibiotics may be indicated:

- Watery diarrhoea with blood and mucus. (Gut-paralysing drugs like Imodium or Lomotil should be avoided in this situation.)
- Watery diarrhoea with fever and lethargy.
- Persistent diarrhoea not improving after 48 hours.
- Severe diarrhoea, if it is logistically difficult to stay in one place.

The recommended drugs (adults only) would be either norfloxacin 400 mg twice daily for three days or ciprofloxacin 500 mg twice daily for three days.

The drug bismuth subsalicylate has also been used successfully. It is not available in Australia. The dosage for adults is two tablets or 30 ml, and for children it is one tablet or 10 ml. This dose can be repeated every 30 minutes to one hour, with no more than eight doses in a 24 hour period.

The drug of choice for children would be co-trimoxazole (Bactrim, Septrin, Resprim), with dosage dependent on weight. A five day course is given.

Ampicillin has been recommended in the past and may still be an alternative.

Dysentery This serious illness is reasonably common in Indonesia. It is caused by contaminated food or water, and is characterised by severe diarrhoea, often with blood or mucus in the stool. There are two kinds of dysentery. Bacillary dysentery is characterised by a high fever and rapid onset; headache, vomiting and stomach pains are also symptoms. It generally does not last longer than a week, but it is highly contagious.

Amoebic dysentery is often more gradual in the onset of symptoms, with cramping abdominal pain and vomiting less likely; fever may not be present. It is not a self-limiting disease: it will persist until treated and can recur and cause long-term health problems.

A stool test is necessary to diagnose which kind of dysentery you have, so you should seek medical help urgently. In case of an emergency the drugs norfloxacin or ciprofloxacin can be used as presumptive treatment for bacillary dysentery, and metronidazole (Flagyl) for amoebic dysentery.

For bacillary dysentery, norfloxacin 400 mg twice daily for seven days or ciprofloxacin 500 mg twice daily for seven days are the recommended dosages. If you're unable to find either of these drugs, a useful alternative is co-trimoxazole 160/800 mg (Bactrim, Septrin, Resprim) twice daily for seven days. This is a sulfa drug and must not be used in people with a known sulfa allergy.

Giardiasis The parasite causing this intestinal disorder is present in contaminated water. The symptoms are stomach cramps, nausea, a bloated stomach, watery, foulsmelling diarrhoea and frequent gas. Giardiasis can appear several weeks after you have been exposed to the parasite. The symptoms may disappear for a few days and then return; this can go on for several weeks. Tinidazole, known as Fasigyn, or metronidazole (Flagyl), are the recommended drugs for treatment. Either can be used in a single treatment dose. Antibiotics are of no use.

Cholera Cholera vaccination is not recommended. However, outbreaks of cholera are generally widely reported, so you can avoid such problem areas. The disease is characterised by a sudden onset of acute diarrhoea, with 'rice water' stools, vomiting, muscular cramps and extreme weakness. You need medical help – but treat for dehydration, which can be extreme, and if there is an appreciable delay in getting to hospital then begin taking tetracycline. See under Dysentery earlier in this section for dosages and warnings.

Typhoid Typhoid fever is another gut infection that travels the faecal-oral route – ie contaminated water and food are responsible. Vaccination against typhoid is not totally effective and it is one of the most dangerous infections, so medical help must be sought.

In its early stages typhoid resembles many other illnesses: sufferers may feel like they have a bad cold or flu on the way, as early symptoms are a headache, sore throat and a fever which rises a little each day until it is around 40°C or more. The victim's pulse is often slow relative to the degree of fever present and gets slower as the fever rises – unlike a normal fever where the pulse increases. There may also be vomiting, diarrhoea or constipation.

In the second week the high fever and slow pulse continue, and a few pink spots may appear on the body; trembling, delirium, weakness, weight loss and dehydration are other symptoms. If there are no further complications, the fever and other symptoms will slowly go during the third week. However, you must get medical help before this because pneumonia (acute infection of the lungs) or peritonitis (burst appendix) are common complications, and because typhoid is very infectious.

The fever should be treated by keeping the victim cool and dehydration should also be watched for.

The drug of choice is ciprofloxacin at a dose of one gram daily for 14 days. It is quite expensive and may not be available. The alternative, chloramphenicol, has been the mainstay of treatment for many years. In many countries it is still the recommended antibiotic, but there are fewer side effects with ampicillin. The adult dosage is two 250 mg capsules, four times a day. Children aged between eight and 12 years should have half the adult dose; younger children should have one-third the adult dose.

People who are allergic to penicillin should not be given ampicillin.

Malaria This serious disease is spread by mosquito bites. If you are travelling in endemic areas, such as Indonesia, it is extremely important to take malarial prophylactics. Jakarta is the only place in Indonesia that has been classified as definitely malaria free. Bali and Java officially fall within the malarial zone but if you are travelling only to the main cities and tourist areas the risk is minimal. Irian Jaya, on the other hand, is definitely a high-risk area, as are some of the more remote parts of the other islands.

Symptoms include headaches, fever, chills and sweating which may subside and recur. Without treatment malaria can develop more serious, potentially fatal effects.

Antimalarial drugs do not prevent you from being infected but kill the parasites during a stage in their development.

There are a number of different types of malaria. The one of most concern is falciparum malaria. This is responsible for the very serious cerebral malaria. Falciparum is the predominant form in many malaria-prone areas of the world, including South-East Asia.

The problem in recent years has been the emergence of increasing resistance to commonly used antimalarials, like chloroquine, maloprim and proguanil. Newer drugs like mefloquine (Lariam) and doxycycline (Vibramycin, Doryx) are recommended for chloroquine and multidrug-resistant areas. Expert advice should be sought, as there are many factors to consider when deciding on the type of antimalarial medication, including the area to be visited, the risk of exposure to malaria-carrying mosquitos, your medical history, and your age and pregnancy status. It is also important to discuss the side-effect profile of the medication, so you can work out some level of risk versus benefit ratio. It is also very important to be sure of the correct dosage of the medication prescribed to you. Some people have inadvertently taken weekly medication (chloroquine) on a daily basis, with disastrous effects. While discussing dosages for prevention of malaria, it is often advisable to include the dosages required for treatment, especially if your trip is through a high-risk area that would isolate you from medical care.

The main messages are:

- Primary prevention must always be in the form of mosquito-avoidance measures. The mosquitos that transmit malaria bite from dusk to dawn and during this period travellers are advised to:
  1. wear light coloured clothing
  2. wear long pants and long sleeved shirts
  3. use mosquito repellents containing the compound DEET on exposed areas (overuse of DEET may be harmful, especially to children, but its use is considered preferable to being bitten by disease-transmitting mosquitos)
  4. avoid highly scented perfumes or aftershave
  5. use a mosquito net – it may be worth taking your own
- While no antimalarial is 100% effective, taking the most appropriate drug significantly reduces the risk of contracting the disease.
- No one should ever die from malaria. It can be diagnosed by a simple blood test. Symptoms range from fever, chills and sweating, headache and abdominal pains to a vague feeling of ill-health, so seek examination immediately if there is any suggestion of malaria.

Contrary to popular belief, once a traveller contracts malaria he/she does not have it for life. Two species of the parasite may lie dormant in the liver but they can also be eradicated using a specific medication. Malaria is curable, as long as the traveller seeks medical help when symptoms occur.

Dengue Fever There is no prophylactic available for this mosquito-spread disease; the main preventative measure is to avoid mosquito bites. A sudden onset of fever, headaches, and severe joint and muscle pains are the first signs before a rash starts on the trunk of the body and spreads to the limbs and face. After a further few days, the fever will subside and recovery will begin. Serious complications are not common.

Eye Infections Trachoma is a common eye infection; it's easily spread by contaminated towels which are handed out by restaurants and even airlines. The best advice about wiping your face is to use disposable tissue paper. If you think you have trachoma, you need to see a doctor – the disease can damage your vision if untreated. Trachoma is normally treated with antibiotic eye ointments for about four to six weeks.

Hepatitis Hepatitis A is a potential problem for travellers to Indonesia. Fortunately, long-term protection is available through the new vaccine Havrix. The alternative to Havrix is the short-lasting antibody gammaglobulin.

The disease is spread by contaminated food or water. The symptoms are fever, chills, headache, fatigue, feelings of weakness and aches and pains, followed by loss of appetite, nausea, vomiting, abdominal pain, dark urine, light coloured faeces, jaundiced skin and the whites of the eyes may turn yellow. In some cases you may feel unwell, tired, have no appetite, experience aches and pains and be jaundiced. You should seek medical advice, but in general there is not much you can do apart from rest, drink lots of fluids, eat lightly and avoid fatty foods. People who have had hepatitis must forego alcohol for six months after the illness, as hepatitis attacks the liver and it needs that amount of time to recover.

Hepatitis B, which used to be called serum hepatitis, is spread through contact with infected blood, blood products or bodily fluids, for example, through sexual contact, unsterilised needles and blood transfusions. Other risk situations include having a shave or tattoo in a local shop, or having your ears pierced. The symptoms of type B are much the same as type A, except that they are more severe and may lead to irreparable liver damage or even liver cancer. Although there is no treatment for hepatitis B, an effective prophylactic vaccine is readily available in most countries. The immunisation schedule requires two injections at least a month apart followed by a third dose five months after the second. Persons who should receive a hepatitis B vaccination include anyone who anticipates contact with blood or other bodily secretions, either as a health care worker or through sexual contact with the local population, particularly those who intend to stay in the country for a long period of time.

Various other new strains have led to a virtual alphabet soup, with hepatitis A, B, C, D, E, G and others. Travellers shouldn't be too paranoid about this apparent proliferation of hepatitis strains; hep C, D, E and G are fairly rare (so far), and following the same precautions as for A and B should be all that's necessary to avoid them.

Sexually Transmitted Diseases Sexual contact with an infected sexual partner spreads these diseases. While abstinence is the only 100% preventative, using condoms is also effective. Gonorrhoea and syphilis are the most common of these diseases; sores, blisters or rashes around the genitals, discharges or pain when urinating are common symptoms.

Symptoms may be less marked or not observed at all in women. Syphilis symptoms eventually disappear completely but the disease continues and can cause severe problems in later years. The treatment of gonorrhoea and syphilis is by antibiotics.

There are numerous other sexually transmitted diseases, for most of which effective treatment is available. However, there is no cure for herpes and there is also currently no cure for AIDS.

HIV/AIDS HIV, the Human Immunodeficiency Virus, may develop into AIDS, Acquired Immune Deficiency Syndrome. Any exposure to blood, blood products or bodily fluids may put the individual at risk. Official HIV figures in Indonesia are pathetically low, though it is widely believed that the real figures are much higher and set to increase significantly unless the promotion of safe sex and hospital practices are improved. The primary risk for most travellers is contact with workers in the sex industry, and in Indonesia the spread of HIV is primarily through heterosexual activity. Apart from abstinence, the most effective prevention is always to practise safe sex using condoms. It is impossible to detect the HIV-positive status of an otherwise healthy-looking person without a blood test.

HIV/AIDS can also be spread through infected blood transfusions; most developing countries cannot afford to screen blood for transfusions. It can also be spread by dirty needles – vaccinations, acupuncture, tattooing and ear or nose piercing can potentially be as dangerous as intravenous drug use if the equipment is not clean. If you do need an injection, ask to see the syringe unwrapped in front of you, or better still, take a needle and syringe pack with you overseas – it is a cheap insurance package against infection with HIV.

Fear of HIV infection should never preclude treatment for serious medical conditions. Although there may be a risk of infection, it is very small indeed.

Rabies Rabies is rare in Indonesia but can be caused by a bite or scratch by an infected animal. Dogs are carriers as are monkeys and cats. Any bite, scratch or even lick from a warm-blooded, furry animal should be cleaned immediately and thoroughly. Scrub with soap and running water, and then clean with an alcohol or iodine solution. If there is any possibility that the animal is infected medical help should be sought immediately to prevent the onset of symptoms and death. In a person who has not been immunised against rabies this involves having five injections of vaccine and one of immunoglobulin over 28 days starting as soon as possible after the exposure. Even if the animal is not rabid, all bites should be treated seriously as they can become infected or can result in tetanus. A rabies vaccination is now available and should be considered if you are in a high-risk category – eg if you intend to explore caves (bat bites can be dangerous) or work with animals.

Fungal Infections Hot weather fungal infections are most likely to occur on the scalp, between the toes or fingers (athlete's foot), in the groin (jock itch or crotch rot) and on the body (ringworm). You get ringworm (which is a fungal infection, not a worm) from infected animals or by walking on damp areas, like shower floors.

To prevent fungal infections wear loose, comfortable clothes, avoid artificial fibres, wash frequently and dry carefully. If you do get an infection, wash the infected area daily with a disinfectant or medicated soap and water, and rinse and dry well. Apply an antifungal powder like the widely available Tinaderm. Try to expose the infected area to air or sunlight as much as possible, and wash all towels and underwear in hot water as well as changing them often.

Cuts & Scratches Skin punctures can easily become infected in hot climates and may be difficult to heal. Treat any cut with an antiseptic such as povidone-iodine. Where possible avoid bandages and Band-aids, which can keep wounds wet. Coral cuts are notoriously slow to heal and if they are not adequately cleaned small pieces of coral can become embedded in the wound. Avoid coral cuts by wearing shoes when walking on reefs, and clean any cut thoroughly with hydrogen peroxide if available. A good dressing is a Chinese preparation called Tieh

Ta Yao Gin which may sting a little, but will dry and heal coral cuts in the warm tropical climate.

Worms These parasites are most common in rural, tropical areas and a stool test when you return home is not a bad idea. They can be present on unwashed vegetables or in undercooked meat and you can pick them up through your skin by walking in bare feet. Infestations may not show up for some time, and, although they are generally not serious, if left untreated they can cause severe health problems. A stool test is necessary to pinpoint the problem and medication is often available over the counter.

Snakes Indonesia has several poisonous snakes (*ular* is the Indonesian word for snake), the most famous being the cobra (*ular sendok*). There are many other poisonous species. *All* sea snakes are poisonous and are readily identified by their flat tails. Although not poisonous, giant-sized pythons lurk in the jungle. They do not generally consume humans but have been known to do so. They do frequently eat pigs, and are thus an enemy of non-Muslim farmers.

To minimise your chances of being bitten always wear boots, socks and long trousers when walking through undergrowth where snakes may be present. Don't put your hands into holes and crevices, and be careful when collecting firewood.

Snake bites do not cause instantaneous death and antivenenes are usually available. Keep the victim calm and still, wrap the bitten limb tightly, as you would for a sprained ankle, and attach a splint to immobilise it. Then seek medical help, if possible with the dead snake for identification. Don't attempt to catch the snake if there is even a remote possibility of being bitten again. Tourniquets and sucking out the poison are now comprehensively discredited.

Jellyfish Heeding local advice is the best way of avoiding contact with these sea creatures with their stinging tentacles. The box jellyfish found in inshore waters in some parts of Indonesia is potentially fatal, but stings from most jellyfish are simply rather painful. Dousing in vinegar will deactivate any stingers which have not 'fired'. Calamine lotion, antihistamines and analgesics may reduce the reaction and relieve the pain.

Women's Health
Gynaecological Problems Poor diet, lowered resistance due to the use of antibiotics for stomach upsets and even contraceptive pills can lead to vaginal infections when travelling in hot climates. Maintaining good personal hygiene, and wearing skirts or loose-fitting trousers and cotton underwear will help to prevent infections.

Yeast infections, characterised by a rash, itch and discharge, can be treated with a vinegar or lemon-juice douche, or with yoghurt. Nystatin, miconazole or clotrimazole suppositories are the usual medical prescription. Trichomoniasis and gardnerella are more serious infections; symptoms are a smelly discharge and sometimes a burning sensation when urinating. Sexual partners must also be treated, and if a vinegar-water douche is not effective medical attention should be sought. Metronidazole (Flagyl) is the prescribed drug.

Pregnancy Most miscarriages occur during the first three months of pregnancy, so this is the most risky time to travel as far as your own health is concerned. Miscarriage is not uncommon, and can occasionally lead to severe bleeding. The last three months should also be spent within reasonable distance of good medical care. A baby born as early as 24 weeks stands a chance of survival, but only in a good modern hospital. Pregnant women should avoid all unnecessary medication, but vaccinations and malarial prophylactics should still be taken where possible. Additional care should be taken to prevent illness, and particular attention should be paid to diet and nutrition. Alcohol and nicotine, for example, should be avoided.

Women travellers often find that their periods become irregular or even cease while they're on the road. Remember that a missed period in these circumstances doesn't necessarily indicate pregnancy. There are health posts or Family Planning clinics in many small and large urban centres, where you can seek advice and have a urine test to determine whether you are pregnant or not.

WOMEN TRAVELLERS

Indonesia is a Muslim society and very much male oriented. However, women are not cloistered or forced to wear purdah and generally enjoy more freedom than in many more orthodox Middle Eastern societies.

Plenty of western women travel in Indonesia either alone or in pairs – most seem to enjoy the country and its people, and most seem to get through the place without any problems, or else suffer only a few minor hassles with the men. Your genetic make-up plays a part – blonde-haired, blue-eyed women seem to have more hassles than dark women. There are some things you can do to avoid being harassed; dressing modestly helps a lot.

Indonesians, both men and women, are generally not comfortable being alone – even on a simple errand they are happier having a friend along. Travelling alone is considered an oddity – women travelling alone, even more of an oddity. Nevertheless, for a woman travelling alone or with a female companion, Indonesia can be easier going than some other Asian countries.

You might spare a thought for Indonesian women, who are given the privilege of doing backbreaking labour and raising children but never trusted in positions of authority. The whole concept of feminism, equality between the sexes etc, would seem absurd to most Indonesians.

GAY & LESBIAN TRAVELLERS

Gay travellers in Indonesia will experience few problems. Physical contact between same-sex couples is quite acceptable, even though a boy and a girl holding hands may be seen as improper. Homosexual behaviour

is not illegal, and the age of consent for sexual activity is 16 years. Immigration officials may restrict entry to people who reveal HIV positive status. Gay men in Indonesia are referred to as *homo* or *gay*.

Indonesia's transvestite/transsexual *banci* community has always had a very public profile. Also known as *waria* – from *wanita* (woman) and *pria* (man) – they are often extrovert performers as entertainers on stage and as street-walkers. Particularly on Java, the banci prostitutes parade their beat at night, provocatively dressed and with great fanfare, attracting primarily heterosexual men seeking oral sex. At performance venues, such as Surabaya's Taman Remaja, the banci mime and perform *dangdut* (popular Indonesian modern music, characterised by wailing vocals and a strong beat) and other music regularly.

Perhaps because of the high profile of the banci, community attitudes to the wider gay community are surprisingly tolerant in a traditional, conservative family-oriented society. Though orthodox Islamic groups are against homosexuality, their views in general are not dominant and there is no queer bashing or campaigns against gays.

There are a few gay organisations, mostly on Java. Gaya Nusantara (☎ (031) 5934924; fax 5939070), Jl Mulyosari Timur 46, Surabaya, coordinates many activities and publishes a monthly magazine *Gaya Nusantara*.

TRAVEL WITH CHILDREN

Travelling anywhere with children requires energy and organisation. The Indonesians are generally very friendly and receptive to children – sometimes too receptive – most Indonesians adore children, especially cute western kids, and children may find the constant attention overwhelming.

Travelling in some areas of Indonesia is hard going, probably too hard for most people to want to tackle with the additional burden of small children. Other areas, such as Bali, are easy. Bali is well set up with resorts, high-quality restaurants, comfortable transport, a ready supply of babysitters and plenty for kids to do. Java doesn't have Bali's mega tourism industry, and so is not as well set up for kids, but it is well developed with a range of amenities, transport, hotel and food options. In the more remote regions, the regional cities are easy to reach by plane, but travel much further afield requires hardiness and experience – both for parents and kids.

Indonesia is not the healthiest country in the world, but with the proper precautions children can travel safely. As with adults, contaminated food and water present the most risks, and children are more at risk from sunstroke and dehydration. Again it depends where you travel and how you travel. Indonesians may have to take their toddlers on gruelling eight hour journeys in stuffy sweltering buses, but you'd be well advised to take a luxury bus or rent a car. Similarly, many adults can comfortably sample warung food, but parents with kids will want to be more careful.

Many inoculations are contraindicated for young children, as are the effective malarial prophylactics. If you're only travelling to the main cities and tourist areas, like the resorts of southern Bali, the malaria risk is minuscule, but in known malarial areas like Irian Jaya or Pulau Nias on Sumatra it is probably not worth the risk.

For more information on travelling with children, with specific examples for Indonesia, Lonely Planet publishes *Travel with Children*.

DANGERS & ANNOYANCES
Theft
While violent crime is very rare in Indonesia, theft can be a problem. If you are mindful of your valuables and take precautions the chances of being ripped off are small. Most thefts are the result of carelessness or naivety. The chances of theft are highest in crowded places and when you are travelling, especially on public bemos, economy buses and trains.

A money belt worn under your clothes is the safest way to carry your passport, cash and travellers cheques, particularly when travelling on the crowded buses and trains. Keep a separate stash of money (say US$200) hidden in your luggage, with a record of the travellers cheque serial numbers and your passport number; you'll need the money if you have got a long trip to the replacement office. If you get stuck, try ringing your embassy or consulate.

Pickpockets are common and crowded bus and train stations are favourite haunts, as are major tourist areas. The thieves are very skilful and often work in gangs – if you find yourself being hassled and jostled, check your wallet, watch and bag. The Indonesian word for thief is *pencuri*.

Don't leave valuables unattended, and in crowded places hold your handbag or day pack closely. Don't carry your passport, travellers cheques or wallet in a bag that can be pickpocketed. Keep an eye on your luggage if it is put on the roof of a bus, but back slashing or theft from bags next to you inside the bus is also a hazard. It is good insurance to have luggage that can be locked. It is worth sewing on tabs to hiking packs to make them lockable.

Always lock your hotel room door and windows at night and whenever you go out, even if momentarily. If you leave small things like sunglasses and books lying around outside your room, expect them to disappear. It's also a depressing reality that sometimes it's your fellow travellers who rip you off. Don't leave valuables lying around in dorms. Bring your own locks for dorm lockers and for those hotel rooms that are locked with a padlock.

Drugs
In most of Indonesia, recreational plants and chemicals are utterly unheard of. Being caught with drugs will result in jail or, if you are lucky, a large bribe. Most marijuana in Indonesia is grown in the north Sumatran province of Aceh, and some of this filters down to tourist resorts such as Danau Toba.

Hotel owners are required by law to turn offenders in. Bali used to be the place to float sky high, but the scene has all but disappeared. You'll still get plenty of offers, but nine times out of ten those 'buddha sticks' are banana leaves, and remember that there are still westerners soaking up the sunshine in Bali's prison.

Crocodiles

The situation here is much like in northern Australia. Crocodiles *(buaya)* mostly inhabit low swampy jungle areas and slow-moving rivers near the sea coast. They wisely avoid contact with humans since they are liable to be turned into fashionable handbags. They *can* be dangerous, but unless you go stomping around the swamps of Irian Jaya you probably won't see one. Still, if you intend to jump into any rivers for a refreshing swim, it would be wise to first make local enquiries.

Noise

If you're deaf, there's no problem. If you're not deaf, you might be after a few months in Indonesia. The major sources of noise are radios and TVs – Indonesians always set the volume knob to maximum. You can easily escape the racket at remote beaches and other rural settings by walking away, but there isn't much you can do on a bus with a reverberating stereo system. In hotels, the lobby often contains a booming TV set, but if you choose your room carefully, you might be able to avoid the full impact. If you complain about the noise, it's likely the TV or radio will be turned down but then turned back up again five minutes later.

Another major source of noise is the mosques, which start broadcasting the calls to prayer at 4 am, repeating the procedure four more times during the day. Again, choose your hotel room carefully.

'Hello Mister' Fatigue

This is the universal greeting given to foreigners regardless of whether the person being addressed is male or female. The less advanced English students know only 'Mister', which they will enthusiastically *scream* in your ear every five seconds – 'Mister Mister Mister!'. Most have no idea what it means, but they have been told by their school teachers that this is the proper way to greet foreigners. After two months of listening to this, some foreigners go over the edge. Try to remember that they think it's polite. It's mainly a problem in the outer islands, not on Java, Bali or the main tourist areas, where foreigners are ubiquitous and English-speaking abilities are higher.

Other Hassles

You tend to get stared at in Indonesia, particularly in places where few foreigners go. But on the whole, the Indonesians stand back and look, rather than gather around you. Those who do come right up to you are usually kids, though some teenagers also do this. Getting stared at is nothing new; almost 500 years ago when the first Portuguese arrived in Melaka the *Malay Annals* recorded that:

...the people of Melaka...came crowding to see what the Franks (Portuguese) looked like; and they were all astonished and said, 'These are white Bengalis!' Around each Frank there would be a crowd of Malays, some of them twisting his beard, some of them fingering his head, some taking off his hat, some grasping his hand.

The insatiable curiosity of Indonesians manifests itself in some peculiar ways. Many Indonesians take their holidays on Bali not for the beach, but so they can stare at foreigners. Sometimes you get people who start following you on the street just to look at you – such people are called *buntut* (tails). If you read a book or write something down, it's not unusual for people to poke their nose right into your book or writing pad, or take it from your hands so that they can have a better look.

The other habit which is altogether ordinary to Indonesians is touching. The Indonesians are an extraordinarily physical people; they'll balance themselves on your knee as they get into a bemo, reach out and touch your arm while making a point in conversation, or simply touch you every time they mean to speak to you or when they want to lead you in a new direction if they're showing you around a house or museum. All this is considered friendly – some Indonesians just have to be friendly regardless of the time or situation, even if it means waking you from your peaceful slumber!

While casual touching among members of the same sex is regarded as OK, body contact between people of different sexes is not. Walking down the street holding hands with a member of the opposite sex will provoke stares, pointing, loud comments and shouting. Public displays of affection (like kissing) may incur the wrath of moral vigilantes.

Sometimes you'll come across young guys who hang around bus terminals, outside cinemas and ferry docks with not much else to do except stir foreigners. They'll crack jokes, laugh and sometimes make obscene gestures. Don't give them their entertainment by chucking a fit – just ignore their puerile antics.

On the whole you'll find the Indonesians (including the army and the police, despite the reputation they have with the locals) *extraordinarily* hospitable and very easy to get on with.

BUSINESS HOURS

Government offices are variable (sometimes very variable) but are generally open Monday to Friday from 7 am to 3 pm. Go in the morning if you want to get anything done. Most post offices have similar opening hours, but central post offices in the large cities often have extended hours and open on weekends for basic postal services. The main Telkom offices are open 24 hours for phone calls, while private telephone agencies are usually open until midnight.

Private business offices have staggered hours: Monday to Friday from 8 am to 4 pm or 9 am to 5 pm, with a break in the middle of the day. Some offices are also open on Saturday morning until noon.

Banks are usually open Monday to Friday from 8 am to 3 or 4 pm. Some banks in major cities also open Saturday mornings, while others may have limited hours for foreign currency transactions, for example, from 8 am to 1 pm. Moneychangers in tourist areas stay open until the evening.

Shops tend to open about 8 am and stay open until around 9 pm. Sunday is a public holiday but some shops and many airline offices open for at least part of the day.

PUBLIC HOLIDAYS & SPECIAL EVENTS

Indonesia has many faiths and many festivals celebrated on different days throughout the country. Islam as the major religion provides many of the holidays. The most important time for Muslims is Ramadan (Bulan Puasa), the traditional Muslim month of daily fasting from sunrise to sunset. Muslim events are affected by the lunar calendar and dates move back 10 or 11 days each year, so it's not easy to list what month they will fall in. Ramadan falls in the ninth month of the Muslim calendar. It's a good time to avoid fervent Muslim areas of Indonesia – you get woken up in your losmen at 3 am in the morning to have a meal before the fasting period begins. Many restaurants shut down during the day, leaving you searching the backstreets for a restaurant that's open. Lebaran (Idul Fitri) marks the end of Ramadan, and is a noisy two day public holiday when half the country seems to be on the move and hotels fill up and prices sky rocket.

January
> New Year's Day (1 January)
> Lebaran (Idul Fitri) – This marks the end of Ramadan and is a noisy celebration at the end of a month of gastronomic austerity. It is a national public holiday of two days' duration.

March-April
> Nyepi – The Balinese New Year marking the end of the Hindu saka calendar.
> Good Friday

April-May
> Waicak Day – This marks Buddha's birth, enlightenment and death.
> Idul Adha – A Muslim festival commemorating Abraham's willingness to sacrifice his son, Isaac, celebrated with prayers and feasts.
> Muharram – The Islamic New Year.
> Ascension of Christ

July
> Maulud Nabi Muhammed (Hari Natal) – This is the birthday of the Prophet Muhammed.

August
> Independence Day (Hari Proklamasi Kemerdekaan) – On 17 August 1945 Soekarno proclaimed Indonesian independence in Jakarta. It is a

national public holiday, and the parades and special events are at their grandest in Jakarta.

December

Isra Miraj Nabi Muhammed – This celebrates the ascension of the Prophet Muhammed (25 December)

Christmas Day (25 December)

With such a diversity of people in the archipelago there are many local holidays, festivals and cultural events. On Sumba, for example, mock battles and jousting matches harking back to the era of internecine warfare are held in February and March. The Balinese have the Galungan Festival, during which time all the gods, including the supreme deity, Sanghyang Widi, come down to earth to join in. In Tanatoraja, in central Sulawesi, the end of the harvest season from July to September is the time for funeral and house-warming ceremonies. On Java, Bersih Desa takes place at the time of the rice harvest – houses and gardens are cleaned, and village roads and paths are repaired. This festival was once enacted to remove evil spirits from the village but it's now used to express gratitude to Dewi Sri, the rice goddess.

A regional *Calendar of Events* is generally available from the appropriate regional tourist office. It lists national holidays, festivals particular to that region, and many of the music, dance and theatre performances held throughout the year. There's also an *Indonesia Calendar of Events* booklet which covers holidays and festivals throughout the archipelago. You should be able to pick up a copy from any of the overseas Indonesian Tourist Promotion Offices, or overseas Garuda Airlines offices.

ACTIVITIES
Scuba Diving

With so many islands and so much coral, Indonesia presents all sorts of possibilities for diving.

For much of Indonesia, diving may not be as good during the wet season, from about October to April, as storms tend to reduce visibility. Bring your scuba certification – most of the main qualifications are recognised,

including those of PADI, NAUI, BSAC, FAUI and SSI.

Bali has the best established dive operators in Indonesia, found in the major resorts and hotels. Baruna Water Sports (☎ (0361) 753820; fax 752779), Jl Bypass Ngurah Rai 300B, Kuta, is one of Bali's most reliable operators. Sanur also has a good selection of dive shops.

Some of Bali's best known dive sites include: Nusa Dua, Sanur, Padangbai, Candidasa, Tulamben (the big attraction is the wreck of the USS *Liberty*), Amed, Lovina Beach and Pulau Menjangan (in the Bali Barat National Park), and perhaps Bali's best diving is on Nusa Penida. Dive operators in Bali's southern tourist area can arrange trips to the main dive sites around the island for US$45 to US$80 per person for two dives with a group of four.

Diving is not as well developed on Lombok, though new diving areas are being explored, such as Gili Petangan off the east coast. Most dive operators are found on Senggigi. Further afield in Nusa Tenggara, Waira near Maumere has dive operators, though much of the nearby reefs suffered damage in the earthquake of 1992. Kupang and more remote Roti also have diving possibilities.

There are the brilliant coral reefs around Pulau Bunaken off Manado in northern Sulawesi, and Sulawesi has many other good dive spots, including the Togian Islands.

In Maluku, the Bandas are popular and Ambon has diving sites and well-established dive operators. Increasingly popular islands are Pulau Halmahera and Pulau Morotai, and around Biak and the Cenderawasih Bay in Irian Jaya, with so many WWII wrecks.

Java is not a great diving destination as the waters tend to be less than clear and it doesn't have the well-developed reefs of some of the other islands. A number of dive operators can be found in Jakarta and in the hotels on the west coast around Carita. Pulau Seribu, just of the coast north of Jakarta, has diving opportunities, as do the waters of West Java, around Krakatau and Ujung Kulon National Park.

On Sumatra, the best diving opportunities are around Pulau We and Pulau Banyak.

Snorkelling

If diving is beyond your budget try snorkelling. Many of the dive sites can also be explored with a snorkel, and there are beautiful coral reefs on almost every coastline in Indonesia. While you can usually buy or rent the gear when you need it, packing your own snorkel, mask and fins is a good idea.

Windsurfing

Obviously, Bali is the place where windsurfing is most common, followed by Lombok. It's caught on in Manado in North Sulawesi too. Indonesians windsurf the Sungai (river) Kapuas at Pontianak in West Kalimantan, and there's a place at Pantai Waiara near Maumere on Flores that rents windsurfing equipment.

Hiking

Despite the fact that Indonesia has numerous opportunities for some superb hiking and jungle trekking, hiking is not well established. Information is lacking and even the national parks often don't have well-maintained trails. Walking in Indonesia is something that poor people have to do, not a recreational activity.

Nevertheless, good hiking can be found, and where demand exists local guide services have sprung up. The national parks, such as Gunung Leuser on Sumatra and Dumoga Bone on Sulawesi, usually have the best hiking possibilities. On Java, the lack of forest means that hiking is mostly limited to short climbs of volcanoes, or Ujung Kulon National Park is the largest wilderness area. Hiking on Bali is similarly restricted mostly to volcanoes, such as Gunung Batur. Gunung Rinjani on neighbouring Lombok is a very popular hiking destination, and the Baliem Valley on Irian Jaya is one of Indonesia's better known walking destinations.

If you hike at high-altitude locations like Gunung Rinjani on Lombok or Puncak Trikora on Irian Jaya, you must be prepared for unstable mountain weather. Sudden rainstorms are common at high altitudes, and

Indonesia is no longer tropical once you get above 3000m. The rain will not only make you wet, but freezing cold. Forget umbrellas – a good rain poncho is essential. Bring warm clothing, but dress in layers so you can peel off each item of clothing as the day warms up. Proper footwear is essential. A compass could be a real life-saver if you're caught in the fog.

Be sure to bring sunscreen (UV) lotion – it's even more essential at high altitudes than in the lowlands.

It should go without saying that you must bring sufficient food and water. Don't underestimate your need for water – figure on about two litres per day, more in extreme heat.

If you haven't done much long-distance walking or jogging recently, work up to it gradually rather than trying to 'get in shape' all at once. Do a few practice runs at home before disappearing into the Indonesian jungles.

Guides A big decision is whether or not you need a guide. Often you do, but be prepared to haggle over the price. Guides in Indonesia sometimes ask for ridiculous amounts of money. Unless hired through a travel agency, a guide will typically cost around 10,000 rp per day. A travel agency may ask 10 times this amount, or more. Take some time to talk to your guide to make sure he (Indonesian guides are always male) really understands the route and won't simply help you get lost.

The Indonesian government has a policy of licensing guides. Licensed guides are not necessarily better than unlicensed ones, but they usually are. If a guide is licensed, he is almost certainly a local, not a transient just passing through looking to pick up some quick cash from tourists. In any event, if your guide claims to be licensed, you should ask to see the licence and copy down his name and number. That way, if you encounter some really big problems (eg the guide abandons you on a mountainside, or rips off your camera and disappears) you can report him. On the other hand, if your guide turns out to be exceptionally good, you can then recommend him to other travellers you meet.

Surfing in Indonesia

Surfing in Indonesia

Dreams of an Indo surf adventure often include wild fantasies of idyllic palm-lined beaches, small bamboo bungalows and perfect barrels peeling around an untouched coral reef. Dreams of a surfing nirvana can come true, but just like anywhere else, Indo is subject to flat spells, onshore winds and, with every new season, more surfers.

In a relatively short time, surfing in Indonesia has experienced tremendous growth, drawing surfers from all parts of the globe. Organised yacht charters and overland tours have become common place, and the pro tour has set up contest sites at Grajagan (G-Land) on Java and the tiny island of Nias in Sumatra.

Crowds can be a problem and, with an increasing number of locals ripping on both small beach-break waves and hollow reef breaks, it can be hard to get waves, particularly on Bali. Treat locals with respect, avoid situations with a smile and you should get lots of waves.

Bali is the focal point and for most surfers the start of their green room search. But from the tip of Sumatra all the way down to West Timor, there is plenty of scope for hardcore surf adventurers to seek out uncrowded waves, hideous tubes and a board bag full of stories to take home.

Weather Conditions

The dry season between May and September is more likely to produce solid ground swell initiated in the Indian Ocean. Trade winds are from the east/south-east, which means winds will be offshore on Bali, from Kuta to Ulu Watu.

During the wet season, between October and April, trade winds will be west/north-west and the other side of Bali (Sanur to Nusa Dua) will be offshore.

Traditionally the months of June and July provide the most consistent and largest swells, but along with the waves come the crowds. Outside the high season, it is still possible to find good waves without the drop-ins and jostling that can go on.

What to Bring

Surfboards On arrival at Denpasar it pays to carry a small amount of Indonesian rupiah, as a 'surfboard tax' (import duty) can sometimes be charged for bringing two or more boards into the country.

Indo's waves mostly break over shallow coral reefs and therefore break more sharply. Given this you will need to have a few more inches underneath you to avoid getting pitched over the falls on the takeoff. Taking a quiver is a good idea. Seven feet to seven feet six inches are the boards most commonly used, but shorter boards are handy for Bali and you'll need every inch of a board around eight feet if you're planning on tackling the big swells.

Board bags holding up to three boards are available, but are expensive. Most Bali-bound airlines are used to carrying this type of board bag but you may be charged for excess luggage at some airports.

Title Page: Shooting the tube can very quickly become a reality in Indonesia, and you'll be stoked about surfing in board shorts and a rash vest (photograph by Martin Tullemans).

Box: Rather than a long paddle, small motorised outriggers have become a common mode of transport in Indonesia (photograph by Martin Tullemans).

Accessories You can buy most surf supplies, including surfboards, at any of the many surf shops in Kuta, although it's better to bring everything you'll need from home. This should include reef boots (preferably hard soled), spare legropes, wax (if you use it), a rash shirt and plenty of full strength sunblock. A set of soft roof racks will make it easier to get around with lots of boards.

Some of the waves in Indo break on super shallow reef, so a surfing helmet and a short arm spring suit will provide protection not only from the reef, but also from the sun.

Most surf shops sell small ding repair kits that are safe to travel with, although local ding repairers are easily found within Kuta or at most of the breaks on Bali.

Organised Tours

Yacht charters and overland tours run throughout the dry season and go to all parts of Indo. Yacht charters allow you to surf breaks that are not accessible by land and offer some of the gnarliest tubes in Indo. They also allow you to escape the overcrowded breaks of Bali.

The Surf Travel Company (STC) offers overland surfaries to G-Land, Sumbawa and Nias. The eight day G-Land trip stays at Bobby's Camp and costs around A$599, including transfers and three meals a day, while the eight day Sumbawa trip stays at Periscope Bungalows for US$350. It also has several yacht charters. Contact its office in Australia for further details: PO Box 446, Suite 2/25, Cronulla Plaza, Cronulla, NSW 2230 (☎ (02) 9527 4722, 9527 4119).

STC's US agent is Waterways Travel (☎ (818) 376 0341) and its contact point for all surfaris on Bali is Wanasari Wisata (☎ 755588), 8B Jl Pantai, Kuta. Daily services run to Nusa Lembongan, Kuta reef, Ulu Watu, Canggu and Medewi.

At Tubes, on Poppies Gang II in Kuta, you can book an eight day G-Land trip staying at The Chinaman's Camp for around A$599, including transfers and three meals a day.

Indo Dreams surf shop (☎ 758650) on Poppies Gang II, opposite Pub Bagus, offers eight day boat trips to Nusa Lembongan, Lombok and Sumbawa with Island Express boat tours for around 900,000 rp.

Daily boat trips to Nusa Lembongan can be booked at most tourist offices on Bali or in Sanur. Boats from Sanur leave around 8.30 am, cost 15,000 rp one way and take around 1½ hours, depending on the conditions.

More Information

As the popularity of surfing in Indo has increased, so has the demand for guides detailing weather conditions and places to surf. See the Books section in this chapter for recommended surfing guides.

The publishers of *Surfer Magazine*, Surfer Publications, publishes *The Surf Report – Journal of World-wide Surfing Destinations*. For a fee of around US$6 per destination it provides detailed information on surf conditions in Indo, maps and the best weather conditions for the various breaks. Order it at PO Box 1028, Dana Point, CA 92629, USA (☎ (714) 496 5922).

Bali

Touted as a surfing Mecca, Bali has much to offer surfers. Though getting to the breaks can be an adventure in itself, the rewards at the end of the road can be well worth the time it takes. If you plan to hire a car or motorcycle, try taking a bemo the first few times you travel to the breaks, just to get familiar with the roads and where the waves are. If you take a hire car, don't leave anything behind in the car – not even your tie downs.

Tubes Bar & Restaurant on Poppies Gang II is a great place for surfers to hang out. It has great meals, surfboards for sale and daily surf movies. Tide charts are also available.

West Coast

Ulu Watu The set up at Ulu Watu is a true surfers' paradise. Warungs line the cliff and look out over the break. The locals at the warung you choose will watch over your gear while you surf and most will let you stay the night if the surf's up.

To paddle out you first have to negotiate the steep path and step ladder that descends down into the cave. At high tide you can paddle out from the cave, but at low tide a walk across the reef will be necessary. The current washing down the reef (particularly when it's big) can be quite strong, so start well right of the cave when you head in to avoid getting swept past it.

The wave has three main sections that are all left-handers: The Peak, Racetracks and Outside Corner. **The Peak** is a high tide wave that handles small and big swells and is directly in front of the cave. **Racetracks**, further down the reef, is a hollow wave that starts to work properly on the mid-tide and gets better as it runs out. It handles up to about six feet and is very shallow. On a big swell and a low tide, try **Outside Corner** for a long ride on a huge face.

Padang Possibly Bali's most hollow wave, Padang is a dangerously shallow left-hander that only works when Ulu Watu is around eight to ten feet. Its jacking takeoff forms into a perilous tube that only experienced surfers should try to exit.

The wave is best surfed on the mid to high tide and will provide top to bottom tube action for the surfer or the spectator. Take the road from Pecatu village to Padang and Bingin.

Bingin & Impossibles Bingin is a short left-hander and its peaky takeoff provides a steep drop followed by a walling barrel section. Be careful not to ride it too far and flick off before the end section closes out on a sharp shallow reef. It will handle around six feet before it starts closing out. The warungs along the beach make food and provide shelter and storage for your gear.

Paddle out to Impossibles from the south end of the warungs at Bingin. The wave looks like you can ride it forever, but it's not called Impossibles for nothing. In bigger swells at low tide you will have the best chance of making longer sections.

Belangan This left-hander is not as top to bottom as Ulu Watu or Padang and needs a high tide, but can be surfed in small or big swells. Although it's not surfed much, this may change when the huge resort on the cliff is completed and beach access is improved.

Airport Rights & Lefts The right-hander breaks on the south side of the airport runway, while the left breaks on the north side. They are best reached by a boat ride from the beach in front of the breaks. The left is usually less crowded than Kuta reef and a little bigger, but not as hollow.

Kuta Reef Take a boat ride from the beach in front of the break (5000 rp return) or paddle out if you're feeling fit. The mid to high tide is best. When it gets big, the wall doubles up on the takeoff and is a fast tubing section all the way to the shoulder. On a high tide the inside reforms and is a bowling wall over a shallow reef. This place is always crowded so you'll need patience.

Kuta & Legian Beach Breaks This is one of the few Indonesian beaches where beginners can learn how to surf. The waves can get big and sometimes the currents are strong, so take care. Hire boards from locals along the beach.

Kuta can provide some fast tubing waves over its sandy bottom and handles some sizeable swells. Any good peak will be crowded, but the beach is long and some less crowded peaks can be found. When Kuta is small, Ulu Watu will be a few feet bigger and Racetracks will be the best option on the mid to low tide.

Legian is usually one or two feet bigger than Kuta and similar peaks and tubing sections can be found on bigger swells. A long walk further north along the beach could provide some waves away from the crowds.

Canggu This is a right-hand reef break good for natural footers. The right is surfable from mid to high tide and holds up to about eight feet. There is a left off the right and another left further north. Canggu will be a foot or two bigger than the Kuta beach breaks. South-east trade winds during the dry season may be side to onshore, so a dawn patrol is the best bet for glassy waves. Canggu has warungs and places to stay.

From Canguu to Medewi, some Legian-style beach breaks and a few reef breaks are reported, but not surfed much.

Medewi Medewi is a long left-hander over a rock and sand bottom. Though a long ride, it's not hollow like the lefts of Ulu Watu, Padang or Bingin. Like Canggu, the trade winds are onshore, so early morning on a mid to high tide will be the best time for a surf. It's about 75 km north of Kuta, so you might need to spend a couple of days there while a swell is running to make the most of the break.

South Coast

Greenball & Nyang Nyang These right and left waves break over reef and sand bottom and need small swells and north winds. During both the dry and wet seasons the wind is cross shore, so a dawn patrol is often the only solution. There can be dangerous currents facing the open ocean. The steep cliffs down to the beach also require careful negotiation, though access to Greenball is via the Bali Cliffs resort and is easier to reach.

East Coast

Nusa Dua Big, thick shifting peaks followed by fast bowl sections characterise Nusa Dua as possibly Bali's best right-hander, usually picking up one to two feet more swell than elsewhere and often overhead. The wave breaks over a more forgiving reef than the lefts on Bali's west coast. It can handle almost any size swell and provides long rides.

During the dry season the wind will be onshore, so it will pay to get there before sunrise. Though offshore during the wet season, waves may be smaller, but good size cyclone swells can provide solid rides.

Take a boat ride to the break from the south end of the golf course as the peak is a long way out to sea.

Sri Lanka A right-hand reef break with a steep bowling takeoff that turns into a very hollow end section. Sri Lanka is more protected in the dry season, but usually smaller than Nusa Dua.

Sanur A fickle, right-hand reef break. Sanur is best on bigger swells and can be surfed on any tide, although mid to high is often better. Its end section is a super shallow almost dry reef excursion that will probably lead to injury, so avoid pulling in.

Between Nusa Dua and Sanur are more reef breaks (**Serangan, Hyatt Reef** and **Tanjung Sari**), but they are a long way offshore and can also be fickle, requiring the right swell and wind direction.

North of Sanur The right-hander **Padang Galak**, **Ketewel**, **Lebih** and **Padangbai** are a combination of beach break and reef waves, although Padang Galak is a sand bottom beach break. These places require big swells from the right direction and even then will be smaller than Sanur, but may be a good option if you are wanting to escape the crowds.

Nusa Lembongan

East across the Badung Strait from Bali is the small island of Nusa Lembongan. The two main breaks are Shipwreck's and Lacerations. They are both right-hand reef breaks and are best surfed in the south to south-east trade winds over the dry season.

Shipwreck's, so named because of the old rusted hull poking precariously up out of the reef, is known for its back door tubes and fast walling sections. You can paddle out at high tide or navigate the small sand trails through the seaweed farm out to the reef at low tide. Wear your reef boots and don't be surprised if you see the odd sea snake wriggle through the patchy seaweed bottom.

Lacerations, also aptly named, is a super shallow tube from takeoff until you're spat into the channel. Usually smaller than Shipwreck's, it needs a bigger swell to work – when it does you should wear reef boots, some rubber and possibly a helmet.

Lombok

The best-known break on Lombok is Desert Point (Bangko Bangko), but waves are increasingly being surfed along the south and west coasts.

Desert Point

Although classic when it works, Desert Point is known as an inconsistent wave that needs a solid ground swell and a dry season south-easterly trade wind. The wave is a left-hander over a coral reef that can get shallow on the inside, so it's best to wear your reef boots. Starting as a smaller peak, the wave builds as it goes down the line and entices you into surprisingly makeable tube sections, but gets faster and shallower the further you go.

Desert Point is best accessed through yacht charters out of Bali or Nusa Lembongan, but it is possible to drive to the break and camp in the small primitive huts on the beach. Bring all of your own supplies.

West Coast

Like Desert Point, the waves on the west coast need a solid ground swell to work properly. **Senggigi** has a right and left reef break that works on dry season trade winds, while further north, **Gili Air** has two breaks. **Pertama** on Gili Air is a very hollow right-hander and, like most hollow Indo waves, breaks over shallow coral reef. The wave can be messy in strong trade winds during the wet and dry season.

South Coast

Working in a variety of changing weather conditions, it's possible to surf the south coast year-round. Some breaks work in the easterly trade winds of the dry season, others work in the westerly trade winds of the wet season, and some work on a northerly wind. Most of the waves break over coral reef, and there are lefts and rights to choose from.

Kuta, on the central south coast, is a good place to begin looking for waves, with a left and a right reef break. Travelling overland by car will get you to most of the breaks, but some will require boat charters for access or an outrigger ride out to the break.

Other places to check include **Semeng**, **Awung** and **Ekas**, all east of Kuta and accessible by car. You may need to charter a yacht and go looking for waves west of Kuta.

Sumbawa

Most surf trips to Sumbawa's west coast (Scar Reef, Supersuck and Yo Yo's) will be organised by yacht charters.

To surf the south-east coast, fly or ferry to Bima and then hire a taxi or negotiate a series of buses to Huu to surf the Periscopes and Lakey Peak area.

Much of the south coast is not surfed and very hard to get to overland, but opportunities for hardened surf adventurers do exist.

West Coast

Scar Reef This left-hander breaks over sharp coral reef and is usually best on the high tide, but needs a solid ground swell to line-up. If it's small at low tide don't despair, the wave often jacks two to three feet on the incoming tide. Beware of the unexpected and unforgiving shutdowns further down the line after the takeoff. The break holds big swells, but the dry season trade winds are mostly cross shore.

You can camp on the beach, but the facilities are nonexistent so you will need to bring all of your own supplies. If you are staying on the beach the paddle out is about one km.

There are a few yacht charters doing this leg now, so don't be surprised to see another yacht anchored at the break.

Supersuck Aptly named Supersuck, this wave turns inside out and is a tube rider's dream. The steep peaky takeoff funnels into a long sucking bowl over a shallow reef. The wave can be surfed on all tides, but is super shallow at low tide. Unfortunately, Supersuck requires a big swell to turn on, but in its favour the dry season trade winds are mostly offshore.

Yo Yo's This right-hand reef break is reasonably deep compared with Supersuck, but the end section gets shallow on a mid to low tide. The wave horseshoes around the reef with some good tubes and walling sections. This bay cops any swell that's around and will be rideable even if Scar Reef is flat. It holds up to about six feet and is best on the high tide. The dry season trade winds are onshore, so early morning surfs are best.

The beach is accessible by land and is about a 20 minute walk off the dirt road that leads south from Maluk village. There is accommodation at Maluk.

South-East Coast

It is possible to surf here year-round as the dry season trade winds tend to cross to onshore. Surfing with fewer people in the water may mean gambling on swell size late in the wet season, but could pay off.

There are plenty of good bungalow-style losmens close to all the breaks.

Lakey Peak A classic A-frame peak with a left and a right. It is usually better for holding big swells and providing good hollow tube sections. Watch out for surfers trying to backdoor the peak. The wave is best surfed at low to mid tide in glassy early morning conditions.

Lakey Pipe is another left over a sucking rock ledge. Deep barrels can be expected.

Nungas On big swells of eight feet plus, this place starts to get good with the sections lining up. It holds almost any size swell and provides big walls and tubing sections.

Periscopes A popular destination for natural footers looking for a right. The wave handles up to about eight feet and can provide excellent tubes over a rock reef. Watch out for the shallow end section bowl before reaching the channel. The wave is best for surfing on the mid to high tide.

It is about two km from Lakey Peak.

Sumba & Timor

Though these islands are being surfed more and more, take a few friends with you, just in case there is no-one out. Yeah!

Around south-western Sumba, **Rua** is a good place to head for. It is a left-hand reef break and the dry season trade winds are cross to offshore. **Tarimbang** on Sumba's central southern coast and **Baing** on the south-eastern coast also have good waves.

STC provides yacht charters to Timor, for surfing at **Roti** and other outer islands. This is possibly the best way to surf Timor. The breaks you'll surf are **T-land** off Roti, **Nusa**, **Ndao**, **Ndana** and **Boa** islands.

T-land is a big left-hander and can be reached by travelling overland to **Nemberala** on Roti. There are several losmens on the beach right in front of the wave.

MARTIN TULLEMANS

More and more Indonesian locals are getting into the water. Here, hot Balinese local Rizal Tanjung throws a good spray at Ulu Watu.

MARTIN TULLEMANS

Surfing a longer board is almost a necessity for negotiating steep drops like this one at Lakey Pipe, Sumbawa.

MARTIN TULLEMANS

When it's working, Super Suck on Sumbawa's southwestern coast is a mechanical tube that barrels from the takeoff all the way down the line.

MARTIN TULLEMANS

After the sucky takeoff, another perfect tube reels across the reef at Lakey Pipe, Sumbawa.

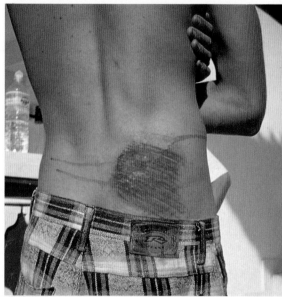

The price you pay for surfing over shallow coral reef is often a scrape similar to this, but it can sometimes be much worse.

MARTIN TULLEMANS

G-land on Java is known for its long rides and deep barrels – this is no exception.

MARTIN TULLEMANS

Java

Grajagan

Alas Purwo National Park on Java's south-east tip is home to what has become a world famous surfing break. Regularly publicised and recently made a leg of the world surfing championships, G-Land is a freight train left-hander that has several takeoff sections, monster barrels and speeding walls. From the camp at Plengkung, the reef stretches east up around the headland as far as the eye can see and, when a ground swell hits and big tubing left-handers line-up all the way round, it's truly a sight to behold.

The only way to surf G-Land is with an organised tour out of Bali (see Organised Tours earlier in this section) or try Wanawisata Alamhayati (☎ 81217), about one km from the centre of Banyuwangi on the road to Carita.

The break has four main sections: Kongs, Moneytrees, Launching Pads and Speedies. **Moneytrees** is probably the most consistent, but **Launching Pads** to **Speedies** starts as a wedging peak and runs into a grinding barrel over the shallow speed reef. The dry season trades are offshore and the wave works best when a solid ground swell over six feet turns on.

If it's too big to paddle out from the edge of the reef, a zodiac will take you around from the channel west of the camp.

A long walk further west of the camp along the beach may provide some good reef breaks if G-Land is 10 feet plus. **Twenty Twenties** is a left-hand reef break and **Tiger Tracks** is a right.

Wanasari Wisata in Kuta has a departure calender outlining the duration and dates of the pro tour contest.

West Java

Gaining popularity among surfers, the south-west beaches of Java offer some excellent opportunities to get good right and left breaks and good beachies. Head for **Pelabuhanratu** where there are quite a few breaks, with **Cimaja** being the most well known. Cimaja is a right-hand reef break that holds big swells.

Further south is **Genteng**, which is usually bigger than Cimaja as it is more exposed to the open ocean. **Ombak Tujuh** is a big left just north of Genteng.

Be wary of strong rips and currents around all of these spots and don't surf alone. It is also a popular surf spot for Jakarta's locals who are mostly friendly – smile and don't hassle for waves.

Pulau Panaitan

Part of Ujung Kulon National Park, Pulau Panaitan is uninhabited apart from a small ranger's station and is only accessible by yacht charter.

The waves here are incredibly hollow breaking over super shallow coral reef and often get faster and more hollow toward the end section. It's advisable to take a spring suit and even a full length wet suit is not out of the question. The No 1 rule for all of the breaks is not to prone out and go straight in front of the white-water. The waves break so close to the reef that if you do go straight you'll be on dry coral in seconds. If the wave looks like closing down and you can't get off, tuck into the tube, it's definitely the safest place to be. This place is for experienced surfers only.

One Palm Point, on the south-eastern corner of the bay, is a merciless tubing left-hander that needs a bigger swell to work and is offshore in the dry season's south-easterly trade winds. Line up with the palm for the takeoff and then flick out in front of the broken surfboard nailed to the tree further down the reef. After the flick-off spot, the wave gets faster and shallower and, though it may look makeable, there is usually no exit. The wave breaks too close to the reef to surf on a small swell, so it has to be around six feet before you can tackle it.

Napalm is another intense left-hander that needs a moderate swell to work and a north wind to be offshore. Best surfed in the early morning in the dry season, it also breaks close to the reef and is most rideable on mid to high tide. The end section bowl is a makeable tube, but is really shallow.

Illusions is a right-hander over coral reef on the western side of the bay that works on a westerly wind. The spot needs a moderate swell and is often onshore in the dry season. It's a fast fun wall with tubing sections and can provide a long ride.

There are other breaks to surf, such as the beach break **Crock n Rolls** and **Pee Pee's**, a left-hander on the western side of Java off Ujung Kulon National Park. Pee Pee's needs a moderate to big swell to work and is offshore in the dry season trades. It's sometimes surfed on the way to Panaitan.

Sumatra

Northern Sumatra's **Nias** is the most visited surfing destination. Like G-Land, the pro tour visits in the dry season for a leg of the contest championships. Getting there can take a while – see the respective Getting There & Away sections in the Sumatra chapter.

There are plenty of cheap losmen nestled among the palm fringed shore at **Lagundri Bay**, with the famous right-hander in full view.

Yacht charters booked through STC leave from Lagundri Bay and visit the neighbouring **Talos**, **Hinakos** and **Mentawai** islands. Tours stay at the more expensive Sorake Beach Resort. Fishing trawlers can also be chartered to the outer islands, but are less comfortable than an organised yacht charter.

The right-hander is a relatively short wave, but at size is a high tight tube from takeoff to finish. The outside reef only starts to work on a solid ground swell of about four to six feet, but holds huge swells and the tubes are perfect. The water is pretty deep and the sets tend to spring up quickly, so keep your eye on **Indicators** further out the back.

In between the main peak and Indicators is a channel in the reef called the **Keyhole**, which provides a safe paddle out to the takeoff area. West to north-westerly winds are offshore and the wave can be surfed on all tides.

On the other side of the bay is a gnarly left-hander that is offshore in easterly winds and provides very hollow tubes. Only surfed on high tides, the famous right needs to be around five feet before this left starts to work.

The outer islands offer some classic tubing rights and lefts over shallow coral reef. This area has been further explored by yacht charter over recent years and new spots are being found all the time.

Whitewater Rafting

Although the art of floating down raging rivers is not well developed in Indonesia, there is great potential. A few commercial operators now cater to this peculiar western custom. The Sungai Hamputung on Kalimantan offers a fairly easy float down a river with an impressive jungle canopy above. The canyon of the Sungai Sadan in Torajaland, Sulawesi, is becoming popular. There are a number of other rivers in Central Sulawesi which are also attracting western tour groups. Enquire with local travel agents if interested. Bali, of course, will pump anything of tourist interest, and hotels and travel agents sell trips down the Ayung River.

Whitewater enthusiasts get quite a thrill out of being the first to raft a particular river, and in this regard Indonesia offers quite a few opportunities. There are a number of unrafted rivers on Irian Jaya, but tackling these will require expedition-style preparations – roads are nonexistent, crocodiles will probably find western food delightful and there may be unexpected surprises like waterfalls. But if you survive all this, it will certainly be the adventure of a lifetime.

COURSES

Many students come to Indonesia to study Indonesian. Most courses are arranged by universities overseas, and are held at the more prestigious universities, including the University of Indonesia in Jakarta and Gajah Mada University in Yogyakarta.

The better private courses can charge US$15 or more per hour, though many offer individual tuition. Jakarta, Yogyakarta and Bali have schools geared for foreigners wishing to learn Bahasa Indonesia.

In Jakarta, some of the cultural centres arrange courses, notably the Perhimpunan Persahabatan Indonesia Amerika (☎ (021) 8583241), Jl Pramuka Kav 30, the French Cultural Centre (☎ (021) 3908585) and the Goethe Institut (☎ (021) 8581139). More expensive private schools include the Indonesian Australia Language Foundation (☎ (021) 5213350), Jl Rasuna Said Kav C6.

Yogyakarta is another favoured place for learning Indonesian. Realia (☎ (0274) 564969), Pandega Marta V/6, Pogung Utara, is highly regarded but expensive. There are plenty of other language schools or even one day courses are arranged for travellers.

Bali Language Training & Cultural Centre (☎ (0361) 239331), Jl Tukad Pakerisan 80, Panjejr, Denpasar, has courses in painting, woodcarving and Balinese dance, as well as Bahasa Indonesia.

There are opportunities for studying Indonesian arts. Batik courses are popular in Yogyakarta and Solo. Mostly they are one day T-shirt making exercises, but more serious study is possible.

WORK

It is possible for foreigners to work in Indonesia, provided you are willing to make some long-term commitments. Although Indonesia is still an underdeveloped country, in some situations you can be paid well. Officially, a work permit is required to work in Indonesia, and these are very difficult to get and should be arranged by your employer.

Indonesia is experiencing an economic boom, and the freeing up of the economy has seen a huge influx of foreign capital and foreign companies, which are the main employers of foreigners. Most positions are managerial, though people with valuable technical skills, such as engineers, computer programmers and the like, may be able to find jobs with foreign multinational corporations. By far the best way to arrange this is through a company overseas. By fronting up in Jakarta and finding work yourself, you may miss out on the benefits that most expats get as standard – accommodation, car and driver etc.

There are jobs available for westerners as chefs and bartenders in five star hotels. The pay is good, but these jobs are usually for men only. It is also possible to pick up work teaching English or another European language, but as a glance at any tourist brochure will show, native speakers of foreign languages are not widely employed in Indonesia. The best opportunities lie in private tutoring in Jakarta, where you can get 30,000 rp per hour or more, but work tends to be part-time only. Many people who take jobs in hotels or teaching English do so on a tourist visa. You run the risk of being fined and booted out of the country if caught, and it also leaves you with little recourse if there is a dispute with your employer over pay and conditions.

Apart from expats employed by foreign companies, most foreigners working in Indonesia are involved in some sort of business, usually exporting clothing, furniture, crafts and the like.

ACCOMMODATION
Mandi & Toilets
One thing you'll have to learn to deal with is the *mandi*. The word mandi simply means to bath or to wash. A mandi is a large water tank beside which you'll find a plastic saucepan. The popularity of the mandi is mainly due to a frequent lack of running water in Indonesia – sometimes the tank is refilled by a hose attached to a hand-pump.

Climbing into the mandi is very bad form indeed – it's your water supply and it's also the supply for every other guest that comes after you, so the idea is to keep the water clean. What you're supposed to do is scoop water out of the mandi and pour it over yourself. Most of the better tourist hotels have showers and hot water, and even bathtubs.

Another thing which may require adjustments to your way of thinking are Indonesian toilets. These are basically holes in the ground, footrests on either side, over which you squat and aim. In some tourist areas, Asian toilets are fading away as more places install western-style toilets. The lack of running water makes flushing toilets a problem, so what you do is reach for that plastic saucepan again, scoop water from the mandi and flush it that way.

As for toilet paper, you'll seldom find it supplied in public places, though you can easily buy your own. In fact, Indonesians seldom use the stuff. This is partly to save money, but mainly because Indonesian plumbing systems don't handle toilet paper too well and easily become clogged up. The Indonesian method is to use the left hand and copious quantities of water – again, keep that saucepan handy. Some westerners easily adapt to this method, but many do not. If you need to use toilet paper, see if there is a wastebasket next to the toilet. If there is, then that's where the paper should go, not down the toilet. If you plug up the hotel's plumbing with toilet paper, the management is going to get really angry.

Kamar kecil is Bahasa Indonesia for toilet, but they usually understand 'way-say' (WC). *Wanita* means women and *pria* means men.

Camping
Camping grounds are relatively rare, but there are plenty of opportunities for back-country camping. It is important that you camp away from civilisation, unless you want Indonesian spectators all night.

You can probably do without a sleeping bag below 1000m, but at higher elevations you'll certainly need one. Rain is a possibility even in the dry season, especially as you gain altitude, so bring some sort of tent or rainfly. You'll also want to guard against insects and other things that crawl and slither in the night, so a tent or mosquito net would be appropriate.

Hostels
Indonesia doesn't have much in the way of hostels, mainly because there are so many low-cost hotels. One exception is Jakarta, where accommodation is relatively dear, so there are a number of places offering cheap dormitory accommodation. There are a handful of hostels in a few other places, like Surabaya and Kupang, but it's entirely possible to travel through Indonesia on a tight budget without ever staying in a hostel.

The main thing to be cautious about in hostels is security. Few places provide lockers, and it's not just the Indonesians you must worry about – foreigners have been known to subsidise their vacation by helping themselves to other people's valuables.

While it's not a huge problem, it is something to be aware of.

If you want to avoid nocturnal visits by rats, don't put food in your room, or at least have it sealed in ratproof jars or containers. Rats have a keen sense of smell, and they can and will chew through a backpack to get at food.

Bedbugs are occasionally a problem in this climate. Examine the underside of the mattress carefully before retiring. If you find it crawling with bugs, either change rooms or have the management spray copious quantities of poison which, hopefully, will eliminate the bugs rather than you.

Hotels

Hotels in Indonesia come in different grades of price and comfort. At the bottom end of the scale is the *penginapan*. A slightly more upmarket penginapan is called a *pondok* or *losmen*. *Wisma* are slightly more upmarket again, but still cheap. Hotel is at the top of the heap.

The Indonesian government has embarked on a campaign to get all penginapan, losmen, wisma and pondok to change their names to 'hotel'. This has largely been successful, but not all the hotel owners are happy about this, since the old naming system gave potential guests some idea of the price. Also, if they are hotels, they have to pay 10% tax.

A hotel can be either a flower *(melati)* or *yasmin* hotel, which is relatively low standard, or a star *(bintang)* hotel, which is more luxurious. A hotel at the bottom of the barrel would be one melati whereas a five star hotel *(lima bintang)* occupies the top end. Most star hotels post signs indicating star rating as set by the government.

All hotels are required to pay a 10% tax to the government, and this may be passed on to the customer, but most cheap hotels either avoid the tax or absorb it into their room rates. Upper-crust places charge a whopping 21% tax and service charge. Why 21%? That's 10% tax, 10% service charge and 10% tax on the service charge, which makes another 1%.

The government, in a show of linguistic chauvinism, has also announced that foreign words are now forbidden to be used in hotel names. This has created a fair amount of confusion. Many hotels have changed their names, but not their signs or letter heads. Others have ignored it, and others don't have to comply because they have copyrighted trademarks. So the thousands of 'Beach' hotels now become 'Pantai' hotels, and the words bungalow, inn, sunset etc are also replaced with their Indonesian equivalents. Nevertheless, everyone in town will still refer to the hotel by its old name.

The real budget hotels are spartan places with shared bath, costing as little as 5000 rp per person. Mid-range hotel rooms often come with private bath and typically cost from 15,000 rp for a single. The five star hotels can match the best in the west, with prices piercing the US$100 level. But in Indonesia, what you pay depends more on where you are; the cost of accommodation varies considerably across the archipelago. If you follow the well-beaten tourist track through Bali to Java and Sumatra, you'll find Indonesia one of the cheapest places in South-East Asia (exceptions like Jakarta apart). Travellers centres like Bali, Yogyakarta and Danau Toba are superb value for food and accommodation. Nusa Tenggara is marginally more expensive than Bali, but cheap by any standards. On the other hand, once you get to some of the outer provinces, like Kalimantan, Maluku or Irian Jaya, you'll pay much more.

If you get into a town and the cheap places mentioned in this book are full, or you have no information on cheap places to stay, then ask taxi drivers, becak drivers or even the police what's available. Other travellers who have come from where you're heading are also good sources of information.

Many hotels have fixed prices and display them, but prices may be flexible, especially in quiet periods. The most polite way to get a cheaper price is to simply ask for a discount. Ask to see the printed price list *(daftar harga)* when you front up at a hotel. For many cheap and mid-range hotels, the price is often fixed to this rate. Seeing the price list will also give you an idea of the range of rooms – many hotels have a huge range of rooms from cheap to expensive, but you may only be offered the most expensive. If there is no price list, there may be room for negotiation.

Ironically, it's high-class places where you can bargain most. They seem to put their prices up every year regardless of occupancy rates or good sense, and accordingly the discounts also grow every year. As a rule, never pay the published rate at a top-end hotel. Always ask for a discount, which are readily available and range from 10% to 50%. On arrival in Indonesia you can book luxury hotels through travel agents for big discounts.

Top-end hotels often quote prices in US dollars, and some mid-range hotels also engage in this dubious practice.

On the whole, it's cheaper if two people travel together and split the cost of the room – the price for a two person room is nearly always well below the cost of two singles. You rarely get dormitory accommodation in Indonesia, although there are a few hotels catering to western budget travellers, notably in Jakarta, that provide dormitory beds.

Even the cheapest hotels tend to be reasonably clean, if spartan, though some stand out as long overdue for demolition. Some places can be abominably noisy, with the inevitable TV booming in the passageway outside your room or punching up through the floorboards until after midnight. Other hotels are just several layers of hot little sweat boxes and slimy bathrooms. The tendency in the last few years has been to tear down the old firetraps and replace them with more wholesome accommodation, but, of course, prices have risen to reflect the improved conditions. The best way to survive some of the more dismal places is to go to Indonesia with a level of saintly tolerance, a good pair of earplugs, or enough money to afford some upper-market accommodation now and then and avoid the worst places.

Staying in Villages

In many places in Indonesia you'll often be welcome to stay in the villages. Ask for the village head – the *kepala desa*. He is generally very hospitable and friendly, offering you not only a roof over your head but also meals. Obviously you don't get a room of your own, just a bed. Your payment for this depends on the bargain you reach with the kepala desa. Sometimes he may offer it to you for nothing but more often some payment will be expected: about 5000 rp a night as a rule of thumb. If you intend to stay with a kepala desa it's a good idea to have one or two gifts to offer – cigarettes, postcards and photographs are popular.

Staying with the Police

In places where there's no accommodation available you can often stay at the local police station. Indonesian police and military are actually quite friendly to foreigners – how they treat the locals is another matter.

Rental Accommodation

Given the wide assortment of cheap hotels, it almost doesn't pay to bother with renting a house or apartment. Trying to find a house for short-term rental – one or two months – is difficult and depends on personal contacts or luck. Real estate agents are virtually non-existent in Indonesia. Ask your Indonesian friends, staff at your hotel, restaurants etc. Something may turn up, but it can take time. Negotiating a proper price may also be difficult, and it's wise to obtain the help of an Indonesian friend.

However, you will want to get your own place if you're working in Indonesia for a long time. Rents vary wildly depending on where you want to live. Jakarta's rates are very high, and rent is required in advance, even for three year leases. Prices are lower elsewhere. More than a few foreigners have taken up semipermanent residence on Bali, either renting houses on long-term lease, or leasing the land and building their own homes with an Indonesian partner.

Indonesian Cuisine

Food

You'll generally eat well in most parts of Indonesia. There are some gastronomic voids in the more poverty-stricken areas, but the variety is stunning in cities like Jakarta and touristy regions like Bali. There are occasional surprises too, like mid-year in Tanatoraja (Sulawesi), when harvest and funeral ceremonies are at their height, and you can try pig and buffalo meat barbecued in bamboo tubes washed down with copious quantities of white and red alcoholic *tuak* tapped from a palm tree. Of course, food like this is not available from your average pushcart.

Jl Malioboro in Yogyakarta is the longest restaurant in the world – lined in the evening with innumerable food stalls serving up genuine Yogya food, which you eat while sitting on mats laid out on the footpath – though the innumerable stalls strung along Pantai Losari in Ujung Pandang also vie for the title. Pontianak and Samarinda on Kalimantan have the biggest river prawns you've probably ever seen in your life; Jayapura has the best selection of barbecued fish *(ikan bakar)*.

Many general books on Asian food include a section on Indonesian cuisine, including *South-East Asia Food* by Rosemary Brissenden. Sri Owen's *Indonesian Food & Cookery* is a straightforward cookery book without the glossy photos, but it gives an excellent rundown on Indonesian food and ingredients and authentic Indonesian recipes.

Restaurants

At the bottom of the barrel in terms of price is the *warung*. This is the poor person's restaurant, which can be seen everywhere in Indonesia. It is usually just a rough table and bench seats, surrounded by canvas strung up to act as walls. In Yogya on Jl Malioboro, they're basically food trolleys and you sit on mats laid out on the footpath. Often the food is as drab as the warung looks, but occasionally you find something outstanding. One thing you can be sure about is that warungs are cheap. A night market *(pasar malam)* is often a congregation point for warungs.

One step up from the warung, sometimes in name only, is the *rumah makan* (literally, house to eat), often only distinguished from the warung by its fixed position and the addition of solid walls – but many such places call themselves warungs so it's a hazy distinction.

A *restoran* is a restaurant – once again often nothing more than the name distinguishes it from a rumah makan. But in many cases a restoran will be an upmarket place, often Chinese-run and with a Chinese menu. Chinese food is nearly always more expensive than Indonesian food, though there is usually a more varied menu.

Kuta Beach and Jakarta are the two main places in Indonesia where western food has grabbed hold. In Kuta you would be forgiven if you thought there was no such thing as Balinese cooking – while the food you get around Kuta is good, traditional Balinese food has just about dropped out of the picture, and Indonesian food is succumbing to the onslaught of hamburgers, steaks, yoghurt, fish and chips, banana muesli and – for homesick Aussies – vegemite on toast, mate!

Jakarta has the most cosmopolitan range of culinary delights in Indonesia, from European and Mexican to Indian, Chinese, Thai, Korean and Japanese. Parts of Indonesia that accommodate large expatriate communities working for foreign firms, Balikpapan for example, are also sources of foreign food.

Title Page: Street cart selling fried noodles and rice, cooked on a kerosene stove inside the cart (photograph by James Lyon).

Box: Indonesian seafood (photograph by Jane Rawson)

Local ingredients, including white pepper corns, snake beans, tomatoes, chillis and limes on a mortar.

JANE RAWSON

Food for gods and humans (clockwise from bottom left) – suncakes (jaje matahari), elephant ears (jaje kuping gajah), pandan crepes filled with palm sugar and coconut (dadar), and rice and palm sugar offering cakes (begina).

JANE RAWSON

Nasi Campur – steamed rice served with pork mince sate (sate lilit), chilli (tabia), soya cake (tempe), beancurd (tahu), shredded coconut, palm sugar and spices (sesaur), snake beans, mung beans, grated coconut and spices (pecel), and spit roasted pork with lemongrass sauce (babi guling).

JANE RAWSON

GLENN BEANLAND

Snack your way through the archipelago at Jakarta's street-side push carts called *kaki lima*. These carts are piled high with delicious snacks from all over Indonesia.

GLENN BEANLAND

Rambutans for sale – get 'em while they're fresh.

SARA-JANE CLELAND

Self-catering is made easy at Indonesia's lively markets, where you'll see stalls spilling over with mouth-watering fresh produce.

Indonesian Food

Some of the dishes you're likely to encounter in Indonesia are listed here:

abon – spiced and shredded dried meat often sprinkled over *nasi rames* or *nasi rawon*
acar – pickle; cucumber or other vegetables in a mixture of vinegar, salt, sugar and water
apam – delicious pancake filled with nuts and sprinkled with sugar
ayam – chicken; *ayam goreng* is fried chicken

babi – pork. Since most Indonesians are Muslim, pork is generally only found in market stalls and restaurants run by Chinese, and in areas where there are non-Muslim populations, such as Bali, Irian Jaya and Tanatoraja on Sulawesi.
bakmi – rice-flour noodles, either fried *(bakmi goreng)* or in soup
bakso or *ba'so* – meatball soup
bawang – onion
bubur ayam – Indonesian porridge with chicken. The porridge is generally sweetened and made from rice, black sticky rice or mung beans.
bubur kacang – mung bean porridge cooked in coconut milk
buncis – beans

cap cai – usually pronounced 'chop chai'. This is a mix of fried vegetables, although it sometimes comes with meat as well.
cassava – known as tapioca to westerners, this is a long, thin, dark brown root which looks something like a shrivelled turnip
cumi cumi – squid

daging babi – pork
daging kambing – goat or mutton
daging sapi – beef
dragonflies – a popular Balinese snack, caught with sticky sticks and then roasted!

emping – powdered and dried *melinjo* nuts, fried as a snack to accompany a main meal
es krim – ice cream. In Indonesia you can get western brands like Flipper's and Peters, and also locally manufactured varieties.

fu yung hai – a sort of sweet and sour omelette

gado gado – another very popular Indonesian dish of steamed bean sprouts, various vegetables and a spicy peanut sauce
garam – salt
gula – sugar
gula gula – lollies (sweets, candy)
gulai/gule – thick curried-meat broth with coconut milk

ikan – fish. Understandably, there's a wide variety to choose from in Indonesia: *ikan laut* is saltwater fish and *ikan danau* is freshwater fish. *Ikan asam manis* is sweet and sour fish and *ikan bakar* is barbecued fish. If you're buying fresh fish (you can often buy it at a market and get your hotel to cook it up), the gills should be a deep red colour, not brown, and the flesh should be firm to touch.
ikan belut – eels. Another Balinese delicacy; kids catch them in the rice paddies at night.

jahe – ginger

kacang – peanuts or beans

kacang hijau – mung bean sprouts. These can be made into a sweet filling for cakes and buns.

kare – curry; as in *kare udang* (prawn curry)

kecap asin – salty soy sauce

kecap manis – sweet soy sauce

keju – cheese

kentang – potatoes; usually the size found in the west and used in various ways, including dishes of Dutch origin and as a salad ingredient

kepiting – crab; features in quite a few dishes, mostly of Chinese origin

kodok – frog; plentiful on Bali and caught in the rice paddies at night

kroket – mashed potato cake with minced meat filling

krupuk – is made of shrimp and cassava flour, or of fish flakes and rice dough, cut in slices and fried to a crisp

krupuk melinjo (emping) – is made of the seeds of the melinjo fruit *(gnetum-gnemon)*, pounded flat, dried and fried to make a crisp chip and served as a snack with a main course

kueh – cake

lemper – sticky rice with a small amount of meat inside, wrapped up and boiled in a banana leaf; a common snack served throughout the country

lombok – chilli. There are various types: *lombok merah* (large, red); *lombok hijau* (large, green); and *lombok rawit* (rather small but deadliest of them all, often packaged with *tahu* etc).

lontong – rice steamed in a banana leaf

lumpia – spring rolls; small pancake filled with shrimp and bean sprouts and fried

madu – honey

martabak – found on food trolleys all over the archipelago. A martabak is basically a pancake but there are two varieties. The one that seems to be everywhere is the sickeningly sweet version guaranteed to set your dentist's bank account soaring when you get back home. But (at least on Java) you can also get a delicious savoury martabak stuffed with meat, egg and vegetables. Some people think the sweet version isn't all that bad.

mentega – butter

mentimun – cucumber

merica – pepper

mie goreng – fried wheat-flour noodles, served sometimes with vegetables, sometimes with meat

mie kuah – noodle soup

nasi campur – steamed rice topped with a little bit of everything – some vegetables, some meat, a bit of fish, a krupuk or two – a good, usually tasty and filling meal

nasi goreng – this is the most common of Indonesian dishes; almost like hamburgers are to Americans, meat pies to Australians, fish and chips to the British – popular at any time of day, including breakfast time. Nasi goreng simply means fried *(goreng)* rice *(nasi)* – a basic nasi goreng may be little more than fried rice with a few scraps of vegetable to give it some flavour, but sometimes it includes meat. *Nasi goreng istimewa* (special) usually means nasi goreng with a fried egg on top. The dish can range from dull and dreary to very good.

nasi gudeg – unripe jackfruit cooked in *santan* (squeezed grated coconut) and served up with rice, pieces of chicken and spices

nasi Padang – Padang food, from the Padang region of Sumatra, is popular all over Indonesia. It's usually served cold and consists of the inevitable rice, with a whole variety of side dishes, including beef, fish, fried chicken, curried chicken, boiled cabbage, sometimes fish

Mangosteen – Round, purple fruit with juicy white flesh shaped like orange segments; has a sweet-sour flavour often likened to a combination of strawberries and grapes.

and prawns. The dishes are laid out before you and your final bill is calculated by the number of empty dishes when you've finished eating. Nasi Padang is traditionally eaten with the fingers and it's also traditionally very hot *(pedas* not *panas)* – sometimes hot enough to burn your fingers, let alone your tongue! It can be wonderful, and it can be very dull. It's also one of the more expensive ways to eat in Indonesia and you generally end up spending a couple of thousand rupiah on a meal, although it can be well worth it.

nasi pecel – similar to gado gado, with boiled papaya leaves, tapioca, bean sprouts, string beans, fried soybean cake, fresh cucumber, coconut shavings and peanut sauce

nasi putih – white *(putih)* rice – usually steamed; glutinous rice is mostly used in snacks and cakes

nasi rames – rice with a combination of egg, vegetables, fish or meat

nasi rawon – rice with spicy hot beef soup, fried onions and spicy sauce

nasi uduk – rice boiled in coconut milk or cream

opor ayam – chicken cooked in coconut milk

pete – a huge broad bean, quite spicy, which is often served in the pod

pisang goreng – fried banana fritters; a popular streetside snack

rijsttafel – Dutch for 'rice table'; Indonesian food with a Dutch interpretation, it consists of lots of individual dishes with rice. Rather like a glorified *nasi campur* or a hot *nasi Padang*. Bring a big appetite.

roti – bread. The stuff you get in Indonesia is nearly always snow white and sweet.

sago – a starchy, low protein food extracted from a variety of palm tree. Sago is the staple diet of the Maluku islands.

sambal – a hot, spicy chilli sauce served as an accompaniment with most meals

sate – one of the best known of Indonesian dishes, sate (satay) are small pieces of various types of meat on a skewer served with a spicy peanut sauce. Street sate sellers carry their charcoal grills around with them and cook the sate on the spot.

saus tomat – tomato sauce; ketchup

sayur – vegetables

sayur-sayuran – vegetable soup with coconut milk

sembal pedis – hot sauce

sop – clear soup with mixed vegetables and meat or chicken

soto – meat and vegetable broth, often a main meal eaten with rice and a side dish of sambal

tahu – tofu, or soybean curd; soft bean cake made from soybean milk. It varies from white and yellow to thin and orange-skinned. It's found as a snack in food stalls and is sometimes sold with a couple of hot chillies or with a filling of vegetables

telur – egg

tempe – made of whole soybeans fermented into cake, wrapped in plastic or a banana leaf; rich in vegetable protein, iron and vitamin B. Tempe goreng is pieces of tempe (tempeh) fried with palm sugar and chillies.

ubi – sweet potato; spindle-shaped to spherical with a pulpy yellow or brown skin and white to orange flesh

udang – prawns or shrimps

udang karang – lobster ■

Durian – Infamous for its smell, this is a large, oval fruit with a hard, spiny shell; though held in high esteem, the pale white-green flesh is definitely an acquired taste – the nearest approximation is onion-flavoured ice cream.

Fruit

It's almost worth making a trip to Indonesia just to sample the tropical fruit – apples and bananas curl and die before the onslaught of nangkas, rambutans, mangosteens, salaks and sirsaks.

apel – apple. Most are imported from Australia, New Zealand and the USA, and are expensive. Local apples grown in mountain areas, such as Malang on Java, are much cheaper and fresher.

apokat – avocado. They are plentiful and cheap; try an avocado and ice-cream combo.

belimbing – the 'starfruit' is a cool, crispy, watery tasting fruit – if you cut a slice you'll immediately see where the name comes from

durian – the most infamous tropical fruit, the durian is a large green fruit with a hard, spiky exterior. Inside are pockets of creamy white fruit. Stories are told of a horrific stench emanating from an opened durian – hotels and airlines often ban them because of their foul odour. Some don't smell so bad – unpleasant yes, but certainly not like holding your nose over an overflowing sewer. The durian season is in the later part of the year.

jambu air – water apple or wax jambu. These glossy white or pink bell-shaped fruit come from a popular street and garden tree found throughout Indonesia. Children can often be seen selling the fruit skewered on a sliver of bamboo. The *jambu air* is crisp and refreshing eaten chilled, but fairly tasteless. The single seed should not be eaten.

jambu batu – guava. Also known as *jambu klutuk*, the guava comes from Central America and was brought to Asia by the Spanish. The fruit comes in many colours, shapes and sizes; the most common are light green and pear-shaped, turning yellow when fully ripe. The pinkish flesh is full of seeds. Ripe guava have a strong smell that some find overpowering. In Asia, the unripe fruit are also popular sliced and dipped in thick soy sauce with sliced chilli; mango can also be served this way.

jeruk – the all-purpose term for citrus fruit. There are several kinds available. The main ones include the huge *jeruk muntis* or *jerunga*, known in the west as the pomelo. It's larger than a grapefruit but has a very thick skin, tastes sweeter, more like an orange, and has segments that break apart very easily. Regular oranges are known as *jeruk manis* – sweet jeruk. The small tangerine-like oranges which are often quite green are *jeruk baras*. Lemons are *jeruk nipis*.

kelapa – coconut; as plentiful as you would expect! *Kelapa muda* means young coconut and you'll often get them straight from the tree. Drink the milk and then scoop out the flesh.

Jackfruit – Similar in appearance to the durian but much easier to develop a taste for; has a large number of bright orange-yellow segments with a slightly rubbery texture.

Western fast food has come to roost in the main cities, complete with air-conditioning, laminex tables and a statue of the ever-smiling Colonel or Ronald the clown. If you made as much money as they do, you'd smile too. Indonesia also has a growing contingent of Pizza Hut, Wendy's and other outlets.

In spite of the wide variety of food, many travellers lose weight, and some say a trip through Indonesia is the best crash diet they know of. This has more to do with illness than the lack of tasty food, so take care – in some places 'hygiene' is just a slogan. As a general guide, the cleanliness of a warung or restaurant is a good indicator as to how sanitary its kitchen is likely to be. A bad meal at the local Rumah Makan

mangga – mango. The mango season is the second half of the year.
manggis – mangosteen. One of the most famous of tropical fruits, this is a small purple-brown fruit. The outer covering cracks open to reveal pure-white segments with an indescribably fine flavour. Queen Victoria once offered a reward to anyone able to transport a mangosteen back to England while still edible. From November to February is the mangosteen season. Beware of stains from the fruit's casing, which can be permanent.

nanas – pineapple
nangka – also known as jackfruit, this is an enormous yellow-green fruit that can weigh over 20 kg. Inside are individual segments of yellow fruit, each containing a roughly egg-shaped seed. The segments are held together by strong white fibres. The fruit is moist and fairly sweet, with a slightly rubbery texture. It is used mostly in cooking. As each nangka ripens on a tree it may be individually protected in a bag. The skin of a nangka is green when young, yellow when ripe. The *cempadak* is a close relative of the nangka, but smaller, sweeter and more strongly flavoured.

papaya – or paw paw are not unusual in the west. It's actually a native of South America and was brought to the Philippines by the Spanish, and from there spread to other parts of South-East Asia.
pisang – banana. The range in Indonesia is astonishing – from midgets to specimens well over a foot long. A bunch of bananas, by the way, is *satu sisir pisang*.

rambutan – a bright red fruit covered in soft, hairy spines – the name means hairy. Break it open to reveal a delicious white fruit closely related to the lychee. From November to February is the rambutan season.

salak – found chiefly in Indonesia, the salak is immediately recognisable by its perfect brown 'snakeskin' covering. Peel it off to reveal segments that, in texture, are similar to a cross between an apple and a walnut, but in taste are quite unique. Each segment contains a large, brown oval-shaped seed. Salaks from Bali are much nicer than any others.
sawo – brown-skinned, looks like a potato and has honey-flavoured flesh
sirsak – the sirsak is known in the west as soursop or zurzak. Originally a native of tropical America, the Indonesian variety is one of the best. The warty green skin covers a thirst-quenching, soft, white, pulpy interior with a slightly lemonish, tart taste. You can peel it off or slice it into segments. Sirsaks are ripe when the skin has begun to lose its fresh green colouring and become darker and spotty. It should then feel slightly squishy rather than firm. ■

Dysentery can spoil your trip – be wary of uncooked vegetables and fruits, rubbery seafood and 'boiled' drinking water straight from the tap.

Snacks

Indonesians are keen snackers and everywhere you'll find lots of street stall snacks, such as peanuts in palm sugar, shredded coconut cookies or fried bananas. Potatoes and other starchy roots are eaten as a snack – either steamed, with salt and grated coconut added, or thinly sliced and fried.

Rambutan – Red, hairy-skinned fruit with lychee-like interior – cool and mouth-watering flesh around a central stone.

Main Dishes

Food in Indonesia, particularly meat dishes, is generally Chinese-influenced, although there are a number of purely Indonesian dishes. Pork is not widely used since it is regarded by Muslims as unclean, but it sometimes appears in Chinese dishes and is eaten in Christian areas. Javanese cooking uses fresh spices and a mixture of ingredients, the chilli mellowed by the use of sugar in many dishes. Sumatran cooking, on the other hand, blends fresh and dry spices to flavour the main ingredient. The types of fresh spices that Indonesians use are known to most westerners only as dried ground powders. There is also some Dutch influence in the use of vegetables from temperate zones in some recipes.

Rice is the basis of the meal, with an assortment of side dishes, some hot (with chilli) and spicy, and some just spicy. Many dishes are much like soup, the water being used to moisten the large quantity of rice eaten. Salad is usually served, along with *sambal* (a spicy side dish) and *acar* (pickles). Many dishes are cooked in *santan*, the liquid obtained when grated coconut is squeezed. *Bumbu* is a combination of pounded ingredients used to flavour a dish. Indonesians use every part of a plant, including the leaves of cassavas, papayas, mangoes and beans.

A few basic words and phrases will help make ordering a meal easier.

makan	to eat	*asam manis*	sweet and sour
minum	to drink	*dingin*	cold
makanan	food	*panas*	hot (temperature)
nasi bungkos	take-away food	*pedas*	spicy hot
minuman	drink	*goreng*	fried
makan pagi	breakfast	*bakar*	barbecued
makan siang	lunch	*rebus*	boiled
makan malam	dinner	*pisau*	knife
enak	delicious	*garpu*	fork
daftar makanan	the menu	*sendok*	spoon
bon	the bill	*Saya mau*	
manis	sweet	*makan.*	I want to eat.

Self-Catering

In any medium to large-sized city you'll find well-stocked supermarkets. It's here that you'll find a wide variety of both local and imported foods. The other alternative is to explore the markets where you'll find fresh fruits, vegetables, eggs, chickens (both living and having recently passed away), freshly ground coffee and just about anything else. There are no price tags in the market and bargaining is often necessary.

An easy guide to the identification of weird-looking food is *A Jakarta Market* by Kaarin Wall, published by the American Women's Association, available in Jakarta and elsewhere. It's got pictures and descriptions of vegetables, roots and herbs, dry goods, fish, fresh fruit and other foods you'll find in the markets in Jakarta, which are also relevant to the rest of Indonesia.

Betel Nut

Not exactly a food, betel nut *(sirih* in Bahasa Indonesia) is popular, especially in the villages. It's what causes that red stain on what's left of the local's teeth and gums. The betel nut *pinang* is chewed in combination with sirih leaf, *kapor sirih* (powdered lime) and a brown substance called *gambir.*

Drinks

Indonesians have enthusiastically embraced western soft drink culture. In a country where delicious, fresh fruit juices are sold you can still rot your teeth on Coca Cola, 7Up, Sprite and Fanta. Prices are typically around 750 rp and up for a bottle, and from 1200 rp for a can.

There is a saying that while the British built roads in their colonies, the Dutch built breweries. Many of these still exist and, while beer is comparatively expensive (normally 3000 rp, often more), it's also good. The three popular brands are Bintang, San Miguel and Anker. Bintang is the most popular. Some other popular Indonesian drinks, both alcoholic and non-alcoholic, include:

air – water. You may get a glass of it with a restaurant meal. It should have been boiled (and may not have cooled down since), but often it won't be boiled at all. Ask for *air putih* (literally, white water) or drink tea. Hygienic bottled water is available everywhere.

air jeruk – citrus fruit juice. *Jeruk manis* is orange juice and *jeruk nipis* is lime juice.

air minum – drinking water

Aqua – the most common brand of mineral water. It is highly recommended if you're dubious about drinking other water, although it's not cheap, costing around 1000 rp for a 1.5 litre bottle.

arak – a stage on from brem (distilled rice wine). It's usually home-produced, although even the locally bottled brands look home-produced. It makes quite a good drink mixed with 7Up or Sprite. Taken in copious quantities it has a similar effect to being hit on the head with an elephant.

brem – rice wine; either home produced or there's the commercially bottled 'Bali Brem'. A bit of an acquired taste, but not bad after a few bottles!

es buah – more a dessert than a drink; a curious combination of crushed ice, condensed milk, shaved coconut, syrup, jelly and fruit. Sickening say some, wonderful say others.

es juice – although you should be a little careful about ice and water, the delicious fruit drinks are irresistible. Just take one or two varieties of tropical fruit, add crushed ice and pass it through a blender. You can make mind-blowing combinations of orange, banana, pineapple, mango, jackfruit, soursop or whatever else is available.

Green Sands – a pleasant soft drink, made not from sand, but from malt, apple and lime juice

kopi – coffee. Excellent coffee is grown in Indonesia. The best comes from Sulawesi, though Sumatra, Bali and Java also produce some mean brews. Like Turkish coffee, it is made from powdered coffee beans, but it is spooned straight into a glass and sugar and boiling water are added. Served sweet and black with the coffee granules floating on top, it is a real kick start in the mornings. Travellers' restaurants have adopted the odd habit of serving kopi without sugar. *Kopi susu* is white coffee, usually made with sweetened, condensed milk.

stroop – cordial

susu – milk. Fresh milk is found in supermarkets in large cities, although long-life milk in cartons is more common. Cans of condensed milk are also sold in Indonesia and are very sweet.

teh – tea. Some people are not enthusiastic about Indonesian tea but if you don't need strong, bend-the-teaspoon-style tea you'll probably find it's quite OK. *Teh tawar* or *teh pahit* is tea without sugar and *teh manis* is tea with sugar.

tuak – an alcoholic drink fermented from the sap tapped from a type of palm tree

Box: Indonesian coffee is usually served sweet and black (photograph by Jane Rawson).

TOBACCO

If you're an anti-smoking activist, you'll have your work cut out for you in Indonesia. Most Indonesian men (rarely women) smoke like chimneys. Some say Indonesian chain smokers only need one match a day – they light the first cigarette in the morning and then continue to light the next cigarette with the one currently being smoked, ad infinitum.

If you have the habit yourself, you might be pleased by the local selection of tobacco products. Indonesia is justly famous for its unique 'kretek' cigarettes, produced by blending cloves with tobacco. The fragrant odour is quite unlike any you've ever smelled before. Imported cigarettes like Dunhill, Lucky Strike and Marlboro are available but more expensive.

ENTERTAINMENT

Cinemas

Indonesians are great movie fans and cinemas can be found in all but the smallest village. In large cities like Jakarta, Surabaya, Denpasar etc, the latest western films can be seen, usually with English dialogue and Indonesian subtitles. They tend to be B-grade adventure flicks but the occasional Hollywood blockbuster is shown. As one gets into the backwaters, the films tend to be of vintage age. Besides western movies, there are plenty of violent kung fu epics from Hong Kong.

Cinemas usually only operate in the evening, starting from 5 pm, but a few places open on Sunday around 1 pm.

Discos

Young Indonesians have taken to disco-dancing like bees to honey. Obviously, discos are easiest to find in large cities like Jakarta, and resort areas like Kuta Beach on Bali. Some discos are independent, but many are located in five star hotels. Prices vary, but generally there's a small cover charge and expensive drinks.

Traditional Performances

Traditional entertainment is easy to see in Indonesia. Wayang, gamelan, traditional theatre and dance performances are held on a regular basis and for special occasions. Tourist offices can tell you what's available. On Bali and other touristy places like Yogya, traditional performing arts can be seen any night of the week, though they may be adapted for foreign audiences and be travesties of the real thing.

The main cities, particularly on Java, have subsidised theatre troupes and performing arts schools where performances are regularly staged.

Spectator Sports

Most of Indonesia's live spectator sports are male-oriented and associated with gambling. You may get the chance to see cockfighting, especially on Bali and Kalimantan. Bull racing, horse racing, ram head-butting and other contests are staged all around the country and are usually designed to improve the breed. Soccer and badminton are the national sporting obsessions. *Pencak silat*, a form of martial arts, is most popular in West Java and West Sumatra. This form of fighting uses not only hands, but also some weapons, including sticks and knives.

THINGS TO BUY

Indonesia is a great place to buy arts & crafts. The range is amazing and the prices cheap.

Souvenir vendors positively swarm around touristy places like Kuta Beach on Bali and Yogyakarta. Off the beaten track, shopping is more relaxed. If you're an art collector, you'll find plenty of chances to stock up on unusual items. Wood carvings are on sale everywhere. Batik and *ikat* (a form of dyed woven cloth) attract a steady stream of foreign art enthusiasts. Good pottery is available, mostly on Lombok and Java. See the Arts & Crafts colour section for an overview.

If you have little or no interest in art, there are still plenty of more practical, everyday items that make good buys. You can even find jackets, ski caps and other winter clothing in Jakarta. Many foreigners get addicted to Indonesian coffee, which is superb. Kapal

Gamelan Instruments

Bonang The bonang consists of a double row of bronze kettles (like small *kenongs*) resting on a horizontal frame; there are three kinds, although the lowest in pitch is no longer used in gamelan orchestras. The bonang is played with two long sticks bound with red cord at the striking end. Although in modern Javanese gamelan the bonang has two rows of bronze kettles, originally it had only one row, as it still does on Bali.

Celempung This is a plucked, stringed instrument, looking somewhat like a zither. It has 26 strings arranged in 13 pairs. The strings are stretched over a coffin-shaped resonator which stands on four legs; the strings are plucked with the thumb nails. The sitar is a smaller version of the celempung, with fewer strings and a higher pitch; the body is box-shaped and without legs.

Gambang The gambang is the only gamelan instrument with bars made not of bronze, but of hardwood, and laid over a wooden frame. They are struck with two sticks made of supple buffalo horn, each ending with a small, round, padded disc. Unlike the *gender* keys, the gambang keys do not need to be damped.

Gender This is similar to a *slentem* in structure, but there are more bronze keys and the keys and bamboo chambers are smaller. The gender is played with two disc-shaped hammers, smaller than those used for the slentem. The hand acts as a damper, so that each hand must simultaneously hit a note and damp the preceding one.

Gong Ageng The gong ageng or gong gede is suspended on a wooden frame. There is at least one such gong, sometimes more, in a gamelan orchestra. The gong is made of bronze and is about 90 cm in diameter. It performs the crucial task of marking the end of the largest phrase of a melody.

Kempul This is a small hanging gong, and marks a smaller musical phrase than the big gong.

GREGORY ADAMS

These bronze gongs are tuned to harmonise with each other, and with other instruments in the gamelan ensemble, by carefully filing the edges until the desired pitch is achieved.

Kendang These drums are all double-ended and beaten by hand (with the exception of the giant drum, the *bedug*, which is beaten with a stick). The drum is an important leading instrument; it is made from the hollowed tree-trunk sections of the jackfruit (nangka) tree with cow or goat skin stretched across the two ends. There are various types of drums but the middle-sized *kendang batangan* or *kendang ciblon* is chiefly used to accompany dance and wayang performances; the drum patterns indicate specific dance movements or movements of the wayang puppets.

Kenong The kenong is a small gong laid horizontally on crossed cord and sitting inside a wooden frame.

Ketuk The ketuk is a small kenong tuned to a certain pitch, which marks subdivisions of phrases; it is played by the kenong player. The sound of the ketuk is short and dead compared with the clearer, resonant tone of the kenong.

Rebab The rebab is a two-stringed bowed instrument of Arabic origin. It has a wooden body covered with fine, stretched skin. The moveable bridge is made of wood. The bow is made of wood and coarse horsehair tied loosely, not stretched tight like the bows of western instruments. The rebab player sits cross-legged on the floor behind the instrument.

Saron This is the basic instrument-type of the gamelan, a xylophone with bronze bars which are struck with a wooden mallet. There are three types of saron: high, medium and low-pitched. The high one is called *saron panerus* or *saron peking* and is played with a mallet made of buffalo horn rather than wood.

Slentem The slentem carries the basic melody in the soft ensemble, as the saron does in the loud ensemble. It consists of thin bronze bars suspended over bamboo resonating chambers; it is struck with a padded disc on the end of a stick.

Suling The suling, or flute, is the only wind instrument in the gamelan orchestra. It is made of bamboo and played vertically.

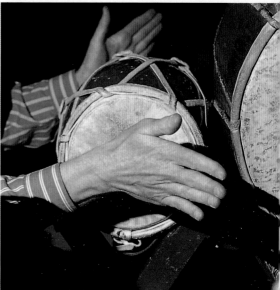

Double-ended drums known as kendang *act as the conductor of all the instruments during a gamelan performance.*

SIMON BRACKEN

Api is a popular brand name for packaged coffee, but the best coffee is the stone-ground stuff you buy in markets. Don't bother buying coffee beans unless you can get it ground to the fine, pulverised powder that gives Indonesian coffee its texture and flavour.

Bali is a shoppers paradise, with crafts from all over Indonesia. Jl Legian in Kuta has km after km of shops selling crafts, antiques, clothes, shoes etc. Sanur, Ubud and other tourist centres are also good, with Yogya the best place to shop on Java, with crafts

from all over Java and a smaller selection from further afield. Jakarta is also very good, with a wide range from all over the archipelago.

Elsewhere in Indonesia you only tend to see local crafts, but of course the price for those items will be much cheaper than in the tourist shops of Bali or Jakarta.

Always bargain for handcrafts. In the more touristed areas prices can be extortionate. Even if price tags are displayed, assume you can bargain. Fixed price art shops are very rare.

Getting There & Away

AIR

The principal gateways for entry to Indonesia are Jakarta and Bali. Jakarta is serviced by more airlines, but with its huge tourist trade Bali gets almost as much traffic.

There are also international flights from neighbouring countries to various cities throughout the country, and a couple of possible land and sea entry routes. Singapore has some of the cheapest flights to Indonesia, and is a major travel hub in the region. It may be cheaper to fly to Singapore, from where you can enter Indonesia by air or ship. The same applies to Penang in Malaysia, from where you can take a short flight or ferry to Medan on Sumatra.

For bargain fares, it is usually better to go to a travel agent than to an airline, as the latter can only sell fares by the book. Budget tickets may come with lots of restrictions. Check for how long the ticket is valid, the minimum period of stay, stopover options, cancellation fees and any amendment fees if you change your date of travel. Plenty of discount tickets are valid for six or 12 months, allowing multiple stopovers with open dates. Make sure you get details in writing of the flights you've requested (before you pay for the ticket). Round-the-World (RTW) tickets may also be worth looking into.

Fares quoted in this chapter are an approximate guide only. Fares vary depending on the season (high, shoulder or low) and special deals are often available. Fares can vary from week to week, and it pays to shop around by ringing a variety of travel agents for the best fare and ticket to suit your needs.

Airports

Indonesian airports are dull affairs. Jakarta's Soekarno-Hatta airport is spacious, modern and surprisingly efficient, but only has a few overpriced food and shopping outlets. Bali's smaller Ngurah Rai international airport is slightly more interesting. Shopping is also overpriced but more varied, and the airport can be exciting if you like crowds. In peak tourist seasons when a few jumbos land, it is standing room only and queues are long. Standard duty-free items are on sale at both airports, but local cigarettes are much cheaper than the duty-free variety, and there are no great bargains for alcohol either.

Buying Tickets

Jakarta is no discount centre, but some reasonably priced tickets can be found. The most popular is the short hop to Singapore costing as little as US$65 with Pakistan Airlines or Gulf Air. Other typical one way return fares are: Bangkok US$200/370; Hong Kong US$310/510; London US$510/820; Los Angeles US$570/1100; Penang US$200/370; Perth US$290/380; and Sydney US$440/630. Travel agents on Bali sell some cheap tickets to Australia – as low as US$550 return to the east coast.

Of most interest to travellers are the short hop tickets, such as Jakarta-Singapore and Kupang-Darwin. Small agents specialising in services for travellers may advertise international tickets, but you will usually get much better discounts at one of the bigger flight specialists. At travel agencies you usually save at least 3% if you pay cash rather than use a credit card.

USA

There are some very good open tickets which remain valid for six months or one year, but don't lock you into any fixed dates of departure. Most of the cheap tickets to Indonesia, either Jakarta or Denpasar, go via Japan, Korea, Taiwan or Hong Kong and will include the country as a stopover (sometimes you have to stopover). Fares to Jakarta or Denpasar start from as little as US$1000 return in the low season (outside summer and Christmas) from the west coast, and around US$1250 from New York. Garuda has the most direct flights to Denpasar and Jakarta.

via Honolulu, but they tend to be slightly more expensive. Garuda no longer flies via Biak.

If you are visiting other parts of Asia, some good ticket deals can be put together. For example, there are cheap tickets between the US west coast and Singapore with stopovers in Bangkok for very little extra money. However, be careful during the high season (summer and Chinese New Year) because seats will be hard to come by unless reserved months in advance.

The *New York Times*, *LA Times*, *Chicago Tribune* and *San Francisco Examiner* all produce weekly travel sections in which you'll find any number of travel agents' ads. Council Travel and STA Travel have offices in major cities nationwide.

The magazine *Travel Unlimited* (PO Box 1058, Allston, Mass 02134) publishes details of the cheapest airfares and courier possibilities for destinations all over the world from the USA.

Canada

Getting discount tickets in Canada is much the same as in the USA – go to the travel agents and shop around until you find a good deal. Again, you'll probably have to fly into Hong Kong or Singapore and carry on from there to Indonesia.

CUTS is Canada's national student bureau and has offices in a number of Canadian cities, including Vancouver, Edmonton, Toronto and Ottawa – you don't necessarily have to be a student. There are a number of good agents in Vancouver for cheap tickets. The *Toronto Globe & Mail* and the *Vancouver Sun* carry travel agents' ads.

Australia

Bali is the major gateway to Australia, with almost all flights to/from Indonesia routed via Denpasar. Direct flights connect Denpasar with Sydney, Melbourne, Brisbane, Perth, Darwin and Port Hedland. Garuda, Qantas and Ansett Australia are the main carriers and compete on most of these runs, but the Port Hedland-Denpasar flight on Saturday is operated only by Merpati. From Denpasar you can connect to other Indonesian cities.

Other direct flights to Indonesia are limited. They include Darwin-Kupang and Melbourne-Jakarta (Merpati); Perth-Jakarta (Garuda and Sempati); and Sydney-Jakarta (Qantas). The cheapest flight is from Darwin to Kupang (on Timor) on Wednesday and Saturday. Merpati's Darwin office (☎ (089) 812727) sells tickets, as do Darwin travel agents. From Kupang, regular flights go to Bali (which is slightly cheaper than flying Darwin-Bali direct) or you can island-hop through the Nusa Tenggara archipelago.

Sample fares in Australian dollars, ranging from the low season to the high season (December and January) are:

From	To	One Way	Return
Melbourne, Sydney, Brisbane	Denpasar	650-800	800-1050
Darwin, Perth	Denpasar	450-500	650-800
Port Hedland	Denpasar	400-450	600-700
Darwin	Kupang	198-248	330-407

Flights to Jakarta cost around A$50 to A$100 more than to Denpasar.

Travel agents are the best place to shop for cheap tickets, but because Bali is such a popular destination flight discounting is not large and most agents prefer to sell Bali packages.

Travel agents to try include the big networks like STA Travel or the Flight Centre, with offices in the main cities, or check the travel pages of the main newspapers. The highest demand for flights is during school holidays and especially the Christmas break – book well in advance.

Of course, Bali is one of Australia's favourite 'OS' holiday destinations and package tours can offer good, cheap deals. Packages including return airfare with five to 10 days accommodation can cost little more than the price of an airfare alone.

New Zealand

Garuda and Air New Zealand have direct flights between Auckland and Denpasar. Air New Zealand's fares are generally a little lower than Garuda's. The return economy airfare from Auckland to Denpasar or Jakarta is about NZ$1200 to NZ$1350, depending on the season.

Check the latest fare developments and discounts with the airlines, or shop around a few travel agents for possible deals. As in Australia, STA Travel and the Flight Centre are popular travel agents.

UK

Ticket discounting is a long-established business in the UK and it's wide open – the various agencies advertise their fares and there's nothing under the counter about it at all. To find out what is available and where to get it, pick up a copy of the giveaway newspapers *TNT, Southern Cross* or *Trailfinder*, or the weekly 'what's on' guide *Time Out*. These days discounted tickets are available all over the UK, they're not just a London exclusive. The magazine *Business Traveller* also covers cheap fare possibilities.

Air Travel Glossary

Apex Apex ('advance purchase excursion') is a discounted ticket which must be paid for in advance. There are penalties if you wish to change it.

Bucket Shop An unbonded travel agency specialising in discounted airline tickets.

Bumped Just because you have a confirmed seat doesn't mean you're going to get on the plane (see Overbooking).

Cancellation Penalties If you have to cancel or change an Apex ticket there are often heavy penalties involved; insurance can sometimes be taken out against these penalties. Some airlines impose penalties on regular tickets as well, particularly against 'no show' passengers (see No Shows).

Check In Airlines ask you to check in a certain time ahead of the flight departure (usually 1½ hours on international flights). If you fail to check in on time and the flight is overbooked, the airline can cancel your booking and give your seat to somebody else.

Confirmation Having a ticket written out with the flight and date you want doesn't mean you have a seat until the agent has checked with the airline that your status is 'OK' or confirmed. Meanwhile you could just be 'on request' (see Reconfirmation).

Cross-Border Tickets Sometimes it is cheaper to fly to countries A, B and C rather than just B to C, usually because country A's airline is desperate to sell tickets or because the currency in A is very weak. Authorities in B can get very unhappy if you turn up for the flight from B to C without having first flown from A to B. Be cautious about discounted tickets which have been issued in another city, particularly in Eastern European cities.

Discounted Tickets There are two types of discounted fares – officially discounted (see Promotional Fares) and unofficially discounted. The lowest prices often impose drawbacks like flying with unpopular airlines, inconvenient schedules, or unpleasant routes and connections. A discounted ticket doesn't necessarily have to save you money – an agent may be able to sell you a ticket at Apex prices without the associated Apex advance booking and other requirements. Discounted tickets only exist where there is fierce competition.

Full Fares Airlines traditionally offer 1st class (coded F), business class (coded J) and economy class (coded Y) tickets. These days there are so many promotional and discounted fares available that few passengers pay full economy fare.

Lost Tickets If you lose your airline ticket, an airline will usually treat it like a travellers cheque and, after enquiries, issue you with another one. Legally, however, an airline is entitled to treat it like cash and if you lose it then it's gone forever. Take good care of your tickets.

No Shows No shows are passengers who fail to show up for their flight, sometimes due to unexpected delays or disasters, sometimes due to simply forgetting, sometimes because they made more than one booking and didn't bother to cancel the one they didn't want.

On Request An unconfirmed booking for a flight (see Confirmation).

A couple of excellent places to look are Trailfinders and STA Travel. Trailfinders is at 194 Kensington High St, London W8 (☎ (0171) 938 3939) and at 46 Earls Court Rd (☎ (0171) 938 3366). It also has offices in Manchester (☎ (0161) 839 6969) and Glasgow (☎ (0141) 353 2224). STA Travel is at 74 Old Brompton Rd, London W7 (☎ (0171) 581 1022) and at Clifton House, 117 Euston Rd (☎ (0171) 388 2261).

Garuda is one of the main discounters to Indonesia, but it only has two flights per week from London via Bangkok. Qantas has daily flights or a travel agent can put together a cheap ticket, usually via Singapore. Rock-bottom one way/return fares (low season) from London to Indonesia are around UK£300/440 to Jakarta and UK£330/590 to Denpasar. Alternatively, you can fly to Singapore for around UK£220/400 and then take a cheap flight to Jakarta, or the ferry to Batam or Bintan islands in Indonesia's Riau archipelago from where there are other ferries. You can get a London-Australia

Open Jaws A return ticket where you fly out to one place but return from another. If available this can save you backtracking to your arrival point.

Overbooking Airlines hate to fly with empty seats, and since every flight has some passengers who fail to show up (see No Shows), airlines often book more passengers than they have seats. Usually the excess passengers balance those who fail to show up but occasionally somebody gets bumped. If this happens guess who it is most likely to be? The passengers who check in late.

Promotional Fares Officially discounted fares like Apex fares which are available from any travel agent or direct from the airline.

Reconfirmation At least 72 hours prior to departure time of an onward or return flight you must contact the airline and 'reconfirm' that you intend to be on the flight. If you don't do this the airline can delete your name from the passenger list and you could lose your seat. You don't have to reconfirm the first flight on your itinerary or if your stopover is less than 72 hours. It doesn't hurt to reconfirm more than once.

Restrictions Discounted tickets often have various restrictions on them – advance purchase is the most usual one (see Apex). Others are restrictions on the minimum and maximum period you must be away, such as a minimum of 14 days or a maximum of one year (see Cancellation Penalties).

Standby A discounted ticket where you only fly if there is a seat free at the last moment. Standby fares are usually only available on domestic routes.

Tickets Out An entry requirement for many countries is that you have an onward or return ticket – in other words, a ticket out of the country. If you're not sure what you intend to do next, the easiest solution is to buy the cheapest onward ticket to a neighbouring country or a ticket from a reliable airline which can later be refunded if you do not use it.

Transferred Tickets Airline tickets cannot be transferred from one person to another. Travellers sometimes try to sell the return half of their ticket, but officials can ask you to prove that you are the person named on the ticket. This is unlikely to happen on domestic flights, but can easily happen on an international flight where tickets may be compared with passports.

Travel Agencies Travel agencies vary widely and you should ensure you use one that suits your needs. Some simply handle tours, while full-service agencies handle everything from tours and tickets to car rental and hotel bookings. A good one will do all these things and can save you a lot of money, but if all you want is a ticket at the lowest possible price, then you really need an agency specialising in discounted tickets. A discounted ticket agency, however, may not be useful for other things, like hotel bookings.

Travel Periods Some officially discounted fares, Apex fares in particular, vary with the time of year. There is often a low (off-peak) season and a high (peak) season. Sometimes there's an intermediate or shoulder season as well. At peak times, when everyone wants to fly, not only will the officially discounted fares be higher but so will unofficially discounted fares, or there may simply be no discounted tickets available. Usually the fare depends on your outward flight – if you depart in the high season and return in the low season, you pay the high season fare. ■

return ticket with a stopover in Jakarta or Bali for around UK£950.

Continental Europe

The Netherlands, Switzerland, Brussels and Antwerp are good places for buying discount air tickets. In Antwerp, WATS has been recommended. In Zurich, try SOF Travel and Sindbad. In Geneva, try Stohl Travel. In the Netherlands, NBBS is a reputable agency.

As well as Garuda and other Asian airlines, KLM and Lufthansa have a number of flights to Indonesia. Usually it is cheaper to fly to Jakarta than Denpasar; for example, Lufthansa's regular discount fares from Germany are around 1600 DM to Jakarta and 1900 DM to Denpasar. The cheapest way to reach Indonesia is often via Singapore, with the East European airlines offering some of the cheapest flights.

Garuda has flight connections between Jakarta and several European cities: Paris, Amsterdam, Zurich, Frankfurt and Rome.

Singapore

There are direct flights from Singapore to Jakarta, Denpasar and several cities in Sumatra, such as Medan, Pekanbaru, Padang and Palembang. Merpati has flights to Pontianak on Kalimantan for around S$260, and to Balikpapan. Silk Air and others fly direct from Singapore to Manado and Ujung Pandang on Sulawesi, and Solo on Java.

Of most interest to travellers are the numerous Singapore-Jakarta tickets which are discounted to as low as US$65.

Singapore is also a good place to buy a cheap air ticket if you're leaving South-East Asia for the west.

Malaysia

The most popular flight is from Penang to Medan on Sumatra with Sempati or Malaysian Air Service (MAS) for around US$75. The number of Sumatran cities with direct flights to Malaysia is growing rapidly. Pekanbaru, Padang and Banda Aceh are all connected by regular flights to Malaysian cities. See the Sumatra chapter later in this book for details.

MAS flies twice weekly between Pontianak on Kalimantan and Kuching in Sarawak for around US$70, and twice weekly between Tarakan and Tawau (and on to Kota Kinabalu), also for around US$70.

For Java, the cheapest connections are from Singapore, though MAS has competitively priced flights from Johor Bahru to Jakarta.

Philippines

Bouraq has a twice weekly flight from Manado on Sulawesi to Davao in the Philippines, as well as regular Manila-Jakarta flights.

Papua New Guinea

From Papua New Guinea there is a once weekly flight between Vanimo and Jayapura on Irian Jaya for US$63. For more details see the Irian Jaya chapter later in this book.

LAND

The only open land crossing is at Entikong, between Kalimantan and Sarawak (eastern Malaysia). This border post on the Pontianak-Kuching highway is now an official international entry point. Visas are not required and a 60 day tourist pass is issued on the spot. See the Kalimantan chapter later in this book for more details.

SEA

Malaysia

Most sea connections are between Malaysia and Sumatra. The comfortable, high-speed ferries from Penang (Malaysia) to Medan (Sumatra) are one of the most popular ways to reach Indonesia. Ferries also connect Medan with Port Kelang and Lumut in Malaysia, and Dumai (Sumatra) with Melaka (Malacca) and Port Kelang. See the Sumatra chapter for full details.

From Johor Bahru in southern Malaysia, daily ferries run to Batam and Bintan islands in Sumatra's Riau archipelago from where there are connections further afield. However, the usual way to reach these islands is from Singapore. A fortnightly passenger ship also runs from Pasir Gudang, about 30 km from

Johor Bahru, to Surabaya. SS Holidays (☎ (07) 2511577), Level 3, 12-13, Kompleks Pusat Bandar, Pasir Gudang, is the agent in Malaysia. See the Surabaya chapter for more details.

Singapore

A popular way to reach Indonesia is via Sumatra's Riau archipelago (see the Sumatra chapter for full details). The main stepping stones are the islands of Batam and Bintan, both only a short high-speed ferry ride from Singapore.

Batam is the bigger travel hub, and from this island speedboats run through to Pekanbaru on the Sumatran mainland.

From Bintan, Pelni ships run to Jakarta, with other regular services from Bintan to Jakarta.

Yachts

With a bit of effort it's still possible to get yacht rides around South-East Asia. Very often, yacht owners are travellers too and need crew members – all it usually costs is the contribution to the food kitty. As for where to look – well, anywhere that yachts pass through or in towns with western-style yacht clubs. We've had letters from people who have managed to get rides from Singapore, Penang, Phuket (in Thailand) and Benoa (on Bali). Other popular yachting places include the main ports in Papua New Guinea and Hong Kong.

It is possible to get a lift as a passenger or crew member from Darwin, especially at the time of the Darwin-Ambon yacht race in July, but make sure you go to a recognised entry port if you don't have a visa. The Darwin Yacht Club at Fannie Bay, Darwin, has a notice board for crews.

DEPARTURE TAXES

Airport tax on international flights from Jakarta and Denpasar is 25,000 rp. On domestic flights, airport tax is between 5500

and 11,000 rp, depending on the airport, but this is normally included in the ticket price.

ORGANISED TOURS

Tours tend to be oriented towards Bali. Most are accommodation and airfare-only packages, which are very popular and can be good value for short stays. Choose your accommodation so that you are not too isolated and forced to rely on expensive hotel services. Other more expensive tours include sightseeing, all transfers, meals etc.

Tours to other parts of Indonesia range from adventure/trekking tours of Irian Jaya and Kalimantan to temple tours of Java. There are so many tours that it's impossible to list them all here. The European market has the biggest selection, especially Dutch tour companies that have very competitively priced tours ranging from big luxury groups to small, interesting off-the-beaten-track tours. Prices range according to the standard of accommodation. Some try so hard to maximise luxury and minimise hassles that participants are hermetically isolated from Indonesia and Indonesians. Smaller groups that provide some independence generally provide a more worthwhile experience.

Some of the more deluxe tours also include luxurious boat trips to neighbouring islands. One note of caution – the more upmarket tours may be comfortable and fun, but some of the staged ceremonies you'll be shown are basically little more than theatre. We ran into one tour group on the island of Lembata while they were attending a 'traditional ceremony' imported from Hawaii, complete with female dancers in grass skirts and flower necklaces, moving to the beat of bongo drums. Nice, but not exactly authentic Indonesian culture.

Of course, you can make your own way to Indonesia and take day tours to surrounding attractions. The major tourist centres, such as Kuta on Bali and Yogyakarta on Java, offer some of the best value tours in Indonesia.

Getting Around

AIR

Indonesia has a variety of airlines, a bizarre collection of aircraft and an extensive network of flights that make some pretty remote corners of the country easily accessible. The main airlines are Garuda, Merpati, Sempati, Bouraq and Mandala, and there are several smaller ones. Ticket prices are fixed and cost the same regardless of the airline. Discounting is officially no longer legal, but some travel agents in the larger cities offer small discounts, especially for return tickets.

On top of the basic fares, 10% tax is charged, along with 1500 rp insurance and domestic departure tax, which varies from 5500 to 11,000 rp, depending on the airport. These taxes are normally paid when you buy the ticket, and will be written on the ticket. Baggage allowance is usually 20 kg, or only 10 kg on the smaller planes. Sometimes a fee is charged for excess baggage.

Most airlines offer student discounts of up to 25%. You need a valid International Student Identity Card (ISIC) to take advantage of this. The age limit for claiming the student discount is usually 26.

Airlines accept credit cards, but don't expect to be able to use them in small offices in the outer islands.

Each airline publishes a nationwide timetable – definitely worth picking up if you're going to do a lot of flying, but not always easy to get. Minor changes to schedules are frequent, so always check with local airline offices about what's available.

Book as far in advance as possible during Indonesian holiday periods and the peak tourist season around August. During these times, flights are often fully booked on the more popular out-of-the-way routes serviced by small aircraft. Indonesian airlines are generally reliable, even efficient these days, but it is essential to *reconfirm*. Overbooking is common and if you don't reconfirm at least a few days before departure you may well get bumped. Expect problems in the outer islands where flights are limited, communications poor and booking procedures haphazard. Here you should reconfirm and reconfirm again.

Travel agents overseas can usually include discounted domestic flights with an international ticket if you enter Indonesia with Garuda. Otherwise domestic tickets bought overseas are quoted in US dollars and cost around 50% more than if bought in Indonesia in rupiah.

Domestic Air Services

Garuda The major national airline is Garuda, named after the mythical man-bird vehicle of the Hindu god Vishnu. Garuda operates most of Indonesia's international flights and has a useful domestic network between the major cities only. Garuda operates wide-bodied jets on the domestic runs and has an efficient booking network. Its air pass can be very good value.

Merpati Merpati runs a mind-boggling collection of aircraft – everything from modern jets to single-engine eggbeaters. It has the most extensive domestic network, and part of its charter is to cover obscure locations that would otherwise be without an air service. It also flies a few back-door international routes, including Darwin-Kupang, Port Hedland-Denpasar and Pontianak-Kuching, and it has recently taken delivery of a new fleet of jet aircraft that will see its network expand to other Asian countries and Australia. Merpati was merged with Garuda for a few years, but now operates independently.

Merpati has a not-undeserved reputation for poor service, bungled bookings and cancelled flights. It provides a reasonable service on the main runs, but in the back blocks flights are subject to frequent and unexplained cancellations. On the less commercial runs, small aircraft may land on grass strips in obscure towns that may not

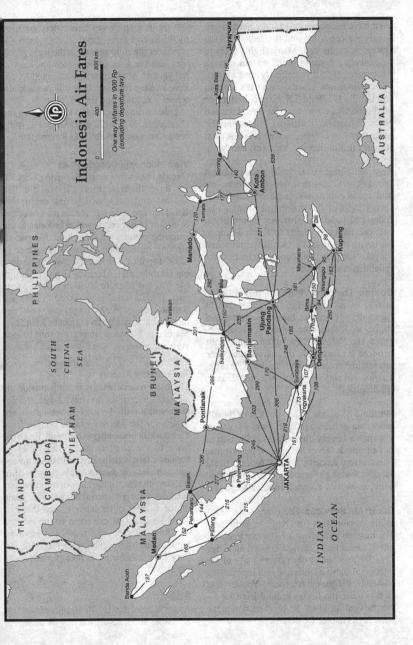

Indonesia Air Fares

*One way Airfares in '000 Rp
(excluding departure tax)*

0   400   800 km

even have telephones. Seats are hard to get, flights are cancelled and the radio booking system is haphazard. Many flights seem to be cancelled because there are not enough passengers, even if you already have a ticket. Hence the airline's theme song: 'It's Merpati and I'll Fly If I Want To'. Expect hassles on the flights that cover Irian Jaya, Maluku and Nusa Tenggara (including some popular tourist runs on Flores), as well as a few rural services in Kalimantan, Sulawesi and Java.

Sempati Sempati is Indonesia's fastest growing airline with a fleet of modern jets and impeccable government contacts. It serves most of the major cities throughout Indonesia, and its growing international network includes flights to Kuala Lumpur, Melaka, Penang, Perth, Singapore and Taipei. Sempati has a good reputation for reliability and service.

Bouraq The network of this privately run airline is nowhere near as extensive as Merpati's or Garuda's, but it has some useful flights in Kalimantan, Maluku, Nusa Tenggara and Sulawesi, including connections between Java and Bali. Bouraq also has some interesting international flights: Tarakan-Tawau (Malaysia) and Manado-Davao (Philippines).

Mandala Mandala is the smallest of the all-Indonesia airlines and apart from a few new jets runs a largely clapped-out collection of rattle traps. It serves a couple of main routes connecting Jakarta with Ambon, Biak, Medan, Padang, Surabaya and Ujung Pandang, as well as Yogya-Denpasar-Kupang.

Other Air Services There are some intriguing possibilities for flying in Indonesia. The mission aircraft which operate in places like Kalimantan, Central Sulawesi and Irian Jaya fly to some really remote parts of the interior of these islands and will take *paying* passengers if they have room. You're most likely to use the flights around Irian Jaya – see the Getting Three & Away section in the Irian Jaya chapter for details.

Various aircraft and helicopters are used by the foreign mining and oil companies – if you meet the right people in the right place, they like the look of your face and they're not yet sick of every self-proclaimed Marco Polo looking for a free ride, you never know where you could end up.

Other airlines include SMAC, Deraya and Dirgantara Air Service (DAS), which fly back routes on Sumatra and Kalimantan.

Visit Indonesia Decade Pass

Garuda issues this air pass, costing US$300 for three flight sectors, US$500 for five sectors and each additional sector for US$110. You must buy the air pass overseas or within 14 days of arrival in Indonesia, and enter the country on Garuda or Merpati. If arriving on another airline, a surcharge of US$50 applies. The Garuda pass can be used on Garuda and Merpati flights, though Merpati has plans to issue its own separate pass. If your travel is restricted to Java and Sumatra these passes might not save any money, but if you're flying out to Irian Jaya, Maluku or Sulawesi, they soon start to look very attractive.

To/From the Airport

There are generally taxis waiting outside the airports – even if the taxi has no meter (*argo*) there will usually be a fixed fare into town; tickets for the journey can be bought from the taxi desk in the airport terminal. From the town to the airport, go by the meter or bargain a fare with the driver. In other towns, local buses or *bemos* may pass within walking distance of the airport; they are considerably cheaper than taking a taxi. In some of the smaller outer islands, like those of Nusa Tenggara, where some of the airports are quite far from the town and have no regular road transport between them, the airlines have minibuses to take passengers to the airport.

BUS

At any time of the day, thousands of buses in all shapes and sizes are moving thousands of people throughout Indonesia. Buses are the mainstay of Indonesian transport.

Classes

Bus services vary throughout the islands, but are usually dependent on the roads. Java, for example, has all types of buses, including luxury air-con coaches that ply the well-paved highways. Luxury buses can also be found on the Trans-Sumatran Highway and the good roads on Bali, Lombok and Sumbawa. The 'Wallace Line' for the evolution of buses lies between Sumbawa and Flores, for luxury buses just don't exist on Flores and the islands further east. Only small, overcrowded rattlers ply the narrow, potholed roads on Flores that would soon wreck an expensive bus. In Indonesia the further off the beaten track you get, the more beaten up the track becomes and the less choice you have in buses.

The bottom line in buses are the ordinary, everyday *ekonomi* buses that run set routes between towns. They stop at bus terminals in every town en route, but will also stop for anyone, anywhere in the search for more paying customers – there is no such thing as 'full'. These buses are the lifeline for many communities, delivering the post and freight, and passengers may include goats, pigs and chickens on the rural runs. They can be hot, slow and incredibly crowded, but they are also ridiculously cheap and provide a never-ending parade of Indonesian life. They are often beat up rattle traps with limited leg room, but if you get a seat and the road is good they can be quite tolerable for short distances, especially on the main highways.

The next class up are the express *(patas)* buses. They can be much the same as the ekonomi buses, but stop only at selected bus terminals en route and don't pick up from the side of the road. Air-con patas buses are more luxurious and seating is often guaranteed. Usually there is no need to book and you can just catch one at bus terminals in the big cities.

The luxury air-con buses come in a variety of price categories, depending on whether they have reclining seats, on-board toilets,

TV, karaoke, snacks etc. These buses should be booked in advance. Ticket agents often have pictures of the buses and seating plans, so check to see what you are getting when you choose your seat. On Sumatra, Java and Bali many of the luxury buses are night buses *(bis malam)*, travelling the highways when the traffic is lighter.

Bring as little luggage as possible – there is rarely any room to store anything on buses. A large pack with a frame will be a positive abomination to find a space for, so if you can travel with a small bag, do so.

Reservations

For short routes on good roads you'll probably find frequent vehicles departing all through the day. For longer routes you'll have to get down to the bus terminal early in the morning to get a vehicle; on bad roads there'll be fewer vehicles, so buying a ticket beforehand can be a good idea. In many places the bus companies will have an office from where you can buy a ticket and reserve a seat; there may be shops which act as agents (or own the buses) from where you can buy tickets in advance. Often, hotels will act as agents or will buy a ticket for you and arrange for the bus to pick you up at the hotel – sometimes they will charge a few hundred rupiah for this service but it's easily worth it.

Costs

Ekonomi buses are ridiculously cheap and you can travel over 100 km for 2000 rp. Prices vary from region to region and with the condition of the road. The daytime buses that depart early in the morning – carrying chickens, pigs and goats – are usually the cheapest. You'll rarely have to pay more than 8000 rp for a full day journey.

By way of comparison, the most luxurious overnight buses from Jakarta to Bali cost around 60,000 rp, including the ferry crossing. A non-air-con express bus will do the same run for around half the price.

MINIBUS (BEMO)

Public minibuses are used both as local transport around cities and towns and on short intercity runs, but their speciality is delivering people out into the hills and villages. They service the furthest reaches of the transport network.

The great minibus ancestor is the bemo, a small three-wheel pick-up truck with a row of seats down each side, but they are more like regular minibuses these days. The word 'bemo' (a contraction of *becak* – three wheeled bicycle-rickshaw and *motor)* is rarely used now but is still applied on Bali and universally understood. In other regions, minibuses go by a mind-boggling array of names, such as *opelet, mikrolet, angkot* or *angkudes*. Just to make things confusing they are called *taksi* in many parts of Irian Jaya and East Java. Often they will be called simply by their brand name, such as Suzuki, Daihatsu or Toyota, but the most popular make by far is the Mitsubishi Colt, and *colt* is widely used.

Most minibuses operate a standard route, picking up and dropping off people and goods anywhere along the way. They can be very cramped with even less room for luggage than the buses, and if there is a choice the buses are usually more comfortable.

Within cities, there is usually a standard fare no matter how long or short the distance. On longer routes between cities you may have to bargain a bit. Minibus drivers often try to overcharge foreigners – more in some places than in others. It's best to ask somebody, such as your hotel staff, about the *harga biasa* (normal price) before you get on. Otherwise see what the other passengers are paying and offer the correct fare.

Beware of getting on an empty minibus; you may end up chartering it! On the other hand, sometimes chartering a bemo is worth considering – for a few people it can work out cheaper than hiring a motorcycle by the day and much cheaper than hiring a car. Regular bemos carry around 12 people, so multiplying the usual fare by 12 should give you a rough idea of what to pay.

As with all public transport in Indonesia, the drivers wait until their vehicles are crammed to capacity before they contemplate moving, or they may go *keliling*, driving endlessly around town looking for a full complement of passengers. Often there are people, produce, chickens, stacks of sarongs, laden baskets and even bicycles hanging out the windows and doors – at times it seems you're in danger of being crushed to death or at least asphyxiated. There's no such thing as air-con on any of these vehicles.

Door-to-Door Minibus

Express minibuses also operate between cities, mostly on Java, but tourist minibuses also run between the main tourist centres on Sumatra and Bali. These minibuses are often luxurious seven or eight seaters with air-con and lots of leg room. Often called *travel*, they will pick you up from your hotel and drop you at your destination at the other end. Cheaper non-air-con minibuses also operate, and sometimes you will have to go to a depot to catch them.

TRUCK

One of the great ironies of Indonesia is that farm animals ride in buses and people ride on the back of farm trucks! Trucks come in many different varieties. The luxurious ones operate with rows of bench seats in the tray at the back of the truck. More likely, you will have to sit on the floor or stand. It's imperative to try and get a seat in front of the rear axle, otherwise every time the truck hits a pothole you'll find out what it's like to be a ping-pong ball. Trucks are most common in Nusa Tenggara, but you'll also find them in other places where the road is so rough as to be impassable to other vehicles. Trucks can even be found in parts of developed Java.

TRAIN

Train travel in Indonesia is restricted solely to Java and Sumatra – for full details see those chapters. Briefly, there is a pretty good railway service running from one end of Java to the other – in the east it connects with the ferry to Bali, and in the west with the ferry to Sumatra. There are a few lines tacked down on Sumatra, but most of that island is reserved for buses. There are no railways on any of the other islands.

Trains vary – they can be slow, miserable and cheap; fast, comfortable and expensive; and in-between.

CAR & MOTORCYCLE
Road Rules

Basically, there aren't any. People in Indonesia drive on the left (usually!) of the road, as in Australia, Japan, the UK and most of South-East Asia. Opportunities for driving yourself are fairly limited in Indonesia unless you bring your own vehicle with you, except on Bali and to a lesser extent Java – see the Bali and Java chapters for more details. In other places where tourists congregate, you can usually hire a jeep or minibus with driver included.

Punctures are usually repaired at roadside stands known as *tambal ban*. Whatever you do, try not to have an accident – if you do, as a foreigner, it's *your* fault.

Petrol

Petrol is reasonably cheap in Indonesia – it's currently around 700 rp a litre. There are petrol stations around the larger towns, but out in the villages they can be hard to find. Small wayside shops sell small amounts of petrol – look for signs that read *press ban* or crates of bottles with a sign saying *bensin*. Some of the petrol from the roadside stands is said to be of dubious quality, so it's probably best to refill whenever you see a petrol station *(pompa bensin)*.

Motorcycle

Motorcycles are readily available for hire right across Indonesia. In the tourist centres, they can be rented from around 10,000 rp per day, but almost anywhere someone will rent you their motorcycle to make a few extra rupiah. Motorcycles are almost all between 90 and 125 cc, with 100 cc as the usual size. You really don't need anything bigger – the distances are short and the roads are rarely suitable for going very fast.

Indonesia is not the place to learn how to ride – inexperienced riders are asking for trouble. The main highways are hectic, especially on Java and Bali, though outside the main cities on the other islands, traffic is usually fairly sedate.

Combined with all the normal hazards of motorcycle riding are narrow roads, unexpected potholes, crazy drivers, buses and trucks that (through size alone) reckon they own the road, children who dart onto the road, bullocks that lumber in, dogs and chickens that run around in circles, and unlit traffic at night. Take it slowly and cautiously around curves to avoid hitting oncoming traffic – this includes very large and heavy buses, buffaloes, herds of stray goats and children. Keep to the back roads as much as possible, where riding can be pleasurable.

A motorcycle is an ideal vehicle to get out into the countryside and day trip to points of interest. A motorcycle gives you enormous flexibility, allowing you to get to places that people without their own transport have to walk to, and it saves having to wait endlessly for transport.

Rental charges vary with the bike and the period of hire. The longer the hire period, the lower the rate: the bigger or newer the bike, the higher the rate. Typically, on Bali you can expect to pay at least 8000 to 12,000 rp per day. Elsewhere it tends to be higher.

In theory you need to have a licence, especially to satisfy travel insurance in case of an accident, though you rarely have to show one. Bring your motorcycle licence if you have one. See the Getting Around section in the Bali chapter for details of how to get a licence and how to rent a motorcycle there.

Some travel insurance policies do not cover you if you are involved in an accident whilst on a motorcycle. Check the small print.

Car

A car offers much the same advantages and disadvantages as a motorcycle. Another major disadvantage is price – at least five times that of a motorcycle.

The price for hiring a car varies according to both location and vehicle. Indonesia has regular car-rental agencies in big cities like

Jakarta, where a car without a driver costs over 100,000 rp per day, or around 150,000 rp with a driver. Bali is one of the cheapest places to rent a car. A Suzuki jeep costs around 35,000 to 40,000 rp a day, including insurance and unlimited km; or a *kijang* (Indonesia's popular family car that is a cross between a sedan and an off-road vehicle) costs from around 55,000 rp per day. In most cases, the price includes unlimited mileage but you supply the petrol.

The major car rental agencies, Hertz, Avis and National, are found in the main cities, such as Jakarta, Bandung, Yogyakarta, Medan, Surabaya and Denpasar, but they are expensive.

Driving yourself is not much fun in many parts of Indonesia. It requires enormous amounts of concentration and the legal implications of accidents can be a nightmare – that is if you survive an angry mob should someone be hurt. It is more common, and often cheaper, to rent a car or minibus with driver.

Renting a minibus can be a particularly good deal for a group. The Mitsubishi Colt L300 is a favourite model – they are sturdy, comfortable, go-almost-anywhere vehicles, and can take up to six people and luggage in comfort.

Travel agents in the travellers centres are good places to try for minibus rental. Go to the cheap tour operators – agents in the big hotels will charge big prices. Through the agents you have a better chance of finding a good, experienced driver that speaks some English and knows what tourists want. Failing that ask at a tourist information centre or your hotel. There is always someone with a vehicle that is looking for work. Bali is a good place for renting on this basis. On Java, Yogyakarta is the best, and on Lombok try around Senggigi. It is less common (and often more expensive) in other parts of Indonesia, but always possible.

Car or minibus rental starts at around 60,000 rp per day, including driver but excluding petrol. Bargaining is usually required. It is harder, but certainly possible, to find a driver for longer trips lasting a few days or even weeks. Negotiate a deal cover-

ing food and accommodation – either you provide a hotel room each night and pay a food allowance, or negotiate an allowance that covers both – figure on about 15,000 rp per day. It pays to see what your driver is like on a day trip before heading off on a lengthy expedition.

BICYCLE

Bicycles can be rented in the main centres of Java, Bali and also Lombok, but they're not used very much by Indonesians or by travellers. A few odd places like Solo are exceptions, with plenty of bicycles in common use.

The main advantage of cycling is the quality of the experience. You can cover many more km by bemo, bus or motorcycle but you really don't see more. Bicycles also tend to bridge the time gap between the rush of the west and the calm of rural Asia – without the noise of a motorcycle engine you can hear the wind rustling in the rice paddies, or the sound of a *gamelan* practising as you pass a village on Bali.

The main problems with seeing Indonesia by bicycle are the traffic on Java and the hills and enormous distances everywhere, which make it rather impractical or tough going to ride all over Indonesia. Bali is more compact and seeing it by pushbike has become much more popular in recent years. More people are giving it a try and more places are renting bikes. At all the main sights on Java there are bicycle parking areas (usually 100 rp), where an attendant keeps an eye on your bicycle.

For serious bicycle touring, bring your own. Good quality bicycles and components can be found in the major cities, particularly on Java and Bali, but are difficult to find elsewhere.

HITCHING

Hitching is not part of the culture in Indonesia but if you put out your thumb someone may give you a lift. Confusion may arise as to whether payment is required or not. On the back roads where no public transport exists, hitching may be the only alternative to walking, and passing motorists or trucks are often willing to help.

Bear in mind, however, that hitching is never entirely safe in any country in the world, and we do not recommend it. Travellers who decide to hitch should understand that they are taking a small but potentially serious risk. People who do choose to hitch will be safer if they travel in pairs and let someone know where they are planning to go.

BOAT

Regular ferries connect all the islands from Sumatra right through Java, Bali and Nusa Tenggara to Timor – see the relevant chapters in this book for details. These ferries run either daily or several times a week, so there's no need to spend days in sleepy little port towns, reading big thick books, waiting for the elusive piece of driftwood to take you to the next island. Almost all of these ferries can transport large vehicles, and all of them will take motorcycles.

To and between Kalimantan, Sulawesi, Maluku and Irian Jaya, the main connections are provided by Pelni, the government-run passenger line.

Pelni Ships

Pelni is the biggest shipper with services almost everywhere. It has modern, all air-con passenger ships and operates regular two weekly or monthly routes around the islands. The ships usually stop for four hours in each port, so there's time for a quick look around.

The fleet is comprised of the ships *Awu*, *Binaiya*, *Bukit*, *Ciremai*, *Dobonsolo*, *Kambuna*, *Kelimutu*, *Kerinci*, *Lambolo*, *Lawit*, *Leuser*, *Raya*, *Rinjani*, *Sirimau*, *Tatamailau*, *Tidar*, *Tilongkabila* and *Umsini*. More are being added to the fleet, and Pelni boats cover virtually all of the archipelago. Routes and schedules change every year. Pick up a copy of the latest schedule from any Pelni office.

Because Pelni ships operate only every two or four weeks, regular ferries are much more convenient. You can travel from Sumatra right through to Timor by land/ferry connections, but Pelni ships are often the only alternative to flying for travel to and between Kalimantan, Sulawesi, Maluku and Irian Jaya.

Travel on Pelni ships is comprised of four cabin classes, followed by Kelas Ekonomi, which is the modern version of the old deck class. There you are packed in a large room with a space to sleep; but, even in ekonomi, it's air-con and can get pretty cool at night, so bring warm clothes or a sleeping bag. It is possible to book a sleeping place in ekonomi – sometimes – otherwise you have to find your own empty space. Mattresses can be rented for 2500 rp and many boats have a 'tourist deck' upstairs. There are no locker facilities in ekonomi, so you have to keep an eye on your gear.

Class I is luxury plus with only two beds per cabin and a price approaching air travel. Class II is a notch down in style, with four to a cabin, but still very comfortable. Class III has six beds and Class IV has eight beds to a cabin. Class I, II, III and IV have a restaurant with good food, while in ekonomi you queue up to collect an unappetising meal on a tray and then sit down wherever you can to eat it. It pays to bring some other food with you.

Ekonomi is fine for short trips. Class IV is the best value for longer hauls, but some ships only offer Class I and II or III in addition to ekonomi. Prices quoted in this book are for ekonomi – as a rough approximation Class IV is 50% more than ekonomi, Class III is 100% more, Class II is 200% more and Class I is 400% more.

You can book tickets up to a week ahead; it's best to book at least a few days in advance. Pelni is not a tourist operation, so don't expect any special service, although there is usually somebody hidden away in the ticket offices who can help foreigners.

As well as its luxury liners, Pelni has Perinitis (Pioneer) ships that visit many of the other ports not covered by the passenger liners. They can get you to just about any of the remote outer islands, as well as the major ports. The ships are often beaten up old crates that also carry cargo. They offer deck class only, but you may be able to negotiate a cabin with one of the crew.

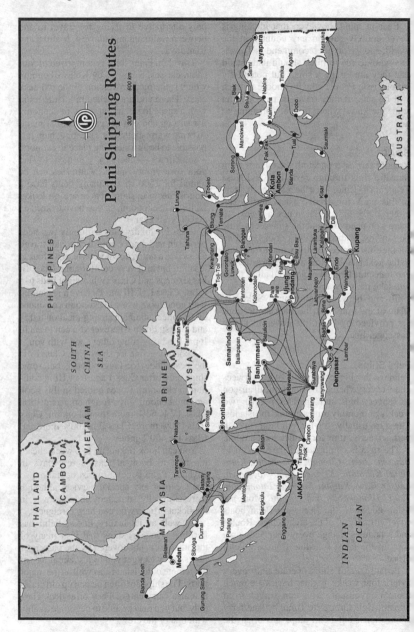

Pelni Shipping Routes

Other Ships

Sumatra, Java, Bali and Nusa Tenggara are all connected by regular ferries and you can use them to island-hop all the way from Sumatra to Timor.

Getting a boat in the outer islands is often a matter of hanging loose until something comes by. Check with shipping companies, the harbour office or anyone else you can think of.

If you're travelling deck class, unroll your sleeping bag on the deck and make yourself comfortable. Travelling deck class during the wet season can prove to be extremely uncomfortable. Either get one person in your party to take a cabin or discuss renting a cabin from one of the crew (it's a popular way for the crew to make a little extra). Bring some food of your own.

It's also possible to make some more unusual sea trips. Old Makassar schooners still sail the Indonesian waters and it's often possible to travel on them from Sulawesi to other islands, particularly Java and Nusa Tenggara.

Small Boats

There's a whole range of floating tubs you can use to hop between islands, across rivers, down rivers and over lakes. Just about any sort of vessel can be rented in Indonesia. Fishing boats or other small boats can be chartered to take you to small offshore islands. Some of these boats are *not* reliable and engine trouble is an occasional problem. Check out the boat before you rent it – it would be nice if it had a two way radio and a lifeboat, just in case.

The *longbot* (longboat) is a long, narrow boat powered by a couple of outboard motors, with bench seats on either side of the hull for passengers to sit on. You find these mainly on the rivers of Kalimantan where they're a common means of transport.

Outrigger canoes powered by an outboard motor are a standard form of transport for some short inter-island hops – like the trip out from Manado in northern Sulawesi to the coral reefs surrounding nearby Pulau Bunaken. On Lombok these elegant, brilliantly painted fishing boats, looking rather like exotic dragonflies, are used for the short hop from Bangsal harbour to the offshore islands of Gili Air and Gili Trawangan. There are standard fares for standard routes, and you can charter these boats.

Speedboats are not all that common, although they are used on some routes on the rivers of Kalimantan, or for some short inter-island hops in some parts of Indonesia. They are, of course, considerably faster than long-bots or river ferries, but considerably more expensive.

River ferries are commonly found on Kalimantan, where the rivers *are* the roads. They're large, bulky vessels that carry people and goods up and down the water network.

LOCAL TRANSPORT

Bus

Large buses aren't used much as a means of city transport except on Java, perhaps because most Indonesian towns aren't that big; smaller vehicles suffice.

There's an extensive system of buses in Jakarta and these are universally cheap, but be *very* careful about pickpockets. They usually work in gangs and can empty your pockets faster than you can say 'gado gado'.

Taxi

Metered taxis are readily available in major cities, especially on Java and Bali. Elsewhere, you may have to bargain the fare in advance. If a taxi has a meter, make sure it is used. Most drivers will use them without fuss, and Indonesian taxi drivers usually provide a good service. Jakarta undoubtedly has the worst taxi drivers in the country.

Metered taxis charge about 1300 rp for the first km, and 550 rp for each additional km.

Minibus

Minibuses are the usual form of transport around Indonesian towns and cities – most run on standard routes with standard fares. They go under a variety of names – bemo, angkot or brand names, like Daihatsu or Colt.

Becak

These are three wheeled bicycle-rickshaws. Unlike the version found in India where the driver sits in front of you, or the Filipino version with the driver at the side, in Indonesia the driver sits at the rear, nosing your life ever forwards into the traffic.

Many drivers rent their machines, but those who own them add personal touches: brightly painted pictures, tinkling bells or whirring metal discs strung across the under-carriage. In Yogyakarta one guy peddled furiously around the streets at night with a tiny flashing light-bulb on the point of his coolie hat!

Whilst becaks are now banned from the main streets of large Javanese cities (they are banned from Jakarta altogether), in just about any town of any size on Java, as well as in some other parts of Indonesia (like Ujung Pandang on Sulawesi), they're the most basic form of transport – for people and anything else that has to be shifted.

Bargain your fare *before* you get in. And make sure, if there are two of you, that it covers both people – otherwise you'll be in for an argument when you get to your destination. Indonesian becak drivers are hard bargainers – they have to be to survive! But they will usually settle on a reasonable fare – around 500 rp per km. Fares vary from city to city, and increase with more passengers, luggage, hills and at night. Hiring a becak for a period of time or for a round-trip often makes good sense if you're planning to cover a lot of ground in one day, particularly in large places like Yogyakarta or Solo.

Bajaj

These are noisy, smoke-belching three wheeled vehicles with a driver at the front, a small motorcycle engine below and seats for two passengers behind. They're a common form of local transport in Jakarta, but you don't see them very often elsewhere.

Dokar

Dokars are the jingling, horse-drawn carts found all over Indonesia. The two wheeled carts are usually brightly coloured with dec-

GLENN BEANLAND

A speciality of Jakarta, the bajaj is a common form of transport, similar to the tuk-tuk of Bangkok or the tempo of Kathmandu. A three wheeled affair, powered by the motorcycle engine, the bajaj takes two passengers and is dirty, noisy and smelly.

orative motifs and fitted with bells which chime when they're in motion. The small horses or ponies that pull them are often equipped with long tassels attached to their gear. A typical dokar has bench seating on either side, which can comfortably fit three people, four if they're all slim; their owners generally pack in as many people as possible plus bags of rice and other paraphernalia. It's a picturesque way of getting around if you don't get upset by the ill-treatment of ani-mals – although generally the ponies are

GREGORY ADAMS

Dokar, the horse-drawn carts found in many areas of Indonesia which typically seat three to four people.

looked after pretty well since they mean the difference between starvation and survival for their owners. The price depends on the colour of your skin – the bidding starts at around 1000 rp. After negotiations, count on paying about 300 rp per person per km.

On Java you also see the *andong* or *delman*, which is a larger horse-drawn wagon designed to carry six people. In some parts of Indonesia like Gorontalo and Manado in northern Sulawesi you also see the *bendi*, which is like a small dokar, designed to carry two people.

Other Local Transport

There are various other ways of getting around.

Ojek (or *ojeg*) are motorcycle riders that take pillion passengers for a bargainable price. They are found at bus terminals and markets, or just hanging around at cross-roads. They will take you around town and go where no other public transport exists. They can tackle roads impassable to any other vehicle. They can also be rented by the hour (starting at around 3000 rp) for sightseeing.

In many of the hill resorts on Java you can hire horses. Likewise, it's often possible to hire one just about anywhere in Indonesia where horses are raised – this is possibly the ideal solution to getting over some of that rough terrain and actually enjoying those abominable roads!

In Jakarta, bicycles with little seats at the rear are used as a taxi service – see them near the Pasar Ikan.

ORGANISED TOURS

A wide range of tours can be booked from travel agents within Indonesia. Most of these take in places where tourists are numerous, such as Jakarta, Yogyakarta, Bali, Lombok and Danau Toba (Lake Toba).

You can be absolutely certain that taking a tour will work out to be more expensive than going by yourself, but some are good value. For example, you can take a day tour to Borobudur and the Dieng Plateau from Yogyakarta, and be picked up and dropped off at your hotel for only 25,000 rp. Yogya and Bali have the cheapest tours and the best range, but cheap tours are available in all the main travellers centres.

Tours are normally much less expensive if you book through a hotel rather than through a travel agent.

There are, of course, expensive all-inclusive tours available from travel agencies in Jakarta, Bali and elsewhere. Some of the major national operators are Vayatour, Pacto and Natour, with offices throughout the country. You can find many other agents by looking in the yellow pages of the telephone directory. Most travel agents have some economy tours, but they prefer to sell packages with accommodation at a luxurious hotel like the Hilton or Sheraton, banquet-style meals and prices beginning at around 200,000 rp per day.

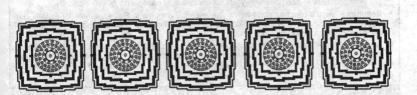

Java is the political, geographic and economic centre of Indonesia. With an area of 132,000 sq km, Java is a little over half the size of the island of Great Britain, but its population of 115 million is almost double Britain's. With such vast human resources, Java is the powerhouse and dictator of Indonesia.

Java presents vivid contrasts of wealth and squalor, majestic open country and crowded filthy cities, quiet rural scenes and bustling modern traffic. The main cities can be overwhelming, but rural Java is still an island of astonishing beauty. A string of high volcanic mountains runs through the centre of the island, providing a smoking backdrop to the fertile green fields and terraces. The rich volcanic soils that have long been the secret to Java's abundance extend north to the flat coastal plain and the murky Java Sea, while the south coast fronts the crashing waves of the Indian Ocean.

It was on plentiful Java that the Hindu-Buddhist empires reached their zenith, producing the architectural wonders of Borobudur and Prambanan. When Islam came to Java, it absorbed rather than banished the existing influences, and Java is a

---

HIGHLIGHTS

- **Yogyakarta** – The cultural centre of Java, Yogyakarta has excellent, cheap facilities and is an ideal base for trips to the awe-inspiring Buddhist pyramid of Borobudur. Nearby, Solo is a quieter court city and a repository of Javanese culture, as is Cirebon on the north coast.

- **Java's Cities** – Jakarta, Bogor, Bandung and Surabaya are intense, crowded and disorienting, but to appreciate contemporary Indonesia, or its Dutch heritage, a visit to Java's cities is essential.

- **Natural Attractions** – A string of volcanoes runs through the island, and Gunung Bromo is one of the most spectacular in Indonesia. Krakatau, Indonesia's most famous volcano, can be visited from the west coast. Java also has the highest concentration of national parks in the country.

- **Beaches** – Java's beaches don't match the superb examples in Sulawesi, Maluku or Bali, but Pangandaran is deservedly Java's No 1 beach resort. The living is cheap and relaxed, and the adjoining national park is good for walks.

- **Seeing it All** – A typical three to four week itinerary starts in Jakarta, continues to Bandung and then heads on to Pangandaran, Yogyakarta, Solo, Surabaya and Gunung Bromo, before hitting Bali. For a whirlwind trip, some just fly into Yogyakarta, with a quick trip out to Borobudur and Prambanan.

blend of cultures and religion. The ready Indonesian images of *wayang* shadow puppets, batik and court dances exist alongside the muezzin's call to the mosque.

Java is a long, narrow island, conveniently divided into three provinces: West, Central and East Java. It also includes the special territories of Jakarta, the teeming capital, and Yogyakarta, a centre for Javanese culture and one of Indonesia's premier tourist destinations.

West Java, home to the Sundanese people, has places of interest such as Bandung in the Sundanese heartland, the court city of Cirebon, the beach at Pangandaran, famous Krakatau and the wilds of the Ujung Kulon National Park.

In Central Java, temples and royal cities plot the rise and fall of the Hindu, Buddhist and Muslim kingdoms, from which the present-day court cities of Yogyakarta and Solo have evolved. Java is people and lots of them, but there are isolated places where you can find yourself out of sight and sound, such as the Dieng Plateau in the beautiful central highlands.

In East Java, spectacular Gunung Bromo volcano is as wild and desolate as you could hope. Off the coast, Madura holds to its independent traditions, and East Java's highlands have some of Java's best hill resorts and hiking opportunities.

HISTORY

The history of human habitation on Java extends back over half a million years when 'Java Man' lived along the banks of Bengawan Solo river in Central Java. Waves of migrants followed, coming down through South-East Asia to inhabit the island. The Javanese are an Austronesian people, closely related to the people of Malaysia and the Philippines.

Early Javanese Kingdoms

The island's exceptional fertility allowed the development of an intensive *sawah* (wet-rice) agriculture, which in turn required close cooperation between villages for the maintenance of the irrigation systems. From this first need for local government small kingdoms developed, but the first major principality appears to have been that of King Sanjaya's. Around the beginning of the 8th century he founded the kingdom of Mataram, which controlled much of central Java. Mataram's religion centred on the Hindu god Shiva, and the kingdom produced some of the earliest of Java's Hindu temples on the Dieng Plateau.

Sanjaya's Hindu kingdom was followed by a Buddhist interlude under the Sailendra dynasty; it was during this time that Mahayana Buddhism was established on Java and work began (probably around 780 AD) on Borobudur. Hinduism continued to exist alongside Buddhism, and the massive Hindu Prambanan complex was built and consecrated around 856 AD. Hinduism and Buddhism often fused into one religion on Java.

Mataram eventually fell, possibly as a result of conflict with the Sumatra-based Sriwijaya kingdom which invaded Java in the 11th century. Sriwijaya, however, also suffered attacks from the Chola kingdom of southern India. Javanese power revived under King Airlangga, a semi-legendary figure who brought much of Java under his control and formed the first royal link between Java and Bali. Airlangga divided his kingdom between his two sons, resulting in the formation of the Kediri and Janggala kingdoms.

Early in the 13th century the commoner Ken Angrok usurped the throne of Singosari (a part of the Janggala kingdom), defeated Kediri and then brought the rest of Janggala under his control. His new kingdom of Singosari expanded its power during the 13th century up until its last king, Kertanegara, was murdered in a rebellion in 1292.

Majapahit Kingdom

Kertanegara's son-in-law and successor, Wijaya, established the Majapahit kingdom, the greatest kingdom of the Hindu-Javanese period. Under Hayam Wuruk, who ruled from 1350 to 1389, the Majapahit kingdom claimed sovereignty over the Indonesian archipelago, although its territorial sovereignty was probably restricted to Java, Madura and Bali. Hayam Wuruk's strongman prime minister, Gajah Mada, was responsible for many of Majapahit's territorial conquests.

While previous Javanese kingdoms based their power on the control of the rich Javanese agricultural areas, the Majapahits established the first Javanese commercial empire by taking control of Java's main ports and the shipping lanes throughout the archipelago.

The Majapahit kingdom began to decline soon after the death of Hayam Wuruk. Various principalities began breaking away from Majapahit rule and adopting Islam.

Islamic Kingdoms

Islam on Java now became a strong religious and political force opposed to Majapahit, making converts among the Majapahit elite even at the height of the kingdom's power.

The 15th and 16th centuries saw the rise of new Islamic kingdoms, such as Demak, Cirebon and Banten along the north coast.

By the end of the 16th century the Muslim kingdom of Mataram had taken control of central and eastern Java. The last remaining independent principalities, Surabaya and Cirebon, were eventually subjugated, leaving only Mataram and Banten (in West Java) to face the Dutch in the 17th century.

Dutch Period

The conquest of Java by the Dutch need not be recounted here, but by the end of the 18th century practically all of the island was under Dutch control. (See the History section in the Facts about the Country chapter for more details.)

During the Dutch period there were strong Muslim powers on Java, most notably Mataram. The Javanese were great warriors who continually opposed the Dutch, but they were never a united force because of internal

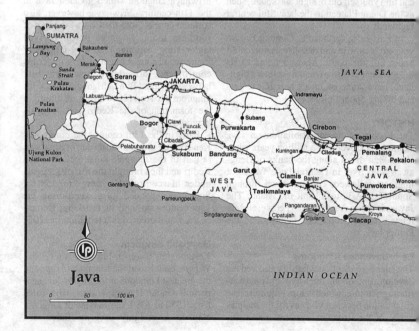

conflict or battles with the Sundanese or the Madurese. The last remnants of the Mataram kingdom survived as the principalities of Surakarta (Solo) and Yogyakarta until the foundation of the Indonesian republic. Javanese kings claimed to rule with divine authority and the Dutch helped to preserve the vestiges of a traditional Javanese aristocracy by confirming them as regents, district officers or sub-district officers in the European administration.

Java Today

Java plays an extraordinary role in Indonesia today. It is more than simply the geographical centre of Indonesia. Much of Indonesian history was hacked out on Javanese soil. The major battles of the independence movement took place on Java and two of the strongest political parties in the first decade of independence – the Nationalist Party (PNI) and the Communist Party (PKI) – drew their support from the Javanese.

To a large extent the rebellions of the Sumatrans, Minahasans and Ambonese in the 1950s and 1960s were rebellions against Javanese domination. Furthermore the Darul Islam rebellion against the new republic broke out in West Java. The abortive Communist coup of 1965 started in Jakarta and some of its most dramatic and disastrous events took place on Java. Java has provided the lead and the leadership for the republic.

It has been said that Soeharto is much more a Javanese king than an 'elected' president, and Indonesia much more a Javanese kingdom than a republic. Admirers of Soeharto compare him to the wise kings of the wayang puppet shows, who turn chaos into order and bring prosperity to the kingdom. Critics respond that he rules much more like a Javanese king or sultan, with systems of palace-centred patronage, favouritism and officially sponsored corruption. The ultimate base for Soeharto's authority is always the military, which is overwhelmingly Javanese at the top level.

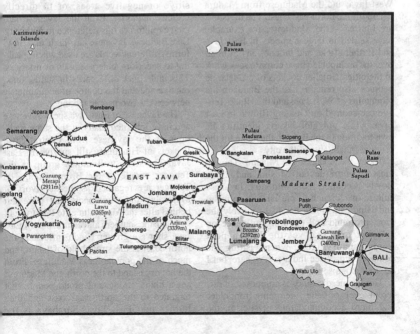

A strong consciousness of ancient religious and mystical thought carries over into modern-day Java, from the peasant farmer to the high-ranking government official. Soekarno identified with Bima, the strong-willed prince of the wayang. Soeharto is said to identify strongly with the clown-god Semar, who in the traditional wayang plays often steps in to save the situation when more refined characters have failed.

Java also dominates economic life in Indonesia. Java has the bulk of Indonesia's industry and is the recipient of most of the new foreign investment pouring into the country. The island is the most developed part of Indonesia by far, but its big test for the future is to manage economic growth and make inroads into the everpresent problems of overpopulation and poverty.

PEOPLE & CULTURE

Java has three main groups of people, each speaking their own language: the Javanese of Central and East Java; the Sundanese of West Java; and the Madurese from Madura island off the north-east coast. The divisions are blurred – the Madurese, for example, have settled in large numbers in East Java and further afield, and Indonesians from all over the archipelago have come to seek work in the cities. Smaller pockets of pre-Islamic peoples also remain, like the Badui in the mountains of West Java and the Hindu Tenggerese centred on Gunung Bromo in East Java, while polyglot Jakarta identifies its own tradition in the Betawi, the name for the original inhabitants of the city.

Today the Javanese are Muslim. Though most are *santri* (devout) Muslim, and Java is slowly becoming more orthodox, Javanese culture owes much to pre-Islamic animism and Hinduism. India has had probably the most profound and enduring influence on religion on Java, yet the Indian poet Rabindranath Tagore, when visiting the country, said: 'I see India everywhere, but I do not recognise it'.

The Javanese cosmos is composed of different levels of belief, stemming from older and more accommodating mysticism, the Hindu court culture and a very real belief in ghosts and numerous benevolent and malevolent spirits. Underneath the unifying code of Islam, magic power is concentrated in amulets and heirlooms (especially the Javanese dagger known as the *kris*), in parts of the human body like the nails and the hair, and in sacred musical instruments. The traditional medicine man *(dukun)* is still consulted when illness strikes.

The *halus* (refined) Javanese is part of the Hindu court tradition, which still exists in the heartland of Central Java. In contrast to Islam, the court tradition is a hierarchical world view, based on privilege and often guided by the gods or nature spirits. Refinement and politeness are highly regarded, and loud displays of emotion and flamboyant behaviour is *kasar* (coarse and rough, bad manners).

Indirectness is a Javanese trait, and stems from an unwillingness to make anyone else feel uncomfortable or ashamed. It is impolite to point out mistakes, embarrassments, sensitive or negative areas, or to directly criticise authority. Even the Javanese language reinforces this deference to authority. Like Balinese, Javanese has 'high' and 'low' forms; different words are used when speaking to superiors, elders, equals or inferiors. This underlines differences in status, rank, relative age and the degree of acquaintance between the two people talking.

The Javanese of East Java speak Javanese and have inherited many of the same traditions as the Javanese from Central Java. Pockets of Hinduism still survive in East Java. The most well-known group is the Tengger people of the Bromo area. The Tengger are regarded as the survivors of Majapahit, the commoners that were left behind after the Majapahit elite fled to Bali.

While the southern and central part of East Java shows a greater Hindu influence, the north coast is the stronghold of Islam, and much of the population is Madurese. From the hot dry island to the north, the Madurese are a blunt, strong and proud people that migrated to the north-east coast and then further into East Java. Surabaya is the melting pot of all East Java, and as the gateway to Madura, shows strong influence from the more devoutly Islamic Madurese. Javanese as spoken in Surabaya is considered very kasar, without the intricacies and deferences of Central Java.

The Sundanese of West Java are likewise less concerned with the flourishes and hierarchies of Central Java. Their culture and traditions have much in common with the Javanese. Sundanese is also a hierarchical language of high and low forms, but Islam has taken stronger root in Sunda, and the people are earthier, more direct and more egalitarian. Yet even in this more Islamic atmosphere, the older traditions remain. The Badui in the western highlands are distinguished by their history of resistance to Islam.

ARTS

Javanese culture is a product of pre-Hindu, Hindu and Islamic influences. The rise of the 16th century Islamic states brought a rich new cultural heritage, but the Hindu heritage also managed to continue its influence.

Wayang

Javanese wayang theatre has been a major means of preserving the Hindu-Buddhist heritage on Java. The most well-known form is the *wayang kulit*, the shadow-puppet theatre using puppets made of leather (*kulit* means leather).

Wayang Kulit In the shadow-puppet theatre, perforated leather figures are manipulated behind an illuminated cotton screen. The stories are usually based on the Hindu epics, the *Ramayana* and *Mahabharata*, although other purely Javanese stories are also performed. In a traditional performance a whole night might be devoted to just one drama (*lakon*) from a legend. A single puppeteer (the *dalang*) animates the puppets and narrates and chants through the entire night to the accompaniment of the *gamelan* orchestra.

Many wayang kulit figures and even whole stories have a specific mystical function; certain stories are performed for the purpose of protecting a rice crop (these incorporate the rice goddess Dewi Sri), the welfare of a village or even individuals.

Shadow-puppet theatre is not unique to Java; it can also be found in Turkey, India, China and parts of South-East Asia, and wayang kulit owes much to Indian tradition.

By the 11th century wayang performances with leather puppets flourished on Java, and by the end of the 18th century wayang kulit had developed most of the details of puppet design and performance techniques we see today. The standardisation of the puppet designs is traditionally attributed to King Raden Patah of Demak, a 16th century Islamic kingdom.

The puppets are made of leather, with water-buffalo leather from a young animal being the most favoured material. The outline of the puppet is cut using a thin knife, and the fine details carved out using small chisels and a hammer. When the carving is finished, the movable arms are attached and the puppet is painted. Lines are drawn in and accentuated with black ink, which is also used to increase the contrast of the carved holes. The *cempurit*, the stick of horn used to hold the puppet upright, is then attached.

The leaf-shaped *kayon* represents the 'tree' or 'mountain of life' and is used to end scenes or to symbolise wind, mountains, obstacles, clouds or the sea. Made of the same flexible hide as the other puppets, the kayon might be waved softly behind the cloth screen while a puppet figure is held horizontally – a surprisingly effective way of indicating flight through the cloudy sky. Symbolic decorations on the kayon include the face in the centre of the tree which symbolises the danger and risk that all people must confront in life.

The characters in wayang are brought to life by the dalang. To call the dalang a puppeteer belittles the extraordinary range of talents a dalang must possess. Sitting cross-legged on a mat before the white screen, the dalang might manipulate dozens of figures in the course of a performance.

The dalang recounts events spanning centuries and continents, improvising from the

The Mahabharata & Ramayana

Ancient India, like ancient Greece, produced two great epics. The *Ramayana* describes the adventures of a prince who is banished from his country and wanders for many years in the wilderness. The *Mahabharata* is based on the legends of a great war. The first story is a little reminiscent of the *Odyssey*, which relates the adventures of Ulysses as he struggles to return home from Troy; the second has much in common with the *Iliad*.

When Hinduism came to Java so did the *Ramayana* and *Mahabharata*. The Javanese shifted the locale to Java; Javanese children were given the names of the heroes and by tradition the kings of Java were descendants of the epic heroes.

The *Mahabharata* and the *Ramayana* are the basis of the most important wayang stories on Java and Bali. While they often come across like ripping yarns, both are essentially moral tales, which for centuries have played a large part in establishing traditional Javanese values.

They are complex tales, and the division between good and evil is never absolute. The good heroes have bad traits and vice versa. Although the forces of good usually triumph over evil, more often than not the victory is an ambivalent one; both sides suffer grievous loss and, though a king may win a righteous war, he may lose all his sons in the process. In the *Mahabharata*, when the great battle is over and the Pandavas are victorious, one of their enemies sneaks into the encampment and kills all the Pandava women and children.

The Mahabharata

The great war portrayed in the *Mahabharata* is believed to have been fought in northern India around the 13th or 14th century BC. The war became a centre of legends, songs and poems, and at some point the vast mass of stories accumulated over the centuries were gathered together into a narrative called the 'Epic of the Bharata Nation (India)' – the *Mahabharata*. Over the following centuries more was added to it until it was seven times the size of the *Iliad* and the *Odyssey* combined!

The central theme of the *Mahabharata* is the power struggle between the Kurava brothers and their cousins, the Pandava brothers. Important events along the way include: the appearance of Krishna, an incarnation of Lord Vishnu, who becomes the adviser of the Pandavas; the marriage of Prince Arjuna of the Pandavas to the Princess Drupadi; the Kuravas' attempt to kill the Pandavas; and the division of the kingdom into two in an attempt to end the rivalry between the cousins. Finally, after 13 years in exile and hiding, the Pandavas realise there is no alternative but war, the great war of the *Mahabharata*, which is a series of bloody clashes between the cousins.

It is at this time that the Pandava warrior Arjuna becomes despondent at the thought of fighting his own flesh and blood, so Krishna, his charioteer and adviser, explains to him the duties and obligations of the warrior in a song known as the 'Bhagavad Gita'. Krishna explains that the soul is indestructible and that whoever dies shall be reborn and so there is no cause to be sad; it is the soldier's duty to fight and he will be accused of cowardice if he runs away.

In the course of the battles many of the great heroes from both sides are slain one by one; many others also lose their lives but in the end the Pandavas are victorious over the Kuravas.

The Ramayana

The *Ramayana*, the story of Prince Rama, is thought to have been written after the *Mahabharata*. Long before Prince Rama was born the gods had determined that his life would be that of a hero – but like all heroic lives it would be full of grave tests. Rama is an incarnation of the god Vishnu, and it is his destiny to kill the ogre king Rawana (also known as Dasamuka and Dasakhantha).

Due to scheming in the palace, Rama, his wife the beautiful Sita and his brother Laksamana are all exiled to the forest, where Sita is abducted by the ogre king. Rawana takes the form of a golden deer, luring Rama and Laksamana into the forest as they try to hunt the deer. Rawana then carries off Sita to his island kingdom of Lanka.

Rama begins his search for Sita, and is joined by the monkey god Hanuman and the monkey king Sugriwa. Eventually a full-scale assault is launched on the evil king and Sita is rescued. ■

basic plot a complex network of court intrigues, great loves, wars, philosophy, magic, mysticism and comedy. The dalang must be a linguist capable of speaking both the language of the audience and the ancient Kawi language spoken by the aristocratic characters of the play. The dalang must also be a mimic capable of producing a different voice for each of the characters, and have great physical stamina to sustain a performance lasting from evening until the early hours of the morning.

The dalang must be a musician, able to direct the village's gamelan orchestra which accompanies the performance, be versed in history, and have a deep understanding of philosophy and religion. The dalang must be a poet capable of creating a warm or terrifying atmosphere, but must also be a comedian able to introduce some comic relief into the performances. Understandably, the dalang has always been regarded as a very special type of person.

The dalang directs the gamelan orchestra using a system of cues, often communicating the name of the composition to be played using riddles or puns. The player of the *kendang* (drum) liaises between the dalang and the other gamelan players by setting the proper tempo and changes of tempo for each piece, and in executing the important signals for ending pieces. The dalang may communicate with the orchestra using signals tapped out with the wooden *cempala* (mallet) held in the left hand. Or there may be other types of cues – for example, one of the clowns in the performance may announce that a singing contest is to be held, then announce the song he intends singing and the gamelan will play that song.

The mass of the audience sits in front of the screen to watch the shadow figures, but some also sit behind the screen with the dalang to watch the expert at work.

Wayang Golek These three dimensional wooden puppets have movable heads and arms, and are manipulated in the same way as shadow puppets – but without using a shadow screen. Although *wayang golek* is found in Central Java, it is most popular among the Sundanese of West Java. Sometimes a wayang golek puppet is used right at the end of a wayang kulit play to symbolise the transition back from the world of two dimensions to the world of three.

Wayang golek uses the same stories as wayang kulit, including the *Mahabharata* and *Ramayana*, as well as stories about the mythical Javanese king Panji and other legendary kings. It also has its own set of stories,

for which there is some direct Islamic inspiration. These include the elaborate romances inspired by legends about the Prophet Muhammed's uncle, Amir Hamzah.

Wayang Klitik In East Java the wayang kulit is replaced by the *wayang klitik* or *keruchil*, a flat wooden puppet carved in low relief; this type of wayang is performed without a shadow screen. The wayang klitik is associated with the Damar Wulan stories which are of particular historical relevance to East Java. The stories relate the adventures of a handsome prince and his rise to become ruler of the Majapahit kingdom.

Wayang Orang Known as *wayang wong* in Javanese, the *wayang orang* is a dance drama in which real people dance the part of the wayang characters.

Wayang Topeng The *wayang topeng* is similar to wayang orang but uses masks. The two forms of dance drama were cultivated at varying times in the courts of Central Java. Wayang topeng is the older of the two and dates back as far as the Majapahit kingdom. In more recent times wayang wong was performed only as the official court dance drama, while wayang topeng was also performed outside the walls of the palace. The stylisation of human features seen in the shadow puppets is also seen in the wayang topeng masks; elongation and refinement are the key notes of the noble (halus) characters, while grotesque exaggeration denotes the vulgar (kasar) characters.

Gamelan

The musical instruments of Indonesia can be grouped into four main strata: those from pre-Hindu days; those from the Hindu period from the first centuries AD until about the 15th century; the Islamic period from about the 13th century AD; and from the 16th century, which is associated with Christian and European influences.

The oldest known instruments in Indonesia are the bronze 'kettle drums' belonging to the Dongson culture which developed in what is now northern Vietnam and spread into the Indonesian archipelago – they are not really drums as they have bronze rather than membrane heads. These instruments have been found on Sumatra, Java, Bali and Kalimantan and in other parts of South-East Asia; among the most curious examples are those of the island of Alor in Nusa Tenggara.

Other instruments, particularly those made of bamboo (like flutes and reed pipes),

are also thought to be very old. By the time of the Hindu period there was a wealth of metallic as well as wooden and bamboo instruments played on Java, and these are depicted on the stone reliefs of Borobudur and Prambanan and other shrines. On Borobudur there are reliefs of drums (waisted, hourglass, pot and barrel-shaped), two stringed lutes, harps, flutes, mouth organs, reed pipes, a keyed metallophone (saron), xylophone, cymbals and others

---

Wayang Characters

The wayang characters are often based on figures from the *Mahabharata* and *Ramayana*. In the *Mahabharata*, the Kuravas are essentially the forces of greed, evil and destruction, while the Pandavas represent refinement, enlightenment and civilised behaviour.

At a wayang or dance performance, if you know the plot well, it is easy to identify the characters, otherwise shape, colour, deportment and voice will help.

The noble (halus) characters tend to be smaller in size and more elegant in proportion; their legs are slender and close together, and their heads are tilted downwards presenting an image of humility and self-effacement. The kasar (coarse, rough) characters are often enormous, muscular and hairy, with their heads upturned.

Eye shape and the colour of the figures, particularly on the faces, are of great importance. Red often indicates aggressiveness, greed, impatience, anger or simply a very forthright personality. Black, and often blue, indicates calmness, spiritual awareness and maturity. Gold and yellow are reserved for kings and the highest nobles. White can symbolise purity or virtue, high moral purpose and the like. Hair styles, ornamentation and clothing are all important in identifying a particular character.

Pandavas

Bima Bima is the second-eldest of the Pandavas. He is big, burly, aggressive, not afraid to act on what he believes; he can be rough, even using the language of the man of the street to address the gods. He is able to fly and is the most powerful warrior on the battlefield, but he also has infinite kindness and a firm adherence to principle.

Arjuna Arjuna is the handsome and refined ladies' man, a representative of the noble class, whose eyes look at the ground because it's kasar to stare into people's faces. He can also be fickle and selfish, but despite his failings, he is halus – refined in manner, never speaking ill to offend others, polite and humble, patient and careful. Arjuna's charioteer is Krishna, the incarnation of the god Vishnu, a spiritual adviser but also a cunning and ruthless politician.

Arjuna

Semar A purely Javanese addition to the story is Arjuna's servant, the dwarf clown Semar. An incarnation of a god, Semar is a great source of wisdom and advice to Arjuna – but his body is squat with an enormous posterior, bulging belly and he sometimes has an uncontrollable disposition for farting.

Semar

Some of these instruments are direct imports from India, while others resemble the instruments now used in the Javanese gamelan orchestra.

One interesting and ancient instrument is the *calung*, a Sundanese instrument which is also found in a few places on Java and in southern Thailand. The basic version consists of a set of bamboo tubes, one end of each tube closed off by the natural node of the bamboo and the other end pared down for part of its length like a goose-quill pen. The instrument is played with one or two sickle-shaped wooden hammers *(panakol)* padded with cotton or rubber. The calung is still commonly found on Java.

The oldest instruments still in use include drums, gongs, various wind instruments and plucked strings. The large Javanese gamelan, whose total complement comprises 60 to 80 instruments, has sets of suspended and horizontal gongs, gong chimes, drums,

Sita

Rama

Kumbakarna

Gareng, Petruk & Bagong Semar has three sons: Gareng, with his misshapen arms, crossed eyes, limp and speech impediment; Petruk, with his hilarious long nose and enormous smiling mouth, lacks proportion in physique and thinking; and Bagong, the youngest of the three, who speaks as though he has a mouthful of marbles. Though they are comic figures, they play the important role of interpreting the actions and speech of the heroic figures in the wayang kulit plays. Despite their bumbling natures and gross appearance they are the mouthpieces of truth and wisdom.

Kuravas
On the Kurava side is Duryudana, a handsome and powerful leader, but too easily influenced by the prevailing circumstances around him and thus often prey to the evil designs of his uncle and adviser, Sangkuni. Karna is the good man on the wrong side, whose loyalty is divided between the Kuravas and the Pandavas. He is actually a Pandava but was brought up a Kurava; adhering to the code of the warrior he stands by his king as a good Javanese should and, as a result, he dies at the hands of Arjuna.

Ramayana Characters
The characters of the *Ramayana* are a little more clear-cut. Like Arjuna, Rama is the epitome of the ideal man – a gentle husband, noble prince, kindly king, brave leader. His wife Sita (or sometimes Shinta) is the ideal wife who remains totally devoted to her husband. But not all chracters are easily defined: Rawana's warrior brother, Kumbakarna, knows that the king is evil but is bound by the ethics of the Ksatria warrior to support his brother to the end, consequently dying a horrible death by dismemberment. ∎

flutes, bowed and plucked string instruments, metallophones and xylophones.

BOOKS

A classic book on Javanese religion, culture and values is *The Religion of Java* by Clifford Gertz, perhaps a rather dated book (it was based on research done in the 1950s) but nevertheless fascinating reading.

Javanese Culture by Koentjaraningrat is one of the most comprehensive studies of Javanese society, history, culture and beliefs. This excellent reference book covers everything from Javanese toilet training to kinship lines.

Two books by Neils Mulder that explore Javanese mysticism are: *Individual & Society in Java* and *Mysticism & Everyday Life in Contemporary Java*. Though concerned primarily with the non-mainstream *kebatinan* mystical movements, they are useful elucidations of Javanese mysticism and world view.

Hindu Javanese: Tengger Tradition and Islam by Robert Hefner is a detailed study on the Tenggerese people of the Gunung Bromo area in East Java.

A classic book on Java's wayang traditions is *Javanese Shadow Puppets* by Ward Keeler. *Wayang Golek* by Peter Buurman is the best book on West Java's wooden puppets. It is well illustrated, covers different styles and everything from puppet making to an explanation of the different characters. *Folk Art of Java* by Joseph Fischer examines wayang puppets, masks, children's toys, ceramics and woodcarving as they relate to village traditions.

The *Oxford in Asia* paperback series (Oxford University Press) has a number of excellent books, including *Javanese Wayang Kulit – An Introduction* by Edward C van Ness & Shita Prawirohardjo, *Javanese Gamelan* by Jennifer Lindsay and *Borobudur* by Jacques Dumarcay.

An excellent way to become familiar with the *Ramayana* and *Mahabharata* epics is to read the English adaptations written by William Buck. His inspired versions read like fantasy novels and will give you a greater appreciation of these Indian epics. They make good train and bus reading.

GETTING THERE & AWAY

Air

Jakarta is Indonesia's busiest entrance point for overseas airlines and, though not in the same class as Singapore, it is the best place in Indonesia to shop around for cheap international air tickets. One of the most popular short-hop international connections is the Jakarta-Singapore run for around US$65.

Jakarta is also the hub of the domestic airline network. Garuda, Merpati and Sempati are the main airlines serving the outer islands from Java, though Bouraq and Mandala also have useful services.

Sea

There are, of course, shipping services from other Indonesian islands, but about the only regular international connection to Java is from Pasir Gudang (just outside Johor Bahru in Malaysia) to Surabaya.

The more usual route to reach Java by sea is to take a ferry from Singapore to Tanjung Pinang on Bintan Island in the Riau archipelago, and then take a ship to Jakarta. Pelni operates boats between Bintan and Jakarta's Tanjung Priok harbour, and the *Samudera Jaya* leaves Bintan every Thursday.

Bali Ferries run round-the-clock between Banyuwangi/Ketapang harbour on Java and Gilimanuk on Bali. Coming from Bali you can take a local bus to Gilimanuk, then catch one of the frequent ferries to Ketapang, from where numerous buses and trains go to the rest of Java. An easier alternative is the through buses from Denpasar to any major city on Java, and these include the ferry journey. From Denpasar you can get a bus straight to Probolinggo (7½ hours) for Gunung Bromo, Surabaya (nine hours), or head through to Yogyakarta (16 hours) or even Jakarta. A few buses also run between Javan cities and Lovina/Singaraja and Pandangbai on Bali.

Sumatra Ferries shuttle 24 hours a day between Merak on Java and the southern Sumatran port of Bakauheni.

Regular buses go to Merak from Jakarta's Kalideres bus terminal. In Bakauheni buses take you north to Bandarlampung's Rajabasa bus terminal, from where other buses can take you all over Sumatra. The easy option are the long-distance buses that run from Jakarta (and other cities on Java) straight through to the main Sumatran destinations, such as Padang, Bukittinggi, Sibolga, Prapat, Medan and even Aceh. Most of these leave from Jakarta's Pulo Gadung bus terminal.

The long bus journeys on Sumatra can take their toll, and as most points of interest are in North Sumatra, many travellers prefer to take a Pelni boat or fly between Jakarta and Padang.

GETTING AROUND

Most travellers going through Java follow the well-worn route from Jakarta to Bogor, Bandung, Pangandaran, Yogyakarta, Solo, Surabaya, Gunung Bromo and on to Bali, with short diversions from points along that route.

Air

There's no real need to fly around Java unless you're in a real hurry or have money to burn, as there's so much transport at ground level. If you do take to the air you'll get some spectacular views of Java's many mountains and volcanoes – try to get a window seat!

Bus

Buses are the main form of transport on Java, and so many operate that you can often just front up to the bus terminal and catch one straight away, especially the big public buses which constantly shuttle between the cities and towns.

Buses are convenient, and quick and comfortable if you pay extra. Java has a huge variety of services from ordinary, public buses that can be very crowded and slow because they pick up and drop off anywhere en route, to super-luxury coaches running

directly between the main cities, sometimes at night to avoid the worst of the traffic.

Tickets for *patas* (express) and luxury buses can be bought in advance at bus terminals, or more conveniently at bus agents in the city centres. Many tourist hotels also arrange tickets.

One drawback to bus travel is that the bus terminal can be a long way from the centre of town, especially in the big cities like Jakarta, Surabaya and Bandung. In these cities, the train is often a better alternative because train stations are conveniently central.

Small minibuses also cover the shorter routes and back runs. They may be called *bemo*, *oplet*, *mikrolet*, *angkot* etc – there is a mind-boggling array of names with many regional variations on Java – but *colt* (after Mitsubishi Colt) is the most common term. Like the public buses, they pick up and drop off anywhere on request, and can get very crowded.

On buses and colts where the fare isn't ticketed or fixed, it's wise to check the price with other passengers – colt drivers are the worst culprits for jacking up fares for foreigners. Beware of the practice of taking your money and not giving you your change until later.

Java also has an excellent system of door-to-door minibuses, which can pick you up at your hotel (though sometimes you have to go to a depot) and will drop you off wherever you want to go in the destination city. These minibuses (usually called *travel*) run all over Java, and are usually roomy, deluxe air-con minibuses.

Train

Java has a pretty good rail service running from one end of the island to the other. In the east (at Ketapang/Banyuwangi) it connects with the ferry to Bali, and in the west (at Merak) it connects with the ferry to Sumatra. The two main lines run between Jakarta and Surabaya – the longer central route goes via Yogyakarta and Solo, and the shorter northern route goes via Semarang.

JAVA

Choose your trains carefully for comfort and speed. Fares and journey times for the same journey and in the same class will vary widely from train to train. Trains range from very cheap squalid cattle trains and reasonably cheap faster trains to very expensive expresses. The schedules change and, although departures may be punctual, arrivals will be late for most services and very late for others, particularly the cheap trains.

Ekonomi trains are no frills with bare wooden seats (if you can get one), hawkers, beggars and all manner of produce. They can be very crowded and horrendously slow. Ekonomi trains on the back runs are to be avoided at all costs, but some of the limited-express ekonomi trains on the main routes, for example, Surabaya-Solo, provide a reasonably efficient service and are fine for shorter hops. Ekonomi trains cannot be booked; just front up before departure time and buy a ticket.

The best trains to catch are the expresses that offer *bisnis* and *eksekutif* carriages. In bisnis class you get a guaranteed, comfortable seat with plenty of room and fans (but not air-con). Eksekutif is similar but with air-con, reclining seats and video (maybe). Both classes may include snacks or dinner in the ticket price. The better trains can be booked up to seven days before departure for an extra 1500 rp booking fee. Outside peak travel times you have a reasonable chance of getting a seat on the day of departure.

Top of the range are the luxury trains that run between Jakarta and Surabaya, such as the new *Argobromo* via Semarang and the *Bima* via Yogyakarta. These trains also have sleeping carriages and are the next best thing to flying, and almost as expensive. They should be booked as far in advance as possible.

When choosing a train, try to get one that begins in the city you are departing from. Seats are more difficult to get on a train coming through from somewhere else, and in ekonomi you may be a standing-room-only sardine. Try also to get a train that ends in the city of your destination. Even if you are only going part of the train's journey, the fare is almost the same for the full journey;

for example, Yogyakarta-Jakarta costs the same as Surabaya-Jakarta on the *Bima*.

Another factor to bear in mind when choosing your trains is that some cities, such as Jakarta and Surabaya, have several stations, some far more convenient than others. Both these cities have convenient central stations, compared to the bus terminals out in the sticks, making the train a good alternative to the buses.

As well as having central train stations, train travel can be less tiring and the better trains can be more comfortable (if slower) than the buses, particularly on long hauls. One drawback is that there are far fewer train departures and while you can get a bus almost any time, you may be in for a long wait at the train station.

Buying tickets is usually straightforward, but ticket windows can be crowded and trying to get information can be a frustrating experience. Some cities, such as Yogya and Bandung, have helpful tourist information booths at the train station, or the station master *(kepala stasiun)* can help. The rail network is slowly upgrading and some stations now have computerised booking offices. Train stations display timetables on boards, and at main stations you can often get a printed timetable *(jadwal)* for that station, but all-Java timetables are almost impossible to get.

Train tickets can also be bought through travel agencies in main cities. They charge for this service, but it can be worth the money to save time and hassle at the train station.

Sector by sector the main train routes through Java are as shown in this section. Scheduled times are given – expect overruns on all trains, more on ekonomi trains. The main drawback to Java's rail network is that only single line tracks exist – breakdowns and delays throw the whole system out.

Jakarta-Yogyakarta All trains between Jakarta and Yogyakarta pass through Cirebon on the north coast, and some continue on through Solo and Madiun to Surabaya.

GLENN BEANLAND

GLENN BEANLAND

SARA-JANE CLELAND

Java

Top: Welcome Monument roundabout in bustling Jakarta.

Middle: Signs of the times, Jakarta.

Bottom: A more relaxed approach to business, Yogyakarta.

PETER TURNER

White Tiger, Taman Safari, Cisarua, West Java.

The luxury, express *Bima* leaves Jakarta at 5 pm for Surabaya and stops in Yogya (70,000 rp eksekutif; 7½ hours), but you'll pay the full fare to Surabaya. Better value are the good *Fajar Utama Yogya* day trains and *Senja Utama Yogya* night services. Between them, departures leave Jakarta (Gambir train station) at 6.10 and 6.30 am, and 7.20 and 8.40 pm. Trains leave Yogya in the other direction at 7 and 9 am, and 6 and 8 pm. Both cost 23,000 rp in bisnis class to 55,000 rp in air-con eksekutif, and the journey time is around 8½ hours.

Other express services include the *Senja Utama Solo* leaving Gambir at 7.40 pm for Yogya (25,000 rp; 8½ hours) and Solo (28,000 rp; 9½ hours), or the slower *Jayabaya* (23,000 rp bisnis; 9½ hours), which runs between Jakarta and Surabaya and stops in Yogya.

At the other end of the comfort scale are the crowded ekonomi class-only trains departing from Jakarta's Pasar Senen train station: the *Gaya Baru Malam Selatan* and *Matamaja*; or the better choice *Empujaya* leaves Pasar Senen at 3.55 pm and terminates in Yogya. The ekonomi trains cost around 14,000 rp and take 10½ hours, but delays are inevitable.

Jakarta-Surabaya The quickest trains between Jakarta and Surabaya are the night trains that take the shorter northern route via Semarang. Trains that take the longer southern route via Yogya include the luxury *Bima* (13½ hours), the bisnis class only *Jayabaya* (26,000 rp; 15 hours) and the ekonomi *Gaya Baru Malam Selatan* (10,000 rp; 16 hours).

The deluxe *Mutiara Utara* takes the northern route from Jakarta (Kota train station) to Surabaya (Pasar Turi train station), departing Jakarta at 4.30 pm, Surabaya at 5 pm. The 12 hour trip ranges from 26,000 rp in bisnis to 94,000 rp for a sleeper.

The cheapest services taking the north coast route are the ekonomi class only *Gaya Baru Malam Utara* (10,000 rp; 14 hours), which goes from Jakarta (Kota) to Surabaya's Pasar Turi train station at 5 pm, and the *Parcel* (10,000 rp; 14 hours) from Jakarta

(Pasar Senen train station) at 5.45 pm. Overruns can turn this into a 20 hour journey on the ekonomi trains.

Yogyakarta-Surabaya There are more than half a dozen trains a day between Yogya and Surabaya. Some of the better trains include the *Bima* (70,000 rp eksekutif A; 4½ hours) and *Mutiara Selatan* (25,000 rp bisnis; five hours). Book as far in advance as possible for these trains. The *Argopuro* (4500 rp; seven hours) is one of the best ekonomi services; it leaves Yogya at 7.30 am, Surabaya at 1.45 pm and continues on to Banyuwangi. The *Prambanan Express* is a good bisnis class train running between Solo and Yogyakarta only.

Car
Self-drive cars can be hired in Jakarta but rates are very high through international companies like Avis and National, typically around US$100 per day. Local companies are slightly cheaper. To hire a car you must have a valid local or international driving licence, and the age limit is usually 19, sometimes higher. Surabaya and Yogya have cheaper car hire.

While it is possible to drive yourself on Java, you need the patience of a saint and the concentration powers of a chess grand master. The main Jakarta-Bandung-Yogya-Solo-Surabaya route is no fun. Apart from a few toll roads and the odd quiet stretch with stunning scenery, driving along this highway is a procession of towns and villages, with constant traffic – buses, trucks, cars, motorcycles, food carts, bicycles, pedestrians and chickens – all competing for the narrow stretch of tarmac.

The usual alternative is to rent a car or minibus with driver, which can be a lot cheaper than hiring a self-drive car. The big car-rental agencies prefer to rent cars with drivers. Much cheaper are the private operators that cost as little as 70,000 rp (US$35) per day with driver. Cars can be hired through travel agents and hotels, who have regular drivers or may know of a driver looking for work. Check out the driver for experience and language ability, and get licence and identity-card details. (See the introductory Getting Around chapter for more information.) Good places for hiring cars on this basis are the main cities and tourist destinations, such as Yogya, Jakarta, Surabaya, Bogor, Bandung, Pangandaran and Malang.

For shorter trips around town you can rent taxis or minibuses quite easily through car-rental companies, some travel agencies and hotels in main cities. Rates vary but it's likely to be around 10,000 rp an hour for a minimum of two hours, or a flat rate for a set route. It is cheaper through the private operators, but heavy bargaining is usually required.

Boat

There are plenty of ferries and boats from Java to the outer islands, but there is also a boat trip across the inland sea between Cilacap and Kalipucang on the south coast which is really worth doing. If you're travelling between Central Java and Pangandaran in West Java the boat is an excellent alternative to taking the bus and/or train all the way.

There are daily boat services to Pulau Seribu in the Bay of Jakarta, but trips to the small islands off the coast usually involve chartering a fishing boat – an outrigger vessel with sails or a motorised boat – which are dependent on the weather. There are regular daily ferries between Java and Madura, Bali and Sumatra.

Local Transport

Taxis are to be found around hotels and at airport, train and bus terminals. Most are metered and drivers will use them – insist if they don't, or catch another. The metered rate is around 1300 rp for the first km and 500 rp for each subsequent km. Private cars and minibuses also operate where taxis don't exist, or in opposition to taxis. Bargaining is definitely the rule with private operators, and taxis are a better alternative for the uninitiated.

Indonesia has all sorts of weird and wonderful means of transport, and most can be found on Java. Bargaining is required for all these forms of transport. The *bajaj* (pronounced 'ba-jai') is a farting, noisy three wheeler, a Jakarta speciality. Java has more *becaks* (trishaws) than just about anywhere in the world. The horse-drawn *andong* can be found throughout Java, or in Jakarta bicycles with passenger seats on the back can take you around the streets. If you really want to get off the beaten track, or simply get home from the market, the *ojek* rider will give you a lift on his motorcycle and go where no buses do or dare.

Jakarta

Jakarta is all Indonesia rolled into one huge urban sprawl of nearly nine million people. Indonesians come from all over the archipelago to seek fame and fortune, or just to eke out a living. Bataks and Minangkabau from Sumatra, Ambonese from Maluku, Dani from Irian Jaya, Minahasans from Sulawesi, Balinese, Madurese and Timorese are all united by Bahasa Indonesia and a desire to make it in the capital. For it is in Jakarta that the latest styles and thoughts are formed, the important political decisions made. Jakarta is the main centre for the economy, the place to find work, do deals and court government officials.

Over the last decade or so, Jakarta has undergone a huge transformation. Once, its miserable poverty and crumbling infrastructure made it one of the hell holes of Asian travel. Now the city's face is being changed by the constant construction of more skyscrapers, flyovers, hotels and shopping malls.

The showpiece of the prosperous new Jakarta is the central business district bounded by Jl Thamrin/Sudirman, Jl Rasuna Said and Jl Gatot Subroto. The 'Golden Triangle', as it is known, is crammed with office towers, luxury hotels and foreign embassies. Viewed from here, Jakarta has all the appearances of a prosperous Asian boom city.

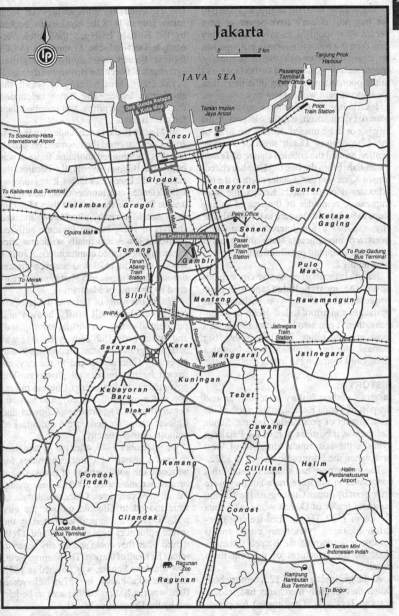

Jakarta

0 1 2 km

JAVA SEA

Tanjung Priok
Harbour

Passenger
Terminal &
Pelni Office

See Sunda Kelapa
& Kota Map

Taman Impian
Jaya Ancol

Priok
Train Station

To Soekarno-Hatta
International Airport

Ancol

Glodok

Kemayoran

Sunter

To Kalideres Bus Terminal

Jelambar

Grogol

Pelni Office

*Kelapa
Gaging*

Ciputra Mall

Senen

See Central Jakarta Map

Pasar
Senen
Train
Station

To Pulo Gadung
Bus Terminal

Tomang

Tanah Abang
Train Station

Gambir

*Pulo
Mas*

To Merak

Slipi

PHPA

Menteng

Rawamangun

Jatinegara
Train
Station

Serayan

Karet

Manggarai

Jatinegara

Jalan Gatot Subroto

Kuningan

*Kebayoran
Baru*

Tebet

Blok M

Cawang

Kemang

Cililitan

Halim

Halim
Perdanakusuma
Airport

*Pondok
Indah*

Condet

Lebak Bulus
Bus Terminal

Cilandak

Taman Mini
Indonesian Indah

Ragunan
Zoo

Kampung
Rambutan
Bus Terminal

Ragunan

To Bogor

Move away from the centre, and much of the city still doesn't have sewerage or a decent water supply. Jakarta has more luxury cars than the rest of Indonesia put together, but it also has the worst slums in the country. Indonesia's biggest city is a vortex that sucks in the poor, often providing little more than the hope of hard work at low pay.

Jakarta is primarily a city of business, not a tourist destination, but the old part of the city is not to be missed. Kota is the heart of the 17th century Dutch town of Batavia, centred around the cobbled square of Taman Fatahillah. From the fine old Dutch architecture of Kota, you can wander north to the old schooner dock of Sunda Kelapa, the most impressive reminder of the age of sailing ships to be found anywhere in the world. The city also has a few interesting museums, oversized monuments, some theme parks and good shopping possibilities to keep visitors amused.

Jakarta is the most expensive city in Indonesia, the most polluted and the most congested, but if you can you withstand its onslaught and afford to indulge in its attractions, then it can also be one of Indonesia's most exciting cities. For this is the 'Big Durian', the foul-smelling exotic fruit that some can't stomach but others can't resist.

HISTORY
Jakarta's earliest history is centred around the port of Sunda Kelapa, in the north of the Kota district of present-day Jakarta. Sunda Kelapa was a bustling port of the Pajajaran dynasty, the last Hindu kingdom of West Java, when the Portuguese arrived in 1522.

The Portuguese had sought to establish a concession in the spice trade but they were driven out by Sunan Gunungjati, the Muslim saint and leader of Demak who took Sunda Kelapa in 1527. He renamed the city Jayakarta, meaning 'victorious city', and it became a fiefdom of the Banten sultanate. None of the structures of this old town remain.

At the beginning of the 17th century both Dutch and English merchants had trading posts in Jayakarta. They jostled for power and exploited the intrigue between local rulers. Late in 1618 the Jayakartans, backed by the British, besieged the Dutch Vereenigde Oost-Indische Compagnie (VOC) fortress. Banten, upset by the unauthorised agreement between the British and the vassal Jayakartans, sent a force to recall the Jayakartan leader. The Dutch celebrated their temporary reprieve and renamed their fortress 'Batavia'.

In May 1619 the Dutch, under Jan Pieterszoon Coen, stormed the town and reduced it to ashes. A stronger shoreline fortress was built and Batavia eventually became the capital of the Dutch East Indies. It was successfully defended on a number of occasions, first against Banten in the west and then Mataram in the east. Mataram's Sultan Agung attacked Batavia in 1628, but the Javanese suffered enormous losses and finally withdrew after executing their failed commanders. Agung's second siege in 1629 was an even greater debacle, and Batavia was never again threatened by an army of Mataram.

Within the walls of Batavia, the prosperous Dutch built tall stuffy houses and pestilential canals on virtual swampland, and by the early 18th century Batavia was suffering growing pains. Indonesians and especially Chinese flocked to the city, attracted by its commercial prospects. The government tried to restrict Chinese migration to the overburdened city, and tensions began to grow. Deportations followed and Chinese gangs created unrest and attacked outposts outside the city.

On 9 October 1740, after the government ordered a search of Chinese premises for weapons, the good citizens of Batavia went berserk and massacred 5000 Chinese within the city. A year later Chinese inhabitants were moved to Glodok, outside the city walls. Other Batavians, discouraged by the severe epidemics between 1735 and 1780, moved when they could and the city began to spread far south of the port. The Koningsplein, now Merdeka Square, was finished in 1818 and Merdeka Palace in 1879; Kebayoran Baru was the last residential area to be laid out by the Dutch after WWII.

Dutch colonial rule came to an end when the Japanese occupied Java and the name Jakarta' was restored to the city. The republican government of the revolution retreated to Yogyakarta when the Dutch returned after the war, but in 1950, after Indonesian independence was finally secured, Jakarta was made the capital of the new republic.

In 1945 Jakarta had a population of *00,000; since then there has been a continual influx of migrants from depressed rural areas and newcomers continue to crowd into the urban slums. Today the population is nearly *ine million, or 17 million, including the surrounding districts that form a greater Jakarta.

Soekarno's image of Jakarta was of a city of grand structures that would glorify the republic and make Jakarta a world centre. The 14 storey Jakarta Hotel broke the skyline, the six lane Jl Thamrin was constructed and a massive sports stadium was erected for the 1962 Asian Games. Work on Jakarta's massive mosque was begun, and the National Monument took root.

With Soekarno's architectural ambitions cut short in 1965, the job of sorting out the city was left to Lieutenant General Ali Sadikin, governor of Jakarta from 1966 to 1977. Although he is credited with rehabilitating the roads and bridges, building several hospitals and a large number of new schools, he also began the campaign of ruthlessly cleaning up the city by clearing out slum dwellers, and banning becaks and street peddlers. He also started the control of migration to the city, to stem hopeless overcrowding and poverty.

New arrivals from the countryside, without Jakarta residence permits, still constantly face the possibility of expulsion from the city. But the lure of the big lights continues, and even a roadside *parkir* directing traffic and parking cars can still earn a good living compared to an existence of village unemployment.

ORIENTATION

Jakarta sprawls over 25 km from the docks to the suburbs of South Jakarta, covering 661 sq km in all. The city centre fans out from around Merdeka Square, which contains the central landmark of Soekarno's towering gold-tipped National Monument (Monas). Merdeka Square itself is just a barren, deserted field, a product of grand urban planning gone wrong. Jakarta's main problem is that it doesn't really have a centre that can be explored on foot, but a number of centres, all separated by vast traffic jams and heat.

For most visitors, Jakarta revolves around the modern part of the city to the south of the monument. Jl Thamrin, running from the south-west corner of Merdeka Square down to the Welcome Monument roundabout, is the main thoroughfare, containing many of the big hotels and a couple of major shopping centres – the Sarinah department store and the Plaza Indonesia.

Just east of Jl Thamrin and south of the National Monument is Jl Jaksa, the main centre for cheap hotels and restaurants.

North of the National Monument, the old city of Jakarta has Jakarta's main tourist attractions. It includes the Chinatown area of Glodok, the old Dutch area of Kota and the schooner harbour of Sunda Kelapa. The modern harbour, Tanjung Priok, is several km along the coast to the east past the Taman Impian Jaya Ancol recreation park.

The main train station, Gambir, is just to the east of the National Monument. The intercity bus terminals – Kalideres in the west, Kampung Rambutan in the south and Pulo Gadung in the east – are on the outskirts of Jakarta.

Jl Thamrin heading south becomes Jl Jenderal Sudirman, home to more hotels, large banks and office blocks. Further south are the affluent suburban areas of Kebayoran Baru, Pondok Indah and Kemang, with their own centres and busy shopping districts, such as Blok M in Kebayoran Baru.

INFORMATION
Tourist Offices

The Jakarta Tourist Information Office (☎ 3142067) is opposite the Sarinah department store in the Jakarta Theatre building on Jl Thamrin. It can answer most queries and has a good giveaway map of Jakarta, and a

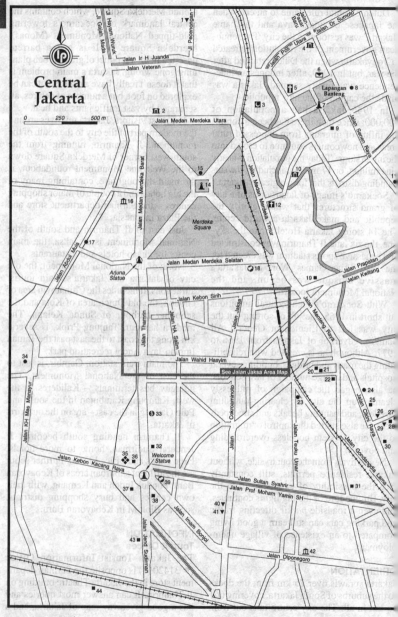

Central Jakarta

0   250   500 m

Merdeka Square

Arjuna Statue

Welcome Statue

See Jalan Jaksa Area Map

Lapangan Banteng

Jalan Medan Merdeka Utara
Jalan Medan Merdeka Selatan
Jalan Medan Merdeka Barat
Jalan Medan Merdeka Timur

Jl Hayam Wuruk
Jl Gajah Mada
Jalan Ir H Juanda
Jalan Veteran
Jl Pecenongan
Jl Gunung Sahari

Jalan Pos Utara
Jalan Dr Sumoto
Jalan Pasar Baru

Jalan Kebon Sirih
Jalan Kebon Kacang Raya
Jalan Wahid Hasyim
Jalan Thamrin
Jalan HA Salim
Jalan Jaksa
Jalan Cokroaminoto
Jalan KH Mas Mansyur
Jalan Abdul Mula
Jalan Teuku Umar
Jalan Sultan Syahrir
Jalan Prof Moham Yamin SH
Jalan Imam Bonjol
Jalan Sudirman
Jalan Diponegoro

Jalan Menteng Raya
Jalan Cikini Raya
Jalan Gondangdia Lama

Jalan Senen Raya
Jalan Prapatan
Jalan Kwitang

PLACES TO STAY
9 Borobudur Inter-Continental Hotel
19 Hotel Aryaduta
20 Sofyan Hotel Betawi
21 Gondia International Guesthouse
22 Hotel Menteng I
25 Sofyan Hotel Cikini
27 Yannie International Guest House
28 Karya II Hotel
30 Hotel Menteng II
31 Hotel Marcopolo
32 President Hotel
36 Grand Hyatt Jakarta Hotel
37 Hotel Indonesia
38 Mandarin Oriental Jakarta Hotel
43 Kartika Plaza Hotel
44 Shangri-La Hotel

PLACES TO EAT
1 Seafood Night Market
26 Raden Kuring Restaurant
29 Oasis Bar & Restaurant
40 Tamnak Thai Restaurant
41 Gandy Steakhouse

OTHER
2 Presidential Palace
3 Istiqlal Mosque
4 Gedung Kesenian
5 Catholic Cathedral
6 Main Post Office
7 Free Irian Monument
8 Mahkamah Agung & Ministry of
   Finance Building
10 Gedung Pancasila
11 Bharata Theatre
12 Emanuel Church
13 Gambir Train Station
14 National Monument (Monas)
15 Entrance to Monas
16 National Museum
17 Tanamur Disco
18 US Embassy
23 Immigration Office
24 Taman Ismail Marzuki (TIM)
33 Bank Internasional Indonesia
34 Pasar Tanah Abang
35 Plaza Indonesia
39 British Embassy
42 Adam Malik Museum

but it has some useful publications, including the *Calendar of Events* and the *Indonesia Tourist Map*, and you might be able to squeeze a copy of the useful *Indonesia Travel Planner* out of the staff. The office is open government office hours only.

Immigration Office
There is a central immigration office (☎ 3909744) at Jl Teuku Umar 1 in Menteng.

Money
Jakarta is crawling with banks offering the best exchange rates in Indonesia, though it pays to shop around. Banks offer better rates than moneychangers.

Most banks are open Monday to Friday from 8 am to 4 pm, and Saturday until 11.30 am. Handy banks to Jl Jaksa are the Lippobank and Bank Duta on Jl Kebon Sirih. In the Plaza Indonesia, the BDNI bank on the 1st level of the Sogo department store is open from 10 am to 9 pm, and offers OK rates. Downstairs, the Bank Internasional Indonesia, Plaza Indonesia LB 17-18, also keeps extended hours and has better rates.

Almost all banks give credit card cash advances over the counter. Bank Internasional Indonesia ATMs (on Jl Thamrin and in the Plaza Indonesia) allow cash advances on Visa and MasterCard. Bank Bali and Lippobank ATMs give cash advances on MasterCard.

Pacto Ltd is the American Express (Amex) agent throughout Indonesia and handles postal services and Amex cheque and card transactions at its Borobudur Inter-Continental Hotel branch (☎ 7975874).

Post & Communications
The main post office, with its efficient poste restante service, is behind Jl Pos Utara, to the north-east of the National Monument. It is open Monday to Friday from 8 am to 8 pm, and on weekends from 8.30 am to 4 pm. It's a good half hour walk from the city centre or you can take a No 12 bus from Jl Thamrin.

For international and intercity phone calls, the efficient Telkom centre is next to the tourist office in the Jakarta Theatre building.

umber of excellent leaflets and publications. It is open Monday to Friday from 8 am to 5 pm, Saturday until 1 pm. It also has a esk at the airport.

The headquarters of the Indonesia Tourist Promotion Organisation is the Directorate-General of Tourism (☎ 3838217) at Jl Merdeka Barat 16-19. This is not the best place to have specific travel queries answered

It's open 24 hours, and has Home Country Direct phones and a fax service. Convenient for Jl Jaksa is the RTQ Warparpostel (☎ 326221; fax 3904503), Jl Jaksa 25, opposite Nick's Corner Hostel. This place offers international and domestic postal, telephone and fax services. You can receive faxes here for 1500 rp per page. Business centres in the major hotels also have more expensive postal and fax services.

Travel Agencies

For international flights, as well as domestic transport, the travel agencies on Jl Jaksa are convenient places to start looking: try Roberto Kencana Travel (☎ 3142926) at No 20B and Flamboyan Prima Wisata (☎ 3151404) at No 33. Other agents worth checking are Natrabu (☎ 3100844), Jl Agus Salim 29A (near Jl Jaksa), and Pacto Ltd (☎ 7975874) in the Borobudur Inter-Continental Hotel.

Indo Shangrila Travel (☎ 6256080), Jl Gajah Mada 219G, is a well-established agent and often has good deals.

Bookshops

Singapore's Times Bookshop chain has a branch in the Plaza Indonesia on Jl Thamrin. It has the best stock of English-language books, and a good range of travel books. The big Indonesian book chains are good for maps, dictionaries and travel books, and also have a few English-language books. Gramedia has shops at Jl Gajah Mada 109 and Jl Melawai IV/13 in Blok M, while Gunung Agung has a huge shop at Jl Kwitang 6, just east of Jl Jaksa. Sarinah department store also has a decent book and map section.

Newspapers

The daily English-language *Jakarta Post* (1000 rp from street vendors) gives a useful rundown of what's on, temporary exhibitions and cinema programmes.

Film & Photography

Jl Agus Salim, between Jl Jaksa and Jl Thamrin, has photographic shops for film, developing and equipment, but 'tourist prices' may apply and bargaining might be necessary. Otherwise, Jakarta has plenty of places for film developing. Fuji is the most common brand of film.

Libraries & Useful Organisations

The Indonesian Heritage Society (☎ 360551 ext 22) at the National Museum is an organisation of volunteer workers that holds weekly lectures or films about Indonesia at the Erasmus Huis (☎ 5252321) on Jl Rasuna Said, beside the Netherlands Embassy in South Jakarta.

The Indonesian/American Cultural Center (Perhimpunan Persahabatan Indonesia Amerika; ☎ 8583241), Jl Pramuka Kav 30, has exhibits, films and lectures related to Indonesia each week. The Australian Cultural Centre (Pusat Kebudayaan Australia) at the embassy on Jl Rasuna Said has a good library, open from 10.30 am to 3.30 pm Monday to Friday. The British Council (☎ 2524115) also has a good library in the Widjojo Centre, Jl Jenderal Sudirman 56. The French Cultural Centre (☎ 3908585), Jl Salemba Raya 25, has a French library and screens French films. The Goethe Institut (☎ 8581139) is at Jl Mataram Raya 23.

Dangers & Annoyances

Jakarta's buses tend to be hopelessly crowded, particularly during rush hours. Its pickpockets are notoriously adept and they're great bag slashers too. So take care. Indeed, if you are carrying a camera or anything else of value, you would be wise to spring for a taxi.

OLD BATAVIA (KOTA)

The old town of Batavia, known as Kota today, is the oldest and finest reminder of the Dutch presence in Indonesia. At one time it contained Coen's massive shoreline fortress the Kasteel, and was surrounded by a sturdy defensive wall and a moat. In the early 19th century Governor-General Daendels did a good job of demolishing much of the unhealthy city but there is still a Dutch flavour to this old part of the town. A few of Batavia's old buildings remain in active use.

although others were restored during the 1970s and have become museums.

The centre of old Batavia is the cobblestone square known as **Taman Fatahillah**. A block west of the square is the **Kali Besar**, the great canal along Sungai (river) Ciliwung. This was once the high-class residential area of Batavia, and on the west bank overlooking the canal are the last of the big private homes dating from the early 18th century. The **Toko Merah**, or Red Shop, now occupied by the Dharma Niaga company, was formerly the home of Governor-General van Imhoff. At the north end of the Kali Besar is a small 17th century Dutch drawbridge, the last in the city, called the **Chicken Market Bridge**.

Jakarta History Museum

On the south side of Taman Fatahillah, the museum is housed in the old town hall of Batavia, which is probably one of the most solid reminders of Dutch rule to be found anywhere in Indonesia. This large bell-towered hall, built in 1627 and added to between 1707 and 1710, served the administration of the city. It was also used by the city law courts and its dungeons were the main prison compound of Batavia. In 1830 the Javanese hero Prince Diponegoro was imprisoned here for a time on his way into exile in Manado.

Today it contains lots of heavy, carved furniture and other memorabilia from the Dutch period. Among the more interesting exhibits is a series of gloomy portraits of all the Dutch governors-general and early pictures of Batavia.

In the courtyard at the back of the building is a strange memorial stone to one Pieter Erbervelt, who was put to death in 1722 for allegedly conspiring to massacre the Dutch inhabitants of Batavia.

Admission to the museum is 1000 rp. It opens every day, except Monday, from 9 am to 3 pm (on Friday to 2.30 pm and Saturday to 12.30 pm).

Wayang Museum

Also on Taman Fatahillah, this museum has one of the best collections of wayang puppets on Java, and includes puppets not only from Indonesia but also China, Malaysia, India and Cambodia.

Formerly the Museum of Old Batavia, the building itself was constructed in 1912 on the site of the Dutch Church of Batavia, which was demolished by Daendels in 1808. In the downstairs courtyard there are memorials to the Dutch governors-general once buried here. These include Jan Pieterszoon Coen, founder of Batavia, who died of cholera in 1629 during the siege by Mataram, and Anthony van Diemen, discoverer of Australia.

Admission and opening hours are the same as the Jakarta History Museum. The best time to visit is Sunday morning. Wayang golek or wayang kulit is performed every Sunday from 10 am to 1.30 pm.

Balai Seni Rupa (Fine Arts Museum)

Built between 1866 and 1870, the Palace of Justice building is now a museum housing a collection of contemporary Indonesian paintings, with works by Indonesia's most prominent painters, including Raden Saleh, Affandi and Ida Bagus Made. Part of the building is also a ceramics museum, with Chinese ceramics and Majapahit terracottas.

The museum is open Tuesday to Saturday from 9 am to 2.30 pm.

Cannon Si Jagur

This huge bronze cannon on Taman Fatahillah is adorned with a Latin inscription, *'Ex me ipsa renata sum'*, which means 'Out of myself I was reborn'. The cannon tapers at one end into a large clenched fist, with the thumb protruding between the index and middle fingers. This suggestive fist is a sexual symbol in Indonesia and childless women would offer flowers and sit astride the cannon in the hope of gaining children. Si Jagur is a Portuguese cannon brought to Batavia as a trophy of war after the fall of Melaka in 1641.

Gereja Sion

On Jl Pangeran Jayakarta, near Kota train station, this church dates from 1695 and is the oldest remaining church in Jakarta. Also known as Gereja Portugis or Portuguese Church, it was built just outside the old city walls for the so-called 'black Portuguese' – the Eurasians and natives captured from Portuguese trading ports in India and Malaya and brought to Batavia as slaves. Most of these people were Catholics but they were given their freedom on the condition that they joined the Dutch Reformed Church, and the converts became known as the Mardijkers, or Liberated Ones.

The exterior of the church is very plain, but inside there are copper chandeliers, the original organ and a Baroque pulpit. Although in the year 1790 alone, more than 2000 people were buried in the graveyard here, very few tombs remain. One of the most interesting is the ornate bronze tombstone of Governor-General Zwaardecroon, who died in 1728 and, as was his wish, was buried among the 'ordinary' folk.

SUNDA KELAPA

Just a 10 minute walk north of Taman Fatahillah, the old port of Sunda Kelapa has more sailing ships, the magnificent Macassar schooners called *pinisi*, than you ever thought existed. This is one of the finest sights in Jakarta. These brightly painted ships are still an important means of transporting goods to and from the outer islands. Most of them come from Kalimantan, spend-

1	Phinisi Café
2	Bandar Kelapa Café
3	Luar Batang Mosque
4	Museum Bahari
5	Watchtower
6	VOC Shipyards
7	Chicken Market Bridge
8	Omni Batavia Hotel
9	Toko Merah
10	Wayang Museum
11	Café Batavia
12	Balai Seni Rupa
13	Jakarta History Museum
14	Gereja Sion

Sunda Kelapa & Kota

ng up to a week in port unloading timber and
hen reloading cement and other supplies for
he return journey.

Old men will take you in row boats around
he schooners for about 3000 rp. You can
pend a good half hour or so rowing around
he schooners, but try to avoid decapitation
y mooring ropes or gangplanks and occaionally having rubbish thrown on you from
he ships.

Entry to the dock is just around from the
Museum Bahari and costs 1000 rp. There are
couple of pleasant tourist cafes at the dock.

Museum Bahari (Maritime Museum) Near
he entrance to Sunda Kelapa, an old VOC
warehouse built in 1645 has been turned into
a maritime museum. It exhibits craft from
around Indonesia, and has an interesting col-
ection of old photographs recreating the
royage to Jakarta from Europe via Aden,
Ceylon and Singapore. The building itself is
worth a visit and the sentry posts outside are
part of the old city wall.

The museum is open every day, except
Monday, from 9 am to 2 pm.

Just before the entrance to the museum is
the old **watchtower** back near the bridge. It
was built in 1839 to sight and direct traffic
to the port. Although there are good views
over the harbour from the top, the watchtower is usually locked.

Further along the same street from the
museum is the early-morning fish market,
Pasar Ikan. Around dawn when the day's
catch is sold it is an intense, colourful scene
of busy crowds. Later in the day it sells
household items and a growing collection of
souvenirs.

GLODOK

After the Chinese massacre of 1740, the
Dutch decided there would be no repetition
and prohibited all Chinese from residing
within the town walls, or even from being
there after sundown. In 1741 a tract of land
just to the south-west of Batavia was allo-
cated as Chinese quarters. The area became

GLENN BEANLAND

The Bahari (or Maritime) Museum is one of the oldest colonial buildings in Jakarta. The Dutch originally
built it to store pepper, tea, coffee and cloth, and named it Westzijdsche Pakhuiszan (Warehouses
on the West Bank). It was expanded from 1663-69 and again in stages from 1718-74. Original sentry
posts can be found outside the building along the old city wall.

Glodok, Jakarta's Chinatown, and the city's flourishing commercial centre.

Glodok is bounded to the east by Jl Gajah Mada, a wide road lined with offices, restaurants and modern shopping plazas. But if you walk in from Jl Pancoran, beside the Glodok Plaza, old Glodok still consists of winding lanes, narrow crooked houses with balconies, slanting red-tiled roofs and tiny obscure shops. In between there are numerous eating places, markets and street hawkers. It can be a fascinating area to wander around. Just south of Jl Pancoran, you'll find the Chinese **Dharma Jaya Temple**, one of the most interesting in Jakarta. Built in 1650 it was the chief temple for the Chinese of Batavia, and was once known for its casino and Chinese wayang kulit.

If you're walking from Glodok back along Jl Gajah Mada, it's worth pausing to have a glance at two old Jakarta buildings along this street. The **Candra Naya** at No 188 was once the home of the Chinese 'captain' employed by the Dutch to manage the affairs of Batavia's Chinese community. Since 1946 the building has housed the offices of a social work society but you may be able to have a short wander inside. Further south at No 111, the **Arsip Nasional** (National Archives) building dates from 1760 and was formerly the country house of Governor-General Reinier de Klerk.

NATIONAL MUSEUM

On the west side of Merdeka Square, the National Museum, built in 1862, is the best museum in Indonesia and one of the best in South-East Asia. Its collection includes a huge ethnic map of Indonesia and an equally big relief map on which you can pick out all those volcanoes you have climbed.

The museum has an enormous collection of cultural objects of the various ethnic groups – costumes, musical instruments, model houses and so on – and numerous fine bronzes from the Hindu-Javanese period, as well as many interesting stone pieces salvaged from Central Javanese and other temples. There's also a superb display of Chinese ceramics dating back to the Han

dynasty (300 BC to 220 AD), which was almost entirely amassed in Indonesia.

One of the best places to start a tour of the museum is the Treasure Room upstairs from the entrance. The gold exhibits are interesting, but the real attraction is the air-con if you have walked to the museum.

Just outside the museum is a bronze elephant which was presented by the King of Thailand in 1871; thus the museum building is popularly known as the Gedung Gajah or Elephant House.

The museum is open daily, except Monday, from 8.30 am to 2.30 pm (on Friday to 11.30 am and Saturday to 1.30 pm). Conducted tours, in a number of languages, are organised by the Indonesian Heritage Society (☎ 360551, ext 22).

OTHER MUSEUMS

Jakarta has a number of other museums apart from the excellent National Museum and those in old Batavia. North-west of the National Museum is the **Taman Prasasti Museum**, or Park of Inscription, on Jl Tanah Abang. This was once the Kebon Jahe Cemetery and some important figures of the colonial era are buried here, including Olivia Raffles (wife of British Governor-General Sir Stamford Raffles) who died in 1814. The cemetery is open from 9 am to 3 pm Monday to Thursday, to 1 pm on Friday and until 2 pm on Saturday. It's closed on Sunday and holidays.

The **Textile Museum** is in a Dutch colonial house on Jl Satsuit Tubun 4, near the Tanah Abang district bus terminal. It has a large collection of batik and woven cloth from all over Indonesia, as well as looms and batik-making tools, and it's well worth a visit. This museum is open from 8 am to 3 pm every day, except Monday (closed) and Friday (8 am to 1 pm).

In Menteng, the **Adam Malik Museum**, Jl Diponegoro 29, was the home of the former vice-president and foreign minister. It's now a museum crammed with his private collection of Indonesian wood carvings, sculpture and textiles, a huge display of Chinese ceramics and even Russian icons from when he was ambassador to Moscow. You can wander around the house, a Dutch villa in the old-money suburb of Menteng not far from Jl Thamrin, and poke into the man's bedroom and even his bathroom, remaining much as he left it in 1984. The museum is open from 10 am to 3 pm every day, except Monday.

NATIONAL MONUMENT (MONAS)

This 132m high column towering over Merdeka Square is both Jakarta's principal landmark and the most famous architectural

extravagance of Soekarno. Commenced in 1961, the monument was not completed until 1975, when it was officially opened by Soeharto. This phallic symbol topped by a glittering flame symbolises the nation's independence and strength (and, some would argue, Soekarno's virility). The National Monument is constructed 'entirely of Italian marbles', according to a tourist brochure, and the flame is gilded with 35 kg of gold leaf.

In the base of the National Monument, the

Soekarno Monuments

Inspired tastelessness – in the Russian 'heroes of socialism' style – best describes the plentiful supply of statues Soekarno left to Jakarta. Many have acquired descriptive nicknames. At the end of Jalan Jenderal Sudirman in Kebayoran, the **Semangat Pemuda (Spirit of Youth) Statue** is a suitably muscular young man holding a flaming dish above his head. He is more commonly known as the 'Pizza Man'.

On Jalan Thamrin, the **Selamat Datang (Welcome) Monument** – 'Hansel and Gretel' – was built by Soekarno as a symbol of Indonesian friendliness for the 1962 Asian Games held in Jakarta. Now that the airport has moved, most visitors' first view is from behind, so it is really the Selamat Jalan (Goodbye), rather than Selamat Datang, Monument.

The propaganda element reaches its peak in the **Free Irian Monument** at Banteng Square near the Borobudur Inter-Continental Hotel. Here another muscle-bound gent breaks the chains around his wrists. He is known as the 'Howzat Man'. An almost identical statue can be found a few thousand km away in Dili where, surprise, surprise, the statue is the Free East Timor Monument.

In Pancoran, the **Dirgantara Statue** is of Hanuman, the monkey god from the *Ramayana* epic. This muscular human body, with the head of a monkey, is mounted on a towering pedestal shaped like a '7'. Hence the '7-Up Man' nickname.

The **Farmer's Monument**, just south of Gambir train station on the Jalan Menteng Raya roundabout, is another heart-rending bronze showing a mother offering rice to her returning hero son after the battle for independence. On the northern side of Merdeka Square, not far from the National Monument, is a more classical statue of freedom fighter, Prince Diponegoro, astride his horse. ■

Free Irian Monument, Lapangan Banteng, Jakarta.

National History Museum tells the history of Indonesia's independence struggle in 48 dramatic dioramas. The numerous uprisings against the Dutch are overstated but interesting, Soekarno is barely mentioned and the events surrounding the 1965 Untung coup are a whitewash.

The highlight of a visit is to take the lift to the top, for dramatic, though rarely clear, views of Jakarta. Avoid Sunday and holidays when the queues for the lift are long.

The National Monument is open every day from 8 am to 5 pm. Admission is 500 rp, including the museum, or 3000 rp for both the museum and the lift to the top.

LAPANGAN BANTENG

Just east of Merdeka Square in front of the Borobudur Inter-Continental Hotel, Lapangan Banteng Square (formerly the Weltevreden) was laid out by the Dutch in the 19th century and the area has some of Jakarta's best colonial architecture.

The **Catholic cathedral** with its twin spires was built in 1901 to replace an earlier church. Facing the cathedral is Jakarta's principal place of Muslim worship. The modernistic **Istiqlal mosque**, a Soekarno construction, is reputedly the largest in South-East Asia.

To the east of Lapangan Banteng is the **Mahkamah Agung**, the Supreme Court built in 1848, and next door is the **Ministry of Finance** building, formerly the Witte Huis (White House). This grand government complex was built by Daendels in 1809 as the administration centre for the Dutch government.

To the south-west, on Jl Pejambon, is the **Gedung Pancasila**, an imposing neoclassical building built in 1830 as the Dutch army commander's residence. It later became the meeting hall of the Volksraad (People's Council), but is best known as the place where Soekarno made his famous Pancasila speech in 1945, laying the foundation for Indonesia's constitution. Just west along Jl Pejambon from Gedung Pancasila is the **Emanuel Church**, another classic, pillared building dating from 1893.

TAMAN MINI INDONESIA INDAH

In the south-east of the city, near Kampung Rambutan, Taman Mini is another of those 'whole country in one park' collections popular in Asia. The idea for the park was conceived by Madame Tien Soeharto, and in 1971 the families inhabiting the land were cleared out to make way for the project (then estimated to cost the awesome total of US$26 million) and the park was duly opened in 1975.

This 100 hectare park has 27 full-scale traditional houses from the 27 provinces of Indonesia, with displays of regional handcrafts and clothing, and a large 'lagoon' where you can row around the islands of the archipelago or take a cable car across for a bird's eye view. There are also museums, theatres, restaurants, an orchid garden and a bird park with a huge walk-in aviary. There's even a mini Borobudur. The park is quite good value and Indonesians will tell you that if you see this there's no need to go anywhere else in the country!

Other attractions include 'Indonesia Indah', a three dimensional screen show of the Indonesian panorama which takes place at the Keong Mas (Golden Snail) Theatre. In 30 minutes the film packs a lot in a special effects travelogue. Admission is 3000 rp and showings are every afternoon and throughout the day on weekends.

You can walk or drive your own car around Taman Mini. Or you can go by horse and cart, take the mini-train service that shuttles around the park or the cable car that goes from one end to the other. The park is open from 8 am to 5 pm daily, the houses and Museum Indonesia from 9 am to 4 pm. Admission is 2000 rp (children 1000 rp). On Sunday mornings there are free cultural performances in most regional houses from 10 am to 2 pm. For other cultural events here, check the Taman Mini monthly programme available from the tourist information office or ring ☎ 8400418 for information.

Taman Mini is about 18 km from the city centre so you need to allow about 1½ hours to get out there and at least three hours to look around. Take any bus to Kampung

GLENN BEANLAND

The imax cinema at Keong Mas (also known as the Golden Snail Theatre from its design), regularly screens an impressive film on the sights of Indonesia. This was once the largest imax screen in the world.

Rambutan bus terminal and from there a T55 metro-mini to the park entrance. A taxi will cost around 15,000 rp from central Jakarta.

TAMAN IMPIAN JAYA ANCOL

Along the bay front between Kota and Tanjung Priok, the people's 'Dreamland' is built on land reclaimed in 1962. This huge landscaped recreation park, providing non-stop entertainment, has hotels, nightclubs, theatres and a variety of sporting facilities.

Taman Impian Jaya Ancol's prime attractions include the **Pasar Seni** (Art Market) (see Things to Buy later in this section), which has sidewalk cafes, a host of craft shops, art exhibitions and live music on Friday and Saturday nights. Near the Pasar Seni is an **oceanarium** (gelanggang samudra), the **Seaworld** walk-through tunnel to view the sealife and an amazing **swimming pool complex**, including a wave pool and slide pool (gelanggang renang). The **Ancol Beach**, so close to the city, is not the greatest place for a swim but you can take a boat from the marina here for day trips to some of Jakarta's Pulau Seribu islands.

The big drawcard at Ancol is **Dunia Fantasi** (Fantasy Land), a fun park that must have raised eyebrows at the Disney legal department. Resemblances to Disneyland start at the 'main street' entrance, and the Puppet Castle is a straight 'it's a small world' replica. But the Indonesian influence prevails – Western World is the old west complete with a 'rumah jahil' for miscreants and a Sate Corner snack bar. Dunia Fantasi is actually very well done and great for kids, with a host of fun rides. Admission (including entry to Ancol) is 21,500 rp on weekdays, 26,000 rp on weekends. Dunia Fantasi is open Monday to Saturday from 2 to 9 pm, Sunday and holidays from 10 am to 9 pm.

Basic admission to Ancol is 2500 rp on weekdays, 3000 rp on weekends. The park is open 24 hours, but most of the attractions, such as the Pasar Seni, open around 10 am and close by 10 pm or earlier. For more information, call ☎ 681511.

To get there, take a No 60 bus or No 22 bus from Pasar Senen, or a bus to Kota and then bus Nos 64 and 65 or a M15 minibus.

The park can be very crowded on weekends, but on weekdays it's fairly quiet and a great place to escape from the hassles of the city.

TAMAN ISMAIL MARZUKI

On Jl Cikini Raya, not far from Jl Jaksa, the Taman Ismail Marzuki (TIM; ☎ 3154087) is Jakarta's cultural showcase. There is a performance almost every night and here you might see anything from Balinese dancing to poetry readings, gamelan concerts to a New Zealand film festival. The TIM monthly programme is available from the tourist office, the TIM office and major hotels, and events are also listed in the *Jakarta Post*.

Jakarta's **planetarium** (☎ 337530) is also here, but shows are generally given in Indonesian. Phone for information about shows in English. The whole complex is open from morning until midnight and there are good outdoor cafes, so it can be a useful place. The No 34 bus from Jl Thamrin stops nearby.

RAGUNAN ZOO

Jakarta's Ragunan Zoo is about 10 km south of the city centre in the Pasar Minggu area. It's large and spacious, but the animal enclosures are shabby and the landscaping consists of half-successful attempts to replace jungle with grass. The zoo has komodo dragons, orang-utans and other Indonesian wildlife. It's open daily from 9 am to 6 pm. Admission is 1500 rp, half-price for children. From Jl Thamrin take bus No 19.

OTHER ATTRACTIONS

Jakarta has several gardens specialising in cultivating orchids and the **Taman Anggrek Indonesia Permai**, just north of Taman Mini, is the best place to see them. Entry is 1000 rp.

Indonesia's independence was proclaimed at **Gedung Perintis Kemerdekaan**, Jl Proklamasi 56 in Menteng, on the site of the former home of Soekarno. A monument to President Soekarno and Vice President Hatta marks the spot.

The **Pasar Burung**, on Jl Pramuka in Jatinegara, is Jakarta's market for captive birds from all over Indonesia.

At Lubang Buaya (literally, crocodile hole),

a few km east of Taman Mini, the **Pancasila Cakti** is a memorial to the six generals and the army officer killed here by the Communists in 1965.

SWIMMING

The swimming pools at Ancol are great, but many of the closer hotels open their pools to the public for a fee – the Hotel Indonesia has a large pool costing 10,000 rp for nonguests (15,000 rp on weekends).

ORGANISED TOURS

Numerous travel agents offer daily tours of Jakarta but they tend to be expensive. Bookings can be made through the tourist office and major hotels. Boca Pirento, Panorama and Buana are the main operators. All tour buses pick up from the major hotels, and tour prices and sights are very similar. A four hour morning city tour, for example, costs US$20, and includes the National Museum, National Monument, Sunda Kelapa and Kota.

There are also a variety of tours to nearby towns in West Java which basically go to Bogor, the Puncak Pass and Tangkuban Prahu volcano near Bandung. An eight hour tour to the Bogor botanical gardens and zoological museum costs US$40; to the Puncak Pass costs US$40.

SPECIAL EVENTS

The Jakarta Anniversary on 22 June celebrates the establishment of the city by Gunungjati back in 1527 with fireworks and the Jakarta Fair. The latter is a fairground event held at the Jakarta Fair Grounds, northeast of the city centre in Kemayoran, from late June until mid-July.

The Jl Jaksa Street Fair features Betawi dance, theatre and music, as well as popular modern performances. Street stalls sell food and souvenirs, and art and photography exhibits are also staged. It is held for one week in August.

Indonesia's independence day is 17 August and the parades in Jakarta are the biggest in the country.

PLACES TO STAY

Jakarta is the most expensive city in Indonesia, and prices are up to double what you'll pay in other parts of Java, especially for bottom-end places. There is a building boom of mid-range and top-end hotels, and competition is keeping the price down. All upper bracket hotels charge 21% tax and service on top of the rates quoted here, but discounts of 20% or more are usually available for the asking. Travel agents in Jakarta and elsewhere also offer the best discounts.

Places to Stay – bottom end

Jalan Jaksa Area Once upon a time, so the story goes, a backpacker arrived at Jakarta's Gambir train station and wandered off looking for a hotel, without success. He chanced down Jl Jaksa and a family took pity on him and gave him a bed for the night. The word spread and soon other backpackers started arriving at the house, so the family decided to open a hostel. Other guesthouses followed and now Jl Jaksa is a lively strip of cheap hotels and restaurants, conveniently central near Jakarta's main drag, Jl Thamrin, and only a 10 to 15 minute walk from Gambir train station.

Wisma Delima (☎ 337026), Jl Jaksa 5, was the original guesthouse and for long the only cheap places to stay. In fact, No 5 would actually be referred to as 'Jl Jaksa' and as a consequence it was often hopelessly crowded and totally chaotic. Now, there are lots of alternatives and Wisma Delima is still popular but quieter. Dorm beds are 7500 rp (6500 rp for Hostelling International members), or small but spotless doubles are 15,000 rp. Food and cold drinks are available, and it has good travel information.

The friendly and well-run *Norbek (Noordwijk) Hostel* (☎ 330392) is across Jl Jaksa at No 14. It's a dark rabbit warren with plywood walls, but many of the rooms have air-con and it has a cafe. Fan rooms start at 9000/12,000 rp, from 25,000 rp with air-con and 30,000 rp with attached bathroom. Down a small alleyway nearby, the *Jusran Hostel* is a smaller, quiet place. Basic plywood rooms cost 17,500 rp with fan.

Nick's Corner Hostel (☎ 3141988) at No 16 is a classier place with mock granite everywhere and it is fully air-conditioned. A bed costs 8000 rp in immaculate, if somewhat cramped, eight and 12 bed dorms. It also has a few rooms with fan for 20,000 to 37,000 rp, and just two rooms with bathroom for 47,000 rp and 65,000 rp. Breakfast is included.

The *Djody Hostel*, Jl Jaksa 27, is another old standby. Enter through the Blue Cafe. Spartan rooms with shared mandi (Indonesian-style bath) cost 15,000/22,000/30,000 rp for singles/doubles/triples. A few doors further up is the related *Djody Hotel* (☎ 315-1404) at No 35, which is a notch above the pack. It is popular with backpackers and also attracts a fair number of local business travellers. Simple rooms without bath cost 16,000/27,000 rp. Rooms with air-con and bath cost 45,000 to 50,000 rp.

The newly renovated *Hotel Tator* (☎ 32-3940), Jl Jaksa 37, is a definite step above the others in quality. Spotless rooms are spartan but comfortable and cost 27,500/42,500 rp with fan, 50,000 rp and 55,000 rp with air-con and telephone. It has a small cafe. Bookings are advisable.

More places can be found in the small streets running off Jl Jaksa. Gang 1 is a small alley connecting Jl Jaksa to Jl Kebon Sirih Timur (running east off Jl Jaksa). A short distance down are two small, quiet places: the *Kresna Homestay* (☎ 325403) at No 175 and the *Bloem Steen Homestay* next door at No 173. They're a bit cramped, but reasonable value for Jakarta. The friendly Kresna has rooms for 15,000/20,000 rp without/with mandi; the Bloem Steen has rooms from 15,000 rp.

At Jl Kebon Sirih Barat 35, running west off Jl Jaksa, *Borneo Hostel* (☎ 320095) is popular, well run and friendly, and has a lively cafe/bar. Well-kept rooms cost 25,000 and 30,000 rp, or 35,000 rp with mandi. The annexe next door is under different management and badly in need of maintenance.

Other places are dotted along this lane, such as *Bintang Kejora* (☎ 323878) at No 52, which has very clean rooms for 20,000/25,000

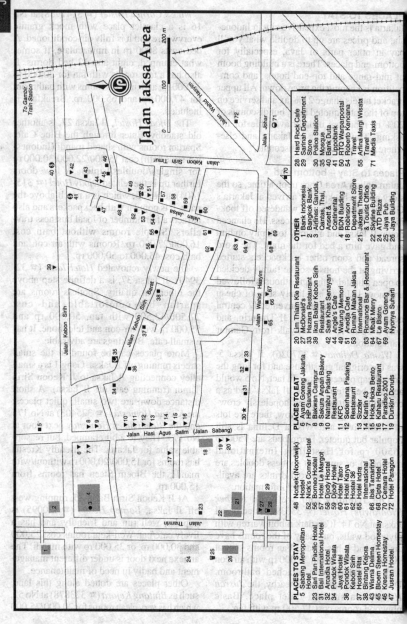

Jalan Jaksa Area

To Gambir
Train Station

0   100   200 m

PLACES TO STAY

5   Sabang Metropolitan
    Hotel
23 Sari Pan Pacific Hotel
31 Bali International Hotel
32 Arcadia Hotel
34 Pondok Wisata
36 Pondok Wisata
    Kebon Sirih
37 Hostel Rita
38 Bintang Kejora
45 Bloem Steen Homestay
46 Kresna Homestay
47 Jusran Hostel
48 Norbek (Noordwijk)
    Hostel
52 Sari Pan Pacific Hostel
56 Borneo Hostel
57 Hotel Le Margot
58 Djody Hostel
59 Djody Hotel
60 Hotel Tator
61 Hotel Karya
62 Hostel 36
65 Hotel Indra
66 Hotel Rita
    International
68 Cipta Tamind
    International
70 Cemara Hotel
72 Hotel Paragon

PLACES TO EAT

6   Ayam Goreng Jakarta
7   Hazara Restaurant
8   Bakwan Campur
9   Sakura Anpan Bakery
10 Natrabu Padang
    Restaurant
11 KFC
12 Sederhana Padang
    Restaurant
13 Sizzler
14 Kantin 43
15 Koka Hoka Bento
16 Bakmi Raya
17 Paradiso 2001
19 Dunkin Donuts
20 Lim Thiam Kie Restaurant
27 McDonald's
33 Ikan Bakar Kebon Sirih
    Restaurant
42 Sate Khas Senayan
44 Angie's Cafe
49 Warung Memori
51 Anedja Cafe
53 Rumah Makan Jaksa
    International
63 Romance Bar & Restaurant
64 Mbak Merry
67 Ie Bistro
69 Ayam Goreng
    Nyonya Suharti

OTHER

1   Bank Indonesia
2   Bangkok Bank
3   Kantor Garuda,
    Qantas & Thai,
    Ansett &
    Continental
4   BDN Building
18 Robinson
    Department Store
21 Jakarta Theatre
    & Tourist Office
22 Skyline Building
24 ATD Plaza
25 Jaya Pub
26 Jaya Building
28 Hard Rock Cafe
29 Sarinah Department
    Store
30 Bangkok Station
40 Mosque
41 Bank Duta
50 Lippobank
54 RTQ Warparpostal
55 Roberto Kencana
    Travel
54 Arfina Margi Wisata
    Travel
71 Media Taxis

p. Further down, there's the *Hostel Rita*, with rooms from 12,000 rp. The *Pondok Wisata Kebon Sirih* at No 16 and the *Pondok Wisata Jaya Hostel* at No 10 are uncomfortably close to the mosque.

Kuningan Apart from Wisma Delima, Jakarta has other youth hostels popular with local school groups and university students, but they tend to be a long way from the city centre. The best and most convenient is the *Graha Wisata Mahasiswa* (☎ 516922), Jl Rasuna Said, in Kuningan about four km south of Jl Thamrin. Good dormitory accommodation costs 7500 rp (2500 rp for students) in six bed dorms. Twin bed, air-con rooms are about the best deal in Jakarta and cost 15,000 rp per person (7500 rp for students). The hostel has a cafeteria and sports facilities. To get there take bus No P11 or 407 from Gambir train station.

Places to Stay – middle

Jalan Jaksa Area Each year new hotels are being built and old ones renovated in the Jl Jaksa area, pushing it slowly more upmarket. All have air-con rooms with hot water, TV and telephone.

The *Hotel Le Margot* (☎ 3913830), Jl Jaksa 15, is a small, new hotel with simple but comfortable rooms, reasonably priced at US$35 (including tax and service). The hotel has a restaurant/bar. The *Hotel Karya* (☎ 3140484), Jl Jaksa 32-34, has had big renovations but still has a few older, overpriced rooms for US$50/55, while new, overpriced rooms cost US$70/75.

Jl Wahid Hasyim has a string of better hotels. The newly renovated *Hotel Indra Internasional* (☎ 3152858) at No 63 is the cheapest. The rooms are good but cheaply furnished and many are internal facing. Rates start at US$50 before discount.

The much more impressive *Arcadia Hotel* (☎ 2300050) at No 114 has modern decor and a pleasant coffee shop/bar. Very comfortable rooms cost US$80 and US$85.

The *Cemara Hotel* (☎ 3149985), on the corner at Jl Cemara 1, has good rooms and service, and is competitively priced with

rooms for US$60 and US$70. The new *Hotel Paragon* (☎ 3917070) at Jl Wahid Hasyim 29 is strangely designed like a multi-storey motel, but has immaculate rooms for US$60/70.

The best hotel by far on Jl Wahid Hasyim is the *Ibis Tamarind* (☎ 3912323) at No 77. Edging into the top end, it has a pool and fitness centre. Rooms cost US$95 and US$130.

Also worth considering is the *Sabang Metropolitan Hotel* (☎ 373933), Jl HA Salim 11. This older high-rise has a pool and the rooms have had a facelift. Rooms cost US$55/70 to US$80/95 – it is good value after discount.

Cikini The Cikini area, east of Jl Thamrin and close to the TIM cultural centre, has a selection of mid-range hotels and some good guesthouses.

The *Gondia International Guesthouse* (☎ 3909221), Jl Gondia Kecil 22, is in a quiet side street off Jl RP Soeroso. Comfortable air-con rooms around small garden areas cost US$37.50/42.50, including breakfast. It has a pleasant, homey atmosphere.

The big *Hotel Marcopolo* (☎ 2301777), Jl Teuku Cik Ditiro 19, is good value. Quite luxurious rooms with fridge, TV and hot water cost 139,000 rp, single or double. The hotel has a swimming pool and a reasonably priced restaurant with excellent buffet breakfasts for only 7000 rp.

Another good and very popular guesthouse near the TIM cultural centre is *Yannie International Guest House* (☎ 3140012), Jl Raden Saleh Raya 35. Spotless, bright rooms with air-con and hot water cost US$35/40, including US breakfast. If it is full, try the *Karya II Hotel* (☎ 3101380) next door at No 37. Air-con rooms range from 66,000 to 105,000 rp. Downstairs rooms are dark – the best value are the upstairs rooms with hot water, TV and phone for 79,000 rp.

At the top of this range are the three star Sofyan hotels: *Sofyan Hotel Betawi* (☎ 390-5011), Jl Cut Mutiah 9, just east of Jl Jaksa, and *Sofyan Hotel Cikini* (☎ 3140695), Jl Cikini Raya 79. The Betawi has well-furnished, classy rooms from US$59/69, but the singles are very small. The Cikini has larger rooms from US$60/72.

Airport If you are just flying in and out of Jakarta, the cheapest hotel near the airport is the *Hotel Bandara Jakarta* (☎ 6191964), Jl Jurumudi Km 2.5, Cengkareng. There's nothing fancy about it – air-con rooms with bath start at US$35/48.50 and there's a 24 hour coffee shop. It usually has a representative at the airport hotel booths offering free transport and discounts.

Places to Stay – top end
The main centre for luxury hotels is the Welcome Statue roundabout on Jl Thamrin. The *Hotel Indonesia*, *Grand Hyatt Jakarta*, *Mandarin Oriental* and *President* are all on the roundabout, and nearby on Jl Thamrin are the *Kartika Plaza* and *Sari Pan Pacific*.

The *Hotel Indonesia* was the first of Indonesia's international hotels, and in the 1960s was the refuge for foreigners surrounded by the turmoil of Soekarno's 'year of living dangerously'. It certainly has history and some nice 1960s touches, but the rooms are increasingly shabby.

Also on the Welcome Statue roundabout, the *Grand Hyatt Jakarta* is widely considered to be the capital's best, and is favoured by many visiting dignitaries and VIPs. Diagonally across from the Hyatt, the *Mandarin Oriental* has no grounds, but it is an excellent business hotel and the well-furnished rooms have good extras. The nearby *President Hotel* is a smaller and more old-fashioned looking hotel. Just south from the Welcome Statue, the *Kartika Plaza* is an older hotel undergoing massive renovations.

More hotels can be found heading south down Jl Thamrin, which runs into Jl Jenderal Sudirman. Just off Jl Thamrin, is the opulent *Shangri-La*, with its impressive lobby of granite, glass and gold. The *Sahid Jaya Hotel* on Jl Jenderal Sudirman is a rambling hotel, while further south, *Le Meridien* is up there with the best. The *Hilton Hotel* is at the bottom corner of the 'Golden Triangle' business district. It has large grounds and a good

range of facilities. Near the Hilton, the *Hotel Atlet Century Park* is a cheaper three star hotel, but it has good facilities and well-appointed rooms.

To the north-east of the city centre near the National Monument, the *Borobudur Inter-Continental Hotel* is one of the older generation of luxury hotels, now undergoing huge renovations. Nearby the *Hotel Aryaduta* is a good business-class hotel.

Other new hotels are springing up everywhere, though these tend to be less central. The *Hotel Equatorial* is a couple of km west of Jl Thamrin in the Tanah Abang area. The *Omni Batavia Hotel* is an excellent new hotel in the historic Kota district, though it's not a great location at night.

Following is a list of the top hotels in Jakarta:

Borobudur Inter-Continental Jakarta, Jl Lapangan Banteng Selatan (☎ 3804444; fax 3805555)
Grand Hyatt Jakarta, Jl Thamrin (☎ 3901234; fax 3906426). Rooms US$290 and US$330. Suites US$570 to US$5400.
Hilton Hotel, Jl Gatot Subroto (☎ 5703600; fax 5733089). Rooms US$180/220 to US$220/235. Suites US$310 to US$2000.
Hotel Aryaduta, Jl Prapatan 44-48 (☎ 3861234; fax 380990). Rooms US$190 to US$220. Suites US$250 to US$1400.
Hotel Atlet Century Park, Jl Pintu Satu Senayan (☎ 5712041; fax 5712191). Rooms US$95/105 to US$130/140. Suites US$250 to US$500.
Hotel Equatorial, Jl Fachrudin 3 (☎ 2303636; fax 2300880). Rooms US$140 to US$175. Suites US$175 to US$750.
Hotel Indonesia, Jl Thamrin (☎ 3140008; fax 3141508). Rooms US$130/140 to US$160/170. Suites US$200 to US$800.
Kartika Plaza Hotel, Jl Thamrin 10 (☎ 3141008; fax 3305301)
Le Meridien Jakarta, Jl Jenderal Sudirman Kav 18-20 (☎ 2513131; fax 5711633). Rooms US$190 to US$230. Suites US$450 to US$750.
Mandarin Oriental Jakarta, Jl Thamrin (☎ 3141307; fax 3148680). Rooms US$180 to US$235. Suites US$480 to US$1500.
Omni Batavia Hotel, Jl Kali Besar Barat 44-46 (☎ 6904118; fax 6904092). Rooms US$120 to US$180. Suites US$200 to US$350.
President Hotel, Jl Thamrin 59 (☎ 2301122; fax 3143631). Rooms US$140/150 to US$220. Suites US$400 and US$450.

Sahid Jaya Hotel, Jl Jenderal Sudirman 86 (☎ 5704444; fax 5733168). Rooms US$150 to US$170. Suites US$190 to US$3000.

Sari Pan Pacific Hotel, Jl Thamrin (☎ 323707; fax 323650). Rooms US$160/180 to US$190/210. Suites US$230 to US$1000.

Shangri-La Hotel, Jl Jenderal Sudirman Kav 1 (☎ 5707440; fax 5703531). Rooms US$200/230 to US$270/300. Suites US$380 to US$1800.

PLACES TO EAT

Jakarta has the best selection of restaurants of any major Indonesian city, although a meal in a better-class restaurant is expensive. Plenty of street hawkers and night markets cater for cheaper meals.

Jalan Jaksa Area

Jl Jaksa's cafes are convivial meeting places dishing out the standard travellers' menu. They are certainly cheap and the breakfasts are very good value. Food is quasi-European or bland Indonesian. The cheapest eats on Jl Jaksa are in the warungs (basic food stalls) at the north end, and in the side alleys towards, Jl HA Salim, but some look remarkably dirty.

Popular places along Jl Jaksa, all dishing out the standard travellers' menu, include *Angie's Cafe*, *Warung Memori* and *Anedja Cafe*. The *Rumah Makan Jaksa International* at No 16-18, next to Nick's, changes name every year but still tops the popularity polls and gets very lively in the main tourist season. *Romance Bar & Restaurant*, Jl Jaksa 40, is the fanciest restaurant in the street, with air-con, a varied menu and a small bar.

At Jl Kebon Sirih 31A on the corner of Jl Jaksa, *Sate Khas Senayan* has air-con and is more expensive, but the food is good and the sate superb. Heading west along Jl Kebon Sirih, on the other side of the street at No 40, the *Ikan Bakar Kebon Sirih* specialises in that popular Sulawesi dish, ikan bakar (Macassar-style roast fish).

Jalan I HA Salim (Jalan Sabang)

The next street west of Jl Jaksa has a string of cheap to mid-range restaurants. Though Jl Sabang was renamed Jl Hasi Agus (HA) Salim years ago, everyone still knows it by its former name.

Throughout Java, Jl Sabang is famed as the sate capital of Indonesia. Dozens of sate hawkers set up on the street in the evening and the pungent smoke from their charcoal braziers fills the air. Most business is take away, but benches are scattered along the street if you want to sit down and eat there.

Restaurants line both sides of Jl Sabang, and the most famous is *Natrabu* at No 29A. This would have to be the classiest Padang restaurant in Indonesia, and if you only try Padang food once then do so here. You can have a filling meal for 10,000 rp.

For standard Chinese fare, the *Lim Thiam Kie* at No 49 has air-con, but the pretensions to being a fancy restaurant stop there. Most dishes are in the 5000 to 10,000 rp range.

Down a little alley off Jl Sabang is the *Paradiso 2001*, an interesting little Chinese vegetarian restaurant. It is nothing fancy but the food is tasty, healthy and cheap, and it does good fruit juices. Other more expensive restaurants range from *Sizzler*, for chain food grills, to the *HP Gardena*, serving Chinese steamboat.

Jalan Thamrin

In the Jakarta Theatre building, the *Green Pub* features Mexican food, with a meal averaging about 25,000 rp, and a popular bar. In the evening, the place is jammed, as Indonesians turn out to enjoy a local country band perform in Mexicano cowboy garb! Also in the Jakarta Theatre building, there's a *California Fried Chicken* joint and a *Pizza Hut*.

Across the road, the Sarinah department store has a very good, but very expensive, food stall area in the basement next to the supermarket. Try the excellent soto betawi – a thick coconut-based offal soup, a Jakarta speciality. Sarinah is also home to Indonesia's first *McDonald's*, the *Hard Rock Cafe*, which is one of the best places for US-style grills and imported steaks and *American Chili's Bar & Grill* for US grills and Tex Mex. The *Jaya Pub* at the back of

JAVA

the Jaya building, Jl Thamrin 12, is another music venue that also puts on good grills.

The Plaza Indonesia further down Jl Thamrin has plenty of other mall-based eateries, including the *Cira Food Court* on the 3rd level, with a range of excellent Asian and western food stalls – Indonesian, Chinese, Thai, Singaporean and Japanese dishes, as well as pizza, French pastries and western fast food for around 6000 rp.

Almost every shopping centre has a supermarket. The Sogo supermarket in the basement of the Plaza Indonesia is one of the best in the city centre and features Japanese groceries. You can also find one in the basement of the Sarinah department store or across the road in the Jakarta Theatre building.

Elsewhere

Street Food Jakarta has plenty of street food, served from push carts called *kaki lima* (five feet) or slightly more permanent warungs with canvas overhangs. As Indonesia's melting pot, Jakarta's street food has specialities from all over the archipelago – delicious srabi pancakes from Solo, sate from Madura or Sulawesi-style ikan bakar. Those new to Indonesia should exercise caution with street food and gradually introduce themselves to the local microbes.

Jakarta's markets always have plenty of street-side warungs. Pasar Tanah Abang, west along Jl Wahid Hasyim from Jl Thamrin, has a collection of cheap and popular night warungs. South of the Welcome Statue roundabout, a string of stalls can be found along Jl Kendal – walk south past the bars on Jl Blora and turn left (where the transvestites hang out) along Jl Kendal, which runs parallel to the train line.

One of the best warung areas is on Jl Pecanongan, about one km north of the National Monument. These night warungs start setting up large marquees around 5 pm and serve excellent Chinese seafood and other dishes at moderate prices.

Restaurants Along Jl Gajah Mada towards Glodok are numerous restaurants, bakeries, and fast food and ice-cream parlours. *Bakmi*

Gajah Mada is a busy noodle-house chain with shops all over Jakarta. The original restaurant at Jl Gajah Mada 92, just south of Arsip Nasional, has been pumping out noodles since the 1950s and is still a very popular, efficient place for cheap eats. The air-con Gajah Mada Plaza shopping centre nearby has fast food.

Right in the middle of historic Kota on Taman Fatahillah, *Cafe Batavia* is very 'in'. Housed in a tastefully renovated Dutch building, good international cuisine will set you back at least 40,000 rp for a main, or you can take in the ambience at the bar. It is open 24 hours.

The historic *Oasis Bar & Restaurant* (☎ 3150646), Jl Raden Saleh 47 in Cikini, is housed in a large, old Dutch villa and has the feel of an extravagant 1930s Hollywood film set, with prices to match. More than a dozen waitresses serve up a traditional rijsttafel, while you are serenaded by a group of Batak singers from Sumatra. Reservations are recommended. It's closed on Sunday.

Restoran Manari (☎ 5204036), Jl Gatot Subroto, on the southern edge of the Golden Triangle district, has dinner and traditional dance performances every night of the week. Prices range from 45,000 to 75,000 rp.

About one km east of Jl Thamrin on Jl Cokroaminoto is the well-to-do Menteng shopping centre, where a number of more upmarket dining possibilities can be found. You can have Thai, Japanese, noodles, seafood or steak (try the *Gandy Steakhouse* or *Black Angus*). *Tamnak Thai*, Jl Cokroaminoto 78, is recommended for good, moderately priced Thai food and Chinese seafood.

The wealthy southern suburbs are the favourite residential district for Jakarta's elite and expatriate community. While the city centre is a much more convenient place to dine, South Jakarta has some excellent restaurants. An expat favourite is the *Orient Express*, Wijaya Grand Centre, Block H37-39, Jl Baramwangsa Raya in Kebayoran Baru. It serves a bit of everything: Indian, seafood, pizza and Mexican. The food is consistently good and the prices moderate.

ENTERTAINMENT

Check the entertainment pages of the *Jakarta Post* for films, concerts and special events. Films, lectures and discussions on Indonesian culture are often sponsored by foreign embassies and the Indonesian Heritage Society, a volunteer organisation devoted to affording an appreciation of the nation's rich cultural heritage.

Cultural Performances

The already mentioned *Taman Ismail Mazurki (TIM)* cultural centre in Menteng is one of the best places to see traditional and modern performing arts and cultural events.

The *Gedung Kesenian Jakarta* (☎ 380-8283), Jl Gedung Kesenian 1, also has a regular programme (see the tourist office) of traditional dance and theatre, as well as European classical music and dance.

The *Bharata Theatre*, Jl Kalilio 15, Pasar Senen, has wayang orang or *ketoprak* (Javanese folk theatre) performances from 8 pm to midnight every evening. Tickets cost 2000 to 5000 rp.

Wayang kulit/golek puppet shows are held at the *Jakarta History Museum* in Kota every Sunday.

Nightlife

Jakarta is the most sophisticated, broad-minded and corrupt city in Indonesia, and has nightlife to match. Hundreds of bars, discos, karaoke lounges and nightclubs range from the sleazy to the refined. Local bands are found in profusion, doing everything from Beatles and Rolling Stones impersonations to jazz and the latest hits. European and Black American bands are definitely in vogue and provide the pick of the music. Bands start around 10 or 11 pm, and continue until 2 or 3 am, sometimes later on the weekends. During the week many places close at 1 am.

Many don't have cover charges, though sometimes a first drink cover charge applies, especially in the discos. A beer or a mixed drink costs from 6000 rp in the cheaper bars, double that in exclusive hotel bars.

Bars & Live Music The *Hard Rock Cafe*, on Jl Thamrin, has the usual blend of rock memorabilia, music and food. It is always lively and has decent bands or occasional top-line imports. The music starts around 11 pm, when dinner finishes, and keeps going until around 3 am. The dance floor is dominated by a huge stained-glass portrait of the King, though this Elvis looks vaguely Indonesian.

The *Jaya Pub*, next to the carpark behind the Jaya building, Jl Thamrin 12, is a Jakarta institution that has live pub music most evenings.

Oreilly's, in the Grand Hyatt, is a salubrious place for a business drink, but it also gets some very good bands on Friday and Saturday nights, when the ties come off, the crowds pack in and the place starts jumping.

The historic, restored *Cafe Batavia* at Taman Fatahillah is another upmarket venue and a popular spot to be seen. The music is mostly jazz and soul from imported bands.

Discos Many discos are found at the big hotels, and dress requirements – no jeans, sneakers, T-shirts – usually apply.

The Glodok area, Jakarta's Chinatown, has an interesting collection. *Stardust*, on Jl Hayam Wuruk next to the Jayakarta Tower Hotel, is very popular with young Chinese and the original disco in the area but it now has lots of competition. Nearby, on the back streets around the Glodok Plaza, unprepossessing entrances and grotty lifts lead to some amazingly sophisticated clubs. *Terminal 1* has three floors of bar girls, karaoke, bands and a disco. The *Kanto Pub* here attracts an ecstatic crowd. *Zodiac* is the biggest and has a huge pumping dance floor. The 9th floor disco of *Sydney 2000* has impressive decor and a dazzling laser show.

Jakarta's most infamous disco is *Tanamur* at Jl Tanah Abang Timur 14. This long-running institution is jammed nightly with gyrating revellers of every race, creed and sexual proclivity, and innumerable ladies of the night. It is unbelievably crowded after midnight on Friday and Saturday nights. Wear what you like here.

THINGS TO BUY

Good buys in Jakarta include batik and antiques but Jakarta has bits and pieces from almost everywhere in Indonesia. If this is your first stop, it's a good place to get an overall view of Indonesian crafts and, if it's your last stop, then it's always a final chance to find something that you missed elsewhere in the country.

A good place to start is Sarinah on Jl Thamrin. The 3rd floor of this large department store is devoted to batik and handcrafts from all over the country. This floor is divided into different concessions sponsored by the big batik manufacturers like Batik Keris and Batik Danar Hadi. Handcrafts are souvenirs rather than true collectibles, but the quality is high and the prices reasonable.

In the same vein, but possibly even bigger, is Pasar Raya Big & Beautiful in Blok M, south of the city centre (see below).

The Pasar Seni, at Ancol recreation park, is an excellent place to look for regional handcrafts and to see many of them actually being made. Whether it's woodcarvings, paintings, puppets, leather, batik or silver, you'll find it here.

In Menteng, Jl Surabaya is Jakarta's famous fleamarket. Here you'll find woodcarvings, furniture, brassware, jewellery, batik, oddities like old typewriters and many (often instant) antiques. It is always fun to browse, but bargain like crazy – prices may be up to five times the worth of the goods.

Jl Kebon Sirih Timur, the street east of Jl Jaksa, has a number of shops for antiques and curios. The quality is high, but so are the prices.

Jakarta has plenty of shopping centres and markets to explore. Clothes and shoes are cheap, but it can take some hunting to find western sizes and styles. Pasar Baru pedestrian mall, just across the canal from the post office, is a good place to shop for cheap clothes and shoes.

Pasar Senen, west of Gambir train station, is another lively shopping area with a large, active market.

Jakarta has plenty of malls. The most exclusive and expensive is the Plaza Indonesia on Jl Thamrin. It's a great place to browse for designer labels, but the prices are very high. Other big, dazzling malls include the Pondok Indah Mall in the southern suburbs and the Ciputra Mall in West Jakarta on the way to the airport.

Blok M is one of the biggest and best shopping areas in Jakarta. Here you'll find the huge Blok M Mall above the large bus terminal. This is a more down-to-earth mall, with scores of small, reasonably priced shops offering clothes, shoes, music tapes, household goods etc. More upmarket shopping can be found at the multi-storey Blok M Plaza just across the way, and Pasa Raya Big & Beautiful department store is also right next to the mall. Jl Palatehan 1, just to the north of the Blok M bus terminal has some interesting antique and craft shops.

GETTING THERE & AWAY

Jakarta is the main international gateway to Indonesia; for details on arriving there from overseas see the introductory Getting There & Away section at the start of this chapter. Travel agencies worth trying for discounted air fares on international flights out of Jakarta are listed under Information at the start of the Jakarta section.

Jakarta is also a major centre for domestic travel, with extensive bus, train, air and sea connections.

Air

International and domestic flights both operate from the Soekarno-Hatta international airport. Airport tax is 25,000 rp on international departures, 11,000 rp on domestic flights. The domestic tax is usually included in the ticket. Flights depart from Jakarta to all the main cities across the archipelago. The main domestic airlines have offices open normal business hours, and usually Sunday morning as well. Travel agents also sell domestic tickets.

Following is a list of the main domestic airlines in Jakarta:

Bouraq, Jl Angkasa 1, Kemayoran (☎ 6295150).
    Bouraq has a useful network.

Garuda, BDN building, Jl Thamrin 5 (☎ 2300925). Garuda flies to the major cities throughout Indonesia; Garuda also has offices at the Borobudur Inter-Continental Hotel (☎ 2310339), Hotel Indonesia (☎ 3200568), Wisma Dharmala Sakti (☎ 2512259), Jl Sudirman 32, and other locations.

Mandala, Jl Garuda No 79 (☎ 4246100). This office is near the Pelni office.

Merpati, Jl Angkasa 2 (☎ 4243608). This office is inconveniently located, but travel agents sell tickets; Merpati is the main domestic carrier with flights throughout the archipelago.

Sempati has several offices, including one at the Plaza Indonesia (☎ 3151612). It has a fleet of jets flying to major cities throughout Indonesia.

Bus

Jakarta has four major bus terminals, all a long way from the city centre. In some cases it can take longer getting to the bus terminal than the bus journey itself, making the trains a better alternative for arriving at or leaving Jakarta. This is especially true for buses to/from Kampung Rambutan bus terminal.

Tickets can be bought from travel agents around town. Jl Jaksa agents not only sell tickets, but can include travel to the bus terminals. Buying tickets through an agent tends to be considerably higher, but can save a lot of hassle. Advance bookings are a good idea for peak-travel periods, but so many buses operate to the main destinations that if you just front up at the bus terminals you won't have to wait long to find one. The bus terminals are:

Kalideres Buses to the west of Jakarta go from the Kalideres bus terminal, about 15 km north-west of Merdeka Square. Frequent normal/air-con buses run to Merak (3000/ 5000 rp; three hours), Labuan (3100 rp; 3½ hours) and Serang (2000 rp; 1½ hours). A couple of midday buses go through to Sumatra from Kalideres, but most Sumatra buses leave from Pulo Gadung bus terminal.

Kampung Rambutan The big, new Kampung Rambutan bus terminal handles buses to areas south and south-west of Jakarta. It was designed to carry much of Jakarta's intercity bus traffic, but it really only handles

buses to West Java, including: Bogor (1200/2500 rp; 40 minutes); Bandung (3500/7500 rp; 4½ hours); Tasikmalaya (6000/10,000 rp; 7½ hours); and Banjar (6500/11,500 rp; nine hours). Buses also go to Sumatra, Cirebon, Yogya, Surabaya and other long-distance destinations, but Pulo Gadung bus terminal still has most of the long-distance services. Kampung Rambutan is about 18 km to the south of the city centre and takes at least an hour by city bus. Take the train for Bogor or Bandung.

Pulo Gadung Pulo Gadung is 12 km to the east of the city centre, and has buses to Cirebon, Central and East Java, Sumatra and Bali. Many of the air-con, deluxe buses operate from here. This wild bus terminal is the busiest in Indonesia, with buses, crowds, hawkers and beggars everywhere.

The station is divided into two sections: one for buses to Sumatra and the other for all buses to the east.

Most buses to Sumatra leave between 10 am and 3 pm, and you can catch a bus right through to Aceh if you are crazy enough. Destinations and fares include: Palembang (32,000 to 42,000 rp); Bengkulu (47,500 to 67,000 rp); and Padang and Bukittinggi (54,000 to 70,000 rp). Prices are for air-con deluxe buses with reclining seats and toilets – well worth it for those long hauls through Sumatra. Putra Rafflesia has the best bus to Bengkulu at 11 am. For Bukittinggi, two good companies are ALS (☎ 8503446), with buses at 12.30, 2.30 and 4 pm, and ANS (☎ 352411), with buses at 10 am, noon and 2 pm. Both charge 70,000 rp for the 30 hour plus journey.

To the east, frequent buses go to Central and East Java and on to Bali. Destinations include: Cirebon (5000 to 10,000 rp; four hours); Yogya (15,000 to 26,000 rp; 14 hours); Surabaya (21,500 to 46,000 rp; 18 hours); Malang (21,000 to 49,000 rp); and Denpasar (48,000 to 62,000 rp; 24 hours). Most buses to Yogya leave between 8 am and 6 pm. Some of the better deluxe bus companies are Raya and Muncul.

Lebak Bulus This bus terminal, 16 km south of the city centre, handles many of the long-distance deluxe buses to Yogya, Surabaya and Bali. Fares are much the same as from Pulo Gadung bus terminal. Most departures are late afternoon or evening.

Train

Jakarta has a number of train stations. The most convenient and most important is Gambir, on the eastern side of Merdeka Square, a 15 minute walk from Jl Jaksa. Gambir handles mostly express trains to Bogor, Bandung, Yogyakarta, Solo, Semarang and Surabaya. Most Gambir trains also stop at Kota, the train station in the old city area in the north. The Pasar Senen train station, to the east, has mostly economy trains to eastern destinations. Tanah Abang train station, to the west, has a couple of slow trains to Merak.

Trains on Java are often subject to delays, but from Jakarta the train stations are much more central than the bus terminals and trains don't have to battle the Jakarta traffic jams.

For longer hauls, the express trains are far preferable to the economy trains, and most have cheaper bisnis class in addition to aircon eksekutif class. For most express trains, tickets can be bought in advance, either at the train station or from some travel agents that arrange tickets for a premium.

From Gambir train station, taxis cost a minimum of 7000 rp from the taxi booking desk. A cheaper alternative is to go out the front to the main road and hail down a bajaj, which will cost at least 2000 rp to Jl Jaksa after bargaining.

Services to Bogor, Bandung, Cirebon, Yogyakarta, Solo and Surabaya include:

Bogor Trains to Bogor (900 rp; 1½ hours) leave every 20 minutes or so from Gambir and Kota train stations. Trains can be horribly crowded during rush hour, but otherwise provide a good service. Best of all are the bisnis trains (2500 rp; one hour) leaving at 7.30, 8.15, 10.35 am, 2.20 and 4.25 pm.

Bandung The efficient and comfortable *Parahyangan* service departs for Bandung (15,000 rp bisnis; three hours) roughly every hour between 5 am and 9.30 pm from Gambir train station. The new, more luxurious *Argogede* departs at 10 am and 6 pm, and costs 30,000 rp in eksekutif class.

Cirebon Most trains that run along the north coast, and those to Yogya, go through Cirebon. One of the best services is the *Cirebon Express* departing from Gambir train station at 7, 9.45 am and 4.30 pm. It costs 12,000 rp in bisnis, 23,000 rp in eksekutif and takes 3½ hours.

Yogyakarta & Solo The *Fajar Utama Yogya* (23,000 rp bisnis; nine hours) departs from Gambir train station at 6.10 am, and the *Senja Utama Yogya* (25,000 rp bisnis) departs at 7.20 and 8.40 pm. The *Senja Utama Solo* is the best option to Solo (28,000 rp bisnis; 10½ hours) and it also stops in Yogyakarta. Expect overruns on the scheduled journey times.

Surabaya Trains between Jakarta and Surabaya either take the shorter northern route via Semarang or the longer southern route via Yogyakarta. Express trains range from the *Jayabaya Utama* (33,000 rp; 12 hours) to the luxurious *Argobromo* (100,000 rp; nine hours).

Minibus

Door-to-door *travel* minibuses are not such a good option in Jakarta because it can take hours to pick up or drop passengers in the traffic jams. Some travel agents book them, but you may have to go to a depot on the outskirts. Media Taxis (☎ 3140343), Jl Johar 15, near Jl Jaksa, has minibuses to Bandung.

Arfina Margi Wisata (☎ 3155908), at Jl Kebon Sirih Barat 39, just off Jl Jaksa near the Borneo Hostel, has convenient buses to Pangandaran (32,000 rp) from Jl Jaksa on Tuesday, Thursday and Saturday. Jl Jaksa travel agents also have direct minibuses to Yogya (35,000 rp) and bus tours to Padang.

Boat

See the Indonesia Getting Around section for information on the Pelni shipping services which operate on a regular two week schedule to ports all over the archipelago. Most of them go through Jakarta (Tanjung Priok harbour). Pelni ships all arrive at and depart from Pelabuhan Satu (Dock No 1) at Tanjung Priok, 13 km north-east of the centre of the city. Take the grey Himpunan bus No 81 from Jl Thamrin, opposite Sarinah department store; allow at least an hour. A taxi will cost around 12,000 rp.

The Pelni ticketing office (☎ 4211921) is at Jl Angkasa No 18, north-east of the city centre. Pelni agents charge a small premium but are much more convenient – try Menara Buana Surya (☎ 3142464) in the Tedja Buana building, Jl Menteng Raya 29, about half a km east of Jl Jaksa.

Ships go from Jakarta to Tanjung Pinang in the Riau archipelago, from where it is just a short ferry ride to Singapore. As well as the Pelni boats, the MV *Samudera Jaya* leaves Jakarta every Saturday and does the trip in 18 hours for 80,000 rp. Bookings can be made through travel agents or PT Admiral Lines, 21 Jl Raya Pelabuhan, right on Tanjung Priok harbour.

The best place to get information on non-Pelni cargo boats is the old harbour, Sunda Kelapa. The staff at the harbour master's office *(kantor syahbander)* are the people to see first. Most of them speak excellent English and they're very helpful. It's also worth going around all the ships at the dock.

GETTING AROUND
The Airport

Jakarta's Soekarno-Hatta international airport is 35 km west of the city centre. A toll road links the airport to the city and a journey between the two takes 45 minutes to an hour, longer in the rush hour.

There's a good Damri bus service (4000 rp) every 30 minutes from 3 am to 7 pm between the airport and Gambir train station (close to Jl Jaksa) in central Jakarta.

Alternatively, a metered taxi costs about 30,000 to 35,000 rp, including the 2300 rp airport service charge and the 6500 rp toll road charges, paid on top of the metered fare. Catch taxis from taxi ranks outside the airport terminal, and avoid offers of 'transport' from unregistered taxis.

Some Jl Jaksa hostels offer minibuses to the airport, but are no bargain if they don't use the toll road.

Bus

In Jakarta everything is at a distance. It's hot and humid, and hardly anybody walks – you will need to use some form of transport to get from one place to another. Jakarta has probably the most comprehensive city bus network of any major Indonesian city.

Buses cost 400 rp, patas (express) buses cost 700 rp and air-con patas buses cost 1800 rp. Jakarta's crowded buses have their fair share of pickpockets and bag slashers. The more expensive buses are generally safer, as well as being more comfortable.

In addition to the big buses, mikrolet and other minibuses operate in some areas. Jakarta still has some Morris bemos, the original three wheelers.

The tourist office has information on buses around Jakarta. Some of the useful buses that operate along central Jl Thamrin include:

No 81
    Blok M to Kota, Ancol and Tanjung Priok Harbour
P11, P10 (air-con)
    Kampung Rambutan to Kota
P1
    Blok M to Kota
P7A
    Pulo Gadung to Kalideres via Jl Juanda

Taxi

Taxis in Jakarta are metered and cost 1500 rp for the first km and 550 rp for each subsequent km. Make sure the meter is used. Many taxi drivers provide a good service, but Jakarta has enough rogues to give its taxis a bad reputation. Tipping is expected, if not demanded, but not obligatory. If good service is provided, it is customary to round the fare up to the next 1000 rp. Carry plenty of small notes – Jakarta taxi drivers rarely give change.

Jakarta has a large fleet of taxis and it's usually not too difficult to find one. Bluebird cabs (pale blue; ☎ 7941234, 7981001) have the best reputation and well-maintained cars. President taxis have the worst reputation.

Typical taxi fares from Jl Jaksa/ Thamrin are: Kota (6000 rp); Ancol (8000 rp); Pulo Gadung (9000 rp); Kalideres (12,000 rp); and Kampung Rambutan or Taman Mini (15,000 rp).

Bajaj & Other Local Transport

Bajaj (pronounced ba-jai) are nothing less than Indian auto-rickshaws: orange three wheelers that carry two passengers (three at a squeeze if you're all dwarf-size) and sputter around powered by noisy two stroke engines. Short trips – Jl Jaksa to the main post office, for example – will cost about 2500 rp. They're good value, especially during rush hours, but hard bargaining is required. Always agree on the price beforehand. Bajaj are not allowed along main streets such as Jl Thamrin, so make sure they don't simply drop you off at the border.

Jakarta has other weird and wonderful means of getting around. 'Morris' bemos are old English Morris vans than operate around Glodok and other parts of Jakarta. In the back streets of Kota, pushbikes with a padded 'kiddy carrier' on the back will take you for a ride! The *helicak*, cousin to the bajaj, is a green motorcycle contraption with a passenger car mounted on the front. They are found only on the back streets of Menteng. Jakarta also has ojeks, motorcycles that take pillion passengers, but weaving in and out of Jakarta's traffic on the back of an ojek is decidedly risky. Becaks have disappeared from the city, and only a few tourist becaks remain at Ancol.

Car

If you feel up to driving yourself around, Jakarta has branches of major rent-a-car operators. Try National Car Rental (☎ 314-3423) in the Kartika Plaza Hotel, Jl Thamrin 10, and Avis Rental Car (☎ 3904745) at Jl

Diponegoro 25. Smaller companies, such as Imperial Rent-A-Car (☎ 323141), Jl Raden Saleh 28, are competitively priced, or enquire at the cheaper travel agents, where a car or minibus with driver may be the cheapest of all.

AROUND JAKARTA
Pulau Seribu (Thousand Islands)

Scattered across the Java Sea to the north of Jakarta are the tropical islands of Pulau Seribu, or Thousand Islands, although they are actually only 105 in number. These beautiful islands have white sand beaches, palm trees, coral reefs and calm waters – just a short ride from Jakarta. The area is a marine national park, though 37 of the islands are permitted to be exploited.

Jakarta's 'offshore' islands start only a few km out in the Bay of Jakarta. The waters closest to Jakarta are murky – the islands are better the further you go from Jakarta. **Pulau Bidadari** is the closest resort island and is popular for day trips with Jakarta residents. It is one of the least interesting resorts, but you can use it to visit other nearby islands like **Pulau Kahyangan**, **Pulau Kelor**, which has the ruins of an old Dutch fort, or **Pulau Onrust**, where the remains of an old shipyard from the 18th century can be explored.

Further north, **Pulau Ayer** is another popular day-trip destination. It has a comfortable resort with a small stretch of good beach, though the waters are still cloudy. **Pulau Laki**, another resort island, is also close to the coast, being about 40 km west of Jakarta.

The entire island group has a population of around 15,000, with the district centre on **Pulau Panggang**, about 15 km north of Jakarta, but most people live on just one island, **Pulau Kelapa**, further north. These poor fishing communities have yet to share in the wealth generated by the resorts. Near Pulau Kelapa, **Pulau Panjang** has the only airstrip on the islands. Around this group of islands are two more resorts on **Pulau Kotok**, which has a good reef for snorkelling and diving, and the Matahari resort on **Pulau Macan Besar**, which is surrounded by a retaining wall. **Pulau Bira** has, believe it or not, a golf course.

The best resorts lie around four km north of Pulau Kelapa, all close to each other. **Pulau Putri** is notable for its aquariums. **Pulau Sepa** is a small sandy island surrounded by wide stretches of pristine sand. Nearby **Pulau Pelangi** also has some good stretches of beach. **Pulau Papa Theo** is a divers' island with a dive camp. **Pulau Antuk Timur** and **Pulau Antuk Barat** are separated by a small channel and both house the fanciest resort on the islands with the best facilities.

Places to Stay All the resorts have individual bungalows with attached bathrooms, and provide water sport facilities, including diving. While comfortable, none are international-standard resorts despite the high prices. Most of the resorts offer packages that include buffet-only meals and transport. Weekends are up to 50% more expensive than prices quoted below.

otok Island Resort, 3rd floor, Duta Merlin Shopping Arcade, Jl Gajah Mada 3-5 (☎ 362948). Packages start at US$75 per person.
Matahari Resort, PT Jakarta International Hotels Management, suite 103, Hotel Borobudur Inter-Continental, Jl Lapangan Banteng Selatan (☎ 3800521). Bungalow rooms cost US$60 to US$80 per person, including all meals.
Pulau Ayer Resort, PT Sarotama Prima Perkasa, Jl Ir H Juanda III/6 (☎ 3842031). Spacious, very comfortable cottages range from US$81 to US$231.
Pulau Bididari Resort, Marina Ancol, Taman Impian Jaya Ancol (☎ 680048). Simple cottages accommodating up to four people cost US$75 to US$100.
Pulau Laki Resort, PT Fadent Gema Scorpio, Jl HOS Cokroaminoto 116 (☎ 3144885). Cottages from US$70 to US$140; packages start at US$60.
Pulau Pelangi Resort, PT Pulau Seribu Paradise, Jl Wahid Hasyim 69 (☎ 335535). Older bungalows cost US$65 to US$110, or full-board packages are US$80 per person.
Pulau Putri Resort, PT Buana Bintang Samudra, Jl Sultan Agung 21 (☎ 8281093). Cottages start at US$60 and go up to US$115 for excellent, Balinese-style cottages; including meals, the package rate is US$70 per person.

Pulau Sepa Resort, PT Pulau Sepa Permai, Jl Kali Besar Barat 29 (☎ 6928828). Air-con bungalows from US$85 to US$105 are comfortable, though fairly basic for the price.
Pulau Seribu Marine Resort, PT Pantara Wisata Jaya, Jl Jen Sudirman Kav 3-4 (☎ 5723161). On Pulau Antuk Timur and Pulau Antuk Barat islands, this is the most upmarket resort; rooms start at US$125/150 and full-board packages are available.

Getting There & Away The resorts have daily boats from Jakarta's Ancol Marina for guests and day trippers, usually leaving around 8 or 9 am and returning around 3 pm. Boats to Pulau Laki Resort leave from Tanjung Kait, 40 km west of Jakarta. The resorts provide speedboats, and even the furthest islands take only a little over two hours to reach. Day trips to the resort include transport, entry and usually lunch – US$15 (US$17.50 weekends) to Pulau Bidadari up to US$60 to Pulau Seribu Marine Resort.

West Java

The province of West Java has a population of 38.3 million, an area of 46,229 sq km and Bandung is its capital. It is historically known as Sunda, the home of the Sundanese people and their culture.

Away from Jakarta and the flat, hot coastline to the north, West Java is predominantly mountainous and agricultural, with lush green valleys and high volcanic peaks surrounding the capital, Bandung, at the core of the region. West Java is also strongly Islamic, yet in the remote Kendeng mountains there is still a small isolated community known as the Badui, believed to be descendants of the ancient Sundanese who fled from Islam more than 400 years ago. The name Sunda is of Sanskrit origin and means 'pure' or 'white'.

For travellers, West Java has tended to be a place to whizz through between Jakarta and destinations east, but, apart from its historic and cultural centres, West Java has a good beach resort at Pangandaran and a fine

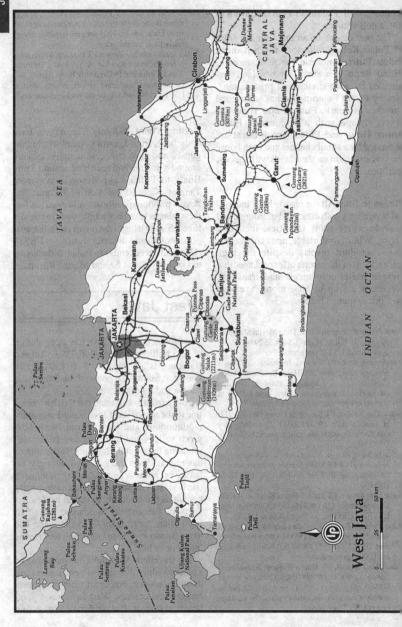

West Java

ackwater trip along the coastal lagoons to Central Java. Other major attractions, though remote and isolated, are the famous Krakatau off the west coast and the unique Ujung Kulon National Park in the south-west of the province.

HISTORY

Early in its history, Sunda was primarily dependent on overseas trade. It was not only an important spice centre in its own right but also a transhipment point for trade with Asia. West Java was the first contact point in Indonesia for the Dutch, and earlier it was one of the first regions to come into contact with Indian traders and their culture.

Ancient stone inscriptions record an early Hindu influence during the reign of King Purnawarman of Taruma, and one of his rock edicts can be seen near Bogor. In the 7th century Taruma was destroyed by the powerful Sumatran-based Buddhist kingdom of Sriwijaya. Much later, Hinduism reasserted itself alongside Buddhism when the Pajajarans ruled the region. They're chiefly remembered for constructing the first trading settlement on the site of Old Batavia when it was called Sunda Kelapa, and for establishing trading relations with the Portuguese.

The first half of the 16th century saw the military expansion of the Muslim state of Demak, and in 1524 Muslim power first made itself felt in West Java. In that year Demak's leader, Sunan Gunungjati, took the port of Banten and then Sunda Kelapa. Some time after 1552 he became the first of the kings of Cirebon, which today is the least visited and thus the most surprising of Java's surviving sultanates. Banten, on the other hand, was the maritime capital of the only Muslim state to remain independent of the great Javanese power, Mataram, but today it is little more than a small fishing village.

After the fall of Melaka in 1511 Chinese, Arabs and Indians poured into Banten, and it became a major trading centre for Muslim merchants who made use of the Sunda Straits (Selat Sunda) to avoid the Portuguese. Gunungjati's successor, Hasanuddin, spread Banten's authority to the pepper-producing

district of Lampung in south Sumatra. His son, Maulana Yusuf, finally conquered the inland Hindu kingdom of Pajajaran in 1579 and so carved out a huge slice of Sunda as Banten's own domain.

Towards the end of the century Banten felt the first impact of a new force – the Europeans. In 1596 the Dutch made their first appearance at Banten, in 1600 the English established an East India Company trading post and two years later the Dutch formed a counterpart company, the VOC. Banten naturally became a centre of fierce Anglo-Dutch competition, and the Dutch soon moved out and seized Jakarta instead, henceforth to be their capital as Batavia.

The VOC's most formidable opponent was the Mataram Empire which was extending its power over parts of West Java, but Banten, so close to their own headquarters, remained a troublesome rival. It not only harboured foreign competitors but a powerful ruling house. Hostilities reached their peak with the accession of Banten's greatest ruler, Sultan Agung, in 1651. With the help of European captains, Agung established an impressive trading network. He defied both Mataram and the VOC on more than one occasion before civil war within the ruling house led to Dutch intervention and his defeat and capture in 1683.

By the end of the 17th century Dutch power had taken a great step forward in the west, and throughout the colonial era West Java remained under more direct control than the rest of the country. It was closer to Batavia but, more importantly, much of the land was ceded to the Dutch by Mataram in return for military aid, while in Central and East Java the kingdoms became Dutch protectorates.

SUNDANESE ARTS
Music

The most characteristic Sundanese instrument is the *kecapi*, accompanied by the *suling*. The kecapi is a type of lute (it looks like a dulcimer) which is plucked; the suling is a soft-toned bamboo flute which fades in and out of the long vibrating notes of the kecapi. Another traditional instrument is the *angklung* – a device of bamboo pieces of differing lengths and diameter loosely suspended in a bamboo frame, which is shaken to produce hollow echoing sounds. Originally the angklung was tuned to a five note scale but it's now being revived using western octaves and can be played by a single performer or a large orchestra. In Cirebon there's a variation on Bandung-style kecapi-suling music, called *tarling* because it makes use of gui*tar* and su*ling*.

Another traditional Sundanese music form is *gamelan degung*. This dynamic gamelan style is played by a small ensemble similar to the Central Javanese gamelan with the addition of the *degung*, which is a set of small suspended gongs, and the suling. It is less soporific and more rhythmic than Central Javanese gamelan music, yet not as hectic as the Balinese forms.

Nowadays, West Java is famous for the more modern music and dance form called Jaipongan, which is found mostly in Bandung and Jakarta. Jaipongan features dynamic drumming coupled with erotic and sometimes humorous dance movements that include elements of *pencak silat* (Indonesian martial arts) and even New York-style break dancing. Jaipongan dance/music is a rather recent derivation of a more traditional Sundanese form called Ketuktilu, in which a group of professional female dancers (sometimes prostitutes) dance for male spectators. The newer form involves males and females dancing alone and together, although in lengthy performances Jaipongan songs are usually interspersed with the older Ketuktilu style.

Other Sundanese dance forms include Longser, Joker and Ogel. Longser and Joker are couples' dances which involve the passing of a sash between the couples. Ogel is an extremely difficult form that features very slow dance movements. Traditional Ogel is in danger of dying out, because few younger performers are patient enough to endure the many years of training required to master the subtle movements.

Wayang Golek

Although the wayang golek puppet play can be seen elsewhere on Java, it is traditionally associated with West Java and the Sundanese prefer it to the shadow play. First used in north-coast towns for Muslim propaganda, this type of puppet play was Islamic and a popular, robust parody of the stylised aristocratic wayang kulit play. In the early 19th century a Sundanese prince of Sumedang had a set of wooden puppets made to correspond exactly to the wayang kulit puppets of the Javanese courts. With these he was able to perform the Hindu epics with the traditional splendour of his rivals, but at the same time preserve his regional identity by using puppets long associated with anti-Javanese art. In West Java the stories are still usually based on the *Mahabharata* and *Ramayana* legends, and the puppets are larger and more vivid than those found in Central Java.

JAKARTA TO MERAK

Most visitors just head straight through from Jakarta to Merak on their way to (or from) Sumatra, but along this route you can also branch off and head for the west coast.

The Jakarta to Merak road runs through flat coastal area with plenty of industrial development. It's one of the busiest on Java, with a great deal of traffic of all types. Getting out of Jakarta from Kalideres can be slow but once on the toll road it is a quick journey.

Serang

Serang, 90 km west of Jakarta, is a crossroads town and the only reason to stop here is if you are visiting Banten. Serang has some very basic hotels, but if you take an early-morning bus from Jakarta and a late afternoon bus back (or on to the west coast) you're going to have all the time in the world to fit in a trip to explore Banten's ruins.

Getting There & Away Buses run to/from Jakarta (Kalideres bus terminal; 2000 rp, 1½ hours) and Merak (1000 rp; one hour). Patas buses between Jakarta and Merak bypass Serang, which is south of the

PETER TURNER

...hip mast, Karimunjawa, Central Java.

Java

Top: Schooners moored at Sunda Kelapa, Kota, Jakarta.
Middle: A fishing boat, Thousand Islands.
Bottom Left: A man cleaning the hull of a schooner, Sunda Kelapa.
Bottom Right: A local woman at Sunda Kelapa.

ighway. From Serang minibuses run to
Banten for 500 rp. Buses also go to Labuan;
or Anyer and the coast road, first take a bus
o Cilegon.

Banten

Due north of Serang, on the coast, are the few
ragments of the great maritime capital of the
Banten sultanate, where the Dutch and
English first landed on Java to secure trade
nd struggle for economic supremacy.

Banten reached its peak during the reign
f Sultan Agung (1651-83) but he unwisely
eclared war on the Dutch in Batavia in
680. Before he could make a move, internal
onflict within the royal house led to Dutch
ntervention on behalf of the ambitious
rown prince. Agung fled Banten but finally
urrendered in 1683 and his defeat marked
he real beginning of Dutch territorial
xpansion on Java. Not only was Banten's
ndependence at an end but its English East
ndia Company rivals were driven out,
vhich effectively destroyed British interests
n Java.

The Dutch maintained trading interests in
Banten for a time, but they did a good job of
emolishing the place in the 19th century.
Then the coastline silted up and Banten
ecame a ghost town. Banten today is just a
mall dusty fishing village.

The chief landmark of a prosperous era is
he 16th century **Mesjid Agung** mosque,
vhich dominates the village. This is the main
ight in Banten, and is a good example of
arly Islamic architecture, though the mos-
ue's great white lighthouse of a minaret was
eputedly designed by a Chinese Muslim.

Next to the mosque is an **archaeological
nuseum** (open from 9 am to 4 pm, closed
Monday), with a modest collection of mostly
lay artefacts found in the area and weapons,
ncluding a few of the long, iron, chained
pikes which the 'Debus players' are famous
or. Banten has long been a centre for prac-
itioners of the Debus tradition, which is
upposed to have come from India. These
slamic ascetics engage in masochistic activ-
ies such as plunging sharp weapons into
heir bodies (without drawing blood!), and

are able to control pain and fear by the
strength of their faith. It's said that in Banten
this was originally part of the training of the
invincible special soldiers to the court.

Directly across from the mosque is the
large grass-covered site of Hasanuddin's fortified palace, the **Surosowan**, which was
wrecked in the bloody civil war during the
reign of Sultan Agung and rebuilt, only to be
razed to the ground by the Dutch in 1832.

Other points of interest around the mosque
include the massive ruins of **Fort Speelwijk**
to the north-west, which now overlook an
expanse of sand-silt marsh, although at one
time it stood on the sea's edge. The fort was
built by the Dutch in 1682 and finally abandoned by Governor-General Daendels at the
beginning of the 19th century. Opposite the
entrance to the fort is a **Chinese temple**,
dating from the 18th century, which is still in
use. Back along the road to Serang are the
huge crumbling walls and archways of the
Kaibon palace, and near it is the **tomb of
Maulana Yusuf**, who died in 1580.

Getting There & Away The usual way to
reach Banten is to take a bus to Serang, 10
km south of Banten, and then a minibus (500
rp; half an hour) which will drop you right
by the mosque. A slightly quicker alternative
is to take any bus between Jakarta and Merak
and get off at the mosque in Kramatwatu
village on the main highway, from where an
ojek (2000 rp) will take you the five km to
Banten.

Pulau Dua Bird Sanctuary

Off the coast at Banten, Pulau Dua is one of
Indonesia's major bird sanctuaries. The
island has a large resident population –
mainly herons, storks and cormorants – but
peak time is between March and July when
great numbers of migratory birds flock here
for the breeding season. At low tide the
island may be accessible by land now that the
mudflats between it and the mainland have
silted up; otherwise it's a half hour boat ride
from the Karanghantu harbour in Banten. A
PHPA (national park) guard is stationed on

the island and there's a watchtower and guesthouse, but if you are planning to stay bring both food and water. Tours are arranged from Carita.

MERAK

Right on the north-western tip of Java, 140 km from Jakarta, Merak is the terminal for ferries shuttling to and from Bakauheni on the south-eastern end of Sumatra. Merak is just an arrival and departure point, and most people pass straight through this small, noisy village.

Pantai Florida is a reasonable beach five km north of Merak, but the west coast beaches to the south have more appeal and plenty of facilities.

Places to Stay

If you do have a reason to stay, the *Hotel Anda* (☎ 71041) on Jl Florida (Pulorida) has reasonably clean rooms with fan and mandi from 10,000 rp, or air-con rooms for 25,000 rp. The *Hotel Robinson* next door is similarly priced but not as good. These standard losmen are just across the train line opposite the bus terminal.

The *Merak Beach Hotel* (☎ 71015) is two km out of town on the road to Jakarta. Comfortable but small air-con units are sandwiched between the bad beach and the noisy highway. Singles/doubles are overpriced at 118,000/168,000 rp.

Getting There & Away

The bus and train stations in Merak are right at the ferry dock. Frequent normal/air-con buses run between Merak and Jakarta (3000/5000 rp; three hours). Most terminate at Jakarta's Kalideres bus terminal, but buses also run to Pulo Gadung and Kampung Rambutan bus terminals. From Merak buses also go to Bogor, Bandung, Cirebon, Yogya, Solo and Banjar.

Local minibuses or larger, more comfortable buses leave from the front of the bus terminal and go to Serang (800 rp) and Cilegon (500 rp). Buses to Labuan via Anyer and Carita leave from the Cilegon bus terminal, or from Merak it is quicker to get down

on the western side of Cilegon at th Simpang Tiga turn-off to Anyer and catch bus from there.

Misnamed *cepat* (fast) trains depart fror Jakarta's Tanah Abang train station fc Merak at 7 am and 2.35 pm, and from Mera they depart at 6 am and 2 pm. They take long four hours.

Boat Ferries between Merak and Bakauher on Sumatra leave every 36 minutes aroun the clock. The trip takes 1½ hours and cos 1500 rp in deck class, 2600 rp in 1st clas The new 'Superjet' service (6000 rp; 3 minutes) leaves every 70 minutes from 8 ar to 4 pm.

WEST COAST BEACHES

At Cilegon, south-east of Merak, the roa branches south to Anyer and runs close to th sea all the way to Labuan. The road passe Cilegon's massive steel works and chemica cement and other industrial plants until reaches Anyer market. From there the roa runs south to Labuan along a flat, gree coastal strip bordered by a rocky, reef-line coast that is punctuated by stretches of white sand beach.

This picturesque coast has masses o coconut palms and banana trees, and becaus of its easy access by toll road from Jakarta it is a popular weekend beach strip. Thoug not world beaters, the beaches are good an make a fine escape from Jakarta's heat an crowds. The main place of interest is Carita where you can arrange tours to Krakatau an Ujung Kulon National Park.

The area is sparsely populated with smal fishing settlements and coconut ports. Thi is perhaps simply because the land isn't suit able for intensive rice agriculture, but it' also said that survivors of the Krakatau erup tion, and succeeding generations, believed i to be a place of ill omen and never returned

Anyer

Anyer, 12 km south-west of Cilegon, is a upmarket beach resort popular with Jakart residents. Anyer was once the biggest Dutc port in Selat Sunda before being totall destroyed by tidal waves generated by Krakatau. The Anyer lighthouse was built by the Dutch at the instigation of Queen Wilhelmina in 1885 after the disaster.

From here you can hire a boat to make the 1½ hour trip to explore the deserted island of **Sangiang**, which has coral reefs.

Karang Bolong

There's another good beach here, 11 km south of Anyer and 30 km north of Labuan, where a huge stand of rock forms a natural archway from the land to the sea.

Carita

This is a popular base for visits to the Krakatau islands and the Ujung Kulon National Park. The wide, sandy beach has good swimming, and there are plenty of opportunities to go wandering along the beach or inland. About two km from Carita across the rice paddies you can see the village of **Sindanglaut** (End of the Sea) where the giant tsunami of 1883 ended.

The **Hutan Wisata Carita** is a forest reserve with walks through the hills and jungle. The **Curug Gendang** waterfall is a three hour return hike through the reserve.

Organised Tours

In Carita, the Black Rhino (☎ 81072), the privately run Tourist Information Service (☎ 81330), opposite Hotel Desiana, and Krakatau Ujung Kulon Tour & Travel (☎ 81124) at the Rakata Hostel have almost identical tours to Krakatau (from 45,000 rp per person), Ujung Kulon (from US$150 per person for four days/three nights) as well as Badui villages, Pulau Dua and even Jakarta. They can also arrange boat hire to nearby coral reefs and islands.

The Pantai Carita hotel in Carita and the Mambruk Quality Resort and Marina Village in Anyer (see below) arrange quite expensive trips to Krakatau and have dive shops. The best diving is in Ujung Kulon National Park, and Krakatau and Pulau Sanghiang also have diving.

Places to Stay

Because of the easy access from Jakarta, the resorts along this stretch of coast are overpriced, but standards are generally high. Dozens of hotels and villas (many private but some for rent) are spaced out along the 30 km stretch from Anyer to Carita. Prices drop the further south you head from Anyer, and the only cheap accommodation is found in Carita.

On weekends the hotels fill up and prices are 20% to 30% more than the weekday rates quoted here, and 21% tax and service is added. During the week, discounts are often available and some bargaining may be required.

Anyer Most hotels in Anyer have swimming pools, restaurants and rooms with air-con, parabola (satellite) TV and hot-water showers. They are spaced out over a five km stretch and start just south of the Anyer market, but the better places are past the Anyer lighthouse. The first one south of the lighthouse is *Mambruk Quality Resort* (☎ 601602), with large gardens, a swimming pool, tennis courts and diving facilities. It is the best in Anyer and excellent rooms with all the trimmings range from US$95 up to the big cottages for US$275. It has manufactured a small beach, but the coast is still rocky here and unsuitable for swimming.

A little further south, *Marina Village* (☎ 601288) is similar but not as good. It has a boat marina and a dive shop. Speedboats can be hired for a mere US$500 per day.

Keep heading south until you reach *Ancotte* (☎ 601556), right on a fine stretch of sandy beach, the best in Anyer. This hotel is moderately priced and very popular with expats, and there is a pool. Rooms cost from US$50, or large, attractive cottages, many with kitchens, are from US$95 to US$120. Rates double on weekends.

The biggest place by far is the *Marbella* (☎ 602756) condominium/hotel, which is nearing completion.

Karang Bolong Coming in to Karang Bolong from Anyer, *Hotel Anyer Hometel*

(☎ 601779) is on the beach and has a pool. Rooms start at US$85. Some need maintenance, but this is still one of the best places in Karang Bolang.

Lalita Cottages (☎ 4806514) is on the beach right next to the recreational park. Large two bedroom cottages with kitchen are quite simple but comfortable and reasonably priced at 130,000 rp.

Closer to Carita, the friendly *Matahari Park Resort* (☎ 42167) has a pool. Well-appointed air-con rooms facing the beach start at 109,000 rp, but discounts are available during the week.

Carita Heading north from Labuan, the usual access point, the four star *Pantai Carita* (☎ 81127) is at the five km mark. It is the most luxurious on the coast, with rooms starting at US$85 (US$110 on Saturday), but the beach fronts a rocky reef.

Further north past Carita village is a sweeping bay with one of the best beaches on the coast and good swimming. This is the area for budget and mid-range accommodation, though prices are still high and new developments are taking over.

Past the eight km mark is the huge, new *Resor Lippo Carita* (☎ 5461180), a product of nonexistent planning regulations and/or bribery. This condominium/hotel complex hogs the best stretch of beach for almost a km, destroying Carita's character in the process. 'Soft opening' rates starting at 120,000 rp are cheap, but expect prices to rise.

Opposite is the popular *Rakata Hostel* (☎ 81171). Bright rooms with bathroom for 35,000 and 65,000 rp are overpriced but a reasonable deal in expensive Carita. A good restaurant is attached, and it runs tours to Ujung Kulon and Krakatau.

Further north is the *Hotel Wira Carita* (☎ 81116), which has a swimming pool. Simple rooms with mandi cost 45,000 rp or 70,000 rp with air-con; cottages are 200,000 rp. Rates rise on weekends and skyrocket during holiday periods.

Around the nine km mark on a good stretch of beach, the friendly *Pondok Pan-dawa* (☎ 82193) has simple, overpriced rooms with mandi for 40,000 rp (50,000 rp on weekends). More expensive cottages are also available.

Nearby, the *Carita Baka Baka* (☎ 81126) also has a good beach and a pleasant restaurant. Three bedroom bungalows with kitchens are way overpriced at 300,000 rp, but it rents good rooms with shower for 48,000 rp (60,000 rp when it's busy).

Just past the Hutan Wisata Carita, across from the public beach park, the *Badak Hitam* (Black Rhino) (☎ 81072) is a budget favourite undergoing renovation. Tours to Krakatau and Ujung Kulon are organised.

Next door is the *Sunset View* (☎ 81075), where clean rooms with mandi cost 20,000 and 25,000 rp, the cheapest in Carita. Next along is the *Ratih Homestay* (☎ 81137), where spartan rooms cost 25,000 rp or 35,000 rp with mandi – try bargaining.

Places to Eat

The coast doesn't have a lot of restaurants and dining is usually done at the hotels, which can work out to be quite expensive at the higher priced establishments. In Anyer and Karang Bolang, unless you have your own transport, you virtually have to eat at your hotel because everything is so spread out.

In Carita, a few places are opposite the Resor Lippo Carita. *Warung Kita* is basic but cheap, or *Restaurant Tetty's* is fancier but still reasonably priced. The beachside restaurant at the *Carita Baka Baka* is very pleasant and the *Rakata Hostel* has decent food. Further north around the 14 km mark, the *Cafe de Paris* is an oddity – it has air-con and European food, and it accepts credit cards.

Getting There & Away

To get to Carita from Jakarta, take a bus to Labuan and then a colt or angkot to Carita (500 rp). Overcharging is common.

Most visitors to Anyer go by car from Jakarta – 2½ to three hours via the toll road and the turn-off at Cilegon. By bus from Jakarta, take a Merak bus and get off at Cilegon from where infrequent buses run to

Labuan via Anyer and Karang Bolong. Minibuses are much more frequent and run to Anyer market from where you can catch other minibuses further south. It usually takes three minibuses to get to Carita and Labuan from Cilegon.

LABUAN

The dreary little port of Labuan is merely a jumping-off point for Carita or the Ujung Kulon National Park.

Ujung Kulon Permits

Wanawisata Alamhayati (☎ 81217), about one km from the centre of town on the road to Carita, is the private company that books the accommodation at Ujung Kulon National Park and will also arrange permits. The Labuan PHPA office, one km further along the same road, is also helpful for information, especially if you want to visit Ujung Kulon independently.

Places to Stay & Eat

The very basic *Hotel Citra Ayu* and the slightly better *Hotel Caringin* are both under the illusion that Labuan is a desirable place to stay and will charge whatever they can – about 15,000 rp per room is reasonable. The *Rawa Yana Hotel* is the best hotel in town and has rooms with bath from 22,500 rp, but Carita is only a few km up the road and has much better accommodation.

Getting There & Away

Frequent buses depart from Kalideres bus terminal in Jakarta for Labuan (3100 rp; 3½ hours) via Serang and Pandeglang. Angkots for Carita (500 rp; half hour) leave from the market, 100m from the Labuan bus terminal, as do minibuses to Sumur (4000 rp; 1½ hours). Other buses to/from Labuan include: Bogor (3500 rp; four hours); Bandung (6000 rp; seven hours); Rangkasbitung (1300 rp; 1½ hours); Serang (1400 rp; 1½ hours); Merak (2000 rp; two hours); and destinations further afield such as Garut, Banjar and Kuningan. Frequent buses go from Labuan to Jakarta, Bogor, Rangkasbitung and Serang, but other departures

are less frequent and usually leave in the morning only.

KRAKATAU

The legendary Krakatau lies in the Selat Sunda straits – 50 km from the West Java coast and 40 km from Sumatra. Today only a small part of the original volcano remains, but when Krakatau blew itself apart in 1883, in one of the world's greatest and most catastrophic eruptions, the effects were recorded

---

The Formation of Krakatau

Thousands of years ago Krakatau built up a cone-shaped mountain which eventually formed a huge caldera over six km across and mostly beneath water level. The peaks of the rim projected as four small islands – Sertung on the north-west, Lang and the Polish Hat on the north-east, and Rakata ('Crab' in old Javanese) on the south-east. Later volcanic activity threw up two cones, Perbunan and Danan, which merged with the Rakata cone to form a single island – Krakatau – that extended almost completely across the caldera. When an eruption in 1883 ended, Lang and the Polish Hat had disappeared and only a stump of the original Krakatau with the caldera of Rakata remained above sea level. ■

Krakatau

······· Islands before 1883 eruption

0   1.5   3 km

far beyond Selat Sunda and it achieved instant and lasting infamy.

For centuries Krakatau had been a familiar nautical landmark for much of the world's maritime traffic which was funnelled through the narrow Selat Sunda straits. The volcano had been dormant since 1680 and was widely regarded as extinct, but from May through to early August in 1883 passing ships reported moderate activity. By 26 August Krakatau was raging and the explosions became more and more violent.

At 10 am on 27 August 1883 Krakatau erupted with the biggest bang ever recorded on earth. On the island of Rodriguez, more than 4600 km to the south-west, a police chief reported hearing the booming of 'heavy guns from eastward'; in Alice Springs, Australia, 3500 km to the south-east, residents also reported hearing strange explosions from the north-west.

With its cataclysmic explosions, Krakatau sent up a record column of ash 80 km high and threw into the air nearly 20 cubic km of rock. Ash fell on Singapore 840 km to the north and on ships as far as 6000 km away; darkness covered the Selat Sunda straits from 10 am on 27 August until dawn the next day.

Far more destructive were the great ocean waves triggered by the collapse of Krakatau's cones into its empty belly. A giant tsunami more than 40m high swept over the nearby shores of Java and Sumatra, and the sea wave's passage was recorded far from Krakatau, reaching Aden in 12 hours over a distance 'travelled by a good steamer in 12 days'. Measurable wave effects were even said to have reached the English Channel. Coastal Java and Sumatra were devastated: 165 villages were destroyed and more than 36,000 people were killed.

The following day a telegram sent to Singapore from Batavia (160 km east of Krakatau) reported odd details such as 'fish dizzy and caught with glee by natives'! Three months later the dust thrown into the atmosphere caused such vivid sunsets in the USA that fire engines were being called out to quench the apparent fires, and for three years it continued to circle the earth, creating strange and spectacular sunsets.

The astonishing return of life to the devastated islands has been the subject of scientific study ever since. Not a single plant was found on Krakatau a few months after the event; 100 years later – although the only fauna are snakes, insects, rats, bats and birds – it seems almost as though the vegetation was never disturbed.

Krakatau basically blew itself to smithereens but, roughly where the 1883 eruption began, Anak Krakatau (Child of Krakatau) has been vigorously growing ever since its first appearance in 1928. It has a restless and uncertain temperament, sending out showers of glowing rocks and belching smoke and ashes.

Boats can land on the east side, but it is no longer possible to climb right up the cinder cones to the caldera, after Krakatau belched a load of molten rock on one unfortunate tourist who ventured too close. Krakatau is still a menacing volcano, and in its more active phases, intermittent rumblings can be heard on quiet nights from the west coast beaches.

Getting There & Away

Most visitors to Krakatau come from Carita or the other beach resorts on the west coast of Java. However, Krakatau officially lies in Sumatra's Lampung Province and it is slightly shorter, and cheaper, to reach Krakatau from the small port of Kalianda, 30 km north of the ferry terminal at Bakauheni (see the Sumatra chapter for details).

During the rainy season (November to March) there are strong currents and rough seas, but even during the dry season strong south-east winds can whip up the swells and make a crossing inadvisable. When weather conditions are fine it's a long one day trip, four hours there and four hours back, but having visited Krakatau we'd say it's definitely worth the effort – if you can hire a safe boat. A few years ago, Lonely Planet almost lost one of its writers, Joe Cummings, who spent the night adrift on such a boat in high swells along with 10 other travellers, though safety standards have since improved. Most boats now at least have life jackets and possibly radios.

By far the easiest way to reach Krakatau is to take a tour from Carita. The tour operators (see under Carita earlier in this section) have a variety of boats, depending on how many people they can band together. Usually it will be on a smaller, adapted fishing boat taking four to 10 people for around 450,000 rp per boat. During the peak July/August tourist season a boat goes every day or two. In the quieter periods, it can take longer to fill a tour and prices may be higher. The large hotels also arrange expensive tours.

It is cheaper to charter a boat yourself from Labuan or Carita, but make sure you get a seaworthy vessel. The PHPA office in Labuan may be able to help.

UJUNG KULON NATIONAL PARK

Ujung Kulon National Park is on the remote south-western tip of Java, covering about 760 sq km of land area, including the large Pulau Panaitan and the smaller offshore islands of Peucang and Handeuleum. Because of its isolation and difficult access, Ujung Kulon has remained an outpost of primeval forest and untouched wilderness on heavily developed Java. The park presents some fine opportunities for hiking and wildlife spotting, and has some excellent beaches with intact coral reefs. Despite its remoteness and the relatively high cost of visiting the park, it is one of the most popular national parks on Java.

Ujung Kulon is best known as the last refuge on Java for the once plentiful one horned rhinoceros, now numbering only around 60. The shy Javan rhino, however, is an extremely rare sight and you are far more likely to come across less-exotic animals such as *banteng* (wild cattle), wild pigs, otters, squirrels, leaf monkeys and gibbons. Panthers also live in the forest, and crocodiles in the river estuaries, but these too are a rare sight. Green turtles nest in some of the bays and there is a wide variety of bird life. On Pulau Peucang, rusa deer, long-tailed macaques and big monitor lizards are

common, and there is good snorkelling around coral reefs.

The main park area is on the peninsula, which is mostly dense lowland rainforest and a mixture of scrub, grassy plains, swamps, pandanus palms and long stretches of sandy beach on the west and south coasts. Walking trails follow the coast around much of the peninsula and loop round Gunung Payung on the western tip.

Information

Secure your permit and book accommodation in Labuan. Pick up a copy of the excellent *Visitor's Guidebook to the Trails of Ujung Kulon National Park*. Entry to the park costs 4500 rp.

The best time to visit Ujung Kulon is the dry season (April to October), when the sea is generally calm and the reserve is not so boggy. Malaria has been reported in Ujung Kulon; antimalarials are advisable, and appropriate measures to prevent mosquito bites should be taken.

Guides must be hired for hiking in the park. The PHPA in Tamanjaya will arrange this for around 10,000 rp per day, plus food. Gili Peucang has a restaurant but otherwise bring your own food for yourself and your guide, which the guide can cook. Bring lightweight food, such as packaged noodles, and drinking water if you will be doing a lot of trekking. Limited supplies are available in Tamanjaya, but it is best to stock up in Labuan.

Exploring the Park

Access to the park is usually by boat from Labuan or Sumur to Gili Handeuleum or Gili Peucang. Alternatively, Tamanjaya can be reached by boat or a bad road. From Tamanjaya it is a three day hike across to the west coast and on to Gili Peucang.

From Gili Handeuleum boats or canoes can be hired for the short crossing to the mainland. From Cigenter, on the mainland opposite Gili Handeuleum, a hiking trail leads six to eight hours along the coast to the Jamang rangers' hut, where it is possible to overnight. From Jamang it is a full day's hike to Cidaon, on the mainland directly opposite Gili Peucang.

Cidaon links up with the trail to Tamanjaya, or another coastal trail leads to the westernmost tip of mainland Java.

From Tamanjaya it is also possible to walk south across the Gunung Honje Range to Cegog village, where homestay accommodation is available, and then along the south coast to Kalejatan or Karang Ranjang and back to Tamanjaya. This is certainly the cheapest way to explore Ujung Kulon, though the main attractions of the park lie to the west.

Remote Pulau Panaitan also has some fine beaches and hiking, though it is known primarily as a surfing destination. Surfing camps accommodate tours.

Places to Stay

Add 15% tax and service to all rates charged in the park.

The guesthouse at Tamanjaya has rooms for US$10/15. The pleasant guesthouse at Gili Handeuleum has doubles/quads for US$15/25, but accommodation is limited and should be booked well in advance. Gili Peucang has doubles in the old guesthouse for US$30, or quite luxurious accommodation with air-con, hot water and refrigerators in the new guesthouses for US$60 and

Rhinoceros: Standing 1½ metres tall and weighing over 1500kg, the javan one-horned rhino once roamed from India through to Java, but now exists only at Ujung Kulon National Park. Sightings are very rare but numbers of this endangered species have increased to around 60.

US$80 a double. Gili Peucang also has a restaurant.

Advance booking is essential for accommodation at both islands, particularly for weekends. Bookings can be made through PT Wanawisata Alamhayati (☎ Labuan 81217 or Jakarta (021) 5710392), a private company which runs the accommodation in conjunction with the PHPA.

You can camp within the park , or wooden huts along the trails accommodate hikers. A tent is handy for the hikes, though not essential for small groups.

Getting There & Away

The easiest way to get to the park is by boat from Labuan or Sumur, if you can afford it. PT Wanawisata Alamhayati has ceased its regular boat service from Labuan to Tamanjaya, Gili Handeuleum and Gili Peucang, and it appears unlikely that it will resume. This means you'll have to charter a boat from Labuan for around 350,000 rp one way. As with boat rides to Krakatau, it can be a rough and dangerous crossing, so make sure you hire a seaworthy boat.

A cheaper but gruelling alternative is to take a colt from Labuan south to Sumur (4000 rp; 4½ hours). From here boats can be hired to Gili Handeuleum for about 150,000 rp, or hunt around for an ojek (10,000 rp; 40 minutes) to Tamanjaya. In Tamanjaya, local boats (maximum 10 people) to Gili Handeuleum can be hired for around 75,000 rp one way.

The expense and hassle of travelling to the park independently soon make a tour look worthwhile. Those from Carita cost around US$150 (minimum four people) for four days/three nights. Accommodation is in tents, and you will be taken to Sumur by car, by boat to Gili Handeuleum, then trek around the northern peninsula and its beaches for two days. (See under Carita earlier in this chapter for details.) Travel agents in Jakarta also arrange tours.

BADUI VILLAGES

When Islam swept through Java, the temples were sacked and the outward manifestations of Hinduism all but disappeared. Although throughout the mountains of Java, small isolated pockets of the old religions remain. The most mysterious of all these groups are the Badui. They have preserved their traditions through a strict policy of isolation, shunning visitors and attempts by the government to make them part of the modern world.

Badui religion is a blend of animism and Hinduism, and the Badui priests are regarded as powerful mystics. This is particularly true of the Badui Dalam (Inner Badui) or 'White Baud' as they are known because of their white dress. The three inner villages of Cibeo, Cikartawana and Cikeusik are off limits to outsiders and are surrounded by Badui Luar (Outer Badui) villages that have contact with the outside world and act as intermediaries for the Badui Dalam.

Permits are required to visit the Badui villages, access is difficult and a guide is necessary. Permits must be obtained from the tourist office (Dinas Pariwisata), Jl Pahlawan 13, Rangkasbitung, 64 km east of Labuan. Cibolger, at the border of Badui territory, is the official entry point. In Cibolger it is possible to stay with the village head.

Getting There & Away
Rangkasbitung is easily reached by bus from Labuan (1300 rp; 1½ hours), Jakarta (2500 rp; three hours), Bogor and Serang. The Rangkasbitung bus terminal is over two km from town (300 rp by angkot).

Most visitors to Cibolger tend to be small tour groups that make the trip by minibus; public transport is infrequent and difficult. Tours can be arranged in Carita.

BOGOR
Bogor, 60 km south of Jakarta, is most famous for its botanical gardens. In the days before independence, however, this was the most important Dutch hill station, midway between the mountains and the heat-ridden plains. Governor-General van Imhoff is credited with its discovery in 1745. He built a large country estate which he named Buitenzorg (Without a Care), but it was not until 1811 that it was first used as a country

residence by Sir Stamford Raffles, during the British interregnum, and not until many years later that Bogor became the semiofficial capital.

Raffles judged it as 'a romantic little village', but Bogor has grown and, other than the botanical gardens, its beauty has faded somewhat. Nevertheless, Bogor has become an important centre for scientific research, including botany, agronomy and forestry. Although the town itself has almost become a suburb of Jakarta, it makes a good base for nearby mountain walks. Many people visit the gardens from Jakarta or stop off on their way to Bandung and points further east, but Bogor could also be used as a Jakarta base since it is only about an hour away.

Though Bogor stands at a height of only 290m it's appreciably cooler than Jakarta, but visitors in the wet season should bear in mind the town's nickname: the 'City of Rain'. Bogor has probably the highest annual rainfall on Java and is credited with a record 322 thunderstorms a year.

Information
Bogor's tourist office (☎ 325701), Jl Merak 1, is north of the town, but it moves every year and provides little information anyway. A small branch is at the entrance to the gardens.

Jl Ir H Juanda has plenty of banks for changing money, such as the BNI bank or Bank Central Asia at No 28.

Kebun Raya (Botanical Gardens)
At the heart of Bogor are the huge, world-class botanical gardens, known as the Kebun Raya (Great Garden), covering an area of around 80 hectares. They are said to be the inspiration of Governor-General Raffles, but the spacious grounds of the Istana Bogor (Presidential Palace) were converted to botanical gardens by the Dutch botanist Professor Reinwardt, with assistants from Kew Gardens (London, UK), and officially opened by the Dutch in 1817. It was from these gardens that various colonial cash crops such as tea, cassava, tobacco and cinchona were developed by early Dutch

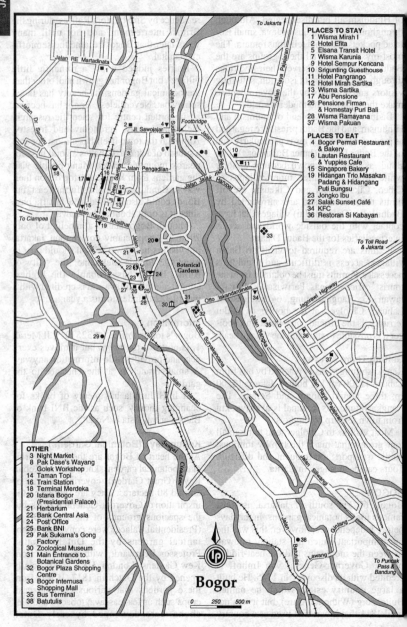

PLACES TO STAY
1 Wisma Mirah I
2 Hotel Efita
5 Elsana Transit Hotel
7 Wisma Karunia
9 Hotel Sempur Kencana
10 Srigunting Guesthouse
11 Hotel Pangrango
12 Hotel Mirah Sartika
13 Wisma Sartika
17 Abu Pensione
26 Pensione Firman
    & Homestay Puri Bali
28 Wisma Ramayana
37 Wisma Pakuan

PLACES TO EAT
4 Bogor Permai Restaurant
   & Bakery
6 Lautan Restaurant
   & Yuppies Cafe
15 Singapore Bakery
19 Hidangan Trio Masakan
    Padang & Hidangang
    Puti Bungsu
23 Jongko Ibu
27 Salak Sunset Café
34 KFC
36 Restoran Si Kabayan

OTHER
3 Night Market
8 Pak Dase's Wayang
   Golek Workshop
14 Taman Topi
16 Train Station
18 Terminal Merdeka
20 Istana Bogor
    (Presidential Palace)
21 Herbarium
22 Bank Central Asia
24 Post Office
25 Bank BNI
29 Pak Sukarna's Gong
    Factory
30 Zoological Museum
31 Main Entrance to
    Botanical Gardens
32 Bogor Plaza Shopping
    Centre
33 Bogor Internusa
    Shopping Mall
35 Bus Terminal
38 Batutulis

To Jakarta

Jalan RE Martadinata

Jalan Jend Sudirman

Jalan Dr Semeru

Footbridge

Jl Sawojajar

Jalan Pengadilan

Jl Dewi Sartika

Jalan Jalak Harupat

Jalan Kapten Muslihat

To Ciampea

Botanical
Gardens

Jalan Ir H Juanda

Jalan Paledang

Jalan Raya Pajajaran

To Toll Road
& Jakarta

Jagorawi Highway

Jl Otto Iskandardinata

Jl Empang

Jalan Surjakencana

Jalan Banjang

Jalan Pahlawan

Sungai Cisadane

Jalan Siliwang

Jalan Raya Pajajaran

Batutulis

To Puncak
Pass &
Bandung

Lawang

Gintang

Bogor

0   250   500 m

researchers during the so-called Forced Cultivation Period in the 19th century. The park is still a major centre for botanical research in Indonesia.

The gardens contain streams and lotus ponds, and more than 15,000 species of trees and plants, including 400 types of magnificent palms. The gardens' orchid houses are reputed to contain more than 3000 orchid varieties, but are not open to the general public. North of the main entrance to the gardens is a small monument in memory of Olivia Raffles who died in 1814 and was buried in Batavia, and further north, near the palace, is a cemetery with Dutch headstones. The cafeteria on the eastern side of the gardens has fine view across the lawns and is a pleasant place for a snack or drink.

The gardens are open between 8 am and 5 pm and, although they tend to be crowded on Sunday, on other days they are a very peaceful escape from the hassles and crowds of Jakarta. The entrance fee is 1500 rp during the week, and 1000 rp on Sunday and holidays. The southern gate is the main entrance; other gates are only open on Sunday and holidays.

Zoological Museum Near the botanical gardens' main entrance, this museum has a motley but interesting collection of zoological oddities, including the skeleton of a blue whale and a stuffed Javan rhinoceros. If you ever heard about the island of Flores having a rat problem, one glance at the stuffed Flores version in the showcase of Indonesian rats will explain why. Admission to the museum is 400 rp, and it's open from 8 am to 4 pm daily.

Istana Bogor (Presidential Palace) In the north-west corner of the botanical gardens, the summer palace of the president was formerly the official residence of the Dutch governors-general from 1870 to 1942. The present huge mansion is not 'Buitenzorg' though; this was destroyed by an earthquake and a new palace was built on the site a few years later in 1856. In colonial days, deer were raised in the parklands to provide meat

for banquets, and through the gates you can still see herds of white-spotted deer roaming on the immaculate lawns. The Dutch elite would come up from the pesthole of Batavia and many huge, glamorous parties were held there. Following independence, the palace was a much-favoured retreat for Soekarno, although Soeharto has ignored it.

Today the building contains Soekarno's huge art collection of paintings and sculptures (which is reputed to lay great emphasis on the female figure), but the palace is only open to the public by prior arrangement. The tourist information centre can arrange tours for groups, or you can write directly to the Head of Protocol at the Istana Negara, Jl Veteran, Jakarta. You need to give at least five days' notice. If a tour is going the tourist information centre will try to include interested individuals. Abu Pensione (see Places to Stay later in this section) also makes regular bookings for tours.

Other Attractions
The **Batutulis** is an inscribed stone dedicated to Sri Baduga Maharaja (1482-1521) by his son King Surawisesa in 1533. Sri Baduga Maharaja was a Pajajaran king accredited with great mystical power. The stone is housed in a small shrine visited by pilgrims. Remove your shoes and pay a small donation before entering. Batutulis is 2.5 km south of the gardens on Jl Batutulis and almost opposite the former home of Soekarno. Soekarno chose this spot for his home supposedly because of the stone's mystical power, but his request to be buried here was ignored by Soeharto who wanted the former president's grave as far away from the capital as possible.

One of the few remaining gongsmiths in West Java is Pak Sukarna, and you can visit his **gong factory** at Jl Pancasan 17. Gongs and other gamelan instruments are smelted over a charcoal fire in the small workshop out the back. A few gongs and wayang golek puppets are on sale in the front showroom. The gong factory is a short walk south from the garden gates down Jl Empang and west

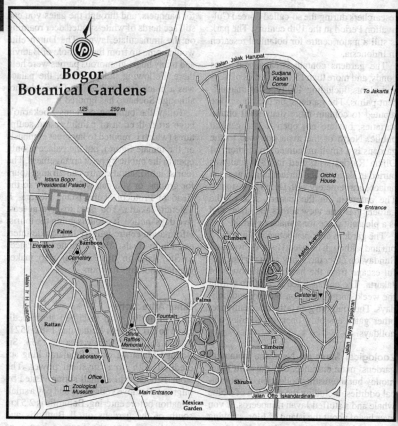

Bogor
Botanical Gardens

0   125   250 m

Jalan Jalak Harupat

Sudjana
Kasan
Corner

To Jakarta

Istana Bogor
(Presidential Palace)

Orchid
House

• Entrance

Palms

• Entrance

Bamboos

Climbers

Cemetery

Jalan H H Juanda

Astrid Avenue

Cafeteria ▼

Palms

Fountain

Rattan

Olivia
Raffles
Memorial

Jalan Raya Pajajaran

Climbers

• Laboratory

Offices

Climbers

Zoological
Museum

Shrubs

Main Entrance

Mexican
Garden

Jalan Otto Iskandardinata

across the river. Look for the 'Pabrik Gong' ('Gong Factory') sign.

Pak Dase makes quality wooden puppets at his **wayang golek workshop** in Lebak Kantin RT 02/VI. You can see them being carved and painted and, of course, they are for sale.

Places to Stay – bottom end

Bogor has a good selection of family-run places which make staying in Bogor a real pleasure, even though a little expensive.

Abu Pensione (☎ 322893), near the train station at Jl Mayor Oking 15, is clean, attractive and pleasantly situated. It overlooks the river and has a good restaurant. It is gradually moving upmarket, and has a variety of rooms starting at 20,000 rp without bath and from 25,000 rp with bath up to 45,000 rp with hot water. It is well set up for travel information and services.

On the other side of the train station, *Wisma Sartika* (☎ 323747), Jl Dewi Sartika 4D, is convenient and well run. Small and dark singles start at 11,000 rp, but doubles from 25,000 to 35,000 rp with shower are better. Breakfast is included.

Just across from the gardens at Jl Ir H Juanda 54, *Wisma Ramayana* (☎ 320364) has the most colonial charm. The rooms from 19,000 to 30,000 rp without bath are average, but rooms with bath from 33,000 to 44,000 rp have style. Breakfast is included.

Around the corner at Jl Paledang 48, the *Pensione Firman* (☎ 323246) is a budget favourite and the cheapest around, with dorm beds at 6000 rp and rooms from 14,000 rp with shared bathroom, from 20,000 rp with bath, all including breakfast. *Homestay Puri Bali* (☎ 317498), next door at No 50, is a quiet place with an attractive garden but is becoming run down. Rooms cost 15,000/20,000 rp with bath.

North of the botanical gardens, *Wisma Karunia* (☎ 323411), Jl Sempur 33-35, is a little out of the way but quiet and reasonably priced at 17,500 rp for doubles with shared bath, and from 25,000 to 35,000 rp for rooms with private bath.

Places to Stay – middle
Wisma Pakuan (☎ 319430), Jl Pakuan 12, is in a large, new family home south-east of the bus terminal. Immaculate rooms with balcony cost 55,000 rp, and 66,000 rp with attached bath and hot water. Breakfast is included.

North-west on the other side of town, *Wisma Mirah I* (☎ 323520), Jl Martadinata 17, is another old-fashioned guesthouse with charm. Rooms range from 28,000 to 60,000 rp.

Two of the best mid-range places can be found near the train station. *Hotel Efita* (☎ 333400), Jl Sawojajar 5, has dazzling, newly renovated rooms for 74,000 rp. VIP rooms with minibar and balcony cost 94,000 rp. *Hotel Mirah Sartika* (☎ 312343), Jl Dewi Sartika 6A, is not as new, but the rooms are spacious and good value. Rooms, all with hot water and TV, range from 40,000 to 71,000 rp, plus 15%.

Places to Stay – top end
The *Hotel Pangrango* (☎ 328670) at Jl Pangrango 23 has a small pool and is currently the best hotel in Bogor. Most air-con rooms

with TV cost 80,000 rp, plus 21% tax and service charge, or suites cost 130,000 rp. Tariffs include breakfast.

Next door, the *Srigunting Guesthouse* (☎ 339661), Jl Pangrango 21, is in a very comfortable house with a garden. Well-appointed rooms cost 75,000 to 125,000 rp, plus 21%.

Places to Eat
Cheap food stalls appear at night along Jl Dewi Sartika and during the day, the Pasar Bogor, the market close to the garden gates, has food stalls and good fruit. In the late afternoon along Jl Raja Permas next to the train station, street vendors cook up delicious snacks such as deep-fried tahu and pisang goreng. Also near the train station, Taman Topi is a recreational park with fun rides for the kids, and the spotless rumah makan here, such as *Tatos Cafe*, have better-than-average Indonesian food and ice juices.

The *Pujasera* is an air-con hawkers' centre on the top floor of the Bogor Plaza shopping centre opposite the entrance to the botanical gardens. *Es Teler KK* is one of the better little eateries, serving inexpensive lunches and good fruit juices.

A good restaurant for Sundanese food is the *Jongko Ibu* opposite the post office at Jl Ir H Juanda 36. Prices are moderate and you can dine buffet-style and try a number of dishes. *Restoran Si Kabayan* (☎ 311849), Jl Bina Marga I No 2, is one of Bogor's most pleasant Sundanese restaurants with individual bamboo huts arranged around an attractive garden. You'll need to order a number of dishes to get your fill, but this restaurant is reasonably priced.

The *Salak Sunset Café*, Jl Paledang 38, attached to the Alliance Française, is a chic little place with river views. Standard Indonesian and European dishes are featured – tasty and cheap enough – but don't expect fine French cuisine.

The *Bogor Permai Restaurant & Bakery*, Jl Jenderal Sudirman 23A, is a large, semi-modern restaurant and bakery complex offering Chinese and western fare, including steaks. The nearby *Lautan Restaurant* at No

15 is just a few tables in a shop serving Chinese cuisine at moderate prices, while most of the building is taken over by the dark, cavernous *Yuppies Cafe*. This bar/restaurant has expensive western dishes, such as steaks and spaghetti, cheaper Chinese and Indonesian food, and nighttime bands.

Bogor also has a *KFC* south of the gardens near the bus terminal, and a *Pizza Hut* in the Bogor Internusa shopping mall on Jl Raya Pajajaran. The Bogor Internusa and Bogor Plaza have supermarkets.

Getting There & Away

Bus Buses from Jakarta (1200/2500 rp aircon) depart every 10 minutes or so from the Kampung Rambutan bus terminal. The trip takes only a little over half an hour via the Jagorawi Highway toll road, but double that time from Kampung Rambutan to central Jakarta.

Buses depart frequently from Bogor to Bandung (3000 to 5000 rp; three hours). On weekends, buses are not allowed to go via the scenic Puncak Pass (it gets very crowded) and have to travel via Sukabumi (3300/5500 rp; four hours). Other bus destinations from Bogor include Pelabuhanratu (2000 rp), Rangkasbitung (2500 rp), Labuan (3600 rp) and Merak (4000 rp).

Air-con, door-to-door minibuses go to Bandung for 12,500 rp, with connections to destinations further afield. Dipo Travel (☎ 331209) has one of the best services, and Erny (☎ 322563) also has buses. Ring for pick-up, or the guesthouses can arrange it.

Angkots to villages around Bogor, including Ciampea (No 5), depart from the Terminal Merdeka near the train station.

Train The easiest way to reach central Jakarta is to take the trains, which run about every 20 minutes until 8.20 pm and take 1½ hours. They cost 900 rp to Gambir train station or 1000 rp to Kota. The ekonomi trains are reasonably efficient but best avoided during peak hours when they can be horribly crowded with commuters. More comfortable *Pakuan* express trains (2500 rp

bisnis class; one hour) leave Bogor at 6.25 7.05 and 9.30 am, 1.10 and 2.30 pm.

Slow ekonomi trains operate between Bogor and Sukabumi. There is no through railway service to Bandung, though plans are afoot to upgrade the line.

Getting Around

Efficient angkots (300 rp) shuttle around town, particularly between the bus and train stations. Most are green, while the blue angkots run to outlying districts and most terminate at Terminal Merdeka, west of the train station. They leave from the street behind the bus terminal, Jl Bangka. Also from the bus terminal, angkot No 3 does an anticlockwise loop of the botanical gardens on its way to Jl Muslihat, near the train station.

Becaks are banned from the main road encircling the gardens – in any case, getting them to go where you want to go is not always easy! Metered taxis are nonexistent, but you can haggle with the minibus drivers that hang out near the entrance to the botanical gardens.

AROUND BOGOR

Purnawarman Stone (Batutulis)

From the village of Ciampea, which is about 12 km north-west of Bogor, you can take a colt to the village of Batutulis, where sits a huge black boulder on which King Purnawarman inscribed his name and made an imprint of his footstep around 450 AD. The inscription on the stone is still remarkably clear after more than 1500 years.

Gunung Halimun National Park

This new national park is home to some primary rainforest, but the park has mixed usage and also includes plantations such as the Nirmala Tea Estate. The dominant feature of the park is the rich montane forest in the highland regions around Gunung Halimun (1929m), the highest peak.

Visitor facilities at the park are not developed, and park administration is handled by the Gede Pangrango National Park at Cibodas. The most easily visited attractions of the park are the waterfalls near Cikidang and those near the Nirmala estate. BJ's Rafting (☎ 7945923), Jl Duren Tiga Pav 42A, Jakarta, organises whitewater rafting on the Class III Sungai Citarak on the south-east edge of the park.

The usual access (you need your own transport) is via Cibadak on the Bogor-Pelabuhanratu road, from where you turn off to Cikadang and then on to Nirmala Tea Estate. Rainfall in the park is around 4000 to 6000 mm per year, most of which falls from October to May, when a visit is more or less out of the question.

SUKABUMI & SELABINTANA

Sukabumi is a thriving commercial town of 110,000 people at the foot of Pangrango and Gede volcanoes. The main reason visitors are likely to come here is to visit Selabintana, a small hill resort seven km to the north of town.

Selabintana is much less developed but much less crowded than the Puncak Pass resort area to the north of Gunung Gede. It is possible to walk up the hillside to **Sawer Waterfall** and on to **Gunung Gede**, but there is no PHPA post in Selabintana. It does have a golf course, swimming pools and a selection of mid-range hotels. Otherwise, it's simply a quiet place to relax and soak up the mountain air.

Places to Stay

Angkots to Selabintana run straight up to the foot of Gunung Gede and terminate at the old-fashioned, slightly faded *Hotel Selabintana* (☎ 221501), Jl Selabintana Km 7. It has a golf course, tennis and volleyball courts, three swimming pools and three restaurants. Rooms start at 50,000 rp and range up to the three bedroom bungalows costing 165,000 rp.

Hotel Selabintana is *the* place to stay, and there is not a lot to do if you stay elsewhere. Nevertheless, Selabintana has plenty of other hotels, such as *Pondok Asri Selabintana*, with modern, well-appointed flatettes from 78,500 rp, or the *Hotel Pangrango*, which has large, musty rooms from 22,000 rp.

The main village, around the six km mark, has cheaper hotels, including the *Pondok Mandari* and *Melinda Hotel*. Cheapest of all is the *Hotel Intan* at 25,000 rp for good, clean rooms with bath.

PELABUHANRATU

Pelabuhanratu, 90 km south of Bogor, is a seaside resort popular with Jakarta residents. On a large horseshoe bay, this small fishing town has black sand beaches and lush scenery, with rice paddies coming almost to the water's edge. Though quiet during the week, it can be crowded at weekends and holidays, and places to stay are quite expensive.

Swimming is possible when the sea is quiet, but like most of Java's south coast, the crashing surf can be treacherous. Drownings do occur in spite of the warning signs.

If you want to enter the realms of legend, Pelabuhanratu (Harbour of the Queen) actually witnessed the creation of Nyai Loro Kidul, the malevolent Goddess who takes fishers and swimmers off to her watery kingdom. Don't wear green on the beach or in the water (it's her colour), and in the Samudra Beach Hotel a room is set aside for offerings to the Queen of the South Seas.

Orientation

Pelabuhanratu is essentially a two street town – Jl Siliwangi, which leads into town and to the harbour, and Jl Kidang Kencana, which runs around the harbour and out to the western beaches. The bus terminal is near the intersection of these two streets. The beach road continues on to Cisolok, 15 km west, and a number of places to stay are scattered along this road.

Things to See & Do

Pelabuhanratu town has little of interest, but the harbour is dotted with brightly painted *prahu* (outrigger boats) and the fish market is lively in the mornings.

The beaches to the west hold the main interest and **Cimaja**, eight km west of Pelabuhanratu, has a pebble beach and good surf. At the 13 km mark, **Pantai Karang**

Hawu is a towering cliff with caves, rocks and pools which were created by a large lava flow that pushed over the beach. According to legend, it was from the rocks of Karang Hawu that Nyai Loro Kidul leapt into the mighty ocean to regain her lost beauty and never returned. Stairs lead up to a small *kramat* (shrine) at the top.

Further west, about two km past Cisolok, are the **Cipanas hot springs**, where boiling water sprays into the river and you can soak downstream where the hot and cold waters mingle. It is a very scenic area, and you can walk a few km upstream through the lush forest to a waterfall.

Further afield **Cikotok**, about 30 km north-west, is the site of Java's most important gold and silver mines. About 80 km south-east, **Genteng** is a turtle-spawning area and also has good surfing at **Ombak Tujuh**.

Places to Stay

Pelabuhanratu has plenty of mid-range accommodation, but only a few vaguely cheap options. The beach, and the best places to stay, start one km west of the town.

Two cheap hotels can be found in town on Jl Siliwangi, a few hundred metres before the harbour: the *Laut Kidul* at No 148 and *Karang Naya* at No 82 both have basic rooms from 15,000 rp.

The *Pondok Dewata* (☎ 41022) is the first place in town on the beach. Air-con Balinese-style cottages are comfortable but expensive at US$25 to US$45, plus 20% tax and service. Rates are up to 100% more in holiday periods.

Next along on a headland, *Buana Ayu* (☎ 41111) has good rooms from 60,000 rp. The rooms and the good seafood restaurant have fine sea views. Further around the headland, the *Bayu Amrta* (☎ 41031), run by the same proprietor, has rooms for 30,000 to 46,000 rp.

In Citepus village, three km from Pelabuhanratu, *Losmen Asry* is a friendly budget place and the owner speaks excellent English. Rooms with bath start at 18,000 rp.

About five km west of town, the best hotel on the coast is the *Samudra Beach Hotel* (☎ 41023), a modern high-rise with several restaurants and a good swimming pool. Singles/doubles cost US$70/80 for slightly faded rooms; those for US$80/90 are better. All rooms face the sea. Add 21% for tax and service, but substantial discounts are available.

Eight km out, Cimaja, the surfing beach, has a couple of very basic, overpriced penginapan (bottom-end hotels) with rooms for 15,000 rp. The *Hotel Mustika Rata* is much better and has rooms from 27,500 rp, more on weekends and holidays.

A few km further towards Cisolok, the *Pantai Mutiara* (☎ 41330) is one of the best hotels. It has a swimming pool, and rooms from 35,000 to 150,000 rp, plus 15.5%.

Getting There & Away

The road from Bogor cuts south over the pass between Gunung Salak and Gunung Pangrango through valleys and hillsides of rubber, coconut, cocoa and tea plantations and terraced rice fields. Local buses run throughout the day from Bogor (2000 rp; three hours) via Cibadak or from Sukabumi (1800 rp; 2½ hours). From Sukabumi buses connect with Bandung. Buses from Sukabumi go on to Cisolok from Pelabuhanratu, or minibuses run between Pelabuhanratu and Cisolok for 600 rp, less for shorter journeys.

From Labuan you can take various buses through the towns of Saketi and Malingping (seven hours) – it's a little-travelled but very scenic route, though new tourism developments are being built along this route.

BOGOR TO BANDUNG
Puncak Pass

If you take the bus from Bogor to Bandung you cross over this beautiful 1500m high pass on a narrow, winding mountain road which passes through small resort towns and tea plantations. At high altitudes it's cool and often misty but in the early morning the views across the valleys can be superb. It is a popular escape from the heat and crowds of Jakarta.

The resort strip, with its hotels and villas,

starts about 10 km out of Bogor at Ciawi, continues up through Cibogo, Cipayung and Cisarua to the Puncak Pass and then over the other side to Cipanas. From Jakarta's Kampung Rambutan bus terminal any Bandung bus can drop you off at any of the resort towns on the highway (but not on Sunday when they aren't allowed to use this highway). From Bogor frequent buses and colts (which do run on Sunday) also ply the highway. While somewhat overdeveloped, the area has fine scenery, a refreshing climate and some good walks, especially from Cisarua on the Bogor side of the pass or Cibodas on the other side. Avoid weekends when the crowds and traffic jams are horrendous.

Cisarua

Ten km from Bogor on the slopes of the Puncak, there are good walks to picnic spots and waterfalls around Cisarua, which has good budget accommodation. **Curug Cilember** is a waterfall about 30 minutes' walk from Cisarua.

Just east of Cisarua is the turn-off to **Taman Safari Indonesia**, a wildlife park. As well as indigenous and African 'safari' animals in the drive-through game park, there is a bird park, white-tiger pavilion, children's rides and a programme of animal shows. This spacious park with its well-cared for animals is streets ahead of any of Indonesia's zoos. Any Bogor-Bandung bus can drop you at the turn-off, from where minibuses go to the park (500 rp; 2.5 km). Entry is 8000 rp for adults, 6000 rp for children; cars are 5000 rp or a minibus is 10,000 rp. A park bus also does tours of the safari park. Park facilities include a swimming pool, restaurants and accommodation.

In the foot hills just before the Puncak summit, you can stop at the huge **Gunung Mas Tea Estate** for a free tour of the tea factory, a couple of km from the highway. Almost at the top of the pass, the Rindu Alam Restaurant has fine views of the surrounding tea estates if it is not shrouded in mist. From there you can walk down through the tea plantations to **Telaga Warna**, a small 'lake of many colours' just below the top of the pass which reflects different colours with changing daylight (if you're lucky).

Places to Stay *Kopo Hostel* (☎ 254296), Jl Raya Puncak 557, is near the petrol station in Cisarua. It's excellent value: the four or six bed dorms cost 8000 rp per person or comfortable rooms cost 21,000 to 49,000 rp, including breakfast. HI cardholders can get a small discount. The hostel has quiet garden grounds, a small restaurant, maps of walks and information on places of interest in the area.

Apart from the Kopo, scores of mid-range hotels and villas are spread out along the highway from Ciawi to Cipanas. Many of the villas are private – quite a few are owned by large corporations and foreign embassies – but some are for rent and worth looking into for longer stays.

The top hotel, in terms of facilities and elevation, is the *Puncak Pass Hotel* (☎ 51-2503), right near the pass itself. Mostly modern bungalows are scattered over the hillside below the old colonial central building. Rates range from US$47 a room up to US$175 for two bedroom bungalows, 20% less during the week.

Getting There & Away From Bogor take a bus or colt to Cisarua (800 rp; 45 minutes) or a bus from Jakarta (1800 rp; 1½ hours). The Kopo Hostel is on the highway, next to the Cisarua petrol station (Pompa Bensin Cisarua).

Cibodas

At Cibodas, over the Puncak Pass, is a beautiful high-altitude extension of the Bogor botanical gardens, the **Kebun Raya Cibodas**, surrounded by thick tropical jungle on the slopes of the twin volcanoes of Gunung Gede and Gunung Pangrango. The 80 hectare gardens were originally planted in 1860. Entry to the gardens is 2200 rp. Beside the entrance to the gardens is the entrance to the Gede Pangrango National Park.

Cibodas has limited facilities and is more difficult to reach than the resort strip along the Puncak Pass Highway. Consequently it gets much fewer visitors, but it has fine scenery and excellent walks.

Places to Stay & Eat In Cibodas village, 500m before the gardens, *Freddy's Homestay* (☎ 515473) is an excellent option. Bright cleans rooms with shared mandi are 15,000 and 20,000 rp, or the dorm is 10,000 rp – breakfast is included. Meals are available and good information is provided.

The modern *Pondok Pemuda Cibodas* (☎ 512807) near the Cibodas PHPA office has large dorms costing 5000 rp per person. It caters mostly to school groups, but outside of weekends and holidays you'll probably have the place to yourself. There's cheap food at the *warungs* near the gardens and in the village.

A truly tranquil place to lodge is within the gardens themselves at the colonial *Cibodas Botanical Gardens Guesthouse* (☎ 512233). You certainly can't beat the surrounding ambience, and large old rooms cost 35,000 to 50,000 rp. Food is also served. Bookings are essential and you can make reservations at the Bogor Botanical Gardens as well as the Cibodas gardens.

Getting There & Away The turn-off to Cibodas is on the Bogor-Bandung highway, a few km west of Cipanas. The gardens are then five km off the main road. Angkots run from Cipanas (500 rp; half hour), or coming from the west you can catch them at the turn-off (400 rp).

Gede Pangrango National Park
The Cibodas gardens are also the main entrance to the Gede Pangrango National Park, the highlight of which is the climb to the 2958m peak of volcanically active Gunung Gede. From the top of Gede on a clear day you can see Jakarta, Cirebon and even Pelabuhanratu on the south coast – well, Raffles reported that he could.

Register for the climb and obtain your permit (4000 rp) from the PHPA office just outside the garden entrance. The office has an information centre and pamphlets on the park.

From Cibodas, the trail passes **Telaga Biru** (15 minutes), a blue/green lake. **Cibeureum Falls** (one hour away) lies just off the main trail. Most picnickers only go this far or some continue on to the **hot springs**, 2½ hours from the gate. The trail continues to climb another 1½ hours to **Kandang Badak**, the saddle between the peaks of Gunung Gede and Gunung Pangrango (3019m). Take the trail to the right for a hard three hour climb to Pangrango. Most hikers turn left for the easier, but still steep, 1½ hour climb to Gede, which has more spectacular views. The **Gede Crater** lies below the summit, and you can continue on to the **Suryakencana Meadow**.

The 10 km hike right to the top of Gunung Gede takes at least 10 hours there and back, so you should start as early as possible and take warm clothes (night temperatures can drop to 5°C), food, water and a flashlight. Most hikers leave by 2 am to reach the summit in the early morning before the mists roll in. Register at the PHPA the day before. The main trails are well maintained and easy to follow. The hike should only be undertaken in the 'dry' season from May to October.

An alternative approach is to climb Gunung Gede from Selabintana to the south, a steep and slippery nine km path. This path joins the main trail at the Suryakencana Meadow, from where a third trail goes to Gunung Putri, west of Cibodas.

Cipanas
Cipanas, five km beyond the Cibodas turn-off, has hot springs noted for their curative properties. The **Istana Cipanas** is another seldom-used summer presidential palace favoured by Soekarno. Built in 1750, it is an elegant country house in beautiful gardens but, like the Bogor palace, it is not normally open to the public. Apart from that, Cipanas is another resort town with plenty of hotels and a few restaurants.

The best place to stay is the *Villa Cipanas*

Indah (☎ 512513), Jl Tengah 8, a 10 minute walk west of the istana. Rooms cost 20,000 rp, and 30,000 rp with hot water. Good information and guides are on offer. The *Hotel Flamboyant* (☎ 512586), Jl Raya Pasekon 69, is one of the cheaper hotels with rooms for 40,000 rp.

BANDUNG

With its population of over two million, Bandung is the capital of West Java and Indonesia's third largest city. At 750m above sea level it has a cool and comfortable climate, and it attracts people from all over Indonesia, and from abroad, seeking work and higher education. The majority of the population are the native Sundanese of West Java, who not only have a reputation as extroverted, easy-going people compared with the extremely refined Javanese, but also as zealous guardians of their own ancient culture. In contrast, the city itself is relatively new.

Bandung was originally established in the late 19th century as a Dutch garrison town of some 90,000 Sundanese, Chinese and Europeans. It rapidly acquired importance as a commercial and educational centre, renowned in particular for its Institute of Technology.

Bandung's most notable entry in the history books was as host of the Asia-Africa conference in 1955, which placed Bandung in the world spotlight. On the industrial front, Bandung has maintained some of its European-created production centres, and its major industries include textiles, telecommunications, tea and food processing. Bandung's multi-million dollar aircraft factory has been promoted by the Minister for Research & Technology, Dr Habibie, despite widespread scepticism about its viability.

Although in the past Bandung was described as the 'Paris of Java', due to its many fine parks and gardens, much of the city's former glamour has faded. Today it is a mishmash of dilapidated colonial architecture and modern buildings, though the northern suburbs still have graceful residential areas.

The Kebun Raja is the focus of the old colonial city and is ringed by Dutch architecture. Art Deco architecture is in abundance, one of the best examples being the Savoy Homann Hotel.

Bandung is an excellent place to visit if you're interested in Sundanese culture; otherwise, its main attractions lie in the beautiful countryside around the city. To the north and south there's a wild tangle of high volcanic peaks, including the famous Tangkuban Prahu, and several huge tea plantations. There are some fine walks in the area – one of the best is the river walk from the village of Maribaya to Dago Hill on the outskirts of Bandung.

Orientation

Bandung sprawls out over the northern foothills of a huge plateau surrounded by high mountain ridges. The main part of the city lies south of the train line, and is centred around Jl Asia Afrika and the city square *(alun alun)*. Along Jl Asia Afrika are the tourist office, post office and most of the banks, airline offices, restaurants and topend hotels. Jl Braga was the ritzy shopping area in Dutch times, and has a few useful shops and cafes. The budget hotel area in Bandung is on the south side of the train station.

In colonial times, the railway tracks divided the riff-raff in the south from the Dutch city in the north. During the transitional independence period after the war, the train line was in fact the official partition line between the reoccupied Dutch city in the north and Republican-controlled Bandung in the south. The railway tracks still provide a social divide. To the north, wealthy residential areas are studded with tree-lined streets and parks, and bordered on the northernmost edge by the hills of Dago.

Information

Tourist Offices The very helpful Bandung visitor information centre (☎ 4206644) at the alun alun on Jl Asia Afrika is the place to go for detailed information and all the latest on cultural events in and around Bandung.

Bandung

To Ledeng, Lembang
& Tangkuban Prahu

To Dago
(2.5km)

Jeans
Shops

Jalan Taman Sari

Jalan Ganeca 3

Jalan Juanda

Jalan Dipati Ukur

Jalan Surapati

4

Jalan Diponegoro

5

6

7

Jalan Sukaladi

Jalan Cipaganti

Jalan Pasteur

To
Airport

Jalan Pajajaran

Jalan Cihampelas

8

9

10

11

Jalan Martadinata

Jalan Pasirkaliki

12

13

Jalan Kebon Kawong

22

21

23

24

14

15

Jalan Merdeka

16

Kebun
Raja

19   18

20

17

Jalan Jawa

Jalan Suniaraja

25

26   28

29

Jalan Kebonjati

32   30   31

33

27

34

Jalan Gardulati

35

Jalan Sumatra

39

Jalan Lembang

40

36

37

Jalan Braga

38

Jalan Tamblong

Jalan Veteran

Jalan Asia Afrika

43

44

42

53   52

54   51

45

Jalan Naripan

Jalan Cibadak

56

55

57

50   48   47   46

Jalan Asia Afrika

41

To
Cicaheum
Bus Terminal

Jalan Dewi Sartika

58

59

Alun
Alun   60

Jalan Dalem Kaum

61

62

Jalan Astana Anyar

Jalan Otto Iskandardinata

Jalan Lengkong Besar

Jalan Karapitan

To Provincial Museum &
Leuwi Pangang Bus Terminal

63

PLACES TO STAY		52	Braga Restaurant &	23	4848 Taxis
4	Wisma Asri		Pub	27	Train Station
11	Bumi Sakinah	54	Night Market Warungs	34	Pasar Baru
14	Wisma Remaja	61	Warung Nasi Mang	35	4848 Taxis
20	Hotel Guntur		Udju	36	North Sea Bar
22	Hotel Patradissa			38	Museum Mandala
25	Hotel Patradissa II	**OTHER**			Wangsit (Army
26	Sakardana Homestay	1	Zoo		Museum)
29	Losmen Sakardana	2	Bandung Institute of	40	Telkom Office
30	Le Yossie Homestay		Technology (ITB)	41	Rumentang Siang
31	By Moritz	3	Kramatdjati Buses	45	Sarinah Department
32	Hotel Surabaya	5	Museum Geologi		Store
33	Hotel Trio		(Geological Museum)	47	Merpati Office
39	Hotel Panghegar	6	Museum Pos dan Giro	48	Wartel
46	Grand Hotel Preanger		(Post & Giro	50	Gedung Merdeka
49	Savoy Homann Hotel		National Stamp		(Freedom Building)
62	Hotel Mawar		Museum)	53	Ramayana
		7	Gedung Sate		Department Store &
PLACES TO EAT			(Regional		Supermarket
10	Tojoyo		Government Building)	55	Bank BRI
24	Rumah Makan	8	Galael Supermarket	56	Main Post Office
	Mandarin	9	Flower Market	57	Golden Megah Corp
28	Warungs &	12	Bandung Cepat Buses		Moneychanger
	Restaurants	13	Bouraq Office	58	King's Department
37	Braga Permai Cafe	15	Plaza Bandung Indah		Store
42	Sindang Reret		Shopping Mall	59	Visitor Information
	Restaurant	16	City Hall (Kantor		Centre
43	Canary Bakery		Walikota)	60	Palaguna Shopping
44	French Bakery	17	Catholic Church		Centre
51	Rumah Makan Tenda	18	Bank Indonesia	63	Kebun Kelapa Bus
	Biru	19	Bethel Church		Terminal
		21	Governor's Residence		

's open Monday to Saturday from 9 am to 5 pm. The knowledgeable Makmun Rustina and staff can organise day trips to Papandayan volcano near Garut and Situ Patengan. Excellent walking tours of the colonial city can be arranged (7500 rp per person for a minimum of two).

A handy tourist information counter, staffed by volunteers, is at the south side of the train station. It is open from 8 am to 5 pm, but usually closes on Sunday and holidays.

Money Bandung has plenty of banks and moneychangers. The Golden Megah Corp moneychanger, Jl Otista 180, usually has the best rates in town and no fees. It is open Monday to Friday from 8.30 am to 4.30 pm, and Saturday until 2 pm.

Post & Communications The main post office at the corner of Jl Banceuy and Jl Asia Afrika is open Monday to Saturday from 8

am to 9 pm. Poste restante is just a tin of jumbled letters out the back. For international telephone calls, the main Telkom office is on Jl Lembong, or the *wartel* on Jl Asia Afrika opposite the Savoy Homann Hotel is central.

Medical Services For medical attention, the Adventist Hospital (☎ 234386) at Jl Cihampelas 161 is a missionary hospital with English-speaking staff.

Gedung Merdeka (Freedom Building)
If you're interested in learning more about the Asia-Africa conference of 1955, visit the Museum Konperensi (Conference Museum) in the Gedung Merdeka on Jl Asia Afrika. There you'll see photographs and exhibits of the meeting between Soekarno, Chou En-Lai, Ho Chi Minh, Nasser and other Third World leaders of the 1950s. The building itself dates from 1879 and was originally the

'Concordia Societeit', a meeting hall of Dutch associations and the centre for high society. The museum is open Monday to Friday from 8 am to 6 pm.

Museum Geologi (Geological Museum)

North across the railway tracks at Jl Diponegoro 57, the museum and the office of the Geological Survey of Indonesia are housed in the massive old headquarters of the Dutch Geological Service. There are some interesting exhibits, such as relief maps, volcano models and an array of fossils, including one of the skull of a *Pithecanthropus erectus*, the famous prehistoric Java man. It's open from 9 am to 2 pm Monday to Thursday, until 11 pm Friday and 1 pm Saturday. Entrance is free. From the train station you can take an angkot bound for 'Sadang Serang' and get off at the Gedung Sate, about 400m from the museum.

Other Museums

The **Museum Negeri Propinsi Jawa Barat** (West Java Provincial Museum), south-west of the city at Jl Oto Iskandardinata 638, has an interesting display of Sundanese artefacts. It is open every day, except Monday, from 8 am to 2 pm.

The **Museum Mandala Wangsit** (Army Museum) at Jl Lembong 38 is devoted to the history and exploits of the West Java Siliwangi division (based in Bandung). It is open Monday to Friday from 8 am to 2 pm.

The **Museum Pos dan Giro** (Post & Giro National Stamp Museum) is in the north-east corner of the Gedung Sate (Regional Government) complex on Jl Diponegoro. As well as thousands of stamps from around the world, the museum has everything from post boxes to pushcarts used since colonial times to ensure that the mail must go through. It is open from 8 am to 2 pm every day, except Sunday.

Bandung Institute of Technology (ITB)

North of town on Jl Ganeca is the Bandung Institute of Technology, built at the beginning of the century. The university has large grounds and gardens, and the main campus complex is notable for its 'Indo-European' architecture, featuring Minangkabau-style roofs.

Opened in 1920, the ITB was the first Dutch-founded university open to Indonesians. It was here that Soekarno studied civil engineering (1920-25) and helped to found the Bandung Study Club, members of which formed a political party which grew as the Indonesian Nationalist Party (PNI) with independence as its goal. The institute's students have maintained their reputation for outspokenness and political activism, and in 1978 they published the *White Book of the 1978 Students' Struggle* against alleged corruption in high places. It was banned in Indonesia but later published in the USA. The ITB is the foremost scientific university in the country but it's also reputed to have one of the best fine arts schools, and its art gallery can be visited. Across from the main gate is a useful canteen in the *asrama mahasiswa* (student dorm complex) where many of the students congregate.

To reach the ITB, take a Lembang or Dago angkot from the train station and then walk down Jl Ganeca.

Zoo

Bandung zoo's spacious, beautifully landscaped gardens make it the most attractive zoo in Indonesia, but the animals are few and most are typically housed in cramped conditions. The zoo is a few minutes' walk from the ITB on Jl Taman Sari – the entrance is down the steps past the toy stalls opposite Jl Ganeca. It's open daily from 7 am to 5 pm and admission costs 1000 rp. Go on Sunday mornings when cultural performances such as pencak silat (Indonesian martial arts) or classical dance are staged.

Dago

At the end of Jl Merdeka, Jl Juanda climbs up to Dago Hill to the north, overlooking the city. The famous Dago Thee Huis (Dago Tea House) offers commanding vistas over the bluff and is a fine place to catch the sunset.

Dago itself is an expensive residential

uburb with some elegant Sundanese-style
estaurants. It's a pleasant tree-shaded area
o walk around. Just behind the tea house is
he Dago Waterfall, and about 2.5 km to the
north is a huge cliff in which the Gua Pakar
Cave was hacked out by the Japanese to store
ammunition in during the war. The latter is
he start (or the end) of the walk between
Maribaya and Dago along Sungai Cikapundung (see under Maribaya Hot Springs
n the North of Bandung section for more
nformation).

Jeans' Street

No discussion of Bandung's sights would be
complete without mention of its famous
eans street, Jl Cihampelas, in the more afflu-
nt northern side of town. Celebrating its
tanding as a major textile centre, shops with
rightly painted humungous plaster statues
of King Kong, Rambo and other legendary
monsters compete with one another for
eenage Indonesian customers. This is the
ltimate in kitsch and has to be seen to be
elieved. Incidentally, the jeans start at
round 25,000 rp, and the shops also have a
abulous collection of T-shirts.

Ram Fights

On most Sunday mornings, noisy traditional
am-butting fights known as *adu domba* are
eld in Cilimus, in the northern suburbs of
Bandung.

To the sound of drums, gongs and hand
lapping, two rams keep charging at each
ther with a head-on clash of horns for 25 or
nore clashes, with a referee deciding the
vinner. If a ram gets dizzy they tweak his
esticles and send him back into combat until
e's had enough! This sport has been popular
n West Java for so long that most villages
ave their own ram-fight societies and there
re organised tournaments to encourage
armers to rear a stronger breed of ram. At
illage level it's just good fun; at district and
rovincial level there's wild betting.

To reach Cilimus, take an angkot or Lembang minibus (400 rp) to Terminal Ledeng
n Jl Setiabudi, the continuation of Jl

Sukajadi. Go down Jl Sersan Bajuri directly
opposite the terminal, turn left at Jl Cilimus
and continue to the bamboo grove.

Places to Stay – bottom end

Bandung's hotels are fairly expensive but Jl
Kebonjati, near the train station and the city
centre, has some good guesthouses, all providing budget rooms, food and information.

The German-run *By Moritz* (☎ 4207264),
Kompleks Luxor Permai 35, Jl Kebonjati, is
a well-managed travellers' guest house with
a good restaurant. Dorm beds cost 8000 rp
and spotless singles/doubles/triples are
12,500/17,000/25,000 rp. Breakfast is included.

Le Yossie Homestay (☎ 4205453), 53 Jl
Kebonjati, is not quite as immaculate but
also good. A dorm bed costs 7000 rp per
person; singles/doubles are 10,000/13,500
rp. The rooms are light, free tea and coffee
are provided and there is a downstairs cafe.

Bandung's original guesthouse, *Losmen
Sakardana* (☎ 4209897) is down a little alley
off Jl Kebonjati beside the Hotel Melati I at
No 50/7B. Basic but well-kept rooms are
8000/12,000 rp. *Sakardana Homestay*
(☎ 4218553), Gang Babakan 55-7/B, further
along the alley, is its more popular copy. It's
friendly and has a good upstairs restaurant.
Now in new premises, the plywood rooms
are still basic, but clean and cheap enough at
10,000/13,000/17,000 rp, or 7000 rp for a
dorm bed.

Jl Kebonjati also has a few hotels. *Hotel
Surabaya* (☎ 444133) at No 71 is a rambling
old hotel with plenty of colonial ambience
(check out the old photographs in the lobby)
but is rather run down. Spartan rooms range
from 11,500/20,000 rp without bath up to
rooms with bath in the 'renovated' section
for 45,000 rp, but they are only marginally
better.

Other places include *Wisma Remaja* in the
Government Youth Centre (Gelanggang
Generasi Muda Bandung) at Jl Merdeka 64.
A bed costs 8000 rp per person in twin or
triple rooms. It is good value, but often full
with school groups.

Places to Stay – middle

North of the train station, the *Hotel Patradissa* (☎ 4206680) at Jl H Moch Iskat 8 has clean, modern rooms with bath. Small singles/doubles are 15,000/20,000 rp, while better doubles with hot water showers start at 35,000 rp. A number of other hotels are nearby.

The *Hotel Patradissa II* (☎ 4202645), Jl Pasirkaliki 12, just around the corner from Jl Kebonjati, has small but spotless rooms with attached bathroom and hot water showers for 30,000 rp, including breakfast. It's a good deal.

At Jl Oto Iskandardinata 20, the *Hotel Guntur* (☎ 4203763) is a large, older hotel with a manicured garden. Doubles with bath, hot water and TV are 51,000 and 54,000 rp.

Wisma Asri (☎ 4521717), Jl Merak 5, is a delightful, older-style guesthouse out near the Gedung Sate. Very comfortable rooms without bath cost 35,000 to 38,000 rp, and deluxe rooms with air-con, fridge, TV and hot water are around 55,000 rp, all plus 16%.

Another old guesthouse is the small *Bumi Sakinah* (☎ 4206842), Jl RE Martadinata 3. It's on a busy road, but provides delightful accommodation for 50,000 and 60,000 rp, including breakfast.

The *Hotel Panghegar* (☎ 432286) at Jl Merdeka 2 is an business hotel spanning the middle and top-end ranges. Rooms cost US$89/99.

Places to Stay – top end

Like most big cities on Java, Bandung is experiencing a luxury hotel boom. The following all have swimming pools, and add an additional 21% tax and service charge. Bookings are advisable for weekends.

The *Savoy Homann Hotel* (☎ 432244) is conveniently central at Jl Asia Afrika 112. Once *the* hotel of Bandung, it is still a stylish old Art Deco building with spacious rooms off a small courtyard garden. Singles/doubles start at US$119/129. The hotel has a garden restaurant and superb Art Deco dining room facing the street.

Built in 1928, the *Grand Hotel Preanger* (☎ 431631) at Jl Asia Afrika 181 competes with the Savoy Homann for colonial style. It doesn't quite match the Savoy Homann on that score but it is Bandung's best hotel. Rooms in the new tower cost from US$120 or the superb rooms in the old wing are US$175.

Many of Bandung's new hotels are found in the north of the city. On the road to Dago the smaller *Sheraton* (☎ 2500303) at Jl Juanda 390 has rooms from US$100, and right near the Dago Tea House, *Hotel Jayakarta* (☎ 2505888), Jl Juanda 381, cost from US$115/125.

North of the zoo on the outskirts of town *Chedi Hotel* (☎ 230333), Jl Ranca Bentang 56-58, is a smaller boutique hotel with countryside views, and unique architecture and furnishings. This is one of Java's most stylish hotels and rooms start at US$150.

Places to Eat

For cheap eats, many travellers don't get past the guesthouses. *By Moritz* has a popular cafe with foreign magazines and local guitar strummers, and *Sakardana Homestay* has a good little cafe upstairs. Between the train station and Jl Kebonjati is a selection of cheap but fairly grotty nighttime warung and restaurants. A lively area for nighttime cheap eats is on Jl Gardujati, just around the corner from Jl Kebonjati, opposite the Hotel Trio. You'll find a whole string of good street-side warungs and a selection of Chinese restaurants.

For excellent warung food head for the night warungs on Jl Cikapundung Barat across from the alun alun near the Ramayana department store. Stalls sell a bit of everything – soto, sate, gado gado, seafood – or try the soto jeroan, intestinal soup with various medicinal properties, mostly designed to stimulate male libido. Nearby on the ground floor in the Ramayana department store is a good, squeaky clean food stall area.

Bandung also has a number of excellent Chinese restaurants. The *Rumah Makan Mandarin* on Jl Kebon Kawung is a no-frills place with excellent dishes served in steaming cast-iron pans. Seafood is a speciality.

nd the restaurant is popular with Bandung's Chinese community.

Jl Braga has a string of fancy coffee shops nd bakeries where you can indulge yourself n a sort of east-west food fantasy. The entre-piece of this quasi-European avenue s the *Braga Permai* sidewalk cafe at No 74, vith a mixed Indonesian and western menu, ·lus a variety of cakes and superb ice cream. \t No 17 is the *Braga Restaurant & Pub*, a hiny place with reasonable Indian, Indones-an and light western meals. On the corner of l Braga and Jl ABC/Naripan is the *Canary Bakery*, with hamburgers and western fare; 1e upstairs balcony is pleasant, if a little oisy. A little further along are the *Sumber Hidangan Bakery* and the *French Bakery*, ood places for a snack or light meal – try roissants, Danish pastries or chicken curry uffs.

Apart from the westernised places along . Braga, the shopping malls also have plenty f fast food. Plaza Bandung Indah on Jl Merdeka has a host of western-style eateries, icluding *McDonald's*.

All the big hotels have restaurants – for a eat with style try the rijsttafel in the *Savoy Homann Hotel* restaurant.

undanese Restaurants Bandung is a ood place to try traditional Sundanese food. he *Warung Nasi Mang Udju*, on Jl Dewi artika just south of the alun alun, is a simple ace, but the food is excellent and you can it well for about 4000 rp. *Rumah Makan Enda Biru* on Jl Braga is a no-frills, cafete-a-style place with good Sundanese food.

Tojoyo, Jl Buah Batu 276A, has a wide inge of Sundanese dishes. It is moderately riced, despite the expensive cars parked out te front.

The *Sindang Reret Restaurant*, Jl Naripan just around the corner from Jl Braga, is :ntral and has good, if slightly expensive, undanese food, and Saturday night cultural erformances.

For a real treat, take a taxi to the Dago area i the north of the city to the lovely *Peni-:ungan Endah*, Jl Tubagus Ismail Raya 60. ere, each party has its own individual

tearoom in which to try Sundanese food, surrounded by Japanese-style gardens bounded by tranquil brooks. From the waters which surround your teahouse, sizeable goldfish are freshly netted to serve as the Sundanese delicacy, ikan mas.

Entertainment
Cultural Performances Bandung is an excellent place to see Sundanese performing arts. Many performances are irregular – the visitor information office can tell you when events are on and can also inform you of special programmes.

Bandung's performing arts centre is the *Rumentang Siang* at Jl Baranangsiang 1. Wayang golek puppet performances are held every other Saturday night from 9.30 pm to 4.30 am. Various other performances, including sandiwara (traditional Javanese theatre), ketoprak folk theatre through to western ballet, are staged. Tickets cost 1500 to 3000 rp.

You can also catch a scaled-down wayang golek exhibition with a meal every Saturday night from 8 to 10 pm at the *Sindang Reret Restaurant*.

Sundanese dance is held every Wednesday and Saturday at 7 pm at the *Hotel Panghegar* for the price of the hotel's expensive dinners. The other large hotels have periodic programmes of Sundanese music and dancing.

Sanggar Langen Setra, Jl Oto Iskandardinata 541A, is a Jaipongan dance club that features Ketuktilu and Jaipongan every evening from 8 pm to 1 am. The club is about one km south of the Kebon Kelapa bus terminal. A cover charge applies and you pay extra to join the performers for a dance. While owing much to traditional dance, Jaipongan is a modern social dance and hostesses dance primarily to entertain male clients – something like traditional bar girls.

Every Sunday at the zoo, from 9 am to noon, traditional performances such as pencak silat or wayang golek are held.

ASTI-Bandung, in the southern part of the city at Jl Buah Batu 212, is a school for traditional Sundanese arts – music, dancing and pencak silat (the art of self defence). Check with the tourist office for events, or it is open to interested visitors every morning, except Sunday. You can get there by Buah Batu angkot from Kebun Kelapa bus terminal.

Angklung performances take place at Pak Ujo's *Saung Angklung* (Bamboo Workshop), Jl Padasuka 118, east of the city on the way to the Cicaheum bus terminal, and you can see the instruments being made. Performances are 12,500 rp and appeal mostly to tour groups.

Nightlife Jl Braga is a good place in the evening for less cultural pursuits. The *North Sea Bar* is a relaxed bar popular with expats that has taken over the mantle from the *Braga Pub* at the southern end of Jl Braga. Opposite the North Sea Bar, *Caesar's Palace* at No 129 is a flash Chinese disco and the place to do business deals, while nearby *Srimpi* is a dangdut hangout. *Polo*, on the 11th floor of the BRI building on Jl Asia Afrika, is a chic disco and an ecstasy hangout. Further out, north-west of the city centre at Jl Dr Junjunan 164, *Laga Pub* is a convivial place that gets some good bands and a fair smattering of expats.

Things to Buy

In the city centre, down a small alley behind Jl Pangarang 22, near the Hotel Mawar, Pak Ruhiyat at No 78/17B produces wayang golek puppets and masks, and you can see them being carved.

The Cupu Manik puppet factory is on Gang Haji Umar, off Jl Kebon Kawung just north of the train station. Traditional Sundanese musical instruments can be bought at Pak Ujo's Saung Angklung (Bamboo Workshop) or the Toko Musik at Gang Suniaraja 3, off Jl ABC.

Jl Cibaduyut, in south-west Bandung, is to shoes as Jl Cihampelas is to jeans, but without the gaudy statues. Dozens of shops sell high-quality shoes and bags at competitive prices.

Jl Braga used to be the exclusive shopping street of Bandung, though it is fairly quiet these days. Jakarta's Sarinah department store has a small branch here with a selection of crafts.

These days the shopping malls dominate the town – Plaza Bandung Indah is Bandung's biggest and brightest mall. For everyday goods, the liveliest shopping district is on Jl Dalem Kaum and nearby streets just west of the alun alun. Supermarkets can be found in the Ramayana department store on Jl Cikapundung Barat and Jl Dalem Kaum, and in the Plaza Bandung Indah.

Pasar Baru is Bandung's big, somewhat grotty central market, with fruit, vegetable and all manner of goods. Bandung's title of the 'City of Flowers' comes true at the flower market on Jl Wastukencana, on the way to the zoo. Pasar Jatayu, one km west of the train station on Jl Arjuna, is a flea market where you may be able to find some collectibles if you sift through the junk.

Getting There & Away

Air Sempati, Bouraq and Merpati fly from Bandung to Jakarta for 67,000 rp. Merpati also flies direct to Yogyakarta (96,000 rp), Palembang, Semarang, Surabaya and Singapore.

The Merpati office (☎ 441226) is at Asia Afrika 73, opposite the Savoy Homann Hotel. Garuda (☎ 4209467) is in the Hotel Preanger on Jl Asia Afrika. Sempati (☎ 420 1612) is in the Grand Hotel Panghegar, Merdeka 2. The Bouraq office (☎ 437896) at Jl Cihampelas 27.

Bus The Leuwi Panjang bus terminal, five km south of the city centre on Jl Soekarno Hatta, has buses to the west to places like Bogor (3000 to 5000 rp; 3½ hours), Sukabumi (2300 rp; three hours) and Jakarta's Kampung Rambutan bus terminal (3500 to 7500 rp; 4½ hours). Buses to Bogor are not allowed to take the scenic Puncak Pass route on weekends. Door-to-door minibuses also go to Bogor (12,500 rp) via Puncak.

Buses to the east leave from the Cicaheum bus terminal on the eastern outskirts of the city. Normal/air-con buses go to Cirebon

2700/5100 rp; 3½ hours), Garut (1400 rp; two hours), Tasikmalaya (2500/3500 rp; four hours) and Yogya (10,800 to 21,500 rp; 12 hours). Most departures to Yogya leave between 3 and 7 pm.

For Pangandaran, a few direct buses go from Cicaheum bus terminal; otherwise take a bus to Tasikmalaya or Banjar and then another to Pangandaran.

A door-to-door taxi service is provided by 848 Taxi, or Sari Harum (☎ 771447) has less cramped, air-con minibuses (15,000 rp; five hours).

For luxury night buses to major Javanese cities and Bali, a conveniently located company is Bandung Cepat (☎ 431333), Jl Doktor Cipto 5.

The old Kebun Kelapa bus terminal on Jl Dewi Sartika, about 10 minutes' walk south of the alun alun, handles a few local buses and colts, such as those to Subang, Ciwidey and Pangalengan.

Train The Bandung-Jakarta *Parahyangan* is the main service with departures to Jakarta's Gambir train station roughly every hour from 4 am to 8.30 pm. Slower trains pass through mid-morning for Jakarta's Pasar Senen train station. The *Argogede* luxury service departs at 6.30 am and 2.30 pm.

Several daily trains also operate between Yogyakarta and Bandung. The journey takes about nine to 10 hours, and the fare varies from around 9000 rp in ekonomi, from 34,000 rp in bisnis. Trains to Surabaya include the *Badra Surya* (10,000 rp ekonomi) and the express *Mutiara Selatan* (28,000 rp bisnis).

Getting Around

The Airport Bandung's Husein Sastranegara airport is four km north-west of town, about half an hour away and 4000 rp by taxi.

Bus, Angkot & Taxi Bandung has a fairly good, if crowded, Damri city bus service which charges a fixed 250 rp. Nos 9 and 11 run from west to east down Jl Asia-Afrika to Cicaheum bus terminal.

Angkots run set routes all over town

between numerous stations. From Stasiun Hall, on the southern side of the train station, angkots go to Dago, Ledeng and other stations. When returning, catch any angkot showing 'St Hall'. Abdul Muis (Abd Muis) at the Kebon Kelapa bus terminal is the other central station, with angkots to Dago, Ledeng, Cicaheum bus terminal and other stations. Angkots cost 250 to 500 rp around town (400 rp for most destinations).

From the terminal outside the train station, colts also run to Lembang and Subang (for Tangkuban Prahu and Ciater).

Becaks have all but disappeared from central Bandung, but taxis are numerous.

NORTH OF BANDUNG
Lembang
On the road to Tangkuban Prahu, 16 km north of Bandung, Lembang was once a hill resort, though most visitors now keep heading further up into the hills.

Places to Stay The *Grand Hotel Lembang* (☎ 2786671), Jl Raya Lembang 272, harks back to the days when Lembang was a fashionable resort for Bandung's Dutch community. It is old fashioned and comfortable, with beautiful gardens, a swimming pool and tennis courts, as well as a pleasant bar and a restaurant. Rooms in the new wing cost 110,000 rp, or faded rooms in the old wing cost 40,000 rp; 55,000 rp with bath.

Maribaya Hot Springs
Maribaya, five km east of Lembang, has a thermal spa, landscaped gardens and a thundering waterfall. It's another tourist spot, crowded on Sunday, but worth visiting. You can extend your Tangkuban Prahu trip by walking from the bottom end of the gardens down through a brilliant, deep and wooded river gorge all the way to Dago. There's a good track and if you allow about two to three hours for the walk (six km) you can be at a Dago vantage point for sunset. From there it's only a short trip by colt back into Bandung.

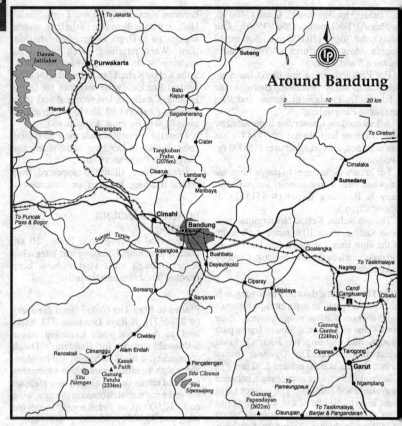

Around Bandung

0   10   20 km

Tangkuban Prahu

The 'overturned prahu' volcano crater stands 30 km north of Bandung. Years ago the centre of Tangkuban Prahu collapsed under the weight of built-up ash and, instead of the usual conical volcano shape, it has a flat elongated summit with a huge caldera.

There is, of course, a legend to explain this phenomenon.

An estranged young prince returned home and unwittingly fell in love with his own mother. When the queen discovered the terrible truth of her lover's identity she challenged him to build a dam and a huge boat during a single night before she would agree to marry him. Seeing that the young man was about to complete this impossible task, she called on the gods to bring the sun up early and as the cocks began to crow the boat builder turned his nearly completed boat over in a fit of anger.

Tangkuban Prahu still simmers and bubbles, sending up noxious sulphurous fumes. Its last serious eruption was in 1969.

Tangkuban Prahu is easily accessible by car, so it's very much a tourist attraction. Up at the crater there are carparks and warungs. A helpful information centre is at the top, and there's a parade of peddlers hustling post-ards, souvenirs and other junk. While the scene is much more commercial than most other Javanese volcanoes, you can escape this bedlam of activity, and Tangkuban Prahu is a spectacular sight.

Kawah Ratu, the huge 'Queen Crater' is at the top, but you can walk around the rim of the main crater (take the safer trail to the right) for about 20 minutes for views of the secondary crater, Kawah Upas. The trail leads further along a ridge between the two craters and returns to the carpark, but it is steep and slippery in parts. Exercise caution. The other main attraction is Kawah Domas, volcanic area of steaming and bubbling geysers that can be reached by a side trail to the top. You can also head off across country towards Ciater or Lembang.

Getting There & Away At 2076m Tangkuban Prahu can be quite cool and around noon the mist starts to roll in through the trees, so try to go early. From Bandung's minibus terminal in front of the train station, take a Subang colt (2000 rp) via Lembang to the park entrance. Alternatively take a Subang bus from Kebun Kelapa (1000 rp).

Entry is 1550 rp per person. Minibuses go to the top for 1500 rp per person – go in the morning when there is a better chance of sharing with other passengers or you'll have to charter. Traffic is heavy throughout Sunday.

Alternatively, you can walk from the gate. It's 4.5 km along the road, or take the more interesting side trail via the Kawah Domas crater and its bubbling hot geysers. It is a very steep one hour walk through the jungle – head up the main road and take the trail that branches off at the first small carpark. It is much easier to walk this trail from the top down – it starts just behind the information centre and is very easy to follow.

An alternative is to get dropped off at Jayagiri, just outside Lembang, and from here you can walk up through the forest to the crater (about eight km). The trail starts just past the Jayagiri fruit market and comes out near the bus parking area, 1.2 km below the main crater. Another less easy-to-follow

trail leads off the main crater to Ciater, a two hour walk through forest and tea plantations.

Drivers in Bandung will charge around 50,000 to 70,000 rp for a visit to Tangkuban Prahu, depending on time spent at the crater, including petrol but excluding entry. From Lembang count on 25,000 to 30,000 rp return.

Ciater Hot Springs
Eight km north-east of Tangkuban Prahu, Ciater is a pretty little place in the middle of huge tea and clove estates. The area has good walks, and a tea factory on the south side of Ciater can be visited.

At the end of the road through the village, Ciater's main attraction is the **Sari Ater Hot Spring Resort**. Although quite commercialised, the pools are probably the best of all the hot springs around Bandung, and if you've been climbing around the volcano on a cool, rainy day there's no better way to get warm. There is a 1500 rp admission into the resort area and it costs extra to use the pool. You can walk to Ciater – about 12 km across country – from Tangkuban Prahu, or flag down a colt at the entrance point.

Places to Stay The extensive *Sari Ater Hot Springs Resort* (☎ 460888) has a variety of rustic, bamboo bungalows spread out in spacious grounds. It has all the facilities of a big hotel, but the rooms are losing their shine. Most cost US$43 to US$100, plus 21%, and around 20% more on weekends.

Ciater has plenty of small penginapan with rooms starting at around 15,000 rp – the ones on the main road are cheaper. *Hotel Permata Sari* (☎ 203891) is close to the hot springs and has rooms for 22,000 rp without bath, from 38,500 rp with bath.

Lake Jatiluhur & Dam
This artificial lake *(waduk in Indonesian)*, 70 km north-west of Bandung in the hills near Purwakarta, is a popular resort for swimming, boating and water-skiing. The tourist blurb certainly raves about the giant Jatiluhur Dam which stretches 1200m across, is 100m high, and has created a lake some 80

hectares in surface area. It's part of a hydro-electric generating system supplying Jakarta and West Java, and also providing irrigation water for a large area of the province. Jatiluhur is also the site of the country's ITT earth satellite station, opened in 1969. The village was built by the French for their staff when they were building the dam. Pur-wakarta is the access point either from Jakarta (125 km by rail or road) or from Bandung (by road).

SOUTH OF BANDUNG

The mountains south of Bandung also have popular weekend retreats, though the area is less developed compared with the resorts north of the city. The road south of Bandung leads to **Ciwidey**, a small town noted for its stylish Sundanese restaurants.

The road winds through the hills to the turn-off to **Kawah Putih**, a volcanic crater with a beautiful turquoise lake. The turn-off is six km before Rancabali, and then it is eight km to the small crater lake just below Gunung Patuha (2334m). Though only a small crater, Kawah Putih is exceptionally beautiful and eerily quiet when the mists roll in and mingle with the steam of the warm lake and the bubbling sulphur deposits.

Back on the road a few km further south are the fairly commercial hot springs at **Cimanggu**.

Rancabali, 42 km from Bandung, is a tea-estate town surrounded by the rolling green hills of the tea plantations. Just two km south of the town is **Situ Patengan**, a pretty lake with tea rooms and boats catering to the Sunday crowds.

Also south of Bandung, **Situ Cileunca** is an artificial lake damned for a hydro-electric scheme, outside the hill town of Pen-galengan.

Places to Stay

Accommodation is limited, and empty during the week. In Ciwidey, *Penginapan Sederhana* on the main road opposite the market has dismal rooms for 7500 rp. The *Sindang Reret Hotel* (☎ 237602) and *Motel Sukarasa Endah* (☎ 9958311) are both on

the highway north of town and have large Sundanese restaurants built over fish ponds. The Sindang Reret is slightly better and has comfortable rooms with hot water shower from 42,000 to 82,000 rp.

At Alam Endah, five km south of Ciwidey, the *Pondok Endah Sari* on the main road has basic rooms from 14,000 rp. *Pondok Taman Unyil Lestari*, half a km from the main road, has rooms and thatched cottages from 32,500 rp. The rooms are expensive, but compensated by fine views, a nice garden and a good restaurant.

Pengalengan has two cheap hotels but the town is of minor interest. At the Malabar tea estate, five km from town, *Malabar Mess* is a delightful colonial guesthouse furnished with Dutch antiques. Rooms cost 75,000 to 150,000 rp. Reservations must be made through Perkebunan XIII (☎ 2502049), Jl I H Juanda 107, Bandung.

Getting There & Away

Frequent buses run between Bandung's Kebon Kelapa bus terminal and Ciwidey (700 rp; 1½ hours). From Ciwidey local angkots run to Situ Patengan (800 rp). Kawah Putih is not serviced by regular public transport, but you'll find plenty of ojeks in Alam Endah.

BANDUNG TO PANGANDARAN

Heading south-east from Bandung, the road passes through a scenic and fertile stretch of hilly countryside and volcanic peaks. This is the Bandung-Yogya road as far as Banjar; the Bandung to Yogya train line passes through Tasikmalaya and Banjar, but not Garut. The district is part of the Parahyangan highlands around Bandung.

Garut & Cipanas

Sixty-three km south-east of Bandung, Garut is a highland town and a centre for vegetable, orange, tea and tobacco growing. The town is ringed by impressive volcanic peaks that have provided the valley's fertility. Garut itself is just another town, but the surrounding area has a number of attractions.

On the outskirts of town, six km north

west, are the hot springs at Cipanas, a small resort at the foot of Gunung Guntur and an ideal base to explore the area. From Cipanas, the **Curug Citiis** waterfall is a three km walk away up the mountain and a four hour walk further on to the peak of Gunung Guntur. It is best to leave by 5 am for good views.

Ngamplang, five km from Garut on the south-eastern outskirts, has a nine hole golf course and resort hotel, and adu domba (ram fights) are held here on the first and third Sunday of the month.

Garut is famed for its *dodol* – a confectionery made of coconut milk, palm sugar and sticky rice. At the bus terminal hawkers selling tubes of sweet dodol besiege the passing buses and it's sold at many shops around town. The 'Picnic' brand is the best quality, and it is possible to visit the Picnic factory on Jl Pasundan.

Places to Stay Garut has plenty of hotels and guesthouses, but Cipanas is the nicest place to stay.

In Garut, *Wisma PKPN* (☎ 231508) at Jl Ciledug 79 has clean rooms with attached mandi for 15,000 rp. *Hotel Kota Baru* is a passable, cheap hotel on Jl Merdeka near the bus terminal. The *Hotel Sarimbit* (☎ 231033), Jl Oto Iskandardinata 236, is on the outskirts of town in Tarogong, on the way to Cipanas. Pleasant rooms with attached bathroom are 27,000 to 40,000 rp.

Cipanas has over a dozen hotels strung along Jl Raya Cipanas, the resort's single road. All have rooms with large baths with water piped in from the hot springs – pamper yourself after a hard day's trekking. Cheap hotels include the basic *Pondok Kurnia Artha* (☎ 232112), which has dark but OK rooms for 15,000 rp. The *Hotel Tirta Merta* (☎ 231422) is cheerier and has singles/doubles from 17,500/22,500 rp. Both hotels charge 5000 rp more on weekends. More expensive, but no better, are the *Hotel Banyu Arta* and *Penginapan Cipta Rasa*, both with rooms from 25,000 rp.

As well as hot baths, the following hotels have swimming pools heated by the springs. *Cipanas Indah* (☎ 233736) is a good mid-

range hotel favoured by tour groups. Rooms start at 30,000 rp and good VIP rooms are 44,000 rp (around 5000 rp more on weekends). The *Sumber Alam* (☎ 231027) is the most attractive hotel, with rooms built over the water ranging from 50,000 to 200,000 rp (40% more on weekends). The big, rebuilt *Tirtagangga* (☎ 232549) is the top hotel, with rooms from 115,000 rp during the week.

Getting There & Away Buses and angkots leave from Garut's Terminal Guntur, in the north of town. Garut is easily reached by bus from Bandung (1300 rp; two hours) and Tasikmalaya (1200 rp; two hours). For Pangandaran take another bus from Tasikmalaya. Buses also go to Jakarta (5000 to 7500 rp).

Regular angkots run around town (350 rp), including Cipanas (angkot No 4) and Ngamplang, and to the nearby villages. A car or minibus with driver can be rented in Cipanas – ask around the hotels. A trip to Papandayan (see below) will cost around 30,000 to 40,000 rp.

Around Garut

Near Leles, about 10 km north of Garut, is **Candi Cangkuang**, one of the few stone Hindu temples found in West Java. Dating from the 8th century, some of its stones were found to have been carved into tombstones for a nearby Islamic cemetery. The small, restored temple lies on the edge of Situ Cangkuang, a small lake, and has become something of a tourist trap. From Garut take a No 10 angkot to Leles on the highway and then an andong for the four km to Candi Cangkuang. Boats across the lake to the temple want 6000 rp.

Twenty-eight km to the south-west, **Gunung Papandayan** (2662m) is one of the most active volcanoes in West Java. Papandayan has only existed since 1772, when a large piece of the mountain exploded sideways in a catastrophe that killed more than 3000 people. It last erupted in 1925. The bubbling yellow crater (Kawah Papandayan) just below the peak is an impressive sight and clearly visible from Garut valley on fine mornings. To get there, take a Cikajang minibus and get off at the turn-off on the outskirts of Cisurupan where you can catch a waiting ojek (2500 rp; 13 km). From the carpark area it is an easy half hour walk to the crater, which is riddled with bubbling mud pools, steam vents and crumbling sulphur deposits. Take care – keep well to the right when ascending through the crater, or it may pay to hire a guide for closer inspection. For fine views, go very early in the morning before the clouds roll in. Gunung Papandayan summit is a two hour walk beyond the crater, and there are fields of Javan edelweiss near the top. Entry is 1000 rp per person at the PHPA hut, and PHPA staff can arrange a camping permit and guide for overnight stays.

To the east of Garut, **Gunung Telagabodas** (2201m) has a bubbling bright-green crater lake alive with sulphur. To get to Telagabodas, take an angkot to Wanaraja (400 rp), then an ojek (2000 rp) and walk to the crater. Other craters to the west of Garut that can be visited are **Kawah Darajat**, 26 km away, and **Kawah Kamojang**, 23 km away, the site of a geothermal plant that has defused the once spectacular geyser activity and replaced it with huge pipes.

Halfway between Garut and Tasikmalaya is **Kampung Naga**, a traditional village and museum piece of Sundanese architecture and village life. The old ways are very much preserved in Kampung Naga – the many tour groups that visit wouldn't come otherwise. Despite the fact that it can be crowded some mornings when the big bus-loads arrive, there's no denying the beauty of the place. Kampung Naga, with its thatched-roof houses, is nestled next to a river and surrounded by steep hills terraced with rice paddies – a photographer's dream. Kampung Naga is 26 km from Garut. From Neglasari on the main highway more than 300 steps lead down into the valley.

Pameungpeuk & Around

The picturesque, twisting road south from Garut leads through vegetable plots, tea plantations and pine forests to Pameungpeuk on the south coast. This area has some reasonable beaches, but it is difficult to get to and not that interesting. Pameungpeuk itself is a fair-sized town, while **Pantai Sayang Heulang**, four km away, has an attractive white-coral beach fronting a reef that will cut swimmers to shreds. Pantai Sayang Heulang has three basic hotels and a few warungs.

Further west, **Pantai Santolo** is the best beach, on a sheltered bay where swimming is possible when the sea is calm. Prahus can take you across the river to a small forest reserve on the headland. *Hotel Citra Agung* two km away on the main road, has rooms for 12,000 rp.

Isolated **Leuweung Sancang**, 35 km east of Pameungpeuk, is a nature reserve noted for its banteng, gibbon and jungle trekking. For permits and information check with the PHPA in Pameungpeuk.

Getting There & Away From Garut, regular minibuses go to Pameungpeuk (2000 rp, three hours). To reach Sayang Heulang or Santolo, you either have to walk from the main road or catch an ojek from Pameungpeuk.

Tasikmalaya

Sixty km east of Garut, Tasikmalaya is the centre for the district of the same name. It is noted for rattan crafts: palm leaf and bamboo are used to make floor mats, baskets, trays, straw hats and paper umbrellas. Tasikmalaya (usually called simply Tasik) also has a small batik industry, and is also noted for its *border* lacework and *kelom geulis* (wooden sandals). For travellers, it is merely a transit town on the way to Pangandaran, but the surrounding area has a few points of interest.

Places to Stay An inexpensive place to stay is the central *Hotel Kencana*, Jl Yudanegara 17, close to the mosque with adequate rooms from 10,000 rp, more on weekends and holidays. Jl Yudanegara has plenty of other hotels, including the *Wisma Galunggung* in an old Dutch house. The best for the price is the *Abadi Hotel* (☎ 332789), Jl Empang 58

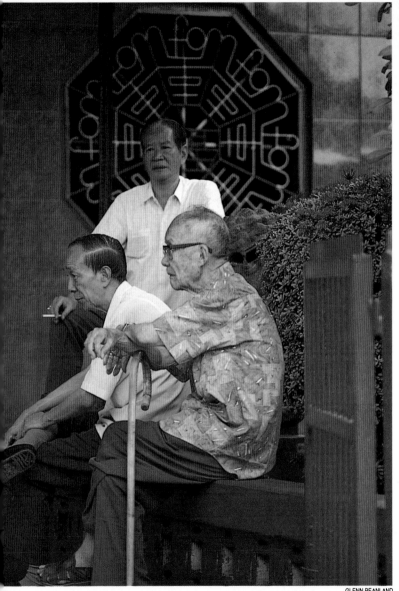

ld men outside the Vihara Dharma Bhakti Temple, Glodok, Jakarta, Java.

Java
Top: Brightly painted becak, Pangandaran, West Java.
Bottom: Fishermen hauling in the nets, Ambunten, Madura, East Java.

Spotlessly clean rooms with bath cost 17,500 rp, including breakfast.

Getting There & Away From Tasikmalaya buses operate to Bandung (2000/3000 rp; four hours), Garut (1200 rp; two hours), Pangandaran (3500 rp; three hours), Banjar, Jakarta, Cipatujah, Cirebon etc. The main bus terminal is four km from the town centre on the eastern outskirts. Tasikmalaya is also on the main rail line.

Around Tasikmalaya

For cheap rattan crafts, visit the village of **Rajapolah**, 12 km north of Tasikmalaya on the road to Bandung, where many of the weavers work.

Cipanas Galunggung, 20 km north-west, is a hot spring at the foot of Gunung Galunggung, a volcano which exploded dramatically in 1982. From the hot springs recreation park, a trail leads to a small waterfall and then on to Galunggung crater, three km away. A road to the crater, suitable only for 4WD vehicles, is an easier walk but less interesting. From Tasikmalaya's main bus terminal take an angkot to Bantar (400 rp) on the highway and then an ojek (3000 rp) can take you the 14 km along a very bad road.

Situ Lengkong, 40 km north of Tasikmalaya and 500m from the village of Panjalu, is a serene lake formed when the Hindu ruler of Panjalu dammed the valley, with a forested island in the middle. Boats can be hired for around 5000 rp to take you around the island. Panjalu village has a small museum containing the heirlooms of the kings of Panjalu. Situ Lengkong can be reached by bus from Tasikmalaya (1000 rp; one hour) or from Terminal Kawali, where angkots run the 20 km to Ciamis.

On the highway to Banjar and Pangandaran, 16 km south-east of Ciamis, **Karang Komulyan** is the excavated site of the ancient Galuh kingdom. Local guides and tourist literature give a glorified account of the Galuh kingdom as both the first Hindu and the first Muslim kingdom on Java, but this neolithic settlement dating from around the 5th century points to the pre-Hindu period. Only a few stone walls and foundations remain of the 'palace', store, prayer and bathing areas, but it is a beautiful walk through the jungle and bamboo groves down to the confluence of the swift Ciliwung and Citanduy rivers. A large carpark and government-built cottages next to the park are attempts to make it a major tourist stop.

Banjar

Banjar, 42 km east of Tasikmalaya, is the junction point where the Pangandaran road branches from the Bandung to Yogya road and rail route. Banjar has some basic hotels if you get stuck en route to Pangandaran – try not to.

Getting There & Away The bus terminal is four km west of town on the highway. Many buses can be caught as they come through the centre of town near the train station. Banjar's reputation (particularly relating to its bus terminal) as a den of thievery and overcharging seems to be improving. From Banjar buses go to Pangandaran (2500 rp; one hour), Bandung, Purwokerto, and Jakarta's Kampung Rambutan bus terminal (10,000 rp air-con; eight hours). Buses also go from the Banjarsari bus terminal, half an hour south of Banjar, to Kampung Rambutan.

Banjar is not a good place to catch trains from. Most are crowded through trains and it is difficult to get on the better express trains, so chances are you'll be stuck without a seat on a slow, crowded rattler. The *Galuh* to Bandung (10,000 rp bisnis; 4½ hours) and Pasar Senen train station in Jakarta (10,000 rp bisnis; nine hours) originates in Banjar and provides a reasonable service, but leaves at 6 am. It leaves Pasar Senen at 2.40 pm.

PANGANDARAN

The fishing village of Pangandaran is Java's most popular beach resort. It lies on the narrow isthmus of a peninsula with broad sandy beaches that sweep back along the mainland. At the end of the bulbous peninsula is the Pangandaran National Park.

Pangandaran has black sand beaches and

Pangandaran

Not to Scale

PLACES TO STAY

2 Pasanggrahan Dewi Laut Kidul (Yuli Beach)
3 Bouganville
10 Bamboo House
11 Mini 3
12 Hotel Citra
13 Surya Pesona Beach Hotel
14 Hideaway
15 Adam's Homestay
16 Duta Beach Hotel
17 Putri Duyung Hotel
18 Hotel Pantai Uni
19 Sandaan Hotel
20 Dahlia Indah Hotel
21 Bulak Laut Bungalows
23 Bulak Laut Bungalows
24 Bayu Indah Hotel
25 Pantai Sari Hotel
27 Lambada Hotel
28 Paradise Hotel
30 Holiday Inn
31 Mutiara Selatan
32 Bimasakti Hotel
41 Hotel Bumi Pananjung
42 Pantai Indah Timur Hotel
44 Losmen Pusaka
46 Wisma Galuh
46 Hotel Mustika Ratu
49 Bumi Nusantara Hotel
51 Dewi Laut
52 Susan's Guest House
53 Losmen Mini II
54 Sari Harum Losmen & Restaurant
55 Samudra Hotel
56 Pantai Indah Barat Hotel
57 Sunrise Beach Hotel
58 Panorama Hotel
59 Adem Ayem Hotel
61 Setia Famili
62 Losmen Mini I
69 Pondok Pelangi
70 Rawamangun Lodge
71 Pondok Pelangi
73 Mangkubumi Beach Hotel
74 Mangkubumi Indah Hotel
75 Nyiur Indah Hotel & Restaurant
76 Penginapan Saputra
77 Hotel Pangandaran
79 Pondok Moris
80 Wismawan Hotel

PLACES TO EAT

7 Hillman's Fish Farm Restaurant
8 Cafe Bagus
22 Skandinavian Restaurant
26 Relax Coffee Shop
29 Bunga Laut Restaurant
33 Rumah Makan Number One
36 Warung Gypsy
40 Pasar Ikan (Fish Market)
60 Chez Mama Cilicap
63 Inti Laut
64 Lonely Planet Restaurant
67 Simpati Cafe
72 Rumah Makan Nanjung

OTHER

1 Sari Bakti Bus Depot
4 Police Station
5 Market
6 Bus Terminal
9 Telkom Office
34 Cinema
35 Agung Travel
37 Luta Travel
38 Villa Electric (Minibus Agent)
39 Post Office
43 Mitra Marsada Utama Travel
47 Pasar Seni (Souvenir Market)
48 Meridien Disco
65 Bookshop
66 Fish Market (Wholesale)
68 Bank Rakyat Indonesia
78 PHPA Office
81 Souvenir Stalls
82 PHPA Office

Jalan Merdeka
To Babakan & Banjar
To Cikembulan
To Cikembulan
Gate
Gate
Jalan Bulak Laut
Jalan Sumadi
Jalan Pramuka
Jalan Talanca
Jalan Kalen Buhaya
Jalan Pananjaten
Jalan Kidang Pananjung
Jalan Pasanggrahan
Jalan Jaga Lautan

Pangandaran National Park

dangerous swimming (except for the more sheltered southern end of the west beach), but despite these drawbacks it is an idyllic place to take a break from travelling; the people are exceptionally friendly, accommolation is cheap and the seafood excellent. If gazing around the beaches and trekking through the jungle of the national park begins to pall, you can head off east or west to other quieter beaches and attractions nearby.

On weekends Pangandaran is very popular with Bandung residents, and during holidays – Christmas and the end of Ramadan in particular – the beaches have a temporary population of literally thousands. At other times this is just an overgrown fishing village, where brightly painted prahu fish the waters and whole families work together to pull in the nets.

Orientation & Information

Pangandaran extends for about three km from the bus terminal and market to the national park boundary in the south. The town is flanked by the west and east beaches, and dissected by the main street, Jl Kidang Pananjung. The west beach is a wide sweep of sand and the main resort strip. The east beach is a quieter, fishing beach, and not much sand remains since a retaining wall was built.

A 1000 rp admission charge is levied at the gates on entering Pangandaran, and it costs another 1250 rp for each visit to the national park.

Tourist Offices Pangandaran has plenty of travel agents and private 'tourist information centres'. They sell bus tickets and arrange tours. Most provide a good service, though you may prefer guides registered with the Indonesian Guide Association. The central office for the association is in the Mangkabumi Beach Hotel on Jl Jaga Lautan.

Money The Bank Rakyat Indonesia on Jl Kidang Pananjung changes most currencies and major brands of travellers cheques at poor rates. It is open Monday to Thursday

from 8 am to noon and on Friday until 11 am. For after hours' transactions, you'll get even poorer rates from moneychangers.

Post & Communications The post office and Telkom office (open 24 hours) are both on Jl Kidang Pananjung.

Things to See & Do

Cloaked in jungle, **Pangandaran National Park** has banteng, *kijang* (barking deer), hornbill and monkeys, including Javan gibbon, and small bays within the park enclose tree-fringed beaches. Well-marked trails can be walked in the main reserve close to the PHPA posts. Further into the headland, trails are less easy to follow and often very muddy. Guides can be hired for longer allday walks, though some trails were closed at the time of writing due to forest degradation.

Like most south coast **beaches**, Pangandaran has black sand beaches and the surf can be treacherous. The northern end of the west beach is dangerous, but the southern end is sheltered by the headland and provides safe swimming. The national park has some sheltered beaches with rocky reefs for snorkelling at high tide, although the main white sand beach of Pasir Putih is now off limits to stop the hordes that have destroyed the reef.

Organised Tours

Pangandaran has a host of tour operators that are constantly thinking up new tours and hyperbole to describe them. Popular tours are to Green Canyon (30,000 rp per person), and 'countryside' or 'home industry' tours (20,000 to 25,000 rp), which take you to plantations and local industries to see the making of tofu, krupuk, sugar etc, as well as a wayang golek maker.

Mitra Marsada Utama (☎ 639733), Jl Kidang Pananjung 163, has tours to the untouched island of Nusa Kambangan (40,000 rp).

Then there are cycling, boating, walking and snorkelling tours to just about anywhere within a 50 km radius of Pangandaran. Tours are usually well run, informative and good value.

Places to Stay

Pangandaran has over 100 places to stay. At Christmas and Lebaran (the end of Ramadan) holidays, Pangandaran is packed and prices sky rocket. It can also get busy during school holidays and in the peak European holiday season, around July/August, but for much of the year most hotels are empty and Pangandaran is quiet. Prices are very seasonal. First night prices are often higher, because of the commission system employed by becak drivers.

Places to Stay – bottom end

Pangandaran The majority of Pangandaran's cheapest hotels are around the main street at the southern end of town.

Losmen Mini I is on the main road, Jl Kidang Pananjung. It is clean, convenient and popular. Singles/doubles with mandi cost 8500/12,500 rp, including breakfast. Across the road, the *Rawamangun Lodge* is very basic but clean, welcoming and cheap at 7500/10,000 rp.

On Jl Kalen Buhaya is a second Mini, *Losmen Mini II*. This long-popular place is a little cramped, but clean and reasonably priced at 8000 rp, or 15,000 rp for more substantial rooms with attached mandi, including breakfast.

On the eastern beach, the *Panorama Hotel* (☎ 639218) straddles the bottom end and mid-range. Pleasant verandah rooms facing the sea cost 25,000 rp with attached bathroom and breakfast, or rooms behind are 20,000 rp with shared facilities.

While the southern end of town has much more of a village atmosphere, the northern end around Jl Bulak Laut is more popular with travellers. Most places tend to be mid-range, but Bulak Laut has some good budget buys.

The popular *Holiday Inn* (☎ 639285), Jl Bulak Laut 50, is one of the cheapest. Bamboo rooms cost 7000/10,000 rp, or rooms with attached mandi are 15,000 rp. Next door at No 49, *Mutiara Selatan* (☎ 639416) is also

good value. Rooms with porch and attached bathroom cost 15,000 rp, including breakfast.

Closer to the beach, the *Pantai Sari Hotel* (☎ 639175) is popular and has a good restaurant. Doubles with fan and mandi cost 15,000 rp, or air-con rooms cost 25,000 rp. It pays to check a few out as the quality varies considerably, as does the price, depending on the season and length of stay.

Bamboo House (☎ 639419) is to the north and away from the beach, but this small family-run place is well worth considering. Attractive singles/doubles with mandi cost 10,000/15,000 rp, including breakfast; or the bungalow costs 20,000 rp.

Around Pangandaran The quiet beaches outside Pangandaran are increasingly popular places to hang out and relax, especially when Pangandaran is crowded during the main holiday periods. Most of the following guesthouses are run by westerners who have settled in Pangandaran, and are on the ball with information and services.

Cikembulan, four km along the beach road to the west, has a small enclave of guesthouses. *Delta Gecko* has a wide variety of bamboo and wood bungalows. A dorm bed costs 7500 rp, singles 10,000 rp, doubles with mandi from 15,000 rp, all including breakfast and free bicycles. It has a restaurant, lots of information and a cultural/BBQ night once a week. Its neighbor, the smaller *Losmen Kelapa Nunggal* is another switched-on place. New, spotless rooms with bathroom cost 12,500/15,000 rp. About half a km back towards Pangandaran on the beach road, *Tono Homestay* is a friendly, cosy place where good rooms with mandi cost 20,000 rp. The *Ibu Iwa Restaurant* nearby has a few rooms at the back but is primarily a good place to eat.

Four km east of Pangandaran in Babakan, the *Laguna Beach Bungalows* (☎ 639761) offers stylish mid-range accommodation and has a good restaurant. Delightful bungalows facing the beach cost 45,000 rp, dropping to 35,000 rp per day for stays of more than two days. Ring for pick-up. Half a km away, andy's Beach (☎ 379085) has bungalows of similar standard and price, but is a little ull.

Places to Stay – middle & top end
The west beach strip along Jl Pamugaran near Jl Bulak Laut is Pangandaran's Riviera, with a host of good value mid-range hotels popular with Europeans.

An oldie but a goodie is the *Bulak Laut Bungalows* (☎ 639377), on the corner of Jl Pamugaran and Bulak Laut, and at the nnexe a few doors further north. Attractive bungalows, most with their own sitting rooms, cost 25,000 and 30,000 rp, including breakfast. Discounts may be available for longer stays, making them exceptional value.

Back from the beach at Jl Bulak Laut 45, he new *Bimasakti Hotel* (☎ 639194) has a restaurant, small pool and immaculate rooms for 66,000 and 88,000 rp (more on weekends).

Further north, *Sandaan Hotel* (☎ 639165) has plain fan rooms with shower costing 5,000 and 50,000 rp, or more luxurious air-con rooms are 80,000 rp, including breakfast. Prices sky rocket in holiday periods. The main attractions are the small swimming pool and the good restaurant.

The delightful *Adam's Homestay* (☎ 63-164) has eclectic architecture, a book shop, good cappuccinos and a small pool. This excellent establishment has large rooms from 29,000/35,000 rp up to 125,000 rp for a luxury two bedroom bungalow.

One of Pangandaran's best, *Surya Pesona Beach Hotel* (☎ 639428) is a big resort hotel with a swimming pool, expensive restaurant and rooms from 95,000 rp.

The *Pasanggrahan Dewi Laut Kidul* better known as Yuli Beach; ☎ 639375) is a long hike from the nearest restaurant, but it is quiet, has a pool and the boutique bungalows with sunken lounge areas offer some of the best accommodation in Pangandaran. Bungalows cost 60,000 rp, but the rate reduces by 5000 rp per night, down to 45,000 rp for stays of three days or more. Rooms

cost 30,000 and 40,000 rp. Tax and service charges apply.

More mid-range hotels can be found towards the southern end of the west beach. Behind the Pasar Seni, the new *Hotel Mustika Ratu* (☎ 639730) has an attractive restaurant and well-presented rooms for 50,000 rp with fan, 80,000 rp with air-con – before discount.

Pondok Pelangi (☎ 639023) has older, self-contained two/three bedroom bungalows in an attractive garden for 200,000/250,000 rp in the high season, negotiable for much less in the low season.

One of Pangandaran's most pleasant hotels is the *Sunrise Beach Hotel* (☎ 639220) at Jl Kidang Pananjung 175 on the east beach. It has a swimming pool and a good restaurant, and attractive, sizeable rooms from US$25/30 for a double with fan, from US$45/50 with air-con, all plus 21%.

Across the street from the Sunrise, the *Pantai Indah Barat* (☎ 639006), along with its plush cousin on the east beach *Pantai Indah Timur* (☎ 630714), offer top-of-the-range accommodation; both are usually empty. The Timur has a huge pool and tennis courts, while the Barat has a more modest pool, tennis courts and a restaurant. Air-con rooms start at 105,000 rp at the Barat and 140,000 rp at the Timur.

Places to Eat
Pangandaran has plenty of restaurants catering to western tastes, with western-style breakfasts, seafood (shrimps, squid and fish), pancakes and a variety of fruit juices and fruit salads. Of course, Indonesian dishes are widely available too, as is Chinese seafood. Seafood is usually very good; other meals are of variable quality.

Popular places for cheap eats are the small, warmly lit warungs on Jl Kidang Pananjung. The basic *Simpati Cafe* is usually packed out because its prices are so reasonable; it serves excellent fruit salads, gado gado and a variety of grilled fish. Over the road, the *Inti Laut* restaurant specialises in superb grilled fish and seafood. On weekends and holidays it turns over more fish than the average fishing boat, but it is often closed in the quiet periods. The nearby *Lonely Planet Restaurant* (no relation!) is on the grotty side but the seafood is cheaper and good.

Chez Mama Cilacap at Jl Kidang Pananjung 187 is one of Pangandaran's best restaurants, despite surly service, with an extensive menu, moderate prices, fresh fish and icy fruit juices.

On the west beach at the southern end, the no-frills *Rumah Makan Nanjung* has a pleasant open-air dining area and good cheap seafood. It really knows how to barbecue fish, and the sauces are excellent, or you could try the 'Fried Frog Balls' for 6000 rp. Further south, the restaurant at the *Nyiur Indah Hotel* is a little more expensive but one of Pangandaran's best Chinese seafood restaurants. Further north, next to the Bumi Nusantara Hotel, is a warung area with cheap Indonesian dishes and sea breezes.

The Bulak Laut area has plenty of eateries. On Jl Bulak Laut, the *Pantai Sari Hotel* has a popular restaurant with Indonesian dishes, reasonable western fare and fish. The *Relax Coffee Shop* is one of Pangandaran's fanciest restaurants and, though overpriced, it is worth shelling out for a weighty slice of its delicious volkenbrot bread. On the other side of the street, the *Holiday Inn* has a typical travellers' menu, is cheap and the breakfasts are good. A few doors along, the *Bunga Laut Restaurant* is shamefully underpatronised because it serves only Indonesian food. Sundanese dishes are a speciality – photographs of the dishes accompany the menu. Further back from the beach *Rumah Makan Number One* has a mixed menu, moderate prices and some style.

The big hotels have restaurants for more-expensive dining. The *Sunrise Beach Hotel* has good food and service, and is recommended for a splurge. *Hillman's Fish Farm Restaurant*, north of the bus terminal, is good for seafood but expensive.

In addition to the restaurants, the excellent Pasar Ikan (Fish Market) on the east beach sells fresh fish, and a selection of good warungs serve seafood according to weight.

The market is to the north near the post offic (not the fish market to the south, which is th wholesale market). The main market near th bus terminal is the place to stock up on frui

Women also do the rounds of the hote with buckets of prawns, lobster, fish, squi or whatever else is in season, and will retur in the evenings with a complete meal cooke up for you.

Getting There & Away

Pangandaran lies halfway between Bandun and Yogya. Coming from Yogya by bus c rail, Banjar is the transit point, though th most popular way to reach Pangandaran i via the pleasant backwater trip from Cilaca to Kalipucang. From Bandung, plenty c direct buses go to Pangandaran, or it's possibl to change for connections in Tasikmalaya.

Pangandaran's long-awaited airport, 2 km to the west, is nearing completion and may soon be possible to fly to Pangandara

Bus Local buses run from Pangandaran' bus terminal to Tasikmalaya (3500 rp; thre hours), Ciamis (3500 rp; 2½ hours), Banja (2500 rp; 1½ hours) and Kalipucang (500 rp 40 minutes). Buses also run along the wes coast as far as Cijulang (750 rp; 40 minutes

The large patas (express) buses leave fror the bus company depots about two km wes of Pangandaran along Jl Merdeka. The Sar Bakti and Budiman companies have frequen buses to/from Bandung (6000/7000 rp ai con; six hours) between 4 am and 6 pm, an also to Bogor (11,500 rp air-con; nine hours Along with the Primajasa company they als have buses to Jakarta for around 12,500 rp but these terminate in Bekasi, 22 km east c Jakarta.

The best option for reaching Jakarta is th Mitra Marsada Utama (☎ 639733) bus tha picks up in Pangandaran and goes right to J Jaksa for 28,000 rp. It leaves Wednesday Friday and Saturday at 9 am, and takes abou 11 hours, longer if Jakarta traffic is bad. I will also drop off in Bogor. The most com fortable way to Bandung is with the Sar Harum door-to-door minibus for 14,000 rp

Agents in Pangandaran sell bus tickets for premium, but they save a lot of hassle and usually include transport to the depots. Commission can be very high – it pays to shop around.

The best way to reach Central Java is via the Kalipucang-Cilacap ferry (see Boat later in this section), with bus connections at either end. If for some reason the boat doesn't appeal, take a bus to Banjar then another bus to Purwokerto for onward buses to Yogya or Wonosobo. You can take the train from Banjar, but economy services heading east are crowded, slow and it is hard to get a seat. Heading to Bandung and Jakarta by train, the *Galuh* originates in Banjar but leaves at 6 am.

Car Most travel agents rent cars with drivers. Most have a list of destinations around Pangandaran and right across Java, but the rates are very high. You are better off trying to organise your own itinerary and negotiate a daily rate.

Boat One of the highlights of a trip to Pangandaran is the interesting backwater trip between Cilacap and Kalipucang. From Pangandaran it starts with a 17 km bus trip to Kalipucang (500 rp; 45 minutes). From Kalipucang the ferry travels across the wide expanse of Segara Anakan and along the waterway sheltered by the island of Nusa Kambangan. It's a fascinating, peaceful trip, hopping from village to village in a rickety 35m wooden boat. As well as carrying a regular contingent of tourists, it's a very popular local service.

Ferries (1300 rp; four hours) leave from Kalipucang at 7 and 8 am and 1 pm (also 6 am and noon if there is demand). Catch one of the early morning ferries to reach Yogya or Wonosobo in one day. Coming the other way, boats depart from Cilacap until 1 pm. From the Cilacap harbour it is about one km to the main road (no more than 500 rp by becak), from where bemos go to the Cilacap bus terminal (300 rp). From Cilacap direct buses go to Yogya or Wonosobo for the Dieng Plateau.

The trip is made very easy by the door-to-door services between Pangandaran and Yogya. Bus-ferry-bus services (15,000 rp; eight hours) are sold all around Pangandaran. Connections to Wonosobo are also advertised, but these are on Yogya buses which will drop you in Purworejo, from where you have to get public buses to Wonosobo. Various extended tours, taking in the ferry then Dieng and Borobudur on the way to Yogya, are also sold and quite popular.

Getting Around
Pangandaran's brightly painted becaks cost a fixed 1000 rp around town regardless of the length of the journey. Bicycles are also an ideal way to get around and can be rented for as little as 4000 rp per day. Motorcycles will cost from around 12,000 rp per day and are ideal for exploring the area around Pangandaran.

AROUND PANGANDARAN
The scenic coast road west from Pangandaran to Cipatujah skirts along the surf-pounded beaches and runs through small villages and paddy fields. **Cikembulan**, four km from Pangandaran, has accommodation (see under Pangandaran) and local industries that can be visited, including the krupuk factory, on the main road just west of the bridge, and a wayang golek workshop.

Karang Tirta, 16 km from Pangandaran and two km from the highway, is a lagoon set back from the beach with *bagang*, night fishing platforms. **Batu Hiu** (Shark Rock), 23 km from Pangandaran and one km from the highway, has a recreational park atop the cliffs with views along the coast.

Inland from Parigi, near Cigugur, **Gunung Tiga** has fine views and is included in many of the tour itineraries. The **Sungai Citumang**, reached by a rough and hard-to-find inland road from Karang Benda, has a small dam from where you can walk upstream to a beautiful gorge – 'Green Canyon II' in Pangandaran tour parlance.

Batu Karas, 42 km from Pangandaran

and 10 km off the highway, is a relaxed fishing village with a surf beach – one of the safest and best on the coast. Accommodation, favoured by Australian surfers, can be found one km beyond the fishing village at the headland beach. *Melati Indah* is the best value and has well-kept rooms for 15,000 and 20,000 rp. *Teratai Cottage* has a run-down swimming pool, and run-down rooms for 25,000 and 40,000 rp. Next door, *Alana's Bungalows* has bamboo decor, surf culture and rooms for 15,000 rp, 30,000 rp with mandi. On the other side of the village to the east, the new *Cijulang Permai* has a pool and very good mid-range rooms for 90,000 rp, but it is a long way from anywhere and the beach is ordinary. Batu Karas can be reached from Pangandaran by taking a bus to Cijulang (750 rp) and then an ojek for 1000 rp.

Pangandaran's No 1 tour is to **Green Canyon**. Many tour operators in Pangandaran run trips here for around 30,000 rp and usually include 'countryside' excursions on the way. To get there yourself, hire a boat from the various jetties on the highway near the turn-off to Batu Karas. A boat will cost 21,000 rp for five people. It travels up the emerald-green river through the forest to a waterfall and a steep rock canyon, and stops here for swimming. Count on two hours for this excellent trip, but it has become so popular that there can be a flotilla of boats on the river.

The coast road ends at the village of **Cipatujah**, which has a wide but uninspiring beach with dangerous swimming, and a

couple of cheap hotels. Five km befor Cipatujah is a small PHPA post that monitor the green turtles that lay their eggs a **Sindangkerta** beach. The post welcome interested visitors.

To the east of Pangandaran, **Karang Nii** is a recreational park perched high on th cliffs. Trails lead down the cliff face to th beach and crashing surf below. Apart fro the occasional pair of young lovers, Karan Nini is deserted during the week. The park i run by the PHPA and it is possible to stay i its guesthouse.

Getting There & Away

Buses run to Cijulang from Pangandaran, bu to get to Cipatujah requires catching a hos of local buses and *angkutan pedesaan* (vil lage bemos). Cipatujah is well serviced b buses from Tasikmalaya and some continu to Ciparanti. From Cipatujah there are eve buses to Jakarta. The best way to see thi stretch of coast is to hire a motorcycle i Pangandaran.

For Karang Nini, take any Kalipucang bound bus to the Karang Nini turn-off (40 rp), nine km east of Pangandaran on th highway. It is then a three km walk to th park.

CIREBON

Few people make the trip out to Cirebon, bu it's an interesting seaport and the seat of a ancient Islamic kingdom with its ow kratons (palaces). On the north coast, nea the border with Central Java, the city

istory has been influenced by both the
avanese and Sundanese with Chinese
ulture thrown in for good measure. A
ulti-ethnic city, the local dialect blends
undanese and Javanese.

Cirebon was one of the independent sul-
anates founded by Sunan Gunungjati of
Demak in the early 16th century. Later the
owerful kingdoms of Banten and Mataram
ought over Cirebon, which declared alle-
iance to Sultan Agung of Mataram but was
nally ceded to the Dutch in 1677. By a
urther treaty of 1705 Cirebon became a
Dutch protectorate, jointly administered by
hree sultans whose courts at that time
valled those of Central Java in opulence
nd splendour. Two of Cirebon's kratons are
pen to visitors and, although not as large as
ne palaces of Yogya and Solo, are well worth
isiting.

During the Dutch Culture System, forced
abour produced a flourishing trade in colo-
ial crops. Cirebon's great wealth attracted
any Chinese entrepreneurs, and the
Chinese influence can still be seen in the
esign of Cirebon's famous batik. The coun-
ryside fared less well under the Culture
ystem – famine and epidemics swept the
egion in the 1840s.

Cirebon has long been a major centre for
atik, and is also famous for its *tari topeng*,
type of masked dance, and tarling music,
lending guitar, suling (bamboo flute) and
oice. Cirebon is also important as the major
ort and fishing harbour between Jakarta and
emarang, with the added bonus that it has
xcellent seafood.

The north coast, particularly in the dry
eason, can be a sweltering contrast to the
ooler heights inland. Other than that,
Cirebon is a well-kept city small enough not
o be overwhelming, and makes a worth-
vhile stopover.

nformation

ourist Office The tourist office is inconve-
iently sited five km out of town on the
ypass road, near Gua Sunyaragi. It has a few
rochures in Indonesian – not worth the trip.

Money Bank Central Asia, Jl Karanggetas
24, changes travellers cheques and foreign
cash at good rates. Bank Bumi Daya, Jl
Siliwangi 137, and Bank Niaga, Jl Siliwangi
110, are also convenient.

Post & Communications Cirebon's main
post office is near the harbour on Jl Yos
Sudarso and a post office branch is just
across the canal on Jl Karanggetas.

For international telephone calls and
faxes, the Telkom office is on Jl Yos Sudarso.
Warpostals at Jl Kartini 7 and Jl Bahagia 40
offer the same services, but don't allow
collect international calls.

Kraton Kesepuhan

At the south end of Jl Lemah Wungkuk, the
Kraton Kesepuhan is the oldest and most
well preserved of Cirebon's kratons. It was
built in 1527, and its architecture and interior
are a curious blend of Sundanese, Javanese,
Islamic, Chinese and Dutch styles. Although
this is the home of the Sultan of Kesepuhan,
part of the building is open to visitors. Inside
the palace is a cool pavilion with whitewashed walls dotted with blue-and-white
Delft tiles, a marble floor and a ceiling hung
with glittering French chandeliers.

The kraton museum has an interesting, if
somewhat run-down, collection of wayang
puppets, kris, cannon, furniture, Portuguese
armour and ancient royal clothes. But the
pièce de résistance of the sultan's collection
is the Kereta Singabarong, a 17th century
gilded coach with the trunk of an elephant
(Hindu), the body and head of a dragon
(Chinese-Buddhist) and wings (Islamic)! It
was traditionally pulled by four white buffaloes. It's near the entrance of the Gedong
Singa carriage museum.

Entry to the kraton is 1000 rp and includes
a guided tour; camera fees are an extra 500
to 2000 rp. The kraton is open from 8 am to
4 pm daily (until 5 pm on public holidays).

Gamelan, wayang and tari topeng performances in the traditional Cirebon style are
sometimes held at the kraton.

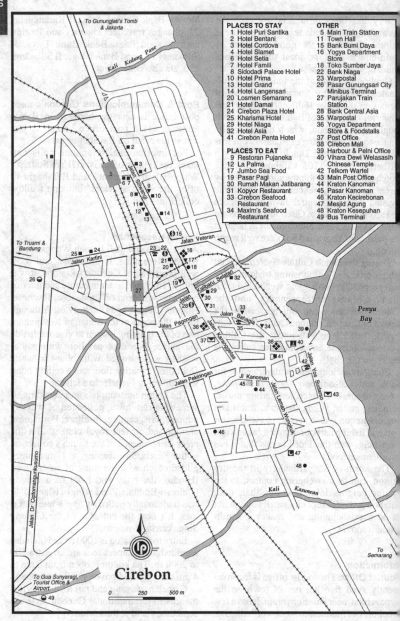

PLACES TO STAY
1 Hotel Puri Santika
2 Hotel Bentani
3 Hotel Cordova
4 Hotel Slamet
6 Hotel Setia
7 Hotel Famili
8 Sidodadi Palace Hotel
10 Hotel Prima
13 Hotel Grand
14 Hotel Langensari
20 Losmen Semarang
21 Hotel Damai
24 Cirebon Plaza Hotel
25 Kharisma Hotel
29 Hotel Niaga
32 Hotel Asia
41 Cirebon Penta Hotel

PLACES TO EAT
9 Restoran Pujaneka
12 La Palma
17 Jumbo Sea Food
19 Pasar Pagi
30 Rumah Makan Jatibarang
31 Kopyor Restaurant
33 Cirebon Seafood Restaurant
34 Maxim's Seafood Restaurant

OTHER
5 Main Train Station
11 Town Hall
15 Bank Bumi Daya
16 Yogya Department Store
18 Toko Sumber Jaya
22 Bank Niaga
23 Warpostal
26 Pasar Gunungsari City Minibus Terminal
27 Parujakan Train Station
28 Bank Central Asia
35 Warpostal
36 Yogya Department Store & Foodstalls
37 Post Office
38 Cirebon Mall
39 Harbour & Pelni Office
40 Vihara Dewi Welasasih Chinese Temple
42 Telkom Wartel
43 Main Post Office
44 Kraton Kanoman
45 Pasar Kanoman
46 Kraton Kecirebonan
47 Mesjid Agung
48 Kraton Kesepuhan
49 Bus Terminal

To Gunungjati's Tomb & Jakarta

Kali Kedung Pane

Jalan Siliwangi

To Trusmi & Bandung

Jalan Kartini

Jalan Veteran

Kaliparu Selatan

Jalan

Jalan Bahagia

Jalan Pagongan

Jalan Karanggetas

Jalan Pekiringan

Jl Kanoman

Jalan Lemah Wungkuk

Jalan Yos Sudarso

Penyu Bay

Jalan Dr Ciptomangunkusumo

Kali Kasunean

To Gua Sunyaragi, Tourist Office & Airport

To Semarang

Cirebon

0   250   500 m

Mesjid Agung

On the west side of the field in front of the Kraton Kesepuhan, the Mesjid Agung, with its tiered roof, is one of the oldest mosques in Java, and is similar in style to the Mesjid Agung in Banten.

Kraton Kanoman

A short walk from Kraton Kesepuhan and approached through Pasar Kanoman, this kraton was constructed in 1588. Kraton Kanoman was founded by Sultan Badaruddin, who broke away from the main sultanate after a lineage dispute to the sixth sultan's heir. Outside the kraton is a red-brick, Balinese-style compound and a massive banyan tree, and further on past the white, stone lions is the kraton, a smaller, neglected cousin of Kraton Kesepuhan.

Go to the right past the lions, sign the register and a guide will unlock the museum. It's worth it – among the museum's small holdings of mostly carved doors is a stunning sultan's chariot, in the same style as the one in the Kraton Kesepuhan. It is claimed that the one in the Kraton Kesepuhan is a newer copy – the rivalry for the sultanate still exists it seems. You can also visit the *pendopo* (large open-sided pavilion) and its inner altar. Antique European plates, some with Dutch Reformist scenes from the Bible, can be seen before entering.

Opening hours are haphazard, but Kraton Kanoman is often open later than Kraton Kesepuhan. The guide's fee is by donation – 1000 rp per visitor is appropriate.

The colourful **Pasar Kanoman** market, just in front of the kraton, is at its most vibrant in the morning and worth a visit in its own right.

Gua Sunyaragi

About four km south-west of town, a not-to-be-missed attraction is this bizarre ruined 'cave' (*gua*) – a grotto of rocks, red brick and plaster, honeycombed with secret chambers, tiny doors and staircases leading nowhere. It was originally a water palace for a sultan of Cirebon in the early 18th century and owes its present strange shape to the efforts of a Chinese architect who had a go at it in 1852.

Other Attractions

Although it's classed as a kraton, **Kraton Kecirebonan** is really only a house occupied by members of the current royal family and is not open to the public. Built in 1839, it is worth a quick look for its exterior architecture, a blend of Dutch and Indonesian styles.

Places to Stay – bottom end

Inexpensive hotels can be found directly opposite the main train station. Very basic rooms can be had in the *Penginapan Budi Asih* and *Penginapan Lesana* for around 10,000 rp. The *Hotel Setia* (☎ 207270), Jl Inspeksi PJKA 1222, is much better but expensive at 20,000 rp a double with mandi.

Jl Siliwangi is the main drag for hotels. On the corner near the main train station, at Jl Siliwangi 66, the *Hotel Famili* (☎ 207935) is another basic place with singles/doubles from 12,500/17,000 rp. Other cheap but uninspiring hotels in the centre of town on Jl Siliwangi are the *Hotel Damai* (☎ 203045), at No 130, where doubles with mandi cost 14,000 to 22,000 rp, and *Losmen Semarang*, next door at No 132, with rooms for 10,000/15,000 rp.

The best bet is the *Hotel Asia* (☎ 202183), Jl Kalibaru Selatan 15, alongside the tree-lined canal near the Pasar Pagi. This fine old Dutch-Indonesian inn has a terraced courtyard where you can sit and have breakfast. It's about a 15 minute walk or 1500 rp by becak from the main train station. This very well-kept and friendly hotel has rooms with shared mandi for 15,000 and 18,000 rp, including breakfast. More expensive rooms with private mandi and fan cost 27,000 to 32,000 rp.

Places to Stay – middle

The *Hotel Grand* (☎ 208867) at Jl Siliwangi 98 is a pleasantly old-fashioned place with a big front verandah. Worn but large rooms with separate sitting areas have air-con, hot water and TV. They cost 43,000 rp for dark internal rooms, 53,000 rp for those with a view of the alun alun and 63,000 rp for suites with office areas.

The *Hotel Cordova* (☎ 204677), Jl Siliwangi 87, near the main train station, is one of the better buys. Good, renovated rooms with air-con and hot water cost 30,000 to 60,000 rp. Older rooms for 12,500 rp, or 17,500 rp with mandi, are tatty but cheap.

The *Sidodadi Palace Hotel* (☎ 202305), Jl Siliwangi 74, is a pleasant motel-style place built around a quiet courtyard. Comfortable rooms with air-con, hot water and parabola TV range from 76,000 to 96,000 rp. The *Hotel Slamet* (☎ 203296) at No 95 is a cheaper hotel, with reasonable fan rooms with mandi from 27,000 rp, air-con rooms with hot water from 38,500 rp.

The *Hotel Niaga* (☎ 206718), Jl Kalibaru Selatan 47, is rather dull but has large, clean rooms with air-con, TV, telephone and hot water for 38,500 and 55,000 rp.

Cirebon has a selection of more expensive mid-range hotels. Most are older hotels that have fallen from grace but offer attractive discounts. The large *Kharisma Hotel* (☎ 20-6795) at Jl Kartini 48 is typical, and has old rooms from US$35/40 or better rooms in the new section from US$70/80 – before discount.

Places to Stay – top end

Cirebon's better hotels charge 21% tax and service, but include breakfast. Competition is stiff and large discounts are readily available, making Cirebon's best hotels good value.

The very central *Cirebon Penta Hotel* (☎ 203328), Jl Syarif Addurakhman 159, is small but classy. Excellent rooms cost from US$65 (only 90,000 rp after discount). The hotel has a rooftop garden and a health centre. It is above the KFC restaurant, opposite the Cirebon Mall.

Close to the train station, *Hotel Bentani* (☎ 203246) at Jl Siliwangi 69 has a variety of rooms from uninspiring mid-range for US$50/60 to newer luxury for US$80/90, and a small pool.

The large *Hotel Prima* (☎ 205411) at Jl Siliwangi 107 has a pool, tennis court, health centre, business centre, restaurants and bar. The rooms, from US$70, are of a high standard but slightly faded. Buffet breakfast is included.

The *Hotel Puri Santika* (☎ 200570), Jl Dr Wahidin 32, is of a similar standard to the Prima, but newer and the best in town. Rooms start at US$85/95.

Places to Eat

Apart from Cirebon's fine seafood, a local speciality to try is nasi lengko, a delicious rice dish with bean sprouts, tahu, tempe, fried onion, cucumber and peanut sauce. The *Rumah Makan Jatibarang*, on the corner of Jl Karanggetas and Jl Kalibaru Selatan, has nasi lengko as well as other Indonesian dishes.

The central market, or Pasar Pagi, has a great array of fruits and basic warungs that stay open until evening. Good warungs serving seafood, ayam goreng and sate can be found along Jl Kalibaru Selatan between the Asia and Niaga hotels. The *Moel Seafood* warung has delicious, cheap prawns in oyster sauce and *Seafood 31* is also good. The Yogya department store on Jl Karanggetas (not the older Yogya store on Jl Siliwangi) has a food stall area on the ground floor, with plenty of the usual Indonesian favourites in squeaky clean surroundings.

Jl Bahagia has a number of seafood restaurants such as *Cirebon Seafood* at No 9. One of Cirebon's best Chinese seafood restaurants is the cavernous *Maxim's* at No 45. Shrimp and crab dishes are a speciality - most dishes are in the 5000 to 10,000 rp range. *Jumbo Sea Food*, Jl Siliwangi 191 next to the Yogya department store, does great seafood grills.

Jl Siliwangi has a few good options. *Restoran Pujaneka* at No 105 is a mid-range buffet-style eatery, with Sundanese and Cirebon specialities as well as western dishes. *La Palma* at No 86 is a very pleasant bakery in an old Dutch villa with tables where you can sit down and enjoy a snack or a drink.

The Cirebon Mall is the place for western fast food, and it features the Hero supermarket for packaged goodies.

Things to Buy

Toko Sumber Jaya, Jl Siliwangi 211, has all sorts of *oleh-oleh* (souvenirs) from Cirebon, mostly of the syrup, dried prawn and krupuk variety, but pottery, bamboo crafts and other interesting knick knacks are on sale.

Cirebon is famed for its rattan work, made in the villages around Cirebon. For some superb and very expensive modern rattan furniture, visit the Yama Mutiara studio in the Hotel Bentani.

Getting There & Away

The road and rail route to Cirebon from Jakarta (256 km) follows the flat north coast, or from Bandung (130 km) the road runs through scenic hilly country. Heading east to Pekalongan (137 km) and Semarang (245 km), the road runs just inland from the coast and is one of the busiest and most traffic-clogged on Java.

Air Cirebon's airport is to the south-west past the bus terminal. Merpati has a limited service from Jakarta for 140,000 rp.

Bus The Cirebon bus terminal is four km south-west of the centre of town.

Regular local buses run between Cirebon and Jakarta (5500 rp; five hours), Bandung (2600 rp; 3½ hours), Pekalongan (3000 rp; four hours), Semarang (5000 rp; seven hours) and Yogya (7500 rp; nine hours; 365 km), as well as Bogor, Solo, Merak, Surabaya and other destinations. Less-frequent, air-con services also operate from the bus terminal on the major routes. For Pangandaran, first take a bus to Ciamis along a winding, but paved, quiet and very scenic road.

For express minibuses from Cirebon, the ACC Kopyor 4848 office (☎ 204343) is conveniently located in town at Jl Karanggetas 7, next door to the Kopyor Restaurant. It has air-con minibuses to Bandung (10,000 rp; 3½ hours), Semarang (15,000 rp; six hours),

Yogya (15,000 rp; eight hours) and Cilacap (9000 rp; five hours). Ring to arrange pick-up from your hotel.

Train Cirebon is on both the main northern Jakarta-Semarang-Surabaya train line and the southern Jakarta-Yogya-Surabaya line, so there are frequent day and evening trains. The better services leave from Cirebon's main train station just off Jl Siliwangi, where you'll find a computerised booking office. Crowded ekonomi trains leave from the Parujakan train station further south.

To Jakarta's Gambir train station, the *Cirebon Express* (15,000 rp bisnis; 3½ hours) departs from Cirebon at 5.50 am, 12.50 and 3.30 pm. It often runs up to an hour over schedule, but is still quicker and more convenient than the buses.

To Semarang, via Tegal and Pekalongan, the *Fajar Utama Semarang* (43,000 rp eksekutif; 4½ hours) departs at 2.20 pm. To Yogyakarta, the *Fajar Utama Yogya* (23,000 rp bisnis; five hours) departs at 9.20 am.

Ekonomi trains include the *Cepat Semarang* (4500 rp; five hours) to Semarang and the *Senja Ekonomi Yogyakarta* (7500 rp ekonomi; seven hours) to Yogyakarta.

Boat The Pelni office (☎ 204300) is at the harbour past the harbour entrance. The KM *Sirimau* stops in Cirebon on its zig-zagging course between Pontianak and Banjarmasin on Kalimantan.

Getting Around

Cirebon's city minibus *(angkutan kota)* service operates from Pasar Gunungsari, a couple of blocks west of Jl Siliwangi. They're labelled G7, GG etc, and charge a fixed 300 rp fare around town – some even offer 'full music'!

Cirebon has hordes of becaks ringing through the streets. A becak from the train station to Pasar Pagi costs around 1500 rp. Taxis congregate around the bus and train stations, but are unwilling to use their meters from these destinations and are hard to find elsewhere. The going rate from the bus terminal to the train station is 4000 rp.

AROUND CIREBON

In the royal cemetery, five km north of Cirebon, is the tomb of Sunan Gunungjati, who died in 1570. The most revered of Cirebon's kings, Gunungjati was also one of the nine *wali songo* who spread Islam throughout Java, and his tomb is still one of the holiest places in the country. The inner tombs are only open once a month on Kliwon Thursday of the Javanese calendar, and at Idul Fitri and Maulud Nabi Muhammed. Pilgrims sit in contemplation and pray outside the doors on other days. Along from Sunan Gunungjati's tomb is the tomb of his first wife, who was Chinese, and this tomb attracts Chinese worshippers.

Trusmi

Some of Cirebon's finest batik is made in the village of Trusmi, five km west of town. Take a G4 or GP angkot from Pasar Gunungsari minibus terminal to Plered, on the Bandung road. Walk past the market from the main road and down a country lane of whitewashed cottages (or take a becak for 400 rp). At the end of the lane, Ibu Masina's is the best known studio where you can see batik tulis being made. Her air-con showroom has a wide range of colours and designs, and excellent silk batik. Also worth visiting is the workshop of Ibu Ega Sugeng – before you enter the lane to Ibu Masina's, follow Jl Trusmi around to the right and continue 200m to No 218.

Surrounding villages, each specialising in their own crafts, include **Tegalwangi**, where rattan workshops line the Bandung road, one km on from Plered.

Linggarjati & Sangkan Hurip

Linggarjati's place in the history books was assured when, in 1946, representatives of the Republican government and the returning Dutch occupying forces met to negotiate a British-sponsored cooperation agreement. Terms were thrashed out in a colonial hotel at the foot of Gunung Cirema (3078m), once a retreat from the heat for Cirebon's Dutch residents. Soekarno briefly attended, but the Linggarjati Agreement was soon swept aside

as the war for independence escalated. The hotel is now the **Gedung Naksa**, a museum recreating the events.

Linggarjati is not one of Java's premier hill resorts, but it has a few mid-range hotels and can still make a pleasant sojourn from the heat of the northern plains. It is possible to climb **Gunung Cirema**, which erupted dramatically last century, but a guide is necessary to negotiate the 10 hour walk through the forested slopes to the crater.

Sangkan Hurip, three km away, is a fairly nondescript hot springs resort, with a large hot water swimming pool, hot baths and a dozen or so hotels in all price ranges.

Getting There & Away Linggarjati and Sangkan Hurip are 23 km south of Cirebon, lying two km to the west of the Kuningan road and one km to the east respectively. From Cirebon take a Kuningan bus to Cilimus (800 rp), and then a colt (300 rp) to either resort. Andongs also go to Sangkan Hurip.

Central Java

Central Java has a population of about 29 million, an area of 34,503 sq km and Semarang as its capital. It's at the heart of Java and is the most 'Indonesian' part of Indonesia. This was the centre of Java's first great Indianised civilisation and much of the island's early culture. Later, the rise of Islam created powerful sultanates centred around the kratons, or palaces, of Yogyakarta and Surakarta (Solo).

Although the north coast was the early Muslims' first foothold on Java, further inland the new faith was gradually infused with strong Hindu-Buddhist influences and even older indigenous beliefs. The old Javanese traditions and arts, cultivated by the royal courts, are at their most vigorous here. The years of Dutch rule made little impact and even though the Indonesian revolution stripped the sultans of their political powers,

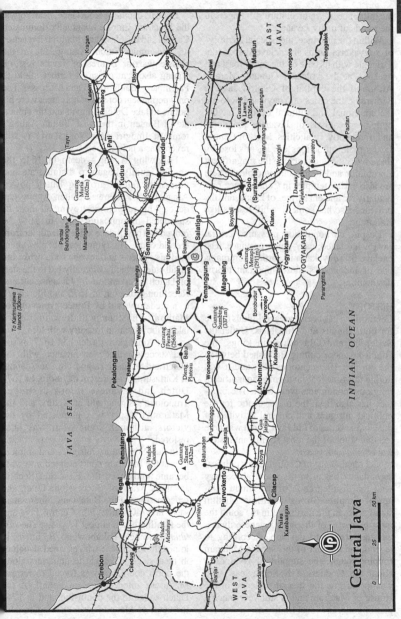

Central Java

the influence of kraton culture still lingers in the minds of many Javanese.

Within the province, the 'special territory' of Yogyakarta forms an enclave shaped like a triangle with its base on the south coast and its apex at the volcano, Gunung Merapi. Although the capital of Central Java is Semarang, the cities of Yogya and Solo are the emotional and cultural centres, having both been capitals of Javanese kingdoms and, frequently, rival cities. Most of Central Java's main attractions are in, or close to, these two cities and include the magnificent Borobudur and Prambanan temples. There are also earlier temples in Central Java, particularly the ancient shrines of Dieng, and the province also has some fine hill resorts like Kaliurang.

Despite its population pressure, Central Java is a relaxed, easy-going province. The enclave of Yogyakarta in particular remains one of Indonesia's most important tourist destinations.

HISTORY

Central Java has been a great religious centre for both Hindus and Buddhists. Under the Sailendra and Old Mataram kings, the Hindu-Javanese culture flourished between the 8th and 10th centuries AD, and it was during this time that Java's most magnificent religious monuments were built. The province has also been the major centre for the political intrigues and cultural activities of the Islamic states of old Java, and it was here too that some of the most significant historical events took place.

The renaissance of Central Java's political ascendancy began in the late 16th century with the disintegration of the Hindu Majapahit Empire. Strong maritime Muslim states arose in the north, but in the south the most powerful of the later Javanese dynasties had started to develop. According to legend, the founder of this second Mataram Empire sought the support of Nyai Loro Kidul, the 'Goddess of the South Seas', who was to become the special protector of the House of Mataram and is still very much a part of court and local traditions.

From its capital at Kota Gede, near Yogya, the Mataram Empire eventually dominated Central and East Java and Madura. It reached its peak under Sultan Agung, one of the classic warrior figures of Java's history. Agung also sent missions further afield to Palembang, Banjarmasin and Macassar. The only permanent defeats of his career were his failure to take Dutch Batavia and the sultanate of Banten in the west. Sultan Agung's tomb at Imogiri near Yogyakarta is still revered as a holy place.

Following Agung's death in 1646 the empire rapidly began to disintegrate and ultimately fell to growing Dutch power. Amangkurat I followed Sultan Agung and devoted his reign to destroying all those he suspected of opposing him. In 1647 he moved to a new palace at Plered, not far from the old court. His tyrannical policies alienated his subjects and revolts soon broke out on all sides, which eventually led to the start of Dutch intervention in Javanese affairs. Rebellion broke out in 1675 and Plered fell to a predatory raid by Prince Trunojoyo of Madura, who then withdrew to Kediri, taking the Mataram treasury with him.

After Amangkurat's death in 1677 his son and successor made an alliance with the Dutch and began his reign from a new capital at Kartasura, near present day Solo. In 1678 Dutch and Javanese troops destroyed Trunojoyo's stronghold at Kediri, and the Mataram treasury was plundered by the victors, although some of it was later restored.

In the 18th century intrigues and animosities at the Mataram court erupted into what became known as the First and Second Javanese Wars of Succession. Later, the repercussions of the Batavian Chinese massacre in 1740 spilled into Central Java and the fighting lasted almost 17 years. The *susuhunan* (king), Pakubuwono II, unwisely joined those Chinese who escaped slaughter in their siege of Dutch headquarters along the north coast, but was forced to retreat. Madurese intervention on behalf of the Dutch added to the confusion, and in 1742 the court of Mataram was once again con quered by Madurese troops. The struggle was finally resolved by the treaty of 1743, by which Pakubuwono II was restored to his battered court but at the cost of enormous concessions to the Dutch.

Kartasura was now abandoned, and in 1745 Pakubuwono II established a new court at Surakarta which is still occupied by his descendants. The new court, however, was no more stable than the old, and in 1746 the Third Javanese War of Succession began and continued until 1757. The Dutch, rapidly losing patience, finally adopted a policy of divide and rule – a tactic which was also adopted by the British when they took control during the five year interregnum from 1811. By 1757 the former Mataram Empire had been split into three rival, self-governing principalities – the realm of Surakarta was partitioned and the Sultanate of Yogyakarta was formed in 1755 and, finally, a smaller domain called Mangkunegara was created within Surakarta (Solo).

The founder of Yogya, Hamengkubuwono I (1755-92), was the most able Mataram ruler since Sultan Agung. During his reign the sultanate was the predominant military power in Central Java. Yet, within 40 years of his death, his successor had brought about the destruction of Javanese independence and the beginning of the truly colonial period of Central Javanese history. The deterioration of Hamengkubuwono II's relations both with his rivals in Surakarta and the Dutch was followed by equal hostility towards the British. In 1812 European troops, supported by the sultan's ambitious brother and Mangkunegara, plundered the court of Yogya, and Hamengkubuwono was exiled to Penang. He was replaced as sultan by his son, and his brother was appointed Prince Paku Alam of a small enclave within the sultanate.

At this time Java was in a state of flux due to corruption at court, continual European interference and increased hardship among the Javanese villagers. Into this turbulent picture stepped one of the most famous figures of Indonesian history, Prince Diponegoro, to launch the Java War of 1825-30. At the end of the war the Dutch held

Yogya responsible and all of its outer districts were annexed. Just to maintain the principle of equality, the outer districts of Surakarta were annexed. Pakubuwono IV was so disturbed by this apparent injustice that he set out for the Indian Ocean to confer with the 'Goddess of the South Seas' but the Dutch, fearing yet more rebellion, brought him back and exiled him to Sulawesi.

The Java War was the last stand of the Javanese aristocracy. For the remainder of the colonial period the courts became ritual establishments and Dutch Residents exercised control. With no real room or will for political manoeuvre, the courts turned their energies to traditional court ceremonies and patronage of literature and the arts. Their cultural prestige among the masses was high and this, combined with their political impotence, possibly explains why the royal elite were not major targets for the nationalist movement which arose in the 20th century. In fact, Yogyakarta became the capital of the Republican government for a period, and the progressive sultan at that time was so popular that he later served in several government posts. The sultanate has also remained administratively autonomous from Central Java as a 'special territory' with the status of a province.

CILACAP

Cilacap, just over the border from West Java, is a medium-sized city in a growing industrial area and has the only natural harbour with deep-water berthing facilities on Java's south coast. Apart from its fort, Cilacap has no real tourist attractions and the main reason to come here is to make the backwater trip to Kalipucang for Pangandaran.

Things to See
Benteng Pendem is an impressive fort complex at the entrance to the old harbour. Though sometimes erroneously referred to as the 'Portuguese fort', it is in fact a Dutch fort built between 1861 and 1879. With intact barracks, gun rooms and massive ramparts, it is one of the best preserved forts on Java, and relatively little stone has been carted off

JAVA

for use in local construction. Bring a flash-light to explore some of the tunnels and rooms, and wear sandals – one tunnel leads to the sea and lies in shallow water.

The fort overlooks a long stretch of dirty sand, **Pantai Teluk Penyu**, which, rather sadly, is a very popular local beach with souvenir stalls selling a dazzling array of shells.

Places to Stay & Eat
In the centre of town at Jl Mayor Sutoyo 61, *Losmen Tiga* is clean and friendly with spartan singles/doubles with shared mandi for 6500/8000 rp. Around the corner at Jl Anggrek 16, *Hotel Anggrek* is also good with slightly larger rooms for 7700/10,200 rp, or 12,000 to 20,000 rp with mandi.

The *Cilacap Inn* (☎ 21543) at Jl Sudirman 1 is a good mid-range hotel. Air-con rooms with hot water, TV and minibar cost from 40,000 rp, including breakfast. At the top end is the *Hotel Wijaya Kusuma* (☎ 22871), Jl A Yani 12A, on Cilacap's main central street. Rates start at 65,000 rp.

The *Restaurant Perapatan/Sien Hieng* at Jl A Yani 62, just around the corner from Losmen Tiga, has a large Chinese menu. Along Jl Mayor Sutoyo, east of Losmen Tiga, are a number of good warungs.

Getting There & Away
Air Merpati has a daily flight between Jakarta's Halim airport and Cilacap for 145,000 rp. Cilacap's airport is 14 km north of the city.

Bus Buses to/from Cilacap include Yogya (4500 rp; five hours; 232 km) and Pur-wokerto (2000 rp; 1½ hours), from where buses run to Wonosobo. The last bus to Yogya leaves around 3 pm. Alternatively, from Yogya take a train to Kroya and then a colt or bus for the one hour ride to Cilacap.

There are also door-to-door minibuses to Yogya and other destinations.

Boat Boats to Kalipucang (1300 rp; four hours) leave from the jetty a few km north-west of town, inland on the river estuary.

Take a bemo (300 rp) to the jetty turn-off and then a becak for the one km or so to the jetty. A becak from the bus terminal or the centre of town all the way to jetty should cost about 2000 rp. The jetty is near the big Pertamina installations – no photography. The last ferry leaves at 1 pm, so start early if coming from Yogya or Dieng unless you want to spend the night in Cilacap. See under Pangandaran in the previous West Java section for full details of this fascinating trip.

PURWOKERTO
This medium-sized city is primarily a trans-port hub, and you may find yourself here en route between Wonosobo or Cilacap, or on the way to Baturaden. Purwokerto is an unhurried, remarkably clean city with some architectural reminders of Dutch colonial-ism.

For a cheap hotel, the clean, well-run *Hotel Sampurna*, Jl Gerilya 47, is near the bus terminal and has good rooms to suit most budgets, or try the *Hotel Baru*, Jl Pasarwage 27, in the centre of town near the market. *Hotel Borobudur*, Jl Yosodarmo 32, is the best hotel in town.

Purwokerto's bus terminal is about two km south of town. Buses run to all major centres, including Cilacap, Wonosobo, Banjar and Yogya. Infrequent direct buses go to Baturaden, or catch a red angkot No B1 to Langentirto and then a minibus to Batur-aden. Purwokerto is also a major rail hub and the train station is close to the centre of town.

BATURADEN
Baturaden, 14 km north of Purwokerto, is one of Java's most attractive mountain resorts on the slopes of Gunung Slamet. Savour the mountain air on quiet weekdays, and go for walks to waterfalls and through the pine-forested slopes. The recreation park also has a swimming pool, boat rides etc.

Gunung Slamet, the second-highest peak on Java at 3432m, is a Fujiesque volcanic cone that dominates the landscape of western Central Java. Trails lead from Baturaden to the peak, but this is a very tough route. The usual ascent is from the north side, from the village of Serang.

Places to Stay

Wisma Kartika Asri has fine views and is in a good position right outside the gates to the recreation park. Comfortable rooms with mandi cost 15,000 rp. Near the bus terminal, the *Kusuma Sari* is similarly priced. The rock-bottom *Losmen Harapan* is one of the cheapest.

Top of the range is the big, modern *Hotel Rosenda* (☎ 32570); the older *Rosenda Cottages* are simpler, homier and better value, with doubles for 80,000 rp.

GUA JATIJAJAR

This huge limestone cave is a popular local tourist attraction, about 130 km west of Yogya and 21 km south-west of Gombong. From the parking area, make your way through the souvenir sellers to the recreation park and up to the cave, which is spattered with graffiti. A concrete path wends its way over natural springs and through the halls of the cave, which are decorated with life-size statues relating the story of legendary lovers Raden Kamandaka and Dewi Ratna Ciptarasa. It is all very tacky, which is unfortunate because this is an otherwise impressive natural cave.

More difficult to explore, but larger and unspoilt, **Gua Petruk** is seven km south of Gua Jatijajar.

Black sand beaches are to the south. **Pantai Indah Ayah** (aka Pantai Logending) is five km beyond Gua Petruk, and at **Pantai Karang Bolong** people make a living collecting the nests of sea swallows from the steep cliff faces above the surf.

WONOSOBO

Wonosobo is the main gateway to the Dieng Plateau. At 900m, in the hills of the central mountain range, Wonosobo has a good climate and is a fairly typical country town with a busy market. For most of the year it's not a particularly interesting place, but on national holidays it comes alive as people from the surrounding villages gather for festivities held in the main square. You might see the Kuda Kepang dance from nearby Temanggung, or the local Lengger dance in which men dress as women and wear masks.

Information

The tourist office (☎ 21194) at Jl Kartini 3 is helpful and has maps of Wonosobo and the Dieng Plateau. The BNI bank on Jl A Yani changes cash and travellers cheques at passable rates. It is open Monday to Friday from 8 am to 3 pm.

Places to Stay – bottom end

Wisma Duta Homestay (☎ 21674), Jl Rumah Sakit 3, is the best budget option, with comfortable, bright rooms with attached mandi for 12,500 rp, including breakfast. It provides good travel information and has tours to Dieng.

Another good guesthouse is the small *Citra Homestay* (☎ 21880), Jl Angkatan 45. Large rooms with shared bathroom cost 15,000 rp and it has a pleasant sitting area. The price includes breakfast, free tea and coffee, and it also offers tours to Dieng.

Wonosobo also has plenty of cheap, uninspiring losmen, such as those on Jl Resimen 18 just south of the Hotel Nirwana. The better *Hotel Jawa Tengah* (☎ 21802), Jl A Yani 45, has basic but clean rooms for 9000 rp, and larger rooms are 12,500 rp with mandi. It is set back from the street down a small alleyway. *Hotel Petra* (☎ 21152), Jl A Yani 97, is good value, with rooms from 5000 rp up to 40,000 rp with air-con. At Jl Sumbing 6, the *Hotel Famili* (☎ 21396) has some old-fashioned style and simple rooms for 8000 rp, or 14,000 rp with mandi.

If you can't be bothered heading into town, you could do a lot worse than the *Hotel Dewi* (☎ 21813), Jl A Yani 90A, right opposite the bus terminal. It has a few economy rooms for 10,000 rp, and mid-range rooms with mandi for 20,000 rp or from 30,000 rp with hot water.

Places to Stay – middle

The long-popular *Hotel Nirwana* (☎ 21066) at Jl Resimen 18 No 34 is secure, quiet and friendly. Comfortable rooms cost 40,000 rp with hot shower, or 70,000 rp for large family rooms with a sitting area. Rates are inflated, but a substantial breakfast is included.

Hotel Parama (☎ 21788), Jl A Yani 96, is reasonable value. Comfortable rooms with hot water showers cost 30,000 rp. A few spartan rooms with cold water are available for 19,000 rp.

The *Hotel Arjuna* (☎ 21389), Jl Sindoro 7A, is further out but it is quiet and pleasant. Rooms around courtyard areas start at 15,000 rp and range up to 40,000 rp.

The *Hotel Sri Kencono* (☎ 21522), Jl A Yani 81, is the best of the older hotels. Well kept rooms with hot water showers and parabola TV cost 44,000 rp. Breakfast is included.

The best hotel by far is the flash, new *Hotel Surya Asia* (☎ 22992), Jl A Yani 137. Well-appointed rooms start at 95,000 rp and a good restaurant is attached.

Places to Eat

The popular *Dieng Restaurant* at Jl Kawedanan 29 has good Indonesian, Chinese and European food served buffet-style. Most dishes cost around 1500 rp per portion. The owner, Mr Agus Tjugianto, is an inspirational source of information on Dieng and sometimes arranges Dieng tours. The photograph albums are worth a look.

The *Asia*, two doors down, is one of Wonosobo's best restaurants and serves Chinese food.

The *Restaurant DHG* at Jl Pasukan Ronggolawe 17 is without a doubt Wonosobo's most stylish restaurant. Set in a nursery it is surrounded by greenery and offers good

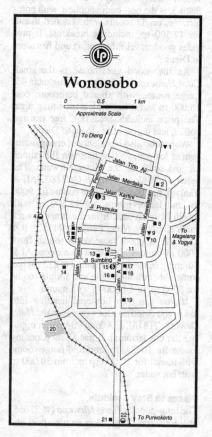

Wonosobo

0   0.5   1 km
Approximate Scale

To Dieng
Jalan Tirto Aji
Jalan Merdeka
Jalan Pemuda
Jalan Kartini
Jl Pramuka
Jl Resimen 18
Jalan Kawedanan
Jalan A Yani
Jl Sumbing
To Magelang & Yogya
To Purwokerto

PLACES TO STAY

2	Hotel Arjuna
5	Hotel Nirwana
6	Losmen Widuri
7	Losmen Rahayu
8	Citra Homestay
12	Hotel Jawa Tengah
13	Hotel Famili
14	Wisma Duta Homestay
16	Hotel Perama
17	Hotel Sri Kencono
18	Hotel Petra
19	Hotel Surya Asia
21	Hotel Dewi

PLACES TO EAT

1	Restaurant DHG
9	Dieng Restaurant
10	Asia Restaurant

OTHER

3	Tourist Office
4	Terminal Dieng
11	Plaza
15	Bank BNI
20	Market
22	Bus Terminal

European food, such as steaks for 11,000 rp, and Indonesian dishes for around 5000 rp. A bar/karaoke lounge is attached.

Getting There & Away

From Yogya take a bus or colt to Magelang (1100 rp; one hour) and from there another bus to Wonosobo (1400 rp; two hours). Door-to-door minibuses also do the Yogya-Wonosobo run. Rahayu Travel (☎ 21217), Jl A Yani 111, has minibuses to Yogya at 7 and 10 am and 2 pm for 5500 rp per person. Hotels can arrange pick-up. Other travel minibuses also go to Semarang, Purwokerto and Jakarta.

Hourly buses go to Semarang (2500 rp; four hours) via Secang and Ambarawa (1700 rp; three hours).

For Cilacap, take a bus to Purwokerto (2400 rp; three hours) and then another to Cilacap. Leave early in the morning if you want to catch the ferry to Kalipucang and on to Pangandaran.

Frequent buses to Dieng (1000 rp; 1½ hours) leave from the Terminal Dieng throughout the day and continue on to Batur.

Getting Around

Yellow angkots run around town and cost 300 rp for most journeys. Andong from the bus terminal to the town centre cost 500 rp per person.

DIENG PLATEAU

The oldest Hindu temples on Java are found on this lofty plateau, 2000m above sea level. The name 'Dieng' comes from 'Di-Hyang', meaning 'Abode of the gods', and it is thought that this was once the site of a flourishing temple-city of priests.

The temples, mostly built between the 8th and 9th centuries, covered the highland plain, but with the mysterious depopulation of Central Java, this site, like Borobudur, was abandoned and forgotten. The holy city reputedly had over 400 temples, but it was

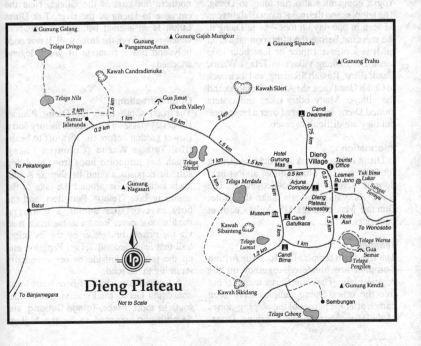

Dieng Plateau

Not to Scale

buried and overgrown, and then plundered for building material. It was not until 1856 that the archaeologist Van Kinsbergen drained the flooded valley around the temples and catalogued the ruins. The eight remaining temples are characteristic of early Central Javanese architecture – stark, squat and box-like.

These simple temples, while of great archaeological importance, are not stunning. Rather Dieng's beautiful landscape is the main reason to make the long journey to this isolated region. Steep mountainsides terraced with vegetable plots enclose the huge volcanically active plateau, a marshy caldera of a collapsed volcano. Any number of walks to cool mineral lakes, steaming craters or other quiet, lonely places can be made around Dieng – to the highest village in Central Java if you're feeling energetic.

To really appreciate Dieng, it is best to stay in Dieng village. Alternatively, Wonosobo has better facilities and can be used as a base. Yogya companies also run tours to Dieng. The temples and the main 'natural' sights can be seen in one day on foot – be in Dieng in the morning before the afternoon mists roll in. It is a pleasant three or four hour loop south from Dieng village to Telaga Warna, Candi Bima, Kawah Sikidang, and then back to Candi Gatutkaca, the Arjuna Complex and the village. Many other lakes and craters around Dieng are scattered over a large area, but they are difficult to reach.

Information

In Dieng village a kiosk sells tickets to Dieng for 2000 rp. The tourist office almost next door is helpful and knowledgeable. The Bank Rakyat Indonesia near the Hotel Gunung Mas changes US dollars cash at poor rates.

Temples

The five main temples that form the **Arjuna Complex** are clustered together on the central plain. They are Shiva temples, but like the other Dieng temples have been named after the heroes of the wayang stories of the *Mahabharata* epic – Arjuna, Punta-dewa, Srikandi, Sembadra and Semar. Raised walkways link the temples (as most of this land is waterlogged), but you can see the remains of ancient underground tunnels which once drained the marshy flatlands.

Just to the south of the Arjuna Complex is **Candi Gatutkaca** and the small site **museum** containing statues and sculpture from the temples. The museum is usually open on weekends only but can be opened upon request at other times. The statuary inside reveals interesting carvings, including an unusual representation of Nandi the bull, Shiva's carrier. Nandi has the body of a man and the head of a bull, a unique representation in Hindu iconography found nowhere else. Another gargoyle-like figure sporting an erection is distinctly animist.

Further south, **Candi Bima** is unique on Java, with its *kudu*, strange sculpted heads like so many spectators looking out of windows.

The restored **Candi Dwarawati** is on the northern outskirts of the village. Near the entrance to Dieng at the river, **Tuk Bima Lukar** is an ancient bathing spring where water spouts from the stone wall. It was once holy and has a fountain of youth legend attached.

Other Attractions

The road south from the Dieng Plateau Homestay passes a mushroom factory and a flower garden before the turn-off to beautiful **Telaga Warna** (Coloured Lake), which has turquoise hues from bubbling sulphur deposits around its shores. A trail leads anticlockwise around the lake to the adjoining lake, **Telaga Pengilon**, and the holy cave of **Gua Semar**, a renowned meditational cave. Return to the main road via the rickety bridge, or by the indistinct trail that leads around Telaga Pengilon and up the terraced hillside before eventually returning to the road.

A turn-off just south of here leads to an unexciting Geothermal station, and further south to another lake, **Telaga Cebong**, and **Sembungan**, reputed to be the highest village on Java at 2300m. The walk to Sembungan to see the sunrise from the hill, one km from the village, is a popular activity. Start at 4 am to reach the top 1½ hours later. The Dieng Plateau Homestay and Losmen Bu Jono both offer guides for 5000 rp per person.

From Telaga Warna, it is one km along the main road to Candi Bima, and then another 1.2 km to **Kawah Sikidang**, a volcanic crater with steaming vents and frantically bubbling mud ponds. Exercise extreme caution here – there are no guard rails to keep you from slipping off the sometimes muddy trails into the scalding hot waters. **Kawah Sibentang** is another less spectacular crater nearby, and **Telaga Lumut** is another small lake.

Other attractions to the west are difficult to reach. **Telaga Merdada** is a large lake with a large mushroom factory alongside. **Kawah Sileri**, two km off the main road and six km from Dieng, is a smoking crater area with a hot lake. The **Gua Jimat** cave is a one km walk through the fields from the main road.

Nine km from Dieng village is the trail to **Kawah Candradimuka**, a pleasant 1.5 km walk to this crater through the fields. Another trail branches off to two lakes, **Telaga Nila** and a longer two hour walk to the further **Telaga Dringo**. Just a few hundred metres past the turn-off to Kawah Candradimuka is **Sumur Jalatunda**. This 'well' (as 'sumur' translates) is in fact a deep hole some 100m across whose vertical walls plunge down to bright green waters.

For breathtaking views of the valley, the viewpoint on the slopes of **Gunung Sondoro** is five km east of Dieng just off the main road towards Wonosobo.

Places to Stay & Eat

Dieng has a handful of spartan hotels. They provide little in the way of amenities, except for blankets, which are essential for the cold nights.

The *Dieng Plateau Homestay* and the *Losmen Bu Jono* next door are the best options. Both charge 7500/10,000 rp for basic singles/doubles with shared mandi,

and they both have cafes, information on Dieng and offer guides to Sembungan. The Bu Jono currently has the edge.

The *Hotel Asri* offers no services but has slightly better rooms for 7500/10,000 rp and larger rooms for 12,500 and 15,000 rp.

Hotel Gunung Mas (☎ 92417) has rooms for 10,000/15,000 rp, which are no better than anywhere else, but they do have rooms with mandi for 20,000 rp, as well as 'VIP rooms' which are the best in town but cost a ridiculous 50,000 rp and the hot water showers are often broken.

Don't expect much in the way of culinary delights – the *Dieng Plateau Homestay* and *Losmen Bu Jono* are the best places to eat.

Getting There & Away

Dieng is 26 km from Wonosobo, which is the usual access point. Buses from Wonosobo run to Dieng village (1000 rp; one hour) and continue on to Batur. From Batur buses go to Pekalongan (1600 rp; four hours; 90 km), but buses are not frequent on the steep, bad road. The usual way to reach the north coast is to head down to Wonosobo and then take a bus to Semarang.

It is possible to reach Dieng from Yogya in one day, including a stop at Borobudur, provided you leave early to make all the connections this venture requires: Yogya-Borobudur-Magelang-Wonosobo-Dieng. To save all this hassle, Yogya travel agents have day tours from 20,000 rp, including Borobudur, or 17,500 rp for Dieng only.

MAGELANG

Magelang was formerly a Dutch military garrison and it was here that the Javanese hero, Prince Diponegoro, was tricked into captivity in 1829. In the house where he was captured is a museum of Diponegoro memorabilia.

Magelang is 42 km north of Yogya, on the main road to Semarang. Shortly before the town is Gunung Tidar, which legend credits as the 'Nail of Java', a mountain planted there by the gods to stop Java from shaking.

Borobudur

From the plain of Kedu, 42 km north-west of Yogya a small hill rises up out of a pattern of palm trees and fields of rice and sugar cane. It's topped by one of the greatest Buddhist relics of South-East Asia – up there with Cambodia's Angkor Wat and Myanmar's Bagan.

Rulers of the Sailendra dynasty built the colossal pyramid of Borobudur sometime between 750 and 850 AD. Little else is known about Borobudur's early history, but the Sailendras must have recruited a huge workforce for some 60,000 cubic metres of stone had to be hewn, transported and carved during its construction. According to tradition, the main architect was Gunadharma. The name Borobudur is possibly derived from the Sanskrit words 'Vihara Buddha Uhr', which means the 'Buddhist monastery on the hill'.

With the decline of Buddhism and the shift of power to East Java, Borobudur was abandoned soon after completion, and for centuries lay forgotten, buried under layers of volcanic ash. It was only in 1815, when Raffles governed Java, that the site was cleared and the sheer magnitude of the builders' imagination and technical skill was revealed. Early in the 20th century the Dutch began to tackle the restoration of Borobudur, but over the years the supporting hill had become waterlogged and the whole immense stone mass started to subside. A mammoth US$25 million restoration project was undertaken between 1973 and 1984.

Although easily forgotten, standing as they do in the shadow of the great Borobudur, two smaller structures – the Mendut and Pawon temples – form a significant part of the complex.

Orientation & Information

The small village of Borobudur consists of warungs, souvenir stalls and a few hotels that face the monument. The bus terminal is less than 10 minutes' walk from the monument.

The temple site is open from 6 am to 5.15 pm, and admission is 5000 rp for foreign tourists (2500 rp for foreign students), 2000 rp for domestic tourists. The higher price includes a guide (in most major foreign languages), camera fees and entry to the museum. Borobudur is Indonesia's single most popular tourist attraction, and it can be crowded and noisy, especially on weekends. The finest time to see Borobudur and

Box: Detail of intricately carved relief, Borobudur (photograph by Peter Morris).

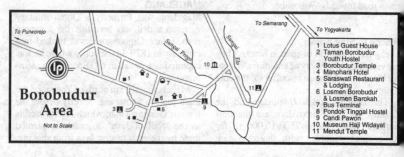

Borobudur Area

Not to Scale

To Purworejo
To Semarang
To Yogyakarta

Sungai Progo
Sungai Elo

1 Lotus Guest House
2 Taman Borobudur Youth Hostel
3 Borobudur Temple
4 Manohara Hotel
5 Saraswati Restaurant & Lodging
6 Losmen Borobudur & Losmen Barokah
7 Bus Terminal
8 Pondok Tinggal Hostel
9 Candi Pawon
10 Museum Haji Widayat
11 Mendut Temple

capture something of the spirit of the place is at dawn or sunset, but you won't have the place to yourself. These are also popular times for the bus-loads of package tourists.

At the entrance to the site are a number of useful books on sale about Borobudur and the Mendut Temple.

Borobudur Temple

Borobudur is a broad, impassive monument, built in the form of a massive symmetrical stupa, literally wrapped around the hill. It stands solidly on its base of 118 by 118m. Six square terraces are topped by three circular ones, with four stairways leading up through finely carved gateways to the top. The paintwork is long gone but it's thought that the grey stone of Borobudur was at one time washed with white or golden yellow to catch the sun. Viewed from the air, the whole thing looks like a giant three dimensional tantric mandala. It has been suggested, in fact, that the Buddhist community that once supported Borobudur were early Vajrayana or Tantric Buddhists who used it as a walk-through mandala.

RICHARD I'ANSON

A Buddha image at Borobudur sits on the upper terraces called the arupadhatu (sphere of formlessness) representing enlightenment. The mudra or position of the hands are symbolically important and here signify reasoning.

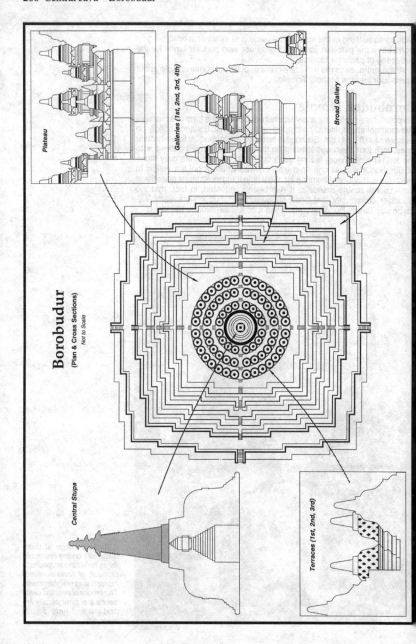

Borobudur
(Plan & Cross Sections)
Not to Scale

Plateau

Galleries (1st, 2nd, 3rd, 4th)

Broad Gallery

Central Stupa

Terraces (1st, 2nd, 3rd)

The entire monument was conceived as a Buddhist vision of the cosmos in stone, starting in the everyday world and spiralling up to nirvana – eternal nothingness, the Buddhist heaven. At the base of the monument is a series of reliefs representing a world dominated by passion and desire, where the good are rewarded by reincarnation as some higher form of life and the evil are punished by a lowlier reincarnation. These carvings and their carnal scenes are covered by stone to hide them from view, but they are partly visible on the south side.

Starting at the main eastern gateway, go clockwise (as one should around all Buddhist monuments) around the galleries of the stupa. Although Borobudur is impressive for its sheer bulk, it is the close-up sculptural detail which is quite astounding. The pilgrim's walk is about five km long. It takes you along narrow corridors past nearly 1460 richly decorated narrative panels and 1212 decorative panels in which the sculptors have carved a virtual textbook of Buddhist doctrines as well as many aspects of Javanese life 1000 years ago – a continual procession of ships and elephants, musicians and dancing girls, warriors and kings. Some 432 serene-faced Buddhas stare out from open chambers above the galleries, while 72 more Buddha images sit only partly visible in latticed stupas on the top three terraces. Reaching in through the stupa to touch the fingers or foot of the Buddha inside is believed to bring good luck.

PETER MORRIS

PETER MORRIS

PETER MORRIS

Top Left: Of the 504 Buddha statues at Borobudur, 432 are contained in open niches on the four galleries leading up to the circular terraces. Water spouting makara gargolyes adorn many of the niches.

Top Right: Aspara (nymph) is shown on the main wall of the base where the world of desire is depicted.

Bottom: Part of a relief showing parasol bearers at a court dance, flanked by horses and elephant.

PETER MORRIS

Candi Pawon

This tiny temple, about one km east of Borobudur, is similar in design and decoration to Mendut. It is not a stupa, but resembles most Central Javanese temples, with its broad base, central body and pyramidal roof. Pot-bellied dwarfs pouring riches over the entrance to this temple suggest that it was dedicated to Kuvera, the Buddhist god of fortune.

Mendut Temple

The Mendut Temple is another two km east, back towards Muntilan. It may be small and insignificant compared with its mighty neighbour Borobudur, but this temple houses the most outstanding statue of any temple on Java that can still be seen in its proper place – a magnificent three-metre-high figure of Buddha, flanked by the Bodhisattvas Lokesvara on the left and Vairapana on the right. The Buddha is also notable for his posture, for instead of the usual lotus position he sits western style, with both feet on the ground.

The Mendut Temple, or the Venu Vana Mandira (Temple in the Bamboo Grove), was discovered in 1836, and attempts to restore it were made by the Dutch between 1897 and 1904. Although parts of the roof and entrance remain unfinished, it is nevertheless a fine temple, and the gracefully carved relief panels on its outer walls are among the finest and largest examples of Hindu-Javanese art.

Top: Many of the Borobudur reliefs feature scenes of everyday life and are interesting as historical documents of 8th to 9th century Java. Shown here are festival celebrations.

Bottom: Mendut Temple was once linked with Borobudur, two km away, by a stone pilgrimage path. This detail shows Atavaka, a human-devouring ogre, who converted to Buddhism. After his conversion he is seen sitting on pots of money and surrounded by happy children.

PETER TURNER

Museum Haji Widayat (Modern Art Museum)

Amongst the antiquities of Borobudur, halfway between the Pawon and Mendut temples on the main road, this museum is incongruously devoted to modern Indonesian art. This small but significant museum is open daily from 9 am to 4 pm, except Monday. Admission is 1000 rp.

Special Events

The Lord Buddha's birth, his enlightenment and his reaching of nirvana are all celebrated on the full-moon day of **Waicak**. A great procession of saffron-robed monks goes from Mendut to Pawon then Borobudur, where candles are lit and flowers strewn about, followed by praying and chanting. This holiest of Buddhist events attracts thousands of pilgrims. Waicak usually falls in May.

Around June, the **Festival of Borobudur** kicks off with a *Ramayana*-style dance, with a cast of over 300, but based on an episode of the Buddhist Manohara. Folk dancing competitions, handcrafts, whitewater rafting and other activities add to the carnival atmosphere.

Places to Stay & Eat

The popular *Lotus Guest House* (☎ 88281), Jalan Medang Kamulan 2, on the east side of the temple near the main parking area, is the place to head for. Singles/doubles with mandi cost 7500/10,000 rp up to 20,000 rp, including breakfast and free tea and coffee throughout the day. This welcoming, well-run losmen has a good cafe, provides information on the things to do in the area, rents bicycles for countryside touring and even organises whitewater rafting trips on the Elo River for US$65 all inclusive.

Other cheap options on the south side directly opposite the temple are the *Losmen Borobudur* and *Losmen Barokah*. Both have dingy rooms from 7500 rp.

The *Saraswati* (☎ 88283), Jalan Bala Putradewa 10, has much better but overpriced rooms with mandi for 20,000 rp, including breakfast. On the same road past the Saraswati, about one km from Borobudur, the lush *Pondok Tinggal Hostel* (☎ 88245) has bamboo-style rooms around an attractive garden. A bed in the spotless, often empty, dorms costs 7500 rp. Comfortable, well-appointed rooms with attached bathroom cost 33,000 rp, or larger rooms with sitting rooms cost from 44,000 rp up to 125,000 rp. Add 10% tax to all rates. It also has a good restaurant.

The top place to stay is the *Manohara Hotel* (☎ 88131), within the monument grounds. Pleasant air-con rooms, most with porches facing the monument, have private bath, hot water and TV for US$33 and US$35 plus 20% tax and service. Breakfast and unlimited entry to Borobudur are included. It also runs the *Taman Borobudur Youth Hostel*, primarily for groups.

Getting There & Away

From Yogya's bus terminal, direct buses go to Borobudur (1200 rp; 1½ hours) via Muntilan. These buses can also be caught at the bus stop on Jalan Magelang. In Borobudur, the hotels are within walking distance of the bus terminal, or a becak will cost no more than 1000 rp anywhere in the village. It's a fine walk to Mendut and Pawon, otherwise a bus or colt is 300 rp to hop from one temple to the next, or hire a becak.

Tours of Borobudur are easily arranged in Yogya at the Prawirotaman or Sosrowijayan agents for as little as 15,000 rp per person.

YOGYAKARTA

Daerah Istimewa (Special District) Yogyakarta is the cultural heart of Java, lying between two of Java's most potent mystical symbols – explosive Gunung Merapi in the north and the Indonesian Ocean, home of the 'Queen of the South Seas', in the south. Yogyakarta, or Yogya (pronounced 'Jogja') for short, is the most active centre for Javanese arts, and spoken Javanese is at its most halus (refined) here. It is also an intellectual centre, crammed with prestigious universities and academies, and Yogya's influence and importance far outweigh its size. Yogya has always strived to maintain its independence, clinging proudly to its traditions, and is still headed by its sultan. The sultan's walled palace, or kraton, remains the hub of traditional life.

The district of Yogyakarta has a population of just over three million and an area of 3186 sq km, while the population of the city itself is around 500,000. No longer the city of bicycles, Yogya has noisy and chaotic traffic like any Javanese city, but just a short stroll behind the main streets are the kampungs where life is still unhurried. Despite its veneer of modernity and westernisation, Yogya clings strongly to its traditional values and philosophies.

The city provides easy access for an insight into Javanese culture. Batik, silver, pottery, wayang kulit and other craft industries are easily visited, traditional Javanese performing arts can readily be seen and the contemporary arts are also flourishing. Yogya is also a good base to explore numerous nearby attractions, including Indonesia's most important and awe-inspiring archaeological sites, Borobudur and Prambanan.

Yogya is Java's No 1 tourist centre and Indonesia's most popular city for visitors. It's easy to see why – apart from its many attractions, Yogya is friendly and easygoing, with an excellent range of economical hotels and restaurants.

History

Yogyakarta owes its foundation to Prince Mangkubumi who, in 1755, after a land dispute with his brother, the susuhunan of Surakarta, returned to the former seat of Mataram and built the kraton of Yogyakarta. He took the title of 'sultan' and adopted the name of Hamengkubuwono, meaning literally 'the universe on the lap of the king' which all his successors have used. He created the most powerful Javanese state since the 17th century. His son was less competent, however, and during the period of British rule the Yogya kraton was sacked, Hamengkubuwono II exiled and the smaller Paku Alam principality created within the sultanate.

For the Javanese, Yogya has always been a symbol of resistance to colonial rule. The heart of Prince Diponegoro's Java War (1825-30) was in the Yogya area. More recently, Yogya was again the centre of revolutionary forces and became the capital of the Republic from 1946 until independence was achieved in 1949. As the Dutch took control of other Javanese cities, part of the kraton was turned over to the new Gajah Mada University which opened in 1946. Thus, as one of the sultan's advisers observed, in Yogya 'the Revolution could not possibly smash the palace doors, because they were already wide open'.

When the Dutch occupied Yogya in 1948, the patriotic sultan locked himself in the kraton, which became the major link between the city and the guerillas who retreated to the countryside. The Dutch did not dare move against the sultan for fear of arousing the anger of millions of Javanese who looked upon him almost as a god. The sultan let rebels, including Soeharto, use the palace as their headquarters, and as a result of this support and the influence of the sultan, come independence Yogya was granted the status of a special territory. Yogya is now a self-governing district answerable directly to Jakarta and not to the governor of Central Java.

Under Soeharto's government, the immensely popular Sultan Hamengkubuwono IX was Indonesia's vice-president until he stepped down in March 1978. The sultan passed away in October 1988 and in March

989 Prince Bangkubumi, the eldest of 16 sons, was installed as Sultan Hamengkubuwono X. The coronation involved great pomp and ceremony, and included a procession of dwarfs and albinos. The new sultan is a member of the National Assembly and, like his father, is intent on preserving the traditions of Yogya.

Orientation

It is easy to find your way around Yogya. Jl Malioboro, named after the Duke of Marlborough, is the main road and runs straight down from the train station to the kraton at the far end. The tourist office and many souvenir shops and stalls are along this street, and most of the cheap accommodation places are just off it, in the enclave near the rain line.

The old, walled kraton is the centre of the intriguing area of old Yogya, where you will also find the Taman Sari, Pasar Ngasem Bird Market) and numerous batik galleries. A second mid-range hotel enclave is south of the Kraton area around Jl Prawirotaman.

Information

Tourist Office The Tourist Information Office (☎ 566000), Jl Malioboro 16, is open Monday to Friday from 8 am to 7.30 pm, Saturday until noon. It has useful maps of the city, produces a number of publications including a calendar of events) and can answer most queries. The train station and the airport also have tourist office counters.

Money Yogya has plenty of banks and moneychangers for changing cash. Banks usually give better exchange rates.

The BNI bank, Jl Trikora 1 opposite the main post office, is efficient and has good rates for most currencies. The BCA bank, just north of the train station on Jl Mangkubumi, gives good rates for major currencies and accepts most brands of travellers cheques. It gives cash advances on credit cards but charges 5000 rp.

PT Baruman Abadi in the Natour Garuda Hotel shopping arcade behind Lippobank is the moneychanger that gives excellent rates. Opposite the train station, PT Haji La Tunrung, Jl Pasar Kembang 17, has passable rates and is open until 9.30 pm every day.

Post & Communications The main post office, on Jl Senopati at the southern continuation of Jl Malioboro, is open Monday to Friday from 8 am to 8 pm, and until 5 pm on Saturday.

For international calls, convenient wartels are those behind the post office at Jl Trikora 2 and opposite the train station at Jl Pasar Kembang 29. The Telkom office, one km east of Jl Malioboro on Jl Yos Sudarso, is open 24 hours and has Home Country Direct phones.

Dangers & Annoyances Yogya has its fair share of pickpockets and thieves. It's not really any worse than many other parts of Indonesia but the high number of tourists means that the 'strike rate' is higher. Be particularly wary when catching buses to Borobudur and Prambanan. Bag snatchings have also been reported.

Compared to Bali, Yogya is relatively free of hawker hassles, but some becak drivers won't take no for an answer. If you want a becak, approach a driver that doesn't hassle.

Yogya is crawling with batik salespeople, who'll strike up a conversation on Jl Malioboro or follow you around Taman Sari, pretending to be guides or simply instant friends. Inevitably you'll end up at a gallery where they'll rake in a commission if you buy. A time-honoured ploy is the special batik exhibition that is being shipped to Singapore and this is your last chance to buy – at maybe 50 times the real price. Get rid of anyone who leads you or follows you to shops, and be wary of anyone who strikes up a conversation on the street.

Kraton

In the heart of the old city the huge palace of the sultans of Yogya is effectively the centre of a small walled-city within a city. Over 25,000 people live within the greater kraton

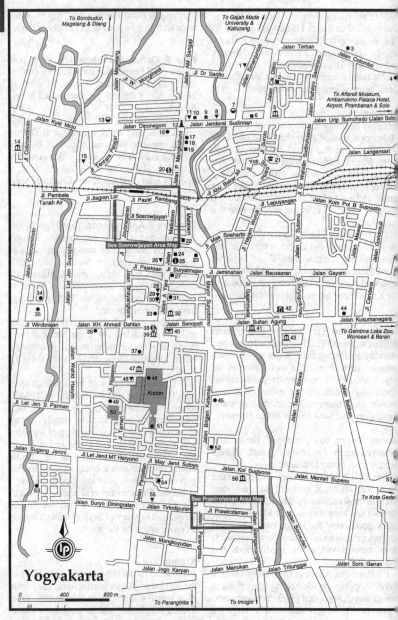

To Borobudur,
Magelang & Dieng

To Gajah Mada
University &
Kaliurang

Jalan Terban

Jalan Colombo

3

Jalan W. Monginsidi

Jalan AM Sangaji

Jalan Magelang

JI Dr Sarjito

Jalan Simanjuntak

Jalan Cik Ditiro

Jalan Raharju Sartono

4

To Affandi Museum,
Ambarrukmo Palace Hotel,
Airport, Prambanan & Solo

1

2

7

Jalan Kyai Mojo

13

Jalan Diponegoro

11 10 9 8

5

6

Jalan Jenderal Sudirman

Jalan Urip Sumoharjo (Jalan Solo

JI Cokroaminoto

14

16

12

17
18
19

Jalan Langensari

15

20

Yos
Sudarso

21

JI Tentara Pelajar

Jalan P Mangkubumi

Jalan Dr Wahidin
Sudirohusodo

JI Pembela
Tanah Air

JI Pasar Kembang

JI Jlagran Lor

JI Sosrowijayan

Joyonegaran

Jalan Abu Bakar Ali

Jalan Lempuyangan

Jalan Kom Pol B Suprapto

JI Cokroaminoto

Malioboro

See Sosrowijayan Area Map

22

Mataran II

JI Mas Soeharto

Jalan Irtayan Wunuk

Jalan Dr Sutomo

Jalan Mewar

Jalan Gondosuli

24
26
25

23

JI Pajeksan

JI Suryatmajan

Jalan Jeminahan

Jalan Bausasran

Jalan Gayam

JI Let Jen Suprapto

27

28

34

29
30

JI A Yani

31

Jalan Mayor Suryotomo

JI Jagalan

42

44

JI Cendana

35

33

32

Jalan Gajahmada

JI Wirobrajan

Jalan KH Ahmad Dahlan

Jalan Senopati

Jalan Sultan Agung

Jalan Kusumanegara

36

38
39

40

41

43

To Gembira Loka Zoo,
Wonosari & Baran

37

Jalan Let Jen S Parman

47

Jalan Taman Siswa

JI Wahid Hasyim

48

46

Kraton

45

Jalan Brigjen Katamso

JI Kasem

49

50

51

Jalan Bantan

JI Taman

JI Let Jend MT Haryono

52

JI May Jend Sutoyo

Jalan Kol Sugiyono

Jalan Menteri Supeno

Jalan Sugeng Jeroni

56

57

53

54

Jalan Panjaitan

Jalan Parangtritis

Jalan Sisingamangaraja

To Kota Gede

55

See Prawirotaman Area Map

Jalan Suryo Diningratan

Jalan Tirtodipuran

JI Prawirotaman

Jalan Mangkuyudan

Jalan Jogo Karyan

Jalan Manukan

Jalan Tritunggai

Jalan Soro Genan

Yogyakarta

0   400   800 m

To Parangtritis

To Imogiri

PLACES TO STAY		5	Army Museum	36	Nitour
2	Indraloka Home Stay	7	Colt/BusTerminal to	37	Mesjid Besar
6	Java Palace Hotel		Kaliurang &	38	BNI Bank
9	Hotel Santika		Prambanan	39	Sono-Budoyo
10	Phoenix Heritage	12	Tugu Monument		Museum
	Hotel	13	Pingit Bus Stop for	40	Main Post Office
18	Arjuna Plaza Hotel		Borobudur	41	Museum Biologi
19	New Batik Palace	14	Museum Sasana	42	Pakualaman Kraton
	Hotel		Wiratama	43	Sasmitaluka
22	Hotel Puri		(Monumen		Jenderal Sudirman
23	Melia Purosani Hotel		Diponegoro)	44	Batik Research
24	Mutiara Hotel	16	Minibus Agents		Centre
		17	Garuda Office	45	Purawisata Theatre
PLACES TO EAT		20	BCA Bank	46	Kraton Entrance
1	Pujayo	21	Telkom Office	47	Museum Kareta
8	Rumah Makan Tio	25	Tourist Information		Kraton
	Ciu		Office	49	Pasar Ngasem
11	Pizza Hut	27	Terang Bulan Batik		(Bird Market)
15	Pesta Perak		Shop	50	Taman Sari
26	Colombo Restaurant	30	Mirota Batik		(Water Palace)
28	Cherry Cafe	31	Pasar Beringharjo	51	Sasono Hinggil
29	Griya Dahar Timur		Market	52	Dalem Pujokusuman
48	Ndalem	32	Benteng Vredeburg		Theatre
	Joyokusuman	33	Gedung Negara	53	Agastya Art Institute
55	Baleanda Restaurant		(Governor's	54	Swasthigita Wayang
			Building)		Kulit Workshop
OTHER		34	Amri Yahya's Gallery	56	Museum Perjuangan
3	ISI Dance Faculty	35	ISI (Fine Arts	57	Umbulharjo Bus
4	RRI Auditorium		Faculty)		Terminal

ompound, which contains its own market, shops, batik and silver cottage industries, schools and mosques.

The innermost group of buildings, where the current sultan still lives, were built between 1755 and 1756, although extensions were made over almost 40 years during the long reign of Hamengkubuwono I. European-style touches to the interior were added much later by the sultans of the 1920s, but structurally this is one of the finest examples of Javanese palace architecture, providing a series of luxurious halls, and spacious courtyards and pavilions. The sense of tradition holds strong in Yogya, and the palace is attended by very dignified and elderly retainers who still wear traditional Javanese dress.

The centre of the kraton is the reception hall known as the Bangsal Kencana, or Golden Pavilion, with its intricately decorated roof and great columns of carved teak. A large part of the kraton is used as a museum and holds an extensive collection, including gifts from European monarchs and gilt copies of the sacred *pusaka* (the heirlooms of the royal family), gamelan instruments, royal carriages and a huge bottle-shaped wooden alarm gong. One of the most interesting rooms contains the royal family tree, old photographs of grand mass weddings and portraits of the former sultans of Yogya.

An entire museum within the kraton is dedicated to Sultan Hamengkubuwono IX, with photographs and personal effects of the great man. Other points of interest within the kraton palace include the small European bandstand with stained-glass images of musical instruments. In another part of the kraton there are 'male' and 'female' entrances indicated by giant-sized 'he' and 'she' dragons, although they look pretty much alike. Outside the kraton, in the centre of the northern square, are two sacred *waringin*, or banyan trees, where, in the days of feudal Java, white-robed petitioners would patiently sit, hoping to catch the eye of the king.

The kraton is open from 8 am to 2 pm

daily, except Friday when it closes at 1 pm. It is closed on national and kraton holidays. Admission is 1500 rp, which includes an excellent guided tour. Booklets about the palace and postcards of the old sultans are on sale inside. In the inner pavilion between 10 am to noon you can see gamelan on Monday and Tuesday, wayang golek on Wednesday, classical dance on Thursday and Sunday, wayang kulit on Saturday, and Mojopait folk singing on Friday.

Taman Sari (Water Castle)

Just west of the kraton is the Taman Sari, or Fragrant Garden. Better known in Yogya as the Water Castle, this was once a splendid pleasure park of palaces, pools and waterways for the sultan and his entourage. The architect of this elaborate retreat, built between 1758 and 1765, was Portuguese and from Batavia, and the story goes that the sultan had him executed to keep his hidden pleasure rooms secret. They were damaged first by Diponegoro's Java War, and an earthquake in 1865 helped finish the job. Today most of the Water Castle has tumbled down amidst dusty alleys, small houses and batik galleries, but it's an interesting place of eerie ruins with underground passages and a large subterranean mosque.

The bathing pools have been restored, not terribly well perhaps, but it is possible to imagine life in the harem. Once surrounded by gardens, the sultan and ladies of the harem relaxed here, and from the tower overlooking the pools the sultan was able to dally with his wives and witness the goings-on below.

The main entrance on Jl Taman leads first to the restored bathing pools, which are open daily from 9 am to 3 pm and cost 500 rp entry. Alternatively, wander through from the Pasar Ngasem (Bird Market) to the old ruins and the underground mosque before proceeding to the bathing pools. Guides will attach themselves to you, and offer a free guided tour that will inevitably end at a batik gallery – either shake them off, establish a price for a guided tour first up or be prepared to put up with the hard sell at the end.

Pasar Ngasem (Bird Market)

At the edge of Taman Sari, the Pasar Ngasem is a colourful bird market crowded with hundreds of budgies, orioles, roosters and singing turtle-doves in ornamental cages. Lizards and other small animals are also on sale, as are big trays of bird feed consisting of swarming maggots and ants. From the back of the bird market, an alleyway leads up to the broken walls of Taman Sari for fine views across Yogya.

Other Palaces

The smaller **Pakualaman Kraton**, on Jl Sultan Agung, is also open to visitors and has a small museum, a pendopo, which can hold a full gamelan orchestra (performances are held every fifth Sunday) and a curious colonial house with fine cast-iron work. The kraton is open Tuesday, Thursday and Sunday from 9.30 am to 1.30 pm.

The **Ambarrukmo Palace**, in the grounds of the Ambarrukmo Palace Hotel, was built in the 1890s as a country house for Hamengkubuwono VII and is another good example of Javanese palace architecture.

Museums

On the north side of the main square in front of the kraton, the **Sono-Budoyo Museum** is the pick of Yogya's museums. Though not particularly well maintained or labelled, it has a first-rate collection of Javanese arts including wayang kulit puppets, topeng masks, kris and batik, and an outside courtyard which is packed with Hindu statuary. Artefacts from further afield are also on display, including some superb Balinese carvings. It's open from 8 am to 2.30 pm daily, except Monday. Entry is 250 rp. Wayang kulit performances are held here every evening from 8 to 10 pm.

Between the kraton entrance and the Sono-Budoyo Museum in the palace square the **Museum Kareta Kraton** holds some opulent chariots of the sultans. It's open from 8 am to 4 pm daily, and admission is 250 rp.

Dating from 1765, **Benteng Vredeburg** is the old Dutch fort opposite the main post office at the southern continuation of Jl

Malioboro. The restored fort now houses a museum with dioramas showing the history of the independence movement. The fort architecture is worth a look, but the dioramas are mostly for Indonesian patriots. Opening hours are 8.30 am to 2.30 pm; closed Monday. Admission is 200 rp.

Up until his death in 1990, Affandi, Indonesia's internationally best known artist, lived and worked in an unusual tree-house studio about six km from the centre of town overlooking the river on Jl Solo. The **Affandi Museum** in the grounds exhibits his impressionist works, as well as paintings by his daughter Kartika and other artists. Affandi is buried in the backyard. It's open from 8 am to 3 pm, and entry costs 1300 rp.

The **Sasmitaluka Jenderal Sudirman** on Jl B Harun is the memorial home of General Sudirman, the commander of the revolutionary forces. Wasted by tuberculosis, Sudirman reputedly often led his forces from a litter. He died shortly after the siege of Yogya in 1948. The house is open every morning, except Monday.

The **Museum Sasana Wiratama**, also known as the Monumen Diponegoro, honours the Indonesian hero, Prince Dipnegoro, leader of the bloody but futile rebellion of 1825-30 against the Dutch. A motley collection of the prince's belongings and other exhibits are kept in a small museum built at the site of his former Yogya residence. There's still a hole in the wall which Diponegoro is supposed to have shattered with his bare fists so that he and his supporters could escape. The museum is open from 8 am to 1 pm daily.

The **Museum Biologi** at Jl Sultan Agung 22 has a collection of stuffed animals and plants from the whole archipelago. It is closed on Sunday. The **Museum Perjuangan**, in the southern part of the city on Jl Kol ugiyono, has a small and rather poor collection of photographs documenting the Indonesian Revolution. The large **Army Museum** (Museum Dharma Wiratama), on the corner of Jl Jenderal Sudirman and Jl Cik Ditiro, displays more documents, home-made weapons, uniforms and medical equipment from the revolution years. Records also trace Soeharto's rise in the ranks of Yogya's Diponegoro Division. It is open from 8 am to 1 pm Monday to Thursday and until noon on weekends.

Kota Gede

Kota Gede has been famous since the 1930s as the centre of Yogya's silver industry, but this quiet old town, now a suburb of Yogya, was the first capital of the Mataram kingdom founded by Panembahan Senopati in 1582. Senopati is buried in the small mossy graveyard of an old mosque near the town's central market. The sacred tomb is open only on Sunday, Monday and Thursday from around 9 am to noon, and on Friday from around 1 to 3 pm. Visitors should wear conservative dress. On other days there is little to see here but a murky mandi and a few goldfish.

The main street leading into town from the north (Jl Kemasan) is lined with busy silver workshops where you're free to wander around and watch the silversmiths at work. Most of the shops have similar stock, including hand-beaten bowls, boxes, fine filigree and modern jewellery. See Things to Buy later in this section for information on Kota Gede's silversmiths.

Kota Gede is about five km south-east of Jl Malioboro – take bus Nos 4 or 8. You can also take a becak, but andong (about 1500 rp) is cheaper, more agreeable and more humane. Cycling is also pleasant on the back road and it is pretty flat all the way.

Other Attractions

In the evenings, if you are bored, you can always head along to the **Purawisata** on Jl Brigjen Katamso. This amusement park is noted more for its dance performances, but there are also rides, fun fair games and a Pasar Seni (Art Market) with a basic collection of souvenirs.

Yogya's **Gembira Loka Zoo** is a spacious but sad affair – dusty and hot in the dry season, muddy in the wet and the rag-bag collection of animals are a miserable-looking bunch.

Organised Tours

Yogya is the best place on Java to arrange tours. Tour agents can be found on Jl Prawirotaman, Jl Sosrowijayan, Jl Dagen and Jl Pasar Kembang – there are so many offering similar tours at competitive prices that it is difficult to recommend one in particular. The big national travel agents are also represented in Yogya – Pacto, Nitour, Natrabu etc – but prices are much higher.

Typical day tours and per person rates through the budget operators are: Borobudur (15,000 rp); Dieng (20,000 rp); Prambanan (15,000 rp); Parangtritis and Kota Gede (25,000 rp); Gunung Merapi (20,000 rp); and Gedung Songo (27,500 rp). Longer tours, such as to Gunung Bromo (80,000 rp; two days/one night) and Bali, are also offered. Tours are often dependent on getting enough people to fill a minibus (usually a minimum of four), and prices will vary depending if air-con and snacks are provided. The prices usually don't include entrance fees.

If you want to put together your own tour, operators also arrange cars with driver at some of the best rates on Java.

Special Events

The three special Garebeg festivals held each year are Java's most colourful and grand processions. Palace guards and retainers in traditional court dress and large floats of flower-bedecked gunungans (mountains) of rice all make their way to the mosque west of the kraton to the sound of prayer and the inevitable gamelan music. These are ceremonies not to be missed if you're anywhere in the area at the time.

Places to Stay – bottom end

Accommodation in Yogya is remarkably good value and the choice is superb. It's certainly the best city on Java for places to stay and places to eat. The central Sosro area has the really cheap places and the best location, while the Prawirotaman area, a couple of km south of the kraton, has mostly mid-range places and a few cheap options. Most of the big hotels are stretched out along Solo.

Fierce competition among the many hotels means that discounts are often available, especially outside the peak July/August tourist season and public holidays.

Sosrowijayan Area Most of the cheap hotels are in the Sosrowijayan area, immediately south of the train line between Jl Pasar Kembang and Jl Sosrowijayan. Running between these two streets are the narrow alleyways of Gang Sosrowijayan I and II with most of the cheap accommodation and popular eating places. More good places to stay are in other small gangs in this area. Despite mass tourism, the gangs are quiet and still have a kampung feel to them. The area is central and Jl Malioboro is a short stroll away.

Gang Sosrowijayan I has some very basic places that cost as little as 4000/6000 rp for singles/doubles, but they are dingy and cater mostly to locals. At the north end, the Losmen Sastrowihadi and Losmen Beta are in this category. A bit further along this gang is the Losmen Superman, behind the restaurant of the same name. Light, clean rooms with shared mandi are 7000 rp, or the rooms with mandi for 10,000 rp are darker but have interesting rock garden bathrooms. New Superman's also has good rooms a couple of doors from the restaurant. Next along is the Sari Homestay, where bright rooms built around a courtyard cost 10,000/12,000 rp with mandi. Just around the corner, the popular Losmen Lucy has good rooms with mandi for 10,000 rp.

On Gang Sosrowijayan II, the Hotel Bagus is a passable cheap place. Clean rooms with fan cost 5000/6500 rp and 6000/8000 rp. Further south, the Gandhi Losmen, in its own garden, has very basic rooms but is friendly and geared to travellers. They don't come much cheaper at 4000 rp per person.

There are a host of small losmen around Gang II and the small alleys off it, most of them in a similar rock-bottom price range. Hotel Selekta is popular and friendly. It's

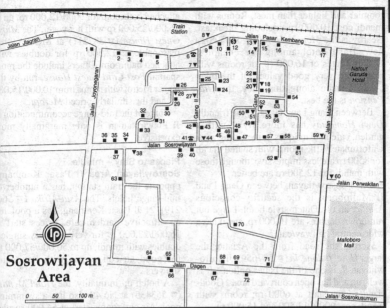

Sosrowijayan Area

0   50   100 m

PLACES TO STAY
1   Hotel Kota
2   Berlian Palace
3   Nusantara
4   Losmen Tugu
5   Hotel Mendut
9   Batik Palace Hotel
10 Hotel Asia-Afrika
11 Hotel Ratna
15 Kencana Hotel
16 Trim Guest House
17 Hotel Trim
19 Sari Homestay
21 Losmen Beta
22 Losmen Sastrowihadi
23 Supriyanto Inn
24 Losmen Setia Kawan
25 Hotel Bagus
26 Losmen Setia
29 Isty Losmen
30 Utar Pension
31 Dewi II
32 Hotel Selekta
33 Monica Hotel
35 Hotel Karunia
36 Yogya Inn
37 Oryza Hotel
39 Wisma Gambira
40 Bakti Kasih

42 Jaya Losmen & Heru Jaya
43 Gandhi Losmen
45 Losmen Atiep
46 Dewi Homestay
47 Losmen Rama
48 Losmen Happy Inn
49 Hotel Jogja
50 New Superman's Losmen
53 Losmen Lucy
54 105 Homestay
56 Lima Losmen
57 Hotel Kartika
58 Hotel Aziatic
61 Marina Palace Hotel
62 Hotel Indonesia
63 Ella Homestay
64 Puntodewo Guest House
65 Wisma Nendra
66 Kombokarno Hotel
67 Peti Mas
68 Blue Safir Hotel
69 Lilik Guest House
70 Hotel Batik Yogyakarta II
71 Wisma Perdada
72 Sri Wibowo Hotel

PLACES TO EAT
7   Cafe Sosro
8   Mama's Warung
13 Borobudur Bar & Restaurant
14 Cheap Warungs
18 Superman's Restaurant & Losmen
20 N & N
27 Anna's Restaurant
28 Budarti
34 Bladok Restaurant & Losmen
38 Caterina Restaurant
44 Restoran Tanjung
51 New Superman's Restaurant
52 Eko Restaurant
55 Bu Sis
59 Prada Cafe
60 Legian Restaurant

OTHER
6   Wartel
12 PT Haji La Tunrung Moneychanger
41 Warpostal

roomier and lighter than most. Rooms with mandi cost 10,000 rp, including breakfast. Nearby is the *Monica Hotel* (☎ 580598), a new, flash hotel among the cheapies. Opening rates of 16,000 rp for rooms with mandi are very good value. Of the other cheap losmen along this alley, the *Utar Pension* is the best.

Between Gang I and Gang II, the friendly *Dewi Homestay* has more style, with a garden, cafe and antiques in the sitting area. Unfortunately, the rooms with shared mandi for 8500 rp are less impressive, though those with mandi for 12,500 rp are better.

On Jl Sosrowijayan, between Gang I and Jl Malioboro, is the security-conscious *Aziatic*, an old Dutch-style hotel. Large but run-down doubles are 10,000 rp, and it has a wide central hallway/cafe.

Across the road from the Aziatic, the larger *Hotel Indonesia* (☎ 587659), Jl Sosrowijayan 9, is one of the better options. It is well run and has open courtyard areas. Good-sized rooms start at 6000 rp; rooms with mandi cost 9000, 12,500 and 15,000 rp.

At the western end of the street, 100m down an alley, another favourite is the friendly *Ella Homestay* (☎ 582219), Gang Sosrodipuran GT I/487. It's good value with rooms from 6500/10,000 rp, or the upstairs rooms with mandi for 16,000 rp are of hotel standard.

Prawirotaman Area This area has some cheaper places like the neat and helpful *Kelana Youth Hostel* (☎ 371207) at Jl Prawirotaman MG III/589. Dormitory beds cost 6000 rp, singles cost from 6500 rp and doubles from 11,500 to 15,000 rp, all with shared mandi. Student and HI card holders can get a small discount.

The quiet *Didi's Hostel*, down an alleyway opposite the Duta Guest House, is part of the Duta chain. The small, clean rooms with outside bath are a little expensive at 9200/11,500 rp, but you can use the pool at the Duta.

The next street south, Jl Prawirotaman II, is quieter and cheaper. *Guest House Makuta* has a pleasant garden and clean rooms with

attached bathroom for 9000/12,000 rp, up 16,000/25,000 rp with hot water. The *Mur Guest House* (☎ 387211) at MGIII/600 reasonable at 12,500 rp for doubles wit attached bathroom. Others include the mo spartan *Post Card Guest House*, run by th bigger Metro, with rooms from 10,000/15,00 rp, and the similarly priced *Merapi*.

Some of the mid-range accommodation i Jl Prawirotaman is only marginally mo expensive.

Places to Stay – middle

Sosrowijayan Area Jl Pasar Kemban opposite the train station, has a number mid-range hotels. The *Asia-Afrika* (☎ 56 219), 21 Jl Pasar Kembang, has a pool an an attractive garden cafe. Prices start 16,000/22,000 rp for very ordinary single doubles with mandi, up to 50,000/57,000 r for good air-con rooms with hot wate showers.

A notch up in quality, the *Hotel Mend* (☎ 563435) at No 49 also has a swimmin pool. Air-con rooms start at 54,000 rp plu 21% tax and service. Expect discounts.

Part of a chain, the *Batik Palace Hot* (☎ 563824), Jl Pasar Kembang 29, has a nic garden and rooms starting at US$22/26. Th sister *New Batik Palace Hotel* (☎ 562229 nearby at Jl Mangkubumi 46 (see the ma Yogya map), has a swimming pool an rooms from US$21/31. Best of the lot, *Hot Batik Yogyakarta II* (☎ 561828) has spaciou grounds and a large pool. It is on the qui back alleys, just north of Jl Dagen and onl a short stroll from Jl Malioboro. Air-co rooms cost US$26/31 or bungalows start US$32/38.

At the western end of Jl Pasar Kemban the small, newly renovated *Hotel Kot* (☎ 515844), Jl Jlagran Lor 1, has oodles colonial charm but you'll pay for it. Room have high ceilings, intricate and origina tilework, air-con and hot water. The single for US$20 and US$30 are very small, but th doubles for US$40 are substantial.

Jl Sosrowijayan also has some good mid range hotels. At No 49, *Oryza Hotel* (☎ 512495 is a renovated villa with some style. Pleasan oms with shared mandi cost 17,500 rp, and oms with private bath cost 20,000 to 7,500 rp. At No 78, the very friendly *Hotel Karunia* (☎ 565057) is a cheaper alternative with a good rooftop restaurant. Fan rooms ost 11,000/13,000 rp, rooms with mandi ost 16,000/18,000 rp or air-con rooms are 0,000 rp, all plus 10% – a pretty good deal. Next door at No 76, the *Bladok Restaurant & Losmen* (☎ 560452) is also good value, nd has a better class of rooms for 20,000/2,500 rp and 32,000/35,000 rp. The restaurant is very good.

Jl Dagen, one street further south from Jl Sosrowijayan, is another mid-range enclave. The stylish, well-kept *Peti Mas* (☎ 561938), Jl Dagen 37, is a European favourite. It has a pool and an attractive garden restaurant. Very ordinary fan rooms cost US$17/19, while better air-con rooms cost US$25/27.50 to US$37.50/40. Nearby at No 23, the *Sri Wibowo* (☎ 563084) has rooms with shared mandi for 20,000 rp, with mandi from 25,000 rp and air-con rooms start at 42,500 rp. The *Wisma Perdada* at No 6, *Blue Safir* at No 34-36 and *Kombokarno Hotel* at No 49

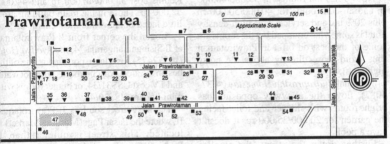

Prawirotaman Area

PLACES TO STAY
1 Indraprastha Homestay
2 Puri Pertiwi
3 Borobudur Guest House
4 Sriwijaya Guest House
7 Didi's Hostel
8 Wisma Harto
10 Mas Gun Guest House
12 Perwita Sari Guest House
14 Kelana Youth Hostel
15 Ayodya Hotel
18 Wisma Gajah
19 Airlangga Guest House
20 Putra Jaya Guest House
22 Prambanan Guest House
23 Wisma Indah
25 Sumaryo Guest House
26 Duta Guest House

27 Rose Guest House
28 Wisma Pari Kesit
30 Prayogo Guest House
31 Galunggung Guest House
32 Kirana Guest House
33 Sartika Homestay
37 Wisma Gajah II
38 Delta Homestay
39 Merapi Guesthouse
40 Muria Guest House
41 Gayatri Guest House
42 Metro Guest House
43 Agung Guest House
44 Kroto Homestay
45 Palupi Guest House
46 Sunarko Guest House
52 Metro Guest House
53 Guest House Makuta
54 Post Card Guest House

PLACES TO EAT
5 Hanoman's Forest Restaurant
6 Griya Bujana Restaurant

9 Putri Restaurant
11 French Grill Restaurant
13 Galunggung Restaurant & Pub
16 Tante Lies (Warung Java Timur)
17 Melati Garden
21 Palm House Restaurant
24 La Beng Beng Restaurant
29 Via Via
34 Going Bananas
35 Little Amsterdam
36 Lotus Garden
48 Bamboo House Restaurant
49 Restaurant Java
50 Ramayana Restaurant
51 Lotus Breeze

OTHER
47 Pasar Pagi (Morning Market)

have a similar range of rooms and prices. Cheaper hotels are the *Wisma Nendra* and the *Puntodewo Guest House*, with rooms for around 20,000 rp.

Prawirotaman Area This street, a couple of km south of the city centre, is a more upmarket enclave than Sosrowijayan but most hotels offer very good value. Many of the hotels are converted old houses that are spacious, quiet and have central garden areas. Swimming pools are the norm.

The *Airlangga Guest House* (☎ 378044) at No 6-8 has fan rooms for 35,000/40,000 rp and air-con rooms for 40,000/50,000 rp plus 20% tax and service. This high-density hotel is somewhat cramped but the rooms are some of the best on offer in Prawirotaman (but avoid those directly above the noisy nightclub).

The small *Indraprastha Homestay* (☎ 37-4087), down the alleyway opposite, has bright rooms with shower and toilet facing the garden for 20,000/25,000 rp. It doesn't have a pool.

Further down the street, the smaller *Prambanan Guest House* (☎ 376167) at No 14 is a newer place with a pool, attractive garden and very comfortable rooms for 25,000/37,500 rp up to 74,000 rp for large doubles with air-con.

At No 26, the big *Duta Guest House* (☎ 372064) is favoured by European tour groups and is often crowded. This is one of the more luxurious places and the garden is very inviting. The cheaper rooms – starting at 28,000/35,000 rp with fan – aren't much but the more expensive rooms – ranging up to 81,000/92,000 rp for the quiet, air-con, garden rooms – are very attractive. Its *Duta Garden Hotel* (☎ 373482), Timuran MG III/103, down a quiet alley just north of Jl Prawirotaman, also has a pool and excellent rooms from US$40/45.

The popular and good value *Rose Guest House* (☎ 377991) at No 28 has a larger than normal pool and a restaurant next to it. A few economy rooms cost 12,500/15,000 rp with shared mandi, but most have attached mandi

starting at 15,000/20,000 rp (5000 rp extr with hot water) up to 45,000/50,000 rp.

A lot of the guesthouses in the old villa are pleasant enough but the rooms can b dingy. *Sumaryo Guest House* (☎ 373507) No 22 is one of the better ones and has a poo Rooms range from 20,000 rp in its annex across the road up to 52,000 rp with air-cor Others with pool in the same price range ar the *Wisma Indah* (☎ 376021) at No 16 an the *Sriwijaya* (☎ 371870) at No 7.

The *Kirana Guest House* (☎ 376600 doesn't have a pool but is furnished wit antiques and has plenty of colonial style Rooms cost 33,000/40,000 rp and 44,000 52,000 rp. Those in the main building are little faded but have the most character.

Around the corner from Jl Prawirotama at Jl Sisingamangaraja 74, the *Ayodya Hote* (☎ 372475) has a large pool and is one of th best in the area. Air-con rooms with hot wate and TV cost US$31/34, or bigger rooms wit mini-bar are US$39/42.

The next street south is Jl Prawirotama II, where the Pasar Pagi (Morning Market) i located. This street is quieter than J Prawirotaman I, and the hotels are not a flash. The *Metro* (☎ 372364) at No 71 is th most popular and has a garden area. Th rooms range from 10,000/12,500 rp t 45,000/50,000 rp with air-con and hot wate showers, but many are looking shabby. Th best value are the mid-priced rooms in th annexe across the street, where you'll fin the pool.

The *Agung Guest House* (☎ 375512) a No 68 has a tiny pool and is also popular fo a cheaper room. It costs from 10,000/12,50 rp to 35,000/42,000 rp with air-con. Th *Delta Homestay* (☎ 378092) at No 597A another in the Duta chain, is good value. I has a small pool and good rooms fo 11,500/18,400 rp, 27,600/32,200 rp wit bathroom or 39,100/43,700 rp with air-con.

Other Areas The *Indraloka Home Sta* (☎ 564341), Jl Cik Ditiro 18, is north of th city centre near the Gajah Mada University so is popular with overseas students and longer term visitors. Singles/doubles with ir-con and hot water in this fine old colonial ouse cost US$18/21 plus 20% tax and ervice. Tours are organised, a travel agent nd wartel are attached, and there is information on other homestay accommodation on ava.

The *Gadjah Mada Guest House* (☎ 59-225), further north, is similar in price and lso popular with students.

On Jl Solo near the airport, *River Castle* ☎ 563526) is an eccentric guesthouse styled fter a castle, overlooking a river. Owned by ffandi's granddaughter and her French diplomat husband, it is plastered with artworks nd the trappings of would-be royalty. It has a swimming pool, and spacious rooms and uites for US$35 to US$100 plus 21%.

Places to Stay – top end

Yogya has a glut of luxury hotels and discounts of 20% to 50% are readily available or the asking. If arriving by air, the hotel ooking desk at the airport often has good eals well below the published rates listed ere. There are two airport booking desks – void the first one. Most of the big hotels are n the Solo/airport road or on Jl Malioboro. All of the following places to stay have wimming pools, and add 21% tax and ervice.

The *Natour Garuda Hotel* (☎ 566353), ight in the action at Jl Malioboro 60, was nce a grand colonial edifice, Yogya's remier hotel in Dutch times. Numerous renvations over the years have seen it lose most f its colonial grace and the rooms will soon eed another renovation, but it is still one of Yogya's better hotels. Singles/doubles are US$100/115 and suites start at US$200.

Further down Jl Malioboro at No 18, the *Mutiara Hotel* (☎ 563814) is also very central. It is a definite notch below Yogya's best otels but is reasonably priced at US$70/80. The old part of the hotel a few doors along as good mid-range rooms for half the price.

Just to the east of Jl Malioboro is the huge, panish-owned *Melia Purosani Hotel* ☎ 589521), Jl Suryotomo 31. This five star otel has all the facilities you would expect of a top international hotel. Rooms start at US$115/125.

Many of Yogya's big hotels are stretched out along the road to Solo. The road changes names many times but is usually referred to simply as 'Jalan Solo'. Close to Jl Mangkubumi and the centre of town, the *Phoenix Heritage Hotel* (☎ 566617), Jl Jenderal Sudirman 9-11, is a smaller hotel with class. Standard rooms cost US$75/80, or much more attractive deluxe rooms are US$85/95.

Nearby and also central, the four star *Hotel Santika* (☎ 563036) is popular with business travellers and noted for its good service. Rooms start at US$100/110.

On Jl Solo about five km from the centre of the city, the *Ambarrukmo Palace Hotel* (☎ 588488) on Jl Adisucipto is a 1960s Soekarno-inspired construction and contains the old Ambarrukmo Palace in its grounds. For long the most prestigious hotel in Yogya, this government-run hotel is now outclassed and looking tired. Singles/doubles begin at US$105/115.

Many new hotels are springing up out towards the airport. The pick of the crop at the moment is the five star *Hotel Aquila Prambanan* (☎ 565005), Jl Adisucipto 48, with rooms from US$100. Other new Yogya hotels include the smaller *Radisson Yogya Plaza* (☎ 584222), Jl Gejayan, closer to the city centre near the RRI Auditorium. Plush rooms start at US$100/110.

Places to Eat

Sosrowijayan Area This area is overrun with cheap eating houses featuring western breakfasts and snacks, as well as Indonesian dishes, and no travellers' menu is complete without fruit salads and banana pancakes. The food is distinguished by big helpings and low prices.

A whole host of good warungs line Jl Pasar Kembang, beside the train line, but *Mama's* is definitely No 1 in the evenings. On Jl Pasar Kembang at No 17, *Borobudur Bar & Restaurant* has average fare at high prices, but it has unlimited cold beer and bands later in the evening.

Gang Sosrowijayan I is a favourite place for cheap eats. The famous *Superman's* is one of the original purveyors of banana pancakes and has been around for decades. The owner, Pak Suparman, adapted his name, and likewise his food, to suit western sensibilities. These days its offshoot, *New Superman's*, a bit further down Gang I, is more switched on with better music and decor, and good apple pie. The *Eko Restaurant* has cheap steaks, and the no-frills *N & N* is very popular for its low prices. *Bu Sis* is another good, cheap eatery. For the cheapest eats on Gang I, head to the little cluster of wall-hugging warungs at the train station end.

Gang II also has some good, cheap places. *Anna's* is very popular, while the *Cafe Sosro* has the best decor but average food. The *Heru Jaya* at the Jaya Losmen has French grills along with Indonesian dishes. *Budarti* is a cheap family-run rumah makan down a side alley.

Jl Sosrowijayan has a number of good restaurants. *Caterina* at No 41 is one of the best. It has a varied menu, good food at low prices and you can dine sitting on mats at the back. *Bladok Restaurant*, opposite at No 76, is a classier little place with predominantly European food. At the other end of the street on the corner of Jl Malioboro, the upstairs *Prada Cafe* has authentic Italian pizzas, calzones and pasta, and video movies are shown in the evening. Higher prices reflect the quality of the food and surroundings.

Jalan Malioboro After 10 pm, the souvenir vendors pack up and a *lesahan* area (where diners sit on straw mats) comes alive along the north end of Malioboro, staying open till early morning. Food stalls serve Yogya's specialities, such as *nasi gudeg* (rice with jackfruit in coconut milk) and *ayam goreng* (fried chicken). Here young Indonesians sit around strumming guitars and playing chess into the wee hours. Dine cross-legged on mats and take in the nightlife.

Hidden away upstairs on the corner of Jl Malioboro and Jl Perwakilan (see the Sosro Area map), the *Legian Restaurant* has

Indonesian, Chinese, French and Italian foc served by Balinese waiters in a roof-garde setting. It's very classy and it does a gre claypot gudeg ayam (chicken with jackfrui The western dishes are less inspiring.

That big new intrusion on Jl Malioboro Malioboro Mall – is not complete witho fast food, and *McDonald's* takes pride place at the front of this monument western consumerism. The mall has som reasonable cafes inside and the top floor ha a squeaky clean food stall area with food variable quality.

Cherry Cafe, upstairs at Jl A Yani 57, tl southern extension of Jl Malioboro, is a excellent little eatery and a great place to s overlooking Jl Malioboro after a hard sho ping session. It serves tasty western, Chine and Indonesian dishes at moderate prices the opor ayam (chicken in coconut milk) particularly good.

Griya Dahar Timur, Jl A Yani 57, is larger place with Chinese, Indonesian an European dishes for around 3000 rp, mo expensive steaks and excellent icy juices.

Prawirotaman Area A few medium-price restaurants along this street seem to specia ise in slow service and mediocre food fc tourists. Fortunately, there are some excep tions. The primary budget recommendatic is *Tante Lies*, also known as *Warung Jav Timur*, at the Jl Parangtritis intersectio Sate, nasi pecel, soto ayam and other Centr; and East Javanese dishes are served at rea sonable prices, and it's a popular meetin place.

Via Via, Jl Prawirotaman 24B, is an exce lent Belgian-run travellers' cafe and meetin spot. As well as providing good food tha includes a daily changing menu of Indonesia dishes, it organises a variety of informativ activities from bicycle trips around Yogya t Indonesian cooking, language and bati courses.

Hanoman's Forest Restaurant feature moderately priced Indonesian and wester cuisine, but the main attraction is the classi cal Javanese dance, wayang golek or wayan ulit shows each night. A cover charge of 000 rp applies for each performance.

On Jl Tirtodipuran, the continuation of Jl rawirotaman, *Baleanda Restaurant* at No 3 see the main Yogya map) is in a beautiful arden setting with an art gallery at the back. he food is good, if a little expensive, but is has to be one of Yogya's most attractive estaurants.

)ther Areas Good eats can be found to the orth of the city out towards Gajah Mada Jniversity. *Pujayo*, Jl Simanjuntak 73, is ogya's best food stall restaurant. A dozen ood vendors split over two floors serve a nind-boggling array of dishes and drinks at ow prices in ultra-hygienic surrounds – and araoke is thrown in as well (6 to 8 pm is the me for songless dining).

The *Pesta Perak*, Jl Tentara Rakyat Mat-ram 8, about one km west of Jl Malioboro, as a delightful garden ambience and some-mes puts on gamelan music. Excellent unch and dinner buffets for 15,000 rp eature a whole range of Javanese dishes. Not surprisingly, it is a very popular tourist estaurant.

In a similar vein, *Ndalem Joyokusuman* ☎ 73520), in a prince's house next to the raton, has lunch buffets for 10,000 rp. Groups can arrange dinner and dance perfor-nances for US$20 a head.

The famous Yogya fried chicken leaves he colonel's recipe for dead. Yogya chicken s boiled in the water of young coconuts and hen deep fried – absolute heaven when done vell. One of the most famous purveyors was Ibok Berek out on Jl Solo just before 'rambanan, and in her wake a host of eater-es have appeared nearby with similar ames. *Nyonya Suharti*, Jl Adisucipto 208, ust past the Ambarrukmo Palace, has restau-ants all over Java and is popular with tour roups.

Intertainment

Yogya is by far the easiest place to see tradi-ional Javanese performing arts, and erformances of one sort or another are held very day of the week. Dance, wayang or gamelan are performed every morning at the kraton (see earlier in this section) and are a good introduction to Javanese arts. Check with the tourist office for any special events.

Most famous of all is the spectacular *Ramayana* ballet held at nearby Prambanan during full moon in the dry season. See under Prambanan later in this chapter for details.

Wayang Kulit Leather puppet performances can be seen at several places around Yogya on virtually every night of the week. Most of the centres offer shortened versions for tour-ists but at Sasono Hinggil, in the *alun alun selatan* of the kraton, marathon all-night per-formances are held every second Saturday from 9 pm to 5 am.

Abbreviated wayang kulit performances are held every day except Saturday, at the Agastya Art Institute, Jl Gedong Kiwo MD III/237, where dalang are trained. The two hour show begins at 3 pm.

The Sono-Budoyo Museum, near the kraton, also has two hour performances every day from 8 pm for 3000 rp.

One hour, tourist-oriented shows are held at the Yogyakarta Craft Centre on Jl Adisucipto near the Ambarrukmo Palace Hotel, about seven km from the city centre. Shows are at 8 pm every day.

Wayang Golek Wooden puppet plays are also performed frequently. The Nitour per-formance, from 11 am to 1 pm every day except Sunday, has a useful handout explain-ing the history of the wayang and the *Ramayana* story. Performances are held at Jl Ahmad Dahlan 71.

On Saturday there are wayang golek per-formances at the Agastya Art Institute from 3 to 5 pm.

Dance Most dance performances are based on the *Ramayana* or at least billed as 'Ramayana ballet' because of the famed per-formances at Prambanan.

Those at the Purawisata theatre in the amusement park on Jl Katamso are excel-lent; they are performed nightly from 8 to 10 pm, and cost 20,000 rp.

Another fine troupe performs at Dalem Pujokusuman at Jl Katamso 45 every Monday, Wednesday and Friday from 8 to 10 pm for 6000 rp. The Ambarrukmo Palace Hotel has *Ramayana* ballet performances most nights at the hotel's Borobudur Restaurant on the 7th floor.

Schools The Indonesia Institute of Arts (ISI) Dance Faculty on Jl Colombo in north Yogya is open to visitors from 8 am to 2 pm, Monday to Saturday. Bagong Kussudiarja, one of Indonesia's leading dance choreographers, has a school at Jl Singosaren 9 (off Jl Wates), where modern and classical dance practice sessions are held. Kussudiarja's main studio is at Padepokan, five km from Yogya, where he runs courses for foreign students.

Other Performances Ketoprak (folk theatre) performances are held at the RRI auditorium, Jl Gejayan, from 8 pm to midnight on the first Saturday of every month.

Some of the big hotels, such as the Ambarrukmo Palace and the Garuda, have gamelan music in their lobbies during the day. Other hotels and restaurants have gamelan or wayang performances. On Jl Prawirotaman, Hanoman's Forest Restaurant has different wayang performances every night of the week.

Things to Buy

Yogya is a noted batik centre, but other craft industries in and around Yogya include silver, leather, pottery and wayang puppets. Even if you don't intend to buy, galleries and workshops are open free of charge for visitors to observe traditional Javanese craftspeople in action.

For serious shoppers, Yogya has a great array of crafts and antiques, primarily from Java, but bits and pieces from all over the archipelago can be found.

Jl Malioboro is one great long colourful bazaar of souvenir shops and stalls, and is a good place to start shopping. The street stalls offer a wide selection of cheap cotton clothes, leatherwork, batik bags, topeng masks and wayang golek puppets. They ar the cheapest place to buy souvenirs, depend ing on your bargaining skills. Look in som of the fixed priced shops on Jl Malioboro t get an idea of prices. Mirota Batik, Jl A Yar 9, is a good place to start. It specialises i batik but also has a wide selection of hand crafts at reasonable prices. Malioboro' labyrinthine and newly renovated marke Pasar Beringharjo, is always worth a brows especially for cheap batik and textiles.

The other major area to shop is . Tirtodipuran, the continuation of Jl Prawirota man. Here you'll find a string of expensiv batik factories, galleries and art shops. Thi is an interesting, more upmarket shoppin stretch, with furniture, antiques and a variet of crafts and curios from Java and furthe afield.

On Jl Adisucipto, opposite the Amba rukmo Palace, the government-promotec fixed price Yogyakarta Craft Centre has a sa collection of overpriced souvenirs. Othe shops can be found nearby, and the hote itself has a few expensive art shops. Th Purawisata amusement park also has souve nirs and crafts, but these are less interestin shopping areas.

Batik Batik in the markets is cheaper than i the shops, but you need to be careful abou quality and be prepared to bargain. A goo place to start looking is the Terang Bula shop, Jl A Yani 108 (just before the marke as you head south on Jl Malioboro), whic will give you an idea of what you should b paying. Other shops in town include Ramay ana Batik, Jl Ahmad Dahlan 21, specialisin; in Yogya-style batik, and the more expensiv Batik Keris, a branch of the big Solo bati house on Jl A Yani 71. Many other reasonabl priced shops are on Jl Malioboro/A Yani.

Most of the batik workshops and severa large showrooms are along Jl Tirtodipuran south of the kraton. Many, such as Bati Indah, Jl Tirtodipuran 6A, give free guide tours of the batik process.

Batik Painting Some artists who pioneere and grew famous from batik painting sti roduce some batik works. Kuswadji, in the orth square next to the Museum Kereta Kraton, has classical batik art on display and new wave' abstract pieces. Tulus Warsito as a gallery with a contemporary orientation at Jl Tirtodipuran 19A. Top of the scale s Amri Yahya's very expensive gallery at Jl Gampingan 67, near Yogya's ISI (Fine Arts faculty), though he mostly produces abstract oil paintings these days.

Prices are high at the well-known galleries and ridiculously cheap at the mass-production galleries, most of which are found round Taman Sari (Water Castle). Styles go through cycles – from the psychedelic mushroom era, to endless birds, butterflies and soaring moons over rice paddies. Now in vogue are more palatable traditional scenes from the wayang, *Ramayana* etc, as well as abstract paintings. Most are very similar, so shop around for something unique and always bargain hard.

Batik Courses If you want to have a go at batik yourself there are lots of batik courses and classes in Yogya. Plenty of places in Sosrowijayan (such as Lucy's) and Prawirotaman (try the Via Via cafe) areas offer short courses of one or two days duration, and you get to make a batik T-shirt. High art they ain't but they provide a good introduction.

Hadjir Digdodarmojo has been teaching batik for years and has three and five day courses. His studio is on the left of the main entrance to the Taman Sari at Taman Kp 3/177. Tulus Warsito (☎ 680093) at Jl Rogokariyan 69B is one of Yogya's top batik artists and also conducts classes. The Batik Research Centre, Jl Kusumanegara 2, may be able to help put you in touch with a teacher for a more comprehensive study of batik.

Antiques, Curios & Furniture While a few antiques can be found, they are best left to collectors who know their stuff. Yogya art shops spend an inordinate amount of time refacing wayang golek puppets and topeng masks in the name of antiquity, and many other items get similar treatment.

Along Jl Tirtodipuran you can buy artefacts from all over Java and Indonesia. Shops to try include Dieng at No 30, Delly at No 22B and its offshoot Hanoman at No 57. Griya Kristaya Nugraha at No 65 has a good collection of old chests and furniture, or Borneo Boutique at No 49 specialises in textiles, particularly ikat from Nusa Tenggara. Prices are generally very high here – bargain furiously, or get an idea of quality and look around for somewhere else to shop.

Silver Silverwork can be found all over town, but the best area to shop is in the silver village of Kota Gede. Fine filigree work is a Yogya speciality but many styles and designs are available. Kota Gede has some very attractive jewellery, boxes, bowls, cutlery and miniatures.

You can get a guided tour of the process, with no obligation to buy, at the large factories such as Tom's Silver, Jl Ngeski Gondo 60, HS at Jl Tegal Gendu 22, and MD, Jl Pesegah KG 8/44, down a small alley off the street. Tom's has an extensive selection and some superb large pieces, but prices are very high. HS is marginally cheaper, as is MD, but always ask for a substantial discount off the marked prices. Kota Gede has dozens of smaller silver shops on Jl Kemesan and Jl Mondorakan, where you can get some good buys if you bargain.

Other Crafts Yogya's leatherwork can be excellent value for money, and the quality is usually high, but always check stitching etc. Shops and street stalls on Jl Malioboro are the best places to shop for leatherwork.

Good quality wayang puppets are made at the Mulyo Suhardjo workshop on Jl Taman Sari and also sold at the Sono-Budoyo museum shop. Swasthigita, Ngadinegaran MJ 7/50, just north of Jl Tirtodipuran, is another wayang kulit puppet manufacturer.

Kasongan, the potters' village a few km south-west of Yogya, produces an astonishing array of pottery, mostly large figurines and pots.

Along Jl Malioboro, *stempel* vendors create personalised stamps hand-carved on

JAVA

leather. Expect to pay 5000 rp or less for a reasonably sized stamp with name, address and a simple design.

Getting There & Away

Air Garuda (☎ 514400), Jl Mangkubumi 52, has direct flights to Jakarta (158,000 rp) and Denpasar (147,000 rp), with onward domestic and international connections.

The Merpati office (☎ 514272) is in the Java Palace Hotel, Jl Jenderal Sudirman 63. Merpati flies directly to Surabaya (80,000 rp), Bandung (97,000 rp) and Jakarta, with connections all over the archipelago.

Sempati (☎ 511612), in the Hotel Garuda at Jl Malioboro 60, has direct flights to Jakarta and Surabaya. Bouraq (☎ 562664), Jl Mataram 60, has direct flights to Jakarta, Denpasar and Banjarmasin. Mandala (☎ 589521), in the Melia Purosani Hotel, Jl Suryotomo 31, also flies to Jakarta and Denpasar.

Bus Yogya's Umbulharjo bus terminal is four km south-east of the city centre. From the station, buses run all over Java and to Bali. Ordinary/air-con buses include: Solo (1500/2500 rp; two hours); Magelang (1100/1500 rp; 1½ hours); Semarang (3000/5000 rp; 3½ hours); Wonogiri (2000 rp; 2½ hours); Purwokerto (3600/6200 rp; 4½ hours); Cilacap (4500/7000 rp; five hours); Bandung (11,000/18,500 rp; 10 hours); Jakarta (13,000/21,000 rp; 12 hours) via Purwokerto and Bogor; Surabaya (7500/13,000 rp; eight hours); Probolinggo (9000/15,000 rp; nine hours); and Denpasar (16,000/27,000 rp; 16 hours).

For the long hauls you are better off taking the big luxury buses. It is cheaper to buy tickets at the bus terminal but it's less hassle to simply check fares and departures with the ticket agents along Jl Mangkubumi, Jl Sosrowijayan, near the Hotel Aziatic, or on Jl Prawirotaman. These agents can also arrange pick-up from your hotel. Typical fares are: Denpasar (35,000 rp); Surabaya and Malang (20,000 rp); Bandung (24,000 rp); Bogor (26,000 rp); and Jakarta (28,000 rp right up to 40,000 rp for super luxury).

Direct minibuses to Pangandaran (17,500 rp air-con) and Gunung Bromo (25,000 rp non air-con) are also arranged.

From the main bus terminal, buses also operate regularly to all the towns in the immediate area: Borobudur (1200 rp; 1½ hours); Parangtritis (1200 rp; one hour); and Kaliurang (600 rp; one hour). For Prambanan (500 rp), take the yellow Pemuda bus. For Imogiri (500 rp; 40 minutes), take a colt or the Abadi bus No 5 to Panggang and tell the conductor to let you off at the *makam* (graves). Buses to Imogiri and Parangtritis can also be caught on Jl Sisingamangaraja at the end of Jl Prawirotaman. You can catch the Borobudur bus going north along Jl Magelang at the Pingit bus stop.

Apart from the main bus terminal, colts operate to the outlying towns from various sub-stations. The most useful is the Terban colt station to the north of the city centre on Jl Simanjuntak. From here colts go to Kaliurang (850 rp) and Solo (2000 rp) passing the airport en route.

Buses, and colts in particular, to the tourist attractions around Yogya are renowned for overcharging. Know the correct fare before boarding and tender the right money, but expect to pay extra if you have luggage taking up passenger space.

Minibus Door-to-door minibuses run to all major cities from Yogya. Many companies are found on Jl Diponegoro, and the Sosrowijayan and Prawirotaman agents also sell tickets. Most will pick up from hotels in Yogya, but not for the short runs like Solo (they will drop off at your Solo hotel however).

On Jl Diponegoro, SAA (☎ 584976) at 9A has minibuses to Solo (5000 rp air-con; two hours), Jakarta (35,000 rp; 12 hours) Malang and Surabaya (20,000 rp; seven hours), Cilacap (7500 rp; five hours) and Semarang (6000 rp; three hours), as well as Purwokerto and Pekalongan.

Rahayu (☎ 561322) is another big agent at No 15, with frequent minibuses to Solo (3500 rp non-air-con), Wonosobo (5000 rp

...on-air-con), Bandung (25,000 rp air-con, ...ine hours) and numerous other destinations.

Train Yogya's Tugu train station is conve-...iently central. See the introductory Getting ...round Java section for details of Jakarta-...ogya and Surabaya-Yogya travel.

For Solo, the best option is the *Pram-...anan Ekspres* departing at 9 am and 3.15 ...m. It costs 2000 rp in bisnis class and takes ...ust over an hour – the quickest and most ...onvenient way to get to Solo.

Six daily trains operate on the Yogya-...anjar-Bandung route. Most trains come ...hrough from Surabaya. The night expresses, ...uch as the *Mutiara Selatan* (25,000 rp) and ...*urangga* (37,000 rp bisnis), provide the best ...ervices and take about 7½ hours. The ...*isadane* ekonomi train originates in Yogya ...nd leaves for Bandung (9000 rp; nine hours) ...t 8.15 am.

Getting Around

The Airport A taxi to Yogya's airport, 10 km ...o the east, will cost around 6000 to 7000 rp. ...axis from the airport operate on a coupon ...ystem.

If you stroll out to the main road, only ...00m from the station, you can get a Solo ...olt to Yogya's Terban colt station (about 1.5 ...m from Jl Sosrowijayan) or a Solo bus to ...he Umbulharjo bus terminal (about one km ...rom Prawirotaman) for 400 rp.

Bus Yogya's city buses *(bis kota)* operate on ...7 set routes around the city for a flat 400 rp ...are. They work mostly straight routes – ...oing out and then coming back the same ...vay – and all start and end at the Umbulharjo ...us terminal.

Bus No 2 is one of the more useful ser-...ices. It runs from the bus terminal and turns ...own Jl Sisingamangaraja, past Jl Prawirota-...nan, then loops around, coming back up Jl ...arangtritis and on to Jl Mataram a block ...rom Jl Malioboro, before continuing to the ...niversity and returning.

For Kota Gede, bus No 4 runs down Jl ...Malioboro and on to Jl Ngeksigondo – get ...ff at Tom's Silver and walk one km south to

the centre of the village. Bus No 8 from the bus terminal runs through the centre of Kota Gede.

Becak & Andong Yogya is overendowed with becaks and it is impossible to go any-where in the main tourist areas without being greeted by choruses of 'becak'. They cost around 500 rp a km, but the minimum fare for tourists is usually 1000 rp and the asking rate is a lot more. The trip from Jl Prawirota-man to Jl Malioboro should cost no more than 2000 rp. Avoid becak drivers who offer cheap hourly rates unless you want to do the rounds of all the batik galleries that offer commission. There are also horse-drawn andong around town, costing about the same, or cheaper, than the becaks.

Car & Motorcycle Travel agents on Jl Sosro-wijayan and Jl Prawirotaman rent out cars from as little as 60,000 rp per day, including driver but excluding petrol. A good minibus will cost a little more. For day trips, agents like to rent on an all-inclusive basis – from 80,000 rp, including driver and petrol for trips around the city, more for long distances. Work out exactly what is included in the price before you hire a car, and be prepared to bargain.

Bali Car Rental (☎ 587548) in front of the Adisucipto airport is a registered car rental agency for self-drive hire.

Motorcycles can be hired for around 10,000 rp a day. An international licence is required by law, but nobody seems to bother.

Taxi Taxis in Yogya are metered, efficient and cost 1300 rp for the first km, then 450 rp for each subsequent km.

Bicycle Yogya traffic is becoming increas-ingly heavy, but a bicycle is still a viable way to explore the city. Pushbikes can be rented from hotels and agents around Jl Sos-rowijayan and Jl Prawirotaman for as little as 2000 rp a day.

AROUND YOGYAKARTA
Imogiri

Perched on a hilltop 20 km south of Yogya, Imogiri was built by Sultan Agung in 1645 to serve as his own mausoleum. Imogiri has since been the burial ground for almost all his successors and for prominent members of the royal family, and it is still a holy place. The cemetery contains three major court-yards – in the central courtyard are the tombs of Sultan Agung and succeeding Mataram kings, to the left are the tombs of the sus-uhunans of Solo and to the right those of the sultans of Yogya. The tomb of Hamengku-buwono IX, the father of the present sultan is one of the most visited graves.

The point of major interest for pilgrims i the tomb of Sultan Agung. The tomb is onl open from 10 am to 1 pm on Monday an from 1.30 to 4 pm on Friday and Sunday, an there is no objection to visitors joining th pilgrims then.

It's an impressive complex, reached by a equally impressive flight of 345 steps. Fro the top of the stairway, a walkway circles th whole complex and leads to the real summi of the hill. Here you have a superb view ove Yogya to Gunung Merapi.

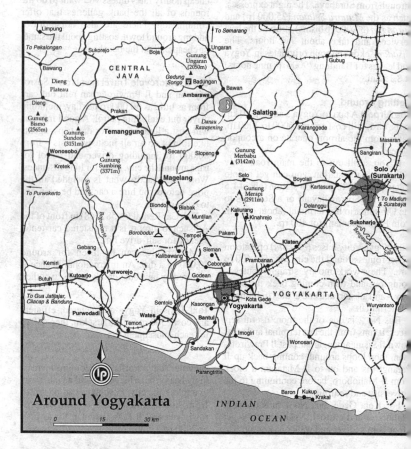

Around Yogyakarta

0   15   30 km

INDIAN OCEAN

Colts and buses from Yogya (500 rp) stop at the parking lot from where it is about 500m to the base of the hill and the start of the steps. Like most pilgrimage sites, there will be various, insistent demands for 'donations'. The only compulsory entry charge (500 rp) is payable when you sign the visitors' book, inside the main compound at the top of the stairs.

To enter the tombs you must don full Javanese court dress, which can be hired for another 1000 rp.

Kasongan

This is Yogya's pottery centre. Dozens of workshops produce pots and some superb figurines, including two metre high dragons and pony-sized horses. Kasongan pottery is sold painted or unpainted – very little glazing work is done.

Getting There & Away Catch a Bantul-bound bus and get off on the main road at the entrance to the village, 6.5 km south of Yogya. It is then about a one km walk to the centre of the village and most of the pottery workshops.

Parangtritis

Twenty-seven km south of Yogya, Parangtritis has rough surf and a long sweep of shifting, black sand dunes backed by high, jagged cliffs. It's a place of superstition and, like so many places along the south coast, a centre for the worship of Nyai Loro Kidul, the 'Queen of the South Seas'. Legend has it that Senopati, the 16th century Mataram ruler, took her as his wife and thus established the strong tie between the goddess and the royal house of Mataram. Their sacred rendezvous spot is at **Parangkusumo**, one km west down the beach, where the sultans of Yogya still send offerings every year at Labuhan to appease this consort of kings. Just beyond Parangkusumo are hot springs at **Parang Wedang**.

The currents and undertows at Parangtritis are reputed to be dangerous, though swimming is sometimes possible. Just don't wear green – Nyai Loro Kidul's favourite colour.

You can swim safely in freshwater pools (*pemandian*) at the base of the hill near the village, where spring water spills out through high bamboo pipes from the hilltop. The beach promenade of straggling warungs and souvenir stalls is nothing to rave about, but this is a quiet, simple place if you want a break from Yogya. Most visitors day trip. Avoid weekends and holidays when the beach is swamped by mobs from Yogya.

Trails along the hills above the sea to the east of Parangtritis lead to caves used for meditation. A couple of km from town is **Gua Langse**, reached by narrow trails, rickety bamboo ladders and ropes down the cliff face to the cave opening. Branches of the cave extend deep into the hillside where would-be mystics sit in contemplation, sometimes for days on end.

Places to Stay & Eat The centre of the village is the plaza, marked by the Diponegoro monument. Leading down to the beach, the main street/promenade has plenty of basic cheap hotels and rumah makan.

Hotel Widodo is the best cheap option with rooms for 15,000 rp, including breakfast and free tea and coffee. It has a good little restaurant and tours are offered along the coast. It has a more basic offshoot behind the main drag, with rooms from 5000 rp per person. The *Agung Garden* is another catering to travellers but it has gone downhill. Dingy rooms range from 10,000 to 35,000 rp with air-con. Other reasonable places are the *Wisma Lukita*, which has rooms with mandi for 10,000 rp, and the *Budi Inn*.

The best hotel by far is the *Queen of the South* (☎ 367196), perched on the clifftops high above town. It has excellent views, a fine pendopo-style restaurant and a swimming pool. Comfortable rooms cost US$82 and US$90 plus 21%.

Getting There & Away Buses from Yogya's Umbulharjo bus terminal, which can also be caught on Jl Parangtritis at the end of Jl Prawirotaman, leave throughout the day for the one hour journey. The last bus back from Parangtritis leaves at around 5.30 pm. The cost is 1200 rp (including 600 rp entry to Parangtritis), but the price is *very* variable. You can also reach Parangtritis via Imogiri, but this is a much longer route.

Other Beaches

Yogya has several other uninspiring beaches besides Parangtritis. The only ones of any minor interest are the isolated beaches to the south-east. **Baron**, 60 km from Yogya, has safe swimming inside a sheltered cove. **Kukup** is a white sand beach one km east of Baron.

Krakal, eight km east of Baron, has a fine, usually deserted, white sand beach, but the shallow reef rules out swimming. If you really want to get away from it all, the *Krakal Beach Hotel* has a restaurant, run-down rooms for 10,000 and 15,000 rp, and cottages with mandi for 25,000 rp.

To reach these beaches, take a bus from Yogya to Wonosari (1000 rp), then an infrequent opelet to the beaches (500 rp), but you will usually have to charter for 5000 rp.

Gunung Merapi

Gunung Merapi ('Fire Mountain'; 2911m) is one of Java's most destructive volcanoes. Standing at the northern pinnacle of Yogya's borders, its towering peak can be seen from many parts of the city on a clear day. The mountain is a source of spiritual power, and every year offerings from the kraton are made to Merapi's destructive power, in conjunction with offerings to the Queen of the South Seas at Parangtritis.

Merapi has erupted numerous times, with at least three major eruptions and dozens of minor ones this century. Some have even theorised that it was a massive eruption of Merapi that caused the sudden and mysterious evacuation of Borobudur and the collapse of the old Mataram kingdom in the 11th century.

Merapi's violent reputation was again confirmed on 22 November 1994, when it erupted killing 69 people. Being so close to major population areas, the volcano is constantly monitored by posts all around the mountain, and advance warnings were issued. Nearby villages were evacuated, bu a wedding party ignored the warning and were caught in the rain of ash. Many of the party were killed by deadly gases escaping through fissures on the flank of the moun tain.

The hill resort town of Kaliurang, 25 km north of Yogya, is the main access point fo Merapi. The small village of Selo, on the other side of the mountain, is an easie staging point for climbing the mountain and currently the only way to get near the top.

Merapi continues to boil away, issuing smoke and a regular stream of lava that flow away down the Sungai Boyong valley from the crater. Check the latest situation in Kaliurang, but with Merapi constantly threatening more eruptions, the climb from Kaliurang is not possible and the peak and crater are off limits.

The good news is that it is possible (and much easier) to go part way up the mountai for spectacular and unique views of Merapi'. lava flows. Only registered rescue guides with radio contact, can undertake the trek to the lava viewpoint. Information and guides can be arranged through Christian Awuy a Vogels Hostel in Kaliurang. The five hou return trek starts at 3 am – to see the lava a its best – and costs 7500 rp per person including lunch.

Climbing Merapi The climb to the top o Merapi from Kaliurang is one of the most difficult on Java and guides are essential When it becomes possible again, the trail up the mountain begins at the main entrance to the forest park. It leads one hour around the mountain to Kinahrejo, and then it is a gruelling five or six hours up to the summit Climbers start around midnight to reach the summit after dawn. The owner of Vogels Hostel, Christian Awuy, has organised climbs for years and is an essential first reference point, and his hikes to see the lava are proving popular.

Because of easy access from Yogya and the availability of reliable information Kaliurang has always been a popular place from which to climb Merapi, but in fact it is easier to climb from Selo, to the north of Merapi.

You can still do the climb from Selo. It takes at least four hours, so a 1 am start is necessary to reach the top for the dawn. After a two km walk through the village to Pos Merapi, the vulcanology post, the steady but steep climb begins. The last stages are through loose volcanic scree, but guides may stop short of the top. Check with your guide if it is possible, or if he is willing, to go to the top before setting off. It is dangerous to go over the summit down to the crater or on to Kaliurang. Climbs from Selo are not always well organised. Some travellers wrote to tell us they were lost on the mountain after becoming separated from their climbing party – and no-one noticed!

Kaliurang

Kaliurang, 25 km north of Yogya, is the nearest hill resort to the city, standing at 900m on the slopes of Gunung Merapi. Pick a clear, cloudless day during the week when it's quiet, and this is a great place to escape from the heat of the plains. There are good forest walks, and superb views of the smoking, fire-spewing mountain.

Day trippers can explore the forest park (Hutan Wisata Kaliurang) on the slopes of the mountain. You can walk to the waterfall but the one hour walk from the park entrance to the observatory at Pos Plawangan (1260m), the vulcanology post that monitors Merapi, is currently off limits.

Kaliurang is a pleasant place to spend a day or two and other mountain walks, including viewing the lava flows of Merapi (see the previous Climbing Merapi section), can still be done.

Places to Stay & Eat *Vogels Hostel* (☎ 89-5208) at Jl Astamulya 76 has deservedly been the travellers' favourite for years. As well as being the local tourist information office, the owner, Christian Awuy, also has one of the best travel libraries in Indonesia, with books on Indonesia and further afield. There is a variety of rooms to suit most tastes and budgets, starting at 3500 rp in the dorm

or doubles from 6000 rp up to good mid-range bungalows at the back with bath for only 22,000 rp. HI card holders get a small discount. The old part of the hostel, the former residence of a Yogya prince, has a good, very cheap restaurant. This is the place to arrange treks to Merapi and other good walks.

In addition to Vogels, Christian has started the nearby *Christian Hostel*. New, spotless rooms with mandi provide excellent accommodation for 12,500 rp (10,000 rp for YHA members). The rooftop sitting area has views of Merapi and the lava flow.

Kaliurang has over 100 other places to stay. Kaliurang is a down-market resort with no star-classified hotels, but some of the guesthouses are pleasant, older-style places. The *Wisma Tamu Gadjah Mada* (☎ 895225) has good views and Indo-European architecture. Run-down rooms cost 12,000 rp or large family rooms cost 40,000 to 60,000 rp, hot water included. *Wisma Wijaya Kusuma* is similar. The *Satriafi* is newer and one of the best in town, with rooms from 20,000 rp up to VIP rooms with hot water for 40,000 rp.

Vogels Hostel has a varied menu, or the *Restaurant Joyo* is a bright, clean place with good Chinese and Indonesian food.

Getting There & Away From Yogya's Terban colt station, a colt to Kaliurang costs 850 rp, or a crowded bus from the main bus terminal costs 600 rp. Buses and colts pass through Pakem before Kaliurang. From Pakem there are buses to Prambanan (750 rp), or for Borobudur take a bus from Pakem to Tempel (400 rp) and then another to Borobudur.

Selo

On the northern slopes of volatile Gunung Merapi, 50 km west of Solo, Selo is just a straggling village with limited amenities, but it has a few basic homestays where guides can be arranged for the climb of Merapi. The views of the mountain from the village are superb.

From Selo it is a four hour trek to the volcano's summit. It is dangerous to attempt the hike around the side of the peak from Selo to see the crater. See the earlier Climbing Merapi section for more details.

Places to Stay The hospitable Pak Darto has been guiding trips to the top for years and runs a popular homestay, known as *Pak Auto*. A misspelling in a French guidebook resulted in Pak Darto assuming the 'Auto' tag rather than confuse his customers. Accommodation is very simple but clean and costs only 5000 rp. Elderly Pak Darto rarely ventures far these days, but his son or other guides can be hired at 15,000 rp for one to three people.

The *Losmen Jaya & Restaurant* has similar basic accommodation and also arranges guides.

The crumbling *Hotel Agung Merapi* is a slight step up in standards and has a restaurant. Singles/doubles cost 10,000/13,500 rp up to 25,000/30,000 rp with mandi. Standards are poor for that price, so try bargaining, or a dorm bed costs 5000 rp. Its guides cost 20,000 rp for two people.

Getting There & Away Selo is most easily reached from Solo. Take one of the six daily Merapi Indah buses from Solo to Magelang, stopping at Selo (1500 rp; two hours) on the way. From Yogya take a Magelang bus to Blabak (800 rp) and then a colt or bus to Selo (1000 rp). Travel agents in Solo and Yogya arrange climbing trips of Merapi via Selo, or the Jaya Losmen on Gang II in Yogya's Sosrowijayan area arranges cheap trips.

PRAMBANAN

On the road to Solo, 17 km east of Yogya, the temples at Prambanan village are the cream of what remains of Java's period of Hindu cultural development. Not only do these temples form the largest Hindu temple complex on Java, but the wealth of sculptural detail on the great Shiva Temple makes it easily the most outstanding example of Hindu art.

All the temples in the Prambanan area were built between the 8th and 10th centuries AD, when Java was ruled by the Buddhist Sailendras in the south and the Hindu Sanjayas of Old Mataram in the north. Possibly by the second half of the 9th century these two dynasties were united by the marriage of Rakai Pikatan of Hindu Mataram and the Buddhist Sailendra princess Pramodhavardhani. This may explain why a number of temples, including the Prambanan Temple and the smaller Plaosan group reveal Shivaite and Buddhist elements in architecture and sculpture. On the other hand, you find this mixture to some degree in India and Nepal, too, so it's hardly a novel idea.

Following this two-century burst of creativity, the Prambanan Plain was abandoned when the Hindu-Javanese kings moved to East Java. In the middle of the 16th century there is said to have been a great earthquake which toppled many of the temples and, in the centuries that followed, their destruction was accelerated by greedy treasure hunters and local people searching for building material. Most of the restoration work of this century has gone into the preservation of Prambanan. Of the outlying temple sites some are just decayed fragments. Perhaps half a dozen are of real interest.

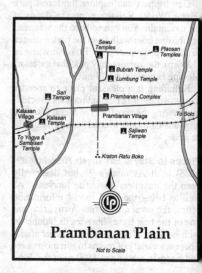

Prambanan Plain

Not to Scale

Orientation & Information

The Prambanan temples *(candi)* can be visited using either Yogya or Solo as a base. The Shiva Mahadeva Temple, the largest of the temples, is locally called Candi Loro Jonggrang, or 'Slender Virgin', and sometimes the entire complex is referred to by this name. Prambanan village is tiny and has little in the way of accommodation facilities. On its northern boundary is the temple complex and the outdoor theatre where the *Ramayana* ballet is performed on full-moon nights. The temple enclosure is open daily from 6 am to 6 pm, with last admission at 5.15 pm. Entry costs 5000 rp and, as at Borobudur, this includes camera fees and a guided tour (if you are prepared to wait to join a large enough group) in most major languages. An audio-visual show on Prambanan plays every 30 minutes for another 2000 rp.

At the temple complex there is little in the way of free brochures or maps – you can buy a copy of *Guide to Prambanan Temple*, which is detailed and covers most of the temple sites on Prambanan Plain.

Most of the outlying temples are spread out within a five km radius of Prambanan village. You'll need at least half a day to see them on foot, or you can hire a horse-drawn cart by the hour in Prambanan. As with any of Java's major tourist attractions, the best time to visit Prambanan is early morning or late in the day when it's quiet, though you can never expect to get Prambanan to yourself. Very few people visit the other sites and the walk can be as much of a pleasure as the temples themselves.

Prambanan Temple Complex

The huge Prambanan complex was constructed in about the middle of the 9th century – around 50 years later than Borobudur – but remarkably little is known about its early history. It's thought that it was built by Rakai Pikatan to commemorate the return of a Hindu dynasty to sole power on Java. Some have even suggested it was intended as a counterpart to Borobudur, but more likely it was a counterpart to Candi Sewu, a Buddhist complex three km away.

Prambanan was in ruins for years and, although efforts were made in 1885 to clear the site, it was not until 1937 that reconstruction was first attempted. Of the original group the outer compound contains the remains of 244 temples. Eight minor and eight main temples stand in the highest central courtyard, and most have been restored.

Shiva Mahadeva The temple dedicated to Shiva is not only the largest of the temples, it is also artistically and architecturally the most perfect. The main spire soars 47m high and the temple is lavishly carved. The 'medallions' which decorate its base have the characteristic 'Prambanan motif' – small lions in niches flanked by 'trees of heaven' (or *kalpaturas*) and a menagerie of stylised half-human and half-bird heavenly beings *(kinnaras)*. The vibrant scenes carved onto the inner wall of the gallery encircling the temple are from the *Ramayana* – they tell how Lord Rama's wife, Sita, is abducted and how Hanuman the monkey god and Sugriwa his white monkey general eventually find and release her. To follow the story, ascend the main eastern stairway and go around the temple clockwise. The reliefs break off at the point where the monkey army builds a bridge to the island of Lanka; the end of the tale is found on the smaller Brahma Temple.

In the main chamber at the top of the eastern stairway, the four armed statue of Shiva the Destroyer is notable for the fact that this mightiest of Hindu gods stands on a huge lotus pedestal, a symbol of Buddhism. In the southern cell is the pot-bellied and bearded Agastya, an incarnation of Shiva as divine teacher; in the western cell is a superb image of the elephant-headed Ganesha, Shiva's son. In the northern cell, Durga, Shiva's consort, can be seen killing the demon buffalo. Some people believe that the Durga image is actually an image of Loro Jonggrang, the 'Slender Virgin' who, legend has it, was turned to stone by a giant she refused to marry. She is still the object of pilgrimage for many who believe in her and the name of the cursed princess is often used for the temple group.

Brahma & Vishnu Temples These two smaller temples flank the large Shiva Mahadeva Temple. The Brahma Temple to the south, carved with the final scenes of the *Ramayana*, has a four headed statue of Brahma, the god of creation. Reliefs on the Vishnu Temple to the north tell the story of Lord Krishna, a hero of the *Mahabharata* epic. Inside is a four armed image of Vishnu the Preserver.

Nandi Temple This small shrine, facing the Shiva Mahadeva Temple, houses one of Prambanan's finest sculptures – a huge, powerful figure of the bull, Nandi, the vehicle of Shiva.

The shrines to the north and south of Nandi may once have contained Brahma's vehicle, the swan, and Vishnu's sun-bird, the Garuda.

Northern Group
Of the northern group of temples, the Sewu and Plaosan temples are the most interesting, and they are within three km of Prambanan. They can be reached on foot by the signposted path leading north from the main Prambanan complex.

Sewu Temples The 'Thousand Temples', dating from around 850 AD, originally consisted of a large central Buddhist temple surrounded by four rings of 240 smaller 'guard' temples. Outside the compound stood four sanctuaries at the points of the compass, of which the Bubrah Temple is the southern one.

All but a few of the minor temples are in various stages of renovation, a great jumble of stone blocks littering the field. The main temple is interesting for the unusual finely carved niches around the inner gallery, with shapes resembling those found in the Middle East. Once these would have held bronze statues but plundering of the temple went on for many years – some of the statues were

melted down and others disappeared into museums and private possession.

Plaosan Temples One or two km east of Sewu, you walk across rice paddies and sugar cane fields to this temple group. Believed to have been built at about the same time as the Prambanan temple group by Rakai Pikatan and his Buddhist queen, the Plaosan temples combine both Hindu and Buddhist religious symbols and carvings. Of the original three main temples, once linked by a multitude of small shrines and solid stupas, one has been reconstructed and is notable for its unusual three part design. It is a two storey, six room structure, with an imitation storey above and a tiered roof of stupas rising to a single larger one in the centre. Inside the temple are impressive stone Bodhisattvas on either side of an empty lotus pedestal within the various cells and intricately carved *kala* (dragon) heads above the many windows. The Buddhas that once sat on the lotus pedestals are now in the National Museum in Jakarta.

Southern Group
Sajiwan Temple Not far from the village of Sajiwan, about 1.5 km south-east of Prambanan, are the ruins of this Buddhist temple. Around the base are carvings from the *Jataka* (episodes from the Buddha's various lives).

Kraton Ratu Boko Perched on a hill overlooking Prambanan, Kraton Ratu Boko, the 'Palace of King Boko', is believed to have been a huge Hindu palace complex dating from the 9th century, the central court of the great Mataram Empire. Little remains from the original complex, though it is possible to get an idea of the scale of this palace complex. Renovations are only partly successful and a lot of new stonework has been included, but you can see the large gateway, walls, the platform of the main pendopo, the Candi Pembakaran (Royal Crematorium) and a series of bathing places on different levels leading down to the nearby village. The view from this site to the Prambanan

Plain is magnificent, especially at sunset, and worth the walk alone.

To get to Ratu Boko, take the road just west of the river 1.5 km south of Prambanan village, and near the 'Yogya 18 km' signpost a steep rocky path leads up to the main site. It is about a one hour walk all up. The site can be reached by car or motorcycle via a much longer route that goes around the back of the mountain.

Western Group

There are three temples in this group between Yogya and Prambanan, two of them close to Kalasan village on the main Yogya road. Kalasan and Prambanan villages are three km apart, so it is probably easiest to take a colt or bus to cover this stretch.

Kalasan Temple Standing 50m off the main road near Kalasan village, this temple is one of the oldest Buddhist temples on the Prambanan Plain. A Sanskrit inscription of 778 AD refers to a temple dedicated to the female Bodhisattva, Tara, though the existing structure appears to have been built around the original one some years later. It has been partially restored during this century and has some fine detailed carvings on its southern side, where a huge, ornate kala head glowers over the doorway. At one time it was completely covered in coloured shining stucco, and traces of the hard, stonelike 'diamond plaster' that provided a base for paintwork can still be seen. The inner chamber of Kalasan once sheltered a huge bronze image of Buddha or Tara.

Sari Temple About 200m north of Kalasan Temple, in the middle of coconut and banana groves, the Sari Temple has the three part design of the larger Plaosan Temple but is probably slightly older. Some students believe that its 2nd floor may have served as a dormitory for the Buddhist priests who took care of the Kalasan Temple. The sculptured reliefs around the exterior are similar to those of Kalasan but in much better condition.

Sambisari Temple A country lane runs to this isolated temple, about 2.5 km north of the main road. Sambisari is a Shiva temple and possibly the latest temple at Prambanan to be put up by the Mataram rulers. It was only discovered by a farmer in 1966. Excavated from under ancient layers of protective volcanic ash and dust, it lies almost six metres below the surface of the surrounding fields and is remarkable for its perfectly preserved state. It has some fine decorations, and in the niches you can see the stone images of Durga, Ganesha and Agastya.

Places to Stay

Very few visitors stay at Prambanan, but there are a few basic hotels, such as *Hotel Muharti*, on the main highway near the entrance, with nondescript rooms from 12,000 rp. Others include *Sari's Hotel* and the quieter *Wisma Ramayana* on the east side of the complex.

Entertainment

The famous *Ramayana Ballet* held at the outdoor theatre in Prambanan is Java's most spectacular dance-drama. The ballet is performed over four successive nights, twice each month of the dry season, from May to October, leading up to the full moon. With the magnificent flood-lit Shiva Mahadeva Temple as a backdrop, more than 100 dancers and gamelan musicians take part in a spectacle of monkey armies, giants on stilts, clashing battles and acrobatics.

Performances last from 7 to 9 pm. Tickets are sold through the Tourist Information Office and travel agents in Yogya at the same price you'll pay at the theatre box office, but they usually offer packages that include transport direct from your hotel. Tickets range from 7500 rp, up to 35,000 rp for VIP. There are no bad seats in the amphitheatre – all have a good view and are not too far from the stage, but the cheapest seats are side on to the action.

Alternatively, the *Ramayana Ballet Full Story* is a good two hour performance, condensing the epic into one night, indoors at Prambanan's Trimurti covered theatre at

7.30 pm every Tuesday, Wednesday and Thursday throughout the year. Tickets range from 10,000 to 15,000 rp.

Also worth seeing is the Tawur Agung festival, held one day before Nyepi, the Hindu new year. It usually falls around March, and thousands flock to see the procession or make offerings to the gods. Tawur Agung is held principally to ward off Ogoh Ogoh, a manifestation of Shiva's fearsome son Kala, who eats children. Kala particularly preys on only children. Families with two children of the same sex, or mixed twins, among other combinations, are also at risk. Kala is appeased by Ruwatan ceremonies, widely held throughout Java when they can be afforded. The children and families of potential victims are invited, and a special dalang will stage a wayang, usually based on stories of the first king of Java.

Getting There & Away

From Yogya, take the yellow Pemuda bus (500 rp; 30 minutes) from the main bus terminal, or a Solo colt from the Terban colt station. From Solo, buses take 1½ hours and cost 1500 rp.

By bicycle, you can visit all the temples. The secret is to avoid as much of the Solo road as possible. Past the Ambarrukmo Palace Hotel in Yogya, turn left down Jl Babarsari, go past the Sahid Garden Hotel and follow the road anticlockwise around the school to the Mataram Canal. You can follow the canal for about six km, most of the way to Prambanan.

SOLO (SURAKARTA)

Only 65 km north-east of Yogya, the old royal city of Surakarta competes with Yogya as a centre of Javanese culture. More popularly known as Solo, Surakarta has two palaces, one even older than Yogya's, for Solo was the seat of the great Mataram Empire before Yogyakarta was split off from it.

Solo, even though it is larger than Yogya, is more traditional and unhurried. It can also rightfully claim to be more Javanese than Yogyakarta, which as a university town has a large population of non-Javanese students.

As well as its palaces, Solo attracts many students and scholars to its academies of music and dance. The city is an excellent place to see traditional performing arts. Traditional crafts are also well represented, especially batik, as Solo is a major centre for high quality batik and other textiles.

While Solo has most of the same attractions as Yogya, it is far less touristed. It can be visited on a day trip from Yogya, but the place is worth far more than a day, and there are a number of attractions outside the city. It has a good range of accommodation, and though tourist services are not as developed as in Yogya, tourism is far less commercialised.

History

Surakarta's founding in 1745 has a mystical past. Following the sacking of the Mataram court at Kartasura in 1742, the susuhunan (king), Pakubuwono II, decided to look for a more auspicious site. The transfer of the capital had something to do with voices from the cosmic world – according to legend the king was told to go to the village of Solo because 'it is the place decreed by Allah and it will become a great and prosperous city'.

But Solo had already reached the peak of its political importance and within 10 years the realm of Mataram had crumbled, split by internal conflict into three rival courts, of which Yogya was one. From then on the rulers of Surakarta and the subsidiary prince of Mangkunegara remained loyal to the Dutch, even at the time of Diponegoro's Java War. During the revolution they fumbled opportunities to play a positive role, and with the tide of democracy in the 1940s the palaces of Solo became mere symbols of ancient Javanese feudalism and aristocracy.

Orientation

The oldest part of the city is centred around the Kraton Surakarta to the east, where the Pasar Klewer, the main batik market, is also located. Kraton Mangkunegara is the centre of Solo. Away from these tranquil palaces Solo can be as busy as any other Javanese city, but it is less congested than its younger ister city, Yogya, and not overwhelmed by ourists. It is perhaps the least westernised of ava's cities, and there are corners with narrow walled streets and a strong village atmosphere.

Jl Slamet Riyadi, the broad tree-lined avenue running east-west through the centre of Solo, is the main thoroughfare. Here the city's double-decker buses run their course. You will also find the tourist office at the west end and most of the banks at the east end, near Kraton Surakarta. Solo's Balapan train station is in the northern part of the city, about two km from the city centre, and the main bus terminal is just a few hundred metres north again. Most hotels and restaurants are on or just off Jl Slamet Riyadi.

Information

Tourist Office The Solo Tourist Office (☎ 711435), Jl Slamet Riyadi 275, has useful pamphlets, a map of Solo and information on cultural events in town and places to visit in the area. The office is open from 8 am to 5 pm. The tourist office also has a helpful stand at the bus terminal.

Post & Communications The efficient main post office on Jl Jenderal Sudirman is open from 8 am to 4 pm Monday to Friday, and until 1 pm on Saturday for international postal services. The Telkom office for international calls is near the post office on Jl Mayor Kusmanto, or there are wartels on Jl Slamet Riyadi, at No 125 at the Hotel Kota and at No 275 at the Sriwedari Amusement Park.

Kraton Surakarta

In 1745 Pakubuwono II moved from Kartasura to Kraton Surakarta (also known as the Kraton Kasunanan) in a day-long procession which transplanted everything belonging to the king, including the royal banyan trees and the sacred Nyai Setomo cannon (the twin of Si Jagur in old Jakarta), which now sits in the northern palace pavilion. Ornate European-style decorations were later added by Pakubuwono X, the wealthiest of Surakarta's rulers, from 1893 to 1939.

Entry to the kraton is through the north entrance, fronting the alun alun. Here the Pagelaran is the main audience hall where the susuhunan held court in front of his people. Crossing over the street behind the Pagelaran is the kraton proper, though the main gateway is not open to the public and entry is from around the east side at the museum/art gallery. Much of the kraton was destroyed by fire in 1985, attributed by the Solonese to the susuhunan's lack of observance of tradition. Many of the inner buildings, including the pendopo (audience hall), were destroyed and have been rebuilt. One that has survived is the distinctive tower known as Panggung Songgo Buwono, built in 1782 and looking like a cross between a Dutch clocktower and a lighthouse. Its upper storey is a meditation sanctum where the susuhunan is said to commune with Nyai Loro Kidul (Queen of the South Seas).

A heavy carved doorway leads through from the museum across the inner courtyard of shady trees to the pendopo, but most of the kraton is off limits and is in fact the *dalem*, or residence, of the susuhunan. The main sight for visitors is the Sasono Sewoko museum/art gallery; exhibits include fine silver and bronze Hindu-Javanese figures, Javanese weapons, antiques and other royal heirlooms.

Admission is 1000 rp, which includes entry to the kraton complex and museum and a guide. A 1000 rp camera fee is extra. Entry is only from the north side opposite the alun alun, and the kraton is open every day, except Friday, from 8 am to 2 pm. Dancing practice classes for children can be seen on Sunday from 10 am to noon, while adult practice is from 1 to 3 pm.

Kraton Mangkunegara

In the centre of the city, Kraton Mangkunegara, dating back to 1757, is the palace of the second ruling house of Solo. It was founded after a bitter struggle against the susuhunan, Pakubuwono II, launched by his nephew Raden Mas Said, an ancestor of Madam Tien Soeharto, the late wife of the president. Though much smaller in scale and

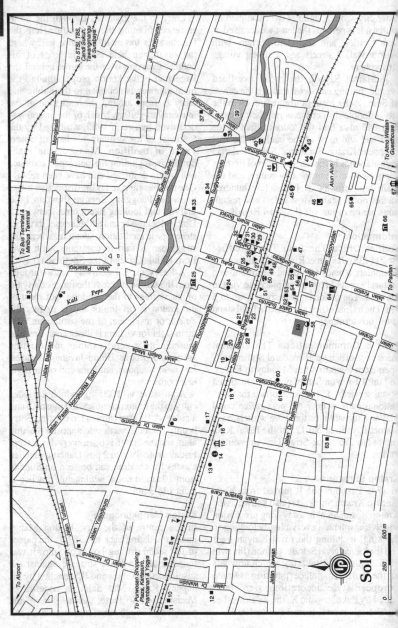

Solo

0   250   500 m

To Airport

To Bus Terminal &
Minibus Terminal

To STSI, TBS,
Candi Sukuh,
Tawangmangu
& Surabaya

To Atmo Wisata
Guesthouse

To Pacitan

To Kraton

To Purwosari Shopping
Plaza, Kartasura,
Prambanan & Yoga

Kali Pepe

Alun Alun

PLACES TO STAY		PLACES TO EAT		15	Radya Pustaka
1	Hotel Agas	7	Adem Ayam		Museum
	International		Restaurant	21	Garuda (Lippobank
3	Hotel Jayakarta	8	Swensen's & KFC		Building)
5	Sahid Raya Solo	16	Pujosari	24	Pasar Triwindu
9	Solo Inn	18	Cipta Rasa	25	Kraton Mangkunegara
10	Hotel Putri Ayu		Restaurant	36	SMKI School
11	Riyadi Palace Hotel	19	Tio Ciu 99	38	Nirwana Disco
12	Ramayana Guest	26	Jalan Teuku Umar	39	Pasar Gede
	House		Warungs	40	Telkom Office
17	Hotel Dana	27	American Donut	41	Main Post Office
20	Java Homestay		Bakery	42	Adpura Kencana
22	Hotel Cakra	28	Warung Baru		Monument
23	Wisata Indah	29	News Cafe	43	Matahari Department
30	Hotel Central	31	Cafe Gamelan		Store
32	Solo Homestay	35	Pringgondani	44	Balai Agung
33	Kusuma Sahid Prince	48	Kasuma Sari	45	BCA Bank
	Hotel		Restaurant	46	Mesjid Agung
34	Griyadi Sahid Kusuma	51	New Holland Bakery	50	Wartel
37	Hotel Trio	52	Kantin Bahagia	55	Batik Keris
47	Mama Homestay	62	Kafe Solo	58	Taxi Stand
49	Hotel Kota			59	Singosaren Plaza
53	Relax Homestay	**OTHER**		60	Batik Danarhadi
54	Cendana Homestay	2	Balapan Train Station	61	Legenda Disco
	& Warung Biru	4	RRI Radio Station	64	Vihara Rahayu
56	Paradise Guest	6	Toko Bedoyo Srimpi		Chinese Temple
	House	13	Sriwedari Amusement	65	Pasar Klewer
57	Westerners		Park	66	Kraton Surakarta
63	Happy Homestay	14	Tourist Office	67	Kraton Museum

design, this kraton is much better maintained and obviously wealthier than the more important Kraton Surakarta. Members of the royal family still live at the back of the palace.

The centre of the palace compound is the pendopo pavilion, bordered on its northern side by the dalem, which now forms the palace museum. The pavilion has been added to over the centuries and is one of the largest in the country. Its high rounded ceiling was painted in 1937 and is intricately decorated with a central flame surrounded by figures of the Javanese zodiac, each in its own mystical colour. In Javanese philosophy yellow signifies a preventative against sleepiness, blue against disease, black against hunger, green against desire, white against lust, rose against fear, red against evil and purple against wicked thoughts. The pavilion contains one of the kraton's oldest sets of gamelan known as 'Kyai Kanyut Mesem', which translates as 'Drifting in Smiles'.

The museum here is a real delight. Most of the exhibits are from the personal collection of Mangkunegara VII. Among the items are gold-plated dresses for the royal Srimpi and Bedoyo dances, jewellery and a few oddities, including huge Buddhist rings and a gold genital cover for a queen. There's also a magnificent collection of masks from various areas in Indonesia, a series of royal portraits and a library collection of classical literary works by the Mangkunegara princes.

The palace is open every day from 8.30 am to 2 pm, except Sunday when it closes at 1 pm. Admission is 1500 rp. At the pavilion, you can see dance practice sessions on Wednesday morning from 10 am until noon. The palace shop sells wayang puppets and other craft items.

Radya Pustaka Museum

This small museum, next to the tourist office on Jl Slamet Riyadi, has good displays of gamelan instruments, jewelled kris, wayang puppets from Thailand and Indonesia, a small collection of wayang beber (scrolls which depict wayang stories) and the Raja Mala, a hairy muppet figurehead from a royal barge. Offerings must be made regularly to the Raja Mala, otherwise it is said it will exude a pungent odour. The museum is open Tuesday, Thursday and Sunday from 8 am to 1 pm, Friday and Saturday until 11 am. Entry costs 500 rp.

Markets

The **Pasar Klewer** is the ever-busy, crowded textile market near the Kraton Surakarta. This is the place to look for batik.

Solo's antique market, **Pasar Triwindu**, is always worth a browse. It sells all sorts of bric-a-brac (not all of it old), though half the market is also devoted to car and motorcycle parts.

The **Pasar Gede** is the city's largest everyday market selling all manner of produce, while the **Pasar Depok** is Solo's bird market, at the north-west end of Jl RM Said.

Other Attractions

On the west side of the alun alun, the **Mesjid Agung** (Grand Mosque) is the largest and most sacred mosque in Solo, featuring classical Javanese architecture.

Sriwedari is Solo's amusement park, with fair rides, side-show stalls and other somewhat dated diversions. Unlike other cities on Java with similar amusement parks, Sriwedari can still draw a crowd on a Saturday night. The main reason to come is for the nightly wayang orang performances and other regular cultural performances.

Swimming

You can use the swimming pool at the Kusuma Sahid Prince Hotel for 7500 rp a day.

Meditation

Solo is a noted centre for contemporary mystical groups, of different philosophies and religions, which come under the broad umbrella of Kebatinan (Mysticism). A few schools in Solo have western followers and most gatherings are generally held informally at private homes. Meditational practices and philosophy are Hindu/Buddhist with a distinct Javanese world view. Islamic mystics also abound in Solo, but they don' attract westerners for some reason.

On the eastern side of the kraton opposite the museum, Pak Hardjanto's Pura Mandira Seta is about as Hindu and as ascetic as they come. Suprapto Suryodarmo (Prapto) follows Buddhist philosophy and practises meditation through movement, something like Tai Chi. Pak Suwondo, on Gang 1 Jl Kratonan teaches the traditional theory and practice of Javanese meditation, and has a reputation a a patient teacher. Ananda Suyono is a Javanese 'New Age' eclectic, who lives at Jl Ronggowarsito 60. The guesthouses ca steer you towards a school.

Batik Courses

You can take batik courses in Solo. Sol Homestay and Mama Homestay (see Place to Stay, below) do short introductory courses.

Organised Tours

Various travel agents around town run tours and many guesthouses and hotels will boo them. City tours cost around 20,000 r (25,000 rp, including Sangiran), Sukuh cost 25,000 rp, Prambanan-Kota Gede-Parang tritis costs 40,000 rp, and there are als Dieng-Borobudur tours for 60,000 rp an others, including Bromo tours. Inta Tour (☎ 56128), Jl Slamet Riyadi 96, is one con veniently located tour operator. Mandir Tours & Travel (☎ 718558), Jl Gajah Mad 77, opposite the Hotel Said Raya Solo, i another well-established operator with wide variety of tours and services.

Warung Baru and some of the homestay run bike tours of Solo and sites outside th city limits. These tours are reasonably price and have earned the praise of numerous trav ellers. For 9000 rp, one full day tour take you through beautiful countryside to se batik weaving, gamelan making, and tofe arak and rice-cracker processing.

Places to Stay – bottom end

Solo has an excellent selection of friendl

omestays. Almost all offer good travel information, tours, bus bookings, bicycles, and breakfast, free tea and drinking water.

The *Westerners* (☎ 633106) at Kemlayan Kidul 11, the first alley north of Jl Secoyudan off Jl Yos Sudarso, is spotlessly clean, well run and secure. Solo's original homestay, it is still popular, though it can be cramped. The dormitory costs 5000 rp per night, small singles cost 6000 rp and doubles range from 7000 to 12,000 rp. Breakfast costs 2000 rp.

On the same alley at No 1/3, the *Paradise Guest House* (☎ 54111) is a classy little place with a pendopo-style lobby/sitting area. The all-white rooms are good, if expensive, at 10,500 to 17,500 rp with shared mandi, 25,000 to 40,000 rp with mandi. Look for the sign offering 'Westerner's' accommodation, an attempt to lure the competition's trade.

A couple of gangs north is *Relax Homestay* (☎ 46417), Gang Empu Sedah 28, one of the best homestays. The rooms are built round a large courtyard garden, and this place has a bar/cafe. Good-sized rooms cost 9500 rp, or more stylish rooms with mandi in the old section are 15,000 and 25,000 rp.

Off the same alley, *Cendana Homestay* (☎ 46169), Gang Empu Panuluh III No 4, is new, so the rooms are a notch ahead of the pack. Rooms cost 7500/10,000 rp (1000 rp extra with fan), and from 15,000 to 20,000 rp with bathroom, all including breakfast. A very good restaurant is attached.

Mama Homestay (☎ 52248), Kauman Gang III, also off Jl Yos Sudarso, has simple rooms for 7000/10,000 rp and 8000/10,000 rp, including breakfast. This is a very friendly, laidback place and offers batik courses. *Solo Homestay*, on an alley near Warung Baru, also has batik courses for 8500 rp per day, and many of the guests stay here just for the courses. It's friendly, if a little dingy, and rooms cost 7000/10,000 rp.

Away from the main guesthouse enclave, but still central, is *Java Homestay* at Jl Jawa 1. The rooms costing from 7000 to 12,500 rp, including breakfast, can be gloomy, but this friendly place is new, so it tries hard.

Further from the city centre, at the south-east corner of the kraton, *Atmo Witatan*

(☎ 54538), Jl Sidikoro 42, is another new place with just a few attractive rooms for 10,000/15,000 rp with outside mandi; it also rents by the week for 60,000/90,000 rp. It is one block south of the Museum Vreteburg.

The small *Happy Homestay* (☎ 57149), Gang Karagan 12, off Jl Honggowongso (look for the sign), has tiny but comfortable singles for 6000 rp or larger doubles for 10,000 rp.

Solo has dozens of hotels, but they tend to be anonymous places. In a more central location, the long-running *Hotel Kota* (☎ 632841), Jl Slamet Riyadi 125, is a double storey place built around a large open courtyard. Rooms cost 8000/12,000 rp to 15,000/20,000 rp for singles/doubles with mandi. At Jl Ahmad Dahlan 32 is the open and airy *Hotel Central* (☎ 712814). It has some fine Art Deco woodwork, but not a lot else. The rooms, all without bath, are 7500 rp for doubles.

Places to Stay – middle

Many of the hotels in this bracket are strung out along or just off Jl Slamet Riyadi, well west of the city centre. The well-maintained *Hotel Putri Ayu* (☎ 711812), Jl Slamet Riyadi 331, is at the bottom of this range. Quiet rooms around a courtyard cost 27,000 rp with mandi, fan and TV, or air-con rooms with bath are 42,000 rp, including breakfast.

Ramayana Guest House (☎ 712814), Jl Dr Wahidin 22, is an attractive house with a garden and stylish dining/lobby area. It has reasonable doubles with bath for 25,000 to 30,000 rp, or rooms with air-con and hot water for 40,000 to 50,000 rp. Add 20% tax and service to the rates, but breakfast is included.

Conveniently located across the street from the tourist office and museum is the *Hotel Dana* (☎ 711976), Jl Slamet Riyadi 286. This fine colonial hotel has undergone extensive renovation, not all of it sympathetic, but it still has plenty of grace, extensive gardens and excellent rooms, most with private sitting areas. Rooms are 85,000 and 109,000 rp, and suites are 125,000 to 217,000 rp, all including breakfast.

JAVA

Solo Inn (☎ 716075), Jl Slamet Riyadi 366, is slightly faded but has well-appointed rooms with fridge, hot water, TV etc from 144,000 rp, before discount.

Close to the city centre, the *Griyadi Sahid Kusuma* (☎ 54122), Jl Sugiyopranoto 8, has well-appointed, quiet rooms for US$15 to US$60. This is the mid-range offshoot of the nearby Kusuma Sahid Prince Hotel, so guests can use the facilities.

At the top of this range, the *Riyadi Palace Hotel* (☎ 717181), Jl Slamet Riyadi 335, is newer, better and well worth considering. Rooms range from 107,500 to 275,000 rp.

Places to Stay – top end

The following hotels all have swimming pools and restaurants, and add 21% tax and service to their rates. With the opening of the new international airport, luxury hotels are being built at a frantic pace in anticipation of a tourism boom that has yet to materialise. Expect big discounts.

The grand *Kusuma Sahid Prince Hotel* (☎ 46356), Jl Sugiyopranoto 20, has been designed around a former Solonese palace and is set in extensive grounds. Older standard rooms cost US$85, or much better bungalow suites cost US$120 to US$250.

The *Hotel Said Raya Solo* (☎ 714144), Jl Gajah Mada 82, is a newly renovated highrise hotel with all the trimmings. It is currently Solo's best. Rooms cost US$95 and US$135.

Hotel Agas International (☎ 720746), Jl Dr Muwardi 44, is a smaller, new hotel without the facilities of the others, but it has a restaurant, pool, bar and excellent rooms for US$75 and US$95, plus 21%.

Luxury hotels nearing completion, most of them on the road to the airport, include the *Marriott*, *Sheraton*, *Novotel* and *Asia*.

Places to Eat

For the cheapest food listen for the weird and distinctive sounds which are the trademarks of the roaming street hawkers. The bread seller sings (or screeches) a high-pitched 'tee'; 'ding ding ding' is the bakso seller; 'tic toc' is mie; a wooden buffalo bell advertises

sate; and a shrieking kettle-on-the-boi sound is the *kue putu*. Kue putu are coconu cakes, which are pushed into small bambo tubes, cooked over a steam box and serve hot, sprinkled with coconut and sugar.

Nasi gudeg is popular, but the specialit of Solo is *nasi liwet*, rice with chicken an coconut milk. Another local speciality to tr at night is *srabi*, the small rice pudding served up on a crispy pancake with banana chocolate or jackfruit on top – best eate piping hot. Lesahan dining (on mats) is ver much a part of eating in Solo.

Jl Ahmad Dahlan is the centre for budge travellers' eateries. At No 23, the mos popular travellers' meeting place is the long running *Warung Baru* which serve substantial breakfasts and Indonesian an western fare at most reasonable price Various travel services, including bike tou of Solo, are also offered.

Across the street, *News Cafe* has stolen th name of the more upmarket chain, but it is i fact a cheap restaurant and bar. It stays ope late and is a good place for a drink whe everything else has closed. Further down a No 28, the friendly *Cafe Gamelan* is the mai competition to Warung Baru for the trav ellers' trade. It has a varied menu o Indonesian and western dishes, and a rang of travel services.

Close to most of the homestays, *Kanti Bahagia* is a pleasant little restaurant wit bamboo decor, cheap Indonesian food an cheap beer. Some of the homestays them selves have good restaurants. The *Warun Biru* at the Cendana Homestay has good foo and vegetarian meals, and the cafe at th Relax Homestay is also popular.

Some of the cheapest and best food is t be found in Solo's numerous warungs Everyone has their favourites and you ca get a feed any time of the night at numerou dusk to dawn warungs.

Pujosari is a good selection of warung next to the museum and tourist office in th Sriwedari Amusement Park area. They offe a wide range of Solonese and other Indones ian dishes. The biggest and best places ar the *Lezat*, a 24 hour lesahan place that some imes has bands on Saturday evenings, and he more restaurant-like *Oriental*. The ayam ampung (village chicken) at Lezat is deli-ious, and the Oriental has a wide range of ood Chinese dishes, including seafood. The nly drawback at both these ever-busy eater-es is that service can be slow.

On fine evenings, straw mats are laid out n the pavement on Jl Yos Sudarso or just round the corner on Jl Slamet Riyadi, and he sate is superb. Or try the warungs on Jl 'euku Umar for an inexpensive taste of local pecialities, including nasi liwet. Wash your neal down with susu segar (fresh milk) – hot r cold milk with optional egg and honey.

On Jl Gatot Subroto, look out for the *Bu Mari* warung, which has miniature chairs round a low table on the footpath. It has reat nasi gudeg and chicken curry with rice nd sambal, open until the wee hours of the norning.

Decent Chinese restaurants along Jl Slamet Riyadi include the *Cipta Rasa* at 245 nd the popular *Tio Ciu 99*. The unpreten-ious Cipta Rasa has cheap, filling fare, hough for a little extra the Tio Ciu 99 is a etter bet for good Chinese food.

Also on Jl Slamet Riyadi at No 342, the *dem Ayam* is split into two restaurants, one erving Chinese food and the other Javanese. 'he gudeg is its best dish. The *Pringgondani*, orth of the river at Jl Sultan Sahrir 79, is a ong-running restaurant with good Solonese pecialties.

Apart from the travellers' places on Jl hmad Dahlan, western food is not widely vailable in Solo. One exception is the *Kusama Sari*, on the corner of Jl Slamet Riyadi and Jl Yos Sudarso, which has seduc-ive air-con, good hot platter grills and ice reams. It is also one of those rarities in ndonesia – a non-smoking restaurant (well, lmost). Another branch is next to the BCA ank.

Bakeries along Jl Slamet Riyadi include he *American Donut* and the *New Holland* *akery*. The latter has a bewildering array of aked goods and delicious savoury martabak olls, as well as a restaurant upstairs.

Kafe Solo on Jl Secoyudan is far and away Solo's most stylish restaurant, housed in a restored colonial building. Food is western with some Solonese specialities.

Entertainment

Solo is an excellent place to see traditional Javanese performing arts.

The Sriwedari Theatre at the *Sriwedari Amusement Park*, Jl Slamet Riyadi, boasts one of the most famous wayang orang troupes on Java. Performances are staged from 8.15 to 10.15 pm Monday to Thursday, and 8.15 to 11.15 pm on Saturday. The theatre is at the back of the park behind the tourist office. Seats cost 850 rp, or 1100 rp for those down the front. There is no need to book – the only time the theatre is even half full is on a Saturday night. On the first Sat-urday night of the month, wayang kulit is also held at Sriwedari, at the open pavilion near the tourist office.

Various cultural performances are held at the broadcasting station of *Radio Republik Indonesia* (RRI), Jl Abdul Rahman Saleh 51. The RRI performances are popular and often excellent. The station has all-night wayang kulit shows on the third Saturday of every month from 9 pm to around 5 am; on the second Tuesday evening of the month there is wayang orang from 8 pm to midnight; and ketoprak (folk theatre) performances are held on the fourth Tuesday of the month from 8 pm to midnight.

At the *Sekolah Tinggi Seni Indonesia* (STSI), the arts academy, you can see danc-ing practice from around 7.30 am to noon from Monday to Saturday. STSI is at the Kentingan campus in Jebres, in the north-east of the city. *SMKI*, the high school for the performing arts on Jl Kepatihan Wetan, also has dance practice every morning, except Sunday, from around 8 am to noon.

Both kratons also have traditional Javan-ese dance practice: Wednesday from 10 am to noon at the *Kraton Mangkunegara*; and Sunday morning and afternoon perfor-mances at the *Kraton Surakarta*.

The tourist office has details of other cul-tural events around Solo. Wayang kulit shows are performed by the famous dalang, Ki

Anom Suroto, at Jl Gambir Anom 100, Notodiningran, in the area behind the Hotel Cakra. You can count on all-night performances there every Tuesday Kliwon in the Javanese calendar, occurring every five weeks. All-night wayang kulit is also held at the *Taman Budaya Surakarta* (TBS), the city's cultural centre at Jl Ir Sutami 57, to the east of the city, on Friday Kliwon of the Javanese calendar. Anom also occasionally performs at the Sriwedari Amusement Park. Ki Mantep Sudarsono is one of Indonesia's most famous dalang and performs all around Java and overseas. He sometimes has performances in his village, 27 km from Solo, near Karangpandan.

Solo's title of the 'city that never sleeps' refers more to its all-night warungs than raging nightlife, but the city has a few lively nightspots. *Nirwana* on the 2nd floor of the Pasar Besar, Jl Urip Sumoharjo, and *Legenda*, Jl Honggowongso 81A, are the city's two most popular discos. The *New Holland Bakery*, Jl Slamet Riyadi 141, has bands upstairs on weekends. *Taven's*, Jl Slamet Riyadi 361, to the west of the city centre just over the train line, is one of the more sophisticated nightspots and has good bands.

Things to Buy

Solo is one of Indonesia's main textile centres, producing not only its own unique, traditional batik but every kind of fabric for domestic use and export. Many people find it better for batik than Yogya, though Solo doesn't have Yogya's range for other handcrafts and curios.

Batik Pasar Klewer, a three storey 'hanging market' near the Kraton Surakarta, has hundreds of stalls selling fabrics. This is a good place to buy batik, mainly *cap* (in which motifs are applied with a metal stamp) but you can also find tulis batik and *lurik* (traditional striped cloth worn by kraton guards) homespun. Bargaining is obligatory, and it pays to know your batik and prices before venturing into the market.

The big manufacturers have showrooms

with a range of often very sophisticate work. You can see the batik process at the bi Batik Keris factory in Lawiyan, west of th city, open Monday to Saturday from 8 am t 5 pm. A showroom is at the factory, or it shop is at Jl Yos Sudarso 62. Another bi Solonese manufacturer is Batik Danarhad with shops at Jl Honggowongso 78 and J Slamet Riyadi 205. It has a good range o batik fabrics and ready-made clothes. Bati Semar, Jl R M Said 148, is good for moder cotton and beautiful silk batiks.

Smaller batik industries include Batik S Senari, Jl Slamet Riyadi 208; Batik Srimp Jl Dr Supomo 25; and Batik Arjuna, Jl D Rajiman 247.

Curios Pasar Triwindu on Jl Diponegoro i Solo's flea market. All kinds of bric-a-bra plus a few genuine antiques are sold here old buttons and buckles, china dogs and fin porcelain, puppets, batik tulis pens, lamp bottles, bell jars and furniture – but if you'r looking for bargains you have to sift care fully through the rubbish and be prepared t bargain hard. Many of the 'antik' (antiques are newly aged. Some of the dealers hav larger collections at their homes, so it i worth asking if they have other pieces.

Toko Bedoyo Srimpi, Jl Ronggowarsit 116, is the place for wayang orang dancers costumes and theatrical supplies, such a gold gilt headdresses and painted arm band It also sells masks and wayang kulit puppet

Jl Dr Rajiman (Secoyudan) is the gold smiths' street. Kris and other souvenirs ca be purchased from street vendors at the eas side alun alun to the north of the Krato Surakarta, and gem sellers have a mind-bog gling array of semi-precious stones. Vendor at Sriwedari Amusement Park also sell sou venirs. Pak Fauzan has a wide variety of kri for sale and you can see the process at hi small home workshop in Kampung Yosorot Rt 09 No 21. It is in the kampung just off . Slamet Riyadi, about 200m from the Riya Palace Hotel.

At the Balai Agung, on the north side the alun alun in front of the Kraton Surakart you can see high-quality wayang kul

uppets being made. Gamelan sets, for
round 40 million rp, are also on sale, but
1ese are produced in the village of
'ekonang, five km from Solo.

ietting There & Away

Air For some reason, Solo now has an international airport in preference to Yogyakarta,
ut flights are still limited. So far the only
international connection is the thrice weekly
lights with Silk Air to Singapore. Garuda
nd Sempati have direct flights to Jakarta,
vhile Merpati flies to Bandung.

The Garuda office (☎ 44955) is in the
.ippobank building, Jl Slamet Riyadi 136.
'empati (☎ 46240) is in the Solo Inn, Jl
lamet Riyadi 366.

Bus The main Tirtonadi bus terminal is just
orth of the train station, three km from the
entre of the city.

Frequent buses go to Prambanan (1000 rp;
½ hours), Yogya (1400 rp; two hours),
emarang (2100/3600 rp air-con; 2½ hours),
alatiga (1200/2000 rp; 1½ hours), Madiun
2400/4000 rp), Bandung (11,000/19,000 rp)
ia Semarang or Yogya, and Jakarta (14,000/
5,000 rp).

Going east, buses include those to Taw-
ngmangu (900 rp; one hour), Pacitan (2600
ɔ; four hours), Blitar (5300 rp; six hours),
urabaya (5600/9500 rp air-con; six hours),
Aalang (7600/13,000 rp; eight hours) and
robolinggo (7500 rp; eight hours). Luxury
uses also do these runs, and agents can be
ound at the bus terminal and in the main
ourist area around Jl Yos Sudarso/Slamet
iyadi; or many of the homestays and
Varung Baru also sell tickets.

Near the main bus terminal, the Gilingan
ninibus terminal has express minibuses to
early as many destinations as the buses.
Deluxe door-to-door minibuses cost 5000 rp
ɔ Yogya (1000 rp extra to pick up from your
otel) or 18,000 rp to Surabaya or Malang.
Iomestays and travel agents also sell tickets.
Bromo Express, Jl Slamet Riyadi 201, has a
ninibus service to Ngadisari (for Gunung
romo) for a hefty 25,000 rp non-air-con or
5,000 rp air-con.

Train Solo is on the main Jakarta-Yogya-
Surabaya train line. The quickest and most
convenient way to get to Yogya is on the
Prambanan Ekspres (2000 rp; one hour)
departing at 7 am and 1 pm.

For Jakarta, the express trains are far preferable to the ekonomi trains. The *Senja
Utama* (28,000 rp bisnis; 10½ hours) departs
at 6 pm and also has air-con eksekutif carriages. The luxury *Bima* and bisnis class
Jayabaya both come through Solo from Surabaya on the way to Jakarta. For Bandung,
the *Senja Mataram* (20,000 rp bisnis; nine
hours) departs at 8.15 pm and the *Mutiara
Selatan* also runs to Bandung.

Numerous trains run between Solo and
Surabaya. They range from the *Argopuro*
(4500 rp; six hours), a reasonable and less-
crowded ekonomi train departing at 9 am, to
the luxury *Bima*.

Ekonomi services also run to Semarang,
Pekalongan, Malang and Kediri.

Getting Around

The Adi Sumarmo airport is 10 km north-
west of the city centre; it's 10,000 rp by taxi
or take a bus to Kartasura and then another
to the airport. A becak from the train station
or bus terminal into the city centre is around
1000 rp, taxis want 5000 rp. The orange
minibus No 06 costs 300 rp to Jl Slamet
Riyadi.

The city double-decker bus runs between
Kartasura in the west and Palur in the east,
directly along Jl Slamet Riyadi, and costs a
flat fare of 300 rp. Bicycles can be hired from
the homestays.

Solo has metered taxis, but the drivers
won't use them from the bus or train station.
The main taxi stand is at the corner of the
Singosaren Plaza shopping centre.

AROUND SOLO
Sangiran

Fifteen km north of Solo, Sangiran is an
important archaeological excavation site,
where some of the best examples of fossil
skulls of prehistoric 'Java Man' *(Pithecanthropus erectus)* were unearthed by a Dutch
professor in 1936.

Java Man

Charles Darwin's *Evolution of the Species* inspired a new generation of naturalists in the 19th century, and his theories sparked acrimonious debate across the world. Ernst Haeckel's *The History of Natural Creation*, published in 1874, expounded further on Darwin's theory of evolution and attributed the evolution of primitive humans from a common ape-man ancestor, the famous 'missing link'.

One student of the new theories, Dutch physician Eugene Dubois, set sail for Sumatra in 1887, where he worked as an army doctor. In 1889 he left his position and went to Java after hearing of the uncovering of a skull at Wajak, near Tulung Agung in East Java. Dubois worked at the dig, uncovering other human fossils closely related to modern man. Later in 1891, at Trinil in East Java's Ngawi district, Dubois unearthed an older skull and other remains that he later classified as *Pithecanthropus erectus*, a low-browed, prominent-jawed early human ancestor, dating from the Middle Pleistocene era. His published findings of 'Java Man' caused a storm in Europe and were among the earliest findings in support of Darwin's theories.

Since Dubois' findings, many older examples of *Homo erectus* have been uncovered on Java. The most important and most numerous findings have been at Sangiran, where in the 1930s Ralph von Koenigswald found fossils dating back to around one million BC; while in 1936 at Perning near Mojokerto the skull of a child was discovered and some, possibly sensationalist, estimates have dated it as 1.9 million years old. Most findings have been along the Bengawan Solo River in Central and East Java, though Pacitan on East Java's south coast is also an important archaeological area.

Discoveries in Kenya now date the oldest hominid human ancestors, *Australopithecine*, to 4.5 million years ago. Ancient man migrated from Africa to Asia and came to Java via the land bridges that existed between the Asian mainland and the now insular Indonesian lands. It is thought that Java Man eventually became extinct, and the present inhabitants are descendants of a much later migration. ■

Pithecanthropus skull found at Sangiran, exhibiting the low brow and prominent jaw of early humans.

Sangiran has a small museum with a few skulls (one of *homo erectus*), various pig and hippopotamus teeth and fossil exhibits, including mammoth bones and tusks. Souvenir stalls outside sell bones, 'mammoth tusks' carved from stone and other dubious fossil junk. Guides will also offer to take you to the area where fossils have been found – it's a hot walk to see a few shells, if you are lucky.

The museum is open daily, except Sunday, from 9 am to 4 pm. Admission is 1000 rp. From the Solo bus terminal, take a Purwodadi bus to Kalijambe (500 rp). Ask for Sangiran and you will be dropped at the turn-off, 15 km from Solo. It is then four km to the museum (1000 rp by ojek).

Gunung Lawu

Towering Gunung Lawu (3265m), lying on the border of Central and East Java, is one of the holiest mountains on Java. Mysterious Hindu temples dot its slopes, and each year thousands of pilgrims seeking spiritual enlightenment climb Lawu's peak.

Though popular history has it that when Majapahit fell to Islam, the Hindu elite all fled east to Bali, Javanese lore relates that Brawijaya V, the last king of Majapahit, went west. Brawijaya's son, Raden Patah, was the leader of Demak and led the conquering forces of Islam against Majapahit, but rather than fight his own son, Brawijaya retreated to Gunung Lawu to seek spiritual enlightenment. There he achieved nirvana as Suna Lawu, and today pilgrims come to seek his spiritual guidance or to achieve magic powers.

The unique temples on the mountain, the last Hindu temples built on Java before conversion to Islam, show the influence of the later 'wayang' style of East Java, though the corporate elements of fertility worship. Most famous is the temple of Candi Sukuh, while Candi Ceto is another large complex that still attracts Hindu worshippers. Some villages in the area have still resisted conversion to Islam.

Climbing Gunung Lawu Colts between Tawangmangu and Sarangan pass Cemoro Sewu, five km from Sarangan. This small village is the usual starting point for the 6.5 km hike to the top. Thousands of pilgrims flock to the top on 1 Suro, the start of the Javanese new year, but pilgrims and holiday-ing students make the night climb throughout the year. Most start around 8 pm, reaching the top around 2 am for meditation. To reach the top for a sunrise free of clouds, you should start by midnight at the latest, though superfit hikers can do the climb in as little as four hours. You can head up during the day, but the mountain is usually covered in mist. The path is easy to follow, but guides should be taken for night climbs. Pak Sardi, the kepala desa of Cemoro Sewu, will arrange a guide, who will also carry your gear, for around 40,000 rp. Sign in at the PHPA post before starting the climb.

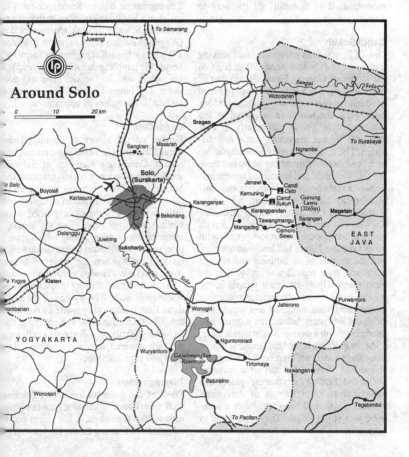

Around Solo

0   10   20 km

The top of the mountain is terraced with ancient stone walls. Pilgrims overnight for meditation at Argodalam Pondok, the largest terrace with a shelter, some 500m before the top. On the way up is Sendangdrajat, a holy spring, where pilgrims should bathe seven times with the icy waters to achieve wealth and influence.

An alternative trail begins at Cemoro Kandang, a few km west on the way to Tawangmangu. The trail to the top is less steep, but much longer. Look out for the *becak lawu* here, a billy cart device which riders use to transport produce down the mountain. It is downhill all the way to Tawangmangu.

Candi Sukuh

One of Java's most mysterious and striking temples, Candi Sukuh stands 900m high on the slopes of Gunung Lawu, 36 km east of Solo. In form it is a large truncated pyramid of rough-hewn stone with a curious Inca look and, while the sculpture is carved in the 'wayang style' found particularly in East Java, the figures are crude, squat and distorted. The temple is hardly as wildly erotic as it is sometimes made out to be but there are fairly explicit and humorous representations of a stone penis or two and the elements of a fertility cult are quite plain.

Built in the 15th century during the declining years of the Majapahit Empire, Sukuh seems to have nothing whatsoever to do with other Javanese Hindu and Buddhist temples, and the origins of its builders and strange sculptural style remain a mystery. It is the most recent Hindu-Buddhist temple in the region, yet it seems to mark a reappearance of the pre-Hindu animism and magic that existed 1500 years before. It's a quiet, isolated place with a strange potent atmosphere.

At the gateway before the temple is a large stone *lingga* and *yoni* (symbolic Hindu penis and vulva). Flowers are still often scattered over it and there's a story that the symbol was used mainly by villagers to determine whether a wife had been faithful or a wife-to-be was still a virgin. The woman had to wear a sarong and stride across the lingga –

if the sarong tore, her infidelity was prove Other interesting cult objects stand further among the trees, including a tall-standir monument depicting Bima, the *Mahabhara* warrior hero, with Narada, the messenger the gods, in a stylised womb followed Bima dropping through at his birth. In the t courtyard three enormous flat-backed turtle stand like sacrificial altars.

From the site the views are superb, to th west and north across terrace fields ar mountains.

Getting There & Away From Solo, take Tawangmangu bus to Karangpandan (7(rp), then a Kemuning minibus to the turn-o to Candi Sukuh (500 rp). On market day (Wage and Pahing in the Javanese calendar a 9 am bus from Karangpandan stops rig beside the temple; otherwise it's a couple km uphill walk to the site. The trip take about 1½ hours in total. The ubiquitou visitors' book makes an appearance.

Candi Ceto

Further up the slopes of Gunung Law Candi Ceto dates from the same era as Can Sukuh. Combining elements of Shivais and fertility worship, it is a larger temple tha Sukuh, spread over terraces leading up th misty hillside. It is a spartan complex, wi little carving, and the closely fitted ston work, some of it new, gives the temple medieval atmosphere. Along with Sukuh, is reputed to be the most recent Hindu temp on Java, built when the wave of Islam conversion was already sweeping the islan

Because of the difficulty in reaching Cet few visitors make it here – one of the attra tions. Ceto is nine km by road past the Suku turn-off. Take a bus as far as Kemuning, the an ojek (3000 rp), or walk the six km throug the hills covered in tea plantations, clov trees and vegetable plots.

Tawangmangu

Trekkers can make an interesting 2½ hou walk from Candi Sukuh along a worn pave path to Tawangmangu, a hill resort on th other side of Gunung Lawu. Or you can g ere by bus from Solo via Karangpandan, hich is just as fine a trip along a switchback ad through magnificent tightly terraced ills. At Tawangmangu is **Grojogan Sewu**, 100m high waterfall and favourite playround for monkeys. It's reached by a long ight of steps down a hillside from the illage and you can swim in the very chilly ool at the bottom.

The cave of **Gua Maria** is a three km walk om the road. Tawangmangu is packed on unday.

laces to Stay & Eat In Tawangmangu, the *ak Amat Losmen* is right by the bus termiL. Rooms with their own enclosed erandahs are good value at 9000 rp, though e attached mandis could do with a good rub. The losmen has a decent restaurant.

Prices and quality increase as you head up e hill. The *Pondok Garuda* (☎ 97239) has od rooms to suit most budgets, ranging om 8000 rp ekonomi rooms, or from 2,000 to big 60,000 rp bungalows with hot ater, TV and breakfast thrown in.

Further up the hill, the friendly *Pondok dah* (☎ 97024) has spacious old rooms ith sitting rooms for 38,000 rp, or new, otel-style rooms from 60,000 rp.

The best place in town is the *Komajaya omaratih Hotel* (☎ 97125), near the turnff to the waterfall. It is favoured by tour oups, and rooms in the old wing cost 5,500 and 57,500 rp, or new rooms accomodating up to four people cost from 5,500 rp.

For good Indonesian dishes, eat at *Sapto go* on Jl Raya Lawu. Continue down Jl aya Lawu and you may dine in the tranquil nbience of *Lesahan Pondok Indah*, while ated cross-legged on bamboo mats overoking the rice paddies.

etting There & Away Buses go to Solo 00 rp) and Sarangan (2000 rp). Mitsubishi inibuses (300 rp) loop through town from e bus terminal up the main road, across to e waterfall and around back to the bus rminal.

Sarangan

An interesting alternative to backtracking to Solo is to take a colt to Sarangan, 18 km from Tawangmangu on the mountain road to Madiun. This picturesque hill town lies on the slopes of Gunung Lawu, with hotels clustered at the edge of Telaga Pasir, a crater lake. At 1287m the climate is refreshing and this is one of the most pleasant hill resorts on Java. It is cooler and more attractive than Tawangmangu, and the lake provides opportunities for boating and water-skiing. You can walk around the lake or it is a pleasant one hour return walk to the Tirtosari Waterfall. Sarangan is also a good base for tackling the ascent of Gunung Lawu. It is just over the provincial border in East Java, though most visitors come via Solo.

Places to Stay This is an upmarket resort without really being luxurious. There is little in the way of budget accommodation. The only cheap places are found away from the lake to the east of town in Ngerong, near the smaller Telaga Wahyu. This lake is less popular because, apart from its poorer aspect, legend has it that courting couples will separate if they visit the lake. On the main road, *Losmen Indrawati* (☎ 98057) is basic but OK for 15,000 rp a double.

The mid-range and expensive hotels are all around Telaga Pasir. *Hotel Sarangan* (☎ 98022) has fine views, colonial atmosphere and is very popular with Dutch tourists. Rooms, most sleeping four or more people, start at 60,000/75,000 rp for singles/doubles and have their own sitting rooms with open fire places. *Hotel Indah* (☎ 98475) is a more modern motel-style place with rooms from 80,000 rp. Right near the entrance to the Hotel Indah, *Penginapan Nusantara* is basic and expensive at 25,000 rp a room, but in a good position near the lake.

Getting There & Away Regular colts run to Tawangmangu (2000 rp) passing Cemoro Sewu (1000 rp) for the climb to Gunung Lawu. Frequent buses run to Madiun, from where there are buses all over Java.

Mangadeg

Near Karangpandan, a road branches south from the main Solo-Tawangmangu highway about five km to Mangadeg, the burial hill of Solo's royal Mangkunegoro family. Make a small donation and visit the graves or simply take in the superb views across the countryside.

A couple of km away in the same sacred hills, the lavish **Astana Giribangun** has been built by the president as the final resting place for himself and the Soeharto family. The president's wife, Madam Tien Soeharto, is buried here and her grave attracts thousands of pilgrims each year.

On the way to Mangadeg is **Pablengan**, the former bathing pools of the Mangkunegoro. The ancient bathing pavilions are in disrepair. The springs emit seven different types of water with various curative powers, though water from one of the springs is drunk to induce abortions.

Salatiga

This provincial city (population 100,000) between Semarang and Solo is noted for its Satya Wacana Christian University and lies at the foothills of Gunung Merbabu. This clean and attractive city has a hill station feel, and some fine colonial architecture. Nearby **Lake Rawapening** is a popular local picnic spot, and **Kopeng** is a small, scruffy hill resort 19 km from Salatiga on the slopes of Gunung Merbabu. Kopeng has a waterfall and dirty hot spring pools, but the main point of interest is the walk to towering **Gunung Merbabu**, a nine hour hike with an overnight on the mountain.

Salatiga has plenty of hotels, or Kopeng has the faded, colonial *Hotel Kopeng* (☎ 26344). Rooms are exceptional value and cost 11,000 rp up to 27,500 rp for a two room flat. Buses between Salatiga and Magelang go via Kopeng.

NORTH COAST

For many centuries Java's north coast was the centre for trade with merchants from Arabia, India and China. Through trade the north coast came in contact with different cultures and ideas, and became the birthplace of Islam on Java. During the 15th and 16 centuries Islam was adopted by the rulers the trading principalities, in opposition to the Hindu kingdoms of inland Central Java.

Islam in Indonesia has immortalised the wali songo, or nine saints, to whom the establishment of Islam on Java is credited. With the exception of Sunan Gunungjati in Cirebon, the tombs of the saints all lie between Semarang and Surabaya, and are important pilgrimage points for devout Muslims. A number of these places lie on the road to Surabaya and can also be visited using Semarang as a base.

While the coast attracts many pilgrims few tourists venture north. The flat, h coastal plain bordered by low hills doesn't have fine beaches or the spectacular scenery of the central mountains. The massive monuments of ancient Java are missing, and apart from some impressive mosques, the reminders of the north coast's trading heyday are not obvious. Yet, while the north coast doesn't have any 'must see' tourist attractions and conspicuously absent from tour group itineraries, it has an interesting mix of cultural influences, a lazy Middle Eastern atmosphere and makes an interesting diversion for the more adventurous with time to spare.

PEKALONGAN

On the north coast between Semarang and Cirebon, Pekalongan is known as Kota Batik (Batik City) and its batiks are some of the most sought after in Indonesia. Positioned on the trading routes between China, India and Arabia, the city absorbed many influences and these are reflected in its style of batik. Pekalongan batik is less formal, more colourful and innovative in design compared the traditional styles of Yogyakarta and Solo.

Pekalongan is a must for batik freaks, but otherwise it is not a tourist destination. The town has a neglected, old-fashioned atmosphere and a mixed population. While the main street, Jl Gajah Mada/Hayam Wuruk can bustle, Pekalongan is a relatively quiet town, especially during the afternoon siesta.

Information

The tourist office in the town hall (Balai Kota) has maps of Pekalongan and will try to answer most queries.

The main post office (Kantor Pos dan Giro) is opposite the Bali Kota, and for international telephone calls, the Telkom office is next door at Jl Merak 2. There is also a warpostal at the train station.

The Bank Expor Impor on Jl Hayam Wuruk is the best place to change money – the other banks in town think foreign currency is the work of the devil.

Things to See

Pekalongan's small **Batik Museum**, two km south of the train station on Jl Majapahit, exhibits examples of different batik styles, with explanations in Indonesian. It's open from 9 am to 1 pm daily, closed Sunday. Of more interest is the **bird market** nearby on Jl Kurinci.

The most interesting area of town is around the **Pasar Banjarsari**, a lively market and a good place for batik shopping. Nearby Jl Blimbing is the old **Chinese quarter**, and along this street is a Chinese temple and old terraced houses. To the east, off Patiunus and the streets leading off it, is the **Arab quarter**, and this is also a good area for batik (see Things to Buy in this section). Facing the alun alun, with its massive banyan trees, is the **Mesjid Jami Yasmaja**. The lighthouse-styled minaret and Arabic architecture enclosing an older Javanese-style mosque is especially impressive when lit at night.

Places to Stay

Pekalongan has decent budget accommodation directly opposite the train station on Jl Gajah Mada. The best is the friendly and very clean *Hotel Gajah Mada* (☎ 22185) at No 11, with doubles for 8500/9500 rp or 2,000 rp with mandi. A few doors along, the *Losmen Damai* is slightly cheaper with rooms from 8000 rp.

In the centre of town, Pekalongan's best budget-to-moderate bet is the *Hotel Hayam Wuruk* (☎ 22823) at Jl Hayam Wuruk 152-

54. A variety of good rooms cost 22,000/ 29,000 rp for singles/doubles with fan and mandi, and with air-con from 28,000/35,000 rp to 42,000/49,000 rp for those with hot water and TV. Breakfast is included.

The *Hotel Istana* (☎ 23581), near the train station at Jl Gajah Mada 23, is a good mid-range hotel with fan rooms from 28,500/ 36,000 rp and air-con rooms from 51,000/ 60,000 rp.

The *Nirwana Hotel* (☎ 22446), Jl Dr Wahidin 11, is the best hotel in town. It has a large pool, coffee shop and restaurant. Air-con rooms cost 57,000/64,000 rp to 92,000/ 99,000 rp, including breakfast.

Places to Eat

Coming into town from the train station, one of the first restaurants you will see signposted on Jl Gajah Mada (there is no number) is *A Karim* in the Pasar THR. It may look like a hole-in-the-wall, but the Madurese sate is superb. The *Purimas Bakery* on Jl Hayam Wuruk has cakes, pastries, cold drinks and a sit-down area to enjoy them. A smaller branch is on Jl Gajah Mada near A Karim.

On Jl Merdeka, the *Mie Rasa* is a spotless little place with noodle dishes and excellent icy fruit juices. At the *Remaja*, Jl Dr Cipto 20, good and reasonably cheap Chinese food is available. Seafood is a speciality. The *Es Teler 77* at No 66 has a selection of Indonesian dishes, cold ice juices and a cool, shady garden.

Things to Buy

Batik, of course. Pekalongan batik is constantly evolving and new designs are more suited to western and modern Indonesian tastes. Traditional batik is still popular, however, and for formal occasions Indonesians are often required to don batik.

Street peddlers casually wave batik from the doorways of hotels and restaurants – mostly cheap clothes and poor quality sarongs. Shops around town, many on Jl Hayam Wuruk, sell ready-made clothes, lengths of cloth and sarongs in cotton and silk.

The Pasar Banjarsari is a great place to browse for cheap, everyday batik, and some better pieces can be found. In the same area, Tobal, Jl Teratai 24, is a large rag trade business that produces clothes for the export market and you can view the process. Jacky, nearby at Jl Surabaya 5A, has a showroom down an alley with a large range of clothes and lengths of good-quality cloth.

Most of the traditional batik is produced in the villages around Pekalongan. In the batik village of Kedungwuni, 17 km south of town, Oey Soe Tjoen's workshop is one of the most famous. Intricate and colourful batik tulis are still produced, and these are regarded as among the highest quality you will find. You can see them being made every day of the week, except Friday.

Getting There & Away

Pekalongan is on the main Jakarta-Semarang-Surabaya road and rail route. There is also a road linking Pekalongan and the Dieng Plateau.

Bus Pekalongan's bus terminal is about four km south-east of the centre of town, 300 rp by colt or 1500 rp by becak. Buses from Cirebon can drop you off in town on their way through.

Frequent buses go to Semarang (2100/3500 rp air-con; three hours). Buses go to Cirebon (2800/5000 rp; four hours) supposedly every hour but chances are you'll first have to take a bus to Tegal (2500 rp air-con; 1½ hours), which leave every half hour, and then another to Cirebon. Most buses to Wonosobo (2500 rp; five hours) go in the morning, or the most direct route to Dieng is to take a bus to Batur (2000 rp; four hours) and then a colt to Dieng, but buses are not frequent and this is a bone-rattling journey along a bad road.

The agents for door-to-door minibuses are clustered together on Jl Alun Alun, just north of the square. Fares and journey times include: Jakarta (30,000 rp air-con; 10 hours); Yogyakarta (9000 rp air-con; five hours); Semarang (6500 rp non-air-con; two

hours); and Bandung (20,000 rp; eig hours). Hotels can ring for pick-up.

Train As Pekalongan is midway for mo train routes, it is hard to get a booking on th better express services, and ekonomi train are crowded. The *Senja Utama* and *Faj Utama* expresses run from Semarang Jakarta and stop in Pekalongan and Cirebo To Semarang and Solo, the ekonomi *Cep* leaves at 3.15 pm.

Getting Around

Pekalongan has plenty of becaks, costi around 500 rp per km. For 1000 rp you ca go halfway across town. Orange bemos ru all over town for a standard 300 rp. F Keduwangi, take a bemo down Jl Mansyu

SEMARANG

The north coast port of Semarang, the capi city of Central Java Province, is a stro contrast to the royal cities of Solo ar Yogyakarta. Under the Dutch it became busy trading and administrative centre, ar great numbers of Chinese traders joined th Muslim entrepreneurs of the north coa Even in the depressed 1950s great weal

JAVA SEA

To Deme & Kudus

See Central Semarang Map

Jamu Nyony Meneer

To Cirebon

Jalan Majapahi

Jl Dr. Wahidin

To Solo

Semarang

1 Terboyo Bus Terminal
2 Airport
3 Puri Maerakaca
4 Gedung Batu
5 Hotel Kesambi Hijau
6 Hotel Candi Baru
7 Patra Jasa Hotel
8 Jamu Jago

0   1.5   3 km

owed through the city, with sugar and other
gricultural produce going out, and indus-
ial raw materials and finished goods
•ming in.

Today, Semarang is the only port open to
rge ships on the central coast. Deep-water
erthing facilities were built so that ocean-
oing vessels no longer had to anchor out in
e mouth of Sungai Kali Baru.

More a commercial centre than a city for
urists, Semarang's main points of interest
e the old city and the famous Chinese
edung Batu Temple. This little-visited city
a good starting point for trips along the
orth coast or south to the central mountains.
can be a pleasant place to stop in for a night
two, for it seems less crowded and more
laxed than its large size and population
ust over 1.3 million) would indicate.

rientation

emarang is split into two parts. 'Old'
emarang is on the coastal plain, sandwiched
etween the two Banjir canals, while the new
wn has spread out to the wealthy residen-
l areas in the southern hills of Candi. An
mportant hub in the old town is the Pasar
har on the roundabout at the top of Jl
muda.

Jl Pemuda, Semarang's premier boulevard
Dutch times, is still a major artery and
opping street, though nowadays the
mpang Lima (Five Ways) square has more
e.

Formation

urist Offices The city tourist office
414332) on the 1st floor of the Plaza
mpang Lima is open every day from 9 am
4 pm. It produces some useful brochures
d can answer most queries.

The Central Java tourist office (DIP-
RDA) has lots of maps and brochures on
province, including a regional *Calendar
Events* and an excellent map of Semarang.
fortunately, it is well out of the city in the
RPP Complex, Jl Madukoro Blok BB, on
way to the Puri Maerakaca.

ney The big banks can be found along Jl

Pemuda. The BCA bank, Jl Pemuda 90-92,
has good rates for cash and travellers
cheques, and will give cash advances on Visa
and MasterCard.

Post & Communications Semarang's main
post office is on Jl Pemuda near the river. The
Telkom office for international calls is at Jl
Suprapto 7, and it has a Home Country
Direct phone. Wartels are found all over
town and there is one directly behind the post
office.

Medical Services The best hospital and first
choice of the sizeable Semarang expat community is RS Saint Elizabeth (☎ 315345) on
Jl Kawi in the Candi Baru district.

Old City

Semarang's decrepit old city has just enough
relics of bygone days to make it an interesting place to wander around. On Jl Let
Jenderal Suprapto, the **Gereja Blenduk** is a
Dutch church built in 1753 and still functioning. It has a huge dome and inside is a
baroque organ. This area was the main port
area in Dutch times, and towards the river
from the church are numerous old Dutch
warehouses, many still housing shipping
companies.

Heading south of the Gereja Blenduk, you
plunge into the narrow streets of Semarang's
old **Chinatown**. The highlight here is the
brightly painted **Tay Kak Sie Temple**, one
of the finest examples of a Chinese temple in
Indonesia. This temple complex dates from
1772 and is on Gang Lombok, the small alley
running along the river off Jl Pekojan. Also
in Chinatown, the **Pasar Cina**, also called
Pasar Gang Baru, is a fascinating market to
wander around. It's a morning market, at its
best before 7 am.

Back towards the centre of the city, **Pasar
Johar** is Semarang's most intriguing market.
You can find a little bit of almost everything
from food to hardware to clothing and it's
worth an hour or so of wandering around.
Facing the market is Semarang's **Grand
Mosque**.

Central Semarang

0   250   500 m

To Demak & Kudus

To Airport & Cirebon

Tawang Train Station

Poncol Train Station

PLACES TO STAY		PLACES TO EAT		18	Tay Kak Sie Temple
1	Losmen Arjuna	17	Loenpia Semarang	19	Pasar Johar
2	Hotel Rahayu	20	Sari Medan	23	Merpati
3	Hotel Oewa Asia	21	Toko Oen	25	BCA Bank
4	Hotel Surya	24	Depot Naga	26	Ngesti Pandowo
5	Losmen Singapore	28	Rumah Makan Tio Cio		Theatre
6	Hotel Blambangan	39	Mbok Berek	27	Bouraq
7	Natour Dibya Puri	40	Timlo Solo	30	Lawang Sewu
8	Metro Hotel	42	Istana & Matsuri	31	Tugu Muda Monumen
12	Hotel Raden Patah		Restaurants	33	Mesjid Baiturrakhman
15	Losmen Jaya			34	Ciputra Mall
16	Hotel Nendra Yakti	**OTHER**		36	Simpang Lima
22	Queen Hotel	9	Main Post Office	37	Plaza Simpang Lima
29	Telomoyo	10	Pelni Office	38	RRI
32	Hotel Graha Santika	11	Gereja Blenduk		
35	Hotel Ciputra	13	Telkom Office		
41	Hotel Santika	14	Minibus Agents		

edung Batu (Sam Po Kong Temple)

nis well-known Chinese temple stands five
n south-west of the centre of the city. It was
uilt in honour of Admiral Cheng Ho, the
mous Muslim eunuch of the Ming dynasty,
ho led a Chinese fleet on seven expeditions
Java and other parts of South-East and
'est Asia in the early 15th century. Cheng
o has since become a saint known as Sam
o Kong and is particularly revered in
elaka, Malaysia. He first arrived on Java
1405, and is attributed with having helped
read Islam. This temple is also revered by
uslims.

The main hall of the temple complex is
uilt around an inner chamber in the form of
huge cave flanked by two great dragons,
nce the temple's popular name, *gedung
tu*, meaning 'stone building'. Inside the
ve is the idol of Sam Po Kong.

To get to Gedung Batu, take Damri bus No
rom Jl Pemuda to Karang Ayu, and then a
uhatsu from there to the temple. It takes
out half an hour from central Semarang.

ri Maerakaca

ten referred to as 'Taman Mini Jawa
ngah', this large theme park is Semarang's
rsion of Jakarta's Taman Mini, with tradi-
nal houses representing all of Central
/a's kabupaten (regencies). While mostly
interest to domestic tourists, it is well done
1 worth a look if you will be exploring
ntral Java in depth. Most houses have a
all display of crafts and a map showing
nts of interest in the regency.

Puri Maerak is open every day from 7 am
6 pm, and entry is 1000 rp, 1500 rp on
nday. It is way out near the airport, and not
:essible by public transport.

nu

narang is known for its two large *jamu*
rbal medicine) manufacturers – **Jamu
onya Meneer**, Jl Raya Kaligawe Km 4,
ir the bus terminal, and **Jamu Jago**, Jl
ia Budi 273, about six km from the city
the Ambarawa road. Jamu Jago is well
wn for its adverts that use a squad of
arfs! Both have museums open Monday

to Friday from 8 am to 3 pm, and tours of the
factories are available upon request.

Other Attractions

The **Tugu Muda**, at the southern end of Jl
Pemuda, is a candle-shaped monument com-
memorating Semarang's five day battle
against the Japanese in October 1945.
Nearby is an impressive European-style
building, known to the Javanese as **Lawang
Sewu** (1000 Doors). It was formerly Dutch
offices, later headquarters of the Japanese
forces and is now Indonesian army offices.

Simpang Lima square is where you'll
find Semarang's cinema complexes and big
shopping malls. Crowds congregate in the
evenings and browse aimlessly at goods they
can't afford to buy.

The **Semarang harbour** is worth a look
to see the pinisi (schooners) and other traditional ocean-going vessels, which dock at the
Tambak Lorok wharfs.

The **Ronggowarsito Museum** is the provincial museum with antiquities from all
over the state. One of the most interesting
exhibits is a recycled stone panel from
Mantingan Mosque. One side shows Islamic
motifs, while the reverse shows a Hindu-
Buddhist scene. The museum is on Jl
Abdulrachman, about one km from the
airport, and is open every day, except Monday, from 8 am to 2.30 pm.

Places to Stay – bottom end

You don't get a lot for your money in Semarang. The cheaper hotels are often dives and
many are full with long-term residents. The
main budget hotel area is close to the city
centre on or just off Jl Imam Bonjol, 15
minutes' walk from the Tawang train station
(1500 rp by becak).

The popular, well-maintained *Hotel Oewa
Asia* (☎ 542547), Jl Kol Sugiono 12, is the
best bet close to the city centre. Large rooms
with fan and mandi cost 20,000 rp and have
some colonial style, or darker air-con rooms
cost 27,500 rp.

Another colonial hotel is the pleasant
Hotel Raden Patah (☎ 511328) at Jl Jend

Suprapto 48. It is further from the city centre but close to the train station. Spartan but good value rooms cost 10,000 rp, or 16,000 rp with mandi and fan. Most rooms ring the inner courtyard and are sheltered from street noise.

If these two are full, and you can speak some Indonesian, Jl Imam Bonjol has a number of other options. The seedy *Losmen Singapore* (☎ 543757) at No 12 has no-frills rooms with shared mandis for 12,500 rp. The similarly priced *Losmen Arjuna* (☎ 544186) at No 51 is a better hotel with character but nearly always full. The *Hotel Rahayu* (☎ 542532) at No 35 has decent rooms with mandi from 17,500 rp, or from 32,500 rp with air-con.

Closer to the action at Jl Pemuda 23A, the *Hotel Blambangan* (☎ 541649) has rooms with mandi from 20,000 rp. Over at Jl MT Haryono 85-87, the *Losmen Jaya* (☎ 543604) is a reasonable budget option with rooms for 12,500 rp, or large doubles/triples with mandi cost 15,000/18,000 rp.

The Chinese-run *Hotel Nendra Yakti* (☎ 542538) at Gang Pinggir 68 is in an interesting area and has a better class of room with fan and mandi for 21,000 to 24,000 rp. Air-con rooms cost 45,000 rp.

Places to Stay – middle

In the city centre, the *Natour Dibya Puri* (☎ 547821) at Jl Pemuda 11 is a rambling old hotel with loads of colonial atmosphere, but badly in need of renovation. Large air-con singles/doubles have terraces overlooking the inner garden, hot water, TV and fridge for 48,000/60,000 rp to 100,000 rp. Bare but big fan rooms without bathroom cost 25,000/30,000 rp.

Also central, Jl Gajah Mada has two good motel-style places. The *Telomoyo* (☎ 545436) at No 138 has a few fan rooms for 22,500 rp, but most are well-appointed air-con rooms for 65,000 to 105,000 rp. The partly renovated *Queen Hotel* (☎ 547063) at No 44-52 is well run and fully air-con. Rooms with a private bathroom cost 62,000 to 98,000 rp, including breakfast and afternoon tea.

The best value in Semarang is found in the tranquil residential districts in the hills to the south of the city. Two excellent options are in Candi Baru, a popular expat suburb about three km south-west of Simpang Lima. Candi Baru can be reached by bus, but be prepared to do a lot of walking or catch taxi.

The *Hotel Kesambi Hijau* (☎ 312642), Kesambi 7, otherwise known as the Green Guesthouse, is a fine old hotel with terrace areas overlooking the city, or the less appealing new section is next to a mosque. Air-con rooms cost 25,000 to 50,000 rp – for 40,000 rp you can have a large bungalow with TV, fridge and hot water.

Hotel Candi Baru (☎ 315272), Jl Rinjani 21, is a magnificent, rambling old villa with even better views of the city. Slightly faded air-con rooms here range from 45,000 95,000 rp, and a few economy rooms cost 22,000 rp, all plus 21%. The On-On Pub at the hotel is the Hash Harrier's hangout and well patronised by expats.

Places to Stay – top end

Add 21% tax and service to the following rates, but discounts usually apply.

Once the top hotel in Semarang, the three star *Metro Hotel* (☎ 547371) at Jl H Agus Salim 2 is right in the city centre. Though now outclassed, and it doesn't have a pool like all the others, renovated rooms from US$48 up to the US$85 suites are good value.

The top luxury hotel in Semarang is the new *Hotel Ciputra* (☎ 449888), with an unbeatable position right on the Simpang Lima, Semarang's showpiece square. Rooms cost from US$115.

The nearby *Hotel Graha Santika* (☎ 318850), Jl Pandanaran 116-120, is an older luxury hotel but well maintained with all amenities and it has a reputation for good service. Singles/doubles cost US$108/117.

The other major hotel is the *Patra Jasa Hotel* (☎ 314441) at Jl Sisingamangaraja Candi Baru, offering fine view of Semarang, a pool, bowling alleys and tennis. Rooms start at US$110/120.

Places to Eat

The *Toko Oen*, Jl Pemuda 52, is not to be missed. It's a large, old-fashioned tea room where white tablecloths, basket chairs and ancient waiters in white jackets are all part of the genteel colonial atmosphere. It has an Indonesian, Chinese and European menu, food grills and a great selection of ice creams. The best deals are the buffet lunches on Monday, Thursday and Friday.

At night you'll find dozens of warungs round Pasar Johar (or Pasar Ya'ik as it is known in the evenings), Semarang's best speciality market. The southern side of Simpang Lima also has plenty of warungs. Of course, Simpang Lima's malls are the place for fast food, including a *McDonald's* in the Ciputra Mall. For something more upmarket, *Parkview Bar-BQ* on the 5th level of the Plaza Simpang Lima has tasty grills, including Korean food, a bar, live music and good views.

Semarang is renowned for its lumpia (Chinese spring rolls). They can be found all over town, but one of the original purveyors is the small *Loenpia Semarang*, near the Tay Kak Sie Temple at Gang Lombok No 11. Other cheap, hole-in-the-wall places are on the same stretch – a good place to have a meal after touring Chinatown.

Another local speciality is wingko babat, delicious coconut cakes – look for them in shops.

Jl Gajah Mada is another hunting ground for Chinese restaurants. Try *Rumah Makan Po Cio*, opposite the Telemoyo hotel, a popular place with reasonably priced seafood. At Jl Gajah Mada 37A, *Depot Naga* is a scrupulously clean, open-sided cafe, with a wide selection of dishes, including excellent grilled fish and sate.

The *Timlo Solo*, Jl A Yani 182, has good, inexpensive Javanese food. Try the lontong culo or nasi timlo. A few doors away, *Mbok Berek* has Yogya-style fried chicken.

Entertainment

The *Ngesti Pandowo Theatre* at Jl Pemuda 116 has wayang orang performances every night from 9 pm to midnight, except Monday

when ketoprak is performed. Tickets range from 1000 to 1500 rp. *RRI* on Jl A Yani puts on wayang kulit shows on the first Saturday of the month. The TBRS amusement park on Jl Sriwijaya, Tegalwareng, has wayang kulit every Thursday Wage and ketoprak every Monday Wage of the Javanese calendar.

Getting There & Away

Air Merpati (☎ 517137), Jl Gajah Mada 11, has direct flights between Semarang and Bandung (110,000 rp), Jakarta (142,000 rp), Pangkalanbun (214,000 rp) and Surabaya (89,000 rp).

Sempati (☎ 414086) is in the Hotel Graha Santika, and has direct flights to Jakarta and Surabaya.

Bouraq (☎ 515921) at Jl Gajah Mada 16D has direct flights to Jakarta, Surabaya and Banjarmasin.

Mandala (☎ 444736), Bangkong Plaza, Jl Haryono, has direct flights to Jakarta.

Deraya Air (☎ 547331), Jl Imam Bonjol 46, has flights to Pangkalanbun, Pontianak and Ketapang on Kalimantan and twice a week to Karimunjawa (57,500 rp).

Bus Semarang's Terboyo bus terminal is four km east of town, just off the road to Kudus. Destinations for non-air-con/air-con buses include: Yogya (2500/5600 rp; three hours); Solo (2100/5000 rp; 2½ hours); Magelang (1600/3500 rp); Wonosobo (2500/5000 rp; four hours); Pekalongan (2100/4000 rp; three hours); Cirebon (4900/11,200 rp; six hours); Kudus (1200/2300 rp; one hour); and Surabaya (7000/15,000 rp; nine hours).

Ticket-agent offices for night and luxury buses can be found on Jl Haryono near the Losmen Jaya. They have departures for all major long-haul destinations, including Jakarta for around 27,000 rp and Denpasar for 31,000 rp. To Jakarta, it's a long 10 hour haul and buses arrive at ungodly hours at Jakarta's remote Pulo Gadung bus terminal.

Agents for express minibuses are found all over Semarang. On Jl Haryono, try the Rahayu agent (☎ 543935) at No 9, or the Nusantara Indah agent (☎ 548648) at No 9B.

Non-air-con/air-con minibuses go to Solo (5000/6000 rp) and Yogya (5000/5500 rp) every hour from 7 am to 6 pm. Other non-air-con services include Kudus (3000 rp) and Wonosobo (6500 rp), or air-con buses include Pekalongan (6500 rp), Surabaya (20,000 rp) and Jakarta (30,000 rp).

Train Semarang is on the main Jakarta-Cirebon-Surabaya train route and there are frequent services operating to and from these cities. Tawang is the main train station in Semarang.

The best trains to take between Jakarta and Semarang are the *Senja Utama* (23,000 rp bisnis; eight hours) and *Fajar Utama* (18,000 rp bisnis; eight hours). They stop in Pekalongan and Cirebon, and usually run over schedule. The luxury *Argobromo* and *Sembani* also pass through Semarang between Surabaya and Jakarta.

To Solo, the *Cepat* (1600 rp ekonomi; four hours) leaves from Poncol train station, but the bus is a much better option.

Boat The Pelni office (☎ 555156) is at Jl Tantular 25, near the Tawang train station. It's open from 8 am to 4 pm Monday to Friday, and to 1 pm on Saturday. Pelni's *Kelimutu*, *Lawit*, *Leuser* and *Bukitraya* run between Semarang and the Kalimantan ports of Pontianak, Kumai, Sampit and Banjarmasin. There are also occasional cargo boats from Semarang to Banjarmasin which take passengers – enquire in the harbour area.

Getting Around
The Airport Ahmad Yani airport is six km to the west of town. A taxi into town costs 7000 rp, less going to the airport. Damri bus No 2 goes to the airport.

Local Transport Semarang has becaks, taxis and a big Damri city bus service, supplemented by orange Daihatsu minibuses. City buses charge a fixed 300 rp fare and terminate at the Terboyo bus terminal. Bus Nos 1, 2 and 3 run south along Jl Pemuda to Candi Baru. Daihatsus cost 400 rp and operate all around town.

A becak from Tawang train station or th[e] bus terminal to the Oewa Asia Hotel will cos[t] about 1500 rp. You shouldn't pay more tha[n] 2000 rp for most becak rides in town. Becak[s] aren't allowed along Jl Pemuda.

Semarang has a limited number of metere[d] taxis, and they can be hard to find on th[e] street. They tend to congregate around th[e] big hotels or in front of the post office. Privat[e] minibuses for hire can be found at the pos[t] office and bus terminal, but bargain furiously[.]

AROUND SEMARANG
Ambarawa
At the junction where the Bandungan roa[d] branches from the Yogya to Semarang roa[d,] this small market town is the site of th[e] **Ambarawa Train Station Museum** (Mus[e]eum Kereta Api Ambarawa). At the o[ld] Ambarawa depot, steam locomotives buil[t] between 1891 and 1928 are on show, inclu[d]ing a 1902 cog locomotive still in workin[g] order. Most of the engines were made i[n] Germany and assembled in Holland. Th[e] museum is open from 7 am to 4.30 pm ever[y] day.

Though the line has closed, groups of u[p] to 100 passengers can charter a train for th[e] 18 km round trip from Ambarawa to Bedon[o] on the old cog railway. Book in Ambaraw[a] or through the Central Java Exploitatio[n] Office (Exploitasi Jawa Tengah; ☎ 524500[)] PJKA, Jl Thamrin 3, Semarang.

Getting There & Around Ambarawa can b[e] reached by public bus from Semarang (or[e] hour; 40 km), and Yogya (2½ hours; 90 km[)] via Magelang. From Solo, you have [to] change buses at Salatiga.

You can get around Ambarawa by doka[r;] they quote around 500 rp from the bus term[i]nal to Pasar Projo or the Railway Museum.

Bandungan
Bandungan at 980m is a pleasant enough hi[ll] resort to savour the mountain air, but th[e] main attraction is nearby Gedung Songo. O[f] Bandungan's main street, just before the roa[d] turns off to Gedung Songo, is an excelle[nt] roadside market with locally grown fruit an[d]

vegetables. In the same area are several cheap eating places. At around 7 am, a flower market gathers here briefly before dispersing to outlying towns and villages.

Places to Stay Bandungan has dozens of losmen and more expensive hotels. There are plenty of dingy losmen; the *Daruki* and *Tiga Dara* are basic but acceptable places with rooms for around 10,000 rp. The *Pura Mandira Karya* (☎ 91454) is a notch up in quality and has rooms from 12,000 to 17,500 rp. Some have hot water – very welcome in the mornings. The *Kusuma Madya Inn* (☎ 91136) has rooms with mandi from 15,000 rp, though most are from 25,000 to 30,000 rp. The hotel has friendly staff and comfortable rooms. Blankets and hot water in the mornings are provided.

About one km out of town towards Gedung Songo, the *Hotel Rawa Pening I* (☎ 91134) is a lovely old colonial-style wood bungalow with a front terrace, fine gardens, tennis courts and a restaurant. This is also *the* place to stay for fantastic views but, as you might imagine, it is often full at weekends. Rooms in the old building start at 75,000 rp and other rooms and cottages cost 63,500 to 81,000 rp. The nearby *Rawa Pening II* is at the more expensive end of the scale, and has a pool and tennis courts.

At the top end is the new *Hotel Nugraha Wisata* (☎ 91501), which has a swimming pool and rooms for 55,000 to 80,000 rp or more expensive suites (50% more on weekends).

Getting There & Away Buses run directly from Semarang to Bandungan, or coming from the south, get off at Ambarawa and then take a colt to Bandungan.

Gedung Songo Temples

These nine small Hindu temples are scattered along the tops of the foothills around Gunung Ungaran. Like those in Dieng, the Gedung Songo are small and simple temples, among the oldest Hindu temples on Java. The architecture may not be overwhelming, but the setting is simply superb. This 1000m

perch gives one of the most spectacular views on Java – south across the shimmering Danau Rawa Pening to Gunung Merbabu and behind it smouldering Gunung Merapi, and west to Gunung Sumbing and Gunung Sundoro.

Gedung Songo means 'nine buildings' in Javanese. Built in the 8th and 9th century AD and devoted to Shiva and Vishnu, the temples are in good condition after major restorations in the 1980s, but many of the carvings have been lost. A well-trodden path ventures up the hill past three groupings – the temples at the third grouping are the most impressive. Halfway, the trail leads down to a ravine and gushing hot sulphur springs, and then up again to the final temple and its expansive views. The three km loop can be walked in an hour, but allow longer to savour the atmosphere. Horses can also be hired.

The site is open from 6.15 am to 5.15 pm every day. Get there early in the morning for the best views.

Getting There & Away

The temples are about six km from Bandungan. From Bandungan's bustling market place, catch a colt for the three km to the turn-off to the temples. From the turn-off, take an ojek for the final three km to Gedung Songo (1000 rp).

Demak

Twenty-five km east of Semarang on the road to Surabaya, Demak was once the capital of the first Islamic state on Java and the most important state during the early 16th century. Demak conquered the great Hindu Majapahit kingdom and helped spread Islam to the interior. At the time this was a good seaport but silting of the coast has now left Demak several km inland.

The **Mesjid Agung** (Grand Mosque) dominates the town of Demak and is one of Indonesia's most important places of pilgrimage for Muslims. It is the earliest mosque known on Java, founded jointly by the wali songo in 1466. Combining Javanese-Hindu and Islamic elements in its architecture, legend has it that it was constructed entirely

JAVA

of wood by the wali songo in a single night. Four main pillars, called the *soko guru*, in the central hall are said to have been made by four of the saints. One pillar, erected by Sunan Kalijaga, is said to be made from pieces of scrap wood magically fused together by the saints when no other wood could be found.

The mosque was extensively restored in 1987. The history and restoration of the mosque is outlined in a small museum to the side, and some of the original woodwork, including some magnificent carved doors, are on display.

The tombs of Demak's rulers are next to the mosque, including Raden Patah, Demak's first sultan, though it is the tomb of Raden Trenggono, who led Demak's greatest military campaigns, that attracts the most pilgrims. During Grebeg Besar, when various heirlooms are ritually cleansed, thousands of pilgrims flock to Demak.

The mausoleum of Sunan Kalijaga is at **Kadilangu**, two km south of Demak.

The mosque is on the main road in the centre of town. Through buses can drop you on the doorstep. The bus fare is 600 rp to Semarang or Kudus.

KUDUS

Fifty-five km north-east of Semarang, Kudus was founded by the Muslim saint Sunan Kudus. Like Demak, it is an Islamic holy city and an important place of pilgrimage. Its name comes from the Arabic *al-Quds*, which means 'holy', and it is the only place on Java that has permanently acquired an Arabic name.

Kudus is strongly Muslim, yet, strangely, some old Hindu customs prevail, such as the tradition that cows may not be slaughtered within the town. Kudus is also a prosperous town and a major centre of Java's kretek (clove cigarette) industry.

Old Town

West of the river on the road to Jepara, **Kauman**, the oldest part of town, can be an interesting place to wander around. Its streets are narrow and winding, stark white and

almost Middle Eastern in atmosphere, crowded with boys in sarong and topi and women in full orthodox Muslim dress. Some of the buildings are colourful traditional houses with ornately carved wooden fronts.

In the centre of the old town, the **Al-Manar** (or Al-Aqsa) **Mosque** was constructed in 1549 by Sunan Kudus. The mosque is named after the mosque of Jerusalem and, like so many of Java's early mosques, it displays elements of Islamic and Hindu-Javanese design, such as the old Javanese carved split doorways. In fact, it was probably built on the site of a Hindu-Javanese temple and is particularly famous for its tall red-brick minaret, or *menara*, which may have originally been the watchtower of that temple.

In the courtyards behind the mosque is the imposing **Tomb of Sunan Kudus**, which is now a shrine. His mausoleum of finely carved stone is hung with a curtain of lace. The narrow doorway, draped with heavy gold-embroidered curtains, leads through to

1 Al-Manar Mosque
2 Garuda Restaurant
3 Telkom
4 Post Office
5 Hotel Slamet
6 BCA Bank
7 Air Mancur Hotel
8 Hotel Notasari Permai
9 Tourist Office
10 Djarum Kretek Factory
11 Tugu Identitas Tower
12 Plaza Kudus
13 Rumah Makan Hijau
14 Kretek Museum
15 Rumah Adat

To Jepara
To Colo
Jl Sunan Muria
Jl Sunan Kudus
Jl Mangga
Jl Jen Sudirman
Jl Mayor H Basuno
Jl A Yani
Jl Pemuda
To Hotel Kudus Asri Jaya, Bus Terminal & Semarang

Kudus

0   250   500
Approximate Scale

in inner chamber and the grave. During Buka Luwur, held once a year on 10 Muharram of the Islamic calendar, the curtains around the tomb are changed and thousands of pilgrims flock to Kudus for the event.

Kretek Production

The main kretek companies are Djambu Bol, Nojorono, Sukun and the Chinese-owned Djarum company which started in 1952 and is now the biggest producer in Kudus. Djarum's modern factory on Jl A Yani is central, but it usually requires a week's notice to tour the factory. Sukun, outside the town, still produce some *rokok klobot*, the original kreteks rolled in corn leaves. For a tour, contact the tourist office for a recommendation of a factory to visit.

Also worth a visit is the **Kretek Museum**, open 9 am to 4 pm, closed Monday and Wednesday. Although explanations are in Indonesian, a number of interesting photo-graphs and implements used in kretek pro-duction are on show.

Other Attractions

Next to the Kretek Museum, the **Rumah Adat** is a traditional wooden Kudus house exhibiting the fabulous carving work for which Kudus is famous. It is said that the Kudus style originated from Ling Sing, a 15th century Chinese immigrant and Islamic teacher. While nearby Jepara is now the famous woodcarving centre, a few work-shops in Kudus still make intricately carved panels and doorways, primarily works com-missioned by architects for public buildings, hotels or Jakarta mansions.

In front of the Plaza Kudus, the **Tugu Identitas**, styled after the menara, can be climbed for views over the town.

Places to Stay

The central *Hotel Slamet* (☎ 37579) at Jl

Kretek Cigarettes

One of those distinctive 'aromas' of Indonesia is the sweet spicy smell, almost like incense, of clove-flavoured cigarettes. The *kretek* cigarette has only been around since the start of the century, but today the kretek addiction is nationwide and accounts for 90% of the cigarette market, while sales of *rokok putih* (ordinary non-clove cigarettes) are languishing. So high is the consumption of cloves for smoking that Indonesia, traditionally a supplier of cloves in world markets, has become a substantial net importer from centres like Zanzibar and Madagascar.

The invention of the kretek has been attributed to a Kudus man, Nitisemito, who claimed the cigarettes relieved his asthma. He mixed tobacco with crushed cloves rolled in corn leaves, and these *rokok klobot* were the prototype for his Bal Tiga brand which he began selling in 1906. Nitisemito was a tireless promoter of his product – on the radio, by air dropping advertising leaflets, and touring in a van, which took a musical troupe across Java in an attempt to sell the new cigarettes.

Kudus on Java became the centre for the kretek industry and at one stage the town had over 200 factories, though today less than 50 cottage industries and a few large factories remain. Rationalisation in the industry has seen kretek production dominated by the big producers such as Bentoel in Malang, Gudang Garam in Kediri and Djarum in Kudus. Nitisemito became a victim of the industry he started and died bankrupt in 1953.

Although filtered kreteks are produced by modern machinery, non-filtered kreteks are still rolled by hand on simple wooden rolling machines. The manual process is protected by law. Women work in pairs with one rolling the cigarettes and the other snipping ends. The best rollers can turn out about 7000 cigarettes in a day.

As to the claim that kreteks are good for smokers' cough, cloves are a natural anaesthetic and so do have a numbing effect on the throat. Any other claims to aiding health stop there, because the tar and nicotine levels in the raw, slowly cured tobaccos used in kreteks are so high that some countries have banned or restricted their import. The Srintil tobacco from Muntilan is said to be the best.

Filtered kreteks now dominate the market and popular brands include Bentoel, Gudang Garam and Sukun. The Bentoel company has even produced a 'light' range of kreteks, Sampoerna, though tar levels are still quite high. For the kretek purist, the conical, crackling, non-filtered kretek has no substitute – the Dji Sam Soe ('234') brand is regarded as the Rolls Royce of kreteks. ■

Jenderal Sudirman 63 is a rambling old place with spartan rooms from 8000 rp. It's just OK – some rooms are better than others. The motel-style *Air Mancur* (☎ 32514) at Jl Pemuda 70 is much better but expensive. Decent doubles with mandi cost 17,000 to 23,000 rp, or air-con rooms are 35,000 and 48,000 rp.

The *Hotel Notasari Permai* (☎ 37245), Jl Kepodang 12, is a good mid-range hotel with a swimming pool, quiet courtyard and restaurant, and the staff are friendly. Comfortable rooms with mandi start at 23,000 rp, including breakfast; air-con rooms start at 42,500 rp, but don't get palmed off with a window-less room.

The *Hotel Kudus Asri Jaya* (☎ 38449) is the best hotel in town. The only drawback is that it is a long way from the town centre, a few hundred metres north of the bus terminal. Rooms with mandi start at 12,500 rp but most are air-con rooms ranging from 65,000 rp to the 125,000 rp suites. It has a pool, bar and restaurant.

Places to Eat

Local specialities to try include *soto Kudus* (chicken soup) and *jenang Kudus*, which is a sweet made of glutinous rice, brown sugar and coconut.

The *Rumah Makan Hijau*, near the Plaza Kudus shopping centre at Jl A Yani 1, is cheap and good for Indonesian food and super-cool fruit juices. It's closed on Friday.

The *Hotel Notasari Permai* restaurant is reasonably priced for the big helpings you get. The *Garuda* at Jl Jenderal Sudirman 1 has Chinese, Indonesian and western food.

Getting There & Away

Kudus is on the main Semarang to Surabaya road. The bus terminal is about four km south of town. City minibuses run from behind the bus terminal to the town centre (300 rp), or you can take an ojek or becak for 2500 rp.

From Kudus you can get buses to Demak (600 rp; half hour), Semarang (1200 rp; one hour; 54 km), Surabaya (5500 rp; 286 km) and Solo (4400 rp; 3½ hours; 156 km). Colts go to Colo for 1000 rp. For Jepara (800 rp;

45 minutes; 35 km) and Mantingan, buses leave from the Jetak sub-station, four km west of town (300 rp by purple minibus).

AROUND KUDUS
Colo

This small hill resort lies 18 km north of Kudus at an altitude of 700m on the slopes of Gunung Muria.

Colo is most famous for its **Tomb of Sunan Muria** (Raden Umar Said), one of the wali songo, who was buried here in 1469. The mosque surrounding the tomb is perched high on a ridge overlooking the plains to the south. It was built around the middle of the 19th century, though it has had many later additions. Pilgrims regularly come to pray at the tomb, and during Buka Luwur, held in Colo on 16 Muharram of the Islamic calendar, up to 10,000 pilgrims line the road to the top.

The **Air Terjun Monthel** waterfall is 1.5 km or about a half hour stroll from Colo village.

Colo has a comfortable, government-run guesthouse for accommodation.

JEPARA

Jepara, only 35 km north-west of Kudus, is famed as the centre for the best woodcarvers on Java. The road into Jepara passes workshops stacked high with furniture, so you get a fair idea of places to visit as you arrive.

Jepara is a small, peaceful country town but it has a colourful history. An important port in the 16th century, it had both English and Dutch factories by the early 1600s, and was involved in a violent dispute between the VOC and Sultan Agung of Mataram. After some of the Dutch reputedly compared Agung to a dog and relieved themselves on Jepara's mosque, hostilities finally erupted in 1618 when the Gujarati (from Gujarat, in west India) who governed Jepara for Agung attacked the VOC trading post. The Dutch retaliated by burning Javanese ships and much of the town. In 1619 Jan Pieterszoon Coen paused on his way to the conquest of Batavia to burn Jepara yet again and with it the English East India Company's post. The

VOC headquarters for the central north coast was then established at Jepara.

Apart from furniture, Jepara is just a conservative small town, but it is undergoing a mini development boom in the wake of the government's decision to build Indonesia's first nuclear power station nearby at the base of Gunung Muria. The proposed plant has put Jepara on the map (though some claim it may wipe it off the map).

Things to See

Kartini's father was regent of Jepara and she grew up in the *bupati's* (regent's) house, on the east side of the alun alun. Though still the bupati's residence, it is possible to visit Kartini's rooms inside if you contact the tourist office. Here Kartini spent her confinement, known as *pingit* in Javanese. Traditionally this was when pubescent girls were forbidden

---

Kartini

Raden Ajeng Kartini (1879-1904) was born in Mayong, 12 km north-west of Kudus on the road to Jepara. She was the daughter of the regent of Jepara and was allowed, against Indonesian custom, to attend the Dutch school in Jepara along with her brothers. As a result of her education, Kartini questioned both the burden of Javanese etiquette and the polygamy permitted under Islamic law. In letters to Dutch friends she criticised colonial behaviour and vocalised an 'ever growing longing for freedom and independence, a longing to stand alone'.

Kartini married the regent of Rembang, himself a supporter of progressive social policies, and together they opened a school in Rembang for the daughters of regents. In 1904 Kartini died shortly after the birth of her son. Perhaps the first modern Indonesian writer, Kartini's letters were published in 1911 in the original Dutch, entitled *Through Darkness to Light*, the English edition is available in paperback.

At Mayong there is a monument to Kartini, which marks the spot where her placenta was buried according to Javanese custom. Jepara and Rembang are other important places where ceremonies are held on 21 April to celebrate Kartini Day. ■

---

to venture outside the house and from 12 to 16 girls were kept in virtual imprisonment.

The small **Museum RA Kartini**, next to the tourist office on the north side of the alun alun, has photos and furniture from the family home. It is open from 7 am to 5 pm every day.

Heading north from the museum, cross the river and veer left up the hill to the old Dutch fort, the **Benteng VOC**. Over the last 50 years the stonework has been pillaged for building material and not much remains, but the site has good views across the town and out to the Java Sea, and the nearby cemetery has some Dutch graves.

Places to Stay

The *Menno Jaya Hotel* (☎ 91143), in the centre of town at Jl Diponegoro 40B, has very basic singles/doubles without mandi for 10,000/15,000 rp. What it lacks in ambience is made up for by the owner, Mr Teopilus Hadiprasetya, an excellent host who speaks good English. He will proudly show you his photo albums and the 'thank you' letter from Prince Charles and Princess Di for a carved plaque he sent them as a wedding present.

Other places include the *Losmen Asia* at Jl Kartini 32, which has rooms from 10,000 rp, or the more expensive *Hotel Terminal* right by the bus terminal, which has rooms from 12,500 rp with mandi, from 25,000 rp with air-con.

The friendly *Ratu Shima* (☎ 91406), Jl Dr Soetomo 13-15, is a good mid-range hotel. Fan rooms start at 15,000 rp, air-con rooms are 40,000 to 55,000 rp. A notch up in quality is the larger *Kalingga Star* (☎ 91054), Jl Dr Soetomo 16. Rooms start at 16,500 rp, from 37,000 rp with air-con. Both have decent restaurants.

To cater to all those engineers and nuclear plant workers, two new hotels have sprung up. *Hotel Segoro* (☎ 91982), Jl Ringin Jaya 2, is a motel with a range of immaculate rooms from 22,000 rp up to suites for 92,000 rp. *Hotel Jepara Indah* (☎ 93548), Jl HOS Cokroaminoto 12, is a cheaply built three star hotel, but far and away the biggest and best in Jepara. Rooms cost US$47/55 and US$68/73, plus 21%.

Places to Eat

Depot Milo, Jl Dr Soetomo 16-19, is a pleasant little restaurant next to the Kalingga Star with bamboo decor and Indonesian/Chinese dishes. Just across the river from the alun alun, the *Pondok Rasa*, Jl Pahlawan 2, has a pleasant garden and a lesahan eating area to enjoy good Indonesian food. The *Saur Kuring* on Jl Sudarso, one block west of the alun alun, has excellent Chinese seafood. The *Ponix Restoran*, next to the Hotel Segoro, is Jepara's flashest restaurant and also specialises in seafood.

Things to Buy

Intricately carved wooden cupboards, divans, chests, chairs, tables, relief panels and the like are carved from teak (*jati*) or sometimes mahogany. Jepara's consumption of teak is so high that demand is outstripping supply on Java. Furniture shops and factories are all around Jepara, but the main centre is the village of **Tahunan**, four km south of Jepara on the road to Kudus.

Brightly coloured ikat weavings using motifs from Sumba are sold on Bali but they come from the village of **Torso**, 14 km south of Jepara, two km off the main road. Other designs are produced and the men do the weaving, allowing broader looms to be used. Srikandi Ratu and Lestari Indah are two workshops with fixed price showrooms.

Pecangaan, 18 km south of Jepara, produces rings, bracelets and other jewellery from *monel*, a stainless steel alloy.

Getting There & Away

From Jepara's conveniently central bus terminal, frequent buses run from Jepara to Kudus (800 rp; 45 minutes) and Semarang (1900 rp; 1½ hours). Buses also go to Surabaya at 6 am, but Kudus has more connections. Night buses to Jakarta cost from 15,000 rp, or Muji Jaya has more luxurious buses.

AROUND JEPARA
Mantingan

The mosque and tomb of Ratu Kali Nyamat are in this village, four km south of Jepara. Kali Nyamat was the great warrior-queen of Jepara who twice laid siege to Portugal's Melaka stronghold in the latter part of the 16th century. The campaigns against Melaka were not successful but she scared the Portuguese witless.

The mosque dating from 1549 was restored some years ago, and the tomb lies around the side. It is noted for its Hindu-style embellishments and medallions.

Mantingan is easily reached from Jepara. *Angkudes* from the bus terminal can drop you outside the mosque for 300 rp.

Pantai Bandengan

Jepara has some surprisingly decent, white sand beaches. Pantai Bandengan, otherwise known as Tirta Samudra, eight km north-east of town, is the most popular beach. The main public section can be littered and is best avoided on weekends, but a short walk away the sands are clean and the waters clear. From Jepara, take a brown and yellow bemo (300 rp) from Jl Patimura, behind the tourist office. To charter a whole bemo costs 2500 rp.

Pondok Bougenville (☎ 92693) has rooms designed for groups, each with four beds or more for 25,000 rp, or 35,000 rp with mandi. Though fairly basic, it has a good beachside restaurant, an excellent stretch of sand out front and windsurfers for rent.

KARIMUNJAWA

These 27 islands, lying around 90 km northwest of Jepara, have been declared a marine national park. Though they are being promoted as a tropical paradise, facilities are limited, the islands are difficult to reach and few visitors make it to this forgotten part of Java.

The main island of **Pulau Karimunjawa** has homestay accommodation, but apart from peace and quiet the island's attractions are few – you can swim in the calm, clear waters but the island is mostly ringed by nangroves and has no decent beaches. Nearby islands do have magnificent beaches and coral reefs but can only be reached by chartered boat.

Pulau Tengah to the north is a small island ringed by a reef and beautiful, sandy beaches. The small resort here has the best accommodation on the islands. Other nearby deserted islands with good beaches are **Pulau Burung** and **Pulau Geleang** to the west.

Places to Stay

It is easy enough to find a homestay in the main village of Karimunjawa. Ask on the boat over or on arrival. Pak Kholik and the Pak Abdul Mu'in have decent accommodation for around 12,000 rp, including all meals. Pak Ipong has the closest thing to a hotel – rooms with mandi cost 17,000 rp with meals. The government-owned *Wisma Pemda* will have the best rooms when it is finished.

Pulau Tengah has quite luxurious, two bedroom cottages with separate sitting areas, but they are only available with expensive tours organised through Satura Tours (☎ 555555), Jl Cendrawasih A-6, Semarang.

Getting There & Away

Deraya Air has flights on Monday and Thursday from Semarang for 57,500 rp. The airstrip is on Pulau Kemujan, which is linked to Pulau Karimunjawa by a bridge across the mangroves.

A well-equipped ferry leaves from Pantai Kartini in Jepara (1500 rp by becak from the town centre) and costs 15,000 rp, or 20,000 rp in air-con (1st class) for the 4½ hour journey. It leaves Jepara at 8 am Monday and 4 pm Thursday, returning from Karimunjawa on Sunday and Wednesday, but schedules change. The much less salubrious MK *Kota Ukir* (7500 rp; seven hours) battles the Java Sea swells and leaves on Monday from Jepara's main harbour by the river, but it doesn't carry life jackets or rafts. Crossings in the wet season are rugged.

East Java

The province of East Java, or Jawa Timur, officially includes the island of Madura off the north-west coast, and has a total population of 33.9 million and an area of 47,921 sq km. The majority of its population are Javanese, but many Madurese farmers and fishermen live in East Java. They are familiar faces, particularly around Surabaya, the capital of the province. In the Bromo area is a small population of Hindu Tenggerese.

Geographically, much of the province is flatter than the rest of Java. In the north-west is lowland with deltas along the Brantas and Bengawan Solo rivers, and km upon km of rice-growing plains. But the rest of East Java is mountainous and hilly, containing the huge Bromo-Tengger Massif and Java's highest mountain, Gunung Semeru (3676m). This region offers a raw, natural beauty and magnificent scenery.

Major attractions for the visitor include the magnificent Gunung Bromo (2392m), still one of Java's most active volcanoes. Then there's a host of other mountains, pleasant walks and fine hill towns, like Malang. In the north-east corner of the province there is also the important Baluran National Park, the most accessible of Java's wildlife reserves. Finally, although East Java is closely related culturally to Central Java, the Madurese are best known for their rugged sport called *kerapan sapi*, the famous bull races which take place on the island during August and September.

HISTORY

East Java's hazy past comes into focus with its political and cultural ascendancy in the 10th century AD, and the reign of Airlangga. Before claiming the throne in 1019 AD, Airlangga had spent many years as a hermit, devoting time to accumulating wisdom through fasting and meditation. Under Airlangga's government, eastern Java became united and powerful, but shortly before his death he divided his kingdom between his two sons,

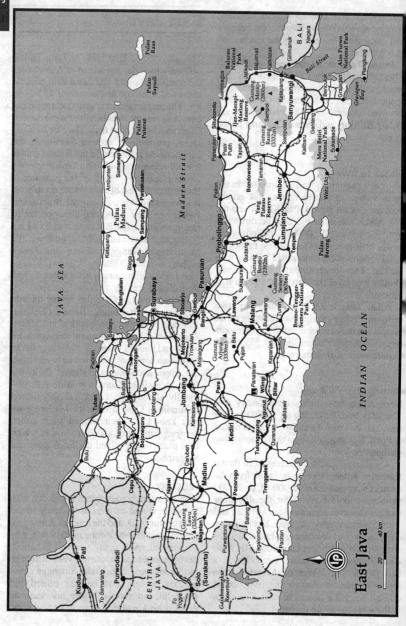

East Java

0   20   40 km

creating Janggala, east of Sungai Brantas, and Kediri to the west. A third kingdom, Singosari, joined in the struggle for the ascendancy.

In 1049 the Kediri dynasty rose to power and continued its rule through to 1222. In 1222 the Singosari kingdom came to power and gradually superseded Kediri under the leadership of the usurper, Ken Angrok. Angrok was a violent man who took the throne by murdering the former ruler of Singosari and then marrying his wife. Legend relates that Ken Angrok first tried out his murder weapon on its maker, who then cursed it with his dying breath, predicting that seven kings would die by the sword. The curse was fulfilled – the rule of Singosari lasted a mere 70 years, but under its kings the Javanese culture nevertheless flourished. East Java inherited some of its most striking temples from that era, and Singosari also pioneered a new sculptural style that owed little or nothing to original Indian traditions. Shivaism and Buddhism evolved into a new religion called Shiva-Buddhism, which even today has many followers on Java and Bali.

Kertanegara (1262-92) was the last of the Singosari kings and a skilful diplomat who sought alliance with other Indonesian rulers in the face of the threat from another great power. In 1292 the Mongol ruler, Kublai Khan, demanded that homage be paid to China. Kertanegara, however, foolishly humiliated the Great Khan by having the nose and ears of the Mongol envoy cut off and sent back to China. This effrontery precipitated the launching of a Mongol invasion of Java, but by the time they arrived Kertanegara had already been killed in a civil war. The new king, Wijaya, defeated the Mongols but the barbaric invasion left such a bitter taste that for nearly 100 years relations between China and Java remained at a standstill.

Wijaya was also the founder of the Majapahit Empire, the most famous of the early Javanese kingdoms. With a capital at Trowulan, the Majapahits ruled from 1294 to 1478, and during the reign of Hayam Wuruk carried their power overseas, with raids into Bali and an expedition against Palembang on Sumatra. Majapahit also claimed trading relations with Cambodia, Siam, Burma and Vietnam, and sent missions to China. When Hayam Wuruk died in 1389, the Majapahit Empire rapidly disintegrated. By the end of the 15th century Islamic power was growing on the north coast, and less than a century later there were raids into East Java by Muslims carrying both the Koran and the sword. Many Hindu-Buddhists fled eastwards to Bali, but in the mountain ranges around Gunung Bromo the Tenggerese people trace their history back to Majapahit and still practise their own religion, a variety of Hinduism that includes many proto-Javanese elements. During the 17th century the region finally fell to the rulers of Mataram in Central Java.

Today, Surabaya, the provincial capital and second-largest city in Indonesia, is a vital centre for trade and manufacturing, but East Java is still a region of agriculture and small villages. In marked contrast to the practically always-wet western end of Java, East Java has a monsoonal climate and a real dry season from April to November.

TEMPLES

Although East Java does not have any monuments that approach the awe-inspiring scale of Borobudur and Prambanan, it does have dozens of small but interesting temples. Around Malang there are several Singosari temples, and near Blitar is the large Panataran complex. All these temples exhibit a strikingly different sculptural style in which figures are exuberantly carved in a two dimensional wayang kulit form. At Trowulan are ruins from the great Majapahit Empire. Overall, the innovative East Javan temple style is an obvious prototype for later Balinese sculpture/architecture.

The decorative imagination of the East Javanese sculptors also found expression in richly ornamented items cast in bronze and more costly metals. A great variety of ritual objects, weapons and other utensils have been preserved, and many can be seen in Jakarta's National Museum.

MALANG

Malang is one of Java's finest and most attractive hill towns. Situated on the banks of Sungai Brantas, it was established by the Dutch around the end of the 18th century when coffee was first grown as a colonial cash crop in the area. In more recent years, local farmers have grown tobacco and apples; cigarette factories and the army have set themselves up here. It's a cool, clean place with a well-planned square, and the central area of town is studded with parks, tree-lined streets and old Dutch architecture.

The main attractions lie outside the city,

but apart from being a good base for many points of interest in East Java, it is also worth a day or two's visit for its own sake. Unlike many Javanese towns, which are planned on a grid pattern, this one sweeps and winds along the river bank, with surprising views and quiet backwaters to explore. The living is good and the atmosphere easy-going.

Orientation

Life in Malang revolves around the alun alun and the busy streets of Agus Salim and Pasar Besar near the central market. Here are the main shopping plazas, restaurants, cinemas

PLACES TO STAY
2 Hotel Graha Santika
4 Regent's Park Hotel
5 Hotel Palei II
6 Hotel Helios
7 Kartika Prince Hotel
12 Hotel Kartika Kusuma
13 Hotel Menara
15 Hotel Aloha
18 Splendid Inn
20 Tugu Park Hotel
21 Montana Hotel
28 Hotel Riche
32 Hotel Pelangi
37 Hotel Santosa
40 Hotel Tosari
41 Hotel Margosuko

PLACES TO EAT
8 Rumah Makan Minang Jaya
23 Jack's Cafe
25 Minang Agung
27 Toko Oen Restaurant
34 Rumah Makan Agung
35 Gloria Restaurant
39 Depot Pangsit Mie

OTHER
1 Gereja Maria Bundel Karmel

3 Army Museum
9 Tourist Office (DIPARDA)
10 BCA Bank
11 Taman Rekreasi Senaputra
14 Tugu Transport Travel Agent
16 City Tourist Office
17 Balai Kota (Town Hall)
19 Wisma IKIP
22 Pasar Senggol & Pasar Bunga
24 BNI Bank
26 Telkom Office
29 Gereja Kathedral Kuno
30 Sarinah Department Store
31 Mosque
33 Main Post Office
36 Mitra & Gajah Mada Plaza
38 Malang Plaza
42 Pasar Besar & Matahari Department Store
43 Eng An Kiong Chinese Temple

and many of Malang's hotels. The alun alun in particular is a very popular area in the evenings, when families and students promenade and buskers perform. North-west of the square along Jl Basuki Rachmat are banks, the Telkom office and restaurants.

Information

Tourist Office The East Java Government tourist bureau (DIPARDA) has a good information centre (☎ 366216) at Jl Semeru 4. It is open from 8 am to 5 pm Monday to Saturday. The city tourist office at Jl Tugu 1 is open Monday to Saturday from 8 am to 2 pm.

Post & Communications The main post office is opposite the alun alun on Jl Kauman Merdeka.

The Telkom office on Jl Basuki Rachmat is open 24 hours and has Home Country Direct phones. The Toko Oen restaurant and the Kartika Prince Hotel also have Home Country Direct phones. You'll find a Telkom wartel on Jl Agus Salim, near the Hotel Santosa.

Money Malang has plenty of banks and moneychangers. Compare the BNI and BCA banks on Jl Basuki Rachmat for the best rates.

Other Services The best bookshops are Sari Agung, next to the Sarinah department store, and Gramedia, on the other side of the street. The Sarinah department store has a small selection of crafts and souvenirs.

Things to See & Do

The major attractions are outside town, but Malang has a few diversions to stave off boredom.

Malang is noted for its colonial architecture. The **Balai Kota** (Town Hall) on Jl Tugu Circle is a sprawling Dutch administrative building, and nearby are some former old mansions, such as the **Splendid Inn** and the **Wisma IKIP** next door on Jl Majapahit. For reliving colonial dreams, nothing beats the **Toko Oen restaurant**. Another good example of Art Deco colonial architecture is the

Hotel Pelangi and its tiled restaurant with scenes of old Holland. Near the Toko Oen, the **Gereja Kathedral Kuno** is the old Dutch Reform Church. **Jl Besar Ijen** is Malang's millionaire's row. Most of the large houses date from the colonial era, but many have been substantially renovated, losing architectural detail in the process.

On the north-west outskirts of town, **Candi Badut** is a small Shivaite temple dating from the 8th century. West of town on Jl Besar Ijen, the modern **Army Museum** is devoted to Malang's Brawijaya Division.

Malang has some good markets. The huge central market, the **Pasar Besar**, is always worth a browse. The flower market, **Pasar Bunga**, has a pleasant aspect down by the river, and it is the place to stroll in the morning. At the same time, you can also take in the nearby **Pasar Senggol**, Malang's bird market. **Pasar Kebalen**, near the Eng An Kiong Chinese temple, is the most active market in the evenings until around 9 pm most nights.

Organised Tours

A number of operators have tours to the Singosari temples, Batu and Bromo (via Tosari for around 50,000 rp per person). The private Tourist Information Service (☎ 36-4052) at Toko Oen restaurant and the cheaper Hotel Helios are two well-known operators, and staff speak Dutch as well as English. They can also arrange car hire with driver from around 70,000 rp per day.

Places to Stay – bottom end

The most popular hotel is the *Hotel Helios* (☎ 362741), Jl Pattimura 37. Doubles cost 14,000 to 20,000 rp with shared mandi, and newer rooms with private bath cost 25,000 rp, or 35,000 rp for three people. It's clean, comfortable and all rooms have balconies overlooking the garden. Good travel information, bus bookings and tours are provided.

Near the Hotel Helios, the *Hotel Palem II* (☎ 25129), Jl Thamrin 15, has clean rooms with mandi for 19,500 to 27,500 rp. The cheaper rooms on the top floor are the best value.

In the lively central area, the rambling *Hotel Riche* (☎ 24560) is well placed near the Toko Oen restaurant at Jl Basuki Rachmat 1, but the rooms are dingy and cost 17,500 rp or from 19,000 rp with mandi.

Other central hotels include the uninspiring *Hotel Santosa* (☎ 23889), in the thick of things at Jl Agus Salim 24, with rooms from 22,000 rp; or a better option is the *Hotel Tosari* (☎ 26945), Jl Achmad Dahlan 31, with bare but very clean rooms for 16,000 rp, or from 24,000 rp with mandi.

Places to Stay – middle

The most fashionable area to stay is in the area around Jl Tugu. This is the old Dutch administrative district with impressive public buildings and old villas. For the colonial feel, the *Splendid Inn* (☎ 366860), Jl Majapahit 2-4, is an expat favourite just off the Jl Tugu Circle. This fine old Dutch villa has worn but very comfortable rooms with hot water, TV and air-con from US$22/26 to US$27/31, including breakfast. It also has a good restaurant and bar, which is the meeting place for the Hash House Harriers.

Nearby at Jl Kahuripan 8, the *Montana Hotel* (☎ 328370) is near the top of this range, but not particularly well maintained and way overpriced with rooms from US$70. For something more modest, and better value, the newer *Hotel Kartika Kusuma* (☎ 352266), Jl Kahuripan 12, has rooms around a courtyard garden for 50,000 rp, or 65,000 rp with air-con.

The friendly, well-run *Hotel Menara* (☎ 362871), Jl Pajajaran 5, has comfortable rooms with mandi from 30,000 rp, or quite luxurious rooms with air-con, hot water and TV for 55,000 rp. The tariff includes breakfast, and there is a good sitting area for meals.

The well-run *Hotel Margosuko* (☎ 325-270), Jl Achmad Dahlan 40-42, is also central. Good rooms with mandi and hot water cost 33,000 and 44,000 rp, or VIP rooms are 66,000 rp. The hotel has a small coffee shop and good service, but can be noisy.

Right on the alun alun, the *Hotel Pelangi* (☎ 365156), Jl Kauman Merdeka 3, is a large, pleasant old Dutch hotel with spacious rooms. Simple 'driver's' rooms cost 20,000 to 30,000 rp, but you'll be directed to the more expensive fan rooms with bath, hot water and TV costing 65,000 and 70,000 rp. Air-con rooms cost 100,000 to 115,000 rp. Add 10% tax to the rates, but buffet breakfast in the delightful hotel restaurant is included.

Places to Stay – top end

All these hotels charge 21% tax and service, but will usually give a similarly sized discount.

The *Tugu Park Hotel* (☎ 363891), Jl Tugu 3, is one of the most delightful hotels on Java. Though neither large nor lavishly appointed, it has real style despite being a modern hotel. Rooms cost US$115, but it is worth the extra for the suites, all furnished in different Asian antique styles, costing US$140 to US$250. It has a pool, business centre, a good restaurant and a tea house facing the Tugu square.

Malang has a couple of older high-rise hotels on Jl Jaksa Agung Suprapto. The *Regent's Park Hotel* (☎ 363388) has worn rooms from US$75. The better maintained *Kartika Prince* (☎ 361900) is a glass-and-marble hotel with good facilities, including a pool, restaurants and bars. Good rooms cost US$90 to US$115.

Straddling the middle and top end, the smaller *Hotel Graha Santika* (☎ 324989), Jl Cerme 16, is a superbly restored Art Deco building converted into a hotel. It is tastefully furnished with antiques, and has a swimming pool and restaurant. Rooms cost US$60 and US$75, suites are US$95 and US$125.

Places to Eat

The *Toko Oen*, opposite the Sarinah department store, is an anachronism from colonial days, with tea tables and comfortable basket chairs. Relax and read a newspaper while being served by waiters in white sarongs and black *peci* hats. It has Chinese and western dishes, plus good Indonesian food and delicious home-made ice cream. This is one of the most relaxing places for a meal and a good place for breakfast. It's open daily from 8.30 am to 9 pm.

For a drink or snack, the *Melati Restaurant* in the Hotel Pelangi is even more architecturally impressive than the Toko Oen. This cavernous colonial relic has towering pressed metal ceilings, and painted tiles around the walls feature picture postcard scenes from old Holland. While guaranteed to make any Dutchman homesick, the Indonesian and western food is only average.

The similarly named *Melati Pavilion Restaurant* in the Tugu Park Hotel restaurant serves good Indonesian, Chinese and Continental cuisine at upscale prices. Dutch dishes are featured, and of course there is rijsttafel. The Tugu rijsttafel for 12,500 rp has a selection of East Javanese dishes.

For cheap and varied eats, head for Jl Agus Salim. The Chinese *Gloria Restaurant* at No 23 specialises in pangsit mie – a bowl of delicious noodles, meat and vegetables served with a side bowl of soup for you to mix. Closer to the alun alun, *Rumah Makan Agung* has excellent savoury murtabak and chicken biryani, as well as Indonesian dishes.

The big shopping centres have a variety of places to eat. The best is the *Food Centre*, sandwiched between the Mitra department store and the Gajah Mada Plaza. The busy food stalls here offer a great selection of dishes, including local specialities such as nasi rawon (beef soup served with rice). Street vendors on Jl Agus Salim also have tasty sweets and dumplings.

The shopping centres on Jl Agus Salim, as well as the Matahari on Jl Pasar Besar, have well-stocked supermarkets. For western fast food, *KFC* and *Swensens* are in the Variety department store building next to the Malang Plaza. *McDonald's* is next to Sarinah on Jl Basuki Rachmat.

Jack's Cafe, Jl Kahuripan 11A, is a hip restaurant with a varied menu, popular with students and an alternative crowd. Bands play downstairs on Thursday, Friday and Saturday.

The *Rumah Makan Minang Jaya* at Jl Basuki Rachmat 111 has good Padang food at reasonable prices.

Entertainment

Taman Rekreasi Senaputra is Malang's cultural and recreational park. Every Sunday morning at 10 am, *kuda lumping* 'horse trance' dances (*jaran kepang* in Javanese) are held here. The dancers ride plaited cane horses until they fall into a trance, allowing them to eat glass and perform other masochistic acts without harm.

On the last Wednesday of the month, wayang kulit is performed at Senaputra from 10 pm. RRI (Radio Republik Indonesia), Jl Candi Panggung, five km north-west of the city, has wayang kulit from 9 pm on the first Saturday of the month.

Getting There & Away

Malang can be approached from a number of directions. The back route between Yogya and Banyuwangi takes you through some beautiful countryside. For an interesting trip, you could take a train from Solo to Jombang, then colts south to Blimbing, Kandangan, Batu and finally Malang.

Air The only commercial flights from Malang's military airport are the daily Merpati flights to Jakarta (225,000 rp).

Bus Malang has three bus terminals. Arjosari, five km north of town, is the main bus terminal with regular buses to northern route destinations, such as Surabaya (1800 rp; two hours), Probolinggo (2100 rp; 2½ hours), Jember (4500 rp; 4½ hours), Banyuwangi (6800 rp; seven hours) and Denpasar (9000 rp; 10 hours). Air-con express buses also cover these routes, and travel to Yogya and Solo. Mikrolet run from Arjosari to nearby villages such as Singosari (500 rp) and Tumpang (600 rp).

The Gadang bus terminal is five km south of the town centre and has buses along the southern routes to destinations such as Blitar (1800 rp; two hours), Tulung Agung (2600 rp; three hours) and Turen (600 rp; one hour).

The Landungsari bus terminal, five km

north-west of the city, has buses to the west to destinations such as Kediri, Madiun and Jombang. Frequent mikrolet run to Batu (500 rp; half an hour).

Malang has plenty of bus companies offering luxury express services for the long hauls. Buses to Bandung (around 40,000 rp), Bogor and Jakarta (35,000 to 50,000 rp) leave around 2 pm. Numerous buses to Solo and Yogya cost from 15,000 rp and leave around 8 pm. Night buses also do the run to Bali for around 22,000 rp, and these continue on to Padangbai and Mataram on Lombok. They leave from the Arjosari bus terminal.

It is easiest to buy tickets from the agents found all over town. There are plenty of agents on Jl Basuki Rachmat, south of the tourist office, or the tourist office itself is helpful. Tugu Transport (☎ 368363), Jl Kertanegara 5, is handy for the Tugu area, or try the travel agent at the Toko Oen restaurant.

Minibus Plenty of door-to-door minibus companies operate from Malang, and hotels and travel agents can book them. Destinations include: Banyuwangi (17,500 rp); Probolinggo (8000 rp); Kediri (8000 rp); Solo (20,000 rp); and Yogya (20,000 rp). Minibuses to Surabaya (6000 to 8000 rp) will drop off at hotels in Surabaya, thus saving the long haul from Surabaya's Ajosari bus terminal.

Train Ekonomi trains run from Surabaya to Blitar via Malang. The *Pattas* express train on this route provides a good service and costs 3000 rp to Surabaya or Blitar. Most other services tend to go via Surabaya. Trains from points west, such as Solo and Yogya, are ekonomi only and very slow. Buses are generally a better choice on these routes.

Getting Around
Mikrolet run all over town from the main bus terminals and to other mikrolet stations. The most useful services are those running between the bus terminals and passing through the centre of town. These are marked A-G (Arjosari to Gadung and return), A-L

(Arjosari-Landungsari), G-L (Gadung Landungsari) etc. A trip anywhere aroun town costs 350 rp.

Becaks and metered taxis are also avai able, but usually not from the bus terminals

AROUND MALANG
Singosari Temples
The Singosari Temples lie in a ring aroun Malang and are mostly funerary temple dedicated to the kings of the Singosar dynasty (1222 to 1292 AD), the precursor of the Majapahit Empire.

Candi Singosari Right in Singosari village 12 km north of Malang, this temple stand 500m off the main Malang to Surabaya road One of the last monuments erected to th Singosari dynasty, it was built in 1304 AD i honour of King Kertanegara, the fifth an last Singosari king who died in 1292 in palace uprising. The main structure of th temple was completed but, for some reason the sculptors never finished their task. Onl the top part has any ornamentation and th kala heads have been left strangely stark with smooth bulging cheeks and pop eyes Of the statues that once inhabited th temple's chambers, only Agastya, the Shiva ite teacher who walked across the water t Java, remains. Statues of Durga and Ganesh were carted off to the Netherlands, but hav since been returned and are now in th Jakarta Museum.

About 200m beyond the temple are tw enormous figures of *dwarapala* (guardian against evil spirits) wearing clusters of skull and twisted serpents. These may have bee part of the original gates to the palace of th Singosari kingdom.

To reach Singosari, take a green mikrole (500 rp) from Malang's Arjosari bus termina and get off at the Singosari market on th highway, then walk or take a becak.

Candi Sumberawan This small, plain Bud dhist stupa lies in the foothills of Gunung Arjuna, about five km north-west o Singosari. Originating from a later perioc than the Singosari temples, it was built t

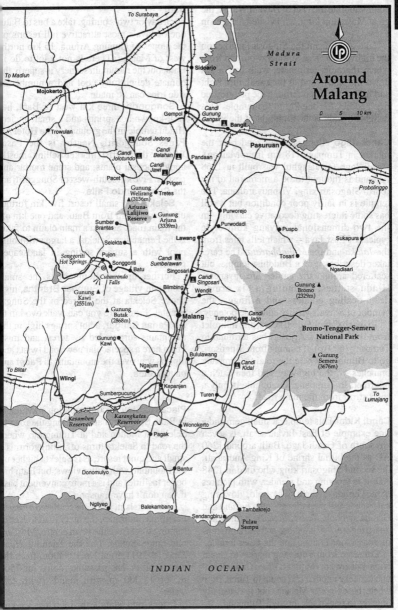

Around Malang

0   5   10 km

Madura Strait

To Surabaya

To Madiun

Mojokerto

Sidoarjo

Gempol

Candi Gunung Gangsir

Bangil

Trowulan

Pasuruan

Candi Jedong

Candi Jolotundo

Candi Belahan

Pandaan

Candi Jawi

Pacet

Prigen

Gunung Welirang (3156m)

Tretes

Arjuna-Lalijiwo Reserve

Gunung Arjuna (3339m)

Purworejo

To Probolinggo

Sumber Brantas

Purwodadi

Puspo

Lawang

Sukapura

Songgoriti Hot Springs

Pujon

Selekta

Batu

Songgoriti

Candi Sumberawan

Singosari

Tosari

Ngadisari

Cubanrondo Falls

Candi Singosari

Blimbing

Wendit

Gunung Bromo (2329m)

Gunung Kawi (2551m)

Gunung Butak (2868m)

Malang

Tumpang

Candi Jago

Bromo-Tengger-Semeru National Park

Gunung Kawi

Bululawang

Candi Kidal

To Bitar

Ngajum

Gunung Semeru (3676m)

Wlingi

Kepanjen

Sumberpucung

Turen

To Lumajang

Kesamben Reservoir

Karangkates Reservoir

Wonokerto

Pagak

Donomulyo

Bantur

Ngliyep

Balekambang

Sendangbiru

Tambakrejo

Pulau Sempu

INDIAN OCEAN

commemorate the visit of Hayam Wuruk, the great Majapahit king, who visited the area in 1359.

Take a colt from the Singosari market on the highway to Desa Sumberawan, and from where the colts terminate, walk half a km down the stony road to the canal, turn right and follow the canal through the picturesque rice paddies for one km to the temple. This delightful walk is the highlight of the visit.

Candi Jago Along a small road near the market in Tumpang (18 km from Malang), Candi Jago (or Jajaghu) was built in 1268 AD and is thought to be a memorial to the fourth Singosari king, Vishnuvardhana. The temple is in fairly poor condition but it still has some interesting decorative carving – in the two-dimensional wayang kulit style typical of East Java – which tells tales from the *Jataka* and the *Mahabharata*. The care-taker describes it as a Buddhist temple, but scattered around the garden are Javanese-Hindu statues, including a six armed death-dealing goddess and a lingga, the symbol of Shiva's virility and male potency.

To reach Candi Jago take a white mikrolet from the Malang's Arjosari bus terminal to Tumpang (600 rp). If coming from Singosari, go to Blimbing where the road to Tumpang branches off the highway, and then catch a mikrolet. In Tumpang, the temple is only a short stroll from the main road.

Candi Kidal This temple, a small gem and a fine example of East Javanese art, is seven km south of Candi Jago. Built around 1260 AD as the burial shrine of King Anusapati, the second Singosari king who died in 1248 AD, it is tapering and slender, with pictures of the Garuda on three sides, bold, glowering kala heads and medallions of the *haruna* and Garuda symbols. Two *kala makara* (dragons) guard the steps – like those at the kraton steps in Yogya, one is male and the other female.

Colts run from Tumpang market to Candi Kidal but are not frequent. From Candi Kidal you can take another colt south to Turen, from where buses go to Malang, but it is usually quicker to backtrack through Tumpang.

Batu

For a day or two's outing, take a bus to Batu, one of Java's most attractive hill resorts on the slopes of Gunung Arjuna, 15 km north west of Malang. There is not a lot to do in Batu, but the mountain scenery is superb, the climate delightfully cool and a number of side trips can be made.

Songgoriti, three km west of Batu, has well-known hot springs and a small ancient Hindu temple in the grounds of the Hotel Air Panas Songgoriti. Nearby is the Pasar Wisata, the tourist market selling mostly apples, bonsai plants, and stone mortar and pestles. Five km south-west of Songgoriti are the **Cubanrondo Falls**.

Selekta is a small resort five km further up the mountain from Batu, and one km off the main road. Selekta's main claim to fame is the Pemandian Selekta, a large swimming pool with a superb setting in landscaped gardens.

Further up the mountain is the small mountain village of **Sumber Brantas**, high above Selekta at the source of the Sungai Brantas. From here you can walk two km to **Air Panas Cangar**, a hot springs high in the mountains surrounded by forest and mist. From here a spectacular new road twists and dips its way over the mountains to **Pacet** and on to **Tretes**.

Places to Stay Accommodation is available in Batu, Songgoriti and all along the road to Selekta at Punten and at Tulungrejo where the road to Selekta turns off. Songgoriti is a small and quiet resort, as is Selekta higher up the mountain with better views, but Batu has better facilities and is a more convenient base if you don't have transport.

Most hotels in Batu are scattered along Jl Panglima Sudirman, the main road to Kediri running west from the town centre. Most are mid-range hotels, but the friendly *Hotel Kawi* (☎ 591139) at No 19, 400m from the central plaza, has passable rooms for 7500 rp, or 15,000 rp with mandi (with *cold* water).

Prices and standards increase as you

roceed up the hill. A better bet for a room
ith bathroom is the cosy *Hotel Ragil*
uning (☎ 593051), half a km further west.
iood rooms with hot water cost 20,000 rp,
ut English is not spoken. Next door the
Iotel Mutiara (☎ 591192) has a few dark
)oms with mandi for 12,000 rp, or better
)oms from 25,000 to 50,000 rp.

Hotel Perdana (☎ 591104) at No 101 is a
ood mid-range hotel. Rooms with shower
nd hot water cost 25,000 rp, or large, newer
)oms at the back cost 42,500 rp.

The upscale *Hotel Kartika Wijaya*
☎ 592600) has a delightful colonial lobby,
nd rooms in the new sections styled after
ifferent regions in Indonesia. Rooms start
t US$53 (more on weekends), and it has a
wimming pool and landscaped gardens.
he newer *Royal Orchids Hotel* (☎ 593083),
earby at Jl Indragiri 4, is of similar price and
andard.

Batu has plenty of other top-end hotels,
icluding the huge *Batu Travelodge*, nearing
ompletion. The *Kusuma Agrowisata*
☎ 593333), Jl Abdul Gani Atas, is a sprawl-
ig place with rooms from US$56 and an
grotourism' apple orchard to visit.

Selekta has a couple of upper-notch
otels, such as the *Hotel Selekta* (☎ 91025),
ear the swimming pool. On the main road
Tulungrejo are the *Hotel Santosa* and
otel New Victory.

laces to Eat Jl Panglima Sudirman also has
lenty of restaurants. At No 7, near the Hotel
awi, *Pelangi Leisure Spot* is an attractive
staurant serving East Javanese and Chinese
eals at reasonable prices, with private bun-
alows around a garden at the back. Further
est, the *Rumah Makan Flamboyant* has
ood cheap Chinese food. Opposite the
letropole Hotel, *Adem Ayem* has fried
icken and the best views of the moun-
ins.

etting There & Away From Malang's
andungsari bus terminal you can take a
ediri bus, or one of the frequent purple
ikrolet to Batu (500 rp; half hour). Batu's
us terminal is two km from the centre of

town, but mikrolet from Malang often continue on to the centre of Batu, otherwise
catch another mikrolet (300 rp) from the bus
terminal. Indah Yana Tour & Travel (☎ 59-
2218) at Jl Agus Salim 2 has travel minibuses
to Surabaya, Madiun and Kediri.

From the bus terminal, orange mikrolet
run through town to Selekta (500 rp; half an
hour) and Sumber Brantas (1000 rp; one
hour), but they often hang out endlessly for
a full complement of passengers. Mikrolet
turn off to Sumber Brantas at Jurangkuwali
village; for Air Panas Cangar continue two
km straight ahead. Cangar can be reached by
car, but public transport won't tackle the
twisting, dipping road.

Gunung Kawi

On Gunung Kawi (2551m), west of Malang
and 18 km north-west of Kepanjen, is the
tomb of a Muslim sage, Mbah Jugo, who
died in 1871. Also buried in the tomb is
Raden Imam Sujono, of Yogya's royal Hamengkubuwono family and grandson of
Diponegoro. From the parking area, a long
path leads up the slope past shops, souvenir
stalls and beggars. Before the tombs at the
top are a Chinese temple and the house of
Mbah Jugo, which attracts non-Muslim,
Chinese worshippers. Legend has it that the
saint will answer the prayers of fortune-
seeking pilgrims, and did so for one Chinese
couple that went on to form one of Indonesia's
biggest kretek companies.

Malam Jumat Legi in the Javanese calendar is the most propitious time, but pilgrims
visit Gunung Kawi throughout the year,
especially at night.

This strange cross-religious mountain
resort can be experienced on a day trip, or
there are plenty of basic penginapan and
restaurants if you want to stay the night.
Gunung Kawi can be reached by taking a
Blitar bus to Kromengan and then a colt to
Gunung Kawi.

South Coast Beaches

The coast south of Malang has some good
beaches, but facilities are limited. **Sendang-**

biru is a picturesque fishing village separated by a narrow channel from **Pulau Sempu**, an island nature reserve with a lake in the middle ringed by jungle.

A few km before Sendangbiru, a rough track to the left leads three km to **Tambakrejo**, a small fishing village with a sweeping sandy bay, which despite the surf is generally safe for swimming.

Balekambang is best known for its picturesque Hindu temple on the small island of Pulau Ismoyo, connected by a footbridge to the beach. This is Java's answer to Bali's Tanah Lot and was built by Balinese artisans in 1985 for the local Hindu communities. Accommodation is limited to the *Pesanggrahan Balekambang*, which has a few rough rooms for 17,000 rp per night. Balekambang is one of the most popular beaches and is crowded on weekends.

Ngliyep further west is a rocky beach and is also very popular. It has a *pesanggrahan* (government rest house) for basic accommodation.

Getting There & Away Minibuses from Malang's Gadang bus terminal go to Sendangbiru (2000 rp; two hours; 69 km), past the turn-off to Tambakrejo; otherwise take a bus to Turen and then another to Sendangbiru.

For Balekambang, first take a minibus to Bantur, and then another along the rough road to Balekambang, or take an ojek (2500 rp). Ngliyep is also reached via Bantur, from where you will usually have to take a bus to Donomulyo first and then another to Ngliyep.

Purwodadi

A few km north of Lawang, the **Kebun Raya Purwodadi** are big dry-climate botanical gardens, open daily from 7 am to 4 pm. The entrance is right on the main highway, and if you want more information and maps of the gardens, visit the garden offices to the south of the entrance. The **Air Terjun Cobanbaung** is a high waterfall next to the gardens.

BLITAR

Blitar is the usual base from which to visit Panataran. It's quite a pleasant country town

to stay in overnight, and is also of interest a the site of President Soekarno's grave.

Blitar is also the home of *ketok magi* (magic knocking), a mystical form of auto motive panel beating that has spread all ove Java and further afield. Leave your dente car at the workshop and behind locked door repairs are 'majikally' made by spiritua intervention, for a very reasonable price.

Information

Change money at the BNI bank at Jl Ker anga 9. The post office is next to the trai station. For international telephone call Telkom is at Jl A Yani 10 (the continuatio of Jl Merdeka), about one km east of th Hotel Lestari.

Makam Bung Karno

At Sentul, about two km north of the tow centre on the road to Panataran, an elabora monument now covers the spot wher former President Soekarno was buried i 1970. Soekarno is looked on by many as th 'father of his country', although he was onl reinstated as a national hero in 1978 by th present regime.

Soekarno was given a state funeral bu despite family requests that he be buried a his home in Bogor, the hero of Indonesia independence was buried as far as possibl from Jakarta in an unmarked grave next t his mother in Blitar. His father's grave wa also moved from Jakarta to Blitar. It was onl in 1978 that the lavish million-dollar monu ment was built over the grave and opened t visitors.

A becak from the town centre will co about 1500 rp, or take a Panataran angkude (yellow minibus) and get off at the rows o souvenir stalls. Entry, amazingly, is free.

Other Attractions

The house that Soekarno lived in as a bo functions as the **Museum Soekarno**. Photo and memorabilia line the front sitting room and you can see the great man's bedroom The house, still owned by relatives o Soekarno, though they now live in Jakarta

at Jl Sultan Agung 59, about 1.5 km from
the centre of town.

The **Museum Blitar**, on the north side of
the alun alun, houses some fine examples of
Hindu statuary removed from Panataran.

Blitar's large **Pasar Legi**, next to the bus
terminal, is also worth a look. In the north-
east corner a few stalls sell kris, woodcarvings
and bronze walking sticks.

Places to Stay & Eat
Blitar is a small compact town and the bus
terminal is very central. Right next to the bus
terminal, the *Hotel Santosa*, Jl Manur 2, is
convenient but no great shakes. Rooms cost
5000 rp or 16,000 rp with mandi.

The best hotel in town, and most popular
place to stay, is *Hotel Sri Lestari* (☎ 81766)
at Jl Merdeka 173, a few hundred metres
from the bus terminal. This good mid-range
hotel has a huge variety of rooms from 9000
to 98,000 rp. The hotel also has a good, if
slightly expensive, restaurant.

The *Hotel Sri Rejeki* (☎ 81770), Jl TGP
3, is cheaper and also worth considering. It
is another mid-range hotel with rooms to suit
most budgets.

Blitar has some good Chinese restaurants
on Jl Merdeka. The no-frills *Rumah Makan
Jaya* is at No 128, the larger *Rumah Makan
Karinah* is at No 170 and the fancier *Ramay-
na* is at No 65, east of the alun alun.

Getting There & Away
Buses from Blitar include: Malang (1800 rp;
two hours; 80 km); Kediri (1500 rp; 1½
hours); Madiun (3400 rp; four hours); Solo
(3300 rp; six hours); and Surabaya (3600 rp;
four hours).

Rosalia Indah (☎ 82149), Jl Mayang 45,
opposite the bus terminal, and Timbul Jaya
(☎ 82583), next door at No 47, have express
air-con minibuses to Solo and Yogya.

Angkudes run from the bus terminal to
Panataran for 750 rp and stop right outside
the temple. They also pass Makam Bung
Karno.

Several trains a day run from Blitar to
Malang; the best one is the *Pattas* express
train (3000 rp; two hours).

AROUND BLITAR
Panataran
The Hindu temples at Panataran are the
largest remaining Majapahit sanctuaries, and
perhaps the finest examples of East Javanese
architecture and sculpture. Construction
began around 1200 AD during the Singosari
dynasty but the temple complex took some
250 years to complete. Most of the important
surviving structures date from the great years
of the Majapahit during the 14th century and
are similar to many temples on Bali.

Around the base of the first level platform,
which would once have been a meeting
place, the comic-strip carvings tell the story
of a test between the fat meat-eating
Bubukshah and the thin vegetarian Gagang
Aking.

Further on is the small Dated Temple, so
called because of the date 1291 (1369 AD)
carved over the entrance. On the next level
are colossal serpents snaking endlessly
around the Naga Temple, which once housed
valuable sacred objects.

At the rear stands the Mother Temple – or
at least part of it, for the top of the temple has
been reconstructed alongside its three tiered
base. Followed anticlockwise, panels around
the base depict stories from the *Ramayana*.
The more realistic people of the Krishna
stories on the second tier of the base show an
interesting transition from almost two dimensional representation to three dimensional
figures.

Behind is a small royal mandi with a frieze
of lizards, bulls and dragons around its walls.

The temple complex is open from 7 am to
5 pm, and entry is by donation.

Getting There & Away Panataran is 16 km
from Blitar, and three km north of the village
of Nglegok. It is possible to see the Panataran
temples comfortably in a day from Malang –
and possibly from Surabaya.

PACITAN
On the south coast near the provincial border,
the village of Pacitan is three km from a large
bay ringed by rocky cliffs. Pacitan's beach,
Pantai Ria Teleng, is one of the best in East

Java, with fine views of the coastline and the hills surrounding Pacitan Bay. Swimming is possible when the seas are calm – the safest area is towards the fishing boats at the end of the bay. Apart from a few day trippers the beach is quiet, and you can wander further along the beach to find a deserted spot.

Information
The Bank Rakyat Indonesia will change US dollars cash and travellers cheques, as well as other currencies (cash only), but the rates are poor.

There is a wartel next to the Hotel Remaja, or the Telkom office is further west on Jl A Yani before the Hotel Remaja.

Places to Stay & Eat
The best place to stay is four km out of town at Pantai Ria Teleng. *Happy Bay Beach Bungalows* (☎ 81474), run by an Australian and his Indonesian wife, has attractive singles/doubles with bathroom for 15,000/20,000 rp, or private bungalows for 27,500 rp. Happy Bay is right opposite the beach, has a good restaurant, and you can rent bicycles or arrange a boat trip. A huge new hotel is planned for this beach, but hopefully it will be some time before it eventuates.

The beach is the main reason to come here, so there is not much point staying in town. Budget hotels in Pacitan are along Jl A Yani, the main street. The *Hotel Remaja* (☎ 81088) at No 67 is a cheap dive, or the *Hotel Pacitan* (☎ 81244) at No 37 is much better.

For food, the *Depot Makan Bu Jabar*, Jl H Samanhudi 3, a block behind the police station on Jl Yani, has excellent gado gado, nasi campur, fish and fruit juices.

Getting There & Away
Pacitan can be approached by bus from Solo (2600 rp; four hours), or along the scenic road to Ponorogo (1800 rp; 3½ hours), just south of Madiun. From Ponorogo, buses run to Surabaya via Madiun, and direct buses to Blitar (2600 rp; four hours) leave Ponorogo in the morning. Otherwise take a bus to Trenggalek and then another to Blitar. From Blitar to Malang take a colt or bus.

For Yogya, take a Solo bus to Baturetno (1200 rp; 1½ hours; 56 km) and then another to Yogya.

Pacitan's bus terminal is half a km from the centre of town on the road to Solo and the beach. When coming from Solo, buses can drop you at the turn-off to the beach. Happy Bay is a 500m walk or becak ride away.

AROUND PACITAN
Other isolated and undeveloped beaches accessible from Pacitan are Watu Karung (27 km) and Latiroco Lorok (41 km).

Just beyond Punung village, 30 km north-west of Pacitan, the **Gua Tabuhan** (Music Cave) is a huge limestone cavern said to have been a refuge for the 19th century guerilla leader Prince Diponegoro. Here you can listen to an excellent 'orchestral' performance, played by striking rocks against stalactites, each in perfect pitch and echoing pure gamelan melodies. You have to hire a guide and a lamp, and the concert lasts about 10 minutes. This is also agate country and there are lots of people at the cave selling very reasonably priced polished stones and rings.

To get to the cave, take a Solo bus to the turn-off, four km beyond Punung, and then an ojek (1000 rp) for the last four km to the cave.

MADIUN
On the Solo to Surabaya road, Madiun is a major travel hub in the western part of East Java. This unhurried city has some interesting colonial architecture and decaying steam locomotives in the rail yard for train buffs, but the real attractions lie outside the city.

AROUND MADIUN
In Ngawi, 33 km north-west of Madiun, the **Benteng Pendem** is an impressive Dutch fort (formerly the Benteng Van Den Bosch) built between 1839 and 1845.

In 1891 at **Trinil**, a Dutchman, Eugen Dubois, unearthed a skull of *Pithecanthropus erectus*, commonly known as Java Man. Dubois' discovery and his 'ape man' revelaons in support of Darwin's theory of evolu-on caused a furore in Europe. A museum isplaying fossils found in the area has been uilt at the site. The turn-off from the main ighway to Trinil is 11 km west of Ngawi nd then it's a further three km.

Ponorogo, 30 km south of Madiun, is amed as the home of the Reyog dance, in vhich gaily costumed performers enact the attle between a court official of Ponorogo nd the *singa barong*, the ruler of the forest. Combining elements of the horse trance ance, the Barong and possibly the Chinese ion dances, the Reyog is performed in 'onorogo's alun alun on 1 Suro (New Year) f the Javanese calendar, falling around May.

SURABAYA

'he capital of East Java, the industrial city f Surabaya is second only to Jakarta in size nd economic importance, and has a popula-on of over four million. For centuries it has een one of Java's most important trading orts, and it is also the main base for the ndonesian navy. Surabaya is a city on the nove, yet the narrow streets in the old part f the city, crowded with warehouses and ostling becaks, contrast strongly with the nodern buildings and shopping centres of he showpiece central city.

For most visitors, Surabaya is merely a ommercial centre or a transit point on the vay to or from Bali or Sulawesi. It has an nteresting old city and if you thrive on big ities, then teeming Surabaya is certainly vely, but otherwise its tourist attractions are ew.

Orientation

he centre of this sprawling city is the area round Jl Pemuda, which runs west from Gubeng train station past the tourist office, laza Surabaya and a number of big hotels nd banks. Jl Pemuda runs into Jl Tun-ungan/Basuki Rahmat, another main ommercial street where you'll find Tun-ungan Plaza. Most of the hotels are in this rea.

The old city is centred around the Jembatan Merah bridge and Kota train station to the

north. Further north is Tanjung Perak har-bour. Surabaya's zoo is five km south of the city centre, and the main bus terminal, Bun-gurasih, is just outside the city limits, 10 km south of the city centre.

Information

Tourist Office The tourist office (☎ 5324499) at Jl Pemuda 118 is open Monday to Satur-day from 9 am to 5 pm. You can get a few maps, some information on places to visit in the province and a regional calendar of events. The head office of the East Java Regional Tourist Office is at Jl Wisata Menanggal, south of the city centre, open government office hours only.

Foreign Consulates As Indonesia's second city, Surabaya has a number of foreign con-sular representatives, such as the USA, the Netherlands and France, but in general they handle only limited functions.

Money Surabaya has more than its fair share of extravagant bank real estate. Jl Pemuda has plenty – Bank Duta and BNI bank usually have good rates and accept credit cards. Jl Tunjungan also has a string of banks.

Post & Communications Surabaya's main post office and poste restante, on Jl Kebon Rojo, is four km north of the city centre.

For telephone calls, a convenient wartel open 24 hours is in the basement level of the Tunjungan Plaza.

Useful Organisations There is a French Cultural Centre (☎ 578639) at the French Consulate, Jl Darmokali 10-12, and a Goethe Institut (☎ 5343735) at Jl Taman Ade Irma Suryani Nasution 15. The British Council (☎ 589957) is at Jl Cokroaminoto 12A.

Other Services For supermarkets, book-shops and everyday shopping needs, Surabaya's huge malls – Plaza Surabaya, Tunjungan Plaza and Surabaya Mall – are well stocked.

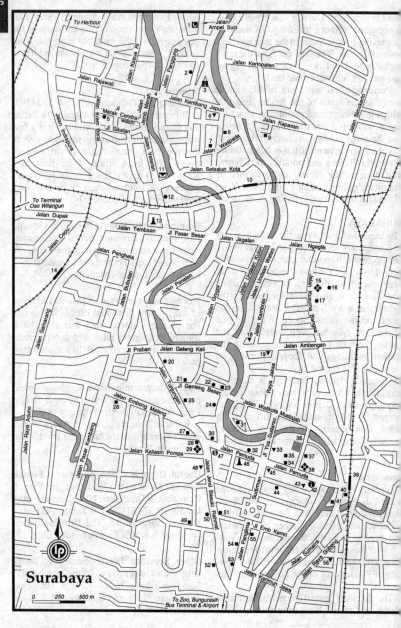

Surabaya

0   250   500 m

To Zoo, Bungurasih
Bus Terminal & Airport

PLACES TO STAY		54	Elmi Hotel	5	Gedung PTP XXII
7	Hotel Semut	55	Tanjung Hotel	10	Kota Train Station
8	Hotel Irian			11	Post Office
9	Hotel Ganefo		PLACES TO EAT	12	Pelni Office
21	Hotel Paviljoen	6	Kiet Wan Kie	13	Tugu Pahlawan
23	Weta Hotel	18	Soto Ambengan	14	Pasar Turi Train
25	Hotel Majapahit	19	Cafe Venezia		Station
26	Westin Hotel	33	Zangrandi Ice Cream	15	Surabaya Mall
27	Sheraton Hotel		Palace	16	TH Amusemen Park
28	Hotel Tunjungan	43	Turin	17	Taman Remaja
30	Natour Simpang	45	Granada Modern	20	Garuda Office
31	Bamboe Denn		Bakery	22	Genteng Market
34	Garden Palace Hotel	48	Galael Supermarket,	24	Andhika Plaza
35	Garden Hotel		KFC & Swensen's	29	Tunjungan Plaza
37	Radisson Plaza Suite	56	Kuningan Seafood	32	Governor's Residence
	Hotel			36	World Trade Centre
40	Sahid Surabaya Hotel		OTHER	38	Plaza Surabayaè
41	Hotel Gubeng	1	Mesjid Ampel	39	Gubeng Train Station
44	Hotel Remaja	2	Pasar Pabean	42	Tourist Office
49	Cendana Hotel	3	Kong Co Kong Tik	46	Joko Dolog
51	Ramayana Hotel		Cun Ong	47	Bank Duta
52	Hyatt Regency	4	Jembatan Mera	50	Minibus Agents
	Surabaya		Bridge	53	Bouraq Office

angers & Annoyances In most large
vanese cities it is hard to cross the street,
t it is almost impossible on Surabaya's big,
ur lane roads which have constant traffic
d few traffic lights or pedestrian bridges.
he only way to cross the street is to wait for
e traffic to subside (it never stops), head
t onto the road and motion with one hand
r the traffic to stop. Cross yourself in
ayer with the other hand.

d City
his is the most interesting part of Surabaya,
eit the grottiest. When the central busi-
ss district was cleaned up all the garbage
ust have been moved here, though recent
eps to improve the area have been taken and
me of the buildings have been renovated.

It was at the **Jembatan Merah** (Red
idge) that Brigadier Mallaby, chief of the
ritish forces, was killed in the lead up to the
oody battle of Surabaya for Indonesian
dependence. Some run-down but good
amples of **Dutch architecture** can be seen
re. Jl Jembatan Merah, running south of
e bus terminal along the canal, is a grungy
plica of Amsterdam. The area further south
ound the post office and Pelni office also
s some fine old buildings, though the most

impressive is the Gedung PTP XXII government office building just west of Jl Jembatan
Merah along Jl Cendrawasih. This superb
building is fashioned in the Indo-European
style.

To the east of the Jembatan Merah is Surabaya's **Chinatown**, where hundreds of small
businesses and warehouses ply their trade.
Becaks and hand-pulled carts are still the best
way to transport goods in the crowded, narrow
streets. **Pasar Pabean** on Jl Pabean is a
sprawling, dark market, where you can buy
everything from Madurese chickens to
Chinese crockery.

Further east, on Jl Dukuh near the canal,
Kong Co Kong Tik Cun Ong temple is
primarily Buddhist but has a variety of Con-
fucian and Taoist altars. On the full moon,
wayang performances are held here at 10 am
and in the evening.

The highlight of a visit to the old city is
the **Mesjid Ampel** in the heart of the Arab
Quarter. From the Chinese temple, proceed
north along Jl Nyamplungan and then take
the second left down Jl Sasak. A crowd of
becaks marks the way to the mosque. Through
the stone entrance is Jl Ampel Suci, a narrow,
covered bazaar lined with shops selling perfumes, sarongs, *pecis* (hats) and other

religious paraphernalia. Follow the pilgrims past the beggars to the mosque. This is the most sacred mosque in Surabaya, for it is here that Sunan Ampel, one of the wali songo who brought Islam to Java, was buried in 1481. Pilgrims chant and offer rose petal offerings at the grave around the back.

From the old city you can then head north to the **Kalimas harbour**, where brightly painted pinisi schooners from Sulawesi and Kalimantan unload their wares.

Surabaya Zoo

On Jl Diponegoro, four km south of Jl Pemuda, the Surabaya Zoo (Kebun Binatang) specialises in nocturnal animals, exotic birds and fish. The animals look just as bored as they do in any other zoo, but the park is quite well laid out, with large open enclosures, a great collection of pelicans and lively otters, and some rather dazed-looking Komodo dragons (a zoo keeper was beating one bedraggled, aged specimen into action for the onlookers when we were there last).

The zoo is open from 7 am to 4 pm. Entry costs 1500 rp. This park is popular with Surabayans, and outside there are warungs and a permanent gaggle of vendors selling drinks and peanuts for the monkeys. Sunday is the big day, and bands play in the afternoon. Any bus heading down Jl Panglima Sudirman will take you to the zoo.

MPU Tantular Museum

Across the road from the zoo, this small historical and archaeological museum has some interesting Majapahit artefacts, and is housed in a superb example of Dutch architecture. It is open from 8 am to 3 pm Tuesday to Thursday, until 2.30 pm Friday, 1 pm Saturday and 2 pm Sunday. The entry fee is 400 rp.

Other Attractions

On Jl Pemuda, across from the governor's residence, is the statue of **Joko Dolog** which dates from 1289 and commemorates King Kertanegara of Singosari. It's known as the 'fat boy'.

The **Taman Remaja** (Youth Park) has occasional dance, theatre and *srimulat* (E Javanese folk comedy) performances, wh next door the Taman Hiburan Rakyat (TH or People's Amusement Park) is Surabaya amusement centre after dark. The near Surabaya Mall shopping centre is usua much livelier, though on Thursday a Sunday evenings the transvestites come (and dangdut music is performed at Taman Remaja.

Places to Stay – bottom end

If you're staying in this busy port town – a many people do at least overnight he between Yogya and Bali – there's really on one very cheap place. The *Bamboe De* (☎ 5340333), Jl Ketabang Kali 6A, a minute walk from Gubeng train station, i Surabaya institution and has been the No travellers centre in Surabaya for over years. Beds in the large dorm are 5500 rp a a few, tiny singles/doubles are 6500/12,5 rp. It can be full in the peak tourist seaso but it will always rustle up a mattress on floor. You may well get roped into a lit English conversation with Indonesian st dents at the language school, which also ru from this youth hostel.

Apart from the Bamboe Denn, Suraba doesn't have a great choice of cheap, cent accommodation. Across the river from t Bamboe Denn on Jl Genteng Besar, t *Hotel Paviljoen* (☎ 5343449) is in an c colonial house at No 94. Renovated roor with mandi are of mid-range standard anc good deal at 27,500 rp, or 35,000 rp wi air-con, including breakfast. The hotel h style and the friendly owners speak Dutch well as English.

The *Hotel Gubeng* (☎ 5341603) at Sumatra 18 is close to the Gubeng tra station if you can't be bothered going ar further. Basic rooms cost 25,500 rp, 30,500 rp with mandi. The *Hotel Olympic*, Urip Sumaharjo 65-67, is decrepit but re sonably priced and close to the city cent (about 500m south of the Bouraq office Jl Panglima Sudirman). Rooms cost 15,00 20,000 rp without mandi, from 21,00 27,000 rp with mandi.

Well north of the town centre, near the
ota train station, *Hotel Ganefo* (☎ 364880),
Kapasan 169-171, is a spacious old hotel
th gigantic ceilings, stained glass, wood
nelling and old furniture. Very simple
oms don't match the lobby and cost 30,000
with shared mandi. Rooms in the new
ction with mandi, air-con, TV and phone
e 50,000 rp. In the same area, another hotel
th some colonial style is the *Hotel Irian*
☎ 20953), Jl Samudra 16, which has
oubles for 15,000 to 20,000 rp with shared
andi.

aces to Stay – middle

hile cheap places are hard to find, Sur-
aya has a wide selection of mid-range
commodation. A number of new two and
ree star hotels are cropping up and compe-
ion is fierce.

Conveniently located, and a good mid-
nge deal in expensive Surabaya, is *Hotel
maja* (☎ 5341359) on quiet little Jl
nbong Kenongo 12, not far from Jl Pemda. Immaculate singles/doubles with
r-con, TV and hot water cost 47,000/50,000
and 57,000/60,000 rp, plus 21% and
cluding breakfast.

Nearby, the *Tanjung Hotel* (☎ 5344032),
Panglima Sudirman 43-45, is a larger hotel
th a variety of rooms, most of which have
d a facelift. Rooms cost 77,000 to 115,000
.

The *Hotel Semut* (☎ 5324578), in the old
rt of town at Jl Samudra 9-15, dates from
e Art Deco era, and has good-sized rooms
cing large verandahs around a central
adrangle. Air-con rooms cost 46,000/
,400 rp up to 72,000 rp, plus 21%.

Surabaya has a number of good new three
ar hotels. The pick of them close to the city
ntre is the *Cendana Hotel* (☎ 5455333), Jl
ombes Pol M Doeryat 6. Well-appointed
oms with minibar cost 110,000/125,000 rp
ter discount. The *Weta Hotel* (☎ 519494),
Genteng Kali 3-11, is similar and costs
4,000/137,000 rp. The *Hotel Tunjungan*
☎ 5466666), Jl Tunjungan 102-104, costs
om 121,000 rp. It is right next to the
unjungan Plaza, but service is lacking.

Surabaya has a number of older three star
hotels all suffering from the competition and
offering discounted rooms for around
125,000 rp. *Natour Simpang* (☎ 5342151),
very central at Jl Pemuda 1-3, has a pool and
faded rooms. The *Sahid Surabaya Hotel*
(☎ 5322711), near the Gubeng train station
at Jl Sumatra 1, has better rooms but no pool.
The *Elmi Hotel* (☎ 5322571), Jl Panglima
Sudirman 42-44, has a fitness centre and a
rooftop swimming pool.

Places to Stay – top end

Surabaya has a glut of luxury hotels, and
more are being built. All hotels in this category have a 21% service charge and
government tax on top of the rates, but discounts from 30% to 50% are offered.

The *Garden Palace Hotel* (☎ 5321001) at
Jl Yos Sudarso 11 is an older four star hotel
with rooms from US$100/110. The adjoin-
ing *Garden Hotel* is its cheaper sister with
slightly run-down rooms from US$80/90.

A newer and better option nearby is the
Radisson Plaza Suite Hotel (☎ 516833), Jl
Pemuda 31-37. This smaller hotel is in an
excellent position. It has a pool (across the
carpark from the hotel), and a variety of
rooms and suites from US$170 to US$550.

The five star *Hyatt Regency Surabaya*
(☎ 5311234) at Jl Basuki Rahmat 124-128
has for long been one of Surabaya's best
hotels. Plush rooms start at US$170 and
suites start at US$375.

The central *Hotel Majapahit* (☎ 5454333)
at Jl Tunjungan 65 is a superb colonial hotel
with a fine garden. Built in 1910, it was
originally named the Oranje Hotel and bears
a striking resemblance to Schomberg's hotel
described in Joseph Conrad's *Victory*.
Recent renovations have restored it to one of
Surabaya's finest hotels. Rooms start at
US$225.

Of all the new hotels, the *Sheraton*
(☎ 546800), Jl Embong Malang 25, has a
great position adjoining the Tunjungan
Plaza, and superior rooms and service.
Rooms cost US$225/245 and the 'towers'
are even more luxurious.

All the other big chain hotels are represented in Surabaya, including the Hilton, Shangri-La, Novotel and Westin.

Places to Eat

For cheap eats, the Genteng Market on Jl Genteng Besar, just across the river from the Bamboe Denn, has good night warungs. Most other eats in the city centre are expensive and found in the shopping malls.

The ground floor of the Plaza Surabaya has the *Food Plaza*, with a range of restaurants serving Korean, Cantonese and Indonesian cuisine, and western fast food. The best deal is the *Food Bazaar* on the 4th floor, with a large variety of moderately priced stalls.

The Tunjungan Plaza is similarly well stocked with restaurants and fast food outlets, starting with a *McDonald's* and *KFC* on the ground floor. The 4th level has the *Mon Cheri* ice-cream parlour, the Chinese *New Singapore* or the cheaper *Es Teler 77*.

The Tunjungan Plaza is similarly well stocked with restaurants and fast food outlets, starting on the lower level with *McDonald's*, *Oh La La* for pastries and *Yashiki* for Japanese food. On the 4th floor *Mon Cheri* is a classy ice-cream parlour with a view, while the *New Singapore* has Chinese dishes and steamboats, or the cheaper *Es Teler 77* has Indonesian dishes. The 5th floor has a host of more expensive restaurants, including the *Tirtomoyo* for East Javanese dishes and *Winda Grill & Steak*.

At Jl Yos Sudarso 15, the *Zangrandi Ice Cream Palace* is an old establishment parlour favoured by wealthy Surabayans. Relax in planters chairs at low tables and somehow ignore the traffic noise. Another good place for ice cream is the *Turin* on Jl Embong Kenongo.

Kiet Wan Kie, Jl Kembang Jepun 51, is an air-con retreat from the Surabaya heat with dark but pleasant decor. This good Chinese restaurant has a varied menu.

For soto famed throughout the island, enjoy Pak Sadi's lemon grass and coriander Madurese chicken soup at *Soto Ambengan*, Jl Ambengan No 3A. Further down the street at No 16, *Cafe Venezia* is a very classy establishment in an old villa with a delightful

garden. Considering the setting, the pric are reasonable. Steaks cost around 10,000 and Japanese grills are also available.

There is plenty of money in Surabaya a plenty of upmarket restaurants to spend it Jl Raya Gubeng has a number of mo upscale possibilities, including *Kuning Seafood*, just off Jl Raya Gubeng at Kalimantan 14.

Entertainment

Surabaya Now! is a monthly giveaw tourist magazine with a good rundown on t latest venues.

Surabayans are big on discos. Popul places include the *Top Ten* and *Fire* Tunjungan Plaza, *Studio Etan* in Andhi Plaza, Jl Simpang Dukuh 38-40, and t huge *Calypso* in the Wijaya Shopping Cent on Jl Bubutan. Otherwise the big hotels ha a selection of bars and Surabaya gets son good bands. The *Tavern* at the Hya Regency is always popular, and *Desperado* at the Shangri-La Hotel, Jl May Jen Su gkono 120 (six km south-west of the ci centre), is a current favourite.

Surabaya's brothels are (in)famous, ar the most well-known of all is Dolly, a re light district named after its madam founde Bangurejo is another large red-light area, b less safe than Dolly.

Getting There & Away

Air Surabaya is an important hub for dome tic flights. There are direct flights to Jakar (227,000 rp), Denpasar (116,000 rp), Ba dung (183,000 rp), Yogyakarta (82,000 rp Solo (75,000 rp), Banjarmasin (171,000 rp Balikpapan (270,000 rp) and Ujung Pandar (257,000 rp), with numerous other connec tions.

Merpati (✆ 588111) is at Jl Raya Darm 111, south of the city centre. Garuda (✆ 534 5886) has offices at Jl Tunjungan 29, th Hyatt Regency Hotel and the Bank Du building on Jl Pemuda. Sempati has an offic in the Hyatt Regency (✆ 5321612), Tur jungan Plaza and elsewhere. Boura (✆ 42383) is at Jl Panglima Sudirman 7(

andala (☎ 578973) is at Jl Raya Dipo-goro 73.

us Most buses operate from Surabaya's ain Bungurasih bus terminal, 10 km south the city centre. Crowded Damri buses run tween the bus terminal and the city centre the P1 service from the bus terminal can op you at the Jl Tunjungan/Jl Pemuda tersection. A metered taxi costs around ,000 rp. Buses along the north coast and Semarang depart from the Terminal Oso ilangun, 10 km west of the city.

Normal/air-con buses from Bungurasih clude: Pandaan (1000 rp; one hour); Ma-ng (1800/3000 rp; two hours); Blitar 800/3600 rp; four hours); Probolinggo 100/3500 rp; two hours); Banyuwangi 500/11,500 rp; six hours); Bondowoso 000/8500 rp; 4½ hours); Solo (7000/ ,500 rp; 6½ hours); and Yogya (7500/ ,000 rp; eight hours). Buses also operate m Bungurasih bus terminal to Madura.

Luxury buses from Bungurasih also do the ng hauls to Solo, Yogya, Bandung, Bogor d further afield. Most are night buses aving in the late afternoon/evening. Book-gs can be made at Bungurasih bus terminal, travel agents in the city centre sell tickets th a fair mark up. The most convenient bus ents are those on Jl Basuki Rahmat. Inter-ty buses are not allowed to enter the city so u will have to go to Bungurasih to catch ur bus.

From Terminal Oso Wilangun buses go to rth coast destinations, such as Gresik (500), Tuban (2400 rp), Kudus (5500 rp) and marang (7000 rp; 13,000 rp air-con).

inibus Door-to-door travel minibuses pick at hotels, thus saving a long haul to the s terminal, but they are not always quicker cause it can take a long time to pick up a ll load of passengers in sprawling Surabaya. Minibuses run from Surabaya to all the ajor towns in East Java and to the rest of va and Bali. Destinations and sample fares clude: Malang (7500 rp); Batu (12,500); enpasar (30,000 rp); Solo (18,000 rp); gya (19,000 rp); and Semarang (20,000

rp). Hotels can make bookings and arrange pick-up, or a selection of agents can be found on Jl Basuki Rahmat, including Surya Jaya (☎ 5342463) at No 72 and Ratna (☎ 531-3672) at No 70.

Train Trains from Jakarta, taking the north-ern route via Semarang, arrive at the Pasar Turi train station. Trains taking the southern route via Yogya, and trains from Banyuwangi and Malang, arrive at Gubeng and most carry on to Kota. The Gubeng train station is much more convenient for central places than Kota or Pasar Turi stations.

The trip from Jakarta takes nine to 17 hours, although in practice the slower ekonomi trains can take even longer. Fares vary from 13,500 rp in ekonomi class, to 33,000 rp in bisnis up to 100,000 rp on the luxury *Argobromo*. The cheapest are the ekonomi services, like the *Gaya Baru Malam Utara* (12 hours) on the northern route or the *Gaya Baru Malam Selatan* (16 hours) on the southern route.

Trains to or from Solo (4½ to six hours) and Yogyakarta (5½ to seven hours) cost from 4500 rp in ekonomi, from 17,000 rp in bisnis. The train is faster and cheaper than the buses. The 8.45 am *Purbaya* and the faster 1.45 pm *Argopura* are good ekonomi services.

Apart from services to the main cities, there are six trains per day to Malang (two hours) and these continue on to Blitar. The *Mutiara* goes to Banyuwangi (4500/9000 rp ekonomi/bisnis; seven hours) at 8 am and 10 pm, or the ekonomi *Argopuro* departs at 2.10 pm.

Boat Surabaya is an important port and a major travel hub for ships to the other islands.

Popular Pelni connections are those to Sulawesi, with at least five Pelni ships doing the Surabaya-Ujung Pandang run, and to Kalimantan, with ships to Pontianak, Kumai, Banjarmasin, Balikpapan, Batu Licin and Sampit. See the Getting Around chapter earlier in this book for Pelni route details.

Ekonomi fares include: Ujung Pandang 65,000 rp; Lembar 40,000 rp; Banjarmasin 46,000 rp; and Balikpapan 103,000 rp.

The Pelni ticket office at Jl Pahlawan 112 is open Monday to Friday from 9 am to 3 pm, and on weekends, if there are ship departures, until noon. The front ticket counter can be chaotic but tourists often get preferential treatment. Boats depart from Tanjung Perak harbour – bus P1 or C will get you there.

Ferries to Kamal on Madura (550 rp; 30 minutes) leave every half hour, also from Tanjung Perak at the end of Jl Kalimas Baru.

Kalla Lines (☎ 335801), Jl Perak Timur 158, also has a passenger ship once every fortnight to Pasir Gudang, just outside Johor Bahru in Malaysia. The cost is 150,000 rp per person for the cheapest berth cabins, and the journey takes 60 hours.

Getting Around

The Airport Taxis from the Juanda airport (15 km) operate on a coupon system and cost 12,000 rp to the city centre. The Damri airport bus drops off in the central city and costs 2000 rp, but departures are not frequent. Going to the airport, buses can be caught in front of the Natour Simpang hotel on Jl Pemuda.

Bus Surabaya has an extensive Damri city bus network, with normal buses (costing 300 rp anywhere around town) and *patas* (express) buses (500 rp per journey). They can be very crowded, especially the normal buses, and are a hassle if you have a lot of luggage.

One of the most useful services is the *patas* P1 bus which runs from Bungurasih bus terminal past the zoo and into the city along Jl Basuki Rahmat. It then turns down Jl Embong Malang and continues on to the Pasar Turi train station, Pelni office and Tanjung Perak harbour. In the reverse direction, it runs to the zoo and Bungurasih bus terminal, and can be caught on Jl Tunjungan or at the bus stop in front of the Natour Simpang hotel on Jl Pemuda. The normal C buses also cover the same route.

Surabaya also has plenty of bemos labelled A, B, C etc, and all charge a standard 350 rp.

Taxi Surabaya has air-con metered taxi charging 1300 rp for the first km and 900 for the next km. Typical fares from centr Surabaya are: Pelni office 4500 rp; Tanju Perak harbour 8000 rp; zoo 5000 rp; Bamb Denn hotel to Gubeng train station 3500 r and Bungurasih 10,000 rp. Surabaya also h yellow *angguna* pick-ups that are no metered taxis and bargaining is required.

AROUND SURABAYA
Gresik

On the road to Semarang, 25 km from Su abaya, this port was once a major centre international trade and a major centre Islam in the 15th century. Close by, at Gi is the tomb of the first Sunan Giri, who regarded as one of the greatest of the ni wali songo. He was the founder of a line spiritual lords of Giri which lasted until was overwhelmed by Mataram in 168 According to some traditions, Sunan G played a leading role in the conquest Majapahit and ruled Java for 40 days after fall – to rid the country of pre-Islamic infl ences. Gresik also has a colourful **pini harbour**.

Pandaan

Pandaan is 40 km south of Surabaya on t road to Tretes. At **Candra Wilwatika Ar phitheatre** (☎ 31841) ballet performanc takes place once a month from June October. The varied programme usually co sists of dances based on indigenous tales a East Java's history. Seats cost 1500 rp. ' reach the amphitheatre take a bus from Su abaya, and then a Tretes-bound colt. Th theatre is one km from Pandaan, right on t main road to Tretes.

Also on the main road to Tretes, a few k from Pandaan before Pringen, **Candi Jawi** an early 14th century Hindu temple. Bas cally a Shivaite structure built to honor King Kertanegara, a Buddhist stupa was lat added on top.

Tretes

This hill town, standing at 800m on t slopes of gunungs Arjuna and Welirang, nowned for its cool climate and fine views. retes also has a reputation as a weekend d-light district. If you have to kill time in urabaya, it can be a pleasant enough place escape to but there's not a great deal to do. he **Kakek Bodo** (Stupid Grandfather), utuh Truno and **Alap-alap** waterfalls are earby, and there are a number of interesting alks around the town, including the trek to e Lalijiwo Plateau and Gunung Arjuna.

The **PPLH Environmental Education entre** (☎ 575884) is near **Trawas**, a few n north-west of Tretes. It has hiking/accomodation packages, mostly for groups, but terested volunteers are welcome and can ay in the dorm for 3000 rp and do self-ided rainforest walks. Take a bus to andaan, then a Trawas bemo (ask for PLH) and then take an ojek (2500 rp).

laces to Stay & Eat Accommodation in retes is overpriced, and haggling seems to ing only minor reductions. Most of Tretes' heap hotels, and many of the more expen-ve hotels, are little more than brothels. nattached males looking for a room to eep are considered an oddity. The best ace to stay is towards the top of the hill, d hotels lower down around Prigen are enerally cheaper. Cottages can be rented for nger stays.

On the main road near the Natour Bath otel, *Mess Garuda* is a reasonable place ith rooms for 15,000 rp during the week. he *Wisma Semeru Indah* (☎ 81701), Jl emeru 7, is below the main shopping area d has overpriced rooms from 32,000 rp.

The three star *Natour Bath Tretes Hotel* ☎ 81776), in a commanding position towards e top of the hill, is the 'old money' hotel ith some style and a good range of facili-es. Large, slightly run-down rooms cost S$60 and US$70, or the smaller, renovated ooms cost US$80. The other luxury hotel is e newer *Hotel Surya* (☎ 81991), a con-ete-and-glass upstart with a huge, heated ol, fitness centre, tennis courts etc, and od rooms from US$95.

For cheap eats, *Depot Abadi*, Jl Raya 27, pposite the Mess Garuda, has standard fare.

A line of mid-range restaurants can be found along the road from the Natour Bath Hotel, including the *Mandarin* for Chinese food and the *Istana Ayam Goreng* for chicken.

Getting There & Away From Surabaya take a bus to Pandaan (1200 rp) and then a minibus to Tretes (500 rp).

Gunung Arjuna-Lalijiwo Reserve

This reserve includes the dormant volcano Arjuna (3339m), the semi-active Gunung Welirang (3156m) and the Lalijiwo Plateau on the north slopes of Arjuna. Experienced and well-equipped hikers can walk from Tretes to Selekta in two days, but you need a guide if you're going all the way. Alternatively, you can just climb Welirang from Tretes.

The easiest access is from Tretes. A well-used hiking path, popular with students on weekends and holidays, begins in Tretes at the Kakak Bodo recreation reserve. Get information from the PHPA post at the entrance to the waterfall before heading off. It's a hard five hour, 17 km walk to the huts used by sulphur collectors, who collect slabs of sulphur from a crater on the side of Welirang.

It is usual to overnight at the huts – bring your own camping gear, food and drinking water, and be prepared for freezing conditions – in order to reach the summit before the clouds and mist roll in around mid-morning. From the huts it is a four km climb to the summit. Allow at least six hours in total for the ascent, 4½ hours for the descent. You can also rent horses – the asking rate is a steep 150,000 rp return.

The trail passes Lalijiwo Plateau, a superb alpine meadow, from where a trail leads to Gunung Arjuna, the more demanding peak. From Arjuna a trail leads down the southern side to Junggo, near Selekta and Batu. It is a five hour descent from Arjuna this way, but a guide is essential.

Gunung Penanggungan

The remains of no less than 81 temples are scattered over the slopes of Gunung Penanggungan (1650m), a sacred Hindu mountain said to be the peak of holy Mt Mahameru, which broke off and landed at its present site when the holy mountain was being transported from India to Indonesia.

This was an important pilgrimage site for Hindus. Pilgrims made their way to the top of the mountain and stopped to bathe in the holy springs adorned with Hindu statuary. The two main bathing places are **Jolotundo** and **Belahan**, the best examples of remaining Hindu art. Both are difficult to reach.

Between Pandaan and Gembol, a rough road leads west and then a turn-off leads south to Genengan village, four km away. From here an even rougher stone road leads two km up through the fields and villages to **Candi Belahan**. The bathing pool is presided over by Vishnu's consorts Sri and Lakshmi, who once flanked the magnificent statue of Airlangga-as-Vishnu, which now lies in the Trowulan Museum. From Lakshmi's cupped breasts (and with the aid of plastic tubing!), water spouts into the pool still used as a bathing spot by the villagers. From Belahan the road continues further up the hill, and the peak of Gunung Penanggungan lies six km away.

Candi Jolotundo is the bathing place on the western side of the mountain. Dating from the 10th century, it is set into the hillside like Belahan but many of its carved reliefs have been removed. It lies about six km south of Ngoro on the Gempol-Mojokerto road. Ojek hang around the turn-off and can take you to the temple along another bad road.

MADURA

Madura is a large and rugged island, about 160 km long by 35 km wide, and separated from Surabaya on the East Java coast by a narrow channel. It is famous for its bull races, the kerapan sapi, but also has a few historical sites, some passable beaches and an interesting, traditional culture. The sarong and peci is still the norm here, mall fever has not found its way to Madura and very few tourists go beyond a day trip to the bull races.

The people of Madura are familiar fac in East Java, particularly in Surabaya whe many have gone to look for work. Sin independence, Madura has been governed part of the province of East Java, but t island has had a long tradition of involv ment with its larger neighbour, Java, a with the Dutch. The Dutch were not int ested in the island itself, which was initia of little economic importance, but rather the crucial role the Madurese played Javanese dynastic politics.

Madurese men claim that the nar Madura is derived from *madu* (honey) a *dara* (girl), and Madura's 'sweet' girls a famed throughout Java for their sexu prowess. Madura is, however, a very trad tional and devoutly Islamic society. T Madurese are rugged *kasar* (unrefine people (according to the Javanese), and a said to be adept at wielding knives wh disputes arise. While the Madurese can disconcertingly blunt at times, and in remo areas you may attract a crowd of curio onlookers, they can also be extremely hos table.

The southern side of the island, facing Jav is shallow beach and cultivated lowlam while the northern coast alternates betwee rocky cliffs and beaches of great rolling sa dunes, the best of which is at Lombang. the extreme east is tidal marsh and vast trac of salt around Kalianget. The interior of th flat and arid island is riddled with limesto slopes, and is either rocky or sandy, so ag culture is limited. There are goat farm tobacco estates, some orchards and extensi stands of coconut palms, but the main indu tries of this dry, sunburnt land are cattle, sa and fishing.

History

In 1624 the island was conquered by Sulta Agung of Mataram and its governme united under one Madurese princely line, th Cakraningrats. Until the middle of the 18 century the Cakraningrat family fierce opposed Central Javanese rule and harass Mataram, often conquering large parts of th

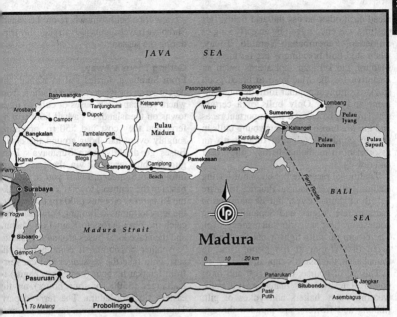

JAVA SEA

Pasongsongan • Slopeng •
Banyusangka • Ambunten •
Arosbaya • Tanjungbumi • Ketapang • Waru • Lombang •
Campor • Dupok • Sumenep • Pulau Iyang
Bangkalan • Tambalangan • Pulau Madura • Karduluk • Kalianget • Pulau Puteran • Pulau Sapudi
Konang • Prenduan •
Kamal • Blega • Camplong • Pamekasan •
Ferry • Sampang • Beach •
• Surabaya

BALI

To Yogya

Madura Strait

SEA

Siboarjo •
Gempol • Ferry Route

Madura

0   10   20 km

Pasuruan •
Panarukan • Jangkar •
Pasir Putih • Situbondo • Asembagus •
To Malang • Probolinggo

---

ingdom. Prince Raden Trunojoyo even managed to carry off the royal treasury of Mataram in 1677, which was restored only fter the Dutch intervened and stormed Trunojoyo's stronghold at Kediri. In 1705 he Dutch secured control of the eastern half f Madura following the conflict of the First avanese War of Succession between Amangkurat III and his uncle, Pangeran Puger. Dutch recognition of Puger was argely influenced by Cakraningrat II, the ord of West Madura. He probably supported Puger's claims simply because he hoped a ew war in Central Java would give the Madurese a chance to interfere but, while Amangkurat was arrested and exiled to Ceylon, Puger took the title of Pakubuwono and concluded a treaty with the Dutch which, along with large concessions on Java, granted them East Madura.

The Cakraningrats fared little better by agreeing to help the Dutch put down the rebellion in Central Java that broke out after

the Chinese massacre in 1740. Although Cakraningrat IV attempted to contest the issue, a treaty was eventually signed in 1743 in which Pakubuwono II ceded full sovereignty of Madura to the Dutch. Cakraningrat fled to Banjarmasin and took refuge on an English ship but was robbed, betrayed by the sultan and finally captured by the Dutch and exiled to the Cape of Good Hope (South Africa).

Under the Dutch, Madura continued as four states, each with its own bupati, or regent. Madura was initially important as a major source of colonial troops, but in the second half of the 19th century it acquired greater economic value as the main supplier of salt to Dutch-governed areas of the archipelago, where salt was a profitable monopoly of the colonial government.

Kerapan Sapi (Bull Races)

As the Madurese tell it, the tradition of bull races began long ago when plough teams raced each other across the arid fields; this pastime was encouraged by an early king of Sumenep, Panembahan Sumolo. Today, when stud bull breeding is big business on Madura, the kerapan sapi are as much an incentive for the Madurese to breed good stock as simply a popular form of entertainment and sport. Only bulls of a certain standard can be entered for important races and the Madurese keep their young bulls in superb condition, dosing them with an assortment of medicinal herbs, honey, beer and raw eggs.

Traditional races are put on in bull-racing stadiums all over Madura. Practice trials are held throughout the year, but the main season starts in late August and September when contests are held at district and regency level. The cream of bulls fight it out for the big prize in October at the grand final in Pamekasan, the island's capital.

This is, of course, the biggest and most colourful festival. As many as 100 bulls, wearing fancy halters and yokes of gilt, ribbons and flowers, are paraded through town and around the open field of the stadium to a loud fanfare of drums, flutes and gongs. For each race two pairs of bulls, stripped of their finery, are matched against each other with their 'jockeys' perched behind on wooden sleds. Gamelan is played to excite the bulls and then, after being given a generous tot of arak, they're released and charge flat out down the track – just as often plunging right into the seething crowds of spectators! The race is over in a flash – the best time recorded so far is nine seconds over the 100m, which is faster than the human world track record. After the elimination heats the victorious bulls are proudly trotted home to be used at stud.

Pamekasan is the main centre for bull races but they can also be seen in the other regency centres, Bangkalan, Sampang and Sumenep, and in the surrounding villages. The *East Java Calendar of Events*, available from the tourist office in Surabaya, has a general schedule for the main races, but if you are on Madura in the main season on a Saturday or Sunday, you can be sure that races will be held somewhere on the island Surabaya travel agents also arrange day trip during the season.

Getting There & Away

From Surabaya, ferries sail to Kamal, the port town on the western tip of Madura, from where you can catch buses or colts to othe towns on the island. It's a half hour trip by ferry and they cost just 550 rp, operating roughly every half hour around the clock Buses go directly from Surabaya's Bun gurasih bus terminal via the ferry righ through to Sumenep, but if you're alread based in the centre of town it's easier to tak the P1 express city bus (500 rp) or C bus to the ferry terminus at Tanjung Perak harbou catch the ferry across to Kamal on Madur and then take local buses around the island

Another possibility, if coming from th east, is to take the passenger and car ferr from Jangkar harbour (near Asembagus) to Kalianget (5500 rp; four hours) on th eastern tip of Madura. The ferry depart Thursday to Monday from Jangkar at 2 pm To get to Jangkar, catch any bus headin along the main highway between Banyu wangi and Situbondo, and get off at the Pasa Kambong in Asembagus. From the market countless becaks make the 4.5 km trip to Jangkar, or take an andong for 500 rp. To Jangkar, the ferry departs from Kalianget a 8 am. To Kalianget take an 'O' colt from Sumenep (500 rp; 11 km).

Getting Around

On arrival on the ferry from Surabaya, nego tiate what can be a wild melee to find a col to your destination. From Kamal, colts run along the main highway to Bangkalan (600 rp; half hour), Pamekasan (2500 rp; 2½ hours) and Sumenep (3500 rp; four hours) Otherwise pick up a through bus from Sur abaya, which are better than the colts.

From Surabaya's Bungurasih bus termi nal, at least a dozen buses a day go to Madura across the island to Sumenep (4600 rp, 7500 rp air-con) and most continue to Kalianget There are also direct buses to/from Banyu wangi via Probolinggo, Denpasar, Malang

Semarang and Jakarta. Colts are much more frequent and run all over the island but can spend a lot of time picking up passengers. Colts travel along the northern route to Arosbaya, Tanjungbumi, Pasongsongan and Ambunten.

To see something of the island, it's interesting to take a colt from Pamekasan inland through tobacco country to Waru, and another to Pasongsongan from where you can head back to Sumenep, via Ambunten and Slopeng.

Madura's roads are almost all paved and in excellent condition with relatively little traffic. As the island is mostly flat, Madura is a good cycling destination, though it does get very hot.

Bangkalan

This is the next town north of Kamal along the coast, and because it is so close to Surabaya many visitors only day trip for the bull races. The **Museum Cakraningrat** is a museum of Madurese history and culture, open from 8 am to 2 pm Monday to Saturday.

Places to Stay & Eat The *Hotel Ningrat* (☎ 3095388) at Jl Kahaji Muhammed Kholil 13, on the main road south of town, is one of Madura's best hotels. It is very clean and comfortable, but expensive for what you get. Small singles/doubles are 11,000/22,000 rp, better rooms with mandi are 22,000/33,000 rp. The much more attractive air-con rooms are decorated in traditional Madurese style and cost 49,600/71,500 rp.

Closer to the centre of town, *Hotel Melati* (☎ 3096457), Jl Majen Sungkono 48, is a basic place with rooms for 10,000 rp, or 15,000 rp with mandi. It is back from the street down an alleyway.

For good Chinese food, try the *Mirasa Restaurant* at Jl Trunojoyo 75A, near the police station.

Sampang

Sampang, 61 km from Bangkalan, is the centre of the regency of the same name and also stages bull races. It has a couple of hotels.

Camplong

Camplong, nine km further east, is a popular, if grungy, beach on the south coast and safe for swimming. The Pertamina storage tanks nearby do nothing for its visual appeal, but it is a breezy oasis from the hot interior of Madura. Impressive flotillas of twin-outrigger dugout canoes are used for fishing along the coast and the prahus carry huge, triangular striped sails.

Places to Stay At Camplong, the *Pondok Wisata Pantai Camplong* (☎ 21569) provides some of the best accommodation on Madura. Attractive cottages on the beach cost 25,000/28,500 rp to 50,000/55,000 rp.

Pamekasan

On the southern side of the island, 100 km east of Kamal, the capital of Madura is a quiet and pleasant enough town, although during October each year it comes alive with the festivities of the Kerapan Sapi Grand Final. Bull races are held in and around Pamekasan every Sunday from the end of July until the big day in early October. To see tulis batik being made, visit Batik Kristal, Jl Jokotole 29, across the road from the BCA bank.

About 35 km east of Pamekasan before Bluto, **Karduluk** is a wood carving centre that produces mostly cupboards.

Information The BCA bank, just east of the alun alun on Jl Jokotole, changes money and travellers cheques at good rates and gives cash advances on credit cards.

Places to Stay In the centre of town opposite the alun alun, *Hotel Garuda* (☎ 22589) at Jl Mesigit 1 has doubles with shared mandi at 4400 rp, and big, old rooms with mandi for 9900 rp up to 22,000 rp with air-con. It's good value but lacks atmosphere.

Nearby on the road to Bangkalan, *Hotel Trunojoyo* (☎ 22181), Jl Trunojoyo 48, is clean, quiet and better. Rooms cost 6000 rp, or 15,000 rp with mandi, and from 20,000 to 35,000 rp with air-con, including breakfast.

Hotel Ramayana (☎ 22406), Jl Niaga 55, is the best in town. A few small rooms with shared mandi cost 7500 rp, but most are bright rooms with mandi from 15,000 rp. Air-con rooms start at 30,000 rp.

Sumenep

At the eastern end of the island, Sumenep is Madura's most interesting town. It is centred around the kraton, mosque and market, and is considered to be the most halus (refined) area of Madura. This small, quiet, easygoing town makes a fine base to explore the island.

Sumenep's decaying villas with whitewashed walls, high ceilings and cool porches give the town a Mediterranean air, which is mixed with the Arabic influence typical of Java's north coast. Sumenep is also a champion bull breeding centre, and on most Saturday mornings practice bull races can be seen at the Giling stadium.

The Festival of Sumenep celebrates the founding of the town on 31 October every year with various celebrations and cultural performances.

Information The post office is on the road to Kalianget, and the Telkom office is further out past the Chinese temple. The BCA bank on Jl Trunojoyo is the best place to change money – the BNI bank changes cash at poor rates.

Things to See The **kraton** and its **taman sari** (pleasure garden) are worth visiting. It was built in 1750 by Panembahan Sumolo, son of Queen Raden Ayu Tirtonegoro and her spouse, Bendoro Saud, who was a commoner but a descendant of Muslim scholars. The architect is thought to have been the grandson of one of the first Chinese to settle in Sumenep after the Chinese massacre in Batavia. The kraton is occupied by the present bupati of Sumenep, but part of the building is a small museum with an interest

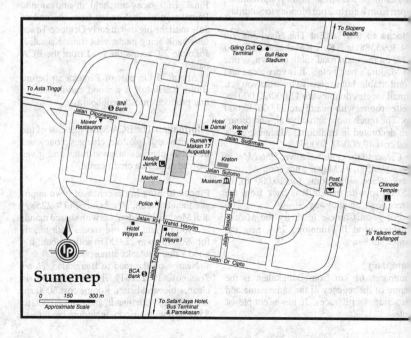

Sumenep

To Slopeng Beach

Giling Colt Terminal — Bull Race Stadium

To Asta Tinggi

Jalan Diponegoro
BNI Bank
Mawar Restaurant

Hotel Damai — Wartel

Rumah Makan 17 Augustus
Jalan Sudirman

Mesjid Jamik
Kraton
Jalan Sutomo
Market
Museum

Police ★

Post Office

Chinese Temple

Jalan KH Wahid Hasyim
Hotel Wijaya II — Hotel Wijaya I

Jalan Basuki Rahmat

Jalan Trunojoyo

To Telkom Office & Kalianget

Jalan Dr Cipto

BCA Bank

0   150   300 m
Approximate Scale

To Safari Jaya Hotel, Bus Terminal & Pamekasan

ng collection of royal possessions, including Madurese furniture, stone sculptures and *inggels*, the heavy silver anklets worn by Madurese women. Opposite the kraton, the royal carriage house museum contains the throne of Queen Tirtonegoro and a Chinese-style bed reputedly 300 years old. Entry is 00 rp to the museum, and from here you will e taken on a guided tour of the kraton. On the first and third Sunday of the month, traditional dance or gamelan practice is held t the kraton.

Sumenep's 18th century **Mesjid Jamik** mosque) is notable for its three tiered Meru-tyle roof, Chinese porcelain tiles and ceramics. Sumenep also has a **Chinese emple.**

The tombs of the royal family are at the **Asta Tinggi cemetery**, which looks out ver the town from a peaceful hilltop two km way. The main royal tombs are interesting, nd decorated with carved and painted anels, two depicting dragons said to represent the colonial invasion of Sumenep. The iggest mausoleum is that of Panembahan Notokusomo (1762-1811), but it is the grave f Tirtonegoro that attracts pilgrims from all ver Madura and Java. One of the small avilions in the outer courtyard still bears the nark of an assassin's sword from an unsuccessful attempt to murder Bendoro Saud.

laces to Stay & Eat The best place to head or is the *Hotel Wijaya I* (☎ 21433), Jl Truno-oyo 45-47. Good clean rooms cost 7000 and 000 rp without mandi, 10,000 and 12,000) with mandi, and air-con rooms cost 2,000 to 60,000 rp. The sister *Hotel Wijaya* ′ (☎ 62532) is also clean and well run. It is uieter, though many of the rooms are dark. 'oubles with common mandi start at 7000). Rooms with mandi are 14,000 rp and ange up to the air-con rooms with mandi, idge and TV for 40,000 rp.

The *Safari Jaya* (☎ 21989), on the south-rn outskirts of town at Jl Trunojoyo 90, is a ig hotel where rooms range from 6500 to 5,500 rp with air-con. It is also good value ut dull and a long way from town. The other ption is the basic and often 'full' *Hotel*

Damai on Jl Sudirman, where rooms cost 8000 rp.

Decent restaurants to try around town include the *Mawar* at Jl Diponegoro 105 and *Rumah Makan 17 Agustus* at Jl Sudirman 34, serving both budget Chinese and Indonesian cuisine. There are good day and night markets in the area around the mosque. The *Hotel Wijaya I* has a good restaurant and ice cold beer.

Things to Buy Sumenep is a centre for batik on Madura, though Madurese batik isn't as fine as that on Java. Try the market or you can visit home workshops around town.

The main business in town is antiques, but unfortunately the best antiques have been carted off by the truck load to Bali and Jakarta. Every second house seems to have something for sale.

Getting There & Away The main bus terminal is on the southern outskirts of town, a 1500 rp becak ride from the town centre. Buses leave roughly every 1½ hours between 6.30 am and 9.30 pm for Surabaya's Bungurasih bus terminal, and there are direct buses to Banyuwangi, Malang, Semarang, Jakarta and Denpasar. Travel minibuses run to Surabaya (7000 rp) and Jakarta – Karina is the main company and hotels can arrange pick-up.

The Giling bus stand for colts to the north is right near the bull-race stadium, 1.5 km from the market, or around 1000 rp by becak. From Giling, colts go to Lombang (1500 rp), Slopeng (1000 rp), Ambunten (1000 rp) and other north coast destinations.

Around Sumenep
From Sumenep, the road to **Kalianget**, 10 km south-east, passes many fine villas with frontages of thick, white Roman-style columns under overhanging red-tiled roofs. Kalianget is a centre for salt production, and from here you can take boats to the other islands of Sumenep district. You can go snorkelling at Pulau Talango just offshore, and the larger islands include Sapudi, Rass and Kangean, well to the east. The ferry from Kalianget to

Jangkar, on the mainland, runs every day except Wednesday and Sunday when it goes to Kangean.

Lombang Beach, 30 km north-east of Sumenep, is one of the best beaches on the island with a sweeping stretch of sand.

North Coast

Fishing villages and their brightly painted prahus dot the north coast. The coast is lined with sandy beaches, but Madura's beaches are not brilliant.

Near Arosbaya, 27 km north of Kamal, the tombs of the Cakraningrat royalty are at **Air Mata** cemetery, which is superbly situated on the edge of a small ravine overlooking a river valley. The ornately carved gunungan headstone on the grave of Ratu Ibu, consort of Cakraningrat I, is the most impressive and is on the highest terrace. The turn-off to Air Mata is shortly before Arosbaya and from the coast road it's a four-km walk inland. *Air mata* means 'tears'.

The village of **Tanjungbumi** is on the north-west coast of Madura, about 60 km from Kamal. Although primarily a fishing village, it's also a centre for the manufacture of traditional Madurese batik and Madurese prahus. On the outskirts is **Pantai Siring Kemuning** beach.

Pasongsongan, a fishing village on the beach, has a homestay run by the friendly Pak Taufik, though it has become run down. Further east, **Ambunten** is the largest village on the north coast and has a bustling market. Just over the bridge, you can walk along the picturesque river lined with prahus and through the fishing village to the beach.

Just outside Ambunten to the east, **Slopeng** has a wide beach with sand dunes, coconut palms and usually calm water for swimming, though the human excrement on the sand put us off the last time we were there. Men fish the shallower water with large cantilevered hand nets which are rarely seen elsewhere on Java. In Slopeng, Pak Supakra continues the tradition of topeng mask-making handed down by his father, Madura's most noted topeng craftsman. Slopeng has an expensive pesanggrahan, but

the beach is better off visited on a day trip from Sumenep, only 20 km away.

Lombang Beach, 30 km north-east of Sumenep, is touted as the best beach on Madura. It has a wide stretch of sand but it's nothing special.

TROWULAN

Trowulan was once the capital of the largest Hindu empire in Indonesian history. Founded by a Singosari prince, Wijaya, in 1294 it reached the height of its power under Hayam Wuruk (1350-89), who was guided by his powerful prime minister, Gajah Mada. During his time Majapahit claimed control over, or at least received tribute from, most of today's Indonesia and even parts of the Malay Peninsula. The capital was a grand affair, the kraton forming a miniature city within the city and surrounded by great fortified walls and watchtowers.

Its wealth was based both on the fertile rice-growing plains of Java and on control of the spice trade. The religion was a hybrid of Hinduism, with Shiva, Vishnu and Brahma being worshipped, although, as in the earlier Javanese kingdoms, Buddhism was also prominent. It seems Muslims too were tolerated and Koranic burial inscriptions, found on the site, suggest that there were Javanese Muslims within the royal court even in the 14th century when this Hindu-Buddhist state was at the height of its glory. The empire came to a sudden end in 1478 when the city fell to the north coast power of Demak and the Majapahit elite fled to Bali, thus opening up Java for conquest by the Muslims.

The remains of Majapahit are scattered over a large area around the small village of Trowulan, 12 km from Mojokerto. The Majapahit temples were mainly built from red clay bricks and did not stand the test of time. Many have been rebuilt and are fairly simple compared to some of Java's other ruins, but you can get an idea of what was once a great city. It's possible to walk around the sites in one day if you start early, but unless you have a strong interest in Majapahit history, this is a very hot way to see a few elatively simple archaeological remains. You really need a car, or hire a becak.

Trowulan Museum

A km from the main Surabaya-Solo road, the museum houses superb examples of Maja-pahit sculpture and pottery from throughout East Java. Pride of place is the splendid statue of Kediri's King Airlangga-as-Vishnu astride a huge Garuda, taken from Belahan. It should be your first port of call for an understanding of Trowulan and Majapahit history, and it includes descriptions of the other ancient ruins in East Java. The museum is open from 7 am to 4 pm; closed Monday and public holidays.

Ruins

Some of the most interesting sites include the **Colam Segaran** (a vast Majapahit swimming pool); the gateway of **Bajang Ratu**, with its strikingly sculptured kala heads; the **Tikus Temple** (Queen's Bath); and the **Siti Inggil Temple**, with the impressive tomb of Wijaya (people still come to meditate here and in the early evening it has quite a strange spiritual atmosphere). The **Pendopo Agung** is an open-air pavilion built by the Indonesian army. Two km south of the pavilion, the **Troloyo cemetery** is the site of the oldest Muslim graves found on Java, the earliest dating from 1376 AD.

Getting There & Away

Trowulan can be visited from Surabaya, which is 60 km to the east. Trowulan has a few restaurants on the highway but no accommodation. If you want to stay nearby, Mojokerto has plenty of cheap hotels.

From the Bungurasih bus terminal in Surabaya it's a one hour trip to Trowulan. Take a Jombang bus, which can drop you at the turn-off to the museum, or a Mojokerto bus which will stop at the bus terminal on the outskirts of town, then another bus or colt to Trowulan. A becak can be hired to get you round the sites.

When leaving Trowulan, flag a bus down on the road from Surabaya to Solo. Heading east to Probolinggo or south to Malang, take a bus or colt to Gempol and continue on from there by public bus, which is cheaper. For Malang, an interesting alternative is to travel by colt via Jombang and the hill town of Batu.

PROBOLINGGO

Probolinggo, on the Surabaya-Banyuwangi coastal road, is a transit centre for people visiting Gunung Bromo. It grows the finest mangos on Java, and its well-stocked fruit stalls are a delight, but otherwise Probolinggo is forgettable.

The main post office and most of the banks, including Bank Central Asia, and government buildings are on Jl Suroyo, which leads off the main street to the train station.

Places to Stay & Eat

Hotels and some cheap restaurants can be found along the main street, Jl Panglima Sudirman.

The *Hotel Bromo Permai* (☎ 22256), Jl Panglima Sudirman 237, is the most popular travellers' hotel, and has comfortable, clean rooms from 8700 to 29,000 rp with air-con. It is on the main road close to the centre of town at the eastern end. The *Hotel Ratna* (☎ 21597) further west at No 16 is one of the best hotels. Good economy rooms cost 8000 and 9000 rp, or rooms with bath range from 22,500 to 50,000 rp with air-con.

On the corner of Jl Panglima Sudirman at Jl Suroyo 1, the renovated but slightly expensive *Victoria Hotel* (☎ 21461) has rooms from 15,000 to 70,000 rp. Further down the street, the *Hotel Tampiarto Plaza* (☎ 21280), Jl Suroyo 16, is the best hotel in town, but only just. Comfortable rooms are from 11,000 to 110,000 rp, and there is a swimming pool.

Most of the hotels have restaurants and there are some good Chinese restaurants elsewhere in Probolinggo. The *Restaurant Malang*, Jl Panglima Sudirman 104, has a wide range of items on the menu and the food is good. You'll find plenty of small restaurants and 'depots' at the night market around Pasar Gotong Royong.

Getting There & Away

Bus Probolinggo's Bayuangga bus terminal is about five km out of town on the road to Gunung Bromo. Yellow angkutan run to/from the main street and the train station for 500 rp. The bus terminal is overrun with 'tourist office' bus agents offering dubious information and some charge outrageous prices for buses. The great Bromo shakedown begins here.

Normal/patas buses include: Surabaya (2100/3500 rp; two hours); Malang (2200/3800 rp; 2½ hours); Yogya (6500/15,000 rp; eight hours); and Banyuwangi (4400/7000 rp; five hours) via Situbondo. Fares for the deluxe night buses are higher, but shouldn't be too much higher. Coming from Bali, night buses cost around 20,000 rp and take eight hours; most departures are around 7.30 to 8.30 pm.

Gunung Bromo Bison minibuses from Probolinggo's Bayuangga bus terminal go to Cemoro Lawang (2500 rp; two hours) via Ngadisari (2000 rp; 1½ hours) until around 5 or 6 pm, as late as 9 pm in the main August tourist season. They sometimes cruise over to the train station in search of passengers, otherwise take a yellow bemo from the train to the bus terminal. To charter a jeep will cost 25,000 rp to Ngadisari, 30,000 rp to Cemoro Lawang.

Buses also run as far as Ngadisari only, but it is better to take the minibus if you are heading straight to Cemoro Lawang. Otherwise you may find yourself at the mercy of the Ngadisari jeep mafia – a jeep from Ngadisari to Cemoro Lawang should cost 1000 rp per person if there is a full load of passengers.

Travel agents in Solo and Yogya sell direct minibus tickets to Bromo for 25,000 rp, or 35,000 rp air-con. These usually stop at the Bromo Home Stay in Ngadisari, which has a deal with travel agents, and other hotels and bus agents won't book these minibuses. Two day/one night tours from Solo and Yogya

cost around 80,000 rp, or from Bali they cos from 100,000 rp.

Train The train station is about six km from the bus terminal. Probolinggo is on the Sur abaya-Banyuwangi train line. The *Argopur* and *Blambangan* are ekonomi trains and tak about two hours to Surabaya (2700 rp), or th *Mutiara* costs 6000 rp in bisnis. Th *Argopuro* continues on to Yogya for a long slow trip. To Banyuwangi takes about fiv hours and costs 2700 rp in ekonomi, but th buses are quicker and better.

GUNUNG BROMO & BROMO-TENGGER-SEMERU NATIONAL PARK

Gunung Bromo (2392m) is an active volcan lying at the center of the Tengger Massif spectacular volcanic landscape and one o the most impressive sights in Indonesia. Th massive Tengger crater stretches 10 kn across and its steep walls plunge down to vast, flat sea of lava sand. From the crate floor emerges the smoking peak of Gunun Bromo, the spiritual centre of the highlands This desolate landscape has a strange end-of-the-world feeling, particularly at sunrise, th favoured time to climb to the rim of Bromo' crater.

Bromo is the best known peak, and ofter the whole area is simply referred to as 'M Bromo', but it is only one of three mountain that have emerged within the caldera of the ancient Tengger volcano, and Bromo i flanked by the peaks of Batok (2440m) anc Kursi (2581m). Further south the whole super natural moonscape is overseen by Gunung Semeru (3676m), the highest mountain on Java and the most active volcano in these highlands. The whole area has been incorpo rated as the Bromo-Tengger-Semeru Nationa Park.

Legend has it that the great Tengger crate was dug out with just half a coconut shell by an ogre smitten with love for a princess When the king saw that the ogre might fulfi the task he had set, which was to be com pleted in a single night, he ordered his servants to pound rice and the cocks started

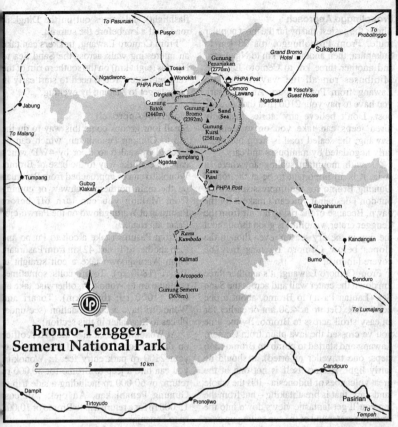

Bromo-Tengger-Semeru National Park

0   5   10 km

to crow, thinking dawn had broken. The coconut that the ogre flung away became Gunung Batok, and the trench became the Sand Sea – and the ogre died of exhaustion.

The Bromo area is also home to the Hindu Tengger people, who cultivate market vegetables on the steep mountain slopes and are found only on the high ranges of the Tengger-Semeru Massif. When the Majapahit Empire collapsed and its aristocracy fled to Bali to escape the tide of Islam on Java, the Tengger highlands provided a haven for Hindus left behind. Hinduism has in fact made a resurgence in the area, with growing cultural ties with Bali and the building of a Hindu temple near the base of Gunung Bromo.

Each year, Bromo is the site for the Kasada festival, with a colourful procession of Tenggerese who come to throw offerings into the crater at sunrise to pacify the god of the volcano.

Access is usually via Probolinggo, but Bromo can be approached from a number of routes. The ideal time to visit is during the dry season, April to November. At any time of year it's cold on these mountains and night temperatures can get down to around 2°C to 5°C.

Probolinggo Approach

This is the easiest and by far the most popular route. From Probolinggo, it's 28 km to Sukapura, then another 14 km to Ngadisari, and another three km to Cemoro Lawang. Minibuses run all the way to Cemoro Lawang from Probolinggo. At Ngadisari, you have to pay your 2100 rp at the entrance post. Don't believe any stories that only hired jeeps can take you on to Cemoro Lawang; the sealed road is steep but regularly negotiated by minibuses and cars.

As with mountain scaling anywhere in Asia, it is all important to be at the top of Gunung Bromo for the impressive sunrise, but don't despair if you can't make it for the dawn. Because of the rising hot air from the Tengger crater, visibility is good throughout the day in the dry season, even though the slopes below Cemoro Lawang may be covered in mist.

From Cemoro Lawang, it's another three km down the crater wall and across the Sand Sea (Lautan Pasir) to Bromo, about a one hour walk. Get up at 4.30 am or earlier for an easy stroll across to Bromo. By the time you've crossed the lava plain from Cemoro Lawang and started to climb up Bromo (246 steps, one traveller reported), it should be fairly light. Bromo itself is not one of the great volcanoes of Indonesia – it is the whole landscape that is breathtaking – but from the top you'll get fantastic views down into the smoking crater and of the sun sailing up over the outer crater. In the wet season the dawn and the clouds often arrive simultaneously, so at that time of year you might just as well stay in bed and stroll across later in the day.

From Cemoro Lawang, it is also possible to walk around the outer crater to **Gunung Penanjakan** (2770m), two hours on foot. This is where those picture postcards shots are taken, with Bromo in the foreground and Semeru smoking in the distance. Walk one hour (or charter a jeep) along the road to the 'Penanjakan II' viewpoint, itself a spectacular vantage point, but it's worth taking the walking trail behind this viewing area one hour more up to Penanjakan proper. The trail is fairly steep but easy to follow (bring a flashlight) and comes out on the Dingklik road, half a km before the summit.

From Cemoro Lawang, trekkers can take an interesting walk across the Sand Sea to Ngadas (eight km) on the southern rim of the Tengger crater. You'd need to start early in order to get to Malang by evening.

Wonokitri Approach

Small tour groups come this way to do the trip to Gunung Penanjakan, which can be reached by sealed road, or by 4WD which can drive all the way to the base of Bromo. Wonokitri can be approached from Pasuruan on the main northern highway, or coming from Malang you can turn off before Pasuruan at Warungdowo on the Purworejo-Pasuruan road.

From Pasuruan take a colt to Puspo and then another to Tosari, 42 km from Pasuruan. From Warungdowo take a colt straight to Tosari (1800 rp). Tosari colts sometimes continue on to Wonokitri, otherwise take an ojek (1000 rp; three km). Tosari and Wonokitri have accommodation (see under Places to Stay later in this section).

At Wonokitri check in at the PHPA office on the southern outskirts of town and pay your 2100 rp park entry fee. In Wonokitri you can hire a jeep to Bromo for 50,000 rp return, or 60,000 rp including a side trip to Gunung Penanjakan. An ojek will cost 15,000 rp for a return trip to Bromo or 10,000 rp to Penanjakan.

From Wonokitri, it is five km along a good road to Dingklik. The views from Dingklik, right on the edge of the outer crater, are superb. From Dingklik the road forks – down to Bromo or four km up along the paved road to Gunung Penanjakan for even better views. From Penanjakan a walking trail leads to Cemoro Lawang.

The paved road from Dingklik six km down to the Sand Sea is hair-raisingly steep. From the bottom it is then three km across the sand to Bromo.

Ngadas Approach

It is also possible to trek into the Tengger crater from Ngadas to the south-west of

Gunung Bromo, although it is more often done in the reverse direction as a trek out from Bromo or as an approach to climbing Gunung Semeru. This is definitely a trek for those willing and able to rough it a bit, but is very rewarding.

From Malang take a mikrolet to Tumpang, or from Surabaya take a bus to Blimbing, just north of Malang, then a mikrolet to Tumpang. From Tumpang take another mikrolet to Gubug Klakah from where you walk 12 km to Ngadas. From Ngadas it is two km to Jemplang at the crater rim, and then three hours on foot (12 km) across the floor of the Tengger crater to Gunung Bromo and on to Cemoro Lawang. From Jemplang, you can also branch off south for the Gunung Semeru climb.

Lumajang Approach

This route to Bromo is rarely used by travellers but is an alternative from the south-east. From Lumajang take a mikrolet to Senduro (500 rp; 18 km). From here you have to charter an ojek (10,000 rp) to Ranu Pani (25 km) via Burno, from where you can walk to Bromo (14 km) or Gunung Semeru.

Climbing Gunung Semeru

Part of the huge Tengger Massif, Gunung Semeru is the highest mountain on Java at 3676m. Also known as Mahameru, the Great Mountain, it has been looked on by Hindus since time immemorial as the most sacred mountain of all and father of Gunung Agung on Bali. It is a rugged three day trek to the summit, and you must be well equipped and prepared for camping overnight. Nights on the mountain are freezing and inexperienced climbers have died of exposure. The best time to make the climb is May to October.

Hikers usually come through Tumpang, from where you can charter jeeps to Ranu Pani, the start of the trek, otherwise take a mikrolet from Tampang to Gubuk Klakah and walk 12 km to Ngadas, and then on to Jemplang. It is also possible to cross the Tengger Sand Sea from Gunung Bromo (12 km) to Jemplang, two km from Ngadas at the Tengger crater rim. From Jemplang, the road

skirts around the crater rim before heading south to Ranu Pani (six km; 1½ hours on foot).

Ranu Pani is a lake with a small village nearby. Pak Tasrep runs a homestay and the warung serves basic meals. He can help organise a climb of Gunung Semeru, and you can rent a sleeping bag and other equipment. Ranu Pani is the usual overnight rest spot, and the Ranu Pani PHPA post is a few hundred metres past the lake. You can also stay here – accommodation is limited and Ranu Pani can be crowded with climbers. Register here and obtain advice on the climb. It can also help arrange guides.

The next day it is a couple of km from the PHPA post to the shelter at the end of the road. Jeeps and motorcycles can make it this far. From here the trail climbs to the beautiful Ranu Kumbolo crater lake (2400m), 13 km or about three hours away. Just past the lake is another shelter and the trail from here climbs to Kalimati (three hours) at the foot of the mountain. From Kalimati it is a steep one hour climb to Arcopodo, where there is a campsite for the second night on the mountain.

The next day from Arcopodo the fun begins. It is a short steep climb to the start of the volcanic sands, the result of Semeru's eruption, and then a struggling three hour climb through loose scree to the peak. Semeru explodes every half hour and sends billowing smoke upwards. The gases and belching lava make Semeru dangerous – stay well away from the vent. From the top on a clear day, there are breathtaking views of Java's north and south coasts, as well as Bali. To see the sunrise it is necessary to start at 2 am for the summit. It is possible to make it back to Ranu Pani on the same day.

Places to Stay & Eat

Sukapura The plush *Hotel Raya Bromo* (☎ 711802) is a few km up the mountain from Sukapura village and a full nine km from the crater. If you want luxury accommodation and have a car this may be your place, otherwise it is too far from the crater to be convenient. Rooms cost US$47 to US$82, or cottages start at US$130, plus

21%. The hostel section next door has large but barren rooms with three beds for 30,000 rp.

Ngadisari From Probolinggo, it's 42 km to Ngadisari, where *Yoschi's Guest House* (☎ 23387), just outside Ngadisari village, is an excellent place to stay. This attractive, friendly inn has singles from 6000 rp, doubles from 7000 to 17,500 rp and comfortable family cottages. It has a great restaurant, and offers tours and cheap transport to Bromo.

A short walk away, the *Bromo Home Stay* (☎ 23484) has rooms with mandi from 15,000 rp, but it caters primarily to the cheap tour operators from Yogya and elsewhere.

Cemoro Lawang Three km from Ngadisari at the lip of the Tengger crater, Cemoro Lawang is right at the start of the walk to Bromo and so is the most popular place to stay.

Cafe Lava Hostel (☎ 23458) is the popular travellers' place. Singles/doubles cost 6000/8000 rp or a dorm bed is 4000 rp. Rooms and shared mandis are very basic, but the hostel is cheap, convivial and has a good restaurant. Its fancier offshoot *Lava View Lodge* is along a side road from the bus terminal and right at the edge of the crater with great views and good rooms with bathroom for 15,000/20,000 rp.

One hundred metres past the Cafe Lava, the *Hotel Bromo Permai I* (☎ 23459) is the fanciest hotel. Rooms with shared mandi cost from 13,500 rp, and with attached bathroom and hot water from 46,500 to 88,500 rp. It has a restaurant and bar.

The *Cemara Indah Hotel* (☎ 23457) is also on the lip of the crater with fantastic views and an excellent, airy restaurant. The large dormitory costs 4000 rp and very spartan rooms are 7000/10,000 rp. Comfortable rooms with bathroom and hot water cost 37,500 and 50,000 rp.

Tosari & Wonokitri The *Bromo Cottages* (☎ Surabaya 336888) in Tosari are perched on the hillside with fine mountain views.

Singles/doubles cost an inflated US$65/70 plus 21%, and expensive meals are available

Wonokitri village has very simple, overpriced homestay accommodation. The going rate is 30,000 rp per night, which includes all meals, but this is very expensive for what you get. It is best to negotiate for a room only, and eat at the couple of basic warungs in town.

Getting There & Away

Most visitors come through Probolinggo (see under Probolinggo earlier in this chapter for transport details). Hotels in Cemoro Lawang and Ngadisari can make bookings for onward bus tickets from Probolinggo for a slight premium.

For Ngadas, frequent mikrolet go to Tumpang from Malang (600 rp). From Tumpang irregular minibuses go to Ngadas, where jeeps go to Ranu Pani for 2500 rp per person. Jeeps can be chartered in Tumpang or Ngadas for high rates. From Tumpang you can even charter a jeep to Bromo for 100,000 rp but this is a long journey there and back.

Bromo tours are easily arranged in Malang, and you can also arrange jeep hire in hotels and travel agents there.

PASIR PUTIH

Roughly halfway between Probolinggo and Banyuwangi, on the north coast road, this is East Java's most popular seaside resort and is mobbed on weekends by sun'n'sand worshippers from Surabaya. It has picturesque outrigger boats and safe swimming, but its name (*pasir putih* means 'white sand') is a misnomer – the sand is more grey-black than white. This quite ordinary beach would make a pleasant enough stopover if the accommodation was better.

Places to Stay

Pasir Putih's hotels, sandwiched between the beach and the noisy main road, are dirty and overpriced. *Hotel Bhayangkara* (☎ 91083) is the cheapest. Dirty, stuffy rooms start at 7000 rp, or dirty, larger rooms with mandi cost 17,500 to 28,000 rp, more for air-con.

The *Pasir Putih Inn* (☎ 91522) is only

slightly better and has singles/doubles with mandi from 12,500/16,000 rp. The *Mutiara Beach Hotel* is similar and has rooms from 15,000 rp.

The *Hotel Sido Muncul* (☎ 91352) is the best hotel – at least it is clean. Rooms with fan and mandi facing the road cost 15,000 rp, or 25,000 to 60,000 rp for those facing the beach.

BONDOWOSO

Bondowoso, 34 km south-west of Situbondo, is one of the cleanest towns on Java, in itself an attraction, but otherwise it is merely a transit point for nearby attractions such as Ijen.

Hotel Anugerah, Jl Sutoyo 12, is a very good cheap hotel, or the *Palm Hotel*, Jl A Yani 32, is the best in town and also exceptional value.

On weekends in **Tapen**, 15 km from Bondowoso towards Situbondo, traditional Madurese horn-locking bullfights (*aduan sapi*) are held.

Getting There & Away

Buses from Bondowoso include: Situbondo (1000 rp; one hour); Jember (750 rp; 45 minutes); Probolinggo (2000 rp; two hours); and Surabaya (4000/7500 rp patas; 4½ hours). For Tapen take any Situbondo bound bus.

JEMBER

Jember is the thriving service centre for the surrounding coffee, cacao, rubber, cotton and tobacco plantations. It has all the amenities of a large city, but is relatively uncongested and competes with Bondowoso for the tidy town award.

From Jember groups can arrange a plantation tour, though Kalibaru is the usual centre for plantation visits. PT Perkubunan XXVI (☎ 21061), Jl Gajah Mada 249, is the state-owned company that controls most of the plantations; it has day or overnight tours with accommodation on the plantations.

The *Hotel Widodo*, Jl Letjen Suprapto 74, about one km south of the town centre, is a good cheap hotel and on the ball with travel information.

Getting There & Away

The main bus terminal, Tawung Alun, six km west of town, has buses to Probolinggo, Surabaya, Malang, Bondowoso, Banyuwangi and Kalibaru, but buses from Bondowoso usually terminate at the sub-terminal, five km north of town, and there are also sub-terminals to the east (for Banyuwangi) and south (for Watu Ulo). Damri city buses and yellow Lin bemos run from the terminals to the centre of town.

Jember is also on the Surabaya-Banyuwangi train line and the station is close to the centre of town.

WATU ULO & PAPUMA

Watu Ulo is a popular weekend resort, but like most of the beaches on Java's south coast, it has grey sands and crashing surf with dangerous swimming. The real surprise lies just west around the headland from Watu Ulo. Papuma is a small beach with white sand, turquoise waters and sheltered swimming. Further around from Papuma, the rugged coastline with spectacular rocky outcrops is again pounded by the surf, but deserted patches of white sand can be found for sunbathing. Nearby **caves** and the **Wana Wisata Londolapesan** forest area can also be explored.

At Watu Ulo, the *Hotel Vishnu* has basic rooms with mandi for 18,000 rp.

Getting There & Away

In Jember, take a city bemo (350 rp) to the Ajung sub-terminal and then a colt to Ambulu (800 rp; 25 km). From Ambulu yellow bemos go to Watu Ulo (400 rp; 12 km). Papuma is then a half hour walk along the paved road over the steep headland.

KALIBARU

The picturesque road from Jember to Banyuwangi winds around the foothills of Gunung Raung (3322m) up to the small hill town of Kalibaru. It has a refreshingly cool climate and makes a pleasant stop on this route. The village itself is unremarkable – the attraction here is the chance to visit nearby plantations around **Glenmore**, 10 km east. Java's finest coffee, both *arabica* and *robusta* varieties, is produced in the Ijen Plateau area, as well as cacao, cloves and rubber. In Kalibaru town, to the north of the train station, are smaller, easily visited plots of coffee and cloves.

Places to Stay & Eat

The only cheap hotel is the *Losmen Darmo*, on the main road at the eastern end of town, but it is a brothel first and a hotel second. If you are desperate, dirty rooms with mandi cost 7500 rp.

Undoubtedly, the best hotel is the delightful *Margo Utomo* (✆ 97123), an old Dutch inn that has maintained its colonial feel. It has new, colonial-style cottages with private balconies built around a pretty garden. Cottages cost US$19/25, including breakfast, and all-you-can-eat meals cost 8000 rp for lunch or 10,000 rp for dinner. Plantation tours and a host of fairly expensive tours to Ijen, Alas Purwo, Sukamade etc are arranged. It also has a new hotel outside of town with comfortable bungalows by the river.

The *Raung View Hotel* (✆ 97314) looks very flash and is comfortable but the rooms from 40,000 rp are quite simple. *Kalibaru Cottages* (✆ 97333) has a swimming pool and all conveniences for US$46/60.

Getting There & Away

Any bus between Jember (1500 rp; one hour) and Banyuwangi (1600 rp; two hours) can drop you near the hotels. The train station is right near the Margo Utomo, and a scenic ekonomi service runs from Kalibaru to Banyuwangi (1100 rp; 2½ hours).

MERU BETIRI NATIONAL PARK

Covering 580 sq km, the Meru Betiri National Park is on the south coast and lies between Jember and Banyuwangi districts. It receives few visitors because access is difficult.

The major attraction is the protected **Sukamade** (Turtle Beach), a three km sand strip where four species of turtle come ashore to lay their eggs. Green turtles are common but the giant leatherbacks have also been reported.

In the mountain forests there are wild pigs, muncaks, squirrels, civets, jungle cats and some leopards; the silvered-leaf monkey and long-tailed macaque are common. Meru Betiri is also said to be the last home of the Javan tiger but chances are it is already extinct.

The reserve contains pockets of rainforest and the area is unusually wet for much of the year. The best time to visit is the dry season from April to October; at other time access can be very difficult because of the condition of the road.

The area has some fine coastal scenery both in the park and along the coast on the approach to the park. **Lampon**, just south of Pesanggaran, is a passable beach that is popular on weekends. **Pancer**, on a sweeping bay, has a fine beach with good swimming and a small island, **Pulau Merah**, at one end. The Hindu community here has a temple and makes offerings at the island. The now rebuilt Pancer was obliterated by the 1994 tsunami with appalling loss of life. At **Rajegwesi**, at the entrance to the park, is a large bay with a beach, though further into the park one of the prettiest spots on the coast is **Teluk Ijo** (Green Bay). The walk between Sukamade and Green Bay makes a good day trip.

Places to Stay

About four km from the beach, *Wisma Sukamade* has very basic accommodation for 11,000 rp per person, plus meals. Visitors can tour the plantations, which include coffee, cacao, coconut and rubber. You can also stay at the PHPA post at Rajegwesi, with food available by arrangement.

Outside the park, the nearest hotels are in Jajag if you get stuck. *Hotel Widodo*, Jl Sudirman 124, is basic but cheap. *Hotel Baru Indah*, right near the bus terminal, has excellent rooms with mandi from 9000 to 25,000 rp, but the nocturnal liaisons can be very noisy. The flash *Hotel Surya* (✆ 94126) has a swimming pool and rooms from 18,000 rp.

Getting There & Away

This is one of the most isolated parts of Java, and it is a long bumpy trip, even by 4WD which is how most visitors travel to the park. By public transport take a bus first to Jajag (south of the highway) from Jember (4000 rp air-con; two hours) or Banyuwangi (1000 rp; one hour). Then take a minibus to Pesanggaran (500 rp; 22 km), or the Minto Putrajaya bus runs direct from Banyuwangi (1500 rp; two hours). From Pesanggaran the road gets progressively worse and the pot holes larger. A morning *taksi* (the confusing name for a public minibus in these parts) leaves Sukamade for Pesanggaran (2500 rp; 2½ hours; 41 km) at 6 am, returning mid-morning. Otherwise trucks also go to Sukamade and cost the same.

An even rougher road to Sukamade runs from Glenmore, but only 4WD vehicles can make the trip and it is quicker to go via Jajag.

ALAS PURWO NATIONAL PARK

Also known as Blambangan, this national park occupies the whole of the remote Blambangan Peninsula at the south-eastern tip of Java. This is perhaps the last area in Indonesia where the fast-dwindling species of Indonesian wild dog (*ajak*, a subspecies of the Indian dhole) still exists in any numbers. The reserve is also noted for its turtle-nesting beaches which, sadly, are often raided by Balinese turtle hunters for grey and green turtles. There are jungle fowl, leaf monkeys, muncaks, rusa deer, leopards and wild pigs.

Entry to the park is via Kendalrejo, where you register at the PHPA office and proceed to Rowobendo (10 km) and then Trianggulasi (two km), a village within the park that has accommodation. Using Trianggulasi as a base it is a three km walk north-east to the viewing tower at **Sadengan**, where wildlife to spot includes banteng, ajak, rusa (deer) and merak (peacocks). From Rowobendo it is an eight km trek to **Ngagelan**, a turtle spawning beach. **Goa Padepokan** cave is inland from the camping ground at Pancur, three km south of Trianggulasi.

Continuing 12 km along the coast from

Pancur, a rugged walking track leads around Grajagan Bay and along some fine beaches to **Plengkung**, otherwise known as Grajagan, or 'G-Land' to the surfing fraternity. The waves at Plengkung have reached legendary proportions among surfers who are willing to pay for the boat tours to Grajagan that operate out of Bali. The beach is superb, but it is the left-hand reef break that has made it world famous among surfers. The Quicksilver Pro surfing championship is held every year at Plengkung around June and is part of the ASP world championships.

Accommodation is in bamboo huts, and controlled access is limited to organised tours – try travel agents in Kuta Beach, or Alam Hayati (☎ 21485), Jl Jenderal Basuki Rachmat, Banyuwangi. Some surfers experienced the terrifying ride of their lives when the 1994 tsunami hit the camp in the middle of the night, carrying huts and surfers 60m back into the jungle.

Places to Stay

The PHPA's *Penginapan Trianggulasi* in Trianggulasi has accommodation in basic rooms for 6000 rp. The surf camp at Plengkung is for tours only. There is also a camping ground at Pancur.

Getting There & Away

From Banyuwangi's Karang Ente bus station, the Purwo Indah company has five taksi (public minibuses) to Kalipahit (1800 rp; 1.5 hours) via Tegaldelimo until mid-afternoon. From Kalipahit occasional trucks battle the bad road to Trianggulasi. Alternatively, take an ojek from Kalipahit to Kendalrejo PHPA (1000 rp) and the rangers can provide transport to Trianggulasi for a small donation.

If coming from Jember, take a bus to Jajag and another to Benculuk (300 rp), from where buses go to Tegaldelimo and Kalipahit or to the town of Grajagan on the northern end of Grajagan Bay. From Grajagan, you can rent a fishing boat or a speedboat to Plengkung. Tours come this way, but this is a very expensive way to reach the park.

BANYUWANGI

Although there are no particular attractions to drag you here, schedules or just the urge to be somewhere different might take you to Banyuwangi, the ferry departure point for Bali. The ferry terminus, main bus terminal and train station are all at Ketapang, eight km north of town, so everyone goes straight though to Gunung Bromo, Yogya or elsewhere. While Bali is teeming with tourists, Banyuwangi, just a stone's throw away, is a quiet, neglected backwater.

Information

The Banyuwangi Tourist Office, Jl Diponegoro 2, is at the cultural centre/sports field. A helpful branch at the LCM Ferry building in Ketapang is open every day from 8 am to 7 pm.

The post office is opposite the tourist office. Change money at the BCA bank on Jl Sudirman.

For information on the national parks and accommodation bookings, the PHPA office (☎ 241119) is at Jl A Yani 108, about two km south of the town centre.

Things to See

The main reason to stay here is to overnight on the way to Kawah Ijen, or the national parks to the south. If you are desperate for something to do, the **Museum Daerah Blambangan**, opposite the alun alun on Jl Sritanjung, has a small collection of artefacts. In **Desa Temenggungan**, the kampung just behind the museum, Banyuwangi-style batik, *gajah oleng*, is produced. Ask around to see it being made. The town's market, **Pasar Banyuwangi**, with its crowded, narrow alleyways, is also worth a look.

Places to Stay

The *Hotel Baru* (☎ 21369), Jl MT Haryono 82-84, is a popular choice. It's friendly and has a good restaurant. Many rooms have private balconies, and singles/doubles with mandi start at 9500/10,600 rp, or with aircon from 25,600/27,000 rp, including breakfast.

Nearby *Hotel Slamet* (☎ 24675), next to

the old train station at Jl Wahid Hasyim 96, is another friendly place with a restaurant. Singles/doubles with mandi start at 10,000/12,000 rp and range up to the new rooms for 35,000 rp with air-con. Some of the rooms are dark, so it pays to check a few out.

For something better, the popular *Hotel Pinang Sari* (☎ 23266) at Jl Basuki Rachmat 116 is a few hundred metres north of the Blambangan bemo station. It has a very attractive garden and a restaurant. Rooms with bath and balcony cost 12,000 to 18,000 rp, or with air-con from 43,000 to 80,000 rp.

The *Hotel Ikhtiar Surya* (☎ 21063), Jl Gajah Mada 9, is the best in the town with large grounds and a huge variety of rooms all with bath, ranging from 14,000 rp up to the 82,500 rp VIP rooms. It is very quiet but a long 1.5 km hike to the centre of town.

The big *Manyar Garden Hotel* (☎ 24741) one km south of the ferry terminal on the road to Banyuwangi, has comfortable motel units but they are in need of maintenance. Rates are from US$30 to US$90 but expect discounts. One km further south, the new *Hotel Ketapang Indah* (☎ 22280) faces the black sand beach and Bali, and is the best in the area. Very good rooms are US$80 and US$100, before discount, and it has a pool.

Places to Eat

For snacks, Jl Pattimura has night food stalls here you'll find delicious air jahe (ginger tea) and dadak jagung (egg and sweetcorn patties), ketan (sticky rice topped with coconut) and fried banana.

The *Rumah Makan Surya* around the corner at Jl W Hasyim 94 has moderately priced Chinese food and serves a good ayam goreng. *Depot Asia*, Jl Dr Sutomo 12, also has good, if slightly expensive, Chinese food and boasts air-con. For the best Madurese-style sate in town, go to Pak Amat's warung on Jl Basuki Rachmat in the evenings.

Getting There & Away

Bus Banyuwangi has two bus terminals. Terminal Seri Tanjung is three km north of the Bali ferry terminal at Ketapang, and 11 km

orth of town. Buses from here go to north-
rn destinations, such as: Baluran (750 rp;
ne hour); Pasir Putih (2500; 2½ hours);
robolinggo (4500/7500 rp patas; three
ours) for Gunung Bromo; Surabaya (6500/
1,500 rp patas; five hours); and Malang
6500/11,500 rp). Buses also go right
irough to Yogya and Jakarta.

Terminal Brawijaya (more commonly
eferred to as Karang Ente) is four km south
f town and has buses to the south. Buses
iclude: Kalipahit (1800 rp; 1½ hours);
esanggaran (2000 rp; two hours); Kalibaru
2000 rp; two hours); and Jember (2400 rp;
iree hours).

rain The main train station is just a few
undred metres north of the ferry terminal at
etapang. Most trains also stop at the
.rgopuro and Karang Asem train stations,
n the northern and eastern outskirts of
anyuwangi respectively, but it is hard to get
ublic transport to either.

Bisnis trains leave at 9.30 am and 10 pm
or Probolinggo (8000 rp; five hours) and
urabaya (9000 rp; seven hours). Ekonomi
ains include the *Blambangan* to Pro-
olinggo (2700 rp; six hours) at 1 pm and *Sri
injung* to Kalibaru (1100 rp; 2½ hours) at
30 pm. The *Argopuro* provides an excruci-
ing trip to Yogya (9000 rp; 15 hours), via
urabaya and Probolinggo, at 6 am. Trains
in be very crowded at peak travel times,
irticularly Sunday.

oat Ferries from Ketapang depart at least
very hour around the clock for Gilimanuk
1 Bali. The ferry costs 1000 rp for passen-
:rs, 3700 rp for motorcycles and 10,550 rp
r cars. Through buses between Bali and
va include the fare in the bus ticket.

Pelni's *Tatamailau* stops in Banyuwangi
1 its route to Nusa Tenggara and Irian Jaya.
docks at Ketapang, along from the Bali
rry dock.

etting Around
anyuwangi has a squadron of minibuses
nning between the bus terminals and ter-
inating at the Blambangan minibus terminal

near the centre of town; they're marked Lin
1, 2, 3 etc, and charge a fixed 400 rp fare
around town. Lin 6 or 12 runs from Blambangan to the ferry terminal and on to the
Terminal Seri Tanjung bus terminal. Lin 2
goes from Blambangan to the Hotel Baru
area. Lin 3 goes from Blambangan to Sasak
Perot, where you get colts to the Ijen Plateau.
Blue kijang sedans at the ferry terminal act
as taxis – they want 5000 rp before they will
move anywhere.

IJEN PLATEAU

The Ijen Plateau, part of a reserve area which
stretches north-east to Baluran, was at one
time a huge active crater complex, 134 sq km
in area. Today Ijen is dormant, not dead, and
the landscape is dominated by the volcanic
cones of Ijen (2400m) and Merapi (2800m)
on the north-eastern edge of the plateau and
Raung (3332m) on the south-west corner.
Coffee plantations cover much of the
western part of the plateau, where there are
a few settlements. The plateau area has a
number of difficult-to-reach natural attractions, but most visitors come for the hike to
spectacular Kawah Ijen.

Kawah Ijen Hike

Kawah Ijen (Ijen Crater) is surrounded by
sheer walls rising up from a magnificent
turquoise sulphur lake. From the crater lip it
is possible to climb down to the smoking
sulphur deposits, and at the south-western
end the crater walls plunge down to a 'safety-
valve' dam which was built to regulate the
flow of water into the Banyu Pahit, the
'Bitter River'. Sulphur is extracted from the
lake and a vulcanology post just below the
crater monitors sulphur collection and is
staffed year-round. There are few people in
this totally unspoilt area.

The best time to make the hike is in the dry
season between April and October. Sulphur
collectors hike up in the morning and return
around 1 pm when the clouds roll in. Trekkers are advised to do the same, but the
clouds often disappear in the late afternoon.

The starting point for the trek to the crater
is the PHPA post at Pos Paltuding, which can

be reached from Banyuwangi or from Bondowoso. The steep well-worn path up to the vulcanology post takes about an hour. Just past the vulcanology post the road forks – to the left is the easy walk to the dam, but the more interesting walk is the right fork another half hour to the top of the crater and its stunning views. From the crater a steep, gravelly path leads down to the sulphur deposits and the steaming lake. The walk down takes about 20 minutes, double the time for the walk back up. The path is slippery in parts and the sulphur fumes towards the bottom can be overwhelming – take care.

Back at the lip of the crater, turn left for the steep half hour climb to the peak and magnificent views of the lake and the surrounding mountains.

You can also keep walking anticlockwise around the crater for equally superb views. On the other side of the lake opposite the sulphur deposits, the trail disappears into crumbling volcanic rock and deep ravines.

Places to Stay & Eat

Most people visit Kawah Ijen on a day trip but it is possible to stay and explore the plateau area. Sempol, 13 km from the Pos Paltuding on the Bondowoso side, has some simple homestays with rooms from as little as 7500 rp and meals can be arranged. Sempol has little else in the way of facilities.

You can always stay at the PHPA posts for a small donation. The enterprising vulcanology post sells drinks and cooks meals, and Pos Paltuding sells provisions.

To the south of Sempol, *Guest House Jampit* provides the best accommodation in the area. It is an old Dutch house in the government-run plantation.

PT Perkubunan (see under Jember earlier in this chapter) run Ijen tours with overnight stays in Jampit, or tours can be arranged through Bondowoso hotels.

Getting There & Away

The starting point for the main trek to Kawah Ijen is at the PHPA post of Pos Paltuding, which can be reached from either Banyuwangi or Bondowoso.

Banyuwangi This is the most popular route. It is shorter and cheaper than coming from Bondowoso, though it is a much longer trek. Start at 5.30 am to reach the crater in time for good views.

From Banyuwangi's Blambangan bemo station, take a Lin 3 bemo to Sasak Perak (400 rp) on the eastern outskirts of town, and then a Licin-bound colt which can drop you off in Jambu (1000 rp) at the turn-off to Kawah Ijen. From here ojek can take you along the paved road for the nine km to Sodong for 4000 rp, though they may not be keen to go further. Sodong is nothing more than a bamboo shed where the sulphur collectors bring their loads to be taken by truck to Banyuwangi. From Sodong the road is paved but very steep and only negotiable by 4WD. The eight km walk to Pos Paltuding goes through some brilliant, dense forest and takes three hours. On the way you will pass another PHPA post, Pos Totogan. You may be lucky enough to get a ride on the truck to or from Sodong but don't count on it. The alternative to all this is to hire a jeep – the tourist office can arrange one for 100,000 rp return to Pos Paltuding.

Bondowoso If you are prepared to charter transport, then the route from Bondowoso is the easiest way to reach Kawah Ijen. From Wonosari, eight km from Bondowoso towards Situbondo, an asphalt road runs via Sukosari all the way to Pos Paltuding. It is potholed in parts but the 64 km trip from Bondowoso to Pos Paltuding can be easily made in about 2½ hours by car.

Colts run from Bondowoso to Sukosari but there is no regular public transport for the remaining 40 km to Pos Paltuding. Irregular public trucks run from Sukosari to Sempol but you may have to charter a pick-up or truck in Sukosari to Pos Paltuding for 50,000 rp return. If you make it to Sempol by public transport, you can then hire an ojek to Pos Paltuding (5000 rp; 13 km).

KALIKLATAK

Kaliklatak, 20 km north of Banyuwangi, is another 'agro-tourism' venture where you ur large coffee, cocoa, rubber, coconut and love plantations. Accommodation is available at the *Wisata Irdjen Guesthouse* (☎ 24061 Kaliklatak, 24896 in Banyuwangi), but is xpensive. Note that tours and accommodation must be booked in advance.

ALURAN NATIONAL PARK

n the north-east corner of Java, Baluran ational Park covers an area of 250 sq km. he parklands surround the solitary hump of unung Baluran (1247m) and contain extensive dry savanna grassland threaded by ony-bedded streams and coastal mangrove. is surprisingly reminiscent of Australia or e African grasslands, and is billed as donesia's 'African safari park'. It is also ery easy to reach, lying on the main Banyuangi-Surabaya highway, and easy car access akes it one of Java's most visited parks.

The main attractions are the herds of feral ater buffalo, banteng (wild cattle), rusa eer, muncaks (barking deer), monkeys, and e wild pigs, leopards and civets that live in e upland forest. Birds include the green nglefowl, peacocks, bee-eaters, kingfish- s and owls.

PHPA staff can arrange a jeep to the more mote parts of the savanna for a price. At ekol, where the main guesthouse is located, ou can see deer and water buffalo at the aterhole, usually in the early morning or e afternoon, so you should stay here for e night. Bekol also has a tower for wildlife otting. From Bekol you can walk or drive e three km to Bama on the coast. Bama also s accommodation, a waterhole and viewg tower, and a half decent beach where you n snorkel. Trails lead around the coast and rough the savanna.

The main service town for Baluran is onorejo, on the main coast road between arabaya and Banyuwangi, where food sup- ies can be bought – the PHPA office and sitor centre is on the highway. Baluran is en daily from 7 am to 5 pm and, if you're t staying overnight, baggage can be left fely at the PHPA office.

Baluran can be visited at any time of the year but the best time is the dry season, between May and November, because this is when the animals come to the park waterholes.

Places to Stay

At Bekol, 12 km into the park, the *Pesanggrahan* has seven rooms and costs 6000 rp per person; there's a mandi and kitchen but you must take your own provisions. *Wisma Tamu* next door has three very comfortable rooms with attached mandi for 10,000 rp per person, and the *Pondok Peneliti* costs 12,500 rp. The canteen at Bekol sells drinks and some provisions, but meals are cooked only for groups if advance notice is given. You might be able to arrange something with the PHPA staff, but you should bring your own food.

Bama Guesthouse is three km east of Bekol on the beach and provides rooms for 6000 rp per person, and there are also cooking facilities here if you bring your own food. Bookings for both can be made in advance at the PHPA office in Banyuwangi or through the Baluran PHPA (☎ 61650). Most visitors tend to day trip so accommodation is not usually full, but it pays to book, especially in the main June/July holiday period when school groups visit the park.

Getting There & Away

Surabaya to Banyuwangi buses, taking the coast road via Probolinggo, can drop you right at the park entrance, and when leaving the park buses are easily flagged down. From Banyuwangi (or Ketapang ferry, if you're coming from Bali) it's only a half hour journey on the Wonorejo bus, which costs 750 rp. Ask the driver to let you off at the park and at the entrance ask a PHPA ranger to arrange an ojek (5000 rp) or car (15,000 rp) to take you the 12 km to Bekol. The park entry fee is 2000 rp. Coming from the west, Baluran is 3½ hours from Probolinggo/ Gunung Bromo.

Bali

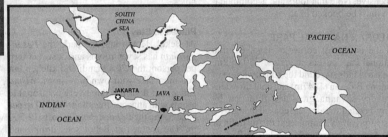

For many westerners, Bali doesn't extend beyond the tourist leaflet: idyllic tropical beaches, lush green forests and rice fields tripping down hillsides like giant steps. This vision of paradise has been turned into a commodity for the hundreds of thousands of tourists who flood into Bali every year. But Bali has much more than this – you can still discover the extraordinary richness of Balinese culture, which remains unique and authentic despite the tourist invasion, and it's not hard to find out-of-the-way places where tourists are a rarity.

HISTORY

It's certain that Bali has been populated since early prehistoric times, but the oldest human artefacts found on Bali are stone tools and earthenware vessels from Cekik, from about 3000 years ago. Other artefacts indicate that the Bronze Age commenced on Bali before 300 BC. Not much is known of Bali during the period when Indian traders brought Hinduism to the Indonesian archipelago, but the earliest written records are stone inscriptions, dating from around the 9th century AD. By that time, rice was being grown with

---

HIGHLIGHTS

- **Something for Everyone** – Bali can be all things to all people: relax in decadence at a luxury beach resort; visit traditional villages; indulge in western comforts after less developed parts of Indonesia; shop until you drop; or experience Bali's dance, music and rich art traditions. You can spend months doing these things, or Bali is compact and developed enough to see a lot in just one day.

- **Beach Resorts** – Bali's most infamous resort, Kuta Beach, has a host of good hotels, restaurants and bars, great shopping and a fine stretch of sand, but the chaotic hustle for the tourist dollar is maddening. Sanur is in the same mould but much quieter, more upmarket and family oriented, while Nusa Dua is more upmarket again. Candidasa and Lovina don't have Bali's best stretches of sand, but are more relaxed and comfortably low key.

- **Natural Attractions** – Bali is wonderfully scenic, with brilliant green sculptured rice terraces, lush jungle gorges and deep blue sea. Some highlights of a trip around the island are the descent from Bedugul to the north coast, the spectacular volcanic crater and lake of Gunung Batur, and the panorama from the southern slopes of Gunung Agung.

- **Balinese Culture** – Head for the hills! Ubud has always been the cultural centre of Bali and the tag still fits despite mass tourism. From here, it is possible to get out and explore the surrounding villages and their rich traditions in music, dance and craftwork. Spectacular temples perch on cliffs over the sea, while hundreds of others come alive during colourful temple festivals.

complex irrigation system, and there were precursors of the religious and cultural tradition which can be traced to the present day.

Hindu Influence

Hindu Java began to spread its influence into Bali during the reign of King Airlangga, from 1019 to 1042. At the age of 16, when his uncle lost the throne, Airlangga fled into the forests of western Java. He gradually gained support, won back the kingdom once ruled by his uncle and went on to become one of Java's greatest kings. Airlangga's mother had moved to Bali and remarried shortly after his birth, so when he gained the throne there was an immediate link between Java and Bali. At this time, the courtly Javanese language known as Kawi came into use among the royalty of Bali, and the rock-cut memorials seen at Gunung Kawi near Tampaksiring are a clear architectural link between Bali and 11th century Java.

After Airlangga's death Bali retained its semi-independent status until Kertanagara became king of the Singasari dynasty on Java two centuries later. Kertanagara conquered Bali in 1284 but his greatest power lasted only eight years until he was murdered and his kingdom collapsed. However, the great Majapahit dynasty was founded by his son. With Java in turmoil, Bali regained its autonomy and the Pejeng dynasty, centred near modern-day Ubud, rose to great power. In 1343 Gajah Mada, the legendary chief Majapahit minister, defeated the Pejeng king Dalem Bedaulu and brought Bali back under Javanese influence.

Although Gajah Mada brought much of the Indonesian archipelago under Majapahit control, this was the furthest extent of their power. On Bali the 'capital' moved to Gelgel, near modern Klungkung, around the late 14th century and for the next two centuries this was the base for the 'king of Bali', the Dewa Agung. As Islam spread into Java the Majapahit kingdom collapsed into disputing sultanates. However, the Gelgel dynasty on Bali, under Dalem Batur Enggong, extended its power eastwards to the neighbouring island of Lombok and even crossed the strait to Java.

As the Majapahit kingdom fell apart, many of its intelligentsia moved to Bali, including the priest Nirartha, who is credited with introducing many of the complexities of Balinese religion to the island. Artists, dancers, musicians and actors also fled to Bali at this time, and the island experienced an explosion of cultural activities. The final great exodus to Bali took place in 1478.

European Contact

The first Europeans to set foot on Bali were Dutch seafarers in 1597. Setting a tradition that prevails right down to the present day, they fell in love with the island and when Cornelius Houtman, the ship's captain, prepared to set sail from Bali, some of his crew refused to leave with him. At that time, Balinese prosperity and artistic activity, at least among the royalty, were at a peak, and the king who befriended Houtman had 200 wives and a chariot pulled by two white buffaloes, not to mention a retinue of 50 dwarfs whose bodies had been bent to resemble kris handles! Although the Dutch returned to Indonesia in later years, they were interested in profit, not culture, and barely gave Bali a second glance.

Dutch Conquest

In 1710 the capital of the Gelgel kingdom was shifted to nearby Klungkung, but local discontent was growing, lesser rulers were breaking away from Gelgel domination and the Dutch began to move in, using the old policy of divide and conquer. In 1846 the Dutch used Balinese salvage claims over shipwrecks as the pretext to land military forces in northern Bali. In 1894 the Dutch chose to support the Sasaks of Lombok in a rebellion against their Balinese raja. After some bloody battles, the Balinese were defeated on Lombok, and with the north of Bali firmly under Dutch control, south Bali was not likely to retain its independence for long. Once again, salvaging disputes gave the Dutch the excuse they needed to move in. A Chinese ship was wrecked off Sanur in

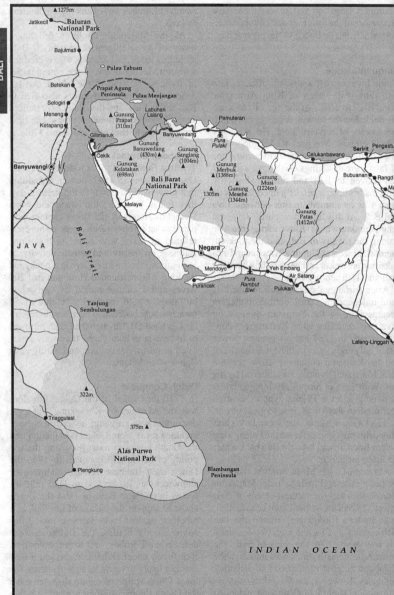

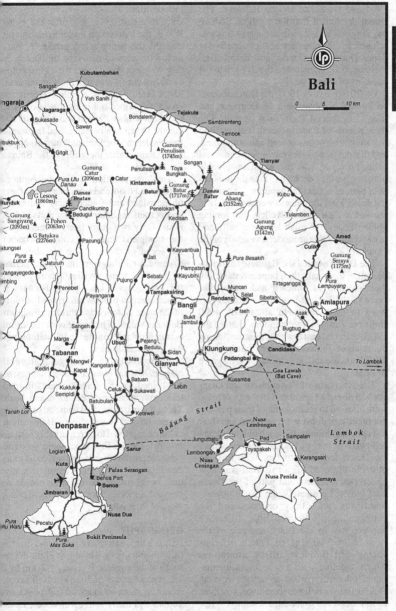

Bali

0   5   10 km

ngaraja
Sangsit
Kubutambahan
Yeh Sanih
Jagaraga
Sukasade
Bondalem
Tejakula
Sambirenteng
Sawan
Tembok
bukbuk
Gitgit
Gunung Penulisan (1745m)
Songan
Tianyar
Gunung Catur (2096m)
Penulisan
Toya Bungkah
Pura Ulu Danau
Catur
Kintamani
Batur
Gunung Batur (1717m)
Danau Batur
Gunung Abang (2152m)
Kubu
Danau Bratan
Candikuning
Tulamben
G Lesong (1860m)
unduk
Bedugul
Penelokan
Amed
Gunung Sangiyang (2093m)
G Pohon (2063m)
Kedisan
Gunung Agung (3142m)
Culik
Gunung Seraya (1175m)
G Batukau (2276m)
Pacung
Kayuanbua
Pura Besakih
atungsei
Pura Luhur
Jatuluh
Jati
Pampatan
Muncan
Tirtagangga
Pura Lempuyang
angayegede
Sebatu
Kayubihi
Selat
Sibetan
mbing
Pujung
Tampaksiring
Rendang
Iseh
Asak
Amlapura
Penebel
Payangan
Bangli
Tenganan
Ujung
Bukit Jambul
Bugbug
Sangeh
Pejeng
Muncan
Marga
Ubud
Bedulu
Sidan
Klungkung
Candidasa
Tabanan
Mengwi
Mas
Gianyar
Padangbai
To Lombok
Kediri
Kapal
Kangetan
Goa Lawah (Bat Cave)
Kukluk
Celuk
Batuan
Lebih
Kusamba
Sempidi
Sukawati
Batubulan
Ketewel
Badung Strait
Nusa Lembongan
Lombok Strait
Tanah Lot
Denpasar
Jungutbatu
Ped
Sampalan
Legian
Sanur
Lembongan
Toyapakeh
Karangsari
Kuta
Nusa Ceningan
Pulau Serangan
Benoa Port
Jimbaran
Benoa
Nusa Penida
Semaya
Pura Ulu Watu
Pecatu
Nusa Dua
Pura Mas Suka
Bukit Peninsula

BALI

1904 and ransacked by the Balinese. The Dutch demanded that the rajah of Badung pay 3000 silver dollars in damages – this was refused. In 1906 Dutch warships appeared at Sanur, Dutch forces landed and, despite Balinese opposition, marched the five km to the outskirts of Denpasar.

On 20 September 1906, the Dutch mounted a naval bombardment on Denpasar and then commenced their final assault. The three princes of Badung (south Bali) realised that they were outnumbered and outgunned, and that defeat was inevitable. Surrender and exile, however, was the worst imaginable outcome, so they decided to take the honourable path of a suicidal *puputan* – a fight to the death. First the palaces were burnt. Then, dressed in their finest jewellery and waving golden krises, the rajah led the royalty and priests out to face the modern weapons of the Dutch.

The Dutch begged the Balinese to surrender rather than make their hopeless stand, but their pleas went unheard and wave after wave of the Balinese nobility marched forward to their death. In all, nearly 4000 Balinese died in the puputan. Later, the Dutch marched east towards Tabanan, taking the rajah of Tabanan prisoner, but he committed suicide rather than face the disgrace of exile.

The kingdoms of Karangasem and Gianyar had already capitulated to the Dutch and were allowed to retain some of their powers, but other kingdoms were defeated and their rulers exiled. Finally, the rajah of Klungkung followed the lead of Badung and once more the Dutch faced a puputan. With this last obstacle disposed of, all of Bali was now under Dutch control and part of the Dutch East Indies. Fortunately, the Dutch government was not totally onerous and the common people noticed little difference between rule by the Dutch and rule by the rajas. Some far-sighted Dutch officials encouraged Balinese artistic aspirations which, together with a new-found international interest, sparked an artistic revival. Dutch rule over Bali was short-lived, however, as Indonesia fell to the Japanese in WWII.

Independence

On 17 August 1945, just after the end of WWII, the Indonesian leader Soekarno proclaimed the nation's independence, but it took four years to convince the Dutch that they were not going to get their great colony back. In a virtual repeat of the puputan nearly half a century earlier, a Balinese resistance group was wiped out in the battle of Marga on 20 November 1946. It was not until 194 that the Dutch finally recognised Indonesia independence. The Denpasar airport, Ngurah Rai, is named after the leader of the Balinese forces at Marga.

The huge eruption of Gunung Agung i 1963 killed thousands, devastated vast area of the island and forced many Balinese t accept transmigration to other parts of Indonesia. Only two years later, in the wake c the attempted Communist coup, Bali becam the scene of some of the bloodiest anti Communist killings in Indonesia, perhap inflamed by some mystical desire to purg the land of evil, but equally because th radical agenda of land reform and abolitio of the caste system was a threat to tradition Balinese values. The brutality of the killing was in shocking contrast to the stereotype c the 'gentle' Balinese.

The tourist boom, which got going in th early 1970s, has brought many changes, an has helped pay for improvements in road telecommunications, education and health Though tourism has had some adverse env ronmental and social effects, Bali's uniqu culture has proved to be remarkably resilien In 1994, for the first time, there was voc public opposition to some controversial touri developments. This may be an indicatio that, in the future, the Balinese people wi demand a more active role in the develop ment of their island.

GEOGRAPHY

Bali is a tiny, extremely fertile and dramati cally mountainous island just eight degree south of the equator. It is only 140 km by 8 km, with an area of 5620 sq km. Bali's centr mountain chain includes several peaks ove 2000m and many active volcanoes, inclue ng the 'mother' mountain Gunung Agung (3142m). Bali's volcanic nature has contributed to its exceptional fertility, and the high mountains provide the dependable rainfall which irrigates the island's complex and beautiful rice terraces.

South of the central range is a wide, gently sloping area where most of Bali's abundant rice crops are grown. The northern coastal strip is narrower, rising more rapidly into the foothills. Here the main export crops of coffee and copra are produced, along with some rice, vegetables and cattle. Bali also has arid areas: the lightly populated western mountain region, the eastern and north-eastern slopes of Gunung Agung, the Bukit Peninsula in the south and the island of Nusa Penida get little rain and have only limited agriculture.

POPULATION & PEOPLE

Bali is a densely populated island, with an estimated 2.9 million people in 1995 – about 520 people per sq km. The population is almost all Indonesian; 95% are of Balinese Hindu religion and could be described as ethnic Balinese. Most of the other residents are from other parts of Indonesia, particularly Java, but also Sumatra and Nusa Tenggara.

The Balinese have a traditional caste system which resembles the Indian Hindu system, although there are no untouchables. Nor is there an intricate division of labour based on caste, except for the Brahman priesthood. Over 90% of the population belong to the common Sutra caste, which now includes many wealthy Balinese. The main significance of caste is in religious roles and rituals, and in the language, but its importance in other aspects of life is declining.

ARTS

The Balinese have no words for 'art' and 'artist' because traditionally, art has never been regarded as something to be treasured for its own sake. Prior to the tourist invasion art was just something you did – you painted or carved as a part of everyday life, and what you produced went into temples or palaces or was used for festivals. Although respect-

ed, the painter or carver was not considered a member of some special elite, the artists' work was not signed and there were no galleries or craft shops.

It's a different story today, with thousands of galleries and craft shops in every possible crevice a tourist might trip into. Although much of Balinese art is churned out quickly for people who want a cheap souvenir, buried beneath the reproductions of reproductions there's still quite a lot of beautiful work to be found – if you dig deep enough.

Even the simplest activities are carried out with care, precision and artistic flair. Just glance at those little offering trays thrown down on the ground for the demons every morning – each one a throwaway work of art. Look at the temple offerings, the artistically stacked pyramids of fruit or other beautifully decorated foods. Look for the *lamaks*, long woven palm-leaf strips used as decorations, the stylised female figures known as *cili* and the intricately carved coconut-shell wall-hangings. At funerals you'll be amazed at the care and energy that goes into constructing huge funeral towers and exotic sarcophagi, all of which go up in flames.

There are, however, some traditional objects which are not only made to last, but are imbued with spiritual significance. An example is the sacred kris, a knife which is thought to contain great spiritual force and thus requires enormous care in manufacture and use. The *wayang kulit* shadow-puppet figures cut from buffalo hide are also magical items since the plays enact the eternal battle between good and evil. The Balinese weave a variety of complex fabrics for ceremonial and other important uses, including *songket* (cloth with gold or silver threads woven into it).

Architecture & Sculpture

Of all the Balinese arts it's said that architecture and stone sculpture have been the least affected by western influence and the tourist boom, because they don't make convenient souvenirs. Traditionally, stone and wooden sculpture were used only for architectural decoration, mostly on temples, so sculpture and architecture are inextricably bound together.

Architecture A basic element of Balinese architecture is the *bale*, a rectangular, open-sided pavilion with a steeply pitched hip roof of palm thatch. A family compound will have a number of bale for eating, sleeping and working. The focus of a community is the *bale banjar*, a large pavilion for meeting, debate, gamelan practice etc. Large, modern buildings like restaurants and the lobby areas of new hotels are often modelled on the bale – they are airy, spacious and handsomely proportioned.

Like the other arts, architecture has traditionally served the religious life of Bali. Balinese houses, though often attractive places, have never been lavished with the architectural attention that is given to temples. Even Balinese palaces are modest compared with the more important temples. Temples are designed to set rules and formulas, with sculpture serving as an adjunct, a finishing touch to these design guidelines.

Sculpture In small or less important temples, the sculpture may be limited or even nonexistent, while in other temples – particularly some of the exuberantly detailed temples of north Bali – the sculpture may be almost overwhelming in its detail and intricacy. A temple gateway, for example, might be carved over every square centimetre, with a diminishing series of demon faces above it as protection. Even then it's not finished without a couple of stone statues to act as guardians.

Door guardians, of legendary figures like Arjuna or other protectors, flank the steps to the gateway. Above the main entrance to a temple is the monstrous face of the guardian temple demon kala, sometimes a number of times – its hands reach out beside its head to catch any evil spirits which try to sneak in. The ancient swastika symbol indicates good fortune and prosperity. Carved panels on the walls may show scenes of local significance or everyday life. The front of a *pura dalem* (temple of the dead) will often feature images of the *rangda* (witch) and sculpture panels may show the horrors that await evil doers in the afterlife.

Painting
The art form probably most influenced both by western ideas and tourist demand is painting. Traditional painting was very limited in style and subject matter, and was used primarily for temple decoration. The arrival of western artists after WWI expanded painting beyond these limitations, introduced new subject matter and brought new materials for artists to work with. The best place to see examples of the various Balinese painting styles is in Ubud at the Puri Lukisan Museum and the Neka Museum.

Traditional Painting Balinese painting was strictly limited to three basic kinds: *langse*, *iders-iders*; and calendars. Langse are large rectangular hangings used as decoration or curtains in palaces or temples. Iders-iders are scroll paintings hung along the eaves of temples. The calendars were usually astrological, showing the auspicious days of each month.

Most of the paintings were narratives with mythological themes, illustrating stories from Hindu epics and literature – rather like a cartoon strip with a series of panels each telling a segment of the story. These paintings were always executed in the wayang style, the flat two dimensional style imitative of the wayang kulit shows, the figures invariably shown in three-quarters view. Even the colours artists could use were strictly limited to a set list of shades (red, blue, brown, yellow and a light ochre for flesh).

In these narratives the same character appeared in several different scenes, each depicting an episode from the story. The individual scenes were usually bordered by mountains, flames or ornamental walls. The deities, princes and heroes were identified by their opulent clothing, jewellery, elaborate headdresses, and their graceful postures and gestures; and the devils and giants by their bulging eyes, canine teeth, bulbous noses and bulky bodies. Klungkung is still a centre or the traditional wayang style of painting and the painted ceiling of the Hall of Justice n Klungkung is a fine example.

Foreign Influences Under the influence of Walter Spies and Rudolf Bonnet, who settled on Bali in the 1930s, Balinese artists started painting single scenes instead of narrative tales, and using scenes from everyday life rather than romantic legends as their themes. More importantly, they started painting pictures purely as pictures – not as something to cover a space in a palace or temple. The idea of a painting being something you could do by itself (and for which there might be a market!) was wholly new.

In one way, however, the style remained unchanged – Balinese paintings are packed full; every spare millimetre is filled in. A forest scene will have leaves and flowers filling every corner, and a whole zoo of birds and other creatures. Other themes include idyllic rural scenes, energetic festivals or engagingly stylised animals and fish.

This new artistic enthusiasm was interrupted by WWII and by the political turmoil of the 1950s and 60s. As the 1930s style degenerated into stale copying, a new style emerged in Ubud, with particular encouragement from the Dutch painter Aries Smit. His 'Young Artists', as they were known (they weren't necessarily young), picked up where those of the 1930s had left off, painting Balinese rural scenes in brilliant technicolour.

Woodcarving

Like painting, woodcarving is no longer done simply for decoration or other symbolic purposes in temples and palaces, but is now created for its own sake. As with painting, influences from outside inspired new subjects and styles, and some of the same western artists provided the stimulus.

Especially around Ubud, carvers started producing highly stylised and elongated figures, leaving the wood in its natural state rather than painting it, as was the traditional practice. Others carved delightful animal figures, some totally realistic and others wonderful caricatures, while other artists carved whole tree trunks into ghostly, intertwined 'totem poles' or curiously exaggerated and distorted figures.

Music, Dance & Drama

Music, dance and drama are all closely related on Bali. In fact, dance and drama are synonymous, though some 'dances' are more drama and less dance, and others more dance and less drama. Most dancers are not specialists, but ordinary people who dance in the evening or in their spare time. They learn the dances by long hours of practice, usually carefully following the movements of an expert.

There's rarely the soaring leaps of classical ballet or the smooth flowing movements often found in western dance. Balinese dance tends to be precise, jerky, shifting and jumpy, like the accompanying gamelan music, which has abrupt shifts of tempo and dramatic changes between silence and crashing noise. There's virtually no physical contact in Balinese dancing – each dancer moves independently, but every movement of wrist, hand and finger is important. Even facial expressions are carefully choreographed to convey the character of the dance.

Balinese dance is not a static art form – old dances fade out and new dances, or new versions of old dances, become popular. The Oleg Tambulilingan, for example, was developed in the 1950s as a solo female dance, but later a male part was added and the dance now mimics the flirtations of two *tambulilingan*, or bumblebees.

The Balinese like a blend of seriousness and slapstick, and their dances show this. Basically, the dances are straightforward ripping yarns, where you cheer on the goodies and cringe when the baddies appear. Some dances have a comic element, with clowns who counterbalance the staid, noble characters. The clowns often have to convey the story to the audience, since the noble characters may use the classical Javanese Kawi language, while the clowns (usually servants of the noble characters) converse in everyday Balinese.

Dances are a regular part of almost every

temple festival and Bali has no shortage of these. There are also dances virtually every night at all the tourist centres; admission to a 1st class performance in Ubud costs around 7000 rp for foreigners. Some performances are offered as entertainment at a restaurant or hotel, often with a mixture of dances – a little Topeng, a taste of Legong and some Baris to round it off. This is not a good way to see Balinese dance, and it's worth looking around for a better performance. The authenticity, quality and level of drama varies widely, but excellent dances can be seen, where the audience includes many appreciative Balinese.

Kecak Probably the best known of the many Balinese dances, the Kecak is unusual because it doesn't have a gamelan accompaniment. Instead, the background is provided by a chanting 'choir' of men who provide the 'chak-a-chak-a-chak' noise which distinguishes the dance. Originally this chanting group was known as the Kecak and they were part of a Sanghyang trance dance. Then in the 1930s the modern Kecak developed in Bona, a village near Gianyar, where the dance is still held regularly.

The Kecak tells the tale of the *Ramayana* (see the Java chapter for a rundown of the story), the quest of Prince Rama to rescue his wife Sita after she had been kidnapped by Rawana, the King of Lanka. Rama is accompanied to Lanka by Sugriwa, the king of the monkeys, with his monkey army. Throughout the Kecak dance, the circle of men, all bare-chested and wearing checked cloth around their waists, provide a nonstop accompaniment, rising to a crescendo as they play the monkey army and fight it out with Rawana and his cronies. The chanting is accompanied by the movements of the monkey army whose members sway back and forth, raise their hands in unison, flutter their fingers and lean left and right, all with an eerily exciting coordination.

Barong & Rangda Like the Kecak, the Barong & Rangda, or kris dance, is a battle between good and evil. Barongs can take

various forms but in this dance it takes th form of the *barong keket*, the most holy o the barongs. The barong keket is a strang creature – half shaggy dog, half lion – and i played by two men in much the same way a a circus clown-horse. Its opponent is th *rangda* (witch).

The barong personifies good and protect the village from the rangda, but is also mischievous and fun-loving creature. flounces into the temple courtyard, snaps it jaws at the gamelan, dances around an enjoys the acclaim of its supporters – a grou of men with krises. Then the rangda make her appearance, her long tongue lolling, he pendulous breasts wobbling, human entrail draped around her neck, fangs protrudin from her mouth and sabre-like fingernail clawing the air.

Now the barong is no longer the clown but the protector. The two duel with thei magical powers, and the barong's supporter draw their krises and rush in to attack th witch. The rangda puts them in a trance an the men try to stab themselves, but th barong also has great magical powers an casts a spell which stops the krises from harming the men. This is the most dramati part of the dance – as the gamelan ring crazily the men rush back and forth, wavin their krises around, all but foaming at th mouth, sometimes even rolling on the groun in a desperate attempt to stab themselves Finally, the rangda retires defeated – goo has won again. Good must always triump over evil on Bali, and no matter how man times the spectators have seen the perfor mance or how well they know the outcome the battle itself remains all-important.

The end of the dance still leaves a larg group of entranced barong supporters to b brought back to the real world. This i usually done by sprinkling them with hol water, sanctified by dipping the barong' beard in it.

Legong This is the most graceful of Balines dances and, to sophisticated Balinese con noisseurs of dancing, the one of most interest

A Legong, as a Legong dancer is always known, is a girl, often as young as eight or nine years and rarely older than her early teens. Such importance is attached to the dance that even in old age a classic dancer may be remembered as a 'great Legong', even though her brief period of fame may have been 50 years ago.

There are various forms of the Legong but the Legong Kraton, or Legong of the palace, is the one most usually performed. Peliatan's famous dance troupe, which visitors to Ubud often get a chance to see, is particularly noted for its Legong. A performance involves just three dancers – the two Legongs and their attendant' known as the *condong*. The Legongs are identically dressed in tightly bound gold brocade. So tightly are they encased that it's something of a mystery how they manage to move with such agility and speed. Their faces are elaborately made up, their eyebrows plucked and repainted, and their hair decorated with frangipanis.

It's a very stylised and symbolic dance – if you didn't know the story it would be impossible to tell what was going on. The dance relates how a king takes a maiden Rangkesari captive. When Rangkesari's brother comes to release her, he begs the king to let her free rather than go to war. The king refuses and on his way to the battle meets a bird bringing ill omens. He ignores the bird and continues on to meet Rangkesari's brother, who kills him. The dance, however, only relates the lead up to the battle and ends with the bird's appearance. When the king leaves the stage he is going to the battle that will end in his death.

The dance starts with the condong dancing an introduction. The condong departs as the Legongs come on. The Legongs dance solo, in close identical formation, and even in mirror image when they dance a nose-to-nose love scene. They relate the king's sad departure from his queen, Rangkesari's request that he release her and the king's departure for the battle. Finally, the condong reappears with tiny golden wings as the bird of ill fortune and the dance comes to an end.

Baris The warrior dance known as the Baris is a male equivalent of the Legong in which femininity and grace give way to the energetic, warlike martial spirit. The solo Baris dancer has to convey the thoughts and emotions of a warrior preparing for action and then meeting an enemy in battle. The dancer must show his changing moods not only through his dancing, but also through facial expression. Chivalry, pride, anger, prowess and, finally, regret, all have to be conveyed. It's said that the Baris is one of the most complex of the Balinese dances, requiring a dancer of great energy, skill and ability.

Ramayana The *Ramayana* is a familiar tale on Bali, but the dance is a relatively recent addition to the Balinese repertoire. It tells much the same story of Rama and Sita as told in the Kecak but without the monkey ensemble and with a normal gamelan orchestra accompaniment. It's also embellished with many improvisations and comic additions. Rawana may be played as a classic bad guy, the monkey god Hanuman can be a comic clown and camera-wielding tourists among the spectators may come in for some imitative ribbing.

Kebyar This is a male solo dance like the Baris, but with greater emphasis on the performer's individual abilities. Development of the modern Kebyar is credited in large part to the famous prewar dancer Mario. There are various forms of the dance, including the seated Kebyar Duduk where the 'dance' is done from the seated position, and movements of the hands, arms and torso plus, of course, facial expressions, are all important. In the Kebyar Trompong, the dancer actually joins the gamelan and plays an instrument called the *trompong* while still dancing.

Janger Both Covarrubias and Powell, in their between-the-wars books on Bali, comment on this strange, new, almost un-Balinese dance which appeared in the 1920s and 30s. Today it is part of the standard repertoire and no longer looks so unusual. It has similarities

BALI

to several other dances including the Sang-hyang, where the relaxed chanting of the women is contrasted with the violent 'chak-a-chak-a-chak' of the men. In the Janger dance, formations of 12 young women and 12 young men perform a sitting dance, where the gentle swaying and chanting of the women is contrasted with the violently choreographed movements and loud shouts of the men.

Topeng The word Topeng means 'pressed against the face', as with a mask. In this mask dance, the dancers have to imitate the character their mask indicates they are playing. The Topeng Tua, for example, is a classic solo dance where the mask is that of an old man and requires the performer to dance like a creaky old gentleman. In other dances there may be a small troupe who dance various characters and types. A full collection of Topeng masks may number 30 or 40.

Another mask dance is the Jauk, but this is strictly a solo performance. The dancer plays an evil demon, his mask an eerie face with bulging eyes, fixed smile and long, wavering fingernails. Mask dances require great expertise because the character's thoughts and meanings cannot be conveyed through the dancer's facial expressions, so the character of the unpleasant, frenetic, fast-moving demon has to be portrayed entirely through the dance.

Pendet This is an everyday dance of the temples, a small procedure gone through before making temple offerings which doesn't require arduous training and practice. You may often see the Pendet being danced by women bringing offerings to a temple for a festival, but it is also sometimes danced as an introduction and a closing for other dance performances.

Sanghyang Dances The Sanghyang trance dances originally developed as a means of driving out evil spirits from a village. The Sanghyang is a divine spirit which temporarily inhabits an entranced dancer.

The Sanghyang Dedari is performed by two girls who dance a dream-like version of the Legong. The dancers are said to be untrained in the intricate pattern of the dance and, furthermore, they dance in perfect harmony but with their eyes firmly shut. A female choir and a male Kecak choir provide a background chant, but when the chant stops the dancers slump to the ground in a faint. Two women bring them around and, at the finish, a priest blesses them with holy water and brings them out of the trance. The modern Kecak dance developed from the Sanghyang.

In the Sanghyang Jaran a boy in a trance dances around and through a fire of coconut husks riding a coconut-palm hobby horse – it's labelled the 'fire dance' for the benefit of tourists. Once again the priest must be on hand to break the trance at the close of the dance.

The Gamelan As on Sumatra and Java Balinese music is based around the gamelan orchestra – for more details see the Java chapter. The whole gamelan orchestra is known as a *gong* – an old fashioned *gong gede* or a more modern *gong kebyar*. There are even more ancient forms of the gamelan such as the *gong selunding*, still occasionally played in Bali Aga villages like Tenganan.

Though the instruments used are much the same, Balinese gamelan is very different from the form you'll hear on Java. The Yogyakarta style, for example, is the most reserved, formal and probably the gentlest and most 'refined' of gamelans. Balinese gamelan often sounds like everyone going for it full pelt. Perhaps a more telling point is that Javanese gamelan music is rarely heard except at special performances, whereas on Bali you seem to hear gamelans playing everywhere you go.

BALINESE SOCIETY

Traditional Balinese society is intensely communal; the organisation of villages, the cultivation of farmlands and even the creative arts are communal efforts – a person belongs to their family, clan, caste and the village as a whole. Religion permeates all aspects of life and ceremonies, and rituals mark each stage in the life cycle. The first ceremony takes place before birth, at the third month of pregnancy, when a series of offerings is made at home and at the village river or spring to ensure the wellbeing of the baby. When the child reaches puberty its teeth are filed to produce an aesthetically pleasing straight line – even teeth symbolise an even temperament, while crooked fangs are characteristic of witches and demons.

Balinese women are not cloistered away, although the roles of the sexes are fairly well delineated, with certain tasks handled by women and others reserved for men. For instance, the running of the household is very much the woman's task, while caring for animals is mostly a male preserve.

Balinese society is held together by a sense of collective responsibility. If a woman enters a temple during menstruation, for instance, it is a kind of irreverence, an insult to the gods, and their displeasure falls not just on the transgressor but on the community as a whole. This collective responsibility produces considerable pressure on the individual to conform to traditional values and customs, called *adat*.

Households

Despite the strong communal nature of Balinese society, traditional houses are surrounded by a high wall and the compound is usually entered through a gateway backed by a small wall known as the *aling aling*. It serves a practical and a spiritual purpose – both preventing passers-by from seeing in and stopping evil spirits from entering. Evil spirits cannot easily turn corners so the aling aling stops them from scooting straight in through the gate. Inside there will be a family temple in one corner, a garden and a separate small building (bale) for each household function: cooking, sleeping, washing and the toilet.

Village Organisation

Each village is subdivided into *banjars*, which all adults join when they marry. It is the banjar which organises village festivals, marriage ceremonies and even cremations.

Throughout the island you'll see the open-sided meeting places known as bale banjar – they're nearly as common a sight as temples. Gamelan orchestras are organised at the banjar level, and a glance in a bale banjar at any time might reveal a gamelan practice, a meeting, food for a feast being prepared, even a group of men simply getting their roosters together to raise their anger in preparation for the next round of cockfights.

One of the important elements of village government is the *subak*. Each individual rice field is known as a *sawah* and each farmer who owns even one sawah must be a member of the local subak. The rice fields must have a steady supply of water and it is the job of the subak to ensure that the water supply gets to everybody. It's said that the head of the local subak will often be the farmer whose rice fields are at the bottom of the hill, for he will make quite certain that the water gets all the way down to his fields, passing through everybody else's on the way!

RELIGION

The Balinese are nominally Hindus but Balinese Hinduism is half a world away from that of India. When the Majapahits evacuated to Bali they took with them their religion and its rituals, as well as their art, literature, music and culture. The Balinese already had strong religious beliefs and an active cultural life, and the new influences were simply overlaid on existing practices – hence the peculiar Balinese interpretation of Hinduism.

The Balinese worship the same gods as the Hindus of India – the trinity of Brahma, Shiva and Vishnu – but they also have a supreme god, Sanghyang Widi. Unlike in India, the trinity is never seen – a vacant shrine or empty throne tells all. Nor is Sanghyang Widi often worshipped, though villagers may pray to him when they have settled new land and are about to build a new village. Other Hindu gods such as Ganesh, Shiva's elephant-headed son, may occasionally appear, but a great many purely Balinese gods, spirits and entities have far more relevance in everyday life.

BALI

The Balinese believe that spirits are everywhere, an indication that animism is the basis of much of their religion. Good spirits dwell in the mountains and bring prosperity to the people, while giants and demons lurk beneath the sea, and bad spirits haunt the woods and desolate beaches. The people live between these two opposites and their rituals strive to maintain this middle ground. Offerings are carefully put out every morning to pay homage to the good spirits and nonchalantly placed on the ground to placate the bad ones. You can't get away from religion on Bali – there are temples in every village, shrines in every field and offerings made at every corner. Although it enforces a high degree of conformity, it is not a fatalistic religion – there are rules and rituals to placate or drive out the bad spirits, and ensure the favour of the gods and the good spirits.

Temples

The word for temple on Bali is *pura*, which is a Sanskrit word literally meaning a space surrounded by a wall. As in so much of Balinese religion the temples, although nominally Hindu, owe much to the pre-Majapahit era. Their alignment towards the mountains *(kaja)*, the sea *(kelod)* or the sunrise *(kangin)* is in deference to spirits which are more animist than Hindu.

There are an amazing number of temples, with almost every village having at least three. The most important is the *pura puseh*, or temple of origin, which is dedicated to the village founders and is at the kaja end of the village. In the middle of the village is the *pura desa* for the spirits which protect the village community in its day-to-day life. At the kelod end of the village is the *pura dalem*, or temple of the dead. The graveyard is also here and the temple will often include representations of Durga, the terrible incarnation of Shiva's wife.

Families worship their ancestors in family temples, clans in clan temples and the whole village in the pura puseh. Certain special temples on Bali are of such importance that they are deemed to be owned by the whole island rather than by individual villages.

These include Pura Besakih on the slopes of Gunung Agung, the most revered place of Bali, often called 'The Mother Temple'.

The simple shrines or thrones you see, for example in rice fields or next to sacred old trees, are not real temples as they are not walled. You'll find these shrines in all sorts of places, often overlooking crossroad intersections or dangerous curves in the road to protect road users.

Temple Design Balinese temples usually consist of a series of courtyards entered from the sea side. In a large temple the outer gateway will generally be a *candi bentar*, modelled on the old Hindu temples of Java. These gateways resemble a tower cut in halves and moved apart, hence the name 'split gate'. The first courtyard is used for less important ceremonies, and will have a number of bale for preparing food and holding meetings. There will also be a *kulkul* (alarm drum) tower in this outer courtyard and perhaps a banyan or frangipani tree.

The innermost and holiest courtyard (small temples may have just two courts) is entered by another candi-like gateway. A passage through the middle of it symbolise the holy mountain through which you must pass to enter the inner court. This gateway will be flanked by statues of guardian figures or by small protective shrines.

In the inner court there will usually be two rows of shrines, the most important on the mountain side and the lesser on the sunrise side. These shrines vary in number and design from temple to temple, although there are detailed rules to cover all of them. In the major temples the shrines will include multiroofed thatched pagodas known as *meru*. The number of roofs are, apart from some rare exceptions, always odd and the holiest meru will have 11 roofs. The inner court may also contain simple little thrones for local and less important gods to use.

Visiting Temples Except on rare occasions anyone can enter a temple, but you are expected to be politely dressed. You should always wear a temple scarf – a sash tied oosely around your waist – and a sarong or ong pants. Many of the larger, more ouristed temples rent scarves to visitors for few hundred rupiah. You can buy one yourelf quite cheaply, and it's a nice thing to ave when visiting temples where sashes are not available for rent. You won't have to pay for renting a sash, but you should still make he appropriate donation to the temple.

Priests should be shown respect, particularly at festivals. They're the most important people and should, therefore, be on the highest plane. Don't put yourself higher than hem by climbing up on a wall to take photographs. There will usually be a sign outside emple entrances asking you to be well dressed, wear a temple scarf and be respectul, and also requesting that women not enter he temple during menstruation.

Nearly every temple (or other site of interst to tourists) will levy an entry charge or sk for a donation from foreigners – any on-Balinese is a foreigner. Usually this is round 1000 rp – occasionally less, occaionally more. If there is no fixed charge and donation is requested, 1000 rp is a suitable mount, though the donation book may indiate that people have paid thousands – zeros re sometimes added.

Temple Festivals For much of the year Balinese temples are deserted, but on holy days the deities and ancestral spirits descend from heaven to visit their devotees, and the emples come alive with days of frenetic ctivity and nights of drama and dance. Temple festivals come at least once every Balinese year – 210 days. Because most illages have at least three temples, you're ssured of at least five or six annual festivals n every village. The full moon periods round the end of September to the begining of October or early to mid-April are often times of important festivals. One such estival is the Galungan, which takes place hroughout the island. During this 10 day period all the gods, including the supreme deity, Sanghyang Widi, come down to earth or the festivities.

Temple festivals are as much a social occasion as a religious one. Cockfights (where two cocks fight with sharp barbs attached to their legs) are a regular part of temple ceremonies: a combination of excitement, sport and illicit gambling. They also provide a blood sacrifice to dissuade evil spirits from interfering with the religious ceremonies that follow. While the men slaughter their prized pets, the women bring beautifully arranged offerings of food, fruit and flowers artistically piled in huge pyramids, which they carry on their heads to the temple. Outside, *warungs* offer food for sale, other stalls are set up to sell toys, trinkets and batik, and there are sideshows with card games, gambling, buskers, mystic healers, music and dancing, while the gamelan orchestra plays on in the outer courtyard.

Inside, the *pemangkus* (temple priests) suggest to the gods that they should come down and enjoy the goings on. The small thrones in the temple shrines are symbolic seats for the gods to occupy during festivals, although sometimes small images called *pratimas* are placed in the thrones to represent them. At some festivals the images and thrones of the deities are taken out of the temple and ceremonially carried down to the sea (or to a suitable expanse of water) for a ceremonial bath. Inside the temple the proceedings take on a more formal, mystical tone as the pemangkus continue to chant their songs of praise before shrines clouded by smoking incense. The women dance the stately Pendet, in itself an offering to the gods through the beauty of their motions.

As dawn approaches, the entertainment and ceremonies wind down, and the women dance a final Pendet, a farewell to the deities. The pemangkus politely suggest to the gods that it's time they made their way back to heaven, and the people make their own weary way back to their homes.

Funerals

A Balinese funeral is an amazing, colourful, noisy and exciting event. Basically it is a happy occasion, as it represents the destruction of the body and the release of the soul so that it can be united with the supreme god.

The body is carried to the cremation ground in a high multi-tiered tower made of bamboo, paper, string, tinsel, silk, cloth, mirrors, flowers and anything else bright and colourful. Carried on the shoulders of a group of men, the tower represents the cosmos, and the base, in the shape of a turtle entwined by two snakes, symbolises the foundation of the world. On the base is an open platform where the body is placed – in the space between heaven and earth. The size

BALI

BALI

of the group carrying the body and the number of tiers on the tower varies according to the caste of the deceased.

On the way to the cremation ground, the tower is shaken and run around in circles to disorient the spirit of the deceased so that it cannot find its way home. A gamelan sprints along behind, providing a suitably exciting musical accompaniment and almost trampling the camera-toting tourists. (Tourists are accepted in the procession because they add to the noise and confusion, further disorienting the spirits.) At the cremation ground the body is transferred to a funeral sarcophagus and the whole lot – funeral tower, sarcophagus and body – goes up in flames. Finally, the colourful procession heads to the sea (or a nearby river if the sea is too far away) to scatter the ashes.

GREGORY ADAMS

Intricate, hand-made offerings, such as this one made from rice, are an important part of the ceremonies during festivals on Bali.

LANGUAGE

Balinese language, as distinct from Indonesian, the national language, reflects caste distinctions. Traditionally there are five forms of the language, with the usage governed by the social relationship between the two people having a conversation. Modern usage is described in terms of three forms. Low Balinese (Ia) is used between intimates and equals and when talking to inferiors. Polite or Middle Balinese (Ipun) is used when speaking about superiors, or when addressing superiors or strangers, mainly when one wishes to be very polite but doesn't want to emphasise caste differences; and High Balinese (Ida) is used when talking to superiors, particularly in the context of religious ceremonies.

FOREIGN CONSULATES ON BALI

The Australian Consulate, in the Renon district of Denpasar, will also help citizens of other Commonwealth countries while they're on Bali, including those from Canada, New Zealand, Papua New Guinea and the UK. Japan also has a full consulate in Denpasar but all the others listed below are consular agents and may offer only a limited range of services. The area code for all telephone numbers listed is ☎ 0361.

Australia
    Jl Mochammad Yamin 51, Renon, Denpasar; PO Box 243, Denpasar (☎ 235092/3; fax 231990)
France
    Jl Raya Sesetan 46D, Banjar Pesanggaran, Denpasar (☎ & fax 233555)
Germany
    Jl Pantai Karang 17, Sanur; PO Box 3100, Denpasar (☎ 288535; fax 288826)
Italy
    Jl Cemara, Banjar Semawang, Sanur Kauh; PO Box 158, Denpasar (☎ 288996; fax 287642)
Japan
    Jl Mochammad Yamin 9, Renon, Denpasar (☎ 234808; fax 231308)
Netherlands
    Jl Imam Bonjol 599, Kuta; PO Box 337, Denpasar (☎ 751517; fax 752777)
Norway & Denmark
    Jl Jaya Giri VIII/10, Renon, Denpasar; Box 188, Denpasar (☎ 235098; fax 234834)

weden & Finland
  Segara Village Hotel, Jl Segara Ayu, Sanur
  (☎ 288407/8)
witzerland
  Swiss Restaurant, Jl Pura Bagus Taruna, Legian
  (☎ 751735; fax 754457)
JSA
  Jl Hayam Wuruk 188, Renon, Denpasar
  (☎ 233605; fax 222426); open from 8 am to 4.30
  pm, Monday to Friday.

BOOKS

There are many publications about Bali. For a detailed travel guide with lots of background information, get Lonely Planet's *Bali & Lombok*.

The classic work is *Island of Bali* by Mexican artist Miguel Covarrubias. First published in 1937, it is still available as an Oxford in Asia paperback. Despite many changes, much of Bali is still as Covarrubias describes it, and few people have come to grips with the island so well.

Colin McPhee's *A House in Bali* is a lyrical account of a musician's lengthy stay in Bali to study gamelan music. *The Last Paradise* by Hickman Powell and *A Tale from Bali* by Vicki Baum also date from that heady period in the 1930s, when so many westerners 'discovered' Bali. K'Tut Tantri's *Revolt in Paradise* again starts in the 1930s, but this western woman who took a Balinese name remained in Indonesia through the war and during part of the subsequent struggle for independence from the Dutch.

Our Hotel in Bali by Louis G Koke tells of the original Kuta Beach Hotel which was established by Americans Robert and Louis Koke during the 1930s. Hugh Mabbett's *The Balinese* is an interesting collection of anecdotes, observations and impressions, and *In Praise of Kuta* is a sympathetic account of that much maligned beach resort.

For a rundown on Balinese arts and culture, look for the huge and expensive *The Art & Culture of Bali* by Urs Ramseyer. An economical and useful introduction to Balinese painting can be found in *The Development of Painting in Bali*, published by the Neka Museum. *Balinese Paintings* by AAM

Djelantik is a concise and handy overview of the field.

Periplus Editions publishes a range of titles on Balinese food, fruit, flowers, textiles etc, which will appeal to those with specific interests. There's a growing number of large-format, well-illustrated coffee-table books on Bali. *Bali High – Paradise from the Air* has some stunning photographs of Bali taken from a helicopter. *Balinese Textiles*, by Brigitta Hauser, Marie-Louise Nabholz-Kartaschoff and Urs Ramseyer, is a large and lavishly illustrated guide to various styles of weaving and their significance.

Bookshops in Kuta, Sanur and Ubud have a wide range of English-language books, particularly on Indonesia. Big hotels, some supermarkets and various tourist shops and galleries have more limited selections, and there are numerous places selling second-hand books.

GETTING THERE & AWAY

Bali has direct international flights from a number of countries, and there are frequent flights to or from Jakarta, which has even more international connections. Regular domestic flights also connect to other centres on Java, Mataram on Lombok and many other islands of Indonesia. Regular ferries go to/from Java and Lombok, which carry vehicles as well as passengers, and there are also fast boat services between Bali and Lombok.

Air

Bali's Denpasar airport is actually a few km to the south, just beyond Kuta Beach. Officially the airport is named Ngurah Rai, after a hero of the struggle for independence from the Dutch.

The airport has a hotel-booking counter, which covers only the more expensive places. There's also a tourist information counter, with some useful brochures and helpful staff, a left-luggage room and a couple of money changing desks.

There's an expensive duty-free shop and some souvenir shops at the airport. The departure lounge cafeteria takes rupiah, but it's much more expensive than the shops outside. You can change excess rupiah back into hard currency at the bank counter by the check-in desks, but keep 25,000 rp for departure tax on international flights. The 11,000 rp domestic departure tax is included in the price if you buy the ticket in Indonesia.

International The number of direct international flights to Bali has increased in recent years. See the introductory Getting There & Away chapter for more details.

If you're flying out of Bali, reconfirm your bookings at least 72 hours before departure. Most travel agents in the main tourist areas can do this, but make sure you get the piece of computer printout that shows you are actually confirmed on the flight. There are Garuda offices in Denpasar, Kuta and Sanur, and most of the other airlines have offices in the Hotel Bali Beach in Sanur. Telephone numbers for international airlines (all in the 0361 area) are:

Air France	☏ 287734
Air New Zealand	☏ 756170
Ansett Australia	☏ 289636
Cathay Pacific	☏ 286001
China Air	☏ 757298
Continental	☏ 752106
Garuda	☏ 235169; reconfirmation ☏ 227825, 222788 or 234606
Japan Air	☏ 287577
KLM	☏ 756126
Korean Air	☏ 289402
Lufthansa	☏ 286952
Malaysian Airlines	☏ 285071
Qantas	☏ 288331
Singapore Airlines	☏ 287940
Thai International	☏ 288141

Domestic Denpasar is a major travel hub with direct flights to Bima, Dili, Jakarta, Kupang, Mataram, Maumere, Surabaya, Ujung Pandang and Waingapu. With connections you can fly to almost anywhere in Indonesia from Denpasar. Most domestic connections are provided by Garuda (which has several Bali offices), Merpati and Bouraq (with offices in Denpasar), and Sempati

(in Sanur's Hotel Bali Beach). Telephone numbers (in the 0361 area) are:

Bouraq	☏ 223564
Merpati	☏ 235358
Sempati	☏ 237343 (open 24 hours every day)

Sea

Java Regular ferries cross the narrow strait between Gilimanuk (western Bali) and Ketapang (East Java) about every 15 to 30 minutes 24 hours a day. See under Gilimanuk in the West Bali section for details.

Frequent direct buses, which include the ferry crossing in their fares, go regularly between Bali and the main cities on Java including Surabaya (10 to 12 hours; 22,400 rp), Yogyakarta (15 to 16 hours; 41,500 rp) and Jakarta (26 to 30 hours; 62,900 rp). Buses will drop you in Probolinggo if you want to climb Gunung Bromo. Generally you have to book a day or more in advance, and air-con and non-air-con buses are available. Check the arrival times to avoid reaching your destination at an absurd pre-dawn hour. Most buses arrive and depart from Ubung terminal in Denpasar, which is the cheapest place to buy tickets, though you can also buy them from agents at Kuta Beach and elsewhere. Direct buses also operate from Singaraja, on Bali's north coast, for similar fares.

Some of the direct bus and ferry services connect with trains at Ketapang, which go to Probolinggo, Surabaya and Yogyakarta (see the Java chapter for details). Train tickets are available from the railways office in Denpasar or from agents in Kuta.

Lombok There are ferries every two hours between Padangbai (Bali) and Lembar (Lombok). See Padangbai in the East Bali section for details. Tourist shuttle buses run between the tourist centres on Bali and Lombok, and include the cost of the ferry – from Kuta or Sanur on Bali to Mataram or Senggigi on Lombok costs 20,000 rp.

The *Mabua Express* is a luxury jet-powered catamaran, providing a fast boat service wice daily between Lembar Harbour on Lom-ok and Benoa Port on Bali. See the Benoa Port section in the South Bali section for de-ails, or call Mabua (☎ (0361) 72370, 72521).

Nusa Tenggara The national shipping line, Pelni, has passenger ships doing regular oops through the islands of Indonesia, typi-ally calling at Benoa once a fortnight. The xact dates and routes can change, so enquire vell in advance. Currently, four Pelni ships top at Benoa: *Kelimutu*, *Awu*, *Tilongkabila* nd *Dobonsolo*. The Pelni office (☎ (0361) 238962; fax 228962) is in Benoa Port at Jl Pelabuhan, Benoa. See the introductory Get-ing Around chapter for further details.

GETTING AROUND

Bali is a small island with good roads and egular, inexpensive public transport. Traffic s heavy from Denpasar south to Kuta and Sanur, east about as far as Klungkung and vest as far as Tabanan. Over the rest of the sland, the roads are remarkably uncrowded. f you rent your own vehicle it's easy to find our way around – roads are well signposted and maps are readily available. Off the main outes, most roads are surfaced but often ery potholed.

Airport

The Ngurah Rai airport is just south of Kuta Beach. There's a taxi counter where you pay or your taxi in advance. Fares from the airport are:

Destination	Price (rp)
Kuta Beach (to Jl Bakung Sari)	6500
Kuta-Legian (to Jl Padma)	8500
Jimbaran	8500
Legian (beyond Jl Padma)	10,000
Denpasar	11,000
Oberoi Hotel (beyond Legian)	11,000
Ubung terminal	12,000
Nusa Dua	15,000
Sanur	15,000
Ubud	40,000

The impecunious should walk across the airport carpark and continue a couple of hundred metres to the airport road, from where public *bemos* go to Denpasar's Tegal terminal via Kuta throughout most of the day. You could walk all the way to Kuta – it's only a few km on the Tuban road or along the beach.

Bemo

Most of Bali's public transport is provided by minibuses, usually called *bemos*, but on some longer routes the vehicle may be a full-sized bus. Denpasar is the transport hub of Bali and has bus/bemo terminals for the various destinations – see the Denpasar section for details. Unfortunately, travel in southern Bali often requires you to travel via one or more of the Denpasar terminals, and this can make for an inconvenient and time-consuming trip.

The fare between main towns may be posted at the terminals, or you can ask around for the right price – it's easier at a terminal as the operators will be competing for your business. You can also flag a bemo down pretty much anywhere along its route, but you may be charged the *harga turis* (tourist price) – Bali bemos are notorious for overcharging tourists. Ask a local the correct fare before embarking on a journey, and pay the exact amount when you get off. If you ask the correct fare, they'll know that you don't know and they may try to overcharge you. It's better to watch what other passengers pay, or make your best estimate of the correct fare.

You can charter a whole vehicle for a trip, which may be more convenient, and between a few people not much more expensive than the standard fare. You can also charter bemos by the day from around 60,000 to 80,000 rp depending on the distance; the price should include driver and petrol. In tourist areas you can only charter vehicles with yellow plates; regular bemos are only licensed to work fixed routes. In non-tourist areas this doesn't seem to be enforced, and bemo charter is cheaper but you have to pay for petrol and buy food for the driver.

Beware of pickpockets on bemos – they often have an accomplice to distract you, or use a package to hide the activity.

Tourist Shuttle Bus

As well as the public buses and bemos, there are a growing number of shuttle bus services between various tourist centres, such as Kuta, Sanur, Candidasa, Kintamani and Lovina – look for the advertisements outside tour and travel agencies. There are also connections to the ports of Gilimanuk, Padangbai and Benoa, and you can book direct tickets to destinations on Java, Lombok and Sumbawa. They are more expensive than the bemos, but much quicker and more convenient. Usually you have to book the day before. The Perama company seems to have the most comprehensive service, but there are others. Make sure that the bus is going direct to your destination and not by some roundabout route. If they promise to deliver you to a specific hotel, have it written on your ticket.

Taxi

Taxis are becoming more common in Denpasar and the tourist areas of south Bali. Praja taxis (☎ 289090) are blue and yellow, and cost 900 rp to start, 900 rp for the first km or part thereof, then around 50 rp per 100m. Bali taxis (☎ 701111) charge similar fares, with a minimum of 2500 rp. They're good, and a lot less hassle than haggling with bemo jockeys and charter bemo drivers. You can always find them at the airport, but taxis can be unpopular in areas where charter operators are trying to hustle tourist business. Taxis probably won't stop on Jl Legian or near Bemo Corner in Kuta. Don't get in a taxi if the driver says the meter isn't working – it may suddenly 'fix' itself, but if not get another taxi.

Car & Motorcycle

Road Rules & Risks Road rules on Bali are the same as for the rest of Indonesia. Remember to have your drivers' licence and the vehicle's registration paper with you at all times. Cops will stop vehicles on some very thin pretexts in order to extract 'on-the-spot fines'. Most matters can be settled for 20,000 to 50,000 rp, but don't make any offers – wait for the cop to ask. Officially, driving withou a licence can get you a 2,000,000 rp fine.

Driving is risky. If you have a seriou accident, it may be wise to go straight to th nearest police station rather than confront a angry mob of locals. If it's a minor accident you may be better off negotiating a cas settlement on the spot than spending the res of your holiday hassling with police an lawyers.

Rental More and more car-rental places ar springing up. The usual rental vehicle is small Suzuki jeep (Jimny), but for more tha two adults a Kijang minibus will be mor comfortable. Typical costs for a Suzuki ar around 35,000 to 40,000 rp a day, includin insurance and unlimited km; a Kijang cost from around 55,000 rp per day. It's substan tially cheaper by the week. You can also fin regular cars, but they cost more and are nc as well suited to steep, rough, winding roads You need to have an International Drivin Permit to rent a car.

Motorcycles are a popular way to ge around Bali, but can be dangerous. Mos rental motorcycles are between 90 and 12 cc, with 100 cc the usual size. Rental charge vary with the bike, period of hire an demand. The longer the hire period the lowe the rate; the bigger or newer the bike th higher the rate. Typically you can expect t pay from around 9000 to 12,000 rp a day This incudes a flimsy helmet, which is compul sory and provides protection against sunbur but not much else.

There are a few places around Kuta whicl specialise in bike hire, but it's often just travel agent, restaurant, losmen or shop witl a sign saying 'motorcycle for rent'. Kuta i the main motorcycle-hire place but you'l have no trouble finding one to rent in Ubuc Sanur, Candidasa or Lovina. Check it ove before riding off – some are very poorl maintained.

You'll need an International Driving Permi endorsed for motorcycles, or you'll have t get a temporary local licence from the polic station in Denpasar, which is easy but time consuming, and costs about 50,000 rp. Th wner of the motorcycle will take you to the lace and help you with the written test (30 nultiple choice questions). You're photo-raphed and fingerprinted, but you don't sually have to do a riding test.

nsurance Insurance for rented cars or notorcycles provides only limited cover and s usually quite expensive. It's not compul-ory, but it's recommended especially for car ental – if you have an accident, insurance vill make it easier for your consulate to get ou out of jail. Your own travel insurance olicy may not cover you for motorcycle ccidents unless you have a home motor-ycle licence, not just a Balinese one.

uel Petrol (bensin) is sold by the govern-nent-owned Pertamina company, at petrol tations on the outskirts of most towns on 3ali, for around 700 rp a litre. Pertamina tations are sometimes out of petrol, out of lectricity or out on a holiday, in which case ook for the little roadside fuel shops where ou fill up with a plastic jug and funnel. They ften have a hand-painted sign saying 'Pre-nium', and they charge a little more – maybe 50 rp per litre.

Bicycle
n the main tourist areas it is quite easy to ent a pushbike by the hour or the day, and t's a good way to get around locally. Mostly hey're 10 speed mountain bikes, and they ent for around 5000 rp per day. You should e able to bargain the price down to about 000 rp per day for a few days or longer. Check the bike carefully – many are in bad ondition and few are perfect.

Touring the island by bicycle is quite opular and a great way to see Bali. If you vant to try it, it's probably best to bring your wn bike with you; airlines will generally arry a bike as part of your 20 kg baggage llowance. Otherwise be prepared to spend ome time looking for a good machine to ent, and/or some effort making it suitable or long-distance touring. Good brakes, seat, tyres and a lock are essential; bells, lights and luggage racks are desirable.

You can usually get a bemo to take you and your bike up the bigger mountains (the bike goes on the roof and costs the same as a passenger), though this is more difficult with the newer minibus bemos. Bicycles are used extensively by the Balinese, and even the smallest village has some semblance of a bike shop. Some shops will allow you to borrow tools to work on your own bike. The best shops for extensive repairs are in Denpasar.

Once you're out of the congested southern region, traffic is relatively light and the roads are not too bad, particularly if you invest in a good, padded seat. You can accomplish a beautiful, 200 km circle trip of Bali, level or downhill almost the whole way, with a coup-le of bemo rides.

Bicycle Tour This 200 km route is designed to take in the greatest number of points of interest with the minimum use of motorised transport and the maximum amount of level or downhill roads. For convenience, the tour is divided into six days of actual riding in a clockwise direction, which takes advantage of evening stops where there are convenient losmen.

Day 1 – Kuta to Bedugul (57 km) The first 37 km is level cycling, but from the village of Luwus it's uphill, so you can catch a bemo – on a good bicycle even this section is quite manageable. Estimated riding time is seven hours.

Day 2 – Bedugul to Singaraja (30 km) Estimated riding time is three hours, a steep climb then downhill most of the way. You can detour to the Lovina beaches.

Day 3 – Singaraja to Penelokan (60 km) The 24 km from the coast up to Penulisan is very steep, so a bemo is recommended. The first 10 km and the final 10 km are fine. Detour down to Lake Batur and Toya Bungkah to climb Gunung Batur.

Day 4 – Penelokan to Klungkung via Rendang (31 km) You can detour to Besakih by bemo, but the direct ride is only about four hours. An alternative would be via Tampaksiring to Ubud.

Day 5 – Klungkung to Denpasar (40 km) Estimated riding time is six hours. This road has heavy traffic.

BALI

Day 6 – Denpasar to Kuta If you go via Sanur and Benoa this is a 24 km ride and estimated riding time is five hours. Again there are some stretches of heavy traffic on this run.

Organised Tours

There are countless tours organised from the main tourist areas, and they can be booked through the many travel agencies or your hotel. Day and half-day tours are offered to all of the tourist attractions on Bali, though they vary widely in price and quality. Some are nothing more than shop crawls, carting you from one warehouse to another, with a brief pause at a temple or an overpriced restaurant. Check the itinerary carefully and compare a few offerings.

A good tour will let you see a variety of hard-to-reach places in a short time. A good day trip might take in silver workshops at Celuk, a hand-weaving factory in Gianyar, the Kerta Ghosa at Klungkung, the 'mother temple' of Besakih, the 'bat cave' of Goa Lawah and a traditional salt-making operation, with some superb rice-field scenery along the way. An excursion to Bona village to see the Kecak dance, the Sanghyang Dedari and the Sanghyang Jaran (fire) dance could make a memorable evening tour. Prices start at around 20,000 rp for a full day trip.

There are also specialist operators, with scuba diving, whitewater rafting, pony trekking, cycling, sailing and surfing tours. Kuta and Sanur are the best places to look for tours.

Tours to Other Islands Tours also go to Mt Bromo in East Java and as far as Yogyakarta, including all accommodation, transport and entry charges. Others take in the main sights on Lombok, and tours to Komodo or Sulawesi are also available. Generally these seem expensive for what they offer. For example: US$125 for a two day, one night trip to climb Mt Bromo; and US$500 for a three day, two night trip to Flores, Komodo and Rinca. It would be much better value to organise your own transport to the area you're interested in, and arrange any sightseeing trips locally.

Denpasar

The capital of Bali, with a population c around 370,000, Denpasar has been th focus of a lot of the growth and wealth ove the last 20 years. It has an interesting museum an arts centre and lots of shops. Denpasa means 'next to the market', and the mai market (called Pasar Badung) is said to b the biggest and busiest on Bali. Denpasa was formerly the capital of the Badung dis trict, but the city and surrounding area including Sanur, Benoa Port and Pulau Se rangan, was split off in 1992 to become self-governing municipality. Denpasar sti has some tree-lined streets and pleasant ga dens, but the traffic, noise and pollutio make it a difficult place to enjoy.

Many of Denpasar's residents are de scended from immigrant groups, such a Bugis mercenaries and Chinese, Arab an Indian traders. More recent immigrants hav been attracted by the wealth in Denpasa including Javanese civil servants, trades people and workers, and Balinese from al over the island. They give the city cosmopolitan air, and it is increasingly Java-oriented modern Indonesian city rathe than a parochial Balinese capital. As the cit grows it is engulfing the surrounding vil lages, but their banjars and village lif continue amid the urbanisation. The recer immigrants tend to occupy detached house outside the family compounds, and may even tually supplant the traditional communal wa of life.

If you feel that Bali is overcrowded wit tourists, you'll find that tourists are vastl outnumbered in Denpasar – it mightn't be tropical paradise, but it's as much a part o 'the real Bali' as the rice fields and temples

Orientation

The main street of Denpasar, Jl Gajah Mada is called Jl Gunung Agung at the west sid of town. It then changes to Jl Wahidin, the Jl Gajah Mada in the middle of town, then J Surapati, then Jl Hayam Wuruk on the eas

ide of town, and finally Jl Sanur before
urning south to a large roundabout, then east
o Sanur. This name-changing is common for
Denpasar streets, and is one source of confu-
ion. Another problem is the proliferation of
ne way traffic restrictions, sometimes for
nly part of a street's length, which often
hange and are rarely marked on maps.
Despite, or perhaps because of, these control
neasures, the traffic jams can be intense.
'arking can also be difficult, so avoid
riving – take taxis, bemos or walk.

Both Kumbasari market and the main
'asar Badung are just south of Jl Gajah
Mada, on the west side of town. The main
hopping centres are between Jl Diponegoro
which is one way, going north towards Jl
Gajah Mada) and Jl Sudirman (which is one
vay going south).

In contrast to the rest of Denpasar, the
Lenon area, south-east of the town centre, is
aid out on a grand scale, with wide streets,
arge carparks and big landscaped blocks of
and – this is the area of government offices.

Information

Tourist Office The Denpasar tourist office
(☎ 234569) is on Jl Surapati 7, just north of
he Bali Museum. A useful calendar of festi-
als and events on Bali, and a pretty good
nap, are usually available. The office may
lso help with information on Bali's bemo
ystem. It is open Monday to Thursday from
am to 2 pm, and on Friday until 11 am. The
Bali government tourist office (☎ 222387),
n the Renon area, is mainly an administra-
ive facility and doesn't provide much
nformation.

Money All the major Indonesian banks have
heir main Bali offices in Denpasar, princi-
ally along Jl Gajah Mada. The Bank
Ekspor-Impor Indonesia, a block to the south
t Jl Udayana 11, is probably the best for
ransfers from overseas.

Post The main Denpasar post office, with a
oste-restante service, is inconveniently
ocated in the Renon area, a long way from
he nearest bemo terminal.

Communications Telkom has an office at Jl
Teuku Umar 6, near the intersection with Jl
Diponegoro. You can make international
phone calls and send telegrams and faxes.
Other Telkom offices are next to the main
post office and on Jl Durian just north of the
tourist office. There's a private telephone
office in the Tiara Dewata shopping centre,
and a Home Country Direct phone at the
museum.

Immigration The kantor imigrasi (☎ 22-
7828) is at Jl Panjaitan 4 in the Renon area,
just around the corner from the main post
office. It opens Monday to Thursday from 8
am to 2 pm, Friday until 11 am and Saturday
until noon.

If you have to visit, make sure you're
neatly dressed. Bemos from Tegal to Sanur
pass within a few blocks of the office.

Medical Services Denpasar's main hospital
(☎ 227911), Rumah Sakit Umum Propinsi
(RSUP), is in the southern part of town in
Sanglah, a couple of blocks west of Jl Diponegoro. It's probably the best place to go on
Bali if you have a serious injury or urgent
medical problem. SOS Gatotkaca Klinik
(☎ 223555), Jl Gatotkaca 21, is a private
clinic with English-speaking staff, open 24
hours a day.

Bali Museum

This museum consists of an attractive series
of separate buildings and pavilions, including examples of the architecture of both the
palace (puri) and temple (pura). Exhibits are
not always well presented, but include both
modern and older paintings, arts & crafts,
tools and various items of everyday use.
Note the fine wood and cane carrying-cases
for transporting fighting cocks, and the tiny
ones for fighting crickets. There are superb
stone sculptures, krises, wayang kulit figures, and an excellent exhibit of dance
costumes and masks. It's a good place to see
authentic, traditional paintings, masks, woodcarving and weaving before you consider
buying something from the craft and antique
shops. There are some excellent examples of

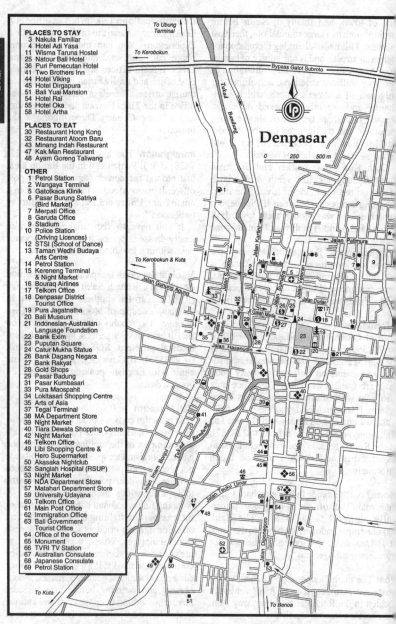

PLACES TO STAY
3 Nakula Familiar
4 Hotel Adi Yasa
11 Wisma Taruna Hostel
25 Natour Bali Hotel
36 Puri Pemecutan Hotel
41 Two Brothers Inn
44 Hotel Viking
45 Hotel Dirgapura
51 Bali Yuai Mansion
54 Hotel Rai
55 Hotel Oka
58 Hotel Artha

PLACES TO EAT
30 Restaurant Hong Kong
32 Restaurant Atoom Baru
43 Minang Indah Restaurant
47 Kak Man Restaurant
48 Ayam Goreng Taliwang

OTHER
1 Petrol Station
2 Wangaya Terminal
5 Gatotkaca Klinik
6 Pasar Burung Satriya
    (Bird Market)
7 Merpati Office
8 Garuda Office
9 Stadium
10 Police Station
    (Driving Licences)
12 STSI (School of Dance)
13 Taman Wedhi Budaya
    Arts Centre
14 Petrol Station
15 Kereneng Terminal
    & Night Market
16 Bouraq Airlines
17 Telkom Office
18 Denpasar District
    Tourist Office
19 Pura Jagatnatha
20 Bali Museum
21 Indonesian-Australian
    Language Foundation
22 Bank Exim
23 Puputan Square
24 Catur Mukha Statue
26 Bank Dagang Negara
27 Bank Rakyat
28 Gold Shops
29 Pasar Badung
31 Pasar Kumbasari
33 Pura Maospahit
34 Lokitasari Shopping Centre
35 Arts of Asia
37 Tegal Terminal
38 MA Department Store
39 Night Market
40 Tiara Dewata Shopping Centre
42 Night Market
46 Telkom Office
49 Libi Shopping Centre &
    Hero Supermarket
50 Akasaka Nightclub
52 Sanglah Hospital (RSUP)
53 Night Market
56 NDA Department Store
57 Matahari Department Store
59 University Udayana
60 Telkom Office
61 Main Post Office
62 Immigration Office
63 Bali Government
    Tourist Office
64 Office of the Governor
65 Monument
66 TVRI TV Station
67 Australian Consulate
68 Japanese Consulate
69 Petrol Station

Denpasar

To Ubung Terminal
To Kerobokun
Bypass Gatot Subroto
Tukad Bandung
Jalan Kartini
Jalan Patimura
Jalan Nakula
To Kerobokun & Kuta
Jalan Sudirno
Jalan Veteran
Jalan Gunung Agung
Jalan Durian
Jalan Surupta
Gajah Mada
Jalan Sumin
Jalan Hasanudin
Jalan Imam Bonjol
Tukad Bandung
Jalan Sudirman
Jalan Teuku Umar
Jalan Diponegoro
To Kuta
To Benoa

0   250   500 m

'double ikat' weaving, a technique in which both the warp and weft threads are resist dyed before being woven.

The museum is open daily, except Monday, from 8 am to 5 pm (to 3.30 pm on Friday). Admission is 500 rp for adults, 200 rp for children.

Pura Jagatnatha

Adjacent to the museum is the state temple Pura Jagatnatha. This relatively new temple is dedicated to the supreme god, Sanghyang Widi and his shrine, the *padmasana*, is made of white coral. The padmasana (throne, symbolic of heaven) tops the cosmic turtle and the *naga* (mythological serpent) which symbolise the foundation of the world.

Taman Budaya Arts Centre

This arts centre (☎ 222776) is quite a large complex on Jl Nusa Indah, in the suburb of Abian Kupas east of Denpasar. It was established in 1973 as an academy and a showplace for Balinese culture, and includes teaching and performance facilities. There are exhibits of traditional and modern painting and sculpture, a dancing stage, craft shop and restaurant. It holds an entertaining Kecak dance every evening at 6.30 pm (6000 rp), as well as frequent special performances and rehearsals, and regular temporary exhibits. The centre is open Tuesday to Sunday from 8 am to 5 pm; 250 rp entry and 200 rp car-parking.

From mid-June to mid-July, the centre hosts a summer **arts festival**, with competitions for the best drama, dance and music performances, and exhibitions of painting and sculpture. You may need to book tickets for the most popular events.

Places to Stay

Most people who stay in Denpasar are Indonesian visitors, mostly business travellers. There are also domestic tourists, especially in July-August, and around Christmas and the end of Ramadan when hotels can fill up. There are plenty of places to stay, however, and you won't be bothered by a surfeit of foreign tourists. Hotels catering to Indonesians often have a wide range of rooms, facilities and prices. If the first room you're offered is too expensive, or too grotty, it's always worth asking for something else.

Places to Stay – bottom end

Hotel Adi Yasa (☎ 222679) at Jl Nakula 23B is a venerable, standard-style losmen, with the rooms facing a central garden – it's OK and quite a few foreigners stay here (one reader suggested that the windows weren't too secure). Rooms are 12,500/17,000 rp for singles/doubles with shared mandi, 15,000/20,000 rp with private bathroom, breakfast included. Just west, on the other side of the same street, *Nakula Familiar* (☎ 226446) at Jl Nakula 4 is a new place, not spacious, but clean, friendly and inexpensive. Tegal-Kereneng bemos go along Jl Nakula.

Near the Tegal terminal, *Two Brothers Inn* (☎ 222704), on a gang off Jl Imam Bonjol, is another old standard losmen, which asks 13,000/18,000 rp for an ordinary room with breakfast and shared bath.

The cheapest accommodation is at the *Hostel Wisma Taruna* (☎ 226913) at Jl Gadung 31, which charges 10,000/12,000 rp with shared bath and no breakfast, or 7500/10,000 rp for Youth Hostel Association (YHA) members. It's friendly enough, and not far from Kereneng terminal, but the rooms are very plain and it's not good value.

The *Bali Yuai Mansion* (☎ 228850), at Jl Satelit 22 in Sanglah, is a good, inexpensive place with a very helpful owner, and clean, comfortable rooms from 10,000/15,000 rp, or 30,000 rp with air-con. It's about 500m from Jl Imam Bonjol – get off the Kuta-Tegal bemo at the roundabout near the Libi shopping centre. You can call for directions, or staff may pick you up from Tegal terminal.

Places to Stay – middle

Mid-range places on or near Jl Diponegoro, the main road coming in from the south of town, cater mainly to Indonesian business travellers. The *Hotel Viking* (☎ 223992) at No 120 has economy rooms from 20,000 rp for singles and air-con rooms up to 50,000 rp. Further south on the eastern side of Jl

Diponegoro is the *Hotel Rai* (☎ 224574), middling to expensive place. Similar hote on the southern part of Diponegoro incluc the *Dirgapura* (☎ 226924), *Artha* (☎ 22737(and *Oka* (☎ 234685).

The *Puri Pemecutan Hotel* (☎ 423491) in the rebuilt palace at the junction of Hasanudin and Jl Imam Bonjol (the road ▪ Kuta), handy to the Tegal terminal. It's n▪ very atmospheric, but there are some inte esting old things there. Rooms with air-co▪ phone, TV and private bath cost 50,000/60,0(rp, 12,000 rp for an extra bed.

Places to Stay – top end

A notch down from luxury standard, th *Natour Bali Hotel* (☎ 225681/5) at Jl Vetera 3 is the former Bali Hotel which dates fro▪ the Dutch days. It was never a masterpie▪ of colonial architecture, but it's a pleasant old-fashioned place with some nice Art Dec details (look at the light fittings in the dinin room), despite recent unsympathetic Bali ese decorations. Standard singles/double start at about US$63/68, including breakfa and air-con; 'executive rooms' cost US$71/7 and a suite is US$105. Some of the room are actually on the other side of Jl Vetera▪ so you'll have to walk across the road to u▪ the dining room, bar and swimming pool.

Places to Eat

The eating places in Denpasar cater for loc people, recent immigrants and Indonesia visitors, so they offer a good selection (authentic food from Indonesia's various cu sines. A number of restaurants along and ne▪ Jl Gajah Mada are operated by and for th Chinese community, and many of them serv excellent Chinese food.

The *Restaurant Atoom Baru* at Jl Gaja Mada 108 is a typical Asian (as opposed ▪ western) Chinese restaurant. Its interestin▪ menu has lots of seafood, and dishes such ▪ beef balls soup and pig's bladder with musl rooms. Other main courses are from 4000 ▪ 9000 rp. Across the road is the *Restaurar Hong Kong*, serving Chinese and Indonesi▪ food. It's a bit classier, with tablecloths, an bit pricier. There are also several Padang ood restaurants along Jl Gajah Mada.

South of Jl Gajah Mada, the Kumbasari market has a *pasar malam* (night market), ith dozens of food stalls. There are other asar malam near the Kereneng and Tegal rminals and along Jl Diponegoro. They rve food until 10 pm or later, after most of e restaurants in town have closed. To try reet-stall type food in a very clean, hyienic setting, try the food hall inside *Tiara ewata shopping centre*. If you can't face at, you may prefer *Dunkin' Donuts*, at the ont of the complex.

Jl Diponegoro has more eating possibilies, like the *Melati Indah*, next to the MA epartment store, and the *Minang Indah*, rther south, with good Padang food. urther south again, the big new NDA epartment store has an excellent array of ateries on its top floor.

A number of *rumah makans* down Jl euku Umar, like *Kak Man*, serve real Balinse food, as well as the standard Indonesian re. *Ayam Goreng Taliwang*, on the same reet, does Lombok-style food – very pedas ot-spicy).

If you want to experience what's left of the utch East Indies colonial style, try the oldshioned dining room at the *Natour Bali otel* on Jl Veteran, where you can have a ne rijstaffel for 10,500 rp.

ntertainment

raditional Performances Dances in and ound Denpasar are mainly for tourists – ere are regular Kejak performances at the *aman Budaya arts centre* (☎ 222776). /ayang kulit performances are often put on : the *Puri Pemecutan* and the *Pura Jagatatha*.

inema The younger, more affluent denins of Denpasar congregate around the opping centres in the evening, and later ound a local *cinema* (bioskop). The ioskop in Denpasar have lost some business TV and videos, but the *Wisata Cineplex* ☎ 423023), on Jl Thamrin near the Lokitari shopping centre, with five screens, is still

a good option. US movies are popular, particularly 'action movies', along with Kung Fu titles from Hong Kong, the occasional Indian epic and some Indonesian productions. Movies are usually in the original language, subtitled in Bahasa Indonesia.

Nightclubs There are a couple of karaoke/ disco/nightclub places; the *Denpasar Moon* (☎ 241337), Jl Sudirman 18A, also called the DM Club; and *Akasaka* on Jl Teuku Umar. For more bars, discos and nightclubs, do as the locals do – go to Kuta or Sanur.

Things to Buy

You'll find some craft shops on Jl Gajah Mada and some more around the corner on Jl Thamrin, but quality is variable. Arts of Asia, just west of Jl Thamrin, is well regarded for its quality Indonesian antiques. Shops often close around 12.30 pm and reopen around 5 or 6 pm.

The colourful and pungent main market, the three storey Pasar Badung, has fruit and vegetables on the ground floor, household goods, foods, spices etc on the 2nd floor, and clothing, sarongs, baskets, ceremonial accessories and other handcrafts on the top floor. It's a great place to browse and bargain, except for the unsolicited guides-cum-commission takers who attach themselves to you.

Kumbasari is another market/shopping centre, on the opposite side of the river from Pasar Badung, with handcrafts, fabrics and gold work. Pasar Satriya, on the corner of Jl Veteran and Jl Nakula, has some good handcrafts too. Kereneng market, just north of the bemo terminal, is much more for everyday fare, selling mainly food and goods for the local community. Pasar Burung Satriya on Jl Veteran is a bird market which will bring no joy to animal conservationists.

Jl Sulawesi, east of Pasar Badung, has many shops with batik, ikat and other fabrics. Gold jewellery is also a speciality in this area.

There's a growing range of western-style shopping centres in Denpasar, with a variety of quality goods. Visitors come to these places for clothing, shoes, toys and electronic goods. Genuine name brands like Calvin Klein, Reebok and Elizabeth Arden are around 20% cheaper than in Australia, competitive with US or European prices (depending on the level of consumer taxes you pay at home). If you're just buying the name, you can get credible fakes in Kuta for a fraction of the price!

The MA department store on Jl Diponegoro was one of the first, but has been somewhat eclipsed by the bigger, newer places. Tiara Dewata shopping centre on Jl MJ Sutoyo incorporates a miniature funfair with amusements which will entertain very young children, and a video arcade and swimming pool (500 rp) for older kids.

Matahari, on Jl Dewi Sartika between Jl Sudirman and Jl Diponegoro, has a wide range of clothes, cosmetics, leather goods, sportswear, toys and baby items. Just opposite is the New Dewata Ayu, or NDA department store, the newest and biggest in town, with an even greater selection of similar goods.

Going west along Jl Teuku Umar you come to the Libi shopping centre, with the Hero supermarket. It's about the cheapest place on Bali to buy groceries, bottled liquor, cigarettes and ingredients for Indonesian cooking.

Getting There & Away

Denpasar is the focus of road transport on Bali, with terminals for buses and bemos to all corners of the island. There are also direct buses to destinations on Java, and agents for boat, bus, train and air tickets.

Air It's not necessary to come into Denpasar to arrange booking, ticketing or reconfirmation of flights. Most of the travel agencies in Kuta, Sanur, Ubud or other tourist areas can provide these services.

The Garuda office (☎ 225245) at Jl Melati 61 is open Monday to Friday from 7.30 am to noon and 1 to 4.45 pm, Saturday from 9 am to 1 pm. Merpati (☎ 235358) is just down the road at Jl Melati 57, and is open every day from 7.30 am to 9 pm; it has flights to Lombok and the other islands of Nusa Teng-

ggara. Bouraq (☎ 223564) at Jl Sudirma 19A has competitive fares to destinations Java and Nusa Tenggara. Sempati (☎ 28851 has its main office in Sanur.

Bus & Bemo For travel within Bali, De pasar has four terminals for bemos ar buses, so in many cases you'll have to tran fer from one terminal to another if you' making a trip through Denpasar. The lon distance terminals are Ubung, Batubulan ar Tegal. Kereneng, Sanglah and Wangaya te minals serve specific destinations close the capital.

Minibuses do the shorter routes betwee towns, while full-size buses are often use on longer, more heavily travelled route Buses tend to be cheaper than smaller veh cles on the same route, but they are le frequent and do not stop at intermedia points.

It's impossible to be precise about th correct fare on any bemo trip. Non-Baline are often charged higher prices, 'officia fares are rounded up to the next 100 rp, an it seems that operators will 'try out' a high fare sometimes, just to see if the market w stand it. The following prices should accurate to within a couple of hundr rupiah, but try to confirm them with a loc before you get on.

Ubung – north of the city centre on t Gilimanuk road, this is the terminal for t north and west of Bali, and also for buses Java – see the Getting There & Away secti earlier in this chapter. To get to Tanah L take a bemo to Kediri, and another one fro there. To get to the Lovina beaches, first ta a bemo to Singaraja.

Destination	Price (rp)
Batubulan terminal	700
Bedugul	3500
Gilimanuk	4500
Kediri	1000
Kereneng terminal	500
Mengwi	900
Negara	3500
Singaraja via Bedugul	3500
Tegal terminal	600

atubulan – this is the terminal for the east and central area of Bali, and it's about six km north-east of Denpasar proper.

estination	Price (rp)
mlapura	3000
angli	1200
andidasa	2200
ianyar	1000
ereneng terminal	500
intamani	2000
lungkung	1200
adangbai	2000
ingaraja via Kintamani	4000
ampaksiring	1200
egal terminal	700
bud	1500
bung terminal	700

egal – south of the city centre on the road Kuta, this is the terminal for the southern eninsula.

estination	Price (rp)
irport	800
atubulan terminal	700
ereneng terminal	600
uta	700
egian	700
anur (blue bemo)	700
usa Dua/Bualu	1000
bung terminal	600
lu Watu	2000

ereneng – east of the city centre, off the 'bud road, this is mainly an urban transfer rminal, but it does have direct bemos to anur (600 rp), Tegal (600 rp), Ubung (500) and Batubulan (600 rp).

anglah – near the market at the south end f Diponegoro, bemos from here go to Suwung nd Benoa Port.

Vangaya – this small terminal on the north de of town has bemos for Sangeh Monkey orest, Pelaga and Petang.

ietting Around

iemo The cute little three wheeled mini- emos *(tiga rodas)* have been phased out of 'enpasar. The main urban transport is in nall, minibus bemos, which take various circuitous routes from and between the main terminals. These transfer bemos line up for various destinations at each of the terminals; they are marked with a letter on the back which indicates the route they take. The tourist office may have a list of these routes, but the best bet is to ask an official at one of the terminals (don't ask a bemo driver or a driver's assistant). The official fare between terminals is around 600 rp.

You can also charter bemos from the various terminals for short trips (from 4000 rp). Agree on prices before getting on board because there are no meters.

Taxi You'll find both blue-and-yellow Praja taxis (☎ 289090) and the white Bali taxis (☎ 701111) in Denpasar. They charge similar fares.

Dokar Despite the traffic, *dokars* (horse-drawn carts) are still used. They should cost the same as a bemo, but tourists are always charged more because of the novelty value; agree on prices before departing. Note that dokars are barred from some streets with heavy traffic.

AROUND DENPASAR
Sidakarya
The only point of interest in this village, about five km south of Denpasar, is the *Bali International Youth Hostel* (☎ 720812) at Jl Mertesari 19. It's adequate, but quite pricey at 12,000 rp per person in a four bed, fan-cooled dorm (16,000 rp with air-con). Not many travellers stay here, and the location is a major drawback, but staff may pick you up from the airport.

Tohpati
About six km north-east of Denpasar, Toh-pati is at the junction of the main roads to/from the south and east of Bali. Sanggraha Kriya Asta (☎ 222942), a government hand-craft and arts centre, is just east of the intersection, with a wide variety of work at marked prices. It's a little expensive, and the quality varies from mediocre to excellent, but it's a good place to get an idea of what's

available and at what prices. It's open weekdays from 8.30 am to 5 pm, and Saturday until 4.30 pm. Catch a Batubulan bemo, or telephone and staff will collect you.

South Bali

The southern part of Bali, south of the capital Denpasar, is the tourist end of the island. The overwhelming mass of visitors to Bali is concentrated down here. Nearly all the package-tour hotels are found in this area

and many tourists only get out on day trips some never get out at all.

KUTA

Kuta is Bali's biggest tourist beach area. Counting the areas of Tuban, Kuta, Legian and Seminyak, the *kelurahan* (local government area) of Kuta extends for nearly eight km along the beach and foreshore. Most visitors come to Kuta sooner or later because it's close to the airport, has the biggest range of cheap tour and travel agents, and the biggest concentration of shops and services. Some

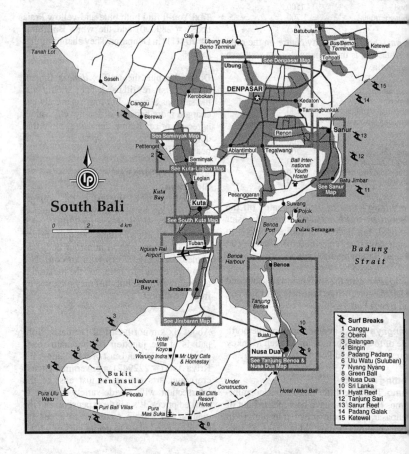

South Bali

0   2   4 km

Surf Breaks
1 Canggu
2 Oberoi
3 Balangan
4 Bingin
5 Padang Padang
6 Ulu Watu (Suluban)
7 Nyang Nyang
8 Green Ball
9 Nusa Dua
10 Sri Lanka
11 Hyatt Reef
12 Tanjung Sari
13 Sanur Reef
14 Padang Galak
15 Ketewel

eople will find Kuta overdeveloped and eedy, but if you have a taste for a busy beach cene, shopping and nightlife, you can have great time here. Just don't expect a quiet, nspoilt, tropical hideaway. It's not pretty, ut it's not dull either, and the amazing rowth is evidence that a lot of people find omething to like in Kuta.

It's still the best beach on Bali, especially ince the activities of the hawkers have been estricted, and watching the spectacular unset is almost an evening ritual. Kuta has he only surf on the island which breaks over and instead of coral, and beginning surfers an wipe out without being cut to pieces on he reefs. Lots of cheap accommodation is vailable, as well as good-value mid-range laces and luxury hotels. There's a huge hoice of places to eat, and a growing number f shops with everything from genuine ntiques to fake fashion items. The tourists hemselves have become a tourist attraction, nd visitors come from Java to ogle the opless bathers, and from the other resorts to ut-tut at the tackiness of it all.

History

Mads Lange, a Danish copra trader and dventurer, established a successful trading nterprise near modern Kuta, and had some uccess in mediating between local rajas and he Dutch, who were encroaching from the orth. His business soured in the 1850s, and e died suddenly, perhaps murdered. His rave, and a monument erected later, are near Kuta's night market.

The original Kuta Beach Hotel was started y a Californian couple in the 1930s, but losed with the Japanese occupation of Bali n 1942. In the late 1960s Kuta became nown as a stop on the hippie trail between Australia and Europe, and an untouched ecret surf spot. Accommodation opened nd, by the early 1970s, Kuta had a delightully laid-back atmosphere. Enterprising ndonesians seized opportunities to profit rom the tourist trade, often in partnership with foreigners who wanted a pretext for taying longer. When Kuta expanded, Legian urther north became the quiet alternative,

but now you can't tell where one ends and the other begins. Legian has now merged with Seminyak, the next village north. To the south, new developments in Tuban are filling the area between Kuta and the airport.

All this development has taken its toll, and the area is now a chaotic mixture of shops, bars, restaurants and hotels on a confusing maze of streets and alleys, often congested with heavy traffic, thick with fumes and painfully noisy. Kuta is trying to move upmarket, and shopping is the big growth area. Nearly all the clothing sold in Kuta is locally made, and a growing Balinese garment industry is exporting worldwide. Lots of expatriate businesspeople rent houses or bungalows around Seminyak; many are married to Balinese and are permanent residents.

Modern Kuta is an international scene, but a traditional Balinese community remains. The religious practices are observed, and the banjars are still active in governing the local community. Temples are impressive and well kept, processions and festivals are elaborate and the offerings are made every day. The observance of *nyepi*, the day of stillness when no work is done, has left many tourists perplexed at the closure of their favourite bar or restaurant.

Orientation

Kuta is a disorienting place – it's flat, with few landmarks or signs other than a riot of advertising; the streets and alleys are crooked and often walled on one or both sides so it feels like a maze; and it's impossible to get a really good map of the place. The main road, busy Jl Legian, runs roughly parallel to the beach from Seminyak in the north through Legian to Kuta. It's a two way street in Legian but in most of Kuta it's one way going south, except for an infuriating block near Jl Melasti where it's one way going north (this seems so crazy that it will probably be changed at some stage). At the south end of Jl Legian is 'Bemo Corner', at the junction with Jl Pantai Kuta (Kuta Beach Rd). This one way street runs west from Bemo Corner then north along the beach to Jl Melasti, which goes back to Jl Legian.

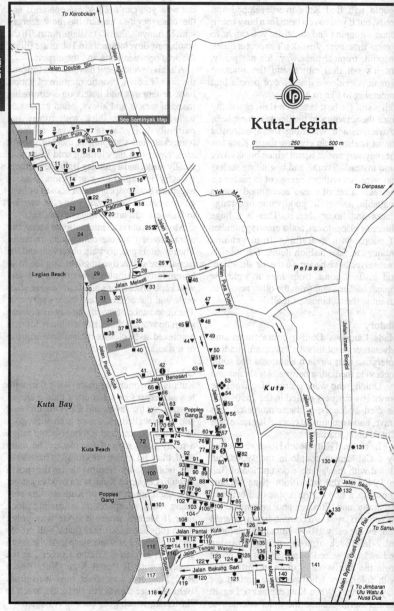

Kuta-Legian

To Kerobokan

Jalan Legian

Jalan Double Six

See Seminyak Map

Legian

Jalan Pura

Jalan Arjuna/Double Six

0   250   500 m

Jalan Padma

Jalan Melasti

Jalan Pantai Kuta

Jalan Legian

Legian Beach

Kuta Bay

Kuta Beach

Poppies Gang II

Poppies Gang

Jalan Benesari

Jalan Pura Puseh

Pelasa

Kuta

Jalan Raya Puri

Yeh Mati

To Denpasar

Jalan Imam Bonjol

Jalan Tanjung Mekar

Jalan Pantai Kuta

Jalan Tengai Wangi

Jalan Bakung Sari

Kuta Square

Jalan Bunisari

Jalan Raya Kuta

Jalan Selasih

To Sanur

Jalan Bypass Ngurah Rai

To Jimbaran
Ulu Watu &
Nusa Dua

PLACES TO STAY

1	Jayakarta Hotel
6	Sari Yasai Beach Inn & Hotel Baleka
10	Sinar Beach Cottages & Adika Sari Bungalows
12	Puri Tantra Beach Bungalows
13	Bali Niksoma Inn & Bali Kelapa Hotel
14	Sinar Indah & Bali Sani Hotel
15	Three Brothers Inn
17	Puri Damai Cottages
18	Legian Beach Bungalows
22	Garden View Cottages
23	Bali Padma Hotel
24	Bali Mandira Cottages
27	Ady's Inn
29	Legian Beach Hotel
31	Bali Intan Legian
34	Kul Kul Resort
35	Legian Mas Beach Inn
36	Puri Tanah Lot Cottages
37	Camplung Mas
38	Bruna Beach Hotel
39	Kuta Jaya Cottage
40	Sayang Beach Lodging
41	Kuta Bungalows
62	Bali Dwipa, Bali Indah, Duta Wisata & Losmen Cempaka
63	Bendesa I & Bendesa II
64	Meka Jaya
67	Suka Beach Inn
69	Kuta Suci Bungalows
71	The Bounty Hotel
72	Sahid Bali Seaside Hotel
73	Poppies Cottages II
74	Palm Gardens
75	Bali Sandy Cottages
77	Ronta Bungalows
78	Jus Edith
86	Komala Indah I
88	Kempu Taman Ayu
89	Puri Ayodia Inn
90	Suji Bungalows
91	Sari Bali Bungalows
92	Sorga Cottages
93	Arena & Mimpi Bungalows
94	Berlian Inn
95	Rita's House & Rempan Accommodation
99	Kuta Puri Bungalows
100	Kuta Segara Caria
101	Aneka Beach Bungalows
103	La Walon Bungalows
106	Poppies Cottages I
107	Budi Beach Inn
108	Kodja Beach Inn
110	Ida Beach Inn
111	Asana Santhi Homestay (Willy I)
112	Suci Bungalows
113	Yulia Beach Inn
115	Natour Kuta Beach
118	Melasti Hotel & Karthi Inn
120	Hotel Ramayana
134	Anom Dewi Youth Hostel
139	Bamboo Inn, Zet Inn & Jesen's Inn II

PLACES TO EAT

2	Topi Koki Restaurant
3	Swiss Restaurant
4	Sawasdee Thai Restaurant
5	Twice Cafe
7	Rum Jungle Road Bar & Restaurant
8	Bamboo Palace Restaurant
9	Glory Bar & Restaurant
11	Poco Loco Mexican Restaurant
16	Warung Kopi
20	Rama Garden Restaurant
21	Joni Sunken Bar & Restaurant
26	Do Drop Inn
30	Karang Mas Restaurant
32	Restaurant Puri Bali Indah & Legian Garden Restaurant
33	Orchid Garden Restaurant
44	Aromas Vegetarian Cafe
47	Yanie's Homestay
49	Gemini Restaurant
50	Mama's German Restaurant
52	Mama Luccia Italian Restaurant
56	Mama's German Restaurant
60	Batu Bulong Restaurant
61	Twice Pub
66	Brasil Bali Restaurant
68	The Corner Restaurant
70	Nana's Swedish Restaurant
80	Mini Restaurant
83	Indah Sari Seafood
85	Poppies Restaurant
87	TJs
96	Nusa Indah Bar & Restaurant & Bamboo Corner
97	Kedin Restaurant
98	Tree House Restaurant
102	Kempu Cafe
104	Fat Yogi's Wood Fired Pizza Restaurant
109	Lenny's Restaurant
119	Singasana Restaurant
122	Dayu I and Wartel
123	Nagasari Restaurant
127	Made's Warung
128	Sushi Bar Nelayan

OTHER

19	Bali Rock
25	Wartel
28	Postal Agent
42	Bali Government Information
43	Bookshop
45	Bounty
46	Peanuts II
48	Legian Mall & ATM
51	001 Club
53	Matahari Department Store, Timezone, & Cinema
54	Jonathon Silver Gallery
55	Norm's Sports Bar
57	Wartel
58	SC (Sari Club)
59	Rudy's Art & Antiques
65	Australian Bungy Jumping Company
76	Tubes Bar
79	BDI Bank
81	Kuta Postal Agency
82	Hard Rock Cafe
84	Perama Office
105	Hanafi Craft Shop
114	Kambodja Wartel
116	Matahari Department Store
117	Kuta Art Market
121	Supermarket & Agung Korean House Restaurant
124	Kul Kul Music
125	The Pub
126	Bemo Corner
129	Duty-Free Shop
130	Fuji Image Plaza
131	KCB Tours & Travel & Dutch Consulate
132	Petrol Station
133	Galeal Supermarket & KFC
135	Casablanca Bar
136	Badung Tourist Information & Sulawesi Tourist Office
137	Police Station
138	Chinese Temple
140	Post Office
141	Night Market (Pasar Senggol)

BALI

Between Jl Legian and the beach is a tangle of narrow streets, tracks and alleys (gangs), with an amazing hodgepodge of big hotels, little hotels, losmen, small shops, restaurants, building construction sites and even a few remaining stands of coconut palms. The grounds of big, expensive hotels front onto the beach, but the beach is still public – you can walk along it for the length of the tourist area. Most of the bigger shops, restaurants and bars are along several km of Jl Legian and on a few of the side streets which head towards the beach. There are also travel agencies, banks, moneychangers, post and telephone offices, doctors, markets, photo shops, motorcycle and car-rental places, and everything else a tourist could possibly need.

Information

Tourist Office The Badung district tourist office (☎ 751419), Jl Bakung Sari 1, opens daily, except Sunday, from 8 am to 6 pm. The Bali government tourist information service (☎ 753540), in the foyer of a modern building on Jl Benesari, opens daily, except Sunday, from 8 am to 2 pm. Both offices have some

printed information, will tell you when an where temple festivals and special events a being held, and can usually answer specifi questions.

Money There are several banks around Kut but the numerous moneychangers are faste more efficient, open longer hours and off equally good rates.

Post There's a post office on a small sic road near the night market. It's small, effi cient and has a sort-it-yourself poste-restan service. There are other postal agencies on Legian, about half a km north of Ben Corner, on Jl Melasti in Legian and on th main road in Seminyak.

Communications There are quite a fe wartels (telephone offices) in Kuta; priva ones are slightly more expensive than thos operated by Telkom. Hours are generall from 7 am to 9 pm but some are open late There are Home Country Direct phones the Natour Kuta Beach Hotel and outside th airport's international terminal.

The whole south Bali tourist area is in th

What's in a Name?

A recent government regulation requires all Indonesian businesses to use an Indonesian name, not a foreign one. For years, many losmen, restaurants and other tourist businesses have operated under English names, or names which are some mixture of local and foreign languages – Bamboo Homestay, The Corner Restaurant, Chez Gado Gado, Susilia Beach Inn, The Jaya Pub and so on. These names are often cute, and are easy for foreign visitors to pronounce and remember, so the name changes are causing a good deal of confusion (not least for guidebook writers). It's not good for business either, as many enterprises have built an excellent reputation under their old names.

The usual response is to translate the old name to Bahasa Indonesia and put that on the street sign with the old name beneath it – Pondok Kelapa (formerly COCONUT COTTAGES) – though there are rules about relative prominence and the size of the lettering. Sometimes the translation doesn't work as well as the original – Wisma Pantai Gembira just isn't as catchy as the old favourite Happy Beach Inn.

International corporations, like the Hilton and Holiday Inn, can use their regular names, and really big businesses like the Bali Cliffs Hotel and the Bali InterContinental don't seem under any pressure to change. It's OK to use your own name – if you are Benny, you can have an eatery with that name but it can't be Benny's Cafe. If the customers sit on benches, it can be Warung Benny, but if there are chairs and tables, it must be Restoran Benny.

One place was very well known to its surfing clientele as Mr Ugly's. The owner was reluctant to change the title of his business, so he had his own name officially changed to Ugly. He was happy to adopt his old nickname, but it may yet prove an embarrassment to his daughter, who can still be grateful her father didn't own Fat Yogi's Restaurant or the Dirty Duck Diner. ■

JAMES LYON

GREG ELMS

JAMES LYON

i

Left: Three tier swimming pool at the luxury Amankila hotel, Padangbai.
Right: Footloose and fancy free.
ttom: The fishing fleet anchors at Jimbaran Bay.

JAMES LYON

GREGORY ADAMS

Bali
Top: Lake Batur sunrise, with Gunung Agung just visible behind Gunung Abang, centra
Bali.
Bottom: Pura Ulun Danau, a Hindu-Buddhist temple, beside Lake Bratan, central Bali.

361 telephone zone. All Kuta numbers have ix digits, usually starting with 7.

Dangers & Annoyances Theft is not an normous problem, but visitors do lose hings from unlocked hotel rooms or from he beach. Always lock your room, even at ight. Valuable items should be checked with eception or, if not needed, left in a security box. There are also some pickpockets and match thieves, so hang on to your bag and keep your money belt under your shirt.

ome years ago Kuta had a number of muggings but he problem was handled with quite amazing efficiency and in a very traditional fashion. The local anjars organised vigilante patrols and anybody they came across who wasn't a tourist or a local Balinese had to have a damn good reason for being there. Thefts in the dark gangs stopped dead and there has been no repeat performance.

Water Safety The surf can be very dangerous, with a strong current on some tides, specially up north in Legian. Lifeguards patrol swimming areas of the beach, indicated by red-and-yellow flags. If they say the water is too rough or unsafe to swim in, they mean it.

Hawkers & Hasslers The activities of hawkers, touts and would-be guides are a major annoyance in Kuta. Beach selling is restricted to the upper part of the beach; closer to the water, you can lie on the sand in peace – you'll soon find out where the invisible line is. The best way to deal with unwanted sales pitches is to ignore them completely – even saying 'no' seems to encourage them.

Places to Stay
Kuta and Legian have hundreds of places to stay, with more still being built. Even cheap losmen have bathrooms these days and the squat toilet is a rarity. Don't be unduly influenced by Kuta hotel names – places with 'beach' in their name may not be anywhere near the beach and a featureless three storey hotel block may rejoice in the name 'cottage'.

Places to Stay – bottom end
Outside busy seasons you can find a good basic losmen for around 15,000 rp a double, with private bathroom, fan, a light breakfast and a pleasant atmosphere. As you move up the price scale you get bigger rooms, better furnishings and a generally less spartan appearance. Bottom-end places usually quote their prices in rupiah, up to about 45,000 rp per night for a double (US$20); above that is mid-range.

The following is a sample, grouped by location, from south of Kuta to north of Legian. If your first choice is full there will be other, similar places within walking distance.

South Kuta There are mostly mid-range to expensive places down Jl Kartika Plaza, but some low-budget places are appearing in the back streets. The location is not central, but it's close to the airport and the beach is good. The streets south-east of Bemo corner are closer to the action and have some of Kuta's longest-running cheapies.

Pendawa Bungalows (☎ 752387) – on a lane east of Jl Kartika Plaza, about 400m from the beach, Pendawa has a spacious garden, pool, big new lobby and a variety of rooms from US$15 to US$45 a double; outside the high season it should be able to give you a good room for about 25,000 rp.

Bunut Gardens (☎ 752971) – just east of Pendawa, with a tiny garden, this is still a good budget option, with doubles from around 22,000 rp.

Bamboo Inn (☎ 751935) – this traditional little losmen is on a gang south of Jl Bakung Sari, on the southern edge of central Kuta but far enough away to be quiet. It's some distance from the beach but close to restaurants and bars. OK rooms cost from 15,000 rp, including breakfast.

Jesen's Inn II (☎ 752647) & *Zet Inn* (☎ 753135) – these are pleasant little places on the same gang as the Bamboo Inn, with double rooms at around 20,000 rp.

Anom Dewi Youth Hostel (☎ 752292) – close to Bemo Corner, this is a cheap but well-run youth hostel-associated losmen, with standard rooms at 12,000/17,000 rp for singles/doubles, superior rooms at 14,000/20,000 rp, plus a 5000 rp high-season supplement but 2000 rp less for YHA members.

BALI

BALI

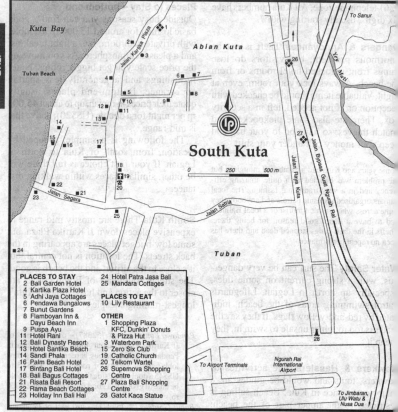

Kuta Bay

Abian Kuta

Tuban Beach

To Sanur

Jalan Kartika Plaza

Jalan Bypass Gusti Ngurah Rai

South Kuta

0   250   500 m

Jalan Raya Kuta

Jalan Segara

Jalan Sattia

Tuban

To Airport Terminals

Ngurah Rai International Airport

To Jimbaran, Ulu Watu & Nusa Dua

PLACES TO STAY	
2 Bali Garden Hotel	24 Hotel Patra Jasa Bali
4 Kartika Plaza Hotel	25 Mandara Cottages
5 Adhi Jaya Cottages	
6 Pendawa Bungalows	**PLACES TO EAT**
7 Bunut Gardens	10 Lily Restaurant
8 Flamboyan Inn &	
Dayu Beach Inn	**OTHER**
9 Puspa Ayu	1 Shopping Plaza
11 Hotel Rani	KFC, Dunkin' Donuts
12 Bali Dynasty Resort	& Pizza Hut
13 Hotel Santika Beach	3 Waterbom Park
14 Sandi Phala	15 Zero Six Club
16 Palm Beach Hotel	19 Catholic Church
17 Bintang Bali Resort	20 Telkom Wartel
18 Bali Bagus Cottages	26 Supernova Shopping
21 Risata Bali Resort	Centre
22 Rama Beach Cottages	27 Plaza Bali Shopping
23 Holiday Inn Bali Hai	Centre
	28 Gatot Kaca Statue

Jalan Pantai Kuta A number of cheap places are on this street between Bemo Corner and the beach. Rooms away from the road aren't too noisy.

Budi Beach Inn (☎ 751610) – an old-style losmen with a garden and pretty ordinary singles/doubles from 15,000/20,000 to 25,000/30,000 rp.

Kodja Beach Inn (☎ 751754) – the rooms here are set well away from the road, and there's a pool; prices range from 20,000/25,000 rp for old fan-cooled rooms to 50,000/66,000 rp for new ones with air-con and hot water.

Suci Bungalows (☎ 751761) – well established with a good restaurant, not too noisy and not far from the beach, with rooms at around 20,000/25,000 rp.

Yulia Beach Inn (☎ 751893) – this standard small hotel has been going for years and offers a ver[y] central location, with cheap rooms from 11,00[0] rp and better bungalows from US$23/28. [It] charges extra for tax, service and breakfast.

Around Poppies Gang I The maze of gang[s] between the beach and Jl Legian have man[y] of the cheapest and best-value places to stay[.]

Komala Indah I (no phone) – on Poppies Gang righ[t] opposite Poppies Cottages I but much mor[e] basic. It's clean and great value for the locatio[n] at 12,000 rp for a room.

Kuta Puri Bungalows (☎ 751903) – well located at the beach end of Poppies Gang, on a large plot of a land with a good pool; fan-cooled cottages here start at 32,000 rp, including tax and breakfast.

Rita's House – on a gang going north of Poppies Gang, this popular little losmen is not fancy but good value at 12,000/15,000 rp for singles/doubles.

Rempan Accommodation (☎ 753150) – squeezed in behind Rita's, this three storey building has plain but clean rooms from 13,000/17,000 rp.

Berlian Inn (☎ 751701) – further up the same gang, with good rooms from 17,000/23,000 rp, including breakfast, this place is good value in a central location.

Arena Bungalows & Hotel (☎ 752974) – a few doors north of the Berlian, and styled like a high-rise Chinese temple, Arena has rooms from 20,000/25,000 rp, or 45,000 rp with air-con, and a small pool.

Sorga Cottages (☎ 751897) – there are quite a few rooms and a swimming pool squeezed onto this site, but it's a quiet location and good value with rooms at 19,000/25,000 rp, or 36,000/46,000 rp with air-con; the open meals area upstairs is a very pleasant bonus.

Suji Bungalow (☎ 752483) – on a lane south of Poppies Gang II, this comfortable family-run place charges US$15/18 to US$22/25, and has a pool, restaurant and quiet location.

Bali Sandy Cottages (☎ 753344) – secluded in one of the last coconut plantations left in Kuta, and close to the beach and Poppies Gang II, the rooms here are pretty nice and good value at 25,000 rp.

Puri Ayodia Inn – this small and very standard losmen is in a quiet but convenient location and has rooms for just 10,000/12,000 rp.

Sari Bali Bungalows (☎ 753065) – nice bungalows in a spacious garden with a good pool, and rooms from 26,000/30,000 rp up to 60,000 rp with air-con.

Jus Edith – a basic place, but very cheap with rooms from 8000/12,000 rp.

Ronta Bungalows (☎ 754246) – good, clean budget accommodation, with a nice garden, central location and rooms at 12,000/17,000 rp.

Around Poppies Gang II The gangs running north of Poppies Gang II, which is also called Poppies Gang II Utara (north), are about the best place to look for cheap accommodation.

Palm Gardens Homestay (☎ 752198) – a neat and clean place on Poppies Gang II, good value from 20,000/25,000 rp for singles/doubles, including breakfast, and popular with surfers; the location is convenient but reasonably quiet.

Bali Dwipa (☎ 751446), *Bali Indah* (☎ 752509), *Bali Duta Wisata* (☎ 753534) & *Losmen Cempaka* (☎ 754744) – these places are on the gang going north of Poppies Gang II. They don't have a lot of character or comfort, but they're central and cheap at around 12,000 rp for a double, including breakfast.

Suka Beach Inn (☎ 752793) – a popular place on the same bottom-end part of Poppies Gang II, with good rooms in a garden setting for around 12,000 rp.

Meka Jaya (☎ 754487), *Bendesa* (☎ 751358) & *Beneyasa Beach Inn* – these places are further north on Poppies Gang II, and also have cheap rooms from 10,000/15,000 rp, including breakfast and tax.

Kuta Suci Bungalows (☎ 752617) – on a cul-de-sac off Poppies Gang II, this is a pleasant two storey place with rooms from 15,000/20,000 rp.

Legian Cheap accommodation in Legian tends to be north of Jl Padma. There's no road along the beach up here, so there are places fronting the beach which you reach on side streets from Jl Legian or back lanes from the side streets. If you really want a beachfront place, walk along the beach and look from that angle.

Sayang Beach Lodging (☎ 751249) – although it's tucked away on a winding lane south of Jl Melasti, this place is handy to the beach and not too far from the action. It has a variety of rooms from small and basic at US$6/8 to larger with air-con at US$25/30, and there is a small pool.

Puri Tanah Lot Cottages (☎ 752281) – on the same back lane, the cheaper rooms from 17,500/25,000 rp are a good budget option, and there's a nice pool here.

Legian Mas Beach Inn (☎ 755334) – a little further up towards Jl Melasti, this simple place is in a quiet location, with clean rooms from 10,000/12,000 rp.

Ady's Inn (☎ 753445) – tucked away off a small street north of Jl Melasti, this is a basic place with a pleasantly overgrown garden. It's nice and cheap with quite good rooms at 10,000/15,000 rp, but breakfast is extra.

Legian Beach Bungalows (☎ 751087) – in the centre of Legian on busy Jl Padma, set back from the street in a nice garden, this places has friendly staff and OK rooms from 20,000 to 25,000 rp.

Puri Damai Cottages (☎ 751965) – also on Jl Padma, this is a traditional-style budget losmen, with rooms from 10,000/15,000 rp and a lot more character than many of the newer places.

BALI

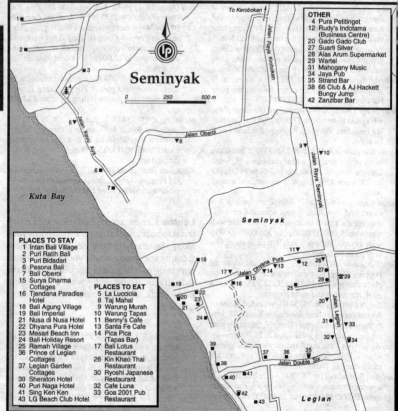

Seminyak

0   250   500 m

To Kerobokan

Kuta Bay

Seminyak

Legian

OTHER
4 Pura Petitinget
12 Rudy's Indotama
   (Business Centre)
20 Gado Gado Club
27 Suarti Silver
28 Alas Arum Supermarket
29 Wartel
31 Mahogany Music
34 Jaya Pub
35 Strand Bar
38 66 Club & AJ Hackett
   Bungy Jump
42 Zanzibar Bar

PLACES TO STAY
1 Intan Bali Village
2 Puri Ratih Bali
3 Puri Bidadari
6 Pesona Bali
8 Bali Oberoi
15 Surya Dharma
   Cottages
16 Tjendana Paradise
   Hotel
18 Bali Agung Village
19 Bali Imperial
21 Nusa di Nusa Hotel
22 Dhyana Pura Hotel
23 Mesari Beach Inn
24 Bali Holiday Resort
25 Ramah Village
36 Prince of Legian
   Cottages
37 Legian Garden
   Cottages
39 Sheraton Hotel
40 Puri Naga Hotel
41 Sing Ken Ken
43 LG Beach Club Hotel

PLACES TO EAT
5 La Lucciola
8 Taj Mahal
9 Warung Murah
10 Warung Tapas
11 Benny's Cafe
13 Santa Fe Cafe
14 Pica Pica
   (Tapas Bar)
17 Bali Lotus
   Restaurant
26 Kin Khao Thai
   Restaurant
30 Ryoshi Japanese
   Restaurant
32 Cafe Luna
33 Goa 2001 Pub
   Restaurant

North Legian & Seminyak Although development up here is quite spread out, and there's not much public transport so getting around can be difficult, there are places within an easy walk of both the beach and the facilities on Jl Legian.

Three Brothers Inn (☎ 751566) – this long-standing and popular place off Jl Legian has rooms scattered around a gorgeous garden, though the newer rooms may have less character than the originals. There's a nice pool, and some rooms are good for families. Prices run from 27,000 to 69,000 rp, plus 10% tax.

Sinar Indah (☎ 755905) – on Jl Padma Utara, the small road between Jl Padma and Jl Pura Bagus Taruna, this standard-style losmen is handy to the beach and asks 25,000 rp for a double room without breakfast; it also has bigger rooms with kitchen facilities.

Sinar Beach Cottages (☎ 751404) – east of Jl Padma Utara, this quiet and pleasant little place asks 20,000 rp for rooms set around the garden.

LG Club Beach Hotel (☎ 751060) – not very well run but with a great location on a spacious lot behind the beachfront restaurants; rooms start at 33,000 rp, but check the room first, because some are a bit run-down.

Mesari Beach Inn (☎ 751401) – one of the few budget places in Seminyak, off Jl Dhyana Pura behind the stables, with rooms for 17,000/20,000 rp and bungalows at around 315,000 rp per week.

Places to Stay – middle

There are a great many mid-range hotels, which at Kuta means something like US$25 to US$55. Prices quoted in US dollars on a printed sheet are the 'publish rates' for the package-tour market – this rate is always negotiable, up to 50% off in the low season, especially when a lot of rooms are empty. All but the cheapest places add a tax and service charge, typically 21%.

The best of the mid-range hotels are former budget places which have improved their facilities. Many of the new package-our hotels are utterly featureless and dull, with air-con, a swimming pool and no Balinese style whatsoever. The following places all have air-con and pools unless otherwise noted. Again, they are listed by location, going from south to north.

South of Kuta The south end of Jl Kartika Plaza is quiet and near the beach, but otherwise not very interesting. The north end is much closer to central Kuta, handy to the beach market and some good shopping areas.

Candi Phala (☎ 753780) – north of Jl Segara, the rooms here are in a neat two storey block facing directly onto the beach. They cost US$25 to US$45, and there's a good pool and a restaurant.

Palm Beach Hotel (☎ 751661) – off Jl Segara and close to the beach, this hotel has nice rooms stacked three storeys high around the swimming pool from US$60.

Adhi Jaya Cottages (☎ 753607) – on Jl Kartika Plaza, this place is nothing special to look at, but it has fan-cooled rooms from US$20/25, air-con suites up to US$42, and a pool.

Karthi Inn (☎ 754810) – at the north end of Jl Kartika Plaza, and surrounded on three sides by the more expensive Melasti Hotel, Karthi is close to the beach and offers all the mod cons in rooms packed around a pool. Standard rooms are US$45, but with a low-season discount they're only US$32, including tax, service and breakfast.

Around Jalan Bakung Sari On the southern fringe of central Kuta, this area is close to the beach and has all the facilities you'll need; the new Kuta Square shopping development may revive this end of town a bit.

Hotel Ramayana (☎ 751864) – on Jl Bakung Sari, a short walk to the beach, this is a long-established place. Lots of rooms are fitted in a limited space, with the cheapest ones around US$45/55.

Asana Santhi Homestay (Willy I; ☎ 751281) – near the heart of Kuta on Jl Tengal Wangi, not far from the beach, this attractive small hotel is unusually quiet and relaxed for its location. The well-kept rooms have interesting furnishings, and there's a good central swimming pool. Air-con rooms are US$30 to US$35.

Ida Beach Inn (☎ 751205) – in a secluded location south of Jl Pantai Kuta, the rooms here fit onto a small site but the place has some style and a nice garden. Rooms are good value at US$30/35 with air-con, or US$25/30 with fan.

Central Kuta The back lanes between Jl Legian and the beachfront road have a mixture of cheap to mid-range places which are handy both to the beach and to shops and restaurants. They don't have much traffic so it's a relatively quiet area.

La Walon Bungalows (☎ 752463) – on Poppies Gang I, handy to the beach and the Kuta scene, La Walon has a pool and some budget rooms with verandahs, open-air bathrooms and ceiling fans from US$21/24 for singles/doubles; air-con rooms cost US$5 more.

Mimpi Bungalows (☎ 751848) – on a back lane north of Poppies Gang I, this small hotel is good value in a pleasant location with a nice little pool. Rooms cost US$30/40.

Aneka Beach Bungalows (☎ 752067) – opposite the beach on Jl Pantai Kuta, the Aneka is quite good value, with nice rooms from US$55 to US$80.

Poppies Cottages II – the original Poppies (despite the name) is not as fancy nor as central as Poppies I. There are only a few cottages, but they are nice and spacious, and reasonably priced at US$23/28. Guests can use the pool at Poppies I.

Legian North of Jl Benesari you're in Legian. There are plenty of mid-range places, some near the beach, others on the lanes behind.

Kuta Bungalows (☎ 754393) – well located on Jl Benesari, the bungalows themselves are a bit stark but quite OK, and the pool, garden setting and general ambience are very nice. Normal price is US$35/40, but in the low season it might offer rooms for as little as US$25.

Bruna Beach Hotel (☎ 751565) – this simple place has a good central location on the beach road, a pool, restaurant and reggae nightclub. The rooms are nothing special but they're cheap, from US$15/18 up to US$30/35 with air-con.

Hotel Camplung Mas – this is marketed to young Aussie package tourists as part of the Ocean Blue Club, and it's quite nice – it's the only place that quotes prices in Australian dollars: A$60/120 (about US$48/96).

Garden View Cottages (☎ 751559) – just north of Jl Padma in Legian, the rooms here have hot water, phone and fridge, but look a little like concrete boxes. Rooms are US$38/42.

Bali Niksoma Inn (☎ 751946) – right on the beach, this hotel is another of the Ocean Blue Club properties, with two storey units in relatively spacious grounds with rooms from US$21/25 to US$60.

Puri Tantra Beach Bungalows (☎ 753195) – the six traditional-style bungalows here provide some of the most tasteful accommodation on Bali, for only US$40. It's often full.

Hotel Baleka (☎ 751931) – at the north end of Legian on Jl Pura Bagus Taruna, this place has a pool and asks from US$15/20 to US$30/35, including breakfast and tax.

Seminyak Some of the best restaurants and nightspots are here, but it's pretty spread out and public transport is nonexistent. There is some good mid-range accommodation – phone first and staff may even pick you up. There are also houses and bungalows to rent by the week or month.

Legian Garden Cottages (☎ 730876) – on Jl Double Six (also called Legian Cottages Rd and Jl Legian Kaja), off Jl Legian but close to the beach, this attractive place is well located, with pool, gardens, and standard rooms from US$38/45 for singles/doubles.

Puri Naga Hotel (☎ 730524) – at the beach end of Jl Double Six, this is a comfortable, well-located hotel with rooms from US$55.

Sing Ken Ken (☎ 752980) – next to Puri Naga, and slightly cramped, this motel-style place has comfortable rooms at US$40/45 in the high season, but only US$26/28 at other times.

Ramah Village (☎ 731071; fax 730973) – for longer stayers, the 16 comfortable bungalows here sleep up to six people from US$140 to US$490 per week. They're well situated, on Gang Keraton, off Jl Legian near the Alas Arum supermarket.

Bali Holiday Resort (☎ 730847) – in a beachfro location south of Jl Dhyana Pura, and close popular restaurants and nightclubs, this very ni place is good value with rooms from US$55/6

Dhyana Pura Hotel (☎ 751422) – on Jl Dhyana Pu in Seminyak, with a beach frontage, this is YMCA-affiliated hotel with air-con rooms ar bungalows in an attractive garden, very reaso ably priced from US$50/60, including tax ar breakfast (15% discounts in the low season).

Nusa di Nusa Hotel (☎ 751414) – right on the beac but some distance from the Jl Legian restauran and shops, it's still in a trendy area. Very pleasa rooms start at US$30/35, but check the roo first.

Places to Stay – top end

Kuta has quite a few places in the top-en category, all with air-conditioning and swim ming pools. As the price goes up, you'll ge TV, telephones, room service and so on. Ad 21% tax and service to the quoted price They nearly all have beach frontage, s they're easy to locate on a map. Going fror south to north, some of the more popular o interesting top-end places include:

Hotel Patra Jasa Bali (☎ 751161), PO Box 312 Denpasar – on the beach at Tuban, this larg deluxe hotel has rooms from US$130. Originall called Pertamina Cottages, it was one of the firs luxury hotels in Kuta and has lovely beachfror gardens and an excellent Japanese restaurant.

Holiday Inn Bali Hai (☎ 753035) – despite being pa of an international chain, this place has excellen Balinese architecture, as well as a beautiful poc and gardens. Rooms cost from US$135, bunga lows from US$200.

Bintang Bali Hotel (☎ 753810) – known for its night time entertainment, this big (400 rooms), top-en hotel also has sports facilities, including a gyr and tennis courts. Rooms start at US$135/145 fo singles/doubles.

Santika Beach Hotel (☎ 751267), PO Box 1008 Tuban – on Jl Kartika Plaza, this place has beach frontage, swimming pools, tennis courts all the usual facilities and a variety of rooms from US$110.

Kartika Plaza Hotel (☎ 751067), PO Box 3084 Denpasar – on Jl Kartika Plaza just south o central Kuta, this large hotel is right on the beac and has rooms from US$135/360.

Natour Kuta Beach Hotel (☎ 751361), PO Box 3393 Denpasar – though it's the successor to the orig inal Kuta Beach Hotel, which was on this site, the rebuilt version has no sense of history at all. The location is excellent at the beach end of Jl Panta

Kuta. Rooms are from US$90/110 up to US$300 for the executive suite.

Poppies Cottages I (☎ 751059) – still setting the standard for what a good Bali hotel should be, Poppies has an exotically lush garden with cleverly designed and beautifully built cottages. It's in the centre of things on Poppies Gang I and has a swimming pool every bit as stunning as the overall design. At US$74/79 for rooms it's cheaper than most top-end places, and with a lot more character. Make a reservation – it's very popular.

The Bounty Hotel (☎ 753030) – centrally located on Poppies Gang II, but away from the beach and not quite as well appointed as the most expensive hotels, this is a nice-looking place with a distinctive black-tiled pool. Free passes to well-known nightspots are given to guests, which might suggest something about the clientele. The published rates start at US$90, including tax and service, but it discounts to as little as US$35 in the low season.

Kul Kul Resort (☎ 752520), PO Box 3097, Denpasar – across the road from the beach, just south of Jl Melasti, this big and popular hotel has two and three storey blocks plus bungalows in relatively spacious grounds. Rooms are around US$90.

Legian Beach Hotel (☎ 751711), PO Box 308, Denpasar – on the beach at Jl Melasti in the heart of Legian, this large, popular hotel has a wide variety of rooms, most of them in three storey blocks, from US$80/90 to US$95/105; recommended for families.

Bali Padma Hotel (☎ 752111), PO Box 1107 TBB, Legian – a big 400 room hotel by the beach, the Padma has lush gardens and lots of lotus ponds. Rooms are in two or three storey blocks or in six room units and cost US$100/110 to US$120/130, with a US$20 high-season supplement; suites are from US$195 to US$1750.

Bali Sani Hotel (☎ 752314) – on Jl Padma Utara (the lane going north of Jl Padma), a short walk from the beach, this small hotel is a bit cramped on the site. Rooms are small but attractively designed, some with a touch of eccentricity, and cost US$60/85.

Bali Imperial Hotel (☎ 754545; fax 751545) – at the beach end of Jl Dhyana Pura in Seminyak, the Imperial is not central but it offers a shuttle service to Kuta. The architecture is very imposing and the prices are substantial, with rooms from US$150, villas from US$400 and the Imperial Villa at US$1600.

Bali Agung Village (☎ 754267; fax 754269) – this small place is off Jl Dhyana Pura, on the northern edge of the tourist area next to the rice fields. It's in a very nice Balinese style, and is quite good value at US$70 to US$150.

Bali Oberoi Hotel (☎ 751061), PO Box 3351, Denpasar – right on the beach at the end of its own road way up beyond Legian, the Bali Oberoi is isolated and decidedly deluxe with beautiful individual bungalows and even some villa rooms with their own private swimming pools. The regular rooms start at around US$200, with the villa rooms more than twice that price.

Persona Bali (☎ 753914; fax 753915) – just north of the Oberoi, this nice-looking beachfront hotel has friendly staff and all the usual luxury facilities. It's quite good value from around US$80.

Places to Eat

There are countless places to eat around Kuta and Legian, from tiny hawker's carts to gourmet hotel restaurants. The cuisine is international and multicultural – you could stay in Kuta for a month, eat in a different place for every meal and never have to confront so much as a nasi goreng. The restaurant business is very competitive and they're quick to pick up on new trends, whether it's sun-dried tomatoes, pad thai or tapas.

If you want to eat cheaply, try the food carts which appear in the afternoon near Legian Beach and the warungs at the night market. You can buy bread, jam, cheese, drinks etc from the bakeries and supermarkets on Jl Legian, and fruit from the public market.

For middle-budget eating, most tourist restaurants have the standard Indonesian dishes (nasi goreng, nasi campur etc), as well as hamburgers, jaffles, spaghetti and salads (2000 and 4500 rp at most places). A pizza or seafood dish will cost between 10,000 and 15,000 rp. The quality varies from indifferent to excellent, and seems to depend as much on when you go and what you order as on the establishment and the price. The very big, barn-like places, often seafood specialists, can be inconsistent.

For fancier food, you'll find some first rate French, German, Italian, Japanese, Korean, Mexican, Swiss, Swedish and Thai restaurants. Wine is expensive, but some places have Australian wine by the glass for around 5000 rp. Beer goes well with most meals, and is a fair index of prices – in cheap places a large beer is around 4500 rp; in expensive places it costs from 6000 rp.

South Kuta On Jl Kartika Plaza, *Café Français*, at the front of the Bali Rani Hotel, is a good patisserie for croissants (1500 rp), coffee and fruit juice. *Bali Seafood*, opposite the Bintang Bali Hotel, is a big place where you can select your main course while it's still swimming. The Cantonese restaurant at the *Bali Dynasty Resort* is pricey, but has an excellent reputation. Further north on this street, a new shopping plaza has *Dunkin' Donuts*, *Pizza Hut* and such like.

Around Kuta The night market, *Pasar Senggol*, at the eastern end of Jl Bakung Sari, has cheap Indonesian food stalls doing sate, noodles, soup etc. The southern section specialises in seafood. In a different style, the new Kuta Square shopping centre has a selection of American-style fast-food places, including a *KFC*. Going east on Jl Bakung Sari there are several reliable, inexpensive restaurants, including *Dayu I* and *Nagasari*, and a supermarket which has many western food items. Above the supermarket, *Agung Korean House* does a popular Korean barbecue.

Jl Buni Sari, which connects Jl Pantai Kuta with Jl Bakung Sari, has some more long-term budget eateries, like the *Bali Indah* and *Dayu II*, and some venerable Aussie-Bali pubs which still serve good tucker.

Along Jl Pantai Kuta, between Bemo Corner and the beach, is the popular *Made's Warung*, a simple open-front place which is good for people-watching – it's been going for years and the food is still excellent, though a touch expensive. The *Suci Restaurant*, at the Suci Bungalows on the south side of the road, is good value and has delicious fruit drinks.

Poppies Gang, the tiny lane between Jl Legian and the beach, is named for *Poppies Restaurant* (☎ 751059), one of the oldest and most popular in Kuta. The prices are quite high (main courses around 10,000 rp) and the menu is not spectacular, but the food is extremely tasty and well presented, and the garden setting and atmosphere are delightful – make a reservation. A few steps west of

Poppies is *TJs* (☎ 751093), a deservedly popular Mexican restaurant, with a good atmosphere and main courses from 9000 to 15,000 rp.

Further west on Poppies Gang, *Bamboo Corner* has a good selection of Chinese and Indonesian dishes for around 5000 rp. *Nusa Indah Bar & Restaurant* is recommended by locals, while the inexpensive *Kempu Café* has some fine vegetarian dishes. The *Tree House Restaurant* is a pleasant place and does an excellent US breakfast for 4200 rp.

On the beach near the end of Jl Pantai Kuta, *Warung PKK* is good for basic, inexpensive food and cold beer. There are kiosks spaced all along the beach serving drinks and snacks, but at slightly higher prices than you'd pay in town. Opposite the beach, on the roof of the Kul Kul Resort Hotel, the *Blue Cactus* Mexican restaurant serves cool margaritas and hot salsa, with a great view and the risk of a mariachi.

Along Jl Legian There are lots of possibilities along Jl Legian, though a table near the road can be noisy. Just north of Bemo Corner, the *Sushi Bar Nelayan* has sushi for 2000 to 5000 rp, and sashimi from around 12,000 rp. Continue north towards Legian and you reach the *Mini Restaurant*, a huge place despite the name, but busy serving good, straightforward food at low prices. The *Sari Club Restaurant*, just north of the Mini, is similar in style, price and quality.

Around the corner, Poppies Gang II has a lot of cheap eateries, like the popular *Batu Bolong*, *Nana's Swedish Restaurant*, *Twice Pub* and *The Corner Restaurant*. Many of these have video movies at night, which can detract from the ambience and the service. The gang going north has also sprouted good, cheap eateries to satisfy those staying in the cheap hotels nearby. Further up Jl Benesari, the *Brasil Bali Restaurant* is reasonably priced, and serves a pretty fair feijoa, and highly alcoholic cachaça.

Continue north to *Mama's German Restaurant*, which offers sauerbraten, bratwurst, pork knuckles and weiner schnitzel for around 8000 rp (Mama has a second restaurant further north). The *Gemini* is an inexpensive, open-roofed place with surprisingly good Indonesian and Chinese food despite its bare and basic appearance. Across the road is *Aromas Cafe*, a mid-priced vegetarian restaurant with good food and a delightful garden setting.

Just east of Jl Legian, *Yanie's* is a popular place with good burgers, pizzas and steaks, as well as Indonesian standards. It's inexpensive, opens till late and has a good, fun atmosphere. Continuing north into Legian, you'll come to *Warung Kopi*, which is well regarded for its varied menu of European, Asian and vegetarian dishes, good breakfasts and tempting desserts. The long-standing *Glory Bar & Restaurant* does various buffets on various nights – its Balinese buffet on Wednesday is one of the few places in Kuta to try 1st class local cuisine.

Around Legian The streets west of Jl Legian have numerous mid-range restaurants and bars. On Jl Melasti is the big *Orchid Garden Restaurant*, the *Legian Garden Restaurant* and the *Restaurant Puri Bali Indah*, with excellent Chinese food. Jl Padma has a number of tourist restaurants, including the *Joni Sunken Bar & Restaurant*, where you can eat and drink while semi-immersed in a swimming pool – if your hotel doesn't run to this indulgence, here's your chance to try it. On the back streets north of Jl Padma, *Poco Loco* is a popular, upmarket Mexican restaurant and bar.

Further north, the standards and the prices get higher. Some of the most interesting places are on Jl Pura Bagus Taruna (also known as Rum Jungle Rd). At the west end, near the big Jayakarta Hotel, the *Topi Koki Restaurant* does pretty good French food and is about the most expensive place around – a full meal for two with drinks will cost over 50,000 rp (still a lot less than in Paris). A little east is the *Swiss Restaurant*, which is adjacent to the Swiss consul so should have some credibility. Other restaurants along this street include the *Sawasdee Thai Restaurant*, *Yudi Pizza* and, nearer to Jl Legian, the distinctive *Bamboo Palace Restaurant*.

Seminyak Good, though not cheap, places to eat here include the *Goa 2001 Pub Restaurant* on Jl Legian, where trendy expats choose from a multicultural menu and a long list of fancy drinks. Further north are the *Ryoshi* Japanese restaurant and *Kin Khao* for Thai food. For something different, *Warung Murah* is an inexpensive Indonesian restaurant.

On Jl Dhyana Pura you'll find *Benny's Cafe*, with pastries and fresh coffee, and the *Santa Fe Cafe* for overpriced south-western US dishes. On a beach track past the Oberoi, near Pura Petitenget, *La Lucciola* is an Italian place with food that people rave about and prices which are expensive but not excessive – main courses around 10,000 rp. Two trendy tapas bars are Pica Pica, on Jl Dhyana Pura, and *Warung Tapas*, a little further north.

Entertainment

Kuta offers plenty of places for drinking, loud music and late nights. It's pretty safe to walk the main streets at night, but avoid isolated parts of the beach. Take a charter bemo or a metered taxi to the more distant venues. Prostitutes, many of them transvestites, are tolerated on the central part of Jl Legian after 11 pm, while 'Kuta cowboys' practise their pick ups in many of the busier tourist bars.

Bars & Clubs Bars are usually free to enter, and often have special drink promotions and 'happy hours' between 6 and 9 pm. The biggest concentration is on Jl Legian. One of the most popular is the *Sari Club* ('SC' for short), with a giant video screen, dance music, a young crowd and lots of local guys. Around the corner is *Tubes Bar*, the surfers' hangout. Further up Jl Legian, the *Bounty* is built in the shape of a sailing ship and easy to spot – it gets people in early with a two-for-one drinks deal, provides passable food, then packs them onto the dance floor till 2 am.

The original Peanuts disco has closed, but *Peanuts II* continues the reputation (or notoriety) of the original. It's on the corner of Jl

Legian and Jl Melasti. There's a large outer bar with pool tables and loud rock music (free), a big dance floor inside with loud dance music (free until midnight, then 5000 rp, including one drink) and even a karaoke bar. The infamous Peanuts Pub Crawl, on Tuesday and Saturday nights, includes transport and entry to three or four local watering holes – it costs 3000 rp (☎ 751333 for all the sordid details).

Some other places to check on Jl Legian include *Lips*, a slightly sleazy C&W bar, the *Double O One Club*, a self-proclaimed rage spot, and *Norm's Sports Bar*, which is a long-established Aussie favourite.

In Legian you'll find a few more down-under drinking places on Jl Padma, like *Bali Rock* and the *Bali Aussie*. Similar places in south Kuta include *The Pub* and *Casablanca*, both on Jl Buni Sari.

The best reggae venue is at the *Bruna Beach Hotel*, which gets some hot local bands doing good covers of reggae classics. There's a roomy dance floor and the crowd is mixed, but enthusiastic.

More upmarket venues, attracting older customers, include the glossy *Hard Rock Cafe* on Jl Legian, with live music, free entry and pricey drinks. Nearby is the new *Studebaker Club*, which is similar in style. *Zero Six*, near the beach down in Tuban, sometimes offers the unusual combination of rock bands and Balinese dancing. Some of the big hotels have discos and/or karaoke bars, but they can be a bit sedate. *Scandal* nightclub, at Tendjana Paradise Hotel, may be more exciting and stays open very late.

The real social scene is centred up north in Seminyak, where fashionable expatriates kick off at the *Goa 2001 Pub Restaurant* on Jl Legian, while the *Jaya Pub* attracts a quieter, older crowd, and *Cafe Luna* has streetside tables where you can see and be seen. Later on, but *never* before 1 am, the action shifts to the beachside *66 Club* (pronounced 'double six') or the chic *Gado Gado* at the beach end of Jl Dhyana Pura; they both have a cover charge (8000 to 12,000 rp) which includes one drink. Both places have sea breezes, good sounds, open-air dance floors, and a trendy, affluent crowd of tourists, expats and Indonesians, with quite a few gays and the occasional, expensive bar girl.

Video Movies Large-screen laser disk video movies are featured at lots of the restaurants/pubs, including the *Batu Bolong*, the *Twice Bar* and the *Bounty*. They're pretty loud and easy to find, and boards outside promote the night's show. The *Topi Koki Restaurant*, on Jl Pura Bagus Taruna, shows French movies and TV shows.

Cinema There's a three screen cinema complex on Jl Legian, in the same building as McDonald's and the Matahari department store. Recent-release movies, mostly from the USA, are usually shown in the original language, with Indonesian subtitles.

Balinese Dance Large hotels and restaurants put on tourist versions of the best known Balinese dances, and tour agents arrange evening trips to dances at Bona, Batubulan and Denpasar, usually charging from around 25,000 rp.

Things to Buy

Shopping is now a major tourist activity in Kuta. For arts & crafts from Bali and all over Indonesia, there are many art and 'antique' shops on the main streets. Countless boutiques for men and women display beachwear and budget Balinese versions of the latest international fashions. Many shops sell silver and jewellery, but the quality is often suspect – well-established places like Jonathon's, Nadya and Mirah are probably best. Simple stalls sell an endless range of souvenirs and T-shirts, especially in the 'art market' at the beach end of Jl Bakung Sari.

For everyday purchases, like food, toiletries and stationery, there are supermarkets on Jl Legian, Jl Bakung Sari and Jl Raya Kuta. The biggest is the Galael supermarket on the road to Denpasar.

The big duty-free shop is nearby, though it is expensive. The department store at Plaza Bali, on the airport road, has a good selection of clothing and leather at reasonable prices.

The new Kuta Square development, near the beach end of Jl Bakung Sari, has several upmarket shops and a Matahari department store. There's another Matahari in Legian.

Music shops have a huge variety of cassette tapes from about 5000 rp. CDs are also available at around 30,000 rp. Mahogany, in Legian, has an excellent selection, including gamelan music on tape and CD. Other good places are Kul Kul and Men at Work, both on Jl Bakung Sari.

Getting There & Away

Air Bali is no place for air-travel bargains, but one of the best places to look for a good airfare is KCB Tours & Travel on the Denpasar road. To reconfirm an onward flight, it's a local call to the airline offices, which are mostly in Sanur (see the earlier Getting There & Away section for details). The myriad Kuta travel agencies will reconfirm your flight for a small fee. Big hotels will reconfirm for their guests.

Bus Lots of agents in Kuta sell bus tickets to Java, although they're cheaper at the Ubung terminal from where the buses depart. Regular tourist shuttle buses go to other resorts on Bali. Perama (☎ 751551) on Jl Legian is the best known operator, but other shuttle bus companies have similar fares and may have more suitable times, or pick up from your hotel. Destinations include Ubud (7500 rp), Candidasa (10,000), Padangbai (10,000 rp), Kintamani (10,000 rp) and Lovina (12,500 rp). Bus-ferry-bus services to Lombok cost 20,000 rp to Mataram or Senggigi Beach.

Bemo Dark-blue public bemos link Kuta to the Tegal terminal in Denpasar (about 700 rp, but they generally charge more for tourists). Some of them do a loop around Kuta and Legian then go back to Denpasar. Others come from Denpasar, pick up passengers just east of Bemo Corner, then continue south to the airport, Jimbaran, and Nusa Dua or Ulu Watu. For all other destinations you'll have to go via Tegal and one of the other Denpasar terminals. You may have to go to Bemo

Corner to catch a public bemo, and even there you will be pressured to charter a whole vehicle.

Car & Motorcycle There are lots of car-rental places, large and small, and they're cheaper here than in Sanur, Ubud or other tourist centres. The moneychanger just up from Bemo Corner (☎ 751738) advertises some of the cheapest rates around and you don't even have to haggle – a Suzuki hardtop jeep with air-con is 35,000 rp per day, including insurance, but 33,000 rp per day if you take it for a whole week. A larger Kijang is around 65,000 rp per day.

Groups of motorcycles for rent are assembled at various points along Jl Legian. They cost about 11,000 rp per day, depending on size and condition; less by the week, perhaps more for one day only. You'll need a valid motorcycle licence (see the introductory Getting Around section).

Getting Around

Kuta is a pain to get around because it's so spread out, and the guys with charter bemos try to preclude any cheaper transport alternatives.

The Airport There are set taxi fares from the airport to Kuta, Legian, Seminyak and as far as the Bali Oberoi Hotel. From Kuta to the airport you should be able to charter a bemo for about the same fares (haggle like crazy), or get a metered taxi. Perama buses to the airport cost 5000 rp. Theoretically, you could get a regular public bemo to the airport, but you'd have to walk to Bemo Corner, and from the airport gates to the terminal building. Public bemos are infrequent in the afternoon and evening too, so this probably isn't a good option.

Bemo Dark-blue bemos do a loop from Bemo Corner, along and up Jl Pantai Kuta, along Jl Melasti and for a short distance up Jl Legian, then return down Jl Legian to Bemo Corner (about 500 rp around the loop). In practice they may be reluctant to pick up tourists on this route, and they are less frequent and more expensive in the afternoon and evening. For many short trips, and certainly at night, you'll probably have to charter transport.

Taxi & Charter Bemo There are plenty of taxis around Kuta Beach. They're blue and yellow, with meters and air-con, and they charge 900 rp flagfall and 50 rp per 100m. The catch is that they won't stop for passengers on Jl Legian or around Bemo Corner, where the transport touts hustle for business.

Bemos for charter are easy to find – listen for the offers of 'transport' which follow any pedestrian. A full day charter should run to about 80,000 rp, and you can estimate a price for shorter trips on a proportional basis but you'll have to bargain hard. The 'first price' for transport can be truly outrageous. A charter bemo shouldn't cost more than an equivalent trip in a metered taxi. Vehicles which can legally be chartered have yellow licence plates – other vehicles offering rides may be a scam.

Bicycle There are lots of places to rent bikes for around 5000 rp per day. Lock your bike when you leave it, and beware of thieves who might snatch things from the basket or luggage rack.

BEREWA
This beach is a few km up the coast from the north end of the Kuta strip, but to reach it you have to take the small roads west of Kerobokan – there's no coast road north of Petitenget. Signs point to *Bolare Beach Hotel* (☎ (0361) 730258), with a great beachfront location, pool, restaurant etc. Standard rates are around US$50/55. *Legong Keraton Beach Cottages* (☎ (0361) 730280) is just next door and not quite as fancy, but still very nice from US$45. The top-end option is the *Dewata Beach Hotel* (☎ (0361) 730263; fax 234990), a member of the Best Western chain.

CANGGU
A well-known surf spot with right and left-hand breaks, Canggu has a nice beach, though there is sometimes polluted water at the river mouth. There's a *warung*, and basic accommodation at the *Canggu Beach Club*. To get there, go east at Kerobokan and follow the signs to Pererenan. There's no public transport.

SANUR
Sanur is a quieter, more upmarket alternative to Kuta for those coming to Bali for sea, sand and sun. Most hotels are more expensive package-tour places, but there are some cheaper places to stay, and there are plenty of good restaurants, so you don't have to swallow the high prices for hotel meals.

An early home for visiting western artists, Sanur is still an artistic centre, famed for its gamelan orchestras. It's also known for black magic and colourful kites.

The beach is pleasant and sheltered by a reef, but shallow at low tide. At high tide the swimming is fine, and there is an array of water sports on offer – windsurfing, snorkelling, water-skiing, parasailing, paddle boards etc – all for a price. The surf break on the reef can be epic in the wet season, but it's fickle.

Orientation
Sanur stretches for about three km along an east-facing coastline, with the landscaped grounds and restaurants of expensive hotels fronting right onto the beach. The conspicuous, high-rise Hotel Bali Beach (now officially the Natour Grand Bali Beach Hotel, but still commonly called by the original name) is at the northern end of the strip. The main drag is Jl Danau Tamblingan, with the hotel entrances on one side, and lots of shops and restaurants on the other.

Information
Sanur has travel agencies, moneychangers, film processing, supermarkets and other facilities, mostly along Jl Danau Tamblingan.

Post Sanur's post office is on the southern side of Jl Danau Buyan (the part of Jl Segara west of the Bypass Rd). If you're an Amex customer you can have your mail sent to it office, c/o PT Pacto Ltd, PO Box 52, Sanur (☎ 288449), which is in the Hotel Bali Beach.

Communications There's a Telkom wartel at the north end of Jl Danau Tamblingan on the corner of Jl Segara, and a private wartel near the south end. A Home Country Direct phone is next to the Malaysian Airlines office in the Hotel Bali Beach.

Museum Le Mayeur

Sanur was one of the places on Bali favoured by western artists during their prewar discovery of the island. The home of the Belgian artist Le Mayeur, who lived here from 1932 to 1958, is now squeezed between the Hotel Bali Beach and the Diwangkara Beach Hotel. It displays paintings and drawings by Le Mayeur, but, unfortunately, many of them are yellowed, dirty and badly lit. They are nevertheless interesting, impressionist-style paintings from his travels in Africa, India, Italy, France and the South Pacific. The more recent works, from the 1950s, are in much better condition, with the vibrant colours of Bali and the scenes of daily life which later became popular with Balinese artists. All the works have titles, descriptions, dates etc in both Indonesian and English. The museum is an interesting example of Bali-esque architecture. Notice the beautifully carved window shutters which recount the story of Rama and Sita from the *Ramayana*.

Admission is 200 rp (children 100 rp), and it's open Sunday, Tuesday, Wednesday and Thursday from 8 am to 2 pm, Friday until 11 am and Saturday until noon.

Places to Stay

Principally, Sanur is a medium to high-price package-tour resort, although there are a few cheapies and a handful of mid-range places.

Places to Stay – bottom end

The cheapest places are away from the beach and at the northern end of town. On Jl Danau Buyan there are three lower-priced places side by side. The *Hotel Sanur-Indah*, closest to Denpasar, is the most basic and the cheapest at about 15,000 rp for a room. The *Hotel Taman Sari* and the *Hotel Rani* (☎ 288578) have singles/doubles for around 15,000/ 20,000 rp up to 55,000 rp with air-con and hot water. Much better located, the *Ananda Hotel* (☎ 288327) is behind the restaurant of the same name, right by the beach. It's neat and clean, and rooms with fan and cold water cost 25,000/30,000 rp.

There are three basic homestays at the north end of Jl Danau Tamblingan, the *Yulia*, *Luisa* and *Coca*, where clean, simple rooms with private bathroom go for around 25,000 rp per night. They're inconspicuously behind shops at Nos 38, 40 and 42. Further south, on a side street west of the main road, the *Bali Wirasana* (☎ 288632) is cheap at 20,000/40,000 rp, or 60,000 rp with air-con; it doesn't have a pool but guests can use the one at Hotel Swastika.

Places to Stay – middle

At the northern end of Sanur Beach, the *Watering Hole Homestay* (☎ 288289), on Jl Hang Tuah (the Sanur to Denpasar road) opposite the Hotel Bali Beach entrance, has clean, pleasant rooms from 25,000 rp for a single. It's a friendly, family-run place, with good food and a bar.

The *Kalpataru Homestay & Restaurant* (☎ 288457), on the west side of Jl Danau Tamblingan, is pleasant and clean with a garden and swimming pool. It's not bad value at US$25/30 for budget rooms, US$30/35 for better rooms with air-con.

A little further south, on a side road, the *Werdha Pura* (☎ 288171) is a government-run 'beach cottage prototype'. The service is OK, and it fronts onto a nice beach. At 35,000/60,000 rp for singles/doubles, including breakfast, tax and service, it's great value; there are good family rooms too.

The more expensive mid-range places quote their prices in US dollars and add 21% tax and service. Starting again from the northern end of town, the *Pura Dalem Hotel* (formerly Sanur Village Club), on Jl Hang Tuah, costs US$50/60 with air-con, but the rooms are crammed onto the site and it is not in a good location.

On Jl Segara, the *Ratna Beach Hotel* (formerly Tourist Beach Inn; ☎ 288418) is clean and well located, but expensive at US$45/50 – in the low season it might come down to US$20.

On Jl Pantai Sindhu, a block further south and right on the beach, the *Baruna Beach Inn* (☎ 288546) has a great location and just nine rooms, from US$40/45, including breakfast, tax and air-con. On the south side of Jl Pantai Sindhu, a bit further from the beach, the Queen Bali Hotel (☎ 288054) has standard rooms at US$25/30 and bungalows at US$30/35; extra beds are US$7.50. The price includes tax, breakfast, air-con and hot water.

Next to the night market and running through to the Bypass Rd, *Abian Srama* has a swimming pool and over 50 rooms on a small site, from US$17/21 or US$25/35 with air-con. It caters mostly to Indonesian guests.

Going down the main drag, you find the *Gazebo Beach Hotel* (☎ 288212), a popular beachfront place with a lush garden and rooms from US$40/45 to US$55/60, US$15 extra in the high season. A small side track west of Jl Danau Tamblingan leads to a T-junction, north of which you'll find *Bumi Ayu Bungalows* (☎ 289101), which cost US$45/50. They're nice but pricey for a place this far from the beach, though the pool is good.

Continuing along Jl Danau Tamblingan, *Laghawa Beach Inn* (☎ 288494) is on the beach side of the road, with air-con rooms for US$40/45; fan-cooled rooms are US$10 less and all prices include continental breakfast. The inn has an attractive garden setting and looks like quite good value.

On the other side of the road, *Hotel Swastika* (☎ 288693) has pretty gardens, two swimming pools and comfortable rooms for US$27.50/35, or US$37.50/45 with air-con. A few metres further south is the *Hotel Ramayana* (☎ 288429), with air-con rooms at US$27.50 for singles or doubles, excluding tax and breakfast. South again is the *Hotel Santai* (☎ 287314), a two storey place with rooms facing inwards to the pool – it's

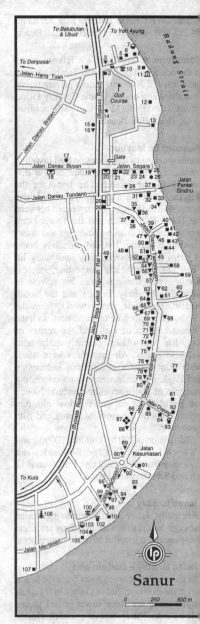

Sanur

0   250   500 m

PLACES TO STAY

1	Pura Dalem Hotel	81	Bali Hyatt	86	Nelaya Restaurant
2	Radisson Bali	84	Hotel Segara Agung	88	Legong Restaurant
5	Watering Hole	91	Hotel Palm Garden	89	Oka's Bar Restaurant
	Homestay & Restaurant	93	Sativa Sanur Cottages	90	Cafe Jepun
6	Alit's Beach	101	Santrian Beach Resort	92	Warung Jawa Barat
	Bungalows & Restaurant	104	Semawang Beach Inn	94	Trattoria da Marco &
8	Ananda Hotel &	105	Hotel Sanur Beach		Italian Consulate
	Restaurant	107	Sanur Bali Travelodge	95	Norman's Bar
9	Diwangkara Beach			97	Alita Garden
	Hotel	**PLACES TO EAT**			Restaurant
12	Grand Bali Beach	3	Si Pino Restaurant	98	Pualam Restaurant
	Hotel & Airline Offices	16	KFC & Swensen Ice	99	Donald's Cafe &
13	Grand Bali Beach		Cream		Bakery
	Hotel - Cottage	19	Splash Bakery		
17	Hotels Sanur-Indah,	25	Warungs	**OTHER**	
	Taman Sari & Rani	28	Borneo Restaurant	4	Bemo & Perama
22	Puri Kelapa Cottages	34	Mango Bar &		Shuttle Bus Stop
23	Ratna Beach Hotel		Restaurant	7	Boats to Nusa
24	Segara Village Hotel	35	Bali Moon Restaurant		Lembongan
27	Baruna Beach Inn	37	Lotus Pond	10	Wartel
29	Abian Srama		Restaurant	11	Museum Le Mayeur
31	Queen Bali Hotel	39	Sindhu Corner	14	Police Station
33	Natour Sindhu Beach		Restaurant	15	Supermarket
38	Homestays Yulia,	46	Kuri Putih Restaurant	18	Post Office
	Luisa & Coca	47	Jak'z Place	20	Postal Agent
40	La Taverna Bali Hotel	49	Sita Restaurant	21	Telkom Wartel
41	Respati Beach Village	53	Cumi Cumi	26	Sanur Beach Market
42	Gazebo Beach Hotel	54	Arena Restaurant	30	Pasar Sindhu Night
43	Hotel Irama	55	Bayu Garden		Market
44	Tandjung Sari Hotel		Restaurant	32	Rumours Nightclub
45	Besakih Beach Hotel	57	Warung Aditya	36	Subec Disco
48	Bumi Ayu Bungalows	62	Laghawa Grill	60	German Consulate
50	Made Homestay & Pub	63	Swastika Garden	64	Temptation
51	Kalpataharu Homestay		Restaurant	70	Handcraft Market
	& Restaurant	65	Swastika II Restaurant	71	No 1 Club
52	Hotel Bumas	68	Nam Ban Kan	73	Petrol Station
56	Prima Cottages		Japanese Restaurant	82	Surya Water Sports
58	Santrian Beach	69	Jineng Restaurant	83	Banjar Club
	Cottages	72	Penjor Restaurant	85	Supermarket
59	Werdha Pura	75	Ryoshi Japanese	87	Double U Shopping
61	Laghawa Beach Inn		Restaurant		Centre
66	Bali Wirasana Hotel	76	Cafe Batu Jimbar, Kiki	96	Asmar Art
67	Hotel Swastika &		Bookshop & Sari Bumi	100	Wartel
	Hotel Ramayana		Ceramics	102	Trophy Pub
74	Hotel Santai	78	Kulkul Restaurant	103	Bemo Stop
77	Hotel Peneeda	79	Melanie Restaurant	106	Pura Belangjong
		80	Telaga Naga		

lean and comfortable, and only US$25/27, ncluding breakfast.

Hotel Segara Agung (☎ 288446) has a ecluded location off Jl Duwung, with a nice ool, plenty of space and new rooms from 0,000 to 60,000 rp per night. At the south-rn end of town, on a small road between the ig hotels, the *Semawang Beach Inn* ☎ 288619) is close to the beach, and offers ;ood facilities and breakfast at US$25 to JS$35 for air-con singles or doubles.

Places to Stay – top end

Most of the top-end hotels are near the beach, and all quote their prices in US dollars, and add about 21% for tax and service. You pay extra for breakfast and everything else. The prices given here are the quoted walk-in rates, but it may be cheaper to book ahead through a travel agency as part of a package.

The Hotel Bali Beach dates from the mid-1960s – a Miami Beach-style block facing the beach. Damaged by fire in 1992, it has been substantially remodelled and renamed the *Natour Grand Bali Beach* (☎ 288511; fax 287917; PO Box 3275, Denpasar), though as a landmark it is more commonly known by its old name. It has all the usual facilities from bars, restaurants and a nightclub, to swimming pools, tennis courts, a golf course and bowling alley. Air-con rooms in the main block cost US$180/190 and there are suites from US$260 to US$600. Adjoining the hotel to the south is the cottage section, in a more Balinese style, from US$150/160. The Presidential Suite is about the most expensive accommodation on Bali at US$3300 per night.

Immediately north of the Hotel Bali Beach and adjacent to the Museum Le Mayeur is the partially secluded *Diwangkara Beach Hotel* (☎ 288577; fax 288894; PO Box 3120, Denpasar). Air-con rooms with breakfast cost US$57 to US$70 a double, and it has a little more character than some of the bigger hotels.

On Jl Segara, the *Puri Klapa Cottages* (☎ 286135; fax 287417) is another small place, a short walk from the beach, with garden cottages for US$60/75, but may discount to US$40 in the low season.

At the beach end of Jl Segara, the *Segara Village Hotel* (☎ 288407/8; fax 287242) has motel-style rooms and two storey cottages from US$75 to US$210. The hotel is in a pleasant landscaped area with swimming pools and a children's playground, and it's one of the few places with an organised programme of kids' activities; US$10 for a 9 am to 1 pm session. Unfortunately, it costs US$20 for an extra bed, which makes it pretty expensive if you have a couple of kids, but it's a nice place with a good atmosphere.

At the inland end of Jl Segara, the new *Radisson Bali* (☎ 281781; fax 281782) has four floors of rooms on either side of a long narrow pool. It's all a bit cramped and it's not a good location, but it compensates with a cultural programme, lots of activities and a kids' club. Rooms start at US$140.

La Taverna Bali Hotel (☎ 288497; fax 287126; PO Box 40, Denpasar), right on the beach, is pretty attractive with air-con rooms

from US$80 and suites from US$160; there' a US$15 high-season supplement.

Continuing south on the main street i *Hotel Irama* (☎ 289060; fax 288300), wit gardens going down to the beach and ver reasonably priced rooms from US$45 double. A little further south is the tree shaded driveway to the *Tandjung Sari Hote* (☎ 288441; fax 287930), one of the origina Balinese beach bungalow places, whic started as an extension of a family home i 1962. Individual bungalows are in tradi tional style and beautifully decorated wit crafts and antiques from US$220 to US$418

Further south, *Santrian Beach Cottage* (☎ 288181; fax 288185; PO Box 3055 Denpasar) has private cottages set in a lus garden with two pools and a beach frontage It's a very attractive place, well located an quite good value at US$70/75 to US$90/95 Keep going to *Hotel Peneeda* (☎ 28842. fax 288300), which has comfortable bunga lows from US$55/65.

Fronting the beach towards the south en of town are the extensive grounds of the *Ba Hyatt* (☎ 281234; fax 287693; PO Box 392 Denpasar), one of the biggest and best hote in Sanur. The Hyatt, with its sloping balco nies overflowing with tropical vegetatio blends in remarkably well – it's an interes ing contrast with the Hotel Bali Beach bui 10 years earlier. Air-con rooms start a around US$140/160 and suites go up t US$685. It has a programme of children activities, and it sometimes offers specia package deals which are great value.

The *Santrian Beach Resort* (☎ 288009 fax 288185) is, if anything, even nicer tha its sister Santrian, with a great beach front age, two swimming pools and tennis courts It's also slightly more expensive, with room from US$80/85 and bungalows at US$100 105. The newer *Sativa Sanur Cottage* (☎ 287881), also near the beach, is attrac tively arranged around a swimming pool an gardens, with stylish air-con rooms from US$66/76; US$15 extra in the high season

As the coast curves around to the wes you'll find the huge *Hotel Sanur Beac* (☎ 288011; fax 287566), with hundreds o air-con rooms from US$140/150 to US$225/260, and suites and bungalows from US$350 to US$900. It has a full range of sporting facilities and entertainment options.

The *Sanur Bali Travelodge* (formerly Surya Beach Hotel; ☎ 288833; fax 287303) is the last place along Sanur Beach, so it's pretty tranquil and facing a quiet beach. Rooms and suites cost US$110/120 to US$650, plus US$20 in the high season.

Places to Eat

All the top-end hotels have their own restaurants, snack bars, coffee bars and cocktail bars, of course – generally with top-end prices too! Tourist restaurants have the standard Indonesian dishes, but for cheaper and more authentic Indonesian food try the rumah makans on the Bypass Rd, the warungs at the night market, and the food carts and stalls at the northern end of the beach, close to where boats leave for Nusa Lembongan.

The *Jineng Restaurant* does Balinese feasts, and quite a few hotels offer Balinese buffet dinners with Balinese dancing from about US$15 to US$75 per head, though you couldn't vouch for the authenticity of either the food or the dancing at some of these functions.

Some reliable places serving inexpensive, tasty, touristy fare include (from north to south): Agung and Sue's *Watering Hole*, opposite the Grand Bali Beach entrance; the *Borneo Restaurant* on Jl Pantai Sindhu, one of several places advertising 'the coldest beer in town', but also recommended for breakfast; *Kalpatharu* on Jl Danau Tamblingan, where you can have a US breakfast, Indonesian lunch and an Italian dinner; *Swastika Garden Restaurant*, a popular place with a nice setting and a reasonable menu; and at the south end of town, *Donald's Cafe & Bakery*, with excellent coffee, pastries, real muesli, yoghurt and fruit drinks.

Trattoria da Marco down at the southern end of the beach road boasts the best Italian food on Bali, though it only opens for dinner. *La Taverna* is recommended for pizza, as is

the *Pualam Restaurant* at the south end of Jl Danau Tamblingan.

The *Kentucky Ayam Goreng* (KFC) and *Swensen's Ice Cream* are next to the supermarket on the Bypass Rd. Also on the Bypass Rd, *Splash Bakery* has a good selection of bread, cakes, and pastries – including Aussie-style meat pies.

For vegetarian and health food, try the *Santai Restaurant* at the hotel of the same name, which does Bali-style vegetarian cuisine with organically grown ingredients. On the corner of Jl Kesumasari, *Warung Jawa Barat* is popular for inexpensive Indonesian food and includes plenty of vegetarian options.

There are several Japanese restaurants, including *Nam Ban Kan*, in the middle of Jl Danau Tamblingan, and *Ryoshi*, nearby in a small shopping centre. *Bayu Garden*, a little further north, serves a good selection of Thai dishes. *Telaga Naga*, opposite the Bali Hyatt which owns it, is about the most expensive place to eat in Sanur, but it offers excellent Szechuan-style Chinese food.

Restoran Segara Agung at the Sanur Beach market is an inexpensive place with tasty food, run by the village co-operative. The best on the beach is possibly the restaurant at *Tandjung Sari*, with an elegant ambience, fine food and regular Balinese dance performances.

Entertainment

Nightlife is not great in Sanur, but there are a few places to go. *Rumours Nightclub* on Jl Pantai Sindhu probably attracts the youngest crowd, mainly tourists plus some local beach boys – call ☎ 288054, ext 71, to be picked up from your hotel. The slick *Subec* disco is popular with Denpasar yuppies, but tourists also come here, along with bar girls and local boys. The *No 1 Club* is one of Sanur's more popular nightspots, with club music, flashy light show and expensive drinks. These three places all have a cover charge of about 6000 to 10,000 rp, and don't get going much before midnight.

For live reggae, try the *Mango Bar*, at the north end of the beach, or the *Banjar Club*, at the south end. *Trophy Pub* at the far southern end of Sanur is a British-style pub with a pool table, bar food and reasonably priced beer. For something different, *LG Club Sehatku* (☎ 287880), just south of the Subec, offers sauna, spa and shiatsu massage from about US$15.

Things to Buy

Sanur shops sell everything from fluoroprint beachwear to the whole range of handcrafts from Bali and other Indonesian islands. The Sanur Beach market, just south of the Hotel Bali Beach, has a variety of stalls so you can shop around. There are plenty of other shops on and near Jl Danau Tamblingan. Some of the art and antique shops have interesting stock. Sanur is close to many of the villages which produce stone and wood carvings, jewellery, weaving, basketry etc, so it's easy to make a shopping trip.

There's a supermarket on the Bypass Rd and another at the southern end of town near the Bali Hyatt. The Pasar Sindhu night market, between the Bypass Rd and Jl Danau Toba near the northern end of Jl Danau Tamblingan, is open most of the day. It caters a bit for tourists, but still sells fresh vegetables, dried fish, pungent spices, plastic buckets and other household goods.

Getting There & Away

Air See the introductory Getting There & Away chapter for information about airlines and flights into and out of Bali.

Bemo There is a bemo stop at the southern end of town near where Jl Danau Tamblingan rejoins the Bypass Rd, and another stop at the northern end of town outside the entrance to the Hotel Bali Beach. There are two different bemos operating between Sanur and Denpasar. Coming from Sanur the blue ones go through the Renon area and across town to Tegal terminal (change here for a Kutabound bemo). The green bemos *sometimes* take a route through town, but usually go through the eastern outskirts straight to Kereneng terminal. The fare is about 600 rp.

Charter Bemo Cars or minibuses for charter congregate outside big hotels and at certain points on Jl Danau Tamblingan. They should cost 4000 rp for a trip to Denpasar, 8000 rp to Kuta and 15,000 rp to Ubud, but you'll have to bargain them down to these prices.

Tourist Shuttle Bus There's no Perama office in Sanur, but Perama buses stop near the entrance to the Bali Beach Hotel. You could book one from the Kuta office (☎ 751551).

Boat Boats to Nusa Lembongan leave from the northern end of the beach. There's a ticket office there, and the fixed price is 15,000 rp (including your surfboard) to get to the island.

Getting Around

The Airport The fixed taxi fare from the airport to Sanur is 15,000 rp, while from Sanur to the airport the meter will come to around 12,000 rp.

Bemo Small bemos shuttle up and down the beach road in Sanur at a cost of 300 rp. Make it clear that you want to take a public bemo, not charter it. Know where you want to go and accept that the driver may take a circuitous route to put down or pick up other passengers.

Car, Motorcycle & Bicycle There are numerous places around Sanur renting cars, motorcycles and bicycles for about 50,000 rp, 12,000 rp and 5000 rp a day respectively. Vehicle hire is more expensive in Sanur than elsewhere and some heavy bargaining may be called for.

PULAU SERANGAN

Very close to the shore, south of Sanur and near the mouth of Benoa Harbour, is Pulau Serangan (Turtle Island). Turtles are fattened here in pens before being sold for village feasts. Eggs are also obtained and hatched, but it's not really a breeding programme – most of the animals (or their eggs) have been taken from the wild, so it's not making any

ontribution to the maintenance of natural
urtle populations and may even be depleting
hem further. The island has an important
emple, Pura Sakenan, noted for its unusual
hrines *(candi)*. Twice a year major temple
estivals are held here, attracting great
crowds of devotees.

Serangan is also the site of a huge tourist
development proposal, including a Disney-
style amusement park. The project is planned
o cover 4800 hectares of land and coastal
waters, and will totally transform the local
environment.

Walking around Serangan is quite pleasant, and the southern end has nice beaches.
The problem is to negotiate a return trip
which gives you enough time to walk the
length of the island, enjoy the beach and then
walk back. You get to Serangan by a char-
ered boat from Suwung – they ask 35,000
rp for the boat but should come down to
around 20,000 rp. They can only do it at high
tide. A public boat costs locals 2000 rp each.

JIMBARAN

Just south of the airport, Jimbaran Bay is a
superb crescent of white sand and blue sea.
Jimbaran itself is a fishing village which has
acquired some luxury hotels over the last few
years, and seems destined to get more.
There's very little budget accommodation,
but it's easily accessible by car or taxi from
Sanur and Nusa Dua, or by bemo from Kuta.
The brilliantly colourful fishing boats at the
north end of the beach are a fine sight, and
the beach itself is perfect. Beachfront restaurants serve cool drinks and fresh seafood,
while you enjoy the scenery.

Places to Stay

The only place resembling budget accommodation, *Puri Indra Prasta*, is away from
the beach on the other side of Jl Ulu Watu at
No 28A. The rooms are pretty unattractive
and overpriced at 35,000 rp. Near the
beachside restaurants, *Nelayan Jimbaran
Cafe & Homestay* (☎ 702253) has small
rooms at 50,000/60,000 rp – at least they're
clean, and the rooftop dining area is a
delight.

Puri Bambu Bungalows (☎ 701377; fax
701440) are on the western side of Jl Ulu
Watu, a short walk from the beach. Air-con
rooms are in three storey blocks around the
pool, but they do have some character and
the staff are friendly. Prices range from
US$55/65 to US$75/90.

The recently renovated *Pansea Puri Bali*
(☎ 701605; fax 701320) has a big swimming
pool, two bars and two restaurants. Accommodation is in air-con bungalows, with
singles/doubles/triples for US$160/180/250,
including breakfast and dinner. A bit to the
north is *Keraton Bali Cottages* (☎ 701961;
fax 701991), with spacious rooms in two
storey cottages surrounded by tastefully
landscaped gardens extending to the beach.
They cost US$120/135 to US$155/175, plus
US$25 in the high season.

Further south you'll find the massive
Hotel InterContinental Bali (☎ 701888; fax
701777), opened in 1993. It has some Balinese features, but it's so big it resembles a

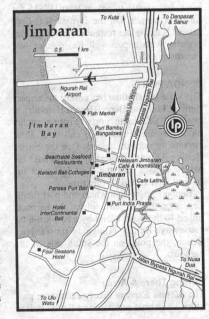

Jimbaran

0   0.5   1 km

To Kuta
To Denpasar & Sanur
Ngurah Rai Airport
Jalan Ulu Watu
Jalan Bypass Ngurah Rai
Fish Market
Jimbaran Bay
Puri Bambu Bungalows
Beachside Seafood Restaurants
Nelayan Jimbaran Cafe & Homestay
Keraton Bali Cottages
Jimbaran
Cafe Latino
Pansea Puri Bali
Hotel InterContinental Bali
Puri Indra Prasta
Four Seasons Hotel
Jalan Bypass Ngurah Rai
To Nusa Dua
To Ulu Watu

fortress. Published room rates are from US$185 to US$340, plus US$30 in the high season.

In a completely different style, the *Four Seasons Hotel* (☎ 701010; fax 701020) has over 100 individual villas spreading down a hillside on the southern edge of Jimbaran Bay – it's like Bali-style tract housing. Guests use little golf buggies to reach the reception area, restaurants and the beach. The villas are delightful, beautifully finished with great views and yours from just US$425 per night.

Places to Eat

About half a dozen open-sided shacks on the beach do great fresh seafood every evening. The standard deal is a whole fish, plus salad and dessert, for around 12,000 rp. You pick your own fish from an ice box and they barbecue it over coconut husks while you wait. Fresh lobster, crabs or prawns are more expensive.

The big hotels all have their own restaurants, but expect to pay at least US$15 for lunch or dinner. On the Bypass Rd, *Cafe Latino* is an Italian restaurant and nightspot popular with expats – it has regular live entertainment.

BENOA PORT

The wide but shallow bay east of the airport runway, Labuhan Benoa (Benoa Harbour), is one of Bali's main ports. Visiting yachts moor here and Pelni ships call in on their circuits through the islands (see the earlier Getting Around chapter). It's also a base for luxury cruises like the *Bali Hai*, and for fishing, diving and surfing trips.

Benoa Port, with a wharf and port facilities, is on the northern side of the harbour, linked to the main island by a two-km-long causeway. Benoa village is on Tanjung Benoa, the point on the south side of the harbour.

Getting There & Away

The *Mabua Express* luxury catamaran provides a fast boat service from Benoa Port to Lembar Harbour on Lombok. It leaves Benoa at 8 am and 2.30 pm, and takes about 2½ hours to reach Lembar. In the other direction, it leaves Lembar at 10.30 am and 5 pm. The fare is US$13.50 in economy, US$20 in 'Emerald Class' and US$27.50 for 'Diamond Class'; the latter two include a snack and soft drink on the boat. Children between two and 12 are charged half price. It costs extra for a surfboard (5000 rp) or a bicycle (20,000 rp).

'Diamond' and 'Emerald' class tickets include pick-up and drop-off service from/to Kuta, Sanur, Nusa Dua, Denpasar and Ubud on Bali, or Mataram, Senggigi or Bangsal on Lombok. The cheaper economy class tickets include pick-up only, but no agents in the tourist areas will sell these tickets – you have to book directly with the Mabua office on Bali (☎ (0361) 72370, 72521) or Lombok (☎ (0370) 81195).

Public bemos to Benoa Port go from Tegal or Sanglah terminals in Denpasar (around 1000 rp). A chartered bemo or taxi to/from Kuta or Sanur should cost around 6000 rp.

TANJUNG BENOA

On the southern side of Benoa Harbour, Tanjung Benoa peninsula extends north from the resort of Nusa Dua, with the village of Benoa at its northern tip. Benoa is one of Bali's multidenominational corners, with a Chinese temple, a mosque and a Hindu temple within 100m of each other.

The peninsula's beaches have several water sports centres. Typical prices are US$14 for an hour of windsurfing or half an hour of snorkelling for two people. A round of parasailing or 15 minutes water-skiing is US$20, and a jet ski is US$20 for 15 minutes. Diving trips and cruises are also available. Beach erosion is occurring, especially towards Nusa Dua.

Places to Stay

Hotels are popping up all along Tanjung Benoa. Up near Benoa village, the *Sorga Nusa Dua* (☎ 771604; fax 771394) is attractive, with pool, gardens and tennis court at US$80/87 for air-con singles/doubles, less

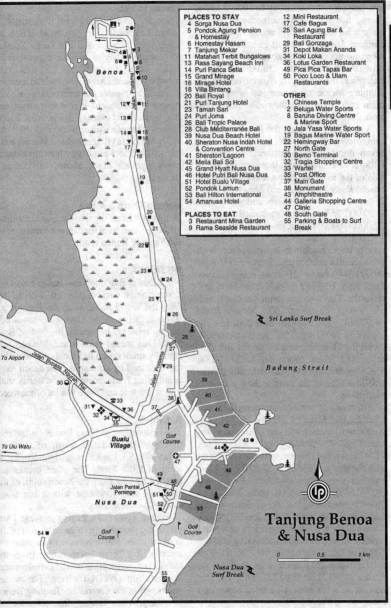

PLACES TO STAY
4 Sorga Nusa Dua
5 Pondok Agung Pension & Homestay
6 Homestay Hasam
7 Tanjung Mekar
11 Matahari Terbit Bungalows
13 Rasa Sayang Beach Inn
14 Puri Panca Setia
15 Grand Mirage
16 Mirage Hotel
18 Villa Bintang
20 Bali Royal
21 Puri Tanjung Hotel
23 Taman Sari
24 Puri Joma
26 Bali Tropic Palace
28 Club Méditerranée Bali
39 Nusa Dua Beach Hotel
40 Sheraton Nusa Indah Hotel & Convention Centre
41 Sheraton Lagoon
45 Melia Bali Sol
46 Grand Hyatt Nusa Dua
46 Hotel Putri Bali Nusa Dua
51 Hotel Bualu Village
52 Pondok Lamun
53 Bali Hilton International
54 Amanusa Hotel

PLACES TO EAT
3 Restaurant Mina Garden
9 Rama Seaside Restaurant

12 Mini Restaurant
17 Cafe Bagus
25 Sari Agung Bar & Restaurant
29 Bali Gonzaga
31 Depot Makan Ananda
34 Koki Loka
36 Lotus Garden Restaurant
49 Pica Pica Tapas Bar
50 Poco Loco & Ulam Restaurants

OTHER
1 Chinese Temple
2 Beluga Water Sports
8 Baruna Diving Centre & Marine Sport
10 Jala Yasa Water Sports
19 Bagus Marine Water Sport
22 Hemingway Bar
27 North Gate
30 Bemo Terminal
32 Tragia Shopping Centre
33 Wartel
35 Post Office
37 Main Gate
38 Monument
43 Amphitheatre
44 Galleria Shopping Centre
47 Clinic
48 South Gate
55 Parking & Boats to Surf Break

Sri Lanka Surf Break

Badung Strait

To Airport
Jalan Bypass Ngurah Rai

To Ulu Watu

Bualu
Village

Golf
Course

Nusa Dua

Jalan Pantai
Peminge

Jalan Pratama

Benoa

Golf
Course

Golf
Course

Nusa Dua
Surf Break

**Tanjung Benoa
& Nusa Dua**

0   0.5   1 km

low-season discounts of up to 30%. *Pondok Agung* has the same management, and is quite a bit cheaper from around 35,000 rp. *Tanjung Mekar* is a small guesthouse, with nice upstairs rooms for about 35,000 rp and downstairs rooms for 30,000 rp. Even cheaper is the *Homestay Hasam*, behind the Tanjung Mekar on a lane just west of the main road, where plain, clean rooms cost from 25,000 rp.

A little further south, the *Matahari Terbit Bungalows* (☎ 771019; fax 771027) has seven comfortable apartments for around US$62. Just down from there, on the cheap side of the road but only a short walk to the beach, *Rasa Sayang Beach Inn* (☎ 771643) is good, friendly and clean, and great value at 20,000/25,000 rp for fan-cooled rooms, or 32,000/40,000 rp with air-con.

Heading towards Nusa Dua, the hotels are mostly upper middle to top-end places with pools and a beach frontage. The *Grand Mirage* (☎ 771888; fax 772148) is a big, luxury hotel from US$162 a double; the hotel features the Thalasso spa, with various health and beauty treatments. The *Mirage Hotel* (☎ 772147; fax 772156) next door has all-inclusive 'club concept' accommodation, including all meals, snacks, drinks and non-motorised water sports for US$117/184. The *Villa Bintang* (☎ 772010), which asks US$110/125, is an unappealing package-tour place.

After passing some construction sites, you reach the *Bali Royal* (☎ 771039; fax 771885), with a pretty garden and just 14 air-con suites from US$140. *Puri Tanjung* (☎ 772121; fax 772424) is a little bigger, with 64 rooms, and a lot cheaper at US$60 to US$90 for doubles, but has very little character. *Puri Joma* (☎ 771526), with only 10 rooms, has a very quiet atmosphere, tasteful Balinese decor and seems like good value for US$55/60. *Taman Sari* (☎ 773953) is a pricey new hotel on the inland side of the road asking US$80/100. The last place before the entrance gate to the Nusa Dua enclave is *Bali Tropic Palace* (☎ 772130; fax 772131), a four star hotel with a big pool, an eroded beach and rooms for US$130/150.

Places to Eat

There are several beachfront restaurants up towards Benoa village, like the *Mini Restaurant*, *Mina Garden* and the *Rama Seaside Restaurant*. They're a little expensive by Bali's usual standards but bargains compared with Nusa Dua prices, and the location is a delight. Nearer the resort entrance, *Sari Agung* is a standard tourist restaurant and bar, while *Bali Gonzaga* is a popular Italian place – cheaper *warungs* cater to the hotel staff. At Benoa village, *Beluga Marina* has a bar with a 5 to 7 pm happy hour, live music every night and dinner shows with Balinese dances.

Getting There & Away

Bemos run from Tegal to the Bualu terminal (1000 rp), and from there green bemos go up the Tanjung Benoa road.

NUSA DUA

Nusa Dua is Bali's top-end beach resort – a luxury tourist enclave planned, with advice from the World Bank, as an isolated luxury resort to bring in the tourist dollars while having minimal impact on the rest of Bali. Nusa Dua means 'two islands', which are actually small raised headlands connected to the mainland by sand spits. The beach itself is suffering from erosion, the water is shallow at low tide and there is a lot of seaweed.

Activities

The best surfing at Nusa Dua is on the reef to the north and the south of the two 'islands'. 'Sri Lanka' is a right-hander in front of Club Med. The other breaks are reached by boat from the beach south of the Hilton. They work best with a big swell during the wet season.

Even if you're not staying in Nusa Dua, you could probably get a game of golf at the country club, rent a bicycle to explore the resort or try some horse riding from the stables behind the Bali Tourist Development Corporation (BTDC) office. For water sports, go to the centres on Tanjung Benoa (see the previous Tanjung Benoa section).

BALI

Places to Stay

The Nusa Dua hotels all have swimming pools, restaurants, bars, sports facilities and all the other international hotel mod cons. They all add 21.5% tax and service, and many charge an extra US$25 to US$50 or so as a high-season supplement. They may be more affordable as part of a package.

Starting at the northern end of the resort, *Club Méditerranée Bali* is strictly a package-tour operation at around US$130 per person per night in the low season, all inclusive.

Next hotel south is the five star *Nusa Dua Beach Hotel* (☎ 771210; fax 771229) which is huge (400 rooms), with all the luxuries you could expect and prices from around US$165. The *Sheraton Nusa Indah Hotel* (☎ 771906; fax 771908) hasn't as many Balinese decorative touches, but it pitches for the conference market with the adjacent Bali International Convention Centre. Prices start at around US$185. The *Sheraton Lagoon* (☎ 771327; fax 772326) has a vast swimming pool, with sandy beaches, land-scaped islands and cascading waterfalls. Rooms start at US$250, but for US$400 you can get one with a balcony from which you can flop straight into the pool. It has a children's programme.

The 500 room *Hotel Melia Bali Sol* (☎ 771510; fax 771360) is run by a Spanish hotel group and has rooms from US$176/98. It's just north of Nusa Dua's 'amenity core', with shopping centre, restaurants, bank, phones etc.

South of the shopping area is the 750 room *Grand Hyatt Nusa Dua* (☎ 771234; fax 772038), which presses for the title of 'best hotel on Bali' and charges US$160/180. South again is the *Hotel Putri Bali Nusa Dua* (☎ 771020; fax 771139), which has 384 rooms, plus suites, cottages and so on from US$130/145 to US$185. It's cheaper than some Nusa Dua palaces. The *Bali Hilton* (☎ 771102; fax 771199) is the most south-erly hotel on the Nusa Dua beach. It's a massive place with a full range of convention and leisure facilities, and rooms from US$145.

Just inland from the Hilton is the smaller *Hotel Bualu Village* (☎ 771310; fax 771313). It was the first hotel at Nusa Dua, and was used as a training facility by the Hotel & Tourism Training Institute (BPLP). It's away from the beach and not as elegant as its newer neighbours, but it has just 50 rooms and a more friendly, informal atmosphere. Prices start at US$80/94.

Close to Hotel Bualu Village is the closest you will come to budget accommodation in Nusa Dua. *Pondok Lamun* (☎ 771983; fax 771985) is the current training ground of the BPLP, and has air-con rooms for 50,000 rp, including tax. The rooms are very ordinary, the location is nowhere and the service could be anything from overattentive to nonexistent.

On a hill overlooking the golf course to the south of the resort area, the *Amanusa* (☎ 772333; fax 72335) is one of Bali's three Aman resorts. Small, understated, with sublime architecture, superb decorations and brilliant views, the individual villas cost from US$430 to US$800.

A new cluster of posh hotels is planned south of the main Nusa Dua resort. The first of these is the *Bali Nikko Hotel*, with 15 levels going down a steep cliff overlooking a private cove with a white sandy beach.

Places to Eat

The Nusa Dua hotels offer a large number of 1st class restaurants, usually several in each hotel. There are several restaurants in the *Galleria shopping centre*, which are excellent but also expensive. In *Bualu Village*, warungs and restaurants cater to hotel staff and to visitors who want better value than they can find inside the resort. These places are emerging almost in defiance of the enclave concept. On the main road, look for *Koki Loka*, for Korean cuisine, or the *Lotus Garden*, both good Kuta-Sanur-style eateries. Warungs at *Depot Makan Ananda* near the Tragia shopping centre serve Indonesian food at Indonesian prices – you can easily fill yourself for under 8000 rp. On the south side of Bualu Village, *Ulam* does quality Balinese seafood, and *Poco Loco* is a Mexican restaurant and bar.

Things to Buy

The large Galleria shopping centre in the middle of the resort enclave has an excellent range of clothing, footwear and leather goods, with lots of big-name brands and occasional sales with bargain prices. A few places have painting, handcrafts and 'antiques' from Bali and all over Indonesia – they're quite expensive, but have some very fine and interesting stock. Unexpected delights, like a barong undulating through the complex, add a touch of fun and remind you that it's not really a shopping mall in California, even if it looks like one.

Just outside the Nusa Dua enclave are a number of tourist shops, and the Tragia supermarket and department store. They're probably a bit cheaper than the Galleria, but not as flashy. There's actually a bit of Kuta bustle out here. If you want to shop for quality goods, you'll probably enjoy a day trip to Nusa Dua.

Getting There & Away

Bemos from Denpasar's Tegal terminal to Bualu Village, just outside the Nusa Dua compound, cost around 1000 rp. There's usually one every hour and more when the hotel staff are finishing their shifts. If you want to shop, call the Galleria (☎ 771662, 771663) or Tragia (☎ 772170, 727172) and they may provide transport.

BUKIT PENINSULA

The southern peninsula is known as Bukit (*bukit* means 'hill' in Indonesian), but was known to the Dutch as Tafelhoek (Table Point). It's dry and was once sparsely inhabited, but is now being developed with a university campus, cement industry and, especially, tourism. The main roads to Nusa Dua and Ulu Watu are quite good, while rougher roads go to some lovely, isolated spots around the coast, many of them targetted for upmarket resorts.

Pura Ulu Watu

The temple of Ulu Watu perches at the southwestern tip of the peninsula, where sheer cliffs drop precipitously into the clear blu sea – the temple hangs right over the edge Ulu Watu is one of several important temple to the spirits of the sea to be found along th coast of Bali. Others include Tanah Lot an Rambut Siwi. Most of them are associate with Nirartha, the Javanese priest credite with introducing many of the elements of th Hindu religion to Bali. Nirartha retreated t Ulu Watu for his final days.

Surfing

Ulu Watu is Bali's surfing mecca, featured i several classic surfing films. Just before th Ulu Watu carpark, a sign indicates the wa to the Suluban Surf Beach (Pantai Suluban Guys on motorcycles will taxi you two o three km down a narrow footpath. From th end of the path, you walk another 250r down to the small gorge which gives acces to the surf. Half a dozen cliff-top warungs o the northern side of the gorge have grea views of the various surf breaks. You can ge wax, ding repair stuff, food, beer or a massage depending on what you need most.

There are other great surf breaks aroun the south-west tip of the Bukit Peninsula notably Padang Padang, Bingin and Balangan On the very south coast are Nyang Nyan and Green Ball. For the latest information ask in the Kuta surf shops or at Tubes Ba Most of the breaks are accessible by roug roads and a short walk. Typically, there is carpark at the end of the road (parking cost a few hundred rupiah), and a warung or tw with snacks and beer. These pretty beache are practically deserted when the surf isn' working.

Places to Stay & Eat

The surf spots have warungs around the clif tops which offer basic Indonesian food (nas and mie), western fare (jaffles and pancakes and expensive beer. Surfers can sometime crash in these warungs to get an early star on the morning waves.

At the very south end of the peninsula, the *Bali Cliffs Resort* (☎ 771992; fax 771993) i a luxury hotel, with rooms from arounc

JS$185. The cliff-top swimming pool looks ood, and a scenic elevator goes down the liff to a restaurant, bar and private beach. A much smaller, more understated, luxury op- on is the *Puri Bali* (☎ 701362; fax 701363), cached by the road to the Nyang Nyang surf oot. It offers about half a dozen large private illas for US$250 per night, each with a nagnificent view to the ocean.

On the road to Ulu Watu, south of Jim- aran, there are a couple places which might e convenient. On the west side of the road, *illa Koyo* (☎ 702927) is a modern mid- ange hotel which asks US$75 for a room, ut may discount to US$40. On the other side f the road, *Mr Ugly's* has five small but omfortable rooms for about 15,000/25,000 o, and the cafe is a good stop for a drink or nack. Other places to eat along this road iclude *Restaurant Puncak Pesona*, which is n expensive tour-group stop, and *Warung idra*, which is more a restaurant than a varung, and has good, cheap food and a nop.

Denpasar to Ubud

he road from Denpasar to Ubud, via Bat- bulan, Celuk, Sukawati, Batuan and Mas, lined with places making and selling hand- rafts. Many tourists stop and shop along this oute, but there are some quieter back roads, here much of the craft work is done in small vorkshops and family compounds. There e regular bemos along this route, but if you vant to stop at craft workshops and buy iings, it's more convenient to have your wn transport.

ATUBULAN

tone carving is the main craft of Batubulan, hich means 'moon stone'. You'll see hun- reds of statues beside the road, and you're velcome to come in and watch the workers, nany of them young boys, chipping away at g blocks of soft volcanic stone. The tem- les around Batubulan are noted for their ne stone sculptures. Pura Puseh, just 200m

to the east of the busy main road, is worth a visit.

Batubulan is also a centre for antiques and a variety of crafts, textiles and woodwork, and has some well-regarded dance troupes. A Barong & Rangda or Kris dance is held in Batubulan at 9.30 am daily. It's touristy, but worth seeing if you won't have a chance to catch a performance elsewhere.

Batubulan also has the main bemo termi- nal for eastern Bali – see the Denpasar Getting There & Away section for details.

CELUK

Celuk is a silver and goldsmithing centre, with numerous jewellery specialists and a wide variety of pieces on sale. The bigger showrooms are for tour groups. Most of the work is done in tiny family workshops in the back streets.

SUKAWATI

Before the turn-off to Mas and Ubud, Suk- awati is a centre for the manufacture of wind chimes, temple umbrellas and *lontar* (palm) baskets, dyed with intricate patterns. Suka- wati has a busy art & craft market, the Pasar Seni, just across from the produce market. It sells semifinished artwork to craft shops who do the final finishing themselves, but has many other things worth seeing. The town has a long tradition of dance and wayang kulit shadow puppet performance.

The small village of **Puaya**, about a km west from the main road, specialises in making high-quality leather shadow puppets and masks.

BATUAN

Batuan is a noted painting centre with a number of galleries. It came under the influ- ence of Bonnet, Spies and the Pita Maha artists' co-operative at an early stage. Tradi- tionally, Batuan painters produced dynamic black-ink drawings, but the newer 'Batuan style' of painting is noted for including a large number of different subjects in a single canvas, even the odd windsurfer or a tourist with a video camera. Batuan is also noted for its traditional dance classes, and is a centre for carved wooden relief panels and screens.

MAS

Mas means 'gold', but it's woodcarving, particularly mask carving, that is the craft here. The road through Mas is almost solidly lined with craft shops which do business by the tour-bus load, but there are plenty of smaller carving operations in the small back lanes. The bigger and more successful outlets are often lavishly decorated with fine woodcarvings. The renowned artist Ida Bagus Tilem, whose father was also a noted woodcarver, has a particularly fine gallery.

If you want to stay in Mas, *Taman Harum Cottages* has elegant individual bungalows, some two storey with balconies overlooking the rice fields, and there's a swimming pool – prices are from about US$40.

BLAHBATUH

Blahbatuh is a detour from the more direct road to Ubud. Its **Pura Gaduh** has a metre-high stone head said to be a portrait of Kebo Iwa, the legendary strongman and minister to the last king of the Bedulu kingdom (see Bedulu and Gunung Kawi in the Around Ubud). Gajah Mada, the Majapahit prime minister, realised that he could not conquer Bedulu, Bali's strongest kingdom, while Kebo Iwa was there, so he lured him away to Java (with promises of women and song) and had him killed. The stone head is thought to be very old, but the temple is a reconstruction of an earlier temple destroyed in the great earthquake of 1917.

KUTRI

Just north of Blahbatuh, near the village of Kutri, on the western side of the road is **Pura Kedarman** (also known as Pura Bukit Dharma). If you climb Bukit Dharma, the hill behind the temple, you'll reach a hilltop shrine with a panoramic view and a stone statue of the eight armed goddess Durga. The statue, in the act of killing a demon-possessed water buffalo, is thought to date from the 11th century and shows strong Indian influences.

Another theory is that the image is of Airlangga's mother Mahendradatta, who married King Udayana, Bali's 10th century ruler. When her son succeeded to the throne she hatched a bitter plot against him and unleashed evil spirits *(leyaks)* upon his kingdom. She was eventually defeated but this incident led to the legend of the rangda, a widow-witch and ruler of evil spirits. The temple at the base of the hill has images of Durga and a bale housing the body of a barong.

Ubud

Perched on the gentle slopes leading up towards the central mountains, Ubud is the centre of 'cultural tourism' on Bali, and it has attracted visitors interested in Balinese art ever since Walter Spies was here in the 1930s. Apart from the many places of interest in Ubud itself, there are also numerous temples, ancient sites and interesting craft centres around the town.

Ubud has undergone tremendous development in the past few years, and now has problems of traffic congestion in the centre and urban sprawl on the edges. It's still a pretty relaxed place though, especially in a secluded family compound or in one of the delightful open-air restaurants, where the fragrant evenings are still quiet enough to hear a frog in a rice field. There's an amazing amount to see in and around Ubud. You'll need at least a few days to appreciate it properly, and Ubud is one of those places where days can become weeks and weeks become months.

Orientation

The once small village of Ubud has expanded to encompass its neighbours – Campuan, Penestanan, Padangtegal, Peliatan and Pengosekan are all part of what we see as Ubud today. The crossroad, where the bemos stop, marks the centre of town. On the north *(kaja)* side is the Ubud Palace, on the south *(kelod)* side is the market. Running south beside the market is Monkey Forest Rd, while the main east-west road is Jl Raya.

West of Ubud, this road drops steeply down to the ravine at Campuan, where an old suspension bridge hangs next to the new one, over the Wos River. On the other side, the Campuan Hotel sits on the site of Walter Spies' prewar home, and the road bends north to pass the Neka Museum. Penestanan, famous for its painters, is just west of Campuan. Further west again, Sayan overlooks the gorgeous valley of the Yeh Ayung Ayung River) – musician Colin McPhee lived here in the 1930s.

East and south of Ubud proper, the Pelliatan, Pengosekan and Nyukuning villages are known variously for painting, traditional dance and woodcarving. The area north of Ubud it's less densely settled, with picturesque rice fields interspersed with small villages, many of which specialise in a local craft or style.

Information

Ubud is just high enough to be noticeably cooler than the coast. It's also noticeably wetter. For getting around Ubud, and especially the surrounding villages, the best map is Travel Treasure's *Ubud Surroundings*, readily obtainable in Bali bookshops – look for its logo, a figure with a pointing hand instead of a head.

Tourist Office The Ubud tourist office (☎ 96285), or Bina Wisata, is on Jl Raya near the main crossroad, and opens daily from 8 am to 8 pm. It doesn't have lots of maps and brochures, but the staff are friendly and can answer most questions, and they sell tickets to cultural performances in Ubud and nearby towns.

The tourist office is a local venture, set up in an effort to protect the village from the tourist onslaught – not by opposing tourism, but by providing a service aimed at informing and generating a respect among visitors for Balinese culture and customs.

The sheer number of tourists, and the insensitivity of a few, can still be intrusive, but to some extent these problems have been alleviated by increasing commercialisation of the tourist industry. Most visitors who witness traditional ceremonies do so through a tour agency or guide. Part of the guide's job is to ensure that his or her charges go only where they are welcome and behave with appropriate decorum. If they don't, the local community holds the guides responsible and will perhaps deny them access in the future. Also, local people make some decisions as to which ceremonies can be open and public, and which must be conducted with discretion; visitors will not learn of the latter ones through the normal sources of information.

Money There are a couple of banks on Jl Raya, and plenty of moneychangers down Monkey Forest Rd.

Post The pleasant little post office, with a poste-restante service, is towards the east end of Jl Raya. Have mail addressed to Kantor Pos, Ubud, Bali, Indonesia. You can also get stamps at a few places around town, identified by a 'postal services' sign.

Communications You can make international direct-dial calls and send faxes from several wartels in Ubud. There's a private one upstairs on Jl Raya, above BCA Bank, and a helpful one near the Puri Lukisan gallery. A cheaper Telkom wartel is at the east end of town, on the road going north towards Penelokan, with a Home Country Direct phone. All of Ubud and the surrounding villages are in the 0361 telephone district.

Bookshops The Ubud Bookshop and the Ganesha Bookshop are close to each other on Jl Raya almost opposite the post office. The Ubud keeps recent newspapers and magazines from Europe, the USA and Australia; the Ganesha has good sections on travel, women's issues, arts and music, including a few in French. Ary's Bookshop, next to Ary's Warung, has a fair stock of books, and maps of Bali and Indonesia.

Medical Services Ubud Medical Service (☎ 974911) at Jl Raya Ubud 36 is used to treating visitors.

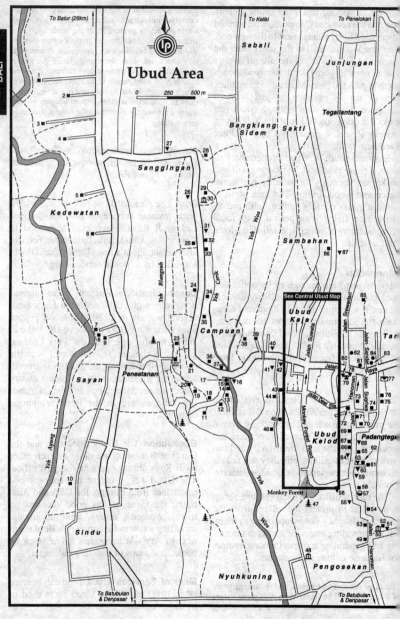

Ubud Area

BALI

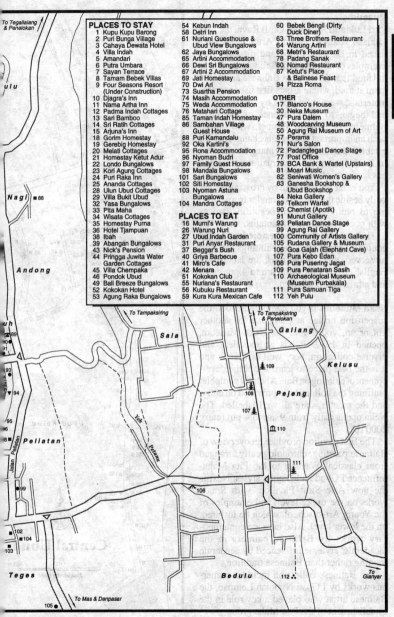

PLACES TO STAY
1 Kupu Kupu Barong
2 Puri Bunga Village
3 Cahaya Dewata Hotel
4 Villa Indah
5 Amandari
6 Putra Umbara
7 Sayan Terrace
8 Tamam Bebek Villas
9 Four Seasons Resort
  (Under Construction)
10 Djagra's Inn
11 Nama Artha Inn
12 Padma Indah Cottages
13 Sari Bamboo
14 Sri Ratih Cottages
15 Arjuna's Inn
18 Gorim Homestay
19 Gerebig Homestay
20 Melati Cottages
21 Homestay Ketut Adur
22 Londo Bungalows
23 Kori Agung Cottages
24 Puri Raka Inn
25 Ananda Cottages
28 Ulun Ubud Cottages
29 Villa Bukit Ubud
32 Yasa Bungalows
33 Pita Maha
34 Wisata Cottages
35 Homestay Puma
36 Hotel Tjampuan
38 Ibah
39 Abangan Bungalows
44 Nick's Pension
44 Pringga Juwita Water
  Garden Cottages
45 Villa Chempaka
46 Pondok Ubud
49 Bali Breeze Bungalows
52 Kokokan Hotel
53 Agung Raka Bungalows

54 Kebun Indah
58 Detri Inn
61 Nuriani Guesthouse &
  Ubud View Bungalows
62 Jaya Bungalows
65 Artini Accommodation
66 Dewi Sri Bungalows
67 Artini 2 Accommodation
69 Jati Homestay
70 Dwi Ari
73 Suartha Pension
74 Masih Accommodation
75 Weda Accommodation
82 Matahari Cottage
85 Taman Indah Homestay
86 Sambahan Village
  Guest House
88 Puri Kamandalu
92 Oka Kartini's
95 Rona Accommodation
96 Nyoman Budri
97 Family Guest House
98 Mandala Bungalows
101 Sari Bungalows
102 Siti Homestay
103 Nyoman Astuna
  Bungalows
104 Mandra Cottages

PLACES TO EAT
16 Murni's Warung
26 Warung Nuri
27 Ubud Indah Garden
31 Puri Anyar Restaurant
37 Beggar's Bush
40 Griya Barbecue
41 Miro's Cafe
42 Menara
51 Kokokan Club
55 Nuriana's Restaurant
56 Kubuku Restaurant
59 Kura Kura Mexican Cafe

60 Bebek Bengil (Dirty
  Duck Diner)
63 Three Brothers Restaurant
64 Warung Artini
68 Metri's Restaurant
78 Padang Sanak
80 Nomad Restaurant
87 Ketut's Place
  & Balinese Feast
94 Pizza Roma

OTHER
17 Blanco's House
30 Neka Museum
47 Pura Dalem
48 Woodcarving Museum
50 Agung Rai Museum of Art
57 Perama
71 Nur's Salon
72 Padangtegal Dance Stage
77 Post Office
79 BCA Bank & Wartel (Upstairs)
81 Moari Music
82 Seniwati Women's Gallery
83 Ganesha Bookshop &
  Ubud Bookshop
84 Neka Gallery
89 Telkom Wartel
90 Chemist (Apotik)
91 Munut Gallery
93 Peliatan Dance Stage
99 Agung Rai Gallery
100 Community of Artists Gallery
105 Rudana Gallery & Museum
106 Goa Gajah (Elephant Cave)
107 Pura Kebo Edan
108 Pura Pusering Jagat
109 Pura Penataran Sasih
110 Archaeological Museum
  (Museum Purbakala)
111 Pura Samuan Tiga
112 Yeh Pulu

To Tegallalang
& Penelokan

Nagi ■88

Andong

To Tampaksiring

Sala

To Tampaksiring
& Penelokan

Galiang

Kelusu

≛109

Pejeng

108 ≛

107 ≛

Yeh Pelanu

Jalan Peliatan

Peliatan

≈ 110

■99

111 ⩎

106

102 ■
104 ■
103 ●

Teges

Bedulu

112 ⩎

To Gianyar

105 ●

To Mas & Denpasar

Museums

Puri Lukisan Museum On Jl Raya, the Puri Lukisan (Palace of Fine Arts) was established in the mid-1950s and displays fine examples of all schools of Balinese art. It was in Ubud that the modern Balinese art movement started, where artists first used modern materials, were influenced by foreign styles and began to depict scenes of everyday Balinese life. Rudolf Bonnet, who played such an important role in this change, helped establish the museum's permanent collection in 1973. It's a relatively small museum and has some excellent art.

You enter the museum by crossing a river gully beside the road and wander from building to building through beautiful gardens with pools, statues and fountains.

The museum has been restored in the last couple of years, and the paintings are well preserved, well lit and most are labelled in English. It's open from 8 am to 4 pm daily, and admission is 2000 rp.

Neka Museum If you continue beyond the suspension bridge at Campuan for another km or so, you'll find the Neka Museum, opened in 1982. It has an excellent and diverse collection, very well exhibited, and it is the best place to learn about the development of painting on Bali. A helpful pamphlet outlining the collection is provided on entry, and the paintings are all well labelled. The Neka opens daily from 9 am to 4 pm (entry 2000 rp).

The first pavilion provides an overview of Balinese painting, chronologically arranged from classical Wayang to the Pita Maha-influenced Ubud and Batuan styles. Next is the new Arie Smit Pavilion, with Smit's works on the upper level, and examples of the Young Artist school, which he inspired, on the lower level. Also here are contemporary works by Balinese painters in the 'academic' style, ie influenced by academic training rather than Balinese tradition.

The Balinese collection includes numerous works by I Gusti Nyoman Lempad, the Balinese artist who played a key role in the establishment of the Pita Maha group.

Central Ubud

PLACES TO STAY
1 Gusti's Garden Bungalows
2 Arjana Accommodation
3 Shanti's Homestay
5 Siti Bungalows
6 Suci Inn
7 Roja's Homestay
10 Mumbul Inn
12 Puri Saraswati Cottages
21 Pondok Wisata Sudharsana
31 Anom Bungalows
33 Happy Inn
34 Canderi's Losmen & Warung
35 Yuni's House
37 Wayan Karya Homestay
38 Shana Homestay
39 Wena Homestay
40 Nirvana Pension
41 Dewi Putra House
42 Sayong's House
43 Sania's House
44 Wija House
45 Bali House
46 Ning's House
47 Devi House
50 Merta House
51 Seroni House
52 Sudartha House
53 Gandra House
54 Pandawa Homestay
56 Gayatri Accommodation
60 Igna Accommodation
61 Puri Muwa Bungalows
62 Alit's House
64 Pondok Wisata Suarsena
65 Oka Wati's Sunset Bungalows
68 Igna 2 Accommodation
70 Bendi's Accommodation
72 Wahyu Bungalows
74 Esty's House

75 Sidya Homestay
76 Ramasita Pension
80 Accommodation Kerta
83 Karyawan Accommodation
85 Frog Pond Inn
86 Pramesti Bungalows
87 Mandia Bungalows
88 Ubud Village Hotel
91 Pertiwi Bungalows
92 Puri Garden Bungalows
93 Rice Paddy Bungalows
94 Sri Bungalows
95 Nani House (Karsi Homestay)
96 Villa Rasa Sayang
97 Jati 3 Bungalows & Putih
100 Jaya Bungalows
101 Ibunda Inn
102 Ubud Bungalows
104 Dewi Ayu Accommodation
105 Ubud Terrace Bungalows
107 Sagitarius Inn
108 Fibra Inn
109 Ubud Inn
110 Lempung Accommodation
111 Pande Permai Bungalows
112 Monkey Forest Hideaway
113 Hotel Champlung Sari

PLACES TO EAT
4 Han Snel's Garden Restaurant
11 Mumbul's Cafe
13 Lotus Cafe
17 Coconut's Cafe
18 Momoya Japanese Restaurant
22 Puri's Bar & Restaurant
27 Ary's Warung

28 Ryoshi Japanese Restaurant
30 Casa Luna
32 Satri's Warung
36 Seroni's Warung
48 Tutmac Cafe
49 Bamboo Restaurant
55 Gayatri Restaurant
63 Ayu's Kitchen
66 Lillies Garden Restaurant
67 Oka Wati's Warung
69 Beji's Cafe
71 Bendi's Restaurant
73 Do Drop In Cafe
77 Cafe Bali
78 Ibu Rai Restaurant
81 Yogyakarta Cafe
82 Dian Restaurant
89 Coco Restaurant
90 Cafe Wayan
98 Mendra's Cafe
99 Jaya Cafe
106 Ubud Restaurant

OTHER
8 Puri Lukisan Museum
9 Wartel
14 Pura Taman Saraswati
15 Pura Desa Ubud
16 Bemo Stop
19 Pura Merajan Agung
20 Ubud Palace & Hotel Puri Saren Agung
23 I Gusti Nyoman Lempad's Home
24 Bemo Stop
25 Tourist Office (Bina Wisata)
26 Ary's Bookshop
29 Toko Tino Supermarket
57 Postal Agent
58 Ibu Rai Gallery
59 Bookshop
79 Bead & Bali
84 Batik Workshop & Crackpot Coffee Shop
103 Meditation Shop
114 Parking

The Contemporary Indonesian Art Hall as paintings by artists from other parts of Indonesia, including Abdul Aziz, Affandi, ullah, Srihadi Sudarsono and Anton Kustia Vijaya, many of whom have worked on Bali. he East-West Art Annexe is devoted to the ork of foreign artists on Bali, including Louise Koke (of Kuta Beach Hotel fame), Miguel Covarrubias, Willem Hofker, Rudolf Bonnet and Theo Meier. More recent artists represented include Australian Donald Friend, Dutchman Han Snell and Spanish/Filipino/Indonesian Antonio Blanco. The temporary exhibition hall has changing displays of mostly contemporary painting, with many paintings available for sale.

Rudana Museum This big, imposing edifice, south-east of Ubud in Teges, opened in 1995. It's worth seeing, but not nearly as good as the Neka. It opens daily, and costs 2500 rp.

Agung Rai Museum of Art Another new art museum recently opened, the ARMA (☎ 97-4228) also has performance spaces and will provide facilities for painting workshops, dance and music classes. It features traditional and contemporary work by Indonesian and European artists from Agung Rai's private collection, as well as temporary exhibitions. It's in Pengosekan, near the Kokokan Hotel.

Galleries

There are countless galleries and shops exhibiting artwork for sale, but a few are particularly worthwhile. The **Neka Gallery**, on Jl Raya Neka near the post office, is owned by Suteja Neka (sponsor of the Neka Museum). It has a huge variety of work, generally of a very high quality, in all the Balinese styles, as well as work by European residents like Snel and Smit. Most works are for sale, often at pretty high prices.

Also important is the **Agung Rai Gallery** at Peliatan, south-east of central Ubud. Again the collection extends for room after room and covers the full range of Balinese styles, plus works by artists like Blanco, Smit, Snel, Meier and Affandi. Some of these may transfer to the new Agung Rai Museum.

The **Seniwati Gallery of Art by Women**, just north of Jl Raya, has a very small permanent collection and a good selection of paintings for sale. There's a variety of style, and a uniformly high standard. Most are by local artists but a few are by visiting women.

Other big commercial galleries include **Munut**, at the east end of Jl Raya, **Rudana**, down in Teges, and the **Pengosekan Community of Artists Gallery.**

Artists' Homes

The home of I Gusti Nyoman **Lempad** is on the main street of Ubud. There are lots of paintings for sale, but the only Lempad works are some attractive but weathered stone sculptures.

Walter **Spies** and Rudolf **Bonnet** both lived for some time at Campuan, near the suspension bridge. Spies' home is now one of the rooms at the Hotel Tjampuan, and can be inspected if it is not in use; you can even stay there if you book well ahead.

Just beside the Campuan suspension bridge, across the river from Murni's Warung, the driveway leads to the superbly theatrical house of Filipino-born artist Antonio **Blanco**. Entry to the beautiful house and gallery is 2500 rp. Blanco's speciality is erotic art and illustrated poetry, though for Blanco, playing the part of the artist is probably just as important as painting.

Arie Smit and Han **Snel** are well-known western artists residing in Ubud. In the 1960s Smit sparked the Young Artists' school of painting in Penestanan. Snel's work can be seen at his restaurant and hotel, just off the main road through Ubud.

Walks Around Ubud

The growth of Ubud has engulfed a number of nearby villages, though they have mostly managed to retain their distinct identities. It's interesting to walk through the fields and the surrounding villages, where you frequently see artists at work in open rooms and verandahs on the quieter streets.

Monkey Forest Monkey Forest Rd is lined with hotels, restaurants and shops for its whole length, but at the far end, at the bottom of the hill, you'll arrive in a small forest. It's inhabited by a handsome band of monkeys ever ready for passing tourists who just might have peanuts available for a handout. Be warned – the monkeys can put on ferocious displays of temperament if you don't come through with the goods, and quick. Don't give any hint that you might have something interesting in a pocket or a bag. You buy a ticket (500 rp) before entering the forest.

GREGORY ADAMS

JAMES LYON

JAMES LYON

GREGORY ADAMS

Bali
Top: Picturesque rice fields near Sideman, East Bali.
Left: Succulent vegetation in East Bali.
Middle Right: The lotus flower is an important symbol in Hindu and Buddhist mythology.
Bottom Right: One of Bali's many species of orchid.

JAMES LYON

GREGORY ADAMS

JAMES LYON

Bali

Top: Some colonial era buildings survive at Toyapakeh, on Nusa Penida.
Bottom Left: Time for a snack, Tampaksiring.
Bottom Right: Dressed in his best for the festival, Sanur.

Ubud's interesting old **Pura Dalem** (Temple of the Dead) is in the forest – look for the rangda figures devouring children at the entrance to the inner temple. The road swings east at the Monkey Forest, and you can follow it around to Padangtegal or Pengosekan. Nyuhkuning is a small village south of the monkey forest, noted for its woodcarving; a small woodcarving museum here keeps irregular hours.

Campuan At the confluence of the Wos and Cerik rivers (Campuan actually means 'where two rivers meet'), and far below the ridges, is the Pura Gunung Labuh, a temple thought to date back as far as 1000 years. From beside the temple a walking track leads away to the north along the ridge between the rivers.

Penestanan The road bends sharply as it crosses the river at Campuan and then runs north, parallel to the river. If you take the steep uphill road which bends away to the left of the main road you reach Penestanan. There are galleries, many of them specialising in paintings of the Young Artists' style, and some losmen and houses to rent.

Sayan & Kedewatan West of Penestanan is Sayan, the site for Colin McPhee's home in the 1930s, so amusingly described in A House in Bali. North of Sayan is Kedewatan, another small village where a road turns east and swings back towards Ubud via Campuan. Just west of the villages and the main road is the Yeh Ayung. The deep gorge of this swift-flowing river offers magnificent panoramas. Several expensive hotels, and the homes of a number of modern-day McPhees, are perched on the edge. Whitewater rafting trips offer another perspective on the river.

Petulu In the late afternoon you can enjoy the spectacle of thousands of herons arriving home in Petulu. They nest in the trees along the road through the village and make a spectacular sight as they fly in and commence squabbling over the prime perching places.

A good route there is along Jl Suweta, north of Ubud's bemo terminal, which continues to the village of Junjungan, heavily into the carving of garudas. Petulu is south-east of Junjungan – the turn-offs are signposted, but ask if you're unsure.

Bird Watching
Bird enthusiasts should enquire about the three hour guided walks departing from the Beggar's Bush Pub (☎ 975009) at 9.15 am on Tuesday, Friday, Saturday and Sunday. They cost US$28, including a guide book and lunch.

Courses
There are quite a few courses on offer – for more information start by asking at the tourist office. Possibilities include Balinese music, dance, painting, woodcarving, mask making, batik, Balinese and Indonesian cooking, meditation, Balinese language and Bahasa Indonesia.

Organised Tours
Numerous tours are offered from Ubud. Those offered by the tourist office are good value – between 15,000 and 30,000 rp for a full day tour, with extensive itineraries which don't include shopping (except tours to craft centres).

Places to Stay – bottom end
Ubud has many small homestays, where a simple, clean room in a pretty garden will cost around 12,000/15,000 rp for a single/double, with private bathroom and a light breakfast. The surrounding villages also have cheap accommodation, often in a much quieter, greener environment. Tax of 10% is added to the cost of a room, and fancier places add 5 to 10% more for service. Some accommodation is geared to longer stayers (several weeks at least) and usually offers cooking facilities, but no meals.

Many budget places are very small, with only two, three or four rooms. The following is just a sample; there are many other excellent places as well.

Central Ubud Close to the top of Monkey Forest Rd, near the market, is one of Ubud's longest-running homestays, *Canderi's* (also Candri's or Tjanderi's depending on which sign or spelling style you choose). It offers typical losmen-style accommodation in a traditional family compound, with singles/doubles at 12,000/15,000 rp. A little further south is *Gayatri*, also in a charming family compound and well priced at 10,000 rp.

On Jl Arjuna, the small street off the west side of Monkey Forest Rd, *Anom Bungalows* are OK at 10,000/14,000 rp. *Pondok Wisata Suarsena* is nice, but asks 15,000/20,000 rp, so it's worth discussing the price. Also west of Monkey Forest Rd, *Igna 2 Accommodation* has a nice quiet location and good rooms for only 10,000/12,000 rp. Look around here for more little places which are secluded but central.

Going down Monkey Forest Rd, cheap places include *Pandawa Homestay* at 10,000/15,000 rp, with nice, traditional-style rooms, and *Igna Accommodation*, with similar prices. South of the football field, the very clean and well-kept *Frog Pond Inn* has a welcoming atmosphere and breakfast, with rooms from 10,000/15,000 to 15,000/25,000 rp. Nearby *Mandia Bungalows*, back from the street, are well kept and friendly, and cost 25,000/30,000 rp with hot water. The inexpensive *Pramesti Bungalows* have also been recommended, as have *Jaya Bungalows* and *Bella House*. Further down is *Ibunda Inn*, a pleasant place with rooms from 10,000/15,000 rp.

The small streets to the east of Monkey Forest Rd, including Jl Karna and Jl Goutama, have heaps of small homestays – just look for the small signs near the gates. They are mostly family compounds with three or four bungalows at around 12,000/15,000 rp, including breakfast and tax, though prices depend somewhat on demand and length of stay. They're very similar, so just wander down the narrow lanes, have a look in a few, compare the rooms and prices, and make

your choice. Both *Seroni House* (☎ 9635?) and *Bali House* have been recommended b readers.

Northern Ubud North of Jl Raya, Jl Kajan has some places with great views west ov the river, including the bargain *Roja's Home stay*, at around 10,000/12,000 rp for goo singles/doubles. Further up is *Gusti's Ga den Bungalows* (☎ 96311), with hot wate and a lovely outlook. Jl Suweta has the *Su Inn* (☎ 975304), across from the banyan tre with simple rooms from 12,000/15,000 r The rooms look out onto the central garde and it's a friendly, relaxed place that's qui yet very close to the action.

Continue along Jl Suweta for about I minutes to Sambahan, where there's a sma group of places, best known of which *Ketut's Place* (☎ 96246), with rooms in family compound from 15,000/20,000 rp f singles/doubles in the front to 25,000/35,00 rp for cottages at the back. Another goo place is the nearby *Sambahan Village Gue House*.

A really secluded place is *Taman Ind Homestay*, with three rooms at 12,000 r From the main road, go north up Jl Sand and keep walking into the rice fields.

South-East of Ubud More accommodatio can be found in Padangtegal, on the stree which run south of Jl Raya; Jl Hanoman, Sugriwa and Jl Jembawan.

On Jl Hanoman, *Jati Homestay* and *Sua tha Pension* are small, cheap, basic homestay *Nuriani Guesthouse* (☎ 975346), just off to th east side in the rice fields, costs 20,000 25,000 rp a double.

The nearby *Ubud View* (☎ 974164) h similar prices, and a similarly attractiv outlook. *Jaya Bungalows* is another goo place to stay, and a little cheaper at 8000 15,000 rp.

Further east is Peliatan, where Jl Tebesay has some possibilities, including popul *Rona Accommodation* (☎ 96229), a ve nice place with rooms from around 15,00 rp, and a book exchange with a good sele tion. It has lots of useful information and c

BALI

rganise tours, car and bike rental, and baby-
tting. A few doors south is *Nyoman Budri*,
ith rooms for only 10,000/12,000 rp, and
ie *Family Guest House* (☎ 974054), also
ell-recommended with a pretty garden and
ood rooms at 15,000/ 20,000 rp.

Going down Jl Peliatan, at the junction
here the road bends sharp left to Denpasar,
ou'll see a sign for the *Sari Bungalows*
☎ 975541), just 100m or so off the road. It's
amily-run, in a pleasantly quiet location,
nd very good value with singles/doubles
om 8000/10,000 rp, including a 'big break-
ast'.

Nearby is the pleasant *Siti Homestay*, with
garden and rooms at 10,000/15,000 rp, and
yoman Astana Bungalows and *Mandra
Cottages*.

Vest of Ubud Heading west on Jl Raya you
ass Jl Bisma on the left, with a few places
> stay – the cheapest is *Pondok Ubud*, which
pretty good for 7000/10,000 rp, including
reakfast. Follow the main road, cross the
uspension bridge and take the steep road
phill on the left to Penestanan, a quiet but
rty area. Along this road you'll find the
ttractive *Arjuna's Inn*, run by Blanco's
aughter, with rooms at 15,000 to 20,000 rp.
earby *Sari Bamboo* (☎ 975597) has rooms
t 20,000 rp, and two storey bungalows,
leal for families, at 30,000 rp.

There are more places further back into the
ce fields – you have to walk to get to them.
nes near this road include *Gerebig*, *Gorim*,
eka and *Made Jagi*. Others are in the rice
addies further north, more easily reached by
limbing the stairs west of the Campuan road
nd following the sign boards. Places to look
or include *Siddharta*, *Danau*, *Pugur* and
ondo. Asking prices are from around
0,000/25,000 rp for singles/doubles, up to
round 40,000 rp per night for a larger
ungalow. Longer stayers negotiate lower
tes – outside peak tourist times, a nice
ungalow should rent for 80,000 to 100,000
> per week, perhaps more with a kitchen.

Further west is Sayan, with great views
ver the Yeh Ayung; one of the few cheap

places is *Putra Umbara*, with rooms for
30,000 rp.

Places to Stay – middle
For 25,000 or 35,000 rp, you can get a very
nice room or bungalow, often decorated with
local arts & crafts, perhaps with a view of
rice fields or garden. Upper mid-range
tourist hotels (with swimming pools, hot
water and US dollar prices) are mostly on
Monkey Forest Rd and near Jl Raya.

Central Ubud The pleasant and well-kept
Puri Saraswati Cottages (☎ 975164), near
the Saraswati palace, has ordinary rooms for
US$19/24, and much nicer ones for US$35/
40. The *Hotel Puri Saren Agung* (☎ 975957),
near the bemo stop in the centre of Ubud, is
part of the home of the late head of Ubud's
royal family. It's not signposted as a hotel,
but walk into the courtyard and enquire – a
bungalow with Balinese antiques, a big
verandah, four poster bed and a full breakfast
costs from US$45 to US$60. Balinese dances
are held regularly in the outer courtyard.

Just west of Monkey Forest Rd, *Oka
Wati's Sunset Bungalows* (☎ 96386) still has
a rice field in view but may be built out soon.
It's pretty quiet, and handy to the centre of
town. The rooms range from US$28/33 to
US$50/55. There's a swimming pool, and a
restaurant presided over by Oka Wati herself,
a familiar face to Ubud visitors since the
early 1970s.

Monkey Forest Rd has a number of newer
mid-range places, although some are very
dull and featureless. One new place with
some imagination and taste is the *Ubud
Village Hotel* (☎ 975069). The pleasantly
decorated rooms, each with a separate
garden entrance, cost US$40/45. There's a
swimming pool with swim-up bar and other
luxuries. *Puri Garden Bungalows* (☎ 975395),
with its lush garden, is a very pleasant place
to stay for 40,000/50,000 rp.

Also on Monkey Forest Rd and almost at
the forest, the well-established *Ubud Inn*
(☎ 975071) has a variety of bungalows and
rooms dotted around a spacious garden with
a pool. Rates are US$30/40 with fan,

US$40/45 with air-con and US$50 for two storey family rooms. Next door, the *Fibra Inn* (☎ 975451) has a pool too, and pretty bungalows from US$30. At the south end of Monkey Forest Rd is the secluded *Monkey Forest Hideaway* (☎ 975354), with rooms from 15,000/20,000 to 30,000/40,000 rp, some romantically overlooking the forest and others far too close to the road. The nicest rooms are often full, so call first.

On Jl Kajeng, north of Jl Raya, one of the nicest places is artist Han Snel's *Siti Bungalows* (☎ 975699). There are seven individual cottages, decorated with the artist's own work, from US$50 to US$60 a night. Some are perched right on the edge of the river gorge – it's worth making a reservation for these.

The *Mumbul Inn* (☎ 975364) is near the Puri Lukisan Museum on Jl Raya in central Ubud. It still has some simple rooms at 30,000 rp, but mostly it's more upmarket, with very nice accommodation at US$30. Further west, another good place is *Abangan Bungalows* (☎ 975082), up a steep driveway north of Jl Raya. It has a pool, and small rooms for US$15/20; larger rooms in the rice-barn style are US$35/45.

Up the slope south of the main road, Jl Bisma has a few mid-range places which are quiet but close to the centre of town. *Pringga Juwita Water Garden Cottages* (☎ 975734) has ponds and a swimming pool in one of the nicest gardens in town; rooms start at US$47/55.

Nearby *Pringga Juwita Inn* is also a nice place to stay, and a bit cheaper at US$25. *Nick's Pension* has a restaurant and pool on Jl Bisma, but the rooms are further back, overlooking a lush river valley; they're pretty good value for 45,000 rp.

East & South of Ubud Most of the places to stay in Padangtegal are budget accommodation, but *Dewi Sri Bungalows* (☎ 975300) is an attractive alternative, with nicely decorated rooms from US$30 to US$50, and there is a pool and a good restaurant. Further east in Peliatan on Jl Raya is *Oka Kartini's*

(☎ 975193), with a family atmosphere an swimming pool, and rooms from US$35/40.

West of Ubud Follow Jl Raya, west an north, towards the Neka Museum and you' reach *Wisata Cottages* (☎ 975017), whic has a wonderful outlook over the Ceri River, though the rooms at US$20/30 ar nothing special. Further on, *Ananda Co tages* (☎ 975376) is quite popular, wit spacious gardens and rooms from US$30/3 to US$35/45.

In the rice fields of Penestanan, up th stairs west of the Campuan road, are cottage with mid-range facilities and prices, incluo ing the charming *Kori Agung* at aroun 50,000 rp. The *Penestanan Bungalows* (☎ 9 5604) has a pool, and costs a bit more, bu you won't even think about money after few days here. For even more rice-fiel luxury, *Melati Cottages* (☎ 974650) also ha a pool, restaurant and quiet location fo US$20/30. Remember that you have to wal to get here.

Further west in Sayan, overlooking th Yeh Ayung, *Sayan Terrace* (☎ 975384) has brilliant view and attractive rooms fo US$25, or bungalows at US$35. Nearby *Taman Bebek Villas* (☎ 976533) has a choic of elegant rooms and villas from US$30 t US$50. Also overlooking the river, *Djagra Inn* (☎ 974343) is a bit hard to get to, bu delightfully secluded, with good-size rooms from US$35 to US$40.

Places to Stay – top end

All the top-end hotels in Ubud have lus landscaping and modern luxuries. The reall expensive places are perched on the edges c the deep river valleys, with spectacula views. The decorations feature artwork which rival many galleries. They all add 21 ° tax and service to the advertised prices.

Most of the top places are well out c town, but there's one within walking dis tance of the centre, down near the Campua bridge. *Ibah* (☎ 974466; fax 974467) has lovely location overlooking a lush valley, ar spacious individual stylishly furnished suite from US$195 to US$250. The delightfu rden is decorated with stone carvings, ndcrafted pots and antique doors, and the vimming pool is set into the hillside neath an ancient-looking stone wall.

Also close to town, the *Villa Chempaka* (96312) on Jl Bisma has very pretty, fully uipped cottages facing a pool for US$75. On the main road, over the suspension idge, is the long-established *Hotel Tjam- han* (975368; fax 975137), beautifully uated overlooking the river confluence d Pura Gunung Labuh. The hotel is built the site of Spies' 1930s home and his all house is now one of the rooms. Indi- dual bungalows in a wonderful garden cost S$50/56 to US$66/82; the Spies room sts US$125 and you'll have to make a servation to get it. Up the steep road oppo- te the Tjampuhan, the *Padma Indah ottages* (& fax 975719) were established a collector of Balinese art, which is dis- ayed in all the cottages and an on-site llery. Rooms with a garden view cost S$90; US$10 more for a rice-field view.

The main road to the Neka Gallery passes new *Pita Maha* (974330; fax 974 329), amatically sited on the edge of the Cerik ver. The individual villas here, each in a all private compound, cost US$250 to S$400 per night, but not all of them enjoy great view. North of the Neka is *Ulun bud Cottages* (975024; fax 975524), th bungalows beautifully draped down the lside overlooking the valley. The whole ace is decorated with wonderful carvings, intings and antiques. Double rooms cost S$55, US$65 or US$90, and there are also ger, two bedroom family units at US$110. ates include breakfast, taxes and service, d there's a restaurant, bar and swimming ol.

Beyond Ulun Ubud Cottages, near the edewatan junction, is Ubud's most beauti- lly designed hotel, the *Amandari* 975333; fax 975335). There are superb ews over the rice paddies or down to the h Ayung, and the main swimming pool ems to drop right over the edge. Accom- odation is in private pavilions at US$430 US$800. They're spacious, exquisitely decorated and the best rooms have a private pool.

North of the Kedewatan junction, *Cahaya Dewata* (975496; fax 975495) overlooks the same magnificent river gorge. The stan- dard rooms are US$55/60 for singles/ doubles, but only the US$80 deluxe rooms have a view. A little north is *Kupu Kupu Barong* (975478; fax 975079). Clinging precariously to the steep sides of the Yeh Ayung gorge, each of the beautiful two storey bungalows has a bedroom and living room; they cost US$335 to US$699 a night – some have two bedrooms and open-air spa baths. The views from the rooms, the pool and the restaurant are unbelievable. Children are not permitted here – they might fall into the view.

In between these two is *Puri Bunga Village* (975448; fax 975073), with a sim- ilarly dramatic location, but less spectacular prices. The rooms, from US$75, don't have a view but are quite comfortable; suites with a view run to US$190. Another place over- looking the Ayung is *Villa Indah* (975490), with just eight rooms for US$120 per night – it may give a discount.

Other expensive hotels are found around the edges of the Ubud area – nowhere is a view of wet-rice cultivation more bankable. The *Hotel Champlung Sari* (975418; fax 975473) at the bottom end of Monkey Forest Rd has nice views, but very ordinary rooms for around US$60/75 for singles/doubles. *Puri Kamandalu* (975825; fax 975851), four km north-east of Ubud, has a wonderful outlook, and attractive, well-decorated, thatched bungalows from US$160 to US$350.

In Pengosekan, *Kokokan* (975742; fax 975332) has a pretty outlook, interesting architecture and fine decor. There's a range of rooms from US$88 to US$180, or US$255 for a complete house.

Places to Eat

Ubud's numerous restaurants offer the best and most interesting food on the island. You can get excellent western food, all the Indonesian standards and Balinese dishes will often be on the menu as well. The very best places might cost 20,000 to 30,000 rp per hungry person (US$9 to US$13), but they are well worth it for the quality, service and atmosphere. Many places will have very fine food for less than half that price. A bottle of wine will cost 80,000 to 120,000 rp, or maybe 6000 rp by the glass.

Jalan Raya West of the tourist office along Jl Raya are some of Ubud's longest-running restaurants. *Ary's Warung* has moved steadily upmarket, but it still serves a wide variety of excellent food, including vegetarian dishes and wholemeal sandwiches, and it has about the longest wine list in town. A little further west is a new Japanese restaurant, *Ryoshi*, which does pretty good sashimi from 7000 to 12,000 rp. Across the road is the *Lotus Cafe* – a leisurely meal overlooking its lotus pond is an Ubud institution, but the food is pricey (main courses from 8000 to 12,000 rp) and not always brilliant. It's worth coming for the ambience, even if you only have a snack – try a Greek salad with fetta cheese and a slice of mango cheesecake.

A little further on, *Mumbul's Cafe* is small, friendly and inexpensive, with good service and excellent food, and even a children's menu. On the other side of the road is *Casa Luna* (☎ 96283), with a superb international menu, including Mediterranean tofu, Vietnamese salad, tandoori chicken and Balinese paella. It also has bread and pastry from its own Honeymoon Bakery, great desserts and half-serves for kids. The service is efficient, the atmosphere is pleasant and friendly, and it's not too expensive. Main courses are 3000 to 8500 rp, and the food is worth blowing your budget on.

Further down, the big *Menara Restaurant* is good for Balinese banquet dishes. Up the slope south of Jl Raya, *Miro's Cafe* is another top place to eat, with a varied menu and a cool garden setting. Well-prepared Indonesian dishes are 5000 rp and other main courses about 8000 rp, and there's a good selection of vegetarian dishes. For carnivores, the *Griya Barbeque*, across the road, does very good pork, chicken, steak and fish in outdoor and indoor settings.

Continuing to Campuan, *Murni's Warun* right beside the suspension bridge, is an o Ubud favourite in a beautiful setting over t river – the lowest level has the nicest outloc It has a diverse menu, but it's a little on t pricey side (main courses from 6000 15,000 rp) and the food is sometimes on average. It's usually pretty good though, a the location makes it worth a visit (clos Wednesday). Above the bridge and acro the river from Murni's Warung, *Beggar Bush Pub* is a British-style pub serving pu style food – it's popular with expats.

The eastern end of Jl Raya has a few plac to eat too. Best known is the *Nomad Resta rant*, which does standard Indonesian a Chinese dishes (4000 to 9000 rp), but mainly a spot for a sociable drink as it sta open late. (Its cocktail list includes the Ub Yuppie, with arak, brem, lime and tonic.) little further east is *Padang Sanak* (al called Dana Corner), a Padang food pla which is one of the cheapest eateries Ubud. Another place for a tasty, inexpensi meal is *Puri's Bar & Restaurant*, opposi the market.

North of Jl Raya One of Ubud's real dini pleasures is *Han Snel's Garden Restaura* north of the main road on Jl Kajeng. It's a b expensive, but the setting is beautiful, t food is good and the servings generous – rijstaffel is famous (closed Sunday).

For a Balinese feast, book into *Ketu Place* (☎ 975304), north of the palace, o km up Jl Suweta. For 20,000 rp per perse you get a great meal of Balinese specialitie and an excellent introduction to Balinese li and customs. There's usually an interestir group there, so it's very sociable.

Monkey Forest Rd Near the northern end Monkey Forest Rd, *Satri's Warung* is inexpensive place with good food, a *Canderi's Warung* is an old Ubud institutio with Indonesian, western and vegetari. dishes.

Just off Monkey Forest Rd, *Oka Wati's* another Ubud institution, with good food a

A Balinese Feast

Traditional Balinese dishes have rarely been served in Bali's restaurants, though they are becoming more common – quite a few places will do delicious Balinese smoked duck for two if you order a day ahead. A complete Balinese feast is something local people would have only a couple of times a year at a major religious or family occasion. Visitors would not normally be able to experience such a feast in a real Balinese home, but Ketut Suartana, who can be contacted at the Suci Inn (☎ (0361) 975304), arranges them regularly in a pavilion in his parents' family compound, about a km north of the main road on Jalan Suweta (Ketut's Place is also a friendly homestay). They're usually held on Sunday, and you have to book the day before. The cost is 20,000 rp, and well worth it.

This is a rare opportunity to sample real Balinese food at its best. Typical meals include duck or Balinese sate, which is minced and spiced meat wrapped around a wide stick, and quite different from the usual Indonesian sate. A variety of vegetables will include several that we normally think of as fruits – like papaya, jackfruit (nangka) and starfruit (blimbing). Paku is a form of fern and ketela potton is tapioca leaves, both prepared as tasty vegetables. Red onions (anyang) and cucumber (ketimun) will also feature. Then there might be gado gado and mie goreng, both prepared in Balinese style, and a special Balinese dish of duck livers cooked in banana leaves and coconut. Of course, there will be prawn crackers (krupuk) and rice, and to drink there will be Balinese rice wine (brem). You'll finish up with Balinese coffee, peanuts and bananas, or Balinese desserts like sumping, a leaf-wrapped sticky rice concoction with coconut and palm sugar or banana and jackfruit.

The dining area is hung with palm-leaf decorations, again as for a Balinese feast, and a gamelan can be heard in the background. It's fun and delicious, and also a great opportunity to learn more about Bali and its customs as Ketut talks about his house, his family and answers all sorts of questions about life on Bali. ■

wonderfully romantic atmosphere, but somewhat higher prices. Nearby *Lillies Garden Restaurant* is less expensive, and almost as atmospheric.

Ibu Rai Restaurant, near the football field, as some good dishes, while *Bendi's Restaurant*, across the road, does authentic Balinese specialities, some of which you may have to order a day ahead.

Further south, *Cafe Wayan* (☎ 975447) is more expensive but has some of the best food in town, with a small room at the front and delightful tables in the open air at the back (a reservation might be worthwhile in the high season). The nasi campur at 6000 rp is terrific, the curry ayam (curried chicken) at 7500 rp superb. Western dishes like spaghetti at 8000 rp also feature. Desserts include the famed coconut pie or you could risk 'death by chocolate'.

Other options on Monkey Forest Rd include *Nyiur Cafe*, with cuisine from all over Asia from 3500 to 7000 rp, and *Mendra's Cafe*, which does Balinese dishes.

Jalan Dewi Sita The side street on the north side of the football field (also called Jl Bima) is breeding new places to eat, drink or snack. *Bamboo Restaurant* has inexpensive Indonesian dishes, while *Tutmac* serves about the best coffee in Ubud – use it to wash down some delicious chocolate cake. The *Do Drop In Restaurant* is also recommended – its video nights are popular.

Around Ubud Anywhere with tourist accommodation will usually have a selection of places to eat. On Jl Karna, east of Monkey Forest Rd, for instance, you'll find quite a few traditional losmen, and also top food at the budget-priced *Seroni's Warung*. *Metri's* on Jl Hanoman is another place recommended for good and tasty tourist fare. Further east in Peliatan, on Jl Tebesaya, are a couple of good, inexpensive places, including *Pizza Roma*, where the Italian food will not disappoint you.

South of Ubud, Padangtegal has some really interesting places. *Bebek Bengil* (The Dirty Duck Diner) does delectable deep-fried duck dishes in a delightful dining area. Going south you pass the *Kura Kura Mexican Cafe*, with substantial Mexican main courses for around 8000 rp.

Around the corner in Pengosekan is a great splurge possibility, the *Kokokan Club*

(☎ 96495). It serves delicious Thai and seafood dishes in opulent surroundings, and the prices are not excessive – soups at 4000 rp, main courses around 8000 rp and desserts at 4000 rp. If you phone first, staff can help with transport.

West of Ubud, you can eat in the restaurants of the hotels overlooking the Yeh Ayung. Try the *Amandari* for excellent food in a sophisticated atmosphere, or *Kupu Kupu Barong* for a brilliant view. They're both very expensive, but so popular that reservations are recommended, especially at lunch time.

Entertainment

Music & Dance The main entertainment in Ubud is Balinese dancing. Most of the regular dances are put on for foreign audiences, adapted and abbreviated to make them more enjoyable. They often combine features of several traditional dances. Nevertheless, they are performed with a high degree of skill and commitment, and usually have appreciative locals in the audience. Competition between the various dance troupes is intense, and locals speculate endlessly about whether the Peliatan troupe is still the best, or if standards have slipped at Bona.

The tourist office has information and a schedule of performances. Tickets are sold there, and are also widely available in town. The usual price is 7000 rp, including transport to performances outside central Ubud. Most start at 7, 7.30 or 8 pm. For out-of-town performances, transport leaves the tourist office at 6 to 6.45 pm. The most central venue, and a very attractive one, is at the Ubud palace, Puri Saren. Other performances at various venues include Kecak, Gabor, Sanghyang, Legong, Mahabharata, Barong & Rangda dances, Ramayana ballet and so on. The women's gamelan at Peliatan is popular, and there is at least one wayang kulit performance per week.

Other Options No-one comes to Ubud for wild nightlife. The *Beggars Bush Pub* has a cosy bar upstairs, and there's also a bar at the *Nomad Restaurant*; they both open till about midnight. A number of restaurants, includir Menara and the Yogyakarta Cafe, sho laser-disk video movies in the evening. Ca Luna sometimes has a kids' session at 4 pr

Things to Buy

The supermarket is on Jl Raya. Ubud's co ourful produce market operates every thi day. It starts early in the morning but pret much winds up by lunch time. The cra market in the building on the corner Monkey Forest Rd and Jl Raya operate every day. Small shops by the market ar along Monkey Forest Rd often have goo woodcarvings, particularly masks. There a other good woodcarving places along th road from Peliatan to Goa Gajah and sou to Mas, and also north around Tegal Lalan Going south, you can browse for crafts an antiques all the way to Batubulan (see th previous Denpasar to Ubud section).

Paintings are sold everywhere. The ma galleries have excellent selections, but pric are often well over US$100. You should able to get better prices direct from the arti or from an artist's workshop. If your budg is limited, look for a smaller picture of hig quality, rather than something that resemble wallpaper in size and originality.

Getting There & Away

In Ubud bemos leave from in front of th market in the middle of town. To get t Denpasar, the southern tourist centres western Bali, you first take a bemo to Ba ubulan terminal for about 1500 rp. Fro there, some bemos go direct to Sanur, but f Kuta you must first transfer to Tegal termina on the other side of Denpasar. To get eastern Bali, get a bemo from Ubud to Gianya where you can change to another bemo fo Klungkung, Candidasa or Kintamani.

To charter transport to Sanur or Denpas will cost about 20,000 rp; to Kuta or th airport is about 28,000 rp.

Tourist shuttle buses go from Ubud t Sanur and the airport (5000 rp), Kuta (750 rp), Kintamani (7500 rp), Padangbai an Candidasa (7500 rp), Singaraja and Lovir Beach (12,500 rp). The Perama offic

BALI

96316) is inconveniently down in Pad-ngtegal, but they will pick up, and maybe rop off, at other points around town. Nomad ransport (☎ 975131) at the Nomad restaurant is more central and has fares which are imilar or slightly cheaper than those men-oned above. There are other services dvertised around town.

Rental cars cost around 40,000 rp for a ay, or 35,000 rp per day for a week or more, cluding insurance – you may have to shop round and haggle. Motorcycle rental costs round 15,000 rp per day, 77,000 rp per week quite a bit more than in Kuta.

Getting Around

emos around town and to the adjacent vil-ges will cost about 300 rp. There are everal places which rent mountain bikes at 000 rp a day, or 4000 rp a day for a longer rm rental – look around the top of Monkey orest Rd.

Around Ubud

he Pejeng region around Ubud encom-asses many of the most ancient monuments nd relics on Bali. Many predate the Maja-ahit era, and raise as yet unanswered uestions about Bali's history.

The majority of sites are found around oa Gajah (south-east of Ubud) and Bedulu, nd near the road from there to Tampaksir-g. This route follows the Pakerisan River, escending from the holy spring at Tirta mpul near Tampaksiring. Some of these tes are heavily overrun by tourist groups, hers are just far enough off the beaten track leave the crowds behind; some lesser sites re overgrown, and so difficult to access that u'd probably need a guide.

You can reach most of the places around bud by bemo, bicycle or on foot. If you're anning to see a lot of them it's a good idea start at Tirta Empul (about 15 km from bud), then any walking you have to do is ack downhill.

GOA GAJAH

Only a short distance beyond Peliatan, on the road to Pejeng and Gianyar, a carpark on the south side of the road marks the site of Goa Gajah (Elephant Cave). The cave is carved into a rock face, reached by a flight of steps down from the carpark. There were never any elephants on Bali; the cave probably takes its name from the nearby Petanu River which at one time was known as Elephant River.

You enter the cave through the cavernous mouth of a demon. The gigantic fingertips pressed beside the face of the demon push back a riotous jungle of surrounding stone carvings. Inside the T-shaped cave you can see fragmentary remains of *lingams*, the phallic symbols of the Hindu god Shiva, and their female counterpart the *yoni*, plus a statue of the ele-phant-headed god Ganesh.

Goa Gajah was certainly in existence at the time of the Majapahit takeover of Bali. One tale relates that it was another example of the handiwork of the leg-endary Kebo Iwa, but it probably dates back to the 11th century, and shows elements of both Hindu and Buddhist use.

The cave was discovered in 1923, but it was not until 1954 that the fountains and pool were unearthed. You can clamber down through the rice fields to the Petanu River where there are crumbling rock carvings of *stupas* (domes for housing Buddhist relics) on a cliff face and a small cave.

Admission to Goa Gajah is 1050 rp, plus 500 rp for a camera, 1000 rp for a video, and you'll have to pay if you use the carpark, and to rent a sash and sarong if you don't have your own. There are some good eateries in the carpark, amidst the slew of souvenir shops.

YEH PULU

Though the path to Yeh Pulu is well marked and easy, you do have to walk to it – just follow the signs off the road beyond Goa Gajah. Eventually, you reach a ticket office at the start of a footpath to the ancient rock carvings (there is a compulsory 'donation' of 1050 rp).

Only excavated in 1925 these are some of the oldest relics in Bali. The carved cliff face is about 25m long and is believed to be a hermitage dating from the late

14th century. Apart from the figure of elephant-headed Ganesh, the son of Shiva, there are no religious scenes here. The energetic frieze includes various scenes of everyday life – two men carrying an animal slung from a pole, a man slaying a beast with a dagger (and a satirical frog imitating him by disposing of a snake in like manner) and a man on horseback, either pulling a captive woman along behind him or with the woman holding the horse's tail.

The Ganesh figures of Yeh Pulu and Goa Gajah are quite similar, indicating a close relationship between the two sites. *Yeh* is the Balinese word for water and, as at Goa Gajah, water and fountains play an important part at Yeh Pulu.

BEDULU

Just beyond Goa Gajah, Bedulu is the road junction where you can turn south to Gianyar or north to Pejeng and Tampaksiring. It's hard to imagine this small village as the former capital of a great kingdom, but the legendary Dalem Bedulu ruled the Pejeng dynasty from here and was the last Balinese king to withstand the onslaught of the powerful Majapahits from Java. He was eventually defeated by Gajah Mada in 1343. The capital shifted several times after this, ending up at Gelgel and later at Klungkung.

A legend relates how Bedulu possessed magical powers which allowed him to have his head chopped off and then replaced. Performing this unique party trick one day, the servant entrusted with lopping off his head and then replacing it unfortunately dropped it in a river and, to his horror, watched it float away. Looking around in panic for a replacement he grabbed a pig, cut off its head and popped it upon the king's shoulders. Thereafter the king was forced to sit on a high throne and forbade his subjects to look up at him; Bedulu means 'he who changed heads'.

The **Pura Samuan Tiga** (Temple of the Meeting of the Three, probably a reference to the Hindu trinity) is about 100m east of the Bedulu junction. This important 11th century temple is packed with Balinese during the Odalan Festival.

The **Bedulu Archaeological Museum** (also called Museum Purbakala and Gedong Arca) is about two km north of Bedulu and includes a collection of pre-Hindu artefacts,

including stone sarcophagi from the tim before cremations were practised on Bal It's not particularly interesting, unless you'r into archaeology.

PEJENG

Continuing up the road to Tampaksiring yo soon come to Pejeng and its famous temple Like Bedulu this was once an important sea of power, the capital of the Pejeng kingdo which fell to the Majapahit invaders in 134

Pura Kebo Edan

Also called the Crazy Buffalo Temple, this not an imposing structure but it's famous fe its three-metre-high statue of Bima, know as the Giant of Pejeng. The temple is on tl western side of the road and you might hav to pay 1000 rp to enter.

There's considerable conjecture over what this fea some image is all about. The dead body which tl image tramples upon appears to relate to the Hinc Shiva cult but it may also have Tantric Buddh overtones. Other figures flank the main one, and ma and female buffaloes lie before it. There is also co jecture about the giant's genitalia – it has either s small penises or one large one, and if that large thin is a penis, the guy must have been heavily into boc piercing.

Pura Pusering Jagat

The large Pura Pusering Jagat (Navel of th World Temple) is said to be the centre of tl old Pejeng kingdom. Dating from 1329, thi temple is visited by young couples who pra at the stone lingam and yoni.

Pura Penataran Sasih

In the centre of Pejeng, Pura Penataran Sasi was once the state temple of the Pejen kingdom. In the inner courtyard, high up i a pavilion where you can't see it properly, the huge bronze drum known as the **Moo of Pejeng**.

The hourglass-shaped drum is more tha three metres long, the largest single-piec cast drum in the world. Estimates of its ag vary from 1000 to 2000 years, and it is nc certain whether it was made locally c imported. The intricate geometrical design

BALI

e said to resemble patterns from as far apart s Irian Jaya and Vietnam.

Balinese legend relates how the drum came to earth s a fallen moon, landing in a tree and shining so ightly that it prevented a band of thieves from going out their unlawful purpose. One of the thieves cided to put the light out by urinating on it but the oon exploded, killed the foolhardy thief, and fell to rth as a drum – with a crack across its base as a result f the fall.

AMPAKSIRING

ampaksiring is a small town with a large nd important temple, and the most impress-e ancient monument on Bali.

unung Kawi

n the southern outskirts of Tampaksiring, a gn points off the road to the right to Gunung awi. From the end of the access road a steep one stairway leads down to the river, at one oint making a cutting through an embank-ent of solid rock. In the bottom of this lush reen valley is one of Bali's oldest, and ertainly largest, ancient monuments.

Gunung Kawi consists of 10 rock-cut ndi – these memorials are cut into the rock ce in a similar fashion to the great rock-cut mples of Ajanta and Ellora in India. Each ndi is believed to be a memorial to a mem-er of the 11th century Balinese royalty but tle is known for certain. They stand in even-metre-high sheltered niches cut into e sheer cliff face. There are four on the west de of the river which you come to first, and ve on the east side. Each of the sets of emorials has a group of monks' cells asso-ated with it. A solitary candi stands further own the valley to the south.

Legends relate that the group of memori-s was carved out of the rock face in one ard working night by the mighty fingernails Kebo Iwa. It's uncertain who the real uilders were but they may date from the dayana dynasty of the 10th and 11th cen-ries. It's said that the five monuments on e eastern bank are to King Udayana, Queen ahendradatta, their son Airlangga, and his rothers Anak Wungsu and Marakata. While irlangga ruled eastern Java, Anak Wungsu

ruled Bali. The four monuments on the western side are, by this theory, to Anak Wungsu's chief concubines. Another theory is that the whole complex is dedicated to Anak Wungsu, his wives, concubines and, in the case of the remote 10th candi, to a royal minister.

Entry to Gunung Kawi is 1050 rp, and they'll charge extra for cameras and sash rental.

Tirta Empul

North of Tampaksiring, the road branches. The left fork runs up to the grand palace, once used by Soekarno, which overlooks the temple and its bathing pools. The right fork dips down past the temple at Tirta Empul and continues up to Penelokan. The holy springs at Tirta Empul are believed to have magical powers, so the temple here is a very impor-tant one.

The springs, used since 962 AD, bubble up into a large, crystal-clear tank within the temple and gush out through waterspouts into a bathing pool. According to legend, the springs were created by the god Indra who pierced the earth to tap the 'elixir of im-mortality', or *amerta*. The temple was totally restored in the late 1960s.

There is an admission charge (1050 rp), parking fee and you have to wear a temple scarf. Come early in the morning or late in the afternoon to avoid the tour-bus hordes.

Other Sites

Between Tirta Empul and Gunung Kawi is the temple of **Pura Mengening**, where you can see a freestanding candi similar in design to those of Gunung Kawi. There is a spring at this temple which, along with Tirta Empul, is the source of the Pakerisan River.

Places to Stay & Eat

Apart from the usual selection of *warungs* there's also the expensive *Tampaksiring Res-taurant* for tourist groups; it's some distance below the village. It's not easy to find a place to stay here, but it's an easy day trip from Ubud or Bangli, or a stopover between Ubud and Batur.

UBUD TO BATUR

The usual road from Ubud to Batur is through Tampaksiring, but there are other lesser roads up the gentle mountain slope. If you head east out of Ubud and turn north at the junction, you'll reach the crater rim just west of Penelokan. Along this road you'll see a number of woodcarvers producing beautiful painted birds, frogs, garudas, flowers and tropical fruit. **Tegallalang** and the nearby village of **Jati** are noted woodcarving centres. Further up, other specialists carve stools, and there are a couple of places where whole tree trunks are carved into whimsical figures.

The *Blue Yogi Cafe* (☎ (0366) 91768) on the west side of the road at Tegallalang is a great lunch stop, and there are a few attractive bungalows for 30,000/35,000 rp.

East Bali

The eastern end of Bali is dominated by mighty Gunung Agung, the 'navel of the world' and Bali's 'mother mountain'. Towering at 3142m, Agung has not always been a kind mother – witness the disastrous 1963 eruption. Today Agung is quiet, but the 'mother temple' Pura Besakih, perched high on the slopes of the volcano, attracts a steady stream of devotees... and tourists.

The main road east goes through Klungkung, the former capital of one of Bali's great kingdoms. It then runs close to the coast passing Kusamba, the bat-infested temple of Goa Lawah and the port of Padangbai. There are lots of beachside places to stay from there to the resort of Candidasa. When you reach Amlapura, another former capital, you can continue past Tirtagangga to the east coast, or return via a route higher up the slopes of Gunung Agung. Bemos from Batubulan go to the towns on this route, and do shorter connections in between.

GIANYAR

Gianyar is the capital of Gianyar district (which includes Ubud). It has some small textile factories, on the Denpasar side of town, where you can see ikat being woven and buy some material made up as shirts, dresses etc, or by the metre. Prices may actually be lower in Denpasar.

The Gianyar royal family saved the palace, and their position, by capitulating the Dutch. The original palace (from 177 was destroyed in a conflict with the Klungkung kingdom in the mid-1880s, was rebuilt and then severely damaged again in the 19 earthquake. It's a fine example of tradition palace architecture, but the royal family still lives there so you can't go inside.

Pondok Wisata (☎ (0361) 942165), just south of the main street, asks 18,000 rp for small, clean double rooms. Gianyar's warungs are noted for their fine roast piglet (babi guling). Eat early though, as the warungs are usually cleaned out by late morning. Excellent traditional food is also available at the night market on the main street.

BONA

The village of Bona, on the back road between Gianyar and Blahbatuh, is credited with being the modern home of the Kecak dance. Touristy Kecak dances are held here regularly, and are easy to get to from Ubud (around 6000 rp, including transport).

Bona is also a basket-weaving centre and many other articles are also woven from lontar (palm leaves). Nearby, Belega is a centre for bamboo work.

SIDAN

Two km east of Gianyar you come to the turn-off to Bangli. Another km north on the road brings you to Sidan's Pura Dalem, a fine example of a 'Temple of the Dead'. Note the sculptures of Durga with children by the gate, and the separate enclosure in one corner, dedicated to Merajapati, the guardian spirit of the dead.

KLUNGKUNG

Bali's most powerful dynasty was based at Gelgel (just south of modern Klungkung) from around 1400 and reached its cultural peak in the late 1550s – Bali's 'Golden Age'

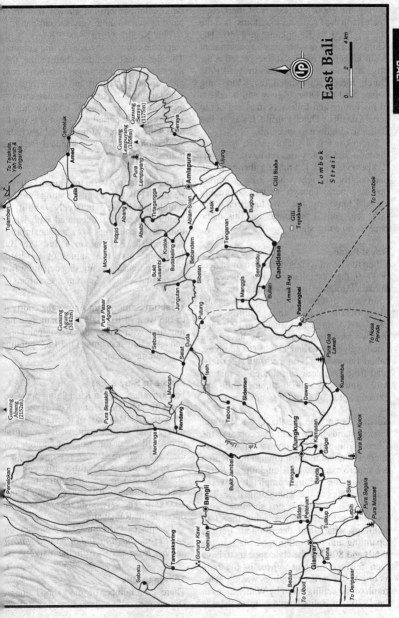

East Bali

During the 1600s successors of the Gelgel line established separate kingdoms, and the court moved to Klungkung in 1710. The Klungkung court never regained a pre-eminent position on Bali, but it is still respected as the original Balinese royal house. In April 1908 Dutch forces surrounded the Klungkung palace, and the Dewa Agung and hundreds of his family and followers marched out to certain death by Dutch gunfire. It was the last Balinese kingdom to succumb.

Klungkung is a major public transport junction and a busy market town. The bus and bemo terminal is a major gathering point, particularly at night when a busy market operates there. Though it's still commonly called Klungkung, the town has been officially renamed Semarapura, and this name appears on some signs.

Royal Palace

When the Dewa Agung dynasty moved here in 1710, they established a new palace, the Semara Pura, laid out as a large square with courtyards, gardens, pavilions and moats. Most of the palace and grounds were destroyed during Dutch attacks in 1908, and the two pavilions you see now have been extensively restored and rebuilt. The complex, called Taman Gili, is on the south side of the road from Denpasar surrounded by a stone wall. Entry costs 1100 rp, including the museum, plus 1000 rp for your camera.

Kertha Gosa The Kertha Gosa (Hall of Justice) stands in the north-east corner of the Taman Gili, a marked contrast to the busy intersection and modern town. The pavilion is a superb example of Klungkung architecture, with the ceiling completely covered with paintings in the Klungkung style. The paintings, done on asbestos sheeting, were installed in the 1940s, replacing the cloth paintings which had deteriorated. Further repainting and restoration took place in the 1960s and 80s, but the style appears to have been fairly consistent. Virtually the only record of the earlier paintings was a photograph of the ceiling taken by Walter Spies in the 1930s. In Bali's humid climate there is

rapid deterioration and already the curren: paintings are looking very second-hand.

The Kertha Gosa was effectively th 'supreme court' of the Klungkung kingdom The defendant, standing before the thre priests who acted as judges (kerthas), coul: gaze up at the ceiling and see wrongdoer: being tortured by demons and the innocer: enjoying the pleasures of Balinese heaven In the colonial period, the court was used t deal with questions of traditional law (adat while colonial law was handled by Dutc courts.

Bale Kambang Also in the Taman Gili is th beautiful Bale Kambang (Floating Pavilion which has been extensively rebuilt thi century. Its ceiling, decorated with Klung kung-style paintings, was redone in 194! Around the Kertha Gosa and the Bal Kambang, note the statues of top-hatte European figures, an amusing departure fror the normal statues of entrance guardians.

Museum Semarajaya Across the courtyar to the west of the Bale Kambang is a ne museum with some archaeological piece and interesting accounts of the 1908 puputar It's nothing special.

Places to Stay & Eat

Few travellers stay in Klungkung but if yo need to, try the Hotel Ramayana Loj (☎ (0366) 21044), east of town on the Can didasa road. It's pleasant, with a restaurar in a pavilion out the back, far enough fror the busy main road to be reasonably quie Its better rooms are quite big and cos 20,000/25,000 rp with a bathroom. Smal spartan rooms with shared mandi cos 10,000 rp. The very basic Bell Inn is almos opposite the Ramayana.

Two places with Chinese-Indonesian foo are Restaurant Bali Indah and Restaurar Sumber Rasa, across from the market.

Things to Buy

There are a number of good shops along . Diponegoro selling classical-style painting:

The 1963 Eruption

The most disastrous volcanic eruption on Bali this century took place in 1963, when Gunung Agung blew its top in no uncertain manner and at a time of considerable prophetic and political importance.

The culmination of Eka Desa Rudra, the greatest of all Balinese sacrifices and an event which only takes place every 100 years on the Balinese calendar, was to be on March 8 1963. At the time of the eruption, it had been more than 100 Balinese years (115 years on the lunar calendar) since the last Eka Desa Rudra, but there was dispute among the priests as to the correct and most propitious date.

Naturally the temple at Besakih was a focal point for the festival, but Agung was already acting strangely as preparations were made in late February. The date of the ceremony was looking decidedly unpropitious, but Soekarno, then the president of Indonesia, had already scheduled an international conference of travel agents to witness the great occasion as a highlight of their visit to the country, and he would not allow it to be postponed. By the time the sacrifices commenced, the mountain was belching smoke and ash, glowing and rumbling ominously, but Gunung Agung contained itself until the travel agents had flown home.

On 17 March Agung exploded. The catastrophic eruption killed more than 1000 people (some estimate 2000) and destroyed entire villages – 100,000 people lost their homes. Streams of lava and hot volcanic mud poured right down to the sea at several places, completely covering roads and isolating the eastern end of Bali for some time. The entire island was covered in ash and crops were wiped out everywhere.

Torrential rainfall followed the eruptions, and compounded the damage as boiling hot ash and boulders were swept down the mountain side, wreaking havoc on many villages, including Subagan, just outside Amlapura, and Selat, further along the road towards Rendang. The whole of Bali suffered a drastic food shortage, and many Balinese were resettled in west Bali and Sulawesi.

Although Besakih is high on the slopes of Agung, only about six km from the crater, the temple suffered little damage from the eruption. Volcanic dust and gravel flattened timber and bamboo buildings around the temple complex but the stone structures came through unscathed. The inhabitants of the villages of Sorga and Lebih, also high up on Agung's slopes, were all but wiped out. Most of the people killed at the time of the eruption were burnt and suffocated by searing clouds of hot gas that rushed down the volcano's slopes. Agung erupted again on 16 May, with serious loss of life, although not on the same scale as the March eruption.

The Balinese take signs and portents seriously – that such a terrible event should happen as they were making a most important sacrifice to the gods was not taken lightly. Soekarno's political demise two years later, following the failed Communist coup, could be seen as a consequence of his defying the power of the volcanic deity. The interrupted series of sacrifices finally recommenced 16 years later in 1979. ■

temple umbrellas and some interesting antiques.

Getting There & Away

Bemos bound for Candidasa and Amlapura all pass through Klungkung. Bemos also shuttle up and down the mountain road from Klungkung to Pura Besakih. The fare to Batubulan is about 1200 rp.

AROUND KLUNGKUNG

Gelgel & Kamasan

South of Klungkung, Gelgel is a quiet, pleasant place with wide streets and some big temples faintly evocative of its past grandeur. Nearby Kamasan is the home of classical Balinese painting, with figures depicted in profile, like wayang kulit shadow puppets. Also called 'wayang' or 'Kamasan' style, classical painting was revived by commissions to restore the royal palace ceilings in Klungkung, and there are several places in Kamasan where you can see artists working and buy classical paintings and calendars.

Tihingan

A couple of km west of Klungkung, the village of Tihingan has a number of workshops making gamelan instruments. It's not really set up for tourists, but the workshops with signs out the front will receive visitors.

Museum Seni Lukis Klasik

The respected modern artist Nyoman Gunarsa established this new museum and arts centre near his home town of Banda. There's a wide variety of old stone and wood carvings, architectural antiques, masks, ceramics and classical paintings, along with a good selection of Gunarsa's own work. The museum opens Tuesday to Sunday from 9 am to 5 pm, and admission is 5000 rp.

Bukit Jambal

The road north of Klungkung climbs steeply to Bukit Jambal, a popular stop because of its magnificent panorama. A couple of large restaurants provide buffet lunches to tour groups. This road continues to Rendang and Pura Besakih (see later in this section).

The Sidemen Road

Just east of Klungkung, a less travelled route goes north-east, via Sidemen and Iseh, to reach the Amlapura-Rendang road east of Selat. It has marvellous scenery and an attractive rural character.

The *Homestay Sidemen* (☎ (0366) 23009) is a delightful place to stay, but a bit expensive at around 60,000 rp per person, though that includes excellent meals. A newer hotel, *Subak Tabola Inn* (☎ (0366) 23015), is on a small track a little further north. It has a pool and a lovely setting, with comfortable rooms from US$35. There are some other small, secluded places to stay in the area.

Kusamba

About six km from Klungkung, a side road goes south to this fishing and salt-making village. You'll see lines of colourful fishing *prahus* (outriggers) lined up on the beach and the thatched huts in which saltwater is rinsed from baskets of sand. The water is then evaporated in rows of shallow troughs, leaving pure salt crystals. Boats from here take supplies to the islands of Nusa Penida and Nusa Lembongan, but are not recommended for passengers.

GOA LAWAH

Beyond Kusamba the road continues close to the coast and after a few km you come to Goa Lawah (Bat Cave). The cave in the cliff face is packed, crammed, jammed full of bats. A distinctly batty stench exudes from the cave, and the roofs of the temple shrines in front of the cave are liberally coated with bat droppings. The cave is believed to lead all the way to Besakih, and is home to a legendary giant snake, Naga Basuki, which lives on bats.

Goa Lawah is open every day (500 rp entry, 200 rp parking), and has extremely pushy souvenir sellers. It's hard to think of a good reason to stop here.

PADANGBAI

Padangbai is the port for the ferry service between Bali and Lombok. It's a couple of km off the main Klungkung to Amlapura

BALI

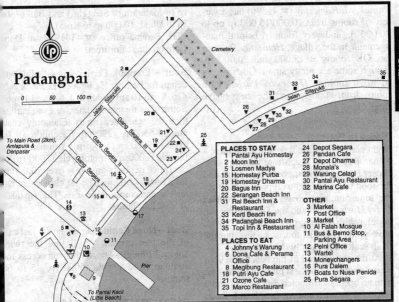

Padangbai

0   50   100 m

To Main Road (2km),
Amlapura &
Denpasar

Cemetery

Jalan Silayukti

Gang Segara

Gang Segara III

Gang Segara II

Jalan Silayukti

Pier

To Pantai Kecil
(Little Beach)

PLACES TO STAY
1 Pantai Ayu Homestay
2 Moon Inn
15 Losmen Madya
15 Homestay Purba
19 Homestay Dharma
20 Bagus Inn
22 Serangan Beach Inn
31 Rai Beach Inn &
 Restaurant
33 Kerti Beach Inn
34 Padangbai Beach Inn
35 Topi Inn & Restaurant

PLACES TO EAT
4 Johnny's Warung
6 Dona Cafe & Perama
 Office
16 Megibung Restaurant
18 Putri Ayu Cafe
21 Ozone Cafe
23 Marco Restaurant

24 Depot Segara
26 Pandan Cafe
27 Depot Dharma
28 Monala's
29 Warung Celagi
30 Pantai Ayu Restaurant
32 Marina Cafe

OTHER
3 Market
7 Post Office
9 Market
10 Al Falah Mosque
11 Bus & Bemo Stop,
 Parking Area
12 Pelni Office
13 Wartel
14 Moneychangers
16 Pura Dalem
17 Boats to Nusa Penida
25 Pura Segara

road, 54 km from Denpasar. There's a perfect little bay, and other pretty and secluded beaches to the north and south (be careful swimming at remote beaches). Padangbai is one of the two main shipping ports in southern Bali, and cruise ships call here, transforming the town into a cacophonous souvenir market.

Information
The tourist information office is in the carpark near the dock. There are moneychangers on the main street, a post office and a wartel.

Diving
There's some pretty good diving on the coral reefs around Padangbai, though the water can be a little cold and visibility is not always good. Most of the Bali dive operations do trips here.

Places to Stay
Most visitors to Padangbai stay at one of the pleasant beachfront places – in the high season accommodation can fill up and prices rise. Closest to the village is the *Rai Beach Inn* (☎ 41385), with two storey cottages in rice-barn style from US$10 up to US$40 with air-con and hot water. More standard single storey rooms with bath cost 16,500/22,000 rp for singles/doubles.

Next along the beach is the *Kerti Beach Inn*, with simple rooms at 12,000/15,000 rp, and also more expensive double storey thatched cottages. The third place in the central beachfront cluster is the *Padangbai Beach Inn* (☎ 41517), with very standard rooms from 12,000/15,000 rp, some with shared bathrooms – it's not great-value accommodation, but most rooms face the sea.

At the east end of the beach, *Topi Inn & Restaurant* has a good location. The bamboo building has small rooms upstairs at 9000/12,000 rp, and some dorm beds for 3000 rp.

Away from the beach there are several alternatives. Back behind the cemetery, the

Pantai Ayu Homestay (☎ 41396) has a variety of rooms from 10,000/15,000 rp up to 30,000 rp, and very friendly, helpful management. In the village, *Homestay Dharma* has OK rooms at 15,000 and 20,000 rp, though some are pretty small. Other places in town include *Homestay Purba*, with rooms from 8000 rp, and the inexpensive *Bagus Inn*.

Places to Eat

Right across from the Rai Beach Inn there's a line-up of simple beachfront warungs – the cheery *Pantai Ayu Restaurant* is popular, and the food is simple and well prepared. Or try the long-running *Warung Celagi*, *Pandan Cafe*, *Marina Cafe* and the *Depot Dharma*, popular with visiting dive groups. They all have pretty standard tourist menus, but the fresh seafood is usually the highlight.

At the eastern end of the beach, the *Topi Restaurant* is the fanciest place in Padangbai, with an open, sand-floored dining area and a colourful menu featuring fish, health foods and the Indonesian regulars.

In the town, but near the beach, there's *Putri Ayu Cafe*, which has seafood specials, and *Marco Restaurant*, with good pizza. The main street has a host of small Indonesian eateries, and *Megibung Restaurant*, past the post office, has also been recommended. The *Ozone Cafe* is something of an evening gathering place.

Getting There & Away

Bus & Bemo Buses direct to Denpasar (Batubulan) cost about 2200 rp. They connect with the ferries and depart from the carpark near the pier. This area is being redeveloped and will eventually be well organised. Direct buses from Padangbai go right through to Surabaya and Yogyakarta on Java. Bemos also leave from the carpark area at the pier, more frequently in the morning. The orange ones go to Candidasa (500 rp) and Amlapura; the blue ones to Klungkung (also called Semarapura).

Tourist shuttle buses connect with some ferries for destinations on Lombok (10,000 rp to Mataram or Senggigi) and Bali (7500 rp to Ubud, 10,000 rp to Kuta).

The Perama office (☎ 41419) is at Dona Cafe on the main street.

Boat – Lombok Ferries are scheduled to depart for Lembar Harbour on Lombok at 2, 4, 6, 8 and 10 am, noon, 2, 4, 6, 8 and 10 pm. Sometimes they leave later, or even earlier than the scheduled times. Economy cost around 5500 rp (2900 rp for children), 1st class is 9000 rp (5000 rp). You can take a bicycle (2000 rp), motorcycle (7000 rp) or car (price depends on size – over 70,000 rp for a Suzuki Jimny). The 1st class cabin has air-con and comfortable seats. The trip takes at least four hours.

Boat – Nusa Penida On the beach just east of the pier carpark you'll find the twin engined fibreglass boats that run across the strait to Nusa Penida (5000 rp; 45 to 60 minutes).

PADANGBAI TO CANDIDASA

It's 11 km from the Padangbai turn-off to Candidasa. After about four km, there's an unmarked turn-off to the very exclusive *Amankila* hotel (☎ (0366) 21993, reservations (☎ (0361) 771267; fax 771266). One of three Aman resorts on Bali, this one features an isolated seaside location and understated architecture which complements the environment. Prices start at US$430, plus 21% tax and service. You can visit for a buffet lunch at its beach club for about US$20 (call first).

Buitan (Balina Beach)

Balina Beach is the name bestowed on the tourist development in the village of Buitan, about five or six km from the Padangbai turn-off, just after the substantial girder bridge. It's a pretty quiet place, which has just acquired its first luxury hotel, but is losing its beach to erosion.

Places to Stay *Balina Beach Bungalows* (☎ (0363) 41002) has a variety of rooms and cottages from US$30/40 to US$50/60. The gardens and pool are very pretty, and dives can be arranged for qualified divers. Directly opposite is *Puri Buitan* (☎ (0363) 41021), with modern, motel-style rooms from US$30/35 to US$65/75, but it gives big discounts. Further east, with its own entrance, is the new *Serai* (☎ (0363) 286543; fax 287065), with elegant, white thatched-roof buildings in a spacious garden facing the beach. Very comfortable rooms cost US$110 to US$200, plus tax and service.

If you walk east along the remains of the beach for 200m, you'll find the *Cangrin Beach Homestay* (☎ (0363) 41029) and *Sunrise Homestay* (☎ (0363) 41008), which have standard losmen rooms for 16,000/20,000 rp a single/double, or 20,000/25,000 rp in the high season.

Other Beach Areas

Coming from the west, there are hotels and losmen off the main road several km before you reach Candidasa. For most of these places, get a bemo which will stop at Sengkidu. Sea walls have been constructed along this coast to limit the damage of beach erosion.

Most places to stay are secluded, mid-range to top-end package-tour hotels like the *Candi Beach Cottage* (☎ (0361) 751711 for information), with all the mod cons and rooms from around US$75/85. To get there, turn right at the volleyball court about two km or so west of Candidasa.

The same side road leads to the *Puri Amarta Beach Inn* (☎ (0363) 41230), which has a great location, a friendly atmosphere and is good value at 15,000/20,000 rp, including breakfast. Opposite, *Anom Beach Inn Bungalows* are a bit fancier, with standard bungalows at US$25/35 and superior air-con bungalows up to US$50/60. In the same area, *Nusa Indah Beach Bungalows* are around 15,000 rp, but it is isolated with no restaurant, so you really need your own transport to get into town for meals.

About one km from Candidasa, *Nirwana Cottages* (☎ (0363) 41136) has only 12 rooms in a quiet location, with rates from US$35/40 to US$50. Another mid-range

place is *Hotel Rama Candidasa* (☎ (0363) 41974), with pool, tennis court, satellite TV etc for US$33/35 to US$70.

As you approach Candidasa there are a few more cheapies on the beach side of the road. *Sari Jaya Seaside Cottage* is OK and quiet, and costs 10,000 rp for singles or doubles, including breakfast. A group of three cheap places, *Pelangi, Tarura* and *Flamboyant*, is just before the bridge but not too far to walk into town.

TENGANAN

At the turn-off to Tenganan, just west of Candidasa, a little posse of motorcycle riders waits by the junction ready to ferry you up to Tenganan for about 1000 rp. Make a donation as you enter the village. There's also a walking path to Tenganan from Candidasa but the trail is sometimes hard to follow.

Tenganan is a Bali Aga village, a centre of the original Balinese who predate the Majapahit arrival. The village is walled, with two neat rows of identical houses stepped up the gentle slope of the hill. The houses face each other across an open central area with the village's public buildings. The Bali Aga are reputed to be exceptionally conservative and resistant to change but even here the modern age has not been totally held at bay – crafts are sold to tourists and TV aerials sprout from the traditional houses.

Tenganan is full of strange customs, festivals and practices. Double ikat cloth known as *gringsing* is still woven here – the pattern to be produced is dyed on the individual threads, both warp (lengthwise) and weft (crosswise), *before* the cloth is woven. It's only produced in small quantities and at great expense, so don't expect to buy some for a bargain price. The magical *kamben gringsing* is also woven here – a person wearing it is said to be protected against black magic! The peculiar, old-fashioned 'gamelan selunding' is still played here, and girls perform the ancient Rejang dance.

At the annual Usaba Sambah Festival, held around June or July, men fight with their fists wrapped in sharp-edged pandanus leaves – similar events occur on the island of Sumba, further east in Nusa Tenggara. At this same festival, small, hand-powered Ferris wheels are brought out and the village girls are ceremonially twirled round.

BALI

CANDIDASA

The road reaches the sea just beyond the turn-off to Tenganan, and runs close to the coast through Candidasa. Not long ago this was a quiet little fishing village; now it's shoulder to shoulder tourist development. Nevertheless, many visitors enjoy Candidasa – it's quieter than Kuta, cheaper than Sanur and a good base from which to explore eastern Bali. It's particularly popular with scuba divers.

The main drawback is the lack of a beach, which eroded away as fast as the new hotels were erected. The erosion started when the offshore coral was dug up to make lime for cement, much of it used to build hotels. Without the protection of the reef the sea soon washed the beach away. Mining the reef stopped completely in 1991, but the erosion continues, even a dozen km along the coast. A series of large and intrusive T-shaped piers have been built (ironically constructed out of concrete blocks), where sand has started to rebuild, providing some nice, sheltered bathing places if the tide is right. It's quite good for kids, but nothing like a wide, white palm-fringed beach.

Information

Candidasa has the full complement of shops, moneychangers, travel agencies, bicycle, motorcycle and car-rental outlets, film developers and other facilities. There are a couple of bookshops and book exchanges and a number of postal agencies. All the services are easily found along the main street.

You can make international phone calls from the private wartel beside the Kubu Bali restaurant. Candidasa is in the 0363 phone district.

Things to See & Do

Candidasa's temple, **Pura Candidasa**, is on the hillside across from the lagoon at the eastern end of the village strip. The fishing village, just beyond the lagoon, has colourful fishing prahus drawn up on the beach. The owners regularly canvas visitors for snorkelling trips to the reef and the nearby islets.

The main road east of Candidasa winds up to the **Pura Gamang** pass (gamang means 'to get dizzy'), from where there are fine views down to the coast. On a clear day Agung rises majestically behind the range of coastal hills.

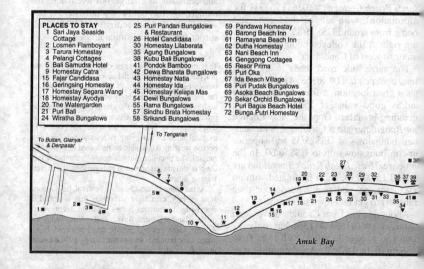

PLACES TO STAY
1 Sari Jaya Seaside Cottage
2 Losmen Flamboyant
3 Tarura Homestay
4 Pelangi Cottages
5 Bali Samudra Hotel
9 Homestay Catra
15 Fajar Candidasa
16 Geringsing Homestay
17 Homestay Segara Wangi
18 Homestay Ayodya
20 The Watergarden
21 Puri Bali
24 Wiratha Bungalows
25 Puri Pandan Bungalows & Restaurant
26 Hotel Candidasa
30 Homestay Lilaberata
35 Agung Bungalows
38 Kubu Bali Bungalows
41 Pondok Bamboo
42 Dewa Bharata Bungalows
43 Homestay Natia
44 Homestay Ida
45 Homestay Kelapa Mas
54 Dewi Bungalows
55 Rama Bungalows
57 Sindhu Brata Homestay
58 Srikandi Bungalows
59 Pandawa Homestay
60 Barong Beach Inn
61 Ramayana Beach Inn
62 Dutha Homestay
63 Nani Beach Inn
64 Genggong Cottages
65 Resor Prima
66 Puri Oka
67 Ida Beach Village
68 Puri Pudak Bungalows
69 Asoka Beach Bungalows
70 Sekar Orchid Bungalows
71 Puri Bagus Beach Hotel
72 Bunga Putri Homestay

To Buitan, Glanyar & Denpasar

To Tenganan

Amuk Bay

BALI

Diving

Two reliable dive operators are Baruna Water Sports, Bali's biggest and most established operator, with a branch at the Puri Bagus Beach Hotel, and Barrakuda, based at Hotel Candidasa, which can offer a full, open-water course with PADI and CAMS certification.

Places to Stay

Candidasa has plenty of low-cost places – basic doubles can be found for less than 12,000 rp. If the first price seems excessive, ask for a discount. A number of newer hotels offer air-con, swimming pools and other luxuries – some are standard package-tour places but a couple are unusual and interesting.

Places to Stay – bottom end

Starting at the Denpasar side, *Sari Jaya Seaside Cottages*, *Pelangi*, *Tarura* and *Flamboyant* are on the beach side of the road just before town. They all charge about 10,000/15,000 rp for singles/doubles, and all offer adequate accommodation within walking distance of Candidasa's restaurant row.

On the right, about 200m from the Tenganan turn-off, *Homestay Geringsing* (☎ 41084) has attractive cottages clustered in a quiet garden from 9000/12,000 rp, or 15,000 rp for a beachfront position – they're very good for the price. Continuing east, the *Puri Bali* (☎ 41063) has simple, clean and well-kept rooms for 9000/12,000 rp, including breakfast, and the cheap rooms at *Wiratha Bungalows* (☎ 41973) are also good value at 9000/15,000 rp, or 5000 rp more with beach frontage.

Further along, also on the beach side, is *Puri Pandan Bungalows* (☎ 41541), which asks from US$10/12 for singles/doubles with breakfast, but gives a 30% discount in the low season. The popular, rock-bottom *Homestay Lilaberata*, with rooms for 10,000/12,000 rp, has a good location, squat toilets and chickens in the garden. *Pondok Bamboo Seaside Cottages* (☎ 41354) is a little fancier, with double rooms from 25,000 to 35,000 rp, and a restaurant overlooking the ocean.

Homestay Ida (☎ 41096), close to the lagoon, has pleasantly airy bamboo cottages dotted around a grassy coconut plantation. Smaller rooms are 17,500/20,000 rp, larger rooms 25,000 rp and family rooms with a

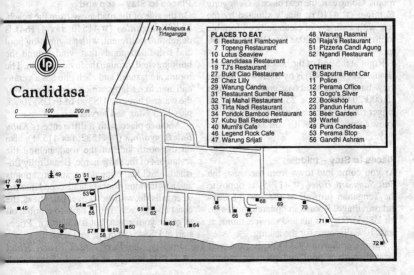

Candidasa

0   100   200 m

To Amlapura & Tirtagangga

PLACES TO EAT
6 Restaurant Flamboyant
7 Topeng Restaurant
10 Lotus Seaview
14 Candidasa Restaurant
19 TJ's Restaurant
27 Bukit Ciao Restaurant
28 Chez Lilly
29 Warung Candra
31 Restaurant Sumber Rasa
32 Taj Mahal Restaurant
33 Tirta Nadi Restaurant
34 Pondok Bamboo Restaurant
37 Kubu Bali Restaurant
40 Mumi's Cafe
46 Legend Rock Cafe
47 Warung Srijati

48 Warung Rasmini
50 Raja's Restaurant
51 Pizzeria Candi Agung
52 Ngandi Restaurant

OTHER
8 Saputra Rent Car
11 Police
12 Perama Office
13 Gogo's Silver
22 Bookshop
23 Pandun Harum
36 Beer Garden
39 Wartel
49 Pura Candidasa
53 Perama Stop
56 Gandhi Ashram

mezzanine level are 40,000 rp, including breakfast and tax. The *Homestay Kelapa Mas* (☎ 41947), next door, is also well kept and spacious, with a range of rooms from around 20,000/25,000 rp – the seafront rooms are particularly well situated.

Beyond the Kelapa Mas is the lagoon, and there are plenty of small losmen further along the beach, as well as some newer, more expensive places. Three fairly standard losmen east of the lagoon are the friendly *Dewi Bungalows* and *Rama Bungalows* (☎ 41778), which are quite good, and the *Sindhu Brata Homestay* (☎ 41825) – they all have rooms from around 15,000/20,000 rp. Nearby *Pandawa Homestay* is a bit cheaper at 12,000/15,000 rp.

The main road to Amlapura swings away from the coast, and a small track, sometimes called Forest Road, branches off giving access to more seafront accommodation. These places face onto what's left of the beach, and they're quiet, but some way from the shops and restaurants. Low-budget options include the *Barong Beach Inn* (☎ 41137), *Ramayana Beach Inn* and *Nani Beach Inn*, all with basic rooms from around 10,000/15,000 rp, as well as more expensive rooms. Going east, the next place is *Genggong Cottages* (☎ 41105), nicely situated by the sea, with a variety of clean and comfortable rooms from 15,000/20,000 to 25,000/30,000 rp.

Right at the end of the beach, *Bunga Putri Homestay* (☎ 41140) is by itself with a great view back along the coast and rooms from 15,000/20,000 rp, or 25,000 rp more for bigger rooms. There's a new restaurant, and a new access road, but it's still a bit out of the way.

Places to Stay – middle

As you come into town from the west, the *Bali Samudra Hotel* (☎ 41795) is opposite the Tenganan turn-off at the start of Candidasa village. Rooms in concrete boxes go for US$55/60, plus tax and service, minus at least 10% discount for the asking.

Fajar Candidasa (☎ 41539) is quite well located, with a pool and pleasant rooms,

somewhat crowded together, for US$25/30 a double, or US$40/50 with air-con, including tax.

Right in the centre of the commercial strip, *Hotel Candidasa* (☎ 41536) is a three storey place which gives the distinct impression that the maximum number of rooms have been crammed into the minimum amount of space. The rooms are quite good though, from US$35/45 for air-con singles/doubles, including a substantial breakfast. *Dewa Bharata Bungalows* has a pool, bar and restaurant, and is good value from US$25/30 with air-con.

Past the lagoon are a number of newer mid-range places, but some of them are uninspiring package-tour places, like *Resor Prima* (☎ 41373), which is overbuilt and overpriced at US$40 a double. Much better value is *Ida Beach Village* (☎ 41118), with architecture based on a traditional Balinese village. Very comfortable, well-decorated cottages in a pretty garden cost US$45 to US$50; US$10 more in the high season. The *Puri Pudak Bungalows* (☎ 41978) are OK, though the service is minimal – at 30,000/35,000 rp it's cheap for a place with a pool.

Places to Stay – top end

On the side of the road away from the beach, *The Watergarden* (☎ 41540; fax 41164) is delightfully different, with a swimming pool and fish-filled ponds that wind around the buildings and through the lovely garden. The rooms are tasteful and each one has a verandah area like a jetty, which projects out over the water. They cost US$60/65 to US$70/75, plus 15.5% tax and service.

Another place with a difference is *Kubu Bali Bungalows* (☎ 41532; fax 41531), also on the north side of the road, behind the restaurant of the same name. Beautifully finished individual bungalows, streams, ponds and a swimming pool are landscaped into the steep hillside, with views over palm trees, the coast and the sea. You'll have to climb a bit to get to your room, but it's worth it. Prices start at US$45/50 in the low season.

Finally, the *Puri Bagus Beach Hotel* (☎ 41131) is right at the end of the beach beyond the lagoon, hidden away in the palm trees. It's a handsome place in the Kuta/Sanur style but without the neighbours. The nicely designed rooms cost US$65/70 plus service and tax, or try a suite from US$125.

Places to Eat

The food in Candidasa is pretty good, particularly fresh seafood. Restaurants are dotted along the main road, mostly on the inland side. The restaurant at *Puri Bagus Beach Hotel* is probably the best in town, and the most expensive.

As you come into town from the west, *Lotus Seaview*, on the right, is an upmarket tourist restaurant with a wonderful outlook. Further along, on the other side, is *TJ's Restaurant*, which is related to the popular TJ's in Kuta, but the food is not as Mexican or as good. Some of the other interesting places are *Bukit Ciao Restaurant*, behind the Pandan Harum dance stage, serving 1st class Italian food, and *Chez Lilly*, which has some imaginative offerings, usually very well prepared. *Warung Candra* and *Taj Mahal* both do reasonably good Indian dishes at reasonable prices. The beachside restaurant at the *Puri Pandan Bungalows* does Balinese feasts, and has better than average Chinese and seafood dishes.

Back on the north side of the road, *Kubu Bali Restaurant* is a big place built around a pond with an open kitchen area out the front – Indonesian and Chinese dishes are turned out with great energy and panache. It's in the middle price range, but usually worth it. For cheaper eating, try *Warung Srijati* and *Warung Rasmini*, on the same side of the road but closer to the lagoon. Just beyond the lagoon, the *Pizzeria Candi Agung* does a good pizza, while *Raja's* has burgers, pasta and other western and Indonesian standards.

Entertainment

Barong, Topeng or Legong dance performances take place at 9 pm on Tuesday and Friday at the Pandan Harum dance stage in the centre of the Candidasa strip (4000 rp). Restaurants like *Raja's* and *Chez Lilly* show video movies most evenings. The *Legend*

Rock Cafe sometimes has live music and dancing, but probably not in the low season when Candidasa is very quiet. *Tirta Nadi Restaurant* has a cheerful atmosphere, a long cocktail list and the occasional band. The *Beer Garden*, which opens later than most places, plays loud dance music but is more a place to hang out than to dance.

Getting There & Away

Candidasa is on the main route between Amlapura and Denpasar. A bus from the Batubulan terminal should cost about 2200 rp. Tourist shuttle buses also operate to Candidasa – to the airport, Denpasar or Kuta it costs 10,000 rp, to Ubud 7500 rp, or to Singaraja and Lovina beaches 20,000 rp. Buy tickets from the agents on the main street. Perama (☎ 41114) is at the west end of the strip, but has a pick-up point near the lagoon. Cars, motorcycles and bicycles can be rented in Candidasa at prices only slightly higher than in Kuta or Ubud.

AMLAPURA

Amlapura is the main town and the capital of the Karangasem district. The Karangasem kingdom broke away from the Gelgel kingdom in the late 17th century and 100 years later had become the most powerful kingdom on Bali, and also ruled much of Lombok. After the 1963 eruption of Agung, lava flows cut the roads and isolated the town, which was then called Karangasem. The name was changed to get rid of any influences which might provoke another eruption!

Information

Amlapura is the smallest of the district capitals and a very quiet place. There are banks (but it's probably easier to change money in Candidasa), a wartel and a couple of post offices.

Palaces

Amlapura's three palaces are decaying reminders of Karangasem's period as a kingdom. They date from the late 19th and early 20th centuries, but only one of the palaces is open for general inspection. Admission to **Puri Agung** (also known as Puri Kanginan) costs 1500 rp, including an explanation sheet which tells you all you'll need to know about the place.

The main building is known as Maskerdam (ie Amsterdam), because it was the Karangasem kingdom's acquiescence to Dutch rule which allowed it to hang on long after the demise of the other Balinese kingdoms. This may be your best opportunity to view a Balinese palace but you won't be overwhelmed. Old photographs and paintings of the royal family are displayed on the verandah. You can see inside several rooms, including the royal bedroom and a living room with furniture which was a gift from the Dutch royal family.

On the other side of this main courtyard is the Balai Kambang, surrounded by a pond. The ornately decorated Balai Pemandesan, in between Maskerdam and the pool, was used for royal tooth-filing and cremation ceremonies. Opposite this, the Balai Lunjuk was used for other religious ceremonies.

There are other courtyards around the main one. It's said that about 150 members of the old family and their servants still live in this slowly deteriorating relic of a now-forgotten era of Balinese history.

Ujung Water Palace

A few km beyond Amlapura, on the road down to the sea, are the remains of the Ujung Water Palace, an extensive and crumbling ruin of a once-grand palace complex. It has been deteriorating for some time but most damage was done by an earthquake in 1979. The last king of Karangasem, Anak Agung Anglurah, was obsessed with moats, pools, canals and fountains, and he had this place finished in 1921. The best view is from a derelict pavilion which overlooks the ruin from the west.

Places to Stay & Eat

Not many travellers stop here – Candidasa is not far away and it's only another six km to Tirtagangga. If you do need to stay, *Homestay*

Lahar Mas (☎ (0363) 21345), on the left as you come in to town, is basic but friendly and quite OK, with rooms at 12,500/15,000 rp for singles/doubles. There's the usual collection of *warungs* around the bus terminal, plus the *Rumah Makan Segar* and the *Sumba Rasa* on Jl Gajah Mada. Amlapura tends to shut down early so don't leave your evening meal until too late.

Getting There & Away

There are buses and bemos on the main road to Denpasar (3000 rp), via Candidasa, Padangbai (1000 rp) and Klungkung (2000 rp). Bemos also take the scenic inland road to Rendang. There are also buses going around the east and north coast from here to Singaraja (about 2500 rp), via Tirtagangga and Tulamben.

TIRTAGANGGA

Amlapura's water-loving rajah, having constructed his masterpiece at Ujung, later had another go at Tirtagangga. This **water palace**, built around 1947, was damaged in the 1963 eruption of Agung and during the political events that racked Indonesia two years later. It's not grand, but it's still a place of beauty and a reminder of the power the Balinese rajahs once had. The palace has a swimming pool as well as the ornamental ponds. Entrance to the water palace is 1000 rp (children 500 rp) and another 2000 rp to use the big swimming pool (children 1000 rp), or 1000 rp for the smaller, lower pool (500 rp for children).

The beautiful **rice terraces** sweep out from Tirtagangga almost like a sea surrounding an island. A few km beyond here, on the road to the east coast, there are more dramatically beautiful terraces, often seen in photographs of Bali. Ask at your losmen for suggested walks in the surrounding countryside. Nyoman Budiasa is another good source of information about the area, and he also arranges and guides climbs up Gunung Agung. He has a small shop opposite the Tirtagangga carpark.

Places to Stay & Eat

Within the water palace compound, the *Tirta Ayu Homestay* (☎ (0363) 21697) has pleasant individual bungalows at 35,000 rp a double, with breakfast, and two large bungalows with great views for 60,000 rp. Prices include admission to the swimming pools.

Near the palace entrance, the peaceful *Losmen Dhangin Taman Inn* (☎ (0363) 22059) has rooms from 10,000/12,000 to 15,000/20,000 rp, including breakfast. It's a pleasant, relaxed place, the owner is a bit of a character and the food is good.

Across the road from the palace, *Rijasa Homestay* (☎ (0363) 21873) is a small and simple place with extremely neat and clean rooms at 10,000/15,000 rp, including breakfast and tea. A little beyond the water palace, on the left, a driveway leads to *Puri Sawah* ☎ (0363) 21847), which has just two large and very comfortable rooms for 50,000 rp.

If you continue for a couple of hundred metres, steep steps on the left lead to *Kusuma Jaya Inn* (☎ (0363) 21250), the 'Homestay on the Hill', with a fine view over the rice paddies. It costs 15,000/20,000 rp for adequate singles/doubles in the low season, 25,000 rp plus in the high season. The staff are not as helpful as they could be, and the caged monkeys might turn you off. About 500m further on is *Prima Bamboo* (☎ (0363) 21316), also up steep steps to the left of the road and also with outstanding views. The rooms are quite OK for 15,000/20,000 rp, including breakfast, and the restaurant is superbly situated.

There are several *warungs* outside the palace, while next to the carpark, *Good Karma* has good food and plays good music.

Getting There & Away

Tirtagangga is on the main road that runs around the eastern end of Bali, about five or six km from the Amlapura turn-off. Bemos from Amlapura cost 500 rp. Going east, you can usually flag down a bemo for transport to Culik or Tulamben – the best time is in the morning. Some buses continue around to Singaraja.

AROUND TIRTAGANGGA

The area around Tirtagangga is very traditional, and some of the nearby villages have special attractions. There are Buddhist communities near **Budakeling**, traditional blacksmiths and silversmiths at **Krotok**, and a unique choral gamelan at **Tanah Lengis**.

Heading north from Tirtagangga, the road starts to climb and a sign points to **Pura Lempuyang**, one of Bali's nine 'directional temples', perched on a hilltop at 768m. Even with your own transport, you have to climb a lot of steps to see the spectacular view.

Further on, the road descends past some of the most spectacular rice terraces on Bali, and gets back down towards sea level at Culik, where there's a turn-off to Amed and the road around Bali's south-east corner. The main road goes north to Tulamben and continues around the east coast to Singaraja.

AMED

This corner of Bali is starting to attract visitors, with secluded seaside accommodation, and quite good diving and snorkelling close to the shore. From the main road at Culik, follow the signs pointing to Hidden Paradise Cottages. There are several small villages along the coast – Amed, Cemeluk, Lipah, Selang – but the general area is called Amed.

The coastline is superb and unspoilt, with views across to Lombok and back to Gunung Agung. Rows of wooden troughs are used to evaporate sea water to extract salt – one of the main industries here.

There are few facilities – no wartels, post offices or moneychangers. The closest dive operations are in Tulamben.

Places to Stay

Try to arrive early, as there are only a few places to stay and no phone connection yet. The first place to try is *Kusumajaya Beach Inn* in Cemeluk, a couple of km past Amed proper. It has a seaside restaurant and some Bali-style bungalows on a slope down from the road – the garden is coming along. Singles/doubles are 25,000/30,000 rp in the low season, 40,000 rp plus in the high season.

Next are the *Hidden Paradise Cottages* in Lipah, which are lovely, isolated and comfortable, with restaurant, pool and a great little beach. It's a quality place, but with rooms from US$35 to US$87, it's not a low-budget option. You can mail a booking to Box 121, Amlapura, or try ☎ (0361) 431273; fax 423820.

Continue south to *Vienna Beach Bungalows*, a cosy complex with bamboo cottages near the water at 35,000 rp, and others closer to the road for about 20,000 rp. It can arrange diving, fishing and sailing trips. Crossing one or two more little hills brings you to *Good Karma*, with classic, basic, bamboo beachside bungalows at 20,000/30,000 rp for a small one, 30,000/45,000 rp for a large one. It's a great place to stay in a lovely location, but the main attraction advertised is 'talking and joking with Baba', the friendly proprietor.

Getting There & Away

It's easy to get here with your own wheels. Public transport is easy to Culik, but it's infrequent from there to Amed, mostly going early in the day. Later on, you should be able to get an ojek for about 2000 rp.

SOUTH-EAST PENINSULA

The road around the south-east peninsula is narrow, winding and hilly, but it's mostly sealed and definitely passable. You might almost be safer with a motorcycle than a car, because you'll have more chance to get out of the way of an oncoming vehicle – be extremely careful. Even if you could find a public bemo, it would be uncomfortable and you wouldn't see the views. Mostly the road follows the slopes of Gunung Seraya, way above the sea, and there's spectacular coastal scenery. It's a pretty dry area with no rice fields, but some places have extensive vineyards and look almost Mediterranean. From Amed around to Amlapura is probably only about 30 km, but allow at least two hours to enjoy the trip.

TULAMBEN

The small village of Tulamben has a good choice of accommodation, a pebble beach, clear water and good snorkelling. It's an interesting place to pause on a trip around the barren east coast. The prime attraction is the wreck of the US cargo ship, USAT *Liberty* which is the most popular dive site on Bali.

Diving

There's a small losmen and restaurant, the Puri Madha, right in front of the wreck site. You can park here, use the change room and rent a snorkel set for 6000 rp per day. Swim straight out from here and you'll see the stern rearing up from the depths. It's heavily encrusted with coral, a haven for colourful fish, and swarming with scuba divers most of the day.

Many divers commute to Tulamben from Sanur, Candidasa and Lovina, and it can get crowded between 11 am and 4 pm, with up to 50 divers on the wreck at a time. It's best to stay the night in Tulamben and dive before or after the crowds. The most comprehensive dive operation here is based at Mimpi Resort but others are OK for certified divers. Dive Paradise at Paradise Bungalows has an SS

USAT Liberty

On 11 January 1942 the armed US cargo ship USAT *Liberty* was torpedoed by a Japanese submarine about 15 km south-west of Lombok. It was taken in tow by the destroyers HMNS *Van Ghent* and USS *Paul Jones*, with the intention of beaching it on the coast of Bali and retrieving its cargo of raw rubber and railway parts. When its condition looked perilous the crew were evacuated and, although it was successfully beached, the rapid spread of the war through Indonesia prevented the cargo from being saved.

Built in 1915 the *Liberty* sat on the beach at Tulamben, a prominent east coast landmark, until 1963 when the violent eruption of Gunung Agung toppled it beneath the surface. Or at least that's one version of the story. Another relates that it sank some distance offshore and the lava flow from the eruption extended the shoreline almost out to the sunken vessel. Whatever the course of events it lies just 40 or 50m offshore, almost parallel to the beach with its stern only a couple of metres below the surface. ■

instructor, and its dive trips are slightly less expensive. Two local dives will cost about US$55.

Places to Stay & Eat

Paradise Palm Beach Bungalows has lots of rooms in a pleasant garden and an inexpensive restaurant right by the sea. They're neat, clean and well kept from 25,000 to 30,000 rp.

Pondok Matahari, a little to the south, has some cheap rooms from 10,000/12,000 rp, but it's not very nice. *Gandu Mayu Bungalows*, a little to the north, has small rooms from 12,000/15,000 rp, and better ones at 20,000/25,000 rp. Right by the wreck is the new *Puri Madha*, with a few small, clean rooms with sea views at 25,000/30,000 rp.

Some better places are appearing here, of which the most attractive is *Mimpi Resort* (☎ (0361) 701070 for reservations), where quite good rooms, well back from the beach, start at US$45, and stylish cottages and suites run from US$105 to US$135.

Getting There & Away

Public buses and bemos around the east coast will stop at Tulamben. Perama buses stop at Gandu Mayu Bungalows.

TULAMBEN TO YEH SANIH

Beyond Tulamben the road continues to skirt the slopes of the eastern volcanoes, Gunung Agung and the outer crater of Gunung Batur. You can still see lava flows from the 1963 eruption. There's very little tourist development, but *Alamanda*, near **Sambirenteng**, is a tasteful new place on the beach with a fine coral reef just offshore. It has its own diving operation and attractive bungalows from US$29 to US$44. The buffet lunch is worth a stop.

Further around is **Les**, where a waterfall is reached via a two km side road and a pleasant 1.5 km walk. The next village is **Tejakula**, which is famous for its horse bath, now the town's public bathing place. The road continues to Yeh Sanih, where there's inexpensive accommodation (see the North Bali section later in this chapter).

RENDANG TO AMLAPURA

A scenic back road goes around the slopes of Gunung Agung from Rendang to near Amlapura. It runs through some superb countryside, descending more or less gradually as it goes further east. It's possible to do this route on public bemos, but you'd enjoy it more with your own wheels. You can do it in either direction, but by bicycle it would be better going eastward.

Starting from the west, **Rendang** is an attractive town, easily reached by bemo from Klungkung or via the very pretty minor road from Bangli. About four km along a very winding road brings you to the old-fashioned village of **Muncan**, with its quaint shingle roofs. East of here the road passes through some of the prettiest rice country on Bali before reaching **Selat**, where you turn north for Sebudi and **Pura Pasar Agung**, a starting point for climbing Agung. You can stay near Selat at *Pondok Wisata Puri Agung*, which has very clean, new rooms for 40,000 rp, though the service may be erratic. Further on is **Duda**, where another scenic route branches south-west via Sidemen to Klungkung.

Two km further is a side road to **Putung**, where you can enjoy the fantastic view down the southern slopes to the coast, with ships anchored off Padangbai and Nusa Penida in the distance. Wonderfully located on the edge of this slope, *Pondok Bukit Putung* (☎ (0366) 23039) has an assortment of not very well-finished bungalows from US$18/20 to US$35. They're a bit overpriced, but the restaurant is good for lunch. The area between this road and the sea has wonderful trekking possibilities.

There's a good track from Putung to Manggis, only eight km down the hill, and a number of very traditional villages south of **Sibetan**. This area is also famous for growing salaks, the delicious fruit with a curious 'snakeskin' covering – you'll get them between December and April.

The scenic road finishes at **Bebandem**, where there's a cattle market every three days, with plenty of other stuff for sale as well. Not far north, **Bukit Kusambi** is a small hill with a big view. There are other interesting villages nearby – see Around Tirtagangga earlier in this section. Two km south of Bebanden at **Abian Soan** is the cheap, basic but delightful *Homestay Lila*, run by a charming and helpful old couple who can tell you a lot about the local area and its customs.

BANGLI

Halfway up the slope to Penelokan, the town of Bangli, once the capital of a kingdom, has a very fine temple. Not many tourists stop here, but it's quite a pleasant place and makes a good base for exploring the area. Bangli is home to a psychiatric institution and a prison, and is therefore the subject of unkind jokes in other parts of Bali.

Three km from Bangli, along the Tampaksiring road, is **Bukit Demulih**, a hill just off the south side of the road. At the top there's a small temple and good views back over Bangli; walk along the ridge line to a viewpoint where all of southern Bali spreads out below.

Orientation & Information

The town is very spread out from north to south; it's nearly 1.5 km from the bus stop to the Pura Kehen temple.

Bangli has a tourist office (☎ 91537), a couple of banks, a post office and a Telkom wartel.

Pura Kehen

At the top end of the town, Pura Kehen, the state temple of the Bangli kingdom, is terraced up the hillside. A great flight of steps leads up to the temple entrance and the first courtyard, which has a huge banyan tree with a kulkul drum entwined in its branches. The inner courtyard has an 11-roofed meru, and a shrine with thrones for the three figures of Brahma, Shiva and Vishnu. The carvings are particularly intricate – this is one of the finest temples on Bali. Entry is 1050 rp, and you'll need the usual temple attire.

Pura Dalem Penunggekan

Beside the road to Gianyar there's an interesting temple of the dead, Pura Dalem Penunggekan. The reliefs on the front depict wrongdoers getting their just deserts in the afterlife.

Places to Stay & Eat

The *Artha Sastra Inn* (☎ (0366) 91179) is a former palace residence and is still run by the grandson of the last king of Bangli. Rooms cost 10,000/12,000 rp for singles/doubles, some with private bathrooms. It doesn't look much from the outside, but it's a pleasant, friendly place, quite popular and very central – right across from the bus terminal and main square.

The *Losmen Dharmaputra*, a short distance up the road towards Kintamani, is a YHA affiliate. It's cheap but very basic and unappealing. Drab double rooms with shared bathroom cost 7000 rp. *Catur Adnyana* (☎ (0366) 91244), near the sportsground, has somewhat better rooms for about 10,000 rp. The new *Bangli Inn* (☎ (0366) 91419), near the market, is the most comfortable place in town and quite good value from 15,000/20,000 to 25,000 rp.

The pasar malam (night market) is in the square opposite the Artha Sastra Inn and there are some great warungs, open till around 10 pm. The *Harmoni Cafe* is good for lunch or dinner.

Getting There & Away

Bangli is on the main public transport route between Batubulan terminal and the Penelokan-Kintamani-Gunung Batur area. You can also get on a Bangli-bound bemo in Gianyar, or at the main-road junction at Peteluan, near Sidan. Tourist shuttle buses between Kintamani and Ubud or Candidasa will probably drop you in Bangli.

BESAKIH

Nearly 1000m up the slopes of Gunung Agung is Bali's most important temple, Pura Besakih. It's actually a complex of some 23 separate but related temples, with the largest and most important being Pura Penataran Agung. It's most enjoyable during a festival, when throngs of gorgeously dressed evotees turn up with beautifully arranged ·fferings. The panoramic view and the nountain backdrop are impressive too.

Despite its importance, Besakih can be a lisappointment to visitors – the architecture s not especially impressive, tourists are not llowed inside any of the temple compounds nd the views are often obscured by mist. Try ɔ arrive early, before the mist and the tour ·uses roll in, and spend some time after-vards exploring the scenic surrounding area.

nformation

`he tourist information office, near the ntrance, can answer specific questions, but as no printed information and does nothing ɔ make the site more comprehensible to ·isitors. Unofficial guides will latch onto ou and tell you about the temple – if you on't want to pay for their services, say so uickly.

There are lots of charges at Besakih. You ·ay to park (600 rp per car; 200 rp for a notorcycle), pay to enter (1100 rp per per-on), pay for your camera (1000 rp) or your ·ideo recorder (2500 rp), pay to rent a sarong 2000 rp) and then brave the rows of souve-ir sellers.

²laces to Stay & Eat

▲bout five km below Besakih, *Lembah Arca* as a restaurant, and rooms from 15,000/ 0,000 to 25,000/30,000 rp, but may give a ·iscount' if it's quiet. It's well situated, but he rooms are just average. There are also ome basic *losmen* at Besakih, between the arpark and the temple – they might be OK you want an early start to climb Agung. `here are several inexpensive *warungs* round the carpark and the approaches to the ∍mple, as well as some pricey places where ɔur buses stop.

;etting There & Away

`he usual route to Besakih is via Klungkung, ·rom where there are regular bemos to the ∍mple. If there are no direct bemos about to lepart, get one to Rendang or Menanga, then nother to Besakih. After about 2 pm you

may have trouble getting a bemo back, so leave early or be prepared to charter or hitch.

GUNUNG AGUNG

Gunung Agung is Bali's highest and most revered mountain, an imposing peak from most of southern and eastern Bali, though it's often obscured by cloud and mist. Most books and maps give its height as 3142m, but some say it lost its top in the 1963 eruption and is now only 3014m. The summit is an oval crater, about 500m across, with the highest point on the western edge above Besakih.

Climbing Agung

It's possible to climb Agung from various directions, but the two shortest and most popular routes are from the temple at Besakih and up the southern flank from Selat, via Sebudi. The latter route goes to the lower edge of the crater rim, and you can't make your way from there around to the very highest point. If that's important to you, climb from Besakih. To have any chance of seeing the view before the clouds form, get to the top before 8 am. Ideally, you should reach the top by 6 am for sunrise. In either case you'll start walking before dawn, so plan your climb when there will be some moonlight, and take a torch. Also take plenty of water and food, waterproof clothing, a warm woollen sweater and extra batteries – just in case.

You should take a guide for either route. Before you start, or early in the climb, the guide will stop at a shrine and make an offering and some prayers. This is a holy mountain and you should show respect. Besides, you will want to have everything going for you on the climb.

It's best to climb during the dry season – July, August and September are the most reliable months. At other times the paths can be slippery and dangerous. Climbing Agung is not permitted when major religious events are being held at Besakih.

Climb from Selat This route involves the least walking because you can go by road to

Pura Pasar Agung, high on the southern slopes of the mountain. From there you can climb to the top in as little as two hours, but allow at least three or four. You should report to the police station at Selat before you start, and again when you return. They may be able to help arrange transport and a guide, but it's rumoured that they usually demand 10,000 rp from prospective climbers.

One recommended guide is Ketut Uriada, a primary school teacher at Muncan, a few km west of Selat. He's well known in Muncan and he can help arrange the practicalities. He'll charge around 40,000/60,000/75,000/80,000 rp for one/two/three/four people, including food, plus whatever it costs for transport etc. The owner of the Pondok Wisata Puri Agung near Selat may act as a guide, and there's also Nyoman Budiasa, who's based in Tirtagangga.

You can stay the night in Selat and drive up early in the morning, or drive up the day before and stay overnight at the temple. Start climbing from the temple at around 3 or 4 am.

Climb from Besakih Leave Besakih at about midnight if you want a clear view from the top. Allow five to six hours for the climb, and four to five for the descent. The starting point is Pura Pengubengan, north-east of the main temple complex, but it's easy to get lost on the lower trails, so hire a guide. The tourist office near the carpark at Besakih will put you in touch with one, who will charge around US$50/75/100 for one/two/three people, plus extra for food and water. Arrange the details the day before, and stay in a losmen near Besakih so you can start early. This climb is even tougher than from Selat.

West Bali

The main tourist attractions in south-western Bali, like Sangeh or Tanah Lot, are easy day trips from Denpasar, Kuta or Ubud. Tabanan district has some fine rice-field scenery and,

further west, spectacular roads head across the mountains to the north. The coast has long stretches of wide, black sand beach with fishing villages that rarely see a tourist.

SEMPIDI, LUKLUK & KAPAL
Kapal is the garden gnome and temple curlicue centre of Bali. Numerous shops line the road displaying the many standard architectural motifs for temples, along with garden ornaments like comic-book deer and brightly painted Buddhas.

Kapal's **Pura Sadat** is the most important temple in the area. Although it was restored after WWII, this is a very ancient temple possibly dating back to the 12th century.

TANAH LOT
The spectacularly placed Tanah Lot is possibly the best known and most photographed temple on Bali. It's also the most touristed and the most commercialised. The temple, perched on a rocky islet, looks superb whether delicately lit by the dawn light or starkly outlined at sunset. But can it ever live up to the hype?

It's a well-organised tourist trap – you pay the parking attendants (350 rp) and they show you where to park. Dozens of souvenir shops are in a sort of sideshow alley, which you can easily bypass. There's a ticket office to collect the entry fee (1050 rp), then you follow the crowd down the steps to the sea. You can walk over to the island at low tide or climb up to the left and sit at one of the many tables along the cliff top. Order a drink (6000 rp for a small beer!) or dinner, get your camera ready and wait for 'The Sunset'.

For the Balinese, Tanah Lot is one of the important and venerated sea temples. Like Pura Luhur Ulu Watu, at the southern end of the island, Tanah Lot is closely associated with the 16th century Majapahit priest Nirartha.

More recently, Tanah Lot is the site of a controversial tourist development, the Bali Nirwana Resort (BNR). The US$200 million project will have a 400 room luxury hotel, 450 residential units and an 18 hole golf course – it's clearly visible just south of the temple.

BALI

n 1994 there were critical articles in the local press
nd public demonstrations opposing BNR. The
roject was subjected to another review, but has been
llowed to proceed. Officially at least, planning and
nvironmental requirements have been made much
tricter, though it remains to be seen whether the
rovincial government can enforce these.

Places to Stay
The *Dewi Sinta Cottages* (☎ (0361) 812933)
are on the souvenir shop alley, not far from
the ticket office. They're clean and quite
good, but unexciting, with rooms from
US$12/16 to US$23/25. Next door is the
newer, and only slightly better, *Mutiara
Tanah Lot* (☎ (0361) 225457), at US$50
with air-con, US$40 without.

Getting There & Away
By bemo, you go from Ubung terminal to
Kediri (1000 rp), then catch another bemo to
the coast (about 600 rp). If you stay for the
sunset, you may have to charter a bemo back.
Tours to Tanah Lot usually take in a few other
sites, like Bedugul (see the Central Mounains section), Mengwi or Sangeh.

MENGWI
The main temple of the kingdom, **Pura
Taman Ayun**, ruled from Mengwi until
1891. The temple was built in 1634 and
extensively renovated in 1937. It's spacious,
and the elegant moat gives it a very fine
appearance. The first courtyard is a large,
open grassy expanse and the inner courtyard
has a multitude of merus.

Across the moat from the temple is a rather
lost-looking **arts centre** and a small **museum** with models and dioramas of Balinese
festivals. Both are unspectacular and not
very informative.

Mengwi is easily reached by road, or public
bemo from Ubung terminal in Denpasar.

BLAYU
In Blayu (or Belayu), a small village between
Mengwi and Marga, traditional songket
sarongs are woven with intricate gold threads.
These are for ceremonial use only, not for
everyday wear.

MARGA
Marga is an attractive area of very traditional
family compounds, west of the road three km
north of Mengwi. North-west of the village
is the **Margarana** memorial, which commemorates the battle of Marga. On 20
November 1946 a force of 96 independence
fighters here was surrounded by a much
larger and better armed Dutch force. The
Balinese leader, Lt Colonel I Gusti Ngurah
Rai, refused to surrender, and, though they
inflicted heavy casualties on the Dutch, Rai
and every one of his men were killed. The
memorial is quite moving, and a small
museum provides some information about
the independence struggle on Bali.

Lots of bemos go up the Mengwi-Bedugul
road, and you can walk west from there to
Marga. It's a good area to walk in, but easier
to get around with your own transport.

SANGEH
About 20 km north of Denpasar, near the
village of Sangeh, stands the monkey forest
of **Bukit Sari**. It is featured, so the Balinese
say, in the *Ramayana*.

To kill the evil Rawana, king of Lanka, Hanuman had
to crush him between two halves of Mahameru, the
holy mountain. On his way to performing this task,
Hanuman dropped a piece of the mountain near
Sangeh, complete with a band of monkeys. Of course,
this sort of legend isn't unique – Hanuman dropped
chunks of landscape all over the place!

There's a grove of nutmeg trees in the monkey forest and a temple, **Pura Bukit Sari**,
with an interesting old garuda statue. Greedy
monkeys will pick your pockets in search of
peanuts, and have been known to steal hats,
sunglasses and even thongs from fleeing
tourists! Local kids may rescue the items, but
they charge a ransom for returning them.

This place is touristy, but the forest is cool,
green and shady, and the monkeys are cute
as well as cheeky. There's a charge for
parking and entry.

Getting There & Away
You can reach Sangeh by bemos which run

direct from Denpasar – they leave from a terminal at Wangaya, on Jl Kartini a block north of Jl Gajah Mada. There is also road access from Mengwi and from Ubud.

TABANAN

The town of Tabanan is the capital of the district of the same name. It's at the heart of the rice belt of southern Bali, the most fertile and prosperous rice-growing area on the island. It's also a great centre for dancing and gamelan playing. It's quite a large town, with shops, banks, hospital, market etc.

Tabanan's only attraction is the **Subak Museum**, with exhibits on the irrigation and cultivation of rice, and the intricate social systems which govern it. The museum is on the left, just before you come into town from Denpasar – look for the sign that says Mandala Mathika Subak. It's supposedly open every day, except Sunday, from 8 am to 6 pm, but hours are somewhat irregular – try before 11 am. A donation of 1000 rp is requested.

If you want to stay here, try *Hotel Taruna Jaya* (☎ (0361) 812478), south of the main road as you come into town from Denpasar. It's basic but OK, with rooms from 15,000 rp.

AROUND TABANAN

Agriculture is much more important tha tourism in the Tabanan district, but the ric fields are very scenic and there's a bit to see At **Kediri**, the Pasar Hewan is one of Bali' busiest markets for cattle and other animal

A little west of Tabanan, a road turns dow to the coast through **Krambitan** (or Keram bitan), a village noted for its old building (including two 17th century palaces), its tra dition of wayang-style painting, and its ow styles of music and dance. One of the palace provides accommodation and meals for vis itors, but it's usually for groups who mak arrangements in advance. Stylish old room cost about 50,000 rp. Phone (☎ (0361) 92667 for details.

A nice, secluded place to stay is *Bee Bee Bungalows & Restaurant* (or Bibi's) at Tibu biyu, four km south-west of Krambitan. charges 32,000/40,000 rp, plus 10,000 rp fc an extra bed, including breakfast. It's sur rounded by rice fields, the beach is close an it serves good meals.

North of Tabanan, the main road branche right to Penebel and continues to Duku village, where you can stay at *Taman Sa Bungalow & Coffee House* (☎ (0361) 812898

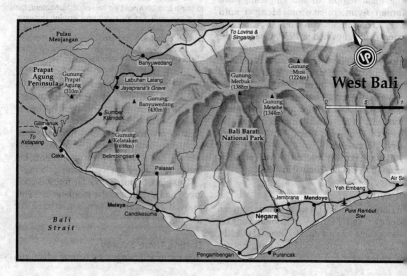

's a bit expensive at 45,000 rp, but a ~~fr~~iendly, out-of-the-way place from which ~~y~~ou can explore the area.

~~L~~ALANG-LINGGAH

~~A~~bout 29 km west of Tabanan near the ~~v~~illage of Lalang-Linggah, *Balian Beach ~~B~~ungalows* overlooks the Balian River (Yeh ~~B~~alian), close to the sea and surrounded by ~~c~~oconut plantations. Most of the accommo-~~d~~ation is in pavilions sleeping from three to ~~s~~ix, costing between 34,000 and 60,000 rp, ~~w~~ith a few cheaper bunk beds, and some ~~r~~ooms from 18,000/24,000 rp. It's a peaceful ~~p~~lace, and the management is friendly and ~~h~~elpful, but not obsessively efficient.

Across the river is a new place with New ~~A~~ge attractions. The *Sacred River Retreat* (☎ (0361) 730904) offers 'transformational ~~s~~eminars', yoga, meditation, massage and a ~~v~~egetarian restaurant in a very pretty setting. ~~S~~imple bamboo bungalows cost from ~~U~~S$20.

~~J~~EMBRANA COAST

~~J~~embrana is Bali's most sparsely populated ~~d~~istrict. The main road parallels the coast ~~m~~ost of the way to Negara, the district capital.

There's some beautiful scenery, but little tourist development along the way.

Medewi
About 25 km east of Negara, a large sign announces the side road south to 'Medewi Surfing Point'. The turn-off is just west of Pulukan village. The beach is nothing, but Medewi is noted for its *long* left-hand wave. It works best at mid to high tide on a two metre swell – get there early before the wind picks up.

Hotel Pantai Medewi (☎ (0365) 40029; formerly Medewi Beach Cottages) is near the beach. The better rooms are on the left side of the road from US$45/50, and there's a good swimming pool. Very ordinary, standard rooms are on the right side of the road for US$10/12.50. Behind these rooms, *Homestay Gede* has some very basic bamboo huts from around 10,000 rp.

The best value is off the main road a little further west, where *Tinjaya Bungalows* has quite pleasant rooms in two storey grass-and-bamboo cottages (20,000 rp downstairs, 25,000 rp upstairs), and some small rooms inside for 15,000 rp. The food here is recommended.

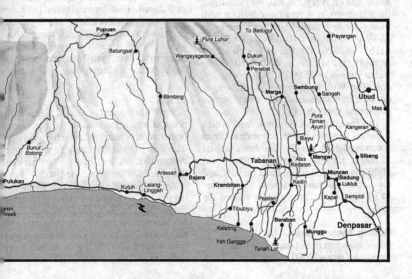

Rambut Siwi

The coastal temple of **Pura Rambut Siwi** at Rambut Siwi is picturesquely situated on a cliff top overlooking a long, wide stretch of beach. A superb temple with numerous shady frangipani trees, this is one of Bali's important coastal temples. It is another of the temples established in the 1500s by the priest Danghyang Nirartha who had such a good eye for ocean scenery (see also Tanah Lot and Pura Ulu Watu).

NEGARA

Negara, the capital of the Jembrana district, comes alive each year when the **bull races** take place around September and October (ask at the tourist office in Denpasar or Kuta for the exact dates). The racing animals are actually water buffaloes, normally docile creatures, which charge down a two km stretch of road pulling tiny chariots. Riders stand on top of the chariots forcing the bullocks on, sometimes by twisting their tails. Style also plays a part and points are awarded for the most elegant runner! Gambling is illegal on Bali but...

Places to Stay & Eat

Hotel Ana on Jl Ngurah Rai, the main street through town, is a very basic losmen with rooms for less than 10,000 rp. Nearby is *Hotel & Restaurant Wira Pada* (☎ (0365) 41161) at Jl Ngurah Rai 107, with rooms from 10,000/12,500 rp, 15,000/20,000 rp with a shower or 25,000/35,000 rp with air-con. The Wira Pada serves good food, as does the *Rumah Makan Puas*, a little further east on the same street.

The Denpasar to Gilimanuk road, which bypasses the town centre, has several cheap accommodation possibilities from around 15,000 rp, including *Hotel Ijo Gading*, west of the town, which is clean and friendly, and the *Losmen & Rumah Makan Taman Sari* (☎ (0365) 41154), on the other side of the road.

Getting There & Away

Public transport from Denpasar's Ubung terminal costs around 3500 rp – try to get a direct bus rather than a bemo that will stop at every village en route.

AROUND NEGARA

There's a bulge in the coastline south of Negara which has quite a few beaches though none are particularly attractive and some are dangerous. There are no tourist hotels here.

Jembrana

The town of Jembrana, once capital of the region, is the centre of the *gamelan jegog*, gamelan using huge bamboo instruments that produce a very low-pitched, resonant sound. Performances often feature a number of gamelan groups engaging in musical contest.

Belimbingsari & Palasari

Christian missionaries were discouraged by the Dutch, but sporadic activity resulted in a number of converts, many of whom were rejected by their own villages. In 1939 they were encouraged to resettle in Christian communities in the wilds of west Bali – Protestants in Belimbingsari and Catholics in Palasari. Both communities have survived, and each has a large and impressive church with distinctly Balinese architectural touches. They're easily accessible from the main road with your own transport, but public bemos are infrequent.

CEKIK

About a km before Gilimanuk, Cekik is the point at which the road to the north coast branches off to the right. Near the junction is a curious pagoda-like structure which commemorates sea battles in 1946 between independence forces and the Dutch.

Archaeological excavations at Cekik during the 1960s yielded the oldest evidence of human life on Bali. Finds include burial mounds with funerary offerings, bronze jewellery, axes, adzes and earthenware vessels from around 1000 BC, give or take a few centuries.

BALI BARAT NATIONAL PARK

On the south side of the road in Cekik is the headquarters of the West Bali National Park (Taman Nasional Bali Barat), open daily from 7 am to 2 pm. The visitors' centre has a little information about birds and animals in the park, and a relief map. This is the place to make arrangements for trekking in the southern part of the park.

In the northern part of the park at Labuhan Lalang, there's another visitors' centre (open daily from 7 am to 4 pm) where you can arrange short treks, but the main attraction is diving and snorkelling on Pulau Menjangan.

The national park covers nearly 20,000 hectares of the western tip of Bali. In addition, 50,000 hectares are protected in the national park extension, as well as nearly 7000 hectares of coral reef and coastal waters.

The main north coast road connects with Gilimanuk through the national park, and you don't have to pay any entrance fees just to drive through. If you want to visit any places of interest (they're called 'visitor objects'), you have to buy an entry ticket – 2000 rp for the day. In addition, you pay for parking at some of the visitor objects.

Flora & Fauna

Most of the natural vegetation in the park is a coastal savanna, with deciduous trees which become bare in the dry season. The southern slopes have more regular rainfall, and hence more tropical vegetation, while the coastal lowlands have extensive mangroves. Over 200 species of plants inhabit the various environments.

Animals include black monkey, leaf monkey and macaque; barking deer, sambar deer, mouse deer, Java deer and muncak; and squirrel, wild pig, buffalo, iguana, python and green snake. The bird life is prolific, with many of Bali's 300 species represented.

Bali Starling Bali's most famous bird is the Bali starling (*Leucopsar rothschildi*), also known as the Bali mynah, Rothschild's mynah or locally as *jalak putih*; it's Bali's only endemic bird. It is a striking white colour, with black tips to the wings and tail,

and a distinctive bright blue mask, and is greatly valued as a caged bird. Its natural population fell as low as 40 pairs, but efforts are being made to rebuild the population by reintroducing captive birds to the wild. Initially this is taking place on the Prapat Agung Peninsula, so trekking in this area is restricted, though you may be able to visit the Pre-Release Centre, where birds are introduced to life outside the cage.

Trekking

All trekking groups must be accompanied by an authorised guide, and you will also need to pay for transport to the starting point of the trek and back from the end point. Costs are 20,000 rp for a two hour trek, 40,000 rp for four hours, 60,000 rp for six hours, plus a park entry fee of 2000 rp per person and 500 rp insurance. Treks start early in the morning, so it's best to arrive the day before to make your arrangements. Alternatively, if you arrive at a visitors' centre before 7 am there will probably be a guide available.

A short two hour trek can be made from Belimbingsari, through thick forest and fruit plantations. A longer trek, about four hours, can be made from the microwave tower up Gunung Kelatakan and down to Ambyasari. A full day trek, around seven hours, is possible from Belimbingsari to Labuhan Lalang on the north coast. Short treks around Labuhan Lalang include mangrove and forest areas, while treks on Prapat Peninsula Agung are good for bird-watchers.

Labuhan Lalang & Pulau Menjangan

At Labuhan Lalang there's a small visitors' centre, a jetty for boats to Pulau Menjangan, a couple of warungs and a pleasant white sand beach. Coral formations close to the shore are good for snorkelling.

Excursions to Menjangan start at 60,000 rp for the half-hour boat trip, three hours on or around the island, and the return trip. If you want to stay longer, each additional hour costs about 5000 rp. Both snorkelling and scuba diving are excellent around the island, with great visibility, superb unspoiled coral, caves, lots of tropical fish and a spectacular

BALI

drop-off. Boats should use fixed moorings, which have been installed to prevent the coral being damaged by anchors. Diving is usually best in the early morning. Diving trips can be arranged from south Bali, but it's a long way to come for a day trip. It's better to go with one of the dive operations at Lovina, on the north coast.

Jayaprana's Grave

A 10 minute walk up some stone stairs from the south side of the road will bring you to this site. Jayaprana, the foster son of a 17th century king, planned to marry Leyonsari, a beautiful girl of humble origins. The king, however, also fell in love with Leyonsari and had Jayaprana killed. In a dream, Leyonsari learned the truth of Jayaprana's death and killed herself rather than marry the king. This Romeo and Juliet story is a common theme in Balinese folklore. From the site, there's a fine view to the north and, according to a national park pamphlet, '...you will feel another pleasure which you can't get in another place'.

Banyuwedang Hot Springs

Coming from the north coast, this is the first 'visitor object' you will encounter. It costs 2000 rp to soak in the hot spring water, which is supposedly therapeutic, but it's not an attractive place.

Places to Stay

There are no lodgings at all in the national park area. The closest places are in Gilimanuk, or at Pemuteran on the north coast. There's a campground near the park headquarters at Cekik.

Getting There & Away

There are frequent public buses and bemos between Gilimanuk and towns on both the south and north coast. These can drop you near the visitors' centres at Cekik or Labuhan Lalang respectively.

GILIMANUK

At the far western end of the island, Gilimanuk is the terminus for ferries across the strait to Java. There's a bus terminal and a market on the main street, as well as shops, cheap restaurants and a couple of places to change money. Most travellers buy combined bus and ferry tickets, and don't need to stop in Gilimanuk. There's little of interest here, but it's the closest accommodation to the national park if you want to trek or dive there early in the morning.

Places to Stay

There are several places to stay along the main street. Lestari Homestay is the closest to the national park (two km away), and can help arrange trekking. It has some basic rooms for around 12,000 rp, and an excellent little restaurant. Nirwana is close to the bemo terminal, and the most popular place for budget travellers – friendly, but nothing fancy, for around 10,000/12,000 rp. Nusantara II is 100m east of the main drag, through a split gate just the south of the ferry port. It's away from the busy road, and has dingy rooms from around 10,000 rp and some larger bungalows for about 25,000 rp. Rumah Makan Bakangun, on the main drag, is about the best place to eat.

Getting There & Away

Bus & Bemo The bus and bemo terminal is about a km south of the ferry port, on the east side of the road. There are direct buses to Denpasar's Ubung terminal (about 4000 rp) and to Singaraja (about 2500 rp), and more frequent bemos to places along the way.

Boat The ferries to Ketapang (near Banyuwangi) on Java leave every 15 to 30 minutes, 24 hours a day. The actual crossing takes under 30 minutes, but you'll spend longer than this loading, unloading and waiting around. One way fares are 1000 rp for an adult, 300 rp for a child, 1400 rp for a bicycle, 2700 rp for a motorcycle and 10,550 rp for a car. See the Banguwangi section in the Java chapter for details about onward connections from Ketapang.

Central Mountains

Bali's mountains are mostly volcanoes, some dormant, some definitely active. Apart from the mighty Gunung Agung (see the earlier East Bali section), the most interesting mountain landscapes are the Gunung Batur crater and the pretty area around Bedugul. A popular round trip goes to the north coast via Batur and returns south via Bedugul, but you can do it just as easily in the other direction. The central mountain range extends west of Bedugul, with some less travelled routes between the south and north coasts.

GUNUNG BATUR AREA

This spectacular area is like a giant dish, with half the bottom covered with water, and a cluster of volcanic cones growing in the middle. It's all in the district of Kintamani, and is often referred to by that name. Unfortunately, the area has a well-deserved reputation as a money-grubbing place where you're badgered to buy things, hassled by would-be guides and where you need to keep an eye on your gear.

Information

You have to buy an entry ticket just to get into the Batur area – 1100 rp per person, plus 400 rp for a car, 1000 rp for a camera and 500 rp for a video camera. Keep the tickets if you plan to drive back and forth around the crater rim or you may have to pay again.

Almost opposite the road down to the lake is a tourist office, Yayasa Bintang Danu (☎ (0366) 23370), which has useful information about transport, trekking and so on. It opens daily from 9 am to 3 pm. Check here before you're taken in by one of the local hustlers. Further west is a bank (which will change travellers cheques), a wartel and a post office.

Penelokan

Penelokan, on the rim of the crater, has superb views across to Gunung Batur and down to Lake Batur. It can get surprisingly chilly up here so come prepared. Clouds often roll in over the crater, obscuring the view and making the crater-rim towns cold and miserable. There's one place to stay, but if you intend to tour around the lake or climb the volcano, accommodation down in either Kedisan or Toyah Bungkah is more convenient.

The *Lakeview Restaurant & Homestay* (☎ (0366) 51464) teeters right on the edge of the crater, with tiny economy rooms with shared bathroom for US$7.50, more comfortable bungalow rooms for US$15 and two large family rooms, with hot water, at US$30. It's not great value, but the view is outstanding. The restaurant is OK and has some well-placed outdoor tables.

Other restaurants around the crater rim are geared to bus-loads of tour groups. Large ones include the *Caldera Batur, Gunawan, Puri Selera, Puri Dewata* and *Kintamani Restaurant*. They all have fine views and prepare buffet lunches from around 15,000 rp. The *Restaurant Rama* is less expensive, and there are also some cheap *warungs*.

Getting There & Away From Denpasar, you can either get a Kintamani-bound bus from Batubulan terminal (2000 rp), which will pass through Penelokan, or take one of the more frequent bemos to Gianyar (1000 rp) or Bangli (1200 rp), then another one up the mountain. From Ubud, go first to Gianyar.

The two main routes to Penelokan, via Bangli or Tampaksiring, are both good roads. The other roads are OK but have very little public transport. The road down to Rendang is rougher, but has great views.

Going to the lakeside, there are public bemos to Kedisan (500 rp), Toya Bungkah (1000 rp) and Songan (1500 rp). They're supposed to run about every half-hour in the morning, and every hour in the afternoon, but at any time they will try to pressure tourists into chartering a whole bemo, which will cost at least 20,000/ 25,000/30,000 rp respectively to the three villages, with a maximum of eight people.

Perama runs two buses a day to Kintamani from Kuta and Sanur via Ubud. They stop at

BALI

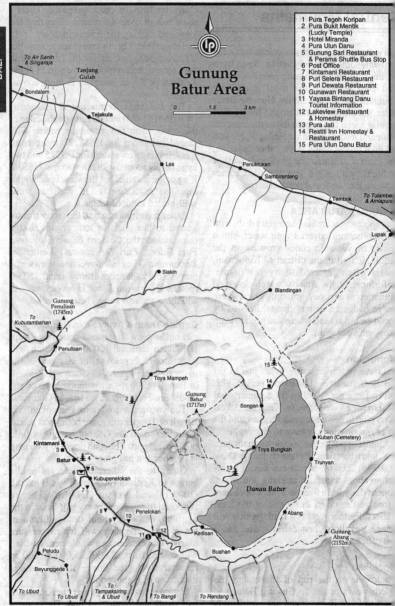

Gunung Batur Area

0   1.5   3 km

1 Pura Tegeh Koripan
2 Pura Bukit Mentik
   (Lucky Temple)
3 Hotel Miranda
4 Pura Ulun Danu
5 Gunung Sari Restaurant
   & Perama Shuttle Bus Stop
6 Post Office
7 Kintamani Restaurant
8 Puri Selera Restaurant
9 Puri Dewata Restaurant
10 Gunawan Restaurant
11 Yayasa Bintang Danu
   Tourist Information
12 Lakeview Restaurant
   & Homestay
13 Pura Jati
14 Restiti Inn Homestay &
   Restaurant
15 Pura Ulun Danu Batur

To Air Sanih
& Singaraja

Tanjung
Gulah

Bondalem

Tejakula

Les

Penuktukan

Sambirenteng

Tembok

To Tulambe
& Amlapura

Lupak

Siakin

Blandingan

Gunung
Penulisan
(1745m)

To
Kubutambahan

Penulisan

Toya Mampeh

Gunung
Batur
(1717m)

15

14

Songan

2

Kintamani

Batur

3

4

5

6

7

Kubupenelokan

8

9

10

Penelokan

11

12

Kedisan

Buahan

Toya Bungkah

Kuban (Cemetery)

Trunyan

Danau Batur

Abang

Gunung
Abang
(2152m)

Peludu

Beyunggede

To Ubud

To Ubud

To
Tampaksiring
& Ubud

To Bangli

To Rendang

e Gunung Sari restaurant, and will help
rrange a charter bemo down to the lakeside
illages. It's a good option if you want to
ninimise hassles.

Getting Around Orange bemos shuttle back
nd forth around the crater rim, running reg-
larly between Penelokan and Kintamani
200 rp).

Batur & Kintamani

The village of Batur used to be down in the
rater. A violent eruption of the volcano in
917 killed thousands of people, and des-
royed more than 60,000 homes and 2000
emples. Although the village was wiped out,
he lava flow stopped at the entrance to the
illagers' temple.

aking this as a good omen, they rebuilt their village,
nly to have Batur erupt again in 1926. This time the
ava flow covered all but the loftiest temple shrine.
ortunately, the Dutch administration anticipated the
ruption and evacuated the village, partly by force, so
ery few lives were lost. The village was relocated up
n the crater rim, and the surviving shrine was also
noved up and placed in the new temple, Pura Ulun
Ďanu, which was commenced in 1927. It's one of
Bali's nine directional temples.

The villages of Batur and Kintamani run
ogether – it's basically one main street
round the western rim of the crater. A large
nd colourful morning **market** is held every
nree days. It's a productive fruit and vege-
able growing area, though the orange crops
ave recently been depleted by disease.

The only recommendable place to stay is
he *Hotel Miranda*, on the west side of the
oad about six km from Penelokan. The
ooms cost 7000 to 12,000 rp for singles/
oubles, including breakfast; the most
xpensive ones have bathrooms. It has good
ood and an open fire at night. Made Senter,
/ho runs it, is very friendly and informative,
nd also acts as a guide for treks into the
rater and around Gunung Batur.

Getting There & Away From Denpasar
Batubulan station) a bemo to Kintamani is
bout 2000 rp, though there will be more

frequent bemos from Gianyar or Bangli.
Buses run between Kintamani and Singaraja
on the north coast for 2000 rp.

Penulisan
The road continues along the crater rim
beyond Kintamani, gradually climbing
higher. If it's clear, there are more fine views
down over the crater. At Penulisan, a steep
flight of steps leads to Bali's highest temple,
Pura Tegeh Koripan, at 1745m. Towering
over the temple is a shrine to a new and
powerful god – Bali's television repeater
mast! The main road descends to the north
coast, but a smaller road does a scenic detour
around the north rim of the crater.

Around Lake Batur
A hairpin-bend road winds its way down
from Penelokan to Kedisan on the shore of
the lake. To get to the hot springs at Toya
Bungkah, take the quaint little road around
the lakeside from Kedisan over many turns
and switchbacks and across the lava field.
The road continues to Songan, under the
north-eastern rim of the crater, and a rough
side road goes right around Gunung Batur to
rejoin the Penelokan-Kedisan road. On the
north-west side of the volcano, near Toya
Mampeh, the road crosses a huge 'flow' of
solidified black lava from 1974. You can
climb to the summit of Gunung Batur in just
a few hours from either Kedisan or Toya
Bungkah.

Expect to be hassled by touts from top to
bottom and around the lakeshore. They will
offer transport or help in finding a place to
stay, but their real objective is to overcharge
you as a trekking guide. Finding a room
yourself is not difficult.

Kedisan Coming into Kedisan from Penelokan you reach a T-intersection. Turning left
towards Toya Bungkah you come first to
Segara Bungalows (☎ (0366) 51136), with
basic rooms from 8000/10,000 rp, and better
rooms with hot water for up to 25,000 rp. A
bit further on is *Surya Homestay* (☎ (0366)
51139), which also has a variety of rooms
from 10,000 to 25,000 rp. Both places are

thick with would-be guides, but are actually some distance from the start of the treks up Gunung Batur. Check the room and discuss the price before you decide.

Buahan Turning right at the bottom of hill you go around to Buahan, where market gardens go down to the lakeshore. *Baruna Cottages* (☎ (0366) 51221) is a peaceful place to stay, with a pleasant restaurant and singles/doubles with mandi from 8000/ 10,000 to 10,000/15,000 rp. The new *Hotel Buahan* (☎ (0366) 51217) is clean but characterless, and charges 20,000 rp for a night or 10,000 rp for a 'short stay'.

Trunyan & Kuban The village of Trunyan is squeezed tightly between Lake Batur and the outer crater rim. This is a Bali Aga village, inhabited by remnants of the original Balinese, the people who predate the Majapahit arrival. It's not an interesting or friendly place. It's famous for its four-metre-high statue of the village's guardian spirit, Ratu Gede Pancering Jagat, but you're not allowed to see it. There are only a couple of the traditional Bali Aga-style dwellings, some old structures in the temple and a huge banyan tree, said to be over 1100 years old.

A little beyond Trunyan, and accessible only by the lake (there's no path), is the village cemetery at Kuban. The people of Trunyan do not cremate or bury their dead – they lie them out in bamboo cages to decompose. A collection of skulls and bones lies on a stone platform. This is a tourist trap for those with morbid tastes.

Getting Around the Lake Boats to Trunyan leave from a jetty near the middle of Kedisan, where there is a ticket office and a secure carpark (and a few persistent hawkers of second-rate souvenirs). The listed price for a boat for a round trip stopping at Trunyan, the cemetery at Kuban, the hot springs at Toya Bungkah and returning to Kedisan is around 37,000 to 44,000 rp depending on the number of passengers (maximum is seven). A group of four people works out at 10,150 rp each, including entry fees, insurance and

a not very informative guide. It's cheape with more passengers, but still not worth i The first boat leaves at 8 am and the last at pm; the complete trip takes about 2½ hour

Don't try hiring a canoe and paddlin yourself – the lake is bigger than it looks an it can get very choppy. A better alternative to follow the track around the lakeside fro Buahan to Trunyan, an easy hour or two walk. The walk will be the best part of th trip. From Trunyan you may be able to nego tiate a cheaper boat to the cemetery and h springs, but don't count on it.

Toya Bungkah (Tirta)

Directly across the lake from Trunyan is th small settlement of Toya Bungkah, als known as Tirta, with its hot springs – *tir* and *toya* both mean 'water'. It's a grubb little village, but many travellers stay here climb Gunung Batur in the early morning and most get out as quickly as possible afte wards. There's a ticket office as you ente which charges 1000 rp for entry into the h springs area, plus 800 rp for a car and 100 for insurance.

The hot springs feed a small bathing po before flowing into the lake. The water soothingly hot, ideal for aching muscles afte a volcano climb, but the pool is not ver attractive and costs 1000 rp. A new an bigger bathing pool is being constructed.

Places to Stay Accommodation here mostly pretty basic. On the left as you ente *Arlina Bungalows* (☎ (0366) 51165) is on of the better places, with clean, good-size rooms at 10,000/15,000 rp for single doubles, and a good restaurant. Next on th left, *Under the Volcano Homestay* (one two by that name) has OK singles/double from around 8000 to 15,000 rp.

Nyoman Pangus Homestay & Restauran on the right as you come in from Kedisan, not bad, with rooms at 10,000 to 15,000 r Down the slope on the right is *Amertha Bungalows*, which are a bit fancier and mor expensive at 20,000/25,000 rp.

The *Balai Seni Toyabungkah* (Toy Bungkah Arts Centre), up the hill on th

vestern side of the village, has the occasional arty group of visitors, but mostly it's
ust a slightly better place to stay, with rooms
rom 15,000 rp and bungalows from 25,000
p, sometimes with hot water. *Laguna Home-
tay* (☎ (0366) 51297) is new, clean and
uite well run, with smallish rooms at around
0,000/12,000 rp.

Awangga Bungalows at the other end of
he village advertises itself as the 'cheapest',
t around 10,000 rp, including breakfast.
Visma Tirta Yastra, right by the lake, also
sks 10,000 rp for rooms with shared bath-
oom. There are a few other places around
ere charging around 10,000 to 15,000 rp for
basic room with a basic breakfast, possibly
nore in the high season. *Abadi Homestay* is
ot a bad choice.

Lakeside Cottages (☎ (0366) 51249), on
he north side of the village, are bigger and
etter built than the standard Toya Bungkah
laces, and quite good value at 20,000/
5,000 rp. The best rooms at US$25 are close
o the lake and have hot water. The new, three
torey *Puri Bening Hayato Hotel* has com-
ortable, characterless rooms with good
iews of the lake for about US$55, and much
maller rooms without a view for about
JS$35.

Places to Eat Fresh fish from the lake is the
ocal speciality, usually barbecued with
nion and garlic – they're tiny but tasty.
Nyoman Pangus and *Arlina* both do a good
ersion of the barbecued fish. *Amertha Res-
aurant* has a great position down by the lake,
slightly more varied menu and slightly
igher prices.

Getting There & Away It's not easy to get a
ublic bemo out of Toya Bungkah. Some
huttle buses go to other tourist areas, but
hey're really charter services – you'll need
t least four passengers.

Songan
he road continues from Toya Bungkah
round the lake to Songan, quite a large
illage with some old buildings, and market
ardens which extend to the edge of the lake.

Not many tourists come this far, but you can
stay at the *Restiti Inn Homestay & Restaurant* (☎ (0366) 51287), north of the village.
It's a neat little place, charging 12,000 rp for
a room with a mandi.

At the end of the road there's a temple at
the crater edge – from there you can climb to
the top of the outer crater rim in just 15
minutes and see the east coast, only about
five km away. It's an easy downhill stroll to
the coast road at Lupak, but there's no direct
public transport back to Toya Bungkah.

Trekking
Soaring up in the centre of the huge outer
crater is the cone of Gunung Batur (1717m).
It has erupted a number of times this century,
most recently in 1971, 1974 and 1994, and
has a number of volcanic features, including
lava flows, lava tubes, parasitic cones and
craters-within-craters. The usual trek is to
climb to the top for sunrise – it's a magnificent sight, though it can get crowded up
there. Wisps of steam issuing from cracks in
the rock, and the surprising warmth of the
ground, indicate that things are still happening down below. At the summit, you can
walk right around the rim of the volcanic
cone and make a longer descent by the new
volcanic cones south of the main peak.

On the way, people with ice buckets sell
cold drinks – it's more than 2500 rp for a
small coke, but it's been carried a long way.
The *warung* at the top has tea and coffee
(1500 rp), sometimes jaffles (2500 rp) and a
brilliant view (free).

If you have a reasonable sense of direction, and it's not totally dark when you start
climbing, you won't need a guide for the
usual routes, but if you're not confident
about it, take a guide. One day the track to
the summit may be properly marked, but the
guides/hustlers do not favour this. In the
rainy season it may be cloudy in the morning
and clear somewhat during the day, so there's
no value in a pre-dawn start.

Information There are two good places to
get information about trekking – Arlina Bungalows, on the left as you come into Toyah

Bungkah, and Jero Wijaya Tourist Service, towards the lake at the other end of town. They both have maps and background information about the area, and can arrange a guide at reasonable rates if you think you need one.

Guides In and around Toya Bungkah you will be hassled by people offering to guide you up the mountain, sometimes asking outrageous prices. You should be able to get someone to guide you up the mountain for about 10,000 rp, with haggling, but they will try to get several people and charge them 10,000 rp each. Treks which take longer, with more interesting routes on the way down, cost more. Jero Wijaya Tours charges US$10 per person for a 'short tour' to the top and back, US$12 for a longer trek, and US$15 for a trip which goes across all the central cones and includes transport back from the far side (minimum four people). Don't pay more than 20,000 rp for a simple trek up the mountain, and don't pay all the money in advance.

Some trips include breakfast at the top, and may include the novelty of cooking eggs or bananas in the steaming holes at the top of the volcano. Some of these holes are extremely hot and it is indeed possible to cook eggs in them. By all means take some food to the top, but please ensure it does not result in any rubbish being left on the mountain.

North-East Route The easiest route is from the north-east, where a new track enables you to take a car to within about 45 minutes' walk from the top. From Toya Bungkah take the road north-east towards Songan, and take the left fork after about 3.5 km. Follow this small road for another 1.7 km to a well-signed track on the left, which climbs another km or so to a parking area. From here a walking track is easily followed to the top. The parking area is not secure, so don't leave anything of value in your car or even a helmet with your motorcycle. It's not easy to get to this trailhead without your own transport.

Toya Bungkah Route From Toya Bungkah walk out of town on the road to Kedisan and turn right just after the office where you buy the entry ticket. There are quite a few paths at first but they all rejoin sooner or later – just keep going uphill, tending south-west and then west. After half an hour or so you'll be on a ridge with quite a well-defined track; keep going up. It gets pretty steep toward the top, and it can be hard walking over the loose volcanic sand. It takes about two hours to get to the top.

Other Routes Other popular routes are from Kedisan or from near Pura Jati, the temple on the Kedisan-Toya Bungkah road. Another possible route is from Kintamani, first descending the outer crater rim and then climbing the inner cone.

For an interesting round trip, climb Gunung Batur from Toya Bungkah, follow the rim around to the other side, explore the new volcanic cones south of the main peak, then go down through the lava fields to Pura Jati. Climbing up, spending a reasonable time on the top and then strolling back down can all be done in four or five hours.

LAKE BRATAN AREA

Approaching Bedugul from the south, you gradually leave the rice terraces behind and ascend into the cool, damp mountain country. There are several places to stay on the southern slopes and near the lake, and Bedugul makes a good base for walking trips around the other lakes and surrounding hills. There is also an interesting temple, botanical gardens, a colourful market, an excellent golf course and a variety of activities on Lake Bratan itself.

Taman Rekreasi Bedugul

The Bedugul Leisure Park (Taman Rekreasi Bedugul) is at the southern end of the lake. It's along the first road to the right as you come in from the south, and it costs 500 rp to get into the lakeside area. Along the waterfront are an expensive restaurant, souvenir shops, a hotel and facilities for a number of water activities. A motor boat is US$15 for lf an hour and a jet-ski costs US$10 for 15 inutes. Water-skiing and parasailing are so available. You can hire a canoe and addle across to the temple – it costs US$10 the ticket office for half an hour, but independent touts come down to 15,000 rp for 'a ong time'; it's cheaper if you go around the ke past the Ashram Guesthouse.

otanical Gardens

Torth of Bedugul the road climbs a hill and escends again to an intersection, conspicuously marked with a large, phallic sculpture f a sweet-corn cob. The smaller road leads est up to the entrance of the Kebun Raya ka Karya Bali, the botanical gardens, established in 1959 as a branch of the national otanical gardens at Bogor, near Jakarta. hey cover more than 120 hectares on the ower slopes of Gunung Pohon, and have an xtensive collection of trees and some 500 pecies of orchid. It's a lovely place – cool, hady and scenic. It's usually quiet, but roups of Balinese like to come for picnics, specially on Sunday when the atmosphere more festive. Some plants are labelled with heir botanical names, but apart from that here is almost nothing in the way of visitor nformation. Some visitors have been annoyed here by stray dogs – carry a stick to deter hem. The gardens open every day from 7 or am to 4.30 pm. Entry is 500 rp and parking s 500 rp for a car, 150 rp for a motorcycle. You can drive a car right into the gardens for 500 rp, but it's better to walk.

Candikuning

Continuing north on the main road, past the botanical gardens turn-off, you'll see the lower and produce **market** on the left. It's t its best early in the morning when truck oads of flowers, fruit and vegetables are dispatched to the hotels and restaurants in outh Bali.

The road swings back to the lakeside past he Ashram Guesthouse, and there's a small anding where you can hire canoes more heaply than in Bedugul – maybe 10,000 rp or half an hour, 15,000 rp for 'a long time',

which should enable you to paddle around most of the lake.

Gunung Catur

It's possible to paddle across Lake Bratan to some caves which the Japanese used during WWII. You can also walk there in about an hour. From the caves a very well-marked path ascends to the top of Gunung Catur (2096m). It takes about two hours for the climb up and an hour back down. The final bit is steep and you should take some water. There is an old temple on the summit with lots of monkeys.

Pura Ulun Danau

Past Candikuning, actually projecting into the lake, is the Hindu/Buddhist temple of Pura Ulun Danau. It's very picturesque, with a large banyan tree at the entrance, attractive gardens and one courtyard isolated on a tiny island in the lake. The temple, founded in the 17th century, is dedicated to Dewi Danau, the goddess of the waters. Ulu Danau has classical Hindu thatched-roof merus and an adjoining Buddhist stupa. There are the usual admission and parking charges.

Around the Lakes

North of Candikuning, the road passes an impressive split gate on the right. This is not a temple, but the entrance to the Bali Handara Kosaido Country Club, with its beautifully situated, world-class **golf course**. Green fees for 18 holes are US$72.50, or US$87.50 on weekends, and you can hire a half-set of clubs for US$12.

Further north is the Pancasari market, with a selection of warungs, and a public bemo stop.

If you continue to Lake Buyan, there's a fine walk around the southern side of Buyan, then over the saddle to the adjoining, smaller **Lake Tamblingan**. From there you can walk uphill, then west to Munduk (see further in this section), or go around the northern side of the lakes back to Bedugul.

BALI

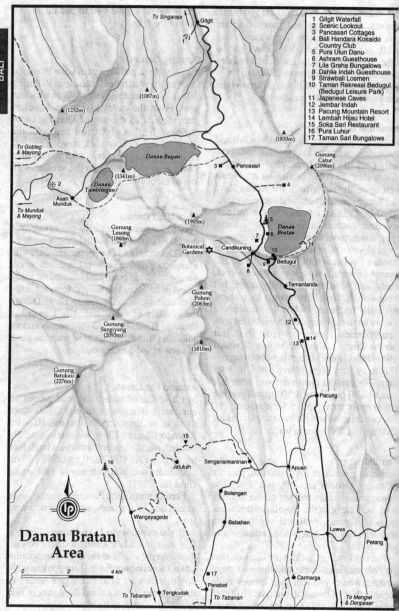

1 Gitgit Waterfall
2 Scenic Lookout
3 Pancasari Cottages
4 Bali Handara Kosaido
   Country Club
5 Pura Ulun Danu
6 Ashram Guesthouse
7 Lila Graha Bungalows
8 Dahlia Indah Guesthouse
9 Strawbali Losmen
10 Taman Rekreasi Bedugul
   (Bedugul Leisure Park)
11 Japanese Caves
12 Jembar Indah
13 Pacung Mountain Resort
14 Lembah Hijau Hotel
15 Soka Sari Restaurant
16 Pura Luhur
17 Taman Sari Bungalows

To Singaraja
Gitgit

(1087m)

(1232m)

To Gobleg & Mayong

(1833m)

Danau Buyan

Gunung Catur (2096m)

3 Pancasari

4

Danau Tamblingan (1341m)

2

Asan Munduk

To Munduk & Mayong

(1905m)

7 5
6
Danau Bratan
10 11

Gunung Lesong (1860m)

Botanical Gardens

Candikuning

8 9 Bedugul

Temantanda

Gunung Pohon (2063m)

12

Gunung Sangiyang (2093m)

(1810m)

13 14

Gunung Batukau (2276m)

Pacung

15

16

Jatuluih

Senganankaninan

Apuan

Bolangan

Luwus

Petang

Wangayagede

Babahan

Danau Bratan Area

0   2   4 km

17

Carmarga

To Tabanan
Tengkudak

Penebel
To Tabanan

To Mengwi & Denpasar

Places to Stay

Accommodation around Bedugul is of indifferent quality, and generally overpriced.

On the road up to Bedugul from the south, *Pacung Mountain Resort* (☎ (0368) 21038) is a top-end place perched on a steep hillside looking west to Gunung Batukau. It has a restaurant, pool and comfortable rooms from US$75/80 to US$95, but it gives a good discount when it's quiet. *Lembah Hijau Hotel* (☎ (0368) 21020), on the other side of the road, has great views, minimal service and very ordinary rooms for 50,000 rp. Further up the hill, *Jembar Indah* (☎ (0368) 21136) is less attractive, a bit cheaper, but still overpriced at 20,000/25,000 rp for singles/doubles with no breakfast.

Opposite the turn-off to the Taman Rekreasi, *Strawbali* (☎ (0368) 23467) is an OK little losmen, with a restaurant and small rooms at 20,000/25,000 rp, including breakfast and hot water. Inside the Taman Rekreasi area, the *Bedugul Hotel* (☎ (0368) 21197) has motel-style rooms near the lake for 35,000 to 45,000 rp, and older, quieter rooms on the slope behind from 40,000 rp.

Continuing north, the road climbs higher up the hillside to the turn-off for the pricey *Bukit Permai Hotel* (☎ (0368) 21443), with rooms from 50,000 to 100,000 rp, including tax, breakfast, TV, hot water, a fireplace and a great view. It's OK, but doesn't look like a fun place to stay.

On a side road near the corn-on-the-cob junction, look for *Dahlia Indah Guesthouse* (☎ (0368) 21233), a neat new place which charges 20,000 rp. It doesn't include breakfast or hot water, but at least it's clean. Just north of the market, *Sari Atha Inn* (☎ (0368) 21011) has adequate rooms from 15,000 to 20,000 rp, but might be noisy.

Back on the lakeside road you come to the *Lila Graha Bungalows* (☎ (0368) 21446), up a steep drive on the left. It was an old Dutch rest house, but the accommodation is in newer buildings from 35,000 to 60,000 rp. It's well located, but the staff can be a bit sleazy. On the other side of the road, right by the lake, is the popular *Ashram Guesthouse* (☎ (0368) 21101), with basic rooms for 15,000 rp with shared bathroom, standard rooms for 30,000 rp, and up to 70,000 rp for the best rooms. It's not very good value.

Top-end accommodation can be found at the *Bali Handara Kosaido Country Club* (☎ (0362) 22646; fax (0361) 287358) from US$75 to US$350, plus 21% tax and service. As well as the golf course, there are tennis courts, a gym and a Japanese bath.

Further north, a driveway goes west of the road to *Pancasari Cottages* (☎ (0362) 21148), with tennis courts and comfortable cottages from US$40 to US$100.

Places to Eat

At the Taman Rekreasi, the lakeside *restaurant* is nicely located but expensive, while the restaurant at the *Bedugul Hotel* specialises in buffet lunches for tour groups. The Candikuning *market* has a few good places for a snack. Further north, the lakeside *Taliwang Bersaudara* is one of the better options, while cheap *warungs* near Pura Ulun Danu should provide a reasonable meal.

Getting There & Away

Buses from Denpasar's Ubung terminal charge about 2500 rp to Singaraja, and no less if you get off at Bedugul. From Singaraja's southern bus terminal, it's about 1200 rp to Bedugul. The Perama stop is at the Pura Ulun Danu restaurant (☎ (0362) 21191), but they'll stop at Bedugul or Candikuning.

MUNDUK

West of Lake Tamblingan, a beautiful winding road goes to Munduk, a ridge-top village with a few old Dutch buildings. *Puri Lumbung Cottages* (☎ (0362) 92810), on the right side of the road as you come into town, can arrange trekking guides, and it has a map which shows nearby waterfalls and the location of seven art installations in the area. It's a delightful place to stay, with well-finished rice-barn bungalows for US$43/50. Its restaurant has a wonderful outlook and serves an excellent lunch or dinner with main courses at around 4000 to 8000 rp.

There is simpler, cheaper accommodation

at three homestays just down the road, the *Guru Ratna*, *Meme Surung* and *Mekel Ragi*, for 20,000 to 30,000 rp, including breakfast. They're a bit pricey, but the excellent location and the ambience of the old Dutch buildings make them worth it. For enquiries and bookings, call the Puri Lumbung Cottages phone number.

About seven km from Munduk, up a steep road, is the village of Gesing, where the *Gesing Inn* is ultra-basic, but superbly located and cheap at 10,000 rp. The owner is friendly, but doesn't speak English.

The easiest way to get to Munduk is with your own transport, but Puri Lumbung Cottages might be able to collect you from the bemo stop in Pancasari, north of Bedugul.

GITGIT

Heading north from the Lake Bratan area, a very scenic road goes to Singaraja, about 30 km away. On the way there's the beautiful **Gitgit waterfall**, west of the road just past Gitgit village. There are plenty of signs and a carpark. You buy a ticket at the office near the west side of the road, and follow the concrete path between the rows of souvenir stalls for about 500m. The *Gitgit Hotel* has clean but uninteresting rooms for 25,000/35,000 rp, or 10,000 rp more with hot water.

GUNUNG BATUKAU

West of the Mengwi-Bedugul road is 2276m Gunung Batukau, the 'coconut-shell mountain'. This is the third of Bali's three major mountains and the holy peak of the western end of the island.

Pura Luhur

Pura Luhur, on the slopes of Batukau, was the state temple when Tabanan was an independent kingdom. The temple has a seven roofed meru to Maha Dewa, the mountain's guardian spirit, as well as shrines for the three mountain lakes: Bratan, Tamblingan and Buyan. It's surrounded by forest, and often damp and misty. There are several routes to Pura Luhur, but the easiest is directly north from Tabanan via the village of Wangayagede.

Jatuluih

A rough but very scenic route to Pura Luhur turns off the Mengwi-Bedugul road near Pacung, and goes via Apuan to Senganan-kaninan. From there an even rougher road goes in a westerly direction to Wangayagede via Jatuluih. There's a good lunch stop at the *Soka Sari Restaurant*, just east of Jatuluih.

ROUTES THROUGH PUPUAN

Less travelled routes over the mountains branch north from the Denpasar-Gilimanuk road, one from Pulukan and the other from Antasari. They meet at Pupuan before dropping down to Seririt, on the north coast to the west of Singaraja.

The Pulukan to Pupuan road climbs steeply up from the coast, providing fine views back down to the sea. The route runs through spice-growing country and you'll often see spices laid out on mats by the road to dry – the smell of cloves rises up to meet you. At one point, the narrow road actually runs right through an enormous bunut tree which bridges the road.

The road from Antasari starts through rice fields, climbs into the spice-growing country, then descends through the coffee growing areas to Pupuan.

If you continue another 12 km or so towards the north coast you reach Mayong, where you can turn east to Munduk and on to the Lake Bratan area.

North Bali

North Bali, the district of Buleleng, makes an interesting contrast with the south of the island. It comprises a narrow coastal plain facing tranquil, reef-sheltered waters, with a steep, hilly backdrop. The capital, Singaraja, is largely untouched by tourism, while the Lovina Beach strip, just to the west, is popular with budget travellers. Many arriving from Java go straight from Gilimanuk to the north coast, avoiding the southern tourist areas.

The Dutch had established control of

north Bali nearly 50 years before their power extended to the south. In 1845 the rajas of Buleleng and Karangasem formed an alliance to conquer other Balinese states, or possibly to resist the Dutch. In either case, the Dutch were worried, and attacked Buleleng and Karangasem in 1846, 1848 and 1849, seizing control of the north in the third attempt. From that time, the Dutch interfered increasingly in Balinese affairs, and Singaraja became the seat of the Dutch administration on Bali.

Buleleng has a unique artistic and cultural tradition. Its dance troupes are highly regarded and a number of dance styles have originated here, including Joged and Janger. Gold and silver work, weaving, pottery, musical-instrument making and temple design all show distinctive local styles. The Sapi Gerumbungan bull race is a Buleleng tradition and quite different from the races of Negara, in south-west Bali. Events are held at Kaliasem, near Lovina, on Independence Day (August 17), Singaraja Day (March 31) and other occasions.

SINGARAJA

In postcolonial Indonesia, Singaraja remained the administrative centre for Bali and the islands of Nusa Tenggara until 1953. It is one of the few places on Bali where there are visible reminders of the Dutch period, but there are also Chinese and Muslim influences.

With a population of around 96,000, Singaraja is a busy town, but orderly, even quiet compared with Denpasar. Some interesting colonial buildings can be seen on pleasant tree-lined streets, and small workshops produce handwoven songket fabric and fine silver work. It's also an educational and cultural centre, with two university campuses giving the city a substantial student population.

For years the port of Singaraja was the usual arrival point for visitors to Bali – it's where all the prewar travel books started. Singaraja is hardly used as a harbour now, due to siltation and lack of protection from bad weather. There are still some old warehouses near the waterfront though, and it's an interesting area to walk around. A conspicuous monument here has a statue pointing out to sea. It commemorates a freedom fighter who was killed by gunfire from a Dutch warship early in the struggle for independence. Nearby is a colourful Chinese temple.

Orientation & Information

The main commercial area is in the north-east part of town behind the old harbour – traffic does a one way loop, clockwise around this block.

The helpful tourist office (☎ 61141) is on Jl Veteran, on the south side of town. It's generally open Monday to Friday from 8 to 11 am. The BCA bank does cash advances on Visa and MasterCard.

The post office and a wartel are near each other on Jl Imam Bonjol, and there's a cheaper Telkom wartel on Jl Udayana.

Gedung Kirtya Historical Library

This small institution has a collection of around 3000 old Balinese manuscripts inscribed on lontar (palm). These lontar books include literary, mythological, historical and religious works. Some older written works, in the form of inscribed metal plates, are kept here, but most valuable works have been transferred to Denpasar. There are also some old publications in Dutch. You're welcome to visit, but it's more a place for scholars than tourists. It opens from 7 am to 1 pm Monday to Friday – donation requested.

Pura Jagatnatha

This is Singaraja's main temple, a new edifice and impressively large. It's not usually open to visitors, but you can see some of the elaborate carved stone decoration from the outside.

Places to Stay

There are plenty of places to stay and eat in Singaraja but most tourists go straight to the beaches, only a few km away. It's a pity because Singaraja is quite an interesting place.

Most of the hotels are principally used by

local business travellers. You'll find a string of hotels along Jl Jen Achmad Yani, starting in the east with the *Hotel Sentral* (☎ 21896), a good choice with basic singles/doubles at 8000/12,000 rp, or 25,000/32,500 rp with air-con. The *Hotel Duta Karya* (☎ 21467), on the other side of the road, is OK at 14,000/16,000 rp, or 27,000/33,000 rp with air-con. Further west again, and handy to the bus terminal, are the *Hotel Saku Bindu* (☎ 21791), at 18,000 rp a double, and the *Hotel Gelar Sari* (☎ 21495).

Wijaya Hotel (☎ 21915), a few hundred metres from the bus terminal on the east side of Jl Sudirman, is the most comfortable place, with standard rooms at 12,000/14,000 rp, up to 65,000/70,000 rp for the best room with air-con and hot water.

Places to Eat

There are plenty of eateries, including a batch of places in a small square on Jl Jen Achmad Yani. You'll find the popular *Restaurant Gandhi* here, with a good Chinese menu and glossy, clean surroundings. Across the road is the *Restaurant Segar II*, where a good Chinese meal will run to about 7000 rp. On the same street, *Cafeteria Koka* is popular with students. In the evening there are *food stalls* in the Jl Durian night market. There are also a few *restaurants* along Jl Imam Bonjol, and some *warungs* near the two bus terminals.

Getting There & Away

Singaraja is the north coast's main transportation centre, with three bus terminals. From the Sukasada terminal, on the south side of town, buses to Denpasar (Ubung terminal) via Bedugul leave about every half-hour from 6 am to 4 pm (around 2500 rp). Buses to/from the west use the Banyuasri terminal, especially to Gilimanuk (2000 rp; two hours). Bemos to Lovina should be 600 rp, but it may be easier to get this price along the road than at the terminal. The eastern terminal, Penarukan, is a couple of km east of town, and has bemos to Air Sanih (500 rp) and Amlapura (via the coast road; 2000 rp). Full-sized buses go to Kintamani (1500 rp) via Kubutambahan. Bemos around town and between the three main terminals cost 400 rp.

There are also direct night buses to Surabaya (Java) from the Banyuasri terminal. They leave at about 5 pm and arrive at about 3 am (approximately 25,000 rp).

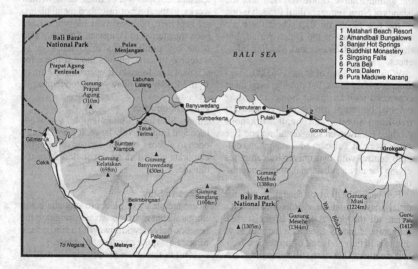

1 Matahari Beach Resort
2 Amandibali Bungalows
3 Banjar Hot Springs
4 Buddhist Monastery
5 Singsing Falls
6 Pura Beji
7 Pura Dalem
8 Pura Maduwe Karang

BALI

EAST OF SINGARAJA

Interesting sites east of Singaraja include some of Bali's best known temples. The north-coast sandstone is very soft and easily carved, so temples are heavily decorated, often with delightfully whimsical scenes. Although temple architecture is similar to that in the south, there are some important differences. In northern temples, there is a single pedestal with 'houses' for the deities to use on their earthly visits, structures for storing important religious relics and probably a *padmasana*, or throne, for the sun god. In southern temples these are all in separate structures.

At Kubutambahan you can turn south to Penulisan and Kintamani, or you can continue east to the lovely spring-fed pools at Yeh Sanih. From there the road continues right around the east coast to Tulamben and Amlapura – see the East Bali section earlier in this chapter.

Sangsit

At Sangsit, only a few km beyond Singaraja, you'll find an excellent example of the colourful architectural style of north Bali. Sangsit's **Pura Beji** is a subak temple, dedicated to the spirits that look after irrigated rice fields. It's about half a km off the main road towards the coast. The sculptured panels along the front wall set the tone with their Disneyland-like demons and amazing nagas. The inside also has a variety of sculptures covering every available space, and the inner courtyard is shaded by a frangipani tree.

Sangsit's **Pura Dalem** shows scenes of punishment in the afterlife, and other pictures which are humorous and/or erotic. It's in the rice fields, about 500m north-east of Pura Beji.

You can stay nearby at *Berdikari Cottages* (☎ (0362) 25195), just north of the main road. It costs 25,000 rp for a reasonably good room, or 45,000 rp with air-con, and you'll probably be the only guest.

Jagaraga

The village of Jagaraga, about 1.5 km south of the main road, has an interesting **Pura Dalem**. The small temple has delightful sculptured panels along its front wall, both inside and out. On the outer wall look for a vintage car driving sedately past, a steamer at sea and even an aerial dogfight between early aircraft. Jagaraga is also famous for its

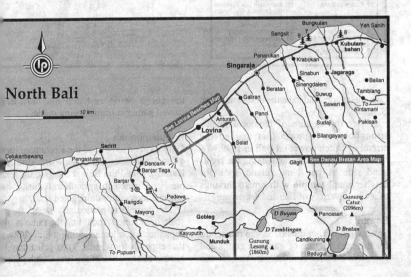

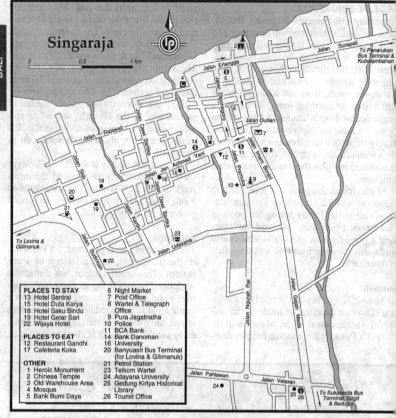

Singaraja

0   0.5   1 km

To Panarukan
Bus Terminal &
Kubutambahan

Jalan Surapati
Jalan Erlangga
Jalan Diponegoro
Jalan Durian
Jalan Rajawali
Jalan Dewi Sartika
Jalan Imam Bonjol
Jalan Jen Achmad Yani
Jalan Dewi Sartika
Jalan Kartini
Jalan Pramuka
Jalan Sila
To Lovina &
Gilimanuk
Jalan Sudirman
Jalan Udayana
Jalan Ngurah Rai
Jalan Gajah Mada
Jalan Pahlawan
Jalan Veteran
To Sukasarda Bus
Terminal, Gitgit
& Bedugul

PLACES TO STAY
13 Hotel Sentral
15 Hotel Duta Karya
18 Hotel Saku Bindu
19 Hotel Gelar Sari
22 Wijaya Hotel

PLACES TO EAT
12 Restaurant Gandhi
17 Cafeteria Koka

OTHER
1 Heroic Monument
2 Chinese Temple
3 Old Warehouse Area
4 Mosque
5 Bank Bumi Daya

6 Night Market
7 Post Office
8 Wartel & Telegraph
   Office
9 Pura Jagatnatha
10 Police
11 BCA Bank
14 Bank Danoman
16 University
20 Banyuasri Bus Terminal
   (for Lovina & Gilimanuk)
21 Petrol Station
23 Telkom Wartel
24 Adayana University
25 Gedung Kirtya Historical
   Library
26 Tourist Office

Legong troupe, said to be the best in northern Bali.

It was the capture of the local rajah's stronghold at Jagaraga that marked the arrival of Dutch power on Bali in 1849.

A few km past Jagaraga, along the right-hand side as you head inland, look for another small **temple** with ornate carvings of a whole variety of fish and fishermen.

Sawan

Several km further inland, Sawan is a centre for the manufacture of gamelan gongs and complete gamelan instruments. You can see the gongs being cast and the intricate carved gamelan frames being made.

Kubutambahan

Only a km or so beyond the Kintamani turn off at Kubutambahan is the **Pura Maduw Karang**. Like Pura Beji at Sangsit, the tem ple is dedicated to agricultural spirits, b this one looks after unirrigated land.

This temple is particularly noted for i sculptured panels, including the famous or depicting a gentleman riding a bicycle wi flower petals for wheels. The cyclist may l Nieuwenkamp, one of the first Dutch peop explore Bali, who actually did get around y bicycle. It's on the base of the main plinth the inner enclosure – other panels are also vorth inspecting.

It's likely that a group of local kids will cite a rote-learned spiel about the carvings s you look at them. Goodness knows who ught them this, but you'd feel pretty stingy you didn't give them a few hundred rupiah r their trouble.

'eh Sanih

bout 15 km east of Singaraja, Yeh Sanih also called Air Sanih) is a popular spot /here freshwater springs are channelled into ome very pleasant swimming pools before lowing into the sea. The area is attractively aid out with pleasant gardens and a restaunt. Admission to the springs and pool is 00 rp (children 200 rp).

laces to Stay & Eat There are a couple of laces to stay near the springs, but they're ot great value and some travellers have xperienced thefts here. The *Bungalow Puri anih* (π (0362) 22990) is actually in the orings complex, with cheap rooms on the est side at 10,000 rp, 15,000 rp and 20,000 b. Better rooms to the west of the pools cost 0,000 to 40,000 rp. Up the steep stairs oppote, *Puri Rena* has double rooms at 15,000 nd 20,000 rp.

The *Archipelago Restaurant*, halfway up ese stairs, is in a handsome bale with a onderful view. It's reasonably priced and e food is usually good. There are also a few heap warungs across the road from the orings.

*Tara Beach Bungalow*s are one km east of 'eh Sanih, with basic beachfront rooms from 2,000/15,000 rp, and a small restaurant.

OVINA

Vest of Singaraja is a string of coastal vilges – Pemaron, Tukad Mungga, Anturan, .alibukbuk, Bunut Panggang and Temukus which have become a popular beach resort ollectively known as Lovina. There are hops, bars and other tourist facilities, but the lace isn't totally dominated by tourist

development. Visitors are hassled by people trying to sell dolphin trips, snorkelling, sarongs and so on, but they don't sell as hard as at Kuta, and the intensity of the harassment seems to wax and wane. Lovina is a convenient base for trips around the north coast, a good place to meet other travellers and there's a bit of nightlife.

The beaches are black volcanic sand, not the white stuff you find in the south. It doesn't look as appealing but it's perfectly clean and fine to walk along. Nor is there any surf – a reef keeps it calm most of the time. The sunsets here are every bit as spectacular as those at Kuta, and as the sky reddens, the lights of the fishing boats appear as bright dots across the horizon. Earlier in the afternoon at fishing villages like Anturan, you can see the boats being prepared for the night's fishing.

Orientation & Information

Going along the main road, it's hard to know where one village ends and the next one begins, but the sign boards for the various places to stay should give you a clue – most of them are marked on the Lovina Beaches map. The tourist area stretches out over seven or eight km, but the main focus is at Kalibukbuk, about 10.5 km from Singaraja. This is where you'll find the tourist office and the police station, which share the same premises. The tourist office is open Monday to Thursday and Saturday from 7 am to 5.30 pm, Friday until 1 pm. The police may be able to help outside these times. There's a moneychanger nearby, and some of the hotels also change money.

Perama is based at the Hotel Perama (π 41161) on the main road. It's a good source of information for tours, and you can also buy stamps and post letters here.

A postal agent is on the main road near Khie Khie restaurant, and local and long-distance telephone calls can be made there, and also at Aditya Bungalows. The private wartel behind Restoran Gandhi may be a little cheaper than the others for international calls. All of Lovina is in the 0362 telephone district.

Dolphins

Dolphin-spotting trips are Lovina's special tourist attraction – so much so that a large concrete statue has been erected in honour of the over-touted cetaceans. At its best, a Lovina dolphin trip is a memorable experience. You take a boat out before dawn and see the sun burst over the volcanoes of central Bali. Then you notice that, despite the ungodly hour, dozens of other boats have gathered beyond the reef and lie there waiting.

Suddenly a dolphin will leap from the waves, to be followed by several more and then a whole school, vaulting over the water in pursuit of an unseen horde of shrimps. The boats all turn and join the chase, sometimes surrounded by dozens of dolphins, till the animals unaccountably cease their sport and the boats wait quietly for the next sighting.

There is a suggestion that the number of dolphins in the morning show has declined and that boats are going further to find them.

Some days, no dolphins at all are sighted b about 80% of the time you'll see at least few. There is no evidence that dolphins a harmed by the attention, and it's clear th they can easily outpace the boats if they fe threatened. The dolphins are such an attra tion that the boatmen have a strong veste interest in conserving the animals in near waters – let's hope they can do so.

At times tourists are hassled by tou selling dolphin trips, but the problem seen to vary. The price of a dolphin trip is fixe by the boat owners' cartel at 10,000 rp p person, and you can buy tickets anywher Occasionally a tout will sell a dolphin trip f more than this rate and pocket the differenc prompting a new and annoying bout of dire marketing.

Snorkelling & Diving

Generally, the water is very clear and the re is good for snorkelling. In many places yo can simply swim out from the beach or get

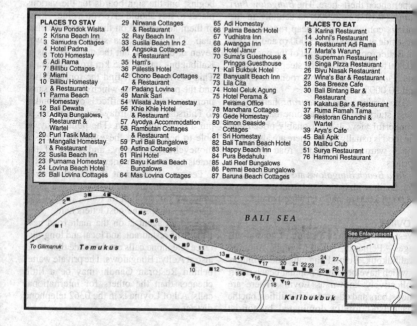

PLACES TO STAY		
1 Ayu Pondok Wisita	29 Nirwana Cottages	65 Adi Homestay
2 Krisna Beach Inn	& Restaurant	66 Palma Beach Hotel
3 Samudra Cottages	32 Ray Beach Inn	67 Yudhistra Inn
4 Hotel Padma	33 Susila Beach Inn 2	68 Awangga Inn
5 Toto Homestay	34 Angsoka Cottages	69 Hotel Janur
6 Adi Rama	& Restaurant	70 Suma's Guesthouse &
7 Billibu Cottages	35 Harri's	Pringga Guesthouse
9 Miami	36 Palestis Hotel	71 Kali Bukbuk Hotel
10 Billibu Homestay	42 Chono Beach Cottages	72 Banyualit Beach Inn
& Restaurant	& Restaurant	73 Lila Cita
11 Parma Beach	47 Padang Lovina	74 Hotel Celuk Agung
Homestay	49 Manik Sari	75 Hotel Perama &
12 Bali Dewata	54 Wisata Jaya Homestay	Perama Office
13 Aditya Bungalows,	56 Khie Khie Hotel	78 Mandhara Cottages
Restaurant &	& Restaurant	79 Gede Homestay
Wartel	57 Ayodya Accommodation	80 Simon Seaside
20 Puri Tasik Madu	58 Rambutan Cottages	Cottages
21 Mangalla Homestay	& Restaurant	81 Sri Homestay
& Restaurant	59 Puri Bali Bungalows	82 Bali Taman Beach Hotel
22 Susila Beach Inn	60 Astina Cottages	83 Happy Beach Inn
23 Purnama Homestay	61 Rini Hotel	84 Pura Bedahulu
24 Lovina Beach Hotel	62 Bayu Kartika Beach	85 Jati Reef Bungalows
25 Bali Lovina Cottages	Bungalows	86 Permai Beach Bungalows
	64 Mas Lovina Cottages	87 Baruna Beach Cottages

PLACES TO EAT
8 Karina Restaurant
14 Johni's Restaurant
16 Restaurant Adi Rama
17 Marta's Warung
18 Superman Restaurant
19 Singa Pizza Restaurant
26 Biyu Nasak Restaurant
27 Wina's Bar & Restaurant
28 Sea Breeze Cafe
30 Bali Bintang Bar &
Restaurant
31 Kakatua Bar & Restaurant
37 Ruma Ramah Tama
38 Restoran Ghandhi &
Wartel
39 Arya's Cafe
45 Bali Apik
46 Malibu Club
51 Surya Restaurant
76 Harmoni Restaurant

BALI SEA

See Enlargement

To Gilimanuk   Temukus

Kalibukbuk

boat to take you out; the skipper should know where the best coral is. The snorkelling trips are controlled by the same cartel which does the dolphin trips, and prices are fixed at 6000 rp per person for an hour, including the use of mask, snorkel and fins. They won't let you see dolphins and snorkel on the one trip – you have to return to shore and do a separate trip to snorkel.

Scuba diving on the reef is nothing special, but it is a good area for beginners. Several local diving operations do trips to other sites in the area, particularly Pulau Menjangan in the Bali Barat National Park (about 60 km to the west), which has some of the best diving on Bali. Dive trips for certified divers include Lovina reef (from US$45), Pulau Menjangan (US$60), the wreck at Tulamben (US$50) and Amed (US$55). Costs are lowest if you can arrange a group of around six people.

Two operators qualified and certified to run PADI open-water courses for beginners are Spice Dive (☎ 41305) on the south side of the main road opposite Johni's restaurant, with an information desk at Arya's Cafe, and Malibu Diving Service (☎ 41671), based at the Malibu Club in central Kalibukbuk. Other operators, like Barrakuda and Baruna, have branches at Lovina, but their headquarters and training facilities are in south Bali. Permai (☎ 41471), based at Permai Beach Bungalows, is another local operator. There's a lot of competition between the diving operations, and the personnel actually running the dive courses and trips can change. Check the qualifications of the instructor or dive master who will be conducting the trip before you sign up.

Glass-Bottom Boat
A glass-bottom boat does a 1½ hour trip from the beach, so you can see some fine coral without getting wet. It costs about 18,000 rp, or 5000 rp for kids. It does a dinner cruise too.

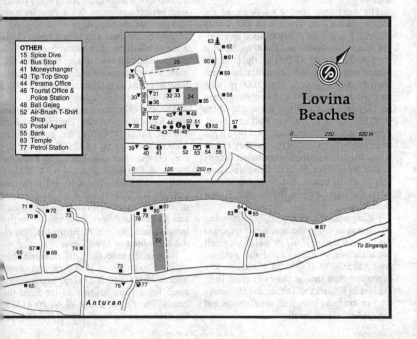

OTHER
15 Spice Dive
40 Bus Stop
41 Moneychanger
43 Tip Top Shop
44 Perama Office
46 Tourist Office &
   Police Station
48 Bali Gejeg
52 Air-Brush T-Shirt
   Shop
53 Postal Agent
55 Bank
63 Temple
77 Petrol Station

Lovina Beaches

To Singaraja

Anturan

Places to Stay

There are so many places to stay along the Lovina Beach strip that it's impossible to give an up-to-date list of them all. During peak times (late July, August and mid-December to mid-January) accommodation can be tight and prices are higher, sometimes even double. Generally the cheapest places are away from the beach, while upstairs rooms are more expensive, especially if they have a view. There's a 10% tax on accommodation, and fancier places add a 10 or 11% service charge as well. Most are budget lodgings, but there are a few mid-range options.

Singaraja to Anturan Starting from the Singaraja end, go past the overpriced *Aldian Hotel* to the nice-looking *Baruna Beach Cottages* (☎ 41745), with rooms and individual cottages from US$17 to US$52, plus tax and service. There's a swimming pool, a bar/restaurant by the beach, and you can also rent water sports equipment and arrange diving trips.

The next side road goes down to the *Happy Beach Inn*, which is in fact a very cheerful place, with delicious food and budget rooms from 8000 to 15,000 rp. Nearby, *Puri Bedahulu* (☎ 41731) is right on the beach, and has stylish, comfortable rooms from 20,000 rp (with fan) to 35,000 rp (with air-con). Just to the east, *Jati Reef Bungalows* are the concrete bunkers by the beach, which cost 12,000 to 15,000 rp. Further inland, *Permai Beach Bungalows* (☎ 41471) has basic rooms from 10,000 rp – but they're free if you do a trip with its dive operation. *Happy Beach Bungalows* are actually quite a long way from the beach, and are trying to cash in on the popularity of the original Happy Beach Inn.

Facing onto the main road, but extending all the way down to the beach, the upmarket *Bali Taman Beach Hotel* (☎ 41126) is small but attractive, with a pool and nice gardens. At US$25/30 to US$45/55 it's much less expensive than similar places in south Bali. Tucked in behind the Taman, *Sri Homestay* is a low-budget place, with small rooms and a great beachfront location.

Anturan Continuing along the road, you come to the turn-off to the scruffy little fishing village of Anturan, which now has an excess of places to stay. Rooms and bungalows are crowded together, competition has led to aggressive touting and some visitors report that the sea water isn't too clean. *Gede Homestay* is one of the friendlier places, with small rooms from 10,000 rp and better rooms up to 25,000 rp. Other possibilities here include *Mandhara Cottages*, with rooms from 10,000 to 30,000 rp, and the slightly upmarket *Simon Seaside Cottages* at 25,000, 30,000 rp – much more in the high season.

Back on the main road, the *Hotel Perama* (☎ 41161) has basic rooms from 8000, 10,000 rp, including breakfast.

Anturan to Kalibukbuk Continuing west from Anturan, the next turn-off goes down to the *Lila Cita*, right on the beachfront. The rooms are plain, but clean and inexpensive with singles/doubles from around 10,000, 15,000 rp – a little more for upstairs rooms with perfect sea views. It's a great location and the staff are helpful.

On the way there you'll pass *Hotel Celuk Agung* (☎ 41039), with rooms from US$25, 30, including air-con, fridge, hot water, satellite TV, tennis courts and a pool. It's rarely busy and you can get discounts of up to 30%, which would make it quite good value.

The next side road down to the beach has quite a few places to stay. The pleasant *Kali Bukbuk Hotel* (☎ 41701) has rooms from 15,000/20,000 rp up to 45,000 rp with air-con. On the other side, back a bit from the beach, is *Banyualit Beach Inn* (☎ 25889), with fan-cooled doubles at 30,000 rp, air-con cottages at 65,000 rp and a range of options in between – it's a well-run place with a pool and gardens, and very good value. Nearby budget places include *Yudhistira Inn*, *Ray II Awangga Inn* and *Hotel Janur*.

Back on the main road, *Adi Homestay* has ordinary rooms from 10,000 rp, and newer ones at 15,000 and 20,000 rp, which seems steep for a plain losmen so far from the beach. The *Palma Beach Hotel* (☎ 41775, fax 41659), on the beach side of the road, has big pool and air-con rooms with fridge, hot water and TV from US$60/67.50 to US$78/85; you can use the pool for just 5000 rp.

On its own side road, *Mas Lovina Cottages* (☎ 41237; fax 41236) are about the most luxurious accommodation in the area, with fully equipped individual cottages at US$75/140 for one or two bedrooms.

Kalibukbuk A little over 10 km from Singaraja is the 'centre' of Lovina – the village of Kalibukbuk. Here you'll find *Ayodya Accommodation*, a traditional place in a big old Balinese house. Rooms cost from 8000 rp and are bare and functional, but you sit and eat outside where it's very pleasant, despite some traffic noise.

Follow the track beside Ayodya down towards the beach and you'll come to the delightful *Rambutan Cottages* (☎ 41388; fax 41057). The beautifully finished rooms cost 30,000/35,000 rp up to 70,000 rp with hot water; 5000 rp more in the high season. It has a swimming pool set in a pretty garden, and a spacious restaurant with ace food. Next along is the *Puri Bali Bungalows* where comfortable rooms cost 12,000/15,000 rp, which is good value for this location.

Down towards the beach is the super-clean and well-run *Rini Hotel* (☎ 41386), with a variety of comfortable rooms from 15,000/20,000 rp in the low season, and big rooms at 50,000 and 65,000 rp. There's a good restaurant, and families with children are welcome. Opposite Rini are the long-standing *Astina Cottages* in a garden setting, with a variety of rooms and bungalows from 10,000/12,000 rp, or 15,000/20,000 rp with private bath; 5000 rp more in the high season. *Bayu Kartika Beach Bungalows* (☎ 41055) is a new establishment facing the beach, with lots of comfortable cottages from 20,000/25,000 rp.

On the south side of the main road, west of Ayodya, *Khie Khie Hotel & Restaurant* has rooms at 20,000 rp, and a not very attractive pool. A bit further along is the small *Wisata Jaya Homestay*, with OK rooms for 11,000/12,000 rp. On the beach side of the road, east of the tourist office, *Bali Gejeg* (☎ 41251) is clean and well run, and good value at 10,000 to 20,000 rp. Further west, *Chono Beach Cottages* are more expensive, and perhaps a bit too squeezed in.

The next turn-off, officially called Jl Bina Ria, goes past some bars and restaurants to the beach. Going off this road is the driveway to rambling *Nirwana Cottages* (☎ 41288), on a large slab of beachfront property. The rooms are pretty good from 10,000/15,000 rp for singles/doubles up to 45,000 rp for comfortable cottages; in the high season this can rise to 20,000 to 60,000 rp. It's not exactly a friendly, family place, but it's well run and the location is perfect.

Another side track, inland from Nirwana, goes to *Angsoka Cottages* (☎ 41841), which has a pool and a couple of rooms at 25,000 rp or less, but most are more expensive – from 35,000 to 70,000 rp. *Susila Beach Inn 2*, on the same track as Angsoka, is a small, friendly, family-run losmen, with cheap little rooms from about 8000 rp. The *Ray Beach Inn* next door has rooms in cell-block style at 8000/10,000 rp. *Palestis Hotel* (☎ 41035) is very colourfully decorated, and only 15,000 rp in the low season.

A small side road next to Palestis leads to some other nice, cheap places, like *Harri's*, *Manik Sari* and *Padang Lovina* – all around 12,500/15,000 rp.

Back on the main road there's a string of cheapies, with low-season prices from about 8000 rp. They include the *Purnama Homestay*, *Mangalla Homestay* and *Susila Beach Inn*, which are all grouped together on the north side of the road. Try to get a room closer to the beach and away from the road noise. *Lovina Beach Hotel* (☎ 41473) has a variety of rooms extending to the beach – pretty basic ones are 17,000 rp; better ones are up to 50,000 rp with air-con and hot water. *Puri Tasik Madu* (☎ 41376) costs 12,000 rp for downstairs rooms, 15,000 rp upstairs, and is friendly and close to the beach.

West of Kalibukbuk Further along there's *Aditya Bungalows & Restaurant* (☎ 41059), a big mid-range place with beach frontage,

BALI

pool, shops and a variety of rooms with TV, phone, fridge etc. Some of the rooms are right on the beach; prices range from US$20 to US$60. Next, there's the *Parma Beach Homestay*, with cottages from 15,000/20,000 rp, set in a garden extending down to the beach. *Bali Dewata* is on the south side of the road – a basic, clean and friendly place for 10,000/12,000 rp.

At the end of town, right on the beach but close to the road, *Toto Homestay* has very basic rooms at 10,000 rp, and a questionable reputation.

Further west are more places, secluded or isolated, depending on your point of view. *Hotel Padma* (☎ 41140) is new, near the road and may be noisy, but until it's better known the rooms are cheap for a mid-standard hotel at 20,000 to 60,000 rp. *Samudra Cottages* (☎ 41571) is another new one, with spotless rooms from 25,000 rp, but maybe more when the pool has water in it. *Krisna Beach Inn* is next, with rooms at 15,000 rp, followed by *Agus* at 15,000/20,000 rp. Expect even more places to spring up west of here.

Places to Eat

Most of the places to stay along the beach strip will serve meals, and there are restaurants as well, some more like bars in the evening. A sample of popular places to eat is listed here, but you'll do well just looking around and eating anywhere that takes your fancy. Even the nicest-looking restaurants will have main courses for under 5000 rp.

Starting from the Singaraja end, the *Harmoni Restaurant* on the main road is a good choice for seafood dishes, but service can be slow. The restaurant at *Happy Beach Inn* is good and friendly – order the Balinese roast duck a day in advance.

In Kalibukbuk village, *Surya Restaurant* is very well regarded and will also do good Balinese dishes, while the restaurant at *Chonos* is popular, as much for its happy hour as its food.

Across the main road, *Arya's Cafe* is an old favourite, especially for cakes and desserts.

On the road down to Nirwana there's the popular *Ruma Ramah Tama*, with a more

imaginative menu than many places, including vegetarian dishes and children's serves. Further down, the *Kakatua Bar & Restaurant* offers western and Indonesian standards in a very convivial atmosphere. At the end of this road, turn left to find the *Sea Breeze Cafe*, right by the beach, with very tasty food and a wonderful outlook. The restaurant at *Nirwana* is pricier, but tables overlooking the beach are very pleasant.

Back on the main road, *Restoran Gana* and *Biyu Nasak* both serve well-prepared and inexpensive western and Asian dishes. Further along are *Singa Pizza Restaurant*, the *Superman Restaurant*, *Marta's Warung* and then *Johni's Restaurant*. All these places are popular in the tourist season but very quiet at other times – their menus and prices are very similar. *Wina's Bar & Restaurant* is more of a nighttime hangout, as is the *Malibu Club*, but they both serve meals.

Entertainment

Some of the hotel restaurants have special nights with an Indonesian buffet meal and Balinese dancing. At about 8000 rp for entertainment and all you can eat, this can be very good value. *Rambutan* does a good one usually on Wednesday and Sunday. *Aditya*, *Bali Gejeg* and *Angsoka* also have buffet nights which are well advertised by leaflets that circulate around the beach and the bars. There's often live music at the *Malibu Club* which has a dance floor and occasional video movies. Other bars, which only seem busy in the tourist season, include the *Bali Bintang* and *Wina's*. *Bali Apik* has about the cheapest beer in town.

The Balinese guys who hang around the bars in Lovina are generally pretty harmless and some of them are a lot of fun. The shameless con-artists of a few years ago have mostly moved on. Nevertheless, you should be very sceptical if local guys offer elaborate pretexts for wanting large amounts of money.

Things to Buy

Lovina has the usual sort of souvenir, sarong and beachwear shops, but for something different, check out Beny Tantra's Air-Brush T-shirt shop on the south side of the main road in Kalibukbuk.

Getting There & Away

From the south of Bali by public transport, you go first to Singaraja, make a local connection to the Banyuasri terminal, then get a bemo west from there. The regular fare from Singaraja to the middle of Lovina's beach strip is 600 rp.

If you're arriving on a bus from Java or Gilimanuk, get off at the Lovina beaches rather than backtrack from Singaraja. Public buses to Surabaya leave Singaraja at around 5 pm; call the ticket office on ☎ 25141 or ☎ 22696 to arrange pick-up in Lovina. Perama (☎ 41161) is based at the Perama Hotel in Anturan. Fares are 12,500 rp to Kuta or Ubud, 20,000 rp to Candidasa or Padangbai, and 30,000 rp to Lombok.

Car & Motorcycle Cars cost from about 35,000 rp per day without insurance. Motorcycles are around 12,000 rp per day. Insurance may need to be arranged separately – there's an agent on Jl Bima Ria.

Getting Around

The Lovina strip is very spread out, but you can get back and forth on bemos, which should cost 400 rp for a short trip (two or three km) or 600 rp all the way to Singaraja - they will try to charge you more if they can. You can also rent bicycles for about 5000 rp

WEST OF LOVINA

The road follows the coast west of Lovina, with several places worth stopping at. It then cuts through the Bali Barat National Park to join the south coast road near Gilimanuk (see the earlier West Bali section). The road is well served by public bemos, which will get you to all of the places mentioned below.

Waterfalls

Five km from Kalibukbuk there's a sign to **Singsing Air Terjun** (Daybreak Waterfall). About one km from the main road you'll see a warung and a carpark. It's a 200m walk along a path to the lower falls, which drop about 12m into a deep pool. The pool is good for a swim, though the water isn't crystal clear. It's much cooler than the sea and very refreshing. Clamber further up the hillside to **Singsing Dua** (the second waterfall), which is slightly bigger and has a mud bath which is supposedly good for the skin.

There are some other falls in the area which you have to walk to – ask at your losmen for details. They may be unimpressive in the dry season.

Banjar

Buddhist Monastery Bali's only Buddhist monastery, Brahma Asrama Vihara, is about 1.2 km beyond the village of **Banjar Tega**, which is about 1.8 km up from the main coast road. It is vaguely Buddhist-looking, with colourful decoration, a bright orange roof and statues of Buddha. There are good views down the valley and across to the sea. You may be charged for parking, and you should wear a sarong or long pants. The road continues past the monastery, winding further up into the hills to Pedewa, a Bali Aga village.

Hot Springs The hot springs *(air panas)* are only a short distance west of the monastery if you cut across from Banjar Tega, rather than return to the main road. From the monastery, go back down the hill and turn left in the centre of the village. The small road runs west for a km or so to the village of Banjar. From there follow the road uphill to the springs. Buy your ticket from the little office (1000 rp, children 500 rp) and cross the bridge to the baths. There are changing rooms under the restaurant on the right side.

Eight carved stone serpents spew water from a natural hot spring into the first bath, which then overflows into a second, larger pool. In a third pool, water pours from three-metre-high spouts to give you a pummelling massage. The water is slightly sulphurous and pleasantly hot, so you might enjoy it more in the morning or the evening than in the heat of the day. You must wear a swimsuit and you shouldn't use soap in the pools, but you can do so under an adjacent outdoor shower.

The area is landscaped with lush tropical plants. The restaurant, a striking Balinese-style building, is not expensive and has good Indonesian food.

You can stay nearby at *Pondok Wisata Grya Sari* (☎ (0362) 92903), where pleasant standard rooms cost US$32/35, including breakfast (perhaps with a 35% discount). The suites are twice as expensive and only slightly better.

Getting There & Away If you don't have your own transport, it's easiest to get a bemo to the Banjar Tega turn-off, then get an ojek to the monastery (1000 rp). From there you can walk to the hot springs (about three km, mostly downhill). From the springs, get an ojek back to the main road.

Seririt

Seririt is a junction town for the roads that run over the mountains via Pupuan to the south coast. Seririt has a petrol station, shops and a market. *Hotel Singarasari* (☎ (0362) 92435), near the bus and bemo stop, has quite good rooms for 9000 rp, or 24,000 rp with air-con and TV.

Celukanbawang

Celukanbawang, the main port for north Bali, has a large wharf. Bugis schooners, the magnificent sailing ships which take their name from the seafaring Bugis people of Sulawesi, sometimes anchor here. The *Hotel Drupadi Indah*, a combination losmen, cinema, bar and restaurant, is the only place to stay. It costs 17,500 rp for a very basic room.

Pulaki

Pura Pulaki is a coastal temple rebuilt in the early 1980s, which has a large troop of monkeys. The village itself is entirely covered with grapevines. A sweet wine is made here, but most of the grapes are exported as dried fruit.

There are two secluded places to stay nearby. *Amandibali Bungalows* (☎ (0362)

25609) are not much to look at, but cost only 15,000/20,000 rp for simple singles/double right by the beach. Much more elegant is th *Matahari Beach Resort* (☎ (0362) 92312) with beautifully finished bungalows in at tractive gardens, a big pool and a privat beach. Rooms cost US$140/160 to US$33C 350. It has its own dive operation, and als offers tennis and windsurfing.

Pemuteran

The Pemuteran temple has hot springs at th front, but is not particularly interesting Nearby is a great place to get away from all, the *Taman Sari Hotel* (☎ (0362) 92623 fronting its own pretty beach. There's a wel placed seafront restaurant, and comfortabl fan-cooled rooms from 35,000 rp. An air-co room with a sea view will run to US$4C Adjacent to this is the *Pondok Sari* (☎ (0362 92337), which is a little less attractive, bt faces the same beach and costs 46,000 rp room, or 65,000 rp with air-con.

Reef Seen Aquatics (☎ (0362) 92339) is dive operation well regarded for its marin conservation programme on the nearb reefs. It runs its own turtle hatching projec It's mainly for experienced, certified divers but may be able to offer an introductory div for beginners.

Nusa Penida

Nusa Penida, an administrative region with in the Klungkung district, comprises thre islands – Nusa Penida itself, the smalle Nusa Lembongan to the north-west and tin Nusa Ceningan between them. The island o Nusa Penida is off the tourist track and ha few facilities. Nusa Lembongan attracts vis itors for its surf, seclusion and snorkelling while Nusa Ceningan is very sparsely inhab ited.

There's some fishing around the islands with sardines and lobster shipped over t Bali. The cultivation of seaweed is now wel established, and the underwater fences o which it is grown can be seen off many of th

Nusa Penida

0   2   4 km

beaches. After harvesting, the seaweed is spread out on the beach to dry, then exported for use in processed foods and cosmetics.

NUSA PENIDA

Clearly visible from Bali's south-east coast, the hilly island of Nusa Penida has a population of around 40,000, and was once used as a place of banishment for criminals and other undesirables from the kingdom of Klungkung. It has been a poor region for many years and there has been some transmigration to other parts of Indonesia. Thin soils and a lack of water do not permit the cultivation of rice, but other crops are grown – maize, sweet potato, cassava and beans are staples, while tobacco is grown for export.

Nusa Penida is the legendary home of Jero Gede Macaling, the demon who inspired the Barong Landung dance. Many Balinese believe the island to be a place of enchantment and evil power *(angker)* – thousands come every year for religious observances

aimed at placating the evil spirits. The island has a number of interesting temples dedicated to Jero Gede Macaling, including Pura Ped near Toyapakeh and Pura Batukuning near Suana.

The north coast has white sand beaches and views over the water to the volcanoes on Bali. This coastal strip, with the two main towns of Toyapakeh and Sampalan, is relatively moist and fertile. The south coast has spectacular limestone cliffs dropping straight down to the sea. The interior is a hilly, rugged landscape, with sparse-looking crops and vegetation, and unsalubrious villages. Rainfall is low, and there are large square tanks called *cabang*, in which water is stored for the dry season.

The population is predominantly Hindu, though there are some Muslims. The language is an old form of Balinese no longer heard on the mainland, and there are also local types of dance, architecture and craft, including a unique type of red ikat weaving.

Most people have had little contact with foreigners, and children are more likely to stare than shout 'hello mister'. They are not unfriendly, just bemused. Many people do not speak Indonesian and almost no-one speaks English.

Toyapakeh

If you come by boat from Nusa Lembongan you'll probably be dropped at the beach at Toyapakeh. It's a pretty town with lots of shady trees. The beach has clean white sand, clear blue water, a neat line of prahus and Bali's Gunung Agung as a backdrop. Step up from the beach and you're at the roadhead, where there will be bemos to take you to Ped or Sampalan (about 400 rp). Few travellers stay here but if you want to, you'll find the *Losmen Terang*, on your right, which has rooms for about 5000 rp.

Sampalan

Sampalan is pleasant enough, with a market, warungs, schools and shops strung out along the curving coast road. The market area, where the bemos congregate, is on the northern side of the road, and Buyuk Harbour, where the boats leave for Padangbai, is a few hundred metres west.

Between the market and the harbour is a small side road, with the friendly, family-run *Losmen Made*, which charges about 11,000/15,000 rp for a small clean room with breakfast. It's opposite the bank, behind a red gate. The town's other accommodation is the government rest house, *Bungalow Pemda,* opposite the police station a few hundred metres east of the market, with rooms for about 12,000 rp. There are a few simple places to eat along the main road and around the market. *Kios Dewi*, east of the market, is the closest thing to a restaurant, with inexpensive Padang-style food.

Around the Island

A trip around the island, following the north and east coasts, and crossing the hilly interior, can be done in a few hours by motorcycle. From Sampalan, follow the coast road southeast. After about six scenic km, steps on the right side of the road lead to the narrow entrance to **Goa Karangsari**, a limestone cave extending over 200m through the hill. It emerges on the other side above a verdant valley. People with a pressure lantern will guide you through the cave for about 5000 rp. During the Galungan Festival there is a torch-lit procession into the cave, with ceremonies held at temples inside it.

Continue south, past a new naval post and several well-located temples, to Suana, where the main road swings inland and climbs into the hills. A rough side track goes south-east, past more interesting temples to **Semaya**, a fishing village with a sheltered beach and one of Bali's best dive sites offshore.

About nine km south-west of Suana you reach **Tanglad**, a very old-fashioned village which is a centre for traditional weaving. Rough roads south and east lead to isolated parts of the coast. There are some experimental wind generators being tested near here.

A scenic ridge-top road goes north-west from Tanglad to Batukandik, where a side road goes two km south to **Air Tejun** on the coast. Sheer limestone cliffs drop hundreds of feet into the sea, with underground streams spilling fresh water into the sea. A pipeline brings water up to the top. You can follow the pipeline down the cliff face on an alarmingly exposed metal stairway. From it you can see the remains of a rickety old wooden scaffolding – women used to clamber down this daily and return with large pots of water on their heads.

Back on the main road, continue to Batumadeg, past **Bukit Mundi** (the highest point on the island at 529m), through **Klumpu** and **Sakti**, which have some very traditional stone buildings. Return to the north coast at Toyapakeh.

The important temple of **Pura Dalem Penetaran Ped** is near the beach at Ped, a few km east of Toyapakeh. It houses a shrine for Jero Gede Macaling, the source of power for the practitioners of black magic, and it's a place of pilgrimage for those seeking protection from sickness and evil.

BALI

etting There & Away

he strait between Nusa Penida and southern
ali is very deep and subject to heavy swells.
oats prefer to run in the early morning.

adangbai Fast, twin-engined fibreglass
oats operate between Padangbai and Nusa
enida. The boats are about eight or 10m
ng and look pretty seaworthy, with a re-
suring supply of life jackets. The trip takes
ss than an hour and costs 5000 rp. It's a
ouncy but exciting ride. At Padangbai, the
oats land on the beach just east of the
arpark for the Bali to Lombok ferry. On
usa Penida, they beach at Buyuk, just west
f Sampalan, or at Toyapakeh.

usamba Traditional boats carry produce
d supplies between Nusa Penida and
usamba, the closest port to Klungkung, the
strict capital. The boats leave when they're
ll, weather and waves permitting, and cost
out 2500 rp one way. They are much
ower than the boats from Padangbai, and
ay be heavily loaded (overloaded?) with
ovisions.

usa Lembongan The boats which carry

local people between the islands usually
leave from Toyapakeh. Get there very early.
You may have to wait a long while, or charter
a boat.

Getting Around

There are regular bemos on the sealed road
between Toyapakeh and Sampalan, on to
Suana and up to Klumpu, but beyond these
areas the roads are rough or nonexistent and
transport is uncertain. You may be able to
rent a motorcycle for about 12,000 rp an
hour, but most of the owners would prefer to
ride themselves and take you as a passenger,
which will cost about the same. A chartered
bemo is another option. If you really want to
explore the island, bring a mountain bike from
the mainland or plan to do some walking.

NUSA LEMBONGAN
Jungutbatu

Most visitors to Nusa Lembongan come for
the surf or the quiet beach, and they stay at
beachfront bungalows north of Jungutbatu.
The surf breaks on the reef, which shelters a
lovely beach with white sand, clear blue
water and superb views across to Gunung
Agung on mainland Bali.

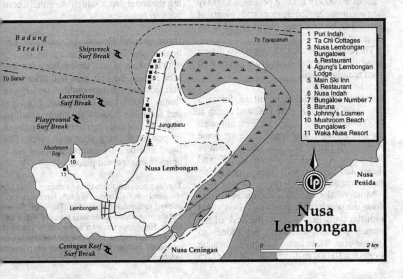

1 Puri Indah
2 Ta Chi Cottages
3 Nusa Lembongan
  Bungalows
  & Restaurant
4 Agung's Lembongan
  Lodge
5 Main Ski Inn
  & Restaurant
6 Nusa Indah
7 Bungalow Number 7
8 Baruna
9 Johnny's Losmen
10 Mushroom Beach
  Bungalows
11 Waka Nusa Resort

Badung Strait
Shipwreck Surf Break
To Toyapakeh
To Sanur
Lacerations Surf Break
Playground Surf Break
Jungutbatu
Mushroom Bay
Nusa Lembongan
Nusa Penida
Lembongan
Ceningan Reef Surf Break
Nusa Ceningan

Nusa Lembongan

0   1   2 km

Apart from the few basic bungalows and some places for visiting cruise boats, there are virtually no tourist facilities. There's no wartel or post office, and the bank doesn't change travellers cheques. The notice board at the Main Ski restaurant advertises excursions and day trips to various locations around the three islands, bicycle and motorcycle hire, and a local doctor who specialises in coral cuts and surfing injuries.

Surfing Waves are best in the dry season (May to September) when the winds come from the south-east. There are three main breaks on the reef, all aptly named. Off the beach where the bungalows are is Shipwreck, a right-hander named for the remains of a wreck that is clearly visible from the shore. South-west of this is Lacerations, a fast right which breaks over shallow coral. Further south-west is Playground, an undemanding left-hander. You can paddle out to Shipwreck, but for the other two it's better to hire a boat (about 3000 to 5000 rp).

Snorkelling & Diving Some good snorkelling spots are accessible from the beach, but for the best spots you'll need to charter a boat – about 10,000 rp for one person, 15,000 rp for two, including equipment and 'plenty of time'. The boatmen are obliging and know the good spots

There are some challenging scuba diving possibilities, but you'll have to organise it all from mainland Bali.

Places to Stay & Eat In the village, *Johnny's Losmen* is basic but quite OK, and cheap at 4000/6000 rp for singles/doubles, although not many people stay here. There are some other small places near the village, such as *Bungalow Number 7*, which is OK and cheap, and *Baruna*, with clean rooms facing the sea for 8000/10,000 rp.

Most of the accommodation is further along the beach to the north-east. Don't deal with the touts here – go to the desk of the losmen yourself, and don't pay money to anyone else. *Nusa Indah* has quite adequate rooms for 10,000 rp downstairs, or 15,000 rp

upstairs. The conspicuous *Main Ski Inn Restaurant* has a two storey restaurant facin the beach, which is a little more expensi than other places, but it serves good food a has a great view. Rooms cost 15,000/20,0 rp upstairs and 10,000/15,000 rp downstai

Agung's Lembongan Lodge has che double rooms from 6000 rp and better on at 17,000 rp. Its restaurant has tasty, inexpe sive food, and it has a happy hour with che drinks from 6 to 8 pm, and sometimes a vid movie. The slightly more expensive *Nu Lembongan Bungalows & Restaurant* is ne door, and then *Ta Chi Cottages* (or Tarc with rooms at 6000/10,000 rp, two stor bungalows at 17,000 rp, and reputedly t best cook on the island.

At the north end of the beach, the new *P Indah* is more upmarket, with smart roor in a solid, two storey block for 35,00 40,000 rp, but some cheaper accommodati at the back.

Lembongan Village

It's about three km south-west along t sealed road from Jungutbatu to Lembong village, the island's other town. It's possib to continue right around the island, follo ing the rough track which eventually com back to Jungutbatu.

Underground House As you enter Ler bongan you'll pass a warung on the rig with a couple of pool tables. For a few tho sand rupiah, the kids here will offer to tal you through the labyrinthine undergrour 'house', 100m back off the road. It's a cra and scramble through the many small pa sages, rooms and chambers, supposedly du by one man. Bring your own torch (flas light) and be very careful as there are b holes in unexpected places.

The story goes that the man lost a dispute with an e spirit and was condemned to death, but pleaded to allowed to finish his house first. The spirit relente and the man started excavating his cave with a sm spoon. He always started a new room before he fi ished the last one, so of course the house was ne completed, and thus his death sentence was postpon indefinitely.

ushroom Bay

his perfect little bay, unofficially named for e mushroom corals offshore, is the focus f Nusa Lembongan's first upmarket tourist evelopment. The *Bali Hai* boat (☎ (0361) 2033) does expensive day cruises around embongan, which now has a 'beach club'. he luxury catamaran will bring you here, here you spend the day lazing around the ool and the beach, doing some snorkelling d enjoying a buffet lunch, all for US$65.

A similar day trip is offered by *Waka ouka* (☎ (0361) 261130) for US$85, a luxu- catamaran that really sails. You can stay very classy thatched bungalows at *Waka 'usa Resort* for US$175 a night. A less xpensive, less luxurious option is the Nusa embongan Express (☎ (0361) 286302), hich does day trips from Sanur for US$20, d you can stay over at *Villa Wayan* for S$28 a night.

There's one budget place to stay, *Mush- om Beach Bungalows*, which are small and lain, but in an excellent location, and well riced from 15,000/20,000 rp. To get there om Jungutbatu, you'll need to walk or take ojek, turning right as you come into embongan village.

etting There & Away

part from the luxury cruises (see Mush- om Bay above), there are regular boats /from Sanur, Kusamba and Nusa Penida. oats pull up on the beach at Jungutbatu and ou have to jump off into the shallows ecause there's no jetty. The boat captains – at's what they're called – might be able to ave you at the northern end of the beach here most of the bungalows are, but other- ise you'll have to walk a km north to get ere.

anur Boats leave from the northern end of anur Beach, in front of the Ananda Hotel. here's a ticket office there; don't buy from tout. The boat captains have fixed the tourist price to Lembongan at 15,000 rp. The strait between Bali and the Nusa Penida islands is very deep, and huge swells develop during the day, so the boats leave before 8.30 am at the latest. Be prepared to get wet with spray. The trip takes at least 1½ hours, more if conditions are unfavourable. For some reason the trip back to Sanur is more expensive (15,500 rp) – be ready by 7.30 am.

Some agents sell a ticket from Kuta to Sanur connecting with the Lembongan boat. Perama charges 22,500 rp for this trip.

Kusamba Most boats from Kusamba go to Nusa Penida, but a few go to Lembongan. Boats from Sanur are safer and quicker.

Nusa Penida Boats take locals between Jungutbatu and Toyapakeh on Nusa Penida, particularly on market days. They leave at 5 am, and will be chock full of people, produce and livestock. The price, for locals anyway, is 2500 rp. Otherwise, it's easy to charter a boat for about 20,000 rp, for up to six or eight people.

Getting Around

You can easily walk around the island in a few hours. You can also hire a motorcycle or get a lift on the back of one. Many are in bad condition, and they're quite expensive at around 10,000 rp per hour.

NUSA CENINGAN

A narrow suspension bridge crosses the lagoon between Nusa Lembongan and Nusa Ceningan, so it's easy to explore its network of tracks on foot or a rented motorcycle – not that there's much to see. The lagoon is filled with frames for seaweed farming, which is the main money spinner here. There's also a fishing village and small agricultural plots, but they don't look too fertile. The island is quite hilly, and you'll get glimpses of great scenery as you go around the rough tracks.

Sumatra

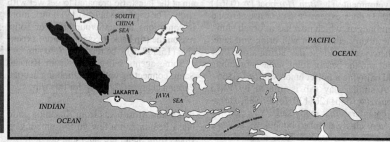

Sumatra is an island with an extraordinary wealth of natural resources, abundant wildlife, astonishing architecture and massive rivers. It is also home to people of diverse cultures: the former head-hunters and cannibals of the Batak regions; the matrilineal Muslim Minangkabau; and the indigenous groups of the Mentawai Islands who, until early this century, had little contact with the outside world.

Sumatra is almost four times the size of neighbouring Java, but supports less than a quarter of the population. During Dutch ru it provided the world with large quantities of oil, rubber, pepper and coffee. Its seemingly inexhaustible resources continue to prop u the Indonesian economy today.

HISTORY

Knowledge of Sumatra's pre-Islamic histor is extremely sketchy. Mounds of stone too and shells unearthed north of Medan sho that hunter-gatherers were living along the Straits of Melaka 13,000 years ago, b

---

HIGHLIGHTS

- **Bukit Lawang** – The famous Bohorok Orang-utan Rehabilitation Centre is at the top of most travellers' itineraries. It is set in the wild and enchanting Gunung Leuser National Park which is characterised by dense jungle and clear, fast-flowing rivers.
- **Danau Toba** – This spectacular lake remains a fine place to unwind, despite large-scale tourism. The largest lake in South-East Asia, it occupies the caldera of a giant volcano that collapsed 100,000 years ago. Pulau Samosir in the lake's centre is the home of the friendly Toba Batak people.
- **Bukittinggi** – This cool mountain town is the cultural heart of Minangkabau in western Sumatra, and is one of the main travellers' centres. It is also the place to organise treks among the isolated villages of the Mentawai Islands.
- **Southern Sumatra** – Few travellers spend much time in the southern part of Sumatra, where the main highlights are Krakatau and the elephant training centre at Way Kambas. Aceh Province in the north is also off the main route, but is becoming increasingly popular. Pulau We is the main attraction.
- **Seeing it All** – The majority of Sumatra's attractions are in the north and most travellers spend about a month taking in the highlights along the well-trodden trail between Medan and Padang. If your time is limited, a week is enough to visit Bukit Lawang and continue to Danau Toba via the highland town of Berastagi.

otherwise there is little evidence of human activity until the appearance about 2000 years ago of a megalithic culture in the mountains of western Sumatra. The most notable remains are in the Pasemah Highlands near Lahat. A separate megalithic cult developed at about the same time on Pulau Nias.

Sumatra had little contact with the outside world until the emergence of the kingdom of Sriwijaya as a regional power at the end of the 7th century. Presumed to have been based near the modern city of Palembang, Sri-vijayan power was based on control of the Straits of Melaka – the main trade route between India and China. At its peak in the 11th century, it controlled a huge slab of South-East Asia covering most of Sumatra, the Malay peninsula, southern Thailand and Cambodia. Sriwijayan influence collapsed after it was conquered by the south Indian king Ravendra Choladewa in 1025. For the next 200 years, the void was partly filled by Sriwijaya's main regional rival, the Jambi-based kingdom of Malayu.

After Malayu was defeated by a Javanese expedition in 1278, the focus of power moved north to a cluster of Islamic sultanates on the east coast of the modern province of Aceh. These sultanates began life as ports servicing trade through the Straits of Melaka. Many of the traders were Muslims from Gujarat (west India) and the animist locals were soon persuaded to adopt the faith of their visitors – giving Islam its first foothold in the Indonesian archipelago.

As well as a religion, these traders also provided the island with its modern name. Until this time, the island was generally referred to as Lesser Java. The name Sumatra is derived from Samudra, meaning 'ocean' in Sanskrit. Samudra was a small port near modern Llokseumawe that became the most powerful of the sultanates. As Samudran influence spread around the coast of Sumatra and beyond, the name gradually came to refer to the island as a whole. Marco Polo spent five months in Samudra in 1292, corrupting the name to Sumatra in his report.

After the Portuguese occupied Melaka (on the Malay peninsula; previously known as Malacca) in 1511 and began harassing Samudra and its neighbours, Aceh took over as the main power on Sumatra. Based close to modern Banda Aceh at the strategic northern tip of Sumatra, it carried the fight to the Portuguese and carved out a substantial territory of its own, covering much of northern Sumatra as well as large chunks of the Malay peninsula. Acehnese power prevailed until the reign of Sultan Iskandar Muda at the beginning of the 17th century, when Dutch traders began their probings into Sumatra. They based themselves in the West Sumatran port of Padang, but made little effort to impose themselves militarily on Sumatra until the post-Napoleonic War phase of their empire building.

After the war, the Dutch returned to find that their influence in Sumatra had all but evaporated. The British still ruled in Bencoolen (modern Bengkulu), founded in 1685, and had also established themselves on the island of Penang in the Straits of Melaka. American traders were monopolising pepper exports from Aceh, and the Chinese were exploiting the rich reserves of tin on the islands of Bangka and Belitung, east of Palembang.

The subsequent Dutch campaign to control Sumatra produced some of the most protracted fighting of the colonial era. They began with a failed attempt to capture Palembang in 1818. A second attempt in 1825 succeeded, but fighting dragged on in the South Sumatran interior until 1847.

In West Sumatra, the Dutch found their designs on the Minangkabau lands threatened by the rise of the Islamic fundamentalist Padri movement. The Padris were so-called because their leaders had made their pilgrimage to Mecca via the Acehnese port of Pedir. They had returned fired up with a determination to establish a true Islamic society, which put them at violent odds with supporters of Minangkabau adat (traditional law). Fighting between the two broke out in 1803, and the Padris had won control of much of the highlands by the time the Dutch entered the fray in 1821 in support of the traditional leaders.

SUMATRA

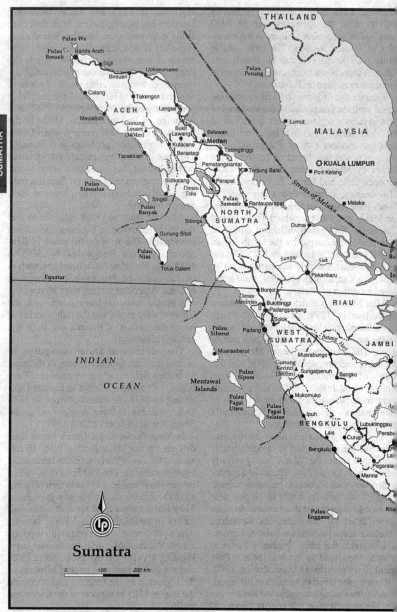

Sumatra

0   100   200 km

Bukittinggi's Fort de Kock was the Dutch headquarters for a war that dragged on until 1837, when they finally captured the equator town of Bonjol, stronghold of the Padri leader Imam Bonjol – whose name adorns street signs all over Indonesia.

The Dutch needed three military expeditions – in 1847, 1855 and 1863 – to establish their authority over Pulau Nias, while diplomacy persuaded the British to vacate Bengkulu, which was traded for the port of Melaka on the Malay peninsula. Treaties and alliances brought other areas of Sumatra under Dutch rule, and the war with the Bataks ended in 1872 – although Batak resistance continued until 1895.

The war with the Acehnese, however, proved both the bloodiest and the longest lasting. The Acehnese turned back the first Dutch attack in 1873 before succumbing to massive assault two years later. They then took to the jungles for a guerrilla struggle that lasted until 1903 when the Acehnese sultan, Tuanku Muhamat Dawot, surrendered. Even then, the Dutch were forced to keep a military government in the area until 1918. They were booted out of Aceh in 1942 immediately before the Japanese WWII occupation of Sumatra and did not attempt to return during their brief effort to reclaim their empire after the war. From 1945 until the rest of Indonesia achieved independence in 1949, Aceh was ruled by Daud Beureueh, the leader of an Islamic modernist movement.

Sumatra provided several key figures in the independence struggle, including future vice-president Mohammed Hatta and the first prime minister, Sutan Syahrir. It also provided the new nation with its fair share of problems. First up was Aceh. The new nation's living-together philosophy didn't go down too well with the staunchly Muslim Acehnese, who rebelled against being lumped together with the Christian Bataks in the newly created province of North Sumatra. Led by Beureueh, they declared an independent Islamic republic in 1953. Aceh didn't return to the fold until 1961, when it was given special provincial status.

The Sumatran rebellion of 1958-61 posed

a much greater threat. Much debate surrounds the true objectives of the rebels when they declared their rival Revolutionary Government of the Republic of Indonesia (PRRI) in Bukittinggi on 15 February 1958. While many local grievances were involved, the main argument with Jakarta concerned the Communist Party's growing influence with President Soekarno. Some have suggested that the rebels had no intention of fighting, and that the Bukittinggi declaration was intended as an ultimatum to Soekarno to back away from the Communists.

The central government showed no interest in negotiations and moved quickly to smash the rebellion, capturing the key cities of Medan and Palembang within a month. By mid-1958 Jakarta had regained control of all the major towns, but the rebels fought on in the mountains of South Sumatra for another three years until a general amnesty was granted as part of a peace settlement.

GEOGRAPHY

Stretching nearly 2000 km and covering an area of 473,607 sq km, Sumatra is the sixth largest island in the world. The island is divided neatly in two by the equator just north of Bukittinggi.

The main feature is the Bukit Barisan mountains which run most of the length of the west coast, merging with the highlands around Danau Toba (Lake Toba) and central Aceh in the north. Many of the peaks are over 3000m (the highest is Gunung Kerinci at 3805m). Spread along the range are almost 100 volcanoes, 15 of them active. The mountains form the island's backbone, dropping steeply to the sea on the west coast, but sloping gently to the east. The eastern third of the island is low-lying, giving way to vast areas of swampland and estuarine mangrove forest bordering the shallow Straits of Melaka. It's traversed by numerous wide, muddy, meandering rivers, the biggest being the Batang Hari, Siak and Musi.

The string of islands off the west coast, including Pulau Nias and the Mentawai Islands, are geologically older than the rest of Sumatra.

CLIMATE

Sitting astride the equator, Sumatra's climate is about as tropical as tropical gets. Daytime temperatures seldom fail to reach 30°C on the coast, but fortunately most of the popular travellers' spots are in the mountains where the weather is appreciably cooler. Places like Berastagi, Bukittinggi and Danau Toba get cool enough at night to warrant a blanket.

The time to visit Sumatra is during the dry season, which runs from May to September. June and July are the best months. The timing of the wet season is hard to predict. In the north, the rains start in October, and December/January are the wettest months; in the south, the rains start in November, peaking in January/February. Bengkulu and West Sumatra are the wettest places, with average rainfall approaching 3500 mm.

FLORA & FAUNA

Large areas of Sumatra's original rainforest have been cleared for plantations, but some impressive tracts of forest remain – particularly around Gunung Leuser National Park in the north and Kerinci Seblat National Park in the central west.

The extraordinary *Rafflesia arnoldii*, the world's large flower, is found in pockets throughout the Bukit Barisan – most notably near Bukittinggi – between August and November.

Sumatra's forests are home to a range of rare and endangered species, including the two horned Sumatran rhino, the Sumatran tiger and the honey bear. Gunung Leuser National Park is one of the last strongholds of the orang-utan, with more than 5000 living in the wild. The rehabilitation centre at Bukit Lawang is one place where you can be sure of seeing one.

ECONOMY

Sumatra is enormously rich in natural resources and generates the lion's share of Indonesia's export income. The biggest earners are oil and natural gas. The fields around the towns of Jambi, Palembang and Pekanbaru produce three-quarters of Indonesia's oil. Llokseumawe, on the east coast f Aceh, is the centre of the natural gas ndustry.

Rubber and palm oil are the next biggest ncome earners. Timber is another heavily xploited resource, and the forests of the astern Sumatran lowland are disappearing apidly into an assortment of pulp mills and lywood factories. Other crops include tea, :offee, cocoa beans and tobacco. Sumatra vas noted as a source of prized black pepper y the Chinese more than 1000 years ago and t remains a major crop in southern Sumatra.

POPULATION & PEOPLE

Sumatra is the second most populous island n the archipelago, with 40 million people. Population density is, however, but a fraction of Bali or Java.

Continuing transmigration from these two slands has added to the remarkably diverse ethnic and cultural mix. (See the entries on he Bataks in the Danau Toba section; the Acehnese in the Aceh section; the Minang-abau in West Sumatra; the Mentawaians in he Mentawai Islands section; and the Kubu under Jambi, all later in this chapter.)

GETTING THERE & AWAY

The international airports at Banda Aceh, Batam, Medan, Padang and Pekanbaru are visa-free, as are the seaports of Belawan Medan); Dumai; Batu Ampar, Nongsa and Sekupang (Pulau Batam); Tanjung Balai Pulau Karimun); and Tanjung Pinang (Pulau Bintan).

Most travellers arrive and depart through Medan, either by air on the daily connections o Kuala Lumpur, Penang and Singapore or oy sea on the high-speed catamarans that run between Penang and Belawan. Most of northern Sumatra's main attractions are within easy reach of Medan.

Another approach is to travel by boat from Singapore to Batam in the Riau Islands (where you clear customs), and then take a boat to the mainland city of Pekanbaru. There are also regular flights from Batam to Medan, Padang and a host of smaller desti-nations.

Coming from Jakarta, the main route is by bus and ferry from Merak to the southern Sumatran ferry terminal of Bakauheni, and then north by bus on the Trans-Sumatran Highway. A popular alternative, which elim-inates the long haul by bus, is to catch the fortnightly Pelni boat from Jakarta to Pad-ang.

If you're heading to Sumatra from the Americas, Europe or Oceania, a good way to travel is to reach Kuala Lumpur, Penang or Singapore first. They are much closer to Medan than Jakarta, and open up more options for onward travel.

Malaysia

Air The number of Sumatran cities with direct flights to Malaysia is growing rapidly. Malaysian newcomer Pelangi Air has done much to expand the range of options. It also offers some good deals for (card-carrying) students, including a 50% standby fare on all flights between Indonesia and Malaysia. The discount drops to 25% for a confirmed seat.

Medan is Sumatra's major international airport and has the widest choice of destina-tions. Both Malaysian Airlines (MAS) and Sempati fly the 40 minute hop to Penang daily for around US$75. MAS and Garuda have daily flights to Kuala Lumpur, while Sempati flies the route three times weekly (all $77). Pelangi flies Medan-Ipoh four times a week (US$70) and Medan-Melaka (US$104) twice a week. Pelangi is the main international operator out of Padang with daily flights to Kuala Lumpur (US$123) and three flights a week to Johore Bahru (US$104). Sempati flies from Padang to Kuala Lumpur twice a week. Pelangi flights to Kuala Lumpur from Padang travel via Pekanbaru (US$107). This company also flies from Pekanbaru to Melaka (US$60) twice a week.

The latest international option to open up is the Pelangi route from Banda Aceh to Kuala Lumpur (US$134), via Penang (US$107).

Boat The most convenient of the many ferry routes operating between Malaysia and

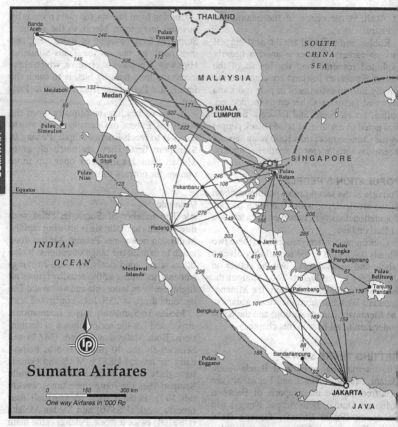

Sumatra Airfares

0   150   300 km

One way Airfares in '000 Rp

Sumatra is the one from Penang to Medan's port of Belawan.

Penang to Belawan The high-speed ferries *Ekspres Selasa* and *Ekspres Bahagia* take about four hours to complete the run across the Straits of Melaka. Between them, there are departures from Penang every day, except Sunday, for RM110, and from Medan every day, except Monday, for 95,000 rp. The fares from Medan include bus transport to Belawan and port tax (7500 rp).

The Express Bahagia's Medan office (☎ 720954) is at Jl Sisingamangaraja 92A,

but tickets can also be bought at Pacto (☎ 510081), Jl Katamso 35G. Its Penang office (☎ (04) 2631943) is on Jl Pasara King Edward.

The Express Selasa's Medan office is Perdana Express (☎ 545803) at Jl Katamso 35C, while in Penang the place to go is the Kuala Perlis-Langkawi Ferry Service (☎ (04) 2625630) on the ground floor arcade of the PPC building on Jl Pasara King Edward.

Lumut to Belawan There are ferries from Belawan to Lumut (200 km south of Penang

n Tuesday and Saturday at 2 pm, returning
n Wednesday and Sunday at 9 am. Fares are
he same as for Penang-Medan. The Lumut
ffice (☎ (05) 934258) is by the jetty.

Port Kelang to Belawan There are ferries
rom Belawan to Port Kelang, near Kuala
umpur, at 11 am on Monday and Wednes-
ay (114,000 rp; six hours). The boats return
t 10 am on Tuesday and Thursday
RM120).

Melaka to Dumai Ferries run from Melaka
o Dumai every Monday and Friday for
RM120, returning on Thursday and Sunday
114,000 rp). Dumai is no more than an
overgrown oil-pumping station, but it's now
. visa-free port.

Singapore
Air Garuda and Silk Air both run daily flights
etween Singapore and Medan for US$140,
vhile Merpati and Silk Air each operate three
lights a week between Padang and Singa-
ore (US$121). Merpati also flies from
Pekanbaru to Singapore (US$102) twice a
veek.

Boat The Riau Islands, immediately south of
Singapore, are convenient stepping stones to
he Sumatran mainland. Pulau Batam and
Pulau Bintan are the main islands, and both
re visa-free entry or exit points.

Batam Pulau Batam, just 45 minutes south
of Singapore by ferry, is the closer island.
There are frequent ferries between Singa-
ore's World Trade Centre and Batam's
ort of Sekupang (S$18, 30,000 rp from
Sekupang). The first ferries leave from Singapore at 8 am and Sekupang. The last ferries
eave at 7 pm in both directions. Batam itself
s deathly dull and very expensive, so few
ravellers stick around. Sekupang's domestic
erry terminal is right next to the interna-
ional terminal – turn right out of the terminal
and walk through the hole in the fence. There
you will find a row of ticket offices offering
speedboat connections to a long list of main-
and towns and other islands. Pekanbaru is

the most popular option, involving a four
hour speedboat trip to the mainland bus/ferry
terminal of Tanjung Buton followed by a
three hour bus trip. Fares for the combined
ticket start at 35,000 rp. Most services leave
before 10 am, so you will need to leave
Singapore early to avoid getting stuck on
Batam.

See the Pulau Batam Getting There &
Away section for more details of services.

Bintan There are three direct services a day
between Singapore and Pulau Bintan, which
is the best place to find boats to the outer
Riau Islands. (See under Tanjung Pinang for
details.)

Java
Air Garuda has five flights a day from Jakarta
to Medan (415,800 rp) and two a day to
Batam (286,000 rp). Merpati has direct
flights from Jakarta to Bandarlampung
(95,700 rp), Batam (286,000 rp), Bengkulu
(192,500 rp), Jambi (212,300 rp), Padang
(300,300 rp) and Palembang (171,000 rp). It
also has daily direct flights from Bandung to
Palembang (174,300 rp), continuing to Batam.

Sempati, Mandala and Bouraq also have
daily direct flights from Jakarta to Batam,
Medan and Padang.

Boat Boat travel can be a pleasant alternative
to the hard grind of bus travel.

Jakarta to Sumatra Pelni has several ships
operating between Jakarta and ports in
Sumatra on regular two weekly schedules.

The Jakarta-Padang-Gunung Sitoli-
Sibolga-Padang-Jakarta route serviced by
both the KM *Lawit* and the KM *Kerinci* is
the one most used by travellers. The journey
from Jakarta to Padang takes 41 hours and
fares vary from 81,500 rp deck class to
230,500 rp in 1st class. See the introductory
Getting Around chapter earlier in this book
for more details of the ships and routes.

Pelni ships also operate weekly services
between Jakarta and Medan (116,500/
330,500 rp; 45 hours), as well as from

Jakarta to Dumai, Kijang (Pulau Bintan) and Mentok (Pulau Bangka). (See the introductory Getting Around chapter for more details of the ships and routes.)

Merak to Bakauheni Ferries operate 24 hours a day between Merak on Java and Bakauheni at the southern tip of Sumatra. They leave every 36 minutes, so there's never long to wait. The trip across the narrow Sunda Strait takes 1½ hours. You're better off travelling deck class (1500 rp) and enjoying the breeze than sitting in the smoke-filled 1st class lounge (2600 rp). If you travel by bus between Jakarta and destinations in Sumatra, the price of the ferry is included in your ticket.

There's also a new 'Superjet' service that does the crossing in 30 minutes for 6000 rp. It leaves Bakauheni every 70 minutes from 8.40 am to 4.50 pm.

The Bahauheni ferry terminal is modern and efficient, and there are buses waiting to take you north to Bandarlampung's Rajabasa bus terminal (1700 rp; two hours). There are also share taxis that will take you to the city destination of your choice for 5000 rp.

Bus If you travel by bus between Jakarta and destinations in Sumatra, the price of the ferry is included in your ticket. Fares from Jakarta to Bandarlampung start at 15,000 rp.

Elsewhere in Indonesia
Air There are occasional direct flights between Denpasar (Bali) and Medan (559,800 rp) and between Pontianak (Kalimantan) and Batam (204,600 rp); otherwise getting to Sumatra by air means changing planes in Jakarta.

Boat Pelni boats can get you from Sumatra to the furthest reaches of the archipelago. The KM *Kambuna,* for example, sails from Medan to Jakarta and then on to Ambon, capital of Maluku, and Ujung Padang on Sulawesi. (See the introductory Getting Around chapter for more details of the ships and routes.)

GETTING AROUND
Travelling around Sumatra is pretty straight forward these days, thanks largely to a greatl improved road network. Most traveller follow a well-trodden trail across Sumatra starting from Medan and stopping at Buk Lawang, Berastagi, Parapat, Danau Toba Pulau Nias, Bukittinggi, Padang and then o to Java.

Air
An hour on a plane is an attractive alternativ to many hours on a bus. Merpati has a com prehensive network of services betwee Sumatra's major cities. Sample fares includ Bengkulu-Palembang for 101,200 rp, Pa lembang-Padang for 179,300 rp, Padang Medan for 172,700 rp and Medan-Band Aceh for 145,200 rp. Bouraq, Mandala an Sempati compete on some of the mos popular routes. Small airlines like SMAC Pelita and Deraya Air fly to minor destina tions that the big airlines don't bother with SMAC, for example, has daily flights from Medan to Gunung Sitoli on Pulau Nias fo 131,300 rp.

Bus
Bus is the most popular mode of transport The old travellers' tales of hours of bone shaking horror on appalling roads are fadin into history – on the main roads, at least. A lot of money has been spent on improvin the island's roads in the last 10 years. If yo stick to the Trans-Sumatran Highway an other major roads, the big air-con buses an tourist coaches make travel a breeze. The best express air-con buses have reclinin seats, toilets, video and even karaoke. The only problem is that many of them do nigh runs, so you miss out on the scenery. The non-air-con buses are in many cases jus older versions of the air-con buses. They rattle more, the air-con no longer works and they can get very crowded, but are fine fo short trips.

There are numerous bus companies cov ering the main routes and prices vary greatly depending on the level of comfort. Ticket

Trans-Sumatran Highway

The sealing of the central southern sections of the Trans-Sumatran Highway means there is now a reasonable sealed road all the way from Bakauheni in the south to Banda Aceh in the north.

The worst section of the highway is now the 10 hour stretch between Bandarlampung and Lubuklinggau in the south, where the surface is badly potholed in places. The sector from Lubuklinggau north to Padang is one of the best stretches of road in Sumatra, as well as being one of the most scenic. It takes about 12 hours.

Most people make one or more stops on the sector between Padang and Parapat, usually at Bukittinggi and/or Sibolga (for Pulau Nias). The road as far as Bukittinggi is excellent and takes about two hours, but the stretch from Bukittinggi to Parapat is the original long and winding road. The air-con buses can do it in 12 to 13 hours, most running at night, while public buses take 16 hours or more. The special tourist minibuses also do the trip in 12 to 13 hours during the day.

The section from Parapat to Medan is plain sailing, taking about four hours. Traffic congestion near Medan is the only problem.

The coast road north from Medan to Banda Aceh is easy going apart from a winding, mountain section between Sigli and Banda Aceh. The air-con buses can do the journey in nine hours at night, while the day buses can stretch it to 12 hours.

Other important roads to have been sealed in recent years are those linking Palembang to the highway at Lubuklinggau, and between Jambi and Muarabunga. ■

Tourist Buses Many travellers take the convenient 'tourist' buses that do the Bukit Lawang-Berastagi-Parapat-Bukittinggi run. You may feel like you're in a tour group at times, and 'tourist' doesn't mean comfortable, but they do take some scenic routes that normal buses don't cover. They also pick up and drop off at hotels, travel during the day so you can see the scenery and stop at points of interest on the way. The cost and journey times are about the same as air-con buses.

Train

Sumatra has a very limited rail network. The only useful service runs from Bandarlampung in the south to Palembang, and then on to Lubuklinggau. There are also passenger trains from Medan to Pematangsiantar, Tanjung Balai and Rantauparapat.

Boat

Sumatra's rivers are also major transport routes which teem with a motley, but colourful, collection of multipurpose vessels: rowing boats; speedboats; outriggers; ferries; junks; and large cargo vessels. Boats are usually available for charter and will take you almost anywhere.

Taking a boat is both a welcome respite from bus travel and another way of seeing Sumatra. There are many places which you can't get to any other way – islands which don't have an airstrip, or river villages not connected by road.

Jambi, Palembang and Pekanbaru are important towns for river transport. There are also regular links to surrounding islands, such as Banda Aceh to Pulau We, Padang to Pulau Siberut, Pekanbaru to Pulau Batam, Sibolga to Pulau Nias and Singkil to Pulau Banyak.

Local Transport

The usual Indonesian forms of transport – *bemos*, *opelets*, *becaks* and *dokars* (horse-drawn carts) – are available for getting around towns and cities in Sumatra. The base rate for a bemo is 300 rp, while the minimum fare for becaks and dokars is 1500 rp.

Hang back and watch what the locals pay

can be bought direct from the bus company or from an agent. Agents usually charge about 10% more, but they are normally more convenient. In some towns, they are the only place to buy tickets. It can pay to shop around, especially in the main tourist areas where agent charges can be excessive.

Travel on the back roads is a different story. Progress can still be grindingly slow, uncomfortable and thoroughly exhausting, particularly during the wet season when bridges are washed away and the roads develop huge potholes. Avoid seats at the rear of the bus where the bouncing is worse.

if you are not certain of the fare, or check the price with other travellers.

North Sumatra

The province of North Sumatra is home to many of Sumatra's most popular attractions, including the jewel in the crown, Danau Toba. Other attractions are the Orang-Utan Rehabilitation Centre at Bukit Lawang, the Karo Batak Highlands around Berastagi and Pulau Nias off the west coast.

The province's 70,787 sq km straddle Sumatra from the Indian Ocean in the west to the Straits of Melaka in the east, bordered by Aceh in the north and West Sumatra and Riau in the south. It has a population of more than 11 million, with Medan and Pematang-siantar the main cities.

The main ethnic groups in North Sumatra are the coastal Malays who live along the Straits of Melaka; the five Batak groups from the highlands around Danau Toba and Pulau Samosir; the Pesisirs (central Tapanuli) along the Indian Ocean coastline; and the people from Pulau Nias. These ethnic groups all have their own dialects, religious beliefs, and traditional customs, arts and cultures.

North Sumatra produces more than 30% of Indonesia's exports. Fine tobacco is grown around Medan. Oil, palm oil, tea and rubber are also produced in large quantities and exported from the port of Belawan, about 26 km from Medan.

MEDAN
Medan is the capital of North Sumatra and the third largest city in Indonesia with a population of around two million.

Apart from some impressive architecture (traditional, colonial and Islamic) and an interesting museum, there is not a lot to hold the traveller's attention.

Most people's abiding memory of Medan is of battered old motorcycle becaks belching fumes into the already heavily polluted air. That and the humidity. Most treat the city strictly as an entry and exit point.

History
Medan is an Indonesian word meaning 'field', 'battlefield' or 'arena'. It was on the fertile swamp, at the junction of the Deli and Babura rivers (near Jl Putri Hijau), that the original village of Medan Putri was founded by Rajah Guru Patimpus in 1590.

From the end of the 16th century to the early 17th century, Medan was a battlefield in the power struggle between the kingdom of Aceh and Deli. It remained a small village until well into the 19th century. In 1823 British government official, John Anderson found a population of only 200.

The town began to grow after the arrival of the Dutch. An enterprising planter named Nienhuys introduced tobacco to the area in 1865 and Medan became the centre of a rich plantation district. In 1886 the Dutch made it the capital of North Sumatra. By the end of Dutch rule, the population had grown to about 80,000 – still a far cry from today's huge, sprawling city.

The solid Dutch buildings of the affluent older suburbs inspire images of bloated bureaucrats and fat European burghers from the colonial era, while jerry-built lean-tos house the bulk of today's population.

Orientation
Finding your way around Medan presents few problems, although the traffic can be horrendous. Most places of importance are on or around the main street, Jl Ahmad Yani, which runs north-south through the city centre. South of the city centre, it becomes Jl Pemuda and then Jl Katamso; to the north, it becomes Jl Soekarno-Hatta and then Jl Putri Hijau (also known as Jl Yos Sudarso).

Travellers arriving in Medan from Parapat and points south will find themselves deposited at the giant Amplas bus terminal, 6.5 km from town on Jl Sisingamangaraja (often written as SM Raja). It runs into the city centre parallel to Jl Katamso.

Information
Tourist Offices The North Sumatran tourist office (☎ 538101) is at Jl Ahmad Yani 107. The staff here are friendly and speak good

English. It's open Monday to Thursday from
.30 am to 4.15 pm, and on Friday until
noon. There is a small information office at
the international arrival terminal at the
airport.

Foreign Embassies & Consulates The following countries have consulates in Medan:

Belgium
    Jl Pattimura 459 (☎ 527991)
Denmark
    Jl Hang Jebat 2 (☎ 323020)
Germany
    Jl Karim MS 44 (☎ 537108)
India
    Jl Uskup Agung Sugiopranoto 19 (☎ 531308)
Japan
    Jl Suryo 12 (☎ 531192)
Malaysia
    Jl Diponegoro 43 (☎ 511567)
Netherlands
    Jl A Rivai 22 (☎ 519025)
Norway
    Jl Zainal Arifin 55 (☎ 510158)
Russia
    Jl Karim MS 17 (☎ 515973)
Singapore
    Jl Tengku Daud 3 (☎ 513134)
Sweden
    Jl Hang Jebat 2 (☎ 538028)
UK
    Jl Ahmad Yani 2 (☎ 518699)
USA
    Jl Imam Bonjol 13 (☎ 322200)

Money Medan has branches of just about
every bank operating in Indonesia. Most of
the major commercial banks are along Jl
Pemuda and Jl Ahmad Yani. The Bank
Negara Indonesia (BNI) branch on Jl Soe-
karno-Hatta doesn't change money. The
branch on Jl Ahmad Yani cashes only Amer-
ican Express (Amex) travellers cheques and
US dollars. Opposite BNI 1946 are Bank
SBU (Amex only) and Bank Duta, which
also accepts travellers cheques backed by
Visa. The best rates are to be found at the
Bank of Central Asia at the junction of Jl
Palang Merah and Jl Imam Bonjol.

Outside banking hours, try one of the
travel agencies on Jl Katamso such as
Trophy Tours at 33D, or one of the big hotels.

Amex is represented by Pacto (☎ 510081)

at Jl Katamso 35G. Diner's Club International has an office (☎ 513331) at the Hotel
Dharma Deli.

If you're heading south, it's a good idea to
change plenty of money because you won't
find good exchange rates again until you hit
Bukittinggi.

Post & Communications The main post
office is a wonderful old Dutch building on
the main square, Kebawan Park, in the
middle of town.

The Telkom office is nearby on Jl Soekarno-Hatta. It has a Home Country Direct
service, as do several popular travellers'
haunts, including the Tip Top Restaurant,
Losmen Irama and Penginapan Tapian Nabaru.

Travel Agencies Jl Katamso is packed with
travel agencies and is the place to buy ferry
tickets. Trophy Tours (☎ 514888) at No 33D
is one of the biggest operators.

Edelweiss Travel (☎ 517297) at Jl Irian-
barat 47-49 is well organised and the
manager speaks fluent English. It has the
best choice of organised tours.

Bookshops Finding anything to read in
English is a hassle. The Toko Buku Deli at Jl
Ahmad Yani 48 has a few books in English,
including a couple of novels. It also sells
Time and *Newsweek*.

The bookshops at the Tiara Medan and
Garuda Plaza hotels both sell a range of
books about Indonesia, as well as a few
expensive 'airport' novels. The Tiara Medan
also has foreign newspapers, such as the
*London Daily Telegraph, International
Herald Tribune* and *Bangkok Post*.

Istana Maimoon & Mesjid Raya

The city's two finest buildings are within
200m of each other. The crumbling Istana
Maimoon (Maimoun Palace) on Jl Katamso
was built by the Sultan of Deli in 1888, and
the family still occupies one wing.

The magnificent black-domed Mesjid
Raya is nearby at the junction of Jl Mesjid

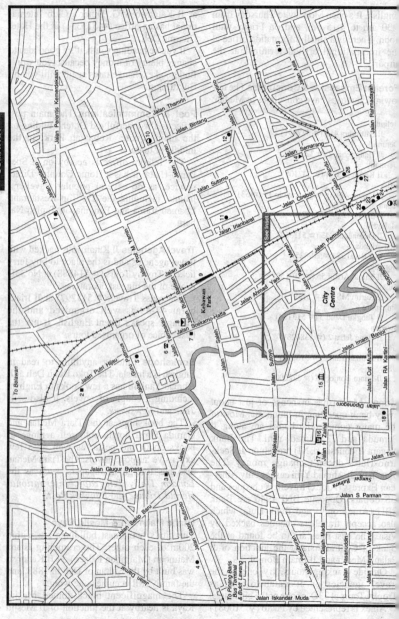

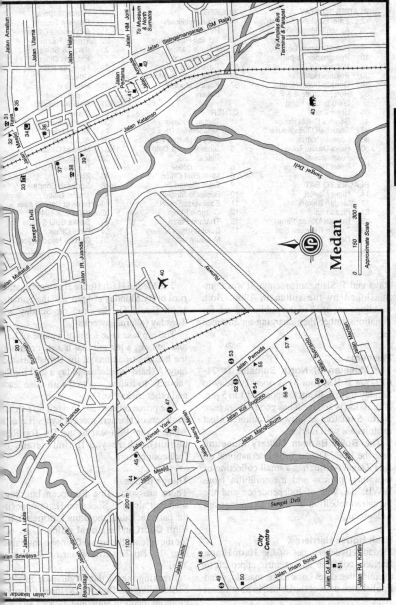

SUMATRA

Medan

Approximate Scale

0   150   300 m

City Centre

Sungai Deli

Sungai Deli

Sungai Deli

PLACES TO STAY		
2	Emerald Garden Hotel	
3	Asean International Hotel	
7	Hotel Dharma Deli	
19	Penginapan Taipan Nabaru	
20	Polonia Hotel	
28	Garuda Plaza Hotel	
30	Hotel Sumatera & Garuda City Hotel	
36	Hotel Zakia	
41	Sarah's Guest House	
42	Shahibah Guesthouse	
48	Losmen Irama	
50	Hotel Danau Toba International	
51	Hotel Tiara Medan	

PLACES TO EAT	
14	Night Market
17	Medan Bakers
21	Pizza Hut
29	Rumah Makan Famili
32	Taman Rekreasi Seri Deli
39	KFC
44	G's Koh I Noor Restaurant
46	Tip Top Restaurant & Lyn's Bar & Restaurant
55	Restaurant Agung
56	Brastagi Fruits Market
57	France Modern Bakery

OTHER	
1	Taman Budaya
4	Amusement Park (Site of Medan Fair)
5	Sinar Plaza & Deli Plaza
6	Telkom Office
8	Main Post Office
9	Train Station
10	Buses to Singkil
11	Edelweiss Travel
12	Olympia Plaza
13	Thamrin Plaza
15	Bukit Barisan Military Museum
16	Parisada Hindu Dharma Temple
18	Governor's Office
22	Trophy Tours
23	Pacto & Selesa Ekspres Office
24	Mandala & Bouraq Offices
25	Inda Taxi
26	Water Tower
27	Gelora Plaza
31	Wartel
33	Istana Maimoon
34	Mesjid Raya
35	ALS Office
37	Merpati Office
38	Wartel
40	Polonia Airport
43	Zoo
45	Souvenir Shops
47	Tourist Office
49	Bank of Central Asia
52	BNI Bank 1946
53	Banks SBU & Duta
54	Pelni Office
58	Garuda Head Office

Raya and Jl Sisingamangaraja. It was commissioned by the sultan in 1906. Both buildings are open to the public and ask for donations rather than charging an entrance fee.

Museums
The **Museum of North Sumatra** (☎ 71-6792) at Jl HM Joni 51 is open Tuesday to Sunday from 8.30 am to noon and 1 to 5 pm. Admission is 200 rp. It has good coverage of North Sumatran history and culture. Most exhibits are well marked.

The **Bukit Barisan Military Museum**, near the Hotel Danau Toba International on Jl H Zainal Arifin, has a small collection of weapons, photos and memorabilia from WWII, the War of Independence and the Sumatran rebellion of 1958. Donations are welcomed.

Hash House Harriers
Medan's two branches of the Hash House Harriers continue an eccentric approach to exercise that dates back to the mad dogs and Englishmen days of the British in South-East Asia.

The Medan Hash House Harriers organis runs every Monday at 4 pm, and the Sumatr Hash House Harriers run on Sunday an Tuesday (alternate weeks).

The run takes the form of a game of har and hounds, a pursuit that has its origins i the hunting traditions of the British aristoc racy. A 'hare' is selected to lay a trail for th 'hounds' to follow – dotted with false lead and other tricks.

The prime objective is to work up a thirs Both sets of Harriers meet at Lyn's Bar at J Ahmad Yani 98 (next to the Tip Top Res taurant), where you'll find details o forthcoming runs.

Things to See
There are some fine European building scattered along Jl Soekarno-Hatta opposit the park, including the **Bank Indonesia**, th **High Court** and the **post office**. Look ou for the splendidly ornate **Chinese mansio** near the Tip Top Restaurant on Jl Ahma Yani.

Breaking the Medan skyline are moder edifices like the **Deli Plaza**, three floors o glittering neon-lit shopping arcades straigh out of Singapore and a nightly hangout for Medan's gays. The top floor has a small **amusement park** with a couple of good rides for small children, as well as dodgem cars for the big kids.

The **Parisada Hindu Dharma** temple is on the corner of Jl Teuku Umar and Jl H Zainal Arifin.

A bemo ride along Jl Katamso is Medan's depressing zoo, the **Taman Margasawata**. The **crocodile farm** at Asam Kumbang, five km from the city centre, is something else to steer clear of.

Places to Stay

Every becak driver in Medan seems to tout for one or other of the travellers' haunts. Their favourite hunting ground is around the travel agencies on Jl Katamso, where buses drop new arrivals at the end of the ferry trip from Penang. They will tell any number of stories to divert you from the hotel of your choice: the place you want to go to doesn't exist; it's either closed for repairs, full, dirty or too expensive; or it's changed its name – to the place they represent.

Places to Stay – bottom end

The best travellers' places are south of the city centre off Jl SM Raja. The *Hotel Zakia* (☎ 722413), right next to the Mesjid Raya on Jl Sipiso-Piso, is a friendly family-run place with a choice of rooms. It has dorm beds for 5000 rp, doubles with fan for 12,500 rp, and doubles with bathroom and fan for 15,000 rp. Prices include a breakfast of roti and coffee.

Further south is *Sarah's Guest House* (☎ 743783), tucked away at Jl Pertama 10. It has doubles with fan for 10,000 rp and doubles with bathroom for 15,000 rp. The owner offers free transport to the airport. This place should not be confused with the nearby *Shahibah Guesthouse* (☎ 718528) at Jl Armada 3, home of the most persistent becak touts. It has dorm beds for 6000 rp and doubles with bathroom for 25,000 rp.

The *Losmen Irama* (☎ 326416), on a little alley at Jl Palang Merah 1125, gets a lot of travellers despite having some of the city's grottiest rooms and laziest staff. Its sole virtue is its proximity to the city centre. It also has a Home Country Direct phone for international calls. It charges 5000 rp per person, but you'll need to fork out another 2500 rp for a fan to have any chance of getting to sleep.

Penginapan Tapian Nabaru (☎ 512155) occupies an old timber house on the banks of the Sungai (River) Deli at Jl Hang Tuah 6. It's a quiet place with dorms for 3000 rp and doubles with shared bath for 6500 rp, but it's a long way off the beaten track.

Places to Stay – middle

There is a string of uninspiring mid-range places north of the Mesjid Raya on Jl SM Raja. The *Hotel Sumatera* (☎ 721551) at No 35 has a range of air-con doubles from 45,000 rp, including breakfast. It offers free transport to the airport.

The formidable-looking *Garuda City Hotel* (☎ 717733), next door, has basic air-con doubles for 55,000 rp and much better rooms in its new wing for 80,000 rp. All prices include breakfast.

Places to Stay – top end

Medan's best hotels are of international standard. They all offer such luxuries as fitness centres, swimming pools and 24 hour room service. They also quote their rates in international currency (US dollars), convertible at the day's rate.

Top of the range is the massive *Hotel Tiara Medan* (☎ 516000) on Jl Cut Mutiah, where prices start at US$105. The *Hotel Danau Toba International* (☎ 557000), on the banks of the Sungai Deli at Jl Imam Bonjol 17, has completed a major renovation job to bring rooms up to the standard of the impressive marble foyer. Doubles start at US$89.

Other international-standard places are the brand new *Emerald Garden* (☎ 611888), Jl Yos Sudarso 1; *Polonia Hotel* (☎ 535111), Jl Sudirman 14; and *Asean International Hotel* (☎ 561965), on the corner of Jl Gatot Subroto and Jl Glugur Bypass.

SUMATRA

SUMATRA

Places to Eat

One of Medan's saving graces is Jl Semarang, east of the train line between Jl Pandu and Jl Bandung. By day it's just a grubby side street, but come nightfall it's jam-packed with food stalls offering great Chinese food.

The *Taman Rekreasi Seri Deli*, across the road from the Mesjid Raya, is a slightly upmarket approach to stall eating. You just sit down and waitresses bring round a menu that allows you to choose from the offerings of about 20 stalls.

The *Tip Top Restaurant* at Jl Ahmad Yani 92 is not the cheapest place in town, but it's an old favourite with foreign visitors. It's a pleasant spot, in spite of the continuous traffic jam outside. It serves European and Chinese food as well as Padang food. It also has a Home Country Direct phone.

There are much better places to eat Padang food than the Tip Top. Try the *Restaurant Agung* at Jl Pemuda 40, or the *Rumah Makan Famili* at Jl SM Raja 21B.

Vegetarians looking for something other than gado gado should check out *G's Koh I Noor*, a family-run Indian restaurant at Jl Mesjid 21.

If you're hanging out for some junk food, there are *KFCs* on the corner of Jl IR Juanda and Jl Katamso and at Deli Plaza. *Pizza Hut* (☎ 519956) on the corner of Jl Multatuli and Jl Suprapto offers free delivery to your home or hotel.

Fruit is surprisingly hard to find. The main fruit market is the *Pasar Ramai*, next to Thamrin Plaza on Jl Thamrin. *Brastagi Fruits Market*, an upmarket, air-con shop rather than a market, is more conveniently located on Jl Kol Sugiono. It has a great selection of both local and imported tropical fruit, as well as apples and oranges.

There are some excellent bakeries awaiting the sweet-toothed traveller. Two to check out are the *France Modern Bakery*, at Jl Pemuda 24C, and *Medan Bakers*, just beyond the Hindu temple at Jl H Zainal Arifin 150.

Entertainment

Cultural performances can be seen at *Taman Budaya* on Jl Perentis Kemerdekaan, near P? Indosat. The tourist office has a list of what' on. The amusement park *(taman ria)* on J Gatot Subroto is also the site for the Medar Fair in August.

Things to Buy

Medan has a number of interesting arts & crafts shops, particularly along Jl Ahmac Yani. Try Toko Asli at No 62, Toko Rufine at No 56 or Toko Bali Arts at No 68. They al have a good selection of antique weaving Dutch pottery, carvings and other pieces.

Getting There & Away

Medan is Sumatra's main internationa arrival and departure point.

Air There are daily international flights from Medan to Singapore, Kuala Lumpur and Penang. See the introductory Getting There & Away section in this chapter for details.

There are numerous direct flights to Jakarta (414,700 rp). Garuda alone does the trip five times daily, Sempati has four flights a day, while Bouraq and Mandala also have five flights daily. Garuda also flies twice daily to Banda Aceh (145,200 rp) and direct to Denpasar (559,800 rp) three times a week Merpati has daily flights to Padang (173,80C rp) and Pekanbaru (159,600 rp). SMAC flies from Medan to Gunung Sitoli (131,300 rp on Pulau Nias at least once a day.

Airlines with offices in Medan are a: follows:

Bouraq
    Jl Katamso (☎ 552333)
Garuda
    Head office: Jl Suprapto 2 (☎ 516066)
    Branch offices: Hotel Tiara Medan (☎ 538527)
    Hotel Dharma Deli (☎ 516400)
MAS
    Hotel Danau Toba International, Jl Imam Bonjo
    17 (☎ 519333)
Mandala
    Jl Katamso 37E (☎ 516379)
Merpati
    Jl Katamso 41J (☎ 514102)
Sempati
    Hotel Tiara Medan (☎ 537800)
    Hotel Dharma Deli (☎ 327011)

ilk Air
    Polonia Hotel, Jl Sudirman (☎ 537744)
MAC
    Jl Imam Bonjol 59 (close to the airport;
    ☎ 537760)
hai International
    Hotel Dharma Deli (☎ 510541)

Bus There are two main bus terminals.
Buses to Parapat, Bukittinggi and other
points south leave from the huge Amplas
terminal, 6.5 km south of the city centre
along Jl SM Raja. The best companies for
long-distance travel south are ALS and ANS.
Their offices are in a separate building
behind the main block. They charge similar
fares – 30,000 rp for air-con services to
Bukittinggi, or 45,000 rp for the deluxe
buses. ALS also has a convenient booking
office in town at Jl Amaliun 2, 150m from
the Mesjid Raya. Almost any opelet heading
south on Jl SM Raja will get you to Amplas.

Buses to the north leave from Pinang Baris
bus terminal, 10 km west of the city centre
on Jl Gatot Subroto. There are buses to both
Bukit Lawang (1500 rp; three hours) and
Berastagi (1400 rp; two hours) every half-
hour between 5.30 am and 6 pm. There are
also frequent buses to Banda Aceh. The
journey takes anything up to 13 hours in
daytime, but the express night buses do the
trip in about nine hours. Fares range from
5,000 to 40,000 rp for the latest luxury
buses with reclining seats.

SMJ Travel (☎ 720652), opposite the
junction of Jl SM Raja and Jl Sipiso-Piso, has
five minibuses a day to Parapat and Sibolga.
Seats cost 15,000 rp, regardless of how far
you go, including hotel pick-up.

Train There are passenger services twice a
day to Pematangsiantar (4000/6000 rp for
konomi/bisnis class), Tanjung Balai (4500/
7500 rp) and Rantauparapat (8000 rp bisnis
class only).

Taxi There are several long-distance taxi
operators in Medan. Inda Taxi (☎ 516615),
Jl Katamso 60, has share taxis to Parapat
(18,000 rp) and Sibolga (20,000 rp). Hotels
can arrange charter taxis for four people to

places like Berastagi (65,000 rp) and Bukit
Lawang (75,000 rp).

Boat The high-speed ferries to Penang can
be booked at the agents on Jl Katamso. Pacto
(☎ 510081), Jl Katamso 35G, handles tickets
for the *Ekspres Bahagia*, which leaves on
Tuesday, Thursday and Saturday at 10 am.
Perdana Express (☎ 545803), Jl Katamso
35C, sells tickets for the *Ekspres Selasa*. It
leaves on Wednesday and Friday at 2 pm, and
on Sunday at 2 pm. Both services cost 95,000
rp, which includes the bus to Medan's port
of Belawan. See the introductory Getting
There & Away section earlier in this chapter
for information on other ferry services to
Malaysia.

Pelni has boats to Jakarta and points
further east every Monday (116,500 rp deck
class; 45 hours). The Pelni office (☎ 518899)
in Medan is at Jl Sugiono 5, one block west
of Jl Pemuda.

Getting Around
The Airport Airport taxis (which operate on
a coupon system) charge a standard 8000 rp
to the city. You'll pay half that if you can find
a regular, metered cab. Becaks are not
allowed into the airport area.

Local Transport Medan's taxis are the best
way of getting around. Flagfall is 1150 rp
and fares work out at about 700 rp per km,
which is a good deal less than you'll pay if
you use the pedal-powered becaks that hang
around the travellers' places.

There are numerous tales of woe involving becak riders and demands for outrageous
amounts of money, almost always as a result
of breaking the golden rule of becak travel:
agree on the fare beforehand and, if there is
more than one passenger, clarify how many
people are covered by the fare. As a general
guide, reckon on paying about 1500 rp per km
– which means that most journeys around the
city centre should cost no more than 3000 rp.

Opelets are the main form of public transport. They cost 300 rp, although you may be

asked to pay double if you have a large backpack. Just stand by the roadside and call out your destination.

There are lots of opelets to Pinang Baris bus terminal along Jl Gatot Subroto. A taxi from the city centre to the terminal costs about 6500 rp.

BUKIT LAWANG

Bukit Lawang, 96 km north-west of Medan, is on the eastern edge of the giant Gunung Leuser National Park. The country is wild and enchanting, with dense jungle and clear, fast-flowing rivers.

It is also the site of the famous Bohorok Orang-utan Rehabilitation Centre, which has made this once-remote village one of the most popular spots in Sumatra. Many tourists opt to spend four or five days here.

It is a very popular weekend destination for Medan people, which means accommodation can be hard to find on Friday and Saturday nights. Foreign tourists have the place pretty much to themselves during the week.

For more information on Gunung Leuser National Park, see the Aceh section later in this chapter.

Orientation

The settlement exists almost solely to service the tourist industry. The bus stops where the road ends: a small square surrounded by shops and a few offices. There are a couple of restaurants by the river where you can sit and take stock. The closest accommodation is on the opposite side of the river, but the prime locations are 15 minutes' walk upstream.

Information

Tourist Office There is a small tourist office in the white building at the back of the bus lot. There is not much information to be gained, but the staff are helpful and speak English.

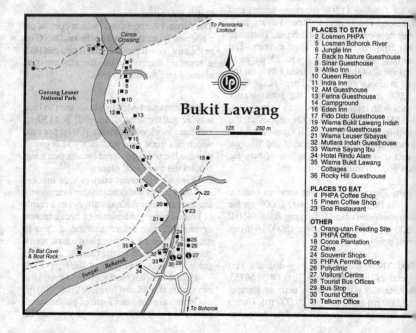

PLACES TO STAY
2 Losmen PHPA
5 Losmen Bohorok River
6 Jungle Inn
7 Back to Nature Guesthouse
8 Sinar Guesthouse
9 Afriko Inn
10 Queen Resort
11 Indra Inn
12 AM Guesthouse
13 Farina Guesthouse
14 Campground
16 Eden Inn
17 Fido Dido Guesthouse
19 Wisma Bukit Lawang Indah
20 Yusman Guesthouse
21 Wisma Leuser Sibayak
32 Mutiara Indah Guesthouse
33 Wisma Sayang Ibu
34 Hotel Rindu Alam
35 Wisma Bukit Lawang Cottages
36 Rocky Hill Guesthouse

PLACES TO EAT
4 PHPA Coffee Shop
15 Pinem Coffee Shop
23 Goa Restaurant

OTHER
1 Orang-utan Feeding Site
3 PHPA Office
18 Cocoa Plantation
22 Cave
24 Souvenir Shops
25 PHPA Permits Office
26 Polyclinic
27 Visitors' Centre
28 Tourist Bus Offices
29 Bus Stop
30 Tourist Office
31 Telkom Office

Bukit Lawang

To Panorama Lookout
Canoe Crossing
Gunung Leuser National Park
To Bat Cave & Boat Rock
Sungai Bohorok
To Bohorok

0   125   250 m

Going Ape

Gunung Leuser National Park is one of world's largest remaining strongholds of the orang-utan, with more than 5000 animals thought to be living in the wild.

The orang-utan is found today only in Sumatra and Borneo, although fossilised remains show that its range once extended to China and Java.

It is the world's largest arboreal mammal, large males weighing up to 90 kg. Despite their size, they move through the jungle canopy with great agility and assurance, swinging on vines and branches, or using their weight to sway saplings back and forth to reach the next.

The name *orang hutan* is Malay for 'person of the forest', and there are numerous myths and legends surrounding the creature. Stories were told of how the orang-utan would carry off pretty girls. Others told of how the orang-utan could speak, but refused to do so because it did not want to be made to work.

The orang-utan has a long life-span, but tends to breed slowly. Females reach sexual maturity at about the age of 10 years. They have few young and stay around their mothers until they are about seven to 10 years old. The females remain fertile until about the age of 30 and, on average, have only one baby every six years. The orang-utan tends to be quite a solitary creature.

They are primarily vegetarians. Their normal diet comprises fruit, shoots and leaves, as well as nuts and tree bark that they grind up with their powerful jaws and teeth. They occasionally eat insects, eggs and small mammals.

Despite its remarkably human expressions, the orang-utan is considered to be the most distantly related to humans of all the great apes.

Apart from Gunung Leuser National Park, orang-utans can also be found in the Tanjung Puting and Kutai national parks and the Gunung Palung and Bukit Raja reserves in Kalimantan, as well as in neighbouring Sarawak and Sabah. ■

Money Change money before you arrive. There are no banks in Bukit Lawang and the rates at the local moneychangers are appalling.

Post & Communications There is no post office, but you can buy stamps from the shops and there are post boxes. The telephone network has finally made it to Bukit Lawang. There is a small Telkom office by the river opposite the Wisma Leuser Sibayak, and Wisma Bukit Lawang Cottages has a card phone.

Medical Services Minor medical problems can be dealt with by the nurse at the small clinic next to the PHPA (national park) permit office.

Dangers & Annoyances The boom has its downside. Petty theft is a problem and visitors are advised to take care with valuables. Use hotel safety boxes where available.

Orang-Utan Rehabilitation Centre
Bukit Lawang's famous Orang-utan Rehabilitation Centre was set up in 1973 to help the primates readjust to the wild after captivity. That was the original intention. These days, the tourist industry that has grown up around the centre would be devastated if the animals actually learned to fend for themselves and failed to front for the cameras.

The orang-utans can be seen every day at a jungle feeding platform in the adjacent national park. Before you set off, get a permit from the PHPA office in Bukit Lawang – open from 7 am daily. The permit costs 4000 rp, plus 500 rp insurance, and is valid for two days. It must be used within three days of issue. In theory, only 40 permits are issued each day, but the numbers swell at the weekend when the Medan crowds arrive.

The feeding site is 30 minutes' walk from the office in town, including a free crossing of Sungai Bohorok in a dugout canoe. The path into the national park from the river crossing can get very muddy.

Feeding times are from 8 to 9 am and 3 to 4 pm. These are the only times visitors are allowed to enter the national park other than with a guide or on an organised trek.

Most days about half a dozen orang-utans turn up to be fed milk and bananas, intended as supplementary feed until they learn to fend fully for themselves. It's best to get there early so that you can see the orang-utans arrive, swinging through the trees. It is forbidden to touch or feed the animals.

The cages by the Losmen PHPA are used to keep new arrivals in quarantine and sick animals under observation.

Occasionally, orang-utans can be seen by the river opposite the Jungle Inn and Losmen Bohorok River, where they come down to check out the tourists.

Bukit Lawang Visitors' Centre

This fine establishment is run by the World Wide Fund for Nature (WWF). It has good displays of flora and fauna in Gunung Leuser National Park and a section to explain the orang-utan rehabilitation programme. It's backed up by some stunning photographs. The centre sells a small, but very informative, booklet about the national park by New Zealand writer and photographer Mike Griffiths. It's a good investment at 12,000 rp if you plan to spend some time in the park.

Rafting

The Back to Nature Guesthouse organises rafting trips down the Bohorok and Wampu rivers for 75,000 rp per day.

Trekking

A lot of people use Bukit Lawang as a base for trekking. Almost every losmen advertises trekking and half the losmen workers seem to be guides – without whom you are not allowed into the park. They offer a range of treks around Bukit Lawang, as well as three and five day walks to Berastagi.

Around Bukit Lawang, expect to pay 25,000 rp for a day trek and 30,000 per day for treks that involve camping out. Prices include meals, guide fees and the cost of the permit to enter the park.

Short Walks

There are a number of short walks that require no guides or permits, including a visit

to a bat cave, 20 minutes' walk to the south west of town. It's signposted behind th Wisma Bukit Lawang Cottages. The two kr walk passes through rubber plantations an patches of forest.

A lot of the forest trees are durians, so tak care in late June and July when the spike fruits crash to the ground (there are sign warning people not to linger). You'll need torch (flashlight) to explore the caves.

There are more bat caves a further four kr downstream at a site called Boat Rock, bu entry is not allowed without a guide.

The Panorama Lookout walk starts jus north of the Jungle Inn. The path through th rainforest is very steep and slippery. Lunt Cave, about 20 minutes' walk from th lookout, is another bat hangout.

Tubing

Many of the losmen rent out inflated truc inner tubes which can be used to ride th rapids of the Sungai Bohorok. Severa people have got into difficulties on the rive People contemplating tubing should b aware that river levels can rise very quickl if it's raining. Life jackets are not available

Places to Stay & Eat

Bukit Lawang has a string of good, chea losmen spread out along the river. Accom modation is concentrated in two main areas along the river bank opposite the town an upstream along the path to the orang-uta feeding site. Like travellers' places else where, most of the losmen have associate restaurants.

The best budget accommodation is up stream near the canoe crossing, about 1: minutes' walk from town. This is also the best spot to go swimming. The *Jungle Inn* with its creative carpentry and incredibl relaxed style, is very popular. It has basi doubles for 5000 rp, as well as rooms wit balconies overhanging the river for 15,00 rp. No doubt the eyes of many will light up on spotting 'extremely herbal jungle tea extra herb' on the menu. It turns out to b very much as described – a drink made from

mixture of jungle herbs, berries, bits of bark
tc.

Some of the Jungle Inn's neighbours offer
etter value. The *Losmen Bohorok River* has
ooms on the river bank for 7000 rp, while
he nearby *Sinar Guesthouse* and *Back to
'ature Guesthouse* both charge 5000 rp. The
'arina Guesthouse, opposite the camp-
round, is good value with large, clean
oubles for 6000 rp.

The downstream accommodation is dom-
nated by the *Wisma Bukit Lawang Cottages*
(☎ 545061) and the *Wisma Leuser Sibayak*
(☎ 550576), two large bungalow complexes
ffering a range of rooms. The Sibayak has
ome cheapies for 5000 rp as well as com-
ortable modern rooms by the river for
5,000 rp, while Bukit Lawang Cottages are
rom 7500 to 20,000 rp. Both also have good
estaurants. Bukit Lawang Cottages has
ome interesting items on the menu like
anana stem curry, while the Sibayak does
xcellent Padang food, as well as travellers'
are.

The most expensive hotel in town is the
ew *Rindu Alam* (☎ 545015), where 70,000
p gets a double with TV and breakfast.

Durian trees can be found everywhere in
nd around Bukit Lawang, and the town is
verflowing with the fruit in late June and
uly. They are as fresh and as cheap as you'll
nd anywhere, from 750 rp for a small one.

Getting There & Away
here are direct buses to Medan's Pinang
aris bus terminal every half-hour between
.30 am and 6 pm. The 96 km journey takes
ree hours and costs 1500 rp. A chartered
axi to Medan costs 75,000 rp.

As elsewhere, the tourist minibuses are
eavily promoted. They leave early in the
norning for Medan (10,000 rp), Berastagi
15,000 rp) and Danau Toba (25,000 rp).

BERASTAGI (BRASTAGI)
Berastagi is a picturesque hill town in the
Karo Highlands, only 70 km from Medan on
he back road to Danau Toba. At an altitude
f 1300m, the climate is deliciously cool
fter the heat of Medan. The setting is dom-

inated by two volcanoes: Gunung Sinabung
to the west and the smoking Gunung Sibayak
to the north.

Few towns in Sumatra are better set up for
travellers, although the town itself is not
wildly exciting. Most people use Berastagi
as a base for trekking and other adventure
activities. Architecture buffs can enjoy trips
to nearby traditional Karo Batak villages.

Orientation
Berastagi is essentially a one street town
spread along Jl Veteran. The hill to the north-
west of town is Bukit Gundaling, a popular
picnic spot and mid-range accommodation
area.

Information
Tourist Office The Karo regional tourist
office (☎ 91084), Jl Gundaling 1, next to the
memorial in the centre of town, is friendly
and well set up. The best source of travellers'
information, however, is the notice boards at
the Wisma Sibayak.

Money You can change US dollars, cash and
travellers cheques at Bank Rakyat Indonesia
at the bottom end of Jl Veteran. You can
change other currencies at any of the many
several moneychangers, but the rates are terrible.

Post & Communications The post office
and Telkom office are side by side near the
memorial at the northern end of Jl Veteran.

Things to See & Do
The town is crawling with guides for treks
along the well-trodden trails through **Gunung Leuser National Park** to Bukit Lawang.
Prices start at 30,000 rp per day for three
days/two nights, staying at villages along the
way.

There's not a lot to do in town. Golfers can
get a game at Hotel Bukit Kubu (see Places
to Stay). Green fees are 10,000 rp for the nine
par-three holes and you can hire a set of clubs
for 12,500 rp.

Kampung Peceren is a cluster of traditional houses on the northern outskirts of

SUMATRA

Berastagi that has almost been absorbed by the town. Most of the houses are still occupied. Any opelet heading north can drop you there (300 rp).

There are good views from **Bukit Gundaling**, particularly at sunset. A round-tour of the hill by horse-drawn *sado* (cart) costs 5000 rp.

Places to Stay – bottom end

The *Wisma Sibayak* (☎ 20953) at the bottom end of the main street is one of the best-run travellers' places in the country. It has dorm beds for 3000 rp and small singles/doubles for 5000/7000 rp, as well as larger rooms for 12,000 rp. It's packed with travellers, and the guest books are full of useful and amusing information about sightseeing, festivals, transport, walks, climbs and other things to

PLACES TO STAY	
2	Rose Garden Hotel
3	Rudang Hotel
4	Hotel Bukit Kubu
6	Demerel Guesthouse
7	Wisma Ikut
10	Crispo Inn
13	Ginsata Hotel
14	Ginsata Guesthouse
15	Losmen TS Lingga
16	Losmen Trimurty
17	Merpati Inn
21	Torong Inn
24	Losmen Sibayak Guesthouse
31	Wisma Sibayak

PLACES TO EAT	
11	Rendezvous Restaurant
22	Asia Restaurant
25	Europah Restaurant

OTHER	
1	Kampung Peceren
5	Power Station
8	Petrol Station
9	Fruit Market
12	Memorial
18	Tourist Office
19	Telkom Office
20	Post Office
23	Public Health Centre
26	Bank Rakyat Indonesia
27	Ria Cinema
28	Market
29	Bus & Opelet Terminal
30	Mini Market

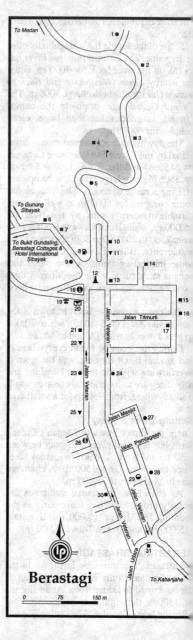

Berastagi

0   75   150 m

To Medan

To Gunung Sibayak

To Bukit Gundaling, Berastagi Cottages & Hotel International Sibayak

Jalan Trimurti

Jalan Veteran

Jalan Veteran

Jalan Masjid

Jalan Perniagaan

Jalan Veteran

Jalan Udara

To Kabanjahe

o in the area. The Sibayak's back-up place s *Losmen Sibayak Guesthouse* in the middle f town on Jl Veteran.

There are several reasonable places at the op end of town. The *Ginsata Hotel* at Jl /eteran 79 has clean doubles with shower for 0,000 rp. Just around the corner is the *Ginsata Guest House*, a pleasant old timber uilding with rooms from 3500/5000 rp. The *Crispo Inn* (☎ 91023) at Jl Veteran 3 has oubles for 5000 rp, or 10,000 rp with hot hower and breakfast.

There is a cluster of small guesthouses round the junction at the eastern end of Jl 'rimurti, a short walk from the memorial. hey include the *Merpati Inn* (☎ 91157), /hich has a few tiny rooms for 4000 rp and arger ones with mandi (small bath) for 7500 p.

There are a couple of old Dutch guest-ouses on the road to Bukit Gundaling. The *Demerel* (☎ 91586) still has a certain dilapi-ated charm and is popular with those /anting to escape the crowds in town. Doubles are 8000 rp. The nearby *Wisma Ikut* s in very poor shape.

Places to Stay – middle

Berastagi's upmarket accommodation is oncentrated around Bukit Gundaling and to ne north of town on the road to Medan.

Kalianda Bungalows, on the road leading /est from the tourist office, is the cheapest f a cluster of bungalow-style places on the pproaches to Gundaling. It charges 20,000/ 0,000 rp for singles/doubles. Further up the ill, and much further upmarket, are the tylish *Berastagi Cottages* (☎ 91725), with choice of rooms from 79,000 rp.

The *Hotel Bukit Kubu* (☎ 20832), just orth of town on Jl Sempurna, was originally guesthouse owned by the Dutch oil com-any Batavia Petroleum. It sits on a small hill et back from the road, surrounded by its wn nine-hole golf course. Rates are 5,000/55,000 rp for large rooms in the old uilding and 65,000/85,000 rp in the new /ing. There are no private bathrooms in the ld building.

Places to Stay – top end

Three and four star hotels are springing up everywhere, aimed largely at the Malaysian and Singaporean package-tour markets. They all come complete with swimming pools, tennis courts and fitness centres. The cheapest doubles are listed at about 120,000 rp, but this is very negotiable. The biggest of them is the *Hotel International Sibayak* (☎ 91301) on the road to Bukit Gundaling.

Places to Eat

Berastagi is famous for its fruit and vegetable markets. The rich volcanic soils of the sur-rounding countryside supply much of North Sumatra's produce. Passionfruit is a local speciality. You'll find both the marquisa bandung, a large, sweet, yellow-skinned fruit, and the marquisa asam manis, a purple-skinned fruit that makes delicious drinks.

At night, try the delicious cakes made from rice flour, palm sugar and coconut, steamed in bamboo cylinders. You can buy them at the stall outside the Ria Cinema.

Most of the budget hotels also operate restaurants. The restaurant at the *Wisma Sibayak* is fast and efficient and serves good food, while the Torong Inn's *Jane & Tarzan Coffee Shop* and the *Ginsata Guest House* serve typical travellers' fare.

There's Padang food at the *Ginsata* and the *Rumah Makan Muslimin*, downstairs from the Torong Inn, where the manager speaks English and is happy to explain his dishes to western novices.

The *Eropah Restaurant* at Jl Veteran 48G does good cheap Chinese food. The air-con *Asia Restaurant* at No 9-10 is bigger and more expensive.

Things to Buy

There are a number of interesting antique and souvenir shops along Jl Veteran. Crispo Antiques has particularly interesting items.

Getting There & Away

Berastagi's bus terminal is on Jl Veteran. There are frequent buses from Berastagi to Medan (1400 rp; two hours).

Getting to Parapat by public bus is a hassle

(see Parapat's Getting There & Away entry later in this section). The easy option is to catch one of the tourist buses making the Bukit Lawang-Parapat run. Berastagi is the midpoint and buses stop for lunch in both directions, leaving at about 1 pm. It costs 15,000 rp to both Bukit Lawang and Parapat.

The Parapat leg includes sightseeing stops at the Sipiso-Piso Waterfall at the northern tip of Danau Toba and the huge king's house near Pematangpurba. Buses follow the winding road along the eastern shore of Danau Toba to Parapat.

The Bukit Lawang leg goes via Medan and includes stops at palm oil and rubber plantations.

Berastagi is the jumping-off point for visits to Kutacane and the Gunung Leuser National Park. For more details, see Kutacane in the Aceh Province section.

Getting Around

Opelets leave from the bus terminal on Jl Veteran. They run every few minutes between Berastagi and Kabanjahe (300 rp), the major population and transport centre of the highlands. You need to go to Kabanjahe, 16 km south of Berastagi, to get to many of the villages mentioned in the following section.

Horse-drawn sados charge from 1500 rp for rides around town.

AROUND BERASTAGI
Gunung Sibayak

Many people come to Berastagi to climb Gunung Sibayak (2094m), probably the most accessible of Indonesia's volcanoes. It's best to avoid going on a Sunday, when day trippers from Medan are out in force.

You need good walking boots because the path is steep in places and is slippery year-round. It can be cold at the top, so bring something warm to wear as well as food, drink and a torch (flashlight), in case you get caught out after dark. The guest books at Wisma Sibayak are full of information about this climb, including numerous warnings about the dangers of sudden weather changes. People are strongly advised not to tackle the climb alone. A lone Danish travel-

ler died on the mountain in July 1995 after getting lost in a storm and falling.

There are three ways to tackle the climb depending on your energy level. The easiest way is to catch a local bus (800 rp) to Semangat Gunung at the base of the volcano from where it's a two hour climb to the top. Alternatively, you can start from Berastagi taking the track leading from the road to Bukit Gundaling. This walk takes about three hours. The longest option is to start from the Panorama Waterfall on the Medan road, about five km north of Berastagi. Allow at least five hours for this walk.

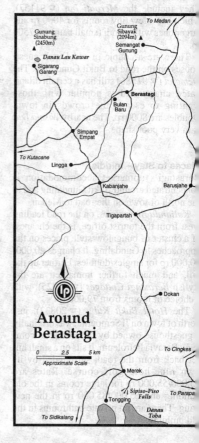

Around Berastagi

0   2.5   5 km
Approximate Scale

Whichever route you choose, on the way own it's worth stopping for a soak in the hot prings (500 to 1500 rp), a short ride from emangat Gunung on the road back to erastagi.

unung Sinabung

unung Sinabung (2450m) is considerably igher than Sibayak and the views from the p are spectacular.

The climb takes six hours up and four ours down, starting from the village of igarang Garang. Sigarang Garang is 30 min- tes by opelet from Kabanjahe (600 rp), so ou will need to start early or join an rganised walk with a guide. Again, you'll eed good shoes, warm clothing, food, drink nd a torch.

ipiso-Piso Waterfall

he impressive Sipiso-Piso Waterfall is at e northern end of Danau Toba, 24 km from abanjahe and about 300m from the main ad. The tourist bus from Bukit Lawang ops at the falls.

raditional Villages

here are some fine examples of traditional aro Batak architecture in the villages round Berastagi. Most of the houses are no ore than 60 years old, or possibly 100, but ertainly not 400 as claimed by some guides. 's surprising that no-one has asked one mily in Cingkes (see further in this section) take down the carved plaque which veals that their ancient-looking home was uilt in 1936!

ingga The best known of these villages is ingga, a few km north of Kabanjahe. Un- rtunately the place is on every tour inerary and is overrun with tourists. There re about a dozen traditional houses with eir characteristic horned roofs. Some, such s the *rumah rajah* (king's house), are occu- ied and in good condition; others, including e *sapo ganjang* (the house for young, nmarried men), have almost collapsed.

Admission to the village is 300 rp. There re English and German-speaking guides

who will show you around for 2000 rp (1000 rp per person for groups). The villagers, especially the women, do not like being photographed. There are regular opelets to Lingga from Kabanjahe (300 rp).

Barusjahe There are only three traditional houses still standing in Barusjahe and their dilapidated condition suggests that they won't be around much longer. It's hardly worth the 30 minute opelet journey from Kabanjahe (600 rp).

Dokan It's amazing that tour groups have yet to discover the charming little village of Dokan, about 16 km south of Kabanjahe. Traditional houses are still in the majority here and most are in good condition.

There are no admission charges, guides or children wanting pens, money etc. You can get there either by the occasional direct opelet from Kabanjahe (600 rp), or by catch- ing any service heading south to Danau Toba and walking the last 1.5 km from the turn-off.

Cingkes Very few travellers make it to Cingkes, about 35 km south-east of Kaban- jahe via Seribudolok. It's the largest of the villages and well worth the effort to get there. At first glance, the place doesn't appear overly exciting, but a bit of exploration reveals at least two dozen houses – all occu- pied and in good condition. There are regular opelets from Kabanjahe (1000 rp; one hour). Wednesday is market day and a good time to visit.

PARAPAT

Tumbling down a hillside on the eastern shore of Danau Toba is the resort town of Parapat, a pleasure spot for the wealthy set from Medan, 176 km to the north. Un- tempted by tourist literature that describes it as the 'most beautiful mountain and lake resort in Indonesia', most travellers linger only long enough to catch a ferry to Samosir.

It is, however, a good place to buy Batak handcrafts, and the lively lakeside markets on Wednesday and Saturday are worth a visit.

SUMATRA

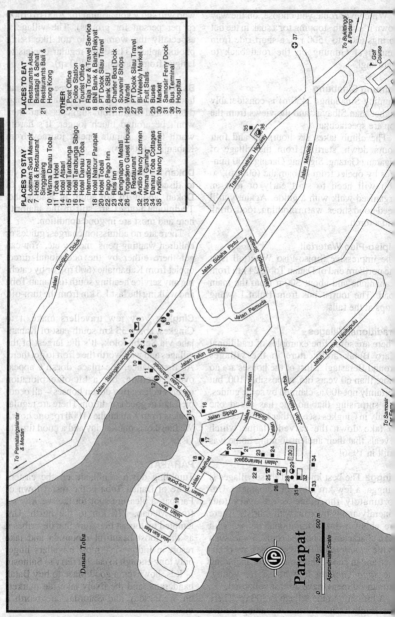

PLACES TO STAY
2 Losmen Sudi Mampir
7 Hotel & Restaurant Singgalang
10 Wisma Danau Toba
11 Toba Hotel
14 Hotel Atsari
15 Hotel Tarabunga
16 Hotel Tarabunga Sibigo
17 Hotel Danau Toba International
18 Hotel Natour Parapat
20 Hotel Tobali
22 Pago Pago Inn
23 Riris Inn
24 Penginapan Melati
26 Trogadero Guest House & Restaurant
32 Andilo Nancy Losmen
33 Wisma Gurning
34 Dinda Town Cottages
35 Andilo Nancy Losmen

PLACES TO EAT
1 Restaurants Asia, Brastagi & Sehat
21 Restaurants Bali & Hong Kong

OTHER
3 Post Office
4 Police Station
5 Tourist Office
6 Raja Tour & Travel Service
8 BNI Bank & Bank Rakyat
9 PT Dolok Silau Travel
12 Bank SBU
13 Charter Boat Dock
19 Souvenir Shops
25 Wartel
27 PT Dolok Silau Travel
28 Bi-Weekly Market & Fruit Stalls
29 Bus
30 Market
31 Samosir Ferry Dock
36 Bus Terminal
37 Hospital

Parapat

Approximate Scale
0   250   500 m

Orientation

Parapat is divided into two parts. The line of restaurants and shops along the Trans-Sumatran Highway are about 1.5 km from the heart of town, the Tiga Raja market place and ferry dock on Danau Toba. The two are linked by Jl Pulau Samosir, which becomes Jl Haranggaol for the final stretch down to the market. The bus terminal is about two km east of town on the Trans-Sumatran Highway.

Information

Tourist Office There is a fairly unhelpful tourist office on Jl Pulau Samosir near the highway.

Money You can change money at the BNI bank on the highway or at Sejahtera Bank Umum (SBU), next door to the Toba Hotel on Jl Pulau Samosir. Rates are poor for currencies other than US dollars, but better than you'll find on Samosir.

Post & Communications The post office is on the Trans-Sumatran Highway. International calls can be made from the *wartel* offices on the highway and by the lake on Jl Haranggaol.

Markets

The produce markets by the ferry dock on Wednesday and Saturday are the main events of the Parapat week. There's always a good selection of fruit.

Organised Tours

PT Dolok Silau, which has offices on the Trans-Sumatran Highway and down by the ferry dock, runs weekly tours to local coffee, tea, ginger, clove and cinnamon farms, as well as other places of interest in and around Parapat.

Special Events

The week-long Danau Toba Festival is held every year in mid-June. Canoe races are a highlight of the festival, but there are also Batak cultural performances.

Places to Stay – bottom end

Travel agent *Andilo Nancy* (☎ 41394) has singles/doubles for 6000/7500 rp above its office by the ferry dock and more rooms next to its office at the bus terminal. There are several places on Jl Haranggaol just uphill from the market. The *Penginapan Melati* (☎ 21174) at No 37 has clean rooms for 7500/10,000 rp. You'll find similar prices at the *Pago Pago Inn*, at No 50, but the rooms are not as flash as the smart bamboo lobby.

Wisma Gurning is a simple, friendly place right by the lake with doubles for 10,000 rp. It's on the street to the left of the ferry dock as you face the lake. The *Trogadero Guest House* (☎ 41148), Jl Harrangaol 112, is a step up from these with small bungalows for 15,000 rp.

There are a couple more budget places near the junction of the highway and Jl Pulau Samosir. Directly opposite the lakeside turn-off is the small and very basic *Losmen Sudi Mampir*, with rooms for 7000/10,000 rp. The *Hotel Singgalang*, uphill on the other side of the road, has much better rooms at 7500 rp per person.

Places to Stay – middle

There are countless mid-range hotels, but nothing outstanding. The *Riris Inn* (☎ 41392), near the ferries at Jl Haranggaol 39, has good, clean doubles from 20,000 rp.

The *Hotel Tarabunga* (☎ 41666) on Jl Pulau Samosir has rooms for 65,000/70,000 rp and a restaurant overlooking the lake. This place is not to be confused with the nearby *Hotel Tarabunga Sibigo* (☎ 41665), a giant concrete box with rooms for 50,000/62,000 rp.

Places to Stay – top end

The *Hotel Natour Parapat* (☎ 41012) at Jl Marihat 1 is the best hotel in town, and also the oldest. It occupies a prime site with fine views over the lake and a private beach. Prices start at 185,000 rp for a double.

Places to Eat

Parapat is dotted with restaurants as well as hotels. The highway strip is well equipped to feed the passing traveller. There are several Padang food places and no less than five Chinese restaurants, the best of which is the *Singgalang* – below the hotel of the same name. There's another string of restaurants along Jl Haranggaol. The *Trogadero Guest House* has a good restaurant right by the lake serving mainly Chinese meals

Getting There & Away

Bus The bus terminal is on the highway, about two km east of town on the way to Bukittinggi. There are frequent buses to Medan (4000 rp; four to five hours), although services taper off in the afternoon. Other destinations include Sibolga (7000 rp; six hours), Bukittinggi (23,000 rp; 18 hours) and Padang (25,000 rp; 20 hours). Most services leave in the morning.

You can cut about five hours off the journey time to Bukittinggi by forking out 30,000 rp for one of the express air-con services. They bypass Sibolga and travel at night, which means you miss out on the scenery. ANS buses have a good name.

Many travellers use the tourist minibuses. There are daily buses north to Berastagi (15,000 rp), Medan (18,000 rp) and Bukit Lawang (23,000 rp), and south to Bukittinggi (27,000 rp) and Sibolga (12,000 rp). Tickets for these services are advertised everywhere in Parapat and on Pulau Samosir.

Getting to Berastagi by public bus is a real hassle. It involves changing buses at Pematangsiantar and Kabanjahe, and can take up to six hours.

Boat See the Danau Toba section for details of ferries to Pulau Samosir.

Getting Around

Opelets shuttle constantly between the ferry dock and the bus terminal (300 rp).

AROUND PARAPAT
Labuhan Garaga

The village of Labuhan Garaga, 25 km south-east of Parapat, is a centre for the weaving of the cotton Batak blankets *(kain*

kulos) that are widely on sale in Parapat an on Pulau Samosir. The colour and pattern vary from group to group, but most hav vertical stripes on a background of ink blu with rust-red and white the predominar colours. They're not cheap, but they ar attractive and practical buys. The price rang is from 30,000 to 70,000 rp; more for goo quality cloth.

DANAU TOBA & PULAU SAMOSIR

Danau Toba is one of Sumatra's most spec tacular sights. It occupies the caldera of giant volcano that collapsed on itself after cataclysmic eruption about 100,000 yea ago. Measurements of ash deposits indica that the blast made Krakatau's 1883 effo look like a hiccup. The flooding of the sub sequent crater produced the largest lake South-East Asia, covering an area of 1707 s km. The waters are 450m deep in places.

Out of the middle of this huge expanse blue rises Pulau Samosir, a wedge-shape island almost as big as Singapore – create by a subsequent upheaval between 30,00 and 75,000 years ago. The island has lon been North Sumatra's premier attraction fc foreign travellers, although it acquired a ba reputation for hustling in the late 1980s an early 1990s. Things have quietened down bit these days and it's a good place to rest u At an altitude of 800m, the air is pleasantl cool – and you couldn't ask for a mor spectacular setting.

Most foreigners stay in Tuk Tuk wher there is nothing much to do but relax. Thos with a serious interest in Toba Batak cultur will gain more satisfaction from scramblin over the mountain ridge to the villages on th other side of the island.

Visitors to the west will discover th Samosir isn't actually an island at all. It linked to the mainland by a narrow isthme at the town of Pangururan – and then c again by a canal.

Danau Toba is the home of the outgoin Toba Batak people. *Horas* is the tradition Batak greeting and it's delivered with gre gusto. Most Toba Batak are Protestant Chri tians.

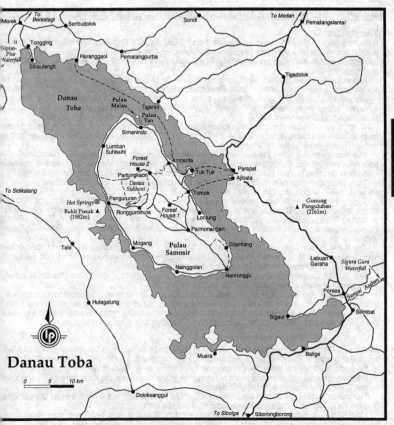

Danau Toba

0   5   10 km

Orientation

Tourist facilities are concentrated around the Tuk Tuk Peninsula (directly opposite Parapat) and nearby Ambarita. Tomok, a couple of km south of Tuk Tuk, is the main village on the east coast.

Information

Money Change money before you get to Samosir. Exchange rates at the island's hotels and moneychangers make the banks in Parapat look like a top deal. The Bank Rakyat Indonesia in Ambarita doesn't change money, but the post office does.

Post & Communications There is a post office in Ambarita. Several shops in Tuk Tuk sell stamps and have post boxes and lists of rates for overseas mail. Many places to stay advertise international phone services. If you want to make a collect call, you will be up for a connection fee of 3000 to 5000 rp.

Bookshops There are several places on the Tuk Tuk Peninsula selling or leasing second-hand books. The Gokhon Library and Bagus Bay Homestay & Restaurant have the best collections.

The Bataks

British traveller William Marsden astonished the 'civilised' world in 1783 when he returned to London with an account of a cannibalistic kingdom in the interior of Sumatra which, nevertheless, had a highly developed culture and a system of writing. The Bataks have remained a subject of fascination ever since.

According to Batak legend, all Bataks are descended from Si Radja Batak, who was born of supernatural parentage on Bukit Pusuk, a mountain on the western edge of Danau Toba (Lake Toba).

According to anthropologists, the Bataks are a Proto-Malay people descended from neolithic mountain tribes in northern Thailand and Myanmar (Burma), who were driven out by migrating Mongolian and Siamese tribes.

When they arrived in Sumatra they did not linger long at the coast but trekked inland, making their first settlements around Danau Toba, where the surrounding mountains provided a natural protective barrier. They lived in virtual isolation for centuries.

The Bataks were among the most warlike peoples in Sumatra – along with the natives of Nias – and their villages were constantly feuding. They were so mistrustful of each other (not to mention outsiders) that they did not build or maintain natural paths between villages, or construct bridges.

They practised ritual cannibalism in which the flesh of a slain enemy or a person found guilty of a serious breach of adat (traditional law) was eaten.

Today, there are more than six million Bataks and their lands extend 200 km north and 300 km south of Danau Toba. They are divided into six main groupings: the Pakpak Batak to the north-west of Danau Toba; the Karo Batak around Berastagi and Kabanjahe; the Simalungun Batak around Pematangsiantar; the Toba Batak around Danau Toba; and the Angkola Batak and Mandailing Batak further south.

The name 'Batak' was certainly in use in the 17th century, but its origins are not clear. It could come from a derogatory Malay term for robber or blackmailer, while another suggestion is that it was an abusive nickname coined by Muslims meaning 'pig eater'.

The Bataks are primarily an agricultural people. The rich farmlands of the Karo Highlands supply vegetables for much of North Sumatra, as well as for export.

In contrast to the matrilineal Minangkabau, the Bataks have the most rigid patrilineal structure in Indonesia. Women not only do all the work around the house, but also much of the work in the fields.

Although there is an indigenous Batak script, it was never used to record events. It seems to have been used only by priests and *dukuns* (mystics) in divination and to record magic spells.

Religion & Mythology The Batak have long been squeezed between the Islamic strongholds of Aceh and West Sumatra. The Karo Batak, in particular, were constantly at odds with the Islamic Acehnese to the north, who several times tried to conquer them and convert them to Islam.

Interestingly enough, after long years of resistance to the Acehnese, the Karo were easily subdued by the Dutch, who brought with them Christianity.

The majority of today's Bataks are Protestant Christians, especially in the north around Danau Toba and the Karo Highlands. Islam is the predominant religion in the south.

Most Bataks, however, still incorporate elements of traditional animist belief and ritual. Traditional beliefs combine cosmology, ancestor and spirit worship and *tondi*. Tondi is the concept of the soul, the spirit – the essence of a person's individuality – which is believed to develop before the child is born. It exists near the body and from time to time takes its leave, which causes illness. It is essential for Bataks to make sacrifices to their tondi to keep it in good humour.

The Bataks regard the banyan as the tree of life and relate a creation legend of their omnipotent god Ompung:

One day Ompung leant casually against a huge banyan tree and dislodged a decayed bough that plummeted into the sea. From this branch came the fish and all the living creatures of the oceans. Not long afterwards, another bough dropped to the ground and from this issued crickets, caterpillars, centipedes, scorpions and insects. A third branch broke into large chunks which were transformed into tigers, deer, boars, monkeys, birds and all the animals of the jungle. The fourth branch which scattered over the plains became horses, buffalo, goats, pigs and all the domestic animals. Human beings appeared from the eggs produced by a pair of newly created birds, born at the height of a violent earthquake.

Architecture Traditional Batak houses are built on stilts one to two metres from the ground. Finishing touches vary from region to region, but all follow the same basic pattern.

They are made of wood (slotted and bound together without nails) and roofed with sugar palm fibre or, more often these days, rusting corrugated iron.

The roof has a concave, saddleback bend, and each end rises in a sharp point which, from certain angles, look like the buffalo horns they are invariably decorated with. The gables are usually extravagantly embellished with mosaics and carvings of serpents, spirals, lizards and monster heads complete with bulbous eyes.

The space under the main structure is used for rearing domestic animals like cows, pigs and goats. The living quarters, or middle section, is large and open with no fixed internal walls and is often inhabited by up to a dozen families. This area is usually sectioned off by rattan mats which are let down at night to provide partial privacy. It is dark and gloomy, the only opening being a door approached by a wooden ladder. A traditional village is made up of a number of such houses, similar to the villages of the Toraja people of central Sulawesi.

There are many interesting traditional villages around Berastagi. The houses have very high roofs and are much larger that those of the Toba Batak. A traditional Toba village *(huta)* was always surrounded by a moat and bamboo trees to protect the villagers from attack. The villages had only one gateway because of this. The houses in the village are lined up to the left and right of the king's house. In front of the houses is a line of rice barns, used for storing the harvest. Even today, walking around Pulau Samosir, you can still see how the villages were designed with defence in mind.

Culture A strong Indian influence on the Bataks is evident in the cultivation of wet field rice, the type of houses, chess, cotton and even the type of spinning wheel.

A purely Batak tradition is the *sigalegale* puppet dance, once performed at funeral ceremonies, but now more often a part of wedding ceremonies. The puppet, carved from the wood of a banyan tree, is a life-size likeness of a Batak youth. It is dressed in the traditional costume of red turban, loose shirt and blue sarong. A red *ulos* (a piece of rectangular cloth traditionally used to wrap round babies or around the bride and groom to bless them with fertility, unity and harmony) is draped from the shoulders.

The sigalegale stand up on long, wooden boxes, through which ropes are threaded and operated like pulleys to manipulate its jointed limbs. This enables the operator to make the sigalegale dance to gamelan music accompanied by flute and drums. In some super-skilled performances the sigalegale weeps or smokes a cigarette. Its tongue can be made to poke out and its eyelids to blink. The sigalegale is remarkably similar in appearance to the *tau tau* statues of Tanatoraja in central Sulawesi, although the tau tau do not move.

One story of the origin of the sigalegale puppet concerns a loving, but childless, couple who lived on Pulau Samosir. Bereft and lonely after the death of her husband, the wife made a wooden image of him. Whenever she felt intensely lonely she hired a *dalang* to make the puppet dance and a dukun to communicate with the soul of her husband through the puppet.

The other story goes that there was once a king who had only one child, a son. When his son passed away the king was grieved because he now had no successor. In memory of his dead son the king ordered a wooden statue to be made in his likeness and when he went to see it for the first time, he invited his people to take part in a dance feast.

Whatever its origins, the sigalegale soon became part of Batak culture and was used at funeral ceremonies to revive the souls of the dead and to communicate with them. Personal possessions of the deceased were used to decorate the puppet and the dukun would invite the deceased's soul to enter the wooden puppet as it danced on top of the grave. At the end of the dance, the villagers would hurl spears and arrows at the puppet while the dukun performed a ceremony to drive away evil spirits. A few days later the dukun would return to perform another ceremony, sometimes lasting 24 hours, to chase away evil spirits again.

Arts & Crafts Traditionally the Bataks are skilled metalworkers and woodcarvers; other materials they use are shells, bark, bone and horns. They decorate their work with fertility symbols, magic signs and animals.

One particularly idiosyncratic form of art developed by the Toba Bataks is the magic augury book called *pustaha*. These books comprise the most significant part of their written history. Usually carved out of bark or bamboo, they are important religious records which explain the established verbal rituals and responses of priests and mourners. Other books, inscribed on bone or bamboo and ornately decorated at each end, document Batak myths.

Porhalaan are divining calendars – 12 months of 30 days each – engraved on a cylinder of bamboo. They are used to determine auspicious days on which to embark on certain activities, such as marriage or the planting of the fields.

Music Music is as important to the Bataks as it is to most societies, but traditionally it was played at religious ceremonies, rather than for everyday pleasure. Today the Bataks are famous for their powerful and emotive hymn singing. Most of their musical instruments are similar to those found elsewhere in Indonesia – cloth-covered copper gongs in varying sizes struck with wooden hammers, a small two stringed violin, which makes a pure but harsh sound, and a kind of reedy clarinet. ∎

Medical Services The small health centre close to the turn-off to Carolina's, at the southern end of the Tuk Tuk Peninsula, is equipped to cope with cuts and bruises and other minor problems.

Emergency There is a small police station at the top of the road leading to Carolina's.

Dangers & Annoyances There have been a number of reports of cash and valuable thefts from rooms – almost always the result of carelessness. It's wise to use hotel safety boxes where available.

Tomok
Although Tomok is the main village on the east coast of Samosir, it is a place to visit rather than a place to stay.

There are many examples of traditional **Batak houses** and also fine old **graves** and **tombs** – sarcophagi decorated with carvings of *singa*, creatures with grotesque three horned heads and bulging eyes. Their faces also decorate the facades of Toba Batak houses.

The grave of King Sidabatu, one of the last Batak animist kings, is 100m up a path that leads from the lake front through the souvenir stalls. His image is carved on his tombstone, along with that of his Muslim military commander and bodyguard, Tengku Mohammed Syed, and the woman he is said to have loved for many years without fulfilment, Anteng Melila Senega. The surrounding souvenir stalls have the best range and prices (after hard bargaining) on the island.

Nearby, a traditional house has bee turned into a small **museum**. There are a fe interesting items among the Christian rel gious photos and paintings.

Tuk Tuk
This once-small village is now a string hotels and restaurants stretching right aroun the peninsula, just above the lake's water Pointed Batak roofs have been plonked c many of the new concrete-block hotels, b otherwise traditional Batak culture is n much in evidence. Still, the living is easy ar very cheap, and Tuk Tuk is a pleasant plac to relax. There are lots of places rentin bicycles and motorcycles, making Tuk Tu a good base from which to explore the re of the island.

Ambarita
A couple of km north of the Tuk Tuk peni sula, Ambarita has a group of **stone chair** where village matters were discussed ar wrongdoers were tried. Guides love to sp a colourful yarn about how serious wrong doers were led to a further group of ston furnishings in an adjoining courtyard ar beheaded. A 'donation' of 1000 rp required.

Simanindo
Simanindo, at the northern tip of the islan can lay claim to being the island's cultur centre.

There's a fine old traditional house th has been meticulously restored and no functions as a **museum**. It was formerly th ome of the Batak king Rajah Simalungun, nd his 14 wives. Originally the roof was ecorated with 10 buffalo horns which represented the 10 generations of the dynasty.

The museum has a very small collection f brass cooking utensils, weapons, Dutch nd Chinese crockery, sculptures and Batak arvings.

There are very polished displays of **Batak Jancing** daily at 10.30 and 11.15 am in an djoining traditional village compound. intry is 3000 rp, or 500 rp to visit just the nuseum.

angururan

amosir's major population centre has virtu-lly nothing of interest to tourists. The town s next to the narrow isthmus connecting amosir to the mainland, so has transport nks to Berastagi. It's not a popular route and ne road is very poor as far as Tele. There are ot springs on the mainland near Pan-ururan.

rekking

here are a couple of treks across the island hat are popular with the energetic. Both are vell trodden and have a range of accommo-ation options, so you can proceed at your wn pace. Gokhon Library at Tuk Tuk has nformation about trekking and a useful map f Samosir.

Most people opt for the short trek from Ambarita to Pangururan. It can be done in a lay if you're fit and in a hurry. The path starts pposite the bank in Ambarita. Keep walking traight at the escarpment and take the path o the right of the graveyard. The climb to the op is hard and steep, taking about 2½ hours. The path then leads to the village of Par-ungkaon (also called Dolok), where there ou can stay at *Jenny's Guest House* or *'ohn's Losmen*. From Partungkaon, it takes bout five hours to walk to Pangururan via Danau Sidihoni.

A longer version of the trek starts from Tomok. It's 13 km from Tomok to Pasang-grahan (Forest House 1) where you can stay f you wish. From here, you can walk along he escarpment to Partungkaon, or cut across

to Ronggurnihuta, almost in the centre of the island. A path leads from Ronggurnihuta to Pangururan via Danau Sidihoni.

You can avoid the initial steep climb on both these treks by starting from Pangururan. Either way, you don't need to take much with you, but wet weather gear may make life more comfortable. The Samosir Bataks are hospitable people and, although there are no *warungs* (food stalls), you can buy cups of coffee at villages along the way. It may also be possible to arrange accommodation in the villages.

Neither walk takes you through jungle or rainforest. In fact, most of Samosir is either pine forest or plantation – cinnamon, cloves and coffee.

Places to Stay & Eat

Samosir has some of the best value accommodation in Indonesia. Losmen have moved steadily upmarket over the years and most places offer a range of rooms. The majority tend to be of the concrete-box variety, but you can still find a good-sized, clean box, usually with attached mandi, for 3000/5000 rp for singles/doubles.

Every losmen or hotel comes with a restaurant, but there are few surprises around and very little difference in prices. The restaurants are good earners, and some places get pretty cranky if you don't eat where you stay.

Tuk Tuk This is where the vast majority of people opt to stay. The shoreline is packed solid with hotels and losmen of every shape and size. The best advice is to wander around until you find something that suits.

Starting in the south, the first stop for the ferries is near the *Bagus Bay Homestay & Restaurant* (☎ 41482). It has large doubles in part-stone, Batak-style houses for 10,000 rp and a good restaurant. Next door is *Tabo Vegetarian Restaurant & Bakery*, with fresh wholemeal bread every day and a range of tasty burgers and snacks. It also has a couple of well-appointed bungalows for 15,000 rp. Uphill from Tabo is *Linda's*, a popular

SUMATRA

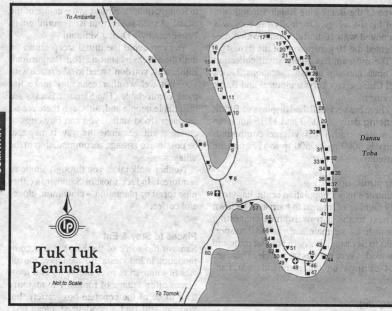

To Ambarita

Danau
Toba

Tuk Tuk
Peninsula

Not to Scale

To Tomok

budget place run by the energetic Linda.
Doubles are 6000 rp.

Second stop for the ferries is the long-
running *Carolina's* (☎ 41520), easily the
most stylish place on the island. Its older
bungalows are from 12,500 rp – for 25,000
rp you get hot water as well. Carolina's also
has a range of modern doubles for 40,000 rp
and family units for 100,000 rp. Beyond
Carolina's is the first of Samosir's new breed
of package hotels, the *Silintong 1*. It looks
like a prison camp with its barbed wire
fencing and guards on the gate.

Next door is *Rumba Homestay* with clean
rooms by the lake for 4000/6000 rp. Its *Pizzeria Rumba* is a popular meeting spot at
night. Further north, the restaurant at *Bernard's* turns out consistently good food.

Romlan (☎ 41557) is a very private place
set on its own small headland with a private
jetty. It has basic rooms for 3000/5000 rp and
better doubles for 7500 rp. Beyond Romlan
is a cluster of big, package-type hotels,

including the giant *Toledo Inn*. Among ther
are a couple of good mid-range places
Samosir Cottages (☎ 41050) and *Anju Cot
tages* (☎ 41348). Both have rooms fo
5000/8000 rp, as well as larger new room
with hot water from 15,000 rp. Nearby i
Leo's Bar & Restaurant, advertising th
cheapest cold beer on the island.

The north-west coast of the peninsul
beyond the Toledo Inn is occupied by a strin
of budget places. *Tony's* (☎ 41209) has quie
rooms right by the lake from 4000/5000 rp
and doubles with hot water for 10,000 rp.

There's half a dozen more places dotte
along the road to Ambarita. *Tuktuk Timbul* i
a great spot for people who want to get awa
from it all. There's a range of rooms fron
4000 to 10,000 rp.

Ambarita If you find Tuk Tuk a bit hectic
there are some quiet guesthouses on th
lakeside north of Ambarita. They includ

PLACES TO STAY	31	Rodeo & France	60	Smiley's
1 Tuktuk Timbal		Restaurant		
2 Mas	32	Hotel Silintong 2		PLACES TO EAT
3 Nina's	33	Rudy's	8	Romlan's Beer Garden
4 Sony	34	Hotel Sumber Polo	16	Reggae Restaurant
5 Yogi		Mas	18	Anju Restaurant
6 Christina's	35	Romlan	19	Leo's Bar &
7 Ho-l'e	36	Marroan		Restaurant
10 Antonius	37	Hisar's	20	Tarian Vegetarian
10 Murni	38	Bernard's		Restaurant
11 Laster Jony	39	Lenny's	22	Baruna Restaurant
12 Sibayak	40	Matahari's	42	Franky's Restaurant
13 Tony's	41	Merlyn	45	Many Toba
14 Abadi's	43	Rumba Homestay		Restaurant
15 Caribien		& Pizzeria	49	Juwita's Restaurant
17 Toledo Inn	44	Hotel Silintong 1	51	Roy's Pub
21 Dewi's	47	Carolina's	57	Tabo Vegetarian
23 Samosir Cottages	50	Mafir		Restaurant & Bakery
24 Anju Cottages	52	Vandu		
26 Popy's	53	Elsina		OTHER
27 Endy's	54	Horas	25	Gokhon Library
28 Lekjon	55	Dumasari	46	Police Station
29 Toledo 2	56	Linda's	48	Health Centre
30 Ambaroba Resort	58	Bagus Bay Homestay	59	Church
Hotel		& Restaurant		

arbara's (☎ 41230), where you'll find a good swimming beach and rooms from 5000) 15,000 rp.

If you're really serious about getting away rom it all, *Le Shangri-La* is the place, six km ast Ambarita (300 rp on a Simanindo-bound us). Clean Batak-style bungalows face a andy beach and cost 4000/6000 rp. You can et there from Parapat on ferries operated by he Nasional co-operative.

omok Few people stay in Tomok, although here are plenty of restaurants and warungs ere for day trippers who come across on the erry from Parapat. *Roy's Restaurant* on the main street has accommodation on the edge f town for 3000 rp per person.

Pangururan Right in the middle of town, *Mr Barat Acomodation* (☎ 20053) at Jl Sising-mangaraja 2/4 has extremely basic rooms or 4000 rp per person and a restaurant with tourist menu. The nearby *Hotel Wisata 'amosir* (☎ 20050) is a better choice. It has conomy rooms for 6000 rp per person, as well as good doubles from 20,000 rp.

Entertainment

The *Bagus Bay Restaurant*, on the Tuk Tuk peninsula, stages Batak dancing on Wednesday and Saturday nights at 8 pm and free videos on other nights. It also offers free transport back to your losmen at the end of the night. *Roy's Pub*, also on the peninsula, pumps out rock music at night and sometimes has bands.

Things to Buy

The souvenir shops of Samosir carry a huge range of cheap cotton goods, starting with dozens of brightly coloured T-shirts that let folks back home know where you've been for your holidays. Most of it is the standard tourist fare found in tourist shops throughout Indonesia.

Something a bit out of the ordinary is the embroidery work produced by locals, such as the Gayo, living north and east of Danau Toba. The work decorates a range of bags, cushion covers and place mats.

Toba Batak musical instruments for sale include the *grantung*, consisting of several slats of wood strung out on a harness and hit with sticks – like a xylophone.

Bamboo divining calendars (*porhalaans*)

are on sale everywhere around Tomok, Tuk Tuk and Ambarita.

Getting There & Away

Bus See the earlier Parapat section for information on bus travel to/from Danau Toba. There are daily buses from Pangururan to Berastagi (5500 rp; four hours) at 8 and 9 am and 3 pm. The buses travel via Sidikalang, from where it's also possible to get buses to Kutacane, Sabulus Salam (for Singkil) and Tapaktuan.

Boat There is a constant flow of ferries between Parapat and various destinations on Samosir. Ferries between Parapat and Tuk Tuk operate roughly every hour. The last ferry to Samosir leaves at about 5.30 pm, and the last one back is at about 4.30 pm. The fare is 1000 rp one way. Some ferries serve only a certain part of Tuk Tuk, so check at Parapat and you will be pointed to the appropriate boat. Tell them where you want to get off on Samosir when you pay your fare, or sing out when your hotel comes around – you'll be dropped off at the doorstep or nearby. When leaving for Parapat, just stand out on your hotel jetty and wave a ferry down.

Some ferries to Tuk Tuk continue to Ambarita, but four or five boats a day go direct from Parapat.

There are hourly ferries to Tomok from Ajibata, just south of Parapat for 500 rp. A vehicle ferry also operates on this route. It leaves Tomok at 7 am and shuttles back and forth all day, with the last departure from Ajibata at 8.30 pm. Cars cost 11,300 rp and places can be booked in advance through the Ajibata office (☎ 41194). The passenger fare is 500 rp.

Every Monday at 7.30 am a ferry leaves from Ambarita to Haranggaol (3000 rp; 2½ hours). There are buses from Haranggaol to Kabanjahe (for Berastagi).

Getting Around

It is possible to get right around the island – with the exception of Tuk Tuk – by public transport. There are regular minibuses between Tomok and Ambarita (500 rp), con-

tinuing to Simanindo (1000 rp) an Pangururan (1750 rp). Services dry up afte 3 pm.

You can rent motorcycles in Tuk Tuk fo 15,000 to 20,000 rp a day. They come wit a free tank of petrol, but no insurance – s take care. There are lots of stories abou travellers who have been handed outrageou repair bills – check the bike over carefull before taking it. Bicycle hire costs from 400 rp a day for a rattler to 8000 rp for a flas mountain bike.

SIBOLGA

It's hard to find a traveller with a good wor to say about Sibolga, a drab little port abou 10 hours north of Bukittinggi. It's the depa ture point for boats to Nias, which is the onl reason people come here.

Orientation & Information

There are two harbours, and the town centr lies midway between the two. Boats to Nia leave from the harbour at the end of Jl Hora You can change money at the BNI bank a the beach end of Jl Katamso.

Bangun, who runs the small Tourist Infor mation Service (travel agency; ☎ 21734) a Jl Horas 78, specialises in dealing with west erners who want to spend as little time i town as possible. He sells tickets for th tourist minibuses and for the boats to Nia and takes travellers to the boats.

Dangers & Annoyances Tales of woe abou rip-offs by becak drivers are a dime a dozer and surfers weighed down with bags an boards are the favourite targets. It is essentia to agree on the fare and destination befor you start – and bargain hard. Becaks theoreti cally cost about 1500 rp for most distance in town.

Beaches

Pantai Pandan is a popular white san beach at the village of the same name, 11 kr north of Sibolga. After a swim, 5000 rp wil buy you a meal of excellent grilled fish at on of the seafood restaurants.

A few hundred metres from Sibolga i

antai Kalangan, where there is a 250 rp ntry fee. Both beaches get very crowded at eekends, but are a good way to pass the me while you're waiting to catch a boat rom Sibolga. Opelets run between Sibolga nd both beaches all day for 300 rp and 400 p respectively.

laces to Stay & Eat

f you need to stay the night, you'll be doing ourself a favour by avoiding the budget otels in the town centre. They are generally irty and/or unfriendly. The better cheapies re along Jl Horas near the port. Both the *Hotel Karya Samudra* at No 134 and *Losmen Tando Kandung* have rooms for 5000 rp.

The best place to head is the *Hotel Pasar Baru* (☎ 22167), a clean place at the corner f Jl Imam Bonjol and Jl Raja Junjungan. It harges 6000 rp for small doubles with fan nd 30,000 rp for air-con doubles. There's Chinese food at the restaurant downstairs. The *Ikan Bakar Siang Malam*, near the BNI ank at Jl Katamso 45, serves delicious rilled fish for lunch and dinner – just as the ame suggests. Reckon on about 6000 rp per ead, including rice and vegetables.

The fanciest place in town is *Hotel Wisata ndah* (☎ 23688), overlooking the sea at the nd of Jl Katamso. It has a range of modern ir-con doubles from 66,000 to 110,000 rp.

Getting There & Away

Bus Sibolga is a bit of a backwater as far as us services are concerned. The express bus-s that travel the Trans-Sumatran Highway ypass Sibolga by taking a shortcut inland etween the towns of Taratung and Padang-idempuan. There are still plenty of buses, ut the going is painfully slow. Typical fares nd journey times from Sibolga are: Bukittinggi (12,000 rp; 12 hours); Medan 11,000 rp; 11 hours); and Parapat (7000 rp; ix hours).

All this makes the door-to-door tourist minibuses an attractive option. There are six a day to Medan (15,000 rp; nine hours) via Parapat (12,500 rp; five hours). There are lso daily buses to Bukittinggi (20,000 rp) nd Padang (25,000 rp). Tickets can be booked through Bangun at the Tourist Information Centre, Jl Horas 78.

Taxi Shared taxis are a good alternative to the buses. Inda Taxi (☎ 22123) at Jl Ahmad Yani 105 has taxis to Medan (20,000 rp) and Parapat (15,000 rp), among other destinations.

Boat Ferries to Nias leave from the harbour at the end of Jl Horas. There are boats to both Gunung Sitoli and Teluk Dalam at 8 pm nightly, except Sunday. The fares are 11,600/18,500 rp for deck/cabin class to Gunung Sitoli, and 12,000/17,000 rp to Teluk Dalam. Agents add a small commission.

Pelni boats sail from Gunung Sitoli to Sibolga every Saturday, continuing to Padang and Jakarta.

PULAU NIAS

Nias is an island almost the size of Bali, 125 km off the west coast of Sumatra. Magnificent beaches and a legendary surf break combine with an ancient megalithic culture and unique customs to make it one of Sumatra's most exotic destinations.

It still takes quite an effort to get to Nias, but it's no longer off the beaten track. Lagundri Bay is now part of the world professional surfing circuit and there's talk of more resorts to follow in the footsteps of the swanky Sorake Beach Resort.

History

Local legend has it that all Niassans are the descendants of six gods who came to earth and settled in the central highlands.

Academics have come up with a host of theories to explain such customs as the use of stone to produce monumental works of art. Niassans have been linked to the Bataks of Sumatra, the Naga of Assam in India, the aborigines of Taiwan and various Dayak groups in Kalimantan.

Head-hunting and human sacrifice once played a part in Niassan culture, as it did in the Batak culture.

The Niassans developed a way of life based mainly on agriculture and pig raising.

Hunting and fishing, despite the thick jungle and the proximity of many villages to the coast, was of secondary importance. The Niassans relied on the cultivation of yams, rice, maize and taro. Pigs were both a source of food and of wealth and prestige; the more pigs you had, the greater your status in the village. Gold and copper work, as well as woodcarving, were important village industries.

The indigenous religion was thought to have been a combination of animism and ancestor worship, with some Hindu influences. Today, most people are either Christian or Muslim – overlaid with traditional belief. Christianity was introduced by the missionaries who followed the arrival of the Dutch military in the 1860s.

Traditionally, Niassan villages were presided over by a village chief, heading a council of elders. Beneath the aristocratic upper caste were the common people and below them the slaves (often used as trade merchandise).

Sometimes villages would band together in federations, which were often perpetually at war with other federations. Prior to the Dutch conquest, inter-village warfare was

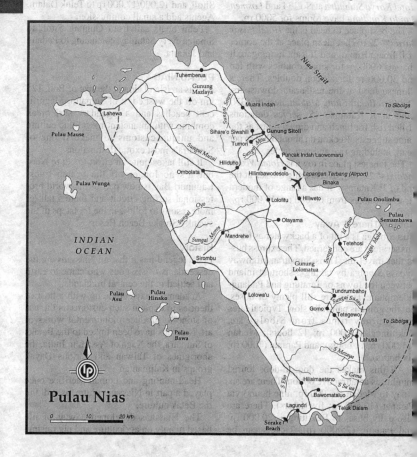

Pulau Nias

0   10   20 km

ast and furious, usually spurred on by the
esire for revenge, slaves or human heads.
Ieads were needed when a new village was
uilt, for the construction of a chief's house
nd for the burial of a chief. In central Nias,
leads were required as part of a wedding
owry. Today you can still see samples of the
veapons used in these feuds: vests of buffalo
ide or crocodile skin; helmets of metal,
eather or plaited rattan; spears; swords; and
hields.

Until the first years of the 19th century,
vhen people like the Englishman Sir Stam-
ord Raffles began to send back reports about
he island, the name of Nias rarely featured.
Vhen it did, it was as a source of slaves.

The island did not come under full Dutch
ontrol until 1914.

Today's population of just under 600,000
s spread through more than 650 villages,
nost inaccessible by road.

Orientation

Most of the interesting places are in the south
nd that's where most travellers head. Teluk
Dalam is the port and main town of the south.
Gunung Sitoli, in the north, is the island's
iggest town. The only airport is near Gun-
ng Sitoli.

Information

Money Changing money is no longer the
assle it once was. Branches of the BPDSU
ank in Gunung Sitoli and Teluk Dalam both
offer respectable rates for US dollars, cash
and travellers cheques.

Health Chloroquine-resistant malaria has
een reported on Nias so take appropriate
precautions.

Organised Tours

Companies like Nias Megalithic Adventures
☎ 21460), at Miga Beach Bungalows just
south of Gunung Sitoli, offer a range of
guided tours and treks. Guides can be hired
hrough the tourist office in Gunung Sitoli if
you want to set your own programme.

Getting There & Away

Air SMAC has daily flights from Medan to
Binaka airport, 17 km south of Gunung
Sitoli, for 131,300/231,000 rp one way/
return. Flights leave Medan at noon and
Gunung Sitoli at 1.10 pm. SMAC also flies
from Padang to Gunung Sitoli on Wednesday (123,600 rp one way).

Boat There are boats to Sibolga from
Gunung Sitoli and Teluk Dalam every night,
except Sunday. In theory, all the services
leave at 8 pm, but in practice they seldom set
sail before 10 pm. The fare from Gunung
Sitoli is 11,600 rp deck class or 18,500 rp for
a bed in a four berth cabin. The trip takes
about eight hours. The trip from Teluk
Dalam takes two hours longer and costs
12,000/17,000 rp.

The ticket office in Gunung Sitoli is opposite the parade ground on Jl Gomo, while the
place to go in Teluk Dalam is PT Simeuleu,
Jl Ahmad Yani 41. Tickets can also be
booked from Lagundri.

Pelni boats provide a weekly link between
Gunung Sitoli and Jakarta (108,500 deck
class/308,500 1st class). They leave Gunung
Sitoli every Saturday at 9 am, and call at
Sibolga and Padang on the way south. The
Pelni office (☎ 22357) is by the seafront on
Jl Lagundri 38.

Getting Around

Getting around Nias is a hassle. The roads
are terrible apart from those around Gunung
Sitoli and Teluk Dalam. Fortunately, most of
the interesting places in the south are fairly
close together.

Government efforts to promote tourism on
the island have included spending a fortune
on upgrading the 'Trans-Niassan Highway'
across the central mountains between
Gunung Sitoli and Teluk Dalam. Although
the journey time for the 128 km trip has been
reduced to manageable levels (around four
hours by bus), unstable soils and heavy rain
mean that the road is constantly under repair
– or in need of it. Road builders are now
concentrating their efforts on a new road
around the east coast, via Tetehosi and

Lahusa. It will supposedly cut the journey to two hours.

Local buses operate around the two major towns; elsewhere you can catch rides on trucks or negotiate pillion rides on motorcycles.

GUNUNG SITOLI

On the north-eastern coast of Nias, this is the island's main town, with a population of about 27,000. It's a fairly innocuous little place with a certain seedy, tropical charm.

Orientation

Most places of importance to tourists are grouped around the parade ground at the northern end of town. The port is about two km north of town, and the bus terminal is on the southern side of town beyond the bridge.

Information

Tourist Office There is a small tourist office

(☎ 21545) behind the parade ground at Soekarno 6. The staff are friendly and couple of them speak English.

Money The best place to change money the BPDSU bank on Jl Hatta. There is also BNI branch on Jl Pattimura.

Post & Communications The post office on the corner of Jl Gomo and Jl Hatta. International phone calls can be made from th Telkom office a few doors away on Jl Hatt where you'll find a Home Country Direc phone, as well as an international car phone.

Medical Services There is a public hospita (☎ 21271) on Jl Ciptmangunkusumo.

Things to See

About the only feature of Gunung Sitoli tha warrants a second look is the bizarre, brigh yellow, corrugated-iron model of a norther

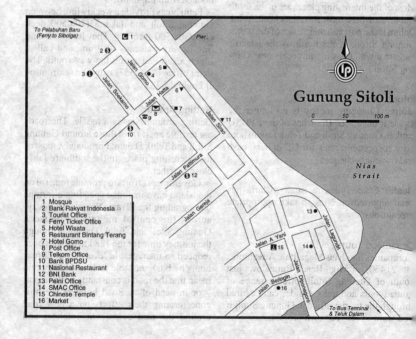

To Pelabuhan Baru
(Ferry to Sibolga)

Pier

Gunung Sitoli

0   50   100 m

Nias Strait

To Bus Terminal & Teluk Dalam

1 Mosque
2 Bank Rakyat Indonesia
3 Tourist Office
4 Ferry Ticket Office
5 Hotel Wisata
6 Restaurant Bintang Terang
7 Hotel Gomo
8 Post Office
9 Telkom Office
10 Bank BPDSU
11 Nasional Restaurant
12 BNI Bank
13 Pelni Office
14 SMAC Office
15 Chinese Temple
16 Market

Niassan home that sits on the roof of the Hotel Gomo.

There are some fine examples of the real thing at the nearby villages of **Sihireo Siwahili** and **Tumori**. Sihireo Siwahili is smaller but easier to get to. Opelets from Gunung Sitoli to Hiliduho can drop you at the turn-off (500 rp), leaving a walk of about 700m.

Places to Stay & Eat

Most travellers head for the *Wisma Soliga* (☎ 21815), four km south of town. It's clean, spacious and has a good restaurant that specialises in seafood. It has a choice of rooms from doubles with mandi and fan for 25,000 rp to air-con doubles for 35,000 rp. The manager can organise tickets and transport. If you're coming from the south, ask to be dropped off, otherwise you will be up for 1500 to 2000 rp for a becak from town – or 700 rp for an opelet.

The same transport arrangements apply to the *Miga Beach Bungalows* (☎ 21460), right by the sea about five km south of town. It has large doubles with mandi and fan for 25,000 rp, and air-con bungalows for 45,000 rp.

The hotels in town are nothing to get excited about – especially cheapies like the filthy *Hotel Beringin*, among the markets on Jl Beringin.

The *Hotel Wisata* (☎ 21858), opposite the parade ground, has doubles with fan for 22,500 rp and air-con doubles with mandi for 37,500 rp. Nearby *Hotel Gomo* (☎ 21926) has doubles with mandi and fan for 15,000 rp, and air-con doubles from 30,000 rp.

There are lots of small restaurants along the main streets. The *Bintang Terang* turns out a decent serve of seafood fried noodles for 3000 rp, while the *Nasional* is the pick of the nasi padang places. Both are on Jl Sirao.

Getting There & Away

Buses to Teluk Dalam (7000 rp; four hours) leave from the bus terminal on the southern side of town. Services dry up in the afternoon, so aim to leave before noon.

Getting Around

SMAC operates a minibus between Binaka airport and Gunung Sitoli for 3000 rp. Buses meet the boats at the port.

GOMO

The most famous reminders of the island's megalithic past are the *menhirs* (single standing stones) and stone carvings around Gomo in the central highlands of southern Nias.

The best examples are at **Tundrumbaho**, five km from Gomo. Some are believed to be more than 3000 years old. There are more carvings at **Lahusa Idanotae**, halfway between Gomo and Tundrumbaho, and at **Tetegewo**, seven km south of Gomo.

Getting There & Away

Unfortunately, Gomo is not an easy place to get to. There's no public transport, and there's no road for the final eight of the 44 km from Teluk Dalam. The last leg to Tundrumbaho involves a tough two hour uphill slog through the steamy jungle.

From Lagundri, it's best to negotiate with the losmen owners for someone to take you there and back by motorcycle.

TELUK DALAM

This nondescript little port is the main town of the south. There's no reason to stop here other than to organise transport to Lagundri, 14 km away. There is always the possibility, however, that you'll return for provisions if you intend staying awhile.

Information

The BPDSU bank on the main street, Jl Ahmad Yani, is the place to change money. The post office is next to the harbour, and there are telephones at Jl Pancasila 1A. Boat tickets to Sibolga can be bought at Pt Simeuleu, Jl Ahmad Yani 41.

Places to Stay

You are better off heading straight to Lagundri. No-one in their right mind would consider staying at the disgusting *Wisma Jamburae* on the waterfront.

Getting There & Away

The principal destination, Lagundri, is about 12 km from Teluk Dalam. It's 1500 rp by truck or opelet, or 3000 rp by motorcycle.

There are also occasional buses to the villages of Bawomataluo and Hilisimaetano (1500 rp).

LAGUNDRI

The perfect horseshoe bay at Lagundri is the reason most people come to Nias. The surfing break is at the mouth of the bay off Sorake Beach, and there is good swimming at the back of the bay on Lagundri Beach.

There's not much to do here except surf, swim, walk and bask in the sun, so bring books, cards and games to keep yourself amused when you get tired of the beach. Lagundri is a good base for treks to traditional villages.

Information

The Nias Surf Club Secretariate, at Sorake Beach, has information on local tours and attractions. SMAC flights from Gunung Sitoli can be confirmed at Sorake Beach Resort.

Lagundri also has a small clinic, which can handle minor medical problems, and a police station.

Dangers & Annoyances Petty theft seems to have reached epidemic proportions. It frequently takes the form of local boys 'finding' valuables and wanting a reward for their safe return. People are advised not to leave *anything* lying around. Security tends to be poorest at the cheaper bungalows.

Surfing

Sorake Beach stages a leg of the World Qualifying Series in June/July, when some of the best young talent in the Southern Hemisphere is on display. The surf is at its best from June to October. For the rest of the year, the waves are perfect for beginners. Boards can be hired from the Nias Surf Club for 5000 rp per day.

Marine Sports Sorake at the Sorake Beach Resort can organise surf excursions to outly-ing islands like Pulau Tello and Pulau As as well as fishing and diving.

Places to Stay & Eat

The bay is ringed by dozens of places to sta You can take your pick of everything fro basic palm-thatch huts to resort-style luxur

Every form of accommodation come with its own restaurant. Some losmen off ridiculously cheap lodging (1000 rp a nigh just to get customers for their restaurant Owners get very peeved if people eat els where. It's worth paying a bit more to be free agent.

The most popular cheapies are thos closest to the surf break, such as *Olayam* and *Sun Beach*. The *Damai*, tucked aroun the corner to the west of the headland, offe comparative seclusion.

The *Sea Breeze* (☎ 21224), close to th judging tower, is a bit upmarket from thes It has decent doubles with mandi and fan f 15,000 rp, and cheaper doubles for 10,00 rp. There's a card phone right on the beac outside the Sea Breeze where you can mak international calls (if it's working).

Non-surfers often prefer to stay near th swimming beach, where the cheapie include the long-running *Risky* and *Magdc lena*. The *Lantana Inn* (☎ 21048), on th Teluk Dalam road, is a mid-range place wit doubles from 33,000 rp and a good seafoo restaurant.

The swanky new *Sorake Beach Reso* (☎ 21195) is on the headland beyond the su break. Listed rates start at US$80 for ver stylish timber bungalows. Most people com on package deals that include pick-up fro the airport at Gunung Sitoli. You can get 50% discount off the listed rates just b walking across the foyer and organising you room through the Marine Sports Sorak office.

In addition to the losmen restaurants, ther are several specialist restaurants. The *Toy Bar & Restaurant*, on the road behind th surf break, does delicious barbecue pork an is very popular in the evenings.

It's also possible to buy fresh fish an

obster cheaply on the beach from local fish-
rmen and get your losmen to cook it for you.

Getting There & Away
Lagundri is about 14 km from Teluk Dalam:
500 rp by truck or bemo, or 3000 rp by
motorcycle.

Buses from Gunung Sitoli usually stop at
the crossroads between Teluk Dalam and
Lagundri Beach, where there are boys on
motorcycles waiting to take travellers the
last six km to Lagundri for 1000 rp. If you're
going to Gunung Sitoli, it's better to go to
Teluk Dalam first as buses are usually full by
the time they reach the crossroads.

SOUTHERN VILLAGES
The architecture of southern Nias is completely different from that of the north.
Whereas the houses of the north are freestanding oblong structures on stilts with
thatched roofs, the more sophisticated
houses of the south are built shoulder to

shoulder on either side of a long, paved
courtyard. Both the northern and southern
houses emphasise the roof as the primary
feature. Houses are constructed using pylons
and cross-beams slotted together without the
use of bindings or nails.

Southern villages were built on high
ground with defence in mind. Often stone
walls were built around the village. Stone
was used to pave the area between the two
rows of houses, the bathing pools and staircases. Benches, chairs and memorials were
also made out of carved stone.

Bawomataluo
This is the most famous, and the most accessible, of the southern villages. It is also the
setting for *lompat batu* (stone jumping), featured on Indonesia's 1000 rp note.

As the name suggests (Bawomataluo
translates as 'sun hill'), the village is perched
on a hill about 400m above sea level. The
final approach is up 88 steep stone steps.

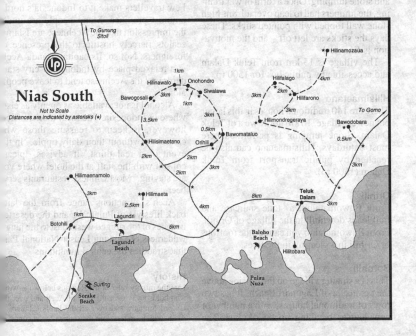

SUMATRA

Houses are arranged along two main stone-paved avenues which meet opposite the impressive chief's house, thought to be the oldest and largest on Nias. Outside are stone tables where dead bodies were once left to decay, and nearby is the 1.8m stone structure for jumping (see below). The houses themselves look like rows of washed-up Spanish galleons.

Although it's still worth exploring, Bawomataluo is on every tourist itinerary and villagers have learned to view foreigners as money jars waiting to be emptied.

Don't arrive expecting to take a casual stroll while studying the architecture; it's likely you'll be hounded by scores of kids trying to unload statues, beads and other knick knacks from the moment you set foot in the village.

The typical tourist fare at Bawomataluo includes fairly half-hearted war dances (traditionally performed by young, single males, but these days by any able-bodied person), and stone jumping. Once a form of war training, the jumpers had to leap over a 1.8m-high stone wall topped with pointed sticks. These days the sticks are left off – and the motivation is financial.

The village is 15 km from Teluk Dalam and accessible by public bus for 1500 rp.

Hilisimaetano

There are 140 traditional houses in this larger but newer village, 16 km north-west of Teluk Dalam. Stone jumping is performed here most Saturdays. Hilisimaetano can also be reached by public transport from Teluk Dalam (1500 rp).

Orihili

From Bawomataluo, a stone staircase and trail leads downhill to the village of Orihili. From Bawomataluo you can see the rooftops of Orihili in a clearing in the trees.

Botohili

This is a smaller village on the hillside above the peninsula of Lagundri Beach. It has two rows of traditional houses, with a number of new houses breaking up the skyline. The

remains of the original entrance way, ston chairs and paving can still be seen.

Hilimaeta

This village is similar to Botohili and als within easy walking distance of Lagundr The stone-jumping pylon can still be see and there are a number of stone monument: including benches and a four legged ston table. In the middle of the paved area stand a two metre-high stone penis. A long path way of stone steps leads uphill to the villag

Hilimaenamolo

This small village is in poor condition. Muc of the paving has been ripped up and man stone monuments have either collapsed c been dismantled.

Aceh

Few travellers make it to Indonesia's north ernmost province. Many people are unde the impression that the Acehnese are Islami zealots fiercely hostile to the presence c foreigners. Not so. Its capital, Banda Acel is a relaxed place by Indonesian city star dards and the Acehnese tend to leave peopl alone.

Alcohol is not available as openly as else where in Indonesia. The local tourist offic however, is keen to reassure those wh cannot do without their daily tipple. 'In th event of a real thirst,' it advises, 'pleas consult with the staff at the hotel where yo are staying.' Most Chinese restaurants serv beer.

Aceh's attractions range from the laic back lifestyle of Pulau We and the deserte beaches of the rugged west coast to the jung wilderness of Gunung Leuser National Par that straddles the central mountains.

History

I am the mighty ruler of the Regions below the win who holds sway over the land of Aceh and over th land of Sumatra and over all the lands tributary Aceh, which stretch from the sunrise to the sunset.

This extract, from a letter sent by the Sultan of Aceh to Queen Elizabeth I of England in 1585, marked the beginning of a trade agreement between Aceh and England that lasted until the 19th century. It also shows the extent of Aceh's sphere of influence as a trading nation, as well as providing a colourful assessment of Aceh's importance.

Years before Melaka fell to the Portuguese, Aceh was Melaka's chief competitor for trade. Rivalry between them was intensified by religious hostility as Aceh was one of the earliest centres of Islam in the archipelago.

Religious differences and the harsh Portuguese rule spurred many traders of different nationalities – Islamic scholars, Egyptians and Arabians, craftspeople from India and goldsmiths from China – to abandon Melaka and set themselves up in Aceh.

The influx of traders and immigrants contributed to Aceh's wealth and influence. Aceh's main exports were pepper and gold; others were ivory, tin, tortoiseshell, camphor, aloe-wood, sandalwood and spices. The city of Aceh was also important as a centre of Islamic learning and as a gateway for Muslims making the pilgrimage to Mecca.

SUMATRA

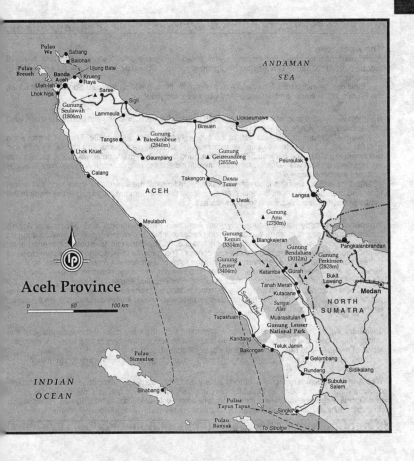

Aceh Province

Aceh is also interesting because, despite its early and strong allegiance to Islam, there have been four women rulers (although it is possible that real power lay with a council of 12 men). However, such a state of 'grace' could not last and in 1699 a legal recommendation from Mecca condemned rule by women as contrary to Islamic practice. The fourth woman ruler was deposed and replaced by a government headed by religious leaders.

Aceh's power began to decline towards the end of the 17th century, but it remained independent of the Dutch for a long time.

Singapore and Aceh were active trading partners with the help of a long-standing secret treaty with Britain.

That came to an end in 1871 when the Dutch negotiated a treaty in which the British withdrew any objections to the possibility of a Dutch occupation of Aceh. The Acehnese tried to counteract this blow by negotiating with both the Italian and US consuls in Singapore. The draft of a US-Acehnese treaty of friendship was sent to Washington. The Dutch, however, forestalled further attempts by declaring war on Aceh in 1873.

The Acehnese

As a result of their history of extensive and mixed immigration, Aceh's population is a blend of Indonesian, Arab, Tamil, Chinese and indigenous groups. Curiously, some of the tallest people in Indonesia live here.

Ethnic groups include the Gayo and Alas in the mountains, the Minangkabau along the west coast, the Kluetin in the south, and Javanese and Chinese throughout.

Religion Aceh is the most staunchly Muslim part of Sumatra, with Christians and Buddhists comprising only a small percentage of the population.

Nevertheless, animism is also part of the everyday fabric of Acehnese life. There is a prevailing popular belief in the existence of spirits who dwell in old trees, wells, rocks and stones. Ghosts and evil spirits are said to be particularly malicious around dusk when they can wreak havoc on all those they come in contact with. *Dukuns* (mystics) are still called in to help solve grievances, cure illnesses and cast spells on enemies.

Offerings and rituals are still observed at significant times of the agricultural year, such as harvest time, and dreams and omens are interpreted. In some parts of Sumatra, pilgrimages are made to the tombs of Acehnese scholars and religious leaders.

Weapons Metallurgy was learned early from Arab and Persian traders and, because of Aceh's continued involvement in wars, weapon-making became a highly developed skill. Acehnese daggers and swords comprise three parts: blade, handle and sheath. The blade can have both edges sharpened or just one, and can be straight, concave or convex. The handles of weapons are usually made of buffalo horn, wood or bone, and are carved in the form of a crocodile's mouth, a horse's hoof or a duck's tail and embellished with gold or silver. The sheaths are made of rattan, silver or wood and fastened with bands of a mixture of gold, brass and copper called *sousa*.

The best example of this art form is the *rencong*, a dagger which has a convex iron and damascene (etched or inlaid) blade with one sharpened edge. Less well-known Acehnese weapons are the *siwah* (knife) and *pedang* (pointed sword).

Jewellery While there is a long tradition – stemming from the early days of the sultanate – of fine artisanship in gold and silver jewellery, there is almost no antique jewellery to be found in Aceh today. Much of it was sold to raise money for the war against the Dutch.

Excellent gold and silver jewellery is still produced, but there is not much variation in design.

Weaving & Embroidery Despite its long history and high reputation, Acehnese weaving is rapidly disappearing. On the other hand, embroidery is a very vital art form. Areas around Sigli, Meulaboh and Banda Aceh are renowned for embroidery using gold-coloured metallic thread *(soedjoe)* on tapestry, cushions, fans and wall hangings. The main motifs are flowers, foliage and geometric designs,

The first Dutch expeditionary force of '000 retreated when its commander, General Kohler, was killed. A new army contingent, wice as large, succeeded in taking the capital, the central mosque and the sultan's palace, but the war went on for 35 years before the last of the sultans, Tuanku Muhamat Dawot, surrendered. Even then, no Dutch area was safe from sabotage or guerilla attack from the Acehnese until the Dutch surrendered to Japan in 1942.

The Japanese were welcomed at first, but resistance soon sprang up when local institutions were not respected. This period saw

the Islamic Party, which had been formed in 1939 under the leadership of Daud Beureueh, emerge as a political force.

In 1951 the central Indonesian government dissolved the province of Aceh and incorporated its territory into the province of North Sumatra under a governor in Medan. Angered at being lumped together with the Christian Bataks prompted Daud Beureueh to proclaim Aceh an independent Islamic Republic in September 1953. This state lasted until 1961 when military and religious leaders had a falling out.

The central government resolved the con-

SUMATRA

and the finished work is also decorated with mirrors, golden pailletes, sequins and beads in an effect known as *blet blot*.

Mendjot beboengo is a kind of embroidery from the Gayo and Alas regions south of Takengon, traditionally done only by men. Stylised motifs of geometric flowers in red, white, yellow and green thread are embroidered on a black background.

Other Crafts Various domestic items are made from coconut husks, tree bark, water buffalo horns, palm leaves and clay. These include spoons, baskets, mats, earthenware pots and dishes.

Music & Dance Every region in Aceh has its local dances, but there are three that are popular throughout the province – the Seudati, Meusakat and Ranub Lam Puan.

Seudati This is a quick-tempoed dance which involves a complicated pattern of forward, sideways and backward leaps. The songs are led by a dancer (called the *syech*) and two narrators *(aneuk syahi)*, and no instruments are used. The rhythm is accentuated by the variation in the movements of the dancers, who also heighten the tension by snapping their fingers and beating their chests. The pace is hotted up even more when contests are held between performing groups.

The traditional Seudati has five parts: the *salaam* (greeting), *likok* (special movements), *kisah* (story), *dhiek* (poetry) and *syahi* (songs). This dance has also been used to disseminate information on government policy and to urge people to become better Muslims.

Meusakat Known as the dance of the thousand hands, Meusakat originated in the region of Meulaboh and is performed by a group of 13 young women. It consists of a series of precise hand, head, shoulder and torso movements. Traditionally, the dance was performed to glorify Allah or to offer prayers.

Like the Seudati, no instruments are used. The songs are led by a girl positioned in the middle of a row of kneeling performers.

Ranub Lam Puan This is a modern adaptation of various traditional dances from throughout Aceh. It is performed to welcome guests and to convey hospitality, which is symbolised in the offering of betel nut or snacks by the dancers.

The *seurene kalee*, a single-reed woodwind instrument, provides the haunting musical accompaniment.

Other typical Acehnese instruments include: a three stringed zither (called an *arbab*) made of wood from the jackfruit tree with strings of bamboo, rattan or horsetail hair; bamboo flutes *(buloh merindu, bangsi, tritit* and *soeling)*; and gongs and tambourines *(rapai)*. The tambourines are made of goatskin, while the gongs are usually brass (sometimes dried goatskin) and are struck with padded wooden hammers. They come in three sizes: *gong, canang* and *mong-mong*. ∎

flict by giving Aceh provincial status and granting autonomy in matters religious, cultural and educational.

BANDA ACEH
Banda Aceh, the capital of Aceh, is a sprawling city at the northern tip of Sumatra. It's an odd mix of faded grandeur and modern architecture. Money is being poured into the region and prestigious building projects – mosques in particular – are everywhere.

Orientation
Banda Aceh is split in two by the Sungai Krueng Aceh. The city's best-known landmark, the Mesjid Raya Baiturrahman (Great Mosque), lies on the southern side. Behind the mosque is the huge central market, and adjoining the market is the main opelet terminal.

The city north of the river is centred around the junction of Jl Ahmad Yani and Jl Khairil Anwar. There are lots of hotels and restaurants in this area.

Information
Tourist Offices The Kanwil Depparpostel (tourist office; ☎ 32417) is near the Mesjid Raya at Jl Ujong Rimba, while the regional office (Diparda; ☎ 23692) is north of the river at Jl Chik Kuta Karang 3.

Money The best rates are to be found at the Bank of Central Asia at Jl Panglima Polem 38-40. The BNI bank 1946 is at Jl Kh Dahlan, and has reasonable rates for Amex US dollar travellers cheques and cash. The Bank Rakyat Indonesia on Jl Cut Meutia will change only US dollar travellers cheques.

Post & Communications The main post office is on Jl Teukuh Angkasah. International phone calls can be made from the Telkom office at Jl Nyak Arief 92.

Mesjid Raya Baiturrahman
With its brilliant white walls and liquorice-black domes, the Mesjid Raya is a truly dazzling sight on a sunny day. The first section of the mosque was built by the Dutch

in 1879 as a conciliatory gesture towards the Acehnese after the original one had been burnt down. Two more domes – one on either side of the first – were added by the Dutch in 1936 and another two in 1957 by the Indonesian government. Two new minarets were added in 1994. Non-Muslims are not allowed to enter any part of the mosque.

Gunongan
For a contrast in architectural styles, visit the Gunongan on Jl Teuku Umar, near the clocktower. This 'stately pleasure dome' was built by Sultan Iskandar Muda (who reigned from 1607-36) as a gift for his wife, a Malayan princess, and was intended as a private playground and bathing place. Its three levels are each meant to resemble an open leaf or flower. The building itself is a series of frosty peaks with narrow stairways and a walkway leading to hummocks, which were supposed to represent the hills of her native land.

Directly across from the Gunongan is a low, vaulted gate in the traditional Pintu Aceh style which gave access to the sultan's palace – supposedly for the use of royalty only.

These architectural curiosities, plus a few whitewashed tombs, are about all that remains to remind today's visitor of the past glories of the Acehnese sultanates.

Dutch Cemetery (Kherkhof)
Close to the Gunongan is the last resting place for more than 2000 Dutch and Indonesian soldiers who died fighting the Acehnese. The entrance is about 250m from the clocktower on the road to Uleh-leh. Tablets implanted in the walls by the entrance gate are inscribed with the names of the dead soldiers.

Museum Negeri Banda Aceh
The museum at Jl Alauddin Mahmudsyah 12 has a good display of Acehnese weaponry, household furnishings, ceremonial costumes, everyday clothing, gold jewellery and calligraphy.

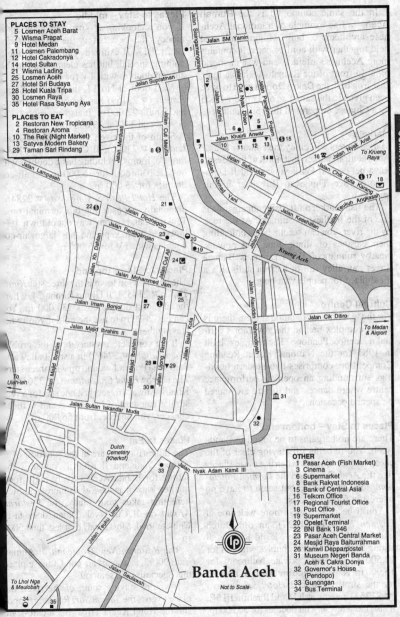

SUMATRA

PLACES TO STAY
5 Losmen Aceh Barat
7 Wisma Prapat
9 Hotel Medan
11 Losmen Palembang
12 Hotel Cakradonya
14 Hotel Sultan
21 Wisma Lading
25 Losmen Aceh
27 Hotel Sri Budaya
28 Hotel Kuala Tripa
30 Losmen Raya
35 Hotel Rasa Sayung Aya

PLACES TO EAT
2 Restoran New Tropicana
4 Restoran Aroma
10 The Rek (Night Market)
13 Satyva Modern Bakery
29 Taman Sari Rindang

OTHER
1 Pasar Aceh (Fish Market)
3 Cinema
6 Supermarket
8 Bank Rakyat Indonesia
15 Bank of Central Asia
16 Telkom Office
17 Regional Tourist Office
18 Post Office
19 Supermarket
20 Opelet Terminal
22 BNI Bank 1946
23 Pasar Aceh Central Market
24 Mesjid Raya Baiturrahman
26 Kanwil Depparpostel
31 Museum Negeri Banda
   Aceh & Cakra Donya
32 Governor's House
   (Pendopo)
33 Gunongan
34 Bus Terminal

Banda Aceh

Not to Scale

In the same compound is the **Rumah Aceh** – a fine example of traditional Acehnese architecture, built without nails and held together with cord or pegs. It contains more Acehnese artefacts and war memorabilia. In front of the Rumah Aceh is a huge cast-iron bell, the **Cakra Donya**, said to have been given to the sultanate of Samudra Pasai by a Chinese emperor in the 15th century.

Markets

Market lovers will enjoy the colourful Pasar Aceh central market, just north of the Mesjid Raya between Jl Perdagangan and Jl Diponegoro. (See Things to Buy later in this section.)

The fish market on Jl Sisingamangaraja is one of the liveliest in Sumatra. At the rear, by the river, you can see the boats unloading their cargoes of shark, tuna and prawns. Nearby, running off Jl SM Yamin, is 'Banana Street', an alley full of banana stalls. It's a great place for people watching.

Cultural Centre

For those with a more cultural bent, there is a new complex behind the governor's official residence, Pendopo. The complex, built in 1981 for the National Koran Reading Competition, comprises two modern buildings surrounding an open-air performance centre where dances and theatre are staged on special occasions.

Places to Stay – bottom end

There are no bargains to be found in Banda Aceh. You're better off staying clear of the cheap losmen along Jl Khairil Anwar. Places like the *Aceh Barat* and the *Losmen Palembang* look interesting, but seem to have no interest in foreign guests.

You'll be made much more welcome at *Losmen Raya* (☎ 21427), an old Dutch building 500m from the Mesjid Raya at Jl Ujong Rimba 30. It has doubles with fan for 12,500 rp and with private bathroom for 15,000 rp. Rates include breakfast. If it's full, try the similarly priced *Hotel Sri Budaya* (☎ 21751), nearby at Jl Majid Ibrahim III 5E. It also has a few air-con doubles for 30,000 rp.

Places to Stay – middle

If you're looking at spending a bit more money, the best bet is the *Hotel Meda* (☎ 21501), Jl Ahmad Yani 15. It looks nothing special, but has clean, comfortab air-con doubles with TV for 45,000 rp.

Next door at No 17, the popular *Wisma Prapat* (☎ 22159) has doubles with man and fan for 22,000 rp. It also has rooms with air-con and TV for 33,000 rp.

South of the river, the sprawling *Wisma Lading* (☎ 23006), Jl Cut Meutia 9, has range of rooms, including basic doubles with outside bathroom for 15,000 rp and air-con doubles for 25,000 rp.

The *Hotel Rasa Sayung Aya* (☎ 22846 diagonally opposite the bus terminal on Jl Teuku Umar, is a long way out of town. It is however, well kept and has large air-con doubles with TV for 55,000 rp.

Places to Stay – top end

The best hotel in town is the three star *Kual Tripa* (☎ 21455), Jl Ujong Rimba 24, wher the cheapest double costs 135,000 rp. Yo can pay 2000 rp to use the pool if you're no staying there.

It's a complete mystery how the grubby *Hotel Sultan* (☎ 22469) in a small alley at Jl Panglima Polem 1 wound up with three stars The nearby *Hotel Cakradonya* (☎ 33633), J Khairil Anwar 10, gets just one star for a ver similar standard of facilities – and is much cheaper with doubles from 56,000 rp.

Places to Eat

The table-filled square at the junction of Jl Ahmad Yani and Jl Khairil Anwar is the setting for Banda Aceh's lively night food market, known as the *Rek*. If there's nothing here that takes your fancy, the *Restoran Aroma* on Jl Cut Nyak Dhien does tasty Chinese food. Most meals cost less than 5000 rp.

The *Restoran New Tropicana*, Jl Ahmad Yani 90-92, is a smart air-con Chinese place that specialises in seafood.

If you're staying south of the river, the place to go is the *Taman Sari Rindang*, opposite the Hotel Kuala Tripa. It's a cafe-style lace that's very popular with Banda Aceh's oung crowd in the evenings. It has cheap leals and a good range of fresh fruit juices.

The Acehnese like their cakes and pastries s much as anyone in Indonesia. The *Satyva lodern Bakery* at Jl Khairil Anwar 3 is a ood place to try.

hings to Buy

ceh is well known for its colourful embroi-ery. You'll find it adorning hats, cushion overs, wallets and bags of every shape and ize. Anita Souvenirs in the Pasar Aceh shop-ing centre on Jl Diponegoro is a convenient lace to look.

There are some interesting places to rowse along Jl Perdagangan on the other ide of the market. H Keucik Leumik at Jl erdagangan 115 specialises in Acehnese ntiques and also has a good selection of old utch and Chinese porcelain. Close by, Toko aud deals in traditional weaponry.

The goldsmiths at the jewellery shops long Jl Perdagangan can turn out any design ou care to nominate.

etting There & Away

ir Pelangi Air has three flights a week from anda Aceh to Penang (US$107) and Kuala umpur (US$134). Pelangi's office (☎ 21705) s at Jl Nyak Arief 163. Garuda has two lights a day from Banda Aceh to Medan 141,900 rp). The Garuda office is at the lotel Sultan (☎ 22469).

Bus The main bus terminal is the Terminal 3us Seuti at the southern approach to town n Jl Teuku Umar. There are numerous buses o Medan. The best way to travel is on the xpress night buses. They do the trip in about line hours and cost 25,000 to 40,000 rp, lepending on the level of comfort. Kurnia nd PMTOH are both recommended, and lave offices in town on Jl Mohammed Jam near the mosque) where you can book. PMTOH is at No 58 and Kurnia is at No 68. The day buses can stretch the journey out to 13 hours.

Heading down the west coast, PMTOH and Aceh Barat run buses from Banda Aceh

to Calang (6500 rp; four hours), Meulaboh (8000 rp; five hours) and Tapaktuan (16,000 rp; 11 hours). From Tapaktuan, it's possible to continue to Sidikalang and then complete a loop of northern Sumatra to Medan via Berastagi.

Getting Around

The Airport Airport taxis charge a standard 15,000 rp for the 16 km ride into town, and 36,000 rp to Krueng Raya (for Pulau We).

Local Transport Opelets (known locally at *labi-labi*) are the main form of transport around town and cost 300 rp. The main opelet terminal is on Jl Diponegoro in the Pasar Aceh central market. This is the depar-ture point for services to Krueng Raya and Lhok Nga.

AROUND BANDA ACEH
Uleh-leh

Five km west of Banda Aceh is the old port of Uleh-leh where you can while away a few interesting hours watching the traders come in from outlying islands. There are some attractive villages around Uleh-leh and an unattractive, exposed black sand beach. In colonial times, the Dutch fenced off part of the beach with metal netting and came here for a dip.

Lhok Nga

Lhok Nga, 17 km west of Banda Aceh, is a popular weekend picnic spot. The beach is dominated by the loading operations of the Semen Andalas Indonesia cement company.

There's a beautiful white sand Indian Ocean beach at nearby **Lampu'uk**. Women should dress modestly – most local women swim fully clothed.

Places to Stay Both the *Pondok Wisata Darlian* and *Pondok Wisata Mitabu* at Lhok Nga have doubles for 7000 rp.

The place to go if you want to relax in comfort is the *Taman Tepi Laut Cottages* (☎ 32029). It has immaculate rooms and cot-tages from 40,000 to 85,000 rp. Facilities include an ocean swimming pool built into the rocky shoreline.

Getting There & Away There are opelets to Lhok Nga (800 rp) from the Pasar Aceh terminal in Banda Aceh.

PULAU WE

This beautiful little island just north of Banda Aceh is the main reason most travellers come to Aceh. It has some magnificent palm-fringed beaches, good snorkelling and a rugged, jungle-covered interior.

There are only 24,000 people on the island, most of them in the main town of Sabang. During Dutch rule, Sabang was a major coal and water depot for steam ships, but it went into decline with the arrival of diesel power after WWII.

During the 1970s it was a duty-free port, but when this status was eliminated in 1986, Sabang once again became a sleepy fishing town. The only industry – other than fishing – is making rattan furniture.

For most people, Sabang is no more than an overnight stop on the way to the beaches at Gapang and Iboih. It's pleasant enough, with some huge tamarind trees dominating the middle of town.

Picking the best time to visit is a bit of a lottery. Rain is never far away – different winds seem to bring rain from different directions. You can, however, be fairly sure that it will rain constantly from November until early January. July is supposedly the driest month.

Malaria has been reported on the island.

Information

The Stingray Dive Centre (☎ 21265), in the centre of Sabang on the corner of Jl Teuku Umar and Jl Perdagangan, doubles as a tourist office. The manager, Mr Dodent, is a good source of information about the whys and wherefores of life on the island. There is also a small collection of second-hand books in English and German for sale or exchange.

The post office is at Jl Perdagangan 66. The telephone office is next door, and is open 24 hours. It has a Home Country Direct phone.

Things to See & Do

The most popular beach is at **Iboih**, about 2 km north-west of Sabang. Opposite Iboih 100m offshore (10,000 rp return by boat) a **Pulau Rubiah**, a densely forested island surrounded by spectacular coral reefs known a the **Sea Garden**. It is a favourite snorkellin and diving spot. The Stingray Dive Centre i Sabang hires out diving gear and snorkellin equipment as well as organising trips to range of diving locations. It also has a 'office' at Iboih.

Adjacent to the Sea Garden is the **Iboih Forest** nature reserve. It has **coastal cave** that can be explored by boat.

Gapang Beach, around the headlan from Iboih, is good for swimming and ther are fewer tourists.

Another beach of note is **Pantai Para diso**, a white sand beach shaded by cocont palms just outside Sabang. Not much furthe away is **Pantai Kasih** and about 30 minute from town is **Pantai Sumur Tiga**, a popula picnic place.

Less than two km from town is a seren freshwater lake called **Danau Anak Laut** the source of the island's water supply. From the nearby hills it is possible to see the por and Sabang Bay.

Gunung Merapi is 17 km from town. Thi semi-active volcano holds boiling water i its caldera and occasionally emits smoke.

Places to Stay

Sabang Sabang has a couple of reasonabl cheapies. Both the *Losmen Irma* (☎ 21148) at Jl Teuku Umar 3, and *Losmen Pulau Jaye* (☎ 21344), further up the street at No 17-25 are well set up for travellers. The Pulau Jay is marginally the better of the two with basi singles/doubles for 4000/7500 rp and larg doubles with bathroom for 20,500 rp.

A step up from these two is the *Holiday Losmen* (☎ 21131), tucked away on a quie lane off Jl Perdagangan. It has large double with mandi for 25,000 rp and air-con double for 40,000 rp.

At the time of research, an old Dutch vill on Jl Diponegoro was being renovated for ew life as the guesthouse-style *Hotel Samdera* (☎ 21503).

boih & Gapang Accommodation at Iboih is n the form of numerous palm-thatch bungaows. *Arena, Dolphin, Fatimah, Mama* and *Mr Afzali* all charge 3000/5000 rp for ingles/doubles. There are similar bungaows at Gapang.

Places to Eat

Sabang Sabang has a remarkable number of estaurants for a town of its size. The majorty are along Jl Perdagangan and serve cheap *Padang* food. The *Dynasty Restaurant* at No ~4 offers something a bit different with pmarket Chinese food. It does a steak for ~000 rp – and you can wash it down with a old beer for 5000 rp.

The *Restaurant Sabang* at No 27 turns out a huge portion of sweet and sour fish for ~000 rp.

Harry's Cafe, downstairs from Losmen rma, has a range of pancakes and breakfast goodies aimed at the tourist trade.

boih & Gapang Each cluster of bungalows at Iboih and Gapang has its own small res-aurant offering basic meals, such as rice, ish and vegetables for 2000 rp.

Getting There & Away

Ferries to Pulau We leave from Krueng Raya, 33 km east of Banda Aceh. There are regular bemos from the central market in Banda Aceh (1500 rp; 45 minutes). Ferries leave Krueng Raya daily at 3 pm, returning at 9 am he next morning. The voyage takes two hours and costs 4250 rp deck class.

Passengers will be reassured to find that the ferry brought in to replace the ill-fated KM *Gurita* is equipped with such basics as ife jackets. As many as 250 people, includ-ng two foreign tourists, drowned when the *Gurita* capsized and sank on 19 January 1996.

Getting Around

The ferries to Pulau We arrive at the port of Balohan, from where there are bemos for the

15 minute ride to Sabang (1500 rp). There are pick-up trucks from Sabang to Gapang and Iboih every day at 10.30 am and 6 pm, returning at 7 am and 4 pm (2000 rp). They leave from outside the Stingray Dive Centre in Sabang.

The island has a good road network and motorcycles are the ideal way to get around if you want to see a bit of the island. They can be rented from Harry's Cafe in Sabang.

BANDA ACEH TO SIDIKALANG

Very few travellers make it to the remote west coast of Aceh, with its seemingly endless deserted Indian Ocean beaches backed by densely forested hills.

The journey from Banda Aceh to Sidi-kalang, in North Sumatra, used to be another endurance test – almost 700 twisting km of potholes and mud or dust, depending on the season. These days, it's plain sailing as far south as Tapaktuan, and even the final stretch from Tapaktuan to Sidikalang isn't too bad. From Sidikalang there is a good road to Medan.

It's best to take the journey in stages, stopping off to enjoy the surroundings en route.

Calang

Calang is a fairly nondescript small town 140 km south of Banda Aceh, but the beaches along this part of the coast are superb.

About 15 km north of Calang is the small village of **Lhok Geulumpang**, home to a small collection of tree houses known offic-ially as *Camp Europa*, but better known as 'Dieter's Farm', after its eccentric expatriate German owner.

The place is pitched at people who want to do nothing more active than meditate. Accommodation is in tree houses, built in littoral rainforest just 100m from a deserted Indian Ocean beach. Doubles are from 15,000 to 40,000 rp, which includes all meals and tea/coffee through the day. The food is very basic.

The place is not set up for crowds. There are only seven tree houses and accommoda-tion for 14 people in all. There are no phones at Camp Europa, but it is possible to book in advance: fax 32139.

If Camp Europa is full, the nearest accommodation is in Calang, where the *Losmen Sri Jaya* has very simple doubles for 5000 rp.

Getting There & Away PMTOH and Aceh Barat operate regular buses to Calang from Banda Aceh (6500 rp; four hours) and Meulaboh (2000 rp; 1½ hours). Drivers know the Camp Europa stop. Some locals know Dieter as 'Daud German'.

Meulaboh

Almost 250 km from Banda Aceh on the south-western coast is the small, sleepy town of Meulaboh.

There's good surf nearby, although the beaches close to town are dangerous for swimming because of strong currents. **Lhok Bubon**, 16 km back towards Banda Aceh, is a safe swimming beach.

Meulaboh has an unusual monument to Acehnese resistance hero Teuku Umar – it's shaped like a traditional Acehnese hat *(kupiah meukeutop)*.

There are half a dozen losmen in Meulaboh. The *Mutiara* (☎ 21531), Jl Teuku Umar 157, has rooms for 5000 rp, as well as rooms with TV and air-con for 50,000 rp. The tiny *Mustika* (☎ 21033) at Jl Nasional 78 has a similar choice.

The *Losmen Pelita Jaya* and *Losmen Erna* on Jl Singgahmata both have doubles for 6000 rp.

Getting There & Away There are regular buses to Meulaboh from Banda Aceh (8000 rp; 5½ hours) and Tapaktuan (8000 rp; six hours). SMAC flies between Medan and Meulaboh on Tuesday, Thursday and Sunday (133,500 rp), continuing from Meulaboh to Sinabang (88,950 rp), on Pulau Simeulue.

Pulau Simeulue

The isolated island of Simeulue, about 150 km west of Tapaktuan, is known for its clove and coconut plantations and not much else. The island is said to be restful and the people friendly. There are few shops and no luxuries, but there is plenty of fruit, coffee, rice, noodles and fish.

Getting There & Away There are occasional boats from Meulaboh to Sinabang, as well as three flights a week from Medan (136,800 rp) via Meulaboh.

Tapaktuan

The sleepy seaside town of Tapaktuan, 20 km south of Meulaboh, is the main town of South Aceh. It's very laid back by Sumatra standards and a pleasant place to hang out for a couple of days.

Information Most places of importance are on the main street, Jl Merdeka, which runs along the coast. Widuri Tours & Travel (☎ 21574) is a good source of information about the town. It also has information about getting to Pulau Banyak.

Things to See The town can be used as a base to explore the lowland **Kluet** region of **Gunung Leuser National Park**, about 40 km south. Kluet's unspoilt swamp forests support the densest population of primates in South-East Asia and are also recommended for bird watching. It may be possible to hire guides through the national park office in **Kandang**, 38 km south of Tapaktuan.

Pantai Tu'i Lhok, 18 km north of Tapaktuan, is the best of several good beaches in the area. There is a small waterfall behind the beach where you can rinse off after swimming. There's a much larger waterfall at **Pantai Air Dingin**, just south of Tu'i Lhok.

Places to Stay & Eat There are half a dozen places to stay along the main coast road, Jl Merdeka.

Tiny *Pondok Wisata Kanada* (☎ 21209) above a shop at No 52, has a few basic doubles for 6000 rp. The *Losmen Bukit Barisan* (☎ 21145) occupies an old Dutch house at No 37. It has cheap doubles out at the back for 7000 rp and better rooms inside for 12,500 rp. *Hotel Panorama* (☎ 21004) is a modern two storey place at No 33, with a range of doubles from 15,000 rp. There are ooms with air-con and TV for 30,000 rp. The best place in town is the new *Hotel Dian Rana* (☎ 21444) on Jl Angkasah. It charges 35,000 rp for large, comfortable air-con doubles.

Jl Merdeka is also a good place to find a site to eat. Being a fishing port, there are several restaurants selling delicious grilled fish. Expect to pay about 4000 rp for a decent feed. After dark, the focus switches to the night market by the main pier, opposite Hotel Panorama.

Getting There & Away Tapaktuan is the major transport centre on the west coast, with good connections to Banda Aceh and Medan.

It's a long haul from Banda Aceh (16,000 rp; 11 hours) and most people prefer to break their journey at Meulaboh (8000 rp; six hours). The journey from Medan (14,000 rp; 10 hours) is about 80 km shorter than from Banda Aceh, going via Berastagi and Sidikalang. Many travellers opt for the night bus that leaves Medan's Pinang Baris terminal at 5 pm.

There are also frequent buses south to Sidikalang; change at Subulus Salem for Singkil.

Teluk Jamin

The tiny coastal village of Teluk Jamin, 70 km south of Tapaktuan, doesn't even rate a mention on most maps. It is, however, one of the departure points for boats to Pulau Banyak, with boats leaving at 9.30 am every Tuesday and Wednesday (10,000 rp; five to six hours).

Pak Ambrin, who operates one of the boats, can reportedly organise a room in a private house if you need somewhere to stay overnight. The nearest losmen is the *Karya Baru* at Bakongan, 11 km north-west.

Getting There & Away Teluk Jamin is on the main coast road so there are frequent buses – both north to Tapaktuan and south to Subulus Salam and Sidikalang. The 5 pm bus from Medan to Tapaktuan passes by at about 4 am. If you're coming from Tapaktuan for

the boat, aim to leave no later than 7 am for the 90 minute ride.

Singkil

Singkil is a remote port at the mouth of the Sungai Alas. It merits a mention only as the main departure point for boats to the Pulau Banyak islands.

Catching a boat will mean spending a night at one of Singkil's four losmen. The *Indra Homestay*, *Harmonis* and *Purnama* have basic doubles for 5000 rp, while the *Favourit* is a shade more upmarket.

Getting There & Away There are daily minibuses from Medan to Singkil, leaving at 11 am from outside the Singkil Raya restaurant on Jl Bintang (behind Olympia Plaza). The trip takes eight hours and costs 15,000 rp. If you're travelling from Berastagi, Danau Toba or Tapaktuan, you will need to change buses at Sidikalang and Subulus Salem.

Boats for Pulau Balai, one of the Pulau Banyak islands, leave on Monday, Thursday and Friday at 8 am. The Monday and Thursday boats take four hours and cost 5500 rp, while the Friday boat takes an hour longer and costs 500 rp less.

PULAU BANYAK

The Banyaks ('many' islands) are a cluster of 99 islands, most of them uninhabited, about 30 km west of the Acehnese port of Singkil. A few years ago, the islands were right off the beaten track; these days the islands are the flavour of the moment and everybody seems to be heading there.

Malaria has been reported on the islands, so take suitable precautions.

Orientation & Information

The village of Desa Pulau Balai on Pulau Balai is where boats from the mainland will deposit you. It is the only settlement of any consequence – it even has electricity in the evenings. It also has a post office and a telegram office, but there is nowhere to change money, so bring enough with you. The Nanda restaurant, close to where the

SUMATRA

boats dock, has information about accommodation and boats to other islands.

Things to See & Do

The setting is perfect for hanging out. The islands are ringed by pristine palm-fringed **beaches** and there is excellent snorkelling on the surrounding coral reefs. Diving can be organised at The Point bungalows (see Places to Stay & Eat) on **Pulau Palambak Besar**. There is good trekking through the virgin jungles of the largest island, **Pulau Tuangku**.

Conservationists are campaigning to save the **turtles** of Pulau Bangkaru from poachers. Green turtles can be seen year-round, and giant leatherback turtles in January and February. A group called the Turtle Foundation organises three day trips to Bangkaru for small groups. They cost 100,000 rp, including food and accommodation, and leave every Saturday. Tours should be booked in Desa Pulau Balai on arrival.

Places to Stay & Eat

New places are opening all the time, and there are now half a dozen islands with accommodation – mostly in small, palm-thatch bungalows by the beach. Every place has its own kitchen, usually charging about 6000 rp for three set meals. Fish, rice and vegetables feature prominently.

Few people bother to stick around on Pulau Balai, although there is some accommodation. *Daer's Retreat* has basic singles/doubles for 3000/5000 rp or 6000/8000 rp with private bathroom.

The most popular destination is Pulau Palambak Besar, which has three good places to choose from. The biggest of them is the aptly named *The Point*, with rooms for 4000/6000 rp . The nine rooms make it one of the few places large enough to offer a choice in its restaurant. It also has a generator, which means cold drinks. *Bina Jaya Bungalows* and *Pondok Asmara Palambak*, normally known as PAP, are the other options.

There's also accommodation on Pulau Palambak Kecil *(Villa Abbas)*, Pulau Rangit Besar *(Coco's)*, Pulau Panjang *(Jasa Baru)*, Pulau Tapus Tapus *(Tap-Tap)* and Pulau Ujung Batu *(Jambu Kolong Cottages)*. Visitors to Pulau Tuangku can stay with the Lukman family at the health centre in Haloban for 2500 rp per person.

Getting There & Away

There are regular boats between Pulau Balai and the mainland ports of Singkil (5500 rp; four hours) and Teluk Jamin (10,000 rp; six hours). Boats to Singkil leave at 8 am on Sunday and Wednesday, returning at the same time on Monday and Thursday. There is an additional slow boat from Singkil on Friday, also at 8 am.

The timetable to Teluk Jamin doesn't appear to make much sense. It lists departures from Pulau Balai at 8.30 am on Tuesday and 7.30 am on Saturday, and from Teluk Jamin at 9.30 am on Tuesday and Wednesday.

The Wisma Sibayak in Berastagi and Widuri Tours in Tapaktuan are places where you can check the latest timetables.

Getting Around

Boats to the various beach bungalows can be arranged through the Nanda restaurant on Pulau Balai. Sample fares include 3500 rp to Pulau Rangit Besar and 5000 rp to Pulau Palambak Besar.

BANDA ACEH TO MEDAN

People who catch the express night buses on this route aren't missing out on a lot.

The first two hours of the journey are slow going as the road twists and turns through the hills south of Banda Aceh. The small hill town of **Saree**, about 1½ hours south of Banda Aceh, sits in the shadow of **Gunung Seulawah** (1806m). One of Sumatra's last wild elephant herds lives around Seulawah for part of the year.

From Saree, the road descends to the coastal town of **Sigli**. According to local tourist literature, there is a factory which produces pre-stressed concrete units for bridges.

Llokseumawe is a major industrial city 274 km south-east of Banda Aceh. Unless ou have an interest in natural gas liquefaction facilities, fertiliser factories or paper mills, there is not much point in stopping here. Don't bother with the footballing elephants at the **Lhok Asan elephant training centre**, 20 km south of the city. You're better off continuing to Medan, another 330 km south-east.

AKENGON TO BLANGKEJERAN

Takengon and Blangkejeran are the main towns of the Gayo Highlands in the central mountains of Aceh Province. The Gayo, who number about 250,000, lived an isolated existence until the advent of modern roads and transport. Farming is the main occupation. Pressure for land to grow coffee and tobacco led to some serious overclearing in the past. The Gayo also grow rice and vegetables.

Like the neighbouring Acehnese, the Gayo were renowned for their fierce resistance to Dutch rule; like the Acehnese, they are also strict Muslims.

It's said that one way of telling you are in Gayo country is from the number of water buffalo, replacing the hump-necked *bentang* cattle preferred by the Acehnese.

Takengon

The Dutch made Takengon, on the shores of Danau Tawar, their base when they arrived at the beginning of this century. Much of the town centre dates from that time. It is the largest town of the highlands, but not wildly exciting. The climate is pleasantly cool at an altitude of 1100m.

The lake is 26 km long, five km wide and 80m deep, surrounded by steep hills rising to volcanic peaks of more than 2500m. Gunung Geureundong, to the north, rises 2855m.

Orientation & Information The Mesjid Raya (Great Mosque) is in the centre of the town on Jl Lebe Kader, which is where you'll find the post office and police station, as well as shops and restaurants. The main bus terminal and the market are closer to the lake. You can change US dollar cash and travellers cheques at Bank Rakyat Indonesia on the road opposite Losmen Danau Laut Tawar.

Things to See There's not much to do in Takengon apart from admire the setting. The intricately carved home of the area's last traditional ruler is open for inspection at the village of **Kebayakan**, on the lakeside just north of Takengon.

There are stalagmites and lots of bats at **Loyang Koro** (Buffalo Caves). The caves are by the lake, six km from town beyond Hotel Renggali. Take a torch (flashlight).

Places to Stay & Eat The best of the cheap losmen is the friendly family-run *Penginapan Batang Ruang* (☎ 21524), Jl Mahkamah 7, close to the cinema. It has clean doubles for 7000 rp.

The *Triarga Inn* (☎ 21073) is a good mid-range place just around the corner from the bus terminal on Jl Pasar Inpres. The cheap (15,000 rp) doubles are not worth looking at, but there are some good doubles upstairs for 25,000 rp – 45,000 rp with hot water. The *Hotel Danau Laut Tawar*, opposite the parade ground at Jl Lebe Kader 35, has rooms for 20,000 rp.

The *Hotel Renggali* (☎ 21144), perched on the lakeside 2.5 km out of town, looks pretty flash from a distance. Close up, it looks too tatty to be charging 75,000 rp for its standard doubles.

There are lots of cheap restaurants serving Padang food and Chinese-style noodle dishes. The main areas are around the bus terminal and on Jl Lede Kader. Delicious fresh Gayo coffee is available everywhere. A local speciality is kopi telor kocok – a raw egg and sugar creamed together in a glass and then topped up with coffee.

Things to Buy This is the place to buy the traditional Gayo/Alas tapestry which is made into embroidered clothes, belts, purses, cushion holders and tapestry. Keramat Mupakat, Jl Lebe Kader 24, has a good range.

It's sometimes possible to buy highly decorative, engraved pottery called *keunire*,

SUMATRA

SUMATRA

which is used in wedding ceremonies, at the market in Takengon.

Getting There & Away There are regular buses to Takengon from Bireuen, on the Trans-Sumatran Highway, 218 km southeast of Banda Aceh. The 100 km journey from Bireuen (3500 rp; three hours) passes through spectacular country.

PMTOH has buses to Medan (15,000 rp; 11 hours) and Banda Aceh (10,000 rp; eight hours). Heading south, there are regular buses on the much-improved road to Blangkejeran (10,000 rp; seven hours) and Kutacane (12,000 rp; 10 hours).

Blangkejeran

Blangkejeran is the main town of the remote southern highlands. The area is known as the Gayo heartland and it is possible to hire guides to take you out to some of the smaller villages.

There are several small guesthouses: *Penginapan Juli* at Jl Kong Buri 12; *Wahyu* at Jl Blawar 9; and *Penginapan Mardhatillah* on Jl Besar.

There are regular buses north to Takengon and south to Kutacane.

KUTACANE & GUNUNG LEUSER NATIONAL PARK

Kutacane, in the heart of the Alas Valley, is the base camp for activities in the surrounding expanses of Gunung Leuser National Park.

Gunung Leuser National Park is one of the great flora and fauna sanctuaries of South-East Asia. Within the park's boundaries can be found four of the world's rarest animals – rhinos, elephants, tigers and orang-utans. There are perhaps 300 elephants, 500 tigers and 100 rhinos living in the park, but your chances of seeing them are extremely remote. You can, however, be sure of encountering plenty of primates. The most common is the white-breasted Thomas Leaf monkey which sports a splendid, crested 'punk' hair-do.

Habitats range from the swamp forests of the west coast to the dense lowland rain-forests of the interior. Above 1500m, the permanent mists have created moss forest rich in epiphytes and orchids.

Rare flora includes two members of the rafflesia family: *Rafflesia acehensis* and *Rafflesia zippelni* which are found along Sungai Alas.

More than 300 bird species have been recorded in the park, among them the bizarre rhinoceros hornbill and the helmeted hornbill, which has a call that sounds like maniacal laughter.

Crocodiles used to be common in the lower reaches of Sungai Alas/Bengkung, but have been virtually wiped out by poachers.

There are two main access points to the park. They are at Bukit Lawang – home of the famous Orang-utan Rehabilitation Centre – and at Kutacane. Kutacane itself has nothing much to offer, as much of the land around the town has been cleared for farming, but it is surrounded by the densely forested hills of the national park.

There is a rainforest research station 40 km north-west of Kutacane at Ketambe, but it is off limits to tourists.

Information

You are not allowed to enter the park without a permit or a guide. Both are available from the PHPA office in Tanah Merah, about 15 minutes by opelet from Kutacane. Permits cost 4000 rp and you will need three photocopies of your passport. Guides cost about 30,000 rp per day and are well worth the investment. They can construct shelters at night, cook food, carry baggage, cut through the trails (or what's left of them) and, possible, show you the wildlife. Guides can also be hired in Kutacane and at Lawe Gurah (see the following entry).

Lawe Gurah

The so-called *hutan wisata* (tourist forest) at Lawe Gurah, opposite the Ketambe research station, is like a park within the national park.

Lawe Gurah's 9200 hectares have been set up to give visitors an introduction to rainforest life with a network of walking tracks and viewing towers. The most popular wa involves a two hour hike from Lawe Gurah **hot springs** by the Sungai Alas. If you want to spend a night in the jungle, there is a campground halfway to the springs. You can hire camping gear and guides at the office.

Lawe Gurah also has a range of bungalow and guesthouse accommodation (see Places to Stay further in this section).

Trekking

As well as supplying guides and permits, the HPA office in Tanah Merah also has information about a wide range of treks, from short walks to 14 day hikes through the jungle to the tops of the park's mountains. Some of the possibilities are listed following.

Gunung Kemiri At 3314m, Kemiri is the second highest of the peaks in Gunung Leuser National Park. The return trek takes five to six days, starting from the village of Kumpang, north of Ketambe. It takes in some of the park's richest primate habitat, with orang-utans, macaques, siamangs and gibbons.

Gunung Leuser The park's highest peak belongs, of course, to Gunung Leuser itself – 3404m. Only fit people with plenty of time on their hands should attempt the 14 day return trek to the summit. The walk starts from the village of Angusan, west of Blanjkejeren.

Gunung Perkinson Allow seven days for the return trek to summit of Perkinson (2828m) on the eastern side of the park. There is a rafflesia site at about 1200m and some spectacular moss forest.

Gunung Simpali The trek to Gunung Simpali (3270m) is a one week round trip starting from the village of Engkran and following the valley of Sungai Lawe Mamas. Rhinos live in this area. The Lawe Mamas is a wild, raging river which joins the Alas about 15 km north of Kutacane.

Rafting

Rafting on the Sungai Alas is widely promoted around the travellers' haunts of North Sumatra. If you're after whitewater thrills, don't bother with the regular US$150 three day/two night trips that start from Muara-situlan, south of Kutacane. There's some magnificent scenery along the way and lots of birds and monkeys, but only one stretch of water vaguely resembling a rapid. You'll be longing for an outboard motor by the time you get to the finishing line at Gelombang on the third afternoon.

Serious whitewater fans should look at arranging to start further upstream – at Angusan, near Blangkejeran, for example.

Places to Stay

There are half a dozen small losmen scattered along Kutacane's main street. You can find basic doubles for as little as 5000 rp at places like *Wisma Renggali* and *Wisma Rindu Alam*. *Wisma Wisata* (☎ 21406) at No 93 is a clean place on the edge of town, with basic doubles for 7500 rp. *Wisma Maroon* (☎ 21078) at No 2 has cheap rooms as well as doubles with mandi and fan for 20,000 rp. The *Hotel Bru Dihe* (☎ 21444), near the mosque on Jl Guru Leman 14, rates as the best place in town. It has large doubles with mandi and fan for 20,000 rp, and air-con doubles for 45,000 rp.

Gurah also has a choice of places to stay, including a forest camping area. There is budget accommodation at places like the *Losmen Pak Ali*, or there's the comfortably appointed *Gurah Lodge*, with air-con doubles for 35,000 rp.

Places to Eat

There are lots of places to eat near the bus terminal along Jl Besar in Kutacane. *Sapo Bawan*, opposite the bus terminal, has good nasi or mie goreng. If you're after Padang food, *Anita*, opposite Wisma Renggali, is worth a try, or you can stroll down Jl Ahmad Yani where there's a choice of the *Roda Baru*, *Damai Baru* or *Nasional*.

Getting There & Away

The Pinem company has daily direct buses from Medan's Pinang Baris bus terminal to Kutacane via Kabanjahe (6000 rp; six hours). Many travellers head to Kutacane from Berastagi, which means catching an opelet to Kabanjahe first. There are frequent services between Kutacane and Kabanjahe (5000 rp; four hours). Along the way, there are fine views of Gunung Sinabung and the Alas Valley. The winding road allows drivers plenty of opportunity to use their favourite toy – the air horn. Every bend, shack and village is an excuse for a triple or quadruple blast.

There are also buses heading north from Kutacane to Blangkejeran and beyond. This road is a lot better than it used to be, but it is still prone to washout in the wet season.

Minibuses run from Kutacane to Tanah Merah (300 rp) and Lawe Gurah (500 rp).

West Sumatra

The province of West Sumatra is like a vast and magnificent nature reserve, dominated by volcanoes, with jungles, waterfalls, canyons and lakes. This is the homeland of the Minangkabau, one of Indonesia's most interesting and influential ethnic groups. They make up 95% of the province's population of 3½ million.

Padang is the provincial capital. The other major cities are Payakumbuh, Bukittinggi, Padangpanjang, Solok and Sawahlunto. There are four large lakes in West Sumatra: Singkarak near Solok; Maninjau near Bukittinggi; and Diatas and Dibawah, east of Padang.

The fascinating Mentawai Islands are also part of West Sumatra. Only recently emerged from their stone-age isolation, the inhabitants of these islands are quite different from the people of mainland Sumatra.

The economy of West Sumatra, although predominantly based on agriculture (coffee, rice, coconuts and cattle), is strengthened by industries like coal mining.

History

Legend has it that the Minangkabau are descended from none other than that wandering Macedonian tyrant, Alexander the Great.

According to legend, the ancestors of the Minangkabau arrived in Sumatra under the leadership of King Maharjo Dirajo, the youngest son of Alexander, more commonly known in Indonesia as Iskandar Zulkarnain. They first settled in the Padangpanjang region and gradually spread out over western Sumatra.

Anthropologists suggest that, in fact, the Minangkabau arrived in West Sumatra from the Malay peninsula some time between 1000 and 2000 BC, probably by following the Sungai Batang Hari upstream from the Straits of Melaka to the highlands of the Bukit Barisan. Little is known about the area's history, however, until the arrival of Islam in the 14th century. The abundance of megalithic remains around the towns of Batusangkar and Payakumbuh show that the central highlands supported a sizeable community some 2000 years ago.

There's evidence that the Jambi-based kingdom of Malayu and its subsequent Majapahit conquerors controlled the area between the 11th and 14th centuries. This tallies with the legend surrounding the origin of the Minangkabau name (see the Minangkabau aside in this section), supposedly stemming from a confrontation with a Javanese king some 600 years ago.

It was about this time that Islam first arrived on the local scene, splitting the region into small Muslim states ruled by sultans. By the time the Europeans arrived in the early 17th century, West Sumatra consisted of little more than a few small-time rajahs ruling over minuscule village-states.

It continued to survive in this form until the beginning of the 19th century, when civil war erupted between followers of the Islamic fundamentalist Padri movement and supporters of Minangkabau adat (traditional law). The Padris were so-called because their leaders were *hajis* (pilgrims) who had made their way to Mecca via the Achenese port of Pedir. They returned determined to establish

true Islamic society. Their frustration at the
lax pre-Islamic ways of their fellows finally
erupted into open conflict in 1803. The
Dutch arrived in 1821 and supported the
traditional leaders against the Padris, who by
this time had won control of much of the
highlands.

The fighting dragged on until 1837 before
the Dutch finally overcame the Padri strongholds. Today, a curious mix of traditional
beliefs and Islam is practised in West Sumatra.

Flora & Fauna

Tigers, rhinoceroses, sun bears, elephants
and various species of monkey and deer are
all native to West Sumatra. Of particular
interest in the Mentawai Islands is a rare
species of black-and-yellow monkey (*siam-
ang kerdil*), usually called *simpai mentawai*
by the locals. Their numbers are small and
they are strictly protected. There is also
diverse bird life.

The *Rafflesia arnoldi* can be seen around
the small village of Palupuh, 16 km north of
Bukittinggi, between August and November.

Strictly speaking, the rafflesia is not a
flower. It's a parasitic fungus specific to a
species of rainforest vine. Whatever its

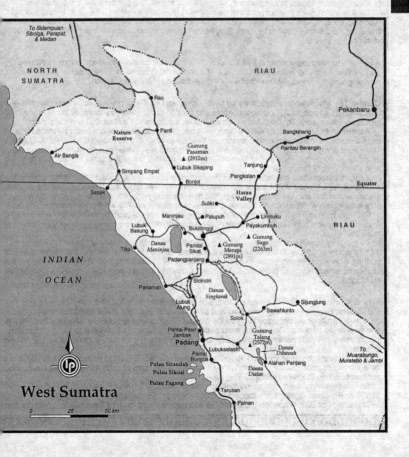

West Sumatra

SUMATRA

The Minangkabau

For centuries, West Sumatrans have built their houses with roofs shaped like buffalo horns and called themselves and their land Minangkabau. They have a long literary tradition which includes many popular and imaginative legends about their origins.

There are several theories on the derivation of the name Minangkabau, but the West Sumatrans prefer a colourful 'David & Goliath' version that also demonstrates their shrewd diplomacy and wit:

About 600 years ago one of the kings of Java, who had ambitions of taking over West Sumatra, made the mistake of sending a messenger to advise the people of his intentions and ordering them to surrender. The wily West Sumatrans were not prepared to give up without a fight. As a way of avoiding bloodshed, they proposed a bullfight between a Javanese bull and a Sumatran bull.

When the time came, the West Sumatrans dispatched a tiny calf to fight the enormous Javanese bull – a ruse which came as a surprise to both the bull and the onlookers. The calf, which appeared helpless, charged straight for the bull and began to press its nose along the bull's belly searching for milk. Soon after, the bull let out a bellow of pain and took to its heels with blood pouring from its stomach and the calf in hot pursuit. When the bull finally dropped dead, the people of West Sumatra were heard to shout, 'minangkabau, minangkabau!', which literally means 'the buffalo wins, the buffalo wins!'.

It seems that the owners of the calf separated it from its mother several days before the fight. Half-starved and with sharp metal spears attached to its horns, they sent the calf into the arena. Believing the Javanese bull to be its mother, the calf rushed to assuage its hunger and ripped the belly of the bull to shreds.

A far more prosaic explanation is that it is a combination of two words – *minanga*, a river in that region, and *kerbau*, meaning buffalo. Another is that it comes from the archaic expression *pinang kabhu*, meaning 'original home' – Minangkabau being the cradle of Malay civilisation.

Culture The Minangkabau are known by their compatriots as the 'gypsies of Indonesia'; they have a reputation as an adaptable, intelligent people and are one of the most economically successful ethnic groups in the country. Though Muslim, Minangkabau society is still matriarchal and matrilineal.

According to Minangkabau adat, a man does not gain possession of a woman by marriage, nor does a woman a man. Men have no rights over their wives other than to expect them to remain faithful. The eldest living female is the matriarch and has the most power in the household, which can number as many as 70 people descended from one ancestral mother, under the same roof. She is deferred to in all matters of family politics.

Every Minangkabau belongs to his or her mother's clan. At the lowest level of the clan is the *sapariouk*, which consists of those matri-related kin who eat together. These include the mother, grandchildren and son-in-law. The name comes from the word *periouk* which means rice pot. A number of genealogically related sapariouk make up a lineage or *sapayung*. The word *payung* means umbrella.

Children born of a female member of the lineage will, by right of birth, be members of that lineage. Ancestral property, although worked collectively, is passed down this female line rather than down the male line.

All progeny from a marriage are regarded as part of the mother's family group and the father has no say in family affairs. The most important male member of the household is the mother's eldest brother, who replaces the father in being responsible for the children's education and offers them economic advice as they grow older. He also discusses and advises them on their prospective marriages.

Arts & Crafts West Sumatra has a reputation for exquisite, handloomed songket cloth and fine embroidery. Songket weaving uses gold and silver threads (imitation these days) to create patterns on a base of silk or cotton, depending on the budget. The designs are usually elaborate floral motifs and geometric patterns. One of the most popular designs, used in both weaving and embroidery, incorporates stylised flowers and mountains in an ornate pattern known as *gunung batuah*, or 'magic mountain'.

The material is traditionally used as a sarong, shawl or wrap. Expect to pay more than 200,000 rp for a sarong of good quality. It's also widely available in the form of such items as cushion covers, bedspreads, handbags, wallets etc.

Songket weaving is widespread in West Sumatra. Kubang, 13 km from Payakumbuh near the border with Riau Province, is the centre for commercial weaving.

The village of Silungkang, on the Agam Plateau near the coal town of Sawahlunto, specialises in vividly coloured silk songket sarongs and scarves. Other weaving villages in this area include Balai Cacang, Koto Nan Ampek and Muara.

Pandai Sikat, near Padangpanjang on the main road between Padang and Bukittinggi, is known for the finery of its cloth. The village is also known for its decorative woodcarving.

The Minangkabau are also known for their fine embroidery. Villages which specialise in this are Koto Gadang, Ampek Angkek, Naras, Lubuk Begalung, Kota Nan Ampek and Sunguyang.

Traditional weavers also used an unusually painstaking technique called 'needle weaving'. The process involves removing certain threads from a piece of cloth and stitching the remaining ones together to form patterns. These patterns include identifiable motifs such as people, crabs, insects, dogs or horses. Traditionally, such cloth is used to cover the *carano* – a brass *sirih* stand with receptacles for betel nut, tobacco and lime – which is used for ceremonial occasions. You're unlikely to find any examples for sale.

Another highly developed art found in West Sumatra is silverwork. Filigree jewellery, as fine as spider webs, is a speciality. Koto Gadang, near Bukittinggi, is the place to go if you're interested.

Dance & Music Dance is an important part of Minangkabau culture. Dances include the colourful Tari Payung (Umbrella Dance), a welcome dance about a young man's love for his girlfriend; the dazzling Tari Lilin (Candle Dance), a miracle of physical coordination where the female dancers are required to rhythmically juggle and balance china saucers with burning candles attached to them while simultaneously clicking castanets; and the dramatic Tari Piring (Plate Dance), which involves the dancers leaping barefoot on piles of broken china.

The most popular of the Minangkabau dances is the Randai, a unique dance-drama performed at weddings, harvest festivals and other celebrations. The steps and movements for the Randai developed from the Pencak Silat, a self-defence routine that comes in various styles. The dance is learnt by every Minang boy when he reaches the age at which he is considered too old to remain in his mother's house, but too young to move into another woman's.

It is the custom for Minang youths to spend some time in a *surau* (prayer house), where they are taught, among other things, how to look after themselves. This includes learning the Pencak Silat. The style of Pencak Silat most often performed is the Mudo, a mock battle which leads the two protagonists to the brink of violence before it is concluded. It is a dramatic dance involving skilled technique, fancy footwork and deliberate pauses which follow each movement and serve to heighten the tension.

Harimau Silat, the most aggressive and dangerous style of Pencak Silat, originated in the Painan district of West Sumatra. The steps for the Harimau Silat imitate a tiger stalking and killing its prey. With their bodies as close to the ground as possible, the two fighters circle around menacingly, springing at each other from time to time.

The Randai combines the movements of Pencak Silat with literature, sport, song and drama. Every village in West Sumatra has at least one Randai group of 20 performers. Both the female and male roles are played by men wearing traditional *gelambuk* trousers and black dress. The traditional version tells the story of a woman so wilful and wicked that she is driven out of her village before she brings complete disaster on the community. The drama is backed by gamelan music.

The percussion instruments used to accompany most of the dances are similar to those of the Javanese gamelan and are collectively called the *telempong* in West Sumatra. Two other instruments frequently played are the *puput* and *salung*, both primitive kinds of flute which are usually made out of bamboo, reed or rice stalks. ∎

atus, it's huge. Some specimens measure as much as one metre across and weigh over even kg. Rafflesia blooms are a gaudy red and white and give off a putrid smell which attracts pollinating flies and insects.

West Sumatra is also famous for its many species of orchids.

pecial Events

addition to the dances performed by the

Minangkabau, there are other important cultural and sporting events in West Sumatra.

Bullfighting Known locally as *adu kerbau*, bullfighting is a popular entertainment in West Sumatra. It bears no resemblance to the Spanish kind – there is no bloodshed (unless by accident) and the bulls, which are water buffaloes *(kerbau)*, don't get hurt.

Two animals (both cows and bulls are used) of roughly the same size and weight are encouraged by their handlers to lock horns for a trial of strength. Once horns are locked, the fight continues until the losing animal tires and runs off pursued by the winner. It often ends up with both beasts charging around a muddy paddock, scattering onlookers in all directions.

The original intention was to help to develop buffalo breeding in the region. As a spectator sport, the local men love to get together for a bet on the buffaloes. It's an interesting insight into local culture and well worth seeing.

The centres for bullfighting are the villages of Kota Baru and Batagak, between Padang and Bukittinggi. The host village in each district is changed every six months or so. The first bullfight in a new location is an important day for the host village, which kicks off proceedings with a meeting of village elders, followed by a demonstration of *pencak silat* dancing.

They're held every Tuesday afternoon at about 5 pm around Kota Baru and every Saturday from 4 pm around Batagak. There are bemos to the bullfights from Bukittinggi's Aur Kuning bus terminal for 600 rp each way. Entry is another 600 rp.

Alternatively, travel agencies in Bukittinggi charge 6500 rp for the round trip plus admission.

Horse Racing Horse racing in Sumatra is a vivid, noisy spectacle and nothing like the horse racing of western countries. The horses are ridden bareback and the jockeys are dressed in the traditional costume of the region or village they come from. The aim is to gain prestige for the district where the horse is bred and raised. Padang, Padangpanjang, Bukittinggi, Payakumbuh and Batu Sangkar each stage one meeting a year, normally over two days.

Tabut Festival The highlight of the West Sumatran cultural calendar is the colourful Islamic festival of Tabut, staged at the seaside town of Pariaman, 36 km north of P dang.

It takes place at the beginning of the mon of Muharam to honour the martyrdom Mohammed's grandchildren, Hassan a Hussein, at the battle of Kerbala. Because t date is fixed by the Islamic lunar calendar, moves forward 10 days each year.

Central to the festival is the *bouraq*, winged horse-like creature with the head a woman, which is believed to have de cended to earth to collect the souls of t dead heroes and take them to heaven.

Nearby villages construct effigies of bou aqs which they paint in vibrant reds, blue greens and yellows, and adorn with go necklaces and other paraphernalia. The ef gies are carried through the streets with mu merriment, dancing and music, and a finally tossed into the sea. Spectators a participants then dive into the water and gr whatever remains of the bouraqs, the mc valued memento being the gold necklac When two bouraqs cross paths during t procession a mock fight ensues. Each gro praises its own bouraq, belittling and insu ing the other at the same time.

So popular has this festival become, pe ple from all over Indonesia arrive to witne or take part in it. Admission to the area is donation.

Other West Sumatran towns also celebra Tabut, but usually on public holidays, su as Independence Day or Hero Day.

PADANG
Padang is a flat, sprawling city (the nar means 'field') on the coastal plains betwe the Indian Ocean and the Bukit Baris mountains. It is the capital of West Suma and its population of almost 700,000 mak it Sumatra's third largest city.

Many travellers use Padang as an ent or exit point for Sumatra, using the Pe boats between the city and Jakarta to byp southern Sumatra. Tabing airport is one Indonesia's visa-free entry points with dire connections to Kuala Lumpur and Sing pore.

Although not particularly inspiring itse

SUMATRA

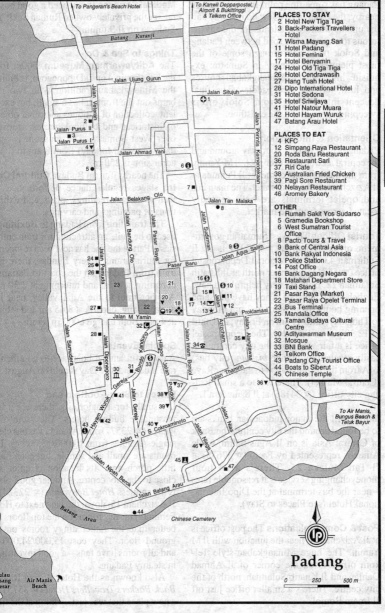

PLACES TO STAY
2   Hotel New Tiga Tiga
3   Back-Packers Travellers Hotel
7   Wisma Mayang Sari
11 Hotel Padang
15 Hotel Femina
17 Hotel Benyamin
24 Hotel Old Tiga Tiga
26 Hotel Cendrawasih
27 Hang Tuah Hotel
28 Dipo International Hotel
31 Hotel Sedona
35 Hotel Sriwijaya
41 Hotel Natour Muara
42 Hotel Hayam Wuruk
47 Batang Arau Hotel

PLACES TO EAT
4   KFC
12 Simpang Raya Restaurant
20 Roda Baru Restaurant
36 Restaurant Sari
37 Riri Cafe
38 Australian Fried Chicken
39 Pagi Sore Restaurant
40 Nelayan Restaurant
46 Aromey Bakery

OTHER
1   Rumah Sakit Yos Sudarso
5   Gramedia Bookshop
6   West Sumatran Tourist Office
8   Pacto Tours & Travel
9   Bank of Central Asia
10 Bank Rakyat Indonesia
13 Police Station
14 Post Office
16 Bank Dagang Negara
18 Matahari Department Store
19 Taxi Stand
21 Pasar Raya (Market)
22 Pasar Raya Opelet Terminal
23 Bus Terminal
25 Mandala Office
29 Taman Budaya Cultural Centre
30 Adityawarman Museum
32 Mosque
33 BNI Bank
34 Telkom Office
43 Padang City Tourist Office
44 Boats to Siberut
45 Chinese Temple

Padang

0   250   500 m

SUMATRA

Padang has some fine palm-fringed beaches nearby, the mountains a few hours away and the unique Mentawai Islands for the adventurous to explore. The road between Padang and Solok takes you through some of the most picturesque scenery in Sumatra: exquisite high-peaked Minangkabau houses and lush, terraced rice paddies. The final descent into Padang from Solok offers sweeping views along the coastline.

Orientation & Information

Padang is easy to find your way around and the central area is quite compact. Jl M Yamin, from the bus terminal corner at Jl Pemuda to Jl Azizcham, is the main street. The main bus and opelet terminals are both centrally located across from the market.

Tourist Offices The West Sumatran government office (Diparda; ☎ 34232) is at Jl Sudirman 43 and the regional Depparpostel office (☎ 55711) is further north at Jl Khatib Sulaiman 22. Both are very helpful and have English-speaking staff. They have the same opening hours: from 8 am to 2 pm Monday to Thursday; until 11 am on Friday; and until to 12.30 pm on Saturday. The Depparpostel office is a fair way from the city centre, but easily reached by orange *biskota* (city bus) 14A from the terminal next to the Pasar Raya (Central Market). There is also a small Padang city office (☎ 34186) at Jl Samudera 1.

Money All the major Indonesian banks are to be found around the city centre. The Bank of Central Asia is on Jl Agus Salim, while Amex is represented by Pacto (☎ 37678) at Jl Tan Malaka 25. There's a 24 hour moneychanging service – at reasonable rates – near the bus terminal at the Dipo International Hotel (see Places to Stay).

Post & Communications The post office is at Jl Azizcham 7, near the junction with Jl M Yamin. The huge Minangkabau-style Telkom office is on the corner of Jl Ahmad Dahlan and Jl Khatib Sulaiman, north of the city centre. There's a smaller office just off Jl Imam Bonjol.

Medical Services If you need a good hosp tal, try the privately owned Ruman Sakit Y Sudarso on Jl Situjuh.

Things to See & Do

The **Adityawarman Museum**, 500m fro the bus terminal on Jl Diponegoro, is built the Minangkabau tradition with two ri barns out the front. It has a small, but exce lent, collection of antiques and other objec of historical and cultural interest from over West Sumatra. The museum is op daily (except Monday) from 8 am to 6 pr admission is 250 rp.

The nearby Taman Budaya **Cultural Ce tre** stages regular dance performances well as poetry readings, plays and exhib tions of paintings and carvings.

The **train line** from Padang to Bukitting used to be quite an attraction for train enth siasts. Part of the line has now been re-open for tourist trains. Every Sunday, there is train from Padang up the coast to Pariam departing at 8 am and returning at 2.30 p Another train to the Anai Valley, near P dangpanjang, departs at 8.45 am and retur at 4 pm. Both charge 6000 rp return.

Special Events

A colourful annual boat race to commem rate Independence Day is held on August 1

Places to Stay – bottom end

Unusually for a major city, there are a fe reasonable budget hotels. The *Hotel S wijaya* (☎ 23577) on Jl Alanglawas has clea singles/doubles from 10,000/15,000 rp. T rooms are small and simple, but each has little porch area. Its location is quiet a close to the city centre. Another good pla is the spotless *Hotel Benyamin* (☎ 22324) Jl Azizcham 15, down the lane next to Ho Femina. The airy rooms on the top floors a better than the rather dingy rooms on t ground floor. They cost 15,000/24,000 and all rooms have fans – a good investme in steamy Padang.

Also known as the Hotel Wisma Rans *Back-Packers Travellers Hotel* (☎ 35751) a new place that was just opening at the tin f writing. Expect to pay about 8000 rp for bed in a spotless air-con dorm, and 30,000 p for air-con doubles with mandi. The hotel s some way from the city centre at Jl Purus ,, but there's free transport from the co-wned Dipo International Hotel (see below).

laces to Stay – middle

f you want to move a little bit upmarket, here are some pleasant old Dutch villas long Jl Sudirman that have been converted nto hotels. The nicest is the friendly guest-house-style *Wisma Mayang Sari* (☎ 22647) t No 19. It has clean, well-appointed rooms vith air-con, hot water and TV from 35,000/-0,000 rp. The nearby *Wisma Anggrek* ☎ 32785) at No 39 has air-con doubles from -0,000 rp. Further south at Jl Azizcham 28, he *Hotel Padang* (☎ 31383) has a range of ir-con rooms from 47,000 to 92,500 rp.

The *Dipo International Hotel* (☎ 34261), l Diponegoro 25, is easily the best of the luster of mid-range places near the bus ter-ninal. It has a range of spotless air-con oubles from 45,000 to 70,000 rp. Other •laces include *Hang Tuah Hotel* (☎ 26556) t Jl Permuda 1 and *Old Tiga Tiga* (☎ 22633) t No 31, both right opposite the bus termi-al.

laces to Stay – top end

he *Hotel Sedona* (☎ 37555) on Jl Bundo Kandung is Padang's No 1 establishment, omplete with swimming pool and flood-lit ennis courts. Room rates start at US$130/-50. The *Natour Muara* (☎ 25600), Jl Gereja 34, and *Pangeran's Beach Hotel* (☎ 51333), l Ir Juanda 79, both have slightly more nodest doubles for around 120,000 rp.

For something a bit different, check out he *Batang Arau Hotel* (☎ 27400). It occu-ies an old Dutch bank, built in 1808, on the iver bank at Jl Batang Arau 33. It's more of a guesthouse than a hotel, with just six rooms - all decorated in traditional Minangkabau style. Some have balconies overlooking the iver. Doubles are US$70, including break-ast.

Places to Eat

The city is famous as the home of Padang food, the spicy Minangkabau cooking that is found throughout Indonesia.

Padang food would have to qualify as the world's fastest fast food. There are no menus in a Padang restaurant. You simply sit down and almost immediately the waiter will set down at least half a dozen bowls of various curries and a bowl of plain rice. You pay only for what you eat, and you can test the sauces free of charge.

The most famous Padang dish is rendang, chunks of beef or buffalo simmered very slowly in coconut milk until the sauce is reduced to a rich paste and the meat becomes dark and dried. Other popular dishes include eggs dusted with red chilli (telor balado), fish baked in coconut and chilli (ikan panggang) and red mutton curry (gulai merah kambing).

The food is normally displayed in the front window so you can take a look at what you're going to eat before entering and go some-where else if you don't like what you see. Don't be overly concerned about the odd fly cruising around the food on display – you'll go hungry if you try to find a restaurant without flies. Fresh fruit, usually pineapple and bananas, is offered for dessert.

Travellers who have acquired a taste for Padang food have hundreds of places to choose. The best places include *Roda Baru*, upstairs in the market at Jl Pasar Raya 6; *Simpang Raya*, opposite the post office at Jl Azizcham 24; and *Pagi Sore* at Jl Pondok 143.

Jl Pondok also has a cluster of Chinese-Indonesian restaurants. The *Riri Cafe* at No 86 is a pleasant little place that opens in the evenings. Immediately opposite is *Austra-lian Fried Chicken* (apparently the owner learned how to fry chicken Down Under). Business hasn't been so good since KFC opened two outlets in town, even though the Aussie portion is twice the size. You can follow up with a choice of fresh ice cream.

The *Restaurant Sari*, Jl Thamrin 71B, is an upmarket Chinese place that also does good seafood. Expect to pay at least 15,000 rp per person. Serious seafood fans should head to the *Nelayan Restaurant* at Jl Hos Cokroaminoto 44. Allow 20,000 rp per head for a meal to remember.

No Sumatran city is without its bakeries and Padang has its share. The *Aromey Bakery* at the southern end of Jl Niaga has a good selection.

Getting There & Away

Air International flights from Padang are covered in the Getting There & Away section at the beginning of this chapter.

Merpati operates a busy domestic schedule with three flights a day to Jakarta (298,100 rp) and daily flights to Pulau Batam (151,800 rp) and Medan (172,700), as well as three weekly to Palembang (179,300 rp). Sempati flies twice a day to Jakarta and four times a week to Pekanbaru (72,600 rp). Mandala also has daily flights to Jakarta, while SMAC flies to Gunung Sitoli on Pulau Nias every Wednesday (123,600 rp).

Merpati, Pelangi Air and SMAC are all based at the Hotel Natour Muara (☎ 38103), while Sempati (☎ 51612) is based at Pangeran's Beach Hotel. Mandala (☎ 32773) is at Jl Pemuda 29A. Silk Air (☎ 38120) has an office at the Hotel Hayam Waruk.

Bus Padang's bus terminal is conveniently central. Every north-south bus comes through here, so there are loads of options.

There are frequent buses to Bukittinggi (2000 rp; two hours). You can get all the way to Jakarta in 30 hours for 45,000 rp, or 70,000 rp air-con. Fares to Parapat (for Danau Toba) and Medan are the same, ranging from 25,000 rp without air-con to 45,000 rp for the best services. Other destinations include Bengkulu (17,500 rp), Sibolga (15,000 rp) and Sungaipenuh (7500 rp).

Boat Pelni ships call at Padang's Teluk Bayur port of every Friday en route to Gunung Sitoli (36,500/100,500 rp for deck/1st class). They stop again every Sunday on the way south to Jakarta (81,500/230,500 rp), Semarang and Pontianak. The Pelni office (☎ 33624) is out at Teluk Bayur, but

you can buy tickets from Ina Tour & Trav at the Dipo International Hotel.

Boats to Pulau Siberut leave from th harbour on the Sungai Batang Arau (als known as the Muara), just south of Padang city centre. See the Mentawai Islands sectio for more details later in this book.

Getting Around

The Airport Tabing airport is nine km nort of the centre on the Bukittinggi road. Airpo taxis charge a standard 10,000 rp for the rid into town. The budget alternative is to wal from the airport terminal to the main roa and catch any opelet into town for 300 r Heading out to the airport, city bus (*biskot* 14A is the best one to get.

Local Transport There are numerous ope lets and *mikrolets* (small opelets) aroun town, operating out of the Pasar Raya termi nal off Jl M Yamin. The standard fare is 30 rp. There's a taxi stand beside the marke building on the corner of Jl M Yamin.

AROUND PADANG
Air Manis

The fishing village of Air Manis is four kr from Padang, just south of the Batang Arau You can get there by opelet, but a mor interesting route is to take a *prahu* (sma outrigger canoe) across the river from whe the boats to Siberut leave. There's a Chines cemetery which overlooks the town, an then it's a one km walk to Air Manis. Accord ing to local mythology, the rock at the end c the beach is the remains of Malin Kundan (a man who was transformed into stone whe he rejected his mother after making fortune) and his boat. There are opelets fron Air Manis back to Padang for 500 rp.

Beaches

There are some good beaches on the coas around Padang. **Pantai Bungus**, 22 kr south of Padang, remains a popular spo despite the huge plywood mill that domi nates the northern end. The southern end palm fringed and postcard pretty. *Losme Carlos* (☎ 30353) is a laid-back place t ang out for a few days. It has basic singles/ doubles for 6000/10,000 rp, and rooms with mandi for 10,000/15,000 rp. Carlos organises snorkelling trips to nearby islands and has information on other local attractions. There are regular opelets from Padang for 700 rp.

Pasir Jambak, 15 km north of town, is the best of several beaches north of Padang. You can stay at *Uncle Jack's Homestay* for 5,000 rp with meals. Jack can organise snorkelling trips to nearby Pulau Sawo. Opelet 423 will get you to Pasir Jambak for 00 rp.

Islands

There are a number of islands close offshore from Padang. **Pulau Pisang Besar** (Big Banana Island) is the closest, only 15 minutes out; boats run there from the Sungai Batang Arau (Muara) harbour. Others islands include **Pagang, Pasumpahan, Sirandah**, and **Sikoai**, where you can stay at the expensive *Pusako Island Resort*. Boats can be chartered from Muara, though Pantai Bunus is the usual departure point.

Contact the tourist office in Padang for more information if you are interested in staying on one of these islands.

PADANG TO BUKITTINGGI

There's some magnificent scenery on the 90 km trip from Padang to the hill town of Bukittinggi, thanks to a combination of rich volcanic soil and ample rainfall. The road climbs through vast patchworks of rice paddy and pockets of lush tropical rainforest. Looming in the background are the peaks of the Merapi and Singgalang volcanoes.

Along the way is the **Lembah Anai Nature Reserve**, renowned for its waterfalls, wild orchids and giant rafflesia flowers.

Padangpanjang

Padangpanjang, 19 km from Bukittinggi, is the main town along the way. It's interesting for its conservatorium (ASKI) of Minangkabau culture, dance and music. This is the best place to get accurate information on live dance and theatre performances. It has a fine collection of musical instruments which includes Minangkabau and Javanese gamelan outfits. There are also excellent costume displays, which are particularly interesting for bridal jewellery and ornaments like the headdress, necklace and the deceptively light bracelet called *galang-gadang*.

Places to Stay Forget about the budget option, the grotty *Hotel Makmur*, Jl Dahlan 34. The modern *Wisma Singgalang Indah* (☎ 82213), on the Padang-Bukittinggi road, has clean doubles with breakfast starting from 35,000 rp.

Getting There & Away Padangpanjang is a comfortable morning or afternoon trip from either Padang or Bukittinggi. There are regular buses between Bukittinggi, Padang and Padangpanjang.

Danau Singkarak

About 15 km south-east of Padangpanjang, Singkarak is the largest of West Sumatra's crater lakes. Despite its easy accessibility, is remains virtually undiscovered by the tourist trail.

Places to Stay The *Singarak Sumpur Hotel* (☎ (0752) 82533) is a small resort hotel at the northern tip of the lake near the village of Sudut Sumpur. It has comfortable doubles overlooking the lake for 50,000 rp and 85,000 rp.

Getting There & Away There are frequent opelets to the villages around the lake from Padangpanjang (500 rp). Most continue to Solok.

BUKITTINGGI

This easy-going hill town is one of the most popular travellers centres in Sumatra. Many travellers heading north from Java make Bukittinggi their first stop. It's easy to spend a week here checking out the town and surrounding attractions. Lying 930m above sea level, it can get quite cold at night.

Bukittinggi was a Dutch stronghold during

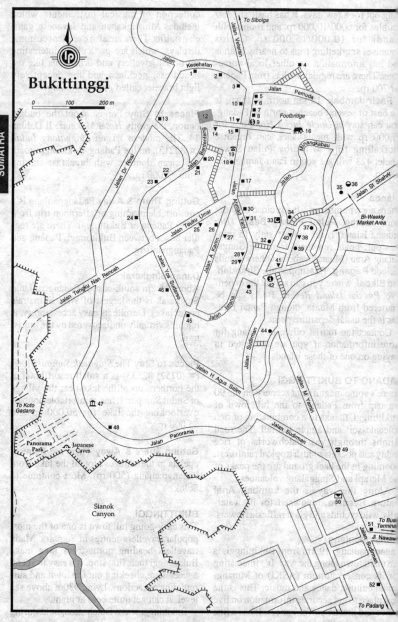

Bukittinggi

0   100   200 m

PLACES TO STAY		52 Hotel Bagindo		12	Fort de Kock
1	Hotel Denai			16	Museum & Zoo
2	Marmy Hotel	PLACES TO EAT		18	Mitra Wisata Tours
3	Sri Kandi Hotel	6 Three Tables			& Travel
4	Hotel Tropic	& Rendezvous		19	Wartel
5	Rajawali Hotel	Coffee Shops		32	Toko Eka
7	Bamboo Homestay	11 Cool Cave		33	Mosque
8	Singgalang Hotel	14 Family Restaurant		34	Gloria Cinema
10	Hotels Murni &	22 Restaurant Sari		35	Pasar Bawah (Market)
	Nirwana	25 Canyon Coffee Shop		36	Opelet Terminal
13	Merdeka Homestay	27 ASEAN Restaurant		37	Pasar Wisata
15	Hotel Yany	28 Selecta Restaurant		39	Pasar Atas
17	Wisma Tiga Balai	29 Kentucky Fried		42	Tourist Office &
20	Benteng Hotel	Chicken			Small Post Office
21	Suwarni Guesthouse	31 Mona Lisa Restaurant		43	Clocktower
23	Mountain View	38 Roda Group		44	Medan Nan
	Guesthouse	Restaurant			Balituduang
24	Wisma Bukittinggi	40 Simpang Raya			(Dance
26	Hotel Surya	Restaurant			Performances)
30	Gangga Hotel	41 Simpang Raya		47	Military Museum
45	Novotel Bukittinggi	Restaurant		49	Telkom Office
46	Hotel Sari			50	Post Office
48	Minang Hotel	OTHER			
51	Dymen's Hotel	9 BNI Bank			

SUMATRA

the Padri Wars (1821-37), and it was here that Sumatran rebels declared their rival government in 1958. Today it is a centre for Minangkabau culture, as well as being a busy market town with a small university.

The town is sometimes referred to as Kota Jam Gadang ('Big Clock Town'), after its best-known landmark – the Minangkabau-style clocktower that overlooks the large market square. Another name is Tri Arga, after the three majestic mountains – Merapi, Singgalang and the more distant Sago – that lie south.

Orientation

The town centre is conveniently compact. Most of the cheap hotels, restaurants and travel agencies are at the northern (bottom) end of the main street, Jl Ahmad Yani. The clocktower and markets are at the top end of Jl Ahmad Yani. Jl Sudirman runs south from the clocktower to the post office and bus terminal.

The rusty iron roofs make Bukittinggi look remarkably like the hill station towns of India. Like them, the changes in level, connected by steps, can be a little confusing.

Information

Tourist Office The tourist office is beside the market carpark, overlooked by the clocktower. The staff are friendly and helpful, although they don't have much other than the standard leaflets and brochures. It's open Monday to Thursday from 8 am to 2 pm, Friday until 11 am, and Saturday until 12.30 pm.

Money A BNI bank, next to the overhead bridge on Jl Ahmad Yani, is the best bank to use. You can also change money at the Bank Rakyat, near the clocktower. After hours, you can change money at places like Toko Eka on Jl Minangkabau, in the market.

Post & Communications The main post office, with its well-organised poste restante section, is on Jl Sudirman. The Telkom office is 150m along the road opposite the post office. It has a Home Country Direct phone. International calls can also be made from the 24 hour telephone office on Jl Ahmad Yani, next to the Grand Hotel.

Travel Agencies There are lots of travel agencies in town. One of the best is Mitra Wisata (☎ 21133) at Jl Ahmad Yani 99. The

SUMATRA

manager, Yan, speaks excellent English and is very helpful. Standard offerings at the various agencies include visits to the bull-fights, full-day excursions to surrounding places of interest and trips to Pulau Siberut.

Market
Bukittinggi's large and colourful market is crammed with stalls of fruit and vegetables, clothing and crafts. The central market is open daily, but the serious action is on Wednesday and Saturday when the markets overflow down the hill. There are some good antiques and arts & crafts to be found around the market.

Fort de Kock, Museum & Zoo
Apart from the defensive moat and a few rusting cannons, not much remains of Bukit-tinggi's old Fort de Kock, built during the Padri Wars (1821-37) by the Dutch. It does, however, provide fine views over the town and surrounding countryside from its hilltop position.

A footbridge leads from the fort over Jl Ahmad Yani to Taman Bundo Kandung, site of the museum and zoo. The museum, which was built in 1934 by the Dutch 'controleur' of the district, is a superb example of Minangkabau architecture with its two rice barns (added in 1956) out the front. It is the oldest museum in the province and has a good collection of Minangkabau historical and cultural exhibits. The zoo is reportedly a disgrace. There's a 1000 rp entry fee to see the fort and zoo, plus an extra 300 rp for the museum.

Panorama Park & Japanese Caves
Panorama Park, on the southern edge of the town, overlooks the deep Sianok Canyon to the west of town. From the park you can enter the extensive grid of caves built by the Japanese using slave labour during WWII. Many of the tunnels open onto the cliff face of the canyon. Entry to the park is 300 rp and entry to the Japanese Caves (Lobang Jepang) costs a further 500 rp. At the entrance there's a bas-relief showing the Japanese herding helpless locals inside.

Military Museum
Next to the Minang Hotel and overlookin Panorama Park is the Military Museum, th final resting place of a collection of fade photographs from the war of independenc against the Dutch. There are also photos of th bodies of five Indonesian generals murdere at the time of the supposed Communist-le attempted coup of 1965, plus war souvenir and photos from Indonesia's war against th Fretilin guerrillas in East Timor.

Organised Tours
Almost every hotel, coffee shop and trave agency offers tours of the district. They rang from trips to the bullfights to full-day tour of the area's attractions to activity tours lik mountain climbing and pig hunting. Se Travel Agencies earlier in this section.

Places to Stay – bottom end
Bukittinggi's budget hotels are a prett charmless lot, but they're certainly cheap Most are close together at the bottom of J Ahmad Yani. The friendly *Bamboo Home stay* has dorm beds for 4000 rp and double with shared mandi for 8000 rp. You will have no trouble finding doubles with share mandi for 7000 rp at places like *Murni*, the decrepit-looking *Rajawali Hotel* and th *Wisma Tiga Balai*. The *Singgalang Hote* (☎ 21576), next to the bank, is a popula place with doubles for 8000 rp.

Many travellers head for the relativ seclusion of the *Hotel Tropic* (☎ 23207), a quiet place down the steps on Jl Pemuda Singles/doubles are 8000/10,000 rp wit shared mandi, 9000/12,000 rp with you own. The *Merdeka Homestay* (☎ 21253), or the corner of Jl Dr Rivai and Jl Yos Sudarso is a solid old Dutch house with large rooms for 10,000/12,500 rp.

There are several good places on the roac to Fort de Kock. The quiet *Suwarni Guest-house* occupies another old Dutch house and has doubles for 10,000 rp. The nearby *Wisma Bukittinggi* has a wide choice o rooms from small singles for 6000 rp to large doubles with a view of Gunung Singgalang fo 15,000 rp.

Places to Stay – middle

The comfortable *Benteng Hotel* (☎ 21115), close to the fort, is easily the best place in this bracket with rooms from 40,000/45,000 p, all including bath, hot water and TV.

The choice is not very exciting elsewhere. The *Marmy Hotel* (☎ 23342) at Jl Kesehatan 30 is a reasonable central option, just around the corner from the budget hotels. It has large doubles with hot water for 45,000 rp. Past the post office, the *Hotel Bagindo* (☎ 23100) at Jl Sudirman 45 is not as bad as it looks (a tacky-looking concrete box with a Minang-kabau-style awning stuck on the front). Doubles with hot water cost from 37,000 rp.

Places to Stay – top end

The *Hotel Denai* (☎ 32920), Jl Dr Rivai 26, was once rated as the top place in town. The older rooms don't measure up to the US$45 price tag, but the so-called superior doubles are large and well appointed. At US$65, they are also better value than you will find at the *Novotel Bukittinggi* (☎ 35000) or the *Hotel Pusako* (☎ 22111), both charging US$95 for standard doubles. Novotel's architects have opted for a curious Arab-Moghul style for their brand-new branch, well located near the clocktower on Jl Istana. The Pusako is an enormous, near-empty complex three km east of town on the road to Payakumbuh.

Places to Eat

The restaurants among the cheap hotels on Jl Ahmad Yani feature all the favourite travellers' fare. There's half a dozen different ways to have your breakfast egg as well as various pancakes, muesli, fruit salad and buffalo yoghurt.

The *Cool Cave*, next to the overhead bridge, is a popular place to hang out, as are the *Three Tables Coffee House* and the *Rendezvous Coffee Shop* at the bottom end of the street. All are also good places to pick up information, although you'll have to deal with all the guides who stop by to offer their services. The Rendezvous has a Home Country Direct phone. The pace is a bit slower at the quiet *Canyon Coffee Shop* on Jl Teuku Umar.

Many travellers reckon the best food in town is at the *Restaurant Sari*, near the fort on Jl Benteng. The menu is predominantly Chinese. It has a good selection of fresh juices. Other places to eat Chinese are the *Selecta* at Jl Ahmad Yani 3 and the long-running *Mona Lisa*, down the street at No 58.

Naturally enough, Padang food is plentiful. The best places are around the market. The *Roda Group* and *Simpang Raya* are big names in the nasi padang business with branches all over Sumatra. Each has two branches in the market. The Simpang Raya also has menus, unusual in Padang restaurants.

A number of places, including the western-oriented coffee houses, do the local speciality, dadiah campur, a tasty mixture of oats, coconut, fruit, molasses and buffalo yoghurt.

Entertainment

There are performances of Minangkabau dance/theatre every night in a hall on the road linking Jl Sudirman and Jl M Yamin. The shows start at 8.30 pm and cost 7500 rp.

Things to Buy

Bukittinggi is a good place to go shopping. There are a number of interesting antique, souvenir and curio shops around. Try Kerajinan at Jl Ahmad Yani 44 or Aladdin at No 14. There are more shops around the market area.

Box collectors can look out for a couple of Minangkabau versions. *Salapah panjang*, or long boxes, are brass boxes used for storing lime and tobacco, and *salapah padusi* are silver boxes used for storing betel nut and lime.

Getting There & Away

The Aur Kuning bus terminal is about two km south of the town centre, but easily reached by opelet. There are heaps of buses south to Padang (2000 rp; two hours), as well as frequent services east to Pekanbaru (6000 rp; five hours).

All buses travelling on the Trans-Sumatran Highway stop at Bukittinggi. Heading south, you can catch a bus right through to Jakarta for 35,000 rp – or 60,000 rp air-con. There are a few buses to Bengkulu, Jambi and Palembang, but most services leave from Padang.

Heading north, you can cut hours off the journey time by catching one of the express air-con buses that bypass Sibolga via a shortcut between Padangsidempuan and Tarutung. They will get you to Parapat in 13 hours for 30,000 rp. The trip to Medan takes 18 hours and costs 30,000 to 45,000 rp. There are also regular buses to Sibolga (12,000 rp; 11 hours). The tourist office has a list of bus companies and ticket prices. Ticket prices vary quite a lot between travel agencies, so shop around. You can also buy tickets at the bus terminal.

Tourist buses leave for Parapat every morning at 7.30 am and cost 27,000 rp. Tickets can be booked at a number of places in town. The buses stop just outside Bonjol at the equator, site of a tacky monument and several stalls selling 'I Crossed The Equator' T-shirts and other souvenirs.

If you're arriving in Bukittinggi from the north (Parapat) or east (Pekanbaru), get off the bus near the town centre and save the hassle of an opelet ride back from the bus terminal.

Getting Around
Opelets around Bukittinggi cost 250 rp for three wheelers or 300 rp for the four wheel variety. The four wheelers run to the bus terminal. *Bendis* (horse carts) cost from 1500 rp depending on the distance.

AROUND BUKITTINGGI
Koto Gadang
This village, known for its silver work, is an hour's walk south-east of Bukittinggi through the Sianok Canyon. Turn left at the bottom of the road just before the canyon and keep going – *don't* cross the bridge.

Pandai Sikat
Its name means 'clever craftsmen' and the village is famous for its songket weaving and ornate woodcarving – too ornate for many

western tastes. The village is only 13 km from Bukittinggi and easily accessible by bemo (200 rp) from Aur Kuning bus terminal.

Ngalau Kamanga
The 1500m long cave at Ngalau Kamanga, 15 km north-east of Bukittinggi, was used a a base for guerrilla attacks against the Dutc in the late 19th and early 20th centuries. Th cave is dripping with stalactites and stalag mites and has a small, clear lake.

Batu Sangkar
The bustling town of Batu Sangkar, 41 kr south-east of Bukittinggi, lies at the heart o traditional Minangkabau country. **Fort de Capellen**, now the police station, was Dutch stronghold during the Padri Wars.

The spectacular **Rumah Gadang Pay aruyung** at the village of Silinduang Bular five km north of Batu Sangkar, features o all the Bukittinggi tour itineraries. The palac is a scaled-down replica of the former hom of the rulers of the ancient Minangkaba kingdom of Payaruyung. The original fea tures on the 100 rp coin.

There are lots of more modest example of traditional architecture in the village around here, particularly at **Belimbing** Anyone who has ever attempted to maintai a timber home will be highly sceptical o claims that these houses were built in th 16th century; early this century would b closer to the mark – for the oldest.

Rafflesia Sanctuary
The sanctuary is signposted near the villag of Palupuh, about 16 km north of Bukittinggi The rafflesia normally blooms betwee August and November. The tourist office i Bukittinggi can tell you if there are bloom around.

Gunung Merapi
Looming large over Bukittinggi to the east i the smouldering summit of Gunung Merap (2891m). Merapi is one of the most restiv of Sumatra's active volcanoes – the las major eruption was in 1979 – and is occa sionally deemed too dangerous to climb. Th

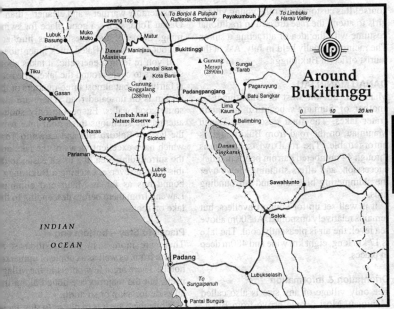

Around Bukittinggi

SUMATRA

tourist office in Bukittinggi can tell you when the mountain is off limits (which probably won't stop the staff offering their services as guides).

The climb begins at the village of Kota Baru (of bullfighting fame on Tuesdays). From Kota Baru, it's a one hour climb to the forestry station (which is no more than a shelter) and then another four hours to the top. Most people climb at night, with the objective of being on the summit at dawn. You'll need good walking boots, warm clothing, a torch (flashlight), and food and drink.

There have been several reports of people getting lost on Merapi. It's very unwise to attempt the climb alone and people are advised to take a guide or join a group. The travel agencies in Bukittinggi offer guided trips to Merapi for 20,000 rp.

Harau Valley

The Harau Valley, 15 km north-east of Payakumbuh, is a popular local beauty spot

that is included on many tour itineraries. The valley is enclosed by spectacular, sheer 100m cliffs. The cliffs are popular with rock-climbers – anyone interested should contact Dodi at the Harau Cliff Coffee Shop in Bukittinggi. Otherwise, there's walks and waterfalls. Harau village is three km up the valley.

Getting There & Away The Harau Valley is not an easy place to get to. The first step is to catch an opelet from Bukittinggi to Payakumbuh (800 rp), and then another from Payakumbuh to the Harau Valley (300 rp) or to Sari Lamak (from where it's a five km walk to the valley). The easiest day to get out there is Sunday, but the place is normally packed with day trippers.

Limbuku

The village of Limbuku, near Payakumbuh, must be the only place on the planet to stage duck racing – the ducks are trained to fly, of course! It is customary for the young village girls to attend the race dressed in traditional costume with the idea of attracting a suitor. The racing is usually held in July. Ask at the tourist office in Bukitinggi.

DANAU MANINJAU
Maninjau, 38 km west of Bukittinggi, is another of Sumatra's beautiful mountain crater lakes. The final descent to Danau Maninjau, on the road from Bukittinggi, is unforgettable. The road twists and turns through 44 numbered hairpin bends in quick succession, and offers stunning views over the shimmering blue lake and surrounding hills.

It is well set up for young travellers, but remains relatively unspoiled. At 500m above sea level, the air is pleasantly cool. The lake is 17 km long, eight km wide and 480m deep in places.

Orientation & Information
The only village of any size is also called Maninjau. Most people arrive from Bukittinggi; the bus stop is at the crossroads where the Bukittinggi road meets the main street.

To the south is Jl H Udin Rahmani. It has most of Maninjau village's shops (which isn't many), several restaurants and three or four guesthouses.

To the right of the crossroads is Jl SMP, which leads off around the lake to the north. It has the majority of Maninjau's 20 odd losmen and numerous coffee shops, as well as the only bank.

Money Bank Rakyat Indonesia will change US dollars only – either cash or travellers cheques.

Post & Communication The post office is opposite the police station on the road running down to the lake. International calls can be made from the telephone office next to the bus stop.

Things to See & Do
Hanging out by the lake is the reason most people come to Maninjau. The waters are considerably warmer – and cleaner – than Danau Toba, so it's a good place for swimming. Some of the guesthouses hire/let dugout canoes or inflated truck inner tubes.

If you're feeling energetic, it takes about six hours to cycle around the lake. The road is fairly flat, but almost three-quarters of the 70 km is on unsealed road. There are also some good walks. Fit people only should attempt the strenuous three hour hike from the lake to **Sakura Hill** and **Lawang Top**, which have excellent views of the lake and the surrounding area. It's much easier to do this hike in reverse, catching a Bukittinggi-bound bus as far as Matur and climbing Lawang from there before descending to the lake on foot.

Places to Stay – bottom end
There are more than 20 guesthouses to choose from, as well as a couple of upmarket hotels. There are a few hotels in the village itself, but the majority are dotted along the lakeside for a km or so north.

While there are lots of places to stay, there is not much between them. The main difference is between those on the shore of the lake and those set back from the water. Those on the water's edge are understandably more popular.

The best place in Maninjau village is the spotless *Pillie Homestay* (☎ 61048), about 200m from the bus stop on Jl H Udin Rahmani. It charges 6000/10,000 rp for singles/doubles.

The nearby *Amai Cheap* (☎ 61054) is a bizarre old Dutch colonial house with a huge balcony and rooms from 5000 to 7000 rp.

Heading north from Maninjau on Jl SMP, there's little to choose between the *Ria Danau*, *Feby's* and the *Beach Guesthouse*, next to each other on the lake's edge 500m from town. All have rooms for 5000/8000 rp.

Further north still, about 1.5 km from town, are the *Palantha Inn* and the *Tropika Baru*. The Palantha Inn is an intriguing old timber rabbit warren that looks like it was built by a dozen carpenters working off different plans. It's rooms cost 5000/7000 rp. If there's nobody home, ask at the Palantha

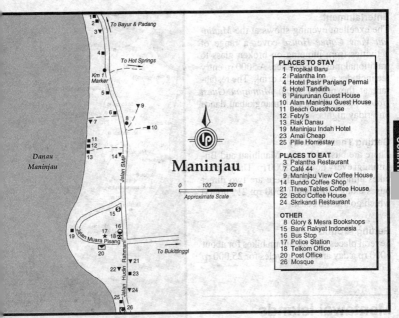

PLACES TO STAY
1 Tropikal Baru
2 Palantha Inn
4 Hotel Pasir Panjang Permai
5 Hotel Tandirih
6 Panuruan Guest House
10 Alam Maninjau Guest House
11 Beach Guesthouse
12 Feby's
13 Riak Danau
19 Maninjau Indah Hotel
23 Amai Cheap
25 Pillie Homestay

PLACES TO EAT
3 Palantha Restaurant
7 Café 44
9 Maninjau View Coffee House
14 Bundo Coffee Shop
21 Three Tables Coffee House
22 Bobo Coffee House
24 Skrikandi Restaurant

OTHER
8 Glory & Mesra Bookshops
15 Bank Rakyat Indonesia
16 Bus Stop
17 Police Station
18 Telkom Office
20 Post Office
26 Mosque

Restaurant. The Tropikal Baru has a few basic doubles for 8000 rp and better rooms overlooking the lake for 10,000 rp.

Places to Stay – middle & top end

New places are springing up all the time. If you want to rest up in a bit more style, the *Hotel Tandirih* (☎ 61253) has comfortable modern rooms with hot water and TV for 50,000 rp. The fanciest place is the *Hotel Pasir Panjang Permai* (☎ 61022), which has doubles from 75,000 to 100,000 rp. All rooms come with hot water and TV, and most overlook the lake. Both places are near the Km 1 marker north of town. The supposedly upmarket *Maninjau Indah Hotel* (☎ 61018), on the lakeside past the post office, looks like it started falling down before it could be finished.

Places to Eat

Most of the guesthouses serve basic meals like mie/nasi goreng. There is more interesting fare to be found elsewhere.

In Maninjau village, the long-running *Three Tables Coffee House* (there are more upstairs) is a good place with an extensive menu geared to western tastes as well as Padang food.

There's good fresh Maninjau fish just down the road at the *Srikandi*. A grilled ikan mas (carp) large enough for two is 8000 rp and a plate of sweet and sour fish is 5000 rp. Sweet and sour spaghetti for 1300 rp is one of several unusual items on the menu.

There are also some good places among the losmen to the north. The *Maninjau View Coffee House*, set back 500m from the lake, is deservedly popular. It has a good menu, cold beer and regular entertainment (see the following Entertainment entry) in the evenings.

Café 44 is a restaurant and party spot on the lakeside, reached down a path next to the Panururan Guest House.

SUMATRA

Entertainment

The excellent evening shows at the *Maninjau View Coffee House* cover a range of activities from jumping on broken glass to traditional music and dance. A 5000 rp entry fee includes a snack and a drink. The restaurant at the nearby *Alam Maninjau Guest House* has displays of Minangkabau dance on Friday nights.

Getting There & Away

There are buses between Maninjau and Bukittinggi every hour for 1000 rp. The journey takes almost an hour. There are two direct buses a day to Padang (3500 rp; 2½ hours) which go via the coast.

Getting Around

Several places rent mountain bikes for about 6000 rp a day and motorcycles for 25,000 rp a day.

Mentawai Islands

The Mentawai Islands are a remote chain of islands off the west coast of Sumatra. The largest island, Siberut, has become a popular destination for trekkers in recent years. Siberut is home to the majority of the Mentawais' population of 30,000. The other islands, Sipora, Pagai Utara and Pagai Selatan, are seldom visited.

After being left quietly on their own for thousands of years, change is now coming at an alarming rate for the Mentawaians. Tourism is but a minor development alongside the transmigration schemes and pro-logging policies of the Indonesian government.

Trekking has become big business on Siberut, with a steady stream of travellers coming to catch a glimpse of a primitive jungle lifestyle that is fast disappearing. The villagers, their bodies covered with ritual tattoos and wearing little but loin cloths and decorative bands and rings, are a photogenic lot who have found tour groups to be good sources of extra income.

In 1864 the Mentawai Archipelago was nominally made a Dutch colony, but it was not until 1901, at the time of the Russo-Japanese War, that the Dutch placed a garrison on the islands to prevent another foreign power using them as a naval base.

Apart from taking a few minor precautions to protect the Mentawai Islands from being taken over by other imperialist nations, the Dutch showed very little interest in them. It was the missionaries who had the most influence on the people, creating fundamental changes in their culture.

The first permanent mission was set up in 1901, on Pagai Utara, by a German missionary August Lett. Eight years later, Lett was murdered by the local people, but the mission survived and by 1916 there had been 11 baptisms recorded. There are now more than 80 Protestant churches throughout the islands. Over half the population claims to be Protestant, 16% Catholic, 13% Muslim, while the rest have no official religion.

It was over 50 years after the advent of the Protestant missionaries that the Catholics moved into the islands to vie for converts. They opened a mission in south Siberut, which combined a church, school and clinic. Free medicines and clothes were given to any islander who became a Catholic and by 1969 there were almost 3000 converts.

The Islamic influence began to make inroads once government officials were regularly appointed from Padang during the Dutch era. To complicate religious matters further, the eclectic Baha'i faith was introduced in 1955.

he growth of bananas is vital to the Mentawaian conomy.

History

Very little is known about the origins of the Mentawaians but it is assumed that they emigrated from Sumatra to Nias and made their way to Siberut from there.

They remained isolated and undisturbed by other cultures until late in the 19th century when the Dutch permitted Protestant missionaries to attempt to convert them to Christianity.

There are several references to the islands before the 19th century. In 1621 it appears that Siberut was the only island inhabited. The Mentawaians are also mentioned in a scientific paper presented in 1799 by the Englishman John Crisp. Sir Stamford Raffles appears to have been particularly impressed by the Mentawaians and their culture. In one of the many reports he wrote urging the British government to compete with the Dutch in colonising Indonesia he states:

Formerly, I intended to write a book to prove that the Niassans were the most contented people on earth. Now I have to acknowledge the fact that the people of the Mentawai Islands are even more admirable and probably much less spoiled than we.

Economy

Taros and bananas are the staple crops of both the Pagai islands and Sipora, while on Siberut, sago is also cultivated. Traditionally, the women own the taro fields and are responsible for planting and maintaining them. The banana plantations belong to the men – some are worked by one or two families, others by an entire *uma* (communal house). The Mentawaians also grow cassava, sweet potatoes and other crops. Their diet is supplemented by hunting and fishing.

SUMATRA

SIBERUT

Although Siberut has been a popular destination for some years now, conditions on the island remain quite basic. Siberut's port of Muarasiberut is the only town of any consequence. It has shops, where you can stock up on provisions, as well as the only losmen.

Despite recent changes, about two-thirds of the island is still covered with tropical rainforest. It's also surrounded by magnificent coral reefs teeming with fish.

When to Go

May is generally the driest month, but it ca

The Mentawaians

Although the distance between mainland Sumatra and the Mentawai Islands is not great, the strong winds, unpredictable seas and coral reefs made navigation to the islands difficult in earlier centuries. The result was that the Mentawaians had very little contact with the outside world and remained one of the purest indigenous Indonesian societies until early in the 20th century when the missionaries arrived. The Mentawaians had their own language, adat and religion. They were skilled in boat building, but had not developed any kind of handcraft nor cultivated rice.

Physically, the Mentawaians are slim and agile. Traditional clothing consists of a loin cloth made from the bark of the breadfruit tree for men and a bark skirt for women. Traditionally they sharpened their teeth and decorated themselves with tattoos which covered part of their faces and most of their bodies. They wear bands of red-coloured rattan, beads and imported brass rings on their arms, fingers and toes. Both men and women often used to thread flowers through their long hair. The government has banned tattoos, sharpened teeth and long hair. Although the ban has not been enforced, it's now rare to see people looking like this, except in the more remote villages.

Culture Villages are built along river banks and consist of one or more uma surrounded by single storey family houses *(lalep)*. A number of families (between five and 10) live in the same building. Bachelors and widows have their own living quarters, known as rusuk, which are identical to the family longhouse except that they have no altar. Traditionally all the houses stand on wooden piles and are designed without windows.

Although essentially patriarchal, society is organised on egalitarian principles. There are no inherited titles or positions and no subordinate roles. It is the uma, not the village itself, which becomes the pivot of social, political and religious life in Mentawai society. It is here that discussions affecting the community take place. Everyone – men, women and children – are present at meetings, but the prominent men make most of the major decisions, including choosing a *rimata* (the person who leads religious affairs and is the community's spokesperson to the outside world), building an uma, clearing forests or laying out a banana plantation.

On such occasions the people of the uma carry out a religious festival known as *punen*. This usually involves ritual sacrifices of both pigs and chickens and, depending on the importance of the occasion, can last for months on end and sometimes years. All kinds of everyday jobs and activities become taboo; work in the fields is stopped and strangers are denied access to the uma – its isolation being marked by a cordon of palm leaves and flowers.

Religion The native Sibulungan religion was a form of animism, involving the worship of nature spirits and a belief in the existence of ghosts, as well as the soul. The chief nature spirits are those of the sky, sea, jungle and earth. There are also two river spirits: Ina Oinan (mother of rivers) is beneficent, while Kameinan (father's sister) is regarded as being evil. Apart from these nature spirits, all inanimate objects have spirits *(kina)* which give them life. There is no hierarchy among the spirits – although the sky spirits are considered the most influential – nor do they have any particular gender, but like human beings there's a mixture of men, women and children.

As with all religions in Indonesia, the worship of the soul is of the utmost importance, being vital to good health and longevity. The soul is believed to depart the body at various times during life before its ultimate escape at death. Sickness, for example, is the result of the temporary absence of the soul from the body, while dreams also signify that the soul is on 'vacation'. When the soul leaves the body at death it is transformed into a ghost *(sanitu)*. Mentawaians try to avoid these ghosts, whom they suspect of malevolently attempting to rob the living of their souls. To protect themselves from such an awful fate, they place fetish sticks at every entrance to the village. This tactic is considered foolproof, provided no-one has committed a ritual sin or broken a taboo. ■

SUMATRA

rain on Siberut at any time of year. The seas between Siberut and the West Sumatran coastline can get very rough in June and July, which means tours may be cancelled if boats aren't running. October and November tend to be the wettest months on Siberut.

What to Bring
If you're heading off independently, you will need your own food supplies – rice, noodles and dried food, as well as tea and sugar. Essential items for jungle living are a mosquito net, insect repellent, torch (flashlight) and plastic bags for keeping things dry. You can buy most supplies in Muarasiberut, but they are much cheaper if bought in Padang.

The smaller your backpack the better. It will be easier to carry in the jungle and to transport in the sampans.

You will also need to bring things for barter and gifts. Pens, pencils and paper are more sound choices than cigarettes, which unfortunately are the accepted gift currency. Medicines should on no account be given away as gifts.

The demand for gifts has become a constant hassle. Most islanders already seem to think that white people are rich fools who will willingly part with anything asked of them. It's wise to give things only to people who have helped.

Information
Information on Siberut is hard to come by. The West Sumatran tourist office in Padang can do little more than advise on boat times and show you a booklet called *Saving Siberut* that was put out by the WWF in the early 1980s. Once you arrive in Muarasiberut, Syahruddin's Homestay is the place to ask questions, organise guides etc.

Permits Permits for the islands are issued on landing in Muarasiberut and cost 2000 rp. Bring three photocopies of your passport details.

Money Bring sufficient cash with you. There are no banks and no official moneychangers, although some cash-strapped travellers have

reported that they managed to change clean US dollar bills in Muarasiberut.

Although some villagers prefer gifts to payment in cash, most places on what is now a well-trodden trail prefer cash. You'll certainly need cash in Muarasiberut.

Post & Communications There is a post office in Muarasiberut. If you're desperate, and very patient, the wartel office may be able to get you a line to the outside world.

Health Chloroquine-resistant malaria is a common problem and each year many locals die from it. There are plenty of snakes around, but they are not likely to be a problem. The rivers are used for washing and as running toilets, and thus are a source of disease. Never drink water unless it has been boiled or purified.

Dangers & Annoyances Theft can be a problem, but normally only small items left lying around go missing. Also remember that elderly people dislike cameras and are afraid of flashes. You will not be well received in a village if you arrive with camera at the ready.

Things to See & Do
The traditional settlement of **Sakelot** is only one km from Muarasiberut and easily accessible on foot. The other villages close to the main town are new – a legacy of the government's policy of moving the people out of the jungle and setting them up in villages along the coastal strip.

The main reason people come to Siberut is to visit the villages of the interior, where the lifestyle is only slowly adapting to the 20th century. One of the easiest villages to get to from Muarasiberut is **Tiap**, which is two hours by boat along a narrow branch of jungle river. A more adventurous, but still comparatively easy, trip is to **Rodok**, where people live in small, traditional houses. It takes between five and six hours to get there and back by boat.

Two more remote villages are **Sakudai** and **Madobak**. The journey to Sakudai takes two days – one day by boat and the other trekking through the jungle. The trip to Madobak takes six hours by boat.

Organised Tours

Most travellers take the easy option of joining an organised tour. It is also the cheap option in view of the costs involved in chartering boats on your own.

You can pay anything from US$150 to US$700 for a 10 day tour, depending on the level of comfort. Seven day tours (US$125) are also available, but given that the tours involve three days in transit, most travellers opt for 10 days. The tour price includes guide service and accommodation (in village huts), food (usually prepared by the guide), local transport and transport to/from the island.

The place to shop for tours is Bukittinggi, where they are promoted in every coffee shop, losmen and travel agency. The best approach is to spend some time in the coffee shops seeking out the experiences of those who have just returned. The comment books run by the agencies can sometimes be helpful, although a glance at the spine of the books shows what happens to pages with negative comments. It's worth asking about the size and composition of a group before signing up.

Some critics claim the Bukittinggi-based tours are no good because they are run by Sumatrans, who are not liked by the Mentawaians. The tour agencies counter that they employ Mentawaian guides. Most people don't seem to notice.

The treks usually include plenty of mud-slogging, river crossings and battles with indigenous insects, so don't set off expecting a gentle jaunt through the jungle.

The return on your suffering is the chance to experience unspoiled rainforest and the local culture of Siberut. Most people come away very happy with their trekking package.

Places to Stay & Eat

The only losmen on Siberut is the friendly *Syahruddin's Homestay* in Muarasiberut. It has good doubles for 10,000 rp. In more

remote areas, it's often possible to stay at missionary buildings, schools or with private families, but don't expect any comforts. Accommodation is usually on the floor. Payment is normally made in the form of gift rather than money.

The situation is much the same for food. There are a few basic restaurants in Muara-siberut; elsewhere you will be expected either to pay or to make a donation for meals.

Getting There & Away

Air The island's only airport is on Pulau Sipora, but there are no scheduled flights.

Boat There are boats to Muarasiberut from Padang's Sungai Batang Arau (Muara) harbour four times a week. PT Rusco Line (☎ 21941), Jl Batang Arau 31, has boats from Padang on Monday and Wednesday, returning on Tuesday and Thursday. The fares are 11,000/16,000 rp for deck/cabin class. The PT Rusco office is to the right through the alleyway next to Elia English Course, opposite the port gates. Mentawai Indah (☎ 28200), Jl Batang Arau 88, has boats from Padang on Thursday and Satur-day, returning on Friday and Sunday. All boats leave at 8 pm and the journey takes 10 to 12 hours.

Sometimes people get groups together to charter a boat across and back, giving them transport around the coast as well.

Getting Around

If you're planning on organising your own way around Siberut, the biggest expense will be the cost of getting around. The roads on the island are little more than logging tracks and there are no buses.

Boats are the main form of local transport. They are used both around the coast and for river transport. Getting to villages that are off the beaten track will mean chartering boats as well as hiring your own guide. Most of the interesting villages will cost at least 100,000 rp to get to. You need to bargain hard.

Riau

The province of Riau is split into two distinct areas, mainland Riau and the Riau Islands.

Mainland Riau covers a huge expanse of eastern Sumatra's sparsely populated east coast and has the modern oil town of Pekanbaru as its capital. It has Indonesia's richest oil fields, as well as huge deposits of tin and bauxite. Much of the land is dense forest or mangrove swamp – too low-lying and poorly drained for agriculture. The jungle is home to such rare creatures as the Sumatran rhinoceros and tiger, as well as bears, tapirs and elephants.

Several animistic and nomadic peoples (including the Sakai, Kubu and Jambisal) still live in the jungle, mostly around the port of Dumai.

Offshore Riau is made up of more than 3000 islands spread over more than 1000 km of ocean. The islands' capital is the town of Tanjung Pinang, on Pulau Bintan south-west of Singapore, although attention is fast turning to the boom island of Pulau Batam next door. The islands are home to a third of Riau province's population of 2.7 million.

Mosquitos are rife throughout Riau and chloroquine-resistant malaria has been reported.

History

Before the advent of air travel, Riau occupied a strategic position at the southern entrance to the Straits of Melaka, the gateway for trade between India and China.

From the 16th century, the Riau Islands were ruled by a variety of Malay kingdoms, who had to fight off constant attacks from pirates and the opportunistic Portuguese, Dutch and English. The Dutch eventually won their struggle with the Portuguese for control over the Straits of Melaka, and mainland Riau (then known as Siak) became a Dutch colony in 1745 when the Sultan of Johore surrendered his claim to the Dutch East India Company.

The Dutch were more interested in ridding the seas of pirates so their fleet could get on with the serious business of trade than in developing the region, so they left Riau alone.

Oil was discovered around Pekanbaru by US engineers before WWII, but it was the Japanese who drilled the first well at Rumbai, 10 km north of Pekanbaru. Rumbai is now the base for Caltex Pacific Indonesia. The country around Pekanbaru is crisscrossed by pipelines connecting the oil wells to refineries at Dumai because ocean-going tankers cannot enter the heavily silted Sungai Siak.

PEKANBARU

Before the Americans struck oil, Pekanbaru was little more than a sleepy river port on the Sungai Siak. Today, it is Indonesia's oil capital – a bustling modern city of more than 500,000 people. There's little reason for travellers to stop there, and most treat it as no more than an overnight stop on the route between Singapore and Bukittinggi.

Orientation

The main street of Pekanbaru is Jl Sudirman. Almost everything of importance to travellers – banks, hotels and offices – can be found on this street or close by. Speedboats leave from the wharf at the end of Jl Sudirman, while the bus terminal is at the other end of town on Jl Nangka, off Jl Sudirman.

Information
Tourist Office The tourist office (☎ 31562) is a long way from the city centre at Jl Merbabu 16.

Money The city's banks are spread along Jl Sudirman. The Bank of Central Asia is at No 448.

Post & Communications The main post office and the Telkom office are on Jl Sudirman, between Jl Hangtuah and Jl Kartini. There is a small post office nearer the port on the corner of Jl Sudirman and Jl Juanda.

Travel Agencies Kota Piring Kencana Travel (☎ 21382), conveniently at Jl Sisingamangaraja

Pekanbaru

0   200   400 m

PLACES TO STAY
1 Hotel Mutiara
  Merdeka
9 Hotel Tasia Ratu
13 Hotel Anom
14 Hotel Dyan Graha
15 Hotel Indrapura
26 Poppie's Homestay
28 Tommy's Place
29 Hotel Linda

PLACES TO EAT
5 Restaurant Asia
  Baru
6 Fruit Shop
8 Seafood Warungs
11 New Holland Bakery
12 Bima Sahti Corner
17 Night Market

OTHER
2 Mesjid Raya
  (Great Mosque)
3 Ferry Wharf
4 Speedboat Wharf
7 BNI Bank 1946
10 Wartel
16 Kota Piring Kencana
  Travel
18 Telkom Office
19 Bank of Central Asia
20 Garuda/Merpati Office
21 Post Office
22 Governor's House
23 Balai Adat Daerah
  Riau
24 University of Riau
25 Police Station
27 Bus Terminal
30 Riau Cultural Park
31 Museum Negeri Riau

3, can handle flight and bus bookings as well as tours.

Things to See & Do

Few people hang around Pekanbaru for long enough to do anything other than buy a ticket out. Not a bad idea, really, but if you've got time to burn there's always the **Museum Negeri Riau** and neighbouring **Riau Cultural Park**, towards the airport on Jl Sudirman. They are open from 8 am until 2 pm Monday to Thursday and Saturday and until noon on Friday.

The **Balai Adat Daerah Riau**, on Jl Dip-

onegoro, has displays of traditional Mala culture and is open the same hours as th museum. The **Mesjid Raya** (Great Mosque near the river on Jl Mesjid Raya, dates bac to the 18th century when Pekanbaru was th capital of the Siak sultans. The courtyar holds the graves of the fourth and fift sultans.

Places to Stay – bottom end

Most people head straight to *Poppie's Home stay* (☎ 33863), an excellent place a fe minutes' walk from the bus terminal on Cempedak II. There are doubles for 10,000 r and dorm beds for 3500 rp, and a small restaurant serving basic meals. The owner speaks good English and can arrange boat tickets to Batam. To get there from the bus terminal, cross Jl Nangka and head up Jl Taskurun. Take the second street on the left (Jl Kuini), and Jl Cempedak II is the first street on the right. If you are coming from the port, phone for a free pick-up.

The alternative is *Tommy's Place*, 400m from the bus terminal on Gang Nantongga, next to Jl Nangka 53. Tommy charges 4000 rp per person and can also arrange tickets for the Batam boats. From the bus terminal, turn right and Gang Nantongga is the second gang (alley) on the right side – opposite Bank Buana. Walk down and ask for Tommy's, which is tucked away on the right after about 50m.

Places to Stay – middle

The *Hotel Linda* (☎ 36915), down a small alleyway opposite the bus terminal, has a good choice of rooms. Doubles with mandi and fan are 20,000 rp, and 65,000 rp gets you a large double with air-con and TV.

The *Hotel Anom* (☎ 30863), on the corner of Jl Sudirman and Jl Gatot Subroto, has OK rooms set around a courtyard. Air-con doubles with mandi start at 35,000 rp.

Places to Stay – top end

Supply far exceeds demand at the top end of the market, which means that there are some good deals to be had. Discounts of 30% on listed rates are freely available at big hotels. The best of them is the *Hotel Dyan Graha* (☎ 26851), conveniently central at Jl Gatot Subroto 7, with doubles from 130,000 to 230,000 rp. Its main rivals in this price bracket are the nearby *Hotel Indrapura* (☎ 36233), Jl Dr Sutomo 86, and the *Hotel Mutiara Merdeka* (☎ 31272), which is a long way from anything else of interest on Jl Dr Pangaitan.

A notch below this lot, but better value, is the *Hotel Tasia Ratu* (☎ 33225), well placed at Jl Hasyim Ashari 10. Doubles here start at 90,000 rp.

Places to Eat

There are innumerable cheap places to eat along Jl Sudirman, particularly at night around the market at the junction with Jl Imam Bonjol. The restaurant at the *Hotel Anom* does good Chinese food, while there's a choice of sate, martabak or Chinese food at *Bima Sahti Corner* on Jl Tangkuban Perahu.

There is cheap seafood at the two *warung makanan laut* on Jl Wolter Monginsidi, easily identifiable by the marine creatures adorning their awnings. The *New Holland Bakery*, Jl Sudirman 153, has a fine selection of cakes and pastries, as well as hamburgers and ice cream. It also does good fresh fruit juices.

Getting There & Away

Air Simpang Tiga is one of the busiest airports in Sumatra. It is also a visa-free entry point. Pelangi Air and Sempati both fly to Kuala Lumpur for US$107, while Merpati flies to Johore Bahru (Malaysia) for US$94 and Singapore for US$102.

Merpati also has direct flights to Jakarta, Batam, Medan and Pangkalpinang. The Garuda/Merpati office (☎ 21575) is at Jl Sudirman 343; Sempati (☎ 21612) is at the Hotel Mutiara Merdeka; and Pelangi Air is represented by Kota Piring Kencana Travel (☎ 21382) at Jl Sisingamangaraja 3.

Bus Bukittinggi is the main destination and there are frequent departures from the bus terminal on Jl Nangka. The 240 km trip takes about five hours and costs from 6000 rp.

Boat Agencies all around town sell tickets for the boats to Pulau Batam. Tickets include the bus fare to Tanjung Buton and the speedboat from there to Batam, usually via Selat Panjang. There is not a lot of difference between the speedboat services, though the prices vary from around 35,000 to 37,500 rp. The journey takes about nine hours, reaching Batam at about 5 pm – in time to catch a ferry to Singapore.

Garuda Express goes by speedboat down the river to Perawang, then by bus to Tanjung Buton and then another speedboat to Batam.

It is an interesting trip, although no quicker despite the claims. Another alternative is the cargo boats which leave on Monday, Wednesday and Friday at 5 pm. They travel down the Sungai Siak and then on to Selat Panjang (9500 rp; 12 hours) before continuing to Batam (25,000 rp; 24 hours) and Bintan. Buy tickets at the wharf – an extra 5000 rp will get you a 'cabin', which is just a bare, wooden sleeping platform, but a luxury compared to deck class.

It's a good idea to take food and drink with you since two meals of boiled rice garnished with a bit of dry, salted fish and a dollop of chilli is all your ticket includes. All is not lost if you forget – or don't have the time – to stock up. The boat stops at various river villages along the way and flotillas of sales people circle around hawking soft drinks, peanuts and fruit.

Getting Around
The Airport Airport taxis charge 10,000 rp for the 12 km trip into town. It's a one km walk to the main road if you want to catch an opelet (300 rp) into town.

Charter Taxi Taxis can be chartered for 8000 rp per hour from Kota Piring Kencana travel agency. There is a two hour minimum.

Local Transport Opelets around Pekanbaru cost a standard 300 rp.

DUMAI
Most of Pekanbaru's oil exits through the port of Dumai, 158 km north of Pekanbaru. Unless you're a fan of oil loading facilities, there's no point in coming here. It is, however, a visa-free entry point with ferry links to the Malaysian port of Melaka. The ferries leave Dumai (114,000 rp) on Thursday and Sunday, and Melaka (RM120) on Monday and Friday. The Pelni boats *Rinjani* and *Umsini* also call at Dumai in the course of their fortnightly circuits out of Jakarta, stopping at Bintan and Bangka

islands. There is a departure from Duma every Saturday at 4 pm.

There are frequent buses from Dumai to Pekanbaru (3500 rp; 2½ hours). If you ge stuck in town, try the *City Hotel* (☎ 21550 on Jl Sudirman. Expect to pay about 15,00 rp for a double with fan and 40,000 rp fo air-con.

SIAK SRI INDERAPURA
Some 120 km down river from Pekanbaru i Siak Sri Inderapura, site of the beautifu **Asserayah el Hasyimiah Palace** built b the 11th sultan of Siak, Sultan Adbul Jali Syafuddin, in 1889. The palace was restore five years ago as a museum. The site als includes a dazzling white **mosque** with silver dome.

The *Penginapan Monalisa*, by the dock i Siak, has basic singles/doubles for 7500 11,000 rp.

Siak can be reached by a variety of rive transport from Pekanbaru, including speed boats that will do the trip in two hours fo 6000 rp.

RIAU ISLANDS
The Riau Islands are scattered across th South China Sea like confetti. There are a many islands, locals say, as there are grain in a cup of pepper (3214 islands in all, mor than 700 of them uninhabited and many o them unnamed).

The term Riau originally applied only t the group of islands immediately south-wes of Singapore, including Batam, Bintan Rempang and Galang islands. The moder administrative region also takes in th nearby Karimun Islands and the Lingg Islands further south, as well as stretchin 1000 km to the north-east to take in th remote South China Sea island groups o Anambas, North and South Natuna an Tambelan.

Tanjung Pinang, on Pulau Bintan, is th traditional capital of the islands, but muc attention is focused these days on Pula Batam, which is rapidly being developed a an industrial extension of Singapore.

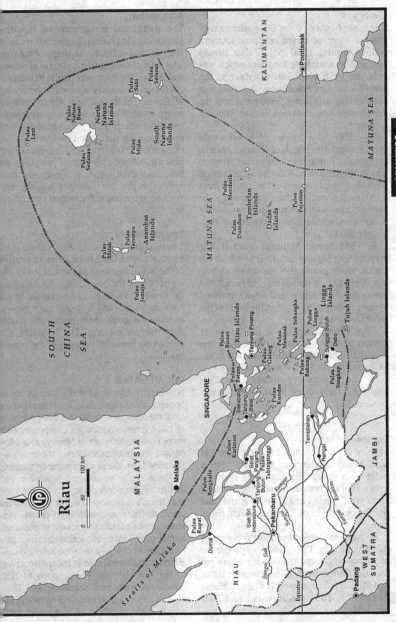

SUMATRA

MATUNA SEA

KALIMANTAN

Pontianak

Pulau Serasan

Pulau Subi

North Natuna Islands

Pulau Natuna Besar

Pulau Laut

South Natuna Islands

Pulau Sedanau

Pulau Midai

Pulau Mendarik

Tambelan Islands

Pulau Dumdum

Dadas Islands

Pulau Pejantan

MATUNA SEA

Anambas Islands

Pulau Terempa

Pulau Matak

SOUTH CHINA SEA

Pulau Jemaja

Lingga Islands

Pulau Lingga

Tujuh Islands

Sungai Buluh

Babo

Riau Islands

Pulau Bintan

Tanjung Pinang

Pulau Sebangka

Pulau Mesanak

Pulau Galang

Pulau Bakong

Pulau Singkep

SINGAPORE

Pulau Batam

Sekupang

Tanjung Balai

Pulau Kundur

Riau

MALAYSIA

Melaka

50   100 km

0   50

Pulau Karimun

Tembilahan

Rengat

JAMBI

Selat Panjang

Pulau Tebingtinggi

Pulau Bengkalis

Tanjung Buton

Pekanbaru

Sungai Kampar

Sungai Siak

Pulau Rupat

Siak Sri Indrapura

Dumai

Sungai Rokan

Sungai Kuantan

Straits of Melaka

RIAU

WEST SUMATRA

Padang

Equator

SUMATRA

History

The early history of the Riau Islands suggests a wave of migration from southern India. Around 1000 AD, Pulau Bintan emerged as a separate kingdom which was enlarged by a propitious marriage to the son of a king of Palembang. A capital was built in Temasik (now Singapore) and the principality was renamed Bintan Temasik Singapura.

By 1500 the kingdom of Melaka held sway through the islands of Kundur, Jemaja, Bunguran, Tambelan, Lingga and Bintan. The Portuguese ruled Riau for a brief period following their conquest of Melaka, but from 1530 to the end of the 18th century the archipelago was a stronghold of Malay civilisation with its main centres at Penyenget and Lingga.

In 1685 Sultan Mahmud Syah II was coerced into signing an agreement with the Dutch which greatly diminished his authority. The Dutch gradually reduced the authority of the rajahs, and finally assumed control of the archipelago on the death of the rajah in 1784.

Opposition to the Dutch did not really re-emerge until the early 1900s when the Rusydiah Club was formed by the last sultan of Riau-Lingga. This was ostensibly a cultural and literary organisation, but later assisted in the struggle for Indonesian independence.

People

Most of the inhabitants of the islands are of pure Malay origins, but there are several indigenous groups like the *orang laut* (sea gypsies) of the Natuna Islands, the Mantang peoples of Penuba and Kelumu islands and the Baruk people of Sunggai Buluh, Singkep.

Bintan is the largest and most populous of the Riau Islands. The majority of people are of Malay origin, but the ethnic melting pot includes Sumatran peoples such as the Batak and Minangkabau, as well as a large Chinese community. The population is about 90% Muslim.

Architecture

The traditional architecture of the Riau Islands is called *rumah lipat kijang*, meaning 'hairpin' and refers to the shape of the roof. The style is undergoing a revival at present and is used for most new public buildings.

Houses are usually adorned with carvings of flowers, birds and bees. Often there are wings on each corner, said to symbolise the capacity to adapt. Four pillars have much the same meaning: the capacity to live in the four corners of the universe. The flowers are supposed to convey a message of prosperity and happiness from owner to visitor, the bird symbolise the one true god and the bees symbolise the desire for mutual understanding.

Special Events

The islanders of remote Pulau Serasan in the South Natuna Islands hold an annual Festival of the Sea. They hang packets of sticky rice on trees near the beach, then cut logs from the forest which they cart down to the beach load into canoes and drop into deep water to appease the gods of the ocean and protect them from drowning. The islanders also uphold the principal festivals of the Islamic calendar.

PULAU BATAM

Nowhere in Indonesia is the pace of development more rapid than on Pulau Batam. Until the island was declared a free-trade zone in 1989, it was a backwater comprising little more than the shanties of Nagoya and a few coastal villages. Several years of frantic construction later, the place is unrecognisable.

There are a number of expensive golf resorts on the north coast, but for the most part there's a distinct frontier town atmosphere to the place, with high prices, ugly construction sites and no reason to pause any longer than it takes to catch a boat out.

Batam has largely usurped neighbouring Bintan's traditional role as the transport hub of the Riau Islands. The seaports of Batu Ampar, Nongsa and Sekupang and Hang Nadim airport are all visa-free entry and exit points.

SUMATRA

rientation
ost travellers arrive on Batam by boat from
ngapore to the port of Sekupang. After you
ear immigration, there are counters for
oney exchange, taxis and hotels. The
mestic terminal for boats to the mainland
right next door. Ferries to Bintan leave
om Telaga Panggur in the south-east.

The main town of Nagoya is decidedly
eazy. It's the original boom town, complete
ith bars and massage parlours. The old
anties can still be seen peeping out be-
een the flash new hotels, offices and
opping centres. Nagoya's port area of Batu
mpar is just north of town.

Batam Centre is a new administrative
ntre that is being built from the stumps up
the north between Nagoya and Hang
adim airport.

The **Nongsa Peninsula** in the north-east
ringed by beautifully manicured golf
sorts built with Singapore visitors in mind.

formation
ourist Office The Batam Tourist Promo-
n Board (☎ 322852) has a small office
tside the international terminal at Sek-
ang. It can help with hotel bookings, and
ts out an enthusiastic brochure describing
atam as a tropical paradise.

oney Singapore dollars are as easy to
end as Indonesian rupiah on Batam. There's
money exchange counter at the Sekupang
rry building, but the rates are better in
agoya where all the major banks are based.
ney include the Bank of Central Asia on Jl
akura Anpan.

ost & Communications The main post
ffice is in Batam Centre, but there is a small
st office near the Nagoya Plaza Hotel on
Imam Bonjol. International phone calls
n be made from the wartel office opposite
e Holiday Inn on Jl Imam Bonjol and from
rd phones everywhere.

aces to Stay – bottom end
udget accommodation on Batam is some of
e worst in Indonesia and another argument

for not sticking around. There is a line-up of
utterly rock-bottom places about one km out
of town at Blok C, Jl Teuku Umar. The
Minang Jaya is the best of a bad bunch with
bare, partitioned singles/doubles for 10,000
rp. The *Wisma Chendra Wisata*, on nearby Jl
Sriwijaya, is marginally better, with singles
for 15,000 rp.

Places to Stay – middle
Mid-range accommodation is similarly uninspiring and overpriced. Prices are quoted in
Singapore dollars, and it's a struggle to find
a double for under S$60. The *Horizona*
(☎ 457111) has rooms for S$45/60 and is
centrally located on Jl S Rahman.

Places to Stay – top end
Flash new hotels and golf resorts are springing up everywhere, even though supply
already appears to far exceed demand. The
only time these places do any business is at
weekends when Singaporeans come over on
packages to play golf and eat seafood.

There are some smart-looking places on Jl
Imam Bonjol in Nagoya. They include *Na-
goya Plaza* (☎ 459888) and *New Holiday
Hotel* (☎ 459308), both charging from
S$110 for the cheapest doubles.

Out at Nongsa, places like the *Palm
Springs Golf & Country Club* (☎ 459899)
and the *Turi Beach Resort* (☎ 310075) won't
give you much change from S$200 for a
double.

Places to Eat
Restaurants on Batam are expensive, much
like everything else, but there are some good
seafood places.

In Nagoya the best place to head is the
night markets along Jl Raja Ali Haji or at the
big and raucous *Pujasera Nagoya* food
centre.

Seafood-loving Singaporeans head for the
kelongs (restaurants built out over the sea on
stilts) that dot the coast. Places like the
Batam View Kelong at Nongsa keep its catch
live in tanks. Everything is charged by the
kg. Allow about 25,000 rp per person for a
decent spread and a couple of cold beers.

SUMATRA

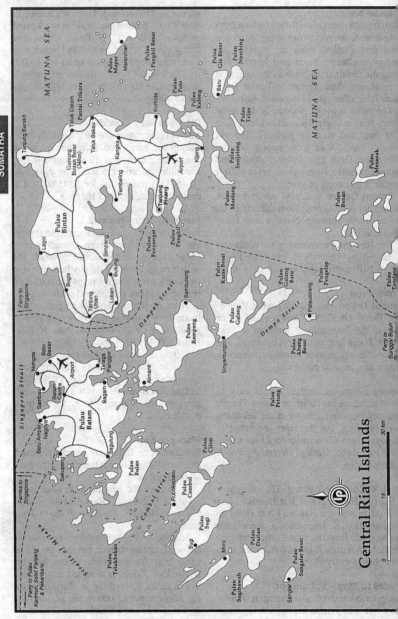

Central Riau Islands

Getting There & Away

Air The brand new airport at Hang Nadim is international in name only. At this stage, there are no international flights.

Garuda, Sempati and Bouraq all have daily direct flights to Jakarta (231,500 rp). Sempati and Bouraq also have daily flights to Medan (193,000 rp). Merpati destinations include Padang, Palembang, Pangkalpinang (Pulau Bangka), Pekanbaru and Pontianak (Kalimantan).

SMAC destinations include Tanjung Pinang (52,100 rp), Pulau Singkep (96,100 rp); Jambi (168,700 rp) and Pangkalpinang (206,100 rp) on Pulau Bangka.

Bouraq (☎ 458344) is at Jl Raden Patah 6; Merpati (☎ 457288) is at Jodoh Square Blok A 1; Sempati (☎ 451612) is at Gedung Astek on Jl Imam Bonjol; and SMAC (☎ 458710) is behind the Bank of Central Asia branch at Complex Sakura Anpan 10.

Boat There are numerous services to Singapore, as well as daily links to the Sumatran mainland.

Singapore Ferries shuttle constantly between Singapore's World Trade Centre and Sekupang. The first ferries leave Singapore at am and Sekupang at 7.45 am, while the last ferries leave at 7 pm in both directions. The trip takes 45 minutes and costs S$18 from Singapore, or 31,000 rp from Sekupang.

There are less frequent services from the World Trade Centre to Batu Ampar and Nongsa.

Pulau Bintan The custom-built ferry dock at Telaga Panggur, 30 km south-east of Nagoya, is the main port for speedboats to Tanjung Pinang on neighbouring Pulau Bintan. There's a steady flow of departures from 8 am to 5.15 pm. The trip takes 45 minutes and costs 10,000 rp one way, plus 1000 rp port tax. There are also three boats a day from Sekupang to Tanjung Pinang.

Elsewhere in Indonesia The main reason travellers come to Batam is to catch an onward boat to Pekanbaru on the Sumatran mainland. Boats leave from the domestic wharf at Sekupang, next to the international terminal. The trip to Pekanbaru involves a four hour boat trip to Tanjung Buton on the Sumatran mainland, travelling via Selat Panjang (on Pulau Tebingtinggi), followed by a three hour bus ride. The combined ticket costs about 35,000 rp. There is no point in breaking the journey en route. Selat Penjang is an oversized water village with a strong Chinese influence, while Tanjung Buton is just a bus/ferry terminal. There are no services to Pekanbaru after 10 am, so you'll need to make an early start if you're coming from Singapore.

Other destinations from Sekupang include: Pulau Karimun (13,000 rp); Pulau Kundur (15,000 rp); Dumai (35,000 rp); and Kuala Tungkal (50,000 rp), on the Jambi coast.

Getting Around

Fixed-fare taxis operate from the ports of Sekupang and Telaga Panggur as well as from the airport. Sample fares from Sekupang include Nagoya for 12,000 rp and Telaga Panggur for 18,000 rp.

There is a token bus service between Nagoya and Sekupang for 600 rp, but most people use the share taxis that cruise the island: just stand by the roadside and call out your destination to passing taxis. Sample fares from Sekupang include 1000 rp to Nagoya and 5000 rp to Telaga Panggur. You will need to make it clear that you are paying for a seat, not the whole taxi.

PULAU BINTAN

Bintan is twice as large as Batam and many times more interesting. Singapore development is very low key on Bintan with the exception of a cluster of golf resorts on the north coast around Lagoi. The main attractions are the old town of Tanjung Pinang (a visa-free entry/exit point), nearby Pulau Penyenget and the relatively untouched beaches of the east coast.

After development-mad Batam, Tanjung Pinang comes as a very pleasant surprise. It may be the largest town in the Riau Islands – being the modern administrative centre – but it retains much of its old-time charm, particularly the picturesque, stilted section of the town that juts over the sea around Jl Plantar II. The harbour sees a constant stream of shipping of every shape and size, from tiny sampans to large freighters.

Orientation

Speedboats from Pulau Batam and Singapore deliver you to the main pier in Tanjung Pinang. Everything of importance is within 10 minutes' walk of the pier.

Information

Tourist Office There's no point in trekkin two km around the coast to the new region tourist office. It hasn't even got a brochur let alone anything useful like a map. Bong Homestay (see Places to Stay in this section is a much better source of information.

Money The Bank of Central Asia has branch on Jl Temiang in Tanjung Pinang while the BNI bank and Bank Dagan Negara are opposite each other on Jl Teuk Umar. Outside banking hours, you will hav

OTHER
2   Taxi Rank
4   Chinese Temple
5   Pelni Office
6   Bank of Central Asia
7   New Oriental Tours & Travel
8   Supermarket
9   Bank Dagang Negara
11 Bus Terminal
12 BNI Bank 1946
13 Volleyball Stadium
15 Mosque
17 Sempati Office
18 Post Office
19 Main Pier: Ferries to Telaga Panggur, Sekupang & Singapore
20 Boats to Pulau Penyenget
21 Shipping Agents
22 Police Station
23 Tickets to Telaga Panggur
24 Souvenir Shop
25 Tennis Court
28 Garuda/Merpati Office
33 Wartel

PLACES TO STAY
1   Hotel Riau Holidays Indah
16 Hotel Surya
26 Johnny's Homestay & Bong's Homestay
27 Rommel Homestay
29 Wisma Riau
30 Hotel Sampurna
31 Hotel Sampurna Jaya
32 Lobo Guesthouse

PLACES TO EAT
3   Fruit Market
10 Night Market
14 Flipper & Sunkist Restaurants

Tanjung Pinang

0   125   250 m

accept the much poorer rates on offer at the numerous moneychangers.

Post & Communications The post office is near the harbour on Tanjung Pinang's main street, Jl Merdeka. International phone calls can be made from the wartel office on Jl Hangtuah.

Pulau Penyenget

Tiny Penyenget, a short hop across the harbour from Tanjung Pinang, was once the capital of the Riau rajahs. The island is believed to have been given to Rajah Riau-ingga VI in 1805 by his brother-in-law, Sultan Mahmud, as a wedding present.

It is a charming place, littered with reminders of its past. The coastline is dotted with silted traditional Malay houses. The ruins of the **old palace** of Rajah Ali and the **tombs** and graveyards of Rajah Jaafar and Rajah Ali are clearly signposted inland. The most impressive site is the sulphur-coloured

mosque with its many domes and minarets. You won't be allowed into the mosque if you're wearing shorts or a short skirt.

There are frequent boats to the island from Bintan's main pier for 1000 rp per person. There's a 500 rp entry charge on weekends.

Beaches

The best beaches are along the east coast, where there is also good snorkelling outside the November to March monsoon period. Getting there can be a battle, but there is a choice of accommodation (see Places to Stay) at the main beach, **Pantai Trikora**. There are buses to Trikora for 2500 rp from the bus terminal in Tanjung Pinang, otherwise you'll be up for 20,000 rp for a taxi.

Senggarang

Senggarang is a fascinating village across the harbour from Tanjung Pinang. The star attraction is an old **Chinese temple** held

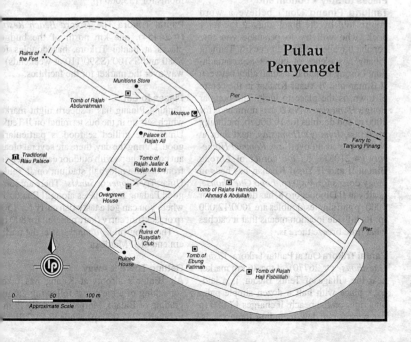

together by the roots of a huge banyan tree that has grown up through it.

The temple is to the left at the end of the pier, coming by boat from Tanjung Pinang. Half a km along the waterfront is a big square with three Chinese temples side by side.

Boats to Senggarang leave from Pejantan II wharf.

Snake River

You can charter a sampan from Tanjung Pinang to take you up Sungai Ular (Snake River) through the mangroves to see the Chinese temple with its gory murals of the trials and tortures of hell.

Organised Tours

There are a couple of tour operators in Tanjung Pinang. Try PT Riau Holidays (☎ 22573) in the Hotel Riau Holidays Indah, or Pinang Jaya Tours & Travel (☎ 21267) at Jl Bintan 44.

Places to Stay – bottom end

Tanjung Pinang Don't believe a word you're told by the hotel touts at the ferry dock, who will try to persuade you that popular travellers' places don't exist. Tanjung Pinang has plenty of budget accommodation. Lorong Bintan II, a small alley between Jl Bintan and Jl Yusuf Khahar in the centre of town, is the place to look. The popular *Bong's Homestay* at No 20 has dorm beds for 5000 rp and doubles for 10,000 rp, including breakfast. *Johnny's Homestay*, next door at No 22, acts as an overflow. *Rommel Homestay* (☎ 21081), on the corner of Lorong Bintan II and Jl Yusuf Khahar, has beds in dingy dorms for 4000 rp. *Lobo Guesthouse*, nearby at Jl Diponegoro 8, has dorm beds for 5000 rp and singles/doubles are 7000/12,000 rp. Its hillside location means that it catches what little breeze there is.

Pantai Trikora Out at Pantai Trikora, *Yasin's Guesthouse* (☎ 26770), at the 36 km marker near the village of Teluk Bakau, is a laid-back place with half a dozen simple palm huts right on the beach. It charges 17,000 rp per person per day, including three meals.

Bukit Berbunga Cottages, right next doo has very similar accommodation. Its room cost 16,000/27,000 rp, including breakfast

Places to Stay – middle

Tanjung Pinang *Hotel Surya* (☎ 21811) o Jl Bintan has clean, simple rooms with fa for 14,000/18,000 rp. *Wisma Riau* (☎ 21023 and *Sampurna Inn* (☎ 21555), side by sid on Jl Yusuf Khahar, have air-con rooms wit TV for 40,000 rp.

Places to Stay – top end

Tanjung Pinang The *Riau Holidays Inda* (☎ 22644), off Jl Plantar II, is an unusu place built on pylons over the water in th midst of the old stilted part of town. It ha comfortable air-con doubles from 58,000 t 80,000 rp. Prices go up 10% at weekends.

The *Hotel Sampurna Jaya* (☎ 21555) at Yusuf Khahar 15 is a reasonable one sta place. It has what it calls 'moderate' air-co doubles for 53,000 rp, and much smarte rooms for 135,000 rp.

Pantai Trikora The *Trikora Beach Reso* (☎ 24454), one km north of the budge places at Pantai Trikora, has doubles fc S$80 and S$100 (S$90/110 at weekends) way over the market for the facilities.

Places to Eat

Tanjung Pinang has a superb night mark which sets up in the bus terminal on Jl Teuk Umar. The grilled seafood is particular good. During the day, there are several pleas ant coffee shops with outdoor eating areas i front of the volleyball stadium on Jl Teuk Umar. Try *Flipper* or *Sunkist*. There are som good Padang food places along Jl Plantar I where you can get a tasty fish curry for 15C rp or jackfruit curry (kare nangka) for 800 r

The colourful *fruit market* is at the north ern end of Jl Merdeka.

Getting There & Away

Air Bintan's airport at Kijang has take something of a back seat following the u grading of Batam. Merpati has daily fligh to Jakarta (287,000 rp), while SMAC flies t remote spots like Ranai (241,300 rp) on Pulau Natuna Besar.

The Sempati office (☎ 21612) is at Jl Bintan 9. The best bet for island hoppers is MAC (☎ 22798), five km from the city centre at Jl Ahmad Yani (Batu 5). It also has regular shuttle which can fly you to Batam (46,700 rp), Dabo (92,900 rp) on Pulau Singkep, Pangkalpinang (128,100 rp) on Pulau Bangka and Tanjung Balai (65,400 rp) on Pulau Karimun, as well as out to Ranai (208,400 rp) in the remote North Natuna Islands. It also flies to Jambi (144,600 rp) and Pekanbaru (113,800 rp).

Boat Although most of the boats to mainland Riau now operate from neighbouring Batam, Tanjung Pinang retains its traditional role as the hub of Riau's inter-island shipping, as well as having international links to Singapore and Malaysia. Most services leave from the main pier at the southern end of Jl Merdeka, but check when you buy your ticket. New Oriental Tours & Travel, Jl Merdeka 61, is a reliable ticket agent.

Pulau Batam There are regular speedboats from Tanjung Pinang's main pier to Telaga Panggur on Batam (10,000 rp; 45 minutes), as well as three boats a day direct to Sekupang (12,000 rp; 1½ hours).

Elsewhere in Sumatra There are two fast boats a day to Tanjung Balai (21,000 rp; 2½ hours on Pulau Karimun), and two a day to Dabo (21,000 rp; four hours) on Pulau Singkep. There's a daily express service to Pekanbaru (51,000 rp), which involves changing boats on Batam. There are also occasional slow boats up the Sungai Siak to Pekanbaru for 31,000 rp.

Malaysia There are two boats a day to Johore Bahru for 48,500 rp.

Singapore There are three boats a day direct to Singapore's World Trade Centre wharf for 49,000 rp.

Jakarta Pelni offers two ways of getting to Jakarta. Either the KM *Rinjani* or KM *Umsini* sails from the port of Kijang, in the south-eastern corner of the island, every Sunday. The journey takes 28 hours and costs 83,000 rp in deck class.

The alternative is the MV *Samudera Jaya*, which leaves Tanjung Pinang every Thursday and does the trip in 18 hours for 95,000 rp. The Pelni office (☎ 21513) in Tanjung Pinang is at Jl Ketapang 8.

Getting Around
Taxis charge a standard 15,000 rp for the 17 km run from the airport to Tanjung Pinang. Buses and share taxis to other parts of Bintan leave from the bus and taxi terminal on Jl Teuku Umar.

PULAU SINGKEP
Few travellers make the trip south from Bintan to Pulau Singkep, the third largest island in the archipelago. The place has become even more of a backwater since the closure of the huge tin mines that provided most of the island's jobs. Much of the former population has now gone elsewhere in search of work.

The main town, **Dabo**, is shaded by lush trees and gardens and is clustered around a central park. A large **mosque** dominates the skyline. **Batu Bedua**, not far out of town, is a white sand beach fringed with palms. It's a good place to spend a few hours. The fish and vegetable **markets**, near the harbour, are interesting, and Jl Pasar Lamar is a good browsing and shopping area.

Information
The Bank Dagang Negara reportedly offers respectable rates for US dollars. The post office is on Jl Pahlawan and there is also an overseas telephone office about three km out of town on the road to Sunggai Buluh.

Places to Stay & Eat
Wisma Sri Indah on Jl Perusalaan has rooms from 15,000 rp. It's spotlessly clean and has a comfortable sitting room. Similar places are the *Wisma Gapura Singkep*, on the opposite side of the street and a bit north, and *Wisma*

SUMATRA

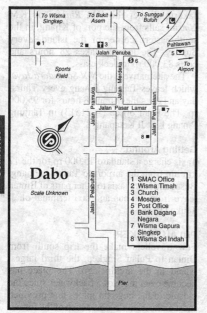

Dabo

Scale Unknown

1 SMAC Office
2 Wisma Timah
3 Church
4 Mosque
5 Post Office
6 Bank Dagang Negara
7 Wisma Gapura Singkep
8 Wisma Sri Indah

Sederhana. Some travellers have reported very good deals at the smartest place in town, the *Hotel Wisma Singkep*, which overlooks the town.

You can eat at the markets behind Wisma Sri Indah or try any of the warungs on Jl Pasar Lama and Jl Merdeka. Food stalls and warungs pop up all over the place at night.

Getting There & Away

Air SMAC is the only airline operating through Singkep. It has flights to Batam (91,700 rp), Jambi (70,800 rp) and Pangkalpinang (117,000 rp) on Pulau Bangka. The SMAC office (☎ 21073) is on Jl Pemandian. The airport is five km from Dabo town.

Boat There are two boats a day to Tanjung Pinang (21,000 rp). Boats dock at Singkep's northern port of Sunggai Buluh, from where there are buses to Dabo. Daily ferries run to Daik on Pulau Lingga.

There's also a weekly boat from Dabo to

Jambi. Several shops in Dabo act as ticket agencies.

PULAU PENUBA

Penuba is a small island wedged between Pulau Lingga and Pulau Singkep. It's an idyllic place to do nothing but swim, walk and read. The main settlement on this island is the village of the same name, which is tucked into a small bay on the south-east coast.

The **Attaqwa Mosque** stands in the centre of the village. Several good beaches are within 10 minutes' walk and there are more fine beaches near the north coast village of **Tanjung Dua**.

A house next to the Attaqwa Mosque is now used as a *guesthouse* for foreign visitors. Expect to pay about 5000 rp for a room. Ask around for the caretaker. There are several *warungs* along Jl Merdeka, the main street.

To get to Pulau Penuba you'll need to charter a boat from Sunggai Buluh (on Pulau Singkep) for the half-hour trip.

PULAU LINGGA

Not much remains of the glory that was once Lingga except a few neglected ruins. The arrival point is Daik, which is hidden one km up a muddy river. It has that all-enveloping atmosphere of oppressive humidity and tropical seediness that pervades many of Somerset Maugham's stories.

Daik is pretty much a single street, some cargo wharves and about a dozen Chinese shops, with dirt roads and tracks branching out to the Malay villages around the island. You must report to the police as soon as you arrive.

Things to See & Do

The main site of historical interest is the ruin of the **old palace** of Rajah Suleiman, the last rajah of Lingga-Riau. Next to the palace are the foundation stones of a building which is said to have housed the rajah's extensive harem. Otherwise there's not much left of the palace. The surrounding jungle hides overgrown bathing pools and squat toilets. The

DUSHAN COORAY

DUSHAN COORAY

DUSHAN COORAY

matra
Left: Traditional Toba Batak house at Ambarita.
Right: Intricately carved monster face decorating the facade of a Toba Batak house.
ttom: Authentic high-peaked Minangkabau house, West Sumatra.

Sumatra

Top: Young Muslim girl.
Bottom: Puppet performance, Simanindo, Pulau Samosir.

Lingga Islands

0   20   40 km

the tomb of Rajah Mahmud I, who ruled in the early 19th century.

Inland is **Gunung Daik**, its three peaks looking like a crown. The central peak is said never to have been climbed.

Places to Stay & Eat

There is one *hotel* in Daik, near the ferry dock on the main street. Expect to pay about 8000 rp for a double. There are a few small *warungs* on the main street.

Getting There & Away

There are daily boats for the two hour trip from Daik to Dabo on Pulau Singkep, and occasional boats between Tanjung Pinang and Daik.

Getting Around

There's no public transport on Lingga, or transport of any sort for that matter.

PULAU KARIMUN

Karimun is a small island to the south-east of Singapore with a few resort hotels that cater to visitors from the city state. The main centre is the port of **Tanjung Balai**.

Tanjung Balai has a few small losmen with doubles from 10,000 rp, as well as the *Hotel Holiday Karimun* (☎ 21065) at Jl Trikora Laut 1, with air-con doubles for 75,000 rp.

Most speedboat services between Batam and Pekanbaru call at Tanjung Balai (13,000 rp) on the way. There are also two boats a day from Tanjung Pinang (21,000 rp; 2½ hours).

EASTERN ISLANDS

These islands are right off the beaten track and difficult to get to, although oil has been found on the largest of the islands, Pulau Natuna Besar in the North Natunas.

The population of the island is fairly small, although there's an extensive transmigration programme on the Sungai Ulu with settlers from Java growing cash crops like peanuts and green peas.

The islands are noted for fine basketweave cloth and various kinds of traditional dance. One particularly idiosyncratic local

ins are a two hour walk from Daik and u'll need someone to guide you through e maze of overgrown forest paths.

Along the same trail is the **tomb** of Rajah Iuhammed Jusuf, who reigned from 1859-9.

A half-hour walk from Daik is the **Makam ukit Cenckeh** (Cenckeh Hill Cemetery), here you'll find the crumbling graves of ajah Abdul Rakhman (who ruled from 812-31) and Rajah Muhammed (who ruled om 1832-41).

On the outskirts of Daik is the **Mesjid ultan Lingga**, in the grounds of which is dance is a kind of *Thousand & One Arabian Nights* saga, incorporating episodes from Riau-Lingga history.

Getting There & Away
There are two flights a week between Tanjung Pinang and Ranai on Pulau Natuna Besar for 241,300 rp.

Jambi

The province of Jambi occupies a 53,435 sq km slice of central Sumatra, stretching from the highest peaks of the Bukit Barisan mountains in the west to the coastal swamps facing the Straits of Melaka in the east.

Jambi's main attractions are natural. Sumatra's highest mountain, Gunung Kerinci (3805m), is on the border of Jambi and West Sumatra, while Sumatran tigers – Jambi's faunal mascot – and rhinos still inhabit the forests of the surrounding Kerinci Seblat National Park.

Huge expanses of rubber and palm oil plantation cover the eastern lowlands. Timber is also big business, with two large pulp mills guzzling up the remaining lowland forest at a frightening rate. Jambi is also emerging as an important oil producer; its main field is south-east of Jambi on the border with South Sumatra.

The province is sparsely populated with around two million people, many of them migrants from Java and Bali.

History
The province of Jambi was once the heartland of the ancient kingdom of Malayu, which first rose to prominence in the 7th century.

Much of Malayu's history is closely and confusingly entwined with that of its main regional rival, the Palembang-based kingdom of Sriwijaya. Most of the little that is known about Malayu has been gleaned from the precise records maintained by the Chinese court of the time.

It is assumed that the temple ruins at

Muara Jambi (see the Muara Jambi ent▮ further in this section) mark the site ▮ Malayu's former capital, the ancient city ▮ Jambi – known to the Chinese as Chan F▮ The Malayu sent their first delegation ▮ China in 644, and the Chinese scholar I Tsin▮ spent a month in Malayu in 672. He reporte▮ that when he returned 20 years later, Malay▮ had been conquered by Sriwijaya.

The Sriwijans appear to have remained i▮ control until the sudden collapse of the empire at the beginning of the 11th centur▮ The Chinese court received numerous dele▮ gations from Chan-Pi during that time, an▮ it appears that at some point the Sriwijaya court was based at Chan-Pi.

After Sriwijaya's demise, Malayu r▮ emerged as an independent kingdom. ▮ stayed that way until it became a dependenc▮ of Java's Majapahit Empire, which rule▮ from 1278 until 1520. It then came under th▮ sway of the Minangkabau people of We▮ Sumatra.

In 1616 the Dutch East India Compan▮ opened an office in Jambi and the Dutc▮ quickly formed a successful alliance wi▮ Sultan Muhammed Nakhruddin to prote▮ their ships and cargoes from pirates. The▮ also negotiated a trade monopoly with Na▮ hruddin and his successors. The predomina▮ export was pepper, which was grown in gre▮ abundance. In 1901 the Dutch moved the▮ headquarters to Palembang and effective▮ gave up their grip on Jambi.

JAMBI
The city of Jambi, capital of the province ▮ the same name, is a busy river port about 15▮ km from the mouth of the Sungai Batan▮ Hari. Unless you're working in the oil ▮ paper industries, there is little reason to g▮ there. It's a long way from anywhere else ▮ interest and the only attraction of any cons▮ quence is the ancient temple complex ▮ Muara Jambi, 25 km downstream.

Orientation
Modern Jambi sprawls over a wide area, ▮ combination of the old Pasar Jambi distri▮ spreading south from the port and the ne▮

The Kubu

The Kubu are the indigenous people of southern Sumatra, nomadic hunter-gatherers who once lived throughout the region's lowland forests. They are descended from the first wave of Malays to migrate to Sumatra.

Today, their domain is restricted to a reserve called Bukit 12 – 287 sq km of forest to the east of the Trans-Sumatran Highway town of Bangko.

The traditional Kubu way of life came to an end when large-scale transmigration from Java and Bali began. The migrants cut down the forests for plantation farming, and brought with them diseases like measles and tuberculosis.

The Kubu steadfastly resisted attempts to persuade them to settle in government-built villages. In 1985 they were granted the forest reserve around Bukit 12. It is home to about 1000 people, divided into five groups. Each group is led by a *temenggung* (chief).

A road leads off towards the reserve from the town of Limbur, on the main highway about 25 km east of Bangko. There are buses to Limbur from Bangko, where you can stay at the *Bangko Indah Hotel* in Jalan Lintas. ∎

...burbs of Kota Baru and Telanaipura to the ...est. Most of the banks, hotels and restau...nts are in Pasar Jambi near the junction of ... Gatot Subroto and Jl Raden Mattaher, ...hile government buildings are out at Kota ...aru.

...formation
...ourist Office It's hardly worth the haul out ... Kota Baru to visit the regional tourist ...ffice (☎ 25330), Jl Basuki Rahmat 11. The ...otel Jambi Raya keeps a stock of bro...hures.

...oney The Bank of Central Asia is conve...iently located on Jl Raden Mattaher. The ...NI has a branch on Jl Sutomo.

...ost & Communications The main post ...ffice is near the port at Jl Sultan Thaha 9. ...ou can make international phone calls from ...e wartel office on Jl Raden Mattaher. The ...ain Telkom office is on Jl Dr Sumantri in ...elanaipura.

Travel Agencies Mayang Tour & Travel (☎ 25450), Jl Raden Mattaher 27, and Saung Bulian Tour & Travel (☎ 25621), Jl Hailim Perdana Kusuma 19, are both reliable.

Things to See
The list is not a long one. The **Museum Negeri Propinsi Jambi** is out in Telanaipura on the corner of Jl Urip Sumoharjo and Jl Prof Dr Sri Sudewi. It has a good section on costumes and handcrafts, as well as a small historical display. It's open Tuesday to Sunday from 8 am to 4 pm. Admission is 200 rp.

Organised Tours
Mayang Tour & Travel (☎ 25450), Jl Raden Mattaher 27, includes the temples at Muara Jambi and the museum in its city tour. It also organises tours to the Kerinci Valley and to the Kubu settlements at Bukit Duabelas.

Places to Stay – bottom end
The cheap hotels are on the market streets by the port. They are rock-bottom, survival-only places. The *Hotel Sumatra* at Jl Kartini 26 has doubles for 10,000 rp and looks marginally less uninviting than the others.

Places to Stay – middle
If you can afford it, step up a notch to somewhere like the *Hotel Pinang* (☎ 23969), 100m from the river at Jl Dr Sutomo 9. It has clean doubles with fan for 21,000 rp, and air-con rooms for 42,000 rp. The *Hotel Kartika Jaya* (☎ 22699), opposite the Pinang on the corner of Jl Hos Cokroaminoto, has air-con singles/doubles from 33,000/44,000 rp.

Places to Stay – top end
The ever-expanding *Hotel Abadi* (☎ 25600), Jl Gatot Subroto 92, is the only three star hotel in town. Its owners have a novel approach to hotel management: don't renovate, just build a new wing. The oldest rooms look decidedly tatty these days, even at 50,000/60,000 rp. The latest wing has comfortable modern rooms for 110,000/125,000 rp. There is a sleazy disco downstairs that belts out rock music until the small hours.

Things are a bit quieter at the nearby *Hotel*

Jambi Raya (☎ 34971), tucked away on a small alleyway at Jl Camar 1. It has small, modern air-con doubles for 65,000 rp and much larger rooms for 95,000 rp.

Places to Eat

There's a reasonable choice of food stalls at the small night *market* on Jl Sultan Iskandar Muda. The market is opposite the well-stocked *Mandala Supermarket*. The *Saimen Perancis* is an excellent bakery on Jl Raden Mattaher that also does meals. The *Simpang Raya*, Jl Raden Mattaher 22, and the *Safari*, Jl Veteran 29, serve good Padang food.

For a blow-out, there is good Chinese food at the *Restaurant Abadi*, adjoining the Hotel Abadi. Allow about 15,000 rp.

Things to Buy

The Sanggar Batik dan Kerajinen (Batik and Art Centre), near the museum on Jl Dr Sri Sudewi in Telanaipura, produces and sells traditional Jambi batik featuring striking floral motifs. The centre also has a range of handcrafts from all over the province, including songket weaving and finely woven split-rattan baskets. The centre was set up by the local PKK (family welfare movement) to provide employment for local women.

Getting There & Away

Air Merpati has two direct flights a day to Jakarta (207,900 rp) and two flights a week to both Batam and Palembang. The Merpati office is at the Hotel Abadi.

SMAC has two flights a week to Pulau Batam (165,400 rp), Pulau Bintan (159,900 rp) and Pulau Singkep (71,900 rp), as well as flights to Pekanbaru (148,500 rp). The SMAC office (☎ 22804) is at Jl Orang Kayo Hitam 26.

Bus Jambi is not on the Trans-Sumatran Highway, but there are good sealed roads linking the city to Palembang in the south, Pekanbaru in the north and the highway at Muarabungo and Saralungun. Intercity services use the Simpang Kawat bus terminal on Jl M Yamin.

There are frequent buses to Palembang,

from 7500 to 13,000 rp depending on th level of comfort, and to Padang (from 17,50 rp; 10 hours). Ratu Intan Permata (☎ 60234 near the bus terminal on Jl M Yamin, h. door-to-door services to Pekanbaru (27,50 rp; eight hours).

Boat Ratu Intan Permata (see above) als operates connecting services from Jambi t the coastal town of Kuala Tungkal (6000 r two hours), from where there's a daily speed boat service to Pulau Batam (50,000 r seven hours).

Getting Around

Airport taxis charge a standard 5500 rp f the eight km run into town. Local transpo comprises the usual assortment of taxi opelets and becaks. Rawasari opelet term nal, off Jl Raden Mattaher in the centre c town, is where all opelets start and finis their journeys. The standard fare is 300 rp.

MUARA JAMBI

The large temple complex at Muara Jamb 26 km downstream from Jambi, is the mo important Hindu-Buddhist site in Sumatra. is assumed that the temples mark the locatic of the ancient city of Jambi, capital of th kingdom of Malayu 1000 years ago. Most c the temples, known as *candi*, date from th 9th to the 13th century when Jambi's powe was at its peak.

For centuries, the site lay abandoned an overgrown in the jungle on the banks of th Batang Hari until it was discovered in 192 by a British army expedition sent to explor the Jambi region.

Things to See

It's easy to spend all day at Muara Jambi. Th site is certainly large enough, stretchin more than seven km along the north bank c the Batang Hari and covering 12 sq kn Much of the area remains covered in fores

Eight temples have been identified so fa each at the centre of its own low-walle compound. Some are accompanied by smalle side-temples, known as *perwara cand* Three of the temples have been restored t

omething close to their original form. The
te is dotted with numerous smaller brick
nounds, called *menapo*, that are thought to
e the ruins of other buildings – possibly
wellings for priests and other high offi-
ials.

The entrance is through an ornate archway
the village of Muara Jambi. Admission is
y donation, although there's a 500 rp charge
bring a vehicle in. Most places of interest
re within a few minutes' walk of here.

The restored temple straight ahead from
e donations office is **Candi Gumpung**.
heck out the fiendish **makara** (demon
ead) that guards the steps. Excavation work
ere yielded some important finds, including
peripih (stone box) containing sheets of
old inscribed with old Javanese characters.
he writing dates the temple back to the 9th
entury. A statue of Prajnyaparamita found
the site is now the star attraction at the
nall **site museum** nearby.

Candi Tinggi, 200m south-east of Candi
ampung, is the finest of the temples uncov-
red so far. It dates from the 9th century, but
built around another older temple. A path
ads east from Candi Tinggi to **Candi Astano**,
5 km away, passing **Candi Kembar Batu**
id lots of **menapo mounds** along the way.
oth temples were being restored at the time
f research.

None of the temples on the western side
the site have been restored and they
main pretty much as they were found –
inus the jungle, which was cleared in the
980s to allow archaeologists to have a look.
he sites are signposted from Candi Gum-
ung. First stop, after 900m, is **Candi
edong Satu**, followed 150m further on by
andi Gedong Dua**. They are independent
mples despite the names. The path contin-
es west for another 1.5 km to **Candi
edaton**, the largest of the temples, and then
further 900m north-west to **Candi Koto
ahligai**.

The dwellings of the ordinary Malayu folk
ave long since disappeared. According to
hinese visitors, they lived along the river
stilted houses or raft huts moored to the
ank.

Getting There & Away

Boats to Muara Jambi leave from the river
bank opposite the Pelni office in Jambi. They
charge 3000 rp one way and take about two
hours. There are lots of boats on weekends,
when Muara Jambi is a popular picnic spot.
On other days, you may be forced to charter
a boat (45,000 rp return).

Another option is to charter a taxi and go
by road. Reckon on paying about 40,000 rp
for the return trip plus two hours waiting time
– the minimum you will need.

KERINCI

Kerinci is a cool mountain valley tucked
away high in the Bukit Barisan on Jambi's
western border. It is one of the most beautiful
places in Sumatra. Towering over the valley
to the north is Gunung Kerinci, an active
volcano and Sumatra's highest mountain at
3805m, while picturesque Danau Kerinci is
nestled at the southern end of the valley. The
Sungai Kerinci waters the rich farmland in
between, and the whole area is surrounded
by the forests of Kerinci Seblat National
Park.

The valley supports a population of almost
300,000, scattered around 200-odd villages.
The main town and transport hub is
Sungaipenuh (Full River). While administratively Kerinci is in Jambi province, the
people are unmistakably Minangkabau West
Sumatran, with the same matrilineal social
structure.

More than 100 people were killed when
an earthquake measuring seven on the
Richter Scale rocked the valley in October
1995, although Sungaipenuh suffered little
damage. Gungung Kerinci last erupted in
1934.

Orientation & Information

Sungaipenuh has all the facilities you'd
expect of a regional centre. Most places of
importance are around the large square in the
centre of town.

You can change US dollars (cash and travellers cheques) at the BNI branch on Jl
Basuki Rahmat on the northern side of the
square. The post office isn't far away at Jl

SUMATRA

Sudirman 1, while the Telkom office is at the south-eastern corner of the square on Jl Imam Bonjol.

If you're heading for Kerinci Seblat National Park, you'll need to call in at the Kantor Taman Nasional Kerinci Seblat (☎ 21692), Jl Arga Selebar Daun 11, for a permit (2500 rp). It's among the government buildings on the road north to Gunung Kerinci. A couple of the staff speak English – a rarity in Sungaipenuh.

Kerinci Seblat National Park

The park protects 1½ million hectares of prime equatorial rainforest spread over four provinces. It covers a 350 km swathe of the Bukit Barisan mountains from near Padang (West Sumatra) in the north to near Curup (Bengkulu) and Lubuklinggau (South Sumatra) in the south. Jambi is the largest contributor, with almost 40% of the park falling within its boundaries, and Sungaipenuh is the only real access point – enabling Jambi's tourist people to promote the park as their attraction.

Unfortunately, there is not much to promote. Facilities within the park are virtually nonexistent. Most of the park is dense rainforest, its inaccessibility being the very reason it is one of the last strongholds of endangered species like the Sumatran tiger and Sumatran rhinoceros. Trekking opportunities are restricted to a few points on the fringe of the park. They are covered below.

If you're planning to visit the park, you'll need to pick up a permit (2500 rp) from the National Parks office (☎ 21692) in Sungaipenuh.

Gunung Kerinci

It's a tough two day climb to the summit of Sumatra's highest mountain, starting from the village of **Kersik Tua**, 43 km from Sungaipenuh among the tea plantations of the 60 sq km Kayo Aro estate.

The mountain lies within the national park, so you'll need to get a permit first – available in Kersik Tua, as well as Sungaipenuh. There is no shortage of would-be guides in Kersik Dua and it is a sensible

precaution to take one along. It is certainl[y] very foolish to tackle the climb alone. A[l]though the path to the top is clearly define[d] weather conditions can change very sud[-]denly on the mountain. You'll need to brin[g] food, a water bottle (water is scarce on th[e] mountain), and a tent and sleeping bag, as [it] is cold (down to 2°C at night).

The 16 km from the village to the top [is] normally tackled in two stages. It takes abou[t] five hours to climb to a campground at abou[t] 3000m, where most people spend the nigh[t] before setting off for the final 90 minut[e] scramble to the summit at dawn. At the to[p] you'll find a crater measuring about 120m b[y] 400m, filled with a greenish lake.

There are **cave paintings** in the **Kasa[h] Cave** on the lower slopes five km fro[m] Kersik Tua. On the way back, you can sto[p] at the **hot springs** near the Kayo Aro plan[-]tation. It's too hot to swim in the main poo[l] but you can get a private room with a ho[t] water mandi.

Danau Gunung Tujuh

Tranquil Danau Gunung Tujuh is the highe[st] lake in South-East Asia at 1950m. It take[s] 3½ hours to climb to the lake from th[e] village of Pelompek, eight km beyond Ke[r]sik Tua. The lake also lies within the par[k] permits are available in Pelompek.

Danau Kerinci

Danau Kerinci, 20 km south of Sungaipenu[h] is a small lake nestled beneath Gunung Ra[ya] (2543m). **Stone carvings** in the village[s] around the lake show that the area supporte[d] a sizeable population in megalithic time[s]. The best known of these stone monuments [is] the **Batu Gong** (Gong Stone) in the villag[e] of Muak, 25 km from Sungaipenuh. It [is] thought to have been carved 2000 years ag[o].

The lake itself is badly clogged with wate[r] hyacinth, which biologists are attempting t[o] control using a fish (*ikan koan*) that feeds o[n] the plant.

Sengering Caves

The extensive network of caves outside th[e] village of Sengering includes the celebrate[d]

Tangko Cave. Obsidian flake tools found in the cave show that it was occupied by some of Sumatra's earliest known residents some 9000 years ago. The caves are also known for their stalactites and stalagmites. Sengering is nine km from Sungai Manau, a village on the road to Bangko.

Mesjid Agung Pondok Tinggi

This fine old mosque, with its pagoda-style roof, stands at the northern edge of Sungaipenuh in the village of Pondok Tinggi. It looks nothing special from the outside, but the interior is a different story with elaborately carved beams and old Dutch tiles. Not a single nail was used when it was built in 1874. You need permission to go inside.

Places to Stay & Eat

There are half a dozen hotels in Sungaipenuh. The best place for travellers is the *Hotel Matahari* (☎ 21061) on Jl Basuki Rahmat. Clean doubles with outside bathroom are 7000 rp, and there is a useful wall map of the area and transport information. The *Hotel Yani* (☎ 21409), Jl Muradi 1, has singles/doubles for 11,000/16,500 rp, including breakfast. There's good Padang food at the *Minang Soto* restaurant next door. The *Dendeng Batokok* restaurant, also on Jl Muradi, is named after the local speciality – harcoal-grilled strips of smoked beef.

There are a couple of small *homestays* in Tersik Dua.

Getting There & Away

The closest major city to Sungaipenuh is the West Sumatran capital of Padang, a journey of 246 km via the coast road (7500 rp; six hours). There is also a scenic back route to Padang that takes the mountain road past Gunung Kerinci and follows the valleys north.

There are also frequent buses east to Bangko (4500 rp; four hours) on the Trans-Sumatran Highway.

Getting Around

You can get almost anywhere in the valley from the bus terminal in Sungaipenuh market. Sample destinations and fares include Danau Kerinci (500 rp), Kersik Tua (1250 rp) and Pelompek (1500 rp).

Dokars cost 1500 rp for most rides around Sungaipenuh.

Bengkulu

The six hour journey through the Bukit Barisan mountains from Lubuklinggau to the town of Bengkulu, capital of the province of the same name, is like taking a journey back in time.

Nothing much seems to have changed in years – except prices. Bengkulu remains Sumatra's most isolated province, cut off from its neighbours by the Bukit Barisan, particularly during the rainy season from December to March when land transport can break down completely.

Few tourists come to Bengkulu. There is not a lot to do apart from adjust to the slower pace of life.

History

Little is known of Bengkulu before it came under the influence of the Majapahits from Java at the end of the 13th century.

Until then, it appears to have lived in something approaching total isolation divided between a number of small kingdoms such as Sungai Lebong in the Curup area. It even developed its own cuneiform script, known as *ka-ga-nga*.

The British moved into Bengkulu, or Bencoolen as they called it, in 1685, searching for pepper after being kicked out of Banten on Java, three years previously. The venture was not exactly a roaring success. Isolation, boredom and constant rain sapped the British will, while malaria ravaged their numbers.

When Sir Thomas Stamford Raffles arrived as Lieutenant-General of Fort Marlborough (as the British called the ruler of Bencoolen) in 1818, the colony still was not a going concern. In the short time he was there, Raffles made the pepper market profitable and planted coffee, nutmeg and sugar cane as cash crops. In 1824 Bengkulu was traded for the Dutch outpost of Melaka and a guarantee to leave the British alone on Singapore.

Bengkulu was a home in domestic exile for Indonesia's first president, Soekarno, from 1938-41.

Flora & Fauna

Bengkulu's rainforests are home to both the *Rafflesia arnoldi* and the world's tallest flower *Amorphophalus titanum*.

While the bizarre rafflesia is found in a number of sites throughout the Bukit Barisan mountains, most notably around Bukittinggi in West Sumatra, it was in Bengkulu that Raffles first set eyes on the flower, in 1818, in company with a British government botanist named Arnold. The rafflesia is found at a number of sites dotted around Bengkulu's mountains, the most accessible being close to the main road halfway between Bengkulu and Curup.

The lily-like *Amorphophalus titanum* flowers only once every three years, when it throws up a spectacular flower spike than can stand over two metres. The flower is a rich red, with a huge yellow stamen protruding from its core. The plant is a member of the same family as the taro, the starchy tuber that is a staple food in parts of Asia and the Pacific islands. The tubers can weigh up to 100 kg. Known locally as *kibut* or *bunga bangkai*, it is Bengkulu's floral emblem, and is found mainly in the Rejang Lebong district north of Curup.

BENGKULU

Capital of the province of the same name, Bengkulu is a relaxed town of about 60,000.

Orientation & Information

Although Bengkulu is by the sea, most of the town is set back from the coast, touching only near Fort Marlborough. The coast is surprisingly quiet and rural, just a km or so from the town centre.

Jl Suprapto and the nearby Pasar Minggu Besar are in the modern town centre, which is separated from the old town area aroun the fort by the long, straight Jl Ahmad Yani/J Sudirman.

Tourist Office The Bengkulu tourist offic (☎ 21272) is inconveniently situated to th south of town at Jl Pembangunan 14. There' not much material in English other than couple of glossy brochures, but the staff ar friendly.

Money The best place to change money i the Bank of Central Asia, near the Gandh Bakery at Jl Suprapto 150. You can als change money at the Bank Dumi Daya at J R Hadi 1, and Amex US dollar cash an travellers cheques at the BNI bank on Jl : Parman.

Post & Communications The main pos office (and poste restante) is south of th town centre on Jl S Parman, but there i another post office on Jl Ahmad Yani. Th Telkom office is just around the corner on J R Hadi. It has a Home Country Direct phone

Travel Agencies Assik Tour & Travel i conveniently located next to Hotel Asia at J Ahmad Yani 922.

Fort Marlborough

Fort Marlborough (Benteng Marlborough) bec??? ?ne seat of British power in Beng kulu after it replaced nearby Fort York i 1719, of which nothing but the foundation remain.

It's curiously unimpressive as British mil itary architecture goes. Opponents clearly weren't that impressed either – the fort fel both times it was attacked. It was overrun b a local rebellion as soon as it was complete in 1719, and was captured briefly by th French in 1760.

The fort was restored and opened to th public in 1984 after a long period of use b the Indonesian army. There are a few smal and uninteresting exhibits about the restora tion, together with a pile of cannon balls. Th old British gravestones at the entrance mak poignant reading. Admission is 250 rp.

Bengkulu has a few other British reminders, including the **Thomas Parr monument**, in front of the Pasar Barukota, erected in memory of a British governor beheaded by locals in 1807. The 'Monumen Inggris' near the beach is to Captain Robert Hamilton who died in 1793 'in command of the troops'.

Soekarno's House

Soekarno was exiled to Bengkulu by the Dutch from 1938 until 1941. The small villa in which he lived on Jl Soekarno-Hatta is maintained as a small museum. Exhibits include a few faded photos, a wardrobe and

even Bung's trusty bicycle. The house is closed on Monday but open other days from 8 am to 2 pm, except Friday when it closes at 11 am and Saturday when it closes at noon. Admission is 250 rp.

Other Things to See

Soekarno, who was an architect, designed the **Mesjid Jamik** mosque at the junction of Jl Sudirman and Jl Suprapto during his stay. It is commonly known as the Bung Karno mosque.

The **Bengkulu Museum Negeri** is near the tourist office on Jl Pembangunan – bring

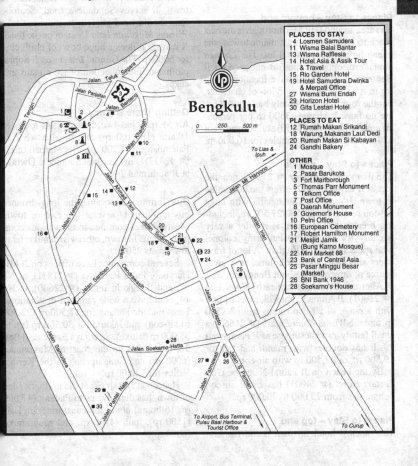

Bengkulu

0   250   500 m

To Lias &
Ipuh

To Curup

To Airport, Bus Terminal,
Pulau Baai Harbour &
Tourist Office

PLACES TO STAY
4 Losmen Samudera
11 Wisma Balai Bantar
13 Wisma Rafflesia
14 Hotel Asia & Assik Tour
   & Travel
15 Rio Garden Hotel
19 Hotel Samudera Dwinka
   & Merpati Office
27 Wisma Bumi Endah
29 Horizon Hotel
30 Gita Lestari Hotel

PLACES TO EAT
12 Rumah Makan Srikandi
18 Warung Makanan Laut Dedi
20 Rumah Makan Si Kabayan
24 Gandhi Bakery

OTHER
1 Mosque
2 Pasar Barukota
3 Fort Marlborough
5 Thomas Parr Monument
6 Telkom Office
7 Post Office
8 Daerah Monument
9 Governor's House
10 Pelni Office
16 European Cemetery
17 Robert Hamilton Monument
21 Mesjid Jamik
   (Bung Karno Mosque)
22 Mini Market 88
23 Bank of Central Asia
25 Pasar Minggu Besar
   (Market)
26 BNI Bank 1946
28 Soekarno's House

SUMATRA

your own lightbulbs if you want to see any-thing. The graves in the **European cemetery**, behind the small church on Jl Ditra, are a reminder of the ravages wrought by malaria among the colonialists.

Bengkulu's main beach, **Pantai Panjang**, hardly rates as an attraction – it's long, grey, featureless and unsafe for swimming.

Dendam Taksudah is an aquatic reserve area eight km south of the town. It's of little interest to travellers in spite of its description as 'exciting' by the tourist brochure. There's not much there other than water snakes and the foundations of a resort hotel.

Places to Stay – bottom end

The area around Fort Marlborough is the best place to look. As in most major towns, the cheap hotels are a dismal lot. The *Losmen Samudera*, opposite the fort entrance on Jl Benteng, does at least have location going for it. It's an old place with lots of character, but the rooms are extremely basic and there are no fans. It charges 3500 rp per person. *Wisma Rafflesia* (☎ 21650) at Jl Ahmad Yani 924 has slightly better doubles for 10,000 rp.

Places to Stay – middle

The *Wisma Balai Buntar* (☎ 21254), near the fort at Jl Khadijah 122, offers the best value in town. It's an old Dutch villa with huge air-con rooms for 20,500/27,500 rp, includ-ing breakfast. The place is run by a very friendly former Indonesian army colonel who speaks excellent English. A lot of trav-ellers stay here and the colonel is a great source of information about Bengkulu.

Alternatives include the nearby *Hotel Asia* (☎ 21901), Jl Ahmad Yani 922, a clean place with a range of air-con rooms from 30,500 rp, and the *Wisma Bumi Endah* (☎ 21665), a small family-run guesthouse at Jl Fatmawati 29. It has doubles with mandi and fan for 19,500 rp, or 27,500 rp with air-con.

By the beach on Jl Pantai Nala, the *Gita Lestari Hotel* (☎ 24001) has small air-con bungalows from 25,000 to 70,000 rp.

Places to Stay – top end

The fanciest hotel in town is the *Horizon*

(☎ 21722) at Jl Pantai Nala 142. Facilities include swimming pool and snooker room. Rooms overlooking the sea cost US$60 and come with satellite TV etc.

The *Rio Garden Hotel* (☎ 21952) at Jl Veteran 63 has air-con doubles from 62,750 rp, and there's also a swimming pool.

Places to Eat

The *Rumah Makan Srikandi*, opposite the Hotel Asia on Jl Ahmad Yani, does excellent southern Sumatran food very cheaply. Locals rate the *Rumah Makan Si Kabayan*, Jl Sudirman 51, as the best restaurant in town. It serves Sundanese food. Seafood fans should head straight to the wonderful *Warung Makanan Laut Dedi*, opposite the Si Kabayan. It does a huge bowl of chilli crab for 6000 rp. The *Gandhi Bakery* on Jl Supra-pto has a fine collection of ice creams and cakes.

Getting There & Away

Air Merpati has two direct flights a day to Jakarta (188,100 rp) and three a week to Palembang (101,200 rp). The Merpati office (☎ 42337) is in the Hotel Samudera Dwinka at Jl Sudirman 246.

Bus Terminal Panorama, the long-distance bus terminal, is several km east of town. Most services continue to the various com-pany depots in town, otherwise a mikrolet to town costs 250 rp.

Several companies have offices on Jl MT Haryono. Putra Rafflesia (☎ 21811), at No 57, and Bengkulu Indah (☎ 22640), at No 14, both have a wide range of destinations. Fares include Padang for 17,500 rp (22,500 rp air-con) and Jakarta for 30,500 rp (up to 55,000 rp deluxe). Sriwijaya Express, Jl Bali 36, runs buses up the coast to Mukomuko (6000 rp) and Sungaipenuh in the Kerinci Valley for 12,500 rp.

Habeco at Jl Bali 67, at the northern edge of town, has daily buses to Padang (17,000 rp; 16 hours) along the coast road via Lais (1500 rp), Ipuh (4500 rp) and Mukomuko (6000 rp).

Boat Ask about services to Pulau Enggano at the Pelni office (☎ 21013), near the fort at Jl Khadijah 10.

Getting Around
Airport taxis charge a standard 10,000 rp to town. The airport is 200m from the main road south and there are regular bemos to town for 300 rp. Tell the driver you want to go to the *benteng* (fort).

NORTHERN BENGKULU
The coast road (Jl Manusurai Pantai), north from Bengkulu to Padang, has a number of possibilities for travellers.

The road is now sealed all the way and takes about 16 hours, making it a reasonable alternative land route to the usual trip inland via Lubuklinggau and the Trans-Sumatran Highway.

The journey can be done as a number of short hops. The first town north of Bengkulu is **Lais**. The beach is only 100m from the road, and you can stay at *Elly's House*, opposite the post office at Jl Utama 21 (the main road).

There is reputed to be elephants further north near **Ipuh**, around the mouth of the Sungai Ipuh. The *Wisma Rindu Alam*, opposite the soccer pitch at Jl Protokol 1, has very basic singles/doubles for 5000/10,000 rp. The owner also rents out a nearby *villa* on the banks of the Sungai Batang Muar. It costs 25,000 rp per night and has four beds.

Mukomuko, 200 km north of Bengkulu, was the northern outpost of the British colony of Bencoolen. **Fort Anna** survives as a reminder.

CURUP
Curup is a small town in the foothills of the Bukit Barisan halfway between Bengkulu and Lubuklinggau. It is a launching pad for the attractions of the surrounding Bukit Barisan. The town itself is set in a valley watered by the upper reaches of the Sungai Musi that eventually flows through Palembang.

There's nowhere to change money in Curup, although it is possible to draw money on Visa or MasterCard from the Bank of Central Asia on Jl Merdeka.

Things to See & Do
There are many fine examples of **rumah adat**, traditional stilted wooden houses, in the villages around Curup.

Volcanic **Gunung Kaba**, 19 km east of Curup, has two large sulphurous craters surrounded by dense rainforest.

The **hot springs** and **waterfall** at Suban are popular with weekend picnickers.

Places to Stay & Eat
There are a number of cheap losmen, including *Losmen Nusantara* at Jl Merdeka 794, which has doubles for 6000 rp.

Much better is the *Hotel Aman Jaya* (☎ 21365) at Jl Dr AK Gani 10. It has standard doubles with shower and fan for 25,000 rp, and huge rooms upstairs with hot water and air-con for 35,000 rp. It's a friendly place with information on surrounding attractions and how to get to them.

The *Restaurant Sari Buan* at Jl Merdeka 120, is a busy Padang food place, while the *Warkop Ramanda*, around the corner at Jl Cut Nyak Dhien 1, does Palembang food.

Getting There & Away
There are frequent connections to Bengkulu and Lubuklinggau. Both cost 2500 rp and take three hours. Buses leave from the busy central market.

PULAU ENGGANO
Pulau Enggano is a remote island with an area of 680 sq km, 100 km off the coast of southern Bengkulu. Its isolation is such that, until as recently as 100 years ago, some Sumatrans believed it was inhabited entirely by women. Apparently, these women managed to procreate miraculously through the auspices of the wind or by eating certain fruit.

The island is featured on a map of Asia drawn in 1593. The name, Enggano, is Portuguese for deceit or disappointment, which suggests that the Portuguese were the first Europeans to discover it. It wasn't until three years later that Dutch navigators first recorded it.

The original inhabitants are believed to be native Sumatrans who fled from the mainland when the Malays migrated there. The present-day inhabitants live by cultivating rice, coffee, pepper, cloves and copra. Wild pigs, cattle and buffalo are abundant.

There are five villages on the island: **Banjar Sari** on the north coast; **Meok** on the west coast; **Kaana** and **Kahayupu** in the east; and **Malakoni**, the harbour. The island is relatively flat (the highest point is Bua Bua which rises to 250m) and the coastline is swampy. It's worth visiting only if you are a keen anthropologist and/or a real adventurer with plenty of time.

Places to Stay

The only place to stay is the *Losmen Apaho* at Malakoni.

Getting There & Away

Pelni operates occasional boats from Bengkulu to the island's port of Malakoni. If the schedules don't work out, you will need to go to the small port of Bintuhan, about 225 km south of Bengkulu, and ask at the harbour.

Getting Around

The villages on the island are connected by tracks originally made by the Japanese and not very well maintained since. The only way of getting around is to walk.

South Sumatra

The province of South Sumatra stretches from the high peaks of the Bukit Barisan mountains in the west to the vast mangrove swamps of the coastal lowlands facing the shallow Bangka Strait in the east. It also includes the large islands of Bangka and Belitung. All roads and rivers (plus the train line) lead to Palembang, the provincial capital.

PALEMBANG

Palembang is a huge, heavily polluted industrial city of almost 1.5 million people – the second largest in Sumatra. The main industries are oil refining, fertiliser production and cement manufacture. The Pertamina refineries at Plaju and Sungai Gerong can handle a combined capacity of 180,000 barrels of oil per day, while the giant Pusri fertiliser plant is the largest producer of urea in South-East Asia. Now there are plans to build the largest pulp mill in the Southern Hemisphere.

People glancing at a map could be forgiven for not realising that Palembang is also a major port, 80 km from the mouth of the Sungai Musi. When Sumatra's oil fields were discovered and opened early in the century, Palembang quickly became the main export outlet for South Sumatra. The port also handles exports from the province' seemingly endless plantations of rubber, coffee, pepper and pineapples.

Palembang has little to offer traveller apart from transport connections.

History

A thousand years ago, Palembang was the centre of the highly developed civilisation of Sriwijaya. The Chinese scholar I Tsing spent six months in Palembang in 672, and reported that 1000 monks, scholars and pilgrims were studying and translating Sanskrit there.

Few relics from this period remain – no sculpture, monuments or architecture of note – nor is there much of interest from the early 18th century when Palembang was an Islamic kingdom. Most of the buildings of the latter era were destroyed in battles with the Dutch.

Palembang translates as 'gold from the ground', which probably stems from the city's name in Sriwijayan times, Swarna Dwipa, which translates as 'Golden Island'.

Orientation

Palembang sits astride the Sungai Musi, once the city's pride, but now suffering badly from the ravages of industrial waste. The city's skyline is dominated by the giant Ampera

SUMATRA

Palembang

0   250   500 m

Seberang Ilir

Seberang Ulu

Sungai Musi

Sungai Ogan

Sungai Ocan

To Museum Sumatera Selatan, Airport & Jambi

To Sumatran Tourist Office

Jalan Veteran

Jalan K. Anwar Sosro

Jalan K. Kapitan Rival

Jalan L Makmun

Jalan Kol Atmo

Jalan Menu

Jalan Segaran

Jalan Dr M Isa

Jalan Cempaka

Jalan Diponegoro

Jalan Sudirman

Jalan Iskandar

Dempo Kematang

Jalan TP Rustam Effendy

Jalan Sayangan

Jalan Tenusan

To Boom Baru (Boat Harbour)

Jalan Dahlan

Jalan K B Duku

Jalan M Lama

Jalan Pasar Baru

Jalan Abdullah Ashan

Jalan Kusuma

Jalan Merdeka

Jembatan Ampera

Jalan Pangeran Ratu

Jalan Ratna

Jalan Kedaton

Jalan II Keronggo

Jalan Makrayu

Jalan Buntung

Jalan Kisonggo Wiro Sentiko

Jalan Ahmad Yani

Train Station

To Perabumulih, Lubuklinggau & Padang

PLACES TO STAY
5 Hotel Sandjaja & Rumah Makan Sari Bundo
6 Sari Hotel
9 Hotel Asiana & Deraya Air Taxi Office
11 King's Hotel
13 Hotel Sriwidjaya
14 Hotels Makasar & Nusantara
16 Hotel Sintera
17 Hotel Lembang
18 Hotel Swarna Dwipa

PLACES TO EAT
7 Restaurant Pagi Sore
8 Fruit Market
12 French Bakery
21 Rumah Makan Mahkota Permai

OTHER
1 Provincial Tourist Office
2 Bank of Central Asia
3 Governor's Office
4 Bank Rakyat Indonesia
10 Bus Company Offices
15 BNI Bank 1946
19 Dutch Fort
20 Mesjid Agung
22 Telkom Office
23 Post Office
24 Garuda Monument
25 Museum Sultan Machmud Badaruddin II & Tourist Office
26 Pasar 16 Ilir
27 Intercity Bus Terminal

SUMATRA

Bridge, built in the 1960s, that links the two halves of the city.

A hodgepodge of wooden houses on stilts crowd both banks of the Sungai Musi. The south side, known as Seberang Ulu, is where the majority of people live. Some of the streams feeding into the Sungai Musi look not merely polluted, but positively corrosive.

Seberang Ilir, on the north bank, is the city's better half where you'll find most of the government offices, shops, hotels and the wealthy residential districts.

The main street is Jl Sudirman, which runs north-south to the bridge. The bus terminal and train station are both on the southern side.

Information
Tourist Office The Palembang city tourist office (☎ 358450) is at the Museum Sultan Machmud Badaruddin II, off Jl Sudirman near the bridge. The South Sumatran provincial tourist office (☎ 357348) is among the government offices on Jl POM IX.

Money Palembang has branches of all the major banks. As usual, head to the Bank of Central Asia for the best rates. Its main office is on Jl Kapitan Rivai. The nearby Bank Rakyat Indonesia also has reasonable rates. The BNI bank is on Jl Sudirman.

Outside banking hours, the bigger hotels are a better bet than moneychangers like Dhrama Perdana, opposite Hotel Lembang at Jl Kol Atmo 446. It will change only cash US and Singaporean dollars at poor rates.

Post & Communications The post office is close to the river, next to the Garuda monument on Jl Merdeka. International phone calls can be made next door at the Telkom office. It has a Home Country Direct phone.

Dangers & Annoyances There are lots of signs around telling people to be beware of pickpockets ('Awas Tukang Copet!'). Locals reinforce the warning, especially at night.

Things to See
The **Museum Sumatera Selatan** is well worth a visit. It houses finds from Sriwijaya times as well as megalithic carvings from the Pasemah Highlands, including the famous *batu gajah* (elephant stone). Check out the magnificent **rumah limas** (traditional house) behind the museum. The museum is about five km from the town centre off the road to the airport. It's open Sunday to Thursday from 8 am to 4 pm and on Friday until 11 am; admission is 250 rp.

You can check out the lifestyle of Palembang's sultans at the **Museum Sultan Machmud Badaruddin II**, near the Ampera Bridge. There is not much else to see. You can also while away an hour or two observing the Sungai Musi life drift by from the middle of the Ampera Bridge, and there's a colourful **floating market** on the river next to the main market, **Pasar 16 Ilir**. The imposing **Mesjid Agung**, at the roundabout near the Ampera Bridge, was built by Sultan Machmud Badaruddin at the beginning of the 19th century.

The remains of the late 18th century **Dutch fort**, occupied today by the Indonesian army, can be seen to the north of Jl Merdeka. Sections of the outside walls still stand.

Special Events
Palembang's annual tourist event is the *bidar* (canoe) race held on the Sungai Musi in the middle of town every August 17 (Proclamation Day). A bidar is about 25m long, one metre wide, and powered by up to 60 rowers.

Places to Stay – bottom end
Palembang's cheap hotels are nothing to look forward to – and they're not particularly cheap either. There are half a dozen rock bottom dives in the market area between Jl Mesjid Lama and Jl Pasar Baru, but they are impossible to recommend. Places like the depressing *Penginapan Kurnia* on Jl Mesjid Lama want 10,000 rp for gloomy little partitioned boxes.

The best place to look is around the junction of Jl Sudirman and Jl Iskandar. The

Hotel Asiana at Jl Sudirman 45E isn't quite as grim as it looks from the street. Basic singles/doubles with fan are 10,000/15,000 rp. The *Hotel Makasar*, tucked away in a quiet cul-de-sac at Jl Iskandar 561, has clean doubles with fan for 15,000 rp.

Places to Stay – middle

You'll have a much wider choice if you're prepared to spend a few thousand rupiah more. The *Hotel Sriwidjaja* (☎ 355555) is a good place to start. It sits at the end of another cul-de-sac at Jl Iskandar 31, which is about 50m from the Hotel Makasar in spite of the street numbers. The huge range of rooms include large doubles with fan for 20,000 rp, and rooms with air-con, hot water and TV for 49,000 rp. All prices include breakfast. The *Hotel Nusantara* (☎ 353306), next to the Hotel Makasar, has air-con doubles for 45,000 rp.

The cheapest rooms at the *Hotel Sintera* (☎ 354618), Jl Sudirman 38, aren't much, but there are large doubles with mandi and fan for 33,000 rp, and air-con rooms for 48,500 rp.

The *Sari Hotel* (☎ 313320), on the corner of Jl Sudirman and Jl Kapitan Rivai, is a rather rundown modern hotel with air-con rooms from 29,500/49,000 rp, including breakfast.

Places to Stay – top end

The four star *Hotel Sandjaja* (☎ 310675), on Jl Kapitan Rivai, is the smartest of a growing band of upmarket hotels catering for businesspeople. It has rooms from US$50/70, a swimming pool and a choice of restaurants.

The central *King's Hotel* (☎ 362323) on Jl Kol Atmo has doubles from US$50. The *Hotel Swarna Dwipa* (☎ 313322) is tucked away at Jl Tasik 2, some distance west of the city centre. Rooms start from US$45/55. Facilities include a gymnasium and swimming pool.

Places to Eat

While Palembang is hardly a name to make the taste buds tingle in anticipation, the city does give its name to the distinctive cuisine of southern Sumatra (including Lampung and Bengkulu) in the same way Padang gives its name to the cooking of West Sumatra.

The best-known dish is ikan brengkes (fish served with a spicy durian-based sauce). Pindang is a spicy clear fish soup. The food is normally served with a range of accompaniments. The main one is tempoyak, a combination of fermented durian, terasi (shrimp paste), lime juice and chilli that is mixed up with the fingers and added to the rice. Sambal buah (fruit sambals), made with pineapple or sliced green mangoes, are also popular.

Another Palembang speciality is pempek, also known as empek-empek, a mixture of sago, fish and seasonings which is formed into balls and deep fried or grilled. They are served with a spicy sauce and are widely available from street stalls and warungs for 250 rp each.

A good place to try Palembang food is the *Rumah Makan Mahkota Permai* at Jl Mesjid Lama 33, near the junction with Jl Sudirman.

If you're hooked on Padang food, the *Rumah Makan Sari Bundo*, part of the Sari Hotel set-up, and the *Pagi Sore*, opposite at Jl Sudirman 96, are both good.

The main night food *market* is on Jl Sayangan, to the east of Jl Sudirman, with dozens of noodle and sate stalls. The *French Bakery*, opposite King's Hotel on Jl Kol Atmo, also does noodle dishes and other simple meals.

For a minor blow-out (20,000 rp for two), check out the air-con Chinese restaurant on the top floor of the *Hotel Sandjaja*.

Getting There & Away

Air Merpati has seven flights a day to Jakarta (168,800 rp) and at least one a day to Pulau Batam (149,600 rp). Other Merpati services include daily flights to Pangkalpinang on Pulau Bangka (70,400 rp), and three flights a week to Bengkulu (103,400 rp), Padang (179,300 rp) and Tanjung Pandan on Pulau Belitung (138,600 rp). The Merpati office is in the Hotel Sandjaja.

Mandala also has two direct flights a day

to Jakarta. Its office (☎ 350634) is also in the Hotel Sandjaja.

Deraya Air Taxi has daily flights from Palembang to the islands of Bangka and Belitung, as well as to Lubuklinggau. Its office (☎ 358038) is at Jl Sudirman 2954.

Bus The main bus terminal is south of the Sungai Musi at the junction of Jl Pangeran Ratu and Jl Kironggo Wiro Sentiko. ANS is a reliable company with daily air-con buses north to Bukittinggi (25,000 rp; 18 hours), Medan (50,000 rp) and through to Banda Aceh (74,000 rp). It also has daily buses to Jakarta (33,000 rp; 20 hours) and points east. ANS has an office in town on Jl Kol Atmo, just north of King's Hotel.

There are numerous services to Jambi; a five hour trip costs 7500 to 13,000 rp with air-con. Bengkulu Indah has daily buses to Bengkulu (15,000 rp; 12 hours).

Train The Kertapati train station is on the south side of the river, eight km from the city centre. There are three trains a day to Bandarlampung – 8.30, 10 am and 9 pm. The 10 am train is ekonomi class only (4500 rp) and takes 7½ hours, while the other services have only bisnis (18,000 rp) and eksekutif class (28,000 rp) and take an hour less. There are also three trains to Lubuklinggau – 8, 10.30 am and 8 pm – which stop at Lahat (for the Pasemah Highlands). It's four hours to Lahat and seven to Lubuklinggau, but the fares are the same: 4500 rp ekonomi (10.30 am service only), 12,000 rp bisnis and 22,000 rp eksekutif.

Boat There are 'jetfoil' services from Palembang's Boom Baru jetty to Mentok on Pulau Bangka daily at 7.30 and 9.30 am. The journey takes about 3½ hours and the fare is 25,000 rp.

There's also a daily slow boat from Palembang to Mentok (14,000 rp; six hours).

Getting Around
The Airport Sultan Badaruddin II airport is 12 km north of town. Taxis cost a standard 10,000 rp.

Local Transport Opelets around town cos a standard 300 rp. There is no city centr opelet terminal. They leave from around th huge roundabout at the junction of Jl Sudir man and Jl Merdeka. There are lots o metered taxis.

DANAU RANAU

Remote Ranau, nestled in the middle of th Bukit Barisan mountains in the south western corner of South Sumatra, is one o the least accessible – and least spoiled – o Sumatra's mountain lakes. It is about 30 km, and about eight hours by bus, fron Palembang.

Temperatures at Ranau seldom get abov 25°C. It is a good place to relax or go hikin in the surrounding mountains. It's possibl to climb Gunung Seminung (1881m), th extinct volcano that dominates the region.

The main town and transport hub of th area is Simpangsender, about 10 km north west of the lake. Bandar Agung, at Ranau' northern tip, is the main lakeside settlement Change money before you get there.

Organised Tours
The Palembang travel agency Varita Tours & Travel (☎ 355669), at Jl Iskandar 16A specialises in tours to Danau Ranau.

Places to Stay & Eat
There are several small hotels in Banda Agung, including the *Hotel Seminung Per mai*, Jl Akmal 89, with clean doubles fo 10,000 rp. Jl Akmal is the main street leading down to the lake. Padang food is about al you'll find in the restaurants.

Tour groups head for the *Wisma Pusri* south of the village of Simpangsender on the lake's western shore. It has lakeside bunga lows for 40,000 rp and large doubles in the main building for 30,000 rp. Rooms can be booked through Varita Tours in Palembang (see the previous Organised Tours entry) Don't bother with the disgusting *Wisma Putri Gunung*, signposted down a muddy track next to the Wisma Pusri.

Getting There & Away

Most routes to Danau Ranau go through the Trans-Sumatran Highway town of Baturaja. There are buses to Baturaja every hour from the main bus terminal in Palembang (6000 rp; 4½ hours). Baturaja is also a stop on the Palembang-Bandarlampung train line, about 3½ hours south of Palembang.

There are regular buses for the remaining 120 km from Baturaja to Simpangsender (3000 rp; three hours), where you can pick up an opelet for the final 18 km to Bandar Agung for 500 rp. It's a good idea to arrive in Baturaja as early as possible to give yourself plenty of time to get a bus out again. If you do get stuck, there are dozens of uninspiring budget losmen to choose from.

PASEMAH HIGHLANDS

The highlands, tucked away in the foothills of the Bukit Barisan west of Lahat, are famous for the mysterious megalithic monuments that dot the landscape. The stones have been dated back about 3000 years, but little else is known about them or the civilisation that carved them. While the museums of Palembang and Jakarta now house the pick of the stones, there are still plenty left in situ.

Orientation & Information

The main town of the highlands is Pagaralam, 68 km and two hours by bus south-west of the Trans-Sumatran Highway town of Lahat.

Lahat's regional tourist office (☎ 22496), Jl Amir Hamzeh 150, is a complete waste of time. The best source of information about the highlands is the Hotel Mirasa in Pagaralam (see Places to Stay in this section). There's nowhere to change money, so bring enough rupiah to see you through.

Megalithic Sites

There are two distinct styles of sculpture to be found in the highlands. The early style dates from almost 3000 years ago and features fairly crude figures squatting with hands on knees or arms folded over chests. The best examples of this type are to be found at a site called **Tinggi Hari**, 20 km

from Lahat west of the small river town of Pulau Pinang.

The later style dates from about 2000 years ago and is far more sophisticated, with expressive facial features. It includes carvings of men riding buffaloes or elephants, groups of people standing next to elephants and buffaloes, two men battling with a snake, a man struggling with an elephant lying on its back, and a couple of tigers – one guards a representation of a human head between its paws. Their makers used the natural curve of the rocks to create a three dimensional effect, though all the sculptures are in bas-relief.

Examples of this style are seemingly everywhere in the villages around Pagaralam, although some take a bit of seeking out. **Tegurwangi**, about eight km from Pagaralam on the road to Tanjung Sakti, is the home of the famous **Batu Beribu**, a cluster of four squat statues that sit under a small shelter by a stream. The site guardian will wander over and lead you to some nearby dolmen-style stone tombs. You can still make out a painting of a dragon and three women in one of them.

The village of **Berlubai**, three km from Pagaralam, has its own **Batu Gajah** (Elephant Stone) sitting out among the rice paddies, as well as tombs and statues. There is a remarkable collection of stone carvings among the paddies outside nearby **Tanjung Aru**. Look out for the one of a man fighting a giant serpent.

Gunung Dempo

This dormant volcano is the highest (3159m) of the peaks surrounding the Pasemah Highlands. It's a tea-growing area, and there are opelets from Pagaralam to the tea factory.

Places to Stay

Pagaralam Few travellers stop overnight in Pagaralam, even though it's much cooler than Lahat and there are half a dozen places to stay. The *Hotel Mirasa* (☎ 21266) is the place to base yourself. There's a range of doubles from 15,000 rp, and the owner can organise transport to the sites. The hotel is on the edge of town on Jl Mayor Ruslan, about two km from the bus terminal. There are cheaper places in town, such as the *Hotel Telaga* (☎ 21236) on Jl Serma Wanar. It has doubles for 8000 rp.

Lahat There are lots of hotels in Lahat. The super cheapies are grouped together close to the train station on Jl Stasiun, but most of them appear to be in the massage business. The places on the main street, Jl Mayor Ruslam III, are much better. The *Hotel Permata* (☎ 21642) at No 31 is conveniently close to both the bus terminal and the train station. It has a few basic doubles for 7000 rp and air-con doubles for 30,000 rp. The best rooms in town are 50m down the road at the *Nusantara Hotel* (☎ 21336), where you can pay up to 60,000 rp for air-con doubles with hot water.

Getting There & Away

Every bus travelling along the Trans-Sumatran Highway calls at Lahat, nine hours north-west of Bandarlampung and 12 hours south-east of Padang. There are also regular buses to Lahat from Palembang (4000 rp; five hours), and the town is a stop on the train line between Palembang and Lubuklinggau. There are frequent small buses between Lahat and Pagaralam (1800 rp; two hours).

Getting Around

There are opelets to the villages around Pagaralam from the *stasiun taksi* in the centre of town. All the local services cost 300 rp.

PULAU BANGKA

Western visitors are few and far between on Bangka, a large, relatively unpopulated island 25 km off the east coast of Sumatra. Tourist authorities are trying hard to promote the place, in particular the beaches of the east coast. They've got their work cut out: the beaches are miles from anything else of interest, a hassle to get to and there are no cheap places to stay. All the beach hotels are priced with wealthy visitors from Singapore and Malaysia in mind, but they, too, appear to be staying away in droves.

The island's name is derived from the word 'wangka', meaning tin, which was dis covered in 1710 near Mentok. The island i covered with old mine workings. Tin is sti mined on the island, although operation have been greatly scaled down in recer years.

There are only small pockets of natura forest left on Bangka. Rubber, palm oil an pepper are major crops.

Orientation & Information

The main town of Pangkalpinang is a bus tling business and transport centre with population of about 50,000. Most places o importance to travellers are close to the inter section of the main streets, Jl Sudirman an Jl Masjid Jamik. The bus terminal and markets are nearby on Jl N Pegadaian.

You can change money at the Bank o Central Asia, Jl Masjid Jamik 15, or at th BNI bank, Jl Sudirman 119. The post offic and telephone office are at the northern en of Jl Sudirman, some way from the tow cen're. Merpati, Sempati and SMAC all hav offices around the central junction, whil local travel specialist Duta Bangka Saran (DBS; ☎ 21698) is at Jl Sudirman 10E.

Sungailiat, 30 km north of Pangkalpinang is the island's administrative centre. There i a small tourist office (☎ 92496) just south o town on the main road to Pangkalpinang Mentok, on the north-western tip of th island, is the port for boats to Palembang.

Pangkalpinang

The fact that the **cemetery** is listed as one o the main attractions is a fair comment on th health of the tourist industry. That said, i is a huge cemetery, divided into section for Muslim, Buddhist and Christians, an there are some extravagant looking graves There are supposedly 100,000 people burie there.

Pantai Pasir Padi is a beach 2.5 km south of town that is easily reached by opelet fo 300 rp. The swimming is poor and the mai attraction is the seafood restaurant.

Travel agents tempt keen Asian golfer with packages that include a round at the **gol**

ourse on the southern edge of town, kindly
onstructed by the island's tin company.
ireen fees are 30,000 rp for nine holes, plus
5,000 rp club hire.

Mentok

`ew people bother to stay here longer than it
akes to catch a bus to Pangkalpinang.

There's a **memorial** close to Mentok's
ighthouse to 22 Australian nurses who were
hot dead by the Japanese during WWII. The
urses had survived the sinking of the SS
`yner Brooke* during the evacuation of Sing-
pore.

The hilltop guesthouse, at nearby **Gun-
ing Menumbing** (445m), served as a home
n domestic exile for future President Soe-
arno and Vice-President Hatta during
egotiations on independence from Febru-
ry until July 1949.

Beaches

`he best are **Pantai Parai Tenggiri**, four km
rom Sungailiat and monopolised by the
Parai Beach Hotel, and the deserted **Pantai
Matras**, five km further up the coast.

Places to Stay

Pangkalpinang There are quite a few cheap
osmen around the centre of town. A good
hoice is the friendly *Penginapan Srikandi*
(☎ 21884) at Jl Masjid Jamik 42. It has
ingles/doubles for 10,000/16,000 rp and
ewer rooms for 12,000/22,000 rp. Both categories come with mandi and fan.

Immediately opposite at No 43 is the *Bukit
Shofa Hotel* (☎ 21062). It's a clean, modern
lace with rooms from 11,000/20,000 rp
with mandi and fan, or doubles with air-con
or 50,000 rp.

The *Sabrina Hotel* (☎ 22424) is a good
mid-range place on Jl Diponegoro, a quiet
ide street off Jl Sudirman. It has comfort-
ble doubles with air-con, TV, hot water and
breakfast for 45,000 rp. Don't bother with
he economy 'Japan-style' rooms (mattress
n the floor). The nearby *Hotel New Wisma
Jaya* (☎ 21656), on the corner of Jl Ahmad

Yani and Jl Mangkol, has spotless rooms for
60,000/70,000 rp.

The *Menumbing Hotel* (☎ 22991), Jl Gereja 5, is supposedly the best hotel in town,
but these days it looks too grubby to justify
two stars. It has rooms for 63,000/76,000 rp
and four-person suites for 115,000 rp. There
is a swimming pool, which non-guests can
use for 2500 rp.

Mentok The *Losmen Mentok*, near the harbour at Jl Ahmad Yani 42, has rooms for
6000 rp. The splendid-sounding *Tin Palace
Hotel*, which overlooks the market place
from Jl Major Syafrie Rahman 1, has rooms
with mandi and fan for 20,000 rp, and with
air-con for 30,000 rp.

Beaches The beaches east of Sungailiat are
tourist resort territory, although there's not
much evidence of tourists. The *Parai Beach
Hotel* (☎ 92335) is the best of this lot, with
accommodation in air-con bungalows by the
beach. Few guests would be paying the
advertised prices, which start from 110,000
rp and peak at 300,000 rp for suites.

Places to Eat

There are lots of small restaurants in Pangkalpinang, including plenty of places to eat
Indonesian and Chinese food along Jl Sudirman and in the markets near the main
junction.

For Padang-style food, try *Sari Bundo* at
Jl Sudirman 77. Nearby, opposite Video
Queen, is a small restaurant serving the Palembang speciality, pempek (fish balls). The
flashiest restaurant in town is the *Tirta
Garden*, an upmarket Chinese and seafood
restaurant about three km from the town
centre at Jl Sudirman 3.

If it's seafood that you're after, the place
to go is the *Restaurant Asui Seafood*, behind
the Bank of Central Asia on Jl Kampung
Bintang. It's the original no-frills restaurant,
but the food is great and the place does a
roaring trade. It's run by a fisherman who
decided that there was more money to be
made from cooking fish than catching them.

Try gebung, known locally as 'chicken fish' because of the firmness of the flesh.

Getting There & Away
Air Merpati has two direct flights a day from Pangkalpinang to Jakarta (159,500 rp) and at least one flight a day to Palembang (68,200 rp). It also flies twice a week to Batam (201,300 rp), as does SMAC. Deraya Air flies daily to the neighbouring island of Pulau Belitung (67,100 rp).

Boat There are two daily jetfoil services between Palembang and Mentok (25,000 rp). They leave Palembang at 7.30 and 9.30 am, and Mentok at 11.30 am and 1 pm. The journey takes between three and 3½ hours, depending on conditions.

There's also a daily slow boat from Palembang (14,000 rp; six hours).

The Pelni liners *Rinjani* and *Umsini* stop at Mentok on the route between Dumai and Jakarta. There are departures to Jakarta (47,500 rp deck class) every Sunday. The Pelni office (☎ 22743) in Mentok is outside the port gates.

Getting Around
The Airport Airport taxis charge 6000 rp for the seven km run into Pangkalpinang, or you can walk to the main road and catch an opelet for 300 rp.

Local Transport There is regular public transport between Bangka's main towns, but most opelets stop running mid-afternoon. After that, taxis are the only option.

There are public buses between Mentok and Pangkalpinang (4000 rp; four hours), but the best way to travel between the two towns is by the private DBS Travel buses that connect with the jetfoil services. They do the journey in 2½ hours for 6000 rp, including hotel pick-up/drop-off. The bus can be booked in Palembang through Carmeta Travel (☎ 314970) at Jl Dempo Luar 29. The buses leave Pangkalpinang at 7.30 and 8.30 am for Mentok.

Lampung

Sumatra's southernmost province was no given provincial status by Jakarta until 1964 The Lampungese, however, have a long history as a distinct cultural entity.

There's evidence that Lampung was par of the Palembang-based Sriwijayan Empir until the 11th century, when the Jambi-based Malayu kingdom became the dominant regional power.

Megalithic remains at Pugungraharjo, o the plains to the east of Bandarlampung, ar thought to date back more than 1000 year and point to a combination of Hindu and Buddhist influences. The site is believed to have been occupied until the 16th century.

From the earliest times, Lampung ha been famous for its pepper, and it was the prized pepper crop that was the target for the West Javanese sultanate of Banten (today no more than a fishing village) when it moved in at the beginning of the 16th century. It wa Banten that introduced the Islamic faith to Lampung.

Lampung pepper also interested the Dutch, and the Dutch East India Company built a factory at Menggala in the late 17th century in a failed attempt to usurp the pepper trade.

When the Dutch finally took control o Lampung in 1856, they began to move larg numbers of people from West Java to farm the fertile plains of eastern Lampung in the first of the transmigration schemes that have sought to ease the chronic overcrowding on Java. The Javanese brought with them the music of the gamelan and *wayang* shadow puppetry.

Transmigration has made east Lampung something of a cultural melting pot. Other newcomers came from Hindu Bali, and trip to 'Balinese villages' are on some organised tour agendas.

The majority of the province's eight million people live in the main city of Ban darlampung and in the transmigration areas to the east. Very few people live on Lampung's gged western seaboard, most of which is ken up by Bukit Barisan Selatan National ark.

Today, coffee is Lampung's most important income earner, closely followed by mber. Pepper remains a major crop, while ere are also large areas of rubber and palm il plantation.

The main tourist attractions are trips to the olcano at Krakatau and the elephants of Vay Kambas National Park.

AKAUHENI

akauheni is the major ferry terminal on umatra's southern tip, and the main transit oint between Java and Sumatra. There is no eason to stay here.

There are 40 ferries a day between Bakaueni and Merak on Java, leaving – according o the timetable – every 36 minutes. The trip cross the Sunda Strait to Merak takes two ours and the cost for ekonomi/1st class is 500/2600 rp.

The Bakauheni terminal is large, modern nd surprisingly efficient. Buses (1700 rp) nd share taxis (5000 rp) are waiting to take assengers to Bandarlampung, two hours' rive away. The taxis are the better bet for ose planning to stay in Bandarlampung. hey will take you directly to the hotel of our choice, thus avoiding the hassles of etting there from Bandarlampung's Rajaasa bus terminal.

RAKATAU VOLCANO

Vhile the movie moguls decided that rakatau was East of Java, they should have pted for South of Sumatra.

The Indonesian government considers rakatau to be Sumatran anyway, and ampung promotes the famous volcano as s attraction. It's certainly cheaper and eportedly safer to get to Krakatau from ampung than from Java.

For the story of Krakatau and details on e area, see the Krakatau section in the Java hapter.

etting There & Away

andarlampung The Lampung provincial

tourist office can arrange speedboat charter for 450,000 rp, which covers up to six passengers. The trip takes 1½ hours each way. Tour operators charge US$75 per person (minimum four) to take you by bus to Canti and then by boat to Krakatau.

Kalianda/Canti The Hotel Beringin in Kalianda is a good place to meet up with other travellers wanting to see Krakatau. The hotel can organise a boat for up to eight people for 160,000 rp. Alternatively, you can head to the small port of Canti nearby and charter a larger boat for about 200,000 rp. The trip takes about three hours each way.

KALIANDA

Kalianda is a quiet little town, 30 km north of the ferry terminal at Bakauheni. It has a great setting overlooking Lampung Bay with Gunung Rajabasa as a backdrop. There are boats to Krakatau and other islands in Lampung Bay from Canti.

Things to See & Do

The main reason for stopping here is to visit Krakatau, but there are a couple of other things you can do while you organise that.

Volcano climbers should add **Rajabasa** (1281m) to their list, while there are hot springs on the tide line at **Wartawan Beach**, just beyond Canti. It costs 300 rp by opelet.

There are scheduled boats from Canti to the nearby islands of **Sebuku** (1800 rp) and **Sebesi** (2500 rp). They leave at 9 am and 3 pm. It is reportedly possible to camp on both islands and there are self-contained bungalows on Sebesi for 75,000 rp.

Organised Tours

The manager of the Hotel Beringin organises a range of tours for small groups, including trips to Krakatau.

Places to Stay & Eat

The *Hotel Beringin* (☎ 2008) is an old Dutch villa with high ceilings and fans slowly stirring the air. It's close to the centre of town at Jl Kesuma Bangsa 75, and has huge rooms with mandi for 9900 rp and smaller rooms without mandi for 6500 rp. The manager is very friendly and has lots of information about local attractions.

The upmarket option is the modern *Kalianda Hotel* (☎ 2392), on the way into town from the highway. It has air-con doubles from 30,000 rp.

The street stalls that emerge in the town centre at night are the best places to eat. There's Padang food at the *Rumah Makan Palapa* on Jl Raya.

Getting There & Away

There are regular buses between Kalianda and Bandarlampung's Rajabasa bus terminal (1700 rp; 1½ hours). There are less regular bemos from the Bakauheni ferry terminal to Kalianda for 1700 rp. It's also possible to get a north-bound bus from Bakauheni to Merak Belantung and then catch an opelet back to Kalianda for 600 rp.

Getting Around

There are regular opelets from Kalianda to Canti (300 rp) and along the road that rings Gunung Rajabasa via Gayam and Pasuruan. Motorcycles can be rented from the Hotel Beringin for 20,000 rp per day.

BANDARLAMPUNG

The major city and administrative centre of Lampung Province is Bandarlampung at the northern end of Lampung Bay.

Bandarlampung is the new name that marks the official merger of the old towns of Telukbetung (coastal) and Tanjungkarang (inland), which have grown together over the years. The merger has produced the fourth largest city in Sumatra, with a population of around 600,000.

When Krakatau erupted in 1883, almost half the 36,000 victims died in the 40m high tidal wave that funnelled up Lampung Bay and devastated Telukbetung. A huge steel maritime buoy, now located on a hillside overlooking the city, was erected as a memorial – in the position it came to rest after the wave had receded. (See Things to See in this section.)

Bandarlampung has acquired a reputation as something of a bogey town for traveller It must be the only place in Sumatra wher you can venture off the beaten track simp by leaving the bus terminal.

In contrast, westerners who live in the cit reckon it is very relaxed by Indonesian urba standards.

Orientation

Most of the places of relevance to travelle are in Tanjungkarang, including the bulk the hotels and the train station. The Rajabas bus terminal is on the northern edge of tow and the airport is 15 minutes' drive furth north.

Information

Tourist Office The regional tourist offic (☎ 251900) is at Jl Kotaraja 12, 150m fro the train station. Several of the staff spea good English and are very helpful. Yama Aziz, of the Lampung Provincial Touri Association (☎ 428565), at Jl WR Supra man 39, also speaks good English.

Post & Communications The main po office is inconveniently located halfway b tween Tanjungkarang and Telukbetung on Kh Dahlan, off Jl Sudirman. There is a sma branch post office on Jl Kotaraja, near th train station. International telephone cal can be made from the 24 hour Telkom offic on Jl Kartini, which has a Home Countr Direct phone.

Money Many banks have branches in bot Tanjungkarang and Telukbetung, includin the Bank of Central Asia. Its Tanjungkaran branch is at Jl Raden Intan 98, and the Teluk betung branch is at Jl Yos Sudarso 100. BN 1946 has a branch on the roundabout in th heart of Tanjungkarang.

Things to See

The city's greatest failing is the absence attractions. The **Krakatau monument**, huge steel maritime buoy washed out Lampung Bay by the post-eruption tid waves, is worth a look to satisfy curiosit about the scale of what happened in 188.

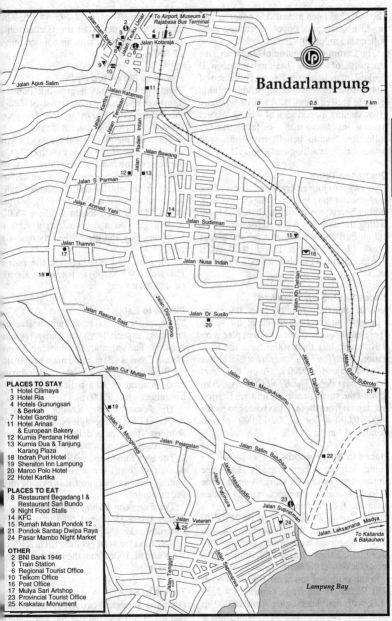

Bandarlampung

0   0.5   1 km

Jalan Imam Bonjol
Jalan Teuku Umar
To Airport, Museum &
Rajabasa Bus Terminal
Jalan Kotaraja
Jalan Agus Salim
Jalan Katamso
Jalan Kartini
Jalan Tendean
Jalan Raden Intan
Jalan Bawang
Jalan S Parman
Jalan Ahmad Yani
Jalan Sudirman
Jalan Thamrin
Jalan Nusa Indah
Jalan Rasuna Said
Jalan Diponegoro
Jalan Dr Susilo
Jalan Cut Mutiah
Jalan Cipto Mangukusumo
Jalan Kh Dahlan
Jalan KH Dahlan
Jalan Garot Subroto
Jalan W Monginsidi
Jalan Pejagalan
Jalan Salim Batubara
Jalan Hasanuddin
Jalan Palimura
Jalan Veteran
Jalan Supratman
Jalan Laksamana Madya
Jalan Saparuna
Jalan Tengiri
To Kalianda
& Bakauheni
Lampung Bay

SUMATRA

PLACES TO STAY
1   Hotel Cilimaya
3   Hotel Ria
4   Hotels Gunungsari
    & Berkah
7   Hotel Garding
11 Hotel Arinas
    & European Bakery
12 Kurnia Perdana Hotel
13 Kurnia Dua & Tanjung
    Karang Plaza
18 Indrah Puri Hotel
19 Sheraton Inn Lampung
20 Marco Polo Hotel
22 Hotel Kartika

PLACES TO EAT
8   Restaurant Begadang I &
    Restaurant Sari Bundo
9   Night Food Stalls
14 KFC
15 Rumah Makan Pondok 12
21 Pondok Santap Dwipa Raya
24 Pasar Mambo Night Market

OTHER
2   BNI Bank 1946
5   Train Station
6   Regional Tourist Office
10 Telkom Office
16 Post Office
17 Mulya Sari Artshop
23 Provincial Tourist Office
25 Krakatau Monument

The buoy has been mounted in concrete and sits in a small park opposite Kupang Kota police station, off Jl Veteran.

The **Lampung Provincial Museum**, five km north of central Tanjungkarang on Jl Teuku Umar, houses a diverse collection of bits and pieces – everything from neolithic relics to stuffed animals. A tourist brochure gives visitors a good idea of what to expect when it announces matter-of-factly that the collection 'would benefit from improved conservation, labelling and display'!

Organised Tours

If you want to join an organised tour it's best to check out the tour companies working at the big hotels; there's more chance of them getting the numbers required for a trip. The Indrah Puri and the Sheraton are the places to ask. Elendra Tour & Travel (☎ 253942), Jl Agus Salim 112, also offers a range of tours.

Places to Stay – bottom end

As is so often the case in big cities, things are a bit grim at the budget end of the scale. There are a couple of rock-bottom places on Jl Kotaraja, less than 100m from the train station. The *Hotel Gunungsari* at No 21 has dingy doubles for 8000 rp. Avoid the *Hotel Berkah* next door. The *Hotel Cilimaya*, 50m beyond the small stream on Jl Imam Bonjol, is a step up from these. It has basic rooms for 5000/10,000 rp, or 10,000/15,000 rp with mandi and fan.

Places to Stay – middle

Things start to improve rapidly if you are prepared to spend a bit more. A good place to look is around the junction of Jl Raden Intan and Jl S Parman.

The *Kurnia Perdana Hotel* (☎ 262030), on the junction at Jl Raden Intan 114, has very clean rooms with air-con starting from 28,900/32,000 rp. You'll find similar rates across the road at the *Kurnia Dua* (☎ 261985).

In the centre of town, off Jl Kartini on Jl Dwi Warna, is the *Hotel Garding* (☎ 255-512), with doubles ranging from 15,000 rp for a basic room to 33,500 rp with shower

and air-con. The *Hotel Ria* (☎ 253974 around the corner from the Garden on Kartini, has doubles with air-con starting 27,000 rp.

Places to Stay – top end

Bandarlampung has a growing band of upmarket hotels. The most stylish of them the impressive *Sheraton Inn Lampun* (☎ 486666). Doubles start at US$90.

There are plenty of good places chargin a lot less. The *Hotel Arinas* (☎ 266778), the heart of town at Jl Raden Intan 35A, ha very comfortable modern rooms from 47,50 52,500 rp, all with air-con, TV and hot wate A bit out of town is the *Marco Polo Hot* (☎ 262511) at Jl Dr Susilo 4, where 45,00 rp will get you a double with a view of Lampung Bay and use of the Olympic-siz pool.

Other top-end offerings are the *Indra Puri Hotel* (☎ 262766) and the *Hotel Kartik* (☎ 487994).

Places to Eat

There are some good restaurants in Banda lampung, especially if you enjoy region cooking. The unremarkable-looking *Ruma Makan Pondok 12*, near the main post offic on Jl Kh Dahlan, specialises in Palemban food. A meal of ikan belida, with all th trimmings, costs 3500 rp.

The *Pondok Santap Dwipa Raya* is a upmarket Palembang-style place on Jl Gate Subroto. It serves a delicious sayur asa (sour vegetable soup) for 900 rp.

The *Sari Bundo* and the *Begadang I* (on of four in town) are a couple of popula Padang restaurants almost side by side on Imam Bonjol.

The *European Bakery & Restaurant* at Raden Intan 35 is particularly strong o chocolate cake.

Fast-food fans can get their fill at *KFC* o Jl Sudirman, 100m from the junction with Raden Intan.

Things to Buy

Lampung produces two types of materia that are worth looking out for. Particular usual are the woven pieces that are known collectively as ship clothes (most feature ships), which use rich reds and blues to create primitive geometric designs. *Kain pis* is a ceremonial cloth elaborately embroidered with gold thread. Mulya Sari artshop at Jl Thamrin 85 has a very good collection of both, but Lampung Art opposite elkom on Jl Kartini is more convenient.

Getting There & Away

Air Merpati operates five flights a day from Bandarlampung to Jakarta (91,500 rp) and two services a week to Palembang (88,200 p). The Merpati office (☎ 263419) is at Jl artini 90.

Bus The city's sprawling Rajabasa bus terminal is one of the busiest in Sumatra. There's a constant flow of departures, 24 hours a day, south to Jakarta and north to all parts of Sumatra.

There are buses to Palembang (from 2,500 rp; 10 hours) and Bengkulu (from 5,000 rp; 16 hours), but most people heading orth go to Bukittinggi; a 22 hour haul that costs 25,000 rp for regular buses to 65,000 for the best air-con services.

The trip to Jakarta takes eight hours and ckets range from 18,000 to 35,000 rp (air-con), which includes the price of the ferry etween Bakauheni and Merak.

Train This is one of the few places in Sumatra where it is possible to catch a train. Unfortunately, the service is only useful if you want to go to Palembang – a place which most travellers avoid.

If you do want to go there, train is definitely the way to go. There are departures at 8.30, 10 am and 9 pm. The 8.30 am and 9 pm trains have bisnis (18,000 rp) and eksekutif (28,000 rp) class only and take 6½ hours, while the 10 am 'market' trains have ekonomi class only (4500 rp) and take an hour longer.

The train station is conveniently located at the end of Jl Kotaraja in the heart of Tanjungkarang.

Taxi There are many share taxis shuttling between Bandarlampung and Bakauheni (5500 rp), Jakarta (32,000 rp) and Palembang (27,500 rp). For Bakauheni, try Taxi 4545 (☎ 252264); for Jakarta or Palembang, try Taxi Dinasty (☎ 445674).

Getting Around

The Airport The airport is 22 km north of town. Airport taxis charge 18,000 rp for the ride to town, while a metered taxi charges about half that for the same trip in the opposite direction.

Local Transport There are frequent opelets between the Tanjungkarang train station and Rajabasa bus terminal. They cost 300 rp.

WAY KAMBAS NATIONAL PARK

This national park occupies 1300 sq km of coastal lowland forest around the Sungai Way Kambas on the east coast of Lampung, 110 km from Bandarlampung.

The park is home to five pairs of rhinos, the occasional Sumatran tiger and – the main attraction – elephants.

Elephants

The elephants in question are Sumatran elephants (*Elephas maximus sumatrensis*), a subspecies of the Asian elephant found only in Sumatra and Kalimantan.

Way Kambas is home to about 350 elephants, about 250 of them still living wild – but don't head out there expecting to see any of them. What you'll find is something much closer to a circus show than a brush with nature: the Way Kambas elephant training centre.

The centre was set up to do something about the 'problem' of wild elephants that has been created by the clearing of elephant habitat for farming.

The elephants are rounded up and get to earn their living by performing useful tricks like playing soccer. Elephantine football is very popular with local tourists. 'It fills my heart with joy to see an elephant playing football' was the overwrought reaction of one visiting Jakarta fan, quite overcome with emotion at the wonder of it all.

It is possible to organise elephant rides through the tourist offices in Bandarlampung given a day's notice. It costs 20,000 rp for an hour's ride, which is quite long enough for the average bum.

Way Kanan

The Way Kanan 'resort', as the tourist blurb rather optimistically calls it, is little more than a small guesthouse and a few ramshackle huts in a jungle clearing on the banks of the Sungai Way Kanan, about 13 km from the entrance to the national park.

An official guide is based at the camp during daylight hours. Guided activities include three hour jungle treks for 15,000 rp, and two hour canoe trips on the Sungai Way Kanan and surrounding waterways for 75,000 rp.

Judging by the piles of evidence on the road, elephants visit Way Kanan from time to time. There's certainly more chance of seeing an elephant than a Sumatran tiger, sightings of which are extremely rare.

What you will see – and hear – is lots of primates and birds.

There is very little virgin forest in the national park. The only parts the loggers left alone were the parts they couldn't get to. They did, however, leave a few big trees. They include some massive scaly barked meranti trees with trunks rising 30m as straight as an arrow before the first branch.

Organised Tours

Prices for day trips from Bandarlampung to Way Kambas and Way Kanan start at about US$60 per person for a minimum of two,

falling to US$30 per person for larger group Some tours also include a stop at the Pugu graharjo archaeological site.

Places to Stay & Eat

There is a small guesthouse at the elepha training centre with basic doubles for 25,0C rp, and there are food stalls to cater for da trippers. They close after dark, so you'll nee to bring food if you're staying the nigh Conditions are even more basic at the *Wa Kanan Guesthouse* and 25,000 rp for double is way over the top. You'll need bring your own food, but cooking facilitie and utensils are provided.

Otherwise, the nearest accommodation the *Losmen Lindung* at Jepara, 10 km sou of the turn-off to Way Kambas, whe singles/doubles are 10,000/15,000 rp.

If you turn up at the park entrance late, th staff will normally let travellers bunk dow somewhere.

Getting There & Away

There are occasional buses from Banda lampung's Rajabasa bus terminal direct Jepara (3500 rp; 2½ hours). They go past th entrance to Way Kambas, an arched gatewa guarded by a stone elephant in the village c Rajabasalama, 10 km north of Jepara. Othe wise, catch a bus to Metro (1500 rp; on hour) and then another to Rajabasalam (2500 rp; 1½ hours).

From the park entrance, it is easy to fin someone to take you into the park by moto cycle. The going rates are 8000 rp to Wa Kambas and 10,000 rp to Way Kanan. Yo will need to negotiate a time to be picked u again.

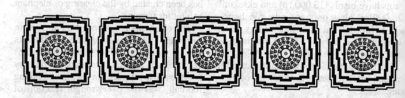

Nusa Tenggara

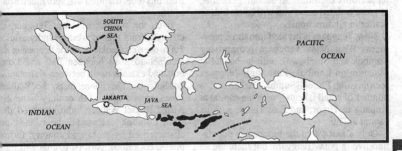

Nusa Tenggara (the name means 'South-East Islands') is quite different from the rest of Indonesia. As you travel east, the climate becomes drier, so people raise corn and sago rather than rice; the flora and fauna are more evocative of parts of Australia than of tropical Bali; the people are poorer than those elsewhere in Indonesia; and there is a great variety of cultures and religions.

Each island has its own peculiar sights, some of which rival anything seen on Java or Bali. The great stone-slab tombs and traditional villages of Sumba, the intricate *ikat* weaving of Sumba and Flores, the brilliantly coloured lakes of Keli Mutu in Flores and the

dragons of Komodo must rate as some of the finest attractions in South-East Asia. Though there are few beaches where you can peel off and lie back undisturbed by a crowd of curious locals, there's fine coral off some of the islands.

Although a steady stream of travellers passes through, until recently the lack of transport confined most of them to a limited route. There are now more opportunities for off-the-beaten-track explorations and the lack of tourists in these places will mean that your reception will be more natural. It does create one problem, though: you will constantly be the centre of attention. It's not

---

HIGHLIGHTS

- **Lombok** – Less frenetic than Bali, Lombok attracts many visitors with its fine beaches, the towering Gunung Rinjani volcano, interesting crafts and a more relaxed approach to tourism.
- **Sumba** – This island has a wonderful mix of the most intact traditional culture in Nusa Tenggara and long white, untouched beaches. Sumba is best known for its spectacular *ikat* weaving in the east and south-east, and its fascinating megalithic cultures.
- **Komodo** – The best-known home of those fabulous dragons; seeing a dragon in the wild is awesome. Rinca, Komodo's smaller neighbour, also has dragons and abundant wildlife.
- **Flores** – A high volcanic island, Flores is famed for the spectacular coloured lakes at Keli Mutu. The Bajawa area has interesting traditional villages, while Labuanbajo and its nearby beaches are the place to kick back for a few days.
- **Timor** – The interior of West Timor still has some interesting traditional areas that are starting to open up and there are other highlights such as the whaling village of Lamalera on Lembata. The towns, villages and beaches of East Timor have been open to travellers since 1989, although tourist infrastructure is poor outside of Dili.

unusual to attract an entourage of 50 children in a small village, all programmed to yell 'hello mister' until either they or you collapse from exhaustion. At the other extreme, in more isolated areas you will cause kids to scatter in all directions!

Nusa Tenggara is divided into three provinces: West Nusa Tenggara (comprising Lombok and Sumbawa), with its capital at Mataram on Lombok; East Nusa Tenggara (comprising Flores, Sumba, Timor and a number of small islands), with the capital at Kupang in Timor; and East Timor, with its capital at Dili.

Only about 4% of the Indonesian population live in Nusa Tenggara, but there are so many different languages and cultures that it's impossible to think of these people as one group. There are several languages on the tiny island of Alor alone, though you won't have any trouble getting by with Bahasa Indonesia anywhere in Nusa Tenggara. Many of its people are now at least nominally Christian; Christians predominate on Flores, Roti and Timor. Muslims form a majority on Lombok and Sumbawa, while in isolated areas such as the western half of Sumba, a large section of the population still adhere to traditional animist beliefs. A layer of anim ism persists alongside Christianity in othe areas, with customs, rituals and festiva from this older tradition still very much a pa of life.

Even the wildlife of Nusa Tenggara different from that of western Indonesia. 300m deep channel (one of the deepest in th archipelago) runs between Bali and Lom bok, and extends north between Kalimanta and Sulawesi. The channel marks the 'Wallac Line', named after 19th century naturali Alfred Russel Wallace, who observed tha from Lombok eastwards, the islands a characterised by more arid country, thorn plants, cockatoos, parrots, lizards and ma supials, while from Bali westwards, th vegetation is more tropical. It's actually ne as clear cut as Wallace thought, but Nus Tenggara is definitely a transition zone be tween Asian and Australian flora and fauna

HISTORY

Despite Portuguese interest in the region i the late 16th century, and Dutch interest fror the 17th century onwards, Nusa Tenggar was never in the mainstream of coloni activity in Indonesia. Because the area offere

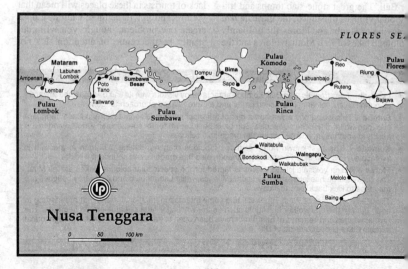

FLORES SE.

Nusa Tenggara

economic temptations, the Dutch largely concentrated on Java, Sumatra and the Spice Islands of Maluku. In Nusa Tenggara they set up trading posts, but didn't find it necessary to exercise much authority. Local rulers and their conflicts, and traditional ways of life (including animist religions), were largely left to run their own course until around 1840. At this time the Dutch were spurred into action for a variety of reasons: to protect their ships from pirates; because of disputes (such as those with the Balinese) over the salvaging of shipwrecks; and to protect their possessions from other colonising powers. As the Europeans scrambled for the last available morsels of territory in Asia and Africa in the last quarter of the 19th century, the Dutch grabbed anything that was left in the archipelago.

Piracy and disputes over shipwrecks motivated the first Dutch assault on Bali, in 1846. When the indigenous Sasaks of Lombok rebelled against their Balinese overlords in 1891 and appealed to the Dutch for help, the Dutch took the opportunity to send in a military expedition to finish off the Balinese and take control of Lombok themselves. Flores, further east, was another target. A desire to

control the slave trade, and disputes over the rights to shipwrecks, led to two Dutch expeditions against the island, in 1838 and 1846. A local rebellion in 1907 prompted a complete takeover. The Dutch waited until the early 20th century to subdue the tribespeople of the interior of the Nusa Tenggara islands, while the eastern half of Timor never fell into Dutch hands (it was a Portuguese colony until 1975, when Indonesia invaded and took it over).

After Indonesia achieved independence in the 1940s, Nusa Tenggara remained a remote and lonely outpost, administered by a handful of Javanese officials and soldiers, who considered themselves virtual exiles. The difficulty of the mountainous terrain, poor communications and, in particular, the islands' location on the path to nowhere, all helped to deter visitors and maintain this isolation, at least until the late 1980s, when regular air connections between Darwin and Timor began.

MONEY

As you travel eastwards, banks are few and far between, and the exchange rate often falls below that on Bali or Java. The safest

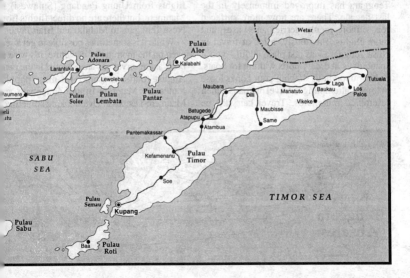

currency to bring is US dollars; travellers cheques should be from the larger companies (such as American Express, Thomas Cook or Bank of America).

Bank Rakyat Indonesia has branches in the main towns, but has always provided low rates and limited exchange facilities. The Bank Negara Indonesia (BNI) has now opened many branches in the main towns, provides better service and cashes most major currencies at reasonable rates, though US dollars still have the edge. Bank Danamon is starting to open branches and promises to provide cash advances on credit cards in the future, but bring travellers cheques or cash. Credit cards are virtually useless between Mataram on Lombok and Kupang on Timor, and most Merpati offices outside those two cities do not accept them.

If venturing away from the major towns, it pays to change larger amounts to tide you over. Banks are usually open Monday to Friday from 8 am to 4 pm, but for foreign currency transactions they may close at 1 pm. Do your banking in the morning.

GETTING THERE & AROUND

The good news is that transport in Nusa Tenggara has improved immensely in the last decade. There are now more surfaced roads, more regular ferries and buses, and more flights. Previously, a lot of travel in Nusa Tenggara was just plain awful – you'd spend days in dreary ports waiting for boats, or hour upon hour shaking your bones loose in trucks, attempting to travel on roads which resembled minefields. Travel can still be arduous, but on the whole, if you stick to the main routes, you shouldn't have much trouble. Most people who travel right through Nusa Tenggara by surface transport are quite happy not to repeat the experience and unless travelling to/from Australia fly back to the starting point.

Air

You can fly direct between Darwin (Australia) and Kupang (Timor) with Merpati, and Kupang is an international gateway (no visa is required for most western nationalities).

Merpati has a good network of flights in Nusa Tenggara. The main hubs are Kupang (Timor), Maumere (Flores) and Mataram (Lombok). These are the easiest places from which to get flights. Other airports tend to be serviced by small aircraft, seats can be harder to get and cancellations are more common. The less used and less profitable the run, the more chance of a cancellation, which Merpati always blames on 'technical problems'. Sempati and Bouraq also fly on some of the main runs and are often more reliable.

Nusa Tenggara is not well connected to the other island groups. Most flights to/from Nusa Tenggara are via Bali. There are direct flights from Ujung Pandang (Sulawesi) to Maumere, but there are no direct flights from Nusa Tenggara to Maluku and Irian Jaya.

While it is sometimes possible to get a seat even on the morning of departure, it's wise to book and reservations are essential in the peak August tourist season. The most popular routes are Mataram-Bima-Labuanbajo and Maumere-Denpasar. Overbooking sometimes

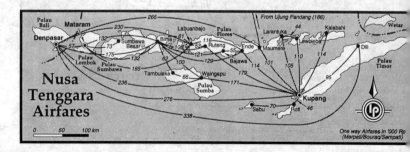

:curs, so make sure your booking has been
1ade when you buy your ticket and always
:confirm. On the other hand, if you've been
1ld a flight is full, it can sometimes be worth
10ing to the airport before the flight leaves,
the airport is easy to get to. Many Merpati
ffices don't have computers, so no-show
:ats are not reoffered.

1oat

1ost of the islands are connected by ferries,
/hich are regular, if rarely comfortable.
here are several trips daily between Bali
nd Lombok, and Lombok and Sumbawa.
.etween Sumbawa and Flores one ferry goes
aily (except Friday), stopping at Komodo
sland along the way. Ferries go twice a week
etween Timor and Larantuka on Flores, and
iree a week go between Timor and Alor and
etween Timor and Sabu. A ferry connects
(upang with Ende (Flores), Waingapu
Sumba) and Sabu once a week. All of these
rries take cars as well as passengers and, in
ddition, there are smaller boats from Flores
) the islands of Adonara, Solor and Lem-
ata, from Kupang to Roti and a few other
ossibilities. Details are provided in the rel-
vant sections.

Nusa Tenggara is serviced by the Pelni
hips *Lambelo*, *Dobonsolo*, *Binaiya* and
ilongkabila. Schedules are provided under
idividual town entries. Pelni's more basic
erintis cargo ships, and freighters, cover
1any routes and are an option if you get
tuck. Ask at the office of the harbour master
syahbandar) or at the shipping offices. Con-
itions are primitive, but you can often
.egotiate to rent a cabin.

For shorter hops, you can often charter
ailing boats or small motorboats. A popular
/ay of travelling between Flores and Lombok
s on a five day boat tour out of Labuanbajo,
:opping at Komodo and other islands along the
/ay. Some Bugis schooners find their way
ight down into Nusa Tenggara, for those who
/ant a really different way of getting to Sul-
.wesi.

3us

.hough the roads have improved enormously,
bus travel is still uncomfortable. Air-con
express coaches run right across Lombok
and Sumbawa, but elsewhere small, hot
buses with limited leg room are crammed
with passengers and all manner of produce.
They constantly stop to drop off and pick up
passengers and, if buses are not full, they will
endlessly loop around town searching for
passengers until they are full. Even if the
road is paved, it is usually narrow and
winding, and there are always sections under
repair that will rattle your fillings. Don't
underestimate journey times – a trip of
only 100 km may take three hours or more
– and don't overestimate your endurance
abilities.

Most buses leave in the morning around 7
or 8 am, so be prepared for early starts.
Where buses leave later in the day, they are
limited and less patronised so they often
spend longer looking for passengers. Some
night buses, leaving around 5 pm, are available between major towns, but you miss out
on the scenery. Long-distance buses usually
meet the main ferries if you want to travel
straight on to other destinations.

Car & Motorcycle

Self-drive cars can be found at reasonable
rates on Lombok. Elsewhere it is much more
difficult and expensive to rent a car. Hotels
are good contact points but they usually
charge hefty commissions. On Flores, asking
rates are exorbitant and you will have to
bargain hard. Expect to pay around 100,000
rp a day, including petrol. *Bemos* can be
chartered for short trips around towns.

If you are an experienced rider, motorcycling is an interesting way to see Nusa
Tenggara, and you can transport your bike
on ferries between most of the islands. It's
best to bring your own machine. It's possible
to find short-term hires in a few large Nusa
Tenggara towns, but it's difficult to convince
anyone to let you take their bikes to other
islands. Traffic is relatively light, even on the
main highways, but the usual hazards of
villages crowded with pedestrians, chickens
and goats apply.

NUSA TENGGARA

Bicycle

Bicycles can be rented around the main centres of Lombok, but they are not a popular form of transport anywhere in Nusa Tenggara. Long-distance cycling is a possibility on Sumba, where there's a lot of flat terrain, but cycling on hilly Flores or Timor requires legs of iron and a state-of-the-art mountain bike. Lombok, with its light traffic, is good for cycling.

Lombok

Lombok has both the lushness of Bali and the starkness of outback Australia. Parts of the island drip with water, while pockets are chronically dry and droughts can last for months, causing crop failure and famine. Recent improvements in agriculture and water management have made life on Lombok less precarious.

The indigenous Sasak people make up about 80% of the population. They follow the Islamic religion, but have a culture and language unique to Lombok. There is also a significant minority who have a Balinese culture, language and religion – a legacy of the time when Bali controlled Lombok. Balinese-style processions and ceremonies are conducted, and there are several Balinese Hindu temples.

History

Islam may have been brought to the island from Java, but there's no firm evidence that Java controlled the island. Not much is known about Lombok before the 17th century, at which time it was split into numerous, frequently squabbling petty states, each presided over by a Sasak 'prince' – a disunity which the neighbouring Balinese exploited.

Balinese Rule In the early 17th century, the Balinese state of Karangasem took control of western Lombok. At the same time, Makassarese crossed the straits from their colonies in Sumbawa and established settlements in eastern Lombok. The war of 1677-8 saw the

Makassarese booted off the island and eastern Lombok temporarily reverted to the rule of the Sasak princes. Balinese control soon extended east and by 1740 or 1750 the whole island was in Balinese hands. Squabbles over royal succession soon had the Balinese fighting among themselves and Lombok split into four separate kingdoms. By 1838 the Mataram kingdom had subdued the other three and reconquered eastern Lombok. Mataram forces then crossed the Lombok Strait to Bali and overran Karangasem, reuniting Karangasem and Lombok.

In western Lombok, where Balinese rule dated from the early 17th century, relations between the Balinese and Sasaks were relatively harmonious. The Sasak peasants assimilated Balinese Hinduism and participated in Balinese religious festivities. Intermarriage between Balinese and Sasak was common, and sasaks were organised in the same irrigation associations (*subak*) that the Balinese used for wet-rice agriculture. The traditional Sasak village government had been done away with and the peasants were ruled directly by the rajah (king) or by a landowning Balinese aristocrat.

Things were very different in eastern Lombok, where the recently defeated Sasak aristocracy hung in limbo. Here the Balinese maintained control from garrisoned forts. Although the traditional Sasak village government remained intact, the village chief became little more than a tax collector for the local Balinese *punggawa* (district head). The Sasak peasants were reduced to the level of serfs while the Sasak aristocracy had their power and land holdings slashed, and were hostile towards the Balinese. This enabled the eastern Lombok Sasak aristocracy to lead several peasant rebellions against the Balinese.

Dutch Involvement In 1855 and 1871 the Balinese suppressed revolts. An uprising in 1891 was almost put down too, but the Sasak chiefs sent envoys to the Dutch officials on Bali, asking for help and inviting the Dutch to rule Lombok. The Dutch were initially reluctant to take military action, but their

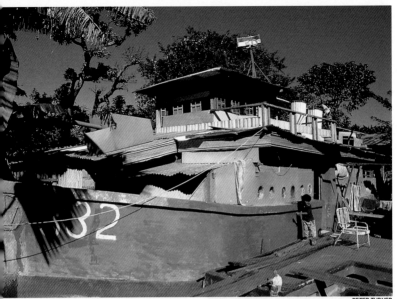

PETER TURNER

SARA-JANE CLELAND

PETER TURNER

Nusa Tenggara
Top: Hotel Anda, Indonesia's most eccentric hotel, Soe, Timor.
Bottom Left: Friendly faces at the small fishing town of Labuanbajo, Flores.
Bottom Right: 27m-high Christ statue, Cape Fatucama, Dili, East Timor.

Nusa Tenggara

Top: The crater lake on Lombok, with Gunung Rinjani (3726m) to the left and the new cone of Gunung Baru (2376m) in the centre.

Left: Keli Mutu (green & turquoise lake), Flores.

Right: A view of rugged Komodo Island over deceptively calm waters.

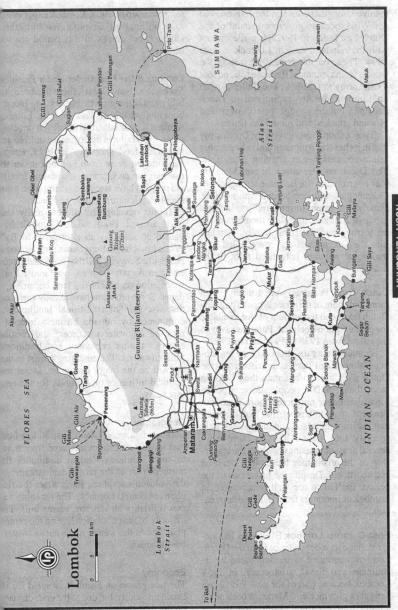

Lombok

resolve strengthened when the ruthless Van der Wijck became governor general of the Dutch East Indies in 1892. He made a treaty with the rebels in eastern Lombok in June 1894. Then, on the pretext of freeing the Sasaks from tyrannical Balinese rule, he sent a large army to Lombok. The Balinese rajah on Lombok quickly capitulated to Dutch demands, but the younger princes overruled him and attacked and routed the Dutch.

It was a shortlived victory; the Dutch army dug in its heels at Ampenan and in September reinforcements began arriving from Java. The Dutch counter-attack began. Mataram was overrun and the Balinese stronghold of Cakranegara was bombarded with artillery. Finally, the rajah surrendered and a large group of Balinese, including members of the aristocracy and the royal family, marched into the Dutch guns and were killed in a traditional *puputan* (ritualised fight to the death).

Dutch Rule Peasants were forced to sell more and more of their rice crops to pay new Dutch taxes and the amount of rice available for consumption declined. Famines ravaged the island from 1938 to 1940 and in 1949.

By maintaining the support of the remaining Balinese and the Sasak aristocracy, the Dutch were able to maintain their hold on more than 500,000 people, using a police force that never numbered more than 250. Peasants wouldn't rebel, for fear of being evicted from their land and losing what little security they had. Although there were several peasant uprisings, without the leadership of the aristocracy these were localised and shortlived. Despite the privations of the period, the Dutch are well remembered in Lombok as liberators from Balinese domination.

Post-Colonial Lombok Even after Indonesia attained its independence from the Dutch, Lombok continued to be dominated by its Balinese and Sasak aristocracy. In 1958 Lombok became part of the new West Nusa Tenggara province and Mataram became its administrative capital. Following the at-

tempted coup of 1965, Lombok experience mass killings of Communists and ethn Chinese, but details of this period are sti obscure.

Lombok & the New Order Under Preside Soeharto's 'New Order', there has been sta bility and some growth, but nothing like th booming wealth of Java or Bali. Lombc remains a poor island with uneven develoj ment. Crop failures led to famine in 1966 ar to severe food shortages in 1973. Peop have moved away from Lombok under th *transmigrasi* programme, and several foreig aid projects have attempted to improve wate supply, agricultural output and health.

Tourist development did not really sta until around 1980, when Lombok fir gained attention as an alternative to Bal While low-budget bungalows proliferated places like Senggigi and the Gili Islands, inte est from outside Lombok was aroused an speculation on beachfront land became ep demic. Some problems have already surface dispossession of traditional landholder dominance by outside business interest pressure on water resources; and confli between tourist behaviour and tradition Muslim values. The emerging tourist indu try will be the major economic, social an political influence on Lombok for the nex few years.

Geography

Lombok is a small island, just 80 km fro east to west and about the same from nort to south. Gunung Rinjani dominates th northern part of the island, and streams o the volcano's southern flank water the ric plains of central Lombok. The far south an east is drier, with scrubby, barren hills. Th majority of the population live on the centra plain and in the wetter, more fertile wester coastal areas.

Economy

The rice grown on Lombok is noted for it excellent quality, but due to the drier climate productivity here is not as high as on Java c

ali. There are also small and large planta-
ons of coconut palms, coffee, kapok and
otton; new crops such as cloves, vanilla,
neapple and pepper have been introduced,
ut tobacco is probably the biggest cash
op. Quarrying of pumice stone has also
een a good earner in recent years.

Attempts are being made to develop up-
arket tourism on Lombok, with a number
f new, expensive hotels on the west coast
nd a grandiose plan for developing the
outh coast.

opulation & People

ombok has a population of 2.4 million
1990 census), the majority living in and
round the main centres of Ampenan, Cak-
negara, Mataram, Praya and Selong. Almost
0% of the people are Sasak, about 10% are
alinese, and there are minority populations
f Chinese, Javanese and Arabs. Some
umbawanese live in the east of the island,
nd Buginese along the coast. There may still
e some isolated villages of the Bodha (or
oda), who are said to be the aboriginal
eople of Lombok.

asaks Physically and culturally, the Sasaks
ave much in common with the Javanese, the
alinese and the Sumbawanese. Basically
ill people, the Sasaks are now spread over
entral and eastern Lombok, and are gener-
lly much poorer than the Balinese minority.
lost Sasaks are nominally Muslims, but
any retain elements of the ancient animist
eliefs.

hinese Most of Lombok's Chinese live in
mpenan or Cakranegara. The Chinese first
ame to Lombok with the Dutch, as a cheap
abour force, but were later fostered as eco-
omic intermediaries between the Dutch and
he Indonesian population and were allowed
 set up their own businesses. When the
utch were ousted in 1949, the Chinese
ayed and continued to expand their busi-
ess interests. Many were killed in the
ftermath of the 1965 attempted coup, but
here are still many Chinese-run shops and
estaurants, especially in Cakranegara.

Arts

Lombok has an indigenous music style and
a number of traditional dances, but they are
mainly performed in the context of seasonal
or life-cycle ceremonies, and have not been
developed as tourist attractions.

Dance The popular Cupak Gerantang tells
the story of Panji, a romantic hero. The
dance, which is usually performed at celebrations and festivals, probably originated
on Java in the 15th century. The Kayak
Sando, another version of the Panji story, in
which the dancers wear masks, is found only
in central and eastern Lombok.

The Gandrung is about love and courtship
– *gandrung* means being in love, or longing.
It's a social dance, usually performed by the
young men and women of the village. Everyone stands around in a circle and then,
accompanied by a full *gamelan* orchestra, a
young girl dances by herself for a time before
choosing a male partner from the audience
to join her. It's performed in Narmada, Lenek
and Praya.

The Oncer is a war dance performed vigorously by men and young boys in central
and eastern Lombok. Participants play a
variety of musical instruments in time to
their movements, and wear severe black costumes with crimson and gold waistbands,
shoulder sashes, socks and caps.

The Rudat, with a combination of Islamic
and Sasak influences, is performed by pairs
of men dressed in black caps and jackets and
black-and-white checked sarongs. They're
backed by singers, tambourines and cylindrical drums called *jidur*.

Music The Tandak Gerok is an eastern Lombok performance which combines dance,
theatre and singing to music played on
bamboo flutes and on the bowed lute called
a *rebab*. The unique feature of the Tandak
Gerok is that the vocalists imitate the sound
of the gamelan instruments. It's usually performed after harvesting or other hard
physical labour, but is also put on at traditional ceremonies.

The Genggong involves seven musicians

using a simple set of instruments, including a bamboo flute, a rebab and knockers; they accompany their music with dance movements and stylised hand gestures.

The Barong Tengkok is the name given to the procession of musicians who play at weddings or circumcision ceremonies.

Handcrafts There's little of the purely decorative art so common on Bali, but traditional Lombok handcrafts are sought after. They are mainly objects for everyday use, like baskets, pottery and textiles, made with great skill using traditional techniques and natural, local materials. The Sweta market has a lot of new handcraft items, while older pieces are sold in Ampenan antique shops. Villages specialise in certain crafts and it's interesting to travel to a number of them, seeing handweaving in one village, basketware in another and pottery in a third.

Society & Conduct

Traditional Culture Traditional law *(adat)* is still fundamental to the way of life on Lombok today, particularly customs relating to birth, circumcision, courtship and marriage.

Sasaks show a fascination with heroic trials of strength, physical prowess and one-on-one contests. The Peresehan is a fight between two men using long rattan staves and small rectangular shields. The Lanca, originally from Sumbawa, is another trial of strength, this time between men who use their knees to strike each other.

Avoiding Offence Most of Lombok is conservative, and immodest dress and public displays of affection between couples can cause offence. Both men and women should cover their knees, upper arms and shoulders – brief shorts and tank tops should not be worn away from the beach areas. Nude or topless bathing is also offensive.

Many people on Lombok fast during Ramadan. During this time it is insensitive and offensive for foreign visitors to eat, drink or smoke in public during the day.

Islamic law forbids drinking alcohol and,

although booze is widely available on Lombok, public drunkenness is frowned on. I[t] particularly offensive near a mosque.

Religion

Islam and Balinese Hinduism are the tw[o] main religions on Lombok (see the introdu[c]tory Facts about the Country chapter and t[he] Bali chapter for details). Wektu Telu is a[n] indigenous religion, unique to Lombok a[nd] thought to have originated in the northe[rn] village of Bayan. The number of adheren[ts] is officially quite small (less than 30,00[0] though this may be understated, as Wek[tu] Telu is not one of Indonesia's official[ly] recognised religions. There are also sma[ll] numbers of Christians and Buddhists.

Wektu Telu In the Sasak language, *wek[tu]* means 'result' and *telu* means 'three'. T[he] name probably denotes the complex mixtu[re] of Hindu, Islamic and animist influences th[at] make up this religion, and the concept of trinity is embodied in many Wektu Te[lu] beliefs, for example the sun, moon and sta[rs] (representing heaven, earth and water) a[nd] the head, body and limbs (representing cr[e]ativity, sensitivity and control). Wektu Te[lu] stresses adat (traditional law and belief[s] while Wektu Lima is a more orthodox for[m] of Islam: *lima* means 'five', referring to t[he] five pillars of Islam (which are considere[d] obligatory for the believer to follow).

The Wektu Telu observe only three day[s] of fasting during Ramadan. They do not pra[y] five times a day as laid down by Islamic la[w] they do not build mosques and they have n[o] objection to eating pork. Their dead a[re] buried with their heads facing Mecca, b[ut] Wektu Telu do not make pilgrimages ther[e.] In fact, the only fundamental tenet of Isla[m] to which the Wektu Telu seem to hold firm[ly] is the belief in Allah and that Muhammed [is] his prophet. They regard themselves a[s] Muslims, but are not accepted as such b[y] orthodox Muslims and relations between th[e] two groups have not always been good. Th[e] number of Wektu Telu has been declining [as] more young people turn to orthodox Islam[.]

eligious Festivals Most of the Wektu Telu
eligious festivals of Lombok take place at
he beginning of the rainy season (from
)ctober to December) or at harvest time
April to May), with celebrations in villages
ll over the island. Many of these ceremonies
nd rituals are annual events but, as they do
ot fall on specific days, getting to see one is
matter of luck and word of mouth. Lom-
ok's Muslims celebrate the various events
n the Islamic calendar (see the introductory
`acts for the Visitor chapter), especially the
nd of Ramadan.

3ooks

here are few books devoted solely to
_ombok. One is _Lombok: Conquest, Coloni-
ation and Underdevelopment, 1870-1940,_
y Alfons van der Kraan, which describes the
conomic destitution of the island during the
)utch administration.

3etting There & Away

_ombok's airport has only a couple of inter-
national connections, but Lombok is very
iccessible by air and sea from neighbouring
ndonesian islands. The vast majority of
ravellers arrive from Bali, which is very
lose, while those island hopping from the
ast reach Lombok from Sumbawa.

Air Agents in Mataram and Senggigi sell air
ickets and reconfirm flights (it's important
o reconfirm). The principal airlines serving
_ombok are:

3ouraq
    Selaparang Hotel, Jl Pejanggik 4, Cakranegara
    (☎ 27333)
3aruda-Merpati
    Nitour agency, Jl Yos Sudarso 6, Ampenan
    (☎ 23235)
Merpati
    (main office) Jl Selaparang, Cakranegara
    (☎ 36745)
3empati
    Cilinaya shopping centre, Mataram (☎ 21612)

Vlore than a dozen flights per day travel
etween Denpasar and Mataram (56,500 rp;
?5 minutes). Other connections are to Sum-

bawa Besar (73,000 rp), continuing to Bima
(132,400 rp); Surabaya (124,700 rp), Yogyakarta (197,700 rp) and Jakarta (311,000 rp)
on Java; and Ujung Pandang (241,700 rp) on
Sulawesi. Some flights are direct, but many
stop at Denpasar.

Silk Air has a daily direct flight to Singapore
– Lombok's first international connection.

Sea Lombok has two main ports: Lembar in
the west; and Labuhan Lombok, on the east
coast.

Bali Ferries run every two hours between
Padangbai (Bali) and Lembar (Lombok),
and the _Mabua Express_ luxury catamaran
provides a faster boat service between Benoa
Port (Bali) and Lembar – see the Lembar
entry in this section for details.

Regular tourist shuttle bus services run
between the main tourist centres on Bali and
Lombok, and the fares include the ferry
ticket and minibus connections at each end.
Perama is the most established operator, but
other companies may have similar services
at similar prices. Tourist shuttles are more
expensive than public transport, but quicker
and more convenient. For example, a Perama
ticket from Ubud to Kuta Lombok costs
27,500 rp, including the ferry to Lombok. On
public transport you could probably do this
trip for about 10,000 rp (if you weren't overcharged), but it would involve at least five
bemo connections as well as the ferry, it
would certainly take longer and you might
have to spend a night in Mataram.

Sumbawa Passenger ferries leave Labuhan
Lombok (in eastern Lombok) for Poto Tano
(Sumbawa) just about every hour from 6 am
to 10 pm, but the exact times vary. See the
Labuhan Lombok entry for details. Direct
buses run from Sweta terminal, near Ampenan, to destinations on Sumbawa, including
Sumbawa Besar (four buses per day, 10,000
rp; 12,000 rp with air-con), Dompu (6 am
and 4 pm, 15,000 rp; 18,000 rp with air-con)
and Bima (9 am, 11 am and 2 pm, 23,000 rp;
26,000 rp with air-con). Fares include the

ferry. Perama also has connections between Lombok and Sumbawa.

Other Islands The national shipping line, Pelni, has passenger ships doing regular loops through the islands of Indonesia, with the *Kelimutu*, *Sirimau* and *Awu* typically calling at Lembar once a fortnight. The exact dates and routes can change, so enquire well in advance. See the introductory Getting Around chapter for details. The Pelni office on Lombok is at Jl Industri 1 in Ampenan (☎ 37212).

Getting Around

There is a good main road across the middle of the island, between Mataram and Labuhan Lombok, and quite good roads in most other populated areas. Public transport is generally restricted to main routes; away from these, you have to hire a pony cart (*cidomo*), get a lift on a motorcycle or walk. In remote regions, food, drinking water and petrol can be scarce, and there are few lodgings.

During the wet season, many roads are flooded or washed away, and others are impassable because of fallen rocks and rubble, making it impossible to get to many out-of-the-way places. The damage may not be repaired until well into the dry season.

Public transport is less frequent in the afternoon and stops completely at 10.30 or 11 pm, or much earlier in more remote areas.

Bus & Bemo There are several bus and bemo terminals on Lombok. The main one is at Sweta, at the eastern end of the main urban area, four km east of Mataram. Others are at Praya, Kopang and Selong. You may have to go via one or more of these terminals to get from one part of Lombok to another. For main routes, fares are fixed by the provincial government and a list should be displayed at the terminals, although it's not always up-to-date. The bus and bemo drivers may still try to overcharge, so check the fare list before setting off. You may have to pay more if you have a big bag.

With a few people together, chartering a bemo by the day can be convenient and quite

cheap – perhaps 60,000 to 80,000 rp per da (from 8 am to 5 pm), including petrol and a English-speaking driver, depending on dis tance. Many vehicles are licensed to opera only in certain areas.

Car & Motorcycle Hotels in Ampena Mataram or Senggigi can often arrange c or motorcycle rental, and there are a fe 'official' car rental companies with a wide range of vehicles, but these tend to be mor expensive. It costs about 45,000 to 50,000 i per day for a small vehicle such as a Suzul Jimny, with a limited insurance cover. If yc rent for a few days or a week, you should g a discount. Large Toyota 4WD vehicles ca actually be cheaper, although you will pa more for petrol. You can rent motorcycles i Mataram and Senggigi from around 12,00 rp per day. Elsewhere, you might find one you ask around.

There are petrol stations around the larg towns, while in rural areas you can only g fuel from small roadside shops. Look for signs that read *premium*, or *press ban* (lite ally, tyre repair).

Bicycle Bicycles can be rented in Ampena and some of the tourist areas, though they' not always in good condition. Lombok, wit its limited traffic, is ideal for bicycle tourin but it might be best to bring your own bike

Organised Tours Specialised tours, such a a 'nature tour' or 'handcraft tour', will giv a quick introduction to a specific aspect c the island and you can revisit your favourit places independently. Costs are from US$1 for a half-day tour, and US$20 to US$35 fo a full day. Many hotels have an arrangemer with a guide or tour operator, or you can as at the tourist office for suggestions.

AMPENAN, MATARAM, CAKRANEGARA & SWETA

Although officially four separate towns Ampenan, Mataram, Cakranegara and Swet merge together, so it's impossible to te where one stops and the next starts. Collec tively, they form the main 'city' on Lombo with banks, travel agencies, markets and some interesting shops, but this urban region is not a major attraction.

Ampenan

Once the main port of Lombok, Ampenan is now not much more than a small fishing harbour. It's a bit run down, but it has character. The main road does not actually reach the coast at Ampenan, but disappears among the ruined port buildings just before it gets to the grubby beach. Apart from Sasaks and Balinese, Ampenan's population includes some Chinese and a small Arab quarter known as Kampung Arab.

Mataram

Mataram is the administrative capital of the province of Nusa Tenggara Barat (West Nusa Tenggara). Some of the public buildings, such as the Bank of Indonesia, the new post office and the governor's office and residence, are substantial. The large houses around the outskirts of town are the homes of Lombok's elite.

Cakranegara

Now the main commercial centre of Lombok, bustling Cakranegara is usually referred to as Cakra. Formerly the capital of Lombok under the Balinese rajahs, Cakra today has a thriving Chinese community, as well as many Balinese residents. Most of the shops and restaurants in Cakranegara are run or owned by Chinese, and there are some Balinese-run *losmen*.

Sweta

Seven km east of Ampenan and only about 2.5 km beyond Cakra is Sweta, the central transport terminal of Lombok. This is where you catch bemos and buses to other parts of the island and on to Sumbawa. Stretching along the eastern side of the terminal is a vast, covered market, the largest on Lombok. If you wander through its dim alleys, you'll see stalls spilling over with coffee beans, eggs, spices, rice, fish, fabrics, crafts, fruit and hardware.

Orientation

The 'city' is effectively divided into four functional areas: Ampenan (the port); Mataram (the administrative centre); Cakranegara (the trading centre); and Sweta (the transport centre and market). The towns are spread along one main road, a one way street running west to east, which starts as Jl Pabean in Ampenan, quickly becomes Jl Yos Sudarso, changes to Jl Langko and then Jl Pejanggik, and finishes up in Sweta as Jl Selaparang, though it's difficult to tell where the road changes names. Indeed, it seems that they overlap, since some places appear to have more than one address.

Traffic going from east to west uses either the main Jl Sriwijaya/Jl Majapahit route, or a series of smaller one way streets – Jl Tumpang Sari, Jl Panca Usaha, Jl Pancawanga and Jl Pendidikan. Bemos shuttle between the bemo terminal in Ampenan and the big terminal in Sweta, about seven km away, so getting back and forth is dead easy. You can stay in Ampenan, Mataram or Cakra, since there are hotels and restaurants in all three places.

The main commercial and shopping area is around the Jl Selaparang/Jl Hasanuddin intersection, with the Cakra market just southeast of there, and other shops further west. The Mataram government buildings are chiefly found along Jl Pejanggik. The main square, Lampangan Mataram, on the south side of Jl Pejanggik, is a venue for occasional outdoor exhibitions and performances.

Information

Tourist Office The main government tourist office, the Kantor Dinas Pariwisata Daerah (DIPARDA; ☎ 31730), is in Mataram at Jl Langko 70, on the north side, almost diagonally opposite the telephone office. The people at the tourist office are friendly, helpful and well informed. The office is open Monday to Thursday from 8 am to 3 pm, and Friday and Saturday until noon.

Immigration Lombok's *kantor imigrasi* (immigration office) is on Jl Udayana, the road out to the airport.

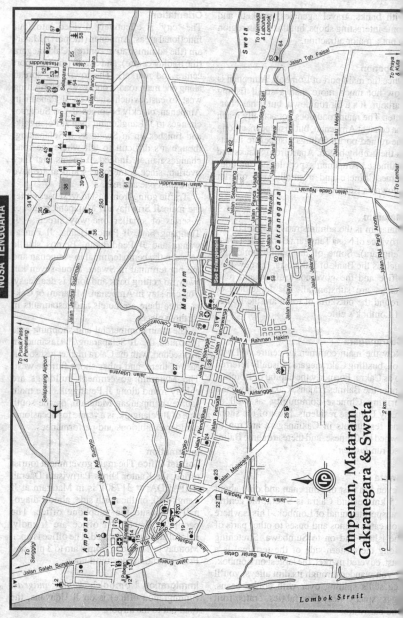

Ampenan, Mataram, Cakranegara & Sweta

PLACES TO STAY		31	Taman Griya Restaurant	26	GPO (Poste Restante)
7	Losmen Angi Mammire	34	Denny Bersaudra	27	Immigration Office
8	Losmen Wisma Triguna		Restaurant	28	Main Square
9	Losmen Horas	39	Friendship Cafe		(Lampangan
14	Hotel Zahir & Wisata	41	Aroma Chinese		Mataram)
	Hotel & Restaurant		Restaurant	29	Governor's Office
16	Nitour Hotel &	52	Rumah Makan Madya	30	Hospital
	Restaurant	53	KFC	33	Perama Office
32	Hotel Kertajoga	54	Sekawan Depot Es	35	Petrol Station
36	Hotel Granada			38	Cilinaya Shopping
37	Hotel Lombok Raya	**OTHER**			Centre
40	Oka Homestay	2	Pura Segara Temple	42	Rinjani Hand Woven
43	Selaparang Hotel	3	Antique Shops	49	Merpati Office
44	Mataram Hotel	4	Ampenan Market	50	Bank Ekspor-Impor
45	Hotel & Restaurant	5	Ampenan Bemo	51	Motorcycle Rental
	Shanti Puri		Terminal	55	Market
46	Losmen Ayu	6	Catholic Hospital	56	Selamat Riady Textile
47	Adiguna Homestay	11	Moneychangers		Factory
48	Astiti Guest House	15	Antique Shops	57	Mayura Water Palace
59	Graha Ayu	17	Tourist Office	58	Pura Meru Temple
60	Puri Indah Hotel	18	Wartel	61	Rungkang Jangkuk
		19	Post Office		Lombok Handicraft
PLACES TO EAT		20	Police		Centre
1	Pizzeria Cafe Alberto	21	Pelni Office	62	Petrol Station
10	Poppy Nice Cafe	22	Museum Negiri	63	Sweta Bus/Bemo
12	Rainbow Cafe	23	Lombok Pottery Centre		Terminal
13	Pabean & Cirebon	24	Mataram University	64	Sweta Market
	Restaurants	25	Petrol Station		

Money There are a number of banks along the main drag, all in large buildings. Most will change travellers cheques, although it can take some time. Moneychangers in Ampenan and in Mataram's Cilinaya shopping centre are efficient, open for longer hours and have similar rates. You can also change travellers cheques at the airport and, sometimes, at the Perama office.

Post Mataram's main post office, on Jl Srivijaya, has the only poste-restante service. It's open Monday to Thursday and on Saturday from 8 am to 2 pm and on Friday until 11 am. For other postal business, there's a more convenient post office opposite the tourist office.

Telephone The Telkom *wartel*, on Jl Langko, has telegram and fax services; it's open 24 hours daily. There's another wartel in the Cilinaya shopping centre in Cakra.

Travel Agency The Perama office (☎ 35936) is at Jl Pejanggik 66. The staff are very helpful and provide good information, organise shuttle bus connections, change money (unless they're out of cash), arrange day tours around Lombok, treks on Rinjani, and try to sell Land-Sea Adventure tours to Komodo and Flores. It's open daily from 6 am to 10 pm.

Museum Negeri
The Museum Negeri Nusa Tenggara Barat is on Jl Panji Tilar Negara in Ampenan. With exhibits on the geology, history and culture of Lombok and Sumbawa, it's well worth browsing around if you have a couple of free hours. If you intend buying any antiques or handcrafts, it might help to start by looking at the *krises* (daggers), textiles, basketware and masks here. The museum is open Tuesday to Sunday from 8 am to 4 pm. Admission is 200 rp (children 100 rp).

Mayura Water Palace
On the main road through Cakra, this 'palace' was built in 1744 and was once part of the royal court of the Balinese kingdom

NUSA TENGGARA

on Lombok. The centrepiece is a large artificial lake with an open-sided pavilion in the middle, connected to the shore by a raised footpath. This *bale kambang* (floating pavilion) was used both as a court of justice and as a meeting place for the Hindu lords. There are other shrines and fountains dotted around the surrounding park. The entrance to the walled enclosure of the palace is on the western side (entry 500 rp). Today the palace grounds are used for offerings and the occasional cockfight. It's a pleasant retreat from Cakra these days, but in 1894 this was the site of bloody battles as Dutch and Balinese forces fought over control of Lombok.

Pura Meru

Directly opposite the water palace, Pura Meru is the largest temple on Lombok, but it's nothing special to look at unless there is a festival on. It's open daily, and a donation is expected. It was built in 1720, under the patronage of the Balinese prince Anak Agung Made Karang of the Singosari kingdom, as an attempt to unite all the small kingdoms on Lombok. Intended as a symbol of the universe, the temple is dedicated to the Hindu trinity of Brahma, Vishnu and Shiva.

The outer courtyard has a hall with *kulkul* drums. In the middle courtyard are two buildings with large raised platforms for offerings. The inner courtyard has one large and 33 small shrines, as well as three *meru* (multi-roofed shrines). The three meru are in a line: the central one, with 11 tiers, is Shiva's house; the one in the north, with nine tiers, is Vishnu's; and the southern one, with seven tiers, is Brahma's. The meru are also said to represent the three great mountains Rinjani, Agung and Bromo.

Pura Segara

This Balinese sea temple is on the beach a few km north of Ampenan. Nearby are the remnants of a Muslim cemetery and an old Chinese cemetery which are worth a wander through if you're visiting the temple.

Places to Stay – bottom end

In Ampenan, only a short stroll from th centre, is *Hotel Zahir* (☎ 34248) at Jl Kc perasi 9. It's a straightforward place wit singles/doubles at 8000/10,000 rp, includin breakfast, and tea or coffee throughout th day. It's a long-standing Balinese-style los men, with rooms facing a central courtyarc The owners are friendly and helpful, and ca arrange cheap motorcycle rental.

Continue to Jl Koperasi 19, where the ne *Wisata Hotel & Restaurant* (☎ 26971) has choice of rooms from 12,000/15,000 t 35,000/40,000 rp – they're clean and com fortable, and the better ones have air-con, bu no character at all. Another few metres bring you to the basic *Losmen Horas* (☎ 31695 where rooms with Indonesian-style batl rooms go for 9000/12,500 rp. Continuin along this road you come to *Losmen Wism Triguna* (☎ 31705), a little over one km fron central Ampenan. It's a quiet, relaxed plac with spacious rooms opening on to a wid verandah and garden. Rooms cost fron 10,000/13,000 rp, including breakfast, an the people here have good information o climbing Gunung Rinjani. Nearby, *Losme Angi Mammire* (☎ 31713) has dark littl rooms, but it's OK, and one of the cheape places, at 6000/12,000 rp.

Even cheaper is *Losmen Pabean* (☎ 21758 at Jl Pabean 146 in the centre of Ampenar It's basic, but a bit better inside than it look from the outside, and only 5000/7500 rp fo rooms with shared mandi (Indonesian-styl bath).

In Mataram, *Hotel Kertajoga* (☎ 21775 at Jl Pejanggik 64, just west of the Peram office, is nothing special, but is good value Rooms are 15,000/18,500 rp with a fan o 20,500/25,500 rp with air-con.

In Cakranegara, south of the main dra and just north of Jl Panca Usaha, are number of Balinese-style losmen which ar good places to stay, despite an inordinat number of mosques within earshot. The *Ok Homestay* (☎ 22406) on Jl Repatmaja has quiet garden and rooms at 9000/12,000 rp including breakfast. *Astiti Guest Hous* (☎ 23670), further east on Jl Subak, ha ooms at around 10,000/12,000 rp, less with shared bathroom, to 35,000 rp with air-con. It's popular with surfers and the staff can help with transport information, rental cars etc.

The *Adiguna Homestay* (☎ 25946) on Jl Nursiwan is another good budget place with rooms from 9000/12,500 rp. The very friendly *Losmen Ayu* (☎ 21761), on the same street, has cheap rooms at about 9000 rp a double and a range of better rooms up to 20,000 rp with air-con. The price includes breakfast and there's a kitchen for guests to use. The bemos from Lembar come close to here; get off on Jl Gede Ngurah and walk west on Jl Panca Usaha, looking for sign boards at the ends of the streets.

In the same area, the *Hotel & Restaurant Shanti Puri* (☎ 32649) at Jl Maktal 15 is almost mid-range quality, with rooms from 15,000/20,000 rp; more expensive rooms are available with air-con and hot water. The management are helpful, and can arrange motorcycle and car hire.

Places to Stay – middle

At Jl Yos Sudarso 4 in Ampenan, *Nitour Motel & Restaurant* (☎ 23780; fax 36579) is quiet and comfortable, with carpets, air-con, telephone etc. 'Superior' rooms are US$30/35 and 'deluxe' rooms US$35/40, but there's a discount of up to 30% at quiet times.

The heavily advertised *Hotel Granada* (☎ 36015) is on Jl Bung Karno, south of the shopping centre in Mataram. There's a swimming pool and all rooms have air-con. It has vaguely Iberian architecture and a depressing caged menagerie. The prices include breakfast and start at 64,500 rp a double plus 10% tax; ask for a low-season discount.

If you want this kind of comfort, the *Puri Indah Hotel* (☎ 37633) on Jl Sriwijaya, Cakanegara, also has a restaurant and a pool, but is much better value at 25,000 rp or 35,000 rp with air-con. It's very clean and well run. The nearby *Graha Ayu* has rooms from 40,000 rp with all mod cons, but doesn't look very appealing.

There are quite a few good-value, mid-

range places in Cakra. The *Selaparang Hotel* (☎ 32670), Jl Pejanggik 40-42, has reasonably sized air-con rooms for 42,500/47,500 rp and fan-cooled rooms for about half the price. Across the road at No 105 is the *Mataram Hotel* (☎ 23411), with a small pool and standard double rooms at 25,000 rp; rooms with air-con, TV and hot water cost up to 50,000 rp. Both have pleasant little restaurants.

Places to Stay – top end

The new *Hotel Lombok Raya* (☎ 32305; fax 36478), Jl Panca Usaha 11 in Mataram, is the only real top-end place, with attractively furnished, fully equipped rooms, conference facilities and a big swimming pool. With rooms from US$50/55, it's pretty good value compared with equivalent three star places on Bali.

Places to Eat

Ampenan Ampenan has several Indonesian and Chinese restaurants, including the popular *Cirebon* at Jl Yos Sudarso 113, with a standard Indonesian/Chinese menu and most dishes from around 3000 rp. Next door is the *Pabean*, with similar food and prices. A little further west is *Rainbow Cafe*, an inexpensive, friendly little place with reggae-inspired decor, a few books, cold beer and OK food. Around the corner, *Rumah Makan Arafat* at Jl Saleh Sungkar 23 has good, cheap Indonesian food and some Middle Eastern dishes. Close to some of the budget accommodation, *Poppy Nice Cafe* on Jl Koperasi is as appealing as its name, with a good range of well-prepared dishes and very hospitable management. *Timur Tengah* at Jl Koperasi 22, right across from the Hotel Zahir, is popular, but closed on Sunday and during Ramadan.

Mataram *Taman Griya* is a pleasant open-air place in a small shopping area by Jl Pejanggik, opposite the hospital. It has very tasty nasi campur, nasi goreng and other standard meals (from 4000 to 6000 rp), as well as home made ice cream. *Denny Bersaudra* on Jl Pelikan, just north of the main road, is famous for Sasak dishes like ayam goreng taliwang – chicken with hot chilli sauce.

Cakranegara In Cakra, handy to the cheap losmen, are the *Friendship Cafe*, on Jl Panca Usaha, and *Aroma*, inconspicuously located on a side street next to the Mataram Hotel off Jl Selaparang. They're cheap Chinese places with stir fried meat and/or vegetable dishes from 3000 to 4000 rp. On the Jl Pejanggik/Jl Selaparang shopping strip is a conspicuous *KFC*, popular with affluent locals, and the more traditional *Sekawan Depot Es*, with cold drinks downstairs and a seafood and Chinese restaurant upstairs. Around the corner on Jl Hasanuddin, *Rumah Makan Madya* serves good, cheap Sasak food. There some bakeries nearby and plenty of food stalls at the market.

Elsewhere North of Ampenan, on the road to Senggigi, the upmarket *Flamboyan Restaurant* is good for Indonesian and seafood, while the *Pizzeria Cafe Alberto* (☎ 36781) offers authentic cucina Italiana – it has a pick-up service.

Things to Buy
Handcrafts & Antiques Two areas in Ampenan have a good selection of handcraft shops and are interesting to browse around. Look on and around the west side of Jl Saleh Sungkar (the road north to Senggigi) for shops like Hery Antiques, Sudirman Antiques, Fancy Art and Musdah. Just north of the bridge, Gang Sunda goes east off Jl Yos Sudarso and has several art-craft-antique shops, including Rora Antiques (with some excellent inlaid wooden boxes, carvings, baskets and traditional Lombok weavings), Renza Antiques and Preti.

Rungkang Jangkuk, the Lombok Handicraft Centre, at Sayang Sayang north of Cakra, has a number of shops with a good selection of crafts from Lombok and elsewhere. An excellent place to look for local products is the Sweta market, next to the Sweta bemo terminal.

Pottery The Lombok Pottery Centre at Jl Majapahit 7 in Ampenan displays and sells good range of Lombok's distinctive hand made earthenware.

Textiles At workshops in Cakranegara yo can see ikat fabric being woven on ancien hand-and-foot powered looms. They'r amazing contraptions, but the complex proc ess of resist dyeing the unwoven thread i even more interesting. Ikat fabric, i mercerised cotton, costs 16,000 to 22,000 r per metre (1200 mm wide), depending on th quality. In silk it's 45,000 to 60,000 rp pe metre. The Selamat Riady factory on J Tanun (a back street east of Jl Hasanuddin is open most mornings, and has a shop wit textiles and a few other crafts. Rinjani Han Woven at Jl Pejanggik 44-46, beside th Selaparang Hotel, has a good range of fab rics, which staff will make into shirts, dresse or cushion covers.

Getting There & Away
Air See the introductory Getting There & Away entry in this section for addresses o airlines serving Lombok.

Bus & Bemo Sweta has the main termina for the island. It's also the eastern termina for the local bemos which shuttle back an forth to Ampenan. The latest official fare should be posted on a notice board near the office in the middle of the terminal, but the following should be accurate within a few hundred rupiah:

Destination	Price (rp)
East (Jurusan Timor)	
Narmada (6 km)	300
Mantang (17 km)	800
Kopang (25 km)	1000
Terara (29 km)	1200
Sikur (33 km)	1100
Pomotong (34 km)	1300
Masbagik (36 km)	1200
Selong (47 km)	2000
Labuhan Haji (57 km)	2200
Labuhan Lombok (69 km)	2500

uth & Central (Jurusan Selatan & Tenggara)

ediri (5 km)	500
mbar (22 km)	700
aya (27 km)	700
ujur (36 km)	1000
uta (54 km)	1500

orth (Jurusan Utara)

nggigi (12 km)	600
menang (31 km)	900
njung (45 km)	1100
ayan (79 km)	2300

he terminal at Ampenan is for local bemos
nd those going up the coast to Senggigi
50 rp).

ar & Motorcycle Some hotels can arrange
ar rental. Metro Rent Car (☎ 32146) at Jl
os Sudarso, Ampenan, rents Suzuki Jimnys
or 45,000 rp per day, including insurance,
ith a US$250 excess. If you rent for more
an three days, it's 40,000 rp per day. Rin-
ni Rent Car (☎ 32259) on Jl Bung Karno
Mataram, opposite the Hotel Granada,
uoted slightly higher rates, but may be
orth checking.

Hotels might also arrange motorcycle
ntal, which can be a pretty informal ar-
ngement. Lots of motorcycle owners hang
ound Jl Gelantik, off Jl Selaparang near the
nction with Jl Hasanuddin, at the Cak-
negara end of Mataram. They rent bikes
ivately for around 15,000 rp for one day,
r maybe 12,500 rp per day for a week.
here's no insurance and they want your
assport for security. Check any bike care-
lly before taking it.

oat The ferry docks at Lembar, 22 km
uth of Ampenan (see the Lembar entry for
etails). The Bali ferry office is at Jl Pe-
nggik 49 in Mataram. The *Mabua Express*
ffice (☎ 81195) is in Lembar. The office of
elni, the national shipping line, is at Jl
dustri 1 in Ampenan (☎ 37212).

etting Around

he Airport Lombok's Selaparang airport is
nly a couple of km from Ampenan. Taxis
om there cost about 7000 rp to Ampenan,

Mataram, Cakra and Sweta; 10,000 rp to
Senggigi; and 22,000 rp to Bangsal. Air-con
taxis are 7500, 12,000 and 26,000 rp respectively. Alternatively, you can walk out of the
airport carpark to the main road and take one
of the frequent No 7 bemos which run
straight to the Ampenan bemo terminal for
300 rp.

Bemo Yellow bemos shuttle back and forth
along the main route between the Ampenan
terminal at one end and the Sweta terminal
at the other. From Sweta, routes D, E and F
all go to Ampenan. The fare is a standard 300
rp regardless of the distance. The bemo terminal in Ampenan is a good place to charter
a bemo.

Bicycle You can rent good bicycles from the
Cirebon Restaurant in Ampenan for about
5000 rp per day.

GUNUNG PENGSONG

This Balinese temple is built, as the name
suggests, on top of a hill. It's nine km south
of Mataram and has great views of rice fields,
the volcanoes and the sea. Try to get there
early in the morning, before the clouds
envelop Gunung Rinjani. Once a year, generally in March or April, a buffalo is taken
up the steep, 100m slope and sacrificed to
celebrate a good harvest. The Bersih Desa
festival also occurs here at harvest time –
houses and gardens are cleaned, fences are
whitewashed, and roads and paths are
repaired. Once part of a ritual to rid the
village of evil spirits, it is now held in honour
of the rice goddess, Dewi Sri. There's no set
admission charge, but you will have to pay
the caretaker 300 rp or so, especially if you
use the carpark.

BANYUMULEK

This is one of the main pottery centres of
Lombok. It's close to Mataram, a couple of
km from the Sweta-Lembar road, and is easy
to combine with a visit to Gunung Pensong.

LEMBAR

Lembar, 22 km south of Ampenan, is the

main port on Lombok. The ferries to and from Bali dock here, as does the *Mabua Express*. There's a canteen at the harbour where you can buy snacks and drinks while waiting for the ferry. The only place to stay, the *Serumbung Indah* (☎ 37153) has rooms from around 15,000 rp and a restaurant, but it's not very convenient, being about two km north of the harbour on the main road.

Getting There & Away
Bemo In theory, you should be able to get a bemo from Lembar to Sweta for about 700 rp; in practice, they will try to get you on a special charter bemo or manage to charge you more – maybe 3000 rp. Get out of the port area and catch a bemo on the main road. Minibuses from the hotels in town sometimes meet the ferry.

Taxi There are set fares for taxis to Mataram – about 20,000 rp with two people.

Boat There are ferries to Padangbai (Bali) at 2, 4, 6, 8 and 10 am, noon, 2, 4, 6, 8 and 10 pm. Sometimes they leave later, or even earlier, than the scheduled times. *Ekonomi* costs 5500 rp (2900 rp for children) and 1st class is 9000 rp (5000 rp for children).

The *Mabua Express* high-speed catamaran leaves Lembar at 10.30 am and 5 pm, and takes about 2½ hours to reach Benoa Port on Bali. The fare is US$13.50 in ekonomi, US$20 in 'Emerald Class' and US$27.50 for 'Diamond Class' (children half-price; surfboard 5000 rp; bicycle 20,000 rp). The price should include transport from Mataram, Senggigi or Bangsal, while the more expensive tickets include onward transport to Kuta, Sanur or Nusa Dua. For the latest details, telephone Mabua's office on Bali (☎ (0361) 72370, 72521) or on Lombok (☎ 81195).

SOUTH-WESTERN PENINSULA
A rough road goes via Sekotong and Taun to Lombok's undeveloped south-western peninsula. Near **Taun**, *Sekotong Indah Beach Cottages* provides comfortable, isolated beachside accommodation. Rooms cost

10,000/15,000 to 25,000/30,000 rp. There no phone here, but you can call a Senggig number (☎ 93040) for bookings. At the en of the road you'll reach **Bangko Bangk** and the famous surf break, **Desert Point**, bu there's no accommodation there.

Two groups of picturesque islands off th north coast of the peninsula can be reache by chartered boat from Lembar for aroun 25,000 rp and from Taun for a little less. Th only tourist accommodation is on **Gili Nan gu**, where *Istana Cempaka* charges aroun 30,000 rp per person, including all meal Enquiries and bookings can be made b phoning a Cakra number (☎ 22898).

SENGGIGI
On a series of sweeping bays between thre and 12 km north of Ampenan, Senggigi is th most developed tourist area on Lombok. A the tourist facilities are here, plus a range c top-end and mid-range accommodation, an some budget places too. There's been a lot c new building in the last couple of years an it shows – landscaping should soften th appearance of the place soon. The mos attractive areas at the moment are the isc lated groups of bungalows north of th central strip.

Senggigi has fine beaches, although the slope very steeply into the water. There some snorkelling off the point and in th sheltered bay around the headland. Th beautiful sunsets over Lombok Strait can b enjoyed from the beach or from one of th beachfront restaurants. As darkness come the lights of the fishing boats look like a littl city just offshore. Later on, there's som nightlife going on at Senggigi and it can b good fun.

Orientation
The area known as Senggigi is spread ou along nearly 10 km of coastal road. Most c the shops, travel agencies and other facil ties, and most of the accommodation, are o the stretch of road near the Senggigi Beac Hotel, about six km north of Ampenan.

NUSA TENGGARA

Senggigi

Senggigi Beach

PLACES TO STAY
1 Hotel Nusa Bunga
2 Windy Cottages
3 Holiday Inn Resort
4 Pondok Damai
5 Hotel Puri Mas
6 Santai Cottages
7 Blue Ocean
9 Bale Kampung
10 Puri Saron
11 Pacific Beach Cottages
12 Sheraton Villas
13 Sheraton Senggigi Beach
14 Puri Bunga Cottages
18 Pondok Sinta Cottages
19 Sonya Homestay
25 Lombok Intan Laguna
27 Hotel Senggigi
   Aerowisata
   (Senggigi Beach
   Hotel)
28 Mascot Berugaq Elen
   Cottages
34 Astiti Guesthouse
35 Pondok Wisata Rinjani
38 Bukit Senggigi
40 Pondok Sederhana
41 Dharma Hotel

42 Lina Cottages
   & Restaurant
46 Graha Beach Hotel
48 Pantai Indah Senggigi
49 Pondok Senggigi
50 Bumi Aditya
51 Pondok Melati Dua
52 Sahid Tamara Resort
   Hotel (Under
   Construction)
55 Batu Bolong Cottages
59 Siti Hawa
61 Atitha Sangraha
62 Pondok Asri

PLACES TO EAT
8 Alang Alang
23 Princess of Lombok
   Pub & Restaurant
26 Gossip Cafe
30 Restaurant & Cafe
   Lombok
33 Arlina Restaurant
43 Sunshine Restaurant
53 Dynasty Restaurant
   & Bar
56 Cafe Wayan

OTHER
15 Telkom Wartel
16 Police
17 Pasar Seni Art
   Market
20 Galleria Shopping
   Centre
21 Pacific Supermarket
22 Ketak Gallery
24 Post Office
29 Kotasi Transport
   Co-Operative
31 Malibu Pub
32 Hero Photo
36 Nazareth Tours
   & Travel
37 Lombok Pub
39 Perama Office
44 Banana Club
45 Wartel
47 Marina Pub
54 Selaparang
   Art Shop
57 Batu Bolong
   Temple
58 Muslim Cemetery
60 Surga Rent Car &
   Motorcycle

To Bangsal & Pemenang
Mangset
Lombok Strait
Lombok Strait
See Enlargement
Batu Bolong
To Hotel Jayakarta & Ampenan

Information

Kotasi, the local transport co-operative, has an office on the side road to the Senggigi Beach Hotel, which is useful mainly for transport information. There's a private wartel and a postal agent on the main street, along with several moneychangers. You can also change money and travellers cheques at most of the big hotels, if they have the cash.

You can make bookings and reconfirm flights for Garuda and Merpati at a number of travel agents, such as Nazareth Tours & Travel (☎ 93033). The Perama office (☎ 93-007/8/9), a bit further south runs tours, tourist shuttle buses, and will also provide information and change money. Other facilities include the supermarket, a Telkom wartel and some photo-processing places.

Batu Bolong Temple

This temple is on a rocky point which juts into the sea about a km south of Senggigi Beach, five km north of Ampenan. The rock on which it sits has a natural hole, giving the temple its name (which literally means 'rock with hole'). Being a Balinese temple, it's oriented towards Gunung Agung, Bali's holiest mountain, across the Lombok Strait. Legend has it that beautiful virgins were once thrown into the sea from the top of the rock. Locals like to claim that this is why there are so many sharks in the water here.

Places to Stay – bottom end

There are a few low-budget places, but expect steep price hikes in the busy tourist season. *Pondok Senggigi* (☎ 93273) advertises rooms at 20,000 rp, but most of them cost from US$15/20 for singles/doubles, plus 15.5% for tax and service. Rooms face an attractive garden, and there's a new pool and a popular restaurant. *Pondok Sederhana* (☎ 93040), a little to the north-west, has good rooms, some with views, for 20,000/25,000 rp. On the beach side of the road, *Lina Cottages* (☎ 93237) is central, friendly and good value at 25,000/35,000 rp, and its restaurant has a good reputation. Its neighbor, the *Dharma Hotel* has rooms and cottages in an open field by the beach for 20,000 / 30,000 rp.

Bumi Aditya, on a grassy slope up behind Pondok Melati Dua, has small, clean and somehow appealing bamboo bungalows from 10,000 to 15,000 rp. *Astiti Guesthouse*, behind Pondok Wisata Rinjani, is less spacious, with ordinary rooms around a small courtyard for 10,000/15,000 rp; friendly local guys hang around here.

Further up the main road, on the left *Sonya Homestay* (☎ 63447) is a basic friendly, family-run losmen with small rooms for 10,000/12,000 rp. Close by, *Pondok Sinta Cottages* are the same price, in slightly more spacious surroundings.

A couple of km further (100 rp by bemo and off to the east in Kampung Krandangan *Bale Kampung* is billed as a backpacker place. It has dorm beds for 6000 rp and rooms for 10,000 and 12,000 rp. It serves cheap food, and has good information about local attractions. Well south of the Senggigi strip, *Siti Hawa* (☎ 93414) is a funky little family-run homestay fronting a fantastic beach. A few, very small, very basic bamboo cottages cost 9000/10,000 rp.

Places to Stay – middle

Coming in from Ampenan, before you hit the main Senggigi strip, are some mid-range places like *Pondok Asri* (☎ 93075) and *Atitha Sangraha* (☎ 93070). They both have cottages that are clean, comfortable and near the beach, but they're nothing special and you'll need transport to Senggigi's facilities and restaurants. Prices start at about 25,000 rp in the low season, considerably more around August.

Much closer to the action, *Batu Bolong Cottages* (☎ 93065) has spacious, well-finished bungalows on both sides of the road from 35,000 to 40,000 rp, including tax which is pretty good value.

On the right as you enter central Senggigi *Pondok Melati Dua* (☎ 93288) has standard cottages at 30,000 rp and better bungalows from 40,000 to 60,000 rp, including tax and breakfast. It's a short walk to the beach, and is generally an OK place. The *Graha Beach lotel* (☎ 93101; fax 93400) has a good central beachside location, but the rooms are small; they cost from US$40/45 (US$5 more for an ocean view), with air-con, phone and TV.

On the side road to the Senggigi Beach Hotel, the *Mascot Berugaq Elen Cottages* (☎ 93365; fax 22314) offers pleasant individual bungalows from US$35 to US$40, plus 21% tax. They have air-con, hot water, and phone, but the best feature is the quiet garden setting which extends to the beach.

At the northern end of Senggigi, *Pacific Beach Cottages* (☎ 93006; fax 93027) has all the standard luxuries – air-con, TV, hot water, swimming pool – but no character at all. Rooms cost US$35 to US$55, plus tax, excluding a discount. The nearby *Puri Saron* (☎ 93424) has the same facilities and asks US$55/65 for unbelievably ordinary rooms.

Further north in Mangset, *Santai Cottages* (☎ 93038) has a family atmosphere, a lush garden and a beachside location. Traditional meals are served in a pleasant pavilion – it's a very peaceful retreat. Most of the cottages cost around 30,000 rp, but there are some cheaper rooms. Next door, the small but stylish *Hotel Puri Mas* (☎ 93023) has attractively decorated bungalows surrounded by trees and shrubs, a pretty pool and a wide range of prices – from 40,000 to 250,000 rp.

Another great place to get away is *Windy Cottages* (☎ 93191), out by itself in spacious grounds five km north of Senggigi. It charges 35,000 to 45,000 rp, and the restaurant has excellent food. Perama will pick up and drop off here on request.

Places to Stay – top end

Senggigi has several luxury hotels, though none of them are well patronised outside the high season. They all add 21% tax and service to their published prices.

Coming north from Ampenan, *Hotel Jayakarta* (formerly the Senggigi Palace Hotel; ☎ 93045; fax 93043) is the first place you'll see. The lobby is massive, but the rooms are plain and clean (sterile?), and cost US$60/70 or US$75/85 with an ocean view.

The first big 'international standard' hotel to be built here, the *Senggigi Beach Hotel* (☎ 93210; fax 93200) is now officially the Hotel Senggigi Aerowisata, but it's usually known by the original name. It has a beautiful garden, tennis courts, swimming pool and other mod cons. Rooms cost US$110 to US$180, or US$550 for the presidential suite. At least as classy is the *Lombok Intan Laguna* (☎ 93090; fax 93185), a large and handsome luxury hotel with a big pool and rooms from US$100/110 and suites from US$250.

Bukit Senggigi (☎ 93173) is a new place on the inland side of the road in central Senggigi, with motel-like rooms staggered up a hillside from US$65/70 (discounted to US$45 or US$50). There's a swimming pool, disco and karaoke lounge – none of them is crowded. A similar, but older, place is *Puri Bunga Cottages* (☎ 93013; fax 93286), also on a hillside on the inland side of the road, with even better views and a lot more character. The published rate is US$60/65, but it discounts to US$35 which makes it reasonable value.

Further north, the *Sheraton Senggigi Beach* (☎ 93333; fax 93140) is the best hotel in Senggigi and the most expensive, with rooms from US$125 to US$170, or US$900 for a suite. Look for the local handcrafts decorating the rooms and public areas; it's all very tasteful, and the pool and gardens are lovely. There's a children's pool and playground, and special family packages.

A new international hotel is the *Holiday Inn Resort* (☎ 93444; fax 93092), which offers all the four star comforts from US$140 to US$450, and may discount 50% in the low season.

Continuing north along the coast, some small, upmarket places offer more character and style. A good one is *Hotel Nusa Bunga* (formerly Bunga Beach Cottages; ☎ 93035), with a splendid beachfront position, a pool and 28 comfortable, air-con bungalows from US$45/50 to US$55/60. *Lombok Dame Indah* (☎ 93246; fax 93248) has good views, and is heavily decorated with Indonesian artefacts. Rooms cost US$140. The new *Hilberon* (☎ 93898; fax 93252), in the Balinese beach bungalow style, has a big pool, and spacious, spotless rooms from US$120.

Places to Eat

You can eat pretty well in Senggigi for a reasonable price, but there's not much at the bottom end of the scale, except for a few food carts down near the beach.

The restaurant at *Pondok Senggigi* is no longer cheap (nasi goreng is around 3000 rp), but it's still popular from breakfast time until late at night, with a convivial dining area and a wide selection of western and Indonesian food.

The restaurant at *Lina Cottages* is also popular, with a big menu and a great location by the beach, and it's a little cheaper. Nearby, the *Sunshine Restaurant* has excellent, slightly westernised Chinese dishes (around 5000 rp) and some seafood specials (9000 rp). *Arlina Restaurant* is also central, OK and reasonably priced. In the art market, *Kafe Alberto* serves pasta, pizza, and barbecued seafood which is a bit better, and a bit pricier, than the standard tourist fare.

The slightly upmarket *Cafe Wayan* (☎ 93-098), south of central Senggigi, is related to the excellent Cafe Wayan in Ubud – the famous, fantastic chicken curry costs 7500 rp, while the home-made bread and yummy desserts are also highlights. Almost in Ampenan, *Pizzeria Cafe Alberto* (☎ 36781) has the most authentic Italian food around, though it's not cheap. Both these places will pick up in the Senggigi area if you call first.

Beachside dining is a Senggigi speciality – try it in the evening at the *Graha Beach Hotel* or *Alang Alang*.

Entertainment

Pondok Senggigi, *Banana Club* and the *Marina Pub* have live music on occasions, with local bands doing good rock and reggae music with an Indonesian flavour. In the busy season, they can all get crowded with tourists and young locals, but at other times only one of them will have any action. A couple of the pubs can be quite sociable – try the *Lombok Pub* or the *Princess of Lombok*.

Getting There & Away

A public bemo to Senggigi is about 450 r from Ampenan and 600 rp from Sweta. Fror the airport, first get a bemo to Ampena terminal (300 rp), then another to Senggig A taxi from the airport to Senggigi is 10,00 rp. To charter a bemo, go to the transpor co-operative (Kotasi) on the side road to th Senggigi Beach Hotel. It can also arrange ca rental.

Perama has good connections from Seng gigi to all tourist centres on Bali and Lombok Lombok Independent (☎ 93447) has simila fares. Most transport to Bangsal will go vi Ampenan rather than going straight up th coast road.

Sunshine Tours (☎ 93029) can arrange boat transfer from Senggigi direct to Gil Trawangan for 7500 rp, but can't take pas sengers in the other direction.

NARMADA

Laid out as a miniature replica of the summi of Gunung Rinjani and its crater lake Narmada is a hill about 10 km east of Cakra on the main east-west road crossing Lom bok. The temple, **Pura Kalasa**, is still used and the Balinese Pujawali celebration is helc here every year in honour of the god Batara who dwells on Gunung Rinjani.

Narmada was constructed in 1805 by the king of Mataram, when he was no longer able to climb Rinjani to make his offerings to the gods. Having set his conscience at res by placing offerings in the temple, he spen at least some of his time in his pavilion or the hill, lusting after the young girls bathing in the artificial lake. Along one side of the pool are the remains of an aqueduct built by the Dutch and still in use.

It's a beautiful place to spend a few hours, but it can get crowded on weekends. Apart from the lake, there are two other pools in the grounds. Admission is 500 rp and there's an additional charge for swimming.

Places to Eat

Right at the Narmada bemo terminal is the local market, which sells mainly food and clothing; it's well worth a look. There are a umber of *warungs* (food stalls) scattered round, offering soto ayam (chicken and egetable broth) and other dishes.

Getting There & Away

There are frequent bemos from Sweta to Narmada (300 rp). Get off at the Narmada bemo terminal and you'll see the gardens directly opposite.

LINGSAR

This large temple complex, just a few km north of Narmada, is said to have been built in 1714 for both the Bali Hindu and Wektu Telu religions. The Hindu *pura* (temple) is in the northern section, a little higher than the Wektu Telu temple in the southern section.

The Hindu temple has four shrines. On one side is Hyang Tunggal, which looks towards Gunung Agung, the seat of the gods on Bali. The shrine faces north-west, rather than north-east as it would on Bali. On the other side is a shrine devoted to Gunung Rinjani, the seat of the gods on Lombok. Between these two shrines is a double shrine symbolising the union between the two islands. One side of this double shrine is named in honour of the might of Lombok; the other side is dedicated to a king's daughter, Ayu Nyoman Winton, who, according to legend, gave birth to a god.

The Wektu Telu temple is noted for its small, enclosed pond which has a number of holy eels. They look like huge swimming slugs and can be enticed from their hiding places by the use of hard-boiled eggs as bait. The stalls outside the temple complex sell boiled eggs, but be there early to see the eels, because they've had their fill of eggs after the first few tour groups. Next to the eel pond is another enclosure, with a large altar or offering place bedecked in white and yellow cloth and mirrors. The mirrors are offerings from Chinese businesspeople asking for good luck and success. Many local farmers also come here with offerings.

At the annual rain festival, held at the start of the wet season (somewhere between October and December), the Hindus and the Wektu Telus make offerings and pray in their own temples, then come out into the communal compound and pelt each other with *ketupat* (rice wrapped in banana leaves). The ceremony is to bring the rain or to give thanks for the rain. Be prepared to get attacked with ketupat from both sides if you visit Lingsar at this time!

Getting There & Away

Lingsar is off the main road. Take a bemo from Sweta to Narmada (300 rp), then catch another to Lingsar village (also 300 rp) and walk the short distance from there to the temple complex. It's easy to miss the temple, which is set back off the road behind the school.

SURANADI

A few km east of Lingsar, Suranadi has one of the holiest temples on Lombok. This small temple, set in pleasant gardens, is noted for its bubbling, icy cold spring water and restored baths with ornate Balinese carvings. The eels here are also sacred and seldom underfed – how many hard-boiled eggs can an eel eat?

You can stop for a swim in the refreshingly cool pool at the hotel (1500 rp, children 800 rp).

Nearby, the small **forest sanctuary**, Hutan Wisata Suranadi *(hutan* means 'forest' or 'jungle'), is sadly neglected. Entry costs 1000 rp.

Places to Stay & Eat

The *Suranadi Hotel* (☎ 33686) has rooms and cottages which are overpriced at US$25 to US$50, but it may give a discount. It's an old Dutch building, but no great example of colonial architecture. There are two swimming pools and tennis courts. Close by, *Pondok Surya* has basic rooms, a nice outlook and excellent food. It's a casual, friendly place and cheap at 15,000 rp per person, including three meals – ask at the warungs to find it.

SESAOT

About five km north of Suranadi, Sesaot is a small, quiet market town on the edge of the forest. Go up the main street and turn left over the bridge, where there's a nice picnic spot and a swimming hole. The water is very cool and is considered holy, as it comes straight from Gunung Rinjani. Another three km up the road is **Air Nyet**, a small village with more places for swimming and picnics.

CENTRAL LOMBOK

Central Lombok, or Lombok Tengah, is the name of one of the three administrative districts (*kabupaten*) on Lombok, but for this section the term is used more generally to cover the inland towns and villages in the rich agricultural area south of Gunung Rinjani. The area is well watered and lush, and offers opportunities for scenic walks through the rice fields and the jungle. Many of the villages specialise in particular handcrafts.

Kotaraja

Kotaraja means 'City of kings', although no kings ruled from here, and it's hardly a city. Apparently, when the Sasak kingdom of Langko (based at Kopang) fell to the Balinese invaders, the rulers of Langko fled to Loyok, the village south of Kotaraja. After the royal compound in that village was also destroyed, two of the ruler's sons went to live in Kotaraja.

Kotaraja sits at a road junction and is the central village of the area, though there's no accommodation here. Various villages around are noted for blacksmithing and basketware. Traditional blacksmiths still use an open hearth and human-powered bellows, but old car springs are the favoured 'raw material' for knives, farm implements and other tools.

Getting There & Away By public transport from Sweta, go first to Pomotong (1300 rp), perhaps via Narmada, then take a bemo or cidomo to Kotaraja (400 rp). If you're staying in Tetebatu or Lendang Nangka, you can take a cidomo, or walk, to Kotaraja. With

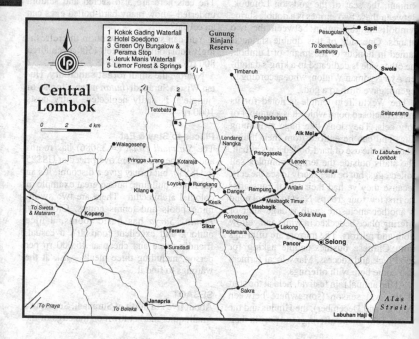

Central Lombok

1 Kokok Gading Waterfall
2 Hotel Soedjono
3 Green Ory Bungalow & Perama Stop
4 Jeruk Manis Waterfall
5 Lemor Forest & Springs

Gunung Rinjani Reserve

To Sembalun Bumbung

Pesugulan — Sapit

Swela

Selaparang

Timbanuh

Tetebatu

Pengadangan

Aik Mel

To Labuhan Lombok

Walageseng

Lendang Nangka

Pringgasela

Lenek

Surabaya

Pringga Jurang

Kotaraja

Loyok — Rungkang

Danger

Rempung

Anjani

Kilang

Kesik

Masbagik Timur

Masbagik

To Sweta & Mataram

Kopang

Pomotong

Suka Mulya

Terara

Sikur

Padamara

Lekong

Suradadi

Pancor — Selong

To Praya

Janapria

Sakra

To Beleka

Labuhan Haji

Alas Strait

our own transport you can easily make a day trip from the capital, but it's worth staying a few days.

etebatu

A mountain retreat at the foot of Gunung Rinjani, Tetebatu is 50 km from Mataram and about 10 km north of the main east-west road. It's quite a bit cooler here and it can be misty and rainy, particularly between November and April.

There are magnificent views and pleasant walks to waterfalls and forests, where lots of jet-black monkeys will shriek at you.

Places to Stay & Eat The original accommodation here is *Soedjono Hotel* (☎ 22159), an old colonial house. Extra rooms and bungalows have been added, and there is a restaurant and a swimming pool. The simplest rooms are rice-barn bungalows for 5,000 rp, while the best rooms are 45,000 and have hot water. The restaurant is quite good and will make a packed lunch.

A crop of inexpensive places is sprouting in the lovely rice fields around Tetebatu. One such place is *Diwi Enjeni* on the south side of town with a nice outlook. Bungalows cost 000/10,000 rp, including breakfast, and there's a small restaurant. *Pondok Tetebatu* is nearby, with cheap rooms at a similar price and much better ones for 8000/12,000 rp. *Mekar Sari* is next door, in a nice location back from the road.

Turn east in Tetebatu along a winding road where there are several new, simple but attractive options. *Green Ory* bungalows costs 12,000/15,000 rp in the low season, and there is a bigger cottage which could sleep several people. Further east is *Pondok Bulan*, with small, cute bungalows for 8000/10,000 rp. Opposite, *Cendrawasi Cottages* is very classy for this area, with an open, upstairs eating area and pleasant rooms for only 12,500/16,500 rp in the low season, which is still good value at the August price of 25,000 rp.

A few more bends bring you to *Hakiki*, with a fine rice field view and double rooms from 12,000 to 15,000 rp. In the next village,

turn right down a dirt track to *Rambutan Garden*, where small cottages for 6000/10,000 rp are nicely spaced in a garden of rambutan trees. It's another peaceful place to stay.

Getting There & Away From Kotaraja, it's just a couple of km up the road to Tetebatu by infrequent bemo, cidomo, *ojek* (motorcycle taxi) or on foot. Perama has one shuttle bus a day to Tetebatu (7500 rp from Mataram).

Loyok

This tiny village, just a few km from Kotaraja, is noted for its basketware and weaving with natural fibres. A handcraft centre has some local products on display, but most of the work is done in family homes.

To get to Loyok, go first to Pomotong, on the main road, then get a bemo to far as Rungkang, the turn-off to the village. From here you can walk the last km or get a cidomo.

Rungkang

Another small village, less than one km east of Loyok, is also known for pottery which is made from a local black clay. The pots are often finished with attractive cane work, which is woven all over the outside for decoration and for greater strength.

Masbagik

Quite a large town on the main road at the turn-off to Selong, Masbagik has a market on Monday morning and a cultural festival every September. There's a post office and a Telkom wartel here. Masbagik Timur, a km or so to the east, is one of the centres for production of pottery and ceramics. A bemo from Sweta to Masbagik (36 km) costs around 1200 rp.

Lendang Nangka

This Sasak village is surrounded by picturesque countryside and has small roads and friendly people. In and around the village you can see blacksmiths who still make knives, hoes and other tools using traditional techniques. Silversmiths also work here.

Lendang Nangka

Jojang, the biggest freshwater spring in Lombok, is a few km away, or you can walk to the gorgeous **Jeruk Manis Waterfall** and look for black monkeys in the nearby forests.

In August you should be able to see traditional Sasak stick fighting at Lendang Nangka. Traditional dances are sometimes performed in the area, but they're not scheduled events – ask at your losmen and you might be lucky.

Hadji Radiah is a local primary school teacher who has been encouraging people to stay in Lendang Nangka. Since Radiah originally wrote to us about the first edition of the *Bali & Lombok* guidebook, his family homestay has become popular among travellers who want an experience of typical Lombok village life. He speaks English very well, and he will often take visitors on a guided walk through the fields, describing and explaining the local crops, agriculture and customs. His family is very hospitable; they have a map showing interesting features in the area and can suggest various walks and day trips.

Places to Stay & Eat *Radiah's Homestay* will cost about 10,000/15,000 rp for a basic single/double or 20,000/25,000 rp in one of the bigger rooms. These prices include breakfast, a good lunch and a communal dinner of authentic Sasak food. Note that this is a Muslim household and alcohol is not available. It's not luxurious, but it's good value and highly recommended. His house is fairly easy to find (see the Lengdang Nangka map, but everyone knows him).

A couple of other places on the outskirts of Lendang Nangka have a more rural setting, but aren't quite as culturally rewarding as Radiah's. About 200m west of town *Pondok Wira* is a friendly place and has nice barn-style rooms, some with views, for 10,000/15,000 rp, including three meals. About 400m north of the crossroads, on a small side track, *Pondok Bambu* is beautifully situated, has a helpful owner and a few simple bamboo bungalows for 15,000/25,000 rp, including three home-cooked Sasak meals.

Getting There & Away Take a bemo from Sweta to Masbagik (1200 rp; 36 km) and then take a cidomo to Lendang Nangka (about four km), which should cost 400 rp per person (but the driver will want at least three passengers) or 1200 rp for the whole cart.

Pringgasela

This village is a centre for traditional weaving of sarongs and blankets, done on simple backstrap looms. The material made here features beautifully coloured stripes running the length of the cloth, with decorative details woven into the weft. You can see the weavers in action and buy some of their beautiful work. Don't bargain too hard – most of the work here is superb quality and takes the women a long time to make.

A few small, friendly homestays in Pringgasela offer simple accommodation usually with typical local food. *Akmal Homestay* is run by a family of weavers and can arrange car and motorcycle rental, and treks to Rinjani. *Rainbow Cottages* is another good place, with similar services. The both cost around 15,000/20,000 rp for singles/doubles.

Lenek

Lenek has a traditional music and dance troupe which performs for tourists on a more-or-less regular basis. Ask at the tourist office in Mataram for the times.

A little north and east of Lenek is the village of **Loang Gali**, where there's a spring and swimming pool in the forest. You can ay here at *Loang Gali Cottages* for about 2,500 rp per person.

Sapit

A side road heads north up the shoulder of Gunung Rinjani, past Swela to Pesugulan, which is the south-eastern entrance to the Gunung Rinjani Reserve. You can walk from ere north to Sembalun Bumbung and from here climb up Rinjani from the east side, but he road is not currently driveable.

Sapit is a little east of Pesugulan, with cool air and stunning views across to Sumbawa, and Rinjani forming a spectacular backdrop. In this splendid location, *Pondok Wisata Jati Suci* has bungalows at 10,000/15,000 rp and 20,000/35,000 rp, including breakfast. There's a restaurant, and the staff can help with information about climbing Rinjani. Get there by bemo from Masbagik or Pringabaya.

Between Swela and Sapit, a side road goes down into the **Lemor forest**, where there's a refreshing spring-fed pool. Further down he road towards Pringgabaya, a side road goes to **Selaparang**, where you can see the burial place of the ancient Selaparang kings. It's nothing exciting, but a good excuse to wander the back blocks.

SOUTH LOMBOK

Praya

This is the main town in southern Lombok. It's quite attractive, with spacious gardens, tree-lined streets, some old Dutch buildings and no tourists. Its bemo terminal, on the north-west side of the town centre, is the transport hub for the area. The *Dienda Hayu Hotel* (☎ 54319), Jl Untung Surapati 28, is new, clean and not a bad place to stay. Rooms cost 20,000 rp, or 35,000 rp with air-con, and he restaurant is good.

Sukarara

A little north-west of Praya, the small village of Sukarara is a traditional weaving centre. It has become rather commercial, but is still worth a visit. Looms are set up outside workshops along the main street, with colourful displays of fabric. Women work out the front, wearing traditional black costumes with brightly coloured edgings, but most of the material is actually made in homes in surrounding villages. The bigger showrooms are geared to tour-bus groups, and have a big range, professional salespeople and higher prices.

There's such a variety of style, quality and size that it's impossible to give a guide to prices, but the best pieces are magnificent and well worth paying for.

Getting There & Away Get a bemo from Sweta to Praya, but get off at Puyung (about 700 rp). From Puyung you can hire a cidomo for about 250 rp to take you the two km to Sukarara.

Penujak

This small village is well known for its traditional *gerabah* pottery made from a local clay with the simplest of techniques. It's a rich terracotta colour, unglazed, but hand burnished to a lovely soft sheen. Some new designs are brightly coloured and geometrically patterned.

It's one of several villages where the Lombok Craft Project, supported by a New Zealand development agency, has done a lot to promote the pottery industry and develop export markets. The main street of Penujak is now lined with showrooms and cute but persistent kids who sell clay whistles and small pots – that's progress.

Penujak is on the main road, six km south of Praya, and any bemo to Sengkol or Kuta will drop you there.

Beleka

The main products here are baskets, mats and boxes made from natural fibres, such as rattan, grass, palm leaf and bamboo. Showrooms along the main road sell some fine examples of this quality work – strong, simple and beautifully made. It's off the main road about 15 km east of Praya.

Rembitan & Sade

The area from Sengkol down to Kuta Beach is a centre of traditional Sasak culture and there are many traditional Sasak villages, including two that are frequently visited by tourists.

Rembitan is about four km south of Sengkol, on a hill just west of the main road. It's a slightly sanitised Sasak village, but has an authentic cluster of thatched houses and *lumbung* (traditional rice barn and an architectural symbol of Lombok) surrounded by a wooden fence. On top of the hill is **Masjid Kuno**, an old thatched-roof mosque. One of the local kids will show you around and it's polite to make a donation, even if they don't ask.

A little further south is Sade, a 'traditional' village which some say was constructed just for tourists, but may have been merely an extensive renovation. It has concrete footpaths and lots of houses display stuff for sale. Hawkers here give the hard sell, and there's no chance you'll forget your donation.

Kuta Beach
The best-known place on the south coast is Lombok's Kuta Beach, a magnificent stretch of white sand and blue sea with rugged hills rising around it, but not much else. It has far fewer tourists than the famous (infamous?) Kuta Beach on Bali, but there are big plans to develop a whole stretch of the superb south coast with luxury hotels. After years of speculation, there are signs of development, with new roads and site works for the first big hotel. Meanwhile, the low budget losmen at Kuta are all on limited leases and seem to be trying to get maximum income from minimum investment. Some of them look decidedly squalid, and travellers are reporting some hassles.

People flock to Kuta for the annual nyale fishing celebration, with visiting celebrities and TV crews, and thousands sleeping on the beach. For the rest of the year it's very quiet.

Surf breaks on the reefs include lefts and rights in the bay in front of Kuta, and some more on reefs east of Tanjung Aan. Local boatmen will take you out for a few thousand rupiah. East of Kuta, there are reef breaks at the entrance of Gerupuk Bay. There are more possibilities from Blongas to Kaliantan, but

nearly all of them are only accessible b boat; the charter rate is about 40,000 r 50,000 rp per day. Bigger yachts from Ba do surf charters along the whole of Lom bok's south coast.

Information You can change money at And Cottages, but the rates are not very goo Wisma Segara Anak is a postal agent and ha a booking desk for Perama. There are tele phones in Kuta, but no wartel. There's market twice a week, on Sunday an Wednesday.

Nyale Fishing Festival On the 19th day o the 10th month in the Sasak calendar – ge erally February or March – hundreds o Sasaks gather on the beach. When night fall fires are built and the young people sit aroun competing with each other in rhyming co plets called *pantun*. At dawn the ne morning, the first nyale are caught, aft which it is time for the Sasak teenagers have fun. In a colourful procession, boys an girls put out to sea in different boats an chase one another with lots of noise an laughter. The worm-like nyale fish are eate raw or grilled and are believed to have aph rodisiac properties. A good catch is a sig that the rice harvest will also be good.

Places to Stay & Eat Most of Kuta's accom modation is along the beachfront road east o the village – all of a similar price and qualit Prices are 5000 rp or so, although higher a busy times. After the police station you pas *Rambutan*, with rooms at 8000 rp, includin tea and breakfast. *Wisma Segara Ana* (☎ 54834), next door, has a restaurant, roug rooms at 6000/7000 rp for singles/double better rooms at 8000/10,000 rp and bunga lows at 12,000/15,000 rp, including breakfas Next along, *Pondok Sekar Kuning* ha double rooms downstairs for 8000 rp an upstairs, with a nice view, for 10,000 rp; it not a bad place. *Anda Cottages* (☎ 54836 next door, has some trees and shrubs, a goo restaurant with Indonesian, Chinese an western dishes, and rooms from 8000 t 10,000 rp, including breakfast.

A bit further along is *Rinjani Agung Beach ungalows* (☎ 54849), with standard rooms om 12,000/15,000 rp, and the *Cockatoo 'ottages & Restaurant* (☎ 54831), the last lace along the beach, with a nice restaurant ea and rooms for 5000/7000 rp, including reakfast.

In the village, *Matahari Inn* (☎ 54832) is somewhat higher standard, with rooms at 5,000/20,000 rp, or 30,000/40,000 rp with r-con, and a pleasant restaurant. A little rther west is Kuta's best hotel to date, the *uta Indah* (☎ 53781), where the rooms ave air-con, hot and cold water and TV for 4,000/55,000 rp, but probably more when completes the swimming pool and the rest f the rooms. It's comfortable, but the loca-on has nothing going for it.

The *Bamboo Restaurant* at the west end f the beach is worth a try, while *Mascot* is place for a beer and music – it's almost a ub.

etting There & Away There is some direct ublic transport from Sweta to Kuta for 1500 , or get a bemo to Praya (700 rp) and nother from there to Kuta (you may have to nange again at Sengkol). Travel early or you ay get stuck and have to charter a vehicle. Perama has connections to Kuta from Iataram and Senggigi (10,000 rp) and other urist areas. Its office in Kuta (☎ 54846) is Wisma Segara Anak. Lombok Mandiri urist buses may be a bit cheaper. If you ave your own transport it's easy – there's a 'ide road, sealed all the way.

ast of Kuta 'uite good roads go around the coast to the ast, passing a series of beautiful bays punc-ated by headlands. There's some public ansport, but you will see more with your vn transport – a bicycle would be good. All e beachfront land has been bought by spec-lators for planned tourist resorts. **Segar each** is about two km east around the first eadland and you can easily walk there. A uge rock about four km east of the village ffers superb views across the countryside if ou climb it early in the morning. The road goes five km east to **Tanjung Aan** (Cape Aan) where there are two classic beaches with very fine, powdery white sand. This is an area slated for upmarket resort hotels.

The road continues another three km to the fishing village of **Gerupuk**, where there's a market on Tuesday. From there you can get a boat across the bay to **Bumgang**. Alterna-tively, turn north just before Tanjung Aan and go to **Awang**, a fishing village which is venturing into the seaweed business. You could get a boat from here across to **Ekas**, and some of the other not-so-secret surf spots in this bay (see the Eastern Lombok section for more information).

West of Kuta

The road west of Kuta is sealed as far as **Selong Blanak**, a lovely sandy bay. The road doesn't follow the coast closely, but there are regular and spectacular ocean vis-tas. In between are more fine beaches like **Mawan, Tampa, Rowok** and **Mawi**, but you have to detour to find them.

Selong Blanak Cottages are 1.5 km north of Selong Blanak Beach, but the manage-ment provides transport to the beach and back free, and to more isolated spots for a small price. It's a very nice place to stay, with a restaurant and a variety of rooms from 20,000 rp; they're 5000 rp more in the high season.

The road north of Selong Blanak is mostly sealed and quite passable to Penujak. To go further west, turn off the Penujak road at Keling 2.5 km from Selong Blanak (you almost double back at the junction). This dirt road goes through the hills to **Montong-sapah** and then swings back to the coast at **Pengantap**. After a few more scenic km you pass the turn-off west to **Blongas** – a very rugged road. The main road north is much better, and brings you to Sekatong and on to Lembar.

It's an excellent trip from Kuta round to Lembar, but there are no phones or facilities en route. It's less than 100 km, but allow plenty of time. It may be impossible in the wet season.

NUSA TENGGARA

EAST LOMBOK

For most travellers, the east coast is just Labuhan Lombok, the port for ferries to Sumbawa, but improvements to the road around the north coast make a round-the-island trip quite feasible. The south-eastern peninsula is also more accessible now for those with their own transport.

Labuhan Lombok

This sleepy little place has concrete houses, thatched shacks and stilt bungalows in the Sulawesi style. From the hill on the south side of the harbour, you look across the Alas Strait to Sumbawa, while Gunung Rinjani looms up behind. Ferries to Sumbawa leave from the port on the east side of the bay.

Places to Stay & Eat There's usually no need to stay overnight here, but if you do, avoid the depressingly basic *Losmen Dian Dutaku* on the main road coming into town – even at 3500/5000 rp it's poor value. On Jl Khayangan, the road to the port, the *Losmen Munawar* is better, with rooms at 5000/10,000 rp. There are a few *warungs* around the bemo terminal and at the port.

Getting There & Away There are frequent buses and bemos to/from Sweta (2000 rp; two hours), Masbagik (1000 rp) and Kopang (1500 rp). Some buses go through to Lembar.

Ferries for Poto Tano (Sumbawa) leave about every hour from approximately 6 am to 10 pm. Try to get to the port before 11 am to make the 1½ hour crossing and the two hour bus trip to Sumbawa Besar before dark. The ferry costs 3600 rp in air-con ekonomi A, 2300 rp in ekonomi B, 3300 rp for a bicycle and 6000 rp for a motorcycle, plus harbour tax.

It's about two or three km from the port to the town of Labuhan Lombok – take a bemo, or die in the heat. The ferry ticket office, with a wartel, warung and waiting room, is beside the carpark.

North of Labuhan Lombok

Foreigners are still a curiosity along this coast. Look for the giant trees about five km north of the harbour. **Pulu Lampur**, 14 k north, has a black sand beach and is popula with locals on Sunday and holidays. You ca stay at *Gili Lampu Cottages*, simple bambo bungalows a bit back from the beach, fo 10,000 rp.

Another few km north, just before th village of **Labuhan Pandan**, you can stay the nicely secluded *Siola Cottages*. It's b itself in a coconut grove on the seashore, an charges 15,000/25,000 rp for singles/ double with three meals. It's a good lunch stop, to You can charter a boat from here to th uninhabited islands of **Gili Sulat** and the **Gi Petangan** group, with lovely white beache and good coral for snorkelling, althoug there are no facilities on them. A boat cos about 30,000 rp, for up to five passenger for a day trip out and back with a few hou on an island. Take drinking water and picnic lunch. Perama has a camp on one o the Gili Petangan islands, which is a stopov on its expensive Land-Sea Adventure tour

The road continues through **Sambelia** an **Sugian** to the north coast. It's all sealed wi good bridges. By public transport, travel on bemo to Anyar (near Bayan) from Labuha Lombok.

1 Ticket Office
2 Warungs
3 Carpark
4 Mosque
5 Bemo Terminal
6 Warungs
7 Post Office
8 Losmen Dian Dutaku
9 Hidayat Restaurant
10 Warung Kelayu
11 Losmen Munawar
12 Cinema

To Sumbawa

Alas Strait

Gate

To Labuhan Pandan

Labuhan Lombok

0   250   500 m

Jalan Khayangan

To Pringabaya & Mataram

outh of Labuhan Lombok

he capital of the East Lombok administra-
ve district is **Selong**, which has a few old
)utch buildings. With recent growth, there
; an almost continuous urban strip from
'ancor to Tanjung. There's actually a tourist
ffice in Selong now, but probably no tour-
:ts. Pancor on the west side of Selong is the
us and bemo terminal for the region, and
ou can change money at the BPD bank.
Visma Erina (☎ 21247) on the north-east
ide of the main road is not a bad place to
tay, but there's no reason to.

On the coast is **Labuhan Haji**, accessible
om Selong and Tanjung by bemo. For-
nerly a port for those departing on a *haj*
pilgrimage to Mecca), its buildings are
bandoned and in ruins. The black sand
each here is a bit grubby and the only
ccommodation is at *Melewi's Beach Cot-
iges*, just north of the Selong road. Doubles
re 20,000 rp, including breakfast (other
neals can be arranged), but it doesn't seem
> be very well run. It would be a good place
> feed mosquitos, so take precautions.

Further south you come to **Tanjung Luar**,
ne of Lombok's main fishing ports, with a
trong smell of fish and lots of Bugis-style
ouses on stilts. From there the road swings
vest to **Keruak**, where wooden boats are
nade, and continues past the turn-off to
;**ukaraja**, a traditional Sasak village which
ourists are welcome to visit, especially if
ney want to buy the local woodcarvings.

Just west of Keruak there's a road south to
erowaru (3.6 km) and the south-eastern
·eninsula, which was inaccessible until
ecently. This peninsula is sparsely popu-
ated with a harsh climate and scrubby
·egetation, but the coastline has some inter-
sting features. You may be able to charter a
emo from Keruak to Ekas (maybe 30,000 rp)
r Kaliantan (40,000 rp). If you want to explore
ou'll need your own transport, but it's easy to
)se your way and the roads go from bad to
vorse. This area feels really remote.

Turn right at Jerowaru and follow the road
bout 16 km to **Kaliantan** and **Serewe**, on
ie far south coast, with brilliant ocean
iews, but no accommodation.

A sealed road branches west 6.4 km past
Jerowaru; it gets pretty rough, but eventually
reaches **Ekas**. There's no accommodation
there, but *Laut Surga Cottages* is on the coast
a few km south. This place had become very
run down and may even have closed. If you
hear the cottages are habitable, you can reach
them by boat from Ekas or from Awang
across the bay. In the dry season you can get
there by road, turning left off the Ekas road
and following the small blue signs. Laut
Surga was mainly a place for surfers and it
has a lovely little beach, but it's a long way
to come if you can't stay there.

On the east coast of the peninsula, **Tanjung Ringgit** has some large caves which,
according to local legend, are home to a
demonic giant. The road to Tanjung Ringgit
may not be passable, so it might be easier to
charter a boat from Tanjung Luar. There's a
cultivated pearl operation at **Sunut** on the
north coast of the peninsula.

NORTH COAST

The road around the north coast is sealed all
the way, with varied scenery and few tourists. You can do it on public transport, but it's
better with your own wheels so you can stop
and detour to the coast, waterfalls and inland
villages.

From Ampenan, the coast road north to
Senggigi, Mangset and Bangsal is very pretty,
but has no public transport. The road north
of Mataram, through the Pusuk Pass to
Pemenang, is also scenic and has regular
bemos (900 rp; 31 km). At Pemenang you
can turn off for Bangsal and the Gili Islands
(see later in this section), or continue to Sira
and the north coast.

Sira

Just a few km north of Pemenang, Sira is a
peninsula with white sand beaches that is
slated for luxury tourist developments. Currently there's no accommodation, but the
new, four star *Mondana Hotel* is a little
further east.

North-West Coast

Tanjung is quite large and interesting, with

NUSA TENGGARA

a big cattle market on Sunday. Just west of Tanjung, *Le Club des Explorateurs* has an eccentric management, a lovely seaside location and four different rooms from 15,000 to 25,000 rp. It offers French-Indonesian cuisine and is definitely not your average Indonesian homestay.

A little further north-east at **Karang Kates**, fresh water bubbles from the sea bed 400m offshore – the local people collect their drinking water from the sea. The sign on the road announcing 'Water in the Sea' is not quite as daft as it appears.

From Godang, you can branch inland to **Tiu Pupas Waterfall**, about four km on a rough track, mostly passable by motorcycle but not by car. There are other waterfalls on the northern slopes of Rinjani, but they're only worth seeing in the wet season.

Segenter

This traditional Sasak village is a bit hard to find, but well worth the effort. The track heads south off the main road by a bridge about one km west of Sukadana. Follow inland through grassy fields for about two km, until you see the village compound. It very neatly laid out, with rows of identical rectangular houses and communal pavilions. Most of the people will be out working during the day, but someone will guide you around. The houses are bamboo, with a stone hearth, and inside you'll see cane baskets and wooden implements. Everything is perfectly made, precisely arranged and very interesting to see. Afterwards you make a donation and sign the visitors' book.

Bayan

This northernmost part of Lombok's coast is the birthplace of the Wektu Telu religion and also a home for traditional Muslims. The mosque at Bayan is said to be the oldest on Lombok – over 300 years old. The stone platform on which it stands may be very old, but the mosque itself seems to have been

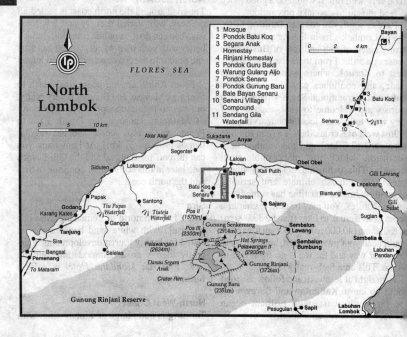

Map legend:
1 Mosque
2 Pondok Batu Koq
3 Segara Anak Homestay
4 Rinjani Homestay
5 Pondok Guru Bakti
6 Warung Gulang Aijo
7 Pondok Senaru
8 Pondok Gunung Baru
9 Bale Bayan Senaru
10 Senaru Village Compound
11 Sendang Gila Waterfall

North Lombok

FLORES SEA

Akar Akar, Sukadana, Anyar, Segenter, Laloan, Obel Obel, Siduten, Lokorangan, Bayan, Kali Putih, Gili Lawang, Papak, Santong, Batu Koq, Senaru, Torean, Blantung, Lepeloang, Gili Sulat, Godang, Tiu Pupas Waterfall, Tiuteja Waterfall, Pos II (1570m), Sajang, Karang Kates, Gangga, Pos III (2300m), Gunung Senkereang (2914m), Sembalun Lawang, Suglan, Tanjung, Sira, Pelawangan I (2634m), Hot Springs Pelawangan II (2900m), Sembalun Bumbung, Sambelia, Bangsal, Pemenang, Selelas, Danau Segara Anak, Gunung Rinjani (3726m), Labuhan Pandan, To Mataram, Crater Rim, Gunung Baru (2351m), Pesugulan, Sapit, Labuhan Lombok

Gunung Rinjani Reserve

NUSA TENGGARA

enovated, or at least re-thatched, quite ecently.

Several buses a day go from Sweta to nyar (2300 rp; three hours) and some con\nue to Bayan, but you'll probably have to hange. More frequent buses go to Pemen\ng, where you can change for Bayan.

East of Bayan

From Bayan, the north-coast road continues bout nine km east to a junction called **Kali Putih**, where there are a couple of warungs. The road south, pretty rough and steep in places, goes 18 km to **Sembalun Lawang** nd another four km to **Sembalun Bum\bung**. These traditional villages are an lternative approach to Rinjani.

East from Kali Putih, 35 km of winding oad passes through landscapes, alternately ush and arid, to Sambelia and Labuhan Pandan on the east coast.

GUNUNG RINJANI

Rinjani is the highest mountain on Lombok nd, outside Irian Jaya, about the highest in ndonesia. At 3726 m it soars above the island nd dominates the landscape, but by mid\norning the summit is usually enveloped in loud. The huge crater contains a large, green rescent-shaped lake, Segara Anak, about six m across at its widest point. The natural hot prings (*air panas*) on the north-eastern side f this crater are said to have remarkable healing powers, particularly for skin dis\bases. The lake is 600 vertical metres below he crater rim, and in the middle of its curve here's a new cone, Gunung Baru (also nown as Gunung Barujari), only a couple f hundred years old. Rinjani is an active olcano and erupted as recently as 1994, hanging the shape of this inner cone and prinkling ash over much of Lombok.

Both the Balinese and Sasaks revere Rinjani. To the Balinese it is, like Gunung Agung, a seat of the gods. In a ceremony alled *pekelan* people throw jewellery into he lake and make offerings to the spirit of he mountain. Some Sasaks make several pilgrimages a year; full moon is the favourite

time for paying respects to the mountain and curing ailments by bathing in its hot springs.

Batu Koq & Senaru

These adjoining villages are spread out along the ridge running up from Bayan and are the usual starting point for a climb up Gunung Rinjani. Homestays in the village are not fancy, but they're friendly and cheap, and some have superb views. Most have places to eat, and sell biscuits, canned fish, eggs, chocolate and other food you can take trek\bking. Most will also store your stuff while you climb, and help arrange transport, equip\bment rental, guides and porters.

Sendang Gila Waterfall It's a very pleasant half-hour walk to this magnificent waterfall. The track goes alongside an irrigation canal which follows the contour of the hill, occa\bsionally disappearing into tunnels where the cliffs are too steep. Watch for the sleek black monkeys swinging through the trees. Another half-hour takes you to some even better falls, further up the hill.

Senaru Village The traditional village com\bpound of Senaru is almost at the end of the road. As late as the 1960s it was completely isolated from the rest of the world and it still seems remote, though trekkers pass by all the time. It's surrounded by a wooden fence and has about 20 thatched wooden houses in neat rows. As you enter there is a visitors' book, a donation tin and a notice indicating how proceeds are used to benefit the village. For all its quaintness, it is obviously a poor village and you should give something, though no-one hassles you at all.

Places to Stay *Pondok Batu Koq* is the furthest from the mountain, but staff here will organise transport to the start of your trek and are very helpful with other trekking arrangements. A single/double room costs only 5000/10,000 rp. Further up the hill, *Segara Anak Homestay* has good views from some rooms, and is also helpful and inexpen\bsive at 7500/10,000 rp. *Rinjani Homestay* is basic but cheap, as is *Pondok Guru Bakti* –

'Guru' Bakti is the school teacher who first helped visitors to discover this area. *Pondok Senaru* has slightly better rooms than most places here for 10,000/15,000 rp, and its restaurant has a wonderful outlook. Closest to the trailhead is *Bale Bayan Senaru*, with helpful management, good food and adequate rooms for 5000/10,000 rp.

Getting There & Away Bemos go from Bayan to Batu Koq, mostly in the morning (about 700 rp).

Sembalun Lawang & Sembalun Bumbung

High up on the eastern slopes of Gunung Rinjani is the cold, but beautiful, Sembalun Valley. The inhabitants of the valley claim descent from the Hindu Javanese, and a relative of one of the Majapahit rulers is said to be buried here.

The Sasak villages of Sembalun Lawang and Sembalun Bumbung are only a 45 minute walk apart, and are surrounded by fields of onion and garlic. There are many pleasant walks and stunning views in the surrounding area.

In Sembalun Lawang, the simple *Maria Guesthouse* costs 7000/10,000 rp. It has some trekking gear to rent and staff can help arrange porters, but bring the food you'll need for your trek.

Getting There & Away From the north-coast road nine km east of Bayan, a rough but useable road climbs to Sembalun Lawang and continues to Sembalun Bumbung. There are a few bemos from Sembalun, mostly in the morning.

From the south you can reach Sembalun Bumbung in a beautiful five hour walk from Pesugulan, near Sapit, which can be reached by bemo from Pringgabaya. The road to Pesugulan has been constructed, washed away and is being rebuilt, but is not currently motorable.

Climbing Rinjani

Many people climb up to Rinjani's crater lake every year; mostly Indonesians making a pilgrimage or seeking the curative power of the hot springs. Many foreign visitor make the climb too, though very few peopl go the extra 1700m or so to the very summ of Rinjani. Even the climb to the crater lak is not to be taken lightly. Don't try it durin the wet season as the tracks will be slipper and very dangerous; in any case you woul be lucky to see any more than mist and cloud There can be big crowds during the fu moon.

Most visitors stay in Batu Koq or Senar climb from there to the crater lake and retur the same way. The other main route is fro Sembalun Lawang on the eastern side. Th northern route is more easily accessible an has better services for trekkers.

Organised Tours A number of agencie mostly in Mataram or Senggigi, organis guided treks, including equipment, foo guides and transport. They seem expensiv at around US$150 per person for a three da two night trek from Senaru, but they ma save a bit of time and trouble. Usually the require a minimum of two people and it cheaper per person if you have a large group. Satisfy yourself that the guide leaders are reliable and knowledgable, as th quality and safety of the trip will depend o them. Established operators include Naza reth Tours & Travel in Senggigi (☎ 93033 and Ampenan (☎ 31705); Discover Lombo (☎ 93390) in the Pasar Seni market at Ser ggigi and Pizzeria Cafe Alberto (☎ 3678 near Ampenan; Perama (☎ 35936, 93007 in Mataram and Senggigi; Lombok Wisa Indah (☎ 32815, 24988), in Senggigi; an Sahir Generations (☎ 21688, 24464) a Masbagik in central Lombok.

Guides & Porters You can trek from Senar to the hot springs and back without a guide From Sembalun Lawang there are a numbe of trails branching off and you could get los You start in the dark when climbing to th summit of Rinjani, so it's good to hav someone who knows the way. Most of th porters know the trails, and will also carr your equipment and cook, even if they don

eak much English. They cost about 15,000
per day and you have to provide food,
ater and transport for them, and probably
garettes as well. A good guide will be infor-
ative, manage all the arrangements and add
eatly to the enjoyment of the trek, but
on't carry anything so you'll have to get at
ast one porter as well. Guides cost around
5,000 rp per day.

quipment There are some very crude shel-
rs, but don't rely on them – a sleeping bag
d tent are essential. Take a stove so you
on't need to deplete the limited supply of
rewood. You'll also need solid footwear
d some layers of warm clothing. In Batu
oq you can rent a two or three person tent
5,000 rp for up to five days), a stove and
ooking gear (3000 rp), and a sleeping bag
d mat (10,000 rp). You could probably get
e whole lot for about 20,000 rp for three
ys. Remember to check the equipment
fore you take it.

ood & Supplies Take rice, instant noodles,
gar, coffee, eggs, tea, biscuits or bread,
me tins of fish or meat (and a can opener!),
ions, fruit and anything else that keeps
ur engine running. It's better to buy most
these supplies in Mataram or the super-
arket in Senggigi, where it's cheaper and
ere's more choice, but you can get a fair
nge in Batu Koq. Take plenty of bottles of
rinking water, matches and a torch.

nvironmental Care A lot of rubbish is
ropped along the route. It would be worse
the student groups from the university
dn't come and clean up every few months.
ring all rubbish out. Don't try to burn it or
ury it. The other problem is firewood –
ere's none left up by the lake. Bring a stove
d fuel for cooking, and enough clothing to
ep warm.

orthern Route This is the most popular
ute; climbing from Senaru to the crater
m, descending to the lake, going round to
e hot springs and returning the same way.
ou can get to the hot springs in one day and

return the next, but this is pretty demanding,
and it means you'll reach the crater rim in the
middle of the day, when much of the view
may be covered by mist. It's better to do it in
three days, spending a night at the base camp
just below the rim and a second night
camping near the springs.

Day 1 If you're staying in Batu Koq, you can
get transport to the trailhead at Senaru (Pos
I on some maps; 860m). From there it's about
2½ to three hours to the first rest stop, (Pos
II; 1570m), where there are two shelters.
Another 1½ hours steady walk uphill brings
you to the 'base camp' (Pos III; 2300m),
where there's another shelter, and a campsite. If you have enough energy left, climb
up to the clearing and watch the sunset.

Day 2 Set off very early to arrive at the crater
rim for sunrise. It takes about 1½ to two
hours to reach the volcano rim, Pelawangan
I, at an altitude of 2634m. ('Pelawangan' means
'gateway' and this is one of the few places
where you can enter the crater.) Above 2000m
the mahogany and teak forest gives way to the
odd stand of pine. As you get closer to the rim
the trees thin out even further and the ground
becomes rockier. There has been some logging
on the slopes of Rinjani, but officially the area
is now protected. Monkeys, wild pigs, deer and
the occasional snake inhabit the forest.

The view from the rim is stunning – it
takes in the amazing crater, the whole north
coast of Lombok and Gunung Agung on
Bali. From the rim, allow at least two hours
to get down to the lake and around to the hot
springs. The narrow path clings to the side of
the cliffs and is quite dangerous. Don't hurry
– some people take much longer to do this
section.

The lake surface is about 2000m above sea
level, with trees right down to the shore.
There are several places to camp, but most
prefer to be near the hot springs, where you
can soak your weary body and recuperate.
There are several waterfalls, pools and
springs to explore, including the 'Milk Cave'
(Goa Susu) which discharges hot, white
water. It's not as cold here as it is at base

NUSA TENGGARA

camp, but it is damp and misty from the steaming springs.

Day 3 Start early to do the hard climb back to the crater rim before it gets too hot – allow at least three hours. Then it's all downhill to Senaru. It's a full day's walk (around five hours), so you'll arrive back in the afternoon. The last bemo down the mountain from Senaru leaves at 4 pm.

Eastern Route The climb from Sembalun Lawang is more difficult to arrange. It's difficult to get there by public transport and there's only a limited amount of equipment available to rent. You can hire porters and get information from the owner of the guesthouse. It will take about eight or nine hours to get to Pelawangan II, the eastern entrance to the crater, at 2900m. Nearby is a crude shelter and a trail junction, with one track climbing southwards to the summit of Rinjani and the other heading west to much more comfortable camp sites near the hot springs, about four hours away. Going the other way, you can get from the crater rim down to Sembalun Lawang in about seven hours. There's no water available along the way.

Across the Crater It's possible to ascend by the northern route and descend by the eastern route, or vice versa, but you'll have to work out how to get yourself, your porter and your rented equipment back to where you started. The best way is probably to go first to Senaru, get your trekking stuff together, then charter transport to Sembalun Lawang and start walking from there.

Night Climb If you travel light and climb fast, you can reach the crater rim from Senaru in about six hours – it's a 1770m altitude gain in 10 km, approximately. With a torch and some moonlight, set off at midnight and you'll be there for sunrise. Coming back takes about five hours, so you can be down in time for lunch. Take lots of snack food and a litre or two of water.

Around the Rim If you reach Pelawangan early in the day, you can follow the crater rim around to the east for about three km to Gunung Senkereang (2914m) at the end of the ridge. From here you can see east to Sumbawa and west to Bali, while Gunung Rinjani looms to the south. It's not an easy walk though, and the track is narrow and very exposed in places.

Other Routes It's possible to climb up to the crater from Torean, a small village just south-east of Bayan. The trail follows the stream that flows from the hot springs, but it's hard to find; you'll need a guide.

On the south side of Rinjani, there are routes from Sesaot or Tetebatu, but they involve at least one night camping in the forest and you won't see any views until you get above the tree line. Again, a guide is essential. A better option from the south is from Pesugulan (near Sapit) towards Sembalun Bumbung, then to Pelawangan II.

Gunung Baru, the cone in the middle of Danau (Lake) Segara Anak, may look tempting, but it's a very dangerous climb. The track around the lake is narrow and people have drowned after slipping off it. The climb itself is over a very loose surface and if you start sliding or falling there is nothing to stop you and nothing to hang on to. Many of the tracks around Gunung Baru were wiped out in the 1994 eruption.

To the Very Top The path to the summit branches off the Sembalun Lawang track near Pelawangan II. From the shelter there allow four hours to reach the summit. Start early in the morning because you have to get to the top within an hour or so of sunrise if you want to see more than mist and cloud.

The view from the rim is great, but it's nothing compared with the view from the very top! From the top you look down into the crater which fills up with 'cotton wool' cloud streaming through the gap in the crater wall at the hot springs. In the distance, you look over Bali in one direction and Sumbawa in the other

It's a difficult three hour climb from the shelter; the air gets thinner and the terrain is horrible to walk on. It's powdery to start with, then you find loose tones on a steep slope (offering little support for your weight). It's a case of climbing one step up, then sliding two-thirds of a step back down, and the peak always looks closer than it is! Climbing without strong-toed shoes or boots would be masochistic.

Richard Tucker, England

GILI ISLANDS

Off the north-west coast of Lombok are three small, coral-fringed islands – Gili Air, Gili Meno and Gili Trawangan – each with superb, white sandy beaches, clear water, coral reefs, brilliantly coloured fish and the best snorkelling on Lombok. Although known to travellers as the 'Gili Islands', *gili* actually means 'island', so this is not a local name. There are lots of other gilis around the coast of Lombok.

A few years ago, descendants of Bugis immigrants were granted leases to establish coconut plantations on the islands. The economic activities expanded to include fishing, raising livestock, and growing corn, tapioca, peanuts and, of course, coconuts. As travellers started to visit Lombok, some came to the Gilis on day trips and then began to stay for longer periods in local homes. Soon, many people on the islands found that the most profitable activity was 'picking white coconuts' – a local expression for providing services to tourists.

The islands have become enormously popular with visitors, especially young Europeans, who come for the very simple pleasures of sun, snorkelling and socialising. It's cheap, and the absence of cars, motorcycles and hawkers adds greatly to the pleasure of staying on the Gilis.

Their very popularity may be a problem, as numbers sometimes exceed the available rooms and put pressure on the island environments, especially water supply and waste disposal systems. The local population is aware of environmental issues, but they do not have the last word on development, and there is always a temptation to build more and better facilities. Gili Meno and Gili Air have retained much of their unspoilt quality, but Gili Trawangan has become much less attractive over the last few years, largely because of external pressures.

There are big plans to develop a luxury resort and golf course on Trawangan and the mainland, which threatens the simple charm which makes the Gilis attractive to current visitors. Ill-conceived plans have already created two costly white elephants: a stone jetty at Bangsal, which local boats can't use because they have outriggers; and an oversize bus terminal, inconveniently located between Bangsal and Pemenang.

Health
Sanitation has improved, but occasional outbreaks of food poisoning have occurred. The islands are definitely in a malaria risk area.

Security
There is the occasional spate of thefts. Make sure your room, including the bathroom, is well secured, even when you're in the room at night. Keep your things locked in a bag and well away from windows, doors or other openings. There are no police on the islands, so if the island *kepala desa* (village head) can't help, go to the police station in Tanjung (on Lombok's north coast) or in Ampenan (which might be easier to deal with).

Avoiding Offence
The islanders are Muslims, and visitors should respect their sensibilities. In particular, topless (for women) or nude sunbathing is offensive to them, although they won't say so directly. Away from the beach, it is polite for both men and women to cover their shoulders and knees. So many insensitive visitors walk around in skimpy clothing that it's easy to get the impression that local people don't mind, but they do.

Activities
A few places rent paddle boards (called canoes) – some even have a window so you can see the coral – or you can rent a boat to go fishing. There are two surf breaks off Gili Air, but they're very fickle.

Diving & Snorkelling Ask locally to find the best snorkelling spots, many of which can be reached from the shore. For scuba divers, the visibility is usually good (best in the dry season). Some excellent coral reefs are accessible by boat. Marine life includes turtles, rays, sharks (harmless) and a giant clam. A particular attraction is the blue coral, with its almost luminous tips. There are qualified dive operators on Gili Trawangan and Gili Air.

Accommodation

A greater variety of accommodation is available now, but there are still lots of basic places. The Gili Islands standard is a plain bamboo bungalow on stilts, with a thatched roof, a small verandah out the front and a concrete bathroom block out the back. Inside, there will be one or two beds with mosquito nets. Prices are around 8000 10,000 rp for singles/doubles in the low season. In the busy seasons (July, August and around Christmas) they ask a lot more – maybe double the prices given here. Most places include a light breakfast.

Touts meet the boats as they land and can be quite helpful. But if you have decided to stay in a particular place, don't let a tout convince you that it's full, closed or doesn't exist.

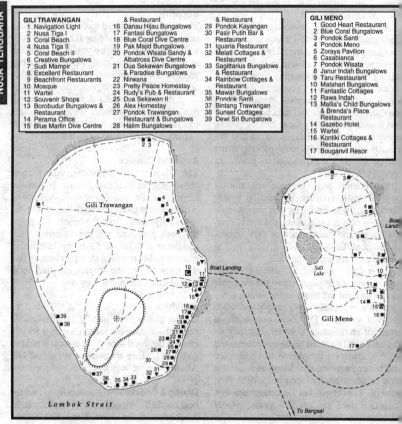

GILI TRAWANGAN
1 Navigation Light
2 Nusa Tiga I
3 Coral Beach
4 Nusa Tiga II
5 Coral Beach II
6 Creative Bungalows
7 Sudi Mampir
8 Excellent Restaurant
9 Beachfront Restaurants
10 Mosque
11 Wartel
12 Souvenir Shops
13 Borobudur Bungalows & Restaurant
14 Perama Office
15 Blue Marlin Dive Centre

& Restaurant
16 Danau Hijau Bungalows
17 Fantasi Bungalows
18 Blue Coral Dive Centre
19 Pak Majid Bungalows
20 Pondok Wisata Sandy & Albatross Dive Centre
21 Dua Sekawan Bungalows & Paradise Bungalows
22 Nirwana
23 Pretty Peace Homestay
24 Rudy's Pub & Restaurant
25 Dua Sekawan II
26 Alex Homestay
27 Pondok Trawangan Restaurant & Bungalows
28 Halim Bungalows

& Restaurant
29 Pondok Kayangan
30 Pasir Putih Bar & Restaurant
31 Iguana Restaurant
32 Melati Cottages & Restaurant
33 Sagittarius Bungalows & Restaurant
34 Rainbow Cottages & Restaurant
35 Mawar Bungalows
36 Pondok Santi
37 Bintang Trawangan
38 Sunset Cottages
39 Dewi Sri Bungalows

GILI MENO
1 Good Heart Restaurant
2 Blue Coral Bungalows
3 Pondok Santi
4 Pondok Meno
5 Zoraya Pavilion
6 Casablanca
7 Pondok Wisata
8 Janur Indah Bungalows
9 Taru Restaurant
10 Matahari Bungalows
11 Fantastic Cottages
12 Rawa Indah
13 Malia's Child Bungalows & Brenda's Place Restaurant
14 Gazebo Hotel
15 Wartel
16 Kontiki Cottages & Restaurant
17 Bouganvil Resor

Gili Trawangan

Boat Landing

Salt Lake

Gili Meno

Boat Landing

Lombok Strait

To Bangsal

Getting There & Away

From Ampenan or the airport, begin with a short bemo ride north to Rembiga (about 300 rp), then a scenic trip to Pemenang (700 rp). Alternatively, get a bemo from Sweta direct to Pemenang (900 rp). From there it's a km or so off the main road to the harbour at Bangsal (200 rp by cidomo). Tourist shuttle buses go from Mataram or Senggigi to Bangsal for 5000 rp and also make direct connections from Bali.

A boat owners' cartel monopolises transport to the Gili Islands – 1200 rp to Gili Air, 1500 rp to Gili Meno and 1600 rp to Gili Trawangan. Buy a ticket at its office in Bangsal and wait until there's a full boat load – about 15 people. If you have almost that number waiting, the boat will leave if you can pay the extra fares between you. It's best to arrive at Bangsal by 9.30 or 10 am.

Alternatively, get one of the scheduled boats at 10 am and 4 pm, which cost 3000 rp to Gili Air, 3500 rp to Gili Meno and 4000 rp to Gili Trawangan, or charter a whole boat, with a maximum of 10 passengers. All the boats pull up on the beaches, so be prepared to wade ashore with your luggage.

Bangsal is not an unpleasant place to hang

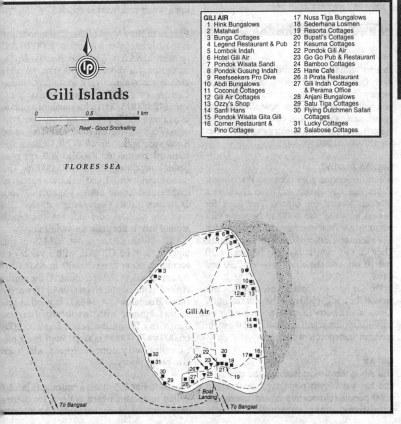

GILI AIR
1 Hink Bungalows
2 Matahari
3 Bunga Cottages
4 Legend Restaurant & Pub
5 Lombok Indah
6 Hotel Gili Air
7 Pondok Wisata Sandi
8 Pondok Gusung Indah
9 Reefseekers Pro Dive
10 Abdi Bungalows
11 Coconut Cottages
12 Gili Air Cottages
13 Ozzy's Shop
14 Sanfi Hans
15 Pondok Wisata Gita Gili
16 Corner Restaurant & Pino Cottages
17 Nusa Tiga Bungalows
18 Sederhana Losmen
19 Resorta Cottages
20 Bupati's Cottages
21 Kesuma Cottages
22 Pondok Gili Air
23 Go Go Pub & Restaurant
24 Bamboo Cottages
25 Harie Cafe
26 Il Pirata Restaurant
27 Gili Indah Cottages & Perama Office
28 Anjani Bungalows
29 Satu Tiga Cottages
30 Flying Dutchmen Safari Cottages
31 Lucky Cottages
32 Salabose Cottages

Gili Islands

0   0.5   1 km

Reef - Good Snorkelling

FLORES SEA

Gili Air

To Bangsal

Boat Landing

To Bangsal

Coral Conservation

In the past there was much damage to coral reefs by fish bombing and careless use of anchors. There is much greater awareness of this now and rehabilitation of damaged reefs is possible. Unfortunately, many visitors are unwittingly causing more damage by standing and walking on the reefs, often while snorkelling, boating or windsurfing. Perfectly formed corals are easily broken and take years to recover; the reef ecology is very sensitive. Please don't walk on coral reefs.

If you're not into conservation, think about the stonefish. These fish are not common, but they do live on the coral reefs here, where they are well camouflaged and almost invisible. If you stand on one, the venomous spines can cause excruciating pain and sometimes death. Don't walk on coral reefs. ■

---

around while you're waiting. The warungs have good food and coffee, and there are moneychangers, shops and travel agents. If you get stuck here, the new *Taman Sari* guesthouse, about 250m east of the Bangsal waterfront, has nice, clean singles/doubles for 15,000/20,000 rp.

Getting Around

A shuttle service goes between the islands, so you can stay on one and have a look, or a snorkel, around the others. The fares for 'island hopping' are 4000 rp between Gili Air and Gili Trawangan; or 3000 rp between Gili Meno and either of the other two islands. They do two runs a day; one between 8.30 and 10 am, and the other between 2.30 and 4 pm.

On the islands themselves, cidomos trot around the tracks (500 rp is the usual charge). If you're in a hurry (almost inconceivable on the Gilis) you can rent a bicycle, but the main mode of transport is walking.

Gili Air

Gili Air is the closest island to the mainland and has the largest population, with about 1000 people. Homes are dotted among the palm trees, along with a few losmen.

Because the buildings are so scattered, the island has a pleasant, rural character and is delightful to wander around. There are plenty of other people to meet, but if you stay in one of the more isolated places, socialising is optional.

Boats beach at the south end of the island and nearby are the boat ticket office and Gili Indah Cottages, with the Perama office (☎ 36341, 37816), wartel and moneychanger.

Diving Reefseekers Pro Dive (☎ 34387), based on the east side of the island, is a very professional operation and does a range of trips for qualified divers (from US$50), as well as introductory dives and full PADI open-water certification courses.

Places to Stay Most of the accommodation is in basic bungalows for about 8000/10,000 rp with breakfast. The cheapest is *Anjani Bungalows*, at about 5000/7000 rp, which is OK, but not attractively located. *Coconut Cottages* (☎ 35365) is a bit better than average at 12,000/15,000 rp for standard bamboo bungalows and 30,000 rp for very nice new ones. They serve great food, including some Sasak specialities. *Pondok Gili Air* has some standard rooms for 8800/13,200 rp, plus better bungalows at 20,000/25,000 rp. The menu is quite varied, and includes vegetarian dishes and home-made yoghurt. *Flying Dutchmen Safari Cottages* is secluded and well run with good food, but the beach around here is not great for swimming.

Gili Indah Cottages (☎ 36341) is the biggest place on Gili Air, with a variety of accommodation from 20,000 to 45,000 rp for a spacious, private pavilion. At the northern end of the island, *Hotel Gili Air* (formerly Han's Bungalows; ☎ 34435) is another up-market option, with beautifully finished bungalows facing the beach from 55,000/66,000 to 77,000/88,000 rp. *Sanfi Hans* has a couple of very attractive rooms, which are also pretty pricey.

Places to Eat *Il Pirata* is a reasonably priced Italian restaurant which is open for dinner only – it's the place that looks like a pirate

p. *The Legend* and *Go Go* are venues for
e island's limited nightlife.

li Meno

li Meno, the middle island, has the small-
t population – about 500. It's the quietest
the islands, with the fewest tourists. It has
salt lake which produces salt in the dry
ason and mosquitos in the wet season. The
ozzies are probably no worse than in other
aces at that time of year, but the usual
ecautions are called for, especially at dusk.
It takes a couple of hours to walk around
e whole island, and you'll feel like Robin-
n Crusoe for most of the way.

The beach on the eastern side of the island
very nice, and there's good snorkelling just
fshore and further north (rent mask,
orkel and fins for 5000 rp).

formation You can make phone calls at the
artel by the Gazebo Hotel, and change
oney at the Gazebo and at Mallia's Child
ongalows.

aces to Stay The accommodation is
ostly on the eastern beach, with several
aces which are pretty fancy by Gili stan-
rds. Good bottom-end places include
ondok Meno and *Mallia's Child*, both at
ound 10,000/15,000 rp for singles/doubles,
t considerably more in the high season.
Zoraya Pavilion (☎ 33801) has interest-
g rooms from US$10/12 to US$30/32 , and
ffers various water sports and a tennis court.
e *Gazebo Hotel* (☎ 35795) has tastefully
corated Balinese-style bungalows with
ivate bathrooms and air-con for US$47/59,
cluding breakfast. *Casablanca* (☎ 33847)
back from the beach and has rooms from
S$10/12 to US$45, but it's not particularly
pealing, even with its tiny swimming pool.
Kontiki (☎ 32824) has good value rooms
12,000/15,000 rp, as well as more expen-
ve ones. At the south end of the island, the
w *Bouganvil Resor* (☎ 27435) features a
rimming pool and large comfortable rooms
th air-con and hot water for US$45 (soon
increase to US$65). The beach down here
neither attractive nor swimmable.

Places to Eat *Brenda's Place*, the beachfront restaurant at Mallia's Child, is one of
the best places to eat and does a tasty pizza.
Kontiki has pretty good food, in a big breezy
pavilion, while *Good Heart*, on the other side
of the island, has a great view at sunset.
Don't expect snappy service or wild nightlife
anywhere on Gili Meno.

Gili Trawangan

The largest island, with a local population of
about 800, Trawangan also has the most
visitors, the most facilities and a reputation
as the 'party island' of the group. The eastern
beach is good for sunbathing and swimming,
the reefs are good for snorkelling and there
are several scuba diving operations.

The island is about three km long and two
km wide – you can walk around it in a few
easy hours. Most of the accommodation and
tourist facilities are on the eastern side of the
island, south of where the boats pull in.
There's a wartel here and a group of shops
which sell basic supplies, souvenirs and
second-hand books. Several places will
change money or travellers cheques, but
you'll get a better rate on the mainland. The
Blue Marlin Dive Centre will give a cash
advance on Visa or MasterCard, deducting a
3% commission.

The hill in the south-west corner is a good
place to enjoy the view across the straits to
Bali's Gunung Agung, especially at sunset.
The sunrise over Gunung Rinjani is also
impressive; one islander described Trawangan's three main attractions as 'sunrise,
sunset and sunburn'!

Diving & Snorkelling The best area for
snorkelling is off the north-east corner of the
island. Beware of strong currents between
Gili Trawangan and Gili Meno. Masks, snorkels and fins can be rented for around 4000
rp per day.

Some excellent scuba diving sites are
within a short boat ride, especially off
Trawangan's west coast. There are several
dive operations, including Blue Marlin
(☎ 32424), Albatross (☎ 30134) and Blue
Coral (☎ 34497). A day trip for a certified

NUSA TENGGARA

NUSA TENGGARA

Gili Trawangan – a paradise lost?

With the simplest of beachfront bungalows, Gili Trawangan attracted an incredible number of visitors but also the attention of the Lombok government and outside business interests. In the early 1990s the government decided that all the small bungalows should be located away from the north-east par of the island, and rumours began to circulate about a proposed luxury hotel and golf course. There was some negotiation and compensation, and alternative leases were offered further south. But some of the people refused to move and, in 1992, after repeated requests, the authorities ordered in the army and closed down the bungalows by the simple but effective means of cutting the posts with chainsaws.

It's not clear whether this was to make way for a grandiose development project, or because the bungalows contravened the lease conditions or environmental standards. A power station has been established at the northern end of the island, but after four years there were still no signs of a new hotel and the whole area, which fronts the best beach on the island, was looking very desolate indeed

Meanwhile, the south end of Gili Trawangan has been neatly subdivided into narrow allotments where most of the accommodation and facilities for low-budget travellers are now concentrated. In 1993 a fire destroyed 15 or 20 bungalows and the authorities encouraged new buildings in brick concrete and tile. The result is reminiscent of Kuta Beach on Bali – charmless concrete boxes are cramped together as closely as possible, with no sense of local architectural style and no sensitivity to the natural environment. ■

diver, with two dives and all equipment, is about US$50. A 'discover scuba' introductory course will cost around US$80 and a four day PADI open-water course is about US$300.

Places to Stay The accommodation here is mostly basic, with bottom-end prices from 8000/10,000 to 12,000/15,000 rp for singles/doubles in the low season, but increasing to as much as 25,000/30,000 rp in the high season. Some of the simple bamboo bungalows are scattered around the coast. The new places tend to be uninspiring concrete boxes cramped in to the tourist area – they're more expensive, but also more secure and with better bathrooms.

Old-style bamboo places in the southern part of the tourist area include *Halim Bungalows* and *Sagittarius*. Newer places are the *Danau Hijau Bungalows* and *Fantasi*, at about 12,000/15,000 rp. *Pak Majid*, *Melati* and *Borobudur Restaurant & Bungalows* are better quality options from 20,000 to 35,000 rp, but without much character. There are some really basic options inland from the main drag, like *Pretty Peace* and *Alex Homestay*, where a room will cost as little as 6000 rp with a shared bathroom.

At the northern end of the island, *Nusa Tiga I* and *Coral Beach* are wonderful isolated, dirt cheap and right by the beach but a bit run down. The south coast does have nice beaches, but there's secluded cheap and adequate accommodation places like *Mawar Bungalows* and *Bintang Trawangan*. *Pondok Santi* is a nice one 17,500/20,000 rp. Right round on the we side, *Dewi Sri* is a tidy place, well away from everything and pretty good value for 800 10,000 rp.

Places to Eat *Borobudur* is a popular re taurant, with a typical menu and prices – great tuna steak costs 5000 rp, plus 2000 for a crisp salad. Your standard mie or na goreng will cost under 2000 rp. *Pond Trawangan*, *Blue Marlin Dive Centre & Re taurant* and *Rainbow Cottages & Restaura* are also popular.

Iguana is a good place to eat, with sor Sasak-style food, seafood specials like squ with garlic butter (3500 rp) and the best be burgers on the island. During the day, there a bunch of simple eateries by the beach ju north of the boat landing.

Entertainment The bigger restaurants ha bars which serve drinks in the evening and few show video movies, which do nothi r conviviality. Party nights, with music, ancing, drinking and the odd mushroom, ternate between *Trawangan*, *Rainbow*, *uana Restaurant* and the *Excellent Restaurant*. The highlight of Trawangan's social alendar is the full moon party, where a fixed rice of about 8000 rp gets you your first rink, food and music.

Sumbawa

etween Lombok and Flores, and separated om them by narrow straits, is the rugged and mass of Sumbawa. Larger than Bali and ombok combined, Sumbawa is a sprawling sland of twisted and jutting peninsulas, with coast fringed by precipitous hills and ngular bights, and a mountain line of weathered volcanic stumps stretching along its ength.

Sumbawa is a scenic island, with plenty of cope for exploring off the beaten track. Few isitors venture beyond Sumbawa Besar, ima or Huu, mainly because once off the ighway, transport is infrequent or excruciatingly uncomfortable. To get out into the ountryside you really need to charter transport or rent a motorcycle.

The mountain and coastal regions in the outh – which were not converted to Islam ntil around the turn of the century – and the ambora Peninsula in the north are rarely isited by travellers. If you're in the right lace at the right time (on holidays and festivals), you might see traditional Sumbawan ghting, a sort of bare-fisted boxing called *erempah*. Horse and water buffalo races are eld before the rice is planted.

Towards the east end of the island, the arrow Bima Bay (Teluk Bima) cuts deep to the north coast, forming one of Indonesia's best natural harbours. It's surrounded y fertile lowlands which reach west into the ch interior Dompu plains.

History

'or centuries Sumbawa has been divided etween two linguistically and, to some extent, ethnically distinct peoples: the Sumbawanese speakers, who probably reached the west of the island from Lombok; and the Bimanese speakers, who independently occupied the east and Tambora Peninsula. The squatter, darker-skinned Bimanese are more closely related to the people of Flores, while the western Sumbawans are closer to the Sasaks of Lombok. Both their languages have considerable variation in dialect, but the spread of Bahasa Indonesia has made communication easier in the last couple of decades.

Sumbawa, with its rich timber resources in the west, was probably an early trading call for Javanese merchants on the way to or from the Spice Islands in Maluku. Bima and parts of western Sumbawa are said to have been under the control of the Javanese Majapahit Empire, although it's more likely that they simply sent tribute.

Along the western coastal lowlands, the local population expanded and petty kingdoms developed along the entire length of the island. In eastern Sumbawa, the areas around Bima Bay and the Dompu plains became the leading centres for the Bimanese-speaking population. Before 1600 these were probably animist kingdoms. By that time, the domestic horse was being used and irrigated rice agriculture, possibly introduced by Javanese traders, was well established. There appears to have been some intermarriage between the Balinese aristocracy and western Sumbawanese aristocracy, which may have linked the islands from the 15th or 16th centuries. In the early 17th century, the Islamic Makassarese states of southern Sulawesi undertook a military expansion, and by 1625, the rulers of Sumbawa had been reduced to Makassarese vassals and had nominally converted to Islam.

Makassar's rise was halted by the Dutch East India Company (Vereenigde Oost-Indische Compagnie; VOC), whose forces occupied it in 1669. Soon afterwards treaties were made between the Dutch and the rulers of Sumbawa by which Dutch hegemony was recognised and tribute was paid to the Dutch. For their part, the Dutch maintained only a

NUSA TENGGARA

distant supervision of what they considered a politically unstable island with poor commercial possibilities, taking more or less direct control only in the 1900s.

The western Sumbawans, meanwhile, held nominal control over neighbouring Lombok from the middle of the 17th century until 1750, when the Balinese took it over. Then followed 30 years of sporadic warfare between the Sumbawans and the Balinese, including at least one large-scale Balinese invasion of western Sumbawa. It was only through the intervention of the VOC, which was interested in maintaining the status quo, that the Balinese were turned back.

Barely had the wars finished, when Gunung Tambora on Sumbawa erupted in April 1815 killing perhaps 10,000 people in a shower of choking ash and molten debris. Agricultural land was wrecked and livestock and crops wiped out throughout the island. It's estimated that another 66,000 people, about two-thirds of Sumbawa's population, either died of starvation or disease or fled their lands.

By the middle of the 19th century, immigrants from other islands were brought in to help repopulate the blighted coastal regions.

The 850,000 people of Sumbawa are therefore a diverse lot. In the coastal regions the are traces of the Javanese, Makassares Bugis, Sasak and other groups who migrate to the island.

In 1908 the Dutch government sent a ministrators and soldiers to Sumbawa Bes and Taliwang to head off the prospect of w between the three separate states that con prised western Sumbawa. This inaugurate a period of far more direct Dutch rule. T sultans kept a fair degree of their pow under the Dutch, but after Indonesian ind pendence their titles were abolished; no their descendants hold official power on when they are functionaries of the nation government.

Little evidence remains of the Dutch pre ence, and the only traces of the old sultanat are the palaces in the towns of Sumbav Besar and Bima.

Climate

Sumbawa is at its best at the end of the w season around April/May. As the dry seaso progresses, the greenery dies off and muc of the island becomes brown and dusty und the increasingly sweltering heat.

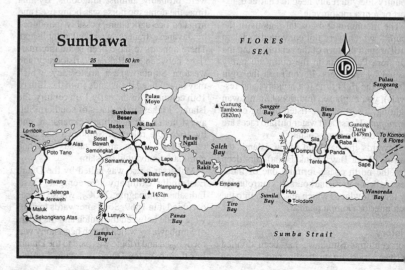

Religion

Sumbawa is the most predominantly Muslim land anywhere east of Java or south of Sulawesi. Christian missionaries never even bothered to try here and Islam seems to have overshadowed Sumbawa's indigenous traditions, though outside the cities older animist traditions still exist under the veneer of Islam.

Special Events

Check out 'horse racing', which is in reality boys on ponies, but still a big local event around Sumbawa from August to October.

Getting Around

Sumbawa's single main road runs all the way from Taliwang (near the west coast) through Sumbawa Besar, Dompu and Bima to Sape on the east coast). It's surfaced all the way. Fleets of buses, some of them luxurious by Nusa Tenggara standards, link all the towns on this road.

POTO TANO

The port for ferries to and from Lombok is a hodgepodge of stilt houses beside a mangrove-lined bay. It's a few km of dirt track away from Sumbawa's single main road.

Getting There & Away

Ferries run hourly from around 6 am to 10 pm between Lombok and Poto Tano (2300 rp; 1½ hours). The through buses from Mataram to Sumbawa Besar or Bima include the ferry fare.

Buses meet the ferry and go to Taliwang (1000 rp; one hour), Sumbawa Besar (2500 rp; two hours) and Bima (8500 rp; nine hours).

TALIWANG

During the 19th century, Taliwang was one of the 'vassal states' of the kingdom of Sumbawa based in Sumbawa Besar. This region has its own dialect and, through migration, is closely linked to Lombok.

Today Taliwang is a sleepy, oversized village, with friendly people and no tourists. It lies close to the west coast of Sumbawa, 30 km south of Poto Tano along a narrow road winding through the hills. **Lebok (Lake) Taliwang**, close to the Poto Tano road near Taliwang, is quite a picture when covered in water lilies.

Poto Batu, six km from Taliwang, is a local sea resort with caves and a decent beach. **Labuhanbalat**, a Bugis stilt fishing community of just eight houses, is seven km from Taliwang; take a truck or bemo there.

Places to Stay & Eat

Taliwang's market is next to the bus terminal. Behind the market and directly opposite the mosque, the friendly but spartan *Hotel Azhar* has rooms for 7500 rp per person. *Hotel Taliwang Indah* on Jl Jenderal Sudirman has a 1st floor porch overlooking the hills and a friendly manager who speaks good English. Rooms cost from 15,000 rp. The attached restaurant has a long menu and excellent food. On the same street, opposite the cinema, *Hotel Tubalong* has rooms with mandi for 10,000/15,000 rp.

Getting There & Away

Buses from Taliwang to Poto Tano cost 1000 rp and you can buy tickets with connections right through to Mataram. Most buses leave in the morning between 6 and 9 am. Direct buses also go from Taliwang to Sumbawa Besar (3000 rp; three hours).

SOUTH-EAST SUMBAWA

Many of the small trickle of visitors who make it to the Taliwang area are surfers in search of the good waves along this coast. The area has many beautiful, but isolated, white sand beaches.

From Taliwang, bemos and trucks run 11 km south over a good, paved road to Jereweh, from where it is six km to the beach at **Jelenga**. The *Pondok Wisata Jelenga* has bungalows for 10,000 rp.

Maluk, 30 km south of Jereweh, has a superb beach and is the best-known surfing destination. *Surya Beach Bungalows* has basic beach bungalows for 5,000 rp per person and its restaurant serves good seafood.

A bus leaves Taliwang for Maluk (2000 rp; 1½ hours) at 8 am every day.

The bus from Taliwang continues on to **Sekongkang Atas**, 10 km further south, where the waves are bigger and more fine beaches can be found around the headland. The bus stops at Sekongkang Bawah village on the highway and it is then a two km walk to the beach. There are no facilities but you can stay with the kepala desa.

SUMBAWA BESAR

At one time the name 'Sumbawa' only applied to the western half of the island, which fell under the sway of the sultan of the state of Sumbawa; the eastern half of the island was known as Bima. Almost all that remains of the old western sultanate is the wooden palace in Sumbawa Besar, the showpiece of the town.

Sumbawa Besar is the chief town of the western half of the island, a laid-back, friendly place where cidomos still outnumber bemos and where Muslims flood out of the mosques after midday prayer. There are some lovely tree-lined boulevards around the new palace, but the town has no remarkable attractions except for the old palace. A trip out to Pulau Moyo or to nearby villages can be rewarding, but they are difficult to reach and for most travellers Sumbawa Besar is just a rest stop on the journey across the island.

Apart from the steady stream of travellers that pass through Sumbawa Besar on their way to or from Komodo and Flores, the area is also popular with luxury cruises from Bali that dock at the small port of Badas, west of the town.

Orientation

Sumbawa Besar is small; you can easily walk around most of it, except maybe to the main post office, which is only a bemo or cidomo ride away.

Information

Tourist Office The tourist office (Dinas Pariwisata Daerah; ☎ 21632) is on Jl Garuda in the large Kantor Bupati offices next to the Hotel Tambora. It has some useful brochures. The office is open Monday t Thursday from 7 am to 3 pm, and on Frida until 11 am.

The PHPA (national parks) office (☎ 2 358) is at the Direktorat Jenderal Kehutana Jl Garuda 12. You can get information he about Pulau Moyo, but you'll probably t referred to one of the tour companies f arrangements. The office is open Monday t Friday from 8 am to 2 pm.

Money Bank Danamon changes a wic variety of currencies and gives credit ca cash advances. The next best option is Bar Negara Indonesia (BNI) at Jl Kartini 1 open Monday to Friday from 7.30 am to 2.3 pm, and until noon on Saturday.

Post & Communications There is pos restante at the main post office, which about 1.5 km from the Hotel Tambora on Kebayan. For stamps, there's a sub-po office near the town centre on Jl Yos Sudars Both are open Monday to Thursday from am to 2 pm, on Friday until 11 am and c Saturday until 12.30 pm.

The Telkom office on Jl Setiabudi is op 24 hours, and there is a Telkom wartel at Hasanuddin 105.

Dalam Loka (Sultan's Palace)

Back in the early 1960s, Helen and Fran Schreider passed through Sumbawa Besar their amphibious jeep and later described th remnants of this palace in their book *Th Drums of Tonkin*:

Sumbawa Besar...had a sultan. A small man wi tortoise-shell glasses and a quiet, friendly dignity...h old palace, now deserted except for a few dista relatives, was a long barn-like structure of unpaint wood that seemed on the point of collapsing. Benea the ramshackle entrance, a rusted cannon from th days of the Dutch East India Company lay half-buri in the ground...Mothers and fathers and naked litt children made the palace shake as they followed up the ramp into a great empty room that was once th audience chamber...Only when the few remaini court costumes, the faded silver brocade kains, t gold-handled krises and the long gold fingernails th were a sign of royalty's exemption from labour we

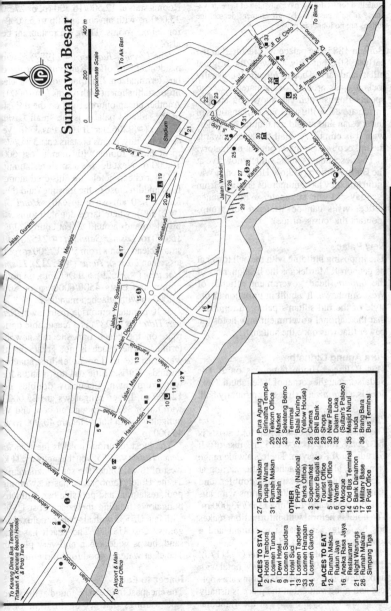

Sumbawa Besar

0   200   400 m

Approximate Scale

PLACES TO STAY
2   Hotel Tambora
7   Losmen Tunas
8   Dewi Hotel
9   Losmen Suudara
11   Hotel Suci
13   Losmen Taqdeer
33   Losmen Harapan
34   Losmen Garoto

PLACES TO EAT
12   Rumah Makan
     Rukun Jaya
16   Aneka Rasa Jaya
     Restaurant
21   Right Warungs
26   Rumah Makan
     Simpang Tiga
27   Rumah Makan
     Puspa Warna
31   Rumah Makan
     Muslin

OTHER
1   PHPA (National
     Parks Office)
3   Supermarket
4   Kantor Bupati &
     Tourist Office
5   Merpati Office
6   Wartel
10   Mosque
14   Old Bus Terminal
15   D Naranamon
     Huda
18   Post Office
19   Pura Agung
     Girinatha Temple
20   Telkom Office
22   Market
23   Seketeng Bemo
     Terminal
24   Balai Kuning
     (Yellow House)
25   Cinema
28   BNI Bank
29   Shops
30   New Palace
32   Dalam Loka
     (Sultan's Palace)
35   Masjid Nurdi
36   Brang Bara
     Bus Terminal

To Karang Dima Bus Terminal,
Tirtasari & Kencana Beach Hotels
& Poto Tano

To Airport & Main
Post Office

To Aik Bari

To Bima

modelled for us did we have any idea of the extravagance of this past era. By government decree, the sultans are no longer in power.

Built in 1885, the palace was restored in the early 1980s, but only a few of the original pillars and carved beams remain. It is usually locked – ask around for the caretaker, who speaks English and can show you around. Inside are a few illustrations, explanations in Indonesian and an old palanquin, but otherwise it is empty. A small donation towards the upkeep is customary, but not obligatory.

The descendants of the sultans now live at the **Balai Kuning** (Yellow House) on Jl Wahidin and they have numerous artefacts from the days of the sultanate. With advance notice, visits can be arranged for groups (contact the tourist office).

New Palace

The imposing building with the bell tower at its gate on Jl Merdeka is the headquarters of the *bupati* (head government official) of West Sumbawa. It's built in imitation of the style of the old sultan's palace; a reminder that the national government now holds the power that was once the sultans'.

Pura Agung Girinatha

This Balinese Hindu temple is on Jl Yos Sudarso, near the corner of Jl Setiabudi. Next door is a *banjar*, a Balinese community hall.

Places to Stay

The place with the best set up for tourists is the *Hotel Tambora* (☎ 21555), just off Jl Garuda on Jl Kebayan. There's a wide range of rooms, all with attached bath, starting at 8250/11,000 rp for singles/doubles and running through to deluxe rooms with air-con, hot water and TV for 77,000/93,000 rp. The hotel is helpful with information, makes bus bookings, and has a restaurant and a small supermarket next door.

Of equal standard, *Dewi Hotel* (☎ 21170), Jl Hasanuddin 60, is a bright, new hotel with stark tilework everywhere. Rooms are spotless and good value, but the place is usually deserted as everyone stays at the Tambora.

Rooms start at 12,500/16,500 rp, or 27,50 33,000 rp with air-con and up to 55,000 for deluxe rooms. There's a restaurant he also.

The *Losmen Taqdeer* (☎ 21987), dowr residential lane off Jl Kamboja near the c bus terminal on Jl Diponegoro, is a cle little establishment with rooms from 6000 Another cheap option, right on the doorst of the sultan's palace, is the small *Losm Garoto* (☎ 22062) at Jl Batu Pasak 48. Ve clean, but tiny, rooms upstairs cost 3500/60 rp or larger rooms with mandi cost 600 10,000 rp. Next door is a small restaurant

Other cheap hotels are clustered along Hasanuddin close to the mosque (and then fore a 4.30 am wake-up call): *Hotel Su* (☎ 21589), where large double rooms wi private mandi around a neat courtyard cc 15,000 rp; *Losmen Saudara* (☎ 21528), wi small, clean rooms from 5000/7500 rp; or t less clean *Losmen Tunas* (☎ 21212). *Losm Harapan* (☎ 21629), 5 Jl Dr Cipto, is anoth option and costs 4500/6000 rp or 800 11,000 rp with attached mandi.

A 10 minute bemo ride from town, *Tirt sari Hotel* (☎ 21987) is a reasonable opti right on the beach opposite the new b terminal. The beach is not great, but t water is clean. The hotel has spacio grounds, but is a little run down and a lo way from town. Economy doubles cc 12,500 rp, larger bungalows are 25,000 with fan or 35,000 rp with air-con, and V bungalows with hot water are 40,000 rp ar 45,000 rp.

The most luxurious hotel is the *Kencar Beach Hotel* (☎ 22555) on the highway, 11 k west of town. Under the same manageme as the Hotel Tambora, it has a swimmir pool, restaurant and poolside bar. Attractiv bungalows fronting the beach cost US$2 with fan, US$35 with air-con, or deluxe bu galows cost US$60. The beach has blac sand, but is wide, clean and very pleasar The clear water is good for snorkelling.

Places to Eat

The cheapest food can be found at the stree side warungs that set up in front of th stadium in the evenings. Soto ayam, sate, bakso and other Madurese fare are sold. The *Rukun Jaya*, on Jl Hasunuddin close to many of the hotels, is a small restaurant with cheap food.

Rumah Makan Mushin, Jl Wahidin 31, is a spotless little cafe with Lombok/Taliwang dishes. Meals are simple, but very tasty, and the ayam bakar (grilled chicken) is excellent. The more adventurous can try the jeroan ayam (chicken intestines).

Sumbawa Besar has two very good Chinese restaurants: the *Aneka Rasa Jaya* at Jl Hasanuddin 14 and the *Puspa Warna* at Jl Kartini 16. Both have extensive menus and specialise in seafood. Grilled whole fish will cost from around 7000 rp and cheaper dishes are on offer.

The restaurant in the *Tambora Hotel* is very good and the *Dewi* and *Tirtasari* hotels also have good food.

Getting There & Away
Air Merpati (☎ 21416) on Jl Diponegoro has four flights a week to/from Mataram (Lombok) and on to Denpasar (Bali).

Bus Sumbawa Besar's main long-distance bus terminal is the new Karang Dima terminal, 5.5 km north-west of town on the highway, although some morning buses to Bima leave from the Brang Bara terminal on Jl Kaharuddin. Fares and approximate journey times from Sumbawa Besar include: Sape (7500 rp; 7½ hours); Bima (6000 rp; seven hours); Dompu (5000 rp; 4½ hours); Taliwang (3000 rp; three hours); and Poto Tano (2500 rp; two hours).

Buses to Bima leave between 7 and 9 am and at 8 pm, but between these times you have to hope for a seat on a bus coming through from Lombok. You can buy combined bus and ferry tickets from Sumbawa Besar through to Mataram (10,000 rp) or Bali. Buses to Lombok leave at 6, 8 and 9 am and 3 pm. Some hotels, such as the Tambora, sell tickets and can arrange pick-up for a slight premium.

Boat Pelni's KM *Tatamailau* stops every two weeks at the small port of Badas, seven km west of Sumbawa Besar, on its loop through the eastern islands. The Pelni office is at Labuhan Sumbawa, the town's fishing port, three km west of town on the Poto Tano road.

Getting Around
The Airport The airport is only 500m from the Hotel Tambora and you can easily walk into town. Turn to your right as you exit the airport terminal and cross the bridge. Alternatively, take a bemo (250 rp).

Bemo The streets here, apart from the bemo speedway along Jl Hasanuddin, are relatively stress free. Bemos and cidomos cost 250 rp for trips anywhere around town.

The local Seketeng bemo terminal is on Jl Setiabudi, in front of the market; cidomos congregate along Jl Urip Sumoharjo near where it meets Jl Setiabudi. For trips to villages around Sumbawa Besar, there should be public bemos. Get to the terminal early in the morning, as sometimes there's only one bemo daily; after that you'll have to charter (prices are negotiable).

AROUND SUMBAWA BESAR
A number of attractions can be visited around Sumbawa Besar if you have time to kill. All are difficult to reach by public transport – hire a motorcycle and preferably a guide in Sumbawa Besar.

Pulau Moyo
Two-thirds of Pulau Moyo, an island off the coast just north of Sumbawa Besar, is a nature reserve with good coral reefs teeming with fish. Moyo rises to 648m; its centre is composed mainly of savanna with stands of forest. The reserve is inhabited by wild domestic cattle, deer, wild pigs and several varieties of birds, though its main attractions are diving and snorkelling.

Accommodation is limited to one ultra-expensive resort, otherwise Pulau Moyo's good diving and snorkelling has to be arranged through operators. It is possible, but difficult, to visit Moyo independently on a day trip. For travel to the island, the PHPA office in Sumbawa Besar has information and a good map of Moyo.

The normal access is from Aik Bari on the coast north of Sumbawa Besar. Public bemos (1500 rp; one hour) run to Aik Bari three or four times daily to no fixed schedule, starting at around 7 am. They leave at the turn-off to Aik Bari at the far end of Jl Sudirman behind the market. Otherwise, you'll have to charter a bemo (around 7500 rp if you bargain hard).

From Aik Bari, you can hire a motorised outrigger or fishing boat for the half-hour, three km crossing to the south coast of the island. You must bargain – 10,000 rp each way is a good price, petrol included. The boats can take you to Aik Manis, which has reasonable snorkelling, or Tanjung Pasir, just to the east, which has better snorkelling. Good reefs with a plunging wall are found all around the island if you are prepared to charter a boat. Some of the best diving is around the Amanwana Resort on the west coast.

If getting there independently sounds like too much trouble, tour operators or the hotels in Sumbawa Besar can arrange trips. The Hotel Tambora's sister hotel, Kencana Beach Hotel, has a good speedboat taking up to 15 people for 350,000 rp per day.

Just to the north-east of Pulau Moyo is the small **Pulau Satunda**, which also has good beaches, snorkelling and a salt-water lake in the middle of the island. It is three hours by boat from Aik Bari.

Places to Stay The only accommodation is at the *Amanwana Resort* (☎ 22330) on the western side of the island. This ultra-exclusive resort is part of the Aman chain and most guests come on packages from the Aman hotels on Bali. Princess Di stayed here and could no doubt afford the US$500 per day rates. The price is incredible when you consider that accommodation is in tents, though admittedly they're luxurious tents on platforms and creature comforts are well catered for. Resort boats run from Badas.

Aik Manis has a small, basic resort, but

after damage by tidal waves it lies deserted and is unlikely to be rebuilt. You could camp in the ramshackle bungalows if you brought your own food and water. Tour operators take guests to camps on other beaches such as Tanjung Pasir.

There are four PHPA guard posts on Moyo; one at the south end, the others in villages, where you can stay overnight for a donation. Take your own food and water.

Other Attractions

Some of the best songket sarongs are made in the village of **Poto**, 12 km east of Sumbawa Besar (600 rp by bus or bemo) and two km from the small town of Moyo. Traditional designs include the *prahu* (outrigger boat) and ancestor head motif. Modern Balinese-style ikat is also woven on handlooms; head into the village across from the football field and ask around to see it being made.

A stretch of the coast near **Lunyuk**, about 60 km south of Sumbawa Besar, is said to be a nesting ground for turtles.

At **Semongkat**, 17 km south-west of Sumbawa Besar in the hills, is an old Dutch swimming pool fed by a mountain river. The hills south of Sumbawa Besar are home to a number of traditional villages and hiking possibilities. One of the more interesting villages is **Tegel**, from where horses can be hired to venture higher into the forest.

Near **Batu Tering** are megalithic sarcophagi believed to be the 2000 year old tombs of ancient chiefs. Footprints in the stones are said to be those of the gods. Batu Tering is about 30 km by bemo from Sumbawa Besar, via Semamung. The sarcophagi are four km on foot from the village, and then it is another two km to **Liang Petang** (Dark Cave).

Aik Beling is a pretty waterfall in the southern mountains. Take the road south through Semamung a further eight km to Brangrea, then the turn-off to the falls, from where it is six km along a rough road with many forks. You need a guide.

Buffalo races, wedding ceremonies and *karaci* (traditional stick fighting) are staged regularly at **Bambunong** village, four km from Sumbawa Besar. They are put on for the cruise ships from Bali, usually on Tuesday and Saturday.

CENTRAL SUMBAWA

It's a beautiful ride from Sumbawa Besar to Bima. After Empang you start moving up into the hills through rolling green country, thickly forested, with occasional sprays of palm trees along the shoreline.

Gunung Tambora

Dominating the peninsula which juts north in central Sumbawa is the 2820m volcano, Gunung Tambora. It can be climbed from the western side. The huge crater contains a two coloured lake, and there are views as far as Gunung Rinjani (on Lombok). The base for ascents is the small logging town of Cilacai, which is eight hours by truck from Dompu or an hour by speedboat from Sumbawa Besar. Not many people bother though, since the climb takes three days.

Tambora's peak was obliterated in the explosion of April 1815 (see Sumbawa History earlier in this section), but since then all has been quiet. The eruption wiped out the entire population of Tambora and Pekat (two small states at the base of the mountain), as well as devastating much of the rest of Sumbawa.

EASTERN SUMBAWA

This part of Sumbawa is little explored by travellers; there aren't many traditional areas left around eastern Sumbawa, but the coastline to the south is quite beautiful and developers are eyeing several sites along it.

Dompu

The seat of one of Sumbawa's former independent states, Dompu is now the third-biggest town on the island. If you're travelling between Sumbawa Besar and Bima, you don't get to see it: buses detour via the lonely Ginte bus terminal (on a hill two km out of Dompu). From there, bemos run into town (250 rp). The town has a big, colourful market snaking around narrow back streets, but otherwise it's just a stopover on the way to the south coast.

The *Hotel Manuru Kupang* (☎ 21387) has gloomy rooms for 11,000 rp or better rooms for 16,000 rp, all with mandi. The more upmarket *Wisma Samada* (☎ 21417) is a spic and span place, but expensive at 20,000 rp for a room with a fan or 35,000 rp with air-con.

Buses run from Ginte bus terminal to Bima (1500 rp; two hours), Sape (2500 rp; 3½ hours) and Sumbawa Besar (5000 rp; 4½ hours). You can get a combined air-con bus/ferry ticket through to Mataram (13,000 rp; 17,000 rp with air-con).

Huu

Huu is best known as a stronghold of one of the most traditional cultures in the world – surf culture. Several hotels have sprung up along Lakey's Beach, three km from Huu village, to cater to surfers who have been coming here since the early 1980s. Lately an attempt has been made to woo the average garden-variety tourist to Huu's long stretch of palm-tree-lined, white sand beach. However, if you're a male and not surfing, be prepared to have your masculinity questioned.

The best waves are between June and August.

Places to Stay & Eat *Mona Lisa Bungalows* is one of the largest places and a good place to start looking. It has a good restaurant and a variety of accommodation, from comfortable economy rooms with outside mandi for 8500/16,000 rp to well-appointed bungalows with bathroom facing the beach for 15,000/20,000 rp and 17,500/25,000 rp. Like all the places here, prices drop outside the May to August peak season.

Right next door is the *Hotel Amangati*, another popular place with new bungalows for 25,000 rp. Next along is *Lakey Peak*, with a dowdy restaurant but stylish bungalows for 15,000/17,500 rp.

Intan Lestari is the one of the original surf camps, with a rustic little restaurant, and rooms for 10,000 rp without mandi and 15,000 rp with mandi. It is popular for the two breaks out front – Lakey Peak and Lakey Pipe – breaking left and right.

Prima Dona is a newer place with a huge restaurant. Bungalows with TV and bathroom cost 17,500/30,000 rp.

There are several other more basic hotels along the beach, such as *Kambera Cottages* with rooms for 10,000/15,000 rp with mandi. *Periscopes* is around 1.5 km from the main beach towards the village, near the surf break of the same name.

A new resort hotel is being built as part of the government's push to develop the area as another Bali (the great dream for provincial tourism everywhere in Indonesia). It is totally out of touch with existing 'surf tourism' and, given Huu's isolation, seems destined to failure.

Getting There & Away It is a god almighty effort to reach Huu by public transport. From Sumbawa Besar or Bima take a bus to Dompu's Ginte bus terminal on the northern outskirts of town, then a bemo (250 rp) to the central market. From here take a cidomo (250 rp per person) to the Lepardi bus terminal on the southern outskirts, from where four buses a day run to Rasabau (750 rp; 1½ hours), starting at 7.30 am. From Rasabau you then have to take an incredibly crowded bemo to the beach.

Try doing this with a surfboard and you'll soon see why everyone takes a taxi from Bima airport. The taxi price is fixed at 54,000 rp, but it may be possible to negotiate a lower price outside the terminal.

Donggo

From Rato/Sila, on the Dompu to Bima road, infrequent buses run to the village of Donggo. It is four km along a good road and then 10 km on a rough road up the mountain. It may be possible to stay with the kepala desa in Donggo. The village has a few traditional houses and superb views. The Dou Donggo ('Mountain People') living in these highlands speak an archaic form of the Bima language and may be descended from the original inhabitants of Sumbawa. Numbering about 20,000, they've adopted Islam and

Christianity over their traditional animism in the last few decades, with varying degrees of enthusiasm; they're being absorbed into Bimanese culture and will probably disappear as a distinct group. The most traditional village is Mbawa where, at least until a few years ago, people still wore distinctive black clothes, and a few *uma leme* (traditional houses whose design was intimately connected with the traditional region) were still standing.

BIMA & RABA

Bima and Raba together form the major town in the eastern half of Sumbawa. Bima, Sumbawa's chief port, is the main centre; Raba, a few km east, is the departure point for buses east to Sape, where you get the ferry to Komodo or Flores.

The Bima region has been known since the 14th century for its sturdy horses, which even then were exported to Java. Local tradition claims that before the 17th century, when Bima fell to the Makassarese and its ruler was converted to Islam, this region had some sort of political control over Timor, Sumba and parts of western Flores.

Today, the former sultan's palace apart, Bima is a rather practical place. It certainly has a good range of services and shops, and the Jl Flores night market is worth a wander.

Information

Tourist Office The tourist information office (Dinas Pariwisata; ☎ 44331) is next to the Kantor Bupati on Jl Soekarno Hatta, about two km from town past the Hotel Parewa. It is open Monday to Friday from 7 am to 3 pm.

Money The BNI bank on Jl Sultan Hasanuddin changes foreign currency and travellers cheques, as does the Bank Rakyat Indonesia on Jl Sumbawa. Both are open Monday to Friday until 1 pm. If you're heading east, this is the last place to change money before Labuanbajo (Flores).

Post & Communications The main post office is on Jl Sultan Hasanuddin, about 500m east of the Hotel Sangyang. Opening

urs are Monday to Saturday from 8 am to
pm. The Telkom office is on Jl Soekarno
atta, about 1.5 km from the town centre,
d is open 24 hours. It's also possible to
ake international calls from the Telkom
arpostel Remaja on Jl Lombok, in the
ntre of town.

ultan's Palace

he former home of Bima's rulers, until they
ere put out of a job after Indonesia's inde-
ndence, is now partly a museum. The
uilding itself is less impressive than its
ounterpart in Sumbawa Besar, but the ex-
bits inside (chainmail shirts, sedan chairs,
attle flags, weapons, a chart comparing the
phabets of Indonesian languages with the
atin alphabet) hold some interest. Built in
27, the palace had fallen into complete
srepair by the late 1950s, but has been
stored. You can see the royal bedchamber
vith its four poster bed, and Koran on the
essing table) and photos of the tombs of

some early Bima rulers which still stand
somewhere in the hills outside town.

The museum is open daily from 7 am to 5
pm. Guides will attach themselves to you and
offer minimal insight, but expect a large
donation – a few hundred rupiah should
suffice.

New Palace

The descendants of the sultan of Bima have
the best collection of artefacts at their house
on Jl Sumbawa. Jewellery, crowns, costumes
and other paraphernalia of the old sultanate
can be seen, but it is open only by appointment. Contact Mr Nasin at the tourist office.

Places to Stay

Bima is compact, and most hotels are in the
middle of town.

An old favourite is the *Hotel Lila Graha*
(☎ 42740) at Jl Lombok 20. It has an excellent restaurant and is still popular, but while
standards gradually slip the prices keep

NUSA TENGGARA

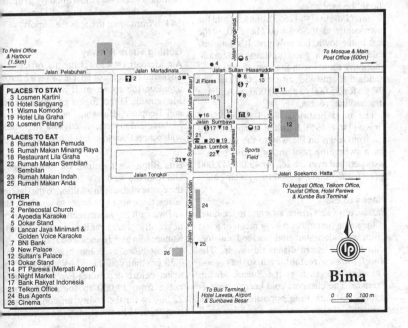

PLACES TO STAY
3 Losmen Kartini
10 Hotel Sangyang
11 Wisma Komodo
19 Hotel Lila Graha
20 Losmen Pelangi

PLACES TO EAT
8 Rumah Makan Pemuda
16 Rumah Makan Minang Raya
18 Restaurant Lila Graha
22 Rumah Makan Sembilan
   Sembilan
23 Rumah Makan Indah
25 Rumah Makan Anda

OTHER
1 Cinema
2 Pentecostal Church
4 Ayoedia Karaoke
5 Dokar Stand
6 Lancar Jaya Minimart &
   Golden Voice Karaoke
7 BNI Bank
9 New Palace
12 Sultan's Palace
13 Dokar Stand
14 PT Parewa (Merpati Agent)
15 Night Market
17 Bank Rakyat Indonesia
21 Telkom Office
24 Bus Agents
26 Cinema

To Peini Office
& Harbour
(1.5km)

Jalan Pelabuhan

Jalan Martadinata

Jl Flores

Jalan Monginsidi

Jalan Sultan Hasanuddin

To Mosque & Main
Post Office (500m)

Jalan Sumbawa

Jalan Sultan Kaharuddin (Jalan Pasar)

Jalan Sultan Kaharuddin

Jalan Lombok

Jalan Sulawesi

Jalan Tongkol

Jalan Sultan Ibrahim

Sports
Field

Jalan Soekarno Hatta

To Merpati Office, Telkom Office,
Tourist Office, Hotel Parewa
& Kumbe Bus Terminal

To Bus Terminal,
Hotel Lawata, Airport
& Sumbawa Besar

Bima

0   50   100 m

rising. Rooms without mandi for 8000 rp are dingy or singles/doubles with mandi for 13,500/16,500 rp are expensive, but better. Air-con double rooms with hot showers go for 42,500 rp. Breakfast is included.

Just next door is the dingy but cheap *Losmen Pelangi* (☎ 42878). Boxy doubles are 6000 rp per person with shared mandi, or 7500 rp with private mandi.

A good option is the friendly *Wisma Komodo* (☎ 42070) on Jl Sultan Ibrahim, which has long been popular with travellers. Good-value doubles are 7500 rp or 12,500 rp with mandi.

The cheapest in town is the seedy *Losmen Kartini* (☎ 42072) at Jl Pasar 11. It rents more than just rooms, but you can stay there for 4000 rp per person.

The ramshackle *Hotel Sangyang* (☎ 42017) on Jl Sultan Hasanuddin was once the best in town, but now looks like a bomb hit it; however, the large, carpeted rooms out the back are quite good and have air-con and hot water for 30,000/35,000 rp. Discounts should be available.

Hotel Parewa (☎ 42652), one km from the town centre at Jl Soekarno Hatta 40, is the best in the town, but only just. It's comfortable and has a good upstairs restaurant. Economy rooms with fan cost 25,000 rp, or standard rooms with air-con, hot water and TV go for 35,000 rp and 40,000 rp. All have attached bathrooms.

The most luxurious hotel is the *Hotel Lawata* (☎ 43696), Jl Sultan Salahuddin, 10 km from town on the way to the airport. It has a swimming pool and attractive bungalows perched over the sea for 42,000/47,000 rp, or from 59,000/65,000 rp with air-con.

Places to Eat
Restaurant Lila Graha, attached to the hotel of the same name, has a long menu of good Chinese, Indonesian and seafood cuisine, with a few western dishes thrown in. The *Hotel Parewa* restaurant also has good Chinese food, as does the *Rumah Makan Pemuda*. The cheapest cold beer in town is at *Rumah Makan Anda*, opposite the cinema.

Rumah Makan Sembilan Sembilan on Jl Lombok near the Hotel Lila Graha specialis in fried chicken and has other good Chine and Indonesian dishes.

The *Rumah Makan Minang Jaya* on Sumbawa is a good, clean Padang restaura while a couple more basic restaurants a along Jl Kaharuddin. The night *market* h stalls selling sate, curry, gado gado, rice cr ations and interesting snacks.

Entertainment
Though Bima is a small, conservative ci like most others in Indonesia, it has undese vedly acquired a reputation as some sort outpost of Islamic fundamentalism. In fa compared to the towns on Flores, it is almc a swinging city. Well, it has a couple slightly seedy karaoke bars if you are despe ate for something to do. Both are on Jl Sult Hasanuddin – the *Ayoedia Karaoke* and t *Golden Voice Karaoke* above the Lanc Jaya Minimart.

Otherwise, horse races are a popul pastime and are held most Sundays in the d season at the horse stadium at Desa Pand 14 km from town towards the airport.

Getting There & Away
Air Merpati (☎ 42697) has its office at Soekarno Hatta 60, or PT Parewa is a Merpa agent on the corner of Jl Sumbawa and Monginsidi. Direct flights go between Bin and Denpasar, Bajawa, Ende, Labuanbaj Mataram, Maumere, Ruteng and Tambulak with connections to points further afield.

Bus Bima bus terminal, for most buses and from the west, is a 10 minute walk fro the centre of town. In addition to the daytim buses, there are night buses to Lombok, Ba or Java with ferry fares included. Several bu ticket offices are near the corner of Jl Sult Kaharuddin and Jl Soekarno Hatta.

Most buses to Lombok leave at arour 7.30 pm, but you should try and book you ticket before departure. Fares to Matara range from 14,000 rp for non-air-con t 22,000 rp for the luxury, air-con buses th take about 11 hours. Bima Setia currently ha e best buses, though Rasa Sayang and ngsung Indah are also good. Many continue on to Denpasar (40,000 to 45,000 rp), riving at 11 am the next morning, or you n even continue right through to Surabaya d Jakarta.

Destinations on Sumbawa are serviced by aller, crowded, non-air-con buses that are e local supply line, stopping anywhere and erywhere. They run between 6 am and 5 n. Destinations from Bima include Dompu 500 rp; two hours) and Sumbawa Besar 000 rp; seven hours).

Buses east to Sape go from Kumbe bus rminal in Raba, a 20 minute (250 rp) bemo le east of Bima. You should be able to pick a bemo easily on Jl Sultan Kaharuddin or Soekarno Hatta. Buses leave Kumbe for ape (1100 rp; two hours) from about 6 am til 5 pm. Don't rely on these local buses to t you to Sape in time for the morning ferry Komodo or Flores. Alternatively, the big ses coming though Bima from Surabaya 4 am will pick up from the hotels and take u through to Sape for 2000 rp. You can range this at the Bima bus terminal the ening before or your hotel might be able arrange it for you. The other alternative is chartered bemo, which will do the run in /2 hours and cost 20,000 to 25,000 rp, pending on your bargaining skills.

oat The Pelni office is at Bima's port at Jl labuhan 103. The *Kelimutu* calls at Bima vice a fortnight; one week sailing on to aingapu, Ende and Kupang, and the next eek sailing to Lembar.

Getting Around

The Airport Taxi prices are fixed at 10,000 rp for the 16 km, 20 minute trip to the town centre or 54,000 rp to Huu, but a price rise is imminent.

The airport is right on the highway, so you can walk out to the main road about 100m in front of the terminal and catch a bus there. Any local bus from Dompu or Sumbawa Besar can take you into town, but they can be very crowded and a taxi may be your best bet.

Local Transport Bemos around town cost 250 rp per person; dokars are 200 rp.

SAPE

Sape is a pleasant little town with amiable people and an immense number of dokars, which the locals call 'Ben Hurs'. These jingling little buggies with their skinny, pompomed horses don't look much like Roman chariots, but the drivers obviously think they're Charlton Hestons as they race each other along the main street after dark.

There are two colourful daily markets in town; one right in its centre and the other behind the bus terminal. Sape has a handful of basic hotels and rumah makan (eating places), but it is a more convenient place to overnight than Bima if you want to catch the ferry to Komodo or Flores. The ferry leaves from Pelabuhan Sape, about four km down the road from Sape. There's lots of boat building going on along the street running down to the port.

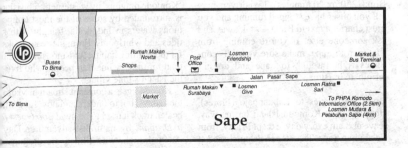

Information

The PHPA office is about 2.5 km from the town centre along the road to Pelabuhan Sape. The office has some interesting brochures and maps, and is open daily until 2 pm.

Places to Stay

The most convenient place to stay if you arrive the night before the ferry leaves is *Losmen Mutiara*, nestled just outside the entrance to the port. The best rooms are upstairs, with access to a back balcony overlooking the harbour. All rooms have shared mandi and cost 7500/10,000 rp. There are a couple of small warungs and shops opposite the hotel, but if you're in Sape for more than a day or so, the four km dokar ride into town could get tiresome.

In town, *Losmen Friendship* lives up to its name. Clean doubles with shared mandi cost 8000 rp (10,000 rp with private mandi). Two cheaper, more basic places are the *Losmen Ratna Sari* and the *Losmen Give* with rooms from 6000 rp.

Getting There & Away

Bus Buses always meet ferries arriving at Pelabuhan Sape; they are usually express services direct to Lombok or Bali. Some sample fares for express air-con buses are: Mataram (26,000 rp); Denpasar (40,000 rp); and Surabaya (50,000 rp).

For most destinations on Sumbawa, you will need to go to Bima for an onward bus. Buses leave from Sape bus terminal every half-hour for Raba (1100 rp; two hours) until around 5 pm. From Raba take a bemo to Bima (250 rp; 20 minutes). Taxi drivers may tell you buses have stopped running and you must charter a taxi to Bima – walk away and ask someone else. If you're coming from Mataram to Sape, make sure your bus continues right through to Sape and doesn't terminate in Bima.

Boat The ferries to Labuanbajo (Flores), stopping in at Komodo Island on the way, leave at 8 am every day, except Friday, from Pelabuhan Sape. Tickets can be purchased at the pier about one hour before departure. both directions, the ferries stop at Komodo but can't dock at the island, so small fishi boats shuttle to Loh Liang for an extra 15 rp. Sape to Komodo costs 10,000 rp, or Labuanbajo 11,500 rp. You can take a cycle from Sape to Labuanbajo for 2000 a motorcycle for 10,000 rp or a car for 97,5 rp.

The duration of the crossing varies w the tides and weather, but allow five to sev hours to Komodo and eight to 10 hours Labuanbajo. Two companies operate alternate days – the *Enlira* leaves Sape Monday, Wednesday and Saturday and is t biggest and fastest. Ferries have been know to break down and be out of action for week and a few years back passengers we stranded at Sape when a party of governme officials commandeered a ferry for a jaunt Komodo. Check schedules in Bima.

You can also charter your own boat Komodo, but this is more easily and cheap done from Labuanbajo.

Getting Around

A dokar between Sape and the ferry pi costs 250 rp per person if you share, b charter rates are more like 1000 rp.

Komodo & Rinca

A hilly, desolate island sandwiched betwee Flores and Sumbawa, Komodo's big attra tion is lizards – three metre, 100 kg monster known as *ora* to the locals and tagge 'Komodo dragons' by westerners. The islan is surrounded by some of the most tempe tuous waters in Indonesia, fraught with r tides and whirlpools. From the sea it looks far more fitting habitat for a monstrous liza than for the few hundred people who live the island's lone village.

Komodo gets a constant stream of visito these days, but to understand how far off th beaten track it used to be, read *Zoo Quest f a Dragon*, by naturalist-adventurer Dav Attenborough, who filmed the dragons

Komodo & Rinca Islands

Sape Strait

FLORES SEA

Labuanbajo

▲ Gunung Satalibo

Pulau Pungut

▲ Gunung Ara (538m) Poreng
● Banu Nggulung

Komodo Loh Liang △

Kampung Komodo ● ● Pantai Merah

▲ Gunung Komodo Pulau Lasa

Lintah Strait

Loh Buaya △

Kampung Rinca

Doro Raja ▲

Padar

Kampung Loh Karora

FLORES

▲ Doro Lankai

Rinca

Pulau Tata

Doro Ora (671m) Kampung Loh Baru

Molo Strait

Gili Dasampi Gili Motong

0   10   20 km

NUSA TENGGARA

1956. Dragons also inhabit the nearby islands of Rinca and Padar, and coastal western Flores. Some people now prefer to visit Rinca than Komodo, since it's closer to Flores, has fewer visitors and dragon-spotting is less organised.

Orientation & Information

Komodo The only village is Kampung Komodo, a fishing village in a bay on the east coast. On the same bay and a half-hour walk north of the village is Loh Liang, the tourist accommodation camp run by the PHPA. You pay a 2000 rp park entrance fee on arrival at Loh Liang, valid for seven days. If you are going on to Rinca, keep your park entrance ticket, as Rinca is part of the same national park.

The PHPA warns you not to walk outside the camp without one of its guides. Longer treks around the island can be organised, and the PHPA office has a list of guides' fees for them. Though the dragons are a docile bunch for the most part, a lot of emphasis is put on 'danger' – this includes encounters with Komodo dragons that can snap your leg as fast as they'll cut a goat's throat, or having a cobra spit poison at you. Several years ago an elderly European did wander off alone and was never found. Locals are attacked periodically, most commonly while sleeping out in the open.

Rinca The PHPA tourist camp is at Loh Buaya and it's possible to camp in some of the villages. The park entrance fee here is also 2000 rp; PHPA guides cost 5000 rp. Again, keep your entrance ticket if you're going on to Komodo.

Dragon Spotting

Komodo You're likely to see dragons all year at Banu Nggulung, a dry river bed about a half-hour walk from Loh Liang. The ritual feeding of dragons with goats provided by tourists is a thing of the past and dragons are now only fed when the PHPA wants to do a head count. The watering hole at Banu Nggulung still attracts dragons, but since the feeding was stopped dragon numbers are now low. More than likely you will see a dragon, but in the future sightings may not be guaranteed as before.

A little 'grandstand' overlooks the river bed where the dragons gather. Spectators are fenced off from the dragons – don't expect to walk up to the dragons and have them say 'cheese'. A telephoto lens is handy, but not essential. A guide costs 3000 rp, or 1000 rp per person for groups of more than three. The

PHPA prefers to organise fixed times and take large groups, though smaller groups are less zoo-like.

You might spot dragons on some of the other walks and a few lazy examples can often be seen around the tourist camp looking for food.

Rinca There are no established dragon feeding places on Rinca, so spotting monitors is more a matter of luck and your guide's knowledge. But other wildlife is much more abundant than on Komodo: there are several monkey colonies, wild water buffalos, deer, horses, pigs, bush turkeys and eagles.

Komodo Dragons

There were rumours of these awesome creatures long before their existence was confirmed in the west. Fishers and pearl divers working in the area had brought back tales of ferocious lizards with enormous claws, fearsome teeth and fiery yellow tongues. One theory holds that the Chinese dragon is based on the Komodo lizard. The first Dutch expedition to the island was in 1910; two of the dragons were shot and their skins taken to Java, resulting in the first published description.

The Komodo dragon is actually a monitor lizard. Monitors range from tiny 20g things just 20 cm long to the granddaddy of them all, the Komodo dragon *(Varanus komodoensis* in science-speak). All monitors have some things in common: the head is tapered; the ear openings are visible; the neck is long and slender; the eyes have eyelids and round pupils; and the jaws are powerful. But the dragons also have massive bodies, four powerful legs (each with five clawed toes) and long, thick tails (which function as rudders and can also be used for grasping or as a potent weapon). The body is covered in small, nonoverlapping scales; some may be spiny, others raised and bony.

The monitors' powerful legs allow them to sprint short distances, lifting their tails as they run. Many species stay in or near the water and can swim quite well, with an undulating movement of the trunk and tail. When threatened they'll take refuge in their normal resting places – holes, trees (for the smaller monitors) or water. They *are* dangerous if driven into a corner and will then attack a much larger opponent. They threaten by opening the mouth, inflating the neck and hissing. The ribs may spread or the body expand slightly, making the monitor look larger. It often rises up on its hind legs just before attacking, and the tail can deliver well-aimed blows that will knock down a weaker adversary. Their best weapons are their sharp teeth and dagger-sharp claws which can inflict severe wounds.

All monitors feed on other animals: small ones on insects; larger ones on frogs and birds; and the ora on deer, wild pig and even water buffalo which inhabit the islands. The ora also eat their own dead. They can expand their mouth cavity considerably, enabling them to swallow large prey; the ora can push practically a whole goat into its throat.

Being such a large reptile, the ora rarely moves until warmed by the sun. They seem to be stone deaf, but have a very keen sense of smell. Of all the monitors, the ora lays the largest eggs – up to 12 cm long and weighing around 200g. The female lays 20 or 30 eggs at a time and usually buries them in the wall of a dry river, where they hatch by themselves nine months later.

Monitors are *not* relics of the dinosaur age; they're remarkably versatile, hardy modern lizards, if not exactly sensitive and new age. Why they exist only on and around Komodo Island is a mystery, as is why males outnumber females by a ratio of 3.4 to one. Populations of the ora vary, though there has been a decline on Komodo from 3336 in 1990 down to an estimated 1600 in 1996. About 800 are found on Rinca and fewer in the other locations.

The villagers never hunted the monitors, which weren't as good to eat as the numerous wild pigs on the island and for other reasons not too hard to imagine! Today the ora is a protected species. ■

other Activities

Most visitors stay one night at Komodo and only visit Banu Nggulung, but Komodo has number of other things to do and it is quite easy to spend two days or more on the island.

Other walks include the climb to **Gunung Ara** (538m). A guide costs 20,000 rp for a maximum of five people and the trip takes ½ hours return. The chances of seeing a dragon are slim, but from the top there are expansive views right across the island.

Poreng Valley, 5.5 km from Loh Liang, is another favourite dragon haunt and has a more out-in-the-wild feeling than Banu Nggulung. Guides cost 12,000 rp for this trip and you can also continue on to Loh Sabita. You may not spot dragons, but you will see other wildlife such as wild buffalos. You'll see plenty of other animals and bird life on Komodo, notably deer and wild pigs, though not all are wild and a number of deer and pigs spend their days hanging out at park headquarters.

Kampung Komodo is a half-hour walk from park headquarters along the beach. It's a friendly Muslim Bugis village of stilt houses infested with goats, chickens and children. The inhabitants are all descendants of convicts who were exiled to the island last century by one of the sultans on Sumbawa. Komodo is very hot most of the year; take water on the walks.

Good snorkelling can be found at **Pantai Merah** (Red Beach) and the small island of **Pulau Lasa** near Kampung Komodo. Boats can be hired at Kampung Komodo – the PHPA isn't very helpful – and if you want to go snorkelling it's best to bring your own equipment. Dolphins are common in the seas between Komodo and Flores, and the area is also on a whale migration route from the Indian Ocean to the South China Sea.

Places to Stay & Eat

On Komodo, the PHPA camp at Loh Liang is a collection of large, spacious wooden cabins on stilts with front balconies. Each cabin has four or five rooms, a sitting area and two mandis. Rooms are spartan with mattresses on the floor, but are comfortable and have plenty of rustic charm. Singles/doubles cost 10,000/15,000 rp, but single rooms are limited and you'll usually have to pay for a double. During the peak tourist season – around July/August – the rooms may be full, but the PHPA will rustle up mattresses to sleep on even if you can't be guaranteed a room. Electricity, produced by a noisy generator, operates from 6 to 10 pm.

There's also a restaurant at the camp, with a limited menu of nasi/mie goreng meals for around 2500 rp, fish and other simple meals, plus some drinks (including beer and drinking water). Bring other food yourself, or pick up basic supplies at Kampung Komodo.

On Rinca, accommodation at the PHPA camp at Loh Buaya is similar to that on Komodo, at the same prices, but there's no restaurant so bring your own food. The PHPA guides are very friendly; they don't get many people staying at the camp and are glad of the company.

Getting There & Away

Komodo From Sape (Sumbawa), a ferry departs at 8 am daily, except Friday, and costs 10,000 rp for the five to seven hour journey, depending on the sea conditions and the ferry (one ferry is faster than the other). Going the other way, the Labuanbajo-Komodo-Sape ferry departs from Labuanbajo at 8 am daily, except Friday, and costs 4000 rp for the three hour journey. Tickets can be purchased from the harbours in Sape and Labuanbajo one hour before departure.

The ferries cannot dock at Loh Liang and stop about one km out to sea, from where small boats transfer you to Komodo for an extra 1500 rp.

Leaving Komodo, the small boats depart at 10 am to meet the Labuanbajo-Sape ferry, and at noon to meet the Sape-Labuanbajo ferry.

Boats to Komodo can be chartered from Labuanbajo or Sape. It is easier and cheaper to arrange in Labuanbajo, although it is becoming increasingly expensive to charter a boat, and hotels and boat operators prefer to sell tours. If you can arrange it yourself, boats start at 60,000 rp for a day trip for up to six people, or about 100,000 rp for a two day trip with an overnight stay on the boat. Labuanbajo to Komodo takes three to four hours in an ordinary boat. Komodo is also included on the boat tours between Lombok and Labuanbajo. See under Labuanbajo in the following Flores section for more details.

Rinca There are no regular passenger ships or ferries to Rinca, so the only option is to charter a boat. It's only about two hours by motorboat from Labuanbajo to Rinca; a charter boat costs around 50,000 rp for up to six people. Ask at the hotels or around the harbour.

Flores

Flores is one of the biggest, most rugged and most beautiful islands in Nusa Tenggara. You'll find some interesting cultures here, with a layer of animism beneath the prevalent Christianity.

The island has a thriving ikat-weaving tradition, a developing beach spot at Labuanbajo and some fine snorkelling off some parts of the coast. The island has attracted a steady flow of visitors in recent years, but has nothing like the tourist scene of Bali or even Lombok.

History

Flores owes its name to the Portuguese, who called its easternmost cape Cabo das Flores, meaning 'Cape of Flowers'. The island's diverse cultures have enough similarities to suggest that they developed from a common type, differentiated by geographical isolation and the varying influence of outsiders. Long before Europeans arrived in the 16th century, much of coastal Flores was firmly in the hands of the Makassarese and Bugis from southern Sulawesi. The Bugis even established their own ports as part of a trading network throughout the archipelago. They brought gold, coarse porcelain, elephant tusks (used for money), a sort of machete known as *parang*, linen and copperware, and

left with rubber, sea cucumber (much of i fished from the bay of Maumere), shark fin sandalwood, wild cinnamon, coconut oi cotton and fabric from Ende. Bugis an Makassarese slave raids on the coasts o Flores were a common problem, forcin people to retreat inland.

Javanese chronicles dating from the 14t century place Flores (rather imaginatively within the Majapahit realm. In the 15th an 16th centuries, most of western and centra Flores is thought to have become a colony o the Makassarese kingdom of Gowa in south ern Sulawesi, while eastern Flores cam under the sway of Ternate in Maluku.

As early as 1512, Flores was sighted b the Portuguese navigator Antonio de Abreu and Europeans had probably landed by 1550 The Portuguese, involved in the lucrativ sandalwood trade with Timor, built fort resses on Solor (off eastern Flores) and a Ende (on Flores), and in 1561 Dominica priests established a mission on Solor. From here the Portuguese Dominicans extended their work to eastern Flores, founding ove 20 missions by 1575. Despite attacks by pirates, local Islamic rulers and raiders from Gowa, the missionaries converted, it i claimed, tens of thousands of Florinese. The fortress at Ende was overrun in 1637 by Muslims and the mission abandoned, a eventually were all the other missions or southern Flores. The growth of Christianity continued, however, and today the church is the centrepiece of almost every village.

In the 17th century, the VOC kicked the Portuguese out of Flores and the surrounding area and concentrated on monopolising the trade in sappan wood (used to make a red dye) and wild cinnamon. The slave trade was also strong; a treaty with Ende outlawed it in 1839, but it was reported to exist into the firs years of the 20th century.

Though Ternate and Gowa ceded all their rights on Solor, Flores and eastern Sumbawa to the Dutch in the 17th century, Flores was too complex and isolated for the Dutch to gain real control. Around 1850 the Dutch bought out Portugal's remaining enclaves in the area, including Larantuka, Sikka and

'aga on Flores. Dutch Jesuits then took over
missionary work on Flores and founded their
new bases in Maumere and Sikka, which are
still their centres on Flores today.

Even into the first decade of this century,
the Dutch were constantly confronted with
rebellions and intertribal wars, until a major
military campaign in 1907 brought most of
the tribes of central and western Flores
firmly under control. Missionaries moved
into the isolated western hills in the 1920s.

Geography

Geographically, the island's turbulent volca-
ic past has left a complicated relief of
V-shaped valleys, knife-edged ridges, and a
collection of active and extinct volcanoes.
One of the finest volcanoes is the caldera of
Keli Mutu in central Flores, with its three
coloured lakes. There are 14 active volca-
oes on Flores; only Java and Sumatra have
nore. The central mountains slope gently to
he north coast, but along the south coast the
spurs of the volcanoes plunge steeply into
he sea.

The island is part of one of the world's
most geologically unstable zones, and earth-
uakes and tremors hit every year. In
December 1992 an earthquake measuring
.8 on the Richter scale, and the massive tidal
wave that followed it, killed around 3000
people in eastern Flores and almost flattened
he large town of Maumere.

The rugged terrain makes road construc-
ion difficult; although Flores is only about
75 km long, its end-to-end road winds,
wists, ascends and descends for nearly 700

km and heavy wet-season rains, as well as
the frequent earthquakes and tremors, mean
that it has to be repaired year-round.

Climate

The rainy season (November to March) is
more intense in western Flores, which receives the brunt of the north-west monsoon
and has the highest mountains. Ruteng, near
Flores' highest peak (the 2400m Ranaka),
gets an average 3350 mm of rain every year,
but Ende has only 1140 mm and Larantuka
just 770 mm.

Population & People

Difficulties of communication have contributed to the diversity of Flores' cultures. In
more remote areas, you'll find older people
who don't speak a word of Bahasa Indonesia
and whose parents grew up in purely animist
societies.

Physically, the people at the western end
of the island are more 'Malay', while the
other inhabitants of Flores are more Melanesian. The island's 1½ million people are
divided into five main language and cultural
groups: from west to east, these are the
Manggarai (main town Ruteng); the Ngada
(Bajawa); the closely related Ende and Lio
peoples (Ende); the Sikkanese (Maumere);
and the Lamaholot (Larantuka).

Religion

Around 85% of the people are Catholic
(Muslims tend to congregate in the coastal
towns), but in rural areas particularly, Christianity is welded onto traditional beliefs.

Animist rituals are still important here for a variety of occasions, ranging from birth, marriage and death to the building of new houses, or to mark important points in the agricultural cycle. Even educated, English-speaking Florinese still admit to the odd chicken, pig or buffalo sacrifice to keep their ancestors happy when rice is planted or a new field opened up. In former times, it took more than animal blood to keep the gods and spirits friendly; there are persistent tales of children or virgin girls being sacrificed.

Getting Around

What one Indonesian tourist leaflet charitably calls the 'Trans-Flores Highway' loops and tumbles nearly 700 scenic km from Labuanbajo to Larantuka, at the eastern end of the island. The road is paved almost all the way now, but bus trips across Flores still rate as some of the most uncomfortable in Indonesia. Small, cramped and overcrowded buses constantly stop to pick up or drop off passengers, and in the towns they will cruise the streets endlessly until they have a full complement of passengers. The road is narrow and forever winding. Floods or landslides in the rainy season are not uncommon, and the latest trouble spots are attended by scores of workers doing back-breaking work in difficult conditions – it must seem like patching a crumbling dyke.

LABUANBAJO

A small Muslim/Christian fishing town at the extreme western end of Flores, this is a jumping-off point for Komodo and Rinca, and also the most popular swimming and sunning spot on Flores. If you've got a few days to while away, Labuanbajo is a pleasant enough town to do it. There aren't any readily accessible walk-on-and-flop beaches, but many of the small islands nearby have white sand beaches and good snorkelling offshore. The harbour is littered with outrigger fishing boats and is sheltered by the islands, giving the impression that you're standing on the shores of a large lake.

Information

Tourist Office The tourist office (Dinas Pariwisata; ☎ 41170) for the Manggarai region is up behind the Telkom office. It has n brochures as yet, but staff are helpful i answering any queries. It is open from 7 a to 3 pm on weekdays until 2.30 pm o Friday.

The PHPA administers Komodo Nationa Park, which takes in Komodo and Rinc islands and other parts of western Flores including the Riung area. The PHPA infor mation booth provides some practica information for Komodo and Rinca island or the main PHPA office is a little out c town.

Money The Bank Rakyat Indonesia is ope Monday to Friday from 7 am to 3 pm. Fc currencies other than US dollars, expect very poor exchange rate. It only accep Bank America, Citibank, Amex and Thoma Cook travellers cheques. If you're headin west, this is the last place to change mone before Bima in Sumbawa.

Post & Communications The post office open Monday to Saturday, is in the centre c the village, while the Telkom office is a bi of a hike from town, near the PHPA office.

Things to See & Do

Walking down the main street of Labuan bajo, you're likely to be offered boats fo charter to the uninhabited island of you choice for swimming and snorkelling. Oth erwise, ask at the hotels. A half-day trip t **Pulau Bidadari**, where there's coral an clear water, costs around 20,000 rp for up t six people. For divers, there's good cora between the islands of **Sabolo Besar** an **Sabolo Kecil**. Operators such as Varanu and Dive Komodo, near the Bajo Beac Hotel, offer dive trips.

Other beaches worth lounging on are a **Batugosok** and on **Kanawa Island**. Bot places have accommodation and transport i free if you stay there. Otherwise, ask aroun where boats for **Weicucu** and **Batugoso** leave at the north end of the main street. Th

rip to Batugosok costs about 4000 rp. **Pan-
ai Weicucu** itself is just a beach, but there's
white sand beach on the small island oppo-
ite.

Batu Cermin (Mirror Rock) is about four
m from town and has a good cave; take a
orch (flashlight). Walk there, or charter a
emo.

Organised Tours

A popular way to travel between Labuanbajo
nd Lombok is on boat tours. A typical itin-
rary takes in one of the offshore islands –
Bidadari or Kanawa – then Rinca. You sleep
vernight on the boat, usually at Pulau
Kalong ('Flying Fox Island', a mangrove
sland covered in bats) then head for Ko-
nodo to see the dragons and take in some
norkelling. The boats then head along the
north coast of Sumbawa making several
norkelling stops off islands, including
Pulau Moyo and Pulau Satunda off Sumbawa, before docking at Labuhan Lombok
Lombok).

The main companies are Sea Transporta-
ion Cooperative (a local concern with a
variety of boats from small to mid-sized),
Suamarnik Kencana and Perama, which
have their own mid-sized boats. They all
have offices in Labuanbajo. Fares are typically around US$95 to US$115 (check their
exchange rates) for a five or six day trip
hough you may end up spending the last day
at Labuhan Lombok, which has little of interest. Bus transfers to Mataram may or may not
be included. Shop around and find out
exactly what is included – entrance frees,
equipment, what sort of food is served,
sleeping arrangements (always on the boat,
but check the cabin) etc.

Independent operators also offer cheaper
ours and it is especially important to check
but arrangements with these. Try to meet the
guides taking the tours, not just the ticket
sellers. Almost all the hotels arrange tours,
either through the main companies or
smaller operators. The cheapest hotels
usually offer the cheapest tours. Travellers
ate the trips from excellent to dismal – it
often depends on the crew and your fellow

travellers, who you are stuck with for almost
a week.

If the ferry schedule to Komodo is not
convenient, tours are available. A two day
tour, sleeping overnight on the boat, to
Komodo, Rinca and Kalong costs around
50,000 rp per person on a fishing boat that
takes eight people. Many hotels can arrange
boats for day trips to Komodo or Pulau
Sabolo, which has good snorkelling. Small
boats for a day trip to Komodo start at around
60,000 rp for up to six people, which will
give you about three hours wandering
around the island. Charter boats can also be

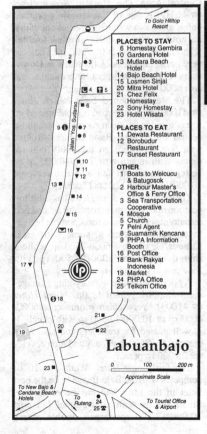

PLACES TO STAY
6 Homestay Gembira
10 Gardena Hotel
13 Mutiara Beach Hotel
14 Bajo Beach Hotel
15 Losmen Sinjai
20 Mitra Hotel
21 Chez Felix Homestay
22 Sony Homestay
23 Hotel Wisata

PLACES TO EAT
11 Dewata Restaurant
12 Borobudur Restaurant
17 Sunset Restaurant

OTHER
1 Boats to Weicucu & Batugosok
2 Harbour Master's Office & Ferry Office
3 Sea Transportation Cooperative
4 Mosque
5 Church
7 Pelni Agent
8 Suamarnik Kencana
9 PHPA Information Booth
16 Post Office
18 Bank Rakyat Indonesia
19 Market
24 PHPA Office
25 Telkom Office

Labuanbajo

0   100   200 m
Approximate Scale

To Golo Hilltop Resort

Jalan Yos Sudarso

To New Bajo & Cendana Beach Hotels
To Ruteng
To Tourist Office & Airport

NUSA TENGGARA

taken to Bidadari and Sabolo – large boats will cost around 50,000 rp.

Places to Stay

You can stay in Labuanbajo itself or at one of the beach hotels. For years a price war between the hotels saw rates drop to ridiculously low levels, especially in the off season, but the hotels have recently banded together to fix prices throughout the year. It remains to be seen if the hotels maintain their spirit of co-operation and the new, non-negotiable rates. All hotel rates include breakfast.

Central Area The *Mutiara Beach Hotel* (☎ 41039) is one of Labuanbajo's original hotels and has a waterfront restaurant with a harbour view. Upstairs singles/doubles without mandi cost 5000/8000 rp. They are very basic, but overlook the harbour. Downstairs rooms are dark, but have mandis, and cost 6000/12,000 rp.

The well-appointed *Bajo Beach Hotel* (☎ 41009) across the road is more upmarket. It has a range of clean rooms set around a central eating area. Basic economy rooms with outside mandi go for 4000/7000 rp, rooms with mandi cost 7000/10,000 rp or better rooms with fan and shower cost 10,000/15,000 to 12,500/17,500 rp.

The popular *Gardena Hotel* has a hilltop position above the main road and an attached restaurant serving good food. Simple bungalows around a garden, some with great harbour views, cost 6000/8500 rp without shared mandi, or 8000/12,500 rp with shower and mosquito nets.

A good, new place with a young management that tries hard is the *Mitra Hotel* (☎ 41003). Very clean rooms cost 6000/8000 rp or 10,000/12,500 rp with mandi. It is well geared for travellers and also rents bicycles for 7500 rp per day and motorcycles for 25,000 rp per day.

The fairly new *Hotel Wisata* (☎ 41020) competes with the Bajo Beach to be the best hotel in the town and has better service. Small rooms with shower and fan cost 10,000/12,500 rp; larger, double rooms

facing the courtyard cost 15,000/20,000 rp. The restaurant here is good.

Labuanbajo also has a number of small homestays. The best of these is *Chez Felix* run by a friendly family that speaks good English. Rooms are clean, with large windows, and there's a pleasant porch area for eating. Singles/doubles are 6000/8000 rp with shared bath, 8000/12,500 rp with mandi and 10,000/15,000 rp with fan and mandi.

Nearby is the quiet *Sony Homestay*, with a nice hilltop view. Basic but clean rooms with private bath are 5000/7500 rp.

Labuanbajo has plenty of other basic anonymous losmen such as the *Bahagia Homestay* and *Homestay Gembira* next to the mosque. They all charge 5000/7000 rp for rooms without mandi.

The *Golo Hilltop Resort*, about one km north of town on a hilltop with spectacular views, was one of the best hotels but has gone bankrupt. Expect it to open again soon.

Beach Hotels You'll need to take a boat ride to get to most of these hotels from Labuanbajo. To get to Weicucu costs 3000 rp, but all the hotels provide free transport for guests.

The *Weicucu Beach Hotel* is a 20 minute boat ride north of Labuanbajo. The beach is dun coloured, but the calm waters are good for swimming and the small island opposite offers a white sand beach and good snorkelling. This has long been a popular budget option because of its price – 7500 rp per person for a basic bamboo bungalow or 10,000 rp with attached mandi, including all meals. Under the new hotel association regime, prices may double, excluding meals, but it won't be worth it and it is unlikely they will rise that high.

Batu Gosok Lodge (☎ 41030) is set on a fine white beach on the mainland, a half-hour boat ride from town. Attractive two storey bungalows cost US$35 per room or separate cottages are US$45. Lunch or dinner costs US$7 per person.

The *New Bajo Beach Hotel* (☎ 41047) is 2.5 km south of town and is the most upmarket hotel in the vicinity. Air-con double ms cost 60,000 rp. The beach is pleasant ough, but no world-beater.

The *Cendana Beach Hotel* (☎ 41125), km past the New Bajo Beach, is on a ndescript beach. This large hotel has come run down, but is now under new nagement. Rooms are very spacious and sonably priced at 10,000/20,000 rp with and shower, or better rooms are 15,000/ ,000 rp.

Kanawa Island Bungalows is on Pulau nawa, one hour by boat from Labuanbajo. e hotel's information centre is in a house posite the Hotel Wisata. The beach and orkelling here are both very good, and nple bungalow accommodation costs ,500/17,500 rp.

Nuca Lala Bungalows on Pulau Pungu is new place with good bungalows a half- ur boat ride from Labuanbajo. Bungalows st 15,000 rp a double. The booking office near the Komodo PHPA information ice.

aces to Eat

buanbajo has a few good restaurants ecialising in seafood at reasonable prices. ck of the crop is the *Borobudur*, set above road with lovely views. It has excellent h, prawns, a few Thai dishes, steaks and en schnitzel. It's more expensive than ost, but worth it.

The *Dewata Restaurant* next door also es good seafood and cheaper Indonesian hes. The *Sunset Restaurant* has a prime sition on the harbour side of the road, erlooking the water, but the menu is ited. Otherwise, the restaurants in the rdena, Bajo Beach and Wisata hotels all ve long menus and reasonable prices.

tting There & Away

 Merpati has direct flights between Lab- nbajo and Ende (116,000 rp), Ruteng ,000 rp) and Bima (61,000 rp), with con- ctions to Mataram (184,700 rp), Denpasar 29,800 rp) and further afield.

The Merpati office is between Labuanbajo d the airport, about 1.5 km from the town.

Bus & Truck Buses to Ruteng (4000 rp; four hours) leave at 7.30 am and around 4 pm when the ferry arrives from Sape and Ko- modo. Other Ruteng buses are supposed to go at 11 am and 2 pm, but don't count on them. Chances are they will cruise town endlessly and, if they still don't have enough passengers, will wait for the ferry. Buses to Bajawa (10,000 rp; 10 hours) leave at 6.30 am and a bus also usually meets the ferry. The Damri bus to Ende (15,000 rp; 14 hours) meets the ferry, if you are desperate to get to Keli Mutu in a hurry and are well stocked with pain killers. You can buy tickets from hotels, or from buses hanging around the pier. If you get an advance ticket, the bus will pick you up from your hotel.

Passenger trucks also ply the route to Ruteng. They are less comfortable, but cost the same. If you do find yourself on a truck, it's imperative to get a seat in front of the rear axle; positions behind give good approxima- tions of ejector seats.

Boat The ferry from Labuanbajo to Komodo (4000 rp; three hours) and Sape (11,500 rp; eight to 10 hours) leaves at 8 am every day, except Friday. You can get tickets from the harbour master's office (in front of the pier) one hour before departure. Bicycles, motor- cycles and cars can be taken on the ferry. See under Sape in the previous Sumbawa section for more details. The ferry doesn't dock at Komodo, but small boats shuttle to the park headquarters for an extra 1500 rp.

The Pelni passenger ship *Tatamailau* stops in at Labuanbajo about once a week.

Getting Around

The Airport The airfield is 2.5 km from the town and hotels can arrange a taxi (5000 rp).

REO

Set on an estuary a little distance from the sea, Reo's focal point is the large Catholic compound in the middle of town. Reo has a couple of cheap losmen and a few small rumah makan. This straggling town used to be important for boat connections. When the highway was impassable in the wet season,

NUSA TENGGARA

regular boats ran between Labuanbajo and the port of Kedidi just outside town, but with the improvement in road transport these boats are now rare. Once a week a boat runs to Riung.

The road from Reo to Ruteng is in bad condition, but is being upgraded. The 60 km trip by bus takes 2½ hours and costs 2000 rp.

RUTENG

A market town and meeting point for the hill people of western Flores, Ruteng is the heart of the Manggarai country, the region extending to the west coast from a line drawn north from Aimere. The town is surrounded by rice fields on gentle slopes beneath a line of volcanic hills. The crisp air gives Ruteng the feeling of a hill town, even though it's quite a sizeable place.

Like Bajawa, Ruteng is a pleasantly cool town with no attractions in itself, but it has points of interest around the town. However, unlike Bajawa which has a well-developed tourist industry, Ruteng only sees overnight visitors who stop to break the bone-shaking bus journey.

Ruteng's lively, sprawling market on Jl Kartini is a meeting place for people from the surrounding hills.

Information

The BNI bank on Jl Kartini has the best rates for cash and travellers cheques. The Bank Rakyat Indonesia on Jl Yos Sudarso is reasonable for US dollars, but has low rates for other currencies. Banks are open Monday to Friday from 7.15 am to noon and 1 to 3 pm.

The post office at Jl Baruk 6 is open Monday to Saturday from 7 am to 2 pm and for limited postal services on Sunday. The Telkom office on Jl Kartini is open 24 hours.

Places to Stay

The *Hotel Sindha* (☎ 21197) on Jl Yos Sudarso is central and a good option. Rooms with outside mandi for 7000/10,000 rp are bright, roomy and better value than those with mandi for 15,000/20,000 rp. Spacious rooms with western bath, TV and balcony

are 20,000/24,000 rp. New VIP rooms w hot water showers cost 35,000 to 40,000 The attached restaurant serves good Chine food and has satellite TV if you're desper for news.

Wisma Agung I (☎ 21080), Jl Waeces is the best hotel in town and is good val although it is a 15 minute walk from the to centre. Pleasant economy rooms with sha mandi are 7000/10,000 rp or good renova rooms with bathroom are 15,000/20,000 The new section next door has spacio well-appointed rooms for 25,000/30,000

Wisma Agung II (☎ 21835), behind To

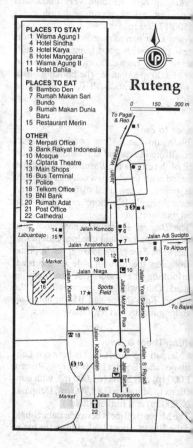

PLACES TO STAY
1 Wisma Agung I
4 Hotel Sindha
5 Hotel Karya
8 Hotel Manggarai
11 Wisma Agung II
14 Hotel Dahlia

PLACES TO EAT
6 Bamboo Den
7 Rumah Makan Sari Bundo
9 Rumah Makan Dunia Baru
15 Restaurant Merlin

OTHER
2 Merpati Office
3 Bank Rakyat Indonesia
10 Mosque
12 Ciptaria Theatre
13 Main Shops
16 Bus Terminal
17 Police
18 Telkom Office
19 BNI Bank
20 Rumah Adat
21 Post Office
22 Cathedral

Ruteng

0   150   300 m

To Pagal & Reo

Jalan Waeces

To Labuanbajo

Jalan Komodo

Jalan Amenehuno

Jalan Adi Sucipto

To Airport

Market

Jalan Niaga

Jalan Kartini

Sports Field

Jalan A Yani

Jalan Motang Rua

Jalan Yos Sudarso

To Baja

Jalan Kabupaten

Jalan Baruk

Jalan S Riyadi

Market

Jalan Diponegoro

The Manggarai

The Manggarai hill people are shy, but friendly – you'll see them in their distinctive black sarongs, trailing droopy stomached black-haired pigs into market or herding beautiful miniature horses. The Manggarai language is unintelligible to the other people of Flores.

Makassarese from Sulawesi have mixed with the coastal Manggarai for well over 100 years and the Bimanese dominated the area for at least 300 years until early this century, when the Dutch took over all of Flores. Christianity now predominates among the upland Manggarai, and Ruteng has several large Christian schools and churches. Traditional animist practices still linger, but are dwindling – traditionally, the Manggarai would carry out a cycle of ceremonies, some involving buffalo or pig sacrifices, to ask favours from ancestor and nature spirits and the supreme being, Mori. In some villages you can still find the compang, a ring of flat stones on which offerings were placed, or you may be shown ritual paraphernalia used during sacrificial ceremonies.

Trials of strength and courage known as caci still take place in Ruteng during the national independence Day celebrations (17 August). The two combatants wear wooden masks like uptilted welder's helmets. One carries a rawhide oval shield and a metre long whip, the other a short, springy stick and a thick cloth wrapped around his forearm.

The Manggarai traditionally practised slash-and-burn agriculture. They were introduced to rice cultivation around 1920 by the Dutch, but only in the last few decades has the area been devoted to permanent rice terraces. Maize (sweet corn) is the other main crop, though other crops (such as coffee and onions) are grown for export. The Manggarai also raise fine horses and large water buffalo, the latter primarily for export. ■

gung on Jl Motang Rua, is basic but clean and right in the town centre. Economy rooms cost 7500/10,000 rp or rooms with mandi are ,500/15,000 rp.

The *Hotel Manggarai* (☎ 21008) on Jl Adi cipto is close to the town centre and reasonable value. Rooms with outside mandi go 8000/10,000 rp or rooms with mandi cost ,000/15,000 rp.

The *Hotel Dahlia* (☎ 21377) on Jl Bhangkari is a fancy-looking hotel, but only the ooms are only average and overpriced at ,000 rp without mandi or 20,000 rp with andi.

The *Hotel Karya* on Jl Motang Rua is the eapest place in town at 5000 rp per person, t it's very dark and often 'full'.

Places to Eat

n Jl Motang Rua, the cosy and friendly *amboo Den* next to the Hotel Karya has ed chicken, sate and other dishes. *Rumah akan Sari Bundo* is a Padang restaurant rving big prawns and good rendang. arungs around the market serve Padang od, buffalo soup and sate.

Ruteng has some good Chinese restaurants, the best of which is the *Rumah Makan Dunia Baru* on Jl Yos Sudarso. The *Restaurant Merlin* on Jl Kartini near the Hotel Dahlia is also good. Many of the hotels have their own restaurants.

Getting There & Away

Air There are direct flights most days to/from Bima, Kupang, Denpasar and Mataram, and a couple a week to Labuanbajo. The Merpati agent (☎ 21197) is out in the rice paddies, about a 10 minute walk from the town centre.

Bus Buses will drop you at hotels on your arrival in Ruteng. Buses to Labuanbajo (4000 rp; four hours), Bajawa (5000 rp; five hours) and Ende (8500 rp; nine hours) leave in the early morning around 7.30 am. There are noon buses to Bajawa and Labuanbajo, and the Agogo bus to Ende at 5 pm costs 10,000 rp, but is quicker than the day buses and will drop you at your hotel in Ende. You can buy tickets for the morning buses at the bus terminal, or ticket agencies are scattered around town, but most hotels will get them for you and arrange for the bus to pick you up.

Buses, trucks and bemos run frequently until noon to Reo (2000 rp; 2½ hours). A

NUSA TENGGARA

front seat will cost an extra 500 rp, but is worth it on the bad road. You can catch buses at the bus terminal or as they circle the streets.

Getting Around
The airport is about two km from the town centre, about a half-hour walk. The Hotel Sindha offers guests free transport to the airport. Otherwise, you can charter a bemo.

AROUND RUTENG
Golo Curu, a hill to the north of Ruteng, offers spectacular early morning views of the hills, valleys, rice paddies, terraced slopes and distant mountain valleys. Go down the Reo road and, 20 minutes past the Hotel Karya, turn right at the small bridge across a stream. There's a derelict shrine on the hilltop, with a statue of the Virgin Mary on a pedestal. Further north, six km from Ruteng near Cancar, is the **Waegarik Waterfall**.

Manggarai sarongs are black with pretty embroidered patterns. You can find them in the main Ruteng market, or visit the weaving village of **Cibal**. Women at Cibal work their looms mainly from May to October. To reach Cibal, there are occasional direct bemos from Ruteng; otherwise, take one to Pagal, 21 km north of Ruteng on the main road to Reo, then walk about three km east over the hill to Cibal.

The 2140m volcano **Gunung Ranaka**, an active volcano that erupted in 1987, can be reached by road – take an eastbound bus along the highway to the turn-off at the eight km mark. It is then a nine km walk along the old Telkom road to the abandoned transmitter station at the top. The road is flanked by two to three metre high regrowth, so views are limited, but it's a pleasant enough walk. You can charter a bemo from Ruteng for around 10,000 rp, but drivers may not be willing to go right to the top. The paved road is in bad repair, especially the last two km. There are good views from the top, but you cannot reach the still-active crater, further down the slopes.

Danau Ranamese, known as 'little Keli Mutu' to locals, is 22 km from Ruteng, right next to the main Bajawa road. This small la is a pleasant picnic spot surrounded jungle-clad hills. A new visitors' centre, w chalet accommodation, is nearing comp tion. A few short strolls can be taken arou the visitors' centre and lake, but no long trails have been developed.

BAJAWA
The small hill town of Bajawa (populati around 12,000) is the centre of the Nga people, one of the most traditional groups Flores. The town is at an altitude of 1100 and is surrounded by volcanic hills, with t 2245m Gunung Inerie (to the south) predo inant. Bajawa is cool, low key and clea It also has a good range of restaurants a accommodation, making it a popular pla to spend a few days exploring the countr side and making trips to the Ngada village

Information
Bajawa has a new tourist office, Dinas Pa wisata, in the government office complex Jl Sugio Pranoto. It collects statistics.

The BNI bank is the best place to chan money, or you can try the Bank Rakyat Ind nesia on Jl Soekarno Hatta. The post offi is close to the latter and is open Monday Saturday from 8 am to 2 pm.

Places to Stay
Bajawa has a surprising number of hotels f its size and new places are opening all t time. All include breakfast in the price.

The long-running *Homestay Sunflow* (☎ 21236), on a small path off Jl Ahma Yani, was one of the first to run trips villages. It is now looking a little run dow but is still an informative place and has pleasant balcony overlooking the valle Small and often dark singles/doubles co 6000/8000 rp or 7000/10,000 rp with a tached mandi.

Not far away, the *Hotel Korina* (☎ 2116 at Jl Ahmad Yani 81 is one of the bett places, with friendly and efficient sta Rooms with outside mandi cost 7000 rp,

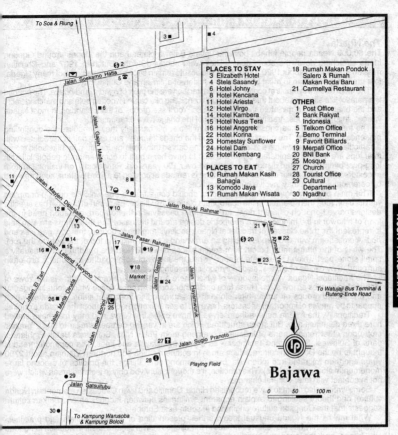

NUSA TENGGARA

Map labels:

To Soa & Riung

Jalan Soekarno Hatta
Jalan Gajah Mada
Jalan Mayjen Dipanjaitan
Jalan Letjend Haryono
Jalan El Tari
Jalan Maria Dinata
Jalan Iman Bonjol
Jalan Satsuitubu
Jalan Basuki Rahmat
Jalan Pasar Rahmat
Jalan Gereja
Jalan Hayamwuruk
Jalan Sugio Pranoto
Jalan Ahmad Yani

Market
Playing Field
Bajawa

To Watujaji Bus Terminal & Ruteng-Ende Road

To Kampung Warusoba & Kampung Bolozi

0   50   100 m

PLACES TO STAY
3 Elizabeth Hotel
4 Stela Sasandy
6 Hotel Johny
8 Hotel Kencana
11 Hotel Ariesta
12 Hotel Virgo
14 Hotel Kambera
15 Hotel Nusa Tera
16 Hotel Anggrek
22 Hotel Korina
23 Homestay Sunflower
24 Hotel Dam
26 Hotel Kembang

PLACES TO EAT
10 Rumah Makan Kasih Bahagia
13 Komodo Jaya
17 Rumah Makan Wisata

18 Rumah Makan Pondok Salero & Rumah Makan Roda Baru
21 Carmellya Restaurant

OTHER
1 Post Office
2 Bank Rakyat Indonesia
5 Telkom Office
7 Bemo Terminal
9 Favorit Billiards
19 Merpati Office
20 BNI Bank
25 Mosque
27 Church
28 Tourist Office
29 Cultural Department
30 Ngadhu

0,000 rp and 15,000 rp with attached mandi. Lucas, one of Bajawa's most experienced guides, speaks excellent English and can be contacted here.

Of the new places in Bajawa, the small *Hotel Ariesta* (☎ 21292) on Jl Diponegoro is right, clean and a good choice. Rooms at the front or around the pleasant courtyard area at the back cost 15,000/20,000 rp with mandi or 10,000 rp with outside mandi.

The *Elizabeth Hotel* (☎ 21223) on Jl Inerie is a fair hike from the centre of town, but worth the effort. Spotless, bright rooms in this family-run establishment cost from 6500/10,000 rp with shared mandi, or very good rooms with shower cost 10,000/15,000 rp and 15,000/20,000 rp.

Nearby, the *Stela Sasandy* (☎ 21198) just off Jl Soekarno Hatta is another friendly, new place, although the rooms for 7000/12,500 rp and 10,000/20,000 rp with mandi are not as good as those at the Elizabeth.

The *Hotel Dam* (☎ 21145) is a quiet and delightful little place near the church, run by a friendly family. Rooms with attached bath cost 15,000 rp and a few cheaper rooms with shared mandi are available.

A group of hotels can be found close to the

The Ngada

The 60,000 Ngada people inhabit both the upland Bajawa plateau and the slopes around Gunung Inerie stretching down the south coast. They were subdued by the Dutch in 1907 and Christian missionaries arrived about 1920. Older animistic beliefs remain strong and the religion of many Ngada, to a greater extent than in most of Flores, is a fusion of animism and Christianity.

The most evident symbols of continuing Ngada tradition are the pairs of *ngadhu* and *bhaga*. The ngadhu is a parasol-like structure about three metres high consisting of a carved wooden pole and thatched 'roof', and the bhaga is like a miniature thatch-roof house. You'll see groups of them standing in most Ngada villages, though in the less-traditional ones some of the bhaga have disappeared.

The functions and meanings of ngadhu are multiple, but basically they symbolise the continuing presence of ancestors. The ngadhu is 'male' and the bhaga 'female', and each pair is associated with a particular family group within a village. Though the carved trunks of ngadhu often feel like solid stone, their tops are usually dilapidated. Some are said to have been built to commemorate people killed in long-past battles over land disputes and may be over 100 years old. Periodically, on instruction from ancestors in dreams, a pair of ngadhu and bhaga is remade according to a fixed pattern, accompanied by ceremonies which may involve buffalo sacrifices.

The main post of a ngadhu, known as *sebu*, should come from a tree which is dug up complete with its main root, then 'planted' in the appropriate place in the village. Each part of the post has specific designs carved on it on different days: an axe and a cassava on the top part; a dragon head in the form of a flower in the middle; and a geometric design around the base. The three parts are also said to represent the three classes of traditional Ngada society: from top to bottom, the *gae*, *gae kisa* and *hoo*. A crossbeam with two hands holding an arrow and a sword links the top of the pole to the roof. The walls of the bhaga must be cut from seven pieces of wood. Near the ngadhu there's usually a small stone post which is the 'gate keeper', while the bases of both ngadhu and bhaga are often surrounded by circles of stones, said to symbolise meeting places.

The traditional Ngada village layout – of which there are still a few examples left – is two rows of high-roofed houses on low stilts. These face each other across an open space which contains ngadhu and bhaga and groups of human-high stone slivers surrounding horizontal slabs. The latter, which appear to be graves of important ancestors, have led to some exotic theories about the Ngada's origins.

Traditionally, the Ngada believe themselves to have come from Java and they may have settled here three centuries ago. But stone structures which are in varying degrees similar to these 'graves' crop up in other remote parts of Indonesia – among them Pulau Nias, Sumatra's Batak Highlands, parts of Sulawesi, Sumba and Tanimbar – as well as in Malaysia and Laos. The common thread is thought to be the Dongson culture, which arose in southern China and northern Vietnam about 2700 years ago then migrated into Indonesia, bringing, among other things, the practice of erecting large monumental stones (megaliths). This practice, it's thought, survived only in isolated areas which were not in contact with later cultural changes.

Some writers also claim to have recognised Hindu, Semitic and even Caucasian elements in Ngada culture; one theory seeking to explain apparent similarities between Indonesian and Balkan culture suggests that the Dongson culture originated in south-east Europe!

What makes the Ngada unusual today is their preservation of animistic beliefs and practices. 'Straight' Christianity has made fewer inroads in the villages than in Bajawa itself. In addition to ngadhu and bhaga and the ancestor worship which goes with them, agricultural fertility rites continue (sometimes involving gory buffalo sacrifices) as well as ceremonies marking birth, marriage, death or house building. The major annual festival is the six day Reba ceremony at Bena, 21 km from Bajawa, held around late December/early January, which includes dancing, singing, buffalo sacrifices and the wearing of special black ikat costumes. The highest god in traditional Ngada belief is Gae Dewa who unites Dewa Zeta (the heavens) and Nitu Sale (the earth). ∎

---

centre of town, just west of the market. The *Hotel Anggrek* (☎ 21172) on Jl Letjend Haryono has clean, reasonably priced rooms with mandi for 10,000/15,000 rp. The restaurant here serves excellent food.

The largest hotel is the *Hotel Kembang* (☎ 21072) on Jl Marta Dinata, which has well-

appointed double rooms with private bath fc 22,500 rp and 25,000 rp.

Other less appealing options are the *Hote Kambera* (☎ 21166), *Hotel Virgo* (☎ 21061) *Hotel Nusa Tera* (☎ 21357) and *Hotel John* (☎ 21079).

At the bottom of the barrel, the *Hote*

Kencana at Jl Palapa 7 is grungy but friendly and they don't come much cheaper at 3000/ 5000 rp with mandi.

Places to Eat

For a small town, Bajawa has a good range of restaurants.

The travellers' favourite is the small and friendly *Carmellya Restaurant*. It has good maps of the area and lots of other information. Oh, and the food isn't bad either, even stretching to a few Indonesian-style Italian, Swiss and Mexican dishes. You'll go a long way for tastier guacamole.

Rumah Makan Wisata, near the market, is another old favourite with Indonesian and Chinese fare. The *Rumah Makan Kasih Bahagia*, a little further along Jl Gajah Mada, is a good Chinese restaurant with cold beer and decent food at reasonable prices. Its offshoot, the *Puteri Cendana*, outside town near the bus terminal, is Bajawa's fanciest restaurant and features karaoke.

The *Komodo Jaya* has an extensive menu with a wide variety of good noodle dishes and seafood. Two smaller Padang restaurants right in the market are the *Rumah Makan Pondok Salero* and *Rumah Makan Roda Baru*.

The *Hotel Anggrek* and *Hotel Kambera* both have attached restaurants with long menus – the Hotel Anggrek, in particular, does excellent home-style cooking.

Things to Buy

Bajawa market is busy and colourful, with lots of women from the Ngada area and further afield wearing ikat cloth, some of which is for sale. The better local stuff is black with white motifs, often of horses. The fruit here is plentiful and of good quality.

Getting There & Away

Air Merpati flies from Bajawa to Bima and Ende, with onward connections. The Merpati office (☎ 21051) is opposite the Bajawa market.

Bus Long-distance buses leave from Watujaji terminal, three km east of town near the

Ende-Ruteng road. The bus to Labuanbajo (10,000 rp; 10 hours) leaves around 7 am. More frequent buses go to Ruteng (5000 rp; five hours). Buses to Ende (5000 rp; five hours) leave at 7 am and noon, and there is a through bus to Moni. Morning buses also run to Riung (2000 rp; 2½ hours) along the newly completed road. Most hotels arrange bus tickets.

Bemo & Truck The town's bemo terminal is on Jl Basuki Rahmat. Regular bemos go from here to Soa, Mangulewa, Mataloko, Langa and Boawae. A bemo to Bena runs perhaps once or twice a day, depending on passenger demand, but not to any schedule. Otherwise, at least one truck a day runs to Jerebuu, passing through Bena. The bemos roam around town a lot, so you can also pick them up on the street.

Getting Around

The Airport The airport is 25 km from Bajawa and about six km outside Soa. Regular bemos go to Soa (1000 rp) from the town's bemo terminal on Jl Basuki Rahmat. You should be able to pick up another from Soa to the airport for 500 rp. Merpati runs a bus (5000 rp).

Bemo There are no regular bemo routes around town, so you'll have to charter.

AROUND BAJAWA

The main attraction of Bajawa is the chance to get out into the countryside and explore the traditional villages. You can visit villages by yourself or guides in Bajawa will offer their services. A guide is well worthwhile – instead of awkwardly fronting up yourself at a village and feeling like a pork chop at a bar mitzvah, a good guide will provide an introduction, explain local customs and give an insight into village life. Members of the local guiding association have banded together to offer similar tours at 20,000 rp per person for a day trip to the villages, including lunch and public transport. You can also charter a bemo for around 60,000 rp per day or a car, such as a kijang, for 100,000 rp. All guides are local and knowledgeable. The main difference is their ability to communicate with you, ie their proficiency in English. Talk to your guide beforehand.

Villages in the area are now quite used to tourists. If visiting independently, it is customary to sign the visitors' book and make a donation of 1000 rp or so. Taking photos is usually not a problem, but ask and remember that entering a village is like entering someone's home.

Bena and Wogo are the most traditional and impressive villages. Bena also has fine views and gets the most visitors by far. Guides can put together interesting tours and include plenty of other options not mentioned here.

Kampung Bolozi

Only a 30 to 45 minute walk from Bajawa, Kampung Bolozi has some ngadhu, a few traditional houses and an old tomb. See the town map for directions; if in doubt, ask for

Kampung Warusoba, which is on the way to Kampung Bolozi.

Langa & Bela

There are ngadhu and bhaga in Langa, seven km from Bajawa, but this is more a modern village. Bemos go here from Bajawa's bemo terminal. More interesting and more traditional is Bela, a couple of km away, off the road. Three km from Langa is another traditional village, **Borado**.

Bena

Underneath the Inerie volcano, 19 km from Bajawa, Bena is one of the most traditional Ngada villages and its stone monuments are a protected site. High thatched houses line up in two rows on a ridge, the space between them filled with ngadhu, bhaga and strange megalithic tomb-like structures. Some of these 'tombs' are said to contain hoards of treasure. The house of the leading family in each part of the village has a little model house on top of its roof. A small Christian shrine sits on a mound at the top of the village, and behind it a recently built shelter offers a spectacular view of Gunung Inerie and the south coast. **Gunung Inerie** can be climbed from Watumeze, between Langa and Bena, in about four hours.

During the day, most of the men and some of the women are out in the fields; only a few mothers and elderly women remain in the village, pounding rice or doing other chores. Try to at least chat to the villagers before wandering around and taking photos. You will probably be shown weavings here as well, some now decidedly commercial. If you want to stay with the kepala desa, you could offer to pay about 5000 rp for accommodation.

Getting There & Away Bena is 12 km from Langa. Occasionally, bemos go from Langa to Bena, but more often they finish in Langa and want you to charter the rest of the way. Otherwise, you have to walk. An easier walk is from Mangulewa, which can be reached by regular bemo from Bajawa. The 10 km walk from Mangulewa to Bena is downhill

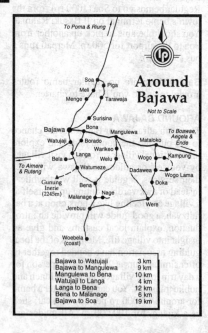

To Poma & Riung

Around Bajawa

Not to Scale

Soa
Meli • Piga
Menge • Tarawaja

Surisina
Bajawa • Bona
Mangulewa   To Boawae,
Watujaji • Borado   Aegela &
Warikeo   Ende
Matatoko
Bela • Langa • Welu   Wogo • Kampung
To Aimere   Watumeze   Dadawea   Wogo Lama
& Ruteng
Doka
Gunung
Inerie   Bena   Nage
(2245m) Malanage
Were
Jerebuu

Woebela
(coast)

Bajawa to Watujaji	3 km
Bajawa to Mangulewa	9 km
Mangulewa to Bena	10 km
Watujaji to Langa	4 km
Langa to Bena	12 km
Bena to Malanage	6 km
Bajawa to Soa	19 km

l the way. There's a daily truck from Bajawa
Jerebuu which passes through Bena usually
arly in the morning or around noon.

age

age is a traditional village on a plateau
oout seven km from Bena, also with great
ews of Gunung Inerie. Several well-main-
ined ngadhu and bhaga and some tombs lie
etween two rows of high-roofed houses.
age has **hot springs** (air panas). Just before
ou reach Malanage on the Bena-Jerebuu
oad, there's a fast-flowing, emerald-green
ot river.

etting There & Away To get to Nage, you
an walk from Bena; just continue on the
aved road through the village. Otherwise,
ne truck to Jerebuu can drop you at Malan-
ge. Nage is a one km uphill walk from there.
his truck returns to Bajawa via Bena and
Iangulewa.

Vogo

Vogo is a large village with eight or nine sets
f ngadhu and bhaga, ringed by traditional
ouses. This is one of the Bajawa's largest
nd most traditional villages, though a few
gns of modernity can be seen. The original
illage, Wogo Lama, was abandoned many
ears ago when the villagers decided to
nove closer to the main road and the delights
f modernity, such as electricity.

About one km further on from Wogo, turn
ff through the bamboo grove at the Dada-
ea sign and follow the track off to the left
> **Wogo Lama**, where vast, jagged groups
f stones jut from the ground. These mega-
thic ancestor tombs are still important for
se in ceremonies.

etting There & Away Wogo is 1.5 km from
Iataloko, which is 18 km from Bajawa on
ne Ende road and easily reached by bus or
emo. Mataloko is famous for its huge sem-
nary on the highway.

oa

oa is about 19 km north of Bajawa. Its main
ttraction is the weekly market (on Thurs-

day), which brings in villagers from a wide
area who tramp into the village with sacks of
rice or lone melons perched on their heads.
There are developed **hot springs** in a river
about a 1.5 km walk from a village six km
beyond Soa. They cost 2500 rp. Soa is easily
reached by bemo from Bajawa for a day trip.

BOAWAE

Forty-one km from Bajawa on the highway
to Ende, Boawae is the centre of the Nage-
Keo people (related to, but distinct from, the
Ngada) and sits at the base of smoking
Gunung Ebulobo. The volcano can be
climbed with a guide hired in the village and
usually involves an overnight stop on the
mountain then a two hour ascent early the
next morning.

Boawae is the source of most of the best
Bajawa-area ikat. Gory buffalo-sacrifice
rituals take place here, and an equally messy
form of boxing called *etu* is part of the May
to August harvest festivities. The boxers
wear garments made of tree bark painted
with animal blood and their gloves may be
studded with broken glass!

Places to Stay

Few visitors bother to stop at Boawae, but
the *Wisma Nusa Bunga* on the highway has
clean, simple rooms from 10,000 rp. A much
better option is the *Hotel Sao Wisata* – take
the road next to the Wisma Nusa Bunga and
follow it for 1.5 km down to the river and
then around to the left near the church. In
lush gardens by the river, this delightful
guesthouse has doubles for 25,000 rp and
meals are available.

RIUNG

This small Muslim/Christian fishing village
is one of the few places on Flores with access
to white sand beaches and excellent snorkelling over intact reefs. The main village itself
is fairly nondescript, although there's a
Muslim Bugis stilt village built around the
harbour. Like Labuanbajo, most of the action
is on offshore islands and getting to them
requires a charter boat. About seven of the

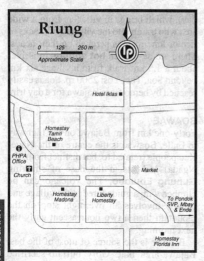

Riung

0   125   250 m

Approximate Scale

Hotel Iklas ■

Homestay
Tamri
Beach

ℹ PHPA
Office

✝ Church

Market

Homestay
Madona

Liberty
Homestay

To Pondok
SVP, Mbay
& Ende

Homestay
Florida Inn

17 uninhabited islands off Riung have white sand beaches. Most of the homestays can arrange day trips to several of the islands (about 20,000 rp for up to six people, including lunch).

Another attraction are the giant iguanas that can be seen further north along the mainland coast at **Torong Padang**. The beasts are more brightly coloured than Komodo dragons, with yellow markings, and some readers reported seeing one three metres long. A combined snorkelling/dragon stake-out day trip can be arranged in Riung.

Watujapi Hill, about three km from Riung, offers a magnificent view of the 17 islands lying offshore. If you count them, there are actually more than 21 islands, but the government authorities decided on the number as a neat tie-in with Independence Day!

Information

The PHPA office is near the Homestay Tamri Beach and is helpful with information about the Riung area. You don't normally have to use one of its guides, but you must sign in and pay 500 rp before going to the islands. The office also rents snorkelling equipment.

Places to Stay & Eat

There are five homestays in Riung, all offering bed-and-meals deals for around 8000 rp per person, though prices are set to rise. The best choice for information and originality *Hotel Iklas*, right next to the harbour, in the Bugis stilt village. The building, originally a traditional stilt house, features precarious stepladders and a large 1st floor balcony. The manager speaks excellent English and has a good boat available for hire.

Liberty Homestay has a nice balcony and large rooms. Nearby, *Homestay Madona* is run by a friendly couple.

Homestay Tamri Beach is popular with travellers and has good maps and information. *Homestay Florida Inn*, on the road into town, is a bit far from the harbour.

The most salubrious accommodation found at the *Pondok SVD*, otherwise known as the 'Missionaries', on the road coming into town. Spacious rooms in the mission cost 25,000 rp.

Getting There & Away

The direct road from Bajawa to Riung is not complete, making access much easier, and buses do the trip in 2½ hours. From Ende (4000 rp; four hours), a bus leaves every morning at 6 am from Ndao terminal. The only other alternative is to take a bus to Mba and then hope to find a truck (ask the driver of every vehicle that comes into the market to Riung from there.

There's a market boat leaving Riung for Reo at around 7 am on Tuesday morning (5000 rp; about six hours).

ENDE

Like their neighbours, the people gathered in south-central Flores in and around the port of Ende have a mix of Malay and Melanesian features. The aristocratic families of Ende link their ancestors, through mythical exploits and magical events, with the Hindu Majapahit kingdom of Java. Today most of the 60,000 people living in Ende are Christians but there are also many Muslims.

Ende is a pleasant enough town, surrounded by fine mountain scenery. The

erfect cone of Gunung Meja rises almost
eside the airport, with the larger Gunung
ya occupying a promontory south of Gun-
ng Meja. Ende is primarily a stopover to
astern Flores, or a launching pad to Sumba,
ough trips to nearby villages are worth-
vhile if you are stuck for something to do,
nd there's interesting weaving from around
lores and Sumba to look at.

The December 1992 earthquake caused
xtensive damage in Ende, but things are
ow back to normal. Ende is very hot and
usty towards the end of the dry season.

Orientation

Ende is at the neck of a peninsula jutting
outh into the sea. The old port of Ende and
most of the shops are on the western side of
he neck; the main port, Pelabuhan Ipi, is on
he eastern side. There are two bus terminals:
Wolowana, about five km east of town (for
buses going east), and Ndao, along the
vaterfront two km north of town (for buses
going west).

Information

Money The Bank Rakyat Indonesia is in the
ame building as the Hotel Dwi Putri on Jl
KH Dewantara.

Post & Communications The main post
office is out in the north-eastern part of town
on Jl Gajah Mada. For stamps, there's a
sub-post office opposite the Bank Rakyat
ndonesia. The Telkom office is on Jl Keli-
nutu, a 15 minute walk from the waterfront.

Things to See

In 1933 the Dutch exiled Soekarno to Ende,
and his house on Jl Perwira is now a **museum**. There's not a lot to see, apart from
some photographs, but the caretaker, a friend
of Soekarno's brother, can tell you a few
stories if your Indonesian is good enough.
It's open Monday to Saturday from 7 am to
noon.

The waterfront **market** on Jl Pasar is a
lively place to wander, and there's an ikat
market on the corner of Jl Pabean and Jl
Pasar which sells a large variety of ikat from

Flores and Sumba. The **Pasar Potulando**
night market on Jl Keli Mutu sells snacks,
fruit and vegetables if you are desperate for
something to do.

The Ende area has its own style of ikat
weaving, mostly using abstract motifs. Some
of the best local stuff comes from the village
of **Ndona**, eight km east of Ende. There are
irregular bemos to Ndona from Ende, but it
might be quicker to go to Wolowana (five km
out) and take another bemo from there to
Ndona.

Wolotopo, about eight km east of Ende,
has traditional houses built on several levels.
Bemos run from Ende about twice a day.
Otherwise, it's a 45 minute walk from Wolo-
wana along the black sand beach of Nanga
Nesa to Wolotopo.

Places to Stay

Accommodation is fairly spread out, but frequent bemos make it easy to get around.

Near the airport, *Hotel Ikhlas* (☎ 21695) on
Jl Jenderal Ahmad Yani is in a 'klas' of its
own – friendly and on the ball with travel
information. There's a range of rooms starting with clean, basic singles/doubles for
3500/6000 rp with shared mandi, to small
rooms with mandi and fan for 7000/10,000
rp and large new rooms for 10,000/15,000
rp. Good, cheap western and Indonesian
food is available.

Next door, the spacious and airy *Hotel
Safari* (☎ 21499) has friendly staff and a
restaurant. Rooms cost 10,000/15,000 rp
with mandi to 35,000/40,000 rp with air-con.

The small *Hotel Amica* (☎ 21683), Jl
Garuda 39, is a good budget hotel. Rooms go
for 10,000/15,000 rp, all with attached bath.
The young manager speaks excellent Eng-
lish and can fill you in on excursions around
Ende.

If you want to be close to the centre of
town near the market, the *Hotel Hamansyur*
(☎ 21373), Jl Loreng Aembonga 11, is reasonable. Dingy rooms in the old building
cost 7000/10,000 rp, or newer, much better
rooms with mandi cost 10,000/15,000 rp.

The *Hotel Flores* (☎ 21075) at Jl Sudirman 28 has a range of rooms starting with

NUSA TENGGARA

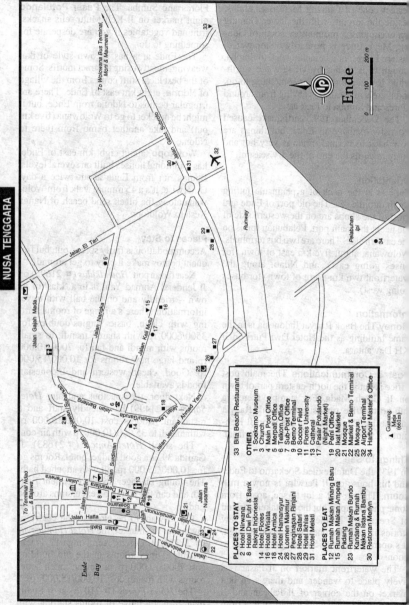

Ende

To Wolowona Bus Terminal,
Moni & Maumere

To Terminal Ndao
& Bajawa

To Terminal Ndao
& Bajawa

Ende Bay

Jalan Gajah Mada
Jalan Gatot Subroto
Jalan El Tari
Jalan Nangka
Jalan Kali Mutu
Jalan Lepembusu
Jalan Jenderal Ahmad Yani
Jalan Banjang
Jalan Sukarno
Jalan Surdiman
Jalan Garuda
Jalan Kartini
Jalan J K K Dewanjara
Jalan Pabean
Jalan Kemakmuran
Jalan Hatta
Jalan Pasar
Jalan Nusantara
Jalan Baki
Jalan Pelawira
Pelabuhan Ipi
Pelabuhan
Runway

▲ Gunung
Meja (661m)

0   100   200 m

PLACES TO STAY
2   Hotel Nirwana
8   Hotel Dwi Putri & Bank
    Rakyat Indonesia
14 Hotel Flores
16 Hotel Wisata
18 Hotel Amica
24 Hotel Hamansyur
26 Pengipapan Rinjani
27 Losmen Makmur
28 Hotel Ikhlas
29 Hotel Ikhlas
31 Hotel Melati

PLACES TO EAT
12 Rumah Makan Minang Baru
15 Rumah Makan Ampera
    Padang
23 Rumah Makan Bundo
    Kandang & Rumah
25 Makan Istana Bambu
30 Restoran Merlyn

OTHER
1   Soekarno Museum
3   Church
4   Main Post Office
5   Merpati Office
6   Telkom Office
7   Sub-Post Office
9   Bemo Terminal
10 Soccer Field
11 Flores University
13 Catheral
17 Pasar Potulando
    (Night Market)
19 Pelni Office
20 Ikat Market
21 Market & Bemo Terminal
22 Mosque
32 Airport Terminal
33 Bita Beach Restaurant
34 Harbour Master's Office

st floor economy rooms with shower for 0,000/15,000 rp, to clean rooms with fan nd mandi for 16,500/22,500 rp and air-con oubles for 40,000 rp. There's a small res- aurant as well.

The large and spotless *Hotel Dwi Putri* ☎ 21685) on Jl KH Dewantara is the best in wn and also has a good 1st floor restaurant. ooms with fan, shower and flushing toilet re 20,000/25,000 rp, air-con rooms are well ppointed and cost 40,000/50,000 rp, and IP rooms are very large and have fridges, ut are not worth 125,000 rp.

The quiet *Hotel Wisata* (☎ 21368) on Jl eli Mutu is another more upmarket hotel nd is reasonably priced. Large, new rooms t the back cost 15,000/20,000 rp with mandi add 2500 rp for rooms with a fan. Huge ir-con rooms are 30,000/40,000 rp and VIP ooms are 45,000/60,000 rp. It also has a TV ounge and a restaurant.

The *Hotel Melati* (☎ 21311) is just around he corner from the airport on Jl Jenderal hmad Yani, but other hotels have more ppeal. The *Hotel Nirwana* (☎ 21199) at Jl ahjawan 29 is a better class of hotel but uiet, while the *Losmen Makmur* and *Pen- inapan Rinjani* are both cheap but seedy ives.

laces to Eat

he market area has the biggest concentra- on of rumah makan. These include the *undo Kandung* for Padang food and the *stana Bambu*, next door, one of Ende's best estaurants with a long menu of Indonesian, hinese and seafood dishes.

Most other restaurants serve Padang cui- ine, such as the *Rumah Makan Minang aru* on Jl Soekarno and the *Rumah Makan mpera Padang* at Jl Keli Mutu 31.

Restoran Merlyn, near the airport on Jl iatot Subroto, is a fancy and slightly expen- ve Chinese restaurant. The remote *Bita each Restaurant*, past the airport down a usty road to the beach, is a local favourite, s much for the karaoke as the food.

etting There & Away

ir Merpati (☎ 21355) is on Jl Nangka, a 15 minute walk from the airstrip. From Ende direct flights go to Bajawa, Bima, Kupang and Labuanbajo. This office is hopeless for organising bookings on through flights orig- inating in other cities. Staff will probably tell you to try your luck at the airport just before departure – seats are often available.

Bus Buses to the east leave from Terminal Wolowana, four km from town. Buses to Moni (2000 rp; two hours) depart between 6 am and 2 pm, or take a Wolowaru bus. Buses to Maumere (6000 rp; five hours) leave around 8 am and 5 pm. Maumere buses will drop you in Moni, but charge for the full fare through to Maumere. A bus to Nggela leaves at 7 am and a through bus to Larantuka leaves at 8 am.

Buses to the west leave from Terminal Ndao, two km north of town on the beach road. Departures are: Bajawa (5000 rp; five hours) at 7 and 11 am; Ruteng (10,000 rp; nine hours) at 7.30 am; Labuanbajo (15,000 rp; 14 hours) at 7 am; and Riung (4000 rp; four hours) at 6 am.

Boat Ships dock at Pelabuhan Ipi, the main port, 2.5 km from the town. The ferry from Kupang (West Timor) to Ende (17,000 rp; 16 hours) departs on Monday, and leaves Ende on Tuesday at 2 pm for Waingapu (12,000 rp; 10 hours) on Sumba then continues to Sabu and return. From Ende to Kupang departures are at 2 pm on Saturday.

Pelni's KM *Binaiya* stops in Ende every two weeks as it comes in from Waingapu on Sumba (15,500 rp ekonomi; seven hours) and continues on to Kupang on Timor (22,500 rp; 10 hours). It runs in the reverse direction one week later. The Pelni office, on the corner of Jl Pabean and Jl Kemakmuran, is open Monday to Friday from 8 am to 4 pm.

Other boats sail irregularly to these and other destinations; ask at the harbour masters' offices at Pelabuhan Ipi.

Getting Around
The Airport You could walk to town, or just walk 100m to the roundabout on Jl Jenderal Ahmad Yani and catch a bemo (400 rp).

Bemo Bemos run frequently just about everywhere in town for a flat fare of 400 rp, even out to Pelabuhan Ipi. You can easily flag one down on the street; if not, pick one up at the bemo stop or on Jl Hatta (near the pier).

Car You can charter a car to Keli Mutu for up to six people for 75,000 rp. Ask at your hotel. The Hotel Ikhlas is particularly well set up for arranging charter minibuses to Keli Mutu, leaving at 3.30 am, and attractions around Ende.

DETUSOKO & CAMAT
Between Detusoko and Camat, 35 km from Ende, *Wisma Santo Fransiskus* is quiet and peaceful. There are some lovely walks around the area; it should even be possible to walk along foot trails all the way to Keli Mutu.

KELI MUTU
Of all the sights in Nusa Tenggara, the coloured lakes of Keli Mutu are the most singularly spectacular. The three lakes, set in deep craters at an altitude of 1600m, near the summit of the Keli Mutu volcano (*keli* means

mountain), have a habit of changing colou Most recently, the largest was a light tu quoise, the one next to it olive green and th third one black. A few years ago the colour were blue, maroon and black, while back i the 1960s the lakes were blue, red-brown an cafe-au-lait. Colours can also change in th rainy season, when they may be less spectac ular.

No-one has managed to explain the caus of the colours, or why they change, except t suppose that different minerals are dissolve in each lake. The moonscape effect of th craters gives the whole summit area an ethe real atmosphere. There's a story among th locals that the souls of the dead go to thes lakes: young people's souls go to the warmt of the green lake, old people's to the cold c the milky turquoise one, and those of thieve and murderers to the black lake.

Keli Mutu has attracted sightseers sinc Dutch times and today there's a paved roa up to the lakes from Moni, 13.5 km away a the base of the mountain. You even get a occasional bus-load of tourists and a sma helipad has been constructed for VIP guests There's a staircase up to the highest looko point, from where you can see all three lakes

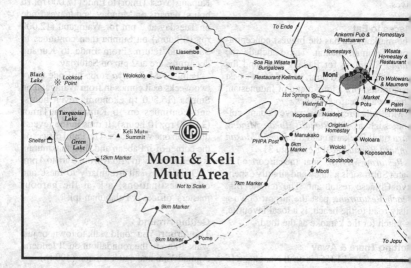

Moni & Keli
Mutu Area
Not to Scale

Fortunately, there's a wonderfully spacious feeling up there and you can scramble round the perimeters of two of the lake craters for a bit of solitude. Hope for a sunny day – sunrise is stunning at the top and the turquoise lake only reaches its full brilliance in the sunlight. If the weather is bad, come back the next day, because it really is worth seeing.

Getting There & Away

Moni, 52 km north-east of Ende, is the usual base for visiting Keli Mutu. From Moni you assess the weather before going up to the lakes for sunrise, though even if it looks clear in Moni, there can be cloud cover at Keli Mutu.

Most visitors make their way up to the top at 4 am by truck or minibus arranged by the hotels for 3000 rp per person. The truck returns to Moni at about 7 am, which can be a little hurried, so you may want to linger until the sun brings out the full brilliance of the lakes, then walk down. The sun rises earlier at the top than in the valley below. Later in the day, clouds roll in and block out the view.

The walk down takes about 2½ hours and isn't too taxing. Some hardy souls also walk up the 13.5 km of winding (but not too steep) road. After about six km there's a PHPA post, where you have to pay 1500 rp per person (more if you've hired a vehicle). Beware of false 'PHPA posts', which have been known to set up lower down the road. A shortcut (jalan potong) leaves the Moni-Ende road about 750m from the centre of Moni and comes out on the Keli Mutu road beside the PHPA post. This cuts about six km off the journey, but is easier to follow in daylight, so most people only use it on the way down unless they've checked it out the day before.

Another path branches off the shortcut at Koposili and goes via the villages of Mboti and Pome, reaching the Keli Mutu road about 5.5 km from the summit. It's no shorter, but it passes through villages where enterprising villagers serve drinks and breakfast.

MONI

Moni is a pretty village and the gateway to Flores' main tourist attraction, Keli Mutu. It is cooler than the lowlands, scenic and a good place for walks.

The village is strung alongside the Ende-Maumere road and is the heart of the Lio region, which extends from just east of Ende to beyond Wolowaru. Lio people, who speak a dialect of the Ende language, are renowned for their ikat weaving, and a colourful market spreads over the playing field in front of Moni's church every Monday morning. The local ikat is attractive, with bands of blue and rusty-red. Cloth from the Nggela and Maumere regions can be bought here.

Things to See & Do

In the kampung opposite the market, the high-thatched *rumah adat* (traditional house) serves as a cultural centre of sorts; traditional dance performances are held in front of it every evening and cost 2500 rp.

Apart from the trek to/from Keli Mutu, there are several other walks from Moni. About 750m along the Ende road from the centre of Moni, paths lead down to a 10m **waterfall**, with a pool big enough for swimming, and a couple of **hot springs**. This is the village mandi and you can also bathe here – men to the left pool, women to the right. Another short walk is out past the church to **Potu** and **Woloara** (about 2.5 km from Moni). From Woloara you could continue on through several villages to **Jopu** (about five km). If you're energetic and well prepared, walk on to **Wolojita** and **Nggela**, or you can loop back to Wolowaru and catch a bus or truck back to Moni.

Places to Stay

Moni has a collection of homestays of a similar basic standard, charging similar prices. New, simple bungalows are sprouting everywhere. The bulk of places are within five minutes' walk of each other, so it's worth checking a few out. The correct price – fixed by the government for all homestays – is 5000 rp per person in a room with outside mandi or 7500 rp per person in a room with

NUSA TENGGARA

attached mandi, plus 10% tax. Breakfast is included. Competition outside the main June to August tourist season has seen prices drop to ridiculously low levels – as little as 3000 rp per person, 10,000 rp or less for a double room with mandi – but it is doubtful those rates can be maintained.

Along the main road opposite the market are several cheap places where beds are rented mostly on a per person basis. *Homestay Daniel* is clean and tidy. *Homestay Amina Moe* is the most aggressive discounter and also has a few rooms with mandi. Next along, *Homestay Sao Lelegana John* is a notch up in standards and has larger rooms with basin and attached mandi. *Homestay Friendly* is another more substantial place with a good aspect and better than average rooms, with and without mandi. *Homestay Maria* just behind it has rooms with attached mandi and verandah. *Homestay Amina Moe II* just off the main road is the most basic of all, but is usually heavily discounted.

More homestays are clustered about five minutes' walk along the road to Ende. They tend to be quieter and less cramped. *Sylvester* has cheap, simple rooms, while *Lovely Rose* has better rooms with mandi and a decent restaurant. *Nusa Bunga*, *Regal Jaya* and *Lestari* are other reasonable places nearby, and *Hidayai* is further up the road.

Another option is the *Wisata Homestay & Restaurant*, which has a large, popular restaurant and rickety bamboo bungalows; it's about 500m back along the road to Maumere.

On the Ende road 1.5 km from Moni, the most upmarket place is the *Sao Ria Wisata*. Bungalows perched on the hillside are the best in Moni and have attached mandis, but are becoming run down and are overpriced at 20,000 rp and 25,000 rp.

Just outside Moni is the quiet *Palm Homestay*, on a side road to Woloara, a few hundred metres past Wisata Homestay. Further past the Palm is the attractive *Original Homestay* in a rural setting. It gets mixed reviews.

Places to Eat
Many of the homestays do simple but tasty buffet meals, usually vegetarian, for around

2500 to 3000 rp. Other good cheap restau rants are the *Restaurant Moni Indah*, next t Homestay Daniel, and the *Nusa Bunga*, nex to Homestay John.

The most popular place for its views an music is the *Ankermi Pub & Restauran* above the main road, between the two clus ters of homestays. The menu is more variec with spaghetti, guacamole and other distrac tions from the usual mie/nasi fare, while th music and cold beer are winners. *Restaurar Kelimutu*, 200m down the road from Sao Ri Wisata, has reasonable food and slov service.

Getting There & Away
Moni is 52 km north-east of Ende and 96 kr west of Maumere. For Ende (2000 rp; tw hours), buses start at around 7 am. Othe buses come through from Maumere or Wolc waru to Ende until about noon. Late buse come through at around 9 pm. Many buse and trucks leave on Monday market day.

For Maumere (5000 rp; four hours) th first buses from Ende start coming though around 9 or 10 am and then later in th evening around 7 am.

As most of the buses stop in Moni mid route they can be crowded and it's first-come first-served for a seat. Sometimes you'll b sitting in the aisle on a sack of rice, or a pi if you're lucky. Some of the homestays mak 'bookings', which usually means they wi just hail a bus down for you.

AROUND MONI
Wolowaru
The village of Wolowaru, straggling alon the Maumere road just 13 km east of Moni can be used as a base for trips to the ikat weaving villages of Jopu, Wolojita an Nggela. The road to these villages branche off from the main road in Wolowaru. Th daily market winds down around 9 am except on Saturday, the main market day.

Hotel Kelimutu is the most convenier place to stay and has simple doubles from 10,000 rp. It is right next to the *Rumah Maka Jawa Timur*, Wolowaru's premier dinin establishment.

Getting There & Away All Maumere-Ende buses stop in Wolowaru, with fares and departure times much the same as from Moni. A few morning buses originate in Wolowaru – ask at the Rumah Makan Jawa Timur. All the through buses stop at the Jawa Timur, usually for a meal break.

Nggela, Wolojita & Jopu

Beautiful ikat sarongs and shawls can be found here and in other villages between Wolowaru and the south coast. Impromptu stalls will spring up before your eyes as you approach the villages.

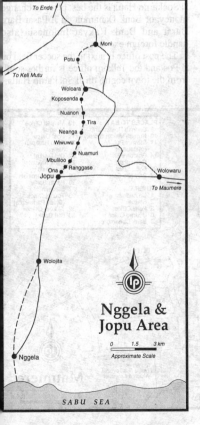

To Ende
Moni
Potu
To Keli Mutu
Woloara
Koposenda
Nuanon
Tira
Neanga
Wiwuwu
Mbuliloo
Nuamuri
Ona
Ranggase
Jopu
Wolowaru
To Maumere

Wolojita

**Nggela &
Jopu Area**

0   1.5   3 km
Approximate Scale

Nggela

SABU SEA

Nggela is worth a visit for its hilltop position above the coast, but the chief attraction is its weaving, usually done by hand and still using many natural dyes. The weaving is among the finest in Flores, and you'll be able to watch women weaving and see at least part of the process that makes up the final product. In former times the size, colour and pattern of the ikat shawls of this region indicated the status of the wearer. Nggela ikat typically has black or rich, dark-brown backgrounds, with patterns in earthy reds, browns or orange. Bargain hard and watch out for synthetic dyes, which are becoming more common (you should pay less if the dyes aren't natural).

In Nggela, the *Homestay Nggela Permai* costs 5500 rp per person.

Wolojita, about seven km inland from Nggela, has similar-quality weavings, but not Nggela's fine location. At Jopu, six km further inland (and the same distance from Wolowaru), weaving has taken a plunge in the last few years. Old weaving may still be worth looking at.

Getting There & Away A road branches off the Ende-Maumere road at Wolowaru to Jopu (six km), Wolojita (12 km) and Nggela (19 km). There's usually a bus or truck every day from Moni at about 8 am (1500 rp), at least as far as Wolojita. This should also pass through Wolowaru. Otherwise, it's a good half day's walk to Nggela from Wolowaru. It's only two or three km further from Moni via Woloara, so you could just as easily start from there. The volcano-studded scenery is beautiful, particularly on the downhill stretch to Nggela. From Wolojita to Nggela, you can either follow the road or take a shortcut past the hot springs (ask for the *jalan potong ke Nggela*). You'd be pushing it to do the return walk the same day, but you might find a truck going back to Wolowaru.

MAUMERE

This seaport is the main town of the Sikka district, which covers the neck of land between central Flores and the Larantuka district (in the east). The Sikkanese language

NUSA TENGGARA

is closer to that of Larantuka than to Endenese. The name Sikka is taken from a village on the south coast controlled by Portuguese rulers and their descendants from the early 17th to 20th centuries.

This area has been one of the chief centres of Catholic activity on Flores since Portuguese Dominicans arrived some 400 years ago. Missionaries were one of the largest groups of foreigners to establish themselves on Flores, and many Dutch, German and Spanish priests spent decades surviving Japanese internment camps, as well as an often-hostile population during the independence wars.

Many of the priests made important studies of the island and its people. They also encouraged local arts & crafts and helped the Florinese with improved tools and seed for agriculture; as recently as two decades ago, many Florinese were still tilling the soil with sharpened sticks, and moving slash-and-burn farming is still common. Today the European priests are being replaced by Florinese.

In December 1992 Maumere was devastated by an earthquake and the ensuing 20m high tidal waves killed thousands. Maumere was only 30 km from the epicentre of the quake, which almost flattened the entire town. Most of the town has now been rebuilt

There's a strong ikat-weaving tradition in the Maumere region, and some interesting trips can be made out of town.

Information

The tourist office (☎ 21652) on Jl Wairklau is well out of the way and has little in the way of literature, but tries hard. The BNI bank on Jl Soekarno Hatta is the best place to change money, or Bank Danamon on Jl Pasar Baru Barat and Bank Rakyat Indonesia also handle foreign exchange.

The post office is next to the soccer field on Jl Pos and the Telkom office is further south from the town centre on Jl Soekarno Hatta.

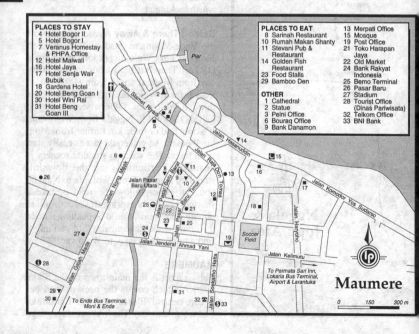

PLACES TO STAY
4 Hotel Bogor II
5 Hotel Bogor I
7 Veranus Homestay & PHPA Office
10 Hotel Maiwali
16 Hotel Jaya
17 Hotel Senja Wair Bubuk
18 Gardena Hotel
20 Hotel Beng Goan I
30 Hotel Wini Rai
31 Hotel Beng Goan III

PLACES TO EAT
8 Sarinah Restaurant
10 Rumah Makan Shanty
11 Stevani Pub & Restaurant
14 Golden Fish Restaurant
23 Food Stalls
29 Bamboo Den

OTHER
1 Cathedral
2 Statue
3 Pelni Office
6 Bouraq Office
9 Bank Danamon
13 Merpati Office
15 Mosque
19 Post Office
21 Toko Harapan Jaya
22 Old Market
24 Bank Rakyat Indonesia
25 Bemo Terminal
26 Pasar Baru
27 Stadium
28 Tourist Office (Dinas Pariwisata)
32 Telkom Office
33 BNI Bank

Maumere

0   150   300 m

Places to Stay

Maumere has a number of hotels, most with a wide variety of rooms. Cheap rooms tend to be dismal, while better rooms with mandi are expensive compared to other towns on Flores.

The *Hotel Senja Wair Bubak* (☎ 21498) on Jl Komodor Yos Sudarso, near the waterfront, is gearing itself to the travellers' trade. It has a travel agent and, like many of the hotels, offers tours and motorcycle and car rental. Nondescript singles/doubles with shared mandi cost 6600/12,100 rp or better rooms with mandi cost 8800/15,400 rp. Other rooms with fan or air-con range from 14,300/20,350 to 27,500/36,300 rp.

Nearby, the small and friendly *Hotel Jaya* (☎ 21292), Jl Hasanuddin 26, is a good buy and has rooms with fan and mandi for 10,000/15,000 rp.

The *Gardena Hotel* (☎ 21489) on Jl Patirangga is on a quiet suburban street but close to the town centre. Clean, if uninspiring, rooms cost 10,000/15,000 rp with mandi and fan or 25,000/30,000 rp with air-con.

The cheapest place in town is the *Veranus Homestay* (☎ 21464), which has a couple of decrepit rooms for 3000/5000 rp. It has a travel agency and could be a good budget place if the damage from the earthquake is repaired as planned.

A little far from the town centre, but close to the Ende (west) bus terminal, the well-run *Hotel Wini Rai* (☎ 21388), Jl Gajah Mada 50, has a wide variety of rooms. Economy rooms with shared mandi are fairly basic for 8250/13,750 rp, while substantial rooms with private mandi and fan are a good mid-range choice for 22,000/27,500 rp or 36,000/42,000 rp with air-con.

The *Hotel Maiwali* (☎ 21220), Jl Raja Don Tomas 40, is the best hotel close to the town centre. Rooms with mandi for 8000/14,000 rp are crappy. Fan rooms for 28,500/42,500 rp and air-con rooms for 42,500/63,500 rp are good, but expensive. It has a restaurant and arranges car hire.

The fanciest place is the *Permata Sari Inn* (☎ 21171) at Jl Jenderal Sudirman 1, on the waterfront about two km from the town centre. Standard rooms with mandi and fan go for 17,500/22,500 rp, while bungalows facing the beach are 30,000/40,000 rp. There's an open-air restaurant near the water. To get there, take a bemo heading east.

Other hotels include the Muslim-run *Hotel Bogor II* (☎ 21137) on Jl Slamet Riyadi, a cheap option if you arrive at the port and can't be bothered walking further. It has rooms with mandi for 10,000/15,000 rp, but is undergoing renovation. It is better than the seedy *Hotel Bogor I* opposite. *Hotel Beng Goan I* on Jl Moa Toda is OK for 11,000/17,500 rp with mandi, but also on the seedy side, while *Hotel Beng Goan III* is finally undergoing post-earthquake restoration, which may make it one of the better hotels.

Places to Eat

The best place to hunt out a restaurant is Jl Pasar Baru Barat, the main street running down to the waterfront. The *Sarinah Restaurant* has Chinese food and does good squid. The *Stevani Pub & Restaurant* has small huts dotted around in a garden setting. It's a pleasant place to sit with a drink, and western and Indonesian dishes are served.

Maumere's old central market, burnt down after a Muslim/Christian flare up, has moved from Jl Pasar Baru Barat to the western outskirts and is being replaced with a shopping centre. A few food stalls can still be found at the southern side of the original site.

Rumah Makan Shanty is spacious and has a long menu of Chinese food and seafood. The *Golden Fish* restaurant, on the waterfront, has good seafood and air-con. The *Bamboo Den* near the Hotel Wini Rai has cheap Indonesian food, good fish and cold beer.

Things to Buy

Toko Harapan Jaya on Jl Pasar Baru Timur has the most comprehensive collection of ikat (from Flores and other islands) that you'll find anywhere in Nusa Tenggara except Sumba. You can also buy carvings and other artefacts here.

NUSA TENGGARA

Getting There & Away

Air Maumere handles bigger aircraft and is the easiest place on Flores to fly into from other islands, but there are no flights to anywhere else on Flores. Bouraq and Merpati fly to Kupang (101,000 rp) and Denpasar (265,000 rp). Merpati flies via Bima (Sumbawa) en route to Bali. Bouraq's office (☎ 21467) is on Jl Nong Meak. Merpati (☎ 21342) is on Jl Raja Don Thomas 18.

Bus There are two bus terminals in Maumere. Buses and bemos east to Larantuka (5000 rp; four hours), Geliting, Waiara, Ipir and Wodong leave from the Lokaria (or Timur) terminal, about three km east of town. Take a bemo (400 rp) there. Buses west to Moni (4000 rp; 3½ hours), Ende (6000 rp; five hours), Sikka and Ledalero leave from the Ende (or Barat) terminal, about 1.5 km south-west of town.

Buses often endlessly do the rounds of the town in their search for passengers. Hotels can arrange pick-up. Ende buses leave at 8 am and 5 pm. For Moni, take an Ende bus. Buses to Larantuka leave throughout the day.

Boat Pelni's KM *Binaiya* sails to and from Ujung Pandang on Sulawesi (41,500 rp; 23 hours) and Dili on Timor (39,500 rp; 18 hours). The Pelni office is on Jl Slamet Riyadi, next to Hotel Bogor II.

Getting Around

The Airport Maumere's Wai Oti airport is three km from town, 800m off the Maumere-Larantuka road. A taxi to/from town is 6000 rp. Otherwise, it's about a one km walk out of the airport to the Maumere-Larantuka road to pick up a bemo (500 rp) into town.

Bemo Bemos run around town regularly and cost 400 rp anywhere within the city.

Car & Motorcycle A car will cost around 80,000 rp per day around town or 120,000 rp further afield. A few places around town hire motorcycles for around 20,000 rp per day; ask at your hotel or the travel agencies.

AROUND MAUMERE
Ledalero & Nita

Many Florinese priests studied at the Roman Catholic seminary in Ledalero, 19 km from Maumere on the Ende road. The chief attraction here is the museum run by Father Piet Petu, a Florinese. It houses a collection of historic stone implements and Florinese ikat – you'll see designs and natural dyes that are either rare or no longer produced, including softly textured, pastel-coloured old Jopu sarongs. It's a good place to try to piece together the jigsaw of Florinese culture. Admission is free, but you might leave a donation.

Nita, two km beyond Ledalero on the main road, has a Thursday market. Bemos to Ledalero and Nita go from Maumere's Ende terminal.

Sikka

On the south coast, 27 km from Maumere, Sikka was one of the first Portuguese settlements on Flores, dating from the early 17th century. Its rulers dominated the Maumere region until this century. Today it's interesting mainly as the home of the distinctive Sikkanese ikat. A lot of Sikka weaving is predominantly in maroons, blues and browns and design has been heavily influenced by the Dutch; you'll see the Dutch coat of arms and pairs of cherubim!

If you're in Sikka overnight, you may be able to stay with the Dutch priest. The road to Sikka leaves the Ende road 20 km from Maumere. Take a bemo from Maumere to Sikka (1000 rp).

About four km before Sikka is **Lela**, another Catholic and weaving centre. It has a few colonial buildings and a long, rocky black sand beach.

Geliting

Geliting, about 10 km east of Maumere on the Larantuka road, has a huge, colourful market on Friday. There's lots of beautiful ikat around – more being worn than for sale – and thousands of people come from surrounding villages. Get there by bemo from Maumere's east terminal.

atublapi

'atublapi, in the hills 20 km south-east of laumere, is a large Catholic mission. From ere, you can walk to **Ohe**, where you can e both coasts of Flores. **Bola** is a large llage six km from Watublapi, and two km rther on is the traditional coastal weaving llage of **Ipir**. Market day in Ipir is Friday, id bemos and trucks go there from Mau-ere (1500 rp; 1½ hours). On other days, ucks usually finish at Bola. You should be ıle to stay with villagers or the kepala desa Bola or Ipir.

antai Waiara

hirteen km east of Maumere, just off the arantuka road, Waiara is the jumping-off oint for the Maumere 'sea gardens'. Unfor-nately, some of the reefs suffered damage the 1992 earthquake.

There are two resorts here. The cheaper ea World Club (☎ 21570) is the friendlier id cleaner. Cabin accommodation starts at),000 rp a double. Snorkelling and dive ackages are arranged.

The newer Flores Sao Resort (☎ 21555) group-tour territory, with prices to match, ut is looking tired. Accommodation starts US$30/40 for singles/doubles with fan and ath.

To get there, catch a Talibura bus from laumere to Waiara (500 rp), or take a bemo Geliting and walk 1.5 km along the arantuka road. You'll see the signs for the ırn-off to Sea World Club first, and Flores ao Resort is about 500m further along the oad.

Vodong

Vodong village is 28 km east of Maumere, short walk off the Maumere-Larantuka oad. A French couple have built lovely bam-oo beachside huts, Flores Froggies, near ie village. Bungalows are 8000/16,000 rp nd some have private mandi. This is an xcellent, well-run place and the French read is a winner. The black sand beach is leasant and the owners have canoes for norkelling and offer boat trips to nearby slands.

Wodong Homestay, another new place a few hundred metres along the beach, has just opened and has bungalows for 7000/12,000 rp.

The main highway runs right out the front – take any Talibura, Nangahale or Larantuka bemo or bus.

LARANTUKA

A busy little port at the eastern end of Flores, Larantuka (population 30,000) nestles around the base of the Ili Mandiri volcano, separated by a narrow strait from the islands of Solor and Adonara. Larantuka is the departure point for boats to the Solor Archi-pelago (east of Flores) and for a twice-weekly ferry to Kupang.

This corner of Indonesia, though always isolated, was one of the first to attract Euro-pean interest. Lying on sea routes used by the Portuguese seeking sandalwood from Timor, the Larantuka-Solor area saw Portuguese forts and over 20 Dominican missions being built by 1575. Portugal even maintained a few enclaves until the mid-19th century, among them Larantuka, which was the centre of a community of Topasses (from *tupassi*, a south Indian word for 'inter-preter'), the descendants of Portuguese men and local women. The Topasses are still a significant group in Larantuka today.

Orientation & Information

Most hotels, the ferry pier, shipping offices and the main bus terminal are in the compact southern part of the town (shown on the Larantuka map). Further north-east are the homes, mosques and fishing boats of the Muslim population, plus the post office, Telkom office and airport. To the south is the pier for boats to Kupang.

The BNI bank and Bank Rakyat Indonesia both change money.

Things to See

Portuguese-style Catholicism flourishes in Larantuka. There's a large **cathedral**, and the smaller **Holy Mary Chapel** (Kapela Tuan Maria) contains Portuguese bronze and silver known as *ornamento*. On Saturday in this chapel, women say the rosary in Portuguese, and on Good Friday an image of the Virgin Mary from the chapel is carried in procession around the town to the accompaniment of songs in Latin.

Larantuka's **market** has some weaving – look for ikat from Lembata, Adonara and Solor.

Places to Stay

The family-run *Hotel Rulies* (☎ 21198) at Jl Yos Sudarso 44 has the best set up for travellers. Clean singles/doubles with shared

bath cost 10,000/16,000 rp and food is avai able. The manager speaks English and sta can answer most queries.

Next door, the *Hotel Tresna* (☎ 21072) a reasonable place catering mainly for bus ness travellers. Rooms with private man are 15,000/25,000 rp or 8000 rp a doub with shared mandi.

The *Hotel Sederhana* right in the midd of town has cheap rooms for 5000 rp, b may not take travellers.

The *Hotel Fortuna I* (☎ 21140) is incor veniently located about two km north-east town at Jl Diponegoro 171 near the Telko office. Rooms for 5000/10,000 rp with mar di are cramped and dreary, while much bett rooms with fan cost 11,000/16,500 rp.

Its new offshoot, the *Hotel Fortuna* (☎ 21383) is a small place directly across th road with the best rooms in town. Larg bright rooms with fan are 20,000/30,000 r or quite plush rooms with air-con are 40,00 60,000 rp.

Places to Eat

Eating possibilities are limited, but a fe warungs set up in the evening along Jl Niag. *Rumah Makan Nirwana* is a decent Chines restaurant and the best in town. Also good the small *Virgo Cafe*, with fish and chips i addition to the usual nasi and mie meals. Th owner speaks excellent English, with a Australian accent, and serves very cold bee

Getting There & Away

Air The Merpati agent's house is at J Diponegoro 64, opposite the cathedral. On flight a week does a Kupang-Larantuka Lewoleba (Lembata)-Kupang loop, but it' often cancelled.

Bus The main bus terminal is five km wes of the town, about one km from Waibalur but you can pick them up in the centre c town or hotels may be able to arrange pick up. Coming into town, buses can drop you a or near your hotel, depending on the one wa street system, though the bemo drivers ma insist that you get down and catch a bem from the terminal (300 rp).

PLACES TO STAY
3 Hotel Sederhana
14 Hotel Rulies
15 Hotel Tresna

PLACES TO EAT
2 Virgo Cafe
4 Rumah Makan Nirwana
6 Warung
10 Rumah Makan & Warungs
11 Rumah Makan & Warungs

OTHER
1 Mosque
5 Merpati Agent
7 Cathedral
8 Statue
9 Harbour Master's Office & Pelni Office
12 Bus & Bemo Stop
13 Bank Rakyat Indonesia
16 Church
17 BNI Bank
18 Kapela Tuan Maria (Holy Mary Chapel)

To Market, Airport, Hotel Fortuna I & II, Telkom Office & Post Office

Cemetery

Arrows indicate direction of town bemos

Jalan Niaga

To Alor, Solor, Adonara & Lembata

Jalan Yos Sudarso

Flores Strait

Larantuka
Not to Scale

To Maumere & Kupang Ferry Pier (Waibalun)

NUSA TENGGARA

The Lamaholot

The Larantuka area has long had closer links with the islands of the Solor Archipelago – Adonara, Solor and Lembata – than with the rest of Flores. It shares a language, Lamaholot, with the islands. The whole area, particularly outside the towns, fascinates anthropologists because of its complex social and ritual structure, which in some parts survives pretty well intact.

There's a web of myths about the origins of the Lamaholot people: one version has them descended from the offspring of Watowele (the extremely hairy goddess of Ili Mandiri) and a character called Patigolo, who was washed ashore, got Watowele drunk, cut her hair (thus removing her magic powers and discovering that she was female) and made her pregnant. Alternatively, locals believe their forbears came from Sina Jawa (China Java), Seram or India – take your pick.

At some stage, probably before the 16th century, the Lamaholot area became divided between two groups known as the Demon and the Paji. The Demon, associated with the 'Rajah' of Larantuka, were mainly grouped in eastern Flores and the western parts of Adonara, Solor and Lembata; the Paji, with their allegiance to the 'Rajah' of Adonara, were centred in the eastern parts of the three islands. Anthropologists tend to believe that the conflict between the two groups was mainly a ritual affair or, as one writer puts it, 'two groups representing the two halves of the universe engaged in regular combat to produce human sacrifices for the securing of fertility and health'. Such a pattern was not uncommon in eastern Indonesia. Today, people still know who is Paji and who is Demon, but ritual warfare has subsided. Other animist rites survive, including those for birth, name-giving, marriage, the building of a new house, the opening of new fields in *ladang* (slash-and-burn) agriculture, and the planting and harvesting of crops. ■

Buses to/from Maumere cost 5000 rp and take about four hours. If you arrive from the Solor Archipelago, enthusiastic bus jockeys will arm-wrestle you into waiting buses and whisk you away to Maumere. Buses leave Larantuka for Maumere hourly throughout the day until around 5 pm.

Boat Ferries to Kupang (14,000 rp; 14 hours) depart Monday and Friday at 2 pm from Waibalun, four km south-west of Larantuka (300 rp by bemo). Going the other way, the ferries to Larantuka leave Kupang on Thursday and Sunday afternoons. Ferries can get crowded, so board earlier to get a seat. Take some food and water.

The Persero passenger/car ferry to Adonara, Lembata and Alor also leaves from Waibalun on Tuesday, Thursday and Sunday at 7 am. More convenient, smaller boats to Adonara, Solor and Lembata leave from the pier in the centre of town. They run twice a day to Lewoleba (3000 rp; four hours) on Lembata at around 8 am and 1 pm, stopping at Waiwerang (Adonara) on the way. A boat goes once a week to Lamalera (5000 rp; seven hours) on Friday at 9 am.

The Pelni passenger ship *Tatamailau* calls in at Larantuka on its route from Labuanbajo on to Dili and Irian Jaya, returning in the opposite direction two weeks later. It's also worth asking around the pier, or at the Pelni and harbour master's office on Jl Niaga for other possibilities.

Getting Around

Bemos run up and down Jl Niaga and Jl Pasar, and to outlying villages. Bemos in town cost 300 rp. A chartered bemo to the airport, 12 km east of town, will cost around 6000 rp.

Around Larantuka

Six km north of Larantuka is a white sand beach at **Weri**; get there by bemo (300 rp) from the central bemo stop in Larantuka. **Lewoloba**, near the village of Oka, puts on traditional dancing once a month when tour boats arrive. **Danau Asmara** is a scenic lake two hours by bus north of Larantuka and is reputed to be home to freshwater crocodiles. Buses (2500 rp) leave from the market in Larantuka at 10 am and can drop you at Riang Kerokok. The lake is 500m from the road. The main problem with a visit is that the bus returns at 1 pm.

NUSA TENGGARA

Solor & Alor Archipelagos

A chain of small islands stretches out from the eastern end of Flores. These volcanic, mountainous specks separated by swift, narrow straits can be visited by a spectacular ferry ride from Larantuka. Andonara and Solor, where the Portuguese settled in the 16th century, are close to Larantuka. Further east, Lembata is the main island of interest because of the traditional whaling village of Lamalera. These islands form the Solor Archipelago, which has close cultural links with the Larantuka area on Flores; together these people are known as the Lamaholot.

Beyond Lembata are the main islands of the Alor Archipelago, Pantar and Alor, whose people were still head-hunting in the 1950s.

The scenery is spectacular, all the islands (notably Lembata) produce distinctive ikat weaving, and there are some traditional, almost purely animist villages, despite the spread of Christianity and (to a lesser degree) Islam.

In remote villages, people are poor and not used to westerners; children will follow you in excited bunches. Food is generally of bad quality. If you can't deal with all this, limit your stay to the urban centres of Kalabahi (Alor) and Lewoleba (Lembata) and make a few day trips into the surrounding countryside.

One thing you should bring is plenty of money. You can only change money in Kalabahi.

History

European contact was made as early as 152[] when the only remaining ship of Magellan[] fleet sailed through the Lembata-Pant[] strait. By the middle of the century, t[] Dominican Portuguese friar Antonio Tavei[] had landed on Solor and set about spreadir[] Catholicism. The Solor mission became t[] base for extending Christianity to mainlar[] Flores and a fort was built to protect t[] converts from Muslim raids. The Portugue[] were eventually kicked out of Solor by t[] Dutch, but until the mid-19th century, Port[] gal held on to Wurek (Adonara) and Pamaka[] (Solor).

Getting Around

Alor has some bemos and ancient buses, b[] most of the islands have only one decent roa[] and transport to more isolated areas is limite[] to a few trucks per week. Asking around th[] ports may prove more fruitful; on Alor ar[] Lembata, the most reliable transport to the[] south coasts is by boat.

SOLOR

Rita-Ebang is the main town on the islan[] Lohajong (towards the eastern end of th[] north coast) has the ruins of the Portugues[] fort. Lamakera (on the north-eastern tip) is [] whaling village, but is losing the batt[] against commercialism of its tradition.

Getting There & Away

From Larantuka there are boats to Pamakaj[] and Lohajong every morning at about 8 an[]

FLORES SEA

Pulau Adonara

Larantuka • Waiwodan • Sago • Lewotolo • Balauring • Wairiang

Pamakajo • Wailebe • Witilama • Lewoleba

Pulau Flores • Lamakera • Walwerang • Puor • Waiteba

Rita-Ebang • Lamalera • Pulau Lembata

Pulau Solor

0   25   50 km

Pulau Pantar

Kabir • Baranusa

Pasirputih • Alor Besar • Mali • Cimbur
Pulau Alor
Moru • Takpala • Taramana
Kalabahi

SABU SEA

Ombai Strait

Pulau Timor

Solor & Alor Archipelagos

rom Waiwerang (Adonara), boats cross to ohajong and Lamakera several times a day.

ADONARA

Adonara was known as the 'Island of Murderers' because of a feud between two clans. The feud apparently ran for hundreds of years, with people in the hills being killed and houses burned year in, year out – very likely a case of ritual conflict between the Demon and Paji groups (see under Larantuka in the previous Flores section). Though extremes of animism have died out, there are villages in the hinterland where Christianity has only the loosest of footholds. One traveller reported placing her hands on a sacred rock above one village and being unable to remove them! The chief settlements are Wailebe (on the west coast) and Waiwerang on the south coast). A few bemos link the main villages.

Waiwerang

There's an uninspiring market every Monday and Thursday – follow the streets about 00m in the Lembata direction from the pier. There are three places to stay in Waiwerang: *Losmen Taufiq*, close to the pier, is run by a friendly Muslim woman and costs 5000/0,000 rp; the more upmarket *Ile Boleng Homestay* is a little out of town. A few rumah makan dot the main street around the pier.

Getting There & Away All the boats to Lewoleba on Solor call in at Waiwerang on the way. They depart from Larantuka at 8 am and 1 pm. The trip takes about 2½ hours. You can pick up boats to Solor and Lembata every day; to Lamalera (on Lembata) on Friday, and to Alor and Pantar perhaps twice a week.

LEMBATA

Lembata is well known for the whaling village of Lamalera and for the smoking volcano, Ili Api, which towers over the main town of Lewoleba. As in the rest of the Lamaholot region, many Lembata villagers still use the slash-and-burn method of clear-

ing land. Corn, bananas, papayas and coconuts are grown; most rice is imported.

Lewoleba

Despite the ominous smoking of Ili Api volcano in the background, the chief settlement on Lembata and 'capital' of Solor regency is a relaxed little town. A couple of larger government buildings and a Telkom office are all that distinguishes it from any other scruffy village.

Boats unload you at a pier about a 10 minute walk west of the town – take a *mikrolet* (small taxi) or *becak* (trishaw) for 500 rp. Below town, on the water, is a Bugis stilt village built out over the sea. Some of its people are pearl divers and you can arrange to go out with them on diving trips. Have a good look at the pearls you're offered in town as many are just shells. Locals will take you out by sampan to a sandbank off Lewoleba – it's the closest place to town for a swim in beautifully clear water.

Orientation & Information The centre of Lewoleba is the market place, which comes alive every Monday evening with buyers and sellers from around Lembata and other islands.

The banks do not change money, so bring sufficient funds with you. The post office is near the south side of the market and the Telkom office is about one km further west along the main street.

Places to Stay & Eat *Hotel Rejeki I* is right in the middle of town, opposite the market. Clean singles/doubles with outside mandi cost 6500/12,000 rp downstairs and are better than the wooden rooms upstairs for the same price. New rooms with attached mandi are being built. Meals are generous and cheap, and there's always fresh seafood on the menu. *Hotel Rejeki II* is about a 10 minute walk south of the market. It's cheaper (5000 rp per person), but a bit out of the way.

The Hotel Rejeki I has the best food in town or a few dismal rumah makan can be found near the market. The *Rumah Makan Hosana* has Padang food.

Getting There & Away Lewoleba is served by air, bus and ferry.

Air Merpati flies Kupang-Larantuka-Lewoleba and return once a week on Thursday, but the flight is often cancelled due to lack of interest. The Merpati agent is in the Hotel Rejeki I.

Bus The main road across the island is now sealed and a host of regular mikrolet and buses run to destinations around Lewoleba, including Waipukang, Loang and Puor (for Lamalera). Buses to the east run to Hakadewa and direct to Balauring (5000 rp; two hours). Some of the rough back roads are plied by infrequent trucks. Buses terminate next to the ferry dock, or you can catch them in Lewoleba in front of the market.

Boat Small passenger ferries daily ply between Lewoleba and Larantuka (3000 rp; four hours). They leave around 8 am and 1 pm from Lewoleba, at the same times from Larantuka, stopping at Waiwerang (on Adonara) on the way. They can be crowded, but there's usually no problem getting a seat. It is a spectacular journey through the islands past smoking volcanoes.

The large passenger/car ferries to Kalabahi (Alor) from Larantuka stop at Lewoleba on Tuesday, Thursday and Sunday. They depart from Lewoleba at 11 am for Balauring (4500 rp; four hours) in north-eastern Lembata where they stop for the night. Balauring has a decent losmen or you can sleep on the deck of the boat. At 7 am the next morning the ferry continues on to Kalabahi (9000 rp; nine hours) via Baranusa (4000 rp; four hours) on Pantar. There are usually plenty of seats, though the ferry can fill up on Pantar. Bring food and water. Coming from Kalabahi, these ferries depart from Lewoleba on Monday, Wednesday and Friday at 11 am for Waibalun harbour (4500 rp; four hours), four km from Larantuka, but the smaller ferries are more convenient and dock in the centre of Larantuka.

Getting Around You can take mikrolet around town and to the ferry dock, o Lewoleba has a few becaks imported fror Ujung Pandang and Java which cost 500 r anywhere around town.

Around Lewoleba

Lembata's best ikat, recognisable by its bur gundy-coloured base and highly detaile patterning, comes from the villages on th slopes of Ili Api, 15 or 20 km from Lewoleb **Atawatun** and **Mawa**, on the north coast, ar two of the best places to see fine ikat. **Jon tona** is on the east side of the deep inlet o Lembata's north coast. It's possible to sta there with the kepala desa. An hour's wal from Jontona towards Ili Api is th **Kampung Lama** (Old Village), with man traditional houses. These contain man sacred and prized objects, including a hug number of elephant tusks, but are occupie by villagers only for ceremonies such as th *kacang* (bean) festival in late Septem ber/early October. It is possible to climb I **Api** – it takes about six hours to the top. Tak a guide.

Lembata has some good **beaches**. Yo can take a mikrolet to Tagawiti and then it i a two km walk to the beach where there i

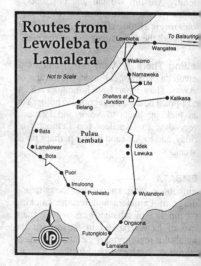

Routes from Lewoleba to Lamalera

Not to Scale

To Balauring
Lewoleba
Wangatea
Waikomo
Namaweka
Lite
Shelters at Junction
Belang
Kalikasa
Bata
Pulau Lembata
Lamalewar
Udek
Lewuka
Bota
Puor
Imuloong
Posiwatu
Wulandoni
Ongaona
Futonglolo
Lamalera

asonable snorkelling out on the reef. The astern bay on the way to Hakadewa also has ome good snorkelling closer to shore. Sunathing is difficult – the crowds of kids block ut the sunlight. It pays to be able to speak ome Indonesian if venturing further afield.

amalera

ike characters out of *Moby Dick*, the people ho live in this village on the south coast of embata still use small boats to hunt whales. he whaling season is limited from May to ctober, when the seas aren't too rough. ven then, the whales are infrequent, with nly about 15 to 25 caught each year. The illagers probably qualify as subsistence halers and are therefore exempt from interational bans on whaling.

The meat is shared according to traditional ictates. The heads go to two families of riginal landowners, a custom observed, it is aid, since the 15th century. The blubber is nelted to make fuel for lamps, and some is

traded for fruit and vegetables in a barteronly market in the hills.

Most whales caught are sperm whales, though smaller pilot whales are occasionally taken. When whales are scarce, the villagers harpoon sharks, manta rays and dolphins, which are available year-round. Using nets is alien to these people and fishing rods are used only for sharks.

The whaling boats are made entirely of wood, with wooden dowel instead of nails. Each vessel carries a mast and a sail made of palm leaves, but these are lowered during the hunt, when the men (usually a crew of 12) row furiously to overtake the whale. As the gap between the boat and the whale narrows, the harpooner takes the three metre long harpoon and leaps onto the back of the whale. An injured whale will try to dive, dragging the boat with it, but cannot escape, since it has to resurface.

Your chances of actually seeing a whale hunt, or the bloody business of butchering a whale, are quite small. Otherwise Lamalera is just another fishing village. A steady trickle of travellers make their way here and tourism is certainly welcome as an attractive economic alternative to whale hunting. For 15,000 rp you can even go out in the boats on a whale hunt.

On Saturday, there's an interesting barteronly market at **Wulandoni**, about a 1½ hour walk along the coast from Lamalera. Another nice walk along the coast is to **Tapabali**, where you can see local weaving. In Lamalera, common ikat motifs are whales, manta rays and boats.

Places to Stay & Eat There are four small homestays in the village, all costing around 7500 rp per day, including meals. *Homestay Ben Guru* is above the village, perched on a hill overlooking the shoreline. The more salubrious *Bapa Yosef's*, also known as the 'White House', is right on the point at the end of the beach. This small house sleeps four and someone will come in three times a day to cook meals. *Mama Maria's Homestay* is right in the heart of the village, behind the shady town square. *Abel Beding* is on the

---

Lamalera

The villagers of Lamalera are thought to have originated from Lapan Batan, a small island in the straits between Lembata and Pantar which was destroyed by a volcanic eruption. The ancestors arrived in boats that each clan has kept as the model for all future boats. While the original boats have been repaired and added to over generations, the villagers consider them to be the same boats. To the villagers, each boat is a living being and a physical link to the ancestors and the ancestral home.

The loss of boats from the village is more than an economic blow to the villagers – it means losing an important part of their heritage. Most recently, in March 1994, two small boats from Lamalera sank after being dragged almost to Timor by a wounded whale, a distance of around 80 km. The crew of the two boats was later picked up by a third boat from the village and the 36 men then drifted for several days before being rescued by the P & O Spice Islands cruise ship.

The loss of the boats sent the village into a two month period of mourning in which no whaling was allowed. When the mourning period finished, a ceremony took place to 'let the boats go'. ■

main path through the village, past the town square, and is on the ball with information.

Getting There & Away The easiest way to get to Lamalera is by boat from either Lewoleba or Larantuka. The boat from Lewoleba to Lamalera (3500 rp; six hours) leaves after the Monday night market (any time between 1 and 5 am). From Larantuka, a boat leaves on Friday at 9 am, stopping in Waiwerang on the way.

Otherwise take a bemo from Lewoleba to Puor, from where it's a three hour walk, mostly downhill. Buses also go to Bota from Lewoleba, an alternative approach, but it is then a harder four hour walk. Bring plenty of water for the walk. It may be possible to charter or hire a motorcycle in Lewoleba.

Balauring

This small, predominantly Muslim town is on the peninsula jutting off the eastern end of Lembata. Ferries linking Alor and Lembata stop here for the night (on Tuesday, Thursday and Sunday), the only reason to visit. There are wonderful views of Ili Api as you come into Balauring.

The town has one place to stay, the welcoming *Losmen Telaga Sari*, though it's in a swampy area and mosquitos are a problem. Walk straight down the road leading off the end of the pier and the losmen is the second last building on the street. It costs 7500 rp per person in dilapidated rooms and meals are provided. Otherwise, you can sleep on the boat – the crew may be able to provide you with a mat to sleep on the deck.

Mikrolet (4000 rp) and buses (5000 rp; two hours) run the 53 km from Balauring over the paved road to Lewoleba. Buses also run to **Wairiang** on the far eastern coast, a 45 minute journey by bus, from where small ferries leave for Kalabahi on Wednesday at 11 am.

ALOR

East of the Solor group are the islands of Alor and Pantar. Alor, in particular, is quite scenic and has a wide mix of cultures in a small area. Diving around the island is reputedly some

of the best in South-East Asia. The island so rugged, and travel there so difficult, th the roughly 140,000 inhabitants of Alor a divided into some 50 tribes, with about a many different languages. To this day the is still some isolated, occasional warfa between the tribes.

Although the Dutch installed local rajah along the coastal regions after 1908, they ha little influence over the interior, whose peopl were still taking heads in the 1950s. Th mountain villages were hilltop fortresse above valleys so steep that horses were useless, and during the rainy season the trail became impassable. The different tribes ha little contact with each other except durin raids.

When the 20th century came, the warrior put western imports to good use by twistin wire from telegraph lines into multibarbe arrowheads, over the tip of which the pressed a sharpened, dried and hollowe chicken bone. When the arrow hit, the bon would splinter deep inside the wound.

The coastal populations are predomi nantly Muslim. Christianity has mad inroads, primarily through Dutch Protestan missionaries, but indigenous animist cul tures still survive, mainly because travel around the island has been very difficul New roads now cross the island, but boat are still a common form of transport.

Kalabahi

Kalabahi is the chief town on Alor, at the en of a long, narrow and spectacular palm fringed bay on the west coast. It's a clich tropical port – lazy and slow-moving, wit wooden boats scattered around the harbou The sea breezes make Kalabahi appreciabl cooler than most other coastal towns in Nus Tenggara.

Kalabahi is relatively prosperous, bu outside the town living conditions are poor There are a few interesting villages and nic beaches nearby. Some of the beaches have spectacular snorkelling and diving, but also dangerous currents.

It's worth strolling around the Pasar Inpre market in Kalabahi. It has a huge variety o

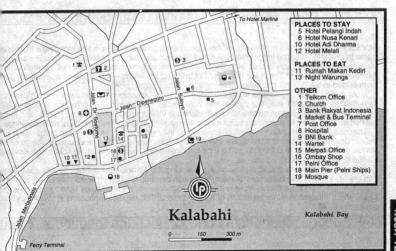

PLACES TO STAY
5 Hotel Pelangi Indah
6 Hotel Nusa Kenari
10 Hotel Adi Dharma
12 Hotel Melati

PLACES TO EAT
11 Rumah Makan Kediri
13 Night Warungs

OTHER
1 Telkom Office
2 Church
3 Bank Rakyat Indonesia
4 Market & Bus Terminal
7 Post Office
8 Hospital
9 BNI Bank
14 Wartel
15 Merpati Office
16 Ombay Shop
17 Pelni Office
18 Main Pier (Pelni Ships)
19 Mosque

Kalabahi

Kalabahi Bay

0   150   300 m

Ferry Terminal

uit and you'll see women making bamboo
ats.

oney Cash and travellers cheques can be
shed at the BNI bank and the Bank Rakyat
donesia. The Ombay shop, one block back
om the port, will also change US dollars
ish outside banking hours at reasonable
tes.

laces to Stay The central *Hotel Adi Dhar-
a* (☎ 21049), Jl Martadinata 12, is on the
aterfront near the main pier. It has the best
tup for travel information and has great
ews across the harbour from the porch,
pecially at sunset. Singles/doubles/triples
ith outside bath are 6000/10,000/12,000
, while large, clean rooms with fan and
ath are 12,500/20,000/24,000 rp.

The nearby *Hotel Melati* (☎ 21073) has a
ady garden and old rooms for 6500/12,000
or 10,000/16,000 rp with mandi. The new
ock has better rooms for 15,000/20,000 rp
25,000/30,000 rp with air-con.

Out near the bus terminal, *Hotel Pelangi
dah* (☎ 21251) at Jl Diponegoro 100 has
e best rooms in town and the attached
staurant is a definite bonus. Spotless rooms

with verandah, fan and mandi cost 15,000/
20,000 rp, while those with air-con and
shower are 35,000/40,000 rp. Any bemo
going to the bus terminal can drop you there.

Nearby, the *Hotel Nusa Kenari* (☎ 21119),
Jl Diponegoro 11, has good rooms for 15,000
rp with mandi, or 25,000 rp and 30,000 rp
with air-con and shower.

The *Hotel Marlina* (☎ 21141) is inconveniently located three km out of town on Jl El
Tari, but you can get there by bemo. Room
rates start at 6000 rp per person in three-bed
rooms with shared bath, or 15,000 rp with
private bath.

Places to Eat Kalabahi has the best dining
in the Solor and Alor archipelagos, which
isn't saying much. The best option and
Kalabahi's only restaurant is at the *Hotel
Pelangi Indah*. Otherwise a few dreary
rumah makan are scattered around town.
They include the *Rumah Makan Kediri*,
close to the pier, which serves reasonable
Javanese food, and there is also a grungy
Padang restaurant opposite the market on Jl
Diponegoro.

At night, a few streetside warungs and
kaki lima food stalls set up on the southern

Moko

Alor's chief fame lies in its mysterious *mokos* – bronze drums about half a metre high and a third of a metre in diameter, tapered in the middle like an hourglass and with four ear-shaped handles around the circumference. They're closed at the end with a sheet of bronze that sounds like a bongo when thumped with the hand. There are thousands of them on the island – the Alorese apparently found them buried in the ground and believed them to be gifts from the gods.

Most mokos have decorations similar to those on bronze utensils made on Java in the 13th and 14th century Majapahit era, but others resemble earlier South-East Asian designs and may be connected with the Dongson culture which developed in Vietnam and China around 700 BC and then pushed its influence into Indonesia. Later mokos even have English or Dutch-influenced decorations.

Theories about the mokos' origins usually suggest they were brought to Alor from further west by Indian, Chinese or Makassarese traders, but this doesn't explain why they were buried in the ground. Maybe the Alorese buried them in some long-forgotten times, as an offering to spirits at a time of plague or to hide them during attacks.

Today mokos have acquired enormous value among the Alorese and families devote great time and energy to amassing collections of them, along with pigs and land. Such wealth is the only avenue to obtaining a bride in traditional Alorese society. In former times, whole villages would sometimes go to war in an attempt to win possession of a prized moko. The export of mokos is restricted by the government. ■

---

side of the sports ground. Sate, soto ayam and other Javanese fare are on offer. This meagre collection is about the closest thing to nightlife in Kalabahi, which otherwise closes down around 8 pm.

Getting There & Away Merpati flies to/from Kupang to Kalabahi (113,500 rp) daily, except Friday.

Kalabahi is linked by passenger/car ferries to Kupang and Atapupu on Timor, and Larantuka on Flores via Baranusa (Pantar), Balauring (Lembata), Lewoleba (Lembata), and Weiwerang (Adonara). These ferries leave from the ferry terminal one km southwest of the town centre. It's a 10 minute walk or 400 rp bemo ride to the Hotel Adi Dharma.

The Perum ASDP ferry leaves Kupang's Bolok harbour on Wednesday and Saturday at 2 pm (16,500 rp; about 16 hours). From Kalabahi to Kupang departures are on Tuesday and Thursday at 2 pm. On Sunday at 10 pm this ferry runs from Kalabahi to Atapupu (8000 rp; eight hours), from where buses run to Atambua with connections to Dili and Kupang. The ferry returns from Atapupu to Kalabahi on Monday.

Ferries leave Kalabahi for Larantuka on Sunday, Tuesday and Thursday at 7 am. They stop at Baranusa (5000 rp; five hours)

and then Balauring (9000 rp; nine hour where they overnight. Balauring has a lo men. The next day at 7 am ferries contin from Balauring to Larantuka (9000 rp; ni hours) via Lewoleba and Waiwerang. Ta food and water, as there's usually none on t boat.

Pelni boats leave from the main pier in t centre of town. The Pelni ship *Binaiya* ca in at Kalabahi twice every fortnight, sailir on to Dili (East Timor) on alternate Frida and to Kupang on alternate Wednesday Pelni cargo ships also regularly run fro Kalabahi to Dili and Kupang and take pa sengers. Check at the Pelni office. They a slow (14 hours to Dili) and conditions are n the best. It pays to rent a cabin from one the crew for around 15,000 rp.

Other small boats from the central wha chug their way to the other islands of the Al archipelago. A boat also travels once a wee to Wairiang on the north-eastern tip Lembata.

Getting Around Kalabahi airport is 28 k from town. Merpati runs a minibus to me flights. Transport around town is by bus a bemo (400 rp), which finish by 7 pm. It's al possible to rent a motorcycle through t Hotel Adi Dharma or the Toko Kencana sho opposite the market on Jl Diponegoro for 5,000 rp per day.

round Kalabahi

akpala is a traditional village about 13 km st of Kalabahi. To get there, take a Mabu us from the Kalabahi market. From where e bus drops you, walk about one km uphill n a sealed road. There are several traditional gh-roofed houses and the view over the lores Sea from the village is stunning. The eople welcome visitors and occasionally ut on dance performances for tour groups.

From Takpala it's possible to continue on Atimelang, another traditional village hich is rarely visited. You can take a bus to labu, but from there it's about a four hour alk; a guide is recommended. It's possible stay with the kepala desa in Atimelang.

The villages of **Alor Kecil** and **Alor Besar** ave good beaches nearby, with excellent norkelling. The water is wonderfully cool, ut the currents are very strong. The diving ound the offshore islands is superb, but is est arranged in Kupang. Alor Kecil has ome weavings and offers great views across other islands. This area is being promoted a potential diving resort. Buses to Alor ecil and Alor Besar leave from the Kala-ahi market or catch them outside the Hotel lelati.

Near the airport at the northernmost tip of e island is **Mali**, a lovely white sand beach ith good snorkelling. It's possible to rent a oat for a tour of the area and at high tide you an walk to **Pulau Suki**, off the beach at Iali. There's an old grave there, said to be at of a sultan from Sulawesi.

ANTAR

he second largest island of the Alor group, antar is about as far off the beaten track as ou can get. The Perum ferries between arantuka and Alor stop at **Baranusa**, the nain town, a somnolent little place with a raggle of coconut palms and a couple of eneral stores. Baranusa's only accommoda-on is at the friendly *Homestay Burhan*, with ist one room, costing 10,000 rp, including neals.

The main reason to visit Pantar is to climb **Gunung Sirung**, an active volcano with an impressive smouldering crater. From Bara-nusa take a truck to Kakamauta (2500 rp), from where it is a three hour walk to Sirung's crater.

The only other island of note is lightly populated **Pulau Pura**, sandwiched between Pantar and Alor. It is dominated by a tower-ing, forested peak topped by a small crater lake.

Timor

If you arrive in Timor from Darwin, it will hit you with all the shock of Asia. Kupang, the main city, is very Indonesian, with its buzzing streets and honking horns and its Third World sights and smells. Away from Kupang, Timor is not very touristy, although it's a scenic island, with some traditional areas in the south-west that are off the track and worth exploring. New interest was added in 1989, when East Timor, a former Portuguese colony, was opened up to foreign tourists for the first time since Indonesia invaded and took it over in 1975.

Timor's landscape is unique, with its spiky lontar palms, rocky soils and central mountains dotted with villages of beehive-shaped huts. The island has some fantastic coastline and rugged, scenic mountains. There are no tourist-type beach spots yet, though you can take trips from Kupang to nearby islands for swimming and snorkell-ing. East Timor's beaches, which attracted travellers before 1975, are again accessible.

Timor is 60% mountainous; the highest peak, Tatamailu, stands at 2963m. Along the north coast, the mountains slope right into the sea. Aggravated by dry winds from north-ern Australia, the dry season is distinct and results in hunger and water shortages. To remedy the water problem, there is an inten-sive programme of small earth-dam building. Maize is the staple crop, but coffee and dry rice are important, and some irrigated rice is grown in the river valleys.

Thanks to Merpati's twice weekly flights between Kupang and Darwin, more travellers to or from Australia are passing through Timor, and there are interesting options for onward travel from East Timor to the Solor and Alor archipelagos, or from Kupang on to Roti, Sabu and Sumba.

Apart from Kupang (one of the most prosperous towns in Nusa Tenggara) and Dili, Timor is poor, especially the eastern half. West Timor has a population of 1.3 million and East Timor about 850,000. Much of Timor – both West and East – is still very traditional. Modern, Indonesian education has permeated the towns, but elsewhere Bahasa Indonesia may not even be spoken. Small children may cry at the sight of an *orang putih*.

Christianity is widespread, though still fairly superficial in some rural areas; the old animistic cultures have not been completely eradicated. In the hills of the centre and the east, villagers still defer to their traditional chiefs. In the mountain areas, traditional ikat dress is common, and betel nut and *tuak* (village liquor) are still preferred. On the southern coast of central West Timor and East Timor, it is rumoured that internecine wars between tribes continue and the occasional head is even still taken.

About 14 languages are spoken on the island, both Malay and Papuan types, though Tetum (the language of the people thought to have first settled in Timor in the 14th century) is understood in most parts.

History

The Tetum of central Timor are one of the largest ethnic groups on the island. Before the Portuguese and Dutch colonisation, they were fragmented into dozens of small states. Skirmishes between them were frequent, with head-hunting a popular activity, although when peace was restored, the captured heads were kindly returned to the kingdom from which they came.

Another major group, the Atoni, are thought to be the earliest inhabitants of Timor. One theory is that they were pushed westward by the Tetum. The Atoni form the predominant population of West Timor an[d] like the Tetum, were divided into numerou[s] small kingdoms before the arrival of Euro[-] peans. It's thought that their tradition[al] political and religious customs were strong[ly] influenced by Hinduism, possibly as a resu[lt] of visits by Javanese traders, but they held [to] a strong belief in spirits, including ancest[or] spirits.

The first Europeans in Timor were th[e] Portuguese, perhaps as early as 1512, th[e] year after they captured Melaka. Like Ch[i-] nese and western Indonesian traders befor[e] them, the Portuguese found the island a plen[-] tiful source of sandalwood (prized in Europ[e] for its aroma and for the medicinal santal[e] made from the oil). In the mid-17th centur[y] the Dutch occupied Kupang, Timor's be[st] harbour, beginning a long conflict for contr[ol] of the sandalwood trade. In the mid-18th century the Portuguese withdrew to th[e] eastern half of Timor. The division of th[e] island between the two colonial power[s,] worked out in agreements between 1859 an[d] 1913, gave Portugal the eastern half plus th[e] enclave of Oekussi (on the north coast of th[e] western half), while Holland got the rest [of] the west. Today's Indonesian province [of] East Timor has the same boundaries as th[e] former Portuguese Timor.

Neither European power penetrated fa[r] into the interior until the second decade of th[e] century and the island's political structure wa[s] left largely intact, with both colonisers rulin[g] through the native kings. Right through unt[il] the end of Portuguese rule in East Timo[r,] many ostensibly Christian villages contin[-] ued to subscribe to animist beliefs. Whe[n] Indonesia won independence, in 1949, th[e] Dutch left West Timor, but the Portugues[e] still held East Timor, setting the stage for th[e] tragedy that continues today.

East Timor (Timor Timur) Until the end [of] the 19th century, Portuguese authority ove[r] their half of the island was never very stron[g.] Their control was often effectively oppose[d] by the *liurai*, the native Timorese rulers, an[d] the *mestico*, the influential descendants [of] Portuguese men and local women. Th[e]

ominican missionaries were also involved
 revolts or opposition to the government.
ventually a series of rebellions between
93 and 1912 led to bloody and conclusive
acification'.

The colony had been on the decline much
rlier, as the sandalwood trade fizzled out,
d when Portugal fell into a depression after
WI, East Timor drifted into an economic
rpor. Neglected by Portugal, it was notable
ly for its modest production of high-
ality coffee and as a distant place of exile
r opponents of the Portuguese regime. The
dinary Timorese were subsistence farmers
ing the destructive ladang (slash-and-
rn) system, with maize the main crop.

In WWII, although Portugal and its over-
as territories were neutral, the Allies
sumed that the Japanese would use Timor
a base from which to attack Australia.
veral hundred Australian troops were
ded in East Timor and, until their evacu-
on (in January 1943), they carried out a
errilla war which tied down 20,000 Japan-
e troops, of whom 1500 were killed. The
ustralian success was largely due to the
pport they got from the East Timorese, for
hom the cost was phenomenal. The Japan-

ese razed whole villages, seized food supplies and killed Timorese in areas where the
Australians were operating. In other areas
the Japanese had incited rebellion against the
Portuguese, which resulted in horrific repression when the Japanese left. By the end
of the war, between 40,000 and 60,000 East
Timorese had died.

After the war the Portuguese resumed full
control. The turning point came in 1974
when a military coup in Portugal overthrew
the Salazar dictatorship. The new government sought to discard the remnants of the
Portuguese Empire as quickly as possible.
With the real possibility of East Timor
becoming an independent state, two major
political groups, the Timorese Democratic
Union (UDT) and the Timorese Social Dem-
ocrats (later known as Fretilin), quickly
formed in the colony. A third group, known
as Apodeti, was a minor player, but its stated
preference for integration with Indonesia
eventually turned it into little more than a
front for Indonesia's goals.

Although both major political groups
advocated independence for East Timor,
Fretilin gained the edge over the UDT, partly
because of its more radical social policies.

NUSA TENGGARA

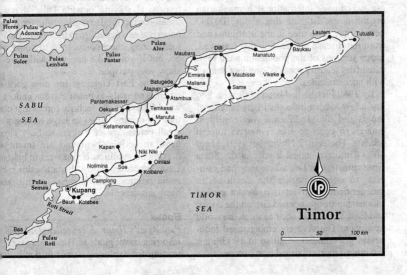

Indonesian leaders had had their eyes on East Timor since the 1940s and, as Fretilin was regarded by them as Communist, they were itching for a reason to step into East Timor.

It came on 11 August 1975, when the UDT staged a coup in Dili which led to a brief civil war between it and Fretilin. Military superiority lay from the outset with Fretilin; by the end of August, the bulk of the fighting was over and the UDT withdrew to Indonesian Timor.

Fretilin proved surprisingly effective in getting things back to normal, but by the end of September Indonesia had decided on a takeover. East Timor and Fretilin now faced Indonesia alone; the Portuguese were certainly not coming back. On 7 December the Indonesians launched their attack on Dili.

From the start the invasion met strong resistance from Fretilin troops, who quickly proved their worth as guerrilla fighters. Though East Timor was officially declared Indonesia's 27th province on 16 July 1976, Fretilin kept up regular attacks on the Indonesians, even on targets very close to Dili, until at least 1977. But gradually, Indonesia's military strength and Fretilin's lack of outside support took their effect.

The cost of the takeover to the East Timorese was huge. International humanitarian organisations estimate that about 100,000 people may have died in the hostilities and from the disease and famine that followed. Large sections of the population were relocated for 'security reasons' and lost contact with ancestral sites.

By 1989 Fretilin had been pushed back to just a few hidden hideouts in the far east of the island and Indonesia was confident enough to open up East Timor to foreign tourists. Then on 12 November 1991, about 1000 Timorese staged a rally at the Santa Cruz cemetery in Dili where they had gathered to commemorate the death of an independence activist two weeks earlier. Indonesian troops opened fire on the crowd and East Timor was once again in the world headlines. The severely embarrassed Indonesian government admitted to 19 killings, but other reports claimed many more.

East Timor remains a political thorn f Indonesia that will not go away. In 19⁘ Bishop Carlos Belo of Dili and Jose Ramc Horta, Fretilin's UN representative, we awarded the Nobel Peace Prize for their wo in highlighting East Timor's struggle. T Indonesian government responded by reite ating its stance that it will never consid independence for East Timor.

Despite East Timor's reputation as one the world's hot spots, the army well and tru controls East Timor. East Timor is not a w zone and there are no official restrictions travel. You can go right through to Tutua East Timor's most easterly point.

You are required to show your passport ⦁ entry into East Timor – on the bus fro Atambua and on arrival by air – but this merely a formality (unless you were si enough to write 'journalist' on your dise⦁ barkation card when arriving in Indonesia

East Timor is crying out for tourists to he its economic development, and visitors a slowly making their way to Dili, especia now that there are better travel connectior Travel to Dili, Nusa Tenggara's most attra tive city, is safe and easy. Outside Di facilities are still limited, but the governme has opened resthouses in some of the old h resorts. If staying outside Dili, you w usually be required to register with the poli on arrival and departure in the towns. On t⦁ roads, army checkpoints tend to come a go, but if you strike one you will have show your passport.

For the East Timorese life now goes ⦁ much as normal – as much as it can under t⦁ watchful eye of the security forces that co tinue to occupy Timor in large numbers. small percentage of visitors to East Tim have an activist bent and are intent ⦁ delving into politics. If you want to help t East Timorese, enjoy the attractions b avoid politics. You only risk getting yo hosts into trouble.

Books

Paul Ryan's *Timor: A Travellers Guide* is inspiring travel guide to Timor and essent reading for exploring Timor in depth. It cked with relevant travel detail and explations of Timorese culture. It is hard to find Timor, but readily available in Darwin, ustralia.

Probably the best account of events surunding the Indonesian invasion of East mor is John Dunn's *Timor: A People Betyed*. Dunn was the Australian consul in st Timor from 1962 to 1964; he was also rt of an Australian government factding mission to East Timor from June to ly 1974, and returned in 1975, just after the etilin-UDT war. *Timor, The Stillborn Nan*, by Bill Nicol, tends to criticise Fretilin's ders and places much more blame on the rtuguese. For the inside story from the etilin point of view, read *Funu: The Unfinhed Saga of East Timor*, by Jose mos-Horta.

JPANG

ough only a small city, Kupang is a oming metropolis compared with the ergrown villages that pass for towns in er parts of Nusa Tenggara. It's the capital East Nusa Tenggara (Nusa Tenggara mur, or NTT) Province, which covers West mor, Roti, Sabu, the Solor and Alor archilagos, Sumba, Flores and Komodo. As ch, it comes equipped with footpaths, ightly coloured bemos with sophisticated und systems and a nightlife of sorts.

The centre is busy, noisy and untidy; the ealthier residential areas are in the suburbs; d the eastern outskirts are experiencing a ilding boom of oversized government ildings.

Merpati's twice weekly Darwin to Kung flights are attracting many short-term urists from Australia and have put Kupang ell and truly on the South-East Asia travlers' route. It's not a bad place to hang ound for a few days – Captain Bligh did ter his *Bounty* misadventures.

istory

ne Dutch East India Company occupied upang in the middle of the 17th century, ainly in an attempt to gain control of the ndalwood trade. The Portuguese had built a fort at Kupang, but abandoned it before the Dutch arrived, leaving the Portuguese-speaking Christian mixed-blood mestico population (or the 'black Portuguese', as they were known) to oppose the Dutch. It was not until 1849, after an attack by the mestico on Kupang had been decisively defeated, that the Dutch went more or less unchallenged in western Timor.

Timor was, however, very much a side-show for the Dutch. Supplies of sandalwood had already dwindled by 1700, and by the late 18th century Kupang was little more than a symbol of the Dutch presence in Nusa Tenggara. Not until the 20th century did they pay much attention to the interior of the island.

The original inhabitants of the Kupang area were the Helong. Squeezed by the Atoni, the Helong had, by the 17th century, been limited to a small coastal strip at the western tip of the island. Later, partly because of the Dutch-supported migration to Kupang of people from the nearby island of Roti, most of the Helong migrated to the small island of Semau (off Kupang). By the mid-20th century they were confined to just one village near Tenau (the port of Kupang) and several villages on Semau.

Orientation

Kupang is hilly and the central area hugs the waterfront. The central bemo terminal, Kota Kupang (or simply Terminal), almost doubles as a town square, though you're not likely to stroll leisurely across it with bemos coming at you from all directions. Many of the shops and restaurants are around here. Kupang's El Tari airport is 15 km east of town; Tenau harbour is 10 km west.

Information

Tourist Office The regional government tourist office (☎ 21540) is way out of town, grouped with other government offices east of Kupang. The office is helpful for maps and a few brochures, but that's about it. To get there, take bemo No 10 or 7. Get off at Jl Raya El Tari at the SMP5 secondary school

NUSA TENGGARA

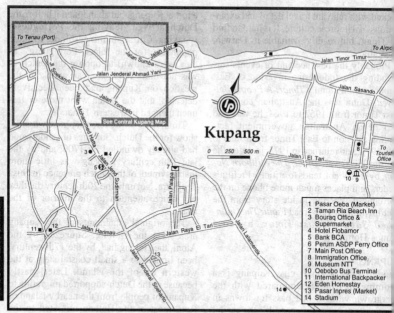

Kupang

0   250   500 m

1 Pasar Oeba (Market)
2 Taman Ria Beach Inn
3 Bourag Office &
  Supermarket
4 Hotel Flobamor
5 Bank BCA
6 Perum ASDP Ferry Office
7 Main Post Office
8 Immigration Office
9 Museum NTT
10 Oebobo Bus Terminal
11 International Backpacker
12 Eden Homestay
13 Pasar Inpres (Market)
14 Stadium

and walk 200m east. The office is open Monday to Thursday from 7 am to 3 pm.

Money Kupang is the best place to change money in Nusa Tenggara outside Mataram on Lombok. The Bank Dagang Negara, Jl Urip Sumohardjo 16, is central, but most banks have good rates. If you want a cash advance on Visa or MasterCard, get it there. The currency exchange office at Kupang airport is open when flights arrive from Darwin.

Post & Communications Poste restante mail goes to the central post office, Kantor Pos Besar at Jl Palapa 1 – take bemo No 5. A branch post office is at Jl Soekarno 29. The Telkom office is at Jl Urip Sumohardjo 11.

Museum NTT

The East Nusa Tenggara Museum, near the tourist office, is worth a look for a taste of what you're heading into, or to round out

your Nusa Tenggara experience. It houses collection of arts, crafts and artefacts fro all over the province. Aurora Arby, an a thropologist, will be happy to show yo around. To get there, take a No 10 bemo fro the Terminal. It's open daily from 8 am to pm. Entry is free, but drop a donation in th box as you leave.

Markets

The main market is the rambling Pasar Inpr off Jl Jenderal Soeharto in the south of th city. To get there, take bemo No 1 or 2 an follow the crowd when you get off. I mostly fruit and vegetables, but some craf and ikat can be found. A lesser market is Jl Alor, two km east of town.

Pulau Semau

Semau, visible to the west of Kupang, h some decent beaches where you can snorke and freshwater springs. Though not one Asia's great island paradises, it makes

leasant day trip from Kupang. International
ackpacker, Eden Homestay and Taman Ria
each Inn all arrange trips (see Places to
tay), as do local tour companies. A day trip
ill cost about 20,000 rp, including lunch.
regular local boats go from Namosaen
illage, west of Kupang. The island has some
an-down bungalows costing 40,000 to
0,000 rp, including meals, built for an
xpected tourism boom that never happened.
he Hotel Flobamor in Kupang books them
nd also arranges diving and fishing trips
om Semau.

Monkey Island (Pulau Kera)
Monkey Island is the blob of trees and sand
isible from Kupang. This small, uninhab-
ed island has sandy beaches and clear
vater. Taman Ria Beach Inn organises day
rips, or talk to the people operating the
shing boats.

Beaches
Kupang's beaches are grubby, but get better
he further you go from town. The beach at
Taman Ria, three km from the town centre,
s OK, or keep heading out to **Pantai La-**
iana, about 10 km east of Kupang by bemo
No 17. It's in a lovely setting, but is a busy
icnic spot on weekends, when drink and
nack stalls and litter are the order of the day.
Outside the wet season, the water is clear.

At Tablolong, 15 km west of Kupang, the
vhite sand beach, **Air Cina**, is good. Take
emo No 8 from the Terminal.

Organised Tours
Village Visits Many fascinating traditional
illages can be visited on Timor, but
ndonesian, let alone English, is often not
poken so a local guide is necessary. Guides
vill find you and will ask around 20,000 rp
er day. You pay for public transport, accom-
nodation and food, or the guide can arrange
motorcycle. Big tour companies include
Pitoby Tours (☎ 32700), Jl Jenderal Sudir-
nan 118. Ultra Tours (☎ 22258), right next
o the bemo terminal at Jl Soekarno 15A, is
ood for air ticketing as well as tours.

Dive Trips Nusa Tenggara has some of Indonesia's best diving and Kupang is a good
place to arrange diving trips. Graeme and
Donavan Whitford (☎ 21154; fax 24833),
two Australian dive masters based in
Kupang, arrange dives to Alor, Dili, Labuanbajo and Komodo.

Places to Stay – bottom end
Accommodation in Kupang is spread out,
and many of the hotels have a range of prices,
so the bottom, middle and top end overlap to
some extent. There are also some good
options a little further out if you want to
escape the bustle of central Kupang. Kupang
is a little more expensive than other cities in
Nusa Tenggara, but the existence of dormitory accommodation seems to be an
extension of the Australian backpackers' network rather than a necessity through high
prices.

Two popular budget options, despite their
distance from town, are found in a quiet area
on Jl Kencil. *Eden Homestay* (☎ 21931) at
No 6 is opposite a shady freshwater pool, the
local swimming spot. Bungalows are about
as basic as they get, but for 3000 rp per
person it is hard to complain. This friendly
place offers meals, cheap tours and has a
shady garden. *International Backpacker* at
No 37B is one street away behind the pool.
Dormitories and small rooms are more substantial, and also cost 3000 rp per person.
This is another friendly place that also has
meals. To get there from the Terminal, catch
a No 3 bemo.

Closer to town at Jl Sumatera 8, *L'Avalon*
(☎ 32278) is Kupang's other main backpacker option. It's a laid-back place run by a
local character Edwin Lerrick and is good for
information on touring Timor. Well-kept
four- and six-bed dorms cost 4000 rp per
person, or the double room costs 10,000 rp.

The *Taman Ria Beach Inn* (☎ 31320) at Jl
Timor Timur 69 is on the beachfront about
three km from the Terminal and gets a steady
trade off the plane from Darwin. The beach
is pleasant enough and the restaurant is good.
Singles/doubles with mandi and fan are
15,500/21,000 rp and they also rent on a

dorm basis at 7500 rp. To get there, catch a
No 10 bemo.

Fateleu Homestay (☎ 31374) at Jl Gunung Fateleu 1 is a friendly place close to the
city centre. Basic rooms cost 8000/12,500 rp
with fan and shared bath; rooms with private
mandi are better, but expensive at 16,000/
21,500 rp.

Sea Breezes Homestay on Jl Ikan Tongkol
(Tuna Fish St), next to Teddy's Bar, is a dive
with rooms from 5000 rp per person.

The central *Hotel Setia* (☎ 23291) at Jl
Kosasih 13 used to be a popular place when
it had good contacts with the Darwin hostels,
but it has changed management and is now
quiet. Nevertheless, it is clean and tidy with
rooms for 8000/16,000 rp or 10,000/20,000
rp with mandi.

Places to Stay – middle

Along the waterfront on Jl Sumatera, a short
bemo ride from the Terminal, are four hotels
– the *Timor Beach Hotel* (☎ 31651) is the
standout for its restaurant with panorami
sea views. Rooms situated around an elon
gated courtyard are a little dark, but goo
value at 12,500/17,000 rp with fan and bath
Air-con rooms go for 24,500/30,000 rp.

Heading back into town, the large *May*
Beach Hotel (☎ 32169) is next to the BN
bank at No 31. This is the best mid-rang
hotel in this stretch with air-con rooms fror
30,000 rp with bath to 50,000 rp with h
water. The others nearby are less inspiring
Hotel Maliana (☎ 21879) at No 35 ha
rooms with mandi for 22,000/25,000 r
while air-con costs another 4000 rp. Th
Hotel Susi (☎ 22172) at No 37 has a rang
of rooms, starting at 15,000/20,000 rp wit
fan and bath.

Clustered on Jl Kelimutu close to the cit
centre is a group of hotels: the *Hotel Keli*
mutu (☎ 31179) at No 38; *Hotel Komod*
(☎ 21913) at No 40; and the *Hotel Lagun*
at No 36. Standards are similar and compe
tition keeps the prices down. The very clea

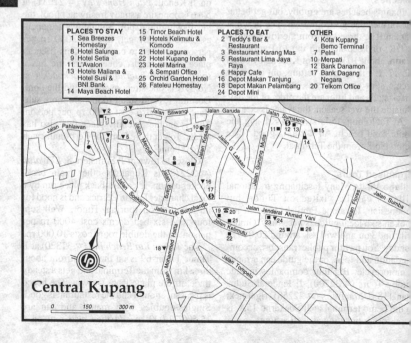

PLACES TO STAY		PLACES TO EAT	OTHER
1 Sea Breezes Homestay	15 Timor Beach Hotel	2 Teddy's Bar & Restaurant	4 Kota Kupang Bemo Terminal
8 Hotel Salunga	19 Hotels Kelimutu & Komodo	3 Restaurant Karang Mas	7 Pelni
9 Hotel Setia	21 Hotel Laguna	5 Restaurant Lima Jaya Raya	10 Merpati
11 L'Avalon	22 Hotel Kupang Indah	6 Happy Cafe	12 Bank Danamon
13 Hotels Maliana & Hotel Susi & BNI Bank	23 Hotel Marina & Sempati Office	16 Depot Makan Tanjung	17 Bank Dagang Negara
14 Maya Beach Hotel	25 Orchid Garden Hotel	18 Depot Makan Pelambang	20 Telkom Office
	26 Fateleu Homestay	24 Depot Mini	

Central Kupang

0   150   300 m

nd relatively new Kelimutu is a notch ahead
f the pack and has good service. Rooms
ith bath and fan cost 20,000/25,000 rp and
r-con rooms cost 27,500/31,500 rp.

Another option is the friendly *Hotel
Marina* (☎ 22566) at Jl Jenderal Ahmad Yani
5. Spacious rooms with fan and shared bath
st 16,500/22,000 rp, or air-con rooms start
27,500/33,000 rp with private bath.

On the waterfront one km west of town is
e *Hotel Ausindo* (☎ 32873) at Jl Pahlawan
1. There's a popular swimming spot across
e road, rooms are spacious and the hotel
ffers full service. Rooms start at 30,000/
5,000 rp. More expensive rooms on the top
or feature balconies with great views.

laces to Stay – top end

otel Flobamor (☎ 33476), Jl Sudirman 21,
a declining hotel that straddles the middle
nge. It has a tiny pool next to the restaurant.
arge rooms are dog-eared, but reasonable
alue at 40,000/60,000 rp and 60,000/
0,000 rp.

At the top of the range is *Orchid Garden
otel* (☎ 33707; fax 33669) at Jl Gunung
ateleu 2. It's a small hotel with excellent
ungalows built around a Balinese-style
arden, and there is a swimming pool.
ooms with hot water, TV and minibar cost
50,000/182,000 rp.

The *Sasando Hotel* (☎ 33334; fax 33338),
RA Kartini, is out in the middle of nowhere
out five km east of town. It is Kupang's
ggest hotel, with a pool, restaurant and
isco. It is built on a ridge with great views
cross the sea. Rooms with all trimmings,
cluding fridge, start at US$50/60. Add
1% to the rates, but similarly sized dis-
unts may be available.

laces to Eat

upang has a greater variety of food than
ost places in Nusa Tenggara, so tuck in
hile you can.

Around the Terminal, *Restaurant Lima
aya Raya*, Jl Soekarno 15, has Chinese and
ndonesian food, and a loud and sweaty
ightclub upstairs. Across the road, the

Happy Cafe at Jl Ikan Paus 3 is a bright place
serving cheap Chinese and Indonesian food.

When you can't eat another noodle or
grain of rice, step into the *Gunung Intan
Bakery* opposite the Happy Cafe and sniff the
air. It has a delicious selection of pastries,
doughnuts and buns.

Visiting Darwinites like to hang out at
Teddy's Bar, Jl Ikan Tongkol 1-3, for a meat
pie and chips (French fries). The expensive
food is compensated for by the excellent
waterside location, with sea breezes and cold
beer. The nearby *Pantai Laut Restaurant* has
seafood and other dishes, and is a better bet
than the grotty *Restaurant Karang Mas*
further along at Jl Siliwangi 88.

Depot Makan Tanjung on Jl Kosasih has
good, cheap Chinese food. The *Depot Mini*
on Jl Jenderal Ahmad Yani is a spotless restaurant with similar fare.

The *Timor Beach Hotel* has one of Kupang's better restaurants, with a varied menu
and an elevated position overlooking the
water. Nearby, at Jl Sumatera 44, *Rujak
Cinjur* has good Javanese food, such as gado
gado and nasi campur, for around 1000 rp.

You'll see night warungs around town,
particularly around the Terminal. Try the
bubur kacang (mung beans and black rice in
coconut milk). Be aware, some of these
warungs sell dog meat.

Things to Buy

Timorese ikat is colourful, with a huge
variety of designs, and there are lots of other
embroidered textiles. Purists will be disappointed that natural dyes are now rare in
Timor, but interestingly, the tourist trade is
starting to create a demand for them. You
may also see some at Kupang's market, Pasar
Inpres, where villagers sometimes bring
their weavings to sell.

Several shops in Kupang sell ikat, handcrafts, old silver jewellery, ornamental *sirih*
(betel nut) containers and more. Bizarre hats
from Roti *(ti'i langga)* make a fun purchase,
but try fitting one in your backpack! These
shops also have ikat from other parts of East
Nusa Tenggara, including Roti and Sabu.
Prices are quite high and bargaining won't

bring them down dramatically, but Timorese crafts are hard to find elsewhere in Nusa Tenggara.

Try Dharma Bakti at Jl Sumba 32, out towards Jl Tim Tim. Toko Sinar Baru, Jl Siliwangi 94, opposite the Terminal, has an interesting range, but it's hard to shift on prices. Ina Koro Artshop on Jl Pahlawan, near the Pelni office, also has a good selection.

Getting There & Away

Kupang is the transport hub of Timor, with buses and flights to/from the rest of the island, plus planes and regular passenger boats to many destinations in Nusa Tenggara and beyond.

Air Merpati (☎ 33833) at Jl Kosasih 2 has direct flights to Denpasar (276,000 rp), Dili (95,000 rp), Waingapu (171,000 rp), Maumere (101,000 rp), Kalabahi (111,500 rp), Larantuka, Ruteng, Ende and Roti.

Merpati also flies to/from Darwin (Australia) on Wednesday and Saturday. From Kupang the fare is US$150 one way – shop around the travel agents. You won't be allowed on the plane without an Australian visa – obtainable in Denpasar or Jakarta, not Kupang.

Bouraq (☎ 21421) at Jl Jenderal Sudirman 20 has direct flights to Waingapu and Maumere, with onward connections. Sempati (☎ 31612) at the Hotel Marina, Jl Jenderal Ahmad Yani, has direct flights to Dili and Surabaya.

There are also numerous ticket agencies around town, including Ultra Tours (☎ 31064), right next to the Terminal at Jl Soekarno 15A.

Bus & Bemo Long-distance buses depart from the Oebobo terminal out near the museum – take a No 10 bemo. Departures include: Soe (4250 rp; three hours) and Niki Niki (5250 rp; 3½ hours) every hour or two from 5 am to 6 pm; Kefamenanu (7500 rp; 5½ hours) from 7 am to 3 pm; and Atambua (10,500 rp; eight hours) and Dili (15,500 rp; 12 hours) at 7.30 and 8 am, 7 and 8 pm.

Bemos to villages around Kupang go fro the central terminal, Kota Kupang.

Boat Pelni passenger ships leave from T nau, 10 km west of Kupang (400 rp by bem No 12). Ferries leave from Bolok, 13 k west of Kupang (550 rp by bemo No 13).

Pelni (☎ 22646) is at Jl Pahlawan 3, ne the waterfront. Pelni's KM *Dobonsolo* rur directly between Banyuwangi (Java) an Kupang, and on to Dili, Ambon (Maluku and Irian Jaya. The KM *Binaiya* stops at a the main islands of Nusa Tenggara and rur to Waingapu-Ende-Kupang-Kalabahi-Dil Maumere, returning on this route two week later.

Perum ASDP (☎ 21140) on Jl Cak Dok is Nusa Tenggara Timur's major ferry com pany, with passenger/car ferries operatin throughout the province. The office sel tickets the day before departure, but it easier to buy a ticket at the harbour. Peru has ferries from Bolok harbour to: Larantuk (14,000 rp; 14 hours) on Thursday and Sur day at 2 pm; Kalabahi (16,500 rp; 16 hour on Wednesday and Saturday at 2 pm; an Ende (17,000 rp; 16 hours) on Monday at pm. The Ende ferry continues on t Waingapu (Sumba) and Sabu.

Perum ASDP also has a ferry to Roti (57C rp; four hours) on Friday at 9 am, and othe daily ferries leave from Bolok at 9 an Ferries leave Bolok for Sabu on Tuesday an Friday afternoon (14,000 rp; nine hours returning to Kupang the following day.

Getting Around

The Airport Kupang's El Tari airport is 1 km east of the town centre. Taxis cost a fixe 12,500 rp. By public transport, turn left o of the terminal and walk a full km to th junction with the main highway, from whe bemos to town cost 500 rp. Going to th airport take bemo No 14 or 15 to the junctic and then walk.

Bemo Around town, bemos cost a standar 400 rp and are fast, efficient, brightly painte and incredibly noisy – drivers like the ba turned up high and a multi-speaker stere

stem is *de rigueur*. They stop running by
pm.

Kupang is too spread out to do much
alking. The hub of bemo routes is the Ter-
ainal Kota Kupang, usually just called
Terminal'. Bemos are numbered, with the
ain bemo routes as follows:

os **1 & 2** Kuanino-Oepura passing the following
hotels: Maya; Maliana; Timor Beach; Fateleu;
Orchid Garden; Marina; and Flobamor
o **3** Aimona-Bakunase to Eden Homestay and
Backpackers
o **5** Oebob-Airnona-Bakunase passing the ferry
office and the main post office
o **6** Oebobo-Oebufu to the stadium but *not* to the
bus terminal
o **10** Kelapa Lima-Walikota from the Terminal to
the Taman Ria Beach Hotel, tourist information
office and Oebobo bus terminal
o **12** Tenau
o **13** Bolok
os **14 & 15** Penfui (useful for getting to the airport)
o **17** Tarus to Pantai Lasiana

Car & Motorcycle It's possible to rent a car
ith driver for around 100,000 rp or a motor-
ycle for 25,000 rp per day. Ask at your hotel
r travel agents such as Ultra Tours.

OEBELO

Oebelo, 22 km from Kupang on the Soe road,
s where Pak Pah and his family have set up
workshop (look for the Home Industri
asando sign) producing the traditional 20
tringed Rotinese instrument, the *sasando*
featured on the 5000 rp note). They also
nake the Rotinese lontar-leaf hat, ti'i langga.
f you're interested, Pak Pah will play the
Rotinese version of *Waltzing Matilda* for
ou.

BAUN

A small, quiet village 30 km south of Kupang
n the hilly Amarasi district, Baun is an ikat-
weaving centre, with a few Dutch buildings.
You can visit the *rumah rajah*, the last rajah's
ouse, now occupied by his widow. She
oves to chat to foreigners and will show you
er weavings and rose garden. Market day in
Baun is Saturday. From Baun to the south

coast is a solid day's hike reportedly; there's
a good surf beach down there.

To get to Baun, take a bemo from Kupang's Pasar Inpres market (850 rp).

CAMPLONG

Camplong, 46 km from Kupang on the Soe
road, is a cool, quiet hill town. One km from
town towards Soe on the highway, the
Taman Wisata Camplong is a forest reserve
that has some caves and a spring-fed swimming pool. It is a tough seven km walk to
Gunung Fateleu, which attracts botanists
interested in the unique montane flora found
on the slopes.

The Camplong convent at the reserve,
Wisma Oe Mat Honis (☎ 6), has excellent
rooms for 5000 rp per person, or 15,000 rp
with meals.

To get there, take a bus from Kupang's
Oebobo terminal (1600 rp).

SOE

The road from Kupang passes through
rugged, scenic hill country, reminiscent of
the Australian bush, to the regional centre of
Soe. At an elevation of 800m, it's cool at
night, but hot enough for shorts and T-shirts
during the day. Soe is an excellent base for
side trips to traditional villages and colourful
markets around the area. Soe itself is a dull
sprawl of modern houses, but has a large
market, where you'll see people in their traditional garb.

Like most of rural Timor, the Soe district
is poor. Australian aid projects in the area
include health education and building dams
to cope with the water shortages.

Outside Soe, you'll see the beehive-
shaped houses *(lopo)* which give the region
a distinctive character. With no windows and
only a one metre high doorway, lopo are
small and smoky and the authorities have
instituted a programme to replace them. The
locals, however, consider their new houses
unhealthy, as they're cold, so they construct
new lopo behind the approved houses. Lopo
are also designed to store grain, particularly
corn, which is kept up high, and the smoke
from kitchen fires keeps the bugs away.

NUSA TENGGARA

Another type of lopo, which acts as a meeting place, has no walls and a toadstool-like roof.

Information

The Tourist Information Centre (☎ 21149) on the main street, Jl Diponegoro, has good information on the surrounding area and can arrange guides. Pae Nope is a knowledgeable guide who can be contacted through the centre. Change money at the BNI bank opposite.

Places to Stay

The travellers' favourite is the *Hotel Anda* (☎ 21323), Jl Kartini 5. This would have to be the most eccentric losmen in Indonesia, with the gaudy statuary and dazzling paint job at the front, and replica of a warship at the back. Rooms with shared mandi are fairly basic, but the rooms in the ship are cute. The cost is 5000 rp per person. Pak Yohannes is a wonderful host, speaks English, Dutch and German, and is a wealth of knowledge on the area's history and attractions.

If this is full, the *Hotel Cahaya* (☎ 21087), next door, has clean rooms with mandi for 7500/15,000 rp.

Soe has a few mid-range hotels. The *Hotel Bahagia I* (☎ 21015), Jl Diponegoro 72, the best value and has rooms with outside mandi for 20,000 rp. Singles/doubles with mandi cost 22,000/25,000 rp and VIP rooms are 35,000 rp. *Hotel Bahagia II* (☎ 21095), on the way in from Kupang, is a long hike from the town centre, but is Soe's best hotel. Air-con rooms range from 32,500 to 65,000 rp.

The *Hotel Makhota Plaza* (☎ 21068) at Jenderal Soeharto 11 is a passable mid-range option with rooms for 22,000/27,500 rp. The *Hotel Sejati* (☎ 21101) at Jl Gajah Mada 1 is dowdy but cheap enough at 7500/12,500 rp, or rooms with mandi cost 10,000/15,000 rp.

Places to Eat

There are a few good restaurants on Jl Jenderal Soeharto, including the *Rumah Makan Padang* and the nearby *Rumah Makan Suka Jadi* (with Javanese food); the *Rumah Makan Harapan* (serving tasty, good-value Chinese food – try the ikan tauco, fish with sweet sauce); and the *Hotel Makhota Plaza*. *Hotel Bahagia I* also has a decent restaurant. Other recommended restaurants are near the

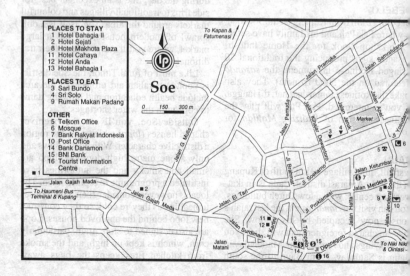

PLACES TO STAY
1 Hotel Bahagia II
2 Hotel Sejati
8 Hotel Makhota Plaza
11 Hotel Cahaya
12 Hotel Anda
13 Hotel Bahagia I

PLACES TO EAT
3 Sari Bundo
4 Sri Solo
9 Rumah Makan Padang

OTHER
5 Telkom Office
6 Mosque
7 Bank Rakyat Indonesia
10 Post Office
14 Bank Danamon
15 BNI Bank
16 Tourist Information Centre

Soe

0   150   300 m

To Kapan & Fatumenasi

To Haumeni Bus Terminal & Kupang

Jalan Gajah Mada

Market

To Niki Niki & Oinlasi

arket on Jl Hayam Wuruk, including the *Sri* *olo* for Javanese food and the *Sari Bundo* r Padang food.

hings to Buy

he shop attached to the Hotel Bahagia I has good, but expensive, range of weaving and arvings. Bargaining is essential. If you are eading out to village markets, wait to see hat's there and, if you don't find what you ant, go back to the shop.

etting There & Away

he Haumeni bus terminal is four km west town (400 rp by bemo). Regular buses run om Soe to Kupang (4250 rp; three hours), efamenanu (3000 rp; 2½ hours) and Oin- si (2500 rp; 1½ hours), while bemos cover iki Niki (1000 rp) and Kapan (800 rp). uses from the east can drop you off at a tel, as can the evening buses from Kupang.

ROUND SOE

inlasi

egular buses from Soe make the 51 km trip ong a winding mountain road to Oinlasi in ound 1½ hours. Its Tuesday market, one of e biggest and best in West Timor, attracts llagers from the surrounding hill districts, any wearing their traditional ikat. Weav- gs, carvings, masks and elaborately carved etel nut containers can be found, but get ere early. The market starts early in the orning and continues until 2 pm, but it is at s best before 10 am. A direct bus from upang makes the trip in about four hours.

oti

an isolated mounted valley, 12 km from inlasi along a rugged mountain road, the illage of Boti is presided over by the rightly 80 year old Rajah of Boti. The rajah eaks only in the local dialect through a anslator, and talks with all the flourish of a lf-styled potentate, even though his 'king- om' comprises only some 220 villagers.

Christianity never penetrated here and the ajah maintains strict adherence to adat radition). Only clothes made from locally rown cotton may be worn, and the villagers

wear homespun shirts, ikat sarongs and shawls. Boti is one of the last remaining villages in Timor where men let their hair grow long, but only after they are married. Indonesian education is shunned, as is Christianity.

The adherence to tradition is a wise one it seems, for the village now attracts a steady stream of visitors, including the occasional tour group. The village welcomes visitors, which provide a welcome source of income.

On arrival you will be lead to the rajah's house where, traditionally, betel nut should be placed in the tray on the table as a gift. It's possible to stay with the rajah in his house, with all meals provided (around 10,000 rp per person) and day trippers are also ex- pected to contribute a sizeable donation. You can see the process of hand weaving ikat in the village's co-operative and, at night, there may be performances of traditional dance.

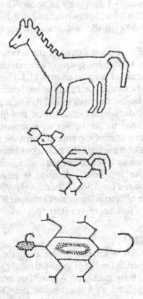

Three of the traditional motifs found on the ikat worn by the local people in the Soe region of West Timor.

Pay at the security post when you sign the visitors' book, or place it in the box provided for offerings at the rajah's house, rather than handing it directly to the rajah.

The rajah will proudly show you his bizarre collection of name cards and photos. If asked to add to the collection, telephone cards, old credit cards, backpackers' discount cards etc would seem to suffice.

The village requests that you bring a guide conversant with Boti adat, though it is unlikely you will be turned away without one. However, a guide really is essential to get there and to converse with villagers. Only a few villagers speak any Bahasa Indonesia.

Getting There & Away From Oinlasi, you can take a bus south on the main road for two km to the turn-off to Boti. It is then nine km on a dry, rocky and hilly road. Motorcycles and cars can negotiate the road, or it is a three hour walk – take plenty of water. The road crosses a wide, stony river bed that may be impassable in the wet season after heavy rain.

The road passes through the seven gates of Bele village. The system of gates and fences is designed to keep the animals in, for in these parts if a farmer catches an animal eating his crops he has the right to kill it. The amount of crop damage is then assessed, and meat is distributed to the farmer as compensation and the owner of the animal keeps the rest.

It is also possible to catch a bus from Soe to Oenai, and then follow the tracks along the river for two hours. A guide is essential. Bring water from Soe. Alternatively, you can charter a bemo in Soe; count on about 80,000 rp for a full day trip to Boti.

Niki Niki

Niki Niki, 34 km east of Soe along the Soe-Kefa road, is the site of some old royal graves. It has a busy market on Wednesday, which is as large and as interesting as the Oinlasi market, but easier to reach, being on the main highway. Niki Niki has a couple of restaurants, but no accommodation. Regular buses and bemos run to Niki Niki from Soe (1000 rp).

Kapan

Twenty-one km north of Soe, Kapan has a interesting market on Thursday, when th roads are blocked with stalls. The village situated on steep slopes, from where you ca see Gunung Mutis (2470m). From Kapa some trucks run to **Futamenasi**, 20 k away, which has even more spectacular a pine scenery, or you can take a bemo the from Soe.

On the way to Kapan is the **Buat Recre ation Park**, which has a swimming poo playground and viewing tower (not that the is a lot to see). The government has recent built two comfortable bungalows there, cos ing US$25 each, but unless you have a c there is little reason to stay way out ther The park is three north of Soe on the Kapa road and then two km west.

Also on the way to Kapan are the **Oahal Falls**, 10 km from Soe. The Kapan buse drop you on the highway, from where it is 2.5 km walk to the falls.

Kolbano

The village of Kolbano, on the south coa 110 km from Soe, has white sand beache and good surf between May and August. Th easiest access is by bus from Noilmina on t Kupang-Soe road (about six hours over decent road). From Soe, there are regula buses to Se'i along a twisting, dipping roa that goes through isolated communities. Se buses sometimes continue on to Kolbano. joint Australian-US-Indonesian oil researc project has begun in the area.

KEFAMENANU

Kefamenanu, 217 km from Kupang, is coo and quiet, with some pleasant walks to th surrounding hills. The town is very Catholi and has a few impressive churches. 'Kefa as it's known to locals, once had a reputatio as a place to buy fine rugs and, though th tradition declined, it is gradually bein revived. Locals bring around reasonable ika to the losmen and you could strike a bargain

Oelolok, a weaving village 26 km fror Kefa by bus and a further three km by bemc has a Tuesday market. The Istana Raja

aolin in Oelolok is a fine Dutch bungalow
at served as the 'palace' of the local rajah.

rientation & Information

efa is fairly spread out; the old market
'asar Lama), a few km north of the bus
rminal, is the town centre. The tourist of-
ce, Dinas Pariwisata (☎ 21520), is on Jl
udirman opposite the playing field north of
e highway, but has little to offer. The post
ffice is on Jl Imam Bonjol, opposite the
arket. The Telkom office is nearby on Jl
udirman.

laces to Stay & Eat

osmen Soko Windu (☎ 21122) is a clean,
iendly place on Jl Kartini, a short bemo ride
om the bus terminal, but close to the centre
f town. Large, clean rooms with shared bath
ost 7500 rp per person. Breakfast is includ-
d.

The Hotel Ariesta (☎ 21002) on Jl Basuki
achmat looks upmarket, but is good value.
lean doubles with shared mandi are 16,500
or 27,500 to 49,500 rp with bathroom. It
so has a good restaurant.

The cool, quiet Hotel Cendana (☎ 21168)
n Jl Sonbay offers rooms with mandi and
an at 15,000 rp, or air-con rooms for 22,000
44,000 rp. The staff can help you charter
emos and rent motorcycles.

Further from the town centre, Losmen
ederhana on Jl Patimura has rooms from
500/12,000 rp.

The Stella Maris, on the corner of Jl El
ari and Jl Sudirman, has good Chinese
ood. On the main road around the centre of
own, try Rumah Makan Sari Bundo for
adang food or the Rumah Makan Kalasan
or good fried chicken. The Hotel Ariesta
nd the Hotel Cendana also serve meals.

etting There & Away

he main bus and bemo terminal, Terminal
us Kefa, is a few km south of the town
entre. Buses to Soe, Kupang and Atambua
eave from there, but the bus to Oekussi
eaves from the Pasar Lama, in the centre of
own. Buses to Kefa leave Kupang early in
he morning. From Kefa to Kupang, there are

several buses in the morning and a few at
night. The last bus leaves at 8 pm from the
Rumah Makan Minang Jaya, near the Hotel
Cendana. Regular buses run to/from Soe
(3000 rp; 2½ hours) and Atambua (3000 rp;
two hours). Buses to Oekussi (3000 rp; three
hours) leave about every two hours from 8
am until 2 pm.

Getting Around

Within Kefa there are no regular bemo
routes; just tell the driver where you are
going. Bemos cost 300 rp around town.

TEMKESSI

Temkessi, a traditional village around 50 km
north-east of Kefa, has seen few travellers
because of its isolation. Sitting high on a
hilltop, its only entrance a small passage
between two huge rocks, the village has
about 18 families and 25 traditional houses.
The rajah's house sits on top of rocks overlooking the village. There's lots of weaving
here, but little Indonesian is spoken, so a
guide may be necessary.

To get there, regular buses run from Kefa
to Manufui, about eight km from Temkessi.
On market day in Manufui (Saturday), trucks
or buses should run through to Temkessi.
Otherwise, it may be possible to charter a
bemo in Manufui.

OEKUSSI

This former Portuguese coastal enclave
north-west of Kefamenanu is part of East
Timor Province. When East Timor was
reopened to tourists in 1989, travellers were
only allowed to pass through Oekussi, but
this restriction has now been dropped.

PANTEMAKASSAR

Pantemakassar, the capital of Oekussi Province, was the first permanent Portuguese
settlement on Timor in the 17th century. The
locals never accepted Portuguese domination, rebelling and forcing the Portuguese to
flee to Dili in 1769. It was later taken back
by the Portuguese, and a fort, garrison and
mission were built. Today Pantemakassar is
a sleepy coastal town of around 8000 people,

NUSA TENGGARA

sandwiched between hills and the coast, and is a pleasant place to wind down for a few days.

Information
The post office is on the corner of Jl Alimurtopo and Jl Jose Osorio. The Telkom office is further east, past the fountain, on Jl Santa Rosa.

Things to See
There are some good **beaches** near Pantemakassar; the black sand beach five km west is where locals say the Portuguese first landed. Many Portuguese buildings are scattered around the town, including the old garrison known as **Fatusuba**, south of town on the hill. **Poto Tano**, 12 km east on the Kefa road, has a large, colourful market on Tuesday, with people coming from all over the region. The market's location is idyllic, nestled under the shade of huge fig trees next to the Sungai Tonor.

Places to Stay & Eat
The town has one hotel, the friendly and clean *Aneka Jaya* on Jl Soekarno, which runs off the beachfront. Doubles with bath are 12,500 rp. The hotel is also an agent for the Dili-Atambua-Oekussi bus. A small restaurant, *Rumah Makan Sri Jaya*, is just around the corner, one block east of the hotel, on Jl Oekussi.

Getting There & Away
Buses run every two hours through the morning to/from Kefa (3000 rp; three hours), starting at 7 am. Regular buses run to/from Dili via Atambua.

ATAMBUA & BELU
Atambua is the major town at the eastern end of West Timor. It's quite a cosmopolitan place; the shops have a wide range of goods and the streets are lively at night. Since the bus route to Dili has changed to the coast road, it's only a three hour journey between the two cities.

Atambua is the capital of Belu Province, which borders East Timor. The district is mainly dry farming, using traditional time consuming methods, though there are some wet paddy lands on the south coast. Belu has some beautiful scenery and traditional villages.

Betun, a prosperous town 60 km south near the coast, has a couple of losmen and restaurants. A few intrepid travellers visit the nearby villages of **Kletuk**, **Kamanasa** and **Bolan** – you can see flying foxes and watch the sun set over the mountains at Kletuk.

Places to Stay & Eat
There are six losmen near the town centre, within walking distance of each other and all offer a free breakfast. You can ask the bus to drop you at a hotel.

Centrally located on Jl Soekarno is *Losmen Nusantara* (☎ 21117), but it's a bit dark and noisy, and rooms are not cheap (12,500/17,500 rp with mandi).

From Losmen Nusantara, walk 200m north-east and turn right at the roundabout onto Jl Merdeka. Along this street are the grungy *Losmen Sahabat*, Jl Merdeka 7, with rooms from 8000/16,000 rp, or the better quality *Losmen Merdeka*, (☎ 21197) at No 37, which has rooms with private mandi for 10,000/15,000 rp. The best of Atambua's hotels is the sparkling *Hotel Intan* (☎ 21343), Jl Merdeka 12. Good, but expensive, rooms cost 15,000/23,000 rp with outside mandi and from 23,000/31,000 rp with attached mandi.

Coming back out of Jl Merdeka, walk through the roundabout and veer to the right onto Jl Jenderal Gatot Subroto. *Hotel Kalapataru* (☎ 21351) at No 5 is a homey place where clean doubles with shared bath cost 15,000 rp.

Jl Soekarno has some reasonable restaurants, all close to the losmen. Try the friendly *Rumah Makan Surabaya*, on the corner of Jl Merdeka and Jl Soekarno, for good, cheap sate, or *Rumah Makan Estry*, at No 11, which has Chinese food.

Getting There & Away
Bus The bus terminal is one km north of town (400 rp by mikrolet No 3 or 4). Buses

clude: Kupang (10,500 rp; eight hours); Dili (5000 rp; three hours); and Atapupu 1500 rp; 40 minutes). Buses to Dili leave regularly until about 11 am and you can easily arrange for the bus to pick you up at our hotel in the morning.

The trip to Dili is quite scenic, hugging the coast most of the way (sometimes closer than you'd like!).

Boat The ferry from the port of Atapupu, 25 km from Atambua, to Kalabahi (Alor) sails Monday morning at 10 am and costs 8000 rp or the eight hour crossing. You might find boats here to other islands.

BATUGEDE, MAUBARA & LICISIA

Batugede, 111 km from Dili, is the border point between West and East Timor. There's a police checkpoint where you'll have to show your passport. Maubara, on the coast 45 km west of Dili, has a 17th century European-built fort. This was the centre of one of the most important old kingdoms in Portuguese Timor, and it was here, in 1893, that a series of revolts took place, eventually leading to the bloody pacification of the island by the Portuguese. Licisia is a cool, green town with some reasonable beaches – mostly black sand – 35 km from Dili. There are regular Dili-Licisia-Maubara return buses for day trips.

MALIANA & ERMERA

Maliana is a large regional capital with one losmen, the *Purwosari Indah*, and a busy market. Ermera, 62 km south-west of Dili, was the main coffee plantation of Portuguese Timor. Both can be reached by bus from Dili.

DILI

Dili was once the capital of Portuguese Timor. Though it had been a popular stop on the Asian trail, it was off-limits from 1975 to 1989 and only now are visitors starting to trickle in again. Dili is a pleasant, lazy city – the most attractive in Nusa Tenggara. Centred around a sweeping harbour, with parkland edging the waterfront on either side, it still has the feel of a tropical Portu-

guese outpost. A number of Portuguese buildings survive, you can sample Portuguese food and wine, and everything closes down for the afternoon siesta from noon until 4.30 pm.

The dry season is *really* dry in this part of Timor, but it makes for some spectacular scenery, with rocky, brown hills dropping right into a turquoise sea lined with exotic tropical plants. To top it off, Dili has some beautiful sunsets over the harbour.

Information

Tourist Office The tourist office, Dinas Pariwisata (☎ 21350), is on Jl Kaikoli. Mr Da Silva speaks good English, and the office has some good brochures and maps.

Money The Bank Danamon on Jl Avenida Sada Bandeira is the best place to change money, but accepts only US or Australian dollar travellers cheques. It will change cash in other currencies. The Bank Dagang Negara, next to the New Resende Inn, also changes money, with the same restrictions.

Portuguese Dili

Dili was never a jewel in the crown of the Portuguese colonial empire, and it lacks lavish public buildings. When the English scientist Alfred Russel Wallace spent several months here in 1861, he noted Dili as:

...a most miserable place compared with even the poorest of Dutch towns...After three hundred years of occupation there has not been a mile of road made beyond the town, and there is not a solitary European resident anywhere in the interior. All the government officials oppress and rob the natives as much as they can, and yet there is no care taken to render the town defensible should the Timorese attempt to attack it.

Despite Wallaces' unflattering assessment, Dili has plenty of reminders of colonial rule. Many Portuguese buildings remain, especially along the waterfront, which was once the preserve of colonial officials and the well-to-do. Most of the buildings are now inhabited by the armed forces, which commandeered them after the takeover. As such, entry is prohibited and photography is generally a no-no.

You can take a pleasant stroll taking in most of the sights, preferably in the morning or late afternoon to avoid the heat of the day.

Starting at the east of the harbour, the old **Chinese Chamber of Commerce** is a delightful Portuguese villa. Dili once had a large Chinese population, and Chinese merchants conducted much of the city's trade, though many fled in 1975. The building has high arches and pillars, decorated in hues of pink and crimson. The scalloped roof tiles around the eaves are typical of Dili's Portu-

guese architecture. The building served as the Taiwanese consulate before the Indonesian takeover and is now naval headquarters. Underneath the Indonesian crest the original Portuguese lettering has been painted over but is still visible.

Further along is the old **Garrison**, built in 1627, with massive, thick walls and heavy wooden-shuttered windows. Portuguese cannons grace the front of the building on Jl Antonio de Corvalho. It now serves as the garrison for the Indonesian army.

The most imposing building in Dili is the **Governor's Office**. It dates from 1960 and

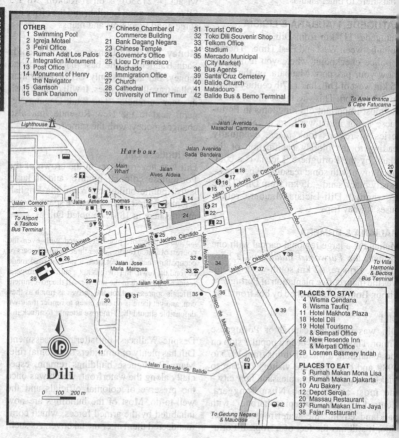

OTHER		
1 Swimming Pool	17 Chinese Chamber of	31 Tourist Office
2 Igreja Motael	Commerce Building	32 Toko Dili Souvenir Shop
3 Pelni Office	21 Bank Dagang Negara	33 Telkom Office
6 Rumah Adat Los Palos	23 Chinese Temple	34 Stadium
7 Integration Monument	24 Governor's Office	35 Mercado Municipal
13 Post Office	25 Liceu Dr Francisco	(City Market)
14 Monument of Henry	Machado	36 Bus Agents
the Navigator	26 Immigration Office	39 Santa Cruz Cemetery
15 Garrison	27 Church	40 Balide Church
16 Bank Danamon	28 Cathedral	41 Matadouro
	30 University of Timor Timur	42 Balide Bus & Bemo Terminal

PLACES TO STAY
4 Wisma Cendana
8 Wisma Taufiq
11 Hotel Makhota Plaza
18 Hotel Dili
19 Hotel Tourismo & Sempati Office
22 New Resende Inn & Merpati Office
29 Losmen Basmery Indah

PLACES TO EAT
5 Rumah Makan Mona Lisa
9 Rumah Makan Djakarta
10 Aru Bakery
12 Depot Seroja
20 Massau Restaurant
37 Rumah Makan Lima Jaya
38 Fajar Restaurant

Dili

0   100   200 m

NUSA TENGGARA

lthough the modern lines are plain, it is built
1 early colonial style with wide, arched
erandahs. In front is the **Monument of
Henry the Navigator**, also erected in 1960
o commemorate the Portuguese presence in
Asia and Henrique's role in opening up the
ea lanes some 500 years earlier. It is one of
he few memorials to the Portuguese pres-
nce still standing in Dili.

On Jl Formosa, a block across from the
Governor's Office, is the solid, neoclassical
Liceu Dr Francisco Machado, a former
chool and now government offices. On the
pposite corner are the old godowns (ware-
ouses) and offices of the former Sociedade
Agricola Patria e Trabacho (SAPT). Similar
odowns can be seen around town.

Back on the waterfront is the **Integration
Monument**, a memorial to Indonesian rule.
A Timorese in traditional costume breaks the
hains of colonialism, in much the same
acky style as the Free Irian monument (the
Jowzat man) in Jakarta. Across from it is the
Rumah Adat, a traditional house from the
Los Palos region that has been taken as the
ymbol of East Timorese architecture.

The waterfront boulevard leads further
vest past the **Igreja Motael**, a modern church
dating from 1955, but built in Portuguese
style. The road runs along the beachside park
and is lined with shady banyan trees. You
pass more whitewashed old villas, some of
Dili's prime real estate, to the still-function-
ng old **lighthouse**.

Back in town towards the stadium, one of
Dili's major attractions is the **Mercado
Municipal** (City Market). From the outside
t looks for all the world like a piece of
Portugal or South America, though renova-
ions to the interior are modern Indonesian
and not *simpático*. The market is a lively
focal point and well worth a browse. It has
only the usual offerings – vegetables, plastic
buckets, clothes etc – but a few peddlers will
sidle up to you offering Portuguese (sometimes Mexican) coins.

Other Portuguese buildings include the
simply styled **Matadouro**, the still-function-
ing city abattoir with tomorrow's *bifstek*
tethered alongside. One of Dili's finest colo-

nial edifices is the **Gedung Negara** to the
south of town not far past the Balide bemo
terminal. This former Portuguese governor's
residence features jutting bay windows,
solid walls and ancient fan palms in the
gardens. Now the government guesthouse,
the Pope stayed here on his visit to Timor.

Areia Branca

About four km east of town, this beach has
white sand (*areia branca* in Portuguese or
pasir putih in Indonesian), clear water, and
sweeping views of the harbour and the hills
to the south. It has the feel of an abandoned
resort, with small thatched shelters. It is a
pleasant escape from the city, but the new
motorcross circuit nearby is noisy when the
budding motorcycle grand prix champions
let rip. A taxi from the town centre costs
around 2000 rp.

Cape Fatucama

At the eastern end of the bay, one km past
Areia Branca, Cape Fatucama is Dili's newest attraction. A massive statue of Christ
occupies the hilltop headland and can be
seen from all around the harbour. Styled after
Rio de Janiero's Christ the Redeemer, 14
stations of the cross line the road to the top,
from where there are magnificent views
across Dili and to the islands. This extravagance is a contentious project. At 27m, its
height symbolises the 27 provinces of Indonesia (including East Timor).

There's a good beach around the headland.

Places to Stay

The only backpackers' hotel is the *Villa Harmonia* (☎ 23595), three km from town on the
way to the Becora bus terminal. This
friendly, well-run establishment is the best
place for travel information and the manager
speaks excellent English. Singles/doubles
with outside mandi cost 10,000/14,000 rp.
Food and drinks are available. Mikrolet I
(300 rp) or bus D (200 rp) run to the Becora
terminal past the Villa Harmonia.

The other vaguely cheap options are
usually 'full'. The *Wisma Taufiq* (☎ 21934)

on Jl Americo Thomas has reasonable rooms for 11,000/18,000 rp or 16,000/22,000 rp with mandi. *Losmen Basmery Indah* (☎ 22151) on Jl Estrade de Balide, opposite the University of Timor Timur, has large but run-down rooms with mandi from 16,000 rp.

Everyone will direct you to *Hotel Tourismo* (☎ 22029) on the waterfront, on Jl Avenida Marechal Carmona. Apart from the Villa Harmonia, almost all foreigners stay here, with good reason. It has a good restaurant with Portuguese, Chinese and Indonesian food, satellite TV and a delightful garden eating area. Good mid-range rooms are reasonably priced for Dili. Singles/doubles with fan and shower go for 25,000/30,000 rp or 35,000/45,000 rp with a sea view; air-con bumps the price up to 45,000/55,000 rp, and more expensive rooms and suites are available.

Hotel Dili (☎ 21871) is nearby on the waterfront at Jl Avenida Sada Bandeira 25. It is deserted most of the time, but the rooms are clean and have their own sitting areas, as well as balconies. Large rooms with fan and bath cost 25,000 rp, or 30,000 rp overlooking the waterfront. Rooms with air-con cost 40,000 rp.

New Resende Inn (☎ 22094) is centrally located on Jl Avenida Bispo de Medeiros 5. Well-appointed rooms are large and it has a restaurant, but the Tourismo has more appeal. Singles/doubles with air-con and bath cost 60,000/65,000 rp.

Wisma Cendana (☎ 21141) on Jl Americo Thomas is a large, government-run hotel with a garden and faded rooms. Doubles with air-con and bath go for 35,000 rp; VIP rooms with TV and fridge are 45,000 rp.

Hotel Makhota Plaza (☎ 21662), right in the town centre on Jl Alves Aldeia, is a big hotel favoured by government officials, and is a bit soulless. Air-con rooms with shower, TV, phone and minibar start at 70,000/75,000 rp, plus 15% tax.

Places to Eat

Dili has a good range of restaurants and some of the best dining in Nusa Tenggara. One legacy of the army is that East Timor imports cheap Portuguese, French and US wines an Tiger beer directly from Singapore. A bottl of tinta (wine) will cost around 20,000 rp i Dili's Chinese shops.

Budget eats are confined to Javanese Padang and other introduced fare. Kaki lim pushcarts offer the cheapest food – sotc bakso, mie etc – and can be found on th waterfront near the Hotel Dili or around th Integration Monument.

The *Rumah Makan Mona Lisa* on Jl Alber queque has cheap and tasty Javanese food - the kering tempe is good. The *Depot Seroj* on Jl Alves Aldeia, next to the cinema, ha reasonable nasi/mie dishes and cold drink in clean surroundings. In the town centre, th more upmarket *Rumah Makan Djakarta*, jus off Jl Alberqueque, has Indonesian food anc a cool interior. For cakes and pastries, try th *Aru Bakery* on Jl Alberqueque.

Portuguese food is a real treat in Dili, anc you can get good steaks, stews and salads with olive oil dressing. Dili's best Portuguese restaurant is the *Massau*, a fair hike from the town centre, or take a taxi. The pleasant bamboo decor and excellent food is best appreciated with a bottle of Portuguese wine brought with you. It is moderately priced.

The *Hotel Tourismo* has one of the bes restaurants in town with a lovely garden setting. As well as Chinese and Indonesian food, Portuguese dishes are featured. The *New Resende Inn* also has a decent restaurant with a similar menu.

Jl 15 Oktober has a few good Chinese restaurants, including the *Lima Jaya* or the fancier *Fajar*, at No 10, which has an extensive menu and dark interior.

On the waterfront, about three km east of town on Jl Metiaut, Sulawesi restaurants such as *Rumah Makan Angin Mamiri* serve delicious ikan bakar (grilled fish). They are great places to sit with a cold drink.

Getting There & Away

Air Merpati (☎ 21088) in the New Resende Inn has daily direct flights to Bali and a Wednesday flight to Kupang. Sempati (☎ 23144) in the Hotel Tourismo has three

lights a week to Kupang (95,000 rp) and on
o Surabaya.

Bus Coming into East Timor on the bus from
West Timor, Indonesians are required to
show their identity cards at police checkpoints along the way, but they don't seem to
bother with foreigners. There is usually one
army checkpoint before Dili where the bus
jockey will take your passport to be inspected.

Terminal Tasitolo, to the west of town past
the airport, has buses to towns in the west,
such as Atambua (5000 rp; 3½ hours) and
Kupang (15,500 rp; 12 hours). Tickets can
be bought in advance from agents opposite
the Mercado Municipal.

Buses east to Baucau (4000 rp; three
hours), Los Palos (7000 rp; seven hours) and
Vikeke (7000 rp; seven hours) leave from
Terminal Becora, four km east of town.
Buses and bemos to Maubisse (3000 rp;
three hours) and Suai (8000 rp; 10 hours)
leave from the Balide Terminal, one km
south of town. Most buses leave before 8 am.

Boat The Pelni office (☎ 21415) at Jl Sebastian de Costa 1 is on the road to the airport
near the town centre. The KM *Binaiya* travels from Kupang to Kalabahi, Dili, Maumere
and Ujung Pandang. The KM *Dobonsolo*
travels from Kupang to Dili and Ambon in
Maluku. The KM *Tatamailau* comes from
Larantuka to Dili and continues on to southern Maluku and Irian Jaya, and then reverses
its route. A regular ferry is scheduled to start
operation to Kalabahi, and Pelni's Perintis
cargo ships also have some interesting
routes.

Getting Around

Dili's Comoro airport is five km west of
town; the standard taxi fare is 5000 rp. Buses
A or B (200 rp) stop on the main road outside
the airport and also go Terminal Tasitolo.
From Terminal Tasitolo, Mikrolet I (300 rp)
or bus D (200 rp) run to the Villa Harmonia
and Becora bus terminal, through the centre
of town.

Dili's beat-up taxis cost a flat 1000 rp
around town.

MAUBISSE

About 70 km south of Dili, the small town of
Maubisse sits high in rugged mountains, surrounded by spectacular scenery.

These old hill towns make a delightful
break from the heat of the coast, and the
government has started renovating the fine
old Portuguese guesthouses, which now cost
25,000 rp. Maubisse's government guesthouse, the former governor's residence,
should still have some charm left after the
renovations, or alternatively *Losmen Udiana*
costs 5000 rp. It gets cold at night in
Maubisse. The town has a couple of small
warung, serving basic meals.

Direct buses leave Balide Terminal in Dili
for Maubisse (3000 rp; three hours) between
6 and 8 am. Later buses may finish in Aileu,
where you should be able to find a truck
going through to Maubisse.

SAME

Same is a further 45 km on from Maubisse
along a scenic route. This was a centre of late
19th and early 20th century revolts led by
Boaventura, the *liurai* (native ruler) of Same.
There's one losmen in town.

Betano, a coastal village about 20 km
from Same, reportedly gets good waves between April and July.

BAUKAU

The second largest centre of what was Portuguese Timor, the charmingly raffish colonial
town of Baukau has many Portuguese buildings (of which the Mercado Municipal is the
most impressive) and Japanese caves left
over from WWII. Baukau once had an international airport, eight km west of the town
centre, but it's now used by the Indonesian
military. The altitude makes Baukau pleasantly cool and the beaches, five km sharply
downhill from the town, are breathtakingly
beautiful. To get to them, you might need to
charter a bemo.

NUSA TENGGARA

Places to Stay & Eat

The Portuguese-built *Hotel Flamboyant* is the only place to stay and rooms cost 20,000 rp. It may have been special once, but now nothing seems to work (though the beds are OK).

There are a couple of restaurants in town and several warung around the market.

Getting There & Away

Dili to Baukau is a three hour bus trip (4000 rp) along the coast. The bus stops briefly at Manatuto on the way. You should check in at the police station when you arrive, otherwise they may come looking for you to give them an English lesson.

BAUKAU TO TUTUALA

There's an old Portuguese fort at **Laga**, on the coast about 20 km beyond Baukau. From Baukau you can continue on to **Los Palos**, the main plateau town of the Lautem regency. The traditional, high-pitched houses of the Fataluku people in the area are a symbol for all East Timor and grace every tourist brochure. The *Losmen Pui Horo Jaya* (otherwise known as the Losmen Verrisimo) is the place to stay and costs 6000 rp. You can hire guides in Los Palos to explore the surrounding countryside. The pretty village of **Rasa**, on the main road 11 km from Los Palos, is easily reached by bemo (500 rp) and has a number of traditional houses.

From Los Palos, early morning buses go along a bad road to **Tutuala** (2000 rp; two hours) on the eastern tip of the island. Tutuala is perched on cliffs high above the sea. The government rest house there has breathtaking views along the coast. A road down the cliffs to the pretty beach leads to caves that house ancient, primitive paintings.

VIKEKE

A road heads south over the mountains from Baukau to Vikeke, which is close to the south coast. The town has one losmen, and there are buses from Dili (7000 rp; seven hours).

Roti & Sabu

The small islands of Roti and Sabu (also spelled Sawu), between Timor and Sumba, are little visited but, with their successful economies based on the lontar palm, have played a significant role in Nusa Tenggara's history and development and now preserve some interesting cultures. Roti, in particular, has a few beautiful coastal villages and some of the best surf in Nusa Tenggara.

ROTI (ROTE)

Off the west end of Timor, Roti is the southernmost island in Indonesia. The lightly built Rotinese speak a language similar to the Tetum of Timor, though Bahasa Indonesia is almost universally understood.

Traditionally, Roti was divided into 18 domains. In 1681 a bloody Dutch campaign placed their local allies in control of the island, and Roti became the source of slaves and supplies for the Dutch base at Kupang. In the 18th century, the Rotinese began taking advantage of the Dutch presence, gradually adopted Christianity and, with

Roti

The Lontar Economy

For centuries, the traditional Rotinese and Sabunese economies have centred on the lontar palm. The wood from this multipurpose tree can be used to make houses, furniture, musical instruments, mats, baskets and even cigarette papers. Its juice can be tapped and drunk fresh, or boiled in a syrup and diluted with water – this syrup formed the staple traditional diet. The juice can be further boiled into palm sugar and the froth fed to pigs and goats. Meanwhile, vegetables were grown in dry fields, fertilised by animal manure and lontar leaves. Basically, it's your average useful tree and, with coconuts in abundance as well, there was no annual period of hunger on Roti or Sabu, as there was on other islands in Nusa Tenggara.

Because the lontar palm required only two or three months of work each year, the women had time for weaving and other handcrafts and the men became the entrepreneurs of Nusa Tenggara. In fact, many Rotinese and Sabunese migrated to Sumba and Timor with Dutch encouragement (it must have been persuasive to leave that set-up!) and, by the 20th century, Rotinese dominated both the civil service and the local anticolonial movements on those islands. ■

utch support, established a school system which eventually turned them into the region's ite.

The Rotinese openness to change is the main reason their old culture is no longer as rong as Sabu's, though there are still ockets of animist cultures and a layer of old eliefs lingers behind Protestantism in the illages. At some festivals, families cut hunks from a live buffalo and take them way to eat.

Ikat weaving on Roti today uses mainly ed, black and yellow chemical dyes, but the esigns can still be complex: floral and atola (traditional geometric ikat design) notifs are typical. One tradition that hasn't isappeared is the wearing of the wide-rimmed lontar hat, ti'i langga, which has a urious spike sticking up near the front like a unicorn's horn (perhaps representing a ontar palm or a Portuguese helmet or mast). Rotinese also love music and dancing; the

traditional Rotinese 20 stringed instrument, the *sasando*, features on the 5000 rp note.

Baa

Roti's main town is Baa, on the north coast. The main street, Jl Pabean, is close to the ocean and there are coral beaches nearby. Some houses have boat-shaped thatched roofs with carvings (connected with traditional ancestor cults) at the ends. Baa's market day is Saturday, when stalls line the area around the central town square. The Bank Rakyat Indonesia in Baa does not change money.

Places to Stay & Eat The best place to stay is *Hotel Wisata Karya* at Jl Kartini 1, just off Jl Pabean. Clean rooms with outside bath are 6000 rp per person. The manager speaks good English and will change money at a reduced rate if you're desperate. Other options are *Hotel Ricki* (on Jl Gereja) and *Hotel Kesia* (on Jl Pabean). Both have rooms with attached mandi from 10,000 rp.

Rumah Makan Karya and *Warung Makan Lumayah*, both on Jl Pabean near the town centre, serve basic meals, and the *Hotel Kesia* has a small restaurant.

Getting There & Away Merpati flies Kupang-Roti-Sabu-Roti-Kupang on Friday (maybe). Kupang to Roti costs 46,000 rp. The Merpati agent is on Jl Pabean.

Direct buses go to Nemberala (5000 rp; five hours) on Wednesday and Saturday, and possibly on other days if there are enough passengers.

The car & passenger ferry from Kupang to Roti (5700 rp; four hours) leaves on Friday at 9 am; smaller daily ferries leave from Bolok at 9 am.

Getting Around The airport is eight km from Baa. A Merpati minibus will meet the flight and drop you in Baa (2500 rp).

The ferry drops you at Pantai Baru, where a pack of buses and bemos will greet you and take you to Baa (2000 rp; 1½ hours).

Nemberala

A surfers' secret for a few years, Nemberala is a relaxed little coastal village with white sand beaches, and good surf between April and July. A long coral reef runs right along the main beach, with snorkelling possibilities.

Boa, about eight km from Nemberala, has a spectacular white sand beach and good surf. You should be able to charter a motorcycle in Nemberala.

The tiny island of **Ndao** is another ikat-weaving and lontar-tapping island. In the dry season, men take off for other islands to sell ikat and to work as gold and silversmiths. You can see weavings and jewellery in Ndao's one large village. It's possible to charter a boat in Nemberala, or you might get a lift on a fishing boat.

Ndana is another island which can be reached by boat from Nemberala. Local legend has it that the island is uninhabited because the entire population was murdered in a revenge act in the 17th century, and the small lake on the island turned red with the victims' blood. The island is now populated by wild deer, a wide variety of birds and (reportedly) turtles, which come to lay their eggs on the beaches.

Boni, about 15 km from Nemberala, is one of the last villages on Roti where traditional religion is still followed. Market day is Thursday. To get there, you can charter or perhaps rent a motorcycle in Nemberala.

Places to Stay & Eat Nemberala has a selection of simple homestays, all charging around 8000 rp per person, including meals. *Ti Rosa*, right on the beach in Nemberala, is run by the kepala desa and his family, who speak good English. The losmen has a generator. *Losmen Anugurah* is close to the main surf break and is a surfers' favourite (the cold beer could come into it, also). *Homestay Thomas*, another small, family-run place, offers a similar deal.

Nemberala Beach, a resortish place on the beachfront a little way outside the village, provides the most comfortable accommodation, with rooms from around 40,000 rp.

Getting There & Away A direct bus Nemberala usually meets the ferry (5000 r five hours). Otherwise, you'll have to org nise transport in Baa. You should be able charter a motorcycle to Nemberala fc 15,000 rp per person.

Papela

This Muslim Bugis fishing village in the fa north of Roti is set on a beautiful harbou Every Saturday, it hosts the biggest mark on the island. There is one losmen, the bas *Losmen Karya*, which costs 5000 rp pc person. Buses go to Papela from Baa an Pantai Baru (1250 rp) over the best road c the island.

SABU (SAWU)

Midway between Roti and Sumba, but wi closer linguistic links to Sumba, the low, ba island of Sabu (also spelled Sawu) is still stronghold of animistic beliefs collectivel known as *jingitui*. These persist, even thoug Portuguese missionaries first arrived befo 1600 and their work was continued by th Dutch.

Sabu's population (about 45,000) is divic ed into five traditional domains; the mai settlement, **Seba** (on the north-west coast was the centre of the leading domain i Dutch times. Sabunese society is divide into clans, named after their male founder but also into two 'noble' and 'commor halves, determined by a person's mother lineage: the halves are called *hubi ae* (greate flower stalk) and *hubi iki* (lesser flowe stalk). Sabunese women have a thriving ika weaving tradition. Their cloth typically ha stripes of black or dark blue interspersed b stripes with floral motifs, clan or hub emblems.

A group of stones near **Namata** is a ritu site: animal sacrifices, with a whole commu nity sharing the meat, take place aroun August to October. Another festival in th second quarter of the year sees a boat pushe out to sea as an offering.

There are three places to stay on Sabu *Ongka Da'i Homestay, Makarim Homesta* and *Petykuswan Homestay*, each costin

ound 12,000 rp, meals included. Seba has
market, and a handful of trucks provides
e island's transport, although you can hire
motorcycle for 15,000 rp per day.

etting There & Away

ir Merpati flies from Kupang to Sabu
5,000 rp) and return via Roti every Friday,
the flights aren't cancelled.

oat Ferries leave Kupang's Bolok harbour
r Sabu on Tuesday and Friday afternoon
4,000 rp; nine hours), returning to Kupang
e following day. The Perum ferry does a
op once a week around Kupang, Ende
lores), Waingapu (Sumba), Sabu and
turn.

umba

great ladder once connected heaven and
rth. By it, the first people came down to
rth on Sumba and settled at Cape Sasar, on
e northern tip of the island – or so the myth
es. Another Sumbanese tale recounts how
mbu Walu Sasar, one of their two ances-
rs, was driven away from Java by the wars.
ransported to Sumba by the powers of
eaven, he came to live at Cape Sasar. The
her ancestor, Umbu Walu Mandoko,
rived by boat, travelled to the east and lived
the mouth of the Sungai Kambaniru.

Such myths may come as near to the truth
s any version of the origins of a people who
e physically of Malay stock with a tinge of
Melanesian; whose language falls into the
ame bag that holds the Bimanese of eastern
umbawa, the Manggarai and Ngada of
estern Flores and the Sabunese of Sabu;
hose death and burial ceremonies are
rongly reminiscent of Torajaland in Sulwesi; and whose brilliant ikat textiles, fine
arved stone tombs and high, thatched clan
ouses suggest common origins with similar
aditions scattered from Sumatra to Maluku.

Wherever they came from, the island on
hich the Sumbanese have ended up lies far
from Indonesia's main cultural currents,
south of Flores and midway between Sumbawa and Timor. Sumba's isolation has helped
preserve one of Indonesia's most bizarre cultures, particularly in its wetter, more fertile
and more remote western half, which is
home to about two-thirds of the island's
400,000 people.

Right up until this century, Sumbanese life
was punctuated by periodic warfare between
a huge number of rival princedoms. Though
Christianity and (to a lesser extent) Islam
have now made inroads, around half the
people in the west and a significant minority
of people in the east still adhere to the animist
marapu religion, and old conflicts are recalled
every year at western Sumba's often-violent
Pasola festivals, which involve mock battles
between teams of mounted horse riders.

The 'mock' battles sometimes become
real, as in August 1992, when two villages
went to war: several people were killed and
over 80 homes were burned down.

Many Sumbanese men still carry long-
bladed knives in wooden sheaths tucked into
their waistbands. They wear scarves as
turbans and wrap their brightly coloured
sarongs to expose the lower two-thirds of
their legs, with a long piece of cloth hanging
down in front. A woman may have her legs
tattooed after the birth of her first child as a
recognition of status; often it will be the same
motifs that are on her sarong. Another
custom, teeth filing, has all but died out, but
you'll still see older people with short, brown
teeth from the time when white teeth were
considered ugly.

The last 20 years have seen an increasing
flow of visitors to Sumba, many attracted by
the ikat cloth of eastern Sumba. Other
Sumbanese traditions are much stronger in
the west, where you'll see exotic houses,
ceremonies and tombs. The tombs are a constant reminder that, for a Sumbanese, death
is the most important event in life. Against
this background, the most recent attraction
of Sumba – surfing – hardly seems to fit.

Despite their warlike past, the Sumbanese
are friendly, but more reserved than many
other peoples in Nusa Tenggara. Foreigners

should consider hiring a guide when going to villages, at least until they learn some visitor behaviour.

Though at least some Bahasa Indonesia is spoken everywhere, Sumba has six main languages. Kambera is spoken throughout East Sumba. The five main languages of West Sumba – Anakalang, Weyewa, Mamboru, Wanukaka and Lamboya – are closely related, but mutually unintelligible.

History

Fourteenth century Javanese chronicles place Sumba under the control of the Majapahits. After that empire declined, the island is supposed to have come under the rule of Bima in Sumbawa, then of Gowa in southern Sulawesi. But Sumbanese history is mostly a saga of internal wars, mainly over land and trading rights, between a great number of petty kingdoms. The most powerful clans claimed direct descent from the legendary original settlers, Sasar and Mandoko.

Despite their mutual hostility, princedoms often depended on each other economically. The inland regions produced horses, lumber, betel nuts, rice, fruit and dyewoods, while the much-valued ikat cloth was made on th coast, where the drier climate was suitab for cotton growing. The coastal people als controlled trade with other islands.

The Dutch initially paid little attention Sumba because it lacked commercial poss bilities. The sandalwood trade conducted i the 18th century was constantly interrupte by wars among the Sumbanese. Only in th mid-19th century did the Dutch arrange treaty permitting one of their representative to live in Waingapu, buy horses and colle taxes. Towards the end of the century Sumba's trade with other islands throug Waingapu led to extensive internal wars various princes tried to dominate it and, i the early 20th century, the Dutch decided secure their own interests by invading th island and placing it under direct militar rule.

Military rule lasted until 1913, when civilian administration was set up, althoug the Sumbanese nobility continued to reig and the Dutch ruled through them. When th Indonesian republic ceased to recognise th native rulers' authority, many of ther became government officials, so their fam lies continued to exert influence.

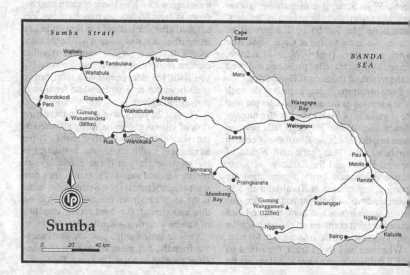

Sumba

Sumba's extensive grasslands made it one
f Indonesia's leading horse-breeding islands.
orses are still used as transport in more
gged regions; they are a symbol of wealth
nd status, and have traditionally been used
s part of the bride-price. Brahmin bulls, first
ought to Sumba in the 1920s, are also bred.

rts

at The ikat woven by the women of eastern
astal regions of Sumba is the most dra-
atic in Indonesia. The colours are mostly
ight (earthy *kombu* orange-red and indigo
ue) and the Sumba motifs are a pictorial
story, reminders of tribal wars and an age
hich ended with the coming of the Dutch –
e skulls of vanquished enemies dangle off
ees and mounted riders wield spears. A
ge variety of animals and mythical crea-
res is also depicted on Sumba ikat,
cluding *nagas* (crowned snake-dragons
ith large teeth, wings and legs), deer, dogs,
rtles, crocodile, apes and eagles.

Traditionally, ikat cloth was used only on
ecial occasions: at rituals accompanying
arvests; as offerings to the sponsors of a
stival; or as clothing for leaders, their rel-
ives and their attendants. Less than 90
ears ago, only members of Sumba's highest
ans, and their personal attendants, could
ake or wear it. The most impressive use of
e cloth was at important funerals, where
ancers and the guards of the corpse were
ressed in richly decorated costumes and
littering headdresses. The corpse itself was
ressed in the finest textiles, then bound with
many more that it resembled a huge
ound. The first missionary on Sumba, DK
ielenga, described a funeral in 1925:

he brilliant examples of decorated cloths were care-
lly kept till the day of the burial. The prominent
ief took 40 or 50 to the grave with him and the rajah
as put to rest with no less than 100 or 200. When
ey appeared in the hereafter among their ancestors,
en they must appear in full splendour. And so the
ost attractive cloths went into the earth.

he Dutch conquest broke the Sumbanese
obility's monopoly on the production of
kat and opened up a large external market,

which in turn increased production. Collected by Dutch ethnographers and museums
since the late 19th century (the Rotterdam
and Basel museums have fine collections),
the large cloths became popular in Java and
Holland. By the 1920s, visitors were already
noting the introduction of nontraditional
designs, such as rampant lions from the
Dutch coat of arms.

A Sumbanese woman's ikat sarong is
known as a *lau*; a *hinggi* is a large rectangular
cloth used by men as a sarong or shawl.

Traditional Culture

Old beliefs fade, customs die and rituals
change: the Sumbanese still make textiles,
but no longer hunt heads; 25 years ago the
bride-price may have been coloured beads
and buffalos, while today it might include a
bicycle. Certainly though, the bride dowry
can be very high and many Sumbanese men
migrate just to find wives that don't expect a
dowry.

Churches are now a fairly common sight,
and in some areas traditions are dying but
elsewhere, particularly in the west, they
thrive.

Villages A traditional village usually consists of two more or less parallel rows of
houses facing each other, with a square
between. In the middle of the square is a
stone with another flat stone on top of it, on
which offerings are made to the village's
protective marapu. These structures, spirit
stones or *kateda*, can also be found in the
fields around the village, and are used for
offerings to the agricultural marapu when
planting or harvesting.

The village square also contains the stone-
slab tombs of important ancestors, usually
finely carved, but nowadays often made of
cement. In former times the heads of slain
enemies would be hung on a dead tree in the
village square while ceremonies and feasts
took place. These skull-trees, called *andung*,
can still be seen in some villages today and
are a popular motif on Sumbanese ikat.

A traditional Sumbanese dwelling is a
large rectangular structure raised on piles; it

NUSA TENGGARA

houses an extended family. The thatched (or nowadays often corrugated-iron) roof slopes gently upwards from all four sides and in the loft are placed *marapu maluri* objects. See Religion in this section for further details.

Rituals accompanying the building of a house include an offering, at the time of planting the first pillar, to find out if the marapu agree with the location; one method is to cut open a chicken and examine its liver. Many houses are decked with buffalo horns or pigs' jaws from past sacrifices.

Visiting Villages Many Sumbanese villages these days are accustomed to tourists, but even those that get a steady stream sometimes have difficulty understanding the strange custom of westerners who simply want to observe 'exotic' cultures. If you're interested in their weavings or other artefacts, the villagers can put you down as a potential trader. If all you want to do is chat and look around, they may be puzzled about why you've come, and if you simply turn up with a camera and start putting it in their faces, they're likely to be offended.

On Sumba, giving betel nut *(sirih pinang)* is the traditional way of greeting guests and hosts, and it's a great idea to take some with you – it's cheap and you can get it at most markets in Sumba. Offer it to the kepala desa or to the other most 'senior'-looking person around.

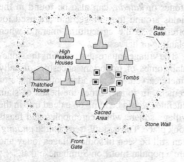

A plan of a traditional Sumbanese village.

Betel Nut – The Peacekeeper

One traditional custom that still thrives in parts of Nusa Tenggara, particularly Sumba and Timor, is the chewing of betel nut, or *siri pinang*. Apart from the obvious reason for chewing it – it gives you a little pep up to help you through the day – there are more complex social and cultural reasons.

Chewing betel is a statement of adulthood, and the three parts that make up the 'mix' that are chewed together have symbolic meaning. The green stalk of the siri represents the male, the nut or pinang the female ovaries and the lime *(kapor)* is symbolic of sperm. The lime causes the characteristic flood of red saliva in the mouth, and when the saliva is spat out, it is believed to be returning the blood of childbirth back to the earth.

Betel nut traditionally played an important role in negotiation and discussion between different clans. Betel nut would always be offered to visitors to a village as a gesture of welcome. If a male entering a village did not accept the betel offered, it was tantamount to a declaration of war.

Even today, if you're offered betel nut never refuse it! Some foreigners have really caused offence by saying, 'No, I don't want to buy it'. If you don't want to chew it, just put it in your pocket or bag. Most foreigners find betel nut pretty disgusting – it tastes a bit like bark. It gives you a mild buzz and a bright red mouth. It also creates an amazing amount of saliva, so if you're going to be embarrassed about spitting constantly, you'd better not have any. Whatever you do, don't swallow it – or you're likely to really embarrass yourself! ∎

Some villages have grown used to foreigners arriving without sirih. In these places appointed representatives keep a visitors book, which they'll produce for you to sig and you should donate 1000 rp or so. I off-the-beaten-track kampungs, offerin money or cigarettes is also OK, especially you make it clear that you're offering because you don't have any sirih. This wa you still conform to the give-and-take prin ciple.

Whatever the circumstances, taking guide, at least to isolated villages, is a bi help. A guide smooths over any languag difficulties and through them you shoul learn enough about the behaviour expecte f guests to feel confident visiting villages lone. No matter where you go, taking the me to chat with the villagers helps them to eat you more as a guest than a customer or lien. Remember that when you enter a illage, you're in effect walking into a home.

eligion

The basis of traditional Sumbanese religion s marapu, a collective term for all the spiritual forces, including gods, spirits and ncestors. The most important event in a erson's life is death, when they join the ivisible world of the marapu, from where ey can influence the world of the living. *Iarapu mameti* is the collective name for all ead people. The living can appeal to them or help, especially to their own relatives, hough the dead can be harmful if irritated. he *marapu maluri* are the original people laced on earth by god; their power is conentrated in certain places or objects, much ke the Javanese idea of *semangat*.

leath Ceremonies On the day of burial, orses or buffalos are killed to provide the eceased with food for their journey to the ind of marapu. Ornaments and a sirih (betel ut) bag are also buried with the body. The ving must bury their dead as richly as posible to avoid being reprimanded by the narapu mameti. Without a complete and onourable ceremony, the dead cannot enter ie invisible world and roam about menacing ie living. It was said the dead travel to Cape asar to climb the ladder to the invisible vorld above.

One Sumbanese custom which parallels ie Torajan customs of central Sulawesi is ie deliberate destruction of wealth to gain restige, often by sponsoring festivals where nany buffalos would be slaughtered. Funerls may be delayed for several years, until nough wealth has been accumulated for a econd burial accompanied by the erection f a massive stone-slab tomb. In some cases ie dragging of the tombstone from outside ie village is an important part of the proceure. Sometimes, hundreds are needed to nove the block of stone and the family of the

deceased feed them all. A *ratu* (priest) sings for the pullers, which is answered in chorus by the group. The song functions as an invocation to the stone.

When the Indonesian republic was founded, the government introduced a slaughter tax in an attempt to stop the destruction of livestock. This reduced the number of animals killed, but didn't alter basic attitudes. The Sumbanese believe you *can* take it with you!

WAINGAPU

The largest town on Sumba, Waingapu (population 25,000) became the administrative centre after the Dutch took over the island in 1906. It had long been the centre of the trade controlled by the coastal princedoms, with textiles and metal goods brought in by traders from Makassar, Bima and Ende, and the much-prized Sumba horses, dyewoods and lumber being exported.

Waingapu is the main entry point to Sumba, but the island's attractions lie elsewhere, in the west and south-east. The town does have a large group of ikat traders who run shops or hang around outside hotels (see Things to Buy later in this section).

Orientation & Information

Waingapu has two centres: the older, northern one focuses on the harbour; the southern one is around the main market and bus terminal, about one km inland.

The BNI bank is on Jl Ampera near the market, or the Bank Rakyat Indonesia is on Jl Ahmad Yani. The post office on Jl Hasanuddin is open Monday to Friday from 8 am to 4 pm. The Telkom office on Jl Tjut Nya Dien is open 24 hours.

Places to Stay

Hotel Permata Sari, otherwise known as Ali's, is handy if arriving by ferry and has harbour views – from the bathrooms! Large rooms with attached mandi are 4500 rp per person. Basic meals are available and Ali, the owner, is a good source of information. A Hindu temple 50m away provides background music in the evenings.

If the Permata Sari is full, as it sometimes

is when the ferries dock, the *Hotel Lima Saudara* (☎ 21083) at Jl Wanggameti 2 is the nearest hotel, but apart from the pleasant front porch, it's an overpriced dive. Singles/doubles with mandi and midget-sized beds are 8800/17,000 rp.

The other hotels are in the new part of town. The *Hotel Elvin* (☎ 22097) at Jl Ahmad Yani 73 is well run, has a good restaurant and large rooms. A few basic rooms without mandi cost 7000/12,500 rp, but most rooms are newly renovated with mandi for 12,500/17,500 to 27,500/35,000 rp with air-con.

The *Hotel Sandle Wood* (☎ 21199) on Jl

WJ Lalaimantik is an attractive, popula hotel close to the bus terminal. It has a land scaped garden, an art shop and a wide variet of rooms. Small, run-down rooms with outsid mandi cost 11,000/16,500 rp, but much be ter rooms with attached mandi for 16,500 22,000 rp are good value; air-con rooms ar 27,500/38,500 rp. It also has a restaurant, bu don't bother.

The *Hotel Merlin* (☎ 21300) on Jl Pan jaitan has better service and is the top hote in town. Rooms start at 16,500/22,000 rp with shower, intercom and comfy beds. Th intercom is not a complete joke, as the stair

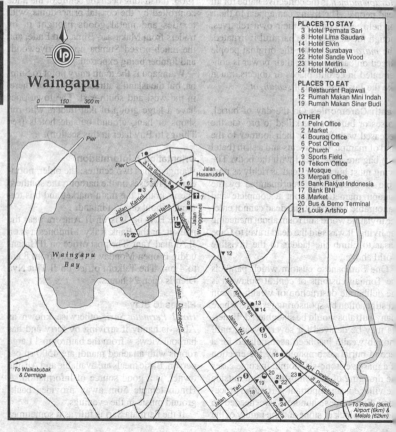

NUSA TENGGARA

Waingapu

0   150   300 m

Waingapu Bay

To Waikabubak
& Dermaga

To Prailiu (3km),
Airport (6km) &
Melolo (62km)

PLACES TO STAY
3 Hotel Permata Sari
8 Hotel Lima Saudara
14 Hotel Elvin
16 Hotel Surabaya
22 Hotel Sandle Wood
23 Hotel Merlin
24 Hotel Kaliuda

PLACES TO EAT
5 Restaurant Rajawali
12 Rumah Makan Mini Indah
19 Rumah Makan Sinar Budi

OTHER
1 Pelni Office
2 Market
4 Bouraq Office
6 Post Office
7 Church
9 Sports Field
10 Telkom Office
11 Mosque
13 Merpati Office
15 Bank Rakyat Indonesia
17 Bank BNI
18 Market
20 Bus & Bemo Terminal
21 Louis Artshop

ere made for a breed of mythical gigantic ourists. Air-con rooms with TV are 27,500/ 8,500 rp, while the VIP rooms at 44,000/ 5,000 rp have hot water. The 4th floor res-aurant has great views, and the hotel has an rt shop attached.

On the same street as the Hotel Sandle Vood is the quiet and friendly *Hotel Kaliuda* ☎ 21264). Rooms with shared bath are 0,000 rp, or 16,000 rp with attached bath.

The *Hotel Surabaya* (☎ 21125) at Jl El ari 2 has efficient service, but is uncomfort-bly close to the mosque. Rooms with attached 1andi go for 10,000/16,000 rp.

laces to Eat

Vaingapu is not over endowed with eateries.

The *Rumah Makan Mini Indah* at Jl Ahmad Yani 27 is a simple place, but has ery tasty food – choose from the selection 1 the showcase. *Restaurant Rajawali* on Jl utomo is a reasonable choice in the old part f town. The *Rumah Makan Sinar Budi*, on ehind the market, serves Padang food.

Otherwise, eat at the hotels. The *Hotel Merlin* has a large 4th floor restaurant with ndonesian and western food, and great iews. The *Hotel Elvin* has a spick-and-span estaurant with a wide variety of good ndonesian and Chinese dishes. The slightly rotty *Hotel Surabaya* has cold beer and heap but small servings of Chinese food.

hings to Buy

Vaingapu has several 'art shops' selling ikat rom the villages of south-eastern Sumba nd artefacts from the west of the island. raders will also set up impromptu stalls in ront of your hotel – some will squat there atiently all day. You can get an idea of the ange of quality, design and price before eading out into the villages. Prices in town re higher, though not necessarily by that nuch, and the range is good.

Two art shops worth a look in Waingapu re Louis, Jl W J Lalaimantik 15, near the Iotel Sandle Wood, and Savana, near the Iotel Elvin on Jl Ahmad Yani. The Hotel andle Wood has a huge collection of ikat

tucked away in a musty back room and the Hotel Merlin also has a decent range.

Getting There & Away

Air Merpati (☎ 21329), Jl Ahmad Yani 73, and Bourag (☎ 21363), Jl Yos Sudarso 57, between them have direct flights to/from Bima (99,500 rp), Kupang (169,000 rp), Tambulaka (Waikabubak, 66,500 rp) and Denpasar (236,000 rp).

Bus The bus terminal is in the southern part of town, close to the market. Buses to Waikabubak (4500 rp; five hours) depart around 7 am, noon and 3 pm. Hotels will book tickets, or go to one of the bus agents opposite the bus terminal. The road to Waikabubak goes through Lewa (long the centre of horse breeding) and Anakalang. It's an excellent road, paved all the way.

Buses also head south-east to Melolo, Rende and Baing. Several travel through the morning and afternoon to Melolo, with a few continuing on to Rende, Ngalu and Baing. Most return to Waingapu the same day.

Car The hotels rent cars with driver for out-of-town trips, but may require bargaining. Count on 100,000 rp for a full day's touring around eastern Sumba, or 80,000 rp to Waikabubak.

Boat The Perum ASDP ferry from Kupang departs from Ende on Tuesday at 2 pm for Waingapu (12,000 rp; 10 hours) and then continues to Sabu (13,500 rp; nine hours) on Wednesday at 2 pm. It returns from Sabu on Thursday and sails from Waingapu to Ende on Friday at 2 pm, continuing to Kupang the next day.

Pelni's KM *Binaiya* calls in every two weeks at the Dermaga dock to the west of town – a bemo to this pier is 300 rp per person. From Waingapu it runs to/from Ende or Bima.

Getting Around

The Airport The airport is six km south of town on the Melolo road. A taxi into town costs 3000 rp, or minibuses from the Elvin,

NUSA TENGGARA

Sandle Wood and Merlin hotels usually meet incoming flights and offer a free ride to intending guests.

Bemo A bemo to any destination around town will cost 300 rp.

AROUND WAINGAPU

Three km out of Waingapu, **Prailiu**, is an ikat-weaving centre that's worth a look. You should be able to see at least some aspects of production going on there. Bemos to Prailiu run from Waingapu's main bus and bemo terminal (300 rp).

Kawangu, 10 km from Waingapu and about 300m off the road south to Melolo, has some stone-slab tombs. Traditional houses may be seen at **Maru**, on the coast north-west of Waingapu. Buses go there every day, and there's a big market (Pasar Belakang) on Monday. **Prailiang**, another traditional village on the road between Waingapu and Maru, sees few visitors.

SOUTH-EASTERN SUMBA

A number of the traditional villages in the south-east can be visited from Waingapu. The stone ancestor tombs are impressive and the area produces some of Sumba's best ikat. The villages are quite used to tourists. Almost every village has a visitors' book, and a donation of 1000 rp or so is expected. Ikat for sale will appear.

Melolo

If you don't want to visit the south-east on a day trip from Waingapu, the small town of Melolo, 62 km from Waingapu and close to some interesting villages, has one losmen, the friendly and security-conscious *Losmen Hermindo*. Clean rooms with mandi cost 6000 rp per person. The losmen can arrange car hire for a day trip around the area. Basic meals are available on request; otherwise there's one small warung in town. Ten minutes' walk through mangroves from Losmen Hermindo, there's a long, sandy beach, although the water's a bit murky.

The market is about three km out of town, in the middle of nowhere on a dusty hill. The main market day is Friday, when you might see some good ikat and also *hikung* cloth (distinguished from ikat by its woven, no dyed, patterns). Bemos run regularly from town to the market (300 rp).

Getting There & Away Buses to Melolo from Waingapu (2000 rp; 1½ hours) run hourly until around 4 pm. It's an excellent paved road and crosses mainly flat grass lands. From Melolo the road continues on to Baing. Another road from Melolo crosses the mountains to Nggongi; trucks run along this road, at least in the dry season.

Rende

Seven km towards Baing from Melolo, Rende has an imposing line-up of big stone slab tombs and makes some fine-quality ikat. You'll be shown some magnificent ikat, but prices are high. Though Rende still has a rajah, other traditions have declined, due to the cost of ceremonies and the breakdown of the marapu religion there.

The largest tomb at Rende is that of a former chief. It consists of four stone pillars two metres high, supporting a monstrous slab of stone about five metres long, 2½ metres wide and one metre thick. Two stone tablets stand atop the main slab, carved with human, buffalo, deer, lobster, fish, crocodile and turtle figures. A massive, newly built traditional Sumbanese house with concrete pillars faces the tombs, along with a number of older *rumah adat* (traditional houses).

It's possible to stay with the rajah, but remember that these are members of a royal family, not hotel staff. Act accordingly!

Getting There & Away A few buses go from Waingapu to Rende, starting at about 7 am, otherwise take a bus to Melolo, from where bemos and trucks run throughout the day.

Umabara & Pau

Like Rende, these two villages about four km south-west of Melolo have traditional Sumbanese houses, stone tombs and weavings. At Umabara, the largest tombs are for relatives of the present rajah, who speaks some nglish and is quite friendly. Weavings, ostly hikung cloth, will make an appear- ıce.

From Melolo, bemos can drop you at the rn-off to the villages on the main Wain- ıpu-Melolo road. After about a 20 minute alk is a horse statue, where you fork right r Umabara or left for Pau, both just a few inutes further. A trail also links the two llages. From Waingapu, ask the bus driver drop you at the turn-off.

angili

ıis village, 38 km from Melolo and a 20 inute walk off the road to Baing, is another gh-quality weaving centre. About six ıses a day from Waingapu and Melolo pass e Mangili turn-off, the first leaving Wain- ıpu at about 7 am and passing through lelolo at about 8.30 am. From Melolo, the ıp takes about 1½ hours and costs 1000 rp.

aliuda

ıis town is reputed to produce the best ikat all of Indonesia. However, you might have ouble finding what you want there – much the best stuff gets bought up in large ıantities and shipped off to Bali! Still, the llagers are happy to chat and you may see ime of the work being produced, even if the ices make you weep. Kaliuda also has ime stone-slab tombs. To get there, take a ıs heading to Baing from Waingapu or lelolo and get off at Ngalu Kaliuda, from here it is about a three km walk.

aing

here's good surf between May and August Kalala, about two km from Baing off the ain road from Melolo. An Australian has t up bungalow accommodation at the *Palm esort*, along the wide, white sand beach for ırfing, which costs 30,000 rp per person per ay. To get there, the same buses you take for langili continue to Baing, about one hour ırther over a rough road. If you get a blank ok when you ask the bus driver for Baing, k for Waijelu, where the buses finish, ırther south of Baing. Baing is about two ours from Melolo and the fare is 2000 rp.

SOUTH-CENTRAL SUMBA

This part of the island is little explored and difficult to access. Although there are regular trucks from Waingapu to Praingkareha, getting around may require a jeep and, often, some hiking.

Praingkareha

The big attraction here is the 100m high **waterfall**. There's a beautiful pool at the base of the falls. By tradition, women are forbid- den to look into it, but an exception is made for foreigners!

You can drive to within eight km of the falls, then you have to walk. A guide is advisable and can be hired for about 5000 rp per day, but you can ask directions to the falls (*air terjun*). It's possible to stay at the kepala desa's house.

Lumbung

As at Praingkareha, the main attraction here is the spectacular 25m high **waterfall**. Al- though the falls are not extremely high, the volume of water is huge and it's crystal clear. At present, you can drive to within eight km of the falls and then you must walk. Road building is continuing, though, and eventu- ally this trip won't require much exercise.

Tarimbang

If you're one of the crazies trudging around the outer islands carrying several surfboards looking for uncrowded waves, you might want to check this place out. Tarimbang has a beautiful surf beach and it's possible to stay with villagers nearby. Trucks from Waingapu can drop you at the Tarimbang turn-off.

WAIKABUBAK

The neat little town of Waikabubak is at the greener, western end of Sumba, where the tropical trees and rice paddies contrast with the dry grasslands around Waingapu. More a collection of kampungs clustered around a main shopping street and market, Waika- bubak has traditional clan houses and small graveyards of old stone-slab tombs carved with buffalo horn motifs. About 600m above sea level, and cooler than the east, it's a good base for exploring the traditional villages of western Sumba.

Information

The tourist office (☎ 21240), Jl Teratai 1, is a fair walk to the outskirts of town, but it has a couple of good publications.

The BNI bank on Jl A Yani changes most major currencies and has the best rates. It's open Monday to Friday from 7.30 am to 4.45 pm, closed for lunch between 12.30 and 1.30 pm.

The post office is open Monday to Friday from 8 am to 3.30 pm. The Telkom office is open 24 hours.

Tombs & Traditional Kampungs

From the main street, Waikabubak looks like any other unprepossessing Indonesian town of shops, houses and concrete, but right within the town are very traditional kampungs with stone-slab tombs and thatch houses.

Kampung Tambelar has very impressive tombs – you could spend days travelling to a remote village and not see better – but the most interesting kampungs are on the western edge of town. It's only a short stroll

from most hotels to Prai Klembung and the up the ridge to Tarung and Waitabar.

Kampung Tarung, reached by a path on Jl Manda Elu, is the scene of an importan month long ritual sequence, the Wula Podh each November. This is an austere perio when even weeping for the dead is prohib ited. Rites consist mainly of offerings to th spirits the day before it ends, hundreds chickens are sacrificed, and people sing an dance for the entire final day. Tarung's mon uments are under official protection.

Plenty of other kampungs are dotte around Waikabubak, such as those on th road to the Hotel Mona Lisa and just off th road at Puunaga, but these are more moden kampungs with concrete tombs.

Other interesting kampungs occupyin ridge or hilltop positions outside town in clude Praijing and Bondomarotto **Kampung Praijing** is especially sceni perched on a hilltop about four km from town. There are five neat rows of tradition houses and large stone tombs. **Kampun Prairami** and **Kampung Primkateti** are als beautifully located on adjacent hilltops. Yo can take a bemo to the turn-off to Praijin (300 rp).

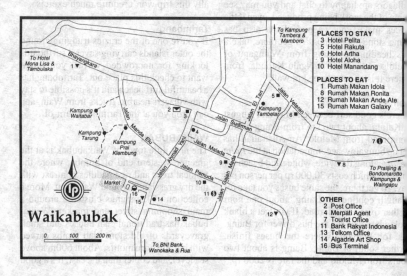

PLACES TO STAY
3 Hotel Pelita
5 Hotel Rakuta
6 Hotel Artha
9 Hotel Aloha
10 Hotel Manandang

PLACES TO EAT
1 Rumah Makan Idola
8 Rumah Makan Ronita
12 Rumah Makan Ande Ate
15 Rumah Makan Galaxy

OTHER
2 Post Office
4 Merpati Agent
7 Tourist Office
11 Bank Rakyat Indonesia
13 Telkom Office
14 Algadrie Art Shop
16 Bus Terminal

Waikabubak

0   100   200 m

To Kampung Tambera & Mamboro

To Hotel Mona Lisa & Tambulaka

Bhayangkara

Kampung Waitabar

Kampung Tarung

Kampung Prai Klembung

Jalan Manda Elu

Jalan Ahmad Yani

Market

Jalan El Tari

Jalan Veteran

Kampung Tambelar

Jalan Sudirman

Jalan Malada

Jalan Pemuda

Jalan Gajah Mada

To Praijing & Bondomarotto Kampungs & Waingapu

To BNI Bank, Wanokaka & Rua

Another major kampung worth visiting is ambera, 10 km north on the road to Mam-oro.

Some of these kampungs are more tradi-onal and visiting them is less formalised an many further out – perhaps because ost can only be reached on foot along arrow paths, while others further out of wn are accessible by vehicle. At most of e kampungs around Waikabubak, locals e accustomed to the eccentric behaviour of urists, so you can see some traditional lture without offending somebody. It is stomary to give 1000 rp and you may be vited to chew betel nut.

laces to Stay
he friendly *Hotel Aloha* (☎ 21024) is a opular budget choice. It has good food and formation on western Sumba. Clean singles/ oubles with shared bath cost 6600/ 8800 rp r 11,000/13,750 rp with private bath.

The cheapest in town is the *Hotel Pelita* ☎ 21104) on Jl Ahmad Yani. Dingy rooms e 5000/8000 rp with shared mandi, while etter rooms with mandi at the back are asonable value at 10,000/15,000 rp.

Just around the corner from the Aloha at Pemuda 4, the *Hotel Manandang* (☎ 21197) the best hotel in town. It has a variety of oms around the garden and a good restau-nt. Large, spotless rooms with washbasin nd comfy beds cost 11,000/16,000 rp. Rooms ith private bath range from 20,000/ 25,000 40,000/45,000 rp. Prices exclude 10% tax.

The *Hotel Rakuta* (☎ 21075) on Jl Veteran friendly and has huge rooms with mandi or 25,000 rp, but it's dowdy and deserted.

The *Hotel Artha* (☎ 21112) on Jl Veteran a quiet, relatively new place. The rooms round the courtyard garden start at 17,500 rp ith private mandi. VIP rooms with fan, show-r and fridge go for 32,500 rp and 47,500 rp.

The *Hotel Mona Lisa* (☎ 21364) on Jl dhyaksa competes with the Manandang to e Waikabubaks's best, but it is 2.5 km from wn. Well-appointed bungalows overlook-g the rice paddies cost 25,000/35,000 to 0,000/55,000 rp with TV and fridge. A few potless rooms with shower cost 15,000/

25,000 rp. Add 10% tax to all prices. The restaurant houses a wonderful collection of photos from around western Sumba.

Places to Eat
The *Hotel Manandang* has the best restau-rant in town, even if it is a little expensive. Otherwise Waikabubak has some decent rumah makan. *Rumah Makan Galaxy* on Jl Ahmad Yani is bright and serves good Indonesian food. *Rumah Makan Ronita* on Jl Basuki Rahmat has a long menu of Indones-ian and western food, and even a karaoke section! *Rumah Makan Ande Ate* near the Hotel Aloha is cheap, and popular with locals. The small *Rumah Makan Idola* on Jl Bhayangkara is a long walk from the centre of town, but has good Chinese and Indones-ian dishes.

Things to Buy
Traders hang around hotels with ikat cloth, nearly all of it from eastern Sumba, and you're better off buying it there. Western Sumba is noted for elaborate bone, wood, horn and stone carvings, and metal symbols and jewellery. There are bone or wooden betel nut and *kapor* (lime) containers with stoppers carved into animal and human heads; knives with Pasola horsemen (see under Pasola Festival in the following Wes-tern Sumba section) or fertility symbols carved into their wooden handles; tobacco and money containers made of wood and coconut shell; stone figures representing marapu ancestors; and metal omega-shaped symbols called *mamuli*, which are worn as earrings and pendants. The one art shop in Waikabubak, Algadrie on Jl Ahmad Yani, is worth checking before you go out to villages. Mostly poor quality souvenirs at high prices are on display – the good stuff is held at the back.

Getting There & Away
Air The Merpati agent (☎ 21051) is at Jl Ahmad Yani 11. Flights between Waingapu and Bima (Sumbawa) stop at Tambulaka, but it is not always easy to get a seat.

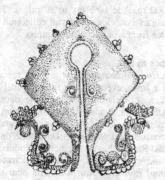

The mamuli symbol is a popular design for metal earrings or pendants in western Sumba.

Bus The bus terminal is central. Buses run to Waingapu (4500 rp; five hours) at 8 am, noon and 3.30 pm, and throughout the day to Anakalang (700 rp; 40 minutes) and Waikelo (1500 rp; 1½ hours). Less frequent and less certain minibuses and trucks run to other villages.

To Waingapu, it's best to book your ticket the day before leaving – your hotel may be able to help, or visit the bus ticket agencies along Jl Ahmad Yani.

Getting Around

The Airport The airport is at Tambulaka, 42 km north-west of Waikabubak. The Bumi Indah bus is supposed to go every flight day at 7 am, but it's not reliable. If it hasn't picked you up at your hotel by 7.30 am, you'd better get a taxi or charter a bemo, which will cost a nasty 45,000 rp. It's not a bad idea to check the flight list at Merpati the day before; if you find out who is going and where they are staying, you can arrange to split the cost.

Bus Minibuses, bemos and trucks service most other towns and villages in western Sumba; for details, see under individual village entries. Generally, it's best to get them early when they tend to fill up and depart more quickly.

Car & Motorcycle The Mona Lisa and Ma andang hotels rent vehicles with driver high rates. They have lists of rates, depen ing on destination, but it may be cheaper ask around elsewhere.

The Hotel Aloha can arrange motorcyc hire for 20,000 rp a day. It's not a bad idea take a guide; you can probably get someor to go with you for around 10,000 rp per da

AROUND WESTERN SUMBA

The traditional village culture of wester Sumba is one of the most intact in Indonesi Kampungs of high-roofed houses are sti clustered on their hilltops (a place of defenc in times past), surrounding the large stor tombs of their important ancestors. Awa from the towns, old women with filed tee still go bare breasted and men in the trad tional 'turban' and short sarong can be see on horseback. The agricultural cycle turns u rituals, often involving animal sacrifice almost year-round, and ceremonies fo events like house building and marriage ca take place at any time. Some kampungs ar unaccustomed to foreigners; taking betel nu and cigarettes is a good way to get a friendl reception.

You should give yourself at least a fe days around western Sumba; once you hav learned some basic manners as a guest arriv ing in a village, hopefully armed with som Indonesian, it's possible to do without guide.

Pasola Festival

The most famous of Nusa Tenggara's festi vals sees large teams of colourfully cla horse riders engaging in mock battles. I pattern is similar to that of other ritua warfare that used to take place in Indonesi – the cause not so much a quarrel betwee opposing forces, as a need for human bloo to be spilled to keep the spirits happy an bring a good harvest. Despite the blur spears that the combatants now use and th efforts of Indonesian authorities to supervis the events, few holds are barred; injuries an sometimes deaths still occur.

The Pasola is part of a series of rituals nnected with the beginning of the planting ason. It takes place in four different areas February or March each year, its exact ning determined by the arrival on nearby asts of a certain type of seaworm called ale. Priests examine the nyale at dawn and om their behaviour predict how good the ar's harvest will be. Then the Pasola can gin: it's usually fought first on the beach d then, later the same day, further inland. ne opposing 'armies' are drawn from astal and inland dwellers.

The nyale are usually found on the eighth ninth day after a full moon. In February sola is celebrated in the Kodi area (centred Kampung Tosi) and the Lamboya area ampung Sodan); in March it's in the anokaka area (Kampung Waigalli) and the mote Gaura area west of Lamboya (Kam-ng Ubu Olehka).

akalang & Around

ght beside the main road to Waingapu at nakalang, 22 km east of Waikabubak, mpung Pasunga boasts one of Sumba's ost impressive tomb line-ups. The grave of rticular interest consists of a horizontal ne slab with a vertical slab in front of it. e vertical slab took six months to carve th the figures of a man and a woman. The mb was constructed in 1926; five people e buried here and 150 buffalo were sacri-ed during its construction. You can see it om the road.

The more interesting villages are south of wn. Walk 10 minutes along the road past e market to **Kabonduk**, home to Sumba's aviest tomb weighing in at 70 tonnes. The nstruction is said to have taken 2000 orkers three years to chisel the tomb out of nillside and drag it to the site.

From Kabonduk, it is a very pleasant 15 inute walk across the fields and up the hill **Makatakeri** and, five minutes further, to **i Tarung**, the original ancestral village for e area. The ancestral village of 12 local ans is now mostly deserted except for a few milies that act as marapu caretakers. There e impressive views over the surrounding

countryside to the coast and several tombs scattered around. There's also a government-built 'showroom' traditional house and some marapu houses. Lai Tarung comes alive for the Purungu Takadonga Ratu – a festival honouring the ancestors – held every year around June.

At **Gallubakul**, 2.5 km down the road from Kabonduk, the Umba Sawola tomb is a single piece of carved stone about five metres long, four metres wide and nearly one metre thick. You'll be asked to sign in and pay 1000 rp to take photos.

Getting There & Away Regular minibuses run between Waikabubak and Anakalang (fewer after 1 pm) or buses to Waingapu can drop you on the highway.

South of Waikabubak

The Wanokaka district, centred around Waigalli about 20 km south of Waikabubak, has numerous traditional kampungs and is the scene of one of the March Pasolas. The Watu Kajiwa tomb in **Praigoli** is said to be one of the oldest in the area. **Kampung Sodan** is the centre for the Lamboya Pasola (further west), but fire destroyed the village some years ago and it is not of interest as a traditional village.

The south coast has some fine beaches. **Pantai Rua** has a beach with swimming spots, but the best beach and surf in the area is at **Pantai Marosi** near Lamandunga – you need a vehicle to get there.

The *Homestay Mete Bulu*, 1.5 km from Pantai Morosi on foot, has rooms for 15,000 rp. The *Homestay Ahong* in the village of Rua is similar. The *Sumba Reef Lodge* is an expensive and exclusive hotel on the south coast – so exclusive that it spends its time chasing unannounced tourists away.

Getting There & Away At least three or four vehicles a day – buses, bemos or trucks – rattle down the road to Waigalli, in the Wanokaka district. From there it's a five km walk to Praigoli. Vehicles usually continue on to Lemboya district via Pandedewatu. It's best to be at Waikabubak bus terminal early,

NUSA TENGGARA

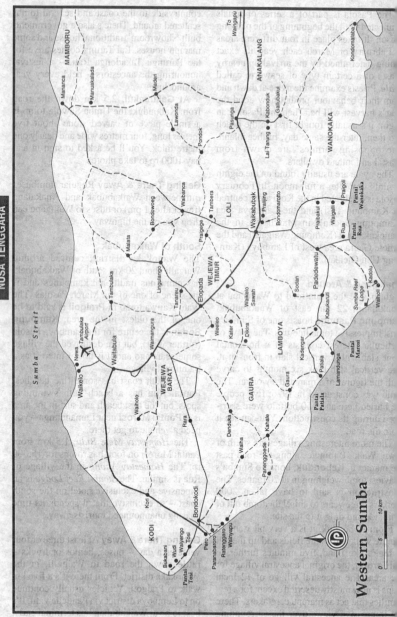

Western Sumba

0   5   10 km

by mid-morning it's all over for transport
the area and you'll have to walk, hitch or
nt a motorcycle.

odi

odi is the westernmost region of Sumba,
nd the small town of Bondokodi, about two
m from the coast, is the centre of this dis-
ict. The Kodi area offers plenty of attractions:
llages with incredible, high-peaked houses
nd unusual megalithic tombs; long, white
nd beaches with waves pounding off coral
efs; and the opportunity to see or buy some
scinating local wood, bone and horn carv-
gs. If you're on foot, you won't see much
the region unless you stay a couple of
ys.

The biggest **market** in the region is at
ori, held every Wednesday; to get there,
eople from around the region hang off any
ehicle they can get hold of, so it must be
ood! A couple of buses run from Bondokodi
the morning, before 8 am.

ero

ero is a friendly coastal village situated
 spectacular coastline just a few km from
ondokodi.

To visit traditional kampungs, go either
orth or south along the coast. To get to
atenggaro, first cross the freshwater pool
at runs to the coast below Pero. At low tide
ou could wade across; otherwise, small
oys will get you across in canoes. From the
her side, follow the dirt track for about
ree km along Pantai Radukapal, a long
retch of white sand beach, until you come
 the fenced kampung of Ratenggaro. It is
ossible to stay with the kepala desa.

The view from Ratengaro along the coast-
ne is breathtaking – coconut palms fringe
e shoreline and the high roofs of Wainyapu
eep out above the trees across the river. On
e near side of the river mouth, unusual
one tombs occupy a small headland. To get
 Wainyapu, you'll probably have to wade
ross the river at low tide.

On the way to Ratenggaro you'll probably
otice the roofs of **Kampung Paranobaroro**
rough the trees about one km inland. Here

are houses with even higher roofs, stone
statues, and an elaborate house with pig jaws
and numerous buffalo horns hanging from its
verandah. During the day, only women and
children are in the village – women are often
weaving and happy to chat.

Another way to reach Paranobararo is to
head south from Bondokodi market for about
one km and take a dirt road to the right past
the school. Keep forking right towards the
coast; you'll reach Paranobararo after about
two km.

To reach **Tosi**, about six km north and the
scene of the Kodi Pasola in February, head
north from Bondokodi market along the
paved road. If you are coming from Pero, it's
simply left at the T-intersection. About one
km along the road you'll see a track on your
left. Follow it for five km, past a series of
tombs. You'll soon see Tosi's roofs on your
right. From Tosi it is a 10 minute walk to the
beach, and a track runs all the way back to
Pero.

Place to Stay The only accommodation in
Pero is the *Homestay Stori*. It's clean and
cosy, but the beds have long since given up
the ghost. The cost is 13,000 rp per person,
including three meals. At night, an impromptu art shop may set up on the front porch. The
bone, horn, wood and stone carvings are
unique to the area.

Getting There & Away From Waikabubak
(2500 rp; three hours) there is usually a direct
bus at around 6 am, which returns to Waikabubak at about 9 am. On market day in Kori,
return buses may finish in Waitabula; you'll
have to change to another bus to continue on
to Waikabubak.

Wejewa Timur

This region less than 20 km west of Waikabubak sees relatively few tourists because
of the lack of transport. You will probably
need a jeep to explore the area. The people
here have maintained their traditional culture
and are very friendly. The villages of **Weeleo**
and **Kater**, both near Elopada, make interesting day trips.

Waikelo

Occasional boats go to Sumbawa, Flores or even further afield from this small port north of Waitabula. More good beaches can be found at Waikelo and one km east of town at

Newa a hotel is being built. Sumba's super beaches are attracting a lot of attention from developers and more hotels are planned especially at this coast with its close proximity to the Tambulaka airport.

Kalimantan

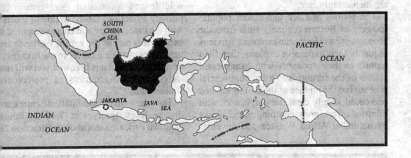

Kalimantan is the southern two-thirds of the island of Borneo. Of the 12 million people in Borneo, about nine million live in Kalimantan, most in settlements along its rivers. Mountains stretch across Borneo's interior, and heavy rainfall and poor drainage have produced a broad rim of dense, inhospitable wetlands along much of the island's coast and river basins.

Timber and mining interests have penetrated deep into Kalimantan, bulldozing and chainsawing at an alarming rate. Growing pressure for tighter controls over natural resource exploitation seems to have spurred fellers and miners to accelerate the pace and make the most of lax environmental law enforcement, as well as to meet the demand

for jobs and development. Indigenous Dayak requests to preserve traditional lands have attracted some government sympathy, yet vast tracts of rainforest continue to fall, rivers are being fouled and indigenous cultures are reeling from the social and economic intrusions of the 20th century.

In fact, deepest, darkest Borneo is becoming increasingly remote. You certainly won't find it on the streets of Balikpapan, Samarinda Banjarmasin or Pontianak, all of which are modern Indonesian cities complete with bustling traffic, department stores and fast-food chains. Travellers in search of unlogged jungle and traditional Dayak hospitality find themselves having to travel further and further afield, often at great expense. There

---

HIGHLIGHTS

- **River Travel** – The rivers of Kalimantan are the major, and sometimes the only, transport routes on the island and reach all the way into the mountains. The bewildering array of watercraft that ply the rivers is a definite highlight, particularly along the Sungai Mahakam.
- **Tanjung Puting National Park** – The Orang-utan Rehabilitation centres at Tanjung Harapan and Camp Leakey are probably the best in Indonesia. The park itself contains reserves of tropical rainforest, mangrove forest and wetlands, and a vast variety of flora and fauna.
- **Balikpapan** – This town and its river life is perhaps the main tourist attraction in Kalimantan and a good place to start exploration of this vast island.
- **Off the Beaten Track** – Kalimantan is one of the least visited parts of Indonesia, mostly because its unique cultures, spectacular flora and unusual wildlife are expensive and time-consuming to reach.

---

are pockets of accessible culture, wildlife and jungle close to major waterways – the highway system of Kalimantan – but these are increasingly rare.

The visions of Eden that colour popular imagery of Borneo probably stem from the accounts of early European explorers. Anxious to justify their expensive exploits, they filed reports to their sponsors with exaggerated claims of the fertility and great commercial potential of the jungles of the east. It seemed one could simply clear the jungle and, with minimal effort, grow anything. Later works by naturalist Alfred Wallace and novelists

such as Joseph Conrad added considerab[...] to Borneo's mystique.

Kalimantan's unique cultures, unusua[...] wildlife and spectacular flora remain th[...] primary attractions for the trickle of touris[...] with the time, money and energy required t[...] explore this part of the world. Wetlands an[...] mountains provide a buffer to the ravages o[...] development, and it is here that you will fin[...] truly wonderful remnants of pre-colonia[...] Kalimantan.

The orang-utan rehabilitation centres an[...] diverse forest reserves at Tanjung Putin[...] National Park are a world-class attraction. S[...]

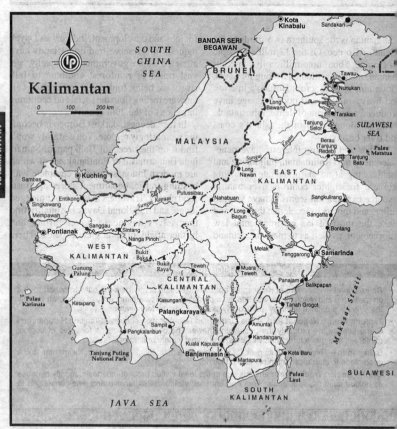

oo is the river life along the Sungai (River) Mahakam and the remote Kayan and Kenyah settlements in the Apokayan and around Long Bawang. Even in tourist precincts such as Tanjung Isuy in East Kalimantan, where visitors pay by the hour to see 'primitive' culture, there are still many who believe in the old ways. Take a walk in any Dayak village late at night, listen for the drumbeat of a healing or harvest ceremony and learn about the old ways first hand.

HISTORY

Although the pace of economic and social change has accelerated dramatically in recent years, there was considerable activity long before the multinationals moved in. The powerful kingdoms of Brunei, Kutai and Banjarmasin were built on a thriving trade in jungle products and, before then, there is evidence that Borneo was an integral part of the Sriwijaya kingdom's 5th century trading network.

Like Sumatra and Java, Kalimantan's place on the India-China trade axis brought Hinduism in by about 400 AD. Hindu temple remains have been unearthed in southern Kalimantan near Amuntai and Negara, and there are Sanskrit tablets from caves at Wahau, East Kalimantan.

Kalimantan was a stopover point on the trade routes between China, the Philippines and Java, and Chinese settlements were established on the island long before Europeans came to the Indonesian archipelago. The coastal ports were Islamic by around the 15th or 16th centuries and some of the sultanates, such as Kutai and Banjarmasin, became major trading centres.

In the early 17th century, Kalimantan became a scene of conflict between the British and the Dutch. The British turned their attention to Banjarmasin, reputedly a great source of pepper. Trade flourished until the British stationed a guard ship at the mouth of the Sungai Barito and recruited Bugis mercenaries to guard their warehouses. Banjarmasin rebelled in 1701, and the British were eventually evicted six years later.

British and Dutch interests on Borneo changed markedly in the 19th century. The British wanted to protect their sailing routes between China and India, while the Dutch wanted to consolidate control over the East Indies. Borneo was a hideout for 'pirates' and the Dutch had some interest in controlling the south and west coasts. By the late 1820s and 1830s, the Dutch had concluded treaties with various small west-coast states. Parts of the Banjarmasin sultanate were signed over to the Dutch in the early 1800s, but the Dutch didn't establish garrisons or administrative offices.

In 1839 the Dutch were jolted by the arrival of English adventurer James Brooke, who established a private colony at Kuching, Sarawak. With Brooke's arrival, the spectre of intervention by other private colonists and European powers suddenly became a reality for the Dutch. In the 1840s and 1850s the Dutch put down several internal disputes and established new treaties with local rulers. From 1846 they opened new coal mines in South and East Kalimantan and gradually the island became more commercially important. War broke out between the Dutch and Banjarmasin in 1859. Within four years the Banjarmasis were defeated, but resistance continued until 1905.

Towards the end of the 19th century the outer islands, rather than Java, became the focus of Dutch commercial exploitation of the archipelago. Rubber and oil became increasingly important, and pepper, copra, tin and coffee plantations were developed. By the end of the century, oil was being drilled in East Kalimantan. To finance the drilling, a British company was set up in London, the Shell Transport & Trading Company. In 1907 Shell merged with the Royal Dutch Company for the Exploitation of Petroleum Sources in the Netherlands Indies (the first company to start drilling in Sumatra) to form Royal Dutch Shell, giving the Dutch the greater share. Shell expanded rapidly and was soon producing oil everywhere from California to Russia. The Russian properties were confiscated in 1917, but by 1930 Shell was producing 85% of Indonesia's oil.

The current division of Borneo between Indonesia and Malaysia originates from the British-Dutch rivalry. After WWII the Brooke family handed Sarawak over to the British government, putting Britain in the curious position of acquiring a new colony at the time it was shedding others. Sarawak remained under British control when Malaya (Peninsular Malaysia) gained independence in 1957.

Sabah was also once part of the Brunei sultanate. It came under the influence of the British North Borneo Company as Brunei declined. In 1888 North Borneo's coast became a British protectorate, although fight-ing did not end until the death of the Sabah rebel leader, Mat Salleh, in 1900. After WWII, the administration of Sabah was handed over to the British government. In 1963 Sarawak and Sabah joined with the Malay peninsula – and, temporarily, Singa-pore – to form the nation of Malaysia.

Indonesia's President Soekarno, suspi-cious of Britain's continuing influence in Malaysia, challenged the newly independent state with military confrontations. Long after 'Konfrontasi' was abandoned, anti-Malay-sian Chinese guerrillas of the Sarawak People's Guerrilla Troops, originally trained and armed by Indonesia, remained in Kali-mantan. The so-called emergency also provided a convenient, officially sanctioned excuse for Dayak people to resume head-hunting.

East Kalimantan has become one of Indo-nesia's prime transmigration targets. The transmigrants tend to settle on marginal lands, replacing diverse tracts of jungle with extensive monocultures of rubber and pulp wood trees. The newcomers also provide the mining and logging industries with a ready supply of willing young labourers. Transmi-grants occasionally clash with Dayak groups whose indigenous land-use regimes and land rights are rarely recognised. A violent out-break in 1997 caused several deaths.

Not everyone goes to Kalimantan on gov-ernment-sponsored schemes. A major group in East Kalimantan are the Bugis of southern Sulawesi, continuing a transmigration tradi-tion 400 years old. The Kahar-Muzakar rebellion in 1951 spurred Bugis movement from Sulawesi. After the rebellion was sup-pressed, another wave of Bugis transmigrants joined their relatives in Kalimantan, tempted by the prospect of a better life.

FLORA & FAUNA

The strangest inhabitants of Kalimantan are the orang-utans, whose almost human ap-pearance and disposition puzzled both Dayaks and early European visitors. The English Captain Daniel Beeckman visited Borneo early in the 18th century and wrote: 'The natives do really believe that these were

---

Borneo's Private Colonists

Kalimantan has had its share of opportunists, including the Bugis pirate Arung Singkang, a descendant of the royal family of Wajo in South Sulawesi. In 1726 he conquered Pasir then Kutai, and in 1733 his forces made an unsuc-cessful attempt on Banjarmasin. Singkang returned to Sulawesi a couple of years later, taking the Wajo throne in 1737 and remaining a political force there until his death 1765.

Less successful was the Briton Erskine Murray, who tried his luck at Tenggarong (the capital of Kutai) in the early 19th century. The incumbent sultan was less than enthused about Murray's plans to rule Kutai and a short battle on the Sungai Mahakam ended in Murray's death and the demise of his private mission.

The waning influence of Banjarmasin, Kutai and Brunei enabled another Briton Alexander Hare to be posted as Resident to the Sultanate of Banjarmasin in 1812. Hare quickly set about creating his own private colony, importing Javanese coolies to work the coal mines and fostering trade in jungle produce. Post-Napo-leonic treaties and the return of the Dutch forced Hare to abandon his colony in 1814.

The most famous of the 'white rajahs' was the English adventurer James Brooke, who in 1839 involved himself in a dispute at Kuching, then part of Brunei. His timely intervention won him the governorship of Sarawak. The new ruler put down the inland tribes, eliminated piracy and founded a personal dynasty. He and his successors forced further territorial conces-sions from Brunei, extending Sarawak to its present expanse. Their rule ended with the Japanese invasion of WWII. ∎

ormerly men, but metamorphosed into
easts for their blasphemy. They told me
nany strange stories of them...'. Today, one
if the last orang-utan refuges is the Tanjung
'uting National Park in Central Kalimantan.

The deep waters of the Sungai Mahakam
n East Kalimantan are home to freshwater
dolphins, and there are gibbons in the
ungles, proboscis monkeys and crab-eating
macaques in the mangrove swamps, plus
crocodiles, clouded leopards, giant butterflies and hornbills, including the legendary
black hornbill.

The Dayaks traditionally believe that the
black hornbill carries the human soul, but
because of its feathers and huge beak it was
almost hunted into extinction. Beaks and
bony humped skulls are still immersed in
water overnight, to give whoever drinks the
water special spiritual powers. Some Dayaks
keep juvenile hornbills as pets, releasing
them when they become old enough to mate.

POPULATION & PEOPLE

The population of Kalimantan is approximately nine million. The three biggest ethnic
groups in Kalimantan today are the recently
arrived Malay-Indonesians who tend to
follow Islam and live in settlements along the
coasts and the main rivers; the Chinese, who
have controlled trade in Kalimantan for centuries; and the Dayaks, the collective name
for the indigenous inhabitants of the island.

The Dayaks

The tribes do not use the term Dayak. It's a
slightly pejorative term often used by Indonesians, or indigenous peoples converted to
Islam (such as the Banjars and the Kutais),
to differentiate non-Muslim from Muslim
inhabitants. Enlightened Indonesians call
them *orang pedalaman* ('inland people') or
orang gunung ('mountain people'). The
tribes prefer to use their separate tribal
names, such as Kenyah, Kayan, Iban and
Punan.

Most were probably coastal dwellers until
the arrival of Malay settlers drove them
inland to the highlands and river banks.
Some also live in neighbouring Sabah and

Sarawak. The Dayaks are generally light-
skinned, somewhat Chinese in appearance
and may be descendants of immigrants from
southern China or South-East Asia. Tribal
dialects show linguistic similarities.

Swidden or so-called 'slash and burn' agriculture is the mainstay of Borneo's agricultural
economy. Dry fields are cleared then burnt
to provide ash to enrich the poor soils, crops
are grown for one or two seasons, then the
blocks are left to fallow for a number of
years. There are also reserves set aside for
hunting, traditional medicines and extraction
of jungle products such as honey and rattan.
Many tribes maintain small reserves of untouched rainforest to provide emergency
food supplies during periods of extreme
drought.

When population growth puts too much
pressure on the land, whole villages can
move to find new land. One such mass migration was the recent exodus of large groups
of Kayan and Kenyah from the Apokayan
Highlands to valleys in the Mahakam basin
or across the border to Sarawak. The
Apokayan's population has dropped from
30,000 in the 1950s to about 5000 today. The
introduction of government-subsidised transport and basic services has stabilised the
situation, but arable land is still scarce and
goods remain prohibitively expensive.

Another, as yet unexplained, migration
started in the mid-16th century when Iban
groups began to abandon their agricultural
settlements in the Kapuas basin in West
Kalimantan and move north, most to the
Batang Lupar region in Sarawak. The pattern
changed again after James Brooke suppressed their 'piracy' and recruited Iban
forces to pacify inland tribes elsewhere in his
expanding colony. Violent Iban incursions
drove other tribes, notably the Kenyah and
Kayan, further upstream.

The most striking feature of many older
Dayak women is their pierced ear lobes,
stretched with the weight of heavy gold or
brass rings. This custom is increasingly rare
among the young. Older Dayaks, influenced
by missionaries, often trim their ear lobes as
a sign of conversion.

KALIMANTAN

It was once the custom for all women to tattoo their forearms and calves with bird and spirit designs. Tattooing of young women has almost disappeared, except in tribes deep in the interior. It is still seen among men, although traditionally men in many Dayak cultures were expected to earn their tattoos by taking heads.

Dayak traditions are being modified by pressure from the Indonesian government and Protestant Christian missionaries. Neither the Muslims nor the Christians seem content to leave the indigenous belief systems, the backbone of these tribal cultures, alone. Plus there is the added pressure of new industries. A miner or sex worker (often mines refuse to employ Dayaks) can bring home much more money than their parents ever could, disrupting traditional roles.

Not all Dayaks live in villages. The Punan are nomadic hunter-gatherers who still move through the jungles, although some stay in longhouses at the height of the rainy season and many have settled in permanent riverside villages. To other Dayaks, the Punan are the ultimate jungle dwellers. As logging and ethno-religious evangelism push them deeper into the interior, they can be difficult to find.

BOOKS

Borneo, Change and Development by Mark Cleary and Peter Eaton is a rich compilation of contemporary research on Borneo and on humanity's accelerating impact on the island. It provides excellent historical and environmental data for researchers or eco-tourists.

A Field Guide to the Mammals of Borneo, Junaidi Payne et al, is another must for eco-tourists.

Stranger in the Forest is an inspiring account of Eric Hansen's six month trek across Borneo in 1982.

Into the Heart of Borneo by Redmond O'Hanlon is an entertaining read, recounting the almost slapstick adventures of a naturalist and an English poet as they made their way to Gunung Batu in Kalimantan, via Sarawak. It gives a good account of interior travel.

GETTING THERE & AWAY

Visa-free entry is now possible for visitors entering Indonesia by road at Entikong or by air at Pontianak and Balikpapan. Tourists enter and leave from Balikpapan so rarely that you can expect delays as the officials ferret around the bottom drawer for that rarely used stamp, but there are no real hassles. To enter or exit Indonesia by air, sea or land elsewhere in Kalimantan you'll need to get a visa in advance. Tarakan, in East Kalimantan, accepts new arrivals as long as they already have visas.

Singapore

Merpati has three flights a week between Singapore and Pontianak, and two flights linking Singapore with Balikpapan. The cheapest fare is the direct Singapore-Pontianak flight for about US$125. Sempati has daily flights (via Jakarta) linking Singapore to Banjarmasin and Balikpapan. There are also daily connections from Tarakan and Palangkaraya to Singapore.

Malaysia

The border post at Entikong became an official international entry point in January 1994. This means the same rules now apply at Entikong as would apply at major airports and seaports. To get a 60 day tourist pass (see under Visas & Documents in the introductory Facts for the Visitor chapter), it's advisable to have an onward ticket. Sarawak has scrapped its 14,000 rp visa fee, but Indonesians can still expect to pay a 50,000 rp *fiskal* to leave the country. Immigration rules can change and Entikong is a long way from anywhere, so double check with Indonesian and Malaysian authorities before setting out from Kuching or Pontianak.

There is still much confusion concerning travel between Sabah and East Kalimantan. There are flights and boats between Tawau and Tarakan, but Tarakan is not yet an official international entry point. This may well change in the near future, as it has become much easier to make the border crossing. In the meantime, Indonesian visas can be obtained at Indonesian embassies in Sabah at

Tawau or Kota Kinabalu. If you entered Indonesia on a 60 day tourist pass and want to leave this way, officially you should do your paperwork in Jakarta before immigration will let you through at Nunukan. Nowadays, however, it seems that most travellers are getting through without this formality – check with the authorities before making the trip.

Air MAS flies twice weekly between Pontianak and Kuching in Sarawak for 179,000 rp, and twice weekly between Tarakan and Tawau (and on to Kota Kinabalu) for M$175.

Bus Air-con buses from Pontianak to Kuching cost 30,000 rp. Bookings can be made at agencies around Pontianak and at some of the mid-range hotels – the Hotel Central sells tickets, and there is also an agency next to the Orien Hotel.

Boat Strictly speaking, to leave Indonesia by sea via Nunukan in East Kalimantan (to Tawau, Sabah), you need an exit permit from the immigration office in Jakarta if you entered Indonesia at a visa-free port (the exit permit isn't necessary if you entered Indonesia on a one month advance paid visa). But in practice this rule doesn't seem to be applied as rigorously as it once was. There is, however, no guarantee you will get through if your paperwork is not in order.

There are longboats from Tarakan to Nunukan for 15,000 rp, and speedboats for 25,000 rp. From Nunukan to Tawau there are speedboats (30,000 rp). Buy tickets from CV Tam Bersaudara on Jl Pasar Lingkas in Tarakan. The boats depart most days between 7 and 8 am, although they may not run on Sunday.

Philippines
Air Bourag flies twice a week between Balikpapan and Davao, via Manado, for US$200.

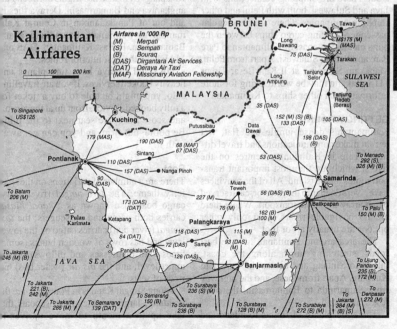

Kalimantan Airfares

Airfares in '000 Rp
(M) Merpati
(S) Sempati
(B) Bourag
(DAS) Dirgantara Air Services
(DAT) Deraya Air Taxi
(MAF) Missionary Aviation Fellowship

0   100   200 km

MALAYSIA
BRUNEI
SULAWESI SEA
JAVA SEA

To Singapore US$125
To Batam 206 (M)
To Jakarta 245 (M) (B)
To Jakarta 221 (B), 242 (M)
To Jakarta 285 (M)
To Semarang 139 (DAT)
To Semarang 150 (B)
To Surabaya 236 (B)
To Surabaya 128 (B) (M)
To Surabaya 236 (S) (M)
To Surabaya 272 (B) (M)
To Jakarta 384 (M) (B) (S)
To Denpasar 272 (M)
To Ujung Pandang 235 (B), 172 (M)
To Palu 150 (M) (B)
To Manado 292 (S), 326 (M) (B)

Tawau
Long Bawang
Long Ampung
Tarakan — MS175 (M) (MAS)
75 (DAS)
Tanjung Selor
Tanjung Redeb (Berau)
Kuching
Putussibau
Data Dawai
35 (DAS)
152 (M) (S) (B), 133 (DAS)
105 (DAS)
179 (MAS)
190 (DAS)
68 (MAF) 67 (DAS)
198 (DAS) (B)
53 (DAS)
Pontianak
Sintang
110 (DAS)
157 (DAS) — Nanga Pinoh
90 (DAS)
Muara Teweh
56 (DAS) (B)
Samarinda
227 (M)
173 (DAS) (DAT)
76 (M)
162 (B) 100 (M)
Balikpapan
Pulau Karimata
Ketapang
Palangkaraya
115 (M)
99 (B)
84 (DAT)
118 (DAS)
93 (DAS)
Pangkalanbun
72 (DAS) Sampit
126 (DAS)
Banjarmasin

KALIMANTAN

Elsewhere in Indonesia

Travel across some parts of Kalimantan is only possible by air or foot. It is usually much easier to go from Kalimantan to Sulawesi or Java, than from one part of Kalimantan to another. For instance, Pelni boats from Tarakan to Balikpapan will take you via Toli-Toli and Palu.

Air Merpati and Sempati have the best connections with the rest of Indonesia, while Dirgantara Air Services (DAS), Deraya Air Taxi and Missionary Aviation Fellowship (MAF) are often your only options on many routes within Kalimantan. Banjarmasin and Balikpapan are the busiest and best-connected airports but, curiously, Bouraq is the only airline connecting the two. Bouraq is prone to cancellations, but it has useful flights between Kalimantan and Sulawesi, including a Banjarmasin-Balikpapan-Palu-Gorontalo-Manado hop.

Boat There are shipping connections with Java and Sulawesi, both with Pelni and other shipping companies. There are also regular passenger-carrying cargo ships between the ports on the east coast of Kalimantan to Pare Pare and Palu in Sulawesi. Apart from Pelni, Mahakam Shipping at Jl Kali Besar Timur 111 in Jakarta may be worth trying for more information on other ships to Kalimantan.

GETTING AROUND

Kalimantan's dense jungle and flat, wet terrain make communications and travel difficult. Life in Kalimantan centres on the rivers, which are the most important transport routes on the island. All of the provinces have rivers deep into the interior, each served by an array of public transport. Where there are no navigable rivers, your only other options are usually air or foot.

The area around Pontianak has the best roads, stretching north along the coast, inland to Sintang and across the border to Kuching. Apart from these, and the highway from Samarinda to Banjarmasin, there are few sealed roads.

There are plenty of flights to inland and coastal destinations, and some shipping along the east coast. Going upriver into some of the Dayak regions is now relatively easy from Pontianak, Samarinda and Banjarmasin, but the further you go off the beaten canal the more time you'll need. For serious forays into the interior, even along the main rivers, you must allow at least two weeks per province.

Air

There are flights around the coastal cities and into the interior of Kalimantan with the regular airline companies. DAS now carries the bulk of the traffic, but Merpati, Sempati, Bouraq and Deraya Air Taxi also have useful routes. Other possibilities include planes run by the missionaries (MAF), which serve the most isolated communities.

DAS's small propeller aircraft fly to all sorts of places, with daily flights from Pontianak to inland West Kalimantan towns like Sintang or south-east to the coastal town of Ketapang. DAS also has flights between Palangkaraya and Banjarmasin. Deraya flies in and out of Pangkalanbun in Central Kalimantan to Pontianak, Palangkaraya and Banjarmasin. In East Kalimantan, DAS and MAF have the best interior routes.

DAS and Deraya have tiny planes and heavily booked services. If you are travelling solo, you might be able to buy a ticket for a fully booked service, front up at the airport and score the spare seat next to the pilot. Be polite, but firm, and you can get away with it.

Boat

There are a number of variations on the river ferry theme. The *feri sungai* (river ferry) cargo boat, also known as a *kapal biasa*, carries both cargo and passengers; the *tax sungai* (river taxi) carries cargo on the lower level and has rows of wooden bunks (sometimes with mattresses and pillows) on the upper level; and the *bis air* (water bus) has rows of seats.

Along Sungai Kapuas in Pontianak are the *bandung*, large cargo-cum-houseboats that take up to a month to move upriver to utussibau. A bis air does the same distance in about four days. A *long bot*, as the name indicates, is a longboat – a narrow vessel with two large outboard motors at the rear and bench seats in a covered passenger cabin. Speedboats commonly ply the Barito, Kapuas, Kahayan and Kayan rivers and seem to be appearing elsewhere. Don't get too hung up on the terminology, as what may be called a bis air in one province may be a taxi sungai in another.

Recent innovations are the coastal jet boat services which fling passengers from Pontianak to Ketapang and from Banjarmasin to Sampit. These big, modern cruisers look more like water-bound planes than boats and are a great way to get around.

West Kalimantan

West Kalimantan is dissected by Indonesia's longest waterway, the Sungai Kapuas (1143 km), which is the main transport artery for rafts of logs and other heavy cargo to and from the interior. Roads and buses are rapidly superseding the river as the main mode of moving people.

The province has about 3.5 million inhabitants, including the highest concentration of ethnic Chinese people in Indonesia. The proportion of Chinese residents in Pontianak is estimated at 35%, and 70% in Singkawang. Everything has a Chinese flavour and even the major Muslim festivals are celebrated with Chinese firecrackers.

Beyond the activity on the coast and along the Kapuas, the province's interior is relatively unexplored. There are many Iban settlements north of the Kapuas, and Punan and Kenyah-Kayan Dayak villages in the mountainous eastern part of the province. Contact with neighbouring Sarawak is increasing now that border restrictions have been relaxed.

PONTIANAK
Situated right on the equator, Pontianak lies astride the confluence of the Landak and Kapuas Kecil rivers. The city was founded in 1770 by Arab trader Abdul Rahman Al Gadri who used a barrage of cannon fire to frighten off the resident *pontianak* (spirits), clearing the way for human settlement. The discovery of sizeable gold deposits north of Pontianak a few decades later gave the young settlement a great economic and demographic boost.

Pontianak is a sprawling city with a giant indoor sports stadium, a sizeable university and two big girder bridges upstream from the city centre. Like Banjarmasin it really needs to be seen from the canals and riverside boardwalks. Charter a sampan (rowboat) or walk over the Kapuas Bridge from Jl Gajah Mada for a sweeping view of the river and brilliant orange sunsets.

From Pontianak you can drive north along the coast to Pasir Panjang, a lovely beach just back from the Pontianak-Singkawang road. (See the Pasir Panjang Beach entry later in this section.) The Mandor Nature Reserve is to the north-east. This is also the starting point for boat trips up the Kapuas, which terminate in Putussibau in the north-eastern corner of the province. From Putussibau, at the edge of Kalimantan's shrinking frontier country, you can walk to the headwaters of Sungai Mahakam in East Kalimantan.

Orientation
The commercial hub of Pontianak is in the north of town, particularly on Jl Rahadi Usman in the area around the city passenger ferry. Here you'll find several markets, the main *bemo* terminal (Kapuas Indah), hotels, airline and Pelni offices, banks and markets.

Information
Tourist Offices The Kalimantan Barat tourist office (☎ 36172) is way out at Jl Ahmad Sood 25. It has fine intentions, but lousy maps and the staff speak little English. Staff at the big hotels and private travel agencies often offer better advice (see Travel Agencies in this section).

The Conservation office (Balai Konservasi Sumber Daya Alam; ☎ 34613), Jl Rahman Saleh 33, has Indonesian-language brochures on nature reserves, and information on getting to them, but its staff's enthusiasm can be misleading. None of its parks cater for visitors.

Foreign Consulates The Malaysian Consulate is at Jl Jen Ahmad Yani 42, but neighbouring Sarawak no longer insists on a visa, nor do visa-free tourists need an exit permit from Indonesian immigration. Consulate hours are Monday to Thursday from 7 am to 3 pm, closed Friday from 11 am to 1.30 pm and weekends.

Immigration The Pontianak immigration office (☎ 34516) on Jl Sutoyo, near the National Museum (Museum Negeri Pontianak), is a bustling, friendly place. For visa extensions it's easier to take a bus to Kuching and get a new two month pass when you return via the border post at Entikong.

Money US and Malaysian cash is easy to change, everything else is not. The bank around the Merpati office on Jl Rahadi Usman handle foreign currency and traveller cheques, and there are moneychangers along Jl Tanjungpura (at Nos 12, 14 and 236B), a

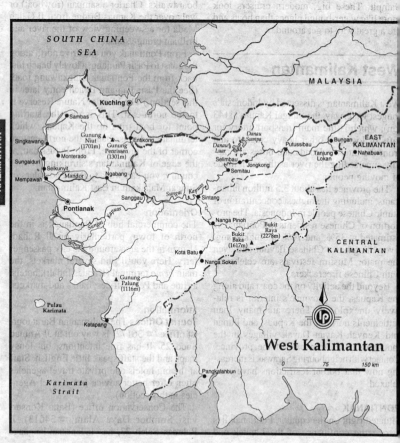

SOUTH CHINA SEA

MALAYSIA

EAST KALIMANTAN

CENTRAL KALIMANTAN

West Kalimantan

Karimata Strait

0   75   150 km

asar Nusa Indah I Blok AA 4 and in the
Kapuas Indah building. As a last resort try
he bigger hotels, though their rates are poor.

ost & Communications You can collect
oste restante mail from the main post office
t Jl Sultan Abdurrakhman 49. It's open
Monday to Friday from 8 am to 7 pm (closed
riday from 11 am to 2 pm), Saturday until
pm and Sunday from 9 am to 2 pm. There's
n older post office on Jl Rahadi Usman, near
he Kartika Hotel, and an agency on Jl
Diponegoro.

There are private telephone agencies next
o the Warung Somay Bandung on Jl Sising-
mangaraja and next to the Hotel Wijaya
Kusuma, but to call collect you must go to
he Telkom office on Jl Teuku.

ravel Agencies PT Asia Jaya Nusantara
☎ 37432), Jl Tajungpura 236B, and Amir at
'T Citra Tour & Travel (☎ 36436), Jl Pak
Kasih 6, can provide general information on
ouring and trekking. The DAS agent, PT
Gajahmada Nusantara (☎ 34383), at Jl Gajah
Mada 67 is good for airline schedules.

River Life
Pontianak's wealth stems from its river trade
nd the best vantage point to view the river
ctivity is from the river itself. Hire a sampan
or an hour or two from next to the ferry
erminals or behind the Kapuas Indah build-
ng for 6000 rp or so. The price depends on
our itinerary and your bargaining prowess,
ut the views are worth every last rupiah.

For an interesting experience of river-
ront life, take a walk from the Mesjid
Abdurrakhman along the wobbly wooden
oardwalks past the stilt houses at washing
ime, either early or late in the day. You will
ind the people of the *kampung* extremely
riendly and curious. Take your camera.
There are plenty of willing models, espe-
ially the kids.

If there is the slightest breeze in the
evening, young men crowd the boardwalks
long the south bank to fly huge paper kites,
many decorated with swastika. They seem
much more interested in the swastika's pattern than its politics.

If you follow Jl Sultan Muhammad south
along the Kapuas Kecil you eventually come
to the *pisini* (schooner) harbour, where you
can see Bugis-style sailing schooners. Also
docked in this area are the large houseboats,
or bandung, peculiar to West Kalimantan.
Bandungs function as floating general stores
that ply Sungai Kapuas, trading at villages
along the way. Their family owners live on
board and a typical run up the Kapuas might
last as long as a month.

Mesjid Abdurrakhman
Also known as the Mesjid Jami, this was the
royal mosque of Syarif Abdul Rahman (in
Indonesian, Abdurrakhman), who reigned as
Sultan of Pontianak from 1770 until his
death in 1808. The Sumatran-style mosque
has a square-tiered roof and is made entirely
of wood. Beautiful inside and out, it's worth
the short canoe trip across the river from the
pisini harbour. Charter a boat for 500 to 700
rp or wait for a shared canoe taxi for only 200
rp per person. The beautiful wooden **Mesjid
Jihad** near the main post office is also a
pleasant stop.

Istana Kadriyah
About 100m behind the sultan's mosque is
his former palace, a double storey ironwood
building which is now an interesting museum. It displays the personal effects of the
sultan's family. Eight sultans reigned after
the death of the first in 1808. The last died in
1978. Visiting hours are from 8.30 am to 6
pm daily. There is no admission fee, but a
donation is encouraged.

Museum Negeri Pontianak
Near Tanjungpura University, south of the
city centre on Jl Jen Ahmad Yani, this recently built national museum has a collection
of *tempayan*, South-East Asian ceramics
(mostly water jugs) from Thailand, China
and Borneo. The jugs displayed vary in size
from tiny to tank-like and date from the 16th
century.

Tribal exhibits include dioramic displays

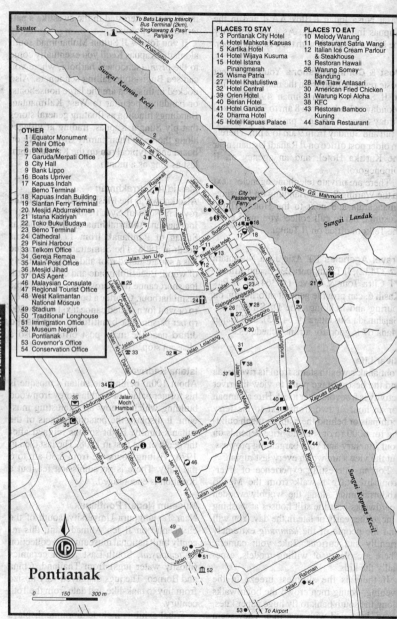

PLACES TO STAY
3   Pontianak City Hotel
4   Hotel Mahkota Kapuas
5   Kartika Hotel
14 Hotel Wijaya Kusuma
15 Hotel Istana
    Pinangmerah
25 Wisma Patria
27 Hotel Khatulistiwa
32 Hotel Central
39 Orien Hotel
40 Berian Hotel
41 Hotel Garuda
42 Dharma Hotel
45 Hotel Kapuas Palace

PLACES TO EAT
10 Melody Warung
11 Restaurant Satria Wangi
12 Italian Ice Cream Parlour
    & Steakhouse
13 Restoran Hawaii
26 Warung Somay
    Bandung
28 Mie Tiaw Antasari
30 American Fried Chicken
31 Warung Kopi Aloha
38 KFC
43 Restoran Bamboo
    Kuning
44 Sahara Restaurant

OTHER
1   Equator Monument
2   Pelni Office
6   BNI Bank
7   Garuda/Merpati Office
8   City Hall
9   Bank Lippo
16 Boats Upriver
17 Kapuas Indah
    Bemo Terminal
18 Kapuas Indah Building
19 Siantan Ferry Terminal
20 Mesjid Abdurrakhman
21 Istana Kadriyah
22 Toko Buku Budaya
23 Bemo Terminal
24 Cathedral
29 Pisini Harbour
33 Telkom Office
34 Gereja Remaja
35 Main Post Office
36 Mesjid Jihad
37 DAS Agent
46 Malaysian Consulate
47 Regional Tourist Office
48 West Kalimantan
    National Mosque
49 Stadium
50 'Traditional' Longhouse
51 Immigration Office
52 Museum Negeri
    Pontianak
53 Governor's Office
54 Conservation Office

Pontianak

0   150   300 m

KALIMANTAN

f the clothing, musical instruments, tools
nd crafts of the Dayak cultures of West
[K]alimantan. All the labels are in Indonesian.
[T]he museum is open Tuesday to Sunday
[f]rom 9 am to 1 pm. Around the corner on Jl
[S]utoyo is a replica of a Dayak longhouse.

[E]quator Monument
[T]he official monument marking the equator
[w]as originally erected in 1928 as a simple
[o]belisk mounted with a metallic arrow. In
[1]930 a circle was welded to the arrow, in
[1]938 another circle was added in the other
[d]irection and its subsequent incarnation is
[u]nintentionally funny, looking like a giant
[g]yroscope on a pillar. The caretakers then
[e]ncased the original in a building in 1991 and
[b]uilt a huge replica. On 23 March and 23
[S]eptember the sun is supposed to be directly
[o]verhead.

[P]laces to Stay – bottom end
[T]he best budget beds are at the *Wisma Patria*
(☎ 36063) at Jl Merdeka Timur 497. Clean
[s]ingles/doubles in a congenial atmosphere
[c]ost from 16,000 rp with fan and mandi
[(]Indonesian-style bath) or 25,000 rp with
[a]ir-con. Another reasonably good budget (by
[P]ontianak standards) option is the *Berian
Hotel* (☎ 32092), which has fan-cooled dou-
[b]les with shared bathroom for 15,000 rp.
[R]ooms with bathroom are 25,000 rp, while
[a]ir-con rooms cost 35,000 rp.

Backing on to the river opposite the Kap-
[u]as Indah bemo terminal is the grim *Hotel
Wijaya Kusuma* (☎ 32547) at Jl Kapten
[M]arsan 51-53. It has barely habitable eco-
[n]omy rooms from 25,000 rp. Smaller and
[c]leaner is the *Hotel Istana Pinangmerah* just
[n]ext door. Rooms start at 25,000 rp; there are
[l]arger air-con rooms for 32,500 rp and VIP
[t]riples at 37,500 rp. The neighbourhood is
[n]otorious for its gambling and prostitution.

The *Hotel Central* (☎ 37444), Jl Merdeka
[T]imur 232, is friendly and has rooms with
[a]ir-con, TV and hot water mandi from
[3]6,000 to 44,000 rp. The rooms suffer from
[t]heir proximity to two busy roads.

Hotel Khatulistiwa (☎ 36773), Jl Dipo-
[n]egoro 151, is a sprawling place with grubby

economy rooms for 22,000 rp. There are
rooms with air-con and TV from 27,500 rp, and
even better rooms with bath for 34,100 rp.

Places to Stay – middle & top end
The *Orien Hotel* (☎ 32650) is in the south of
town on Jl Tanjungpura. It's a good mid-
range place; rooms with fan, video and bath
are 34,000 rp, or 42,000 to 54,000 rp with
air-con. The *Pontianak City Hotel* (☎ 32495)
at Jl Pak Kasih 44 is up in the north of town.
It has economy air-con rooms with TV from
36,000 to 48,000 rp and standard rooms at
54,000/60,000 rp.

The *Kartika Hotel* (☎ 34401), on the river
across from the city hall, is a feeble attempt
at a top-end hotel, but it has good views of
the river and its cheaper rooms function as a
good mid-range option. Rooms start at 75,000/
85,000 rp and go as high as 110,000/120,000
rp for 'panorama' singles/doubles with sweeping river views.

The *Hotel Kapuas Palace* (☎ 36122; fax
34374) is just off Jl Pahlawan. It has a 100m
swimming pool. Rooms in the main building
start at 120,000 rp and range to 240,000 rp
for business suites. Not far away, the *Hotel
Garuda* (☎ 36890; fax 39001) at Jl Pahlawan
8 is an upmarket mid-range hotel with karaoke
and so on. Standard rooms cost 65,000 rp,
deluxe are 85,000 rp and superior rooms are
128,000 rp.

The *Hotel Mahkota Kapuas* (☎ 36022;
fax 36200) at Jl Sidas 8 is the best place in
town. Rooms start at US$40 plus tax or
US$55/65 for standard singles/doubles.
Suites cost US$125. The Mahkota has a
couple of bars, an excellent restaurant, a disco
and a swimming pool, and often discounts its
rooms.

Places to Eat
The local coffee is excellent and the numerous warung kopis around town are central to
life in Pontianak. The best place to seek them
out is in the centre of town on the side streets
between Jl Tanjungpura and Jl Pattimura.
The *Warung Kopi Aloha* is a good place for
coffee and snacks.

The clean little *Warung Somay Bandung*,

in the theatre complex on Jl Sisingamang-araja near Jl Pattimura, serves delicious Chinese-style bubur ayam (sweet rice porridge with chicken) and the house speciality, somay, a tasty concoction of potatoes, tofu, hard-boiled egg and peanut sauce for 1300 rp. It also serves good ice drinks.

The best fare (and good coffee) is at the countless warungs. Those in the Kapuas Indah bemo terminal offer a great choice, but this neighbourhood gets pretty smelly when it rains. Try the night warungs on Jl Sudirman and Jl Diponegoro for steaming plates of rice noodles, crab, prawns, fish and vegetables, and goat sate – all fried up in a wok for 2000 rp.

Pontianak has a big Chinese population and excellent Chinese food. The speciality of *Mie Tiaw Antasari* on Jl Antasari 72 is its fabulous beef mie tiaw (fried or rapid-boiled noodles). It also offers tasty bihun (beef noodle dish, fried or boiled), bakso (meatball soup) and yellow noodles. There are several similar restaurants on nearby Jl Diponegoro, including the *Mie Tiau Sam* at No 63, with its popular bakso, beef and bean noodle soup.

The *Restoran Hawaii* on Jl Pasar Nusa Indah is a good choice for Chinese, as is *Restaurant Satria Wangi* on Jl Pasar Nusa Indah II. There's a Chinese flavour to everything – even the gado gado is served on noodles rather than rice.

For a western food fix, there's a *KFC* on Jl Gajah Mada and the *Italian IceCream Parlour & Steakhouse* on Jl Pasar Nusa Indah – this place has good hamburgers for 5000 rp. *American Fried Chicken* is on Jl Diponegoro, opposite the Hotel Khatulistiwa. There is also good, but expensive, western fare at the *Hotel Mahkota Kapuas*.

Things to Buy

It's worth looking out for *kain songket*, a material from Sambas with silver or gold thread woven into it. It is available from souvenir and material shops around the old market area, often at prices better than those at Sambas. These shops also stock selections of old (and reproduction) trading beads, cheap bags of rough-cut gems, and beautifu old Chinese and Dutch china and glassware

Getting There & Away

Air Garuda/Merpati (☎ 34142), Jl Rahac Usman 8A, is open Monday to Friday fron 8 am to 4 pm, Saturday until 1 pm, and Sunda and holidays from 9 am to noon. DA (☎ 32313), Jl Veteran Baru Blok B/1; Boura (☎ 37261), Jl Pahlawan 3A; and Deray (☎ 32835; office at airport) also service Por tianak.

Flights between Pontianak and Jakart cost 245,000 rp on Merpati and Bourac Merpati has five flights daily and same-da connections via Jakarta to Bandarlampung Bengkulu, Jambi, Padang, Palembang Pekanbaru and Tanjung Pandan (all on Su matra), plus Semarang (Java).

Merpati has flights to Medan and Batar (206,000 rp), and to Singapore three days week for US$125. There are also direc Merpati flights to/from Balikpapan (266,00 rp) twice a week.

MAS flies to/from Kuching on Monda and Thursday for US$74 (179,000 rp), an has connections to Kuala Lumpur (US$185 and Singapore (US$154).

DAS has three flights a day to Ketapang and daily services between Pontianak an Sintang (116,000 rp), Putussibau (190,00 rp), Pangkalanbun (173,000) and on to Sam pit (72,000). DAS flies from Nanga Pinoh t Pontianak every day (157,000 rp), but onl three days a week in the other direction Deraya has a similar schedule and prices t DAS, and better planes.

MAF (☎ 30271; fax 32757), Jl Veteran 9 goes to big centres which don't have com mercial services. If you are planning o trekking, it is worth flying into the jungl with MAF and coming out by foot or boat If you are hiking to East Kalimantan, MA has monthly flights as far as Tanjung Lokan It regularly flies to Kelansan, Serawai Sungai Ayak and Sandai in the south, and i considering adding villages in the northern hills of Central Kalimantan to its network.

Bus Pontianak's intercity bus terminal i

atu Layang, north-west of town. Take a erry to Siantan (150 rp) and a white bemo ɔ Batu Layang (350 rp). From there you can atch buses north along the coast to Singkaⱱang (4000 rp; 3½ hours) and Sambas 5000 rp), inland to Sanggau (7000 rp) or intang (10,000 to 13,000 rp), or over to ʼemangkat (7000 rp), Tebas (6000 rp) or ⸺artiasa (7000 rp). Singkawang buses leave ɪroughout the day. Others are less frequent, ut the mornings are busiest.

For the longer hauls to Kuching (30,000 ɔ; 8½ hours), Sintang and Putussibau, book arly at bus offices such as SJS at Jl Sisingmangaraja or Sinar Indah at Jl Machmut 68 (Siantan) for the best seats. Luggage is ɔaded at these offices, but you must be ⸺rried by bemo to Batu Layang to actually ⸱oard the bus. Buses arriving at Pontianak in ɪe wee hours will cut laps of the city until ʼ very last passenger is delivered to their loorstep.

ʼaxi There are scheduled taxi fares to destiⱭations such as Singkawang (85,000 rp), ʲambas (150,000 rp), Entikong (200,000 rp) ɪnd Sintang (250,000 rp). Ask at the taxi ʆffice in front of the Kartika Hotel.

ʲar & Motorcycle Renting a car in Ponɪanak is the perfect way to see coastal West ⸺alimantan at your own pace. Road condiɪions are good and traffic is relatively light. ʲitra Tour & Travel (☎ 36729), Jl Pak Kasih ʒ, rents a minibus or jeep for 120,000 rp per Ꮮay with a driver. Motorcycles are an option ʆor experienced riders only and cost around ʲ0,000 to 30,000 rp a day.

ʒoat There are five Pelni ships that regularly ʽonnect Pontianak with Jakarta are the ʆortnightly *Lawit, Sirimau, Binaiya* and ʒukitraya*, and the monthly *Tatamailau*. The ʼelni office is on Jl Pak Kasih on the southⱭrn bank of the river at the Pelabuhan Laut ᎠEwikora, and ticket sales are only in the ᵯorning.

For other ships ask at the entrance to the ʲort adjacent to the Pelni office. At least two ᵯon-Pelni cargo ships also take passengers on the Pontianak-Jakarta run daily (around 30,000 rp), but you might have to sleep on deck. Travellers have reported miserable conditions and long delays on some of these ships.

There are six daily jet boats to Ketapang (36,000 rp; six hours). This is more like a plane trip than a boat. The coastal boat leaves from just downstream of the Siantan car ferry.

Riverboats up Sungai Kapuas leave from behind the Kapuas Indah bemo terminal near the Hotel Wijaya Kusuma. Some, like the houseboat bandungs, leave from the pisini harbour near the end of Jl Sultan Muhammed. Bandungs don't usually take passengers, but they may make exceptions for curious foreigners. There are a few deluxe bandungs available for rent by upmarket tourists.

Getting Around

The Airport A counter at the airport sells tickets for taxis into town (15,000 rp). Alternatively, walk down the road in front of the terminal building to the main road in Pontianak, from where you should be able to get a bemo for 500 rp. It is a half-hour drive from the airport to the Kapuas Indah bemo terminal. Ticketing agencies in Pontianak can organise lifts to the airport for 5000 rp.

Local Transport The two main bemo terminals are in the middle of the city: the Kapuas Indah terminal near the waterfront, and the other on Jl Sisingamangaraja. There are taxis for hire next to the Merpati office and *becaks* (bicycle rickshaws) aplenty – the drivers overcharge, but they're not too difficult to bargain with. Should you wish to tour the city and environs with a taxi, the set tariff is 10,000 rp per hour with a two hour minimum.

Outboard motorboats depart from piers next to the Kapuas Indah building on the river. They cross the river to the Pasar Lintang and Siantan ferry terminal for 300 rp per person. A car & passenger ferry 100m downstream will take you to the other side for 150 rp.

KALIMANTAN

SUNGAI KAPUAS

Pontianak is the launching point for river-boat services along Indonesia's longest river. The Kapuas basin is broad and flat, making it hard to pick where the river ends and the surrounding countryside begins. The primary attraction is the river itself and the many vessels using it. As elsewhere in Kalimantan, take a slow boat to see and photograph the river activity.

Boats of all shapes and sizes journey the Kapuas, but the standard is a double-deck bandung with beds on the upper deck which takes passengers from Pontianak to Putussibau for 33,000 rp. Allow five days. A boat to Sintang (about 700 km by river from Pontianak) costs 15,000 rp per person and takes two days and one night. This includes basic meals, but you're well advised to supplement the meagre fish and rice diet with food from Pontianak.

Cheap, fast and reliable buses from Pontianak to Sintang (12,500 rp; seven hours) are rapidly superseding the regular passenger services along the lower Kapuas; however, boats remain the dominant mode of moving people beyond Sintang. Daily speedboats ferry passengers from Sintang to the larger centres of Putussibau (43,000 rp; eight hours) and Nanga Pinoh, as well as Semitau, Merakai, Separk and Mengkirai, or there are the irregular slow boats.

On your return to Sintang from upstream, there will be touts aplenty to meet the speedboats and shove Pontianak bus tickets into your hand. Prices and departure times vary widely, so go instead to the ticket sellers at the town bus terminal to hunt out the best deal.

Sintang

A wave of transmigration brought 15,000 new farming families to the Sintang area in the early 1980s, but most migrants come to this area to service the logging boom. Sintang, situated halfway up the Kapuas between Pontianak and Putussibau, has better accommodation than you might expect for such a small town.

The nearby **Gunung Kelam** monolith of-

1 Sesean
2 Losmen Setia
3 Ranah Minang
4 Losmen Central
5 Warkop Valentine
6 Flamboyan
7 Bemo Terminal
8 Bakso 33
9 Market
10 Bus Terminal

Speedboats to
Putussibau &
Nanga Pinoh

To Intercity
Bus Terminal
(5km)

Sintang

0   50   100 m

fers a challenging hike, jungle, a waterfall butterflies and panoramic views of the surrounding countryside. Take a white bemo to Pasar Impres (400 rp) and then a Kelam bemo to the base (2000 rp). A road circles the hill and you can be dropped off at the gaudy park entrance. The stepped path to the top, including steel ladders over more difficult rock faces, is one of the best you will find anywhere, but it takes hours and the going is difficult.

Places to Stay The *Sesean*, a friendly place on the waterfront, has tiny singles from 6500 rp, doubles for 8500 rp and rooms with bath for 23,000 rp. The *Flamboyan* charges 9000 rp for a double, 12,000 rp for a double with fan, 28,000 rp with private bath, and 35,000 rp with bath and air-con. The *Losmen Setia* and *Losmen Central* are both a little cheaper.

Places to Eat For strong coffee, reasonable food and a view of the riverside activity, join the rest of the gossips at *Warkop Valentine. Bakso 33* has conventional Indonesian fare and *Ranah Minang* has passable Padang food. Otherwise there are coffee and cake stalls around the market.

Putussibau

The Dutch were conspicuous by their absence from much of inland Kalimantan until the turn of the century. Even then, the colonial presence tended to be for security rather than economic reasons. The first district officer was stationed in Putussibau in 1895

Today Putussibau is an important market

wn, pretty and quiet. A few km upstream
ere traditional attractions, such as the long-
use villages of **Melapi I** and **Sayut** on the
apuas. Along the Sungai Mendalam there
a new longhouse at **Semangkok I** and a
uch older one just upstream at **Semang-
ok II**. Get there by speedboat for 15,000 to
0,000 rp.

laces to Stay The *MESS Pemdaer* governent hostel on Jl Merdeka is frequented by
ad contractors. Apart from a noisy TV
unge at the front, it is great value with
ean rooms with private mandi for 12,000
 15,000 rp.

The *Marisa Hotel* on Jl Melati has a sad-
oking bar downstairs, and rooms upstairs
r 12,000 rp, 20,500 rp with mandi and
5,500 rp with air-con. The sleazy *Losmen
arapan Kita*, Jl Pelita, faces the river and
as small rooms from 7500 rp.

One option for solo women travellers is to
ut up at the Catholic mission school of the
uster Belanda. Offer to pay.

laces to Eat The unnamed 'Muslim' eatery
Jl Melati 5, next door to the Hotel Melati,
as excellent sate, green vegetables, rice and

mixed dishes; it's great value. There is OK
bakso and coffee in the small Chinese
warung on the boardwalk behind the DAS
agent, and strong coffee and cake from the
warung on the corner of Jl Pelita and the
boardwalk.

Getting There & Away There are various
transport options to/from Putussibau.

Air MAF, better known locally as 'air missi',
flies between Putussibau and Sintang, while
DAS flies direct to Pontianak (190,000 rp).
Occasionally, MAF flies beyond Putussibau
to Tanjung Lokan.

Bus Pioneering souls might like to try the
buses between Sintang and Putussibau, or
hitch a ride with the road contractors. Good
luck. Let us know if the 'road' improves.

Boat Arriving speedboats will drop you off
at the dock in front of the house of the *bupati*
(district head); however, boats heading
downstream depart from Terminal SDS, 4.5
km from town. Bemos to the terminal usually
cost 300 rp, but if you are rushing to catch
that 6 am boat, haggle for a 2000 rp charter.
It is possible to connect with a bus from
Sintang and be in Pontianak, Entikong or
Singkawang that night.

Putussibau to Long Apari
The hardy, intrepid and wealthy can begin a
river and jungle trek eastwards from Putussibau, across the West-East Kalimantan
border through the Muller Range to Long
Apari at the headwaters of the Mahakam.
The going is arduous and expenses can be
considerable. It is easier and probably
cheaper to do this trek in reverse from Samarinda, where there are experienced
guides.

From Putussibau, the first step is to arrange a knowledgeable guide – the bupati
can assist. There will be plenty of guides
willing to take your cash, but few with
detailed knowledge of the track and local
languages. If guides cannot be found in
Putussibau, you can postpone this until you

KALIMANTAN

To SDS Terminal
(Speedboat
Departures: 4.5km)

Jalan Merdeka

To MAF
Terminal
(300m)

Jalan Pelita

Jalan Melati

Sungai Sibau

To Melapi I

Sungai Kapuas

To Airport
& Sintang

Putussibau
Not to Scale

1 MESS Pemdaer Hostel
2 Bemo Terminal
3 Bupati's House
4 Market
5 Police Post
6 Muslim Restaurant
7 Marisa Hotel
8 Bakso Warung
9 Losmen Harapan Kita
10 DAS Agent &
   Speedboat Bookings
11 Coffee & Cake Warung
12 Dock (Speedboat
   Arrivals)
13 Mosque

reach the village of Tanjung Lokan. Do not attempt the trip beyond Tanjung Lokan alone, as the trails are not well marked.

In Putussibau, stock up on provisions for you and your guide(s) – allow about 100,000 rp for rice, sugar, coffee, eggs, canned fish and tobacco. Then charter a motorised canoe for 350,000 to 450,000 rp – bargain hard – to make the one day trip to Nangabungan. From there you must charter a smaller canoe for 75,000 rp for another day's travel to **Tanjung Lokan**. Fuel is *very* expensive.

In Tanjung Lokan, find guides to lead you through the jungle into East Kalimantan. Some claim the walk takes two or three days, but allow five or six. Guides will ask for around 60,000 rp each, often more. Once you reach the logging camp west of Long Apari, the guides will turn around – you must offer them a substantial amount of rice for their return journey. From the logging camp it's a four hour walk plus a three hour boat ride to the village of **Long Apari**. You should be able to charter a canoe for the trip for about 35,000 rp.

This is rough country so travel light. You need food, a set of dry clothes to sleep in, basic medicines, cooking equipment and a sheet of strong waterproof material for shelter. Allow plenty of time each day for your guides to set up camp and hunt or fish for extra protein. You will almost certainly hanker for variation in your diet.

An added warning: many travellers report thefts on this route. To avoid disappointments lock up anything of value, including food, before handing your pack over to an assistant. If you get 'ripped off', you might just have to put it down to experience.

NANGA PINOH
An interesting side trip off Sungai Kapuas is from Sintang along Sungai Melawai to Nanga Pinoh. There are four losmen in Nanga Pinoh with rooms for 5000 to 20,000 rp. From Nanga Pinoh catch boats further south on the Sungai Sayan to the villages of **Kota Bahru** and **Nanga Sokan**. The journey entails riding sections of thrilling rapids and spending nights in Ngaju Dayak villages.

Boat fares from Nanga Pinoh to Nanga Sokan should be about 12,000 rp. Allow a week to do the trip from Sintang. You can fly back to Pontianak from Nanga Pinoh (book ahead), or hire guides for the difficult two or three day trek to Central Kalimantan. (See the following section.)

NANGA PINOH TO PANGKALANBUN
This route is an option for those travelling light. Take a speedboat from Nanga Pinoh to **Nanga Sokan** (25,000 rp; four hours), and stay with the hospitable *camat*, the subdistrict head. (Just 2½ hours walk from Nanga Sokan is a modern longhouse at **Batu Begansar**.) The walk from Nanga Sokan to Central Kalimantan is a two day adventure across hills and rivers. Guides from Nanga Pahan cost 40,000 rp for two.

A speedboat from Nanga Sokan to **Nanga Pahan** is 50,000 rp. From Nanga Pahan walk about four hours to **Kediman** and then another five hours on to a logging base camp of the Corindo group. If the guides tell you after two hours of strenuous walking that you've reached Kediman (two huts in the forest), don't believe them. It will take at least three hours. After Kediman, it takes another two hours to reach the main logging road and another three to get to the base camp. From the base camp, hitch a lift to logging camps further south, then take a 15,000 rp taxi to **Pangkalanbun**. (See Pangkalanbun in the Central Kalimantan section for more information.) The path between Nanga Pahan and the logging road crosses various rivers about 20 times. It is impossible to find your way without a guide. Beware of dehydration.

SINGKAWANG
This predominantly Hakka Chinese town boomed in the early 18th century when minefields from Sambas to Pontianak were realising about one-seventh of total world gold production. Powerful Chinese associations ran the show, especially on the rich Montrado fields, and an agricultural infrastructure soon sprang up to supply the miners. Hakka is still the *lingua franca*.

New, some say illegal, open-wash mining Montrado is stimulating some activity, but otherwise Singkawang is pretty quiet. If you've travelled along the west coast of West Malaysia, the atmosphere and colonnaded shop architecture will seem familiar. If nothing else, it's probably the cleanest town in Indonesia. It's a day trip from Pontianak and a good base for a day trip to Sambas.

Singkawang's main attraction is nearby Pasir Panjang beach, a three km stretch of white sand and calm water with few people except on public holidays. Pasir Panjang is a 20 minute drive out of Singkawang just off the Singkawang-Pontianak road. (See Pasir Panjang Beach later in this section.)

Places to Stay

Singkawang is best avoided by budget travellers, or visited as a day trip from Pontianak: accommodation tends to be expensive.

The hotel precinct is in the noisy commercial hub at the northern end of Jl Diponegoro

near the main mosque and Chinese temple. The *Hotel Khatulistiwa Plaza* (☎ 31697) at Jl Selamat Karman 17 has decent rooms from 10,500 rp with private mandi. Across the road, the *Hotel Pelita* has surly staff and rundown rooms from 12,000 rp.

The best hotel in this price range is the *Hotel Duta Putra Kalbar* (☎ 31430) at Jl Diponegoro 32, diagonally opposite the Khatulistiwa Plaza. The 10,000 rp rooms are small, but all have fans and clean mandi. Larger rooms are 13,000 rp and for an extra 25,000 rp you get air-con.

In the Kal-Bar Theatre complex on nearby Jl Kepol Machmud, the *Hotel Kalbar* (☎ 31404) has reasonable rooms for 15,000 rp. There's a fridge in the lounge area stocked with cold beer – a rarity in Singkawang. Air-con rooms cost 26,000 rp.

About one km south of town is Singkawang's best mid-range accommodation, the *Hotel Palapa* (☎ 31449) on Jl Ismail Tahir. It's a pleasant, clean place, if a little isolated,

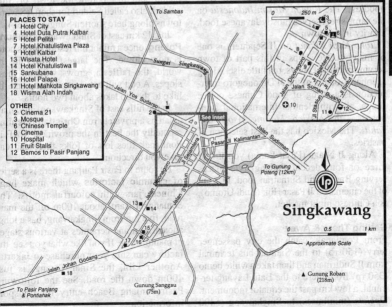

PLACES TO STAY
1 Hotel City
4 Hotel Duta Putra Kalbar
5 Hotel Pelita
7 Hotel Khatulistiwa Plaza
9 Hotel Kalbar
13 Wisata Hotel
14 Hotel Khatulistiwa II
15 Sankubana
16 Hotel Palapa
17 Hotel Mahkota Singkawang
18 Wisma Alah Indah

OTHER
2 Cinema 21
3 Mosque
6 Chinese Temple
8 Cinema
10 Hospital
11 Fruit Stalls
12 Bemos to Pasir Panjang

Singkawang

Approximate Scale

▲ Gunung Roban (218m)

with economy rooms with air-con and TV from 32,000 rp, to VIP rooms for 70,000 rp. Just opposite is the depressingly quiet *Sankubana*, with rooms from 17,500 rp (28,500 rp with air-con).

The top accommodation in town is the *Hotel Mahkota Singkawang* (☎ 31244; fax 31491) on Jl Diponegoro 1. It has a swimming pool, disco and air-con rooms from 90,000 to 250,000 rp.

Places to Eat

Chinese food is your best bet. The *Rumah Makan Tio Ciu Akho* at Jl Diponegoro 106 serves fabulous kue tiaw goreng (fried rice noodles), loaded with shrimp, squid, wheat gluten and freshly made fishballs. Most of its dishes are prepared in the savoury Chiu Chao (Chao Zhou, Tae Jiu) style and the beer is ice cold (3000 rp). Look for the giant wood stove at the front.

Also on Jl Diponegoro are the *Bakso 68* and *Bakso 40* noodle shops, serving variations on bakso with mie (wheat noodles), bakmi (egg noodles) and kue tiaw (rice noodles). The *Rumah Makan Indonesia* on the same street serves mostly Javanese food, a rarity in this town.

Toko Kopi Nikmat on Jl Sejahtera is one of many coffee shops in this part of town serving excellent brews, but little else. Along Jl Johan Godang at the Jl Diponegoro intersection is a string of good Chinese coffee shops, all with Bentoel International signboards – the *Mexico, Malang, Asoka* and *Tahiti*. The Mexico has the best selection of pastries.

Along Jl Niaga (Pasar Lama) you'll find three or four decent Padang-style places serving Banjar and Sumatran food. In front of the cinema, on Jl Pasar Hilir (Budi Utomo), is a Chinese night market.

Getting There & Away

From Pontianak, catch the city passenger ferry (150 rp) to the Siantan bus terminal from Jl Sudirman and then take a white bemo (350 rp) from there to the Batu Layang terminal, a few km past the equator monument. *Opelets* (minibuses) to Singkawang (5400

rp; 3½ hours) leave throughout the day There is no longer a main depot in Sing kawang, so let your driver know where yo want to get off. When leaving town, you wi find buses outside Rumah Makan Asu Rumah Makan Aheng or along Jl Niaga.

From Singkawang to Gunung Poteng (se the following Around Singkawang entry catch a Bengkayang bus east for the 12 k trip (700 rp). Let the driver know whe you're going and he'll let you off at the fo of the hill. Or offer him a little extra to tak you up the hill to Wisma Gunung Poteng, t closed hotel.

Beyond Singkawang there are opelets a far as Sintang, a nine hour ordeal for a me 12,500 rp. You can also get *colts* (minibuse north-east to Sanggau (5200 rp), north Pemangkat (700 rp) and Sambas (see later this section) or east to Mandor (2200 rp).

AROUND SINGKAWANG

On the road to Singkawang from Pontiana you could stop at **Pulau Kijing**, a seasid picnic spot just before the town of Sur gaiduri, also called Seiduri for short. (Sever towns along here shorten Sungai to Sei.)

Just 12 km east of Singkawang is **Gunun Poteng**, once a minor hill resort, but its hote is now closed. The largest flower in th world, the rafflesia, grows wild on thes slopes. A colt will get you to Poteng and th hike to the top takes about two hours.

In the hills east of Singkawang, at Sama antan, is a privately run **Christian hospita** reputedly the best in the province. MAF i Pontianak flies lots of folks there and ca give you directions.

En route to Pasir Panjang there is a serie of **ceramic factories** which make hug Chinese jars with colourful motifs. Th Semanggat Baru, about 100m off the mai road, five km from Singkawang, has a long ancient kiln and ceramics at various stage of manufacture. If you like what you see, th factory can ship your purchase to Jakarta Another kiln, the Sinar Terang, is jus 400m down the road. See the followin Pasir Panjang Beach entry for transpor information.

ASIR PANJANG BEACH

st 12 km south of Singkawang, this mar-
llous stretch of sand and flat grassy picnic
eas is deserted on weekdays and in the
ornings. However, the locals dress up and
scend en masse on weekends and public
lidays. At the northern end of the beach is
ecreational park, the Taman Pasir Panjang
dah, with a swimming pool, disco and
arung area.

norkelling

eyond Pasir Panjang, Hotel Palapa runs
vernight snorkelling tours to a tiny, deserted
land beyond Pulau Lemukutan. Facilities
e basic, so bring your own food. It is a great
cape.

laces to Stay

otel Palapa has shabby rooms/cottages for
n outrageous 28,000/35,000 rp. Much
etter are its cottages set back from the beach
 its 'motel' section for 45,000 rp, or 56,000
 on weekends and public holidays.
amping is an attractive option, particularly
nong the casuarina trees that line the beach
 the quieter southern end.

etting There & Away

o get there from Singkawang take a bemo
om Toko Olimpik on the corner of Jl Su-
an Bajang and Jl Sintut (700 rp; 15 to 20
inutes) and get off at the Taman Pasir Pan-
ng gate or at the warung 200m further on.
rom there, you'll have a 500m walk to the
each.

AMBAS

rchaeological finds of Indian materials
dicate Sambas had connections with the
riwijaya kingdom and perhaps India in the
th century, and became an important port
ity in its own right from the late 13th
entury. The Dutch established a factory in
ambas from 1608-10, but showed little
nterest in colonising the area.

Palace ruins show a hint of the city's
ormer prosperity, but Sambas is now better
nown for its cloth – kain songket – a mat-
rial with silver or gold thread woven into it.

Check the prices in Pontianak before taking
on the weavers or vendors at Sambas market.
It might still be cheaper down south.

Colts from Singkawang to Sambas cost
2200 rp.

Central Kalimantan

Central Kalimantan was formed in 1957, after
a Dayak revolt calling for greater autonomy
from centuries of domination by Banjarmasin. It remains the only province with a
predominantly Dayak population, mostly
Ngaju, Ot Danum and Ma'anyan peoples. It
is also the least populated, with just 1.4
million people.

Bahasa Ngaju is the most widely spoken
dialect, and is the language of the Kapuas,
Palangkaraya and southern Barito regencies.

The main faith is nominally Islam, but
kaharingan is still widely observed. Kaharingan, which means 'life', is an indigenous
tradition passed from generation to generation through story telling, rituals and festivals.
Jakarta recognises the creed as a kind of
'Hinduism', the name used for any religion
that won't fit neatly into an officially recognised category. Every few years a major
intertribal religious festival called a *tiwah*
takes place in Central Kalimantan (see the
following Society & Conduct entry) and features a month of feasting, drinking and ritual
dancing.

The northern reaches of Central Kalimantan are mountainous, while most of the
province is low, flat and poorly drained.
Timber extraction has stripped most of the
province. Natural attractions include the
mountains north of Muara Teweh and Tanjung Puting National Park near Pangkalanbun
in the south.

The major river thoroughfares run roughly parallel from the northern hills to the
coast. Five canals built in the Dutch era join
the Kahayan with the Kapuas and two lower
branches of the Barito, cutting km off the
route from Banjarmasin to Palangkaraya.
The bigger rivers also carry phenomenally

KALIMANTAN

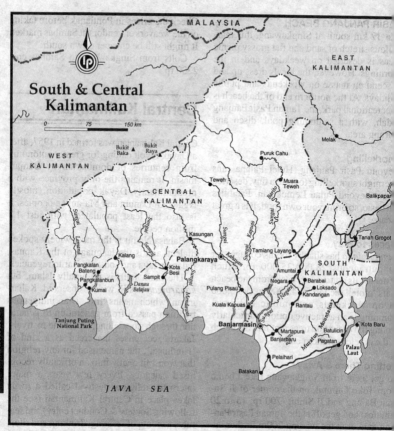

South & Central Kalimantan

0   75   150 km

MALAYSIA

EAST KALIMANTAN

WEST KALIMANTAN

CENTRAL KALIMANTAN

SOUTH KALIMANTAN

Melak

Puruk Cahu

Teweh

Muara Teweh

Balikpapan

Bukit Baka

Bukit Raya

Kasungan

Tamiang Layang

Tanah Grogot

Kalang

Palangkaraya

Kota Besi

Amuntai

Barabai

Loksado

Kandangan

Pangkalan Bateng

Pangkalanbun

Kumai

Sampit

Danau Belajau

Pulang Pisau

Kuala Kapuas

Negara

Rantau

Tanjung Puting National Park

Banjarmasin

Martapura

Banjarbaru

Batulicin

Pagatan

Kota Baru

Palau Laut

Pelaihari

Batakan

JAVA SEA

Sungai Lamandi, Sungai Arut, Sungai Sampit, Sungai Katingan, Sungai Kahayan, Sungai Kapuas, Sungai Barito, Sungai Mendawai, Sungai Negara, Muratus Mountains

long rafts of logs, some stretching almost a km and requiring three tugs to keep them in line.

Society & Conduct

Tiwah, Ijambe & Wara The region is famous for its *tiwah*, colourful interment ceremonies in which dozens of Ngaju Dayak families retrieve the remains of their dead from temporary graves and send them on their way to the next life according to the traditions of the kaharingan faith. Groups of villages participate, dispatching 60, 100, 150 or more long-dead 'spirits' in a month of feasting and ceremonies. The peak of activity is whe bones are taken from the graves, washed an purified to cleanse the spirit of sins. Wate buffalo, pigs, chickens and everything els needed for the journey to the next life a tethered to a totem then slaughtered. Afte more feasting, dancing and ceremonies, th purified human remains are transferred to th family *sandung*, house-shaped boxes o stilts.

Most tiwah occur along the Sungai Ka hayan, where there is one or two a year, an a major one every four or five years. Every one is welcome, even foreigners. Introduc

urself to the chief of the organising com-
ttee, explain why you are there, ask
mission to take photos, then enjoy the
spitality. Nothing happens in a hurry, so
n't be too surprised if the organisers are a
vague about the programme.

The *ijambe* is a Ma'anyan and Lawangan
ayak variation on the tiwah. In sending
eir dead relatives on the journey to the next
e, the bones are cremated and the ashes are
red in small jars in family apartments.

Wara is the funeral ritual of the Tewoyan,
yan, Dusun and Bentian Dayak people of
e northern Barito. They are far less con-
rned about the physical remains; instead,
ey use a medium in the wara ceremony to
mmunicate with the dead and show their
rits the way to Gunung Lumut, the nirvana
this branch of the kaharingan faith.

tong Pantan Another kaharingan tradi-
n is the *potong pantan* welcoming ceremony
which important guests are met by the head
the village, offered a machete and invited to
through *pantan*, lengths of wood blocking
entrance to the village. As they cut, guests
roduce themselves and explain the purse of their visit to purge themselves of bad
rits. *Tapung tawar* is an extension of the
tong pantan, in which guests have their
es dusted with rice flour and their heads
rinkled with water to protect them from
d spirits and illness.

LANGKARAYA

langkaraya (population approximately
0,000) was considered during the Soekar-
period for development as Kalimantan's
pital city. It is a large, clean inland town on
e Sungai Kahayan surrounded by an extra-
dinarily flat expanse of heath forests and
led transmigration settlements.

Palangkaraya, meaning 'great and holy
ce', was built on the site of the village of
handut and quickly developed into a
dern, regional centre. Literacy is gener-
y high and you will find some of the best
glophones in Indonesia here.

The town's chief attraction is the road
nnecting it to the nearby village of Tan-

gkiling. Built by the Russians during the
Soekarno period, this surfaced road leads 35
km to nowhere and appears to have no use to
justify the extravagance of building it. Eventually it will form part of a highway linking
Banjarmasin to Sampit and Pangkalanbun.

Information
The Dinas Pariwisata regional tourist office
(☎ 21416) at Jl Parman 21 has helpful,
English-speaking staff with brochures and
useful information on tiwah. Take an A or C
taxi (350 rp) and get out just west of the
stadium. Enter the office at the rear, from a
small street which runs parallel with Jl
Parman.

The local guide association has English-
speaking members who are often a step
ahead of the tourist office. Association sec-
retary Yusuf Kawaru (☎ 23341; fax 21254)
at the Dandang Tingang hotel can refer you
to helpful guides such as Aprianus Dulimar.
These people are young, educated and artic-
ulate, with an obvious affection for their
province.

Things to See
There is a lively **market** south of Dermaga
Flamboyan (the upstream ferry pier), a traditional house and art centre near the post
office, the sort of monuments and public
buildings that befit a well-planned regional
capital, lots of river traffic to watch, and a
string of souvenir shops between the Laris
and Melati Halmahera hotels. Other than
that, Palangkaraya is just a place to recharge
your batteries before launching inland.

The **museum** on Jl Cilik Riwut (Km 2½)
is open daily from 8 am to noon and 4 to 6
pm (closed Monday); admission is free. Take
an A taxi (350 rp) to Km 2½.

Places to Stay
There's a cluster of cheap hotels by Rambang Pier where the longboats, river ferries
and speedboats depart for Banjarmasin.
Even the cheapest places provide 'breakfast', usually sweet tea and banana in sticky
rice.

KALIMANTAN

Hotel Mina (☎ 22182), Jl Nias 17, is cool, clean and friendly. Singles/doubles with fan go for 10,000/15,000 rp, 20,000/27,500 rp with air-con; it's recommended. Next door is the *Losmen Putir Sinta* (☎ 21132) at Jl Nias 15. It's a good budget option – rooms with shared mandi range from 5000/7000 rp.

Losmen Mahkota (☎ 21672), across the road at No 5, has old rooms from 6000/9500 rp with shared bath, and new rooms out the back with mandi and car parking for 26,500/37,500 rp.

Losmen Ayu (☎ 34747) at Jl Kalimantan 147, near Rambang Pier, is small and grotty, but cheap. Singles start at 5000 rp and doubles from 7000 rp. *Losmen Harapan* (☎ 34047), Jl Nias 18, is markedly nicer – a tiny, family place with clean rooms, fan, and shared mandi for 5600/9000 rp.

Hotel Laris (☎ 34674) at Jl Darmasugondo 78 is friendly, airy and clean, although it overlooks a noisy intersection. It has great rooms for 11,500/14,000 rp. *Hotel Yanti* (☎ 21634), Jl Ahmad Yani 82A, is smart and clean with rooms from 14,000/17,000 rp; air-con suites with TV and hot water cost 27,000/30,000 rp.

The overpriced *Hotel Virgo* (☎ 21265) at Jl Ahmad Yani 7B has fan-cooled roo[?] ranging from 22,000 to 38,500 rp. The *A[?]das Hotel* (☎ 21770) at Jl Ahmad Yani 90[?] preferable. Decent air-con rooms here c[?] 46,750 rp.

Dandang Tingang (☎ 21805) at Jl Y[?] Sudarso 13 is Palangkaraya's luxury hot[?] with cheery, helpful staff who speak Engli[?] Japanese and basic French. It's a long hi[?] from the centre of town, but C taxi buses r[?] straight past the front. The hotel has a resta[?] rant, bar and disco. All air-con rooms star[?] 42,000/60,000 rp; it's highly recommende[?]

Places to Eat

Fish and freshwater cray hold pride of pla[?] in Banjarmasin cuisine. *Depot Makan[?] Sampurna*, Jl Jawa 49, serves some of [?] best barbecued fare, including delicio[?] river cray and patin fish. The patin is cons[?] ered a delicacy upriver, selling at markets [?] up to 20,000 rp a kg. Nearby *Rumah Mak[?] Almuminum* on Jl Halmahera reputedly [?] the best fish place in town.

Both restaurants face stiff competiti[?] from a lively, colourful night *market* on [?] Halmahera and Jl Jawa where there [?] plenty of cheap noodle and rice dishes, p[?]

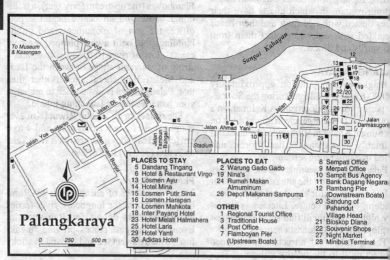

Palangkaraya

0   250   500 m

PLACES TO STAY
5 Dandang Tingang
6 Hotel & Restaurant Virgo
13 Losmen Ayu
14 Hotel Mina
15 Losmen Putir Sinta
17 Losmen Harapan
18 Inter Payang Hotel
23 Hotel Melati Halmahera
25 Hotel Laris
29 Hotel Yanti
30 Adidas Hotel

PLACES TO EAT
2 Warung Gado Gado
19 Nina's
24 Rumah Makan Almuminum
26 Depot Makanan Sampurna

OTHER
1 Regional Tourist Office
3 Traditional House
4 Post Office
7 Flamboyan Pier (Upstream Boats)
8 Sempati Office
9 Merpati Office
10 Sampit Bus Agency
11 Bank Dagang Negara
12 Rambang Pier (Downstream Boats)
20 Sandung of Pahandut Village Head
21 Bioskop Diana
22 Souvenir Shops
27 Night Market
28 Minibus Terminal

colourful range of very cheap seasonal
uit. There are coffee *warungs* around the
ocks.

For moderately priced Indonesian fare, try
ina's at Jl Murjani 14A, the *Sampaga* at Jl
urjani 100 or the *Virgo Restaurant* at the
tel of the same name on Jl Ahmad Yani 7B.
ose to the Hotel Virgo, you will find decent
dang food at *Simpang Raya*. For Chinese
od try the *Tropicana* on Jl Darmasugondo
the *Depot Gloria* on Jl Murjani.

For breakfast, consider *Warung Gado
ado* near the regional tourist office. Its one
ole has a smorgasbord of fried banana,
mpe (fermented soybean cake) cakes,
nanas wrapped in rice and other cheap
odies, washed down with coffee. Alter-
tely, opt for gado gado (the house speciality)
choose fresh eggs from the basket on the
ble and order accordingly.

etting There & Away
r Sempati (☎ 21612) is at Jl Ahmad Yani
  Merpati (☎ 21411) has an office at Jl
hmad Yani 69A, DAS (☎ 21550) is at Jl
ilono 2 and Bouraq (☎ 21622) is at Jl
hmad Yani 84.

Bouraq flies from Palangkaraya to Ban-
rmasin and Sampit twice daily and to
ngkalanbun daily.

Merpati connects Palangkaraya with Ba-
:papan, Banjarmasin, Buntok, Jakarta,
uara Teweh, Surabaya and Tubangsamba.
DAS flies daily to Pangkalanbun with
nnections to West Kalimantan and Kuala
urun. Sempati has daily flights to Balik-
pan and Surabaya, and connections to
rious other destinations.

us & Jeep
Patas Tours (☎ 23307), Jl Yani
, has jeeps leaving for Kuala Kapuas twice
ily (four hours; 20,000 rp). Alternatively,
ke a regular minibus to Pulang Pisau (7000
), cross the river for 500 rp, then take
other regular bus to Kuala Kapuas for
'50 rp. From there you can connect with
gular buses to Banjarmasin (5600 rp).

Patas claims it can get you to Sampit in
ss than seven hours (15,000 rp), weather
rmitting.

Dimendra Perkasa Travel at Jl Yani 30
charges 17,000 rp to Sampit and 41,000 rp
to Pangkalanbun. Wet-season trips require
three vehicle changes and 20 plus hours. It is
probably better to wait until roads are built.

Boat Boats downstream to Banjarmasin leave
from the Dermaga Rambang (Rambang Pier)
near the hotel cluster. Speedboats to Banjarmasin cost 27,000 rp (and take about six
hours), 20,000 rp to Kuala Kapuas and
17,000 rp to Pulang Pisau. Buy your ticket
from the little office at the pier. The river
ferries (bis air) take about 18 hours to Banjarmasin, but they're much cheaper – 6500 rp.
Buy your ticket from the larger office at the
dock.

Boats heading upstream leave from Dermaga Flamboyan. Two daily speedboats
terminate at Tewah, six hours (35,000 rp)
upstream. The slow boats take two days and
cost 25,000 rp.

To go beyond Tewah, you can charter a
small boat. Tewah to Tubangkurik will cost
about 50,000 rp, or up to 200,000 rp by
klotok (motorised canoe). Your choices
usually depend on the condition of the water:
too high is dangerous, too low is too much
like hard work.

Getting Around
The Airport The airport is on the edge of town,
but there are no direct roads. Taxis cost 9000
rp, but you can share with up to four others.

Local Transport Efficient taxi buses –
marked A, B, C or D – cost just 350 rp.
Choose your destination, then ask a local
which taxi will get you there. You can charter
a colt for 4000 rp an hour, or a motorcycle
for about half that. Hotels all advertise the
recommended rates. Becak drivers congregate around the dock and along Jl Halmahera
at the night market.

The terminal for bemos to Tangkiling is
way past the western boundary of Palangkaraya. It's a long way and it seems to take
ages to catch a bemo. There are frequent
bemos for the 25 minute trip from the terminal to Tangkiling.

KALIMANTAN

AROUND PALANGKARAYA

Around 35 km north of Palangkaraya is the **Tangkiling National Park**. The only thing of note out here is **Tangkuban Parahu**, a ship-shaped rock on the northern face of the hill with sweeping views of the surrounding countryside. Not far from Tangkiling is **Danua Tahai**, a lake, recreation area and nature reserve.

INTO THE INTERIOR

The main challenge is to get beyond the logging areas or find sections which have escaped the ravages of the chainsaw. Palangkaraya guide association members (see the earlier Palangkaraya Information section) can assist at a reasonable price, but travel to the interior is always an uncomfortable, expensive proposition.

One route is to take a speedboat from Palangkaraya to **Tewah** (35,000 rp, more in the dry season), charter a klotok to **Batu Suli Hill** and on to the longhouse settlement of **Tumbang Korik** (200,000 rp), hike from there to **Tubang Mahuroi** (spending a night in the jungle), and then head back downstream to Tewah or on to **Kuala Kurun**.

Another option involves motorcycles. Go from Tewah to **Tubang Miri**, by motorcycle south to **Tubang Rahuyan**, by klotok to **Tumbang Baringei**, by motorcycle to **Tubang Malahoi** (the site of a longhouse) and then by klotok or speedboat south to **Tangkiling**.

Alternatively, take motorcycles from Kuala Kurun north to **Seihanyu**, a klotok up the upper reaches of the Kapuas to **Seimandown** and on to **Jakarta Masupa**. Hike from there to **Masupa Rai**, a gold-rush field in a natural depression in the jungle, continue by motorcycle to **Tubang Masao** then by klotok downstream. It is also possible to take a boat from Tubang Masao to the Sungai Barito headwaters, past a series of rapids north of Tubang Tuan, and into territory so far untouched by the logging companies. These last options are the most difficult and expensive, but well worth considering if you have the cash and the stamina.

MUARA TEWEH AREA

Muara Teweh is the last riverboat stop Sungai Barito. Beyond Muara Teweh, trav is then by speedboat to **Puruk Cahu** in t foothills of the Muller Range. Hire Day guides for treks into the mountains in Pur Cahu. Near Gunung Pancungapung, at t border of Central and East Kalimantan, cement pillar marks the geographical cent of Borneo.

There is a bat cave, **Liang Pandan**, 10 k from Muara Teweh, while the **Bukit Par rawan** forest reserve and lookout is 40 k from town. The area is also known for gold and diamond mining, particularly arou Tumbang Lahung.

Places to Stay

Muara Teweh The *Barito* and the *Perm* have adequate rooms for 7000 rp per nig The Barito also has more expensive roo with private mandi. The *Gunung Sintuk* slightly better at 10,000/14,500 rp and rooms have private mandi.

Puruk Cahu In Puruk Cahu you can stay a longhouse.

Getting There & Away

Air Merpati links Muara Teweh with P angkaraya (76,000 rp) and with Banjarmas (115,000 rp). There are also flights fro Muara Teweh to Balikpapan.

Boat It's 56 hours by longboat from Banja masin to Muara Teweh. The fare is 17,000 per person and most boats have beds and warung. Speedboats from Muara Teweh Puruk Cahu take about 2½ hours and co around 20,000 rp.

MUARA TEWEH TO SAMARINDA

From Muara Teweh you can trek overland **Long Iram** in East Kalimantan and the catch a boat down the Sungai Mahakam Samarinda. (See Samarinda and Long Ira in the East Kalimantan section.) The tr takes up to two weeks and can be done your own, following logging roads – a d pressing way to see the jungle. Be sure

KALIMANTAN

ke sun protection and iodine to purify your ater. You can trek along more interesting ails if you hire a guide in Banjarmasin or uara Teweh.

NGKALANBUN

ngkalanbun is a dusty stopover where you gister with the police if you intend to visit njung Puting National Park. It is a fairly portant harbour for the cargo boats that n from here to Java. Very few ply the alimantan coast. Most travellers avoid ngkalanbun.

rientation & Information

ngkalanbun is little more than an over-own village with a small central area tween Jl P Antasari and Jl Kasumayuda. any businesses, banks, the post office, avel agencies and mosques are along these reets. There are also several cafes, a few otels and a large, swampy market. Bank egara Indonesia (BNI) near the passenger er on Jl P Antasari will change US dollar avellers cheques.

Try PT Dimendra Travel (☎ 22954) at Jl angga Santrek 11 for air tickets, and Yessoe ravel, nearby, for overland travel to Sampit d Palangkaraya.

laces to Stay – bottom end

he choice is not brilliant at this end of the arket. Once you have restocked and made nward travel arrangements, consider stay-g at Kumai. (See the following Tanjung uting National Park section.)

Losmen Selecta (☎ 21526), behind the emo terminal for Kumai, is central, very asic and one of the only friendly budget smen in town. Singles/doubles cost 7200/ 2,000 rp. Also recommended is the *Losmen andi Agung* (☎ 21183) on Jl P Suradilaga. has two wings, on either side of the road, d a restaurant. Rooms are 11,000/17,500 with private mandi. Triples are also avail-le at 22,500 rp.

On Jl P Antasari is the *Losmen Abadi* ☎ 21021), with fan-cooled singles starting 7000 rp, better singles/doubles for 14,000/

18,000 rp, and air-con ones for 30,000/ 35,000 rp. The *Losmen Mawar* (☎ 21358), around the corner on Jl Blimbing Manis, is a grungy option with rooms from 7000 rp.

The *Losmen Bahagia* (☎ 21226) is slightly expensive at 15,000 rp for basic rooms with mandi.

Losmen Rangga Santrek (☎ 21125) on Jl Kasumayuda is only worth checking out if everything else is full – it's not very welcoming to foreigners. Rooms cost from 7000 rp.

Away from the town centre is *Losmen Anda*, next door to the Hotel Blue Kecubung, with clean rooms from only 6500 rp.

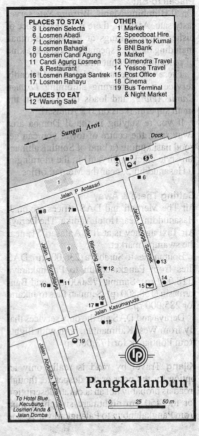

PLACES TO STAY	OTHER
3 Losmen Selecta	1 Market
6 Losmen Abadi	2 Speedboat Hire
7 Losmen Mawar	4 Bemos to Kumai
8 Losmen Bahagia	5 BNI Bank
10 Losmen Candi Agung	9 Market
11 Candi Agung Losmen	13 Dimendra Travel
& Restaurant	14 Yessoe Travel
16 Losmen Rangga Santrek	15 Post Office
17 Losmen Rahayu	18 Cinema
	19 Bus Terminal
PLACES TO EAT	& Night Market
12 Warung Sate	

Pangkalanbun

To Hotel Blue Kecubung, Losmen Anda & Jalan Domba

0   25   50 m

KALIMANTAN

Places to Stay – top end

The *Hotel Andika* (☎ 21218), Jl Hasanuddin 51A, is on the road from the airport into town. It's clean, the staff are helpful and the restaurant is good. Rooms range from 24,000 to 50,000 rp plus tax.

The *Hotel Blue Kecubung* (☎ 21211; fax 21513), Jl Domba 1, has well-kept economy rooms for 44,000/55,000 rp and standard rooms from 63,000/88,000 rp. All rooms have air-con. Given the state of the hotel, it's a little overpriced, but still the best in town. The Blue Kecubung has its own place to stay – Rimba Lodge – in the national park.

Places to Eat

On Jl Blimbing Manis, *Warung Sate* serves tasty sate. At night, there is a great choice of dishes from warungs at the bus terminal, including the local speciality, es kolak, a kind of pineapple-coconut smoothie.

There is barbecued chicken and friendly service at the warung adjoining *Losmen Candi Agung*, and loads of snacks in the small supermarkets on Jl P Antasari.

If you're staying in the Jl Domba area away from the centre of town, you can get good nasi kuning (a kind of South Kalimantan-style chicken biryani) in the morning at Jl Hasanuddin 2, near the Merpati office.

Getting There & Away

Air The Merpati and DAS offices are on Jl Hasanuddin, near Hotel Andika. The Deraya Air Taxi agency is at Jl P Antasari 51, near the swampy market.

Bouraq flies to Surabaya (236,000 rp). DAS flies from Pangkalanbun to Palangkaraya (118,000 rp), Sampit (72,000 rp), and Banjarmasin (158,800 rp). Sempati flies to Jakarta for 285,000 rp.

Deraya and DAS are the only services that fly from West Kalimantan, both with flights from Pontianak for 173,000 rp.

Kijang Travel by road is really only an option for the poor or the desperate, though 'road' is probably not an accurate description for the 450 km nightmare stretch of mud from Pangkalanbun to Palangkaraya. Yessoe

Travel can get you to Palangkaraya via Sar pit for 45,000 rp, but be prepared to sha your six seat *kijang* (4WD) with a doz other adults, plus children and luggage.

Boat Pelni passenger ships from Semara and Surabaya (both on Java) call at Kuma the access point for the Tanjung Puti National Park (see the following sectio every two weeks. The trip takes a full d and night from either Semarang or Surabay and the *ekonomi* fare is 33,000 rp.

If you can find a boat to Pontianak, expe to pay about 35,000 rp, including meals. T trip takes three days and two nights. For extra 15,000 rp you can usually get a bed a crew cabin; otherwise you sleep on t deck. If you can find a boat to Banjarmas you'll pay around 25,000 rp. Failing th catch a boat to Semarang, and get a Pel boat to Pontianak or Banjarmasin from the Pelni ships to Pangkalanbun leave every days and cost 23,000 rp in ekonomi a 31,000 rp with a cabin.

Getting Around

From the airport it's 10,000 rp to your des nation in town, or 30,000 rp for a two ho charter. If you are going direct to Kumai, y could charter a taxi at the airport for 30,0 rp – this includes a stop at the Pangkalanbu market to photocopy your passport and vis and at the Pangkalanbun police station f your registration to enter the reserve. Pangkalanbun, the easiest way to get arour is to flag down an *ojek* (motorcycle taxi) f around 500 rp. An ojek out to Kumai cos around 5000 rp.

TANJUNG PUTING NATIONAL PARK

The orang-utan rehabilitation camps Tanjung Harapan and Camp Leakey are li nowhere else in Indonesia: a sanctuary f humans and primates alike. Juvenile oran utan orphaned or rescued from captivity a reintroduced to the jungle at these centre under the supervision of rangers. As the grow and learn to live in the wild, the form captives spend longer and longer away fro the camps. However, some adults can't ki

e habit and usually return at dawn and dusk
eding times.

What sets Tanjung Puting apart is the
nse of refuge, absence of litter and the
vious affection the staff have for the ani-
als they work with. Canadian researcher Dr
irute Galdikas – known locally as 'the
rofessor' – founded the rehabilitation pro-
ammes in the early 1970s with the assistance
˙ the Leakey Foundation, the US philan-
ropic foundation which sponsors research
1 all of the great apes.

The orang-utan in Kalimantan and Su-
atra are the only great apes outside Africa,
1d Dr Galdikas knows more about them
an anyone. In the early days of her re-
arch, she would spend weeks tracking wild
rang-utan and was the first to document, for
stance, that the birth interval for orang-
an is about once in every eight years,
aking them vulnerable to extinction. Despite
eir playful antics in the camps, adult orang-
an are solitary in the wild.

Tanjung Puting National Park, now an
donesian conservation showpiece, encom-
asses 305,000 hectares of tropical rainforest,
angrove forest and wetlands. It is home to
vast variety of fauna, including crocodiles,
rnbills, wild pigs, bear cats, crab-eating
acaques, orang-utan, proboscis monkeys,
bbons, pythons, dolphins and mudskippers
kind of fish that can walk and breathe on
nd). This is also a habitat for the dragon
sh, an aquarium fish worth 700,000 rp and
ghly valued by Chinese collectors through-
ut South-East Asia. Unfortunately, both the
ragon fish and the crocodiles are occasion-
ly prey to poachers.

Most visitors go straight to the research
entre at Camp Leakey, or the quieter reha-
ilitation centre at Tanjung Harapan which
as established in 1989 to cope with the
xcess from Camp Leakey. At Natai Leng-
uas, further up the Sungai Sekonyer, there
a project to research the large populations
f proboscis monkeys and gibbons. Another
lea is to follow Sungai Kumai south into
umai Bay to visit the deserted beach of Tan-
ng Keluang, which is said to be a fine vantage
oint to enjoy a lovely sunrise and sunset.

Supporters of the orang-utan research and
rehabilitation work in Tanjung Puting could
send donations to Orang-Utan Fund Australia Inc, PO Box 447, St Leonards NSW
2065 (☎ (61-2) 9489 6341).

Orientation & Information
A trip into the park begins at the Pangkalanbun police station, where you must register
and give the friendly cop a bit of English
practice. Make sure you have photocopies of
the photo page of your passport and of the
page with your current immigration stamp.

Then head to Kumai, on the banks of
Sungai Kumai about 25 km south-east of
Pangkalanbun, and register at the riverside
conservation office (PHPA) north of town.
It's open Monday to Friday from 7 am to 2
pm and Saturday until 1 pm (closed Sunday).
If you're not planning to spend the night in
the park it's best to register a day in advance,
as the whole procedure takes at least an hour.

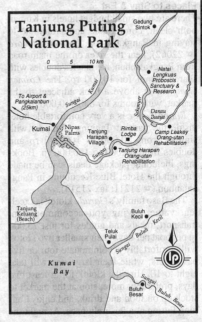

Registration costs 2000 rp per person per day, 2000 rp a day for a boat 'parking' fee, plus life insurance of 2500 rp (you can talk your way out of this one). You *must* provide a copy of your police letter from Pangkalanbun and a copy of your passport. The park office will give you three letters: one for you; one for the ranger stationed at Tanjung Harapan (or whichever other post you choose to visit inside the park); and the third for the ranger at the Orang-Utan Research & Conservation Project at Camp Leakey.

Guides

The PHPA may try to talk you into hiring a guide or two, but they're really not necessary as the boatmen know where to go and the rangers in the park are happy to accompany you on walks. However, some PHPA guides speak a little English and will also cook on overnight trips. The official PHPA guide rate is a bargain 7500 rp per day, but they may ask more. Use your discretion.

Places to Stay & Eat

There are two small budget hotels in Kumai, both clean, comfortable and preferable to staying in Pangkalanbun. *Losmen Kumara* (☎ 22062), near the river on the main road from Pangkalanbun, has singles/doubles with shared mandi for 10,000 rp. The *Losmen Cempaka* is above a bank adjacent to the market, with rooms for 8500/10,000 rp.

Rimba Lodge is a very comfortable hotel inside the park at Tanjung Harapan, with singles from 50,000 to 100,000 rp and doubles from 80,000 to 150,000 rp. Bookings, including package deals, can be made through the Hotel Blue Kecubung in Pangkalanbun (☎ 21211; fax 21513).

The Baso family's *Garuda* klotok is excellent value, giving you accommodation, transport, meals and guides for just 75,000 rp per boat per day. Their smaller two klotok will comfortably accommodate four or five passengers, while their large one will take eight to 10. Hire the klotok for at least two days, preferably more, stop at the market to stock up on food and drink, and enjoy Tanjung Puting at a leisurely pace. At night the

crew moors the boat well away from settlements, allowing passengers to enjoy the sunsets and wildlife in peace. Sleep on mattresses on the lower deck, wake to the haunting cries of gibbon at dawn and watch for the telltale splash of big crocodiles. Swim and wash in the river pool at Camp Leakey but be wary of the mercury-contaminated waters of Sungai Sekonyer. Allow time to explore the glorious jungle reserves around the rehabilitation camps and plan your river movements for dawn or dusk, when various primates come down to the river's edge.

The Basos' boats are in high demand around school and public holidays – the only time you will need a reservation. To book write to *Boat Garuda*, Baso (Yatno), Jl Idris Rt 6, No 507, Kumai Hulu 74181, Pangkalanbun, Kalimantan Tengah. Agencies handling bookings (and charging commissions) are Loksado (☎ 64833) and Arjuna (☎ 54927), both in Banjarmasin, and Ethanika Expresindo (☎ 4216373) in Jakarta.

Getting There & Away

Colt Kumai is about 30 minutes away from Pangkalanbun by colt. You can catch colts to Kumai (1000 rp) near the market by Sungai Arot in Pangkalanbun, or on the road to Kumai, which skirts the northern end of Pangkalanbun. This is the same road that goes to the airport. A detour to the airport will cost a little extra. Haggle hard.

Boat Pelni ships from Semarang and Surabaya call at Kumai every two weeks. Enquire at the Kumai and Pangkalanbun docks.

Getting Around

Klotok Public klotok, overloaded to within an inch or two of sinking, carry passengers to the tiny village at Tanjung Harapan for 2000 rp and to the illegal gold-mining fields upstream for 3000 rp.

Klotok hire costs 75,000 rp a day, takes four to five hours to reach Camp Leakey (plus stops along the way) and is considerably more pleasant. The added bonus of this option is that the klotok doubles as comfortable

ry accommodation and as your restaurant.
ee the earlier Places to Stay & Eat entry.)

peedboat Speedboat charter to Camp Lea-
y costs 100,000 rp a day and will get you
om Kumai to Tanjung Harapan in 45
inutes, to Camp Leakey in 90 minutes or
atai Lengkuas in 90 minutes. Most day
ppers opt for this.

ugout Canoe Dugout canoes with crew
in be hired in Tanjung Harapan for 7500 to
,000 rp per day. This is a better way around
ingai Sekonyer and its shallow tributaries.
ie canoes are also much quieter so you're
kely to see more wildlife. It is not unusual
see three to four metre crocodiles in this
ea.

South Kalimantan

outh Kalimantan (Kalimantan Selatan, or
al-Sel) is Kalimantan's smallest and most
ensely populated province with an area of
7,660 sq km and a population of 2.8
illion. Kal-Sel is an important centre for
amond mining, rattan processing and, of
ourse, timber. It is also the centre of Banjar-
se culture and a good starting point for treks
ito Central and East Kalimantan.

Traditional Banjarese clothing is made
om *kain sasirangan*, cloth produced by a
riking tie-dyeing process. The traditional
anjar-style house is the 'tall roof' design
id the best examples can be seen in the town
f Marabahan, 50 km north of Banjarmasin
n Sungai Barito. There are still a few around
anjarmasin and Banjarbaru, the remains of
ome in Negara and some impressive public
uildings such as the governor's office on Jl
ali which draw on this style.

In the mountainous north-eastern interior
f South Kalimantan are groups of Dayaks
aid to be descendants of the original Banjar
ace. These original Banjars may have been
imilies from the Barito delta area who fled
o the mountains to avoid Muslim conversion
1 the 15th and 16th centuries. Communal

houses *(balai)* accommodate up to 30 or
more families and serve as a ritual centre for
these mountain villages.

The province also has one million hectares
of wetlands, including 200,000 hectares of
tidal marshlands, and 500,000 hectares of
freshwater swamps. As elsewhere in Kalimantan, these rich reserves are heavily
exploited and becoming degraded, but their
sheer size still makes them a valuable refuge
for wildlife.

BANJARMASIN

Banjarmasin is far and away Kalimantan's
most interesting city. Indeed it is the only city
in Kalimantan worth lingering in for a few
days. The main attraction is the city's water-
logged suburbs traversed by canals; the
residents of Banjarmasin are up to their
floorboards in water and much of the city's
commerce occurs on water. Many houses are
perched on stilts or ride the tides on bundles
of floating logs. Don't leave town without
taking a tour of the canals and an early
morning visit to the floating market.

History

The upstream city of Negara is the site of the
region's first kingdom. Banjarmasin rose to
prominence in 1526 when Pangeran Samudera, a descendant of one of Negara's Hindu
kings, overthrew the ruler in Negara and
moved the capital to Bandar Masih, the
present site of Banjarmasin. The sultanate
became an important commercial power, on
a par with Brunei.

Competing English and Dutch interests
each established factories in Banjarmasin
between 1603 and 1814. Trouble erupted in
1701 after the British stationed a warship on
the Sungai Barito to guard their warehouses.
The Banjars revolted, and took six years to
evict the foreigners.

The Dutch felt the sting of Banjar resistance after placing an unpopular prince on
the Banjarmasin throne in 1857. A full-
blown rebellion followed, leading to the
Banjarmasin War of 1859-63. Rural Islamic
leaders led a courageous resistance, heavily
taxing Dutch financial and human resources.

KALIMANTAN

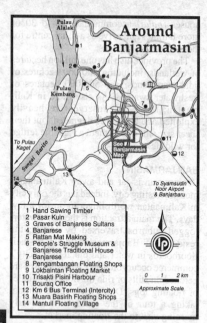

Around Banjarmasin

1 Hand Sawing Timber
2 Pasar Kuin
3 Graves of Banjarese Sultans
4 Banjarese
5 Rattan Mat Making
6 People's Struggle Museum &
   Banjarese Traditional House
7 Banjarese
8 Pengambangan Floating Shops
9 Lokbaintan Floating Market
10 Trisakti Pisini Harbour
11 Bouraq Office
12 Km 6 Bus Terminal (Intercity)
13 Muara Basirih Floating Shops
14 Mantuil Floating Village

0   1   2 km

Approximate Scale

The Dutch declared the sultanate to be 'lapsed' in 1860. By 1863 they were back in control, but sporadic resistance continued until 1905.

Orientation

Banjarmasin is big, but just about everything you'll need is packed into the city centre around the Pasar Baru markets along Jl Pasar Baru. There are two cheap 'homestays' just off Jl Hasanuddin and most of the big banks are along Jl Lambung Mangkurat. Travellers arriving by ship can catch small yellow *bis kota* (literally, city minibus) direct to Jl Hasanuddin (300 rp), but most others terminate at the Antasari market, a few hundred metres east of the city centre. The Sungai Barito lies to the west of the city centre.

Information

Tourist Offices The South Kalimantan regional tourist office (☎ 68707) at Jl Panjaitan 3, near the Grand Mosque, is open Monday to Thursday from 7.30 am to 2.[ ] pm and until 11.30 am Friday; it's closed[ ] weekends. The helpful staff can put you [ ] touch with the South Kalimantan Tour Guide Association and its adventure/jung[ ] guides. There is also a city tourist office ne[ ] to the Banjarmasin city hall on Jl Pasar Bar[ ] and an information counter at the airport.

Money Bank Dagang Negara, next to t[ ] Telkom office on Jl Lambung Mangkur[ ] has the best rates for travellers cheques, b[ ] insists on seeing your purchase agreeme[ ] Rates are less generous at the moneychang[ ] next to Diamond Homestay, and even wor[ ] at Lippobank and the handful of other ban[ ] willing to handle travellers cheques [ ] foreign currency.

Post & Communications The Telko[ ] office for long-distance phone calls is on [ ] Lambung Mangkurat, and the main po[ ] office is further south at the Jl Pangera[ ] Samudera intersection. There is a Hom[ ] Country Direct-Dial phone in the departu[ ] lounge of Banjarmasin's airport.

Travel Agencies Adi Angkasa Travel (☎ 5[ ] 131), Jl Hasanuddin 27, is run by the friend[ ] and informative Pak Mariso who, along wi[ ] his staff, speaks English. It also accep[ ] credit cards. The Borneo Homestay has [ ] travel agent, Indo-Kalimantan Tours, whic[ ] can book air tickets and arrange inexpensiv[ ] local tours and trekking. Other good age[ ] cies are Arjuna (☎ 54927), on Jl Lambun[ ] Mangkurat, and Loksado (☎ 64833), on [ ] Seberang Mesjid.

Guides The going rate for guides is abo[ ] 7000 rp per hour for local tours (includin[ ] transport to nearby Pulau Kaget, the floatin[ ] markets or Pulau Kembang) or 40,000 [ ] 50,000 rp per day for jungle tours (eg t[ ] Loksado). Johan of the Borneo Homesta[ ] and Indo-Kalimantan tours is the best loca[ ] source of trekking information and also ha[ ] a small team of excellent guides. At th[ ] regional tourist office, Akhmad Arifin speak[ ]

ry good English and moonlights as a guide
weekends and holidays.

ookshops Detailed blueprint maps of
uth and Central Kalimantan are available
Toko Cenderawasih Mas, Jl Hasanuddin
, between the Garuda/Merpati office and
Pos. Across the street a bookshop sells
ek-old copies of *Newsweek* and *Asiaweek*,
d there is a Gramedia bookshop in Mitra
aza for maps and magazines.

esjid Raya Sabilal Muhtadin

Jl Jenderal Sudirman, this is a giant mod-
n mosque with a copper-coloured flying
ucer dome and five minarets with lids and
ires. Also called the Grand Mosque, it was
mpleted in 1981 at the monumental cost
US$4.5 million and is the second largest
Indonesia. Despite the gaudy exterior, the
terior is a work of art.

oating Markets

he floating markets are groups of boats,
rge and small, to which buyers and sellers
ddle in canoes. Trading begins at dawn
d is usually over by 9 am. **Pasar Kuin** at
e junction of the Kuin and Barito rivers is
particularly fine floating market with canoe
fes among the hundreds of boats that con-
rge here. Pull up beside the canoe cafe and,
ing a bamboo pole with a nail pushed
rough the end, spike your choice from the
nerous smorgasbord.

anal Trips

verything happens on or around the water-
ays, so hire someone to take you around for
00 rp per hour in a motorised canoe. Allow
o or three hours, including a dawn visit to
e of the two floating markets. Start from
e mosque, go to Pasar Kuin where the
ngai Kuin runs into the Barito, perhaps
p at Pulau Kembang (see the next section),
ad past the sawmills of the Sungai Alalak
d back to town via the Sungai Andai. Johan
Borneo Homestay will provide a boat, or
k around the wharf near the junction of Jl
ambung Mangkurat and Jl Pasar Baru.

Don't hire a speedboat – they go too fast to
observe or photograph anything.

The kampung of **Muara Mantuil** is a floating village of houses and shops built on logs
lashed together. It's on a tributary of the
Barito close to the Trisakti pisini harbour.

Borneo Homestay has inexpensive tours
of the canals that are very worthwhile and get
rave reviews from travellers.

Pulau Kembang

Pulau Kembang is an island 20 minutes from
the city centre by boat. It's home to a large
tribe of long-tailed macaques who congregate at a decrepit Chinese temple near the
shore. On Sunday, Chinese families descend
on the place bearing gifts of eggs, peanuts
and bananas for the monkeys. The temple is
a decidedly minor attraction and, if you've
fed monkeys with peanuts before, it can be
safely dropped from your itinerary.

If you haven't fed monkeys peanuts before, hold on to your peanuts tightly or keep
them in your pockets if you don't want to be
mugged. The macaques here can be quite
aggressive when they're feeling peckish.

Pulau Kaget

About 12 km downstream from Banjarmasin
is a wetland reserve inhabited by the comical
long-nosed proboscis monkeys. Indonesians
call them *kera belanda*, or Dutch monkeys,
because of their long noses, red faces and pot
bellies. Borneo Homestay or the tourist office
can tell you the best time to leave Banjarmasin (this depends upon the tide) so you can
reach the island when the monkeys come out
to feed. Because they're very shy creatures the
boat pilots should cut the engines and glide
beneath tree perches so the monkeys won't
flee. Avoid boats with loud sound systems.

Speedboats at the pier at the end of Jl Pos
ask 45,000 to 50,000 rp for a round trip, or
you can pay 25,000 to 30,000 rp for a round
trip in a klotok, two hours each way. Smaller
boats can take you via south Banjarmasin's
narrow canals. You will also pass Banjarmasin's giant plywood mills, most of which
were built after a total ban on log exports in
the late 1980s.

KALIMANTAN

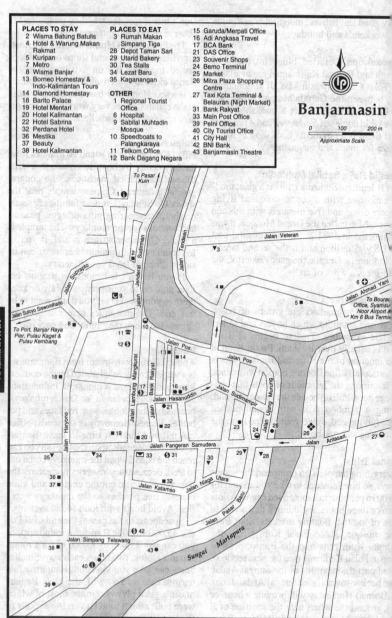

PLACES TO STAY
2 Wisma Batung Batulis
4 Hotel & Warung Makan Rakmat
5 Kuripan
7 Metro
8 Wisma Banjar
13 Borneo Homestay & Indo-Kalimantan Tours
14 Diamond Homestay
18 Barito Palace
19 Hotel Mentari
20 Hotel Kalimantan
22 Hotel Sabrina
32 Perdana Hotel
36 Mestika
37 Beauty
38 Hotel Kalimantan

PLACES TO EAT
3 Rumah Makan Simpang Tiga
28 Depot Taman Sari
29 Utarid Bakery
30 Tea Stalls
34 Lezat Baru
35 Kaganangan

OTHER
1 Regional Tourist Office
6 Hospital
9 Sabilal Muhtadin Mosque
10 Speedboats to Palangkaraya
11 Telkom Office
12 Bank Dagang Negara

15 Garuda/Merpati Office
16 Adi Angkasa Travel
17 BCA Bank
21 DAS Office
23 Souvenir Shops
24 Bemo Terminal
25 Market
26 Mitra Plaza Shopping Centre
27 Taxi Kota Terminal & Belauran (Night Market)
31 Bank Rakyat
33 Main Post Office
39 Pelni Office
40 City Tourist Office
41 City Hall
42 BNI Bank
43 Banjarmasin Theatre

Banjarmasin

0   100   200 m

Approximate Scale

Special Events

During Ramadan, the Muslim fasting month, Banjarmasin is the site for the festive *pasar wadai* or cake fair. Dozens of stalls sell South Kalimantan's famous Banjarese pastries near the city hall or the Grand Mosque. Muslims don't eat these delicious pastries until after sundown, of course, but non-believers can gorge themselves all day. The cake fair is at its most lively at the beginning and the end of Ramadan.

Places to Stay – bottom end

The *Borneo Homestay* (☎ 57545; fax 57515) in an alley just off Jl Pos is a good information centre and excellent place to be based. The owner, Johan, speaks English and knows South and Central Kalimantan well. There is a bar and rooftop lounging area upstairs overlooking the river. Single rooms without fan cost 7500 rp, with fan 10,000 rp and with private mandi 20,000 rp. At the time of writing Johan was installing air-con for two of the rooms.

The *Diamond Homestay* (☎ 50055) on the next alley is another friendly budget option. It is run by terrific staff at the moneychanger next door. Ring the bell above the door at the homestay on Jl Simpang Hasanuddin or knock on the blue shutters at No 58. This pleasant place charges 12,000/18,000 rp for singles/doubles.

Just over the iron bridge, the *Hotel Rakmat* (☎ 54429) at Jl Ahmad Yani 9 is sizeable with a friendly manager. Rooms cost 10,500/7,500 rp with shared mandi and no fan, or 14,000/17,000 rp with fan and no mandi. The *Hotel Kalimantan* on Jl Haryono near Jl Simpang Telawang (not to be confused with the luxury hotel of the same name) has rooms for 9000/15,000 rp.

The popular *Wisma Banjar* (☎ 53561), 500m from the Grand Mosque on Jl Suprapto, is a slightly more expensive option. Rooms range from 12,500 to 25,000 rp with air-con.

Places to Stay – middle

The comfortable *Hotel Sabrina* (☎ 54442), Jl Bank Rakyat 21, has rooms for 20,000/25,000 rp with fan, and 32,000/38,000 rp with air-con and TV; prices include breakfast. If it's full, you'll probably be directed to the nearby *Perdana Hotel* (☎ 68029) at Jl Katamso 3. Perdana has economy singles for 31,500 rp, doubles with fan for 37,000 rp and air-con doubles for 48,000 rp.

The city has a pleasant government guesthouse near the Grand Mosque, the *Wisma Batung Batulis* (☎ 53458). It has large air-con rooms with hot water for 48,000/65,000 rp. Foreigners are welcome. Also near the Grand Mosque, *Metro* (☎ 52427), Jl Sutoyo Siswomiharjo 26, has big fan-cooled rooms at 20,000/27,000 rp and air-con rooms at 42,000 rp.

The *SAS Hotel* (☎ 53054) on Jl Kacapiring has loads of character and pleasant staff. Singles start at 25,500 rp or 38,500 rp with air-con.

Once Banjarmasin's top hotel, the *Hotel Mentari* (☎ 68944) at Jl Lambung Mangkurat 32 is now sliding into decrepitude. There's a noisy disco on the 6th floor. Standard rooms cost 65,000 rp and deluxe rooms are 85,000 rp.

Places to Stay – top end

The *Hotel Kalimantan* (☎ 66818) on Jl Lambung Mangkurat is popular with tour groups, offering restaurants and a pool among its amenities. Its rates start at US$70.

The *Barito Palace* (☎ 67300; fax 52240) at Jl Haryono 16-20 has similar standards, but probably has the edge on the Kalimantan (there's little between them). Standard doubles start at US$70, while deluxe rooms are US$100. Discounts of 35% are often available for walk-in guests.

Places to Eat

Banjarmasin's excellent array of kueh (cake) includes deep-fried breads – some with delicious fillings – and sticky banana rice cakes; a cheap but tasty option for breakfast at the tea stalls. Stuff yourself for 300 to 400 rp, or even less at the canoe warung at the floating markets. Another breakfast option is nasi kuning (a local rice and chicken dish) from the *Warung Makan Rakmat*, next door to the Hotel Rakmat on Jl Ahmad Yani; it's open between 6 and 10 am. Across the street is a no-name *warung* that serves cheap and tasty soto banjar, another local dish.

A local speciality is ayam panggang (chicken roasted and served in sweet soy), but fish and freshwater cray hold pride of place in Banjar cuisine. There are a string of eateries along Jl Pangeran Samudera – try the *Kaganangan* at No 30 for local dishes. As with most regional cuisine, you only pay for what you eat. The *Lezat Baru* on the same street is reckoned to have the best Chinese food in town – it's not expensive.

Behind the Hotel Rakmat (Jl Veteran) is a string of moderately priced Chinese rumah makan – such as *Rumah Makan Sari Wangi* at No 70, the *Flamingo* across the road and *Rumah Makan Simpang Tiga* at No 22.

Depot Miara, on the corner diagonally opposite the Flamingo on Jl Veteran, has good bubur ayam, as does the *Rumah Makan Jakarta* on Jl Hasanuddin near the Garuda/Merpati office.

If you're on a tight budget or want a taste of street culture, eat at the tea stalls along Jl Niaga Utara between Jl Katamso and Jl Pangeran Samudera near Pasar Baru. There is a friendly tea stall next to the Jl Ahmad Yani bridge and another at Jl Hasanuddin.

Kalimantan's version of night markets is called *belauran*. Banjarmasin's is a huge affair at the Antasari terminal, another cheap eatery.

The Arjuna Plaza complex on Jl Lambung Mangkurat offers some superlative non-Indonesian fare for those willing to spend more. Carnivores will love the *Rama Steak House*, where grilled fillets cost from 10,000 rp. Cheaper here are char-grilled hamburgers and hot dogs. Japanese businesspeople congregate at the Arjuna's *Hakone Restaurant* for a taste of home.

The Mitra Plaza shopping centre has a popular restaurant, the *Steakhouse*. It's a little pricey, but worth splurging on if you've been trekking. Those craving western fare will find the Hotel Kalimantan complex on Jl Lambung Mangkurat harbours a *KFC* and a *Swenson's Ice Cream*.

For pastries, check out the famous *Utarid*

(also called the Menseng) bakery at Jl Pas Baru 22-28, near the Jl Antasari bridge. Th Utarid has cakes, whole wheat bread, a rang of biscuits and ice cream. The best views a from a rooftop cafe next to the Jl Antasa bridge, *Depot Taman Sari*, where you ca bring pastries from the Utarid and hav coffee or tea – the owners don't mind. In th evenings this place turns into a rather seed drinking spot.

The Mitra Plaza's *Hero Supermarket* is good place to stock up on goods for trekkir and the complex also has several fast-foc places.

Things to Buy

The central market (Pasar Baru) area sel hats of every shape, colour and material – th locals love them.

The city is famous for its kain sasiranga a kind of colourful tie-dye batik. A few shop along Jl Hasanuddin and some stalls in th market near the Jl Antasari bridge sell sas rangan. Otherwise troop out to the Cit factory at Km 12 to see the dyeing proces and make your purchases there.

Polished stones are a hot item on th streets of Banjarmasin. Just as touts flin boxes of wrist watches at you in Kuta, th touts here will show you their stones. Mos are polished and cut for bulky jewellery, bu some offer cut crystals, agates and othe interesting bits. Don't fork out more than yo can afford if you don't know much abou stones – there are a lot of fakes about.

The Malabar souvenir shops, adjacent t the bemo terminal off Jl Pangeran Samudera offer a rag-tag selection of worm-ridde carvings, but the occasional real antiqu appears on their shelves too. Bargain ver hard.

Getting There & Away

Air Garuda/Merpati (☎ 54203) at Jl Hasan uddin 31 is open Monday to Thursday from 7 am to 4 pm, Friday until noon and 2 to 4 pm Saturday until 1 pm, and Sunday and holi days from 9 am to noon. Bouraq (☎ 52445 is inconveniently situated at an office fou

n from the city centre at Jl Ahmad Yani
43. DAS (☎ 52902), Jl Hasanuddin 6, Blok
is across the road from Garuda/Merpati.

Bouraq has daily flights to Balikpapan
15,000 rp). It also services Surabaya
70,000 rp), Semarang (198,000 rp), Den-
asar (via Surabaya; 277,300 rp) and Jakarta
?98,700 rp). Occasionally there aren't
hough passengers and flights are delayed a
ay or so.

Merpati has direct flights to Surabaya
69,800 rp net) and Jakarta (298,500 rp),
nd connecting flights from there. Sempati
so has direct flights to its Surabaya hub,
here it offers same-day connections across
adonesia. DAS has handy flights to Pal-
ngkaraya, Muara Teweh, Pangkalanbun
58,800 rp), and on to Kalimantan Barat.

Adi Angkasa Travel at Jl Hasanuddin 27
a good place to buy air tickets and offers
ome discounts.

us Buses and colts depart frequently from
he Km 6 terminal for Martapura and Banjar-
aru (1600 rp). Night buses to Balikpapan
6,000 rp or 22,000 rp with air-con) leave
aily between 4 and 4.30 pm and arrive in
anajan, across the river from Balikpapan,
bout 12 hours later, where you must take a
peedboat across the river – the cost should
e included in your bus ticket.

You can break the trip from Banjarmasin
Balikpapan halfway by spending the night
n Tanjung. From Banjarmasin to Tanjung
osts 8500 rp and takes five hours. Tanjung
Panajan/Balikpapan costs 8500 rp and
akes six hours.

Regular day buses from Km 6 go to Balik-
apan via Rantau, Amuntai and Tanjung, and
here are buses to other destinations in the
outh-east corner of the island. To get to the
Km 6 terminal, take a yellow minibus (400
p) from the newspaper kiosks behind the
BCA bank.

oat All sorts of vessels leave from Banjar-
asin. From here you can travel by ship to
nother island or head inland by river. The
nain terminal for longboats heading upriver

is conveniently located on the Sungai Martapura, adjacent to the Grand Mosque.

Passenger Ship Ships leave for Surabaya
twice a week (16 hours) and Semarang once
a week (20 hours). The ships dock at Trisakti
pisini harbour. To get there take a bemo from
the taxi kota terminal on Jl Antasari for 400
rp. The bemo will take you past the harbour
master's and ticket offices.

The harbour master's office (☎ 54775) is
on Jl Barito Hilir at Trisakti. Opposite is a
line of shops with several agencies which sell
boat tickets to Surabaya, but Pelni fares are
cheapest from the Pelni counter inside the
harbour master's office. It's also possible to
book tickets at Borneo Homestay. Pelni fares
from Banjarmasin to Surabaya range from
50,000 rp in ekonomi, 103,000 rp in 2nd
class and 136,000 rp in 1st class. Fares to
Semarang are 58,000/118,000/156,000 rp.

Another agency for these ships is at the
Km 6 bus terminal and others can be found
off Jl Pasar Baru near the Jl Antasari bridge.
The Pasar Baru agents also sell less expensive passenger tickets for cargo boats that
leave about every two days – fares are
usually around 20,000 rp to Surabaya.

Pelni also sells tickets to Pangkalanbun in
Central Kalimantan. The ship leaves every
11 days and costs 26,000 rp in ekonomi.

Sailboat Schooners constantly ply the route
from Banjarmasin to Surabaya. First, go to
the harbour master's office for information
and for permission to sail. You are more
likely to get permission if you have a demonstrated interest in sailing, or want to
photograph or write about the trip. Then
approach the individual captains for permission to board.

Ferry & Speedboat Heading inland, one of
the more obvious courses to take is from
Banjarmasin to Palangkaraya, a journey of
18 hours in a bis air (river ferry) or about six
hours in a speedboat. You go up three rivers
– the Barito, Kapuas and the Kahayan – and
through the two artificial canals that link
them.

Speedboats to Palangkaraya leave from a dock at the mosque end of Jl Pos. From Banjarmasin to Palangkaraya is 27,000 rp and there are boats daily.

Bis air to Palangkaraya depart from the Banjar Raya pier on the Sungai Barito for 7500 rp.

Long-distance bis air which journey up the Barito leave from the river taxi terminal near the Banjar Raya fish market. To get there take a yellow colt (400 rp) to the end of Jl Sutoyo Siswomiharjo west of the city centre. The end of the route is the town of Muara Teweh in Central Kalimantan, 56 hours away and costing only 17,500 rp. The tariff includes the price of a bed.

Getting Around

The Airport Banjarmasin's Syamsudin Noor airport is 26 km out of town on the road to Banjarbaru. To get there take a bemo from Pasar Baru to the Km 6 terminal. Then catch a Martapura-bound colt, get off at the branch road leading to the airport and walk the 1.5 km to the terminal. A taxi all the way to the airport will cost you 12,500 rp. They cluster near the Garuda/Merpati office and the Hotel Sabrina.

From the airport to the city, buy a taxi ticket at the counter in the terminal, or walk out of the airport, through the carpark, past the MIG aircraft, turn left and walk to the Banjarmasin-Martapura highway. From here pick up one of the frequent colts to Banjarmasin.

Local Transport You can hire a boat operator to navigate the canals. Expect to pay about 7500 rp per hour without a guide.

On dry land, the area around Pasar Baru is very small and easy to walk around. You don't need wheels since the hotels, taxi terminal, airline offices etc are all grouped together. For longer trips there are taxis (60,000 rp a day, 12,000 rp for two hours), bemos (400 rp), becaks (1000 rp minimum), ojeks (500 rp minimum) and *bajaj* (three wheel motorised taxis, 1000 rp minimum). A bajaj from the city centre to Banjar Raya pier

is around 1500 to 2000 rp; by motorcycle costs 1000 rp.

Bemos go to various parts of town, including the Km 6 terminal, which is the departure point for buses to Banjarbaru, Martapura and Balikpapan. The standard fare is 400 rp.

Banjar becak drivers aren't predatory, b they are hard to bargain with. The baj drivers work the same way. Motorcycle tax wait at Pasar Baru and the Km 6 terminal an will take you anywhere. If you're travellir light this is a good way to get to the airpor

MARABAHAN & MARGASARI

For a glimpse of river life, take a speedbo from Banjarmasin to Marabahan, 65 k (7500 rp) up the Barito. It is a small tow with old houses, including traditional Ban jar-style wooden houses. The losmen on th river, such as the *Hotel Bahtera*, have room from 7000 to 15,000 rp.

From Marabahan there are charter boats Margasari (17,500 rp), a handcraft villag which produces lots of rattan and bambo products, such as fans, hats and maps. Fro there you can take a colt to Rantau (1500 rp and another colt back to Banjarmasin (250 rp), or hang around for a riverboat up Negara.

BANJARBARU

The chief attraction of this town, on the roa from Banjarmasin to Martapura, is its museur collection of Banjar and Dayak artefacts, an statues found at the sites of Hindu temples i Kalimantan. Exhibits include a replica of Bar jar riverboat equipment used in tradition Banjar circumcision ceremonies (includin an antibiotic leaf and a cut-throat razor cannons, swords and other artefacts fror wars with the Dutch, a small cannon used b British troops in Kalimantan, Dayak an Banjar swords, knives and other point things.

Probably the most interesting exhibit is c items excavated from the Hindu Laras Templ and Agung Temple in East Kalimantar including a Nandi bull and a *lingam* (th phallic symbol of the Hindu god Shiva). Th remains of the Laras Temple are in Margasa llage, near Rantau. Agung Temple is near muntai, 150 km from Banjarmasin. Unless ou're a hard-core archaeology freak, it's not orth going all the way to these villages to ew what are mainly heaps of rubble.

The museum is on the Banjarmasin to Martapura highway. Ask the colt driver to rop you off. It is open from 8 am to 1 pm, loses earlier on Friday and is closed on Monday. Dance performances are occasionally held on Sunday at 9 am, but it's a rare ning nowadays.

MARTAPURA

Continuing on from Banjarbaru you come to Martapura. The large market here is at its usiest on Friday when it is a photographer's aradise, with every type of food on sale and ots of colourfully dressed Banjar women. Unfortunately, the diamond mines do not perate on Friday.

A section of the market sells uncut gems, ilver jewellery and trading beads – the hoice, both strung and unstrung, is excel-ent. Be prepared to bargain diligently. The narket is behind the Martapura bus terminal. A few minutes' walk diagonally across the ports field near the bus terminal is a diamond-polishing factory and shop. Visitors can go through to the back, where the diamond polishers work. Don't think about spending too much money on diamonds unless you know what you're doing.

Backing on to the market is *Wisma Penginapan Mutiara*, Jl Sukaramai, where quite decent rooms start at 6000 rp.

Frequent colts leave from the Km 6 terminal in Banjarmasin. The fare is 1100 rp and it takes about 45 minutes along a good surfaced road.

CEMPAKA

A must-see are the Cempaka diamond fields, a short detour off the Martapura road. It is one place where you can see some of the smaller diamond and gold digs. The mines are, in fact, silt-filled, water-logged holes dug from muddy streams. The diggers spend the day up to their necks in water, diving below and coming up with baskets of silt which is washed away to separate the gold specks, diamonds or agates.

There are records of 20 carat diamonds from these fields as far back as 1846 – a 106.7 carat monster in 1850 and, the biggest

KALIMANTAN

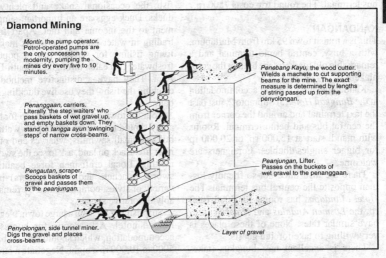

Diamond Mining

Montir, the pump operator. Petrol-operated pumps are the only concession to modernity, pumping the mines dry every five to 10 minutes.

Penanggaan, carriers. Literally 'the step waiters' who pass baskets of wet gravel up, and empty baskets down. They stand on *tangga ayun* 'swinging steps' of narrow cross-beams.

Pengautan, scraper. Scoops baskets of gravel and passes them to the *peanjungan*.

Penyolongan, side tunnel miner. Digs the gravel and places cross-beams.

Penebang Kayu, the wood cutter. Wields a machete to cut supporting beams for the mine. The exact measure is determined by lengths of string passed up from the *penyolongan*.

Peanjungan, Lifter. Passes on the buckets of wet gravel to the *penanggaan*.

Layer of gravel

of all, the 167.5 carat Tri Sakti (Thrice Sacred) found in August 1965. Most diamonds are a fraction of the size, but the hope of another big find keeps the miners focused on the job.

Diggers usually work in teams of 10 to 15, digging one day, sluicing the next, with men and women sharing the back-breaking work. Typically, there is a 'chief' who pays the miners 2000 rp a day lunch money to work the claim. If and when there is a find, 10% of the dividend usually goes to the land owner, 10% to the chief, 15% to the pump operator and wood cutter, 10% for tax and the remaining 55% is divided between the team. By-products such as sand and large stones are sold for building and road construction. The activity on the fields tends to follow the big finds. There are touts aplenty to show you the way, give you a lift and sell you polished stones.

Note that the diamond mines and polishing centres are closed on Friday. Take a Banjarmasin-Martapura bemo and ask to get off at the huge roundabout just past Banjarbaru (1600 rp). From here take a green taxi to 'Alur' (500 rp) and walk the last 500m from the main road to the diamond digs. Bemos leave infrequently from Martapura; otherwise charter a bemo from Martapura bus terminal. The round trip costs 7500 rp.

KANDANGAN

This is a transit town 95 km from Martapura, with a busy, central bemo terminal and a remarkable old marketplace built in the colonial era.

Kandangan has excellent accommodation at the *Bangkau Hotel*, Jl Suprapto 2, just past the taxi terminal and around the corner from the central bus and bemo terminal. Rooms with mandi start at 15,000 rp, or 20,000 rp for bigger singles/doubles. Foreigners are welcome.

There are also three not-so-friendly losmen opposite the central bus terminal. The *Hotel Mandapas* has rooms for 5000/7000 rp; the *Losmen Andalas* and *Hotel Sentosa* have similar rates. None of these places is very willing to take foreign guests.

There is excellent nasi bungkus (take-away rice parcels) with chicken or liver at th barrow stalls that set up at the bemo termin after 3 pm.

The bus from Banjarmasin's Km 6 term nal to Kandangan costs 4000 rp and take about three hours.

NEGARA

The north-western section of South Kal mantan is mostly wetlands and, towards th end of the wet season, they surround Negar making the city look like a very waterlogge island. The only land above water is th roads, but even they disappear occasionall

Negara was the capital of South Kaliman tan's first kingdom, the Hindu realm Negara Dipa, first ruled by Maharaja Emp Jatmika. In 1526 Pangeran Samudera, descendant of one of Negara's Hindu king overthrew his uncle – Pangeran Tumeng gung – and moved the capital to Band Masih, the present site of Banjarmasin.

One amazing Negara custom is the raisin of water buffalo herds on wooden platform They are released daily for grazing an drinking, swim up to five km and are herde home by 'canoe cowboys'. The wetlands ar also remarkable for their prolific bird lif fish, the occasional snake and plenty c ducks. Duck eggs are an important supple ment to the income and diet. Apart fron trading in water buffalo the locals make living fishing for serpent fish, a popula freshwater fish eaten throughout South-Eas Asia. They have a distinctive method c catching the fish – they use live ducklings a bait.

Tour the town by boat – 10,000 rp for hal a day should be enough to visit the wetlan buffalo, small sawmills, wharves and othe river life. Back on land, ask to see the sword making. Local craftsmen forge beautifu swords, machete and *kris* (daggers) in variety of styles, complemented by remark ably decorative sheaths.

Surprisingly for such a large town, Negar has no hotel. Ask around for homesta accommodation, which should set you bac 5000 to 10,000 rp a night. Negotiate a rate i

dvance. The cafes opposite the tiny cinema
erve a delicious ayam panggang, chicken
pasted and served in sweet soy. For break-
ast, look out for the eateries with trays of
oughnut-style kueh.

Getting There & Away

he bus from Banjarmasin to Kandangan
osts 4000 rp and takes 2½ hours. From
Kandangan to Negara you have the option of
us (1500 rp), shared taxi (2500 rp per per-
on), chartered taxi (20,000 rp) or ojek (7500
b). Twice weekly boats (Wednesday and
riday), direct from the Banjarmasin river
axi pier, cost 7000 rp and take a day and a
ight to reach Negara.

LOKSADO

Last of Kandangan in the Muratus Mounains is a collection of villages which are the
emnants of an animist Banjar society that
may have moved here from the Barito delta
o avoid the Javanese immigration of the
5th and 16th centuries. About 20 villages
re spread over about 2500 sq km between
Kandangan and Amuntai to the west and the
outh Kalimantan coast to the east.

Loksado is an important market village in
he area and a good base from which to
xplore. One of the best times to be in
Loksado is market day, on Wednesday.

Places to Stay & Eat

There's good accommodation at the government cottages on a river island in the village
10,000/15,000 rp a single/double). The
Loksado kepala desa (village head) takes
guests for 7500 rp a night, but charges a
ortune for food. Many of the villages in this
rea – such as Niih, to the south-west of
Loksado – will take guests for 5000 to
0,000 rp per night.

Those looking for a little luxury in this
neck of the woods should check out the
ecently established Amandit Lodge. The
pleasant rooms are fan-cooled and there's a
garden and a coffee shop. Rates range from
0,000 to 50,000 rp. Reservations can be
made at Ajuna Travel in Banjarmasin.

Eateries along the main lane from the suspension bridge are basic and shut down
shortly after dusk. The best breakfast is roti
fresh from the wok at a warung about 20m
from the bridge.

Getting There & Away

There is a good road to Loksado, terminating
just before the suspension bridge. Bemos
and pick-ups leave Loksado for Kandangan
first thing in the morning, and return from
Kandangan later in the day (4000 rp).

Coming back from Loksado, many travellers charter a bamboo raft and pole down
Sungai Riam Kiwa. The usual drop-off point
is Tanuhi, two hours downstream (35,000
rp), but it is much nicer to stay on board for
eight hours and get off at Bubuhi (45,000 rp).
From the nearby road, you can catch a bemo
or ojek back to Kandangan.

AROUND LOKSADO

From Loksado there are hundreds of paths
through mountain garden plots to other villages over the hills, many crossing mountain
streams via suspension bridges. Locals
bound across effortlessly, but the rest of us
manage to send the tangle of wire and planks
into a frenetic rhythm.

Follow the path upstream on Sungai Riam
Kiwa for three hours to a series of **waterfalls**
just past Balai Haratai. It is easy enough to
find the first waterfall, but local knowledge
is handy if you want to climb to the middle
and top falls, and find the nearby cave. Ask
at Haratai or get someone from Loksado to tag
along in exchange for some English practice.

Malaris

A 30 minute walk through a bamboo forest
south-east of Loksado brings you to the
village of Malaris, where 32 families (about
150 people) live in a large balai (communal
house). Stay the night at the invitation of the
village head (balai kepala) and offer to pay
7500 rp or so.

Treks

There is an excellent three day trek through
primary forest, via Haratai and Hudjung, to
Pagat and **Barabai**. Start from either end,

take guides and stay at longhouses along the way. Expect to pay 7500 rp a day per guide for assistance, plus 5000 rp for their return fares (by public transport). There are plenty of places to stay in Barabai, most of which look much nicer from the outside than inside. Try the *Fusfa*, where doubles start at 15,000 rp. Doubles elsewhere cost around 6000 rp per room.

There are also paths over the hills from Loksado to the coast. The trek to **Kota Baru** on Pulau Laut takes three or four days by a combination of foot, bemo and boat. It takes you through hillside gardens, forests and over Gunung Besar, the province's highest peak at 1892m.

There are also other treks downstream to Kandangan.

SUNGAI BARITO

From Banjarmasin, you can travel by river-boat up Sungai Barito all the way to **Muara Teweh** in Central Kalimantan and then by speedboat to the Dayak village of **Puruk Cahu**. From Puruk Cahu a logging road leads to **Long Iram** in East Kalimantan.

A boat from Banjarmasin to Muara Teweh costs 17,500 rp and takes about 56 hours. There are several budget hotels in Muara Teweh where you can stay for about 6000 rp. You can charter a speedboat to Puruk Cahu for 30,000 rp one way and stay in longhouses there. See the Muara Teweh Area entry in the earlier Central Kalimantan section for more information.

SOUTH COAST

An alternative route between Banjarmasin and Balikpapan is the coastal route via **Pagatan** and **Batulicin**. Set out from Banjar-masin's Km 6 terminal before 7 am, take a Batulicin air-con bus (8000 rp) and get out at Pagatan. Get a 1000 rp becak to the losmen on the beach. Nearby, there are schooners under construction. On 17 April each year, local Bugis make offerings to the sea at the end of week-long celebrations.

From Pagatan, take a bemo to Batulicin and then 75 km further to **Bangkalan**. Get out at Km 325 and ask locals to direct you to

nearby caves, where cave swiftlet nests are collected. The nests are used to make birds nest soup and medicine. Black ones sell for 300,000 rp and white ones for 800,000 rp, or up to 1.5 million rp in Surabaya.

Local transport connections continue through to Balikpapan in East Kalimantan.

East Kalimantan

East Kalimantan is the largest (202,000 s km) and richest province in Kalimantan with a population of 2.1 million people. Indonesia earns a big share of its export income from East Kalimantan's lucrative oil, timber and natural gas industries, plus its rapidly expanding coal and gold ventures.

While most commercial activity is along the coast and the Sungai Mahakam valley, far into the interior once-thriving Dayak cultures are confronting dramatic change in the face of logging and mining activity. With time and planning you can reach places that rarely see a foreign face, and enjoy pockets of wilderness, but loggers and the military are ever-present.

Fifth century Sanskrit inscriptions found in the Wahau Valley north of Tenggarong are all that remains of one of Indonesia's oldest Hindu kingdoms and its contact with Indian and Sriwijaya merchants. Its successor, the Sultanate of Kutai, was founded in the 13th century with the assistance of refugees from strife-torn East Java. Kutai became an important regional trading power and its capital, Tenggarong, remained East Kalimantan's largest and busiest urban centre until eclipsed by Samarinda and Balikpapan this century.

The region has had its share of opportunists, such as the pirate Arung Singkang, a descendant of the Bugis royal family of Wajo in Sulawesi Selatan. (See the 'Borneo' Private Colonists' aside at the beginning of this chapter.)

Full-scale exploitation of the Mahakam delta's oil reserves began in 1897, shifting the focus of commerce to the oil refineries at

likpapan. By 1913 the province was pro-
cing more than half of the East Indies' oil
tput and Balikpapan has been riding the
oms and busts of the oil market ever since.
Government transmigration schemes ac-
unted for 114,000 newcomers to East
alimantan (Kalimantan Timur or Kal-Tim)
tween 1954 and 1985, with over half set-
ng in the Kutai regency. Despite an acute
ortage of arable land, transmigration still
counts for a significant share of population
owth.

The various Dayak tribes have adapted to
e scarcity of arable land through swidden
techniques in which plots of secondary jungle are slashed, burnt to provide ash to enrich
the poor soils, sown for one or two seasons,
then left fallow for years. Logging, population growth and competition for arable land
has shortened the fallow periods in some
areas, giving the land less time to recover.
Unsustainable logging and farming has been
blamed for degrading 200,000 hectares of
the province's forests to poor grassland.

Even when areas are set aside for conservation, competing demands can still exact a
heavy toll. The Kutai Game Reserve, established as a nature reserve in 1936, was cut by

East
Kalimantan

100,000 hectares in 1968 when the park's whole coastal frontage was opened for logging and oil exploration. Within a few years this area, which had been severely degraded, was returned to the park as 'compensation' for a new logging concession excised from the park – 60,000 hectares of primary forest in the south. Fires in 1982-83 then claimed a big share of the remnants of the park's undisturbed forests.

DAYAK VILLAGES

Probably the best starting point for visits to inland Dayak villages is Samarinda. Longboats leave from here to ply the Mahakam, Kedang Kepala and Belayan rivers. DAS flies from Samarinda to Long Ampung, close to the mouth of the mighty Sungai Kayan.

There is also the relatively acculturated Kenyah Dayak village of **Pampang**, 26 km from Samarinda. You can travel there in a rented car or the yellow shared taxis which depart from Samarinda's Segiri terminal.

Guides

Even those fluent in Indonesian will find guides a must in some areas. The drill is to introduce yourself to the camat or kepala desa, explain where you are trying to go and ask for assistance. The money you pay for guides is one of the few opportunities many folk get to supplement their subsistence incomes, but if you arrive at harvest time or other busy periods, you might have trouble.

Your other option is to take a guide from Balikpapan or Samarinda. If you meet someone you like, consider taking them with you. Even in easily accessible areas, it can be nice just to let someone else do the haggling, travel and other arrangements.

Organised Tours

Professional tour agencies in Balikpapan include Kaltim Adventure (☎ 33408) in Komplek Balikpapan Permai (ask to see Tour Manager Antoni), or PT Tomaco Tours (☎ 21747) in the Hotel Benakutai building, Jl Ahmad Yani. These agencies have good reputations for Mahakam and Kedang Kepala river trips. They have three and six day tours

---

The Great Fires

Farmers and loggers blamed each other for the great fires of 1982-83, in which 35,000 sq km or 17% of the province's total land area was ravaged by 11 months of wildfire. There was a similar disaster in neighbouring Sabah that year. Both followed severe drought, and the damage was considerable.

Three months of fire in 1991 claimed another 500 sq km of East Kalimantan's forests and created a haze that disrupted air traffic as far away as Singapore. Kalimantan and Sumatran wildfires in 1994 created similar havoc over Singapore and Malaysia, reducing visibility over Singapore to just 300m and prompting a Malaysian appeal to the United Nations for assistance.

Swidden farmers undoubtedly start many of the fires through their age-old practice of slash and burn cultivation. But heavily logged, degraded forest was the worst affected, indicating that the volume of combustible material left behind by loggers, and the damage done by logging, had made the jungle vulnerable to fire damage. ■

---

going as far as Rukun Damai on the Mahakam and Tanjung Manis on the Kedang Kepala.

Rates start at about 900,000 to one million rp per person with 10 or more on the tour including accommodation, river transport, meals, village performances, and transport between Balikpapan and either Loa Janan or Tenggarong (the tours' starting points).

BALIKPAPAN

Balikpapan is an air-con oil boomtown with little to recommend it to the average traveller. Accommodation is expensive and there's little to see around town. For upmarket travellers, on the other hand, Balikpapan has the best hotels and restaurants in Kalimantan. also has an active nightlife scene.

Balikpapan's oilfields made it a strategic target in the Japanese invasion of 1941, and again in the Allied advances in 1944-45. Australians occupied Balikpapan after a bloody invasion and suppressed anti-colonial unrest.

Balikpapan's fortunes soared with the oil price shocks of the 1970s, but then plummeted with an oil glut and falling prices in the 1980s, crippling the city's enclave economy. The current upturn in oil, coal and timber prices has restored confidence and stimulated new activity.

Today Balikpapan has an air of easy affluence that you won't find anywhere else in Kalimantan. The central area is mainly given over to shops, hotels and restaurants. The Pertamina, Union Oil and Total residential areas are insulated from the rest of town. The suburban area bounded by Jl Randan Utara and Jl Pandanwanyi near the fruit market north of the oil refinery is by far the most interesting precinct. It is built on stilts over tidal mudflats, with uneven, lurching wooden walkways.

The huge oil refinery dominates the city and, while flying in, you can see stray tankers and offshore oil rigs. This is the centre of Kalimantan's oil business and the chief city of the province. There are 12 Jakarta-Balikpapan flights a day, a couple of five star hotels with world-class standards, and nearly as many American and European faces as there are Japanese motorcycles.

Orientation & Information
The best landmark is the beachfront Balikpapan Centre on the corner of Jl Sudirman and Jl Ahmad Yani. This large shopping complex is at the axis of the commercial and hotel district. Head north along Jl Yani to find the restaurants, east along the shore front to get to the airport, or west along Jl Sudirman to find the immigration, government and post offices. Jl Sudirman joins Jl Yos Suarso, which loops past the seaports and oil refinery areas.

Money The BNI bank on Jl Pengeran Antasari changes major travellers cheques and cash currencies. The bank is open Monday to Friday from 8 am to noon and 1.30 to 3 pm, and on Saturday until 11 am. The branch office at Seppingan airport also changes cash and travellers cheques.

Bank Dagang Negara on Jl Ahmad Yani offers good rates, but insists on seeing your purchase agreement. There are fewer hassles at the nearby BCA bank.

Post & Communications The office is on Jl Sudirman, east of the city centre. It is open Monday to Friday from 8 am to 6 pm, and on Saturday, Sunday and holidays until 5 pm.

Organised Tours
Several travel agencies in Balikpapan organise all-inclusive visits to Dayak villages. See under Dayak Villages at the beginning of this section for details.

Places to Stay – bottom end
Budget travellers are better off skipping Balikpapan altogether and heading up to Samarinda, where there are much better deals. In Balikpapan the cheaper accommodation is inconveniently located far north of the city centre on Jl Ahmad Yani. Even here there are no great deals to be had.

The *Hotel Aida* (☎ 21006) has airless singles/doubles from 12,000/18,000 rp and air-con rooms at 38,000 rp. Close by, the *Hotel Murni* has rooms from 18,000/22,000 rp and looks OK, but get a room at the back away from the main road.

The *Penginapan Royal*, near the Pasar Baru, is at the start of the airport road near the Jl Ahmad Yani corner. It's a grim place and it's unlikely you'll get a room here. Rooms start from 8500 rp.

Places to Stay – middle
The *Hotel Sederhana* (☎ 22564) at Jl Sudirman 7 is a reasonable mid-range option. Rooms start from 50,400/55,600 rp.

Better value is the very central *Hotel Gajah Mada* (☎ 34634) at Jl Sudirman 14, with economy rooms for 22,500/27,500 rp and standard ones at 45,000/50,000 rp, all with private mandi. The 2nd floor terrace overlooks the sea. Unfortunately, this hotel is often full.

Hotel Budiman (☎ 36030) on Jl Ahmad Yani 18 has rooms with air-con and TV for 45,000 rp, plus tax. Close by is the *Hotel Tirta* (☎ 22772), a basic mid-range option

KALIMANTAN

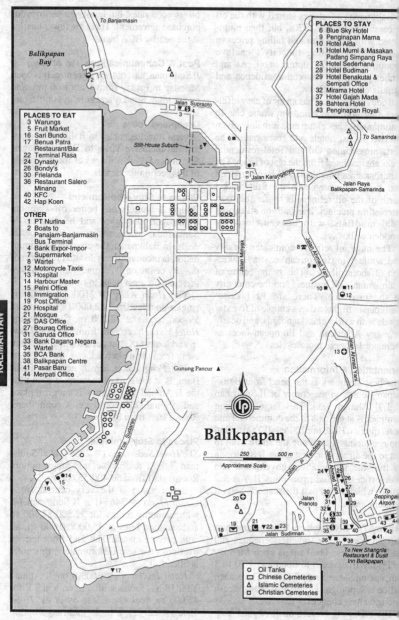

To Banjarmasin

Balikpapan Bay

Jalan Suprapto

Stilt-House Suburb

To Samarinda

Jalan Karanganyar

Jalan Raya
Balikpapan-Samarinda

PLACES TO STAY
- 6 Blue Sky Hotel
- 9 Penginapan Mama
- 10 Hotel Aida
- 11 Hotel Murni & Masakan Padang Simpang Raya
- 23 Hotel Sederhana
- 28 Hotel Budiman
- 29 Hotel Benakutai & Sempati Office
- 32 Mirama Hotel
- 37 Hotel Gajah Mada
- 39 Bahtera Hotel
- 43 Penginapan Royal

PLACES TO EAT
- 3 Warungs
- 5 Fruit Market
- 16 Sari Bundo
- 17 Benua Patra Restaurant/Bar
- 22 Terminal Rasa
- 24 Dynasty
- 26 Bondy's
- 30 Frielanda
- 36 Restaurant Salero Minang
- 40 KFC
- 42 Hap Koen

OTHER
- 1 PT Nurlina
- 2 Boats to Panajam-Banjarmasin Bus Terminal
- 4 Bank Expor-Impor
- 7 Supermarket
- 8 Wartel
- 12 Motorcycle Taxis
- 13 Hospital
- 14 Harbour Master
- 15 Pelni Office
- 18 Immigration
- 19 Post Office
- 20 Hospital
- 21 Mosque
- 25 DAS Office
- 27 Bouraq Office
- 31 Garuda Office
- 33 Bank Dagang Negara
- 34 Wartel
- 35 BCA Bank
- 38 Balikpapan Centre
- 41 Pasar Baru
- 44 Merpati Office

Gunung Pancur ▲

Jalan Minyak

Jalan Ahmad Yani

Jalan Ahmad Yani

Jalan Yos Sudarso

Balikpapan

0   250   500 m

Approximate Scale

Jalan P. Tendean

Jalan Ahmad Yani

To Seppinang Airport

Jalan Pranoto

Jalan Sudirman

To New Shangrila Restaurant & Dusit Inn Balikpapan

○ Oil Tanks
□ Chinese Cemeteries
△ Islamic Cemeteries
□ Christian Cemeteries

with rates from 75,000 rp for a standard room. The *Mirama Hotel* (☎ 33906), Jl Praoto 16, is the pick of the mid-range hotels, with a restaurant, chemist and barber shop. Its air-con rooms cost 60,000 to 90,000 rp.

The *Blue Sky Hotel* (☎ 22268) is inconveniently located in the north of town. It's comfortable, but expensive. Doubles cost 45,000 to 135,000 rp. All rooms are air-con, and there is a sauna, gym and billiard room.

Places to Stay – top end

The top hotel in Balikpapan, and indeed in Kalimantan, is the *Dusit Inn Balikpapan* (☎ 20155; fax 20150). It has a fitness centre, tennis courts, a jogging track, swimming pool, Chinese, Thai, Indonesian and western dining, one of the more popular bars in town and top-notch service standards. Rack rates start from US$130 plus taxes, though discount deals are sometimes available.

Hotel Benakutai (☎ 31896; fax 31823), Jl Ahmad Yani (PO Box 299), was formerly the best hotel in town and still maintains high standards. Rooms range from US$95/110, plus tax. Substantial discounts are occasionally available. There's an international-style bar/restaurant with pleasant surrounds and great coffee.

The central *Bahtera Hotel* (☎ 22563; fax 31889) at Jl Sudirman 2 has a popular disco and Chinese restaurant. Economy rooms cost US$50, standard rooms US$70 and superior rooms US$85.

Places to Eat

Balikpapan has some excellent restaurants. *Bondy's* on Jl Ahmad Yani offers seafood and hearty serves of western fare in an open courtyard. It's not cheap, but well worth a splurge. Venture through the sterile streetfront bakery to the courtyard and its broad balconies where you'll find good food, attentive staff and a pleasant atmosphere. The seafood is much better than the steaks.

There is plenty of inexpensive Indonesian-style Chinese fare around town. One of the best areas is the string of restaurants, including *Frielanda*, opposite the Mirama Hotel.

For slightly more authentic Chinese food try the *Atomic* on a little alley near the Hotel Benakutai, the *Dynasty* on Jl Ahmad Yani, or the *Hap Koen* on Jl Sudirman. The best Chinese food is at the *New Shangrila* on the road out to the airport, about halfway between the city centre and the Dusit Inn. Its crab in Singapore sauce is messy, but unbeatable, or there is a savoury hot-plate special with pigeon eggs, vegetables and your choice of meat, chicken or seafood. The es campur here is pretty good too. Get there before 7 pm or you may have a considerable wait.

For Padang food, try the *Masakan Padang Simpang Raya* next to the Hotel Murni. The *Restaurant Salero Minang* at Jl Ahmad Yani 12B is similarly priced, as is the *Restaurant Sinar Minang* on Jl Sudirman. The latter serves udang galah (giant river prawns) and is marginally better than the Salero Minang.

If you are willing to spend an average of 30,000 rp for an excellent meal with a splendid view of the ocean, visit the *Benua Patra* on Jl Yos Sudarso. A potpourri of cuisines, including western, Japanese, Korean and Chinese, is skilfully prepared and oriented to please the palates of expats.

Both the Dusit Inn and the Benakutai hotels have excellent upmarket western and Asian restaurants. For fast food there's a *KFC* next door to the Bahtera Hotel and a *Texas Fried Chicken* in the Balikpapan Centre. The *Hero Supermarket*, also in the Balikpapan Centre, is a good place to shop for a do-it-yourself meal.

Entertainment

Balikpapan is an R&R centre for oil workers and other expats working in mining and logging upriver, and consequently there is a large number of bars and discos in town. Some of these places tend to be a bit seedy. One of the better options is the *Borneo Pub* at the Dusit Inn. The bar at the *Bahtera Hotel* was once popular, but is generally deserted these days. If you want to do a bit of a pub crawl, there are places such as *Tom's Bar* and *Joy's Bar* scattered along the waterfront.

For late night entertainment, most people

gravitate either to *Panorama*, a huge open-sided affair with dancing on the waterfront, or the *Pinisi Pub & Disco* at the Bahtera Hotel. Both these places have minimal cover charges.

Getting There & Away

Air Garuda (☎ 22300), Jl Ahmad Yani 14, is diagonally opposite the Hotel Benakutai. Sempati (☎ 31612) is in the Hotel Benakutai, Merpati (☎ 24477) is at Jl Sudirman 22 and Bouraq (☎ 23117) has an office next to Hotel Budiman.

Garuda flies to Denpasar (271,000 rp), Jakarta (384,000 rp), Pontianak (266,000 rp), Surabaya (277,000 rp) and Ujung Pandang (194,000).

Merpati has useful flights to Pontianak (266,000 rp), Singapore, weekly flights to Batam and on to Medan, Ujung Pandang (194,000 rp), Ambon, Maumere, Kupang, Palu and Manado, Surabaya (277,000 rp) and on to Bandung, Denpasar (271,000 rp), Semarang and Yogyakarta. Its only intra-provincial flight is to Tarakan (201,000 rp).

Bouraq has a smaller inter-island schedule, but it is the only airline linking Kalimantan's two busiest airports, Balikpapan and Banjarmasin (115,000 rp). Its other useful routes include Berau, Muara Teweh, Kota Baru, Palangkaraya and Tarakan. Both Bouraq and DAS fly to nearby Samarinda (56,000).

Bus From Balikpapan you can head either north to Samarinda or south to Banjarmasin. Buses to Samarinda (3000 rp, 4000 rp air-con; two hours) depart from a bus stand in the north of the city accessible by a No 2 or 3 bemo for 700 rp (it's a long way out). Buy your ticket on the bus or at the terminal.

Buses to Banjarmasin (16,000 rp, 22,000 rp air-con; 12 hours) depart from the bus terminal on the opposite side of the harbour to the city. To get there, take a colt from the Rapak bus and bemo terminal to the pier on Jl Mangunsidi. Charter a speedboat to take you to the other side (the speedboat drivers will mob you). It costs 1500 rp per person, or around 5000 rp to charter, and takes 10

minutes. Alternatively, a motorised longboat costs 1000 rp and takes 25 minutes.

Boat The Pelni liners *Kambuna, Umsini,* an *Tidar* call in fortnightly, connecting Balik papan to Tarakan, Pantoloan, Ujung Pandang Surabaya and beyond.

In Balikpapan the Pelni office (☎ 21402 is on Jl Yos Sudarso 76. For regular ships t Surabaya try PT Elang Raya Abadi for th MV *Hafag* services to Ujung Pandang (35,00 to 68,000 rp), or Surabaya (55,000 to 90,00 rp). Alternately try PT Ling Jaya Shippin (☎ 21577) at Jl Yos Sudarso 40 and PT Suc Jaya Agung (☎ 21956) at Jl Pelabuhan 39 Fares are around 35,000 rp.

A recently added service is the *Paradipt Darma,* which leave three times a week fo Mamoju in southern Sulawesi. The eigh hour trip costs 22,000 rp in ekonomi.

Getting Around

The Airport Seppingan airport is a 15 minut fast drive from Pasar Baru along a surface road. A taxi from the airport to town costs standard 11,000 rp if you buy your taxi ticke in the terminal. Walk outside and you ca bargain your fare down to around 9000 rp.

In town you should be able to charter bemo to the airport for less – from Pasar Bart for 5000 to 6000 rp, or less by ojek. Char tered bemo or taxi seems to be the only way to the airport.

Bemo Bemos cut a circular route; 400 rp get you anywhere around town. The chief termi nal is the Rapak bus and bemo terminal at th end of Jl Panjaitan. From here, bemos run circular route around Jl Ahmad Yani, J Sudirman, Jl Yos Sudarso and Jl Suprapto Ojeks will take you anywhere as a pillior passenger for 1000 rp (minimum).

SAMARINDA

Balikpapan for oil, Samarinda for timber Both cities are important trading ports, bu just a couple of hours from Balikpapan by bus, Samarinda is worlds away from Balik papan. Samarinda is less affluent, less expat more Indonesian than its neighbour. For ravellers it's a good place to arrange inland journeys up the Sungai Mahakam to Dayak areas. See under Dayak Villages at the beginning of this section.

Most of the people who have settled in Samarinda are Banjars from South Kalimantan, so the main dialect is Banjarese. There are also many Kutais, who include the indigenous people of this area.

On the south side of Sungai Mahakam, in the part of town called **Samarinda Seberang**, you can visit cottage industries where Samarinda-style sarongs are woven. The traditional East Kalimantan wraparound is woven from *doyo* leaf.

Orientation

The main part of Samarinda stretches along the north bank of the river. The best orientation point is the enormous mosque on the river front. Jl Yos Sudarso runs east from here and Jl Gajah Mada runs west. Most of the offices and hotels are along these two streets or in the streets behind them.

Information

Tourist Office The Kantor Pariwisata tourist office (☎ 21669) has good maps, can quote tour prices and refer travellers to decent guides. It is just off Jl Kesuma Bangsa at Jl Suryani 1.

Money The BNI bank, on the corner of Jl Sebatik and Jl Panglima Batur, only changes US dollars (cash and travellers cheques). It is open Monday to Thursday from 8 am to 12.30 pm, Friday from 1.30 to 4.30 pm and Saturday from 8 to 11.30 am. Bank Dagang Negara on Jl Mulawarman is the only bank in Samarinda that changes travellers cheques in other currencies.

Post & Communications The main post office is on the corner of Jl Gajah Mada and Jl Awanglong, opposite the Bank Rakyat Indonesia.

Guides Guides seem to keep a check on who is in town through the budget hotels. Mokhta, who works out of the Aida Hotel, is a

reliable and enthusiastic guide and a mine of information on treks upriver. Rates for guides vary enormously depending on the kind of trip you are planning. If you are looking for real adventure, don't expect anything in the way of a bargain.

Things to See

Samarinda is not an unpleasant place to stroll around, but there's little to see. Beside the Mahakam Cinema is an old Chinese temple. About 500m north of the Hotel Mesra is a large morning market, open from 5 to 10 am. Arrive before 7 am to see it at its best.

Places to Stay – bottom end

The central *Hotel Hidayah II* (☎ 41712), Jl Hahlid 25, is spartan but clean. Rooms start from 17,500/22,500 rp, or 20,000/25,000 rp with mandi. Rates include a small breakfast. The *Hotel Hidayah I* (☎ 31210) on Jl Temenggung is cheaper: rooms with mandi cost 18,150/21,175 rp; or air-con doubles from 40,000 rp.

Next door, the *Aida* (☎ 42572) is a good place to be based. It has a coffee shop verandah area, and rooms cost 19,000/22,000 rp or from 38,000 rp with air-con.

Hotel Andhika (☎ 42358), Jl Agus Salim 37, has noisy, stuffy economy rooms from 19,000/22,990 rp. Next door is *Hotel Maharani* (☎ 49995), where basic rooms cost 15,000/20,000 rp.

On a quiet street are *Wisma Pirus* (☎ 21-873) and *Hotel Hayani* (☎ 42653), both on Jl Pirus. Stuffy rooms in the old wing of the Pirus start from 20,000 rp, while air-con rooms in the new wing range from 60,000 rp. The Hayani, across the street at No 31, is also good, with doubles ranging from 22,990 to 54,540 rp.

Hotel Mesir (☎ 42624), Jl Sudirman 57, is an unfriendly larger cheapie with rooms from 15,000 to 20,000 rp. This place is best avoided except as a last resort.

Places to Stay – middle & top end

Hotel Mesra (☎ 32772; fax 35453), Jl Pahlawan 1, is inconveniently located, but offers value for money with the full complement of

KALIMANTAN

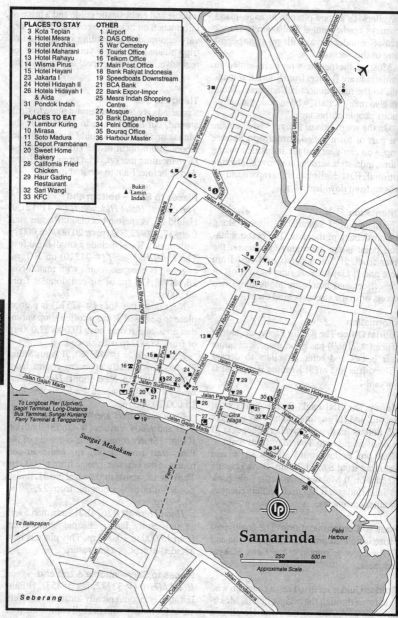

PLACES TO STAY
3 Kota Tepian
4 Hotel Mesra
8 Hotel Andhika
9 Hotel Maharani
13 Hotel Rahayu
Wisma Pirus
15 Hotel Hayani
23 Jakarta I
24 Hotel Hidayah II
26 Hotels Hidayah I
& Aida
31 Pondok Indah

PLACES TO EAT
7 Lembur Kuring
10 Mirasa
11 Soto Madura
12 Depot Prambanan
20 Sweet Home
Bakery
28 California Fried
Chicken
29 Haur Gading
Restaurant
32 Sari Wangi
33 KFC

OTHER
1 Airport
2 DAS Office
5 War Cemetery
6 Tourist Office
16 Telkom Office
17 Main Post Office
18 Bank Rakyat Indonesia
19 Speedboats Downstream
21 BCA Bank
22 Bank Expor-Impor
25 Mesra Indah Shopping
Centre
27 Mosque
30 Bank Dagang Negara
34 Pelni Office
35 Bouraq Office
36 Harbour Master

Bukit
▲ Lamin
Indah

Jalan Sutomo
Jalan Camar
Jalan Gatot Subroto
Jalan Gatot Subroto
Jalan Kalakuka
Jalan Sanga
Jalan Pahlawan
Jalan Suksari
Jalan Kesuma Bangsa
Jalan Bayangkara
Jalan Agus Salim
Jalan Bhayangkara
Jalan Abdul Hasan
Jalan Imam Bonjol
Jalan Hidayatullah
Jalan Gajah Mada
Jalan Awanglong
Jalan Pirus
Jalan Sudirman
Jalan Haidir
Jalan Diponegoro
Sulawesi
Jalan Panglima Batur
Jalan Mulawarman
Jalan Niaga Timur/Sebelak
Jalan Yos Sudarso
Jalan Nakhoda
Jalan Gajah Mada
Citra
Niaga

To Longboat Pier (Upriver),
Segiri Terminal, Long-Distance
Bus Terminal, Sungai Kunjang
Ferry Terminal & Tenggarong

Sungai Mahakam

To Balikpapan

Ferry

Seberang

Jalan Hasanuddin
Jalan Cokroaminoto
Jalan Bendahara

Pelni
Harbour

Samarinda

0   250   500 m
Approximate Scale

KALIMANTAN

rvices, including tennis courts, a large
vimming pool, restaurants and golf links.
conomy rooms cost US$37/48, standard
oms are US$47/56, superior are US$64/71
d cottages are also available at US$102/
15, plus tax.

The *Hotel Bumi Senyur* (☎ 41443; fax
8014) is the latest addition to Samarinda's
otel scene. It tries hard, has some good
staurants and amenities, such as tennis
ourts, a business centre, sauna, pool and
ven a golf course, but it doesn't quite match
e standards at the Mesra. Room rates start
US$65 for standard rooms, US$85 for
perior rooms and US$155 for executive
ites.

The *Kota Tepian* (☎ 32513; fax 43515) at
Pahlawan 4 is close to the Mesra and has
r-con rooms from 50,000 to 130,000 rp.

laces to Eat

amarinda's chief gastronomic wonder is the
dang galah (giant river prawns) found in the
cal warungs. The Citra Niaga hawkers'
entre off Jl Niaga, a block or two east of the
osque, is a pleasant pedestrian precinct
ith an excellent range of seafood, Padang,
ate, noodle and rice dishes, fruit juices and
arm beer. Establish prices in advance.

At the Mesra Indah shopping centre, close
the Hotel Hidayah II on Jl Hahlid, are two
ecent food centres and, upstairs overlook-
g the street, an ice-cream parlour.

For excellent Chinese breakfasts your best
et is the spotless *Depot AC*, behind the
ella Beauty Salon off Jl Mulawarman. If
ou prefer Indonesian soups for breakfast,
ere's the efficient *Warung Aida* on the
uth side of Jl Panglima Batur at the Jl
alimantan intersection. For savoury beef
up for lunch or dinner, eat at *Soto Madura*
n Jl Agus Salim.

For good, albeit not cheap, Chinese fare
ine at *Lezat* on Jl Mulawarman. The *Sari
angi*, on Jl Niaga Utara, also has good
hinese fare and it's cheaper than Lezat.

For a splurge, the Hotel Bumi Senyur has
good range of restaurants, including the
aisaku Japanese Restaurant* and the
hiang Palace Chinese Restaurant*. The

Hotel Mesra often has a barbecue grill for
pool-side dining. The fanciest restaurant in
town is the *Haur Gading Restaurant* off Jl
Sulawesi. It specialises in seafood, but was
closed for renovations at the time of writing.

If you like sticky pastries try the *Sweet
Home Bakery* at Jl Sudirman 8, west of Jl
Pirus on the left. For the best kueh outside
Banjarmasin, try the warung opposite Mesra
Indah which has a fabulous selection, includ-
ing custard star cakes. Alternatively, there is
a tempe stall in the lane behind Mesra Indah.

Travellers craving a fast-food fix will find
a *California Fried Chicken* joint on Jl Sulawesi and the new *KFC* on Jl Mutawarman.

Entertainment
Several bars and discos are tucked away
throughout the Kaltim Theatre complex
across from the sleazy Sukarni Hotel. Most
are fairly hard-core hostess bars, but the *Blue
Pacific* is a slightly upmarket disco where
couples are welcome. The cover charge is
5000 rp and includes a small beer.

For young Indonesians, the place to dance
the night away is the floating disco, *Restoran
Terapung*, upstream, picturesquely situated
at the foot of the Mahakam bridge. There is
a cover charge.

Things to Buy
Rattan goods, doyo leaf cloth, carvings and
other jungle products are available from a
string of souvenir shops along Jl Slamat
Riadi and Jl Martadinata. Forget the poorly
stocked souvenir and antique shops along Jl
Mulawarman. Those with an environmental
conscience should consider the beautiful
tubular rattan baskets and wild honey which
the environmental group Plasma buys direct
from the isolated communities it works with.
The group (☎ 35753) runs on a shoestring
budget and its volunteers are busy, so only
call if you are serious about buying.

Sleeping bags are essential for anyone
travelling to the interior, either as a sleeping
mat on the boats or for those cold nights on
the verandahs of mountain longhouses. Toko
Venus (☎ 33255), Jl Citra Niaga, Blok C1,

has sleeping bags for 75,000 rp, as well as masks, snorkels and other gear.

Getting There & Away
Air DAS (☎ 35250), Jl Gatot Subroto 92, has heavily subsidised and heavily booked flights to the interior. Fares are just 53,000 rp (plus tax) to Data Dawai, 35,000 rp to Long Ampung in the Apokayan, 198,000 rp to Tarakan and 75,000 rp from there to Long Bawang. As a general rule, the cheaper the flight, the heavier the bookings. Apart from seats set aside for VIPs and those on urgent business, you need to book weeks in advance. Telephone about a month before you want to fly.

MAF (☎ 43628), Jl Rahuia Rahaya I, also has regular flights to Long Ampung and Data Dawai. Check for other destinations.

Merpati (☎ 43385), Garuda and Sempati are all at Jl Sudirman 20, and can be contacted on the same telephone number.

Bus From Samarinda you can head north-west to Tenggarong or south to Balikpapan. The long-distance bus terminal is adjacent to the riverboat terminal, on the west side of the river a couple of km upstream from the bridge. Bemos run between the centre of town and the bus terminal for 500 rp. There are daily buses to Tenggarong (1700 rp; one hour) and Balikpapan (3000 rp, 4000 rp aircon; two hours) along well-surfaced roads.

Taxi You can be driven direct to your destination in Balikpapan in less than two hours by chartering a taxi for around 40,000 rp, depending on your bargaining skills.

Boat Many vessels leave from Samarinda, including coastal ships and riverboats.

Passenger Ship Pelni (☎ 41402) is at Jl Yos Sudarso 40-56, or ask at the nearby Terminal Penumpang Kapal Laut Samarinda and the Direktorat Jenderal Perhubungan Laut – both on Jl Yos Sudarso. The *Leuser* does a fortnightly run from here to Toli-Toli and Nunukan, and south to Pare Pare, Batulicin and Surabaya. Ekonomi fares are 92,000 rp

to Nunukan, 81,000 rp to Tarakan and 49,00 rp to Toli-Toli.

There are many non-Pelni boats fro Samarinda to other ports along the Kaliman tan coast, including weekly boats to Bera (aka Tanjung Redeb; 28,000 to 45,000 r about 36 hours) and occasionally to Taraka If you can't get a ship to Tarakan then tak one as far as Berau. From there it's easy get a boat to Tarakan.

For information on what leaves whe check with the harbour master at the Adp office on the corner of Jl Yos Sudarso and Nakhoda.

Riverboat Boats up the Sungai Mahaka leave from the Sungai Kunjang ferry term nal south-west of the town centre. To g there take a green city minibus A (called ta A) west on Jl Gajah Mada and ask for 'feri The regular fare is 500 rp, but if you get an empty taxi they may try to make yo charter – insist on *harga biasa* (the usu price).

A boat to Tenggarong takes four hours, Melak one day and a night (10,000 rp) an to Long Bagun two days and a night (cond tions permitting). Most boats have a sleepin deck upstairs, which costs extra, and wa ungs downstairs.

Speedboats will get you to Melak an back for just one million rupiah, including two night stop upstream.

Getting Around
The Airport The airport is quite literally i the suburbs. From the taxi counter in th terminal, you pay 8000 rp for a taxi into th centre of town. Alternatively, walk 100r down to Jl Gatot Subroto, turn left and catc a reddish-brown colt – a taxi B – all the wa to the waterfront (400 rp).

Public Taxi City colts, called taxi, run alon several overlapping routes designated A, and C. Route C goes past Hotel Mesra an the university area, route B goes past th airport. Most short runs cost 350 rp. It's standard 500 rp to the ferry pier for boat going upriver and 350 rp to the airport.

ROUND SAMARINDA

utai Game Reserve

his wildlife reserve is home to orang-utan
nd other exotic species, and can be visited
ther via a tour booked through agencies in
alikpapan and Samarinda or on your own.
ther than a monument to Bontang's loca-
on on the equator, some wooden houses on
ilts and an immense liquefied natural gas
lant, there is little reason to spend much
me in the town. Guide services cost about
2,000 rp.

laces to Stay If you stay overnight in
ontang, the best place is the comfortable
quator Hotel. Air-con bungalows start at
5,000 rp with TV and private mandi. There
e also a few cheap hotels in town. The
overnment *Kutai Guesthouse* in the reserve
fers beds for 5000 to 7000 rp. There is
asic Indonesian food here, but it is recom-
nended that you bring some of your own.

etting There & Away Independent travel-
rs can take a bus from Samarinda to
ontang for 3000 rp (three hours) and then
harter a boat from the PHPA office (50,000
o for the round trip).

ENGGARONG

)n the Sungai Mahakam, 39 km from Sam-
rinda, Tenggarong was once the capital of
ne sultanate of Kutai. Today it's a little
verside town cut by dirty canals. Like many
mall towns along the Mahakam, wooden
valkways lead from each house to the toilet
hacks built on stilts over the waterways.
3oth river and canals function as a combined
oilet, washroom and well.

)rientation & Information

he chief attractions of Tenggarong are its
nnual Erau Festival and the former sultan's
alace museum, built earlier this century
vith the royalties from early oil exploitation.
ome travellers prefer to start long river trips
rom here, but you can save a lot of travelling
me if you catch a bus to Kota Bangun and
atch a boat from there.

A tourist office next to the sultan's palace

has information on river trips and the Kutai
Game Reserve.

Mulawarman Museum

The former sultan's palace is now a museum.
It was built by the Dutch in the 1930s in a
futurist, monolithic, modernist style. It holds
a collection of artefacts from the days of the
sultan and many Dayak artefacts. Sadly,
there are few of the former sultan's furnishings or personal relics remaining.

The palace is open Tuesday to Thursday
from 8 am to 2 pm, Friday until 11 am,
Saturday to 1 pm and Sunday and holidays

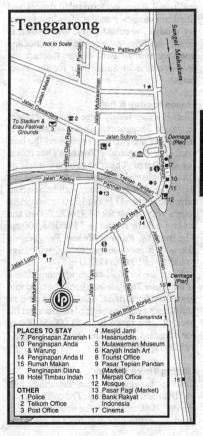

Tenggarong

Not to Scale

PLACES TO STAY
7 Penginapan Zaranah I
10 Penginapan Anda
   & Warung
14 Penginapan Anda II
15 Rumah Makan
   Penginapan Diana
18 Hotel Timbau Indah

OTHER
1 Police
2 Telkom Office
3 Post Office
4 Mesjid Jami
   Hasanuddin
5 Mulawarman Museum
6 Karyah Indah Art
8 Tourist Office
9 Pasar Tepian Pandan
   (Market)
11 Merpati Office
12 Mosque
13 Pasar Pagi (Market)
16 Bank Rakyat
   Indonesia
17 Cinema

KALIMANTAN

until 2 pm; it's closed on Monday. The sultan's fine porcelain collection is only exhibited on Sunday (although if you pay the guard a tip he might show you the porcelain on other days). Admission to the museum is 500 rp. On some Sundays, Dayak dancing is performed; it can be arranged on other days for a good sum – say 100,000 rp.

Special Events

Once a year, Dayak people travel to Tenggarong from various points in Kalimantan to celebrate the Erau Festiva. Although the festival is somewhat touristy, it will give you a good opportunity to see the Dayaks in their traditional finery perform tribal dances and ritual ceremonies. Plus it is a fabulous excuse for a huge intertribal party. The festival is usually held the last week in September and goes for one to two weeks. Contact the tourist office in Samarinda for the exact dates.

Places to Stay & Eat

There is a surprisingly large number of places to stay in Tenggarong. Down on the waterfront there are two places right on the boat dock. The *Penginapan Zaranah I* has rooms for 5000 rp. The *Penginapan Anda & Warung* costs 7500 rp. The *Penginapan Anda II* is a better option, with basic economy rooms for 11,000/13,750 rp, standard rooms with mandi for 18,150/22,000 rp and air-con deluxe rooms at 33,000/38,500 rp. The nearby *Rumah Makan Penginapan Diana* is a good budget option, with large rooms from 10,000/15,000 rp.

There's good mid-range accommodation at the *Hotel Timbau Indah*, on the road into town from Samarinda. All rooms are air-con, and there's a coffee shop and restaurant at the back. Rooms range from 48,000/54,000 rp for standard rooms (no TV) to 108,000/121,000 rp for suites.

Getting There & Away

Colts to Tenggarong from Samarinda take one hour and cost 1700 rp. The colt pulls into the Petugas terminal on the outskirts of Tenggarong. From here you have to get a taxi

kota (another colt) into the centre of Tenggarong for 300 rp.

Ojeks will also take you into town for 500 rp. City taxis run between 7 am and 6 pm. takes about 10 minutes to get from Petugas terminal to Pasar Tepian Pandan, where you get off for the boat dock, palace and tourist office.

There are no direct buses or colts from Tenggarong to Balikpapan, but you can get out south of Samarinda, a couple of km before the bridge, and hail a bus from the roadside.

SUNGAI MAHAKAM

Rivers are the highways of Kalimantan and the Sungai Mahakam is the busiest of all. Daily longboats ply the Mahakam from Samarinda all the way to Long Bagun, three days and 523 km upstream. When conditions are right, four or five motorised canoes week link Long Bagun to Long Pahangai, one to two day trip through gorges and rapids (40,000 rp). The return trip to Long Bagun takes just six or seven hours. *Never* tackle this stretch without local assistance. These waters can be lethal.

Beyond Long Pahangai, there are motorised canoes through to Long Apari, and from there it is possible to walk through to Tanjung Lokan on the Sungai Kapuas head waters in West Kalimantan.

If the Mahakam is low, you might not be able to get any further than Long Iram, 11 km short of Long Bagun. If the river's too high, the same may apply if the currents are too swift.

Many of the towns and villages along the Mahakam are built over wooden walkways that keep them above water during the wet season. Often there will be a budget hotel or a longhouse where travellers can stay – the standard price everywhere is 5000 rp per person. Alcoholic beverages can be hard to come by upriver so, if you want to, bring along your own supply from Samarinda.

Kota Bangun

Kota Bangun is a dusty stop at the start of the Mahakam lake country, about three hours by

...us from Samarinda along a rapidly improv-
...g road. Coal, rubber and transmigration are
...ie major local activities.

Penginapan & Rumah Makan Mukjizat, Jl
...lesjid Raya 46, is directly opposite the main
...iosque. It has small rooms for 5000/9000
..., great river views, nice people, and is just
...short walk to the bus terminal and motor-
...ed canoe dock, the Liang dock. Hire a
...iotorised canoe to Muara Muntai for 20,000
..., or charter for two days for a trip to Muara
...luntai, Tanjung Isuy, Mancong and back to
...ota Bangun for 120,000 rp.

The people at Sri Bagun Lodge can run
...oats to the lakes at dawn and dusk to see the
...ird life, proboscis monkeys and other wild-
...fe plus, if you are lucky, *pesut* – the
...eshwater dolphins this area is famous for.

There are five buses a day to Samarinda,
...ie first at 7 am and the last at 3 pm (3500
...).

¡uara Muntai

...luara Muntai is a Kutai market town built
...ver mudflats in the heart of the Mahakam's
...ike country. The streets are spotlessly clean
...oardwalks, but mind the mosquitos. The
...own is little more than a transit stop, but its
...eautifully built and maintained boardwalks
...re an attraction. Join the hordes promenad-
...ig at night, and check out the deputy
...upati's fine old wooden house and huge
...ortico, straight ahead from the dock. There
...s a market by the dock, as well as canoes
...vhich trade directly on the water.

Places to Stay & Eat There are two losmen.
...urn left at the boardwalk parallel to the
...ock and you will find the first, the *Pen-
inapan Nita Wardana,* about 20m further.
...iny, grubby rooms cost from 6000 rp per
...ead. *Penginapan Etam Sri Muntai Indah*,
...0m down the boardwalk, is run by fun folk
...vho don't hassle their guests. Singles/
...oubles cost 4500/9000 rp.

The warung between the two losmen
...erves sop Muara Muntai, a filling soup with
...ice, chicken, noodles, cabbage and a squeeze
...f lime. Warungs opposite the Nita Wardana
...ell fried rice, noodles etc. For breakfast, buy

kueh and return to the losmen, or go to the
warung on the dock for nasi kuning and a
great choice of roti and kueh.

Getting There & Away Public boats leave
for Tanjung Isuy via Jantur and Danau Jem-
pang every morning. They leave at 7.15 am
(be there at 7 am) and return from Tanjung
Isuy at 1 pm. The price is 3000 rp, provided
there are five or more passengers. If there are
four, each person pays 5000 rp. If there are
just two, you need to charter for 25,000 to
30,000 rp. A full day on the lakes costs about
60,000 rp.

The boat from Samarinda to Muara Muntai takes 13 hours on the 7 am express boat
or 18 hours (overnight) on the 9 am boat. The
fares are 5000 rp, more or less. The slower
boat has mattresses on the upper deck and its
own warung.

Tanjung Isuy

Tanjung Isuy is on the shores of Danau Jem-
pang in Banuaq Dayak territory. Half the fun
is getting there, via spectacular wetlands,
shallow lakes and **Jantur**, a Banjar village
built on a flooded mudflat. Jantur's mosque
stands alone on a bend in the river, accessible
only by boats and high gangplanks. Beside
it is the cemetery, the highest point in town
but still just 20 cm above the water table at
the end of the wet season. Bodies buried here
must be anchored in their watery graves to
prevent them bobbing to the surface.

There is plenty of bird life on **Danau
Jembang**, but sadly no pesut (freshwater
dolphin) have been seen here since the
drought and fires of 1982-83.

Tanjung Isuy is a favoured destination for
packs of aging tourists in search of an
'authentic' Dayak experience. Most arrive in
speedboats from Samarinda, mob the souvenir stalls in the longhouse, watch a mix of
Dayak dancing and zoom back the next day.
Activity focuses on the **Taman Jamrot
Lamin**, a longhouse vacated in the late
1970s, and rebuilt by the provincial government as a craft centre and tourist hostel.
Despite the commercial nature of these pay-
by-the-hour performances, they are lively,

KALIMANTAN

rhythmic and loads of fun for the whole town. The mix of Kenyah, Kayan and Banuaq dancing is confusing, but very entertaining.

The older, original longhouse is an inauspicious-looking building near the jetty. Unlike the other, it is in bad repair and a 50m section has been demolished. Two families live here, but many more use it as a craft centre, meeting hall and cultural centre. You can often find healing and harvest ceremonies in progress. The carvings on display are about 20% to 30% cheaper than at the hostel.

Places to Stay & Eat The best place to stay is the *Taman Jamrot Lamin* on Jl Indonesia Australia, 500m from the jetty. Unlike a real longhouse it has private guest rooms and comfortable beds at 5000 rp per person.

Another option is the one budget hotel in Tanjung Isuy – the *Penginapan Beringan*, which also costs 5000 rp per person. The couple who run the Beringan also prepare and serve food downstairs.

A *cafe* a few doors down from the Taman Jamrot Lamin has basic fare, or very tough chicken if you order a few hours ahead.

Getting There & Away Riverboats leave for Samarinda each Monday and Thursday. *Ces* (motorised canoe) to Muara Muntai leave daily at 1 pm (2500 to 20,000 rp), or you could charter a ces direct to Kota Bangun (50,000 rp), catch a bus and be in Samarinda or Balikpapan that night.

Mancong

Hire a ces to get from Tanjung Isuy to nearby Mancong via the Sungai Ohong, past flocks of magnificent water birds and a gorgeous stretch of riverside jungle. Pay 20,000 to 30,000 rp, allowing for two or three hours in each direction. It is essential to go slowly to spot the many proboscis monkeys, snakes (if you are lucky) and bird life, including hornbills. You'll pass villages with houses fronted by carved statues, folk weaving baskets and cloth, schools with steps leading into the water, and the odd ibis hanging around the house docks, hoping for a free feed.

In Mancong there is a grand wooden two storey **longhouse**, built by the government as a tourist attraction in 1987. The locals will gladly show you around. You can also see Banuaq weaving cloth from doyo leaf, have the process explained to you and buy some at very reasonable prices. Folk dances are occasionally held at the longhouse for ritual purposes or for tourist groups. You can stay for 5000 rp per person. Return to Tanjung Isuy by ces, or by motorcycle (5000 rp).

THE UPPER MAHAKAM
Melak & Around

Melak is the biggest town on the upper Mahakam, famous for the nearby **Kersik Luwai Orchid Reserve**, where 72 different species of orchid grow, including the extremely rare green-black *Cologenia pandurata* orchids. The best time to see the orchids is supposedly January to February, but the visitors' book indicates that you never see more than a few at any time of the year. The reserve is about 16 km from Melak and may be reached via jeep or ojek charter. Pak Banen shows you around for 1000 rp per person – walk slowly and ask questions.

Enquire whether any funerals, weddings or harvest ceremonies are being held while you are there – they can be fascinating experiences, often including the ritual slaughter of water buffalo. Healing ceremonies are most frequently held in March, April and June, according to locals.

Barong Tongkok is a small village at the centre of the plateau. There are five warungs in town, most serving Padang food, plus a losmen.

In nearby **Eheng** there is an unusually long Banuaq longhouse and cemetery. The longhouse was started in the 1960s, and may well be the last real Kalimantan longhouse built without government subsidy. Market day is Tuesday, the best day to visit. The final stretch of road from Mencimai to Eheng is appalling, ensuring the village's continued isolation. You can walk there, or rent a jeep or ojek from Melak. Locals sell carvings and rattan goods, and know the Melak shop prices better than most tourists.

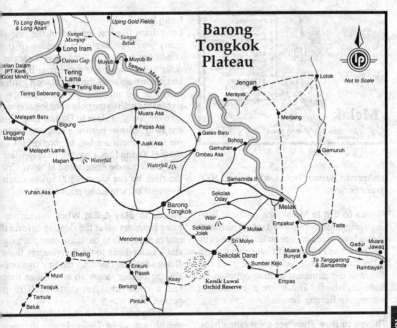

Barong Tongkok Plateau

Not to Scale

Mencimai has an excellent museum with detailed explanations in English and Indonesian of the local systems of swidden, or shifting, agriculture. The Museum Mencimai Papatn Puti was set up by a Japanese student of agricultural economics to explain the Banuaq systems of land use, methods for collecting wild honey, traps for pigs and monkeys, and bark cloth production (revived during the Japanese occupation of WWII). It also has relics, including excellent old *mandau* (machetes) and rattan ware. This tiny museum is easily one of the best in Indonesia.

PT Kem, Indonesia's biggest **gold mine**, an Australian-run operation at Kalian Dalam which employs 800 workers. Apart from the parade of prospective employees trooping via Melak and Tering, and the occasional waste spill, you wouldn't know it was here. The shanty town at the gates is as close as you will be allowed to get without prior approval.

Guides If you need a guide for trekking beyond Melak, travellers have recommended Agus Noto from Rojok, who can be contacted through the Penginapan Rahmat Abadi in Melak. He charges around 50,000 rp a day for local jungle treks or to Long Ampung, about five days away via Sungai Boh by boat and foot. Avoid the November-January wet season.

Places to Stay There are three losmen in Melak, each as good as the next, and all charging 5000 to 6000 rp per person. *Penginapan Rahmat Abadi*, Jl Piere Tendean, is the most foreigner-friendly place and is close to the dock. *Penginapan Bahagia* is deserted, clean and overlooks the dock. *Penginapan Flamboyan* faces the river about 100m upstream from the dock.

In Eheng, you may be allowed to stay in the longhouse.

In the village of Barong Tongkok, there is

the spartan *Wisma Orchid*, which costs 5000 rp per person.

Places to Eat In Melak, the riverside *Warung Pangkalan* serves good sate. The owner does a brisk trade in beer on ice. Warungs by the market sell coffee with hot pancakes and cakes for breakfast, and there are good rice dishes at the nameless warung opposite the Rahmat Abadi. There are a number of warungs in Barong Tongkok.

Things to Buy There are great rattan bags, hats, baskets etc for 10,000 to 30,000 rp, depending on size and quality. There are a few old mandau (machetes) – mostly working knives, but a few good old ones for up to 300,000 rp. There are also beautiful trading beads, but most are not for sale. Locals know the shop prices and are canny hagglers.

Getting There & Away Boats from Samarinda leave for the 325 km trip at 9 am and arrive in Melak at around 10 am the next day. The fare is 8000 rp per person. The fare back to Muara Muntai is 5000 rp.

Getting Around Transport charter is expensive – about 100,000 rp a day for cars or jeeps and 25,000 to 30,000 rp a day for motorcycles. Use a map, and be explicit about where you wish to go, or go solo.

There are regular bemos between Melak and Tering, the only decent road in the area. The fare is 1500 rp to Sekolat Darat, 5000 rp to Tering (one hour) and 10,000 rp to the gates of the big gold mine, PT Kem.

Long Iram

Long Iram is often the end of the line f many would-be explorers because of riv conditions or lack of time. It is a pleasar quiet village with a few colonial building and it's an easy walk through market garde to Tering. Go north along Jl Soewondo, tu right at the path to the police station and wa on over pretty bridges to **Danau Gap**, thr km away. Hire or borrow a canoe to explo the lake – there are lots of monkeys. Co tinue to Tering Lama and see its magnifice new church at the eastern end of town. Cro the river by *cat* (canoe, 500 rp) or catch riverboat back to Long Iram (1000 rp).

Places to Stay & Eat When you arrive Long Iram, get off at the floating cafe on t east bank, climb to the main road, turn rig and wander down to the *Penginapan Waht* Jl Soewondo 57 (look for the tiny sign opp site the double storey shops). Clean room and a good breakfast costs 7500 rp p person.

For the best food on the Mahakam, eat the *Warung Jawa Timur*. Ignore the men Dinner is whatever's on the stove – perha a curry of jackfruit and pumpkin, rice and t fattest, juiciest chicken anywhere in t tropics for 3000 rp.

Getting There & Away Long Iram is 409 k from Samarinda, 1½ days by riverboat. Th fare is usually 10,000 rp.

Long Iram to Banjarmasin

A few intrepid travellers have trekked ove land west of Long Iram (a week to 10 day to a tributary of the Sungai Barito in Centr Kalimantan and, from there, worked the way downriver to South Kalimantan an Banjarmasin. It's not exactly a jungle exper ence, as much of this area has been logge and travel is often via logging roads. Ther is a logging road from nearby Tering to Ta **jung Balai** in Central Kalimantan. You ma be able to hitch a ride to Tanjung Balai an then to **Muara Teweh**. From there regula longboats ply the Barito all the way to Ba jarmasin.

Path to Danau
Gap & Tering

Police ★

Floating
Penginapan
& Warung

Kueh & Bakso
Vendors

▼ Warung Jawa Timur

Market

Row of
Shops

Penginapan
Wahtu

Long Iram

0   50   100 m

Sungai Mahakam

Jalan Soewondo

Datah Bilang to Muara Merak

If conditions allow you to ferry upriver beyond Long Iram, places of interest include Datah Bilang, where there are two Bahau Dayak longhouses, one of which is heavily decorated. A reader has recommended the Dayak village of **Long Hubung**, 45 minutes north of Datah Bilang by motorised canoe (7500 rp per person). Yusram, the kepala desa, welcomes visitors.

Between Datah Bilang and Long Bagun is **Rukun Damai**, surrounded by rainforest and home to Kenyah people who migrated here from the Apokayan in 1973. Many still hold fast to their traditions. There are five Kenyah amin (longhouses), including one 250m long.

Less than 25 km downstream is Muara Merak, a Punan settlement. There is good trekking in this area, especially along the Merak to the north-east. With a Punan guide hired in Muara Merak, you could trek overland east for three to four days to Tabang and then travel down the Sungai Belayan to Kota Bangun, where you can catch a boat or bus back to Samarinda.

Long Bagun to Long Apari

Long Bagun is a longhouse settlement and the end of the line for regular longboat services from Samarinda along the Mahakam. The journey costs 15,000 to 20,000 rp and takes three days, conditions permitting. The boat docks in Long Iram one night each way while the crew sleeps, since night navigation can be tricky this far upriver.

Long Bagun to Long Apari

From Long Bagun you must charter motorised canoes from village to village or trek through the forests. River conditions must be optimal because of river rapids between Long Bagun and the next major settlement, **Long Pahangai**. Under normal conditions, it's a one or two day canoe trip from Long Bagun to Long Pahangai (40,000 rp), then another day to Long Apari. **Long Lunuk**, between Long Pahangai and Long Apari, is a good place from which to visit Kenyah villages. At Long Lunuk, stay with Luhat Brith and his family. He can take you upriver to Long Apari. It helps financially to go with four other travellers as you are unlikely to encounter other foreigners here.

Long Apari is the uppermost longhouse village on the Mahakam and it is beautiful. The longboat trip from Long Lunuk takes five to six hours. It's tiring and a stopover in Long Apari is recommended. Join the villagers for a night of dancing. Dinner is often greasy pig and bony fish – tasty supplements from the city make welcome presents. Long Apari is the stepping off point for treks to West Kalimantan.

Getting There & Away To start your trip from the top, fly to Data Dawai, an airstrip near Long Lunuk. DAS flies four times a week (53,000 rp each way), but you need to book weeks in advance. From there you can work your way downriver back to Samarinda, or trek overland to the Apokayan highlands.

One way to save a considerable amount of money going downriver is to buy a canoe and paddle yourself. The price will depend on the size and condition of the canoe – a decent used canoe costs 35,000 to 75,000 rp without an engine. If you want an engine it will cost

KALIMANTAN

considerably more, as much as double. But *never* tackle the lethal rapids between Long Pahangai and Long Bagun on your own. In fact, it would be best not to start a self-paddled trip above Long Bagun. Downriver from Long Bagun it's a pretty straightforward trip as long as you check in at villages along the way to make sure you haven't taken a tributary of the Mahakam by mistake.

SUNGAI TELEN

There are regular longboat services up the Telen, which branches north off the Mahakam near **Muara Kaman**, from Samarinda to **Muara Wahau**. This trip takes three days and two nights, and goes via the Kenyah and Bahau villages of **Tanjung Manis**, **Long Noran** and **Long Segar**. The boat fare from Samarinda to Muara Wahau is 16,500 rp. Nearby caves were the site of 5th century Sanskrit finds, now in the museum at Tenggarong.

An alternative route from Samarinda to Berau (see the Berau entry further in this section) is to take a boat north from Muara Wahau to **Miau Baru**, where you can stay with the Dutch-speaking kepala desa and his English-speaking son. Then travel by local school bus to a lumber camp four km north and hitch a ride on a jeep to the Dayak village of **Marapun**, two hours away. From Marapun, get a 12 hour boat ride down the Kelai to **Berau/Tanjung Redeb**.

SUNGAI BELAYAN

Another adventurous trip is up the Sungai Belayan to **Tabang**. The Belayan branches north-west off the Mahakam at Kota Bangun and longboats take about three days to reach Tabang from Samarinda.

You can also reach Tabang on foot from the town of **Muara Merak** on the Mahakam. You can hire a Punan guide in either Tabang or Muara Merak to lead you north of Tabang into extensive rainforests that are nomadic Punan territory.

SUNGAI KAYAN & THE APOKAYAN

South of Tarakan is **Tanjung Selor** at the mouth of the mighty Sungai Kayan. There are regular longboat services up the Kayan as far as the Kenyah villages of **Mara I** and **Mara II**, but a long section of rapids – Kalimantan's wildest whitewater – further on prevents boats from reaching the headwaters of the Kayan in the Apokayan Highlands.

There is good trekking in the Apokayan Highlands; you could also trek overland to the Mahakam headwaters from here in about a week with a guide from Long Ampung. Guides in Samarinda lead easy or vigorous treks to Dayak longhouses from Long Ampung.

One of Jailani's most picturesque tours consists of the following itinerary: first flight from Samarinda to Long Ampung on DAS, then a 2½ hour easy walk to stay overnight at the longhouse of **Long Uro**. The next day involves a 45 minute walk to the longhouse of **Lidung Payau** where you catch a boat back to Long Ampung for your flight back to Samarinda. Hardy travellers may include a difficult five hour jungle walk from Lidung Payau to **Long Sungai Barang**. Nights are cold and longhouse verandahs can be hard, so pack a sleeping bag.

A Kenyah godly mask from the Apokayan region

etting There & Away

AS flies from Samarinda to Tanjung Selor aily, and has a government-subsidised ight from Samarinda to Long Ampung in e Apokayan area four times a week for 6,000 rp.

ONG BAWANG

nother inland option is the picturesque area round Long Bawang. Like the Apokayan, it too far above the rapids to be of much terest to logging companies – yet. Also like e Apokayan, there is a noticeable military resence and high prices for even the sim est commodities. Any presents from the ty will be welcome – booze, toys, sweets, gar etc.

etting There & Away

ir DAS flies to Long Bawang from Tarakan or 75,000 rp.

oat Riverboat trips are a slow but very laxing way to travel into the interior. Gen ally, you sleep on a covered deck with an nobstructed view of every sunset and sun se. Every few hours, boats without cooking cilities pull in at a village dock and those ho haven't brought their own food get off eat in a warung.

Some boats have warungs on board and an pstairs sleeping area with mattresses and ockers. Either way it's a good idea to bring nacks and plenty of bottled water. Also, take eading or writing material to help pass the me when you tire of viewing river life.

Fares vary according to conditions. When ney're just right the fare is lower, and when e water level is too low or too high the fare a bit higher. The boat dock in Samarinda at the Sungai Kunjang pier outside town, ached by a taxi kota A for 500 rp.

ERAU (TANJUNG REDEB)

eople use the names Berau and Tanjung edeb interchangeably. Strictly speaking, anjung Redeb is the spit of land between ungai Segan and Sungai Kelai, whereas erau refers to the whole urban area. It oesn't seem to matter which you use. These days Berau is best known for its riverside coal fields downstream from the city.

Berau was once the seat of two minor kingdoms, Gunung Tabur, with its palace (kraton) on the banks of the Segan, and Sambaliung, with a palace on the Kelai. Both face each other across Tanjung Redeb. Gunung Tabur's moment in history came towards the end of WWII when the palace was mistaken for a Japanese military post and flattened by Allied bombers. The Sambaliung palace was untouched, supposedly because of the spiritual power of cannon swaddled in the belfry.

The Gunung Tabur palace was rebuilt, and is now the **Museum Batiwakkal**. It contains a few relics, including an old cannon found in the jungle by the very first rajah; however, its spiritual powers have been in doubt since the Allied bombing. Another back-room relic is the yellow birthing table in the next room, a slanted wooden bed.

In the bungalow beside the palace lives A Putri Kanik Sanipan, the daughter of the last rajah of Gunung Tabur. She is a graceful woman in her 70s, speaks fluent Dutch and Indonesian, and occasionally takes tea with visitors and talks of the old days. Her collection of photographs includes many of the former palace and of state occasions. Locals often ask her to bless their children, light incense and say prayers in the traditional Gunung Tabur way. Get there by regular canoe ferry (300 rp).

The **Sambaliung Kraton** is now a private residence, occupied by the grandson of the last rajah and his relatives. It is an old building with loads of character and a belfry which once overlooked the palace grounds. There are photographs of the royal cemetery at Batu Putih, 48 km from Talisayan.

Places to Stay

Hotel Citra Indah, Jl Soetomo, is a cavernous place built in the former Soviet style. Large clean rooms cost from 12,000/14,500 rp with shared mandi and 15,000/17,500 rp with private mandi, ranging to 40,000/44,000 rp with air-con and TV. The staff are friendly.

KALIMANTAN

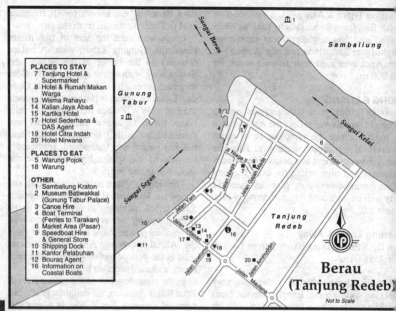

PLACES TO STAY
7   Tanjung Hotel &
     Supermarket
8   Hotel & Rumah Makan
     Warga
13 Wisma Rahayu
14 Kalian Jaya Abadi
15 Kartika Hotel
17 Hotel Sederhana &
     DAS Agent
19 Hotel Citra Indah
20 Hotel Nirwana

PLACES TO EAT
5   Warung Pojok
18 Warung

OTHER
1   Sambaliung Kraton
2   Museum Batiwakkal
     (Gunung Tabur Palace)
3   Canoe Hire
4   Boat Terminal
     (Ferries to Tarakan)
6   Market Area (Pasar)
9   Speedboat Hire
     & General Store
10 Shipping Dock
11 Kantor Pelabuhan
12 Bouraq Agent
16 Information on
     Coastal Boats

Berau
(Tanjung Redeb)

Not to Scale

Kalian Jaya Abadi, Jl Antasari, is a tourist-friendly place with basic accommodation for 7500 rp per person, including bath.

The *Hotel Sederhana*, Jl Antasari, has old losmen rooms from 15,000 rp and a much brighter hotel section with rooms from 18,000 rp plus tax, or 30,000 rp with air-con. *Wisma Rahayu*, Jl Antasari, is drab but has some economy rooms from 8000 rp. *Tanjung Hotel & Supermarket*, Jl Niaga II, focuses more on its grocery lines than guests. Rooms cost 8500/13,000 rp. *Hotel & Rumah Makan Warga* on the same street is better, with rooms from 12,000/18,000 rp.

Places to Eat

The *warung* at Jl Yani 16, between Toko Medan Raya and Toko Logam Murni, has superb rice, curries and home-made roti and kueh. Nasi kuning or campur with cake and coffee costs 2500 rp. It's great for breakfast or takeaways.

The *warung* opposite the Citra Indah keeps odd hours, serving excellent soup an sate at night, and soto ayam (chicken an vegetable broth) and nasi pecel (similar gado gado) for breakfast.

Another dinner option is the martaba (pancake) stalls on Jl Yani. Eat on the ha bour wall and chat with the passers-by.

The *supermarket* at the Tanjung Hotel c Jl Niaga II stocks everything from chocola to infant formula. Stock up on snacks f long journeys upriver or up the coast.

Getting There & Away

Air The DAS agent is in the Hotel Sederhar on Jl Antasari. Bouraq's is nearby on Niaga. Both airlines fly from Samarind along the coast and over the LNG and po facilities at Bontang, and the coal mines Sanggata.

Boat Passenger boats to Tanjung Batu (12,50 rp; four hours) and on to Tarakan (25,000 r leave daily. You buy your tickets on the boa

alimantan

p: Workers at a diamond mining site, Cempaka, South Kalimantan.

p Left: Scaling and gutting the catch, Sungai Mahakam, East Kalimantan.

ttom Left: Banuaq women preparing doyo leaf for dying and weaving, Kalimantan.

ght: Orang-utan at the Tanjung Puting National Park, Central Kalimantan.

Dayak dancing, Tanjung Isuy, East Kalimantan.

here are also weekly boats to Samarinda. ervices and departure times are advertised n the boards outside the small dock. From 'anjung Batu, hitch a lift with a local boat oing to Pulau Derawan. To charter a speed-oat direct from Berau to the dive resort at ulau Derawan costs 350,000 rp. Ask at the 'itra Indah *wartel* or at Toko Tiga Berlian.

'etting Around

'he **Airport** Shared taxis from the airport ost 2500 rp each, or 500 rp if you catch the emo from the road at the end of the airstrip.

'ULAU DERAWAN

)erawan is part of the Sangalaki Archipel-go, a marine reserve off Tanjung Batu 'etween Berau and Tarakan. There are dive esorts on Derawan and Sangalaki islands, nd their popularity is growing despite their solation.

Derawan is a beautiful tear-shaped speck f land with a village around the fringe, potless white sand beaches, coconut planta-ions in the centre and a good supply of fresh vater. Schools of tuna surround the island, ongkol fish create feeding frenzies near the urface where birds dive for spoils and at full noon rare green turtles lay eggs on the beach ear the Derawan Dive Resort.

There are no cars, no motorcycles and lectricity generators run only for a few ours in the evening. The main entertainment s the volleyball and badminton matches in the arly evening, and a couple of satellite TVs. 3y some miracle of modern planning, the nly losmen is just in front of the only nosque, but the dawn call to prayer is a tame ffair, thanks to the absence of electricity for he amplifier.

Other islands in the group include **San-**alaki, which divers visit to see manta rays nd green turtles; **Karaban**, which has a lake n the centre, caves with swallows' nests and population of huge coconut crabs; and **Maratua**, which has 2100 people in four villages, set around a lagoon. There's also a nilitary patrol stationed here to keep 'pirates' n check.

Activities

The island's main attractions, snorkelling and diving, are conducted from the Derawan Dive Resort (see the following Places to Stay & Eat entry). The charge for two dives off Pulau Derawan, plus tanks and equipment hire, is 165,000 rp. Two dives off Pulau Sangalaki and other outer islands costs 308,000 rp.

Places to Stay & Eat

Pulau Derawan Most visitors to Pulau Derawan come on package diving tours and stay at the *Derawan Dive Resort* (☎ 20293; fax 20258), which has an office in the Hotel Benakutai in Balikpapan. Four day, three night packages cost US$470 with three dives per day, accommodation and meals. Seven day, six night packages cost US$1130 for the same deal. A minimum of two people is required.

Private accommodation is also available. *Losmen Ilham*, at the western end of the island, is run by Pak Herman and Ibu Suryati. They charge 17,000/23,000 rp, plus 3500 rp per person for generous serves of grilled fish. Pak Herman itemises everything, charging 800 rp for coffee etc. He also has a karaoke machine and adores singing at ear-splitting volumes.

The other option is to stay with the kepala desa, a friendly man with a spare room, for around 5000 to 10,000 rp a night.

The only commercial eateries are at the losmen and dive resort. There is a tiny warung near the dive resort which serves roti and kueh in the morning. Fruit, other than coconuts, is scarce and expensive.

Tanjung Batu The *Losmen Famili* has rooms for 10,000/15,000 rp or 15,000/ 25,000 rp with meals.

Getting There & Away

The daily Berau-Tarakan boat drops passen-gers at Tanjung Batu, a fishing village with a couple of warungs and a losmen (see under Places to Stay & Eat).

There are no regular services to Derawan from Tanjung Batu, just fisherfolk heading

KALIMANTAN

to and fro. Ask *'Boleh saya ikut?'* ('Can I tag along?') if you see a group with bags heading towards either pier. Offer to chip in for the fuel, say 5000 rp. Otherwise you need to charter a boat, which will cost 20,000 to 25,000 rp.

TARAKAN

Just a stepping stone to other places, Tarakan is an island town close to the Sabah border. It was the site of bloody fighting between Australians and Japanese at the end of WWII. Unless you're really enthusiastic about Japanese blockhouses, or want to try exiting Indonesia to Sabah, there's little of interest. It's not a bad town, just dull. Some of the houses have old Japanese cannon shells painted silver and planted in their front yards like garden gnomes.

The battle at Tarakan was one of a series of battles fought by Australian soldiers in Indonesia and New Guinea from mid-1944 onwards. There's an interesting argument put forward by Peter Charlton in *The Unnecessary War – Island Campaigns of the South-West Pacific 1944-45* that these battles had no value in the defeat of the Japanese. By that time the Japanese in Indonesia were already effectively defeated, reluctant to fight and incapable of being either evacuated or reinforced; they fought only when they were forced to.

The capture of Tarakan (after six weeks of fighting and the deaths of 235 Australians) was carried out to establish an air base which was never used. After the Tarakan operation Indonesia was effectively bypassed, yet in July 1945 an assault was made on Balikpapan. This last large amphibious landing of the war managed to secure a beach, a disused oil refinery, a couple of unnecessary airfields and the deaths of 229 Australians.

Information

Bank Dagang Negara on Jl Yos Sudarso will change US travellers cheques and currency.

Places to Stay

Hotel Taufiq (☎ 21347), Jl Yos Sudarso 26, is a huge rambling place near the main

mosque. It is basic, but affordable at 800(9000 rp, 14,500/17,500 rp with mandi c 28,500/29,750 rp with air-con.

There's a line of cheap and mid-rang hotels along Jl Sudirman, including *Losme Jakarta* (☎ 21704) at No 112, the friendlies of the cheap digs with rates from 3800/660 rp. Nearby *Losmen Herlina* is basic, but hab itable, at 5500/6400 rp.

Barito Hotel (☎ 21212), Jl Sudirman 13: has basic but clean rooms for 13,750/16,50 rp or 33,000 rp with air-con. Next door, th sleazy *Hotel Orchid* (☎ 21664) has grott rooms from 11,000/15,000 rp.

PLACES TO STAY
1 Mirama Hotel
5 Losmen Jakarta
7 Losmen Herlina
9 Barito Hotel
10 Hotel Orchid
17 Hotel Tarakan Plaza & Bulungan Restoran
20 Hotel Taufiq
28 Hotel Bunga Muda

PLACES TO EAT
2 Rumah Makan Cahaya
8 Restoran Kepeting Saos
11 Depot Gembira
12 Turi
18 Antara Restoran
19 Phoenix Restaurant
23 Bagi Alam

OTHER
3 MAF Office
4 Wartel
6 DAS Office
13 Police
14 Bouraq Office
15 BNI Bank
16 Bank Dagang Negara
21 Mosque
22 Merpati Office
24 Bank Rakyat Indonesia
25 Pasar Sebengkok
26 Bemo Terminal
27 Post Office

To Immigration Office

To Airport

Tarakan
Not to Scale

Boardwalk

To Port & Pelni Office

Pier

Further along Jl Sudirman near the Jl Mulwarman intersection at No 46 is the *Wisata Hotel* (☎ 21245), which has basic but pleasant rooms from 8500/10,900 rp, or 14,000/20,000 rp with mandi and fan.

Nearby is the slightly more upmarket *Hotel Nirama* (☎ 21637), where rooms with air-con, TV and hot water cost 42,350/48,400 rp.

The big *Hotel Tarakan Plaza* (☎ 21870), Jl Yos Sudarso, is the best in town. It comes complete with restaurant and expats held up by a bar. Doubles with air-con, hot water and TV cost 77,000 to 99,000 rp. The delightful, informative staff know Tarakan and the interior well; ask for Yusuman.

Further down Jl Yos Sudarso towards the Melni harbour is the *Hotel Bunga Muda* (☎ 21349) at No 78, a newish concrete block with fairly clean rooms at 8500/11,000 rp.

Places to Eat

There is a good choice of cafes and mobile warungs selling fried rice and noodles at night. The lane off Jl Sudarso near Jl Sudirman has a wide choice after dark.

Turi on the corner of Jl Sudirman and Jl Yos Sudarso is the popular choice for ikan bakar (barbecued fish), a Tarakan favourite. *Antara* and *Bagi Alam* are the other good ikan bakar places.

Rumah Makan Cahaya on Jl Sudirman opposite the Losmen Jakarta is pretty good; the menu includes octopus, cap cai (fried vegetables) and nasi goreng. The *Phoenix Restaurant* on Jl Yos Sudarso is another good choice for Chinese.

Restoran Kepeting Saos, near Losmen Herlina on Jl Sudirman, specialises in crab dishes and does them well.

At night the happening place is *Depot Theola* on Jl Sudirman, where the local speciality, nasi lalap (battered, fried chunks of chicken served with rice and soup), is served. It also offers cold beer, ice cream, fruit juices and jamu (medicinal herbal drinks). There are only one or two tables downstairs, but there's an upstairs area with several more.

The *Nirwana* on the airport side of Jl Yos Sudarso has OK alfresco dining, but most patrons come here after 11 pm for the bar, disco and other diversions.

If you are craving for different food, try the *Bulungan Restoran* in the Hotel Tarakan Plaza. Its impressive array of Chinese banquet food is very tasty.

Getting There & Away

Air Sempati, Bouraq, DAS and Merpati all fly to Tarakan from Balikpapan or Samarinda. All airline flights from Tarakan to Balikpapan connect with onward flights across Indonesia and internationally.

In Tarakan, Sempati (☎ 21870) is in the Tarakan Plaza on Jl Yos Sudarso. Merpati (☎ 21911) is at Jl Yos Sudarso 10. Bouraq (☎ 21248) is at Jl Yos Sudarso 9B, across from the Tarakan Theatre. DAS (☎ 51612), at Jl Sudirman 9, has useful flights inland, as does MAF (☎ 51011), the missionary airline in the tax building at Jl Sudirman 133. See the Kalimantan Airfares chart in the Getting Around section at the start of this chapter for routes and fares.

Boat The Pelni office is at the main port – take a colt almost to the end of Jl Yos Sudarso. The Pelni ship *Tidar* calls into Tarakan on its Pantoloan-Balikpapan-Pare Pare-Surabaya run. There's another Pelni boat, the *Leuser*, which goes straight from Toli-Toli to Nunukan and Tawau.

From Tarakan you can catch boats to other parts of East Kalimantan. There are daily boats to Berau from the pier near Pasar Sebengkok. Other longboat destinations include: Tanjung Selor (5000 rp, or 10,000 rp by speedboat); Nunukan (15,000 rp, or 25,000 to 30,000 rp by speedboat); and Pulau Bunju (7000 rp). There are also weekly boats to Toli-Toli.

Getting Around

The Airport Taxis (3000 rp) or chartered bemo (1000 rp) are your only option from town to the airport (five km) for those dawn flights. At all other times, bemos pass the terminal gate about 200m from the terminal, and can get you to/from town in 10 minutes for 300 rp.

KALIMANTAN

Colt Transport around town is by colts, which cut a circular route via Jl Sudirman and Jl Yos Sudarso. A 300 rp flat rate gets you anywhere.

TARAKAN TO MALAYSIA

For boats on to Tawau in the eastern Malaysian state of Sabah, go to Pelabuhan Tarakan. Longboats leave daily at around 9 am and arrive in Nunukan 12 hours later for 15,000 rp per person. In **Nunukan** you can catch a speedboat to Tawau for 21,000 rp – it takes about four hours. You can also spend the

night at the *Losmen Nunukan* for 5000 rp and get a speedboat the next day.

There is an Indonesian immigration office in Nunukan where you must finalise your paperwork. Note that if you got a two month tourist visa on arrival in Indonesia, you will need an exit permit from the immigration office in Jakarta. If you obtained a one month tourist visa before coming to Indonesia, immigration at Nunakan can stamp your passport without an exit permit from Jakarta. Some travellers report an easy exit via this route, but most get turned back.

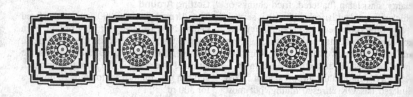

he strangely contorted island of Sulawesi
(formerly Celebes) sprawls across the sea
between Borneo and Maluku. It was first
referred to as Celebes by the Portuguese but
the origins of the name are unclear. One
derivation is from the Bugis *selihe* or *selire*,
meaning 'sea current', or from *si-lebih*,
meaning 'more islands'. Others say Celebes
could be a corruption of *Klabat*, the name of
the volcano which towers over Minahasa in
the north. The modern name Sulawesi (and
possibly Celebes too) seems to come from
sula (island) *besi* (iron), a reference to the
iron deposits around Danau (Lake) Matano,
the richest in South-East Asia.

The 227,000 sq km island is divided into
four provinces: South; South-East; Central;
and North Sulawesi. Most visitors head to
Tanatoraja in South Sulawesi, but more are
venturing beyond the tourist precincts.

HISTORY

Protected by mountains and walled in by
thick jungle, the interior of the island has
provided a refuge for some of Indonesia's
earliest inhabitants, some of whom preserved
elements of their idiosyncratic cultures well
into the 20th century. The Makassarese and
Bugis of the south-west peninsula and the
Christian Minahasans of the far north are the
dominant groups of Sulawesi. They have
also had the most contact with the west, but
it's the Christian-animist Toraja, of the Tanatoraja district of the central highlands, who
attract large numbers of visitors every year.

Other minorities, particularly Bajau sea

HIGHLIGHTS

- **Tanatoraja** – The colourful funerals of Tanatoraja, a highland region in the south-western peninsula, are Sulawesi's best-known attraction. Throngs of tourists tail a mass migration of expatriate Toraja living all over Indonesia, who return each dry season (June-August) for these festive events.

- **Natural Attractions** – The mountains of Tanatoraja are serenely beautiful, as are those of Central Sulawesi. Many hikers are venturing further afield to explore the island's natural beauty, as well as the unusual megaliths of the Bada Valley, south of Palu, and the unique wildlife of Sulawesi's richly diverse parks.

- **Beaches** – Sulawesi also has some superb beaches and coral reefs. The 'sea gardens' off Manado, particularly around Pulau Bunaken, offer some of the best snorkelling and diving in Indonesia, while the pristine reefs around the Togian Islands are an untouched tropical wonder.

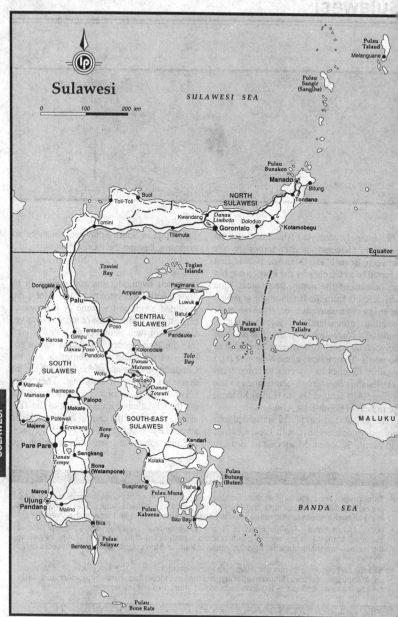

Sulawesi

0   100   200 km

SULAWESI SEA

Pulau
Talaud
Melanguane

Pulau
Sangir
(Sangihe)

Pulau
Bunaken
Manado
Bitung
Tondano

**NORTH
SULAWESI**

Buol
Toli-Toli
Kwandang *Danau* Doloduo
Limboto
Tomini **Gorontalo** Kotamobagu
Tilamuta

Equator

*Tomini
Bay* *Togian
Islands*

Donggala Pagimana
Ampana Luwuk
Palu Batui
Poso **CENTRAL
SULAWESI** Pandauke
Tentena Pulau Pulau
Gimpu Banggai Taliabu
Karosa *Danau Poso* Kolonodale
Pendolo *Danau* *Tolo
Wotu* *Matano* *Bay*
**SOUTH
SULAWESI** Saroako
*Danau
Mamuju* *Towuti*
Mamasa Rantepao
Palopo
Makale **SOUTH-EAST
SULAWESI**
Polewali
Enrekang *Bone*
Majene *Bay* Kendari
Pare Pare Kolaka
Sengkang Pulau
Danau Bone Butung
Tempe (Watampone) (Buton)
Buapinang Pulau Muna Raha
Maros Pulau
Ujung Malino Kabaena Bau Bau *BANDA SEA*
Pandang
Bira
Benteng Pulau
Selayar

MALUKU

Pulau
Bone Rate

nomads, have played an integral role in the land's history. The rise of Gowa – Sulawesi's first major power – from the mid-16th century was partly due to its trading alliance with the Bajau. The Bajau supplied much-sought after sea produce, especially *trepang* sea cucumbers; a Chinese delicacy), tortoiseshell, birds' nests and pearl, attracting international traders to Gowa's capital Makassar (now Ujung Padang).

Makassar quickly became known as a cosmopolitan, tolerant and secure entrepôt which allowed traders to bypass the Dutch monopoly over the spice trade in the east. This was a considerable concern to the Dutch. In 1660 they sunk six Portuguese ships in Makassar Harbour, captured the fort and forced Gowa's ruler, Sultan Hasanuddin, into an alliance. Eventually, the Dutch managed to exclude all other foreign traders from Makassar, effectively shutting down the port.

Even after Indonesia won its independence, ongoing civil strife stultified Sulawesi's attempts at post-war reconstruction until well into the 1960s. Sulawesi is now enjoying its first decades of uninterrupted peace, peace that has delivered unprecedented and accelerating development. This rapid growth is particularly evident in Ujung Pandang, which is rapidly reasserting its place as the entrepôt for eastern Indonesia.

CLIMATE

Although temperatures are relatively constant all year, Sulawesi's mountainous terrain plays havoc with local rainfall patterns. The wettest months along Sulawesi's west coast tend to be around December, when north-westerly and westerly winds prevail, while south-easterly winds dump heavy falls along the eastern regions around May.

Mountain ranges at right angles to the prevailing winds tend to have heavy rainfall on the windward side and little on the leeward. So, while Maros cops over 500 mm of rainfall per month between December and February, towns on the leeward side of the peninsula are relatively dry.

Valleys with a north-south orientation receive little rain at any time of year, making the Palu Valley in Central Sulawesi one of the driest areas in Indonesia, with an average annual rainfall of less than 600 mm.

FLORA & FAUNA

Sulawesi's landscape is strikingly beautiful and the island, a transition zone between Asia and Australia, is home to some peculiar animals. Of the 127 indigenous mammals, 61% are found only on Sulawesi. If you exclude 62 species of bats, the proportion of endemic mammal species rises to 98% and many of these are in danger of extinction.

Wallace's Line

Detailed surveys of Borneo and Sulawesi by English naturalist Alfred Wallace in the 1850s resulted in some inspired correspondence with Charles Darwin. Wallace was struck by the marked differences in wildlife, despite the two islands' proximity and similarities in climate and geography. His letters to Darwin, detailing evidence of his theory that the Indonesian archipelago was inhabited by one distinct fauna in the east and one in the west, prompted Darwin to publish similar observations from his own travels. The subsequent debate on species distribution and evolution revolutionised modern thought.

Wallace refined his theory in 1859, drawing a boundary between the two regions of fauna. Wallace's Line, as it came to be known, divided Sulawesi and Lombok to the east, and Borneo and Bali to the west. He believed that islands to the west of the line had once been a part of Asia and those to the east had been linked to a Pacific-Australian continent. Sulawesi's wildlife was so unusual that Wallace suspected it was once a part of both, a fact that geologists have since proven to be true.

Other analyses of where Australian-type fauna begin to outnumber Asian fauna have placed the line further east. Much depends on what groups of animals are included, as M Weber found in using molluscs and mammals. Lydekker's Line, which lies east of Maluku and Timor, is generally accepted as the western boundary of strictly Australian fauna, while Wallace's Line marks the eastern boundary of Oriental fauna. The zone in between includes large groups of endemic species that challenge the notion of a gradual transition from one region to the next. ■

The biggest (and among the rarest) mammal is the metre high dwarf buffalo, or *anoa*, found in both lowland and highland jungle. There are also curly tusked *babirusa*, or 'pig-deer', which have long legs and tusks which curve upwards like horns, and various other critters, including primates such as the *tarsier* – the world's smallest primate at just 10 cm long.

Of the 328 known species of birds on Sulawesi, 27% are endemic. The best known and most vulnerable is the *maleo*, a megapode about the size of a chicken, which builds mounds near hot springs, volcanic vents and hot sandy beaches to incubate its eggs.

Popular locals not yet considered at risk of extinction include the shy, but very cute, cuscus and the slightly punk-looking black-crested macaque.

LANGUAGE

Sulawesi's 12 million residents speak dozens of dialects; at least two of the nine language groups in western Malayo-Polynesia are found only on Sulawesi. Indonesian is, at best, a second or third language for most, and foreign languages barely rate a mention except in the Minahasan region of North Sulawesi, where most older people speak fluent Dutch and younger folk have a better than average grasp of English.

MONEY

US travellers cheques are the only useful foreign denomination and even those can only be changed in provincial capitals and larger towns, such as Rantepao and Poso. A few banks in Manado and Ujung Pandang will accept cheques in other currencies, notably British, but not many.

BOOKS & MAGAZINES

Sulawesi: Indonesia, edited by Toby Volkman, Ian Caldwell and Eric Oey, revised by Kal Muller, is a guide book with plenty for readers to chew on.

Nigel Barley's *Not a Hazardous Sport* is the larger than life account of an anthropological 'plunge' into Tanatoraja. Barley's irreverent, self-deprecatory humour shed new light on the frustrations of travel i Indonesia.

White Stranger – Six Moons in Celebes by Harry Wilcox, a British army officer wh spent six months in the Rantepao district i the late 1940s.

The Ecology of Sulawesi, by Anthon Whitten, Muslimin Mustafa and Gregor Henderson, is heavy to carry, even heavier t read, but a bonanza of useful data on ever thing that grows, crawls, swims or flies c Sulawesi.

DANGERS & ANNOYANCES

Road blocks Most road blocks, such a police 'licence checks', inflate drivers' cos by around 1000 rp per stop. Others stin travellers directly with official charges t enter areas such as Bira beach (1000 rp Tanatoraja (3500 rp) and anywhere else th draws a crowd.

Diving courses Crash courses for divers ca be lethal. Some are better than others, bu most are very expensive and none match th standard of professionally recognise courses run over several months. Lear before you go to Sulawesi.

Money Travellers who make a spectacle c haggling to save 100 rp on fruit at a marke but happily pay the inflated costs of set-pric establishments, are another annoyance. Sim ply ask around for the going price of marke produce and save the foot stomping for res tauraateurs commanding 6000 rp for bottle of warm beer.

HIKING

Central Sulawesi is becoming a Mecca fo novice trekkers attracted by ancient mega liths, good paths, intact jungle and isolatec easy-going locals. A huge area between Tan atoraja and Palu is only accessible by foot c light aircraft, as are the nature reserves of th eastern peninsula.

SULAWESI

GETTING THERE & AWAY
Air

Garuda, Merpati, Sempati, Bouraq and Mandala all fly to Sulawesi, with most connections via Ujung Pandang. Singapore's regional carrier Silk has direct flights from Singapore to Ujung Pandang and Manado, and Malaysia Airlines now links Kuala Lumpur to Ujung Pandang. The Philippines city of Davao is serviced by Bouraq flights to and from Manado twice a week. Manado and Ujung Pandang are approved gateways for visa-free tourists.

Sea

North Sulawesi's Bitung sea port is approved for visa-free entry, but there are no ferry services from the Philippines.

Sulawesi's domestic ferry connections are the best in Indonesia. Nine Pelni ships call at Ujung Pandang, including five which sail on to Bitung in North Sulawesi, and each year Pelni adds to its fleet. The KM *Tilongkabila* goes a fortnightly hop up and down Sulawesi's isolated east coast, and then on to the Sangir (Sangihe)-Talaud islands.

GETTING AROUND
Air

Garuda, Sempati and Bouraq fly the busier, more profitable routes, while Merpati takes care of the rest. The Missionary Air Fellowship (MAF) services remote communities, but its cheap flights are usually booked well in advance.

Bus

Regions around Ujung Pandang in the southwest and Manado in the north-east have excellent roads and frequent buses. Other thoroughfares include the well-maintained Trans-Sulawesi Highway from Ujung Pandang to Manado via Rantepao and Poso, however, landslides often block the mountainous stretches in central and north Sulawesi.

Boat

Pelni ships call regularly at all big ports, providing a comfortable alternative to long hours by road. Smaller ferries bridge Sulawesi's characteristically long peninsulas, including regular boats across Tomini Bay from Pagimana to Gorontalo, and another across Bone Bay from Bajoe to Kolaka.

Sulawesi Seafarers

The Bugis are Indonesia's best-known sailors, trading and carrying goods on their magnificent wooden schooners throughout Indonesia. The Bugis' influence expanded rapidly after the fall of Makassar resulting in a diaspora from southern Sulawesi in the 17th and 18th centuries. They established strategic trading posts at Kutai, Johor and Selangor, and traded freely throughout the region. Bugis and Makassarese boats are still built along Sulawesi's and Kalimantan's south coasts, using centuries-old designs and techniques.

The Bajau, Bugis, Butonese and Makassarese seafarers of Sulawesi have a 500 year history of trading and cultural links with the Aborigines of northern Australia. British explorer Matthew Flinders encountered 60 Indonesian schooners at Melville Bay in 1803 and many more are still making the risky journey to fish reefs in a cyclone belt off the north Australian coast today.

In a 1981 treaty which considerably extended Australia's territorial waters, Indonesia traded as much as 80% of the sea area between its southernmost islands and Australia's northern shores, in return for generous promises of aid. This agreement was the culmination of series of measures which gradually excluded (without compensation) Indonesia's traditional seafarers from the reefs they had been fishing for centuries. Australia still allows sail-powered vessels to continue the tradition in certain areas, but fiercely protects vaguely marked and ever-expanding conservation zones. 'Offenders' caught on these reefs are jailed or repatriated and have their boats burnt.

The Minahasans of North Sulawesi, relative newcomers to sailing folklore, are found working on international shipping lines across the world. Like their Filipino neighbours, the Minahasans' outward looking culture, plus their language and sailing skills, make them the first choice of many captains. ■

SULAWESI

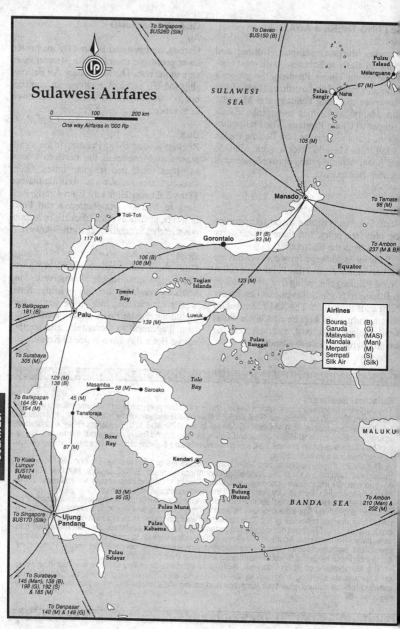

Sulawesi Airfares

0   100   200 km

One way Airfares in '000 Rp

SULAWESI SEA

To Singapore
$US260 (Silk)

To Davao
$US150 (B)

Pulau
Talaud

Melanguane

67 (M)

Pulau
Sangir   Naha

105 (M)

Manado

To Ternate
98 (M)

Toli-Toli

117 (M)

Gorontalo   91 (B)
93 (M)

To Ambon
237 (M & B)

106 (B)
108 (M)

Equator

Togian
Islands   123 (M)

Tomini
Bay

To Balikpapan
181 (B)

Palu   139 (M)   Luwuk

Pulau
Banggai

To Surabaya
305 (M)

129 (M)
138 (B)

Masamba   58 (M)   Saroako

Tolo
Bay

To Balikpapan
164 (B) &
154 (M)   45 (M)

Tanatoraja

Airlines

Bouraq   (B)
Garuda   (G)
Malaysian   (MAS)
Mandala   (Man)
Merpati   (M)
Sempati   (S)
Silk Air   (Silk)

87 (M)

Bone
Bay

Kendari

MALUKU

To Kuala
Lumpur
$US174
(Mas)

Pulau
Butung
(Buton)

93 (M)
95 (S)

To Ambon
210 (Man) &
202 (M)

To Singapore
$US170 (Silk)   Ujung
Pandang

Pulau Muna

BANDA SEA

Pulau
Kabaena

Pulau
Selayar

To Surabaya
145 (Man), 138 (B),
198 (G), 192 (S)
& 185 (M)

To Denpasar
140 (M) & 149 (G)

SULAWESI

South Sulawesi

outh Sulawesi Province covers the south-
western peninsula, a lush, mountainous
egion of caves, waterfalls and large (but
urprisingly shallow) lakes. Irrigated-rice
griculture is widely practised. Coffee,
otton and sugar cane are also important
rops. The 6.5 million inhabitants include
bout four million Bugis, two million Mak-
ssarese and around 500,000 Toraja.

Descendants of the region's earliest tribes
till existed until fairly recently. Groups like
he Toala (meaning 'forest people') had
windled to a couple of villages near Maros
y the 1930s and have now vanished. Other
ribes have been subsumed by the dominant
groups.

Torajan mythology suggests that its ances-
ors came by boat from the south, sailed up
he Sungai Sa'dan and initially dwelled in
he Enrekang region, before being pushed
nto the mountains by the arrival of other
groups.

The Bugis and the Makassarese are the
nain groups on the coast. The Makassarese
are concentrated in the southern tip, centred
on the port of Makassar. The Bugis and
Makassarese have similar cultures. Both are
seafaring people who for centuries were
active in trade, sailing to Flores, Timor and
Sumba, and even as far south as the northern
coast of Australia. Islam became their dom-
nant religion, but both retain vestiges of
heir traditional beliefs.

History

Much of South Sulawesi's history has been
shaped by the conflict between the Bugis,
Makassarese and Toraja. Pushed north-
wards, the Toraja built their villages high in
the mountains of central Sulawesi to guard
against the marauding Bugis. Despite the
constant threat they never formed a united
front against the common enemy. Compli-
cating the story was the continuing rivalry
between the Bugis and the Makassarese.

The southern peninsula was divided into
petty kingdoms, the most powerful being the
Makassarese kingdom of Gowa (centred on
the port of Makassar) and the Bugis kingdom
of Bone. Around 1530, before its conversion
to Islam, Gowa started to expand. By the
mid-16th century it had established itself at
the head of a major trading bloc in eastern
Indonesia. The king of Gowa adopted Islam
in 1605, and between 1608 and 1611 Gowa
attacked and subdued Bone, spreading Islam
to the whole Bugis-Makassarese area.

The Dutch Vereenigde Oost-Indische
Compagnie (VOC) found that Gowa was a
considerable hindrance to its plans to
monopolise the spice trade. They found an
anti-Gowa ally in the exiled Bugis prince
Arung Palakka. The Dutch sponsored
Palakka's return to Bone in 1666, prompting
Bone and Soppeng to rise against the Makassarese. A year of fighting ensued, and Sultan
Hasanuddin of Gowa was forced to sign the
Treaty of Bungaya in 1667. Under the treaty,
Makassarese claims to Minahasa, Butung
and Sumbawa were abandoned and European traders (other than the VOC) were
expelled. Gowa's power was broken and in
its place Bone, under Palakka, became the
supreme state of southern Sulawesi.

The closure of Makassar prompted many
Bugis – particularly from Wajo – to emigrate
throughout the region and establish sultanates in Kutai (Kalimantan), Johore (near
Singapore) and Selangor (near Kuala Lumpur).

Rivalry between Bone and the other Bugis
states continually reshaped the political
landscape. After their brief absence during
the Napoleonic Wars, the Dutch returned to
a Bugis revolt led by the Queen of Bone. This
was suppressed, but rebellions continued
until Makassarese and Bugis resistance was
finally broken in 1905-06. In 1905 the Dutch
also conquered Tanatoraja, again in the face
of bloody resistance. Unrest continued until
the early 1930s.

The 20th century has had a mixed effect
on the people of South Sulawesi. Under
the Dutch, the Toraja came down from
their hilltop forts into the valleys and adopted wet-rice cultivation. The efforts of the

SULAWESI

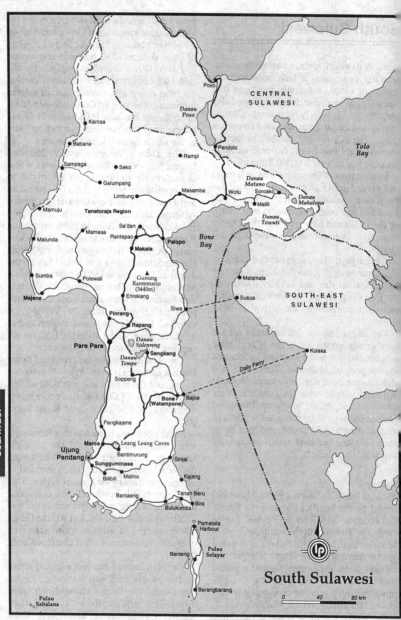

South Sulawesi

0   40   80 km

missionaries have given a veneer of Christianity to their traditional beliefs and customs, although extravagant funeral ceremonies continue. The Makassarese and Bugis remain Indonesia's premier seafaring people. Their schooners probably comprise the biggest sailing fleet in the world today. The people are staunchly Islamic and independently minded – revolts against the central government on Java took place in the 1950s. In 1996 a central government proposal to permit public transport price hikes of up to 60% triggered mass protests on the streets and university campuses of Ujung Pandang. Several students died in the ensuing military crackdown.

UJUNG PANDANG

Once known as Makassar, this great city-port of 800,000 people on the south-western limb of Sulawesi has been the gateway to eastern Indonesia and the 'Spice Islands' (Maluku) for centuries. From Makassar, the Dutch could control much of the shipping that passed between western and eastern Indonesia. The direct territorial control required to maintain this hegemony was very small.

Today, Ujung Pandang is regaining its prominence as a major regional port with the reconstruction of its main shipping docks and the installation of container facilities. An investment boom is reshaping the centre of town, with new hotels, offices and shopping centres, and satellite suburbs are springing up to the east of town.

Elements of the past remain intact. The Muslim Bugis are known for their magnificent sailing ships that trade extensively throughout the Indonesian archipelago. You can see some of these *prahu* at Paotere harbour, a short *becak* (bicycle-rickshaw) ride north of the city centre.

The impressive Fort Rotterdam stands as a reminder of the Dutch occupation and there are many other colonial buildings, including the governor's residence on Jl Jen Sudirman. Ujung Pandang is also the last resting place of Sultan Hasanuddin and of the Javanese prince Diponegoro. In the surrounding area are the palace of the Gowanese kings, waterfalls where the naturalist Alfred Wallace collected butterflies, and cave-paintings left by the first inhabitants of Sulawesi.

Orientation

Ujung Pandang is a busy port with its main harbour in the north-west of the city. The streets immediately east of the harbour are where you'll find the cheapest accommodation and a seedy Chinatown. Further east is the local transport hub and main shopping centre, the Makassar Mall.

Fort Rotterdam is in the centre of the older commercial hub, and the nearby Makassar Golden Hotel dominates the beach front. The esplanade stretching south of the hotel is one of Indonesia's finest hawker strips and claims to be the longest dining table in the world.

Information

Tourist Office The South Sulawesi tourist office (☎ 443355) is at Jl Pettarani, near the corner of Jl Rappocini, several km south-east of the centre. The staff are friendly, but their information is limited.

Money The Bank Rakyat Indonesia (BRI), Bank Danamon and Bank Niaga are on Jl Ahmad Yani, and Bank Negara Indonesia (BNI) is on the corner of Jl Ahmad Yani and Jl Sudirman. The moneychanger at the airport, 22 km east of town, gives the same rates as the banks. Haji La Tunrung Star Group (☎ 872910), Jl Monginsidi 42, just north of the fort, gives similar rates to the banks and is open on public holidays.

Post & Communications The post office is on the corner of Jl Supratman and Jl Slamet Riyadi, south-east of the fort. *Wartel* offices are everywhere, but the beachfront Wartel Metro (☎ 314514) at Jl Penghibur 42 is cheaper and better than Telkom. Card phones have international access, and the Marannu Hotel and Legends Hostel have Home Country Direct phones for collect and credit calls.

SULAWESI

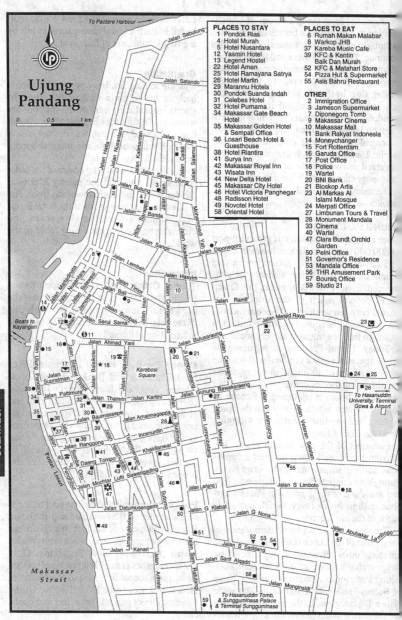

PLACES TO STAY
1 Pondok Rias
4 Hotel Murah
5 Hotel Nusantara
12 Yasmin Hotel
13 Legend Hostel
22 Hotel Aman
25 Hotel Ramayana Satrya
26 Hotel Marlin
29 Marannu Hotels
30 Pondok Suanda Indah
31 Celebes Hotel
32 Hotel Purnama
34 Makassar Gate Beach Hotel
35 Makassar Golden Hotel & Sempati Office
36 Losari Beach Hotel & Guesthouse
38 Hotel Riantira
41 Surya Inn
42 Makassar Royal Inn
43 Wisata Inn
44 New Delta Hotel
45 Makassar City Hotel
46 Hotel Victoria Panghegar
48 Radisson Hotel
49 Novotel Hotel
58 Oriental Hotel

PLACES TO EAT
6 Rumah Makan Malabar
8 Warkop JHB
37 Kareba Music Cafe
39 KFC & Kantin Baik Dan Murah
52 KFC & Matahari Store
54 Pizza Hut & Supermarket
55 Asia Bahru Restaurant

OTHER
2 Immigration Office
3 Jameson Supermarket
7 Diponegoro Tomb
9 Makassar Cinema
10 Makassar Mall
11 Bank Rakyat Indonesia
14 Moneychanger
15 Fort Rotterdam
16 Garuda Office
17 Post Office
18 Police
19 Wartel
20 BNI Bank
21 Bioskop Artis
23 Al Markas Al Islami Mosque
24 Merpati Office
27 Limbunan Tours & Travel
28 Monument Mandala
33 Cinema
40 Wartel
47 Clara Bundt Orchid Garden
50 Pelni Office
51 Governor's Residence
53 Mandala Office
56 THR Amusement Park
57 Bouraq Office
59 Studio 21

Medical Services

Of the several hospitals in town, the biggest and best is the Rumah Sakit Umum (General Hospital) adjacent to the Hasanuddin University way out on the eastern outskirts of town.

Fort Rotterdam

One of the best preserved examples of Dutch architecture in Indonesia, Fort Rotterdam continues to guard the harbour of Ujung Pandang. A Gowanese fort dating back to 1545 once stood here, but that failed to keep out the Dutch. The original fort was rebuilt in Dutch style after the Treaty of Bungaya in 1667. Parts of the crumbling wall have been left pretty much as they were, and provide an interesting comparison to the restored buildings. The fort now bears the rather more nationalistic title of Benteng (Fort) Ujung Pandang. Admission costs 1000 rp.

Of the two **museums** in the fort, the larger, more interesting one is on the right as you enter. It is open Tuesday to Thursday from 8 am to 1.30 pm, Friday until 10.30 am, weekends until 12.30 pm and closed Monday. It has an assortment of exhibits, including rice bowls from Tanatoraja, kitchen tools, musical instruments and various costumes.

The other museum is Speelman's House, completed in 1686 and the oldest of the fort buildings. The building itself is beautiful; not so the shoddy display of stamps and coins.

Every Sunday, the **Benteng Conversation Club** turns the fort into a type of open university for students to practise their English. Dozens of youths meet around midmorning, canvass a topic, then break up into small groups for sometimes heated debates – in English – on everything from politics to shotgun weddings. It is a terrific way to hear what young locals have to say about a whole range of issues.

Diponegoro Tomb

Prince Diponegoro of Yogyakarta led the Java War of 1825-30, but his career as a rebel leader came to a sudden halt when he was tricked into going to the Dutch headquarters to negotiate peace. He was taken prisoner and exiled to Sulawesi. He spent the last 26 years of his life imprisoned in Fort Rotterdam. His grave and monument can be seen in a small cemetery on Jl Diponegoro.

Paotere Harbour

This anchorage north of town is where the Bugis sailing ships berth. There is usually lots of activity on the dock and in the busy fish market a few streets south of the port.

Chinese Temples

You'll notice a large number of ethnic Chinese Indonesians in Ujung Pandang. Both new and old Chinese temples can be seen along Jl Sulawesi, but the most ornate is the brilliantly coloured building on the corner of Jl Sulawesi and Jl Serui Sama.

Clara Bundt Orchid Garden

This well-known orchid garden and shell collection is almost an institution of the city, hidden away behind a home at Jl Mochtar Lufti 15. It's a little oasis in the middle of Ujung Pandang, founded by the late Clara Bundt as a hobby but subsequently developed into a business famous for its exotic hybrids. Some specimens grow up to five metres high. There's a huge collection of shells, including dozens of giant clams. This is a private garden, but visitors are welcome. Admission is free.

Monument Mandala

This scaled-down version of Jakarta's Monas (National Monument) obelisk celebrates the 'liberation' of Irian Jaya. Its completion in 1996 coincided with an Organisasi Papua Merdeka (OPM) guerilla campaign in Irian Jaya drawing world attention to Indonesia's 'occupation' of the territory.

Al Markas Al Islami Mosque

This impressive new mosque east of town is to be complemented by a university and Islamic education centre.

Nearby Islands

A speck of land just off Ujung Pandang, **Samalona Island** is a popular spot for fishing and snorkelling. Legend Hostel and Kareba Cafe both run Sunday excursions there; the price depends on the number of people to share the costs.

Ceria Nugraha at Jl Usman Jafur 9 runs tours to Samalona, **Barranglompo** (a fishing and silversmith island), **Kudingakang Keke**, and other islands and sand bars. Or you can charter a boat from beside the Kayangan jetty (opposite the fort) for around 30,000 rp a day.

Pulau Kayangan is more of a promenading circuit than a beach and is not really a place to swim. The main interest lies in its Sunday discos, karaoke and other entertainment. Boats at the jetty opposite the fort ferry sightseers to and fro for 5000 rp per person.

Old Gowa

Remnants of the former kingdom of Gowa on the south-eastern outskirts of Ujung Pandang include the **Tomb of Sultan Hasanuddin** (1629-70), ruler of Gowa in the mid-17th century. Hasanuddin is a revered figure among the Makassarese because of his struggle against the Dutch. Outside the tomb compound is the **Pelantikan Stone**, on which the kings of Gowa were crowned.

About 15 minutes' walk from the tomb of Sultan Hasanuddin is the site of the **Katangka Mosque**. A mosque was first built here in 1603, but a modern building now occupies the site. More interesting is the attached cemetery with its large crypts, each containing several graves.

Sungguminasa Palace, once the seat of the Sultan of Gowa, is a few km further south at Sungguminasa. The former royal residence, now known as **Museum Ballalompoa**, houses a collection of artefacts similar to those in the Fort Rotterdam museums. Although the royal regalia can only be seen on request, the wooden Bugis-style palace itself is the real attraction. It was constructed in 1936 and raised on stilts. To get there take a *pete-pete* (bemo; 350 rp) or Damri bus (250 rp) from Makassar Mall.

Tallo

The Tallo dynasty was a junior, but influential, partner in the Gowa-Tallo alliance that founded Makassar in the 16th century. Tallo's spiritual centre was a seaside fort on the banks of Sungai Tallo, three km north east of the centre of modern Ujung Pandang. Little remains other than a few royal tombs amid rice fields off Jl Tallo Umar.

Places to Stay – bottom end

Legend Hostel (☎ 328203), Jl Jampea 5G, is cheap, clean and friendly, with small doubles for 12,500 rp, dorm beds for 5500 rp and 3000 rp crash mats when all else is full. There is a cafe-lounge, maps, advice, books of tips from other travellers, and a Home Country Direct telephone for international collect and credit calls.

Hotel Ramayana Satrya (☎ 442478), Jl Gunung Bawakaraeng 121, has rooms from 15,000 rp, plus tax. It's clean, conveniently located and popular with travellers. There are also rooms from 25,000 rp with air-con and private bath. Take mosquito coils. Diagonally opposite is the similarly priced *Hotel Marlin*.

Pondok Rias at Jl Bontomarannu 7 has singles/doubles for 15,000/17,500 rp, or 20,000/25,000 rp with air-con.

The *Mandar Indah Inn* (☎ 875548) at Jl Anuang 17, to the south of town, is not so convenient, but is better value at 9000 rp for a double, or 15,000 rp for a double with mandi (Indonesian-style bath).

The other cheapies are far less impressive and many don't take foreigners. The bottom of the line is *Hotel Nusantara* (☎ 323163) Jl Sarappo 103, where hot, noisy little sweatboxes go for 7000 rp. Just across the road at No 60 is the slightly better appointed *Hotel Murah* (☎ 323101), with windowless rooms for 15,000 rp and 'boxes' from 10,000 rp.

Rates for the dimly lit *Hotel Purnama* (☎ 323830), just south of the fort at Jl Pattimura 3, start at 16,500/22,000 rp.

Ujung Pandang Backpackers (☎ 322-417), Jl Lompobattang 3, next to the Bioskop Artis, has dorm bunks from 8000 rp. It's a good new facility, but was struggling to get its act together.

Places to Stay – middle

The choice of mid-range hotels is excellent, especially in the residential precinct south of the fort. *Pondok Suanda Indah* (☎ 312857) at Jl Hasanuddin 12, opposite the Marannu, is highly recommended. This small, airy hotel is new, but has the feel of a classic colonial guesthouse. Singles/doubles start at 32,350/48,400 rp.

Wisata Inn (☎ 324344), just down the road at No 36, has small rooms out the back with a shared mandi for 27,500/37,500 rp. Better value are the bigger air-con rooms from 50,000/60,000 rp which overlook a courtyard garden. The *New Delta Hotel* (☎ 312711), opposite the Wisata at No 43, is friendly and similarly priced at 42,500/55,000 rp plus tax.

The five storey *Surya Inn* (☎ 327568), Jl Daeng Tompo 3, offers breezy high-rise views of the city and harbour islands. Second floor rooms are 52,500/ 65,000 rp. Prices drop as you climb the stairs. Rooms are small, but comfortable.

The nearby *Makassar Royal Inn,* also on Jl Daeng Tompo, has so-so economy air-con rooms for 34,500 rp, including breakfast, but you might need a map to find your way through the warren of extensions.

The *Hotel Karuwisi Indah* at Jl Sumoharjo 225, the road to the airport, has basic rooms from 20,000 to 40,000 rp.

The *Makassar Cottages* (☎ 873363), Jl Dangko 52, are less conveniently located south of town, but offer top-value Balinese-style cottages for 27,500 to 32,000 rp. To get there take a Jl Dangko mikrolet (bemo) from Makasar Mall for 300 rp.

Hotel Afiat (☎ 510724) is a 10 minute walk from the airport, facing the main road into Ujung Pandang, with singles from 26,000 rp.

Places to Stay – top end

Boom times in Ujung Pandang have spurred a spate of hotel building. Prices yo-yo as each newcomer floods the market with extra capacity.

The expanding choice now includes the fine and friendly *Yasmin Hotel* (☎ 320424; fax 328283) at Jl Jampea 5, with rooms from $US45/50 to $US105, less discounts.

The *Radisson Ujung Pandang* (☎ 333111; fax 333222), Jl Somba Opu 235, is leading the brigade of big-name chains chasing corporate business in Ujung Pandang. Room rates range from US$140 to $350, with discounts of up to 50%. The Novotel and construction plans by other large chains should keep the discounting competitive.

On the waterfront is the *Losari Beach Hotel* (☎ 326062) at Jl Penghibur 10, with rooms from 87,000/114,000 rp. The best views are reserved for the expensive suites. Try for a 'low season' discount, or check out the *Losari Beach Guesthouse* next door.

Makassar Golden Hotel (☎ 314408; fax 320951), on the shore at Jl Pasar Ikan 50, is an enormous hotel with rooms from US$66/83. *Makassar Gate Beach Hotel* (☎ 325791), a couple of doors down the road, is similar value with rooms from 140,000/ 165,000 rp, including tax.

The renovated and extended *Marannu City Hotel* (☎ 315087; fax 311818) at Jl Hasanuddin 3 has rooms from $US48/55, and suites from $US70, with discounts of up to 50%. The adjoining *Marannu Tower* starts at 155,000/175,000 rp. The complex also has a small swimming pool open to the public for 7000 rp a day. The *Marannu Garden Hotel* (☎ 852244), Jl Baji Gau 52, opens its big pool to visitors for 7000 rp a day.

The classy new *Celebes Hotel* (☎ 320770) at Jl Hasanuddin 2 has rooms from 75,000/108,000 rp. Check the view from the rooftop restaurant.

Hotel Victoria Panghegar (☎ 311556; fax 312468), Jl Jen Sudirman 24, has standard rooms for 65,000/75,000 rp (plus tax) in its pavilion, and rooms from 135,000/140,000 in the tower. Bands play in a cafe overlooking the pool.

Places to Eat

Home to Indonesia's foremost seafaring peoples, this place has good seafood in abundance. Barbecued fish and octopus are especially popular. Because of the sizeable Chinese population, Ujung Pandang is also a good place for Chinese food. Local specialties include soto makassar, a soup made from buffalo innards, and the odd, but very tasty, blend of avocadoes, condensed milk and chocolate syrup.

The dozens of evening food trolleys along the waterfront south of the Makassar Golden Hotel make Pantai Losari (Losari Beach) the longest dining strip on Sulawesi, and also the best spot to watch Ujung Pandang's famous sunsets.

If the hustlers get too much for you, retreat to *Kios Semarang*, or the *Minasa* or *Fajar* rooftop cafes south of the Kareba Music Cafe. The food is so-so, but the views are great.

There are good, cheap restaurants along Jl Sulawesi. *Rumah Makan Malabar*, Jl Sulawesi 264, specialises in Indian curries and martabak. Try the goat head curry, cow tail soup, sate or the tastiest chicken curry east of Singapore.

The vegetable curry puffs at *Warkop JHB* on the corner of Jl Sulawesi and Jl Lembah are delicious. This sunny little co-operative also dishes up wanton noodles, nasi kuning and hot, strong filtered coffee. It's very busy on Sunday.

Asia Bahru Restaurant, near the corner of Jl Latimojong and Jl G Sala, specialises in seafood and when you order a big fish you get a very big fish! But the best and cheapest fish, as well as excellent fried duck, can be found at the *warung* opposite the hotel.

Rumah Makan Ujung Pandang, Jl Irian 42, is an air-con restaurant with a mixed Chinese and Indonesian menu, and very large servings.

The great junk food hunt might lead you to *KFC* or the *Kantin Baik dan Murah* (Good & Cheap Canteen) above the supermarket diagonally opposite the Marannu Tower Hotel. The supermarket downstairs panders to the tastes of homesick westerners with imported cheese, chocolates and other overpriced goodies. *Pizza Hut* sells expensive wedges of pizza out the front. *KFC* has a new outlet at the huge Makassar Mall and shares the Latanete Plaza precinct on Jl S Saddang with its clone *CFC*, *Pizza Hut* and several other fast-food chains.

Entertainment

The *Kareba Music Cafe* is a bar and rockin live band venue on Jl Penghibur – admissio prices include drink coupons.

Ujung Pandang's Hash House Harrier drink to their jogging mania at Pak Amin' *Kios Semarang*, Jl Penghibur 20, while mos others go there for cheap beer, views of th sunsets and to prime themselves for a bi night out.

Nightlife options also include the *Zig Za* disco at the Makassar Golden Hotel, seed bars for sailors along the waterfront an occasional live shows at bigger hotels.

Film buffs should rug up before headin to the chilly modern *Studio 21* on Jl San Ratulangi. There's also the *Makassar* on J Bali, and older places such as the *Bioskop Artis* and *Benteng*. Check Ujung Pandang' daily *Fajar* newspaper for screening detail and admission prices.

Things to Buy

Jl Sombu Opu, south of the fort, has shop with great collections of jewellery and 'an tiques'. Toko Kerajinam at No 20 is good fo touristy souvenirs. CV Kanebo, on the J Pattimura corner, has crafts from all ove Indonesia and the nearby Makassar Handi craft Centre is a good starting point fo jewellery.

Ujung Pandang is supposed to be a goo place for buying Kendari filigree silver jewellery. Again, Jl Sombu Opu has a wide selection and is a good starting point.

Other possible buys include Torajan handcrafts, Chinese pottery, Makassarese brass work, silk cloth from Sengkang and Soppeng and mounted butterflies from Bantimurung.

Shopping centres are appearing everywhere, from the amorphous bazaars in and around Makassar Mall, to the huge Matahari department store on Jl S Saddang. The pace of development will accelerate as the new container port, tourism and infrastructure projects bring more commerce to the city.

Getting There & Away

Ujung Pandang is the gateway to southern Sulawesi and is connected to many other arts of Indonesia by air and sea. There are numerous buses to various destinations on the south-western peninsula, although for most people the next stop is the Tanatoraja district in the central highlands.

Air Shop around and check current prices with both airlines and agents. There is plenty of competition and agents can discount heavily. One of the biggest and best discounting shops is Limbunan Tours and Travel (☎ 315010) at Jl G Bawakaraeng 40-42. Anta Travel (☎ 321440) on Jl Irian is another discounter.

Garuda (☎ 322543), Jl Slamet Riyadi 6, flies direct to Manado, Jakarta and Denpasar.

Merpati (☎ 24114) at Jl Gunung Bawakaraeng 109 has the most comprehensive network within Sulawesi, particularly in the south and south-west. For destinations and indicative prices, see the Sulawesi Airfares map at the start of this chapter.

Bouraq (☎ 452506) at Jl Veteran Selatan has useful hops to Balikpapan, Banjarmasin and Samarinda on Kalimantan. Mandala (☎ 324288), Jl Saddang, flies to Jakarta, Surabaya and Ambon. Sempati (☎ 324116) also flies from Ujung Pandang to Denpasar and Surabaya, with connecting flights to Jakarta and beyond.

Malaysia Airlines (☎ 331888) has an office on the ground floor of the Marannu City Hotel and flies to Kuala Lumpur for US$174. Silk Air's office is in the Makassar Golden Hotel.

Bus & Bemo The Gowa terminal for north-bound buses is a few km out on Jl Gowa Jaya, the main airport road. Get there by pete-pete (bemo) for 300 rp. South-bound buses leave from the terminal at Sungguminasa. To get there, take a red pete-pete from Jl Lompobattang east of Karebosi Square for 400 rp.

From Ujung Pandang most people head north to Pare Pare and inland to Rantepao in Tanatoraja. Buses to Makale and Rantepao leave at 8 am (10,000 rp; 10 to 12 hours), plus there are buses in the afternoon and early evening. Liman (☎ 315851) also has buses from Ujung Pandang to Palopo and

Malili. A number of other companies run buses and minibuses to Tanatoraja and other parts of South Sulawesi.

An alternative path to Rantepao is via the south coast road to Bantaeng, Bulukumba and Bira beach. From Bulukumba, turn north to Bone (Watampone), and head north via the highland silk areas of Sengkang and Soppeng.

Taxi Shared taxis to Pare Pare leave from Jl Sarappo, on the same block as the Hotel Nusantara. There are also shared taxis to other places around Ujung Pandang.

Boat Pelni (☎ 331393), Jl Sudirman 38, has nine modern liners which make regular stops in Ujung Pandang on their various loops around Indonesia. For full schedules, visit the Pelni office or the photocopy shop adjacent to Warkop JHB on Jl Sulawesi.

Other possibilities include the cargo ships which leave Ujung Pandang for various Indonesian ports. For inter-island shipping, try PT PPSS at Jl Martadinata 57. If it's not helpful, find out what ships are in port, where they're going and negotiate directly with the captains.

Getting Around

The Airport Pete-pete from Makassar Mall to Ujung Pandang's Hasanuddin airport (22 km east of town) run via Terminal Daya for 1000 rp. From the airport, walk 500m to the main road for pete-pete to the city.

The set taxi fare from the airport to the city centre is 14,300 rp, or 10,000 to 12,000 rp using the meter. Groups can charter minibuses parked opposite the arrivals area for around 10,000 rp, a good option for those rushing to connect with early morning buses to Tanatoraja.

Local Transport Ujung Pandang is too hot to do much walking – you'll need becak and pete-pete. The main pete-pete terminal is at Makassar Mall, and the standard fare is 300 rp or 400 rp to the suburbs. Big old Damri buses take you any distance for 250 rp.

Becak drivers kerb-crawl for custom and

are hard bargainers – the shortest fare costs 500 rp. Some enterprising drivers offer menus of tours around town at set prices.

Taxis run on argo meters – 1500 rp will get you three to four km.

AROUND UJUNG PANDANG
Bantimurung

About 45 km north-east of Ujung Pandang, Bantimurung Falls are set amid lushly vegetated limestone cliffs. Bantimurung is crowded with Indonesian day trippers on weekends and holidays; at other times it's a wonderful retreat from the congestion of Ujung Pandang. Entrance to the reserve costs 2050 rp.

Upstream from the main waterfall there's a smaller waterfall, a pretty but treacherous pool and a **cave** at river level. Bring a torch (flashlight) to look inside. Beyond the upper falls is a quiet, rocky gorge.

There are many other caves in these cliffs, including the 'Dreaming' and 'Toakala Palace' caves, but apart from the scenery the area is also famous for its numerous beautiful **butterflies**. The naturalist Alfred Wallace collected specimens here in the mid-1800s.

To get to Bantimurung, take a Patas bus from in front of Ujung Pandang's BRI bank. The trip takes a bit over an hour. If you can't find a direct bus then take one to Maros (1000 rp; one hour) and another from there for the rest of the way (500 rp; 30 minutes).

Leang Leang Caves

A few km before the Bantimurung turn-off is the turn-off for the Leang Leang Caves, noted for their ancient paintings. The paintings in Leang Pettae and Leang Peta Kere caves are images of human hands. The age of the paintings is unknown, but other relics from nearby Leang Burung II, Ulu Leang and Leang Burung I caves have provided glimpses of life from 8000 to 30,000 years ago.

There are 60 or so known caves in the Maros district. Most are inactive or dry. A notable exception is the recently discovered Salukan Kalang, the largest known cave on Sulawesi at 11 km long; access is restricted.

To get to the Leang Leang caves, take a pete pete from Maros to the 'Taman Purbakala Leang-Leang' turn-off on the Bone roa (250 rp), then walk the last couple of km.

Malino

Malino is a hill resort 74 km east of Ujun Pandang on the pine-covered slopes o Gunung (Mount) Bawakaraeng. Its momen in history was in July 1946, when a meetin of Kalimantan and East Indonesian leader in Malino endorsed the Netherlands' ill-fate plans for a federation.

The Dutch influence is still highly visibl in Malino's architecture and there are man scenic walks. Deer hunting on horseback i these parts was once a favoured sport of th Makassarese royalty.

The spectacular **Takapala Waterfalls** are set amid rice fields four km east of town There are two small *losmen* charging 6000 to 10,000 rp a night. To get there, take a pete pete from Ujung Pandang's Gowa termina for 2500 rp.

SOUTH COAST

South Sulawesi's south coast is remarkably barren compared to the peninsula's rich agricultural hinterland. The climate is drier, rice gives way to maize and lontar palm, and traditional boat building and fishing are the main focus of activity. The landscape is unique, with salt pans by the sea and occasional stands of cactus.

Minibuses and 4WDs run from Ujung Pandang's Sungguminasa terminal to the ports of Bulukumba and Bira. The wide flat road is also an increasingly popular cycling route.

Bantaeng

Bantaeng (also known as Bontain), 123 km from Ujung Pandang, is a Makassarese boat-building centre with a rich maritime history. It was noted as a dependency of the Javanese kingdom of Majapahit, and its ships were mentioned in 14th century Javanese poetry. It was ceded to the Dutch under the Treaty of Bungaya in 1667 and became an administrative centre. These days it is a town much like any other, with fairly ordinary homestay accommodation. North of town, near the village of **Bissapu**, is a 100m-high waterfall.

Bulukumba

The Bugis and Makassarese villages on the coastline near Bulukumba are known for their traditional boat building. The biggest sail major trade routes through Indonesia and beyond, but the main commissions these days seem to be for smaller fishing boats. Bulukumba is also the port for the Pulau Selayar ferry when the May-July currents close Bira's jetty. For cheap accommodation try the grotty *Sinar Jaya* (☎ 81032) on Jl Sawerigading 4, which has dorm beds for 4000 rp, or rooms from 10,000 rp.

Tanah Beru

Tanah Beru is the undisputed capital of traditional south-coast boat building. Recent commissions include full-size boats for foreign customers. Tanah Beru is a fishing village with many of the attractions of Bira, including a beach, but none of the facilities. *Losmen Anda* on the main road has very basic singles/doubles for 6000/8000 rp, including breakfast.

BIRA

Fishing, boat building and weaving are the primary commercial activities in Bira. Its white and beaches are now drawing travellers off the main Ujung Pandang to Tanatoraja tourist trail, but Bira has neither the beauty nor the comfort of Bali's beach resorts. There is swimming, snorkelling, fishing and dolphin watching (if you can find them), but most people peg out a shady corner of the long west beach and drift off with a book.

Bira's facilities are basic, the food is functional and the beach often disappears under feral tides. Those same tides occasionally dump alarming mounds of garbage on the beach. The locals are used to it. Indeed, beachcombing is a time-honoured pastime, and in an area with little of its own timber, the currents' supply of driftwood for fires and other general use is invaluable. Note the artistically sculptured lines of driftwood fencing around houses in Tanateng village.

Fresh water is scarce – most has to be trucked in each morning. Theoretically, this should cap the frenetic tourist development on Paloppalakaya Bay, but unless areas are set aside for conservation, it is likely developers will keep on building. The main spin-off for locals not directly involved in the tourist trade is a new market for the district's cottage industries, especially weaving.

Information

New arrivals at Bira Beach must pay 1000 rp per head at a road block as they enter the beach area. There is an expensive radio telephone and fax link from the wartel at Bira Beach Hotel (☎ (0413) 81515), and travel agencies at the Bira Beach Hotel and Bira View Inn. The souvenir booth near the gate to Bira Beach can change foreign currency, but don't rely on it.

Things to See & Do

Boat builders use age-old techniques to craft **traditional ships** at Marumasa beach near Bira and along the coast at Tanah Beru. Boats of various sizes are at various stages of construction. Natural attractions include dolphin spotting from **Lasa Cape**, butterflies and panoramas at **Pua Janggo**, a small rise above Tanateng village, and snorkelling from the beach in front of Bira View Inn.

Places to Stay

Bira View Inn has a row of 14 Bugis-style cottages on a cliff overlooking Paloppalakaya Bay and is the only sea-front hotel to exploit its superb location. Singles/doubles with breakfast go for 35,000/45,000 rp, or less for longer stays or rooms out the back. Bira View has a shop, snorkelling gear for rent (5000 rp a day) and a restaurant.

Anda Bungalows' gritty thatched-roof cottages cost 8000/10,000 rp a night, including a doughy pancake breakfast. The manager can organise snorkelling and fishing trips. It's quiet and cheap.

Riswan Bungalows is nicer, but rooms all face the main road. The 13,500 rp singles and 17,000 rp doubles include breakfast. If you need to hire a snorkel, mask and fins (7500 rp), negotiate these with the room price. You can find overpriced postcards here too.

The very popular *Riswan Guesthouse* is a

SULAWESI

Bugis house with a cool, breezy porch looking out to the sea. On the quiet rise behind Anda Bungalows, Riswan charges 14,000 rp for singles with shared bath, including three meals. Top value. *Riswan Homestay* in Tanateng village near East Beach takes guests in June/July.

Yaya Homestay, in Bira village, has rooms and three meals for 12,000 rp per person.

Bira Beach Hotel (☎ (0413) 81515) has modern doubles for 45,000 rp, including breakfast, but the price is negotiable. It has a good restaurant and friendly staff.

Hotel Sapolohe next door has a beautiful new Bugis-style house with a 75,000 rp suite and 60,000 rp doubles with ocean views, plus a neat row of clean, comfortable bungalows (40,000 rp) out the back, all with views of the rear of the hotel.

New places include the big, lifeless *Nusa Bira Indah* guesthouse and restaurant, with rooms for 25,000/40,000 rp, including breakfast; the noisy *Pondok Wisata Bahagia*; and the *Pondok Wisata Purnama Bira* – a fine new guesthouse nearing completion with rooms for 20,000 rp.

Tanjung Bira Cottages was also nearing completion at the time of writing, and has an unbeatable location at the north-western end of Paloppalakaya Bay.

For good views and a pleasant setting, *Sunrise Guesthouse* is on a cliff overlooking East Beach. Follow the street that runs past Riswan Homestay right to the end. This area is better known for its dawn views and for the monkeys that appear in the wee hours.

Places to Eat

Bira is no gastronomic getaway. Fish, rice and chilli are the order of the day, but the choice is expanding. *Warung Melati* between Bira Beach Hotel and Riswan's is the cheapest and best, serving simple Indonesian fare, plus the cheapest beer. The *Rumah Makan Sederhana*, a few doors down, offers similar fare.

The restaurant at *Bira Beach Hotel* has a long menu and is happy to fry any fish you drag in. The cooks have garlic, oil and good intentions, but lack imagination.

The restaurants at most guesthouses are open to the public. The *Anda* is the oldest, serving reasonably priced Indonesian dishes. There are fabulous views from the restaurant at *Bira View Inn*.

Things to Buy

Weavers gather under raised Bugis houses to work and gossip. You can hear the click clack of their looms as you walk along the streets. Show an interest, wait for an invitation to take a closer look and, if you like what you see, make an offer. For many women weaving provides a useful cash supplement for school fees and other essentials.

Getting There & Away

Kijang & Bemo From Ujung Pandang's Sungguminasa terminal there are *kijang* (4WD taxis) that go the full 195 km direct to Bira for 7000 rp, but most terminate at Bulukumba (5000 rp). From there you can go to the market to find very crowded bemo to Tanah Beru (25 km; 1200 rp), then wait at the five way intersection at the centre of town for a lift to Bira (18 km; 700 rp). Kijang travelling direct to Bulukumba and Ujung Pandang leave from outside the Bira Beach Hotel every morning.

Bemos between Bira and Bira Beach cost 200 rp.

Bemos from Bulukumba's intercity terminal to Bone (4500 rp) take you through lush, pretty countryside, a stark contrast to the barren limestone surrounding Bira. The road is good.

Boat Ferries from Bira to Pamatata Harbour on Pulau Selayar (4000 rp) depart from the East Beach jetty at 2 pm daily. When the seasonal currents bring waves to Bira, usually between May and July, the ferry service switches to Bulukumba and goes direct to Benteng on Pulau Selayar (5000 rp).

AROUND BIRA
Pulau Lihukan

Weavers at **Ta'Buntuleng** on Pulau Lihukan make heavy, colourful cloth on hand looms.

under houses in the village. On the beach west of the village there is an interesting old graveyard, and off the beach there are acres of sea grass and coral, but mind the currents and snakes. To see the best coral further out, you need fins or a boat to get back to the island.

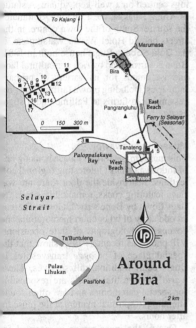

Around Bira

1 Yaya Homestay
2 Market
3 Tanjung Bira Cottages
4 Riswan Homestay (Seasonal)
5 Sunrise Guesthouse
6 Hotel Sapolohe
7 Bira Beach Hotel
8 Warung Melati
9 Riswan Bungalows
10 Rumah Makan Sederhana
11 Souvenirs
12 Pondok Wisata Purnama Bira
13 Anda Bungalows
14 Riswan Guesthouse
15 Nusa Bira Indah
16 Pondok Wisata Bahagia
17 Bira View Inn

Kajang

There are people inland from Kajang supposedly living at one with nature with no modern equipment or mechanised transport, under the leadership of a man known as Ammatoa. To visit this community, you are obliged to wear black and can hire appropriate attire at the entrance to the village. These days, however, you and Ammatoa are likely to be the only ones respecting the traditional ways. En route to Kajang, stop over at **Ara** north of Bira to see the caves. The rubber plantations in this area are quite interesting too.

PULAU SELAYAR

This long, narrow island lies off the tip of the south-western peninsula of Sulawesi and is inhabited by Bugis and Makassarese people. Most reside along the infertile west coast and **Benteng** is the chief settlement. Like Bira, Selayar's long coastline is a repository of flotsam from nearby shipping lanes, perhaps accounting for the presence of a 2000-year-old Vietnamese Dongson drum. This metre wide bronze drum was excavated more than 300 years ago and is now kept in an annexe near the former Bontobangun Palace, a few km south of Benteng.

Another explanation for the drum is that Selayar once supported a significant population which traded with Dongson, in present day Vietnam, 2000 years ago. Interestingly, motifs on Dongson drums are similar to the designs found on *tongkonan* (traditional houses) in Tanatoraja.

Selayar's other attraction is its sandy beaches and picturesque scenery. Try renting a prahu and snorkelling near small **Pulau Pasi** opposite Benteng.

Few foreigners visit Selayar. When they do, most stay at the *Hotel Berlian* in Benteng, which has rooms for 8000/10,000 rp. There is no set price at the older *Harmita Hotel* but expect to pay around 8000 rp a double. Benteng's newest hotel is the *Selayar Beach*.

Getting There & Away

Take a bus or kijang from Bone or Ujung Pandang to Bira (4000 rp) and a boat from

SULAWESI

Bira to Pamatata Harbour (4000 rp) at the northern end of Pulau Selayar. Seasonal currents around May-July often force the ferry operators to reroute the ferry from Bulukumba to Benteng (5000 rp). If this is the case, there will be plenty of people telling you so when you get to Bulukumba.

TAKA BONE RATE

South-east of Pulau Selayar and north of Pulau Bone Rate is the 2220 sq km Taka Bone Rate, the world's third largest coral atoll. The largest is Kwajalein in the Marshall Islands, just 20% bigger. Taka Bone Rate's extensive patch and barrier reefs are now a marine reserve, and the focus of conservation projects working with the atoll's inhabitants to document and preserve the area's rich variety of marine and bird life. One threat is cyanide, used in diluted doses to stun rare and beautiful tropical fish for aquariums. Even if the fish survive, the coral usually dies. Nine of the atoll's 21 islands are inhabited.

Getting There & Away

Pelni's KM *Kelimutu* now breaks its journeys between Ujung Pandang and Maumere with weekly stops at Bone Rate. Inter-island traders and fishing boats are the only other alternative.

BONE (WATAMPONE)

Bone, also known as Watampone, became a major centre of power under the authoritarian rule of Arung Palakka in the 17th century. Bone had been a semi-autonomous state under the overlordship of Gowa, the strongest anti-Dutch power in the East Indies. Palakka and his followers returned from exile in 1666 and rallied the Bugis of Bone and Soppeng for a long overland campaign, forcing Hasanuddin to cede territory, including Bone. Palakka emerged the most powerful man in South Sulawesi, creating a system of unprecedented autocratic rule.

Information

Change your travellers cheques and cash in Tanatoraja or Ujung Pandang. It is hopeless trying to change foreign currency in Bone. The Telkom office on Jl Manginsidi is open 24 hours.

Things to See

Bone is a modern town with the bupati' residence, museum and other public buildings centred on a well-kept square. A statue of Arung Palakka, the 15th king, dominate the square. South of the town centre, in the streets behind Hotel Wisata Watampone, i the **Bola Soba**, a Bugis house built in 1881 Bone is surrounded by rich agricultural land and is famous for its variety of primary industries, including prawn farming and processing, crab farms at Pallime and a suga estate.

Museum Lapawawoi

This museum is a former palace housing one of Indonesia's most interesting regional collections. Just inside the door there are wa flags featuring cocks, remarkably similar to flags flown by Bone's rival, Gowa. There i an odd array of other court memorabilia and dozens of photographs of state occasions VIP photos as recent as 1993 show that the special place of *pajogge* transvestites in Bugis court tradition still survives. These *waria* (transvestite) priests are responsible for special ceremonies and are often found attending to spiritual matters at the museum after hours.

One of the inner rooms is reserved for offerings to Bone's former kings; visitors may enter, but please don't take photographs. On the wall to the right is a complex family tree. Lines of royal succession can be hard to follow. For instance, Toappainge, the 24th raja, had two wives, 200 consorts and dozens of children. The museum is open daily from 8 am to 2 pm.

Bajoe

The nearby harbour of Bajoe is a busy centre of commerce, five km (500 rp) from Bone Charter a canoe from the wharf to see the floating village and port area.

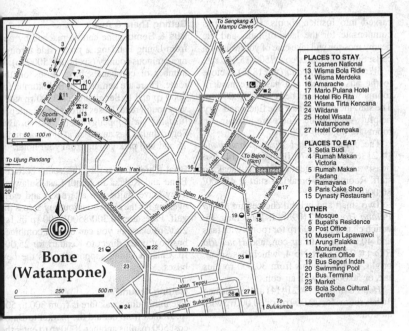

PLACES TO STAY
2 Losmen National
13 Wisma Bola Ridie
14 Wisma Merdeka
16 Amarache
17 Mario Pulana Hotel
18 Hotel Rio Rita
22 Wisma Tirta Kencana
24 Wildana
25 Hotel Wisata
   Watampone
27 Hotel Cempaka

PLACES TO EAT
3 Setia Budi
4 Rumah Makan
   Victoria
5 Rumah Makan
   Padang
7 Ramayana
8 Paris Cake Shop
15 Dynasty Restaurant

OTHER
1 Mosque
6 Bupati's Residence
9 Post Office
10 Museum Lapawawoi
11 Arung Palakka
   Monument
12 Telkom Office
19 Bus Segeri Indah
20 Swimming Pool
21 Bus Terminal
23 Market
26 Bola Soba Cultural
   Centre

**Bone
(Watampone)**

Mampu Caves

James Brooke (later the Raja of Sarawak) visited these caves, 40 km north-west of Bone, in 1840 hoping to find remnants of an ancient civilisation. The statues he had been told of turned out to be fallen stalactites. According to legend, these figures were living in the court of Mampu, but were suddenly turned to stone through a curse. One story goes that the princess dropped a spool and promised to marry whoever could return it. The spool was retrieved by a dog, which demanded the princess honour her promise. Chaos erupted. Many were caught unawares by the disaster.

A tour of the caves requires imagination as the guides point out the buffalo, a ship on a river of stone, the prince, a crocodile (by far the most convincing), a woman in labor, a deer, a party of wedding guests near two eloping lovers, a chamber of judges and, of course, the dog with the princess. The whole lot is covered by slippery, smelly bat guano.

Women scrape the guano to fertilise nearby fields.

To get to the caves, take a bemo to **Uloe**, 34 km north-west of Bone. The caves are seven km south of Uloe, past two boom gates where villagers demand a 'toll'. It is easier to have your own transport.

Places to Stay

Wisma Bola Ridie on Jl Merdeka is a former royal residence, built in Dutch style and 'royal' yellow throughout. Small 10,000 rp rooms with a mandi face a rear courtyard, or there are huge rooms in the main building for 20,000 rp.

Wisma Merdeka next door at No 4 – a former army hostel – is more modern, with huge rooms in the main house for 15,000 rp, and smaller ones out the back for 8000 to 10,000 rp.

Losmen National, Jl Mesjid Raya 86, is an old-style mansion built in 1952 and recently carved into losmen rooms. High ceilings compensate for the lack of fans, and the nearby mosque will take care of your wake-up calls. Singles/doubles cost 7500/15,000 rp.

Wisma Tirta Kencana (☎ 21838) is close to the bus terminal and has large modern rooms with king-size beds from 15,000 rp. The staff includes at least one fluent and very helpful Anglophone. There are also air-con rooms for 40,000/45,000 rp.

The upmarket *Hotel Wisata Watampone* (☎ 21362; fax 22367), Jl Sudirman 14, also boasts a fair contingent of English-speaking staff. Rooms with breakfast start at 45,000/ 80,000 rp plus tax.

Two smart and helpful choices are *Mario Pulana Hotel* (☎ 21098), Jl Kawerang 15, which charges 30,000 rp for rooms with fans and 40,000 rp with air-con, and *Hotel Rio Rita* (☎ 21053) at No 4, which has small, bright, modern rooms from 30,000 rp plus tax, or 50,000 rp with air-con.

Hotel Cempaka (☎ 21414) at Jl Sudirman 36 has rooms for 20,000 rp, or 30,000 rp with air-con.

Places to Eat

There is a cluster of eating houses in the main shopping centre. The *Rumah Makan Victoria* on Jl Tanah Bangkalae serves generous plates of standard Chinese-Indonesian fare, including fu yung hai (an omelette stuffed with seafood and vegetables).

The *Rumah Makan Padang* and the *Setia Budi* are nearby, and piles of fresh fare at the *Ramayana* across the road.

By far the best are the *Restaurant Pondok Selera* at Jl Biru 28; the *Dynasty Restaurant* at Jl Thamrin 8, which has a menu longer than its karaoke song list; and the cheap martabak and kueh (cake) stalls that set up next to the town square. Wandering vendors also sell Javanese cat (rice-flour cakes) steamed over humming barrows and lots of fried goodies.

If you are invited home you might get to try some of the many Bugis-style cakes. Otherwise you'll find a few in the windows of *Paris*, the corner shop next to Ramayana.

Getting There & Away

Bus & Bemo Bone can be reached by bus from Ujung Pandang, a pretty ride through mountainous country (six hours; 5000 rp). A number of companies have buses on the route. There are bemos from Bulukumba for 4000 rp and to Sengkang for 2500 rp via a very rough road. Buses through to Rantepao (usually via Soppeng) cost 9000 rp. Bus Segeri Indah has an office at Jl Hasannudin 16 and will pick you up from your hotel.

Boat Three ferries ply the route between Bone and Kolaka in South-East Sulawesi. They leave Bajoe late afternoon and early evening for the eight hour journey across the gulf. Fares are 10,300/8500/6800 rp in 1st/ 2nd/3rd class, or you can book a combined bus/boat ticket direct to Kendari for 25,000 rp. Cahaya Ujung supposedly has the best buses.

Getting Around

The minimum becak fare is from 300 to 500 rp. Bemos from behind the market to Bajoe cost 500 rp, plus another 1000 rp to enter the dock area.

SENGKANG

The lakeside resort of Sengkang between Bone and Pare Pare has only recently been discovered by foreign tourists. Scenic Danau Tempe, a large shallow lake fringed by wetlands, is the main attraction and is best admired by taking a boat trip. Geologists believe the lake was once a gulf between southern Toraja and the rest of South Sulawesi. As they merged, the gulf disappeared and it is thought the lake will eventually disappear too.

There are floating houses, magnificent bird life and a range of commercial activities on the lake. Lake tours usually take in Batu Batu on the other side, but the most interesting part is along the river around Sengkang. Boats can be chartered for 10,000 to 15,000 rp each.

Sengkang's other main attraction of is *sutera* (silk) weaving industry. You can visit the silk villages or go to the factories and get hings made to order. Most visitors buy ready-made silk products at bargain prices in the own's silk market, but be very wary of otton and synthetic blends. To get an idea f the quality and prices available, visit the eputable Toko Sumber Sutera (☎ 21383) at l Magga Amirullah 140.

Places to Stay

Hotel Apada (☎ 21053) at Jl Durian 9 is a pleasant place with a gorgeous courtyard restaurant serving traditional, but expensive, Bugis food in the evenings. The manager

speaks English and can arrange tours. Doubles cost 25,000 to 35,000 rp.

Pondok Eka (☎ 21296) at Jl Maluku 12 is just as nice and much cheaper with roooms for 10,000/15,000 rp, including breakfast. Eka has large rooms and a wide front veran-dah. The kitchen backs onto the town cinema so you can preview the films from the window – just behind the rear stalls. Bargain for a bed, breakfast and escorted tour to see silk production and the lake for around 20,000 rp.

Hotel Al'salam II (☎ 21278) at Jl Emmi Saelan 8 also assists with tours. The hotel is clean and efficient, with rooms for 8500/12,500 rp with shared mandi, standard for 12,500/20,000 rp and air-con for 30,000/35,000 rp.

Penginapan Merdeka, Jl Latainrilai, has box-like rooms for 2500/5000 rp. *Wisma Ayuni* (☎ 21009) at Jl Ahmad Yani 31 in an old Dutch house is better value and quieter at 5000/10,000 rp. *Wisma Herawaty* down the road at No 20 has spacious rooms for 10,000/15,000 rp. *Pondok Indah* on Jl Sudir-man looks OK for 8000/ 10,000 rp.

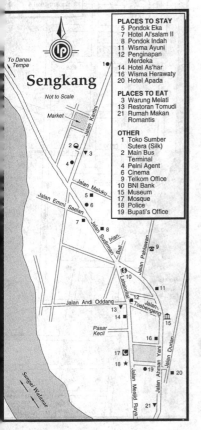

PLACES TO STAY
5 Pondok Eka
7 Hotel Al'salam II
8 Pondok Indah
11 Wisma Ayuni
12 Penginapan Merdeka
14 Hotel As'har
16 Wisma Herawaty
20 Hotel Apada

PLACES TO EAT
3 Warung Melati
13 Restoran Tomudi
21 Rumah Makan Romantis

OTHER
1 Toko Sumber Sutera (Silk)
2 Main Bus Terminal
4 Pelni Agent
6 Cinema
9 Telkom Office
10 BNI Bank
15 Museum
17 Mosque
18 Police
19 Bupati's Office

To Danau Tempe

Sengkang

Not to Scale

Market

Jalan Kartini
Jalan Maluku
Jalan Emmi Saelan
Jalan Sudirman
Jalan Bali
Inan
Jalan Pahlawan
Jalan Andi Oddang
Jalan Toebengeng
Latainrilai
Pasar Kecil
Jalan Ahman Yani
Jalan Mesjid Raya
Jalan Durian
Sungai Walanae

Places to Eat

Warung Melati, opposite the bus terminal on Jl Kartini, has fresh Indonesian fare, includ-ing chunky serves of tasty nasi campur and western-style dishes such as potato fries and scrambled eggs. The martabak from the night stall in front of the bus terminal is also good.

There's a cluster of eating houses on the corner of Jl Latainrilai and Jl Andi Oddang, the best of which is *Restoran Tomudi* at Jl Andi Oddang 52. *Rumah Makan Romantis* at Jl Petterani 2 has good cheap food and cold beer in an upmarket setting.

Getting There & Away

Sengkang is readily accessible from Pare Pare by bus or bemo (two hours; 2500 rp). If you're heading to/from Rantepao, bemos go through Palopo and take about six or seven hours. There are plenty of buses south to Bone (horrible road, 2000 rp) and the port of

SULAWESI

Bajoe, plus bemos from Bone to Bulukumba
and Bira (4000 rp).

SOPPENG (WATANSOPPENG)

The pretty town of Soppeng, or Watan-
soppeng, is the other big silk producer in this
region and the source of silk-worm eggs for
Sengkang's silk industry. The breeding cycle
is the same as Sengkang's, so you will see
the same thing at either area. It is a pleasant
detour and easy to get to by bemo from either
Pangkajene or Sengkang.

There is a small choice of places to stay.
Hotel Kayangan at Jl Kayangan 4 has basic
rooms from 12,500 to 22,500 rp with air-con.
Hotel Makmur (☎ 21038), Jl Kemakmuran
104, is nicer with rooms from 20,000 rp, and
Hotel Aman (☎ 21206), Jl Merdeka 92, is an
old Dutch house with rooms from 15,000 rp.

PARE PARE

The second largest city in South Sulawesi is
a smaller, greener version of Ujung Pandang.
Pare Pare is a seaport through which a good
deal of the produce of southern Sulawesi
(rice, corn, coffee etc) is shipped out. It's a
quiet stopover between Tanatoraja or Mamasa and Ujung Pandang. There are also
frequent ships to the east coast of Kalimantan
and to northern Sulawesi from here.

At **Bangange**, a few km south of Pare
Pare, there is a small museum housing a
collection of cloth, ornaments, tools and
other remnants of the royal house of Bac-
ukiki. About 10 km further south there is a
quiet, swimmable beach, much cleaner than
the effluent pools around Pare Pare.

Orientation & Information

Pare Pare is stretched out along the waterfront. At night, the street by the water turns
into a lively pedestrian mall with warungs
and stalls. Most of what you need (hotels,
restaurants etc) is on the streets running parallel with the harbour.

Bank Negara Indonesia is the only bank in
town that changes money. It's right next to
the large mosque (see the Pare Pare map).
The Haji La Tunrung moneychanger at Jl
Hasanuddin 59 has competitive rates.

PLACES TO STAY
2 Hotel Siswa
9 Tanty Hotel
13 Hotel Gandaria
17 Hotel Cahaya Ujung
20 Hotel Gemini

PLACES TO EAT
1 Restaurant Asia
3 Warung Sedap

OTHER
4 People's Struggle
    Monument
5 Night Market
6 Moneychanger
7 Main Mosque
8 BNI Bank
10 Post Office
11 Harbour Master
12 Wartel
14 Pelni Office
15 Cinema
16 Rattan Goods
18 Ujung Cahaya
    Supermarket
19 Supermarket &
    Department Store

Pare Pare

Not to Scale

Places to Stay

The *Hotel Gandaria* (☎ 21093) at Jl Bau-massepe 171 is clean, comfortable and run by friendly people. Economy singles with attached toilet and shower cost 15,000 rp. Air-con singles cost 25,000 rp.

The *Hotel Gemini* (☎ 21754) at Jl Bau-massepe 451 has small rooms from 6500 rp, rooms with mandi for 8500 rp and newly renovated airy rooms with TV for 16,500 rp.

Hotel Cahaya Ujung (☎ 22810), Jl Mang-a Barat 2, is above a new shopping centre on the corner of Jl Baumassepe. New rooms with old mandi cost 10,000 rp, up to 45,000 rp with air-con.

Tanty Hotel (☎ 21378), Jl Sultan Hasa-uddin 5, has clean, basic rooms from 10,000 rp.

Nurlina Hotel (☎ 21278) at Jl Pawero 10, off Jl Andi Makassau north-east of the town centre, boasts antechambers for all its rooms even the 20,000 rp economy ones.

Places to Eat

Restaurant Asia has Chinese food and excellent, but pricey, seafood from 8000 to 14,000 rp per serve. There are a couple of vegetarian dishes and fresh, meaty corn and crab soup. *Warung Sedap*, next door to the Asia, serves ikan bakar.

Restaurant Sempurna, a few km south of town on Jl Baumassepe, is good value serving both Indonesian and Chinese food. There are many small warungs along the main street in the vicinity of the Hotel Siswa, and at night there's a string of warungs along the waterfront, each with exactly the same choice of mie, rice and bakso dishes.

Getting There & Away

Bus Pare Pare is on the road from Ujung Pandang to Rantepao. The bus fare from Ujung Pandang is 6000 rp. From Pare Pare, most travellers head north-east to Rantepao (four to five hours), but there are also excellent roads inland to Sengkang (2500 rp; two hours), north to Polewali and Mamasa – Polmas' – or around the coast to Majene and Mamuju. There are buses from the new bus terminal several km south of the city, but it

is much easier to just hail them as they fly through town.

Boat The main reason to come to Pare Pare is to catch a ship to the east coast of Kalimantan. There are daily boats to various ports. There are also ships once or twice a week from Pare Pare along the coast to Pantoloan (the port of Palu) and North Sulawesi.

Pelni (☎ 21017) at Jl Andicammi 130 has regular ferries to Pantoloan and Kalimantan. The harbour master's office is near the waterfront on Jl Andicammi, and several shipping companies have their offices here.

MAJENE

Most of the pleasure in visiting Majene is getting there, via a coast road with stunning vistas of sand, sea and mountains. The town itself is a centre for fishing and boat building, and whatever other commerce such a small, isolated market town can support. Few tourists come this way and the town is ill-equipped to handle visitors. Travellers say the best place to stay is with the local doctor. Ask at the market for directions. The moderately priced *Wisma Cahaya*, Jl Rahman 2, and *Penginapan Abrar*, Jl Sudir-man 49, also take guests. Dine at the small *warung* on Jl Syukur Rahim.

MAMUJU

Mamuju used to be the end of the road, literally and metaphorically. Regular bus services still terminate here, but the steady advance of a new coastal road through to Palu is opening this isolated region to the outside world. Mamuju has a couple of reasonable places to stay. *Wisma Rio* (☎ 21014) at Jl Kemakmuran 28 has rooms from 10,000 rp, or 30,000 rp with air-con. *Wisma Kencana Sakti* (☎ 21039) at Jl Langsat 2 charges 10,000 rp, or 25,000 rp with air-con.

MAMUJU TO MASAMBA

From Mamuju there are bemos to **Tarailu**. Stay at the losmen there for 2500 rp, then get a motorised canoe to **Galumpang** on the Sungai Karama, where archaeologists have excavated remains of Neolithic villages. Galumpang to **Tambing, Bau, Seko, Emo, Seka Tenggah** and **Seko Padan**g is a three or four day walk. You might be able to fly from Seko Padang to Masamba by MAF. If you head this way, travel light, pay around 5000 rp a night for accommodation and leave gifts – pencils, cards, tobacco, batteries, cheap copy watches from Bali etc.

Tanatoraja

Despite long conflict with their Bugis neighbours to the south, it was only in the early years of this century that the Toraja came into serious contact with the west. Torajan life and culture had survived the constant threat from the Bugis, but in 1905 the Dutch began a bloody campaign to bring central Sulawesi under their control. The Toraja held out against the Dutch for two years, until the last substantial resistance was wiped out in the mountains around Pangala, north-west of Rantepao.

The missionaries moved in on the heels of the troops, and by WWII many of the great Torajan ceremonies (except for their remarkable funeral celebrations) were already disappearing. Tourism, mining and migration have aided the work the missionaries began.

The busiest time of year in Tanatoraja is the height of funeral season in July and August. Toraja working throughout Indonesia return home for the celebrations, followed by hoards of tourists whose presence sends Rantepao hotel prices into orbit. To avoid the big tour groups (and big prices), visit Tanatoraja in the gap between the end of the wet season and the onset of the tourist season. The wet season usually begins in December and ends in March – although there can still be a considerable amount of rain after that. The rice crops are harvested (from May to August) and the ceremonies begin.

The Toraja

Despite the isolation caused by the rugged landscape of central Sulawesi, similar cultures have existed in the territory bordered by the Bugis to the south-west, the Pau district in the north, and the Loinang and Mori peoples in the east. The people in this vast area are collectively referred to as the Toraja. The name is derived from the Bugi word *toriaja* (literally, 'men of the mountains'), but the connotations of the name are something like 'hillbilly' – rustic, unsophisticated, oafish highlanders.

The Bugis traded Indian cloth, Dutch coins and porcelain with the Toraja in return for coffee and slaves. The Bugis are even said to have introduced cockfighting to the Toraja, who incorporated the sport into the death rituals of their noble class. Islam brought a new militancy to the Bugis, and under Arung Palakka they attacked the Toraja in 1673 and 1674. However, Islam never spread much further than the southern Toraja areas because, it is said, of the people's fondness for pork and palm wine.

Customarily the Toraja have been split by ethnologists into western, eastern and southern groups. To some extent these divisions represent the varying degrees of influence the old kingdoms of Luwu, Gowa and Bone have had on the Toraja. It *doesn't* reflect any political organisation among the Toraja. In the past there had been no organisation beyond the level of the local village or small groups of villages. Sometimes villages would band together in federations to resist the Bugis invaders, but there have never been any large Torajan states.

Of all the Toraja peoples the best known to the western world are the southern Toraja, also known as the Sa'dan or Saqdan Toraja. Most live in and around the towns of Rantepao and Makale. Like Bali, the impact of tourism is evident in the rapid emergence of hotels, losmen and restaurants around Rantepao. The area, however, is unspoilt and the tourist trade is peripheral.

The introduction of wet-rice cultivation after the Dutch conquest has sculpted and terraced the slopes of the steep mountainsides, with streams originating near the hilltop harnessed to flow in a succession of little

Pulu Pulu
Sapan
Baruppu
Gunung
Sesean
(2150m) ▲
Pangala
Sa'dan
Batutumonga
Bate Bambalu
Deri
Rantetondan
Lokomata
Palawa
Lempo
Balusu
Pana
Pangli
Bori
To
Palopo
Tikala
Nanggala
To
Mamasa
Marante
Tallunglipu
Siguntu
Rantepao
Tandung
Mendoe
Bunte
Karre
Pune Kete
Sullukang
Kesu
Paniki
Palatokke
Labo
Bittuang
Londa
Madandan
Langda
Seseng
Tilanga
Airport
Buntao
Tangratte
Randanbatu
Tembamba
Lemo
Rembon
Bokin
Sangalla
Tampangallo
Kambira
Suaya
Makale
Tondon
Makula
Sa'dan
Bera
Buakayu

Tanatoraja

0   5   10 km
Approximate Scale

waterfalls before escaping once more into
the natural rivers below. Toraja villages were
once built on the summits, sometimes surrounded by fortified walls with the settlement
itself reached by tunnels. This was partly for
protection and partly because the clan ancestors were supposed to have arrived from
heaven on hilltops.

Before the Dutch there were several
groups of head-hunters in the archipelago,
including the Toraja. Their head-hunting was
not on any great scale and their raids were
basically tests of manhood for the young
men of the tribe. Head-hunting was also

necessary to find heads for a chief's death-
feast to provide slaves for his afterlife. If
enough enemies could not be captured in
raids, the chief's family would buy slaves
and sacrifice them. Under Dutch rule the
wars and raids came to an end, and the
Sa'dan were ordered to build their villages
on the river flats.

Buffaloes are a status symbol for the
Toraja and are of paramount importance in
various religious ceremonies. Pigs and chickens are slaughtered at many rituals, such as
the consecration of new *tongkonan* (traditional houses), but buffalo are usually saved

Torajan Cuisine

Food Visiting ceremonies provides a chance to try Torajan food. The best-known is *pa'piong*, the spinach-like vegetable with pork, chicken or fish cooked in bamboo tubes. The chicken pa'piong has the added flavour of coconut. If you want to try it in a warung, order several hours in advance as it takes hours to cook. The pork pa'piong tends to have a high fat content, because fat is considered as tasty as the meat. *Pamerasan*, buffalo meat in a black sauce, is delicious if the meat is tender.

Fresh fish is rushed from Palopo on ancient motorcycles, laden with huge pannier baskets. They fly down the two hour stretch of twists and turns to Palopo often twice a day, returning with glittering baskets of silver fish. *Ikan mas* (gold fish) and *ikan belut* (eels) are caught in padi fields and barbecued.

Indulge your sweet tooth with *kue baje*, cakes of sticky rice and palm sugar rolled in a dry corn leaf like a Christmas cracker. They go off quickly, so it's a good idea to try before you buy. *Kue deppa* are triangular rice flour cakes bought loose from street stalls, and *kacang goreng* is an over-sweet concoction of peanuts and treacle wrapped in corn leaves. A hard to find delicacy is *kolak*, a kind of sweet banana soup based on coconut milk and palm sugar, and spiced with ginger.

The cool climate makes Toraja ideal for fresh vegetables, such as cabbage, beans and spinach-type leaves. See tiny women carrying huge baskets of these vegetables to market early in the morning.

Drinks Rantepao and Makale markets have whole sections devoted to the sale of the alcoholic 'palm wine' known locally as *balok*. Balok is actually sap from the sugar palm and is probably the strongest proof yet of a benevolent creator.

Every few months the palm, with its huge, dark metallic-green fronds and untidy black-haired trunk, produces a great cluster of round, dark fruit. The stem is pierced close to the fruit and if sugary sap flows from the wound the fruit cluster is cut off and a receptacle is hung to catch the juice dripping from the amputated stump. This ferments naturally, producing one of creation's finest brews. The sap can also be boiled down to produce crystalline red sugar – *gula merah*.

Balok, known nationally as *tuak* and internationally as *toddy*, is sold in huge jugs in tiny warungs around town. It comes in a variety of strengths and ranges from lemonade coloured to orange or red – made by adding tree bark. It also ranges from sweet to bitter, depending on its age. It doesn't keep for more than a day, so be wary of buying blends of old and new.

Coffee is Toraja's other famous brew, an excellent antidote to a night of balok tasting. Robusta is the most widely available variety, drunk strong and black with equal portions of coffee and sugar. The aromatic arabica is also available at much higher prices. It is largely produced for export, and you can see the whole process of growing, harvesting, drying and roasting throughout Tanatoraja. In villages, coffee is sometimes roasted with ginger, coconut or even garlic for an unusually fragrant taste. For souvenirs, buy carved boxes and fill them with coffee yourself – the pre-packaged ones in the shops are usually only half full. ■

for the biggest celebrations of all – the funeral feasts. Dogs are eaten in some parts of Tanatoraja and sold for meat like regular livestock. Coffee (reputedly the best in Indonesia) is the main cash crop and fish are farmed in ponds in the rice fields.

Religion

Despite the strength of traditional beliefs, the Christian Church of Toraja is a very active force. One of the first questions asked is your religion, and Protestants are given immediate approval as *'saudara'* (sister/brother).

Physical isolation and the lack of a written language resulted in considerable variations in beliefs, customs and mythology, although the ancestor cult has always been ver strong. Prior to the arrival of Christianity, th Toraja believed in many gods, but wo shipped one in particular as the special go of their family, clan or tribe. Puang Matu was the nearest the Toraja originally came t the concept of a supreme being and earl missionaries began prayers in their churche with his name.

The Toraja have a long and involved cre ation mythology dividing creation into thre worlds, each watched over by its own go The Sa'dan Toraja also had a rigid cast system and a slave class. Although the Dutc abolished slavery, its effects continued lon after. There is also a class of nobles whic

BRENDAN DELAHUNTY

SIMON ROWE

ulawesi
op: Live pigs for sale at the Makale market.
ottom: A traditional Torajan dwelling, Mamasa Valley.

SIMON ROWE

SIMON ROWE

Sulawesi
Top: The buffalo is a status symbol for the Toraja in Tanatoraja.
Bottom: Funeral ceremonies are a vital part of Torajan culture.

ntinues to be important. Christianity under-
ined some traditional Toraja beliefs, but
e ceremonies are still a vital part of life.

Although it is one of the five pillars of the
ancasila that every Indonesian must believe
one god, the Toraja gained official sanc-
on to maintain their polytheistic beliefs
Alulh Todolo), possibly due to the tenuous
gument that Toraja beliefs were similar to
ose of the Balinese for whom an exception
ad already been made. People who believe
the old ways are rare. Like the followers
traditional faiths elsewhere in Indonesia,
ey are officially listed as Hindu.

ouses

ne of the first things you notice about Tana-
raja is the size and grandeur of the
ngkonan, the traditional houses, raised on
les and topped with a massive roof. The
ngkonan houses of Tanatoraja are closely
ound up with Torajan traditions – one of
eir important functions is as a constant
minder of the authority of the original noble

families whose descendants alone have the
right to build such houses. The state of a
tongkonan also symbolises the unity of a
clan. They are the meeting place for family
gatherings and may not be bought or sold.

Tanatoraja is one of the few places in
Indonesia where traditional houses are still
being built and the skills to make them
survive. The owners often live in modern
houses, keeping the tongkonan for ceremonies and as a symbol of the family's status.
The tourist trade has also inspired the renovation of some older houses and construction
of new ones. There are a number of villages
in the region still composed entirely of traditional houses. Most tongkonan have rice
barns, surrounded by several ordinary bungalows on stilts, like the houses of the Bugis
and Makassarese.

The roof, rearing up at either end, is the
most striking aspect of a tongkonan. Some
say the house represents the head of a buffalo
and the rising roof represents the horns.
Others suggest that the roof looks more like

Graves & Tau Tau

The Toraja believe you can take possessions with you and the dead generally go well equipped to
their graves. Since this led to grave plundering, the Toraja started to hide their dead in caves or hew
niches out of rock faces.

These caves were hollowed out by specialist cave builders who were traditionally paid in buffaloes
– and since the building of a cave would cost several buffaloes, only the rich could afford it. Although
the exterior of the cave grave looks small, the interior is large enough to entomb an entire family. The
coffins would go deep inside the caves and you can see, sitting in balconies on the rock face in front
of the caves, the *tau tau* – life-size, carved wooden effigies of the dead.

Tau tau are carved only for the upper classes. Their expense alone rules out their use for poor
people. Traditionally, the statues only showed the sex of the person, not the likeness, but now they
attempt to imitate the likeness of the person's face. The making of tau tau appears to have been a
recent innovation, possibly originating in the late 19th century. The type of wood used reflects the
status and wealth of the deceased, nangka (jackfruit) wood being the most expensive. After the
deceased has been entombed and the tau tau placed in front of the grave, offerings are placed in the
palm of the tau tau. You can see the carvers at work at Londa, across the padi opposite the caves.

Apart from cave graves there are also house graves – houses made of wood in which the coffin is
placed when there is no rocky outcrop or cliff face to carve a niche in. Most of the hanging graves in
which the wooden coffins were hung from high cliffs have rotted away. Sometimes the coffins may be
placed at the foot of a mountain. Babies who died before teething were placed in hollowed-out sections
of living trees; such graves can be seen at Suaya and Pana (see the Around Rantepao & Makale
section).

Most tau tau seem to be in a permanent state of disrepair, but in a ceremony after harvest time the
bodies are re-wrapped in new material and the clothes of the tau tau replaced. Occasionally left lying
around the more obscure grave caves is the *duba-duba*, a platform in the shape of a traditional house
which is used to carry the coffin and body of a nobleman to the grave. ∎

SULAWESI

Funerals

Tomate (funeral) literally means 'dead person', and of all Torajan ceremonies the most important are those concerned with sending a dead person to the afterworld. Without proper funeral rites the spirit of the deceased will cause misfortune to its family. The funeral sacrifices, ceremonies and feasts also impress the gods with the importance of the deceased, so that the spirit can intercede effectively on behalf of living relatives. Funerals are sometimes held at the *rante*, funeral sites marked by one or more megaliths. In Tanatoraja there are several arcs or groups of roughly hewn stone slabs around villages, and it is said that each stone represents a member of the noble class who lived and died there. Some are as high as four metres, symbolising the importance of the deceased. The efforts to raise even one stone involves scores of men dragging the stone to the designated place with ropes and a sacrificial slaughter to celebrate the new megalith – part of the complex funeral preparations for nobles.

At a funeral, bamboo pavilions for the family and guests are constructed around a field. The dead person is said to preside over the funeral from the high-roofed tower constructed at one end of the field. Like the Balinese, the Toraja generally have two funerals, one immediately after a death and an elaborate second funeral after sufficient time has elapsed to make the preparations (raise the necessary cash, obtain livestock, gather relatives from afar and so on). For this reason tomate are usually scheduled during the dry season from July to September, when family members have free time. The Toraja cheerfully refer to this period as 'party season'.

The corpse remains in the house where the person died. These days it is preserved by injection instead of traditional embalming herbs. Food is cooked and offered to the dead person; those of noble birth have attendants who stay in their immediate presence from the hour of death to the day of their final progress to the tomb. An invitation to visit the deceased is an honour. A polite refusal won't cause offence. If you accept, remember to thank the deceased and ask permission of the deceased when you wish to leave – as you would a living host. You won't be expected to pray, but might be invited to take photos, an indication that the deceased is still an important part of the family.

The souls of the dead can only go to Puya, the afterworld, when the entire death ritual has been carried out. A spirit's status in the afterlife is the same as its owner's status in the present life; even the souls of animals follow their masters to the next life – hence the animal sacrifices at funerals. It is believed that that the soul of the deceased will ride the souls of the slaughtered buffaloes and pigs to heaven. The trip to Puya requires a strong buffalo because the long and difficult journey crosses hundreds of mountains and thousands of valleys.

Sons and daughters of the deceased have an equal chance to inherit their parents' property, but their share depends on the number of buffaloes they slaughter at the funeral feast. The buffalo has traditionally been a symbol of wealth and power – even land could be paid for in buffaloes. A modelled buffalo head, fitted with real horns, is the figurehead of traditional Toraja houses; buffalo motifs are carved or painted on the walls of houses; and horns decorate gable poles.

The more important the deceased, the more buffaloes must be sacrificed: one for a commoner,

a boat and that the raised ends represent the bow and the stern. The houses all face north – some say because the ancestors of the Toraja came from the north, carrying their boats to the safety of the hills and inverting them to use as shelter. Others maintain that the north (and the east) are regarded as the sphere of life, the realm of the gods.

The high gables are supported by poles and the wall panels are decorated with painted engravings. Each geometrical design has an individual name and meaning. On these panels red is meant to symbolise human life, as red is the colour of blood; white is the colour of flesh and bone, and a symbol of purity; yellow represents God's blessing

and power; and black symbolises death an darkness. Traditionally the colours were a natural – black is the soot from cooking pot yellow and red are coloured earth, and whi is lime. *Balok* (palm wine) was used improve the staying power of the colour Artisans would decorate the houses and t paid in buffaloes. A realistic carving of buffalo's head decorates the front part of th house. Numerous buffalo horns, indicatir the wealth of the family, are attached to th front pole which supports the gable.

The beams and supports of Torajan hous are cut so that they all neatly slot or a pegged together; no metal nails are used. Th older houses have roofs of overlappir four, eight, 12 or 24 as you move up the social scale. The age and status of the deceased also determines the number of animals slaughtered. Large *pesta*, where more than 100 buffalo are slaughtered, are talked of with awe for years afterwards. The type of buffalo is also significant – the most prized being the *tedong bonga* (spotted buffalo), which may cost many millions of rupiah per head.

The temptation to sacrifice dozens of buffalo to honour the dead and impress the living prompted the Indonesian government to levy a tax on each slaughtered animal to limit the destruction of wealth. However, funeral ceremonies have lost none of their ostentation and are still a ruinous financial burden on families. Some now refuse to hold tomate, despite their social obligation to do so.

Those with strong stomachs can see freshly killed pigs roasted on open fires to scorch the skin before the pig is gutted and the meat mixed with piles of vegetables and stuffed into bamboo tubes. The bamboo tubes are cooked slowly over low flames to produce tasty pa'piong. Cuts of buffalo meat are also distributed – the funeral season is the only time of year families are guaranteed regular supplies of meat.

Funerals can be spread out over several days and involve hundreds of guests. The wooden effigies *(tau tau)* alone can cost nearly a year's wages for most Indonesians. Bamboo pavilions are constructed specially for the occasion, with a death tower at one end.

After the guests display their presents of pigs and buffaloes, the traditional Mabadong song and dance is performed. This is a ceremonial re-enactment of the cycle of human life and the life story of the deceased. It is a slow-moving circular dance performed by men in black sarongs, who stand shoulder to shoulder and chant for hours. It also bids farewell to the soul of the deceased and relays the hope that the soul will arrive in the afterworld safely.

Cigarettes are circulated, and endless supplies of food and tuak *(palm wine)* are served to the guests by immaculately clad women. Each family member is responsible for a pavilion and its kitchen. Women recruited from friends and family cater for the constant flow of guests.

Ceremonies last from one to seven days, depending on the wealth and social status of the deceased. There may be buffalo fighting in which the bulls, agitated by the insertion of chilli up their behinds, lock horns and strain against each other. The winner is the one which makes its opponent slide backwards. The crowd urges them on with frenzied whoops and yells, but is ready to scatter in case one breaks loose and charges in panic. You might also see *sisemba* (kick-fighting) and maybe cockfights at the end of the ceremony.

As well as the Mabadong, you might see orchestras of Sunday school children playing painted bamboo wind instruments. Reward their serious performing by putting a donation on the ground in front of them – there will be donations from other spectators, in response to your effort if not the children's. The programme might also include dances like the Maranding, a war dance performed at the burial service of a patriotic nobleman to remind the people of his heroic deeds, or the Makatia, which reminds the people of the deceased's generosity and loyalty. Songs may also be sung to console the bereaved family or convey their grief to the other guests at the funeral. ■

ieces of bamboo, but newer houses use orrugated metal sheets. Standing on thick olid piles, the rectangular body of the house s small in contrast to the roof, and consists f two or three dark rooms with low doors nd small windows. If necessary the whole ouse can actually be put on runners and oved to another location.

Torajan houses always face a line-up of ce barns – wealthy owners may have a hole fleet of barns. The barns look like iniature houses and, like the living area in house, the rice storage area is surprisingly mall considering the overall size of the ructure. The barn has a small door at one nd, and the surface of the walls and the high

gables are usually decorated. The rice storage chamber is raised about two metres off the ground on four smooth columns of wood, polished to prevent rats climbing up them. About 60 cm from the ground is a wooden platform stretched between the pillars, an important meeting place to sit and wile away the hours, as well as a shelter from downpours. Who sits where depends on their status, so be careful not to offend elders by taking their place at ceremonies. The boat-shaped roof shelters an area about twice the size of the rice chamber.

The Toraja have a number of ceremonies connected with the construction of a tongkonan. Construction is preceded by the sacrificial killing of a chicken, pig or buffalo; its successful completion is celebrated with a large feast in which many pigs and at least one buffalo are killed.

Traditional Sports

There's a unique form of man-to-man combat in Tanatoraja, an unarmed contest called *sisemba*. The aim of the game is to kick your opponent into submission. It's something like Thai boxing except that use of the hands is banned and you can't kick your opponent when he is down (very sporting). More a feat of strength and endurance now, the original aim of the contest was to instil courage in Torajan youths – a useful attribute for a people once hemmed in by their coastal enemies and occasionally at war with each other.

The fights are held at the time of the rice harvest or just after (June to early August), which is also the most popular time for funerals and house ceremonies. Fights are held between individuals or teams of two or more, and the women look on and cheer their favourites. When the men of one village challenge another, anything up to 200 a side is possible.

The Toraja had another contest known as the *sibamba*, in which the contestants used wooden clubs to hit each other, protectin[g] themselves from the blows with a bull-hi[de] shield (very similar to the contests found o[n] Lombok, eastern Bali and Sumbawa). Appa[r]ently it was banned during Dutch rule.

A more docile sport is the game known a[s] *takro*, where a rattan ball is kicked an[d] bounced over a metre high bamboo stic[k] fixed parallel to the ground. It's somethin[g] like volleyball, but uses only two or thre[e] players, and only the head, legs and feet ca[n] touch the ball.

Books

The locally produced *A Guide to Toraja* b[y] AT Marampa is available in some Rantepa[o] shops in English, German and French. It lis[ts] dances, ceremonies and some local walk[s] and is quite useful.

Also locally produced is *Toraja – A[n] Introduction to a Unique Culture* by LT Ta[n]gdilintin and M Syafei in their own uniqu[e] style. Much more readable is *Life & Dea[th] of the Toraja People* by Stanislaus Sa[n]darupa. Both are sold in Rantepao's souven[ir] shops.

Tales from the Tuak Tree is a collection o[f] Torajan superstitions put together by Gera[l]dine Sheedy and the students of the SM[A] Barana as a fundraiser for REPAIDS Toraj[a]

Language

The weary 'Hello misters' will instantly change to radiant grins if you attempt a word or two of the Torajan dialect. Bahasa Toraja and its variations remains the predominant language, despite the lack of books written in Bahasa Toraja. Many villages and older people do not speak Bahasa Indonesia at all. The following phrases will guarantee instant laughter and appreciation. If you can't get your tongue around the characteristic glottal stop (indicated with an apostrophe), there will be a crowd of teachers to help.

How are you?	*Apa kareba?*
I'm well.	*Kareba melo.*
Good/fine.	*Melo.*
Thank you.	*Kurre sumanga.*
You're welcome.	*Bole paria.*
How much is this?	*Se pira te' indok?*
Very expensive!	*Masuli' liu!*
Where are you going?	*Umba me sule?*
I'm just going for a walk.	*Su malong-malong.*
I don't have any sweets!	*Ta'e ku ampui gula-gula!*

local HIV/AIDS education project. The booklet's pearls of wisdom, in English and Indonesian, provide some daring conversation starters.

RANTEPAO

Rantepao, with a population of about 20,000, is the largest town and commercial centre in Tanatoraja. It is also the main travellers' centre on Sulawesi. The places to see are scattered around the lush, green countryside surrounding Rantepao. This area has cool evenings and rain throughout the year – even in the 'dry' season.

Information

Tourist Office The government tourist office on Jl Niaga in the town square opens from 7.30 am to 2 pm Monday to Friday. It's helpful, has maps of the area, and lists dates and locations of ceremonies.

Money Bank Rakyat Indonesia and Bank Danamon on Jl Jen Ahmad Yani both give lower exchange rates than banks in Ujung Pandang. The best rates are available from the moneychanger at the Hotel Indra II, Haji La Tunrung, at Jl Diponegoro 4, and Abadi, at the intersection of Jl Diponegoro and Jl Jen Ahmad Yani.

Post & Communications The post office is on Jl Jen Ahmad Yani opposite the Bank Rakyat Indonesia. Next door is the Telkom office, open 24 hours, with telephones, a Home Country Direct service, facsimile and information. There are card phones in foyers of banks and hotels, and several pricey wartels along the main north-south thoroughfare.

Travel Agencies Private agencies such as JET on the corner of Jl Jen Ahmad Yani and Jl Landorundun provide bicycles, motorcycles, cars, guides and trekking advice. Toraja Permai Tours and Travel (☎ 21784; fax 21236) offers trekking and rafting tours.

Guides Readily available for 30,000 to 35,000 rp a day, guides are only needed for an introduction to the funerals and other traditional celebrations. Guides plus car hire cost 50,000 to 60,000 rp a day. Be very wary of guides who offer to take care of gift giving on your behalf, then short-change your hosts by turning up to ceremonies with dozens of guests and just a few packs of cigarettes as presents. Private agencies such as JET can introduce you to Torajan guides who are sensitive to the culture. If you happen to pay a deposit but have to cancel the trip, you are entitled to a refund.

Tourist Tax Since mid-1995, tourists entering Tanatoraja by road must pay a 3500 rp 'entry' charge at a road block south of Makale. This is in addition to the service tax now levied on hotel beds and meals.

Things to See

Rantepao's **market day** is held every six days. These are very big, very social occasions which attract crowds from far afield. The commerce is lively, but incidental to the real business of the day – endless coffee, *kretek* (clove cigarettes) and gossip. Ask around Rantepao for the exact day, or seek out markets elsewhere in the valley. Rantepao's market is two km north-east of the town centre, easily reached by minibus from the bridge.

Special Events

To get the most out of Tanatoraja, attend the funeral and other ceremonies. Otherwise what you see is a lot of nicely decorated houses, caves full of coffins and *tau tau* (carved wooden effigies of the dead). Seek out locals to take you to the ceremonies and explain what's happening – you won't have to search hard, but you will need to fend off opportunists from out of town to find a local. Generally the further you venture from main roads to get to a ceremony, the less likely the funeral will be overrun with tour groups.

Also ask around about weddings, new house or harvest ceremonies, each with special traditions and a bit of ritual slaughter.

SULAWESI

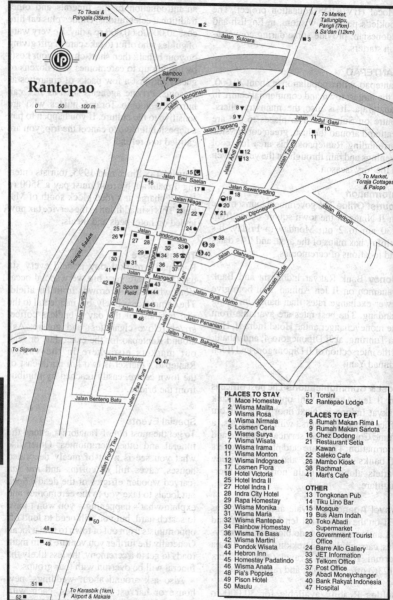

Rantepao

0   50   100 m

To Tikala &
Pangala (35km)

To Market,
Tallunglipu,
Pangli (7km)
& Sa'dan (12km)

Jalan Suloara

Bamboo
Ferry

Jalan Monginsidi

Jalan Abdul Gani

Jalan Tappang

Jalan Andi Mappanyuki

Jalan Tanaa

To Market,
Toraja Cottages
& Palopo

Jalan Emi Saelan

Jalan Sawerigading

Jalan Beringin

Jalan Niaga

Jalan Diponegoro

Jalan Landorundun

Jalan Pasuan Kude

Jalan Olahraga

Sungai Sadan

Jalan Pembangunan

Jalan Mangadi

Jalan Budi Utomo

Jalan Kartika

Jalan Siem Ratulangi

Sports
Field

Jalan Jen Ahmad Yani

Jalan Merdeka

Jalan Penanian

To Siguntu

Jalan Taman Bahagia

Jalan Pantekesu

Jalan Pao Pura

Jalan Benteng Batu

Jalan Pong Tiku

To Karasbik (1km),
Airport & Makale

PLACES TO STAY
1 Mace Homestay
2 Wisma Malita
3 Wisma Rosa
4 Wisma Nirmala
5 Losmen Ceria
6 Wisma Surya
7 Wisma Wisata
10 Wisma Irama
11 Wisma Monton
12 Wisma Indograce
17 Losmen Flora
18 Hotel Victoria
25 Hotel Indra II
27 Hotel Indra I
28 Indra City Hotel
29 Rapa Homestay
30 Wisma Monika
31 Wisma Maria
32 Wisma Rantepao
34 Rainbow Homestay
36 Wisma Te Bass
42 Wisma Martini
43 Pondok Wisata
44 Hebron Inn
45 Homestay Padatindo
46 Wisma Anata
48 Pia's Poppies
49 Pison Hotel
50 Maulu

51 Torsini
52 Rantepao Lodge

PLACES TO EAT
8 Rumah Makan Rima I
9 Rumah Makan Sarlota
16 Chez Dodeng
21 Restaurant Setia
   Kawan
22 Saleko Cafe
26 Mambo Kiosk
38 Rachmat
41 Mart's Cafe

OTHER
13 Tongkonan Pub
14 Tiku Lino Bar
15 Mosque
19 Bus Alam Indah
20 Toko Abadi
   Supermarket
23 Government Tourist
   Office
24 Barre Allo Gallery
33 JET Information
35 Telkom Office
37 Post Office
39 Abadi Moneychanger
40 Bank Rakyat Indonesia
47 Hospital

SULAWESI

You need to be invited, not formally, but at least by someone who knows someone. Dress conservatively.

These celebrations offer a chance to see traditional Torajan dancing, graceful routines to the beat of a large drum (or sometimes to taped music). What the dance lacks in complexity is more than made up for by the enthusiasm of members of the audience who dash forward to stuff 5000 rp and 10,000 rp notes into the performers' headbands. The women's clothes accentuate the strength of Torajan women: they wear flame-coloured dresses with beaded decoration hanging from the waist and shoulders. The family kris (dagger) is tucked into the waistband – in other areas of Indonesia only men may wear a kris.

Places to Stay – bottom end

Rantepao has a competitive selection of cheap hotels and comfortable homestays, but all prices rise in the peak tourist season of June to August. Many private homes take in guests during the high season.

Losmen Ceria on Jl Monginsidi is a clean, basic losmen with bed and breakfast from 5000 rp.

North of the bridge is *Wisma Rosa* (☎ 21-075), Jl Sa'dan 28, a pleasant, older place with singles/doubles from 10,000/12,000 rp, including breakfast, and rooms with hot water from 15,000 rp.

Herds of backpackers mob the *Wisma Malita* (☎ 21011), Jl Suloara 110, which has basic rooms from 10,000/12,000 rp, and rooms with hot water for 20,000/25,000 rp.

Nearby *Mace Homestay* (☎ 21852) at Jl Tenko Saturu 4 is set in a pretty garden on a quiet street. The delightful women who run it have four rooms for 12,500 rp in the low season and variable surcharges in the high season. Around the corner at Jl Tandung is *Melo Homestay*, with four twin rooms in a garden by the river for 25,000 rp, including breakfast and hot running water.

Wisma Wisata (☎ 21746) and *Wisma Surya* (☎ 21312) are neighbours and back on to the river, and both charge 10,000/15,000 rp.

The Wisata at Jl Monginsidi 40, is modern and quiet, with back rooms overlooking the river. The Surya at No 36 charges 2500 rp for breakfast, but is flexible with its pricing.

Wisma Maria (☎ 21165) on Jl Ratulangi looks on to a garden and has a collection of Torajan artefacts in its foyer. It's cheap, central and clean, with rooms from 10,000/15,000 rp, but the staff tend to be aloof.

Much more hospitable is the *Wisma Monika* (☎ 21216) across the road, with rooms from 15,000 to 20,000 rp with breakfast.

Further south at No 62 is *Wisma Martini* (☎ 21240). It's tattered, but friendly, and all rooms have private bath starting at 7500/10,000 rp.

Wisma Nirmala (☎ 21319) on Jl Andi Mapanyuki is relatively quiet and near the river. Rooms with private bath cost 15,000/17,500 rp.

Wisma Rantepao (☎ 21397) on Jl Landorundun is central, with reasonable rooms ranging from 10,000 to 25,000 rp.

The *Rapa Homestay* (☎ 21517) on Jl Pembangunan has two rooms. Bed and breakfast costs 10,000 rp, or 15,000 rp in the high season. *Rainbow Homestay*, almost opposite at No 11A, has modern and quiet rooms for 15,000/20,000 rp. *Homestay Padatindo*, a few doors down on the corner of Jl Merdeka, has 10,000 rp rooms.

Wisma Indograce on busy Jl Andi Mapanyuki suffers from street noise, but has rooms with private bath for 10,000/12,500 rp.

Losmen Flora (☎ 21586), right next to a mosque, is basic but cheap with 5000 rp for singles. The nearby *Hotel Victoria* (☎ 21038) on Jl Sawerigading is on a busy street and is a bit noisy, but all rooms have private bath costing 11,000/15,000 rp.

A few km north of town, restaurateur Pak Bitty runs *Homestay Chez Dodeng* at the village of Tallunglipu, with rooms from around 10,000 rp.

Ibu Martha's *Gardenia Homestay* on the Palopo road has exceptionally clean rooms with hot water for 25,000/35,000 rp. Entertainment is either the satellite TV or long chats under the rice barn in the secluded garden.

Places to Stay – middle

The *Indra City Hotel* (☎ 21060) at Jl Landorundun 55 is an old place with good carpeted rooms at 30,000/35,000 rp in the low season.

Pondok Wisata (☎ 21595) is a large place on Jl Pembangunan 23, with spotless rooms from 20,000 rp, or 45,000 rp for a large room with balcony – add 5000 rp in high season. Just a few doors south on the same street is *Hebron Inn* (☎ 21519), a clean and quiet place with doubles for 49,000 rp.

Around the corner is *Wisma Te Bass* (☎ 21415), an old but pleasant place run by a couple – the husband speaks English and the wife speaks Dutch. Rooms are 15,000/20,000 rp, or 25,000 rp in the high season.

A little further south at the end of the street is *Wisma Anata* (☎ 21356), where all rooms are triples and cost 20,000 rp for one or two persons, 25,000 rp for three.

Wisma Irama (☎ 21371) at Jl Abdul Gani 16 is a quiet hotel with a large garden. It's north-east of the town centre and has rooms with mandi for 20,000/25,000 rp. Deluxe rooms with hot showers go for 40,000/50,000 rp.

Wisma Monton (☎ 21675; fax 21665) at Jl Abdul Gani 14A is in an alley behind the Irama. Its clean modern rooms start at 20,000 rp, or 25,000 rp with hot running water, all including breakfast. The capable manager speaks English.

Less conveniently located, but recommended, are *Wisma Maria II* (☎ 21288), on the Makale road two km south of town, with rooms from 17,500/22,000 rp; the *Pison Hotel* (☎ 21344), Jl Pong Tiku 8, with rooms from 15,000/27,500 rp; and marginally cheaper *Pia's Poppies* (☎ 21121) across the lane at No 27A.

Places to Stay – top end

The *Hotel Indra II* (☎ 21583) is the new wing of the Hotel Indra complex on Jl Sam Ratulangi, with rooms from $US32/40, including breakfast and tax. The rooms face a pleasant courtyard garden. *Hotel Indra I* (☎ 21163) across the road was being rebuilt to Indra II standard and prices.

Rantepao's main tourist hotel is *Toraja Cottages* (☎ 21089), a collection of well appointed bungalows on Jl Diponegoro three km north-east of town. Rooms start at 125,000/140,000 rp.

The *Toraja Prince* (☎ 21458), adjacent to Toraja Cottages, has all the mod cons for 130,000/150,000 rp.

Novotel was planning to swell the ranks of Tanatoraja's upmarket hotels with a resort development – expect all the top-end hotels to discount heavily to maintain patronage.

Places to Eat

Many of the eateries around Rantepao serve Torajan food. A local speciality is pa'piong, a mix of fish or meat (usually pork or chicken) and leaf vegetables smoked over a low flame for hours. Order a couple of hours in advance and enjoy it with black rice.

Some smaller, unmarked warungs along Jl Andi Mapanyuki and Jl Suloara offer 1st class barbecued fish and other local staples for considerably less than the restaurants. It's best to go with a local rather than barging in uninvited. So, too, the many balok (palm wine) bars around town, which welcome foreigners (especially those with musical talents), but not in big numbers. Local by-laws now stipulate that warungs must not serve tuak after 9 pm and owners risk steep fines if you are still tippling after last orders.

Kiosk Mambo, Jl Ratulangi, serves Indonesian and Torajan food, but is also great for western breakfasts. Nearby *Hotel Indra I* has an upmarket Indonesian and Torajan restaurant – the chicken pa'piong is especially recommended.

The classy restaurants at *Pia's Poppies* and *Pison* hotels serve Torajan food (order in advance). The former also dishes up Continental breakfasts, yoghurt, juices and other goodies, and is worth the wait despite the very slow service.

Rumah Makan Rima I at the northern end of Jl Andi Mapanyuki is an old favourite, offering generous serves of Indonesia fare, as well as the best banana pancakes north of Bali. Its neighbours *Rumah Makan Sarlota* and *Lisher Restaurant* offer tasty Indonesian dishes, while *Drisno's* across the road serves excellent gado gado and nasi campur. Check out the *Padang restaurant* on Jl Diponegoro for its bamboo vegetable dish and perkedel potato cakes).

Pak Bitty's *Chez Dodeng* on Jl Emi Saelan is a Rantepao landmark serving basic warung fare. *Restaurant Setia Kawan* (☎ 21-264), Jl Andi Mapanyuki 32, does good Chinese food, as does *Wilsma Indograce* a block or so north.

Mart's Cafe on the corner of Jl Ratulangi and Jl Mangadi has an ambitiously long menu, with Indonesian dishes starting at 3000 rp and plenty of tourist food, including breakfast cereals.

Island Cafe is a professional outfit a few km north of town, with huge serves of Indonesian and other fare, including rich, tasty Mexican dishes. The breezy dining deck overlooks small rapids and a river flat where men spend hours washing and grooming their buffaloes. There are crafts and antiques from across eastern Indonesia in the gallery next door, and accommodation is being built downstairs.

If you want to self-cater, Toko Remaja and Toko Abadi are the main grocery and department stores. Both are on Jl Jen Ahmad Yani, near the Restaurant Setia Kawan.

Entertainment

The *Tongkonan Pub* on Jl Andi Mapanyuki features disco, karaoke and the occasional live performance. Opening hours are from around 8 pm until midnight or 1 am.

Saleko Cafe, above the souvenir shops on the corner of Jl Andi Mapanyuki and Jl Niaga, is a quiet breezy cafe alternative to the pubs. It's open Friday to Sunday.

The restaurant at *Hotel Indra II* puts on a traditional Torajan menu with dancing and flute music for diners and guests on Saturday nights.

Things to Buy

Woodcarving, weaving and basketry are the main crafts of Tanatoraja – some villages are noted for particular specialities, such as Mamasan boxes (used to store magic, as well

as salt, betel nut etc), huge horn necklaces and wooden figurines. Woodcarvings include panels, clocks and trays, carved like the decorations on traditional houses and painted in the four traditional colours – black, white, yellow and brown.

Look for carvings being hand etched at Kete Kesu, where nobleman Pak Jinting runs a skillshare project for unemployed youths. Pak Jinting, an authority on Torajan carving, regularly travels to Japan to maintain a Torajan house in a museum. His trainees' bamboo containers with designs carved and burnt on them are decorative as well as functional; formerly used for storing important documents, they are ideal for keeping spaghetti.

Other artefacts sold in the souvenir shops include mini replicas of Torajan houses with incredibly exaggerated overhanging roofs. Other interesting pieces include hand spun Toraja weaving, especially from Sa'dan, and the longer cloths of the Mamasa Valley. Necklaces made of plant seeds and chunky silver and amber or wooden beads festoon the gift shops, but the orange beaded necklaces are the authentic Torajan wear. Black and red velvet drawstring bags are popular with tourists, much to the amusement of locals who use them for carrying betel nut ingredients to funerals.

The Barre Allo gallery above the souvenir shops has an impressive range, priced and beautifully displayed (unlike the souvenir shops below). Note that the prices are not fixed, and ask about packaging and shipping. The Tengko Situru workshop, one km out on the Tikala road, sells crafts from local villages as part of a handcraft development scheme.

Shops along Jl Landorundun sell locally woven blankets, a reasonable alternative to Sa'dan's weaving centre.

Getting There & Away

Air Flying gives you an idea of the dramatic contrasts in South Sulawesi geography and thrilling descents over tongkonan villages amid bamboo groves. The airport is near Makale, 25 km south of Rantepao. Merpati

SULAWESI

(☎ 21485), Jl Pao Pura, flies daily from Ujung Pandang and twice on Sunday. The fare is 87,000 rp. Be prepared for delays and always reconfirm flights – staff often double book. The runway has been extended to cater for more flights.

Bus & Bemo There are regular buses between Ujung Pandang and Rantepao. In Rantepao the bus company offices are around Jl Andi Mapanyuki in the centre of town. The main bus companies on the Rantepao-Ujung Pandang route are Litha, Liman and Alam Indah. Departures in each direction are typically at 7, 10 and 11 am, and 1, 6 and 9 pm. The trip to Ujung Pandang (330 km) costs 10,000 rp (13,000 rp for the Alam Indah executive bus or 14,500 rp on Litha, with air-con, TV and leg room). Pare Pare to Rantepao takes four to five hours and costs 6000 rp.

Litha, Alam Indah, Damri and other buses heading north to Tentena, Poso and Palu tend to leave Rantepao at 10 am. Fares to Pendolo (10 hours), Tentena (12 hours) and Poso (13 hours) are all 20,000 rp. To Palu (20 hours), it's 25,000 rp.

Bemos run down to the coastal city of Palopo (4500 rp), taking two hours for the journey or 2½ hours in the uphill direction. There are daily buses from Rantepao to Soroako on Danau Matano, leaving at about 10 am from Rantepao from the corner of Jl Landorundun and Jl Jen Ahmad Yani (10 hours; 8000 rp); the road is surfaced all the way.

Getting Around
The Airport A Merpati bus collects passengers from their hotels and guarantees that you will reach your flight on time, but costs a steep 5000 rp.

Local Transport Central Rantepao is small and easy to walk around. Becaks start at 500 rp, and the bamboo raft ferry behind Wisma Surya offers a 100 rp shortcut across the river.

The closure of the central market and bemo terminal has rather inconveniently dispersed the transport points. Kijang opposite the post office run almost continuously from Rantepao south to Makale (500 rp), and you can get off at the signs for Londa (400 rp) Tilanga (400 rp) or Lemo (400 rp) and walk. From Jl Diponogoro there are frequent bemos east towards Palopo for the sights in that direction, such as Nanggala (500 rp) Bemos north to Lempo start from Jl Monginsidi. Others leave from Jl Tappang and the bridge – to Sa'dan costs 800 rp. Regular services stop at 6 pm. Makale-bound punters can sometimes hitch a free lift on a 9 pm Ujung Pandang bus.

Motorcycles can be rented for 3000 rp per hour, or 10,000 to 20,000 rp per day. Allow for two days of recovery after one day of riding! It can be cheaper for a group to charter a bemo or a 4WD.

Apart from the well-beaten paths to Makale, Palopo, Sa'dan, Kete Kesu and a few other places, most of the roads around Rantepao are constructed out of compacted boulders – you don't get stuck, but your joints get rattled loose. If trekking, take good footwear, a water bottle, something to eat, a torch (flashlight) in case you end up walking at night, and an umbrella or raincoat. Even in the dry season it's more likely than not to rain.

MAKALE
Makale is the administrative capital of Tanatoraja, but has few of the amenities of Rantepao. It is a small, pretty town built around an artificial lake and set amid cloud-shrouded hills. There are whitewashed churches atop each hill and a good market, and Dutch houses in the older part of town.

Things to See
Makale's **market**, held every six days, is a blur of noise, colour and commotion. There are pigs aplenty, strapped down with bamboo strips for buyers' close inspection, buckets of live eels, piles and piles of fresh and dried fish, and a corner of the market reserved for balok (palm wine) sales. The balok women are constantly mixing and blending fresher, sweeter *induk* with the

lder more alcoholic brews. Taste before you buy, either by pouring the proffered capful in to your palm and slurping from there, or by flicking the lot into your mouth. When you find the perfect brew, pay around 5000 to 10,000 rp for five litres, including the container.

Heading out of the market towards Tondon, there are a few **tau tau** hidden in a rock face. Then explore the hills behind the town, or continue along the road to **Sangalla**, which is two hours by foot.

Places to Stay

There are simple, but clean, places near the town centre. *Wisma Bungin* (☎ 22255) at Jl Pongtiku 35 is a modern place with airy rooms for 10,000 rp, with private mandi. Bungin's neighbour, *Wisma Yani Randanan* (☎ 22409), Jl Nusantara 3, is also good value, with rooms for 15,000 rp.

Losmen Indra (☎ 22022), Jl Merdeka 11, is on the south side of town. It is a clean place

with friendly people. Rooms with shared bath are 10,000 rp, or 15,000 with private bath.

Losmen Merry (☎ 22013) on the corner of Jl Yamin and Jl Musa has rooms for 5000/10,000 rp with shared bath. It is very central, and above a shop. *Losmen Litha* (☎ 22009) is on noisy Jl Pelita, but is OK for a night. The small rooms with shared bath go for 10,000 rp per person.

Further north on Jl Pongtiku is *Losmen Marga* (☎ 22011), which looks a bit tattered, but has friendly management and rooms with private bath for 5000 rp per person.

Wisma Merry II (☎ 22174), Jl Pongtiku 100B, is a big, homey place north of town, with quiet rooms for 10,000 rp.

About three km north of the town centre is the elegant *Wisma Puri Artha* (☎ 22047), where rooms are 38,500/45,500 rp. Next door is Makale's expensive tourist resort, the *Marannu City Hotel* (☎ 22028), with rooms for 95,000/108,000 rp. This place comes complete with tennis courts and a swimming pool. At 1500 rp, the pool provides welcome refuge from the attentions of the local kids, except on Sunday. Tennis court hire is 5000 rp, including racquet hire.

Places to Eat

Dining out is limited to basic warungs. Self-caterers can supplement market purchases with goods from Toko Sahabat or Sinar Muda. The main alternatives are the hotel restaurants at the *Wisma Puri Artha* (ordinary menu) or the *Marannu City Hotel* (expensive, tasty western food, but slow service).

Pa'piong is the local speciality, smoked in bamboo tubes in the market through the day, and sold in the *warung* around the market at night. Eat there or take some back to your hotel. The tiny *warung* next to Telkom has good chicken soup and hot, spicy saraba, that tasty ginger/coconut alternative to coffee.

Throughout the day seasonal fruit and kueh (cakes), such as banana fried in a shortcrust pastry, are available from the stalls along the lanes near the market.

Rumah Makan Bira, overlooking the river

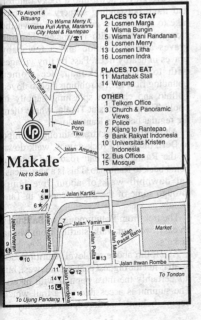

PLACES TO STAY
2 Losmen Marga
4 Wisma Bungin
5 Wisma Yani Randanan
8 Losmen Merry
13 Losmen Litha
16 Losmen Indra

PLACES TO EAT
11 Martabak Stall
14 Warung

OTHER
1 Telkom Office
3 Church & Panoramic Views
6 Police
7 Kijang to Rantepao
9 Bank Rakyat Indonesia
10 Universitas Kristen Indonesia
12 Bus Offices
15 Mosque

Makale
Not to Scale

SULAWESI

about midway between Rantepao and Makale, has fabulous baked chicken and barbecued fish at restaurant prices.

Getting There & Away

Makale shares its airport with Rantepao, and airline offices are in Rantepao.

From dawn to dusk, kijang race between Rantepao and Makale (40 minutes, 500 rp). However, the last kijang from Rantepao leaves around dusk, making dining out in Rantepao a tricky proposition.

From Makale you can get buses to the same places (and for the same prices) as you can from Rantepao. The bus offices and agents are all in the middle of Makale, clustered near the corner of Jl Merdeka and Jl Ihwan Rombe.

AROUND RANTEPAO & MAKALE

The following places are all within fairly easy reach on day trips, but you can make longer trips by staying overnight in villages or camping out. If you take advantage of Torajan village hospitality, bring gifts or pay your way. Guides are useful if you have a common language, but in some ways it's better without a guide. The Toraja are friendly and are used to curious travellers, and the quiet beauty of the hills around Rantepao is a real tonic. If you're really short of time you could hire a car or motorcycle and whip around the main sites in a day or two – but that's not the way to see this place.

Batutumonga

Batutumonga, north of Rantepao, is a haven on the slopes of Gunung Sesean, with panoramic views of Rantepao and the Sa'dan Valley, including stunning sunrises. There are several losmen, but no telephones, so get there by afternoon to secure a room. The electricity cuts out at midnight. From Rantepao, take a bemo to **Lempo** (11 km; two hours) via a very bumpy trail and walk from there to Batutumonga (half an hour).

Places to Stay *Mama Siska's* is up a small track to the right as you enter Batutumonga from Lempo. Her outstanding cooking easily compensates for the gloom of the creaky bamboo house. Prices average around 15,000 rp per head for bed, breakfast, lunch and dinner.

Londoruden Homestay has its own generator, restaurant, a few tongkonan rooms and amazing views over the valley. Rooms with private mandi and garden settings cost 7000 to 10,000 rp per head, including breakfast. Ask Aras to explain the name.

Betania Homestay (Mama Rina's) offers top views, and comfortable beds in traditional tongkonan. Prices per head are 12,000 rp for dinner, bed and breakfast, 7000 rp for bed and breakfast, or 5000 rp for bed and coffee.

Mentirotiku has tongkonan and conventional rooms, a pricey restaurant and plans for a karaoke bar. The 15,000 rp asking price for bed and breakfast is negotiable.

Around Batutumonga

From Batutumonga you can walk to **Lokomata** and return on the same day. Lokomata has cave graves hewn into a rocky outcrop and more outstanding scenery. The return hike to Rantepao is an easy hike down the slopes to **Pana**, with its ancient hanging graves among bamboo and a few baby graves in nearby trees. Pass by tiny villages with towering tongkonan, see women pounding rice, men scrubbing their beloved buffalo and children splashing happily in pools. The path ends at **Tikala**, where there are regular bemo to Rantepao.

Alternatively, backtrack through Lempo to **Deri**, the site of rock graves, walk down to the Rantepao-Sa'dan road and catch a bemo back to Rantepao. This is a very pleasant downhill walk of about five hours through some of the finest scenery in Tanatoraja.

The trek from Batutumonga to **Sa'dan** is an easy two hour walk, starting from Mama Siska's.

At 2150m above sea level, **Gunung Sesean** is not the highest peak on Sulawesi, but it's certainly the most popular with hikers. The summit is accessible via a trail which begins behind Londoruden Homestay in

Batutumonga. The return trip to the summit takes five hours. A guide might be useful, but you can manage on your own.

Beyond Gunung Sesean, the sleepy village of **Pangala** (35 km from Rantepao) is noted for its fine dancers, as is nearby **Baruppu**, the place made famous by Nigel Barley's book *Not a Hazardous Sport.* Pangala is a hair-raising 2½ hour bemo ride from Rantepao, starting by the river then up a pot-holed road for as far as you can bear. Eventually walking seems a better option.

Pangala's only losmen, *Losmen Sando,* is a surprisingly elegant place with comfortable rooms, clean mandi, carved doors and a roomy lounge-restaurant with big windows looking out to the owner's coffee plantation. Peter charges about 10,000 rp per person, and offers free advice on treks back to Rantepao, across to Batutumonga, or to Rongkong.

A traditional Toale village, **Rongkong** is a difficult four day trek across the mountains north of Baruppu. From Rongkong there is occasional transport to Limbung, which has regular buses east to Masamba.

North of Rantepao
The traditional village of **Palawa**, two km north of Pangli, is just as attractive but less popular than Kete Kesu, with tongkonan houses and rice barns. In the dry season you can walk to **Bori**, fording a river and walking through padi fields. Bori is the site of an impressive *rante* (ceremonial ground) and some towering megaliths. A km south is **Parinding**, which has tongkonan houses and rice barns which you pass on the two hour walk from Bori to Tikala. Rantepao-bound bemos occasionally go this way.

Pangli, seven km north of Rantepao, has tau tau and house graves. House graves are an interesting innovation used when there are no rock faces available for carving out burial niches. Graves are dug in the earth and a small Toraja-style house is built over the top. Each grave is used for all the members of the family, and the bodies are wrapped in cloth and entombed without coffins.

Further north is the weaving centre of **Sa'dan**, where local women have a market to sell their woven cloth. It is all handmade on simple, back-strap looms, but not all is produced in the village. Many of the large, earthy blankets come from the west, particularly Mamasa. You can see the Sa'dan women making cloth using traditional techniques. Bemo from Rantepao go direct to Sa'dan, 13 km along a surfaced road (500 rp). Stop for dinner and drinks at the *River Cafe* on the way back, then check out the crafts next door to the cafe.

West of Rantepao
Just a km west across the river from Rantepao, **Gunung Singki** is a rather steep hill. There's a slippery, somewhat overgrown trail to the summit with its panoramic view across the town and the surrounding countryside. Rantepao looks surprisingly large from high up.

From Singki you can continue walking down the dirt road to **Siguntu**, seven km from Rantepao and an interesting walk past the rice fields. The path is not obvious so keep asking directions. From Siguntu to the main road at Alang Alang is also a pleasant walk. Stop on the way at the traditional village of **Mendoe**, six km from Rantepao. At **Alang Alang**, where a covered bridge crosses the river, you could head to **Londa** or back to Rantepao or Makale or, alternatively, remain on the west side of the river and continue walking to the villages of **Langda** and **Madandan**.

South of Rantepao
On the outskirts of Rantepao, just off the road leading to Makale, is **Karasik**, with traditional-style houses arranged in a horseshoe around a cluster of megaliths. The complex of houses may have been erected some years ago for a single funeral ceremony, but some are now inhabited. In the past, temporary houses were built around a *rante* (funeral site) for use at a funeral and would be demolished or burnt when the funeral was finished.

Just off the main road south of Rantepao (on the way to Kete Kesu) is **Buntu Pune**,

SULAWESI

where there are two tongkonan houses and six rice barns. The story goes that one of the two houses was built by a nobleman named Pong Marambaq at the beginning of this century. During the Dutch rule he was appointed head of the local district, but planned to rebel and was subsequently exiled to Ambon where he died. His corpse was brought back to Toraja and buried at the hill to the north of this village.

A km or so further along the road is **Kete Kesu** (six km from Rantepao), reputed for its woodcarving (see Things to Buy in the previous Rantepao section). On the cliff face behind the village are some grave caves and very old hanging graves. The rotting coffins are suspended on wooden beams under an overhang. Others, full of bones and skulls, lie rotting in strategic piles. If you continue along the vague trail heading uphill you'll come to another grave cave. There are no tau tau, just coffins and bones, similarly neglected. One of the houses in the village has several tau tau on display.

The houses at Kete Kesu are decorated with enough handcrafts to fill a souvenir floor at Harrods. The village is a tourist museum no-one seems to live here any more, but there are surfaced paths to the main caves and it's still an interesting site. To get there take a bemo from Rantepao.

From Kete Kesu you can walk to **Sul-lukang**, which has a rante marked by a number of large, rough-hewn megaliths, and on t **Palatokke** (nine km from Rantepao). In thi beautiful area of lush rice paddies and trad tional houses there is an enormous cliff fac containing several grave caves and hangin graves. Access to the caves is difficult, bu the scenery alone makes it worthwhile.

From Palatokke you could walk to Lab and then to **Randanbatu**, where there ar more graves, then continue to Balik, San galla, Suaya and Makale.

Six km south of Rantepao is the ver extensive burial cave of **Londa** at the base o a massive cliff face. A bemo from Rantepa heading towards Makale will drop you at th turn-off, two km from the cave.

The entrance to the cave is guarded by balcony of tau tau. Inside the cave is a col lection of coffins, many of them rotted away with the bones either scattered or thrown int piles. Other coffins hold the bones of severa family members – it's an old Toraja custom that all people who have lived together in on family house should also be buried togethe in a family grave. There are other cave grave in Tanatoraja where no coffin is used at all the body is wrapped in cloth, placed in a niche in the rock face and then the door o the niche is tightly closed. A local myth says that the people buried in the Londa caves are the descendants of Tangdilinoq, chief of the Toraja at the time when they were pushed ou of the Enrekang region by new arrivals and forced to move into the highlands.

Kids hang around outside the Londa caves with oil lamps to guide you around (3000 rp). Unless you've got a strong torch you really *do* need a guide with a lamp. Inside the caves, the coffins (some of them liberally decorated with graffiti) and skulls seem to have been placed in strategic locations for the benefit of sightseers. Ask to see 'Romeo and Juliet' and (if you are thin and don't suffer from claustrophobia) squeeze through the tunnel connecting the two main caves. It is a 10 minute crawl past some interesting stalactites and stalagmites. Walk up the path by the padi opposite to where tau tau are carved. New red coffins up the nearby cliff show the old traditions are continuing.

The Palatokke Story

There is a story among the Toraja that Palatokke is the name of a person who was able to climb the rock face, his palms being like those of a gecko and able to cling to walls. When he died, it is said, his corpse was put into an *erong* (wooden coffin) and hung on these cliffs. In another part of Tanatoraja there is a story that Palatokke refers to a group of people who were able to climb the rock face like geckos. These people are said to have been a special class of workers whose job it was to hang the erong of noblemen on the cliff face by climbing the cliff without using ladders. ■

Close to the Londa graves is **Pabaisenan** (Liang Pia), where the coffins of babies can e found hanging from a tree.

Further south, just off the Rantepao-Makale road, is **Tilanga**, a pretty, natural ool-water swimming pool. Coming from Makale, it's an interesting walk along the muddy trails and through the rice paddies rom Lemo to Tilanga, but keep asking directions along the way. The natural pool at Tilanga is uphill from a derelict concrete swimming pool and decaying changing rooms.

Lemo (11 km south of Rantepao) is probably the most interesting burial area in Tanatoraja. The sheer rock face has a whole series of balconies for the tau tau. The biggest balcony has a dozen figures, with white eyes and black pupils and outstretched arms like spectators at a sports event.

There is a story that the graves are for descendants of a Toraja chief who, hundreds of years ago, reigned over the surrounding district and built his house on top of the cliff into which the graves are now cut. Because the mountain was part of his property only his descendants could use it. The chief himself was buried elsewhere, as the art of cutting grave caves had not been developed then.

It's a good idea to go early in the morning so you get the sun on the rows of figures – by 9 am their heads are in the shadows. A bemo from Rantepao will drop you off at the road to Lemo. From there it's a 15 minute walk to the tau tau.

Apart from those at Lemo, it is becoming increasingly difficult to see tau tau in Rantepao. This is because so many of them have been stolen that the Toraja now keep the remaining ones in their own homes.

East of Rantepao

Marante is a fine traditional village close to the road to Palopo. Near Marante there are stone and hanging graves with several tau tau, skulls on the coffins and a cave with scattered bones. From Marante you can cross the river on the suspension bridge and walk to the village of **Ba'ta**, which is set in attractive padi fields.

In the same direction, but further off the Palopo road, is the traditional village of **Nanggala** (16 km from Rantepao). It has a particularly grandiose traditional house and an impressive fleet of 14 rice barns. The rice barns have a bizarre array of motifs carved into them, including soldiers with guns, western women and cars. Bemos from Rantepao take you straight there for 300 rp. Keep an eye out for a colony of huge black bats hanging from trees at the end of the village. Children bait kites to pull down bats to sell for traditional medicine.

From Nanggala you can walk south to **Paniki** and **Buntao**, a very long walk along a dirt track up and down the Torajan hills. The trail starts next to the rice barns. It's a three hour walk from Nanggala to the Paniki district, and along the road you'll see coffee-plantation machines grinding and packing coffee into sacks. It's a long, long trudge and can be very hot, so take lots of water.

From Paniki it's a two hour walk to Buntao, which has some house graves and tau tau. Alternatively, catch a bemo from Paniki to Rantepao. Buntao is about 15 km from Rantepao. Two or three km beyond Buntao is **Tembamba**, which has more graves and is noted for its fine scenery.

East of Makale

South of Buntao and 22 km from Rantepao is **Sangalla**, which has a simple homestay, the *Homestay Kalembang Indah*. From there head south-east to the hot spring at **Makula**, west of the Rantepao-Makale road, or north to Labo and the road to Kete Kesu. There are occasional bemos from Makale and Rantepao to Sangalla.

One place where you can still see substantial numbers of tau tau is **Tampangallo**, close to Suaya. Turn off the Suaya to Sangalla road about a km from Suaya, and walk 500m through the rice fields to a place where there are over 40 tau tau. The graves belong to the chiefs of Sangalla, descendants of the mythical divine being, Tamborolangiq, who is believed to have introduced the caste system, death rituals and agricultural techniques into Torajan society. The former royal families of Makale, Sangalla and Menkendek all claimed descent from Tamborolangiq, who is said to have descended from heaven by a stone staircase.

Sungai Sa'dan

The canyon of Sungai Sa'dan makes for an interesting white-water rafting trip that can be completed in one day. There are over 20 rapids, including a few class three and four rapids. All equipment, transport and guides can be provided by Sobek Expeditions (☎ (0423) 22143), a professional US-Indonesian outfit with bases on Bali, Ujung Pandang and soon in Central Sulawesi. It runs trips down the Maulu and Sa'dan rivers through beautiful valleys. One day excursions cost US$50, or three day trips cost from US$225. Toranggo Buya (☎ (0411) 858836) is Sobek's affiliate at Jl Bulukunyi 9A, PO Box 107, Ujung Pandang 90131.

Toraja Permai Tours and Travel (☎ 21784; fax 21236) offers various trekking and rafting combinations around the area and down the nearby Madong and Sa'dan rivers for around US$65 a day.

PALOPO

This Muslim port town is the administrative capital of the Luwu district. Before the Dutch this was once the centre of the old and powerful Luwu Kingdom. The former palace is now the tiny **Museum Batara Guru** at Jl Andi Jemma 1, opposite the police station, and contains relics of the royal era. On the waterfront is a Bugis village and a long pier where you can get a closer look at the fishing boats.

Places to Stay

The best place by far is the quiet, relaxed *Hotel Pusma* (☎ 21178/22373) at Jl Andi Jemma 14. Its clean, new single rooms with shared mandi cost 5000 rp. There are doubles with mandi at 20,000 rp and air-con for 30,000 rp. Prices include breakfast.

Buana Hotel (☎ 22164), Jl Dahlan 89, is an attractive place, with rooms from 10,000 to 24,000 rp.

Wisma Kumala Indah (☎ 22488) at Jl Opu Tosappaile 77 is clean and friendly, with rooms from 12,500/20,000 rp.

The *Palopo Hotel*, Jl Kelapa 11, opposite the bus terminal, is not recommended. Very grubby doubles go for 15,000 rp, or 25,000 rp with air-con.

Hotel Bumi Sawerigading is an old echo chamber, but it's not bad and all rooms have private bath from 10,000 rp. It's about a 1 minute walk from the bus terminal. *Hotel Adifati I*, Jl Andi Jemma, is a noisy truckers stop. *Hotel Adifati II* is newer and classier, with budget rooms from 10,000 rp.

Places to Eat

There are dozens of warungs around the market and the new Plaza Luwu shopping centre. *Warung Segeri* on Jl Kelapa, opposite the bus terminal, has outstanding grilled fish with sate sauce, soup and rice for 4000 rp.

The *Rumah Makan Padang* on Jl Sudirman has an array of good but cold grub, and the *Borobudur* near Hotel Adifati II is clear and cheerful, with better than average vegetables. The *Aroma Sulawesi* around the corner on Jl Kartini has pricey but huge serves of Chinese-style Indonesian food and fruity es jeruk. Good value.

Palopo's flashiest eatery, *Celebes Restaurant*, is built on stilts over the sea a few km from town. The food is more expensive but good value, with big meaty serves and seafood aplenty, plus half-decent chips (fries). Wash it down with cold beer, karaoke on Friday and Saturday, and the occasional band. By day there are views of Palopo, the mountains and life on the water.

Getting There & Away

The frequent bemos from Rantepao twist and turn their way down to the coast in 2½ hours. The fare is 4500 rp and the views are spectacular. Kattun, a cafe-stop midway between Rantepao and Palopo, has superb views, six pricey rooms at 45,000 rp, lovely walks and an adjacent orchid garden. There are buses and bemos from Palopo's main market to Pare Pare and Ujung Pandang, Soroako and Malili, Pendolo and Poso, and to Sengkang and Bone (Watampone).

SULAWESI

From Rantepao you could take a bus to Palopo and then head down the east coast back to Ujung Pandang, via Sengkang and Bone (Watampone). Palopo to Bone takes six hours. The road is good for the first half of the journey, but disappears into huge pot-holes for the last two hours.

There are irregular boat services from Palopo to Malili, but the buses are faster and more frequent. A useful ferry connection is the service between Siwa, south of Palopo, and isolated Susua on the south-east penin-ula.

MALILI & SOROAKO

Any town as isolated and forgotten as Malili is hardly a candidate for a colourful history, but thanks to the rich iron deposits around nearby Danau Matano, that's what it has.

A thriving Dutch settlement at Malili was largely destroyed by the Japanese during WWII, and the town was levelled again during separatist upheaval in the 1950s. Kahar Muzakar, a Luwu local who played a key role in anti-Dutch resistance on Java during Indonesia's war of independence, later led Southern Sulawesi in a revolt against central rule. Sent to Sulawesi in June 1950, Muzakar teamed up with guerrillas fighting for greater autonomy. Their discontent with the infant republic's frequent crises was accentuated by Javanese and Minahasan domination of the civil and military services. By 1956 Kahar Muzakar's guerrillas con-rolled most of the southern Sulawesi countryside and the rebellion continued until Muzakar was killed by government troops in 1966.

Next came the mining company PT Inco, which officially opened its US$850 million nickel mining and smelting project at Soroako in 1977. The project converts low-grade ore (a nickel content of only 1.6%) into a high-grade product with a nickel content of 75%. The company not only built a smelting plant, but also towns at Malili and Soroako for its employees, an airport (at Soroako), administration buildings, a road to connect Soroako and Malili with Bone Gulf, a wharf and a satellite station to link PT Inco directly

with its offices in Ujung Pandang and Jakarta.

Danau Matano, Mahalona & Towuti
The most striking natural feature of this area is the series of mountain-fringed lakes linked by rivers and streams. Soroako is on the shores of the 16,400 hectare Danau Matano. It is Sulawesi's deepest lake, with depths of up to 540m. It forms the headwaters of the Sungai Malili system, with overflows pour-ing into Mahalona, then into Towuti and finally out into the rivers.

Danau Towuti is the second largest lake in Indonesia, with an area of 56,100 hectares and depths of up to 203m – only Sumatra's Danau Toba is bigger. Towuti is still quite elevated, so the outflow passes through a series of rapids and waterfalls before reach-ing the sea near Malili. The lakes support impressive bird life and other fauna.

Getting There & Away
There is a great road between Palopo and Soroako via Malili, with regular bemos and buses from Rantepao. Those travelling light could take the ferry across Danau Matano to Nuha, then hitch or hire a ride on the back of a motorcycle north to Beteleme. From there, squeeze your way on to buses or bemos to Kolonodale, or west to Tentena. Merpati also flies to Soroako via Masamba every Sunday.

Mamasa Valley

The Mamasa Valley is often referred to as West Tanatoraja, but this probably overstates the connection between Mamasa and the area around Rantepao. A key factor distin-guishing the people of Mamasa from their more famous neighbours is isolation. There is no air access and the recently sealed road linking Mamasa to Polewali is closed by mud slides almost every time there is heavy rain. The provincial government is funding construction of an all-weather road from Mamasa to Bittuang, near Rantepao, but it is likely Mamasa will retain its Shangrila-like isolation for a few years yet.

Mamasans have embraced Christianity with unfettered enthusiasm, or at least they have embraced that aspect of Christianity which encourages hymn singing. Choir groups meet up and down the valley every dawn and dusk, flexing their vocal chords in praise of god. Interest in the old ways is waning. Tongkonan are falling into disrepair and no new ones are being built. Mamasan tongkonan have heavy, wooden roofs, quite different from the exaggerated U-shaped bamboo roofs to the east. Torajan ceremonies survive, notably funerals, but on the whole these are far less ostentatious affairs than those around Rantepao.

Sambu weaving is a craft which still thrives in the hills around Mamasa. These long strips of heavy woven material are stitched together to make blankets, ideal insulation for the cold mountain nights. Most use factory-dyed thread, but ask around and you can find the few still using the old time-consuming natural-dye techniques.

Like Tanatoraja, the best way to see this area is by foot. Paths tend to follow the ridges, giving hikers stunning views of the clean, mountain-fringed countryside. There are few roads and far too many paths to choose from. The only sensible way to choose between the dozens of alternatives is to constantly ask directions as you go. Open-ended questions (such as: 'Where does this path lead to?') are better than those requiring a yes or no. The other source of confusion is that village districts, such as Balla, cover broad areas and there are few villages per se. Even centres within the village area, such as Rante Balla, Balla Kalua and Buntu Balla, are very spread out. There are frequent invitations to sit, drink the local coffee and talk. Take your time, listen and enjoy.

MAMASA

Mamasa, population 2000, is the only large town in the valley. The air is cool and clean, and the folk hospitable – everyone makes time for a chat. The rhythm of life has a surreal, fairytale-like quality for those used to the hustle of Indonesia's big cities. The town wakes to choirs at dawn, prayer groups punctuate the daily routine, electricity runs from 6 pm to midnight and dogs roam misty streets in the wee hours. The highlight of the week is the **market**, where hill people trade

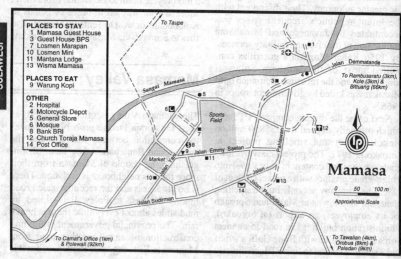

PLACES TO STAY
1 Mamasa Guest House
3 Guest House BPS
7 Losmen Marapan
10 Losmen Mini
11 Mantana Lodge
13 Wisma Mamasa

PLACES TO EAT
9 Warung Kopi

OTHER
2 Hospital
4 Motorcycle Depot
5 General Store
6 Mosque
8 Bank BRI
12 Church Toraja Mamasa
14 Post Office

To Taupe

Jalan Demmatande

To Rambusaratu (3km),
Kole (3km) &
Bittuang (66km)

Sungai Mamasa

Sports Field

Jalan Emmy Saelan

Market

Pahlawan

Jalan Sudirman

Jalan Pendidikan

Mamasa

0   50   100 m

Approximate Scale

To Camat's Office (1km)
& Polewali (92km)

To Tawalian (4km),
Orobua (8km) &
Paladan (9km)

heir produce. Look for locally made woven
lankets, a must for those cold mountain
ights. Trekkers will also be offered plenty
f fine-looking blankets direct from weavers
/hile walking through hill villages, so take
noney or gifts to barter with.

Places to Stay & Eat

1amasa has several lodging houses, all
lean, comfortable and cheap. Most serve
easonably priced food. *Losmen Mini* on Jl
/ani is a rambling mountain lodge in the
eart of town, with sunny upstairs doubles,
nandi and bibles for 15,000 rp, or darker
ooms out the back for 10,000 rp – wake to
he lilting voices of a gospel choir which
neets a few doors down.

Mantana Lodge on Jl Emmy Saelan has a
ery bright tiled interior. Singles start at
0,000 rp, and doubles range from 15,000 to
5,000 rp. There is a good restaurant, cold
eer, souvenir sales and an English-speaking
nanager.

Guest House BPS off Jl Demmatande is a
ig old-fashioned place run by the Mamasa
Toraja church, with 5000 to 7500 rp rooms
eacking on to the gurgling waters of Sungai
Mamasa.

Losmen Marapan, Jl Yani 39, is one of the
older penginapan. Its small clean doubles
vith mandi cost 9000 rp, or there are economy rooms for 6000 rp. If antiques take your
ancy, ask to see Papa's collection in the attic.

Mamasa Guest House, a pleasant place
near the hospital, has views of the surround-
ng mountains and Mambulilin Waterfall.
Doubles cost 15,000 rp. *Wisma Mamasa*, an
old Dutch house on the rise overlooking the
own, is 10,000 rp a double.

Mamasa Cottage is an ambitious hotel
oroject built over hot springs at Kole, three
cm north of Mamasa, with lovely rooms for
around 95,000 to 113,000 rp. Hot spring
vater flows to every room.

Getting There & Away

Take a bus from Pare Pare to Polewali and
hen a bum-numbing bemo to Mamasa.
There is a track east to Bittuang, best traversed by foot. Getting to Ujung Pandang is

comfortable and easy if you can score a seat
on one of the express buses that leave from
in front of the market early in the morning
(10,000 rp). These buses occasionally drop
passengers at Pare Pare (7000 rp), but prefer
passengers bound for Ujung Pandang.

AROUND MAMASA

The countryside surrounding Mamasa is
strikingly beautiful. You can hire motorcycles from the guys hanging around the
garage on Jl Demmatande in Mamasa or
hitch along the valley's couple of roads, but
footpaths and very slender suspended
bridges are the only access to most villages.
The following places (with distances in km
from Mamasa in brackets) are within easy
reach, but take warm clothes and gifts for
your hosts if you plan to stay overnight in the
hills. As most people grow their own coffee
here, put condensed milk, chocolate, sugar,
kreteks and other goods from town on your
gift list. Souvenirs such as copy watches from
Bali (*do* tell people they are just cheap copies)
or T-shirts from abroad are also popular.

North of Mamasa

Rante Buda (four km) has an impressive
25m-long tongkonan house known as Banua
Layuk (High House), an old chief's house
with colourful motifs. Visitors are invited to
inspect the *tado*, the reception room at the
front. Beyond that is a *ba ba* (guestroom),
tambing (the owners' private quarters) and a
lombon (kitchen area at the rear). This
tongkonan is one of the oldest and best preserved in the valley, built about 300 years
ago for one of five local leaders, the chief of
Rambusaratu. Exit is by donation.

At **Kole** (one km) there are hot springs,
now tapped for the paying guests of Mamasa
Cottages.

Loko (four km) is a traditional village with
old houses, set in the jungle. Get there by foot
via Kole or Tondok Bakaru. Hardy hikers
can continue up the steep hill to the **Mambulilin Sarambu** (Mambulilin Waterfall)
and on to the peak of Gunung Mambulilin
(nine km).

SULAWESI

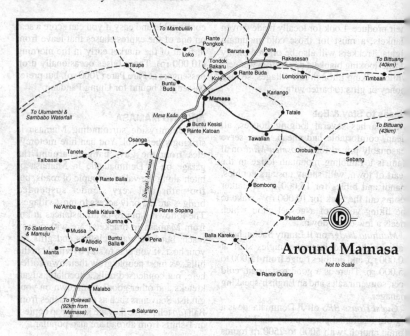

Around Mamasa

Not to Scale

Taupe (five km) is a traditional village with jungle walks and panoramic views.

South of Mamasa

Rante Sopang (nine km) is a busy centre for weaving and retailing crafts. Take the path up the hill from the roadside craft shop to see women working in open-sided shelters in the village, weaving long strips of heavy cloth for Mamasa's distinctive, colourful blankets. Others work from home – listen for the clack of hand looms as you walk through the village and check out what's on offer.

Osango (three km) is the site of *tedong-tedong* (burial houses), supposedly up to 200 years old. There are lots of paths and the village is *very* spread out, so ask for directions along the way.

Mesa Kada (two km) are hot springs which look more like a municipal swimming pool than fresh water from the earth, but are still nice for a swim.

Tanete (eight km) has mountain graves

under a cave. Tanete and nearby **Taibassi** are also centres for traditional weaving and carving.

Rante Balla (12 km) has big beautiful tongkonan, many with dozens of buffalo horns adorning the front, honouring the former residents. The village is also a centre for traditional weaving and there are fantastic weaved baskets from this area.

Buntu Balla (15 km) is another section of Balla, with traditional houses, beautiful vistas, traditional weaving and tedong-tedong burial sites. On a nearby peak there's a church with a spire. A few km further west you will find a waterfall at **Allodio**, a traditional village at **Balla Peu**, megalithic remains at **Manta** and views back along the whole valley from **Mussa**.

Malabo (18 km) has tedong-tedong burial sites. The village is on the main Polewali-Mamasa road and is the turn-off for those hiking to Mamuju, a full week's hike from Mamasa.

Orobua (nine km) has a fine old tong-
onan, one of the best in the area. There are
wo others at **Tawalian**, en route from Ma-
iasa; one in good condition and the other in
nany pieces. There are more sweeping
iews from nearby **Paladan** further south.

Iikes from Mamasa

Mamasa to Bittuang This 66 km hike takes
ibout three days. It's not too difficult as it's
nostly downhill. The hills get quite chilly at
ight, so come prepared. Also take coffee,
ugar, small toys, pens, sweets, kretek and
andles as gifts. The track is easy to follow,
nd there are plenty of hamlets along the way
or food and accommodation. You can hire a
iorse and guide for around 20,000 rp a day
- enquire at Mantana Lodge in Mamasa. A
ample itinerary could be as follows:

Day 1 – Mamasa to Timbaan (26 km) This trek is
mostly uphill. Take a tea break at Rakasasan, two
hours up the road, then lunch at Lombonan. Cross
the peak and stop for the night at Timbaan. There
are two homestays: *Ibu Kaka's* for 10,000 rp,
including dinner and breakfast; or mattresses on
the floor of a place behind the village shop.

Day 2 – Timbaan to Paku (24 km) Have tea and
coconut (1000 rp) from a house at Bau, and swim
at a crossing 2½ hours down the road. Stay at
Homestay Papasado in Ponding (10,000 rp per
night, including two meals; it's next to the traditional house), or continue to Paku and stay at
Mountain Homestay for 10,000 rp. It is run by a
young couple with children, and has a clear view
of the perfect sunsets.

Day 3 – Paku to Bittuang (16 km) Three hour walk
or half an hour by car (2500 rp) over a rough
track; it's better to walk. There are three losmen
at Bittuang; try *Losmen Pabongian* (5000 rp a
night, plus 5000 rp for meals and drinks). There
are bemos from Bittuang to Makale.

Mamasa to Mamuju The hike to Mamuju
akes from three days to a week, depending
on your luck with transport. Salarindu, the
aalfway mark, can be reached by a road of
sorts. The trail from there to Mamuju is
somewhat rougher. You'll need a guide, plus
some fluency in Indonesian, to find your
vay. Try to persuade someone in Salarindu
o join you.

South-East Sulawesi

South-East Sulawesi rewards the handful of
travellers prepared to venture a little off the
beaten track with some stunning scenery,
hospitable cultures, surprisingly good infrastructure and excellent transport links. The
province, including the Buton (Butung) and
Tukangbesi island groups off its southern tip,
has an area of 38,000 sq km and just 1.2
million inhabitants – sparsely populated by
Indonesian standards. It is inhabited by
diverse ethnic groups, including both seafaring and land-oriented cultures. Islamic
influence from neighbouring sultanates was
also strong and Islam now predominates.

History

Some of the earliest records of life in South-
East Sulawesi are depicted in prehistoric
paintings on the walls of caves near Raha, on
Pulau Muna. The red ochre paintings include
hunting scenes, boats and warriors on horse
back. There were also carved coffins and
skeletons, but visiting archaeologists in the
1980s deemed, in their wisdom, that these
and other remains should be buried in a
museum archive.

South-East Sulawesi's most powerful pre-
colonial kingdom was Buton, based at
Wolio, near Bau Bau. Its influence over vassal states in Muna, northern Muna, northern
Buton and the Tukangbesi island of Kale-
dupa was noted by Dutch traders who (for
their own strategic reasons) supported
Buton's struggle for autonomy from the expansionist powers of Makassar and Ternate
early in the 17th century. Buton came under
direct Dutch rule after the fall of Makassar
in 1669 and was granted limited self-govern-
ment by the colonial administration in 1906.

Other local trading centres maintained a
low profile, probably for reasons of self-
defence. Kendari was one of the busiest, but
the island of Bungkutoko at the mouth of
Kendari harbour hid the port so well that
only select traders knew of its existence until
a Dutch explorer 'discovered' the thriving

SULAWESI

South-East Sulawesi

0   25   50 km

trading post in 1830. At that time the inland regions were dominated by the Tolaki, traders of agricultural and forest produce who originated in the Konaweha valley upstream from Una'aha and gradually forced other inland tribes southwards.

The civil strife of the 1950s and 1960s was a time of extreme hardship for the people of South-East Sulawesi. Farms and villages were plundered by rebel and government forces alike, decimating the region's agricultural sector.

The restoration of order has been accompanied by unprecedented development.

South-East Sulawesi's varied agricultural base is supplemented by lucrative cash crops, forest industries and small scale mining. Considering its relatively sparse population, the province's communications, transport and other infrastructure is among the best in Indonesia.

Flora & Fauna

Perhaps the best documented and most accessible area is the 96,800 hectare **Aopa Wetlands** between Kendari and Kolaka. Aopa consists of two shallow lakes both about 25 km across, containing a rich array f aquatic plant life and birds. The lakes and nearby Gunung Watumohai form the Rawa Aopa Watumohai National Park, home to noa, macaques, maleo, deer and the unusual ail-fin lizard – a metre-long aquatic lizard with a distinctive crested tail.

Special Events

omeone discovered that the government gives grants to organise festivals and the partying hasn't stopped since. Kendari has oat races each April, there is horse fighting and kite flying at Raha in June, and cultural estivals at Una'aha and Bau Bau each September. While the accent is on socialising ather than spectacle, it is still a fun time to be there.

Getting There & Away

Despite its isolation, South-East Sulawesi is well-connected to the outside world. Merpati and Sempati flights from Kendari to Ujung Pandang connect with services to the rest of Indonesia. Bouraq also plans to fly this route.

There are daily ferries across the Bone Gulf from South Sulawesi to Kolaka, on South-East Sulawesi's west coast, and Pelni ships call regularly at Bau Bau, Raha and Kendari en route to/from Ujung Pandang, Central Sulawesi and Ambon.

KOLAKA

The port town of Kolaka is readily accessible by boat from Bajoe, the port of Bone, making it the main gateway to South-East Sulawesi. The Pomalaa nickel mine north-west of Kolaka was once a major regional industry, but these days cocoa, cloves and other agricultural produce are the primary source of income.

The district's few attractions include Lamadai Game Reserve, a 500 hectare ironwood and wildlife sanctuary, 40 km from Kolaka, and Tamborasi Beach, on the main road to Wolo, which claims to have the world's shortest river – 150m long. Visits to the Pomalaa nickel mine and the Japanese processing plant built in 1942 can be arranged by contacting the tourist office director at the bupati's office (☎ 21433).

Places to Stay

Kolaka has several budget losmen. The centrally located Losmen Rahmah (☎ 21036), Jl Kadue 6, at 10,000 rp per head is better than most. Losmen Alkaosar at Jl Sudirman 20, with rooms from 8000 rp, is also worth considering.

Other choices include Monalisa (☎ 21-035), Jl Konggoasa 67, with rooms for 10,000 rp, the central Mustika (☎ 21038), Jl Replita 22, for 8500 rp, and the Aloha, Jl Kewanangan 19, from 8000 rp.

Getting There & Away

Ferries from Bajoe to Kolaka leave nightly (7500 to 9600 rp; eight hours), or you can book a combined bus/boat ticket from Ujung Pandang to Kendari for 23,000 rp. From the harbour in Kolaka there are hordes of minibuses eager to take you to Kendari (5000 rp; four hours).

UNA'AHA

Blink and you might miss this dusty stop on the road from Kolaka to Kendari, except in September when the town hosts the annual Festival Budaya Tolaki – the Tolaki cultural festival. The Tolaki people originate from mountainous regions upstream from Una'aha and are now the province's predominant inland group. They celebrate their culture each September with several days of dance and music, traditional sports and other festivities.

Getting There & Away

Una'aha is on the busiest road in South-East Sulawesi. There are frequent buses and bemos east to Kendari (1000 rp; 1½ hours) and west to Kolaka (2000 rp; 1½ hours).

KENDARI

This small provincial capital (population 150,000) on the east coast of the peninsula has long been the key port for trade between the inland Tolaki people and seafaring Bugis and Bajau traders. Little is known of Kendari's history before its 'discovery' by a Dutch explorer in 1830, and its isolation continues to cushion it from dramatic developments elsewhere. The pro-development orientation

SULAWESI

of Soeharto's New Order has fostered a small, but sophisticated, enclave around Kendari, with good facilities and excellent infrastructure.

Kendari is more akin to a series of *kampung* along a highway than a city. It begins in a tangle of lanes in the old 'Kota' precinct adjacent to the original port in the east and becomes progressively more modern as each era has tacked another suburb to the west.

Orientation & Information

Kendari has one very, very long main street which changes name every kilometre or so. It runs from east to west along the full length of Kendari Bay, then veers south-west from Kendari's only major intersection at the western end of the bay. Almost all transport, accommodation, offices and commerce are scattered along this thoroughfare, including Kendari's three main markets. The main street's many names can be confusing, especially at the Kota end where 'Jl Sudirman' and 'Jl Sukarno' are used interchangeably for the same stretch.

Tourist Office For unusually informative tourist brochures visit the regional Dinas Pariwisata (☎ 26634) at Jl Tebau Nunggu 2, near the governor's office. Ask for Pak Burhanuddin, who speaks English and is a more reliable source of information than any of his 'superiors'.

Money Until recently, there were no money-changing facilities in the province. A few Kendari banks now accept US currency and travellers cheques at competitive rates, including the BNI bank on Jl Diponegoro, across the road from the city police. Banks close all weekend.

Post & Communications Telephone and fax facilities are 1st class. The 24 hour Telkom office is on Jl Sudirman (Sukarno), west of the central market. The main post office is on Jl Sam Ratulangi, near the main intersection.

Things to See & Do

There is little of interest in Kendari itself apart from the **Kambu Cascade** at the foot of Gunung Kambu, 3 km upstream from the new campus of Haluoleo University. Walk from the university or negotiate a charter direct.

Far more impressive is the multi-tiered **Morame Waterfalls**, 100m of tumbling water set amid ebony, teak and banyan trees on the Sungai Kali Osena, 65 km south of the capital. It takes over an hour to get there by bus from Pasar Baru terminal (3000 rp) or one to two hours by chartered boat. There is a deep pool at the base of the falls, which is excellent for swimming. Those with the energy can beat their way through the bush to mountain lakes 10 km upstream. If returning to Kendari by boat, stop off at **Lapuko Bay**, a good swimming and snorkelling spot with white sand beaches and clear water.

Hari Island is a nature reserve just off the Kendari coast, with a white sand beach, snorkelling and walks. To get there, get a group together and charter a boat for around 50,000 rp for the day.

There is a hill resort and beach 20 km north of Kendari, **Toli-Toli Hill** and **Batu Gong beach**, worth a visit if you have time to kill. There is also a bathing beach much closer to Kendari at **Maya Ria**, a 600 rp bemo ride east from Kendari Theatre.

Places to Stay

Bottom end The cheapest losmen are near the older 'Kota' area near the port, and get progressively more expensive further west.

Hotel Mutiara (☎ 21319) at Jl Hatta 61A, which backs onto a junior high school (classes start at 6 am), has airy rooms with fans for 15,000 rp, or mosquito pits out the back for 10,000 rp.

Closer to the port, but not so flash, are the genial but dingy *Penginapan Noer Empat* (☎ 21327), Jl Sudirman (Jl Soekarno) 120 at 8250 rp per head; *Losmen Murni*, Jl Sudirman 40, at 7500 rp per head; and the similarly priced, rambling *Wisma Nirwana* across the road at No 115.

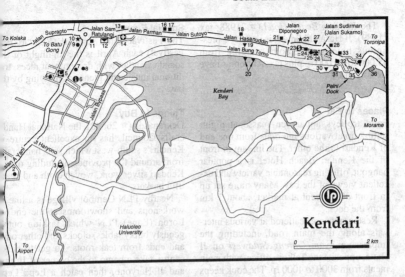

Kendari

PLACES TO STAY		20	Floating Bars &	9	Sempati Office
11	Hotel Duta		Discos	10	Regional Police
13	Hotel Memilwin	27	Ruma Maka Ayam	12	Post Office
15	(New) Nusa Indah		Goreng Sulawesi	14	Provincial Hospital
16	(Old) Nusa Indah	30	Night Food Stalls	22	City Police
17	Kartika Hotel			23	BN Bank
18	Kendari Beach Hotel	**OTHER**		25	Travel Agent
21	Hotel Cendrawasih	1	Loron PLN	26	Telkom Office
24	Hotel Mutiara	2	Dekranasda	29	Pasar Sentral
28	Noer Empat	3	Pasar Baru Terminal	31	Central Bemo
32	Wisma Nirwana	4	Governor's Office		Terminal
33	Losmen Murni	5	Al-Kautbar Mosque	34	Pelni Office
		6	Tourist Office	35	Kendari Theatre
PLACES TO EAT		7	Merpati Office	36	Kapal Kayu Dock
19	Night Food Stalls	8	Pasar Mandonga		

SULAWESI

Hotel Cendrawasih (☎ 21932), Jl Diponegoro 100, 2 km from the main dock, is clean, comfortable and good value, with singles/doubles from 16,500/27500 rp, or rooms with air-con for 38,500/44,000 rp.

Middle to Top end *Hotel Duta* (☎ 21053), Jl A Silondae 1, is on a hill 8 km from the dock, overlooking Kendari's only big intersection. Grubby rooms start at 20,000 rp, but the 30,000 to 35,000 rp rooms are infinitely more user-friendly.

The gloomy 'old' *Hotel Nusa Indah*

(☎ 21146), Jl Parman 88, has rooms from 30,000/35,000 rp, or from 40,000/45,000 rp with air-con. The 'new' *Hotel Nusa Indah* (☎ 22970) across the road at No 87 is brighter and has better rooms from 30,000/35,000 rp, ranging to 75,000 rp, plus a 10% tax.

The friendly and cheerful *Kartika Hotel* (☎ 21088), Jl Parman 84, next door to the old Nusa Indah, is one of the smartest places in town. It has rooms from 55,000/66,000 rp, ranging to 110,000 rp for suites, including breakfast and tax.

The *Kendari Beach Hotel* (☎ 21988; fax 21989), Jl Hasanuddin 44, is the city's prestigious hotel, with rooms ranging from 65,000 to 95,000 rp plus tax. All rooms have air-con and TV.

Places to Eat

Food trolleys appear en masse at night, setting up at various intervals from one end of Kendari to the other. The line-up in front of the Kendari Beach Hotel is a popular hangout, offering reasonable variety and excellent views of the bay. Many more set up in front of the central market, about 1 km from the dock.

Restaurants are scattered at various intervals along the main road, including the impressive *Ayam Goreng Sulawesi* on Jl Hatta, opposite the Telkom office, with main meals from 3000 to 4000 rp. The cook keeps two huge woks simmering at the front, delivering tasty dishes in an instant. Cashews from Pulau Muna are also available here: 12,500 rp per kg; or 8000 rp for 500g of fried and seasoned cashews.

The upstairs restaurant at the *Kendari Beach Hotel* overlooks the bay and offers an extensive menu at surprisingly competitive prices, with rice and noodle dishes for 2500 to 4000 rp, chicken dishes at 5500 to 6500 rp and seafood for 6000 to 7500 rp.

Entertainment

If you look like you are from out of town (white skin or fair hair can be a dead giveaway), *you* will be the main entertainment – all the more so if you can speak some Indonesian and entertain the crowds.

The well-heeled can head to either the *Kendari Lady* or *Bright Gold* 'floating' restaurants moored in front of the Kendari Beach Hotel. For 600,000 rp, 10 or more diners can arrange to cast off for a night of eating, karaoke and Molulo folk dancing on Kendari Bay. Cheaper, but no less entertaining, are the B Grade action movies at the *Kendari Theatre*, the cinema in the Kota area.

Special Events

The Festival Teluk Kendari (Kendari Bay Festival) each April is the highlight of the social calendar, with dragon boat races, traditional music and plenty of partying by the bay.

Things to Buy

Dekranasda (☎ 26533), the National Handicrafts Council, has an excellent centre in Kendari's south-west which sells handcraft from around the province, including ornate Kendari silver work, woven cloth and beautiful baskets.

Nearby PLN Gembol village is a line of workshops and showrooms at the end of Loron (Lane) PLN which fashion outrageously bulky tables, clocks and other odds and ends from teak roots. To get to either centre, take a bemo to the corner of Jl Yani and Jl Haryono, then catch a Lepo Lepo bemo to the PLN or Dekranasda turn-offs.

Elaborately carved model sailing ships can be found at the main gate of the Pelni dock whenever a Pelni ferry comes to town. Or there are fresh and fried cashew nuts from Pulau Muna at shops and restaurants, including Rumah Makan Ayam Goreng Sulawesi on Jl Hatta.

Getting There & Away

Air Both Sempati (☎ 22600), Jl A Silondae 26, and Merpati (☎ 22242), Jl Soekarno 84 have daily flights to Ujung Pandang for just under 100,000 rp (including airport tax), both with onward connections throughout Indonesia and beyond. Agents tend to offer 3 to 5% discounts on the listed prices. Bouraq was planning to start servicing this already competitive route in 1996.

Bus & Bemo Buses and bemos to and from Una'aha (1000 rp; 1½ hours), Kolaka (3000 rp; three hours) and beyond to Bone and Ujung Pandang, terminate at Puwatu terminal on the western outskirts of Kendari. Travellers arriving by the slow boats (*kapal kayu*) from Bau Bau and Raha will be hustled by bus company touts within moments of docking at Kendari.

Southbound minibuses start from the ~~P~~asar Baru terminal at 6 to 6.30 am and 11 ~~a~~m to noon, heading to the south coast port ~~o~~f Torobulu (3000 rp; two hours) in time to ~~m~~eet the 10 am or 3 pm ferries to Tampo on ~~P~~ulau Muna (3200 rp; 2½ hours) and on to ~~R~~aha (1000 rp; one hour).

~~B~~oat Pelni's *KM Tilongkabila* stops at Kendari ~~o~~n its fortnightly run up and down Sulawesi's ~~e~~ast coast, calling at Bau Bau and Raha to the ~~s~~outh, and Kolondale, Luwuk and Gorontalo ~~t~~o the north. Three others also call at Bau Bau. ~~T~~he Pelni office (☎ 21935) is adjacent to the ~~c~~hurch on top of the hill behind the Kendari ~~T~~heatre.

PT Nyiur Tapau Permai (☎ 25838) at Jl ~~L~~onggoasa 2 runs a daily fast boat *(kapal cepat)* service between Bau Bau and Kendari's main Pelni dock. Kendari to Raha costs 25,000 rp, Kendari-Bau Bau 35,000 rp and Raha-Bau Bau 15,000 rp. The daily schedule is: Bau Bau to Raha 6.30 to 7.30 am; Raha-Kendari 8.15 to 10.45 am; Kendari-Raha 1 to 3 pm; and Raha-Bau Bau 3.45 to 4.45 pm.

Slow, noisy old ferries (kapal kayu) chug out from Kendari every afternoon, calling at Raha and arriving at Bau Bau the following dawn. These boats stop for eight hours at Bau Bau, then return by the same route and all meet at Raha for a noisy reunion between 8 to 10 pm. Kendari to Raha costs 7500 rp deck class, or 13,000 rp for a room; Raha-Bau Bau costs 3500 rp deck class, or 7500 rp for a room. To reserve a room (you get no sleep and no views in deck class), you usually need to buy a ticket the night before departure.

Getting Around

The Airport The airlines run shared taxis to and from the airport (30 km south-west of Kendari) for 6000 rp a head, or you can charter for 10,000 rp.

Local Transport Becak start at 500 rp, and mikrolet – known locally as *pete pete* – will take you from one end of town to the other for just 300 rp. Even if you miss your stop, you can't get lost. From Puwatu or Pasar Baru terminals, drivers heading straight through to the market near the port will call out 'Kota' as they inch by.

RAHA

Raha, the main settlement on Pulau Muna, is famous for its horse fighting, prehistoric cave paintings and lagoons. The horse fighting is a Muna tradition with a robust following – not for tender-hearted foreigners.

Horses of a different kind can be viewed at caves and rock shelters near **Mabolu** village, about 10 km from Raha. An hour's walk from Mabolu are a dozen or more caves with **prehistoric ochre paintings** depicting hunting scenes, warriors on horses and even boats.

The prettiest spot on Muna is the clean, green **Napabale & Motonunu lagoons**, 15 km south of Raha. See the following Around Raha section for details.

Places to Stay

Hotel Tani (☎ 21168), Jl Sutomo 18, with good sized rooms with fan and bath, is already good value at 12,500 rp per head, but is prepared to discount. Check out the teak root furniture.

The ageing *Penginapan Napa Bale* (☎ 21-276) at Jl A Yani 29 features views of the sea – such as they are – and cheap, clean rooms at 10,000 rp a head.

Hotel Raudhah (☎ 21088), opposite the port at Jl Yos Sudarso 25, is run by a couple of capable women and charges 17,500/25,000 rp for singles/doubles.

Hotel Anuggerah (☎ 21019), Jl Dewi Sarika 12, has rooms for 15,000/20,000 rp. Air-con and higher rates are on the way.

Andalas Hotel (☎ 21071), Jl Sukowati 62, is pleasant enough at 27,500 rp a room, or 40,000 rp with air-con, including breakfast, but take any travel advice you get with huge grain of salt.

The owner-operated *Hotel Ilham* (☎ 21-072), Jl Jati 15, has quality accommodation at 35,000 rp for a room and breakfast, or 50,000 rp with air-con, and it serves superb meals by arrangement.

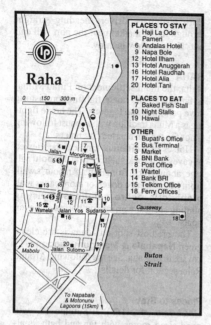

PLACES TO STAY
4 Haji La Ode
   Pameri
6 Andalas Hotel
9 Napa Bole
12 Hotel Ilham
13 Hotel Anuggerah
16 Hotel Raudhah
17 Hotel Alia
20 Hotel Tani

PLACES TO EAT
7 Baked Fish Stall
10 Night Stalls
19 Hawai

OTHER
1 Bupati's Office
2 Bus Terminal
3 Market
5 BNI Bank
8 Post Office
11 Wartel
14 Bank BRI
15 Telkom Office
18 Ferry Offices

Other possibilities include the *Hotel Alia* (☎ 21218), Jl Sudirman 5, big and empty with rooms from 17,500/35,000 rp, and *Penginapan Haji La Ode Pameri* (the former Berlian Hotel), overlooking the market area, with rooms for 8000 rp a head.

Places to Eat

Apart from the home cooking of *Hotel Ilham*, pickings are slim. The best of several Chinese places along Jl Sudirman is the *Hawai*, or there are a handful of shabby warungs at the base of Raha's long jetty which serve hot drinks and very basic fare.

Things to Buy

Raha is known for its gaudy tables fashioned from teak roots, available from the shop opposite the Hawai restaurant. Far more portable souvenirs are the cashew nuts at 12,000 rp a kg from the grocer a few doors down from the teak place.

Getting There & Away

Boat Pelni's *KM Tilongkabila* stops in th middle of the strait a few km off the coa twice a fortnight to exchange passengers an goods via a small launch from Raha.

There are nightly kapal kayu (slow boats to Kendari which take seven hours and co 7500 rp deck class, or 13,000 rp in a cabi Others head to Bau Bau (3500 rp deck clas 7500 rp cabin). The Saudara Jaya kapal cep (fast boat) leaves for Kendari at 8 am eac day (22,000 rp; three hours) and to Bau Ba at 4.30 pm (15,000 rp).

Bus Kendari buses depart from Raha's ma ket terminal each morning in time to meet th daily ferry across the Tiworo Strait to To obulu. The five hour trip to Kendari cost 8000 rp. Buses to Bau Bau cost 6000 rp.

Getting Around

Becak can get you around Raha for 300 t 500 rp. There are bemos to Mabolu for 40 rp and to the lagoons for 1500 rp. Motorcyc charter can sometimes be arranged throug your hotel for 30,000 to 40,000 rp a day.

AROUND RAHA

Napabale & Motonunu lagoons

Raha's main attractions lie well beyond th suburbs. The most impressive is the inter linked Napabale and Motonunu lagoons, jus 15 km south of Raha. The swimming i excellent in both and you can also hir canoes to paddle around. Napabale is at th foot of a hill and linked to the sea via a natura tunnel, which you can paddle through whe the tide is low. The other entrance to Moto nunu is via an opening to the sea. Bemo from Raha to Napabale cost 1500 rp, or les on a Sunday when the crowds head ther with picnics.

Mabolu Caves

While Mabolu might be the nearest drop-of point, the caves are a solid 10 km wal through plantations and pretty walled garden from Mabolu village. It is best to leave earl

efore the sun gets too hot and carry plenty
f water.

From Raha take a bemo to Mabolu for 400
), or charter for 3000 rp, and get the driver
) let you out at the path to the caves (*gua*).
he paths are far from clear and you will
eed kids from Mabolu to show you the way
) Pak Lahadha or Pak Lajiwa, the 'key
olders' who live near the caves.

The walk through cashew plantations,
ver countless rock walls via rickety stiles
nd through garden compounds surrounded
y rock walls to keep the babirusa at bay, is
s interesting as the caves themselves. Look
or long ropes that stretch from the high
vatch towers over the gardens to old pieces
f corrugated iron on the far side of the plot.
'hose on watch duty occasionally tug the
ope to make the tin crash against rocks to
righten foraging animals.

The key holders can show you to a selec-
ion of the best caves, starting with **Liang
Metanduno** which includes paintings of a
norse with two riders, headless warriors,
logs hunting babirusa and some boats. The
only disappointment is that Indonesians'
ove affair with the bag of cement has trans-
ormed the entrance to the cave to a stepped
uditorium. There used to be coffins and
ones in some of the caves, until scientific
apers describing the caves in 1983-84
rompted a team of Jakarta archaeologists to
olunder the site.

There are a dozen or so other caves with
paintings, including a couple of rock shelters
along the path from Mabolu. You should find
hat three or four are enough to visit. For an
explanation of the caves' history and local
raditions, get in touch with Haji Sido Thamrin (☎ 21283) in Raha, who often takes
groups to the caves. It is expensive, but
nformative.

Horse Fighting

This is too cruel for many, but a thriving
element of local culture. The Festival Danau
Napabale each June features horse fighting
as well, as the more gentle spectacle of kite
flying, at the village of Latugho, 20 km
inland from Raha.

BAU BAU

Bau Bau is the main settlement on Pulau
Buton and is strategically situated at the
southern entrance of the Buton Strait. It was
once a fort, the seat of the former sultanate
of Wolio which reigned over the scattered
settlements on Buton and the neighbouring
islands of Muna, Kabaena, Wowini and
Tukangbesi. Wolio's political history is
punctuated by the competing territorial
ambitions of Makassar and Gowa to the west
and Ternate in the east. It enjoyed relative
autonomy after the subjugation of Makassar
in the 17th century.

The people of this island group are all
closely related culturally and speak similar
languages. As in South Sulawesi, many of
the cultural influences seem to have come
from the Bugis. The Butonese are Muslim,
and they were noted sailors and traders who
emigrated widely, especially to Maluku. The
Buton island group was also once a pirate
bastion and a slave-trading centre.

Things to See & Do

The main attraction is the **Wolio Museum** in
the partly restored palace and fort on the hill
2 km behind town. The former palace complex is also the focal point of Bau Bau's
annual Festival Kraton each September, a
celebration of the craft, culture and former
glory of the Wolio kingdom. Another hangout is **Pantai Nirwana**, a beach near Bau
Bau.

Places to Stay

If you are inclined to stay, try the grubby
Losmen Deborah (☎ 21203) at Jl Kartini 15,
with rooms from 15,000 rp, the slightly more
commodious and similarly priced *Liliana*
(☎ 21197) on the same street at No 18, or the
Elizabeth at No 21.

Getting There & Away

Bau Bau is one of the big winners from the
expansion of Pelni's national fleet. Four
inter-island ferries call regularly on their way
from Ujung Pandang (29,500 rp economy;
14 to 19 hours) to Bitung in the north or
Ambon in the east. There are also daily slow

SULAWESI

boats, speed boats and buses to Kendari via Raha – see the earlier Raha section for details.

Central Sulawesi

With most of Central Sulawesi's 1.6 million people living in its coastal cities and towns, the province's 63,000 sq km hinterland is sparsely populated. Yet it is these mountains and valleys that attract most of the visitors to the province.

While the star attraction are the Bronze Age megaliths around Bada and Besoa, it is the rugged landscape and hospitable highland cultures throughout Central Sulawesi that make such a difficult detour worthwhile. Few other places can boast such an interesting and accessible juxtaposition of nature, culture and history.

History

Evidence of Neolithic settlements found along Sungai Karama north of the Quarles mountain range and undated remains from a cave near Kolonodale indicate a long history of human settlement. But by far the most spectacular prehistoric remains are the Bronze Age megaliths found throughout Central Sulawesi. The meaning and creators of these statues, cylindrical vats, urns and mortars are unknown. The highest concentration is along Sungai Lariang in the Bada Valley and near the village of Besoa, but there are others from this era throughout the region and down to Tanatoraja.

There was no single dominant power on the coast. The Portuguese built a fort at Parigi at the eastern end of Tomini Bay in 1555, and were followed by two Muslim Minangkabau traders who settled in Palu and Parigi in 1602 to trade gold and propagate their faith. Ternate, competing with Gowa for dominance of Sulawesi, had extended its influence over Palu and Toli-Toli by 1680.

The inland people in this era tended to live in fortified settlements because of recurrent inter-tribal unrest. The earthworks surrounding their stockades are still visible in Besoa, Padang Lolo and Bala. Remains of Chinese porcelain are evidence of their trade with the outside world.

Ternate held some sway over the Banggai Islands off the eastern peninsula of Sulawesi. Banggai's inhabitants are a diverse bunch but include a large number of Bajau sea traders. At one time a royal dynasty of Javanese origin ruled here, subject to the sultanate of Ternate. After the Dutch took over in 1908 indigenous rulers were set up to run the islands.

The period of Dutch rule was brief. Their earliest settlements on Tomini Bay were on the north coast at Gorontalo in North Sulawesi in the late 17th century and another at Parigi at the western end of the bay in 1730. Along with Makassar, these were the principle Dutch settlements of the time. The rest of the island was controlled by local tribes. In the late 1780s the Dutch attempted to take Toli-Toli (because of its fine harbour), but without success.

Hiking

Central Sulawesi offers some of the best trekking in Indonesia, giving hikers relatively easy access to networks of jungle, megalithic remains and confident, friendly cultures. Timber companies are opening up the interior, but the province's mountainous, rugged terrain has mitigated the damage from these activities – for now.

Information

Money Palu and Poso are the only two centres where travellers cheques can be changed, so you may need to carry wads of rupiah. Bank branches in smaller centres such as Ampana, are starting to accept US cash, but at a punitive exchange rate.

PENDOLO

Pendolo is a sleepy village on the southern shore of beautiful Danau Poso. The highway south to Wotu is a nicely paved shelf carved out of the mountains, but is subject to landslides. As the road improves, traffic along this route will increase.

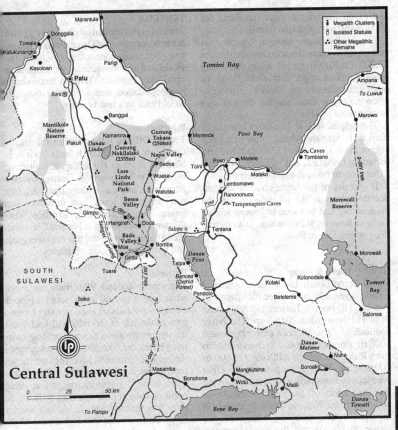

Central Sulawesi

0   25   50 km

To Palopo

Danau Poso and its beaches are the main attraction – although the beaches disappear under rising waters towards the end of the wet season. You can swim, see the lake by boat or hike in the surrounding countryside. The lake is 600m above sea level, so the evenings are pleasantly cool without being too cold. The area is also famous for its wild orchids, especially on the western shores near **Bancea**.

Places to Stay & Eat

The *Pondok Wisata Masamba* and the *Pondok Wisata Victory* on Jl Pelabuhan overlook the beach adjacent to the jetty and have small rooms with tiny mandis from 7500 rp. Each have pavilions on the beach for pleasant lakeside dining. The food is good and the prices reasonable. Both also offer good travel advice.

Pamona Indah, on the beach behind the Masamba in a quieter locale, and *Homestay Petezza* at Jl Pelabuhan 216, a couple of doors up from the Victory, are also good value at 7500 rp per head.

Penginapan Danau Poso, about 100m back from the jetty, has singles/doubles for 5000/10,000 rp. The homey *Penginapan*

Sederhana across the road has beds for 4000/8000 rp with shared mandi.

The *Mulia Hotel*, about a km out, has comfortable lakeside accommodation for 25,000 to 35,000 rp per room, including breakfast. You might hear about floods or other calamities at the losmen in town to discourage you from staying there. Don't believe these stories.

The helpful folk at *Pendolo Cottages*, Jl Yani 441, near the Mulia, offer beachside accommodation for 15,000/17,500 rp, including breakfast, and will carry your bag to the jetty in town to meet the ferry.

If you tire of the home cooking and unbeatable views of the lakeside losmen, the main eatery and bus stop is *Rumah Makan Cahaya Bone* on Jl Pelabuhan, just up from Penginapan Danau Poso.

Getting There & Away

Bus & Bemo Damri, Litha, Acam Indah and others have daily buses from Rantepao to Pendolo (10 hours), Tentena (12 hours) and Poso (13 hours) for 20,000 rp. The buses continue to Palu, an extra seven hours and 5000 rp. Another option is to charter a bemo from Rantepao, which will cost 175,000 to 200,000 rp. Split among seven or eight people, this costs only a little more than the bus, cuts hours off the journey and allows you to do the Wotu to Pendolo stretch in daylight hours, stopping whenever you please to photograph the rugged ranges, huge butterflies and monster spiders.

You can also reach Tentena by bus and bemo. Right near the beach at Pendolo is a sign indicating the Jawa Indah bus company. The fare to Tentena is 2500 rp, or 5000 rp to Poso. There is a track along the western edge of the lake, but only for hikers and cyclists.

Boat Tentena, at the northern end of the lake, is larger and prettier than Pendolo. Most people take the ferry to enjoy the spectacular vistas, but in rough weather this trip is no fun. It leaves daily at 8 am from Pendolo (2000 rp; three hours).

TENTENA

Tentena is surrounded by clove-covered hill at the northern end of Danau Poso. It has lon had good roads connecting it to the outsid world and is consequently far more deve oped than Pendolo. Tentena has exceller accommodation and a varied cuisine, bu lacks Pendolo's fine beaches.

Information

Tourist Offices Ebony Visitor Informatio Centre (☎ /fax 21232), Jl Setia Budi 6, be hind the Horison Homestay, has a treasur trove of information on Central Sulawes attractions, and can arrange transport, orga nise treks and tours, and introduce loca guides. Tentena's other tourist office, Wisat Gautama Putra Indah, at Natural Cottages, i pretty casual, but a good place to meet guide and mull over trekking itineraries.

Waterfalls

The nearby **Salopa Waterfalls** are a clas attraction, a crystal clear series of pools cascades and falls set amid unspoilt forest. A path to the left of the falls will lead you to the upper levels and to some pristine swim ming holes, but take care not to get caught in the tumbling currents. Mornings are the bes time to catch the cascades on film. Take a bemo to the Balinese transmigration village north of Tonusu (750 rp), then walk the las three km through padi fields and winding lanes. Bemo charter will cost around 15,00 rp – perhaps prearrange a chartered bemo to meet you for the return journey, or hope to hitch a lift.

There is another waterfall at **Sulewana**, a sunken gully of steaming white water 12 km north of Tentena that has been surveyed as a potential site for a hydroelectric power station. Take a bemo to Watunoncu, then walk three km west.

Danau Poso

Indonesia's third largest lake, Danau Poso covers an area of 32,300 hectares and reaches 450m in depth. There's a handful of narrow **beaches** around Tentena, but these disappear when levels are high. Bathing

PLACES TO STAY

1	Pondok Wisma Ue'Datu
12	Wisata Remaja
13	Horison Homestay
15	Losmen Victory
16	Wasantara Hotel
17	Pamona Indah Hotel
18	Natural Cottages

OTHER

2	Telkom Office
3	Hospital
4	Danau Poso Festival Grounds
5	MAF Airstrip
6	Pamona Cave
7	Market
8	Post Office
9	Police
10	Church
11	Jeeps to Bada Valley
14	Mosque

pots include a sandbar near the big silver esus south of town and the stretch of sand near Siuri Cottages on the western shore. The water is clear, cold and clean; hire a boat and go exploring.

The lovely old covered bridge marks where the lake ends and the outflowing Sungai Poso begins its journey to the coast. V-shaped eel traps north of the bridge snare

the two metre monsters Tentena is famous for. Live specimens are available for inspection and sale at the warung next to the bridge.

Caves

Near Panorama Hotel, off the Kolonodale road, **Latea Cave** contains bones and skulls from burials long ago. Closer to town is the **Pamona Cave**, just across the big covered bridge near the missionary airstrip.

Special Events

The undisputed highlight of Central Sulawesi's social calendar is the annual Danau Poso Festival in late August. Villagers from far afield gather for a colourful celebration of culture, with dancing, song, traditional sports and other activities in which everyone has a damn fine time.

Places to Stay

The *Losmen Victory* (☎ 21392) at Jl Diponegoro 18 is run by the friendly and capable Bu Doris. It's doing a brisk trade, with spotless rooms for 15,000 rp with breakfast, or from 25,000 rp in the high season.

The *Pamona Indah Hotel* (☎ 21245), adjacent to the lakeside jetty, has economy rooms from 12,000 rp, doubles for 25,000 rp with breakfast, and to 35,000 rp with TV, hot water and other amenities. The staff are fun.

Pondok Wisma Ue'Data (☎ 21222) is a delightful place with a cafe in pleasant surrounds overlooking the river north of the main bridge. Rooms cost from 20,000 rp.

The *Wasantara Hotel* (☎ 21345) by the lake is large and cheery. Room cost from 16,000 rp. *Natural Cottages* (☎ /fax 21356), Jl Yani 32, is also by the lake, with singles/doubles from 10,000/16,500 rp.

The quiet, clean *Horison Homestay* (☎ 21038) at Jl Setia Budi 6 has small 10,000 rp rooms, and larger rooms with mandi for 12,500 rp. *Penginapan Wisata Remaja* has doubles for 5000 to 7500 rp. *Penginapan Panorama* is on a hill set back from the lake and affords fine views, with rooms from 15,000 rp. *Penginapan Tiberius* charges 10,000 rp per room.

SULAWESI

Siuri Cottages, 19 km from town on a beach past Tonusu, provides a little luxury with rooms from 30,000/35,000 rp, or US$50 for red carpet treatment. Good for those with spare days and dollars.

Places to Eat

The local speciality is sugili (eel), one to two metre monsters from the river flowing out of the lake. These 10 to 20 kg beasties sell for up to 5000 rp a kg from the stall next to the bridge, but it is much easier to get the competent cooks at *Pamona Indah* or *Wisma Ue'Data* to do the shopping and cooking for you. And it's worth every last rupiah. Pamona Indah also does a rich ikan mas (gold fish) in arak.

For fabulous pisang molen (banana fried in a sweet pastry), try the stalls in front of the fish boxes at the bridge.

Getting There & Away

Air MAF's (☎ 21020) six seat Cessna flies folk between isolated villages. This is a charitable service which struggles to keep pace with local demand, but sometimes carries travellers, space permitting. From Tentena, MAF flies to Bada (51,000 rp, plus baggage penalties), Besoa (51,000 rp), Rampi or Wuasa (60,000 rp), Seko (94,000 rp), Rantepao (154,000 rp) and a host of other wonderful places. There are waiting lists for most flights.

Bus & Bemo Bemos and buses make the run to Poso for 2000 rp in about two hours. Set out early from the Tentena bridge, or be prepared for a long wait. There is a long-distance bus terminal at a fork in the road, two km north of the town centre, and bus agents near the bridge. Buses to Kolonodale (152 km, 8000 rp) originate in Poso, but seats can be reserved through Ebony Visitor Information Centre for a 3000 rp booking fee.

Car Availability and prices of jeeps to Gintu in Lore Lindu National Park depend on the condition of the road. The price should be around 25,000 rp a head by public jeep, 250,000 rp to charter, or 700,000 rp for a five day trip, but as this neglected 70 km stretch sinks into the mud, fewer drivers are prepared to endure the trip. Walking takes a couple of days, and is often just as fast. Can hire around Tentena costs 75,000 rp a day, or pool resources to hire a car to Palu (175,000 rp), Toraja (300,000 rp), Manado (500,000 rp), Ampana (150,000 rp) or Kolonodale (100,000 rp).

Boat Boats across the lake to Pendolo (2000 rp; three hours) leave from Tentena at 3 pm and return at 8 am the next day. (See under Pendolo earlier in this section for more details.)

AROUND TENTENA

Tentena is the starting point for treks west to Lore Lindu National Park and through to Palu (see under Palu later in this section), east to the Morowali Reserve and along Sulawesi's eastern peninsula, or south-west through rugged countryside to Rampi or Seko in South Sulawesi and back to Tanatoraja. All require energy, planning and various degrees of local assistance.

Guides

Guides can save a lot of time and hassle, and cut through regional language barriers, but beware of inexperienced 'cowboys' from out of town. Tentena's two private tourist offices can point you in the right direction (see Tourist Offices in the previous Tentena section). A fair price is around 40,000 rp a day plus expenses (remember that transport can be prohibitively expensive).

Contact Manuel, a veteran of the business whose erratic ways get very mixed press from travellers, but whose knowledge of Morowali Reserve is second to none. A veteran of Lore Lindu treks, Karel at Losmen Victory in Tentena is widely applauded as a well-organised and knowledgeable porter ('Don't call me a guide, I don't speak English', he says).

Others recommended by travellers include Rudy Ruus, a laid-back Minahasan who knows Lore Lindu; Simson Onara at the Homestay Petezza in Pendolo; Marther

Gonti, a fun and informative Mori man at the Pamona Indah; Jeng, a woman who knows Morowali, its people and customs; and Jeng's colleague at Ebony Visitor Information Centre, Dina Sawuwu, who leads extended treks to Bada Valley and south to Masamba.

LORE LINDU NATIONAL PARK

Covering an area of 250,000 hectares, this large and remote national park has been barely touched by tourism. It's a wonderful area for trekking – the park is rich in exotic plant and animal life, including incredible butterflies larger than your hand. It is also home to several indigenous tribes, most of whom wear colourful clothing, at least for traditional ceremonies. Other attractions include ancient megalithic relics, mostly in the Bada, Besoa and Napu valleys. It's even possible to climb remote peaks, as high as 2613m above sea level.

There are two main approaches to the park – from Palu to the north or from Tentena on the east side of the park. From Palu, it's 100 km or 2½ hours by car south to Gimpu, from where the road deteriorates into a track with deep muddy chasms. The other approach, from Tentena, usually takes visitors by 'road' 73 km to the isolated village of Gintu. Roads within the park consist chiefly of mud and holes, and transport is usually by jeep, horseback and foot.

Getting to the park is a bit of an expedition, but you are likely to meet some of the friendliest people in Indonesia here. A permit and a guide are required, but not compulsory. The government tourist office in Palu can put you on to some licensed tour operators, though it tends to recommend its most expensive friends. Otherwise wait until you get into the park and contract a local for around 15,000 to 20,000 rp a day. You will need help to find the megaliths, most of which are concentrated around Gintu and Doda.

Food is readily available, but it's wise to bring other necessities such as mosquito repellent and sunblock lotion, plus presents if you end up staying in someone's home.

Accommodation in the Lore Lindu area ranges from nights huddled under the roofs of covered bridges (hard and cold) to homestay accommodation throughout the park.

Trekking

The main trail is from Tentena to Palu, either via Tuare and Goa on Sungai Lariang, or via Doda and Hangirah. Travel light. Unless you are planning to return to your starting point, send all non-essential gear ahead by car or bus via the main highway.

Tentena to Gintu hikers can start from Tonusu and walk for two days, sleeping under covered bridges. You'll need to carry food and water-purification tablets. You could shorten the hike by chartering a motorcycle to Peatua (26 km) and walking to the Malei bridge (four hours). The next day, hike from Malei to Bomba (18 km; five hours), and get a local guide to help you find the Bomba, Bada and impressive Sepe megaliths (10,000 to 15,000 rp per day). At Bomba, stay at the friendly *Ningsi Homestay* for 11,000 rp, including breakfast, lunch and dinner.

At Gintu the *Losmen Merry* has five clean rooms at 10,000 rp, including three meals. *Losmen Sanur* is also clean and friendly, charging 7500 rp with two meals, 10,000 rp with three – two of the rooms have their own mandi. Seek out the knowledgeable Pak Agus at Gintu for assistance to find the megaliths.

Gintu to Tuare is an easy three hour walk. Tuare's kepala desa (village head) takes guests for 7500 rp, including breakfast and dinner. **Moa** is several hours beyond Tuare, over two difficult rivers. Moa's kepala desa takes guests for 10,000 rp, including dinner, bed and breakfast.

Moa to Gimpu is a strenuous eight hour hike, again over two rivers with broken bridges. Gimpu's kepala desa offers the same deal as Moa's. From **Gimpu to Palu** there are five buses a day, starting at 7.30 am (4000 rp; three to six hours).

An alternative from Gintu might be to take horses through jungle to Gimpu. Horses and

SULAWESI

handlers are available for 30,000 to 60,000 rp a day. You need a guide for this section. There is also a path to **Doda**, a lesser centre for megalithic remains, where you can stay (if you must) at the *Losmen Rindu Alam* for 7500 rp, including three meals. Other paths from Gintu cross the peaks to Gimpu, or north to Watutau. The bird sanctuaries in the north of the park are easier to get to from Palu.

Sungai Lariang

Ebony Tours in Tentena and Palu were planning to offer rafting tours along Sungai Lariang, which flows through a series of forested mountainous gorges along the south-western edge of the Lore Lindu national park. At 225 km, the Lariang is the longest river on Sulawesi. The plan is to start at Gintu and come ashore at Tuare, one day west, or to offer a four day tour through a 'Royal Flush' of five class IV rapids and get out near Gimpu.

KOLONODALE

Kolonodale is a small tangle of long, dusty streets set on Tomori Bay, arguably the prettiest natural harbour in Indonesia. The town is the gateway to Morowali Reserve on the other side of the bay, and a stepping-off point for ferries along the eastern peninsula or south to Kendari. Rainfall in the bay area is heavy and constant, with average falls of more than 200 mm for 10 to 12 months of the year. The best time to visit is September to November, the peak of the east coast 'dry' season.

Orientation

Most services are adjacent to the main dock, including accommodation, shops and a market. The intersection in front of the market is the departure point for buses and bemos, and a meeting place for work gangs each morning.

Information

Local guide Jabar Lahadji runs a kind of information service called Sahabat Morowali (Friends of Morowali; ☎ 21225) from an office at the Penginapan Sederhana on Jl Yos Sudarso.

There is a small post office behind the main mosque, and a 24 hour Telkom exchange at Jl Trundungi 11, up the hill from the Pelni kiosk.

Tomori Bay

While most travellers catch the first ferry out or head straight to Morowali, the stunning beauty of the islands and inlets of Tomori Bay warrant closer inspection. Limestone cliffs plunge into emerald waters, unbroken forests cover islands and surrounding hills and there are fishing canoes everywhere. For around 40,000 rp you can charter a small wobbly 'Johnson', a dugout canoe with an outboard motor, to spend a day on the bay. Large boats could cost up to 100,000 rp.

Sights include a limestone cliff across the water from Kolonodale with faint painted outlines of prehistoric handprints and fossils embedded in the rock, the oddly shaped 'mushroom rock', tiny fishing villages and some fine beaches on uninhabited islands at the mouth of the bay. There are coral reefs with plenty of life, but visibility can be poor. By far the busiest spot on the bay is the main dock at Kolonodale, especially when the fishing canoes bring the dawn catch to market.

Places to Stay & Eat

Losmen Jungpandang (☎ 21091), Jl Yos Sudarso, is close to the dock, with small rooms at 5000/10,000 rp for singles/doubles with shared bath, including basic breakfast. Its restaurant offers a simple selection. *Penginapan Sederhana* (☎ 21124) a few doors down is basic, with rooms at 5000 rp.

About 200m north of the Sederhana, *Penginapan Lestari* (☎ 21044), Jl Yos Sudarso, is infinitely nicer. It is an old place with rooms for 12,500 rp a head, including two meals.

Penginapan Rejeki Jaya, 250m south of the centre at Jl Hasanuddin 73, offers clean old rooms and two meals for 8800 rp a head.

Salon Prima Melayani on Jl Yos Sudarso, opposite the Pa'antobu bus office, is a hair

...alon which supplements its income by ...erving hot drinks, including saraba telur, a ...elicious Bugis concoction of ginger, palm ...ine sugar, coconut, water and egg.

Getting There & Away

Bus The main road from Tentena to Kolon-...dale passes through a series of desperate ...ransmigration settlements, enters a pretty ...imestone gully in the hills near Kolonodale, ...hen crosses a rise with spectacular views of ...he port and bay area.

Pa'antobu has daily buses to Kolaki (5000 ...p), Tomata (6500 rp), Tentena (8500 rp; six ...ours), Poso (10,000 rp; eight hours) and ...alu (16,000 rp). Other companies such as ...umbur Rejeki run direct to Palopo, Pare ...are and Ujung Pandang.

It is possible to reach Kolonodale from the ...outh. From Soroako, cross Danau Matano ...y boat to Nuha, then rent a motorcycle to ...eteleme (15,000 rp; two hours if the road is ...ood), or go by jeep – price and availability ...epends on condition of the track. From ...eteleme to Kolonodale there are daily ...uses for 2000 rp, or try hailing buses along ...he main Poso to Kolonodale route as they ...rop off passengers.

Boat Pelni's *KM Tilongkabila* checks in at ...olonodale once a fortnight en route to ...uwuk and Bitung in the north, then stops ...gain five days later on its way south to ...endari and Ujung Pandang. The Pelni ...ffice (☎ 21186) is on a corner at Jl Pat-...imura 5.

Prahu leave from the main dock at 11 pm ...or an overnight trip east to Baturube and on ...o Pandauke for 5000 rp, where you can ...atch buses (5000 rp; five hours) to Luwuk ...t 10 am and noon.

MOROWALI RESERVE

This 225,000 hectare nature reserve was ...stablished in 1980 on the eastern shore of Tomori Bay in the wake of Operation Drake, a British-sponsored survey of the endan-...gered species of the area. It rises from islands ...on the bay and accessible lowland plains, to densely vegetated peaks of up to 2630m high.

The reserve is home to around 5000 Wana people, who live mostly by hunting and gath-ering, and through shifting agriculture. There are small Wanu settlements at Ranu and Kayu Poli on the Morowali Plain, but most live in the isolated highlands.

The park is rich in wildlife, such as anoa, maleo birds, babirusa and several primate species, as well as flora and fauna unique to Morowali, but unless you are lucky dense jungle is often all you will see.

Trekking

You need at least three days to enter the park, and the going can be tough. Treks of the area usually take four or five days, and can be organised through guides in Tentena, Pen-dolo or through Jabar Lahadji's Sahabat Morowali office in Kolonodale (see the pre-vious Kolondale section). Permits to enter the park must be arranged through Pak Ar-min at the PHPA office in Kolonodale.

From Kolonodale it's a two hour boat trip across Tomori Bay and up Sungai Morowali to drop-off points that will allow you to hike to Kayu Poli. You could stay there, or at another Wana village, and spend some time with the locals to observe their way of life. Walk two to three hours west of Kayu Poli to the eerily silent Rahu lakes and allow half a day to cross the lakes by tiny canoe. Leave the park via Sungai Rahu and return to Kolonodale by boat.

The further you trek, the more difficult the terrain and the longer you will need. For instance, from Kayu Poli you could hike east to Taronggo and spend five to seven days trekking to visit highland villages. Another useful starting point is to catch the regular night ferry from Kolonodale to Baturube and enter the reserve from the east. Particularly hardy trekkers can hike (with a guide) north across the peninsula all the way to Ampana in nine days.

LUWUK

Luwuk is the biggest town on Sulawesi's seldom-visited eastern peninsula, and the stepping-off point for the Banggai Islands. Attractions include the 75m-high **Heng-ahenga Waterfall**, three km west of Luwuk; the **Suaka Margasetwa Reserve**, eight km north; and the daily ferries to the Banggai Islands. **Bangkiriang Wildlife Reserve**, home to Central Sulawesi's largest maleo bird population, is near the coast 80 km south-west of Luwuk.

Peleng is the biggest and most populous island, and **Banggai**, which is on Pelni's *KM Ciremai* ferry route, has sandy beaches. There is a pearl-diving site at **Kokungan**, near Bandan, and good snorkelling at **Muk-alayo** reef. **Pulau Tikus**, three hours from Banggai, was an uninhabited snorkelling spot making a name for itself as a secluded getaway, but has been snapped up by specu-lators.

Places to Stay
The *Hotel Kota* near the bus terminal charges 8000 rp per head. Other cheapies include the *Rahmat* (5500 rp), The *Senang Hati* (4500 rp) and *Sadar* (4000 rp). The *Ramayana Hotel* (☎ 21073) on Jl Danau Lindu and its harbour-side restaurant comes highly recom-mended, with singles/doubles from 17,500/30,000 rp. The *Safari Beach* is similarly priced.

Getting There & Away
Merpati (☎ 21123), Jl Imam Bonjol SK-3, has flights from Palu (139,000 rp) and weekly flights from Manado (123,000 rp). Luwuk's connections with the outside world also include daily buses from Poso 390 km away (17,500 rp; 20 hours) and ferries from Pagimana which travel to/from Gorontalo in North Sulawesi every second day. Pelni's *KM Tilongkabila* calls at Luwuk on its fort-nightly hop up and down the east coast.

POSO
Poso is the main town and port on the north-ern coast of central Sulawesi. For most travellers it's just a transit point and a place to change currency. Poso itself is not rich in sights. Most folk head for the beaches which unfortunately, are not within walking dis tance.

Information
Tourist Office One of Sulawesi's few infor mative tourist information services (☎ 21211 is at Jl Sudirman, behind the central tele phone exchange.

Money Poso is the last chance for Togian c Tentena-bound travellers to change travel lers cheques. Try the BNI bank on Jl Yo Sudarso, open Monday to Friday from 8 an to 4 pm.

Things to See
Pantai Madale is a snorkelling spot five km east of Poso (350 rp by bemo). **Pantai Ma tako** is a white sand beach 25 km east (100€ rp), and **Tombiano**, 40 km east, has huge we caves occupied by bats (1500 rp by bemo).

Pantai Toini, seven km west of Pos (5000 rp), has a great seafood dining spo back from the beach. A further 40 km west **Maranda** offers a small waterfall, a hot water spring and a swimming spot (1500 rp)

Lembomawo village, four km south o Poso, is known for its ebony carving. To ge there take a bemo from the main terminal ane cross two hanging bridges on foot. A circula route from Lembomawo to Ranononucu wil bring you back to the main road and to the roadside stalls selling the carvings.

Gua Tampenaporo is a cave off the mair road to Tentena, 22 km south (1000 rp by bemo).

Places to Stay
Poso's hotels tend to be cheap and func-tional. One spot which stands out from the rest because of its superb location is a breezy guest wing being built over the water at the *Losmen Lalango Jaya*, near the dock.

The *Hotel Kalimantan* (☎ 21420), Jl Haj Agus Salim 14, is old but airy. It's also relatively cheap at 8500/14,500 rp for rooms with bath.

Hotel Alamanda (☎ 21333) at Jl Bali 1 is better value than most at 5000 rp per person.

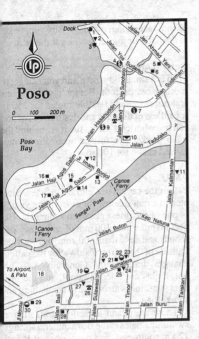

Poso

0   100   200 m

Poso
Bay

To Airport,
& Palu

The *Losmen Alugoro* (☎ 21336), Jl Sumatera 20, has rooms from 5000/7000 rp, and from 7500/10,000 rp with bath.

Up the road at the corner of Jl Haji Agus Salim and Jl Imam Bonjol is the *Penginapan Sulawesi* (☎ 21294), which has singles for 4000 rp – tiny, but clean.

Anugrah Inn (☎ 21820), Jl P Samosir 1, is around 500m south of the main market. It's friendly and quiet, with doubles for 16,500 rp, or 27,500 rp with air-con.

Bambu Jaya Hotel (☎ 21570), Jl Haji Agus Salim 101, was built in the charmless style once favoured by Soviet architects, but has great bayside views from the breezy rear terrace. Rooms are from 22,500 rp.

Hotel Nels (☎ 21013) is in the northern part of town on Jl Yos Sudarso. It's old and travellers frequently complain about the manager. Rooms are 7500/12,500 rp. Other central, cheap and functional options include *Hotel Wisata*, *Penginapan Beringin*, *Penginapan Poso*, *Penginapan Sederhana* and *Penginapan Ideal*. None will be a highlight of your travels.

Kartika Beach Hotel, three km north-west of the market, is Poso's only upmarket hotel. Like most so-called 'beach' hotels on Sulawesi, there is no beach.

Places to Eat
Warung Lalango Jaya, near the dock on Jl Yos Sudarso, offers cold beer, fresh juice, reasonably priced food, friendly service and unbeatable views of the harbour activities.

Restaurant Depot Anugrah (☎ 21586) is a Chinese-Indonesian restaurant offering good cheap food. It's above a shop on Jl Sumatera on the south side of town. Less appealing, but well priced, are the *Jawa Timur* and the *Rumah Makan Pemuda* just down the road. Padang food lovers should try the *Padang Raya* near the bridge.

SULAWESI

Getting There & Away

Air Merpati (☎ 21274) has an office at Jl Yos Sudarso 9, but has suspended its air services to Poso.

Bus & Bemo There are regular buses from Poso to Tentena (2500 rp). Buses from Palu to Rantepao come through Poso, but don't count on being able to board. Your best bet for seats to Palu (8500 rp; six hours) is to try Jawa Indah (☎ 21560), Alugoro (☎ 21336) or Sinar Sulawesi (☎ 21298), all with offices on Jl Sumatera. Jawa Indah and Pa'antobu (based at the bus terminal) have daily buses to Kolonodale (10,000 rp), and the Ampana Express and Morowo Indah have daily buses to Ampana (5500 rp) each morning.

Boat Ferries depart from Poso for Gorontalo, on the northern peninsula, at least once a week. The trip via Ampana and the Togian Islands takes about two days. Buy your ticket at the harbour master's office at the port.

Getting Around

Poso is a small, tidy town and you can get to most places on foot. Bemos ply the streets and run extremely flexible routes for 350 rp regardless of distance and destination, or you can take shortcuts across the river behind the main market and further upstream by motorised canoe for 100 rp.

PALU

Palu is the capital of Central Sulawesi. Situated in a rain shadow for most of the year, it is one of the driest places in Indonesia. Expect no more than 100 mm of rain in any one month and less than 600 mm over a year. Outside of the narrow Palu Valley the pattern changes dramatically. Generally days are hot, nights are tolerably cool, and the brilliant sunshine is amenable to sunbathing and snorkelling.

There are inland attractions too, such as swimming holes at the **Bora** mineral springs, 12 km south-east, and the springs at **Mantikole Nature Reserve**, 25 km south of town.

Orientation

Palu is spread out and the street names constantly change. The town is split neatly in two by the Sungai Palu and the airport is on the south-eastern outskirts. The commercial centre is either side of Jl Gajah Mada and north of Jl Hasanuddin.

Information

Tourist Office The regional tourist office, on Jl Raja Moili, has plenty of brochures and good maps of the city, kept securely locked away from prying eyes. A better bet is to engage the staff in chat about hiking itineraries. The office is open from around 7.30 am until 2 pm.

Post & Communications The post office is way out on Jl Yamin and the main Telkom office is at the southern end of Jl Ahmed Yani.

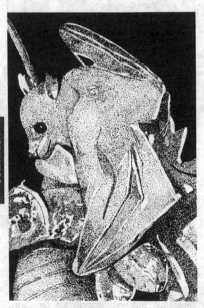

Bats are found in the caves in Central Sulawesi and the local people provide a once-in-a-lifetime culinary opportunity – bat stew.

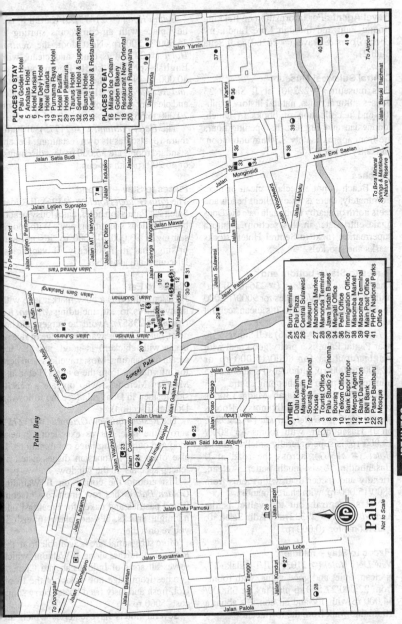

PLACES TO STAY
4 Palu Golden Hotel
5 Buana Hotel
6 Hotel Karsam
7 New Dely Hotel
13 Hotel Ganuda
19 Purnama Raya Hotel
21 Hotel Pasifik
29 Hotel Patimura
31 Taunus Hotel
32 Sentral Hotel & Supermarket
33 Buana Hotel
35 Kartini Hotel & Restaurant

PLACES TO EAT
16 Milano Ice Cream
17 Golden Bakery
18 Restaurant New Oriental
20 Restoran Ramayana

OTHER
1 Datu Karama Mausoleum
2 Souraja Traditional House
3 Central Sulawesi Museum
8 Tourist Office
9 Palu Studio 21 Cinema
10 Bourisu
11 Telkom Office
12 Bank Expor Impor
14 Merpati Agent
15 Bank Danamon
22 BNI Bank
23 Pasar Bambaru Mosque
24 Buru Terminal
25 Palu Plaza
26 Central Sulawesi
27 Manonda Market
34 Manonda Terminal
34 Jawa & Sibah Buses
36 Merpati Office
37 Peini Office
38 Immigration Office
39 Masomba Market
40 Masomba Terminal
41 Main Post Office
PHPA National Parks Office

Jalan Yamin

Jalan Juanda

Jalan Kartini

Jalan Basuki Rachmat

To Airport

Jalan Setia Budi

Jalan Thamin

Jalan Tadulako

Jalan Emi Saelan

Jalan Monginsidi

Jalan Letjen Suprapto

Jalan MT Haryono

Jalan Cik Ditiro

Jalan Mawar

Jalan Bali

Jalan Maluku

To Bora Mineral Springs & Mantikole Nature Reserve

Jalan Sisinga Mangaraja

Jalan Sam Ratulangi

Jalan Ahmad Yani

Jalan Adin Saleh

Jalan Suharso

Jalan Sudirman

Jalan Hasanuddin

Jalan Wahidin

Jalan Sulawesi

Jalan Patimura

To Pantoloan Port

To Pantoloan Port

Sungai Palu

Palu Bay

Jalan Pala Molli

Jalan Wachid Hasim

Jalan Gajah Mada

Jalan Gumbasa

Jalan Poso Dolago

Jalan Lindu

Jalan Umar

Jalan Cokroaminoto

Jalan Imam Bonjol

Jalan Said Idus Aldjufri

Jalan Karama

Jalan Datu Pamusu

Jalan Sapi

Palu
Not to Scale

Jalan Diponegoro

Jalan Barittan

Jalan Supratman

Jalan Tanggo

Jalan Kunduri

Jalan Lobe

Jalan Palola

To Dongala

To Dongala

SULAWESI

Travel Agents For information on trekking around Palu and through Lore Lindu, try Ebony Tours & Travel (☎ 26260) at Jl Setia Budi 21.

Central Sulawesi Museum

This museum (☎ 22290) at Jl Sapiri 23 houses cultural relics, natural history exhibits, and a collection of books in Dutch, Indonesian and English. Its opening hours are from approximately 8.30 am until noon, and entry is free.

Beaches

Palu Beach is not especially clean or nice. Fortunately, there is an excellent beach and reefs north of nearby Donggala (see the Donggala entry later in this section). Sentosa supermarket (next to Sentral Hotel) stocks masks and snorkels.

Places to Stay – bottom end

The *Purnama Raya Hotel* (☎ 23646), Jl Wahidin 4, has singles/doubles for 9000/15,000 rp, all with private bath. It's clean, central and recommended.

Hotel Karsam (☎ 21776) at Jl Suharso 15, near Pantai Palu, is a pretty good deal with singles/doubles for 8000/15,000 rp or 12,500/20,000 rp, although it's about a 15 minute walk from the shopping centre.

Hotel Pasifik, Jl Gajah Mada 130, is central, but supernaturally noisy. Rooms start at 6000 rp. *Hotel Garuda* (☎ 252994), on Jl Hasanuddin, with rooms for 8000/12,000 rp, is supernaturally smelly. *Taurus Hotel* (☎ 21567), across the road at Jl Hasanuddin 36, is much better – clean, friendly and soccer mad, with rooms from 8800/15,000 rp, with shared mandi.

Not so central, but top value, is the *Andalas Hotel* (☎ 22332) at Jl Adin Saleh 50, with rooms for 10,000 rp.

Places to Stay – middle

New Dely Hotel (☎ 21037), Jl Tadulako 17, is clean, quiet and good value, with rooms from 22,000/27,500 rp plus tax, or 38,500/44,000 rp with TV and air-con. It's about a 10 minute walk from the town centre.

Buana Hotel (☎ 21475), Jl Kartini 8, is a tidy place with air-con rooms starting at 35,000/37,500 rp. Next door, the *Sentral Hotel* (☎ 22789) is quiet and clean, with English-speaking staff. Rooms start at 40,000 rp. Next in the row is *Kartini Hotel and Restaurant* (☎ 21964), a smaller, older and pleasant enough place with doubles from 20,000 to 55,000 rp.

The *Hotel Pattimura* (☎ 21775), Jl Pattimura 18, also has its own restaurant. Decent standard rooms are 35,000 rp, less discounts or 46,200 rp with air-con.

Places to Stay – top end

The *Palu Golden Hotel* (☎ 21126), Jl Rader Saleh 22, Palu's top hotel, has a lousy beach, but a fabulous swimming pool. With rooms starting at 93,000/146,000 rp, it's not surprising that it has plenty of vacancies. Discounts are available.

Places to Eat

Jl Hasanuddin II is a busy market lane with many places to eat, including *Milano Ice Cream* (☎ 23857). Avoid the burgers and hot dogs, but the bubur ayam (porridge of rice or beans with chicken) is good, and the ice cream outstanding. Most travellers stop here for information from the owners, Peter and Maureen Meroniak, who operate a beachside losmen in Donggala (see the following Donggala section).

The *Restaurant New Oriental* (☎ 23275), across the lane, serves excellent Chinese food and outstanding juice combinations. It also often has Indonesian dishes listed as 'cheap specials' in the window.

Just around the corner on Jl Wahidin, *Golden Bakery* has row upon row of confected pastries and cakes for breakfast and midnight snacks. It's no place to visit if you're on a diet.

More substantial fare is available from the *Ramayana*, further along Jl Wahidin, which serves all sorts of Indonesian and Chinese goodies from huge hot woks out the front. Hot, fresh and tasty fried laksa (curry soup) costs 5000 rp.

Several hotels have eateries which are

open to the public, including the *Andalas Hotel* which serves mouth-watering Padang fare.

If you want to self-cater, *Sentosa* is a busy supermarket at the Sentral Hotel complex.

Entertainment

The slim pickings include discos, barbecues and other social activities at the *Palu Golden Hotel*, or occasional concerts at the stadium. The *Palu Studio 21* cinema on the corner of Jl Juandas and Yamin is a more reliable choice.

Getting There & Away

Air Aside from the usual daytime office hours, Merpati, Garuda and Bouraq also sell tickets in the evening from about 7 pm until the staff feel like going home.

Bouraq (☎ 21195), Jl Juanda 87, offers flights west to Balikpapan and Banjarmasin, or east to Gorontalo, Manado and the Philippines.

Merpati (☎ 21271), Jl Monginsidi 71, has the broadest network and oldest planes, with direct flights to Toli-Toli (117,000 rp), Luwuk (139,000 rp), Gorontalo (108,000 rp) and Ujung Pandang (145,000 rp). Merpati's busy agent (☎ 21295) at Jl Hasanuddin 33 also keeps extended hours.

Sempati (☎ 21612), at the Sentral Hotel, Jl Kartini 6, has flights to Ujung Pandang and beyond. Garuda (☎ 21095) has an office at the airport.

Bus Buses to Gorontalo, Poso, Palopo, Manado and Rantepao all leave from the Inpres terminal. At Masomba terminal you can get buses to inland cities. Palu to Gorontalo takes 1½ days over a bone-jarring road. Jawa Indah buses depart from the company's Jl Hasanuddin office to Poso (8500 rp; six hours), Kilo (6500 rp), Tambarana (6000 rp), Sausu (5000 rp), Tolai (4500 rp) and Parigi (4000 rp).

Boat There are three ports near Palu. Larger vessels, such as Pelni, dock at Pantoloan north-east of Palu, and some dock at Donggala north-west of Palu. Smaller ships dock at Wani, two km past Pantoloan.

Pelni (☎ 21696) has an office at Jl Kartini 96 and another at Pantoloan, opposite the road to the wharf. The offices of the other shipping companies are at the various ports. Three modern Pelni boats now call at Pantoloan – see the introductory Getting Around chapter for Pelni's ferry routes.

You can avoid the long and uncomfortable bus ride through central Sulawesi by taking a ship from Palu to Ujung Pandang or Pare Pare.

Getting Around

The Airport Palu's Mutiara airport is seven km east of town, not far past the post office; take a bemo (2000 rp; 10 minutes) or taxi (5000 rp). For the brave or the desperate, *ojek* (motorcycle taxis) hang around the corner of Jl Hasanuddin and Jl Sudirman. Bargain hard.

Local Transport Transport around town is by bemo – 350 rp gets you anywhere. Routes are flexible so flag down one that looks like it is going your way and state a landmark near your destination. Buru terminal near Pasar Bambaru has kijang to Donggala for 1500 rp, or 4000 to 6000 rp to charter all the way to the beach at Tanjung Karang.

DONGGALA

As the administrative centre under the Dutch, Donggala was briefly the most important town and port in central Sulawesi. When the harbour silted up, the ships switched to the harbours on the other side of the bay and Palu became the regional capital. Today Donggala is a quiet backwater.

Diving & Snorkelling

The main attractions are sun, sand and water at **Tanjung Karang** (Coral Peninsula) north of town. The reef off the Prince John Dive Resort is a delight for snorkellers and beginner divers. The losmen is run by a German expat Peter Meroniak and his Indonesian wife, Maureen. Bring your own gear, buy the basics at Sentosa supermarket in Palu, or rent

SULAWESI

a mask and fins for 10,000 rp per day. There are also tanks and weights (40,000 rp), regulators (10,000 rp), BCDs (10,000 rp) and wetsuits (5000 rp). It all adds up. Day dives cost 65,000 rp, and night dives 75,000 rp. Beginners can dive for 95,000 rp, including tuition. Donggala caters well for experienced divers, not so well for beginners – especially when Peter is away. Do your dive training *before* coming to Sulawesi.

Towale, 12 km south-west of Donggala, is another excellent swimming and snorkelling spot, especially in the lagoons around Bukit Pusentasi. This is an easy excursion from Tanjung Karang. Boat-based diving excursions from Prince John Dive Resort include nearby wrecks, drop-offs on the other side of the bay and plenty of reefs.

Trekking
Donggala is also a good place to meet guides touting for business, gather groups for excursions and discuss itineraries with travellers convalescing from a few days in the jungle. Like elsewhere on Sulawesi, you need plenty of luck and patience to spot much wildlife and good hiking boots are essential. Do not try make do with trainers or joggers.

Places to Stay & Eat
Prince John Dive Resort offers simple, clean accommodation set in pleasant gardens. Singles cost 25,000 to 45,000 rp, including three basic meals. Everyone gathers for communal dining at dusk.

Natural Cottages (☎ 21235) is an excellent spot run by Oge right on the tip of the peninsula, a five minute walk past the dive resort. Beach cottages cost 15,000 rp, including three very good meals. The downside is that Prince John refuse to rent any of its diving gear to Oge's guests.

Getting There & Away
From Palu, you can catch a *taksi Donggala* for 1500 rp (40 minutes). It's another 20 minutes on foot to the beach. Alternatively, you could charter to Tanjung Karang beach for 4000 to 6000 rp.

AMPANA
Ampana, a port on Sulawesi's eastern peninsula, is the stepping off point for ferries and chartered boats to the Togian Islands. There is a small market and dock, then a continual string of fishing villages around to **Tanjung Api** (Cape Fire), a nature reserve east of town. Its wildlife includes anoa (dwarf buffalo), babirusa (pig-deer), crocodiles, snakes and maleo, but most people come to see the burning coral cliff fuelled by a leak of natural gas. Try cupping the gas bubbling through the water and putting a match to it! To get there, you need to charter a boat around the rocky peninsula. Try to get there at night.

Places to Stay
There are four losmen within easy walking distance from the Ampana market. On weekends in wedding season they are flat out catering for wedding receptions and accommodating guests, a fun time for all.

Losmen Irama, Jl Kartini 11, about 200m west of the market, is a modern place run by pleasant people with a better than usual appreciation of music and volume control. Rates are 6000 rp per person per night, or 10,000 rp with breakfast. There is an air-con room for 25,000/30,000 rp.

Penginapan Rejeki (☎ 21274) at Jl Talatako 45, about 400m south of the market, is the other relatively modern place, with pleasant singles for 5000 rp.

Penginapan Mekar, Jl Kartini 5, is the cheapest at 4500 rp for old singles, or 5500 rp per person for quieter rooms out the back.

Hotel Plaza (☎ 21091), Jl Kartini 45, is airy and pleasant, with a stock of English-language magazines. Singles cost 5000 rp, or 15,000 rp with meals.

Places to Eat
For dining out, the pokey *Rumah Makan Melati* at the beach end of Jl Kartini has great gado gado, or try the coffee shops in the market.

Getting There & Away
Bus Ampana is on the main road from Poso

5500 rp; five hours) to Luwuk (eight hours from Amapana).

Boat The weekly ferry from Poso chugs on to Gorontalo via the Togian ports of Wakai, Katupat and Dolong. Boats drop in and out of service, so check with other travellers along the way for updates. Another route to Gorontalo is by bus to Pagimana (7000 rp) and by ferry from there (see Gorontalo in the North Sulawesi section later in this chapter). There are smaller public boats from Ampana to Bomba (2500 rp; three hours) or to Wakai (2000 to 3000 rp) daily, more or less, or groups can charter for around 50,000 rp.

Togian Islands

This archipelago of pristine coral and volcanic isles in the middle of Tomini Bay is a riot of blue, gold and green. Undisturbed jungle shelters a variety of wildlife, reefs around the islands support rich marine life, and the seven or so ethnic groups sharing this place are extraordinarily hospitable.

This is the only place in Indonesia where you can find all three major reef environments – atoll, barrier and fringing reefs – in one location. Two atolls and their deep lagoons lie off the north-west of **Pulau Batu Daka**, barrier reefs surround the islands at the 200m depth contour (five km to 15 km offshore) and fringing reefs surround all of the coasts, merging with sea grass and mangroves. There are few beaches, and none near any of the major settlements, but there is more colour and movement in these reefs to make up for a lifetime of beaches.

The mix of coral and marine life is unusually diverse. The more conspicuous residents include gaily marked coral lobsters, a colony of dugong (the world's only vegetarian marine mammal), schools of dolphins numbering 100 or more, the occasional great whale, commercially important species of trepang, natural pearls, plus fish, fish and more fish.

On land, there is a cave with a colony of bats in the hills behind **Bomba** on Pulau Batu Daka, as well as pleasant walks and prolific bird life. Even smaller islands such as **Pulau Malenge**, north-east of Katupat, support diverse fauna, including the babirusa, hornbill, very cute cuscus, salamander and even a species of primate just 'discovered' in the early 1990s.

The islands are part of an active volcanic belt. **Pulau Una Una**, which consists mostly of Gunung Colo, was torn apart in 1983 when the volcano exploded for the first time in almost 100 years. Ash covered 90% of the island, destroying all of the houses, animals and most of the crops. Una Una's population had been safely evacuated and access to the island remains restricted. Islanders return to tend their crops, but no-one may live there. Subsequent eruptions in 1996 ensure the ban on resettlement stayed in place.

The Bajau

Nomadic Bajau 'Sea Gypsies' dive for trepang, pearl and other commercially important marine produce, just as they have done for hundreds, perhaps thousands, of years. Unlike the Bugis, Sulawesi's other famous seafarers, the Bajau are hunter-gatherers who spend more or less their whole lives on boats, travelling as families wherever they go. There are several permanent Bajau settlements on the Togians, and even some stilt villages on offshore reefs, but the itinerant character of Bajau culture still survives. Newlyweds are put in a canoe and pushed out to sea to make their place in the world. When they have children, the fathers dive with their three-day-old babies to introduce them to life on the sea.

Intrusions from the outside world are rare and the consequences are sometimes tragic. When Bugis and Chinese traders introduced air compressors to enable the Bajau to dive longer and deeper for their trepang, no-one explained the lethal nature of caisson disease ('the bends'), which killed 40 or more in one area and crippled many others. These days Bajau divers' only concessions to modernity are goggles fashioned from wood and glass, and handmade spearguns. Many Madurese

SULAWESI

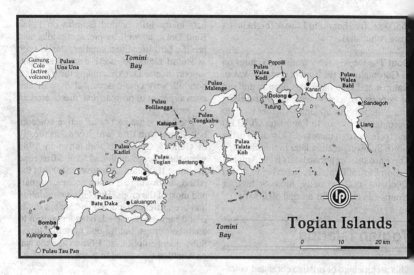

Togian Islands

0   10   20 km

divers working the Togian reefs still use compressors.

Information

There is nowhere to change foreign currency in the Togians. Cash up with wads of rupiah in Gorontalo or Poso, or you may have to do without.

Getting There & Away

There are small public boats (known locally as *bodi*) from Ampana to Bomba or Ampana to Wakai every day or two for 2000 to 3000 rp per head. There is also a ferry service which originates in Poso, and calls at Ampana, Wakai, Katupat and Dolong en route to Gorontalo. These ferries drop in and out of service, and sometimes there are none at all.

If the ferries to Gorontalo are out of service, catch a public boat to Ampana, and a bus east to Pagimana (5000 rp; five hours) or Luwuk (a further three hours). Pagimana has a ferry every second day to Gorontalo (10,000 rp), while Pelni's *KM Tilongkabila* calls at Luwuk on its fortnightly run up and down the east coast. Carrying a current Pelni timetable helps.

For 250,000 rp, groups can also charter a boat to Marisa on the northern peninsula (10 hours) then try to catch a bus to Gorontalo (three to four hours). This is the least reliable and most expensive option, and boat crews often lose their way. It is also very dangerous during 'wave season' (usually around December/January).

Getting Around

Transport within the Togians is a chronic problem. Regardless of where you stay, you need boats to get there and away, and to reach swimming and snorkelling spots.

A convenient (but not cheap) solution is to charter a boat for a few days. There are a few ancient craft in Ampana and on the islands – price and availability depends on the season, number of people, your itinerary and whether the crew like the look of you. Facilities are basic – sleep at least a few nights on the boat – and be prepared to hang out the back for the call of nature. There is usually no shelter, often not even a platform, just a slim handhold as everything else stretches over the churning water.

Another option is to base yourself at Bomba, Wakai, Katupat, Malenge islands or

Tongkabu and do short snorkelling and whale-watching excursions from there. Lone travellers will need all their powers of persuasion to reduce the usual 20,000 to 40,000 rp asking price, but may be able to get fishing boats for as little as 10,000 rp.

The cheapest way to get from one place to another is to look out for cargo boats heading in your direction. A boat going from Wakai to Dolong, for instance, will usually be happy to drop passengers at Katupat or Pulau Malenge for around 3000 rp. Otherwise you might need to spend 40,000 to 50,000 rp on a charter. If you do charter, start early in the day and include a snorkelling detour to one of the reefs in the deal.

BOMBA

Bomba is a tiny outpost at the south-eastern end of Pulau Batu Daka. Borrow a canoe to get to good snorkelling spots around the Island Homestay or adjacent to the fish co-operative on the island offshore. Chartering a boat to offshore reefs will cost 20,000 to 40,000 rp a day, or 50,000 rp if you continue on to Wakai at the end of the day. To find your way to the **bat cave** in the hills behind Bomba, you will need to ask around for a guide. It is a pleasant walk. Take a flashlight for the cave.

Places to Stay

Business is booming for Pak Ismail, Bomba's paramedic turned guesthouse proprietor. His homestay accommodation can be crowded at times, and as close to village life as you could get (note the mosque), but at 10,000 rp per head, including three basic meals, he remains a popular choice. The construction of a purpose-built guesthouse over the water will extend the options and the price.

Pak Amah runs the *Island Homestay*, a pleasant place on stilts adjacent to a speck of land a few hundred metres offshore. Stay for 10,000 rp a day, including meals. Either get your boat to drop you there, borrow a canoe or enquire at Pak Amah's house in Bomba. Signs at the base of Bomba's pier will point you to his home, a green house on the foreshore path about 50m from the pier.

WAKAI

There is little of interest in Wakai itself, except the port, two fine hotels and some well-stocked general stores. The proprietors of the Togian Islands Hotel seem to own half the town, such as the main shop which also trades in a variety of local produce, including cloves, pearl shell, trepang and coconut crabs. The huge crabs are kept out the back in holding boxes, ready to sell to travelling traders.

The world's largest terrestrial arthropod, **coconut crabs** once lived on islands throughout the western Pacific and eastern Indian oceans, but unsustainable human exploitation has reduced stocks to a handful of isolated islands, including the Togians. Mature crabs weigh up to five kg and their large-clawed legs can span 90 cm. Despite popular myth, there is little evidence to support stories of crabs climbing trees to snip coconuts off, removing the husk, then carrying the nut up again to drop from a great height. However, there *is* evidence that humans are eating these crabs to the edge of extinction, so please make a more sustainable choice from the menus.

For a pleasant walking excursion, visit the small **waterfall** a few km inland from Wakai.

Places to Stay & Eat

The friendly and very capable Tante Yani runs *Wakai Cottages*, a professional outfit with singles/doubles for 16,500/30,000 rp, including three excellent meals. She even packs superb picnics for day excursions and takeaways for those bound elsewhere. Fin and mask hire costs 4000 rp, and boat hire is 20,000 rp a day for the noisy old diesel boat or more for the faster boat.

Togian Islands Hotel is an airy weatherboard hotel built over the water near Wakai jetty. Prices range from 7500 rp up to 50,000 rp for the big rooms over the water, excluding meals. The kitchen here will cook the fish and lobsters you bring in from the reefs, as well as generous serves of rice and noodles. There's a small selection of dodgy diving gear available for hire – 75,000 rp for two dives (unescorted), including lunch and boat.

SULAWESI

The Togian Islands Hotel and Wakai Cottages have basic huts on a sandy beach at Pulau Kadiri, both for 15,000 rp a day. The seclusion, beach and adjacent snorkelling make up for what you lose in creature comforts, and the sunsets are fantastic. The boat to Kadiri will cost 2500 rp and pre-arranged excursions to atoll reefs to the north are about 25,000 rp a day.

A walk west of the beach huts will eventually bring you to a series of craggy coral cliffs, home to coconut crabs the size of small footballs. Put your hand in an occupied burrow and you are likely to lose a finger.

KATUPAT

Katupat is a relaxed village on Pulau Togian in the heart of the Togians and the closest port to the atoll reefs. It has simple accommodation, a small market and a couple of shops, plus some decent walking for those who need exercise. The big ferries call here: Katupat to Gorontalo costs 17,500 rp, or double if you hire a bed in one of the crew's cabins.

Places to Stay & Eat

Losmen Bolilanga Indah is built over the water adjacent to Katupat's main jetty, with bed and meals for 15,000 rp a head. However, travellers complain of constant money hassles here and few enjoy their stay.

A better option is *Losmen Indah Tongkabu* on nearby Pulau Tongkabu, which gets consistently good press. It offers friendly homestay accommodation for 11,000 rp, including three meals (more fish and rice, I'm afraid). Guides and transport are readily available at reasonable prices.

PULAU MALENGE

Malenge supports a microcosm of diverse wildlife, which recent surveys have shown includes a 'new' species of primate apparently unique to the island. The more researchers study islands such as Malenge, the more we realise how little we know about less accessible ecosystems elsewhere on Sulawesi.

The *Malenge Indah Losmen* near the pier charges 10,000 rp a night, including plenty of food. It is run by friendly, not pushy, folk who can organise day trips to the atoll lagoons for around 20,000 rp, but you will need to bring your own snorkelling gear. If you find these people touting for guests in Wakai or Katupat, negotiate commitments on price and transport before you go.

DOLONG

Dolong, on Pulau Walea Kodi, is one of the largest towns on the islands and the last port of call for Ampana to Gorontalo ferries. It is set in a sheltered harbour, but has no commercial accommodation. There are several restaurants that thrive on the rush of hungry ferry passengers who arrive late at night.

North Sulawesi

North Sulawesi is the most developed region on Sulawesi and probably the most egalitarian in Indonesia. Its people have a long history of trade and contact with the outside world. Together with the Sangir-Talaud island group, North Sulawesi forms a natural bridge to the Philippines, providing a causeway for the movement of peoples and cultures. Language and physical features related to the Philippines can be found among the Minahasans at the tip of the peninsula, and the Minahasans also share the Filipinos' love of music.

The three largest distinct groups of people in North Sulawesi are the Minahasans, Gorontalese and Sangirese, but there are many more dialects and subgroups. The kingdoms of Bolaang Mongondow, sandwiched between Minahasa and Gorontalo, were important political players too.

The Dutch have had a more enduring influence on this isolated northern peninsula than anywhere else in the archipelago. Minahasans held privileged positions in the Dutch East Indies civil service, Dutch is still widely spoken among the older generation throughout the province and well-to-do families

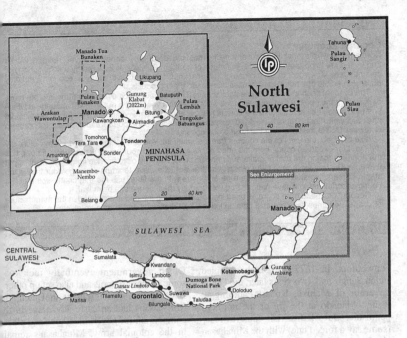

North Sulawesi

SULAWESI

often send their children to study in the Netherlands.

History

As most Minahasans will proudly tell you, they have never been subject to dynastic rule. Pressure to institute royalty led to a meeting of the linguistically diverse Minahasan states around 670 AD at a stone now known as Watu Pinabetengan. That meeting paved the way for a durable system of independent states. Subsequent, highly symbolic meetings at Watu Pinabetengan kept the system intact.

Threats from outside forces, notably the neighbouring kingdoms of Bolaang Mongondow, unified the Minahasans from time to time. Bolaang Mongondow expansionism led to a strong Minahasan backlash in 1655; one of the few occasions when the independent states were forced into a defence alliance.

At the time of the first contact with Europeans in the 16th century, North Sulawesi had strong links with the sultanate of Ternate and Bugis traders from South Sulawesi. The Portuguese used the Minahasan port of Manado as a supply stop, and Portuguese missionaries had some success in Minahasa and Sangir-Talaud in the 1560s. Even today there are subtle reminders of their presence: Portuguese surnames and various words not found elsewhere in Indonesia, like *garrida* for an alluring woman and *buraco* for a bad man, can still be found in Minahasa.

The Spanish, who had set themselves up in the Philippines, had colonial designs on the area. Spanish envoys and missionaries established their influence, but an abortive attempt to impose a half-Spanish king on the Minahasans in 1643 provoked violent insurrection and pushed the Minahasans closer to the Dutch.

The Dutch had already toppled the Ternate sultanate, and were keen to collude with local powers to throw out their European

Coconut Economy

Northern Sulawesi's inhabitants are among the most prosperous in Indonesia. Cloves, nutmeg, vanilla and coffee are important cash crops, but much of northern Sulawesi is covered by a solid canopy of coconut trees. The coconut palm is one of the most important plants in the tropical economy, not only producing edible fruit but also oil, waxes, fibres and other products.

The coconut flesh is enclosed in a light-coloured inner shell, which eventually turns into the hard, dark shell of the ripe nut that you see in the west. It takes a year for the nut to reach maturity, at which point the hard-shelled nut within the fibrous husk is about 12 cm in diameter, and full of sweet liquid and hard, white flesh. Copra is the dried flesh and the second most important export product of northern Sulawesi. Coir is the fibre from the husk of the coconut.

Like bamboo, the uses of the coconut tree are manifold. You can eat the meat, drink the juice, dry the meat for export as copra, burn the dried husks as fuel, build your house with coconut timber, use the fronds to thatch the roof or make mats and baskets, burn the oil to provide lighting at night or put it in your hair to keep it moist and glossy, use the leaf as a sieve to strain the sago flour that is the staple of many isolated areas, make rope and mats with the fibre, use the thin centre spine of the young coconut leaf to weave hats, or bag your midday meal of rice in a palm leaf.

Coconut oil, made from copra, is used instead of cooking fat, and is also used in the manufacture of soaps, perfumes, face creams, tanning lotions, hair dressings and even nitro-glycerine. ■

---

competitors. In 1677 the Dutch occupied Pulau Sangir and, two years later, the Dutch governor of Maluku, Robert Padtbrugge, visited Manado at the tip of the northern peninsula. Out of this visit came a treaty (some say a forced one) with the Minahasan chiefs, which led to domination by the Dutch for the next 300 years.

Although relations with the Dutch were often less than cordial (a war was fought around Tondano between 1807 and 1809) and the region did not actually come under direct Dutch rule until 1870, the Dutch and the Minahasans eventually became so close that the north was often referred to as 'the twelfth province of the Netherlands'. A Manado-based political movement called Twaalfe Provincie even campaigned for Minahasa's integration into the Dutch state in 1947.

Christianity became a force in the early 1820s when a Calvinist group, the Netherlands Missionary Society, turned from an almost exclusive interest in Maluku to the Minahasa area. Wholesale conversion of the Minahasans was almost complete by 1860. With the missionaries came mission schools, which meant that, as in Ambon and Roti, western education in Minahasa started much earlier than in other parts of Indonesia. The Dutch government eventually took over some of these schools and also set up others. Because the schools taught in Dutch, the Minahasans had an early advantage in the competition for government jobs and place in the colonial army. Minahasans remain among Indonesia's educated elite today.

The Minahasans fought alongside the Dutch to subdue rebellions in other parts of the archipelago, notably the Java War of 1825-30. They seemed to gain a special role in the Dutch scheme of things, and their loyalty to the Dutch as soldiers, their Christian religion and geographic isolation from the rest of Indonesia all led to a sense of being 'different' from the other ethnic groups of the archipelago.

The Minahasan sense of being different quickly became a problem for the central government after independence. As in Sumatra there was a general feeling that central government was inefficient, development was stagnating, money was being plugged into Java at the expense of the outer provinces and that these circumstances favoured the spread of Communism.

In March 1957 the military leaders of both southern and northern Sulawesi launched a confrontation with the central government with demands for greater regional autonomy ore local development, a fairer share of venue, help in suppressing the Kahar Mukar rebellion in southern Sulawesi, and at the cabinet of the central government be d jointly by Soekarno and Hatta. At least itially the 'Permesta' (Piagam Perjuangan emesta Alam) rebellion was a reformist ther than a separatist movement.

Negotiations between the central governent and the Sulawesi military leaders revented violence in southern Sulawesi, but he Minahasan leaders were dissatisfied with he agreements and the movement split. aspired, perhaps, by fears of domination by he south, the Minahasan leaders declared heir own autonomous state of North Sulwesi in June 1957. By this time the central overnment had the situation in southern ulawesi pretty much under control, but in he north they had no strong local figure to ely upon and there were well-founded umours that the USA was supplying arms to he Minahasan rebels.

The central government sought a military olution, bombing Manado in February 958. By May the Minahasans had given up ope of military support from southern Sulwesi and Permesta forces were driven out of Central Sulawesi, Gorontalo, the Sangir slands and Maluku. US policy shifted, avouring Jakarta, and in June 1958 central overnment troops landed in Minahasa. The Permesta leaders retreated into the mounains and the rebellion was finally put down n mid-1961.

The rebellion strengthened exactly those rends the rebels had hoped to weaken. Cenral authority was enhanced at the expense of ocal autonomy, radical nationalism gained over pragmatic moderation, the power of the Communists and Soekarno increased while hat of Hatta waned, and Soekarno was able o establish 'guided democracy' in 1959.

Like most export-oriented commodity producing regions in Indonesia, North Sulawesi has done well under the stability and pro-development orientation of Soeharto's 'New Order'. The province's infrastructure s second to none, and export demand for its varied cash crops has offset the disadvantage of distance from domestic markets. Fleeting booms, such as when clove prices soared to dizzy heights in the 1970s, have been complemented by shrewd business acumen and forward thinking, making North Sulawesi a model of economic development.

GORONTALO

The port of Gorontalo, population 120,000, is the second-largest centre in North Sulawesi and has the feel of a large, friendly country town. Islam probably arrived here with Bugis traders and became established when the Ternate sultanate extended its influence over the tribes of the Gorontalo region in the 16th century.

Orientation

Although rather spread out, most of the hotels, shops and other life-support systems are concentrated in a small central district. The intercity bus terminal is three km north of the city and the port is 2.5 km south-east. Mikrolet fan out in all directions from the terminal opposite the main market on Jl Sam Ratulangi.

Information

Money The banks along Jl Yani cash travellers cheques and foreign currency. Manado, Poso and Palu are the next closest places to change money.

Post & Communications The post office is two blocks east of the Telkom office and is supplemented by a mobile postal service which sells stamps in the Jl Pertiwi night market after hours. There is an excellent Telkom office on Jl 23 Januari which is open 24 hours.

Things to See & Do

Gorontalo features some of the best preserved colonial houses on Sulawesi. The town's local hero is **Nani Wartabone**, an anti-Dutch guerilla, and there is a large statue of him dressed like a boy scout in the sports field adjacent to the Melati Hotel.

On the outskirts of Gorontalo are two fortresses. **Otanaha Fort**, on a hill at Le-

SULAWESI

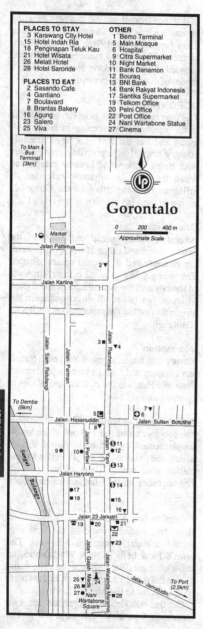

PLACES TO STAY
3 Karawang City Hotel
15 Hotel Indah Ria
18 Penginapan Teluk Kau
21 Hotel Wisata
26 Melati Hotel
28 Hotel Saronde

PLACES TO EAT
2 Sasando Cafe
4 Gantiano
7 Boulavard
8 Brantas Bakery
16 Agung
23 Salero
25 Viva

OTHER
1 Bemo Terminal
5 Main Mosque
6 Hospital
9 Citra Supermarket
10 Night Market
11 Bank Danamon
12 Bouraq
13 BNI Bank
14 Bank Rakyat Indonesia
17 Santika Supermarket
19 Telkom Office
20 Pelni Office
22 Post Office
24 Nani Wartabone Statue
27 Cinema

Gorontalo

0   200   400 m
Approximate Scale

kobalo overlooking Danau Limboto, wa
probably built by the Portuguese and suppos
edly used by Gorontalo kings as a bastion
against the Dutch when relations soured
Today there is just the remains of three tow
ers. To get there take a *bendi* (pony cart) o
a mikrolet from the market terminal, to a par
at the foot of the hill. There is another fort o
the shore of the lake to the south-eas
Otanaha also offers panoramic views o
Danau Limboto, a 5600 hectare lake with
maximum depth of just 2.5m.

Pantai Lahilote is the name of the whit
sand beach near Pohe's Ikan Tuna harbou
two km south of Gorontalo. Local musician
occasionally perform here. You can get ther
by bendi or mikrolet. On the opposite shor
of Gorontalo bay, the **Du Panggola Ceme
tery** in Leato has mystic significance for th
locals, who visit on special occasions fo
good luck.

The **Lombongo** hot springs are 17 kr
from Gorontalo, at the western edge o
Dumoga Bone National Park. There is
swimming pool filled with hot spring wate
but a much nicer spot is the **swimming hol**
at the foot of a 30m waterfall about three kr
past the springs. It is a solid walk, so brin
good footwear. To get to Lombongo, take th
'Suwana' mikrolet from in front of the Go
rontalo hospital.

The **swimming pool** near Gorontalo'
stadium is a fun choice and opens till 9 pm
Get there by bendi (300 rp) or mikrolet (25(
rp) from the market terminal, and pay 750 r
to enter.

Beyond Lombongo is the **Dumoga Bon**
National Park – a large reserve with th
highest conservation value in North Sul
awesi. Illegal gold miners working dee
inside the park occasionally enter from th
west, but this is bandit country. The onl
safe, accessible and legal way in is vi
Doloduo to the east of the park.

Places to Stay – bottom end
Melati Hotel (☎ 21853), Jl Gajah Mada 33
is a lovely old place facing the Nani War
tabone square. It was built around the turn o
the century for the then harbour master

hose grandson, Alex Velberg, has opened
ae house to guests. Large airy rooms with
aared bath cost 9000/14,000 rp for singles/
oubles, plus 1500 rp per person for break-
ist. Alex's advice in English, Dutch or
idonesian is accurate and free.

Hotel Saronde (☎ 21735) at Jl Walanda
Maramis 17, just across the square, has
ooms with fan from 13,200/19,000 rp, and
ir-con for 35,750/43,000 rp. Breakfast is
icluded.

Penginapan Teluk Kau at Jl Parman 42 has
irge rooms with high ceilings and big dou-
le beds for 6600/ 13,000 rp. It's rundown
nd noisy, but helpful.

Hotel Wisata (☎ 21736), Jl 23 Januari 19,
s good value, helpful and the location of the
Merpati office. Rooms with shared mandi
ost 11,000/12,000 rp, or 32,500/42,500 rp
ith air-con, TV and mandi.

The *Hotel Indah Ria* (☎ 21296) at Jl Yani
0 has rooms with mandi from 25,300/40150
. It's a congenial place.

laces to Stay – middle
he *Hotel Saronde II* (☎ 21735), Jl Walanda
Maramis 17, is attached to the Hotel Sa-
onde, with rooms from 57,750 rp. All rooms
re big and bright, with refrigerator, TV and
ir-con.

Karawang City Hotel, Jl Rachmad 31, has
nodern rooms for 44,000 rp, including tax
nd breakfast. It's cool, clean and pleasant.

laces to Eat
he local delicacy is milu siram, a corn soup
vith grated coconut, fish, salt, chilli and
me. Look for it at stalls and warung along
l Pertiwi at night.

Brantas Bakery on Jl Sultan Hasanuddin,
pposite the main mosque, is a depot of
elights with an exquisite selection of cakes
nd pastries. Wash them down with coffee
ack at your losmen or pack them for your
nward journey. The *warung* next door has
imple fare - pricey, but good.

The *Boulavard* has a varied selection of
ish and Chinese food and is well worth
eeking out. *Gantiano* across the street from
ie Karawang City Hotel is a Padang restau-

rant with an airy seating area. It's worth a
visit, as is *Salero,* the Padang place just south
of the post office, and the flashy *Sasando
Cafe* at Jl Panjaitan 3.

Viva, next door to the Melati Hotel, has
functional fare, and *Agung* around the corner
at Jl Januari 23 is not bad either.

Things to Buy
Souvenirs of the area include the soft and
very colourful *krawang* embroidery, available at Toko Kerawang Lasui Indah, Toko
Delilah Krawang and Toko Palapa. That
most useful of tropical accessories, the mosquito net, is available from Toko Bin Yusuf.

Getting There & Away
Air Merpati (☎ 21736) is in the Hotel Wisata
at Jl 23 Januari 19 and Bouraq (☎ 21070) is
at Jl Ahmad Yani 34, next to the BNI bank.
Both have frequent connections to Manado
and Palu.

Bus The main bus terminal is three km north
of town. There are direct buses to Palu
(22,500 rp), Poso (32,500 rp) and Tentena
(40,000 rp) in Central Sulawesi, one day
away. Buses to Manado take 10 hours if the
road is clear; if it rains, mud slides frequently
cause delays. There are small, crowded buses
(13,000 rp), air-con buses (17,500 rp) and
top-of-the-range Tomohon Indah buses
(30,000 rp). Tomohon Indah tends to run on
time, but at heart-stopping speeds and with
many near misses. It is not recommended.
An option for groups is to charter a taxi to
Manado from Merit Taxi (☎ 25421). Paris
Express air-con buses get you to Kotomo-
bagu for 10,000 rp.

Boat Pelni's *KM Tilongkabila* calls at a dock
just a few km south-east of town, and is
easily the most comfortable way to get to
Bitung (near Manado) or to Luwuk and
beyond. Pelni (☎ 20419), Jl 23 Januari 31,
also has an office at the port in Kwandang,
which is a stop for the *KM Umsini*.

Gorontalo's ferry dock, Pelabuhan Feri, is
about five km past the Pelni dock. PT ASDP
(Persero) runs a ferry across the gulf to

SULAWESI

Pagimana every second day, leaving at 9.30 pm and arriving at 6 am. Tickets cost 10,000 rp, plus 25,000 rp if you want a cabin for two. Connecting buses in Pagimana go straight to Luwuk or Ampana.

Old, but not so faithful, ferries chug between Gorontalo and Poso via the Togian Islands. At the time of updating, there was just one boat dropping in and out of service. Its timetable depends on how many others are serving the route.

Getting Around

The Airport The shared Merpati and Bouraq bus will transport you from town to the airport 32 km away (5000 rp; half an hour).

The Port Mikrolets direct from the port to the main bus terminal cost 1500 rp per person. Allow plenty of time to get to a departing ferry as mikrolet from the central terminal across from the market are usually full by the time they reach the post office corner. Leave early, set out from the central terminal or hang around the BNI bank to get the last available seats. The long bumpy track precludes bendi as an option.

Local Transport Gorontalo is rather spread out and you really need the horse-drawn bendi – 300 rp will get you almost anywhere. For longer routes take mikrolets which cruise the streets and can also be found at the central terminal across the road from the market.

KWANDANG

Kwandang is a port on the north coast of the peninsula, not far from Gorontalo. On the outskirts of Kwandang are the remains of two interesting fortresses of obscure origins. While the town itself is nothing special, the forts are worth checking out. Both are just off the Gorontalo to Kwandang road as you enter Kwandang.

Fort Ota Mas Udangan stands on flat ground and at first glance appears to be ill-placed to defend anything. One suggestion is that the ocean once came right up to the fort but has since receded. All that remains of the once-sizeable fort are the ruins of a tower alongside the road, a gateway further back and traces of the walls.

Fort Oranje lies on a hill some distance back from the sea and just a short walk from the Gorontalo-Kwandang road. It's been partly restored, though Fort Ota Mas Udangan is probably the more interesting of the two.

To get to Kwandang, take a bus from the Gorontalo bus terminal (2500 rp; two hours).

KOTAMOBAGU

Kotamobagu or 'Kota' is a prosperous market town set in a fertile valley of towering coconut plantations. Neat rows of bungalows in manicured gardens line well-sealed streets, and friendly locals are intensely curious about the handful of travellers who bother to stop here.

Kotamobagu was once the seat of power for the pre-colonial Bolaang Mongondow kingdoms, and more recently the rebel capital of the failed Permesta movement. Transmigration schemes have successfully transformed the area, providing an abundance of irrigated produce for export to other regions. The need for large, erosion-free water catchments to supply the irrigation schemes led to the creation of the Dumoga Bone National Park – another of Bolaang Mongondow's impressive assets.

Kotamobagu is a useful supply stop, with two supermarkets and a busy market. There is also a small cinema in town.

Things to See

Twenty-three km east of Kotamobagu, **Danau Mooat** is a crater lake 800m above sea level. The lake is surrounded by dense forest providing refuge for a variety of birds and other fauna.

There is also a small crater lake at **Gunung Ambang**, a large nature reserve north of Kotamobagu. The summit area, about 2 km from Kota via Bongkudai Baru, features sulphur fumaroles, hot mud pools, pigafetta palms, tree ferns and flowering shrubs.

Places to Stay

The apparent shortage of tourists has had little effect on Kotamobagu's bustling hotel sector. There are plenty of places to stay, and they all seem to be doing a steady trade.

The *Ramayana* (☎ 21188), Jl Adampe Dolot 50, the main road from the bus terminal, has singles/doubles from 7500/13,500, plus 10,000 rp for three meals. Although basic, the Ramayana is better value than the similarly priced *Hotel Tentram* and *Losmen Viduri* nearby.

New, busy and popular is the *Hotel Wijaya* (☎ 21621), Jl Adampe Dolot 193, with doubles from 13,000 to 30,000 rp.

Hotel Ade Irama (☎ 21216), Jl Ade Irama, is a pleasant place on a quiet street a couple of blocks behind the Bank Rakyat Indonesia, with big doubles for 16,500 rp and nice rooms out the back for 8800 rp. It's recommended.

The nearby *Hotel Wisata* (☎ 21603) at Jl Sutoyo 174 is also quiet, with rooms from 6,500 rp. *Hotel Molosing* (☎ 21121), a few doors down, is run by the erratic, but friendly, Ibu Dilapanga. Rooms cost from 2,500 rp.

The large, comfortable *Kotamobagu* and *Indang Rahayu* (☎ 22094) on Jl Yani are neighbouring hotels run by the same manager. Air-cooled rooms cost 10,000/15,000 to 20,000/30,000 rp. Even fancier is the *Tamsya Hotel* (☎ 21195), Jl Sutoyo, with rooms from 22,000/27,500 rp with fan, or from 49,500/55,000 rp with air-con.

There are loads of cafes along the main street, but they tend to be very lonely at night. The *warung compound* adjacent to the main mosque is the best place with the broadest selection. Try the fresh, crunchy gado gado (2000 rp) and half a dozen sate (1000 rp). The *Rumah Makan Sudi Mampir* on the corner of Jl Sutoyo and Jl Ade Irma serves great nasi kuning for breakfast.

Getting There & Away

Bus The inter-city bus terminal is at the edge of town, a few km north-east of the business district. Manado is three hours by bus via a pretty coastal road. Paris Ekspress, with a ticket office at Kotamobagu's Paris Supermarket, has the best buses (5500 rp with air-con). Damri is cheaper at 4750 rp. Travellers to Gorontalo can catch daily Paris Ekspress buses for 8500 rp, or 10,000 with air-con. The trip, via the main highway, takes eight hours.

Car Bintang Harapan (☎ 22477), next door to the Hotel Ide Irama, has a fleet of kijang which ferry passengers in relative comfort to/from Manado (7500 rp). Chartering a taxi costs around 20,000 rp.

Getting Around

Mikrolet from the central market head off in all directions, taking passengers around town for 300 rp. Once full, they stop for no-one. Ojek and horse-drawn bendi rates depend on your bargaining skills.

DUMOGA BONE NATIONAL PARK

About 50 km west of Kotamobagu, Dumoga Bone is a national park with the highest conservation value in North Sulawesi. The 300,000 hectare park is large, but mostly inaccessible. Only the illegal goldminers working deep within the reserve seem to have the means (and determination) to venture beyond the handful of established tracks.

The national park is at the headwaters of Sungai Dumoga, and was established to protect large irrigation projects downstream from flooding, silting and poor water quality. Like reserves elsewhere, your chances of seeing rare fauna require a little luck and a lot of patience, but it is a great place to look for cuscus, maleo and countless other bird species, as well as a rich array of colourful flora. You should at least get to see a waterfall, plenty of hornbills, macaques and tiny tarsier. Present, but fairly people-shy, are anoa, babirusa, wild pigs and a recently discovered species of giant fruit bat.

Trekking

From Doloduo continue by foot or bemo to the ranger station at Kosinggolan just inside the park to purchase a 1000 rp permit to enter

SULAWESI

the park. You will also be required to hire a guide: 15,000 rp per excursion, or 45,000 rp for overnight trips.

One option is to base yourself at Kosing-golan, staying at *Ibu Niko Homestay* for 20,000 rp a night, including meals, or at a cheaper, unnamed *homestay* near the dam for 7500 rp, excluding meals – there is a *warung* nearby with dishes from 1500 rp.

Another option is for you and your guide to walk, catch the very occasional bemo (500 rp) or hitch the nine km through the jungle to Toraut, and stay at the ranger's lodge there for 30,000 rp a head, or 10,000 rp in the pits with no windows. Breakfast costs 3000 rp and dinner 7500 rp. While not cheap, this option is marginally more comfortable than sleeping in the jungle and is very convenient for dawn treks.

For those with a hammock, mosquito net and other camping accessories, take an extended trek and stay overnight in the jungle itself.

Getting There & Away

There are buses directly from Manado's Malalayang bus terminal to Doloduo for 6500 rp and frequent connections from Kotamobagu. Improvements to the rough coastal road from Bilungala to Molibagu south of the park are creating a Gorontalo-Doloduo shortcut, but connections and road conditions are less than reliable.

MANADO

When the naturalist Alfred Wallace visited in 1859 he described Manado as 'one of the prettiest in the East'. Only 14 years earlier Manado had been levelled by earthquakes, enabling the Dutch to redesign the thriving settlement from scratch.

Today neat rows of wooden houses with picket fences line orderly streets. This provincial capital of 290,000 people is clean, confident and cosmopolitan, with the highest standard of living in eastern Indonesia. The locals are affable, the kids won't hound you and westerners can mingle freely without constant assaults of 'Hello Misteerrrr'.

Manado is the centre of Minahasa, the name given to the collective of independent states that once dominated Sulawesi's northern peninsula. Minahasa literally means 'united, becomes one', referring to a pre-colonial defence pact which united clans against the neighbouring Bolaang Mongondow regency.

History

The original Minahasans are said to originate from Lumimuut, who rose from the sea and gave birth to Toar. After many years' separation, mother and son met again. Not recognising each other, they married and their descendants populated the region. Minahasan lands and languages were divided by the god Muntu Untu at Watu Pinabetengan (the 'dividing stone'), a carved rock on the foothills of Gunung Soputan.

Rice surpluses from Minahasa's volcanic hinterland made Manado a strategic port for European traders sailing to and from Maluku's Spice Islands. Spain established a fort at Manado in 1627, but by 1643 the Manado rulers wanted their unruly and corrupt Spanish guests out and appealed to the Dutch VOC in Ternate for help. The Dutch and their Minahasan allies eventually gained the upper hand in 1655, built their own fortress in 1658 and expelled the last of the Spaniards a few years later.

The Dutch helped unite the linguistically diverse Minahasan confederacy, and in 1694 the Minahasans scored a decisive military victory against the Bolaang to the south. Dutch influence flourished as the Minahasans embraced European goods and gods. Missionary schools in Manado in 1881 were among the first attempts at mass education in Indonesia, giving their graduates a considerable edge in gaining civil service, military and other positions of influence.

By the mid-1800s compulsory cultivation schemes were producing huge crops of cheap coffee for a Dutch-run monopoly. Minahasans suffered immensely from this 'progress', yet economic, religious and social ties with the colonists continued to intensify. Minahasan mercenaries put down anti-Dutch rebellions on Java and elsewhere urning them the name *'anjing Belanda'* – Dutch dogs'.

The Japanese occupation of 1942-45 was period of deprivation, and the Allies ombed Manado heavily in 1945. During the ar of independence that followed, there as bitter division between pro-Indonesian nitarians and those favouring Dutch-sponored federalism. The appointment of a Manadonese Christian Sam Ratulangi as the rst republican governor of eastern Indone-a was decisive in winning Minahasan upport for the republic.

As the young republic lurched from crisis crisis, Jakarta's monopoly over the copra ade seriously weakened Minahasa's econo-y. Illegal exports flourished and in June 956 Jakarta ordered the closure of Manado ort, the busiest smuggling port in the repub-c. Local leaders refused and Jakarta backed own. Soon the Permesta rebels confronted e central government with demands for olitical, economic and regional reforms. akarta responded in Manado by bombing e city in February 1958 then invading in ine.

Manado has prospered under Indonesia's ew Order, which implemented many of the conomic reforms (but few of the political forms) sought by the Permesta rebels. The ty has a tolerant, outward-looking culture ith a promising future. The development of itung's deep sea port and the establishment f direct air links with the Philippines and ingapore are opening Manado to the out-de world and fostering trade and tourism.

rientation

Iikrolets from every direction loop around asar 45, a block of shops, fruit stands and epartment stores in the heart of town. The narket backs on to Jl Sam Ratulangi, the nain road running south, where you will find pmarket restaurants, hotels and supermar-ets. Pasar Jengki fish market, north of the entre, is the main launching place for boats Bunaken Island.

nformation

ourist Offices These are places of obscure purpose and much confusion. Mikrolets marked '17 Aug Wanea' from Pasar 45 will get you to the North Sulawesi Tourism Office (☎ 64299) on Jl 17 Agustus. They can also drop you near the National Parks Office (☎ 62688) at Jl Babe Palar 67. More convenient is the information and booking centre at the Nunaken Souvenir Shop at Jl Sam Ratulangi 178.

Immigration Manado's immigration office (☎ 63491), near the tourist office on Jl 17 Agustus, is more helpful than most. There's another at Bitung to process sea-bound travellers. The Philippines has a consulate general (☎ 62365; fax 55316) at Jl Lumimuut 8.

Money Manado is overflowing with banks, most of which can change money. Bank Rakyat Indonesia is on Jl Sarapung and Bank Expor Impor Indonesia is on Jl Sudirman. The Bank Central Asia on Jl Lolong Lasut is probably unique in its willingness to change French Franc travellers cheques.

Post & Communications The post office is on Jl Sam Ratulangi 21. The Telkom office is at Jl Sam Ratulangi 4, there are card phones all over town and wartel offer competitive long-distance rates.

Things to See

There are good movies, shopping and food in Manado, discos aplenty and a busy new esplanade bustling with vendors, but otherwise the main attractions are outside the city.

The **Provincial Museum of North Sulawesi** on Jl Supratman is worth a look, as is the **Kienteng Ban Hian Kiong** Confucian-Buddhist temple, a colourful landmark on Jl Panjaitan.

There are monuments on every second corner dedicated to Minahasan and Indonesian heroes. The **Sam Ratulangi** monument on the street bearing the same name honours the first republican governor of east Indonesia, hailed as the 'father to the Minahasan people' after his death in June 1949.

The **Toar Lumimuut** monument at the

SULAWESI

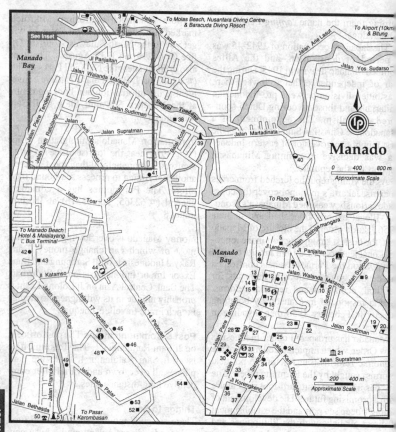

Manado

0   400   800 m
Approximate Scale

Manado Bay

0   200   400 m
Approximate Scale

eastern end of Jl Sudarso depicts the Adam and Eve characters of Minahasan mythology, Lumimuùt and her son-husband, Toar. On the same street is a monument to **Ibu Walanda Maramis**, a pioneer of the Indonesian women's movement, and the grave of **Imam Bonjol**, hero of the Padri War (1821-38) and just one of many anti-Dutch rebels to die in exile in Manado during the 19th century.

Special Events

Minahasans love an excuse to party. Watch out for festivals, such as Tai Pei Kong festi-

val at Ban Hian Kong temple in February; Pengucapan Syukur (Minahasan Thanksgiving Day) in June/August; Bunaken Festival in July; the Anniversary of Manado on 1 July; traditional horse races in the second week of August; and the anniversary of North Sulawesi Province on 23 September.

Places to Stay – bottom end

Smiling Hostel (☎ 68463), Jl Rumambi 7, in a charmless cement block backing on to the old harbour, is cheerful, cheap, central and spotlessly clean. There is a comfortable rooftop cafe and, best of all, information

PLACES TO STAY		18	Rumah Makan Ria	21	Museum
3	Losmen Jakarta		Rio	24	Garuda
	Jaya	19	KFC & Gelael	25	Silk Air
4	Crown Hotel		Supermarket	26	Ocean Night Club
5	Smiling Hostel	20	Rumah Makan Raja	27	Pelni Office
9	Rex Hotel		Oci	28	Telkom Office
10	Manado Plaza Hotel	35	Restoran Surabaya	30	Matahari Department
17	Kawanua Sahid	48	Manado Hilltop		Store
	Hotel, Shopping		Restaurant	31	BCA Bank
	Centre & Sempati			32	Post Office
	Office			34	Bouraq
22	Kawanua Kecil	**OTHER**		39	Toar Lumimuut
23	Manado Bersehati	1	Pasars Bersehati &		Monument
29	Novatel Hotel		Jengki	40	Paal 2 Terminal
33	Hotel Mini Cakalele	2	Boats to Bunaken	41	Philippines Consulate
36	Hotel Jeprinda	6	Ferry Ticket Offices	42	Mandala Airlines
37	Hotel New Queen		& Port	44	Philippines Consulate
38	Ahlan City Hotel	7	President Complex	45	Governor's Office
43	Hotel Minahasa		(Shops & Cinema)	46	Immigration
52	Manado Homestay	8	Ban Hian Kiong	47	Tourist Office
54	Garden Hotel		Temple	49	Studio 21 Cinema
		11	Town Square	50	Wartel
PLACES TO EAT		12	Pasar 45	51	Sam Ratulangi
13	CFC & Jumbo	14	Hot Gossip		Monument
	Supermarket	15	Benteng Cinema	53	National Parks Office
		16	Bank Rakyat		
			Indonesia		

plenty from the staff, other travellers and cooks of tips. Dorm beds cost 5500 rp and basic single rooms start from 7500 rp. The cafe does a brisk trade in jaffles, pancakes, fried rice or noodles, and beer – all the basic food groups.

The friendly *Rex Hotel* (☎ 51136) at Jl Sugiono 3 is modern and clean, with economy singles/doubles for 9000/15,000 rp, and air-con rooms for 30,000 rp.

Manado Bersehati Hotel (☎ 55022), Jl Sudirman 1, is a Minahasan-style house set about 20m off the main road. Rooms with shared mandi go for just 8500/14,000 rp.

Manado Homestay (☎ 60298), Wanea Lingkungan III, Komplek Diklat Rike, is less conveniently located, but compensates with comfort, information, tours and rooms from 5,000 rp per night. To get there, take a 'Teling' mikrolet from Pasar 45 and ask to get off at Komplek Diklat.

An old favourite with travellers is *Crown Losmen* (☎ 66277), Jl Hasannudin 28, with rooms for 6000/10,000 rp, or 15,000 rp with mandi. It's basic but hospitable. Another is the marginally cheaper *Losmen Jakarta Jaya* (☎ 64330) across the road.

The once-popular *Hotel Kawanua*, now the *Kawanua Kecil* (☎ 63842), Jl Sudirman 40, is run down and depressing. Singles start at 12,500 rp. *Ahlan City Hotel* (☎ 63454) is in the same neighbourhood at Jl Sudirman 103. It's spartan but clean, with singles from 10,000 rp. The cheery *Hotel Jeprinda* (☎ 64049), Jl Sam Ratulangi 33, has rooms for 25,000/29,000 rp. The manager speaks English.

The comfortable *Hotel Mini Cakalele* (☎ 52942) is at Jl Korengkeng 40, south of the main post office. Rooms with fan are 20,900 rp, or from 29,700 rp with air-con.

The *Hotel Minahasa* (☎ 62059), Jl Sam Ratulangi 199, is an elegant hotel with an old colonial feel. The friendly manager speaks Dutch and English. Spotlessly clean rooms cost from 22,000/27,500 rp, or 35,000/42,500 rp with air-con.

Places to Stay – middle
Kolongan Beach Hotel (☎ 53001) is seven km south of the city and is the last stop for many of the mikrolets. Rooms start at 30,000 rp. This is a good place for snorkelling and diving.

SULAWESI

Hotel New Queen (☎ 65979; fax 65748), Jl Wakeke 12-14, is clean and even has an award to prove it. It's on a quiet street and is one of the best mid-range places in Manado, with rooms from 65,250/ 78,300 rp, plus tax. All rooms have air-con.

The *Manado Plaza Hotel* (☎ 51124), Jl Walanda Maramis 1, is an ageing landmark in the heart of town. Motel-style rooms start at 75,000 rp, plus tax.

The *Nusantara Diving Centre* (NDC; ☎ 63988) at Molas Beach, five km north of town, attracts diving groups and has a popular disco. Tiny, grotty rooms start at $US10, or $US40 with air-con. There are discount packages for snorkellers and divers.

The similarly priced *Baracuda Diving Resort* (☎ 62033) just past NDC is clean, modern and has prime views of the sunset. It also has dive packages from $US70 to US$100.

Places to Stay – top end

The Kawanua Sahid Hotel (☎ 67777; fax 65220), Jl Sam Ratulangi 1, is Manado's top establishment, complete with swimming pool. Rooms range from $US90/100 to $US375 for suites, plus tax.

The *Manado Beach Hotel* (☎ 67001; fax 67007) is 22 km south of the city. Rooms start at $US110/120, plus tax.

Novotel was nearing completion of a huge new hotel on the esplanade near Matahari department store at the time of writing.

Other places to spoil yourself include a five star resort at Likupang on the northern tip of North Sulawesi, with rooms from $US125, and a resort at Kunkungan Bay (see Bitung later in this section).

Places to Eat

Manado is a Mecca for adventurous diners. Regional delights include kawaok, translated into Indonesian as tikus hutan goreng or 'fried forest rat'. The name is unfortunate because this heavily spiced dish of bones and lean meat (something akin to possum) actually tastes sensational. There's also tough, gamy rintek wuuk (spicy dog meat), lawang pangang (stewed bat), the tender and tasty

freshwater ikan mas (gold fish) and tinutua (vegetable porridge).

Tinoor Jaya on Jl Sam Ratulangi, south the Matahari department store, is one of th few restaurants in Manado serving region cuisine. But to eat really well, stop at the ro of restaurants in the Lokon foothills, ju before Tomohon. The food at *Tinoor Inda* and the *Pemandangan* is as incredible their spectacular views over Manado. Get th Tomohon bus to drop you there.

The drinks of choice are saguer, a ve quaffable fermented sago wine, and Ca Tikus (literally 'rat brand'), the generic nam for distilled saguer. Cap Tikus is sold as N 1, No 2 or No 3, referring to its strength an when it was removed from the distillatio process. It is best diluted and served over ic For durian lovers, try crushed durian i saguer.

The esplanade near Pasar 45 attracts good selection of night warungs sellin cheap Indonesian food. A local English-la guage conversation club meets here o Monday, Wednesday and Friday.

For fresh hot seafood, try the *Ria Rio* at Sudirman 5, or the *Raja Oci* up the road. E well for 2000 to 4000 rp. The *Restoran Sur abaya* on Jl Sarapung has a long, varie menu, and the *Xanadu* at the southern end c Jl Sam Ratulangi is a Chinese restaurant fo smartly dressed diners on that special nigl out. Dishes cost 4000 to 6000 rp.

The ubiquitous *KFC* is above Gelae supermarket on Jl Sudirman, and there's smaller outlet next to the Matahari depart ment store opposite the post office. There also a *CFC* outlet above the Jumbo super market behind Pasar 45. For pastries an desserts to die for, check out the restaurar opposite the Bioskop Manado on Jl Sutomo

Also, check out the Warong Nusa Inda and Warong Souvenir, both on Jl Panjaita near the temple, for candied nutmeg frui canary halua, bagea (happiness) cake an other Manado delicacies.

Entertainment

As in the nearby Philippines, music is a wa of life for the Minahasans. They love jazz d there are always small concerts and ackroom gigs, so ask around. Discos tend look like crowded airport lounges early in e evening. Be patient. When the smuggled asks of Cap Tikus are drained, the crowds osen up and mob the dance floor.

The young crowd heads to *Hot Gossip* xt to the Benteng cinema, with its upstairs sco and downstairs karaoke. Arrive late. *bony Disco* in the Manado Plaza Hotel mplex can be a bit of a pick-up joint, or ere's a disco out at NDC, which starts at 8 n.

Pub options include the very expensive *rsius* on the esplanade, which charges 00 rp for a beer; the better value *Bosita*, xt door; and the *Oriental* bar and karaoke n Jl Sudirman near Gelael supermarket. The *cean* restaurant and nightclub offers 'menu' tertainment, with a bizarre mix of dancing, shion shows, drinking competitions, aerobic splays and other events.

Cinema options are expanding. *Studio 21* the southern end of Jl Sam Ratulangi is odern, cold and tends to have more recent eleases. There's also the *Plaza* at the lanado Plaza Hotel, *President* and *Benteng* nemas. Check the local *Manado Post* daily r screening details.

etting There & Away

ir Like Ujung Pandang, there are huge discrepancies between airlines' listed prices and e discounts some agents are prepared to ffer. Enquire at Limbunan (☎ 52009), Jl am Ratulangi 159, or Pola Pelita Express ☎ 60009), Jl Sam Ratulangi 113, and shop round.

You'll find airlines in Manado at the folowing locations: Garuda (☎ 51544), Jl iponegoro 15; Merpati (☎ 64027), near aal 2; Bouraq (☎ 62757, Jl Serapung 27B; empati (☎ 51612) in the Kawanua City lotel; and Mandala at the southern end of Jl am Ratulangi.

Useful connections include Bouraq's vice weekly flights to Davao in the Philipines ($US150 – less if you can persuade it give student or other discounts), direct ights to Singapore on Singapore's carrier

Silk Air ($US260), Bouraq and Merpati's flights to Gorontalo and Palu, and daily flights to Ujung Pandang by all the big domestic carriers. Garuda was planning to service a new route from Manado to Japan, and other new Asian routes should open as tourism and economic interest in Sulawesi grows.

Bus Fares to Gorontalo (10 hours) range from 13,000 to 30,000 rp – the mid-range 17,500 rp older air-con buses are the best. Buses go around the gulf to Palu for 37,500 rp and all the way to Ujung Pandang for 70,000 rp – if you can tolerate the three day haul. Allow for delays during wet weather. These and the Kotamobagu-bound buses (5500 rp) all leave from the Malalayang bus terminal south of Manado.

Boat Pelni (☎ 62844) at Jl Sam Ratulangi 7 opens Monday to Friday from 8 am to 2 pm. It has several large boats calling at the deepwater port of Bitung, near Manado, plus there are smaller ferries out of Manado itself. They tend to call at ports along the coast, go north to Tahuna (Pulau Sangir) and Lirung (Pulau Talaud), or over to Ternate and Ambon. There has long been talk of a regular boat service from Manado to Davao in the Philippines, but only for Indonesian and Filipino nationals.

From Bitung, 1st class/economy fares on the *KM Kerinci* include 175,500/60,500 rp to Ambon and 337,500/114,500 rp to Ujung Pandang. First class/economy fares on the *KM Ciremai*, which sails from Jakarta to Jayapura, include Ternate 87,000/31,000 rp, Banggai 83,500/31,500 rp, Bau Bau 279,000/95,000 rp, Ujung Pandang 286,500/97,500 rp and Jayapura 361,500/122,500 rp. *KM Kambuna* sails westwards, stopping at Toli Toli 109,500/38,500 rp, Pantaloan 156,000/54,000 rp and Balikpapan 205,500/70,500 rp. The *KM Tilongkabila* cruises north to Siau 45,500/20,000 rp, Tahuna 65,300/23,000 rp and Lirung 90,000/32,000 rp; and down Sulawesi's east coast to Gorontalo 63,000/25,000 rp, Luwuk 103,500/36,500 rp,

SULAWESI

Kolonodale 138,000/48,000 rp and Kendari 196,500/67,500 rp and beyond.

Tickets for slow, ageing ferries from Manado are available from stalls outside the port compound north of Pasar 45. Destinations include boats to Tahuna (17,500 rp; 12 hours), Pulau Siau (7500 rp; 10 hours), Lirung (25,000 rp; 11 hours), Ternate (14 hours) and Ambon (28 hours).

Getting Around

The Airport Mikrolets from Sam Ratulangi airport go to Paal-2 (350 rp), where you change mikrolets for Pasar 45 (250 rp) or elsewhere in the city. Taxis run on argo meters. From the airport to the city (13 km) costs 6000 to 7500 rp. There are also infrequent Damri buses from Pasar 45.

Local Transport Transport around town is by mikrolet for a flat fare of 250 rp. Destinations are shown on a card in the front windscreen. There are various bus terminals around town for destinations outside Manado – get to any of them from Pasar 45. Mercifully, the vehicles do not do endless pick-up rounds. Another option for touring the area is to hire a car for 8000 rp per hour. Boats for Pulau Bunaken leave from the fish market.

PULAU BUNAKEN

The wildly varied shapes and colours of the fringing coral off Pulau Bunaken have become an international snorkelling and scuba-diving attraction. The flat coral off **Pantai Liang** takes a dramatic 90 degree turn about 100m offshore, plummeting from one to two metre depths to dark oblivion. Floating over the edge is akin to floating from the top of a skyscraper.

Unfortunately, tourism and plastic have exacted a heavy toll. Westerly winds sweep alarming piles of garbage on to Pantai Liang, turning picturesque tropical beaches into refuse heaps overnight. Unchecked development on the beach has increased the boat traffic across the shallows, destroying acres of flat coral.

Despite the damage, Bunaken remains a world-class attraction. Its dramatic drop-of are largely intact and easily accessible, a there is plenty of good diving on other rec off Bunaken and neighbouring islands. remains to be seen whether the governmen conservation plan for the island group c slow the degradation.

The 800 hectare Pulau Bunaken has abo 2000 residents, most living in **Bunake village** at the southern tip. There is also small settlement on neighbouring **Pula Siladen**. The scarcity of fresh water h limited development and villagers must ir port their drinking water from Manad Washing water is drawn from small, bracki wells. Fishing, coconuts, fruit and now tou ism provide much of Bunaken's income.

There are other coral reefs around t Minahasan peninsula. **Manado Tua**, or 'O Manado', is a dormant volcano you can s off the coast. The Portuguese and Spani once based themselves here to trade betwe northern Sulawesi and Maluku. Nowaday like Pulau Bunaken, it's the coral reefs th pull in visitors. Other coral reefs lie off Pula Mantehage and Bitung.

Diving & Snorkelling

Get your feet wet and float over some of t world's most spectacular and accessib coral drop-offs, caves and valleys. You c buy snorkelling gear from sport shops Manado, such as Toko Akbar Ali on t western boundary of Pasar 45, or hire wel worn masks and snorkels from warung along the beaches on Pulau Bunaken.

The going rate for dive excursions, inclu ing equipment hire and lunch, is arour $US50 in the low season and $US65 in t June-July high season. Fatalities from divin accidents have turned the spotlight on safe and fostered plenty of scuttlebutt as eac operator points to the flawed practices of t others. Much depends on the competence the dive instructors, so be sure to quiz the carefully on equipment maintenance, div planning and other fundamentals. If yc haven't already done your dive training home, snorkelling is a safe and enjoyab option.

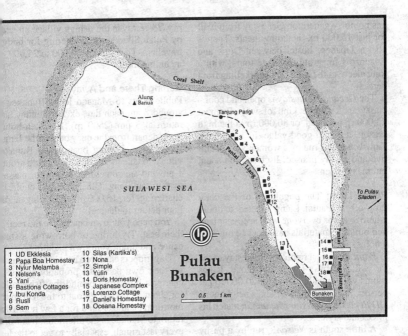

Coral Shelf

Alung
▲ Banua

Tanjung Parigi

SULAWESI SEA

To Pulau
Siladen

**Pulau
Bunaken**

1 UD Ekklesia	10 Silas (Kartika's)
2 Papa Boa Homestay	11 Nona
3 Nyiur Melamba	12 Simple
4 Nelson's	13 Yulin
5 Yani	14 Doris Homestay
6 Bastiona Cottages	15 Japanese Complex
7 Ibu Konda	16 Lorenzo Cottage
8 Rusli	17 Daniel's Homestay
9 Sem	18 Oceana Homestay

0   0.5   1 km

The Nusantara Diving Centre (NDC;
63988; fax 63707) on Molas Beach, Ma-
ado, caters for beginners but not very well.
ay around $US500 for video tuition,
struction, 11 dives and accommodation.

The similarly priced Murex (☎ 66280), Jl
udirman 28, also caters for beginners, while
e swish Baracuda Diving Resort (☎ 62033;
x 64848) at Molas Beach is another com-
ned resort/dive centre. This is the most
xpensive dive school, but has had good
ports.

Bunaken-based operators include the
uch-applauded Ronny at MDC, near
aniels Homestay, and the much-maligned
icki at the similarly priced Riantama Dive
entre in Bunaken village. Judge for yourelf.

Samurindah Paradise Dive Manado
☎ 65298), the Tarsius Celebes Diving Club
☎ 61764), Jl Mongisidi 333, and Manado Sea
arden Diving Club (☎ 66231) at Malalayang
re among the other local operators.

Places to Stay & Eat

There is a range of hastily built homestays
and cottages along Pantai Liang, and a few
more on the quieter, less crowded Pantai
Pangalisang near Bunaken village. Popular
places, such as Daniel's Homestay, set the
standard and smaller ones adapt their rates
accordingly. Most tariffs are negotiable and
all include food.

Pantai Pangalisang *Daniel's Homestay* is
the biggest, most popular place on Pantai
Pangalisang and is heavily promoted by
touts on commission. The cheapest beds are
17,500 rp, including three big meals, or
20,000 to 25,000 rp for bungalows.

Lorenzo Cottage next door is smaller, with
cottages for 17,500 rp per person, including
meals (20,000 rp in the high season), and
15,000 rp (more or less) for homestay rooms.
Lorenzo is a friendly, easy-going guide born-
and-bred on Bunaken.

Doris Homestay at the far end of the beach

SULAWESI

has no noisy generator. Get away from it all for just 15,000 rp, including meals. There's also a Japanese hostel between Doris and Lozenzo's for group package tours, with a long pier over the coral. Try snorkelling from here.

The *Oceana Homestay* is open and cool – classy in a simple kind of way. Even at 25,000 rp per head, or 30,000 rp in the high season, it is still good value. Its neighbour, *Tuwokona*, was run by a women's co-operative and highly praised. It closed too soon, but may reopen.

Pantai Liang The popularity of the coral drop-off at Pantai Liang created a boom where it seems everyone with access to land and building materials has knocked together a homestay.

Papa Boa's is a rambling homestay at the far end, run by a lovely old bloke. It has rooms with outside mandi for 20,000 rp per person, including meals. Papa's neighbours, *UD Ekklesia* and *Nyiur Melambai*, match his prices and style.

A little south is *Nelson's*, run by a pushy character who is quick to find fault with the competition. Rooms cost from 15,000 rp, or cottages up the hill for 50,000 rp.

The next in line, *Yani* is clean and comfortable, with simple quiet rooms from 15,000 rp per person. *Bastiona Cottages* are pretty flash by Bunaken standards – and ask 40,000 rp per head. Negotiate.

Ibu Konda's is the only place with a little distance from its neighbours. Her good cooking and hospitality – not to mention the 15,000 rp tariff – compensate for the sand floors.

Rusli has nicer rooms and mosquito nets at 15,000 rp a night, and *Sem* right next door asks 15,000 rp (more or less), including mask hire and meals. *Kartika's*, *Nona* and *Simple* are three small, similarly priced homestays clustered at the southern end of the beach. Rooms are solid and clean, and cost 15,000 rp per person. *Yulin*, set apart from the rest on its own little stretch of sand, has simple rooms for 15,000 rp.

There is also *Martha Homestay* and *Sting-*

ray Homestay in the fishing village on near by Pulau Siladen, both catering for budg travellers. They charge 20,000 to 25,000 r including meals.

Getting There and Away
Public boats to Manado leave Bunaken around 8 am each day, except Sunday, an return at 3 pm (2500 rp). Bunaken-boun boats depart from the quay behind the Jeng fish market. Fishing boats leave Bunake village to take their catch to Manado arou 1 pm and are sometimes happy for passe gers to tag along. Otherwise you could t chartering for 15,000 rp, including a o hour detour to the reefs.

You need your own boat to see the reefs their best. Try hiring or borrowing a sm canoe and doing your own paddling.

Day trippers can hire a boat in Manado ar set their own pace. It's probably easiest charter a boat from behind the fish mark for about 25,000 rp, go out to the reef in th morning, paddle around for a few hours an return to Manado in the afternoon. It is wor every last rupiah, especially to get to the le crowded islands and reefs, such as tho around Manado Tua.

TOMOHON
Minahasa's extraordinary cuisine is serve in a string of restaurants on a cliff overlool ing Manado, just a few km before Tomoho (see Manado's Places to Eat section earlic in this chapter).

Tomohon has a **vulcanology centr** which monitors and advises on the safety o active volcanoes in the area. Seek advic there and see its monitoring equipmer before tackling gunungs Soputan, Lokon Mahawu. It also has information and spec tacular photographs of other volcanoes, fro Gunung Colo on the Togians, to the leth Gunung Awu on Pulau Sangir. Awu kille 7300 people in an eruption in 1870. Th work of Tomohon's vulcanology centr attempts to averts similar disasters.

About midway between Tomohon an Lahendong, there's the extensive Huta Minahasa, or **Lahendong hot springs**. Als near Lahendong is **Danau Linow**, a small highly sulphurous lake which changes colours with the light. It is possible to hike via small footpaths to **Danau Tondano**, seven km east – ask directions along the way. There are also hot springs, private mineral baths and nice walks near **Langowan**.

Several km out of Tomohon on the road to Tara Tara are some **caves** used by the Japanese forces during WWII. Take a mikrolet from Manado's Pasar Karombasan (Wanea terminal) to Tomohon and another mikrolet towards Tara Tara. There are also mikrolets between Tomohon and Tondano, and between Kawangkoan and Tomohon. Tomohon is the site of a Christian college and a centre for the study of Christian theology in Minahasa.

Places to Stay

The *Happy Flower Homestay* at the foot of the Gunung Lokon volcano is justifiably applauded by all who stay. Simple accommodation, a pretty garden with ponds, cool nights, communal dining and the cheerful hospitality of Tommy and his hard-working mother make this place a delightful refuge. At 7500/9000 rp for singles, and 13,500 rp for doubles, including a cheese and egg jaffle breakfast, the price is unbeatable. See the informative Tommy for advice on climbing Gunung Lokon and other hikes in the area. To get there from Manado, take a Tomohon-bound bus and get out at 'Gereja Pniel', a few km before the centre of town. Take the path opposite the church, walk 300m, cross a stream and look for the homestay tucked away in trees to the right of the path.

The *Lokon Resting Place* (☎ 51203) at Kakaskassen I, Tomohon, is set amid well-groomed gardens with doubles from 75,000 rp and cottages from 125,000 rp.

Kawanua Cottages (☎ 52060), Jl Raya Tomohon, is a new place on the south side of Tomohon, near the Pertamina office. Very comfortable cottages start at 35,000 rp, including breakfast.

SONDER

The people of Sonder are famous for their business acumen. When Minahasan incomes soared during the clove boom of 1970s, Sonder's canny business people diversified their investments and survived the subsequent drop in prices. For a while, they had the highest per capita income in Indonesia. Their wealth and industry shows today in Sonder's architecture.

The town's concession to tourism is the Komplex Walepapetaupan Toar-Lumimuut, a park, swimming pool and landscaped gardens dedicated to the Minahasans' origin myth. Guest accommodation is available for 25,000 rp, or 45,000 rp for bed and breakfast in new rooms overlooking the park. The park also has a guesthouse, *Pondok Wisata Toar Lumimuut*, 100m down the road, opposite the unusual white gothic Sion Protestant church. Large rooms overlooking a pond cost 30,000 to 40,000 rp.

As elsewhere, the easiest way around is by chartered transport, but there are mikrolets from Manado for 1000 rp. En route to Sonder, look out for **Leilem**, a village famed for furniture making.

KAWANGKOAN

During the Japanese occupation in WWII, they dug caves into the hills surrounding Manado to act as air-raid shelters and storage space for ammunition, food, weapons and medical supplies. One such **cave** is three km from Kawangkoan on the road to Kiawa. There are mikrolets to Kawangkoan from Pasar Karombasan (the Wanea terminal) in Manado.

Close to Pinabetengan village, about 40 km from Manado and five km from Kawangkoan is **Watu Pinabetengan**, a place of immense spiritual significance for the Minahasans. It is a stone on a summit, said to be the place where the lands of Minahasa were first divided around 670 AD in a pact to establish the region's system of independent states. There were subsequent meetings to discuss unity, plan insurrection against the Spanish in 1643, organise resistance to Bolaang Mongondow's kings in 1655, attack the Dutch in 1939 and to unite resistance leaders in 1945. Unfortunately, much of the stone and its obscure markings have been smothered by Indonesia's love affair with the bag of cement.

To get there, take a mikrolet to Kawangkoan from Manado's Wanea terminal, then a bendi to Desa Pinabetengan. The bendi takes you as far as the turn-off road that leads to Watu Pinabetengan and then walk the last half hour.

TONDANO

Danau Tondano, a crater lake in an extinct volcano, is 30 km south-west of Manado. It's 600m above sea level, making it pleasantly cool, scenic and an excellent place to visit. In addition, some of the best **Japanese caves** are just outside Tondano on the road to Airmadidi. A bus from Airmadidi to Tondano will get you to the caves in 45 minutes. From the caves you can hitch or walk (one hour) to Tondano mikrolet station and get a mikrolet back to Pasar Karombasan in Manado. Mikrolets from Tondano to Tomohon take 30 minutes.

AIRMADIDI

Airmadidi (literally, boiling water) is the site of mineral springs. Legend has it that nine angels flew down from heaven on nights of the full moon to bathe and frolic here. One night a mortal succeeded in stealing a dress belonging to one of them – unable to return to heaven she was forced to remain on earth. The public baths make a refreshing stop after an overnight hike to the peak of nearby Gunung Klabat.

Airmadidi's real attraction is the odd little pre-Christian tombs known as *waruga*. Corpses were placed in these carved stone boxes in a foetal position with household articles, gold and porcelain – most have been plundered. There's a group of these tombs at **Airmadidi Bawah**, a 15 minute walk from Airmadidi bemo terminal. You can see more warugas at Sawangan and Likupang, and at Kema on the south coast near Bitung.

Mikrolets go to Airmadidi from Manado's Paal-2 terminal (400 rp). From Airmadidi you can also take a mikrolet to Tondano

(1000 rp; 45 minutes) or to Bitung (1000 rp; 40 minutes).

GUNUNG KLABAT

At 2022m, Gunung Klabat is easily the highest peak on the peninsula. The pre-dawn hike to the crater at the top is a hard five hours, but the view across the whole peninsula is spectacular. Within an hour or two of sunrise, the clouds rise and obscure the view, but the hike back to Airmadidi is a bonus because of the rainforest flora and fauna en route. This was the last hideout for the Permesta rebels. It is easy to see how they evaded capture for so long.

BITUNG

Sheltered by Pulau Lembah, Bitung is the chief port of Minahasa and lies to the east of Manado. Many ships dock at Bitung rather than at Manado. There are also many factories here because of the port facilities. Despite its spectacular setting, the town is not very attractive. The Pelni office (☎ 21167) is in the harbour compound.

Places to Stay & Eat

The *Samudra Jaya* (☎ 21333), Jl Sam Ratulangi 2, is cheap and central, with rooms from 15,000 rp, including breakfast. *Penginapan Sansarino* near the main market has rooms for 15,000 rp and a downstairs restaurant. *Penginapan Minang* (☎ 21333) is a dark hovel above a restaurant by the same name at Jl Sam Ratulangi 34. The fanciest place in town is *Dynasty Hotel* (☎ 22111), Jl Sudarso 10, with doubles from 60,000 rp.

A few km north of Bitung is the *Kunkungan Bay Resort*, a swanky diving resort amid coconut plantations on a secluded bay. There is helpful staff, an American dive master and excellent diving. Packages, including accommodation and meals, cost around $US170.

Getting There & Away

Bitung is 50 km from Manado and is connected by a surfaced racetrack along which mikrolet drivers attempt to break land speed records. There are regular departures from

Manado's Paal-2 terminal (1000 rp; one hour). The mikrolet drops you off at the Mapalus terminal just outside Bitung, where you catch another mikrolet into town (300 rp; 10 minutes).

AROUND BITUNG

Tangkoko-Batuangas Dua Saudara

Tangkoko is one of the most impressive and accessible nature reserves in Indonesia. Thirty km from Bitung, it is home to black apes, anoas, babirusa and maleo birds, among others. This national park, an amalgam of several reserves, also includes the coastline and coral gardens offshore.

To enter the park you need a permit from the national parks office, plus 10,000 rp for guides to point the way. Exhausting day trips with knowledgeable guides will lead you to a variety of fauna. Sometimes the rewards are excellent. It is worth taking both dawn and dusk excursions, as each features different fauna.

Stay with *Mama Ruus* for 20,000 rp, including three meals, or at the ranger-run accommodation just inside the park for 15,000 rp. Neither will be a highlight of your travels, but both are conveniently placed for the 5 am rises needed to see the wildlife – the real reason for staying here.

The easiest way to Batuputih, the main entrance to Tangkoko, is by jeep from the Girian (one hour), a terminus on the main road from Manado to Bitung.

SANGIR-TALAUD GROUP

Strewn across the straits between Indonesia and the southern Mindanao region of the Philippines are the island groups of Sangir and Talaud. These small and volcanically active islands are at the end of the long chain of volcanoes that stretches from the western highlands of Sumatra, east through Java and Nusa Tenggara, and then north through the Banda Islands of Maluku to north-east Sulawesi. One of the more recent volcanic eruptions in northern Sulawesi was Gunung Api on Pulau Siau in 1974, which compelled the temporary evacuation of the entire population of the island (then 40,000 people).

The main islands in the Sangir group are Sangir Besar, Siau, Tahulandang and Biaro. The Talaud group consists of Karakelong, Salibabu, Kabaruan, Karatung, Nanusa and Miangas. Despite their tiny size, around 300,000 people live on these islands. The capital of the Sangir-Talaud group is Tahuna on Sangir Besar.

History

Once upon a time these islands were subject to strong Islamic influence from the Ternate sultanate to the south. That was checked by the Christian missionaries who followed in the wake of the Dutch takeover in 1677. Most of the population was converted to Christianity. Prior to the arrival of the missionaries, ancestral spirits were important and some women (and occasionally men) became possessed by spirits. Human sacrifice at various ceremonies was also reported.

Not only did the Dutch bring a new religion, but they also encouraged the local population to raise coconuts (for copra) and nutmeg. The island economy came to rely heavily on trade in these products, chiefly carried on with Ternate and Manado. Today the main industries are copra and cloves.

Getting There & Away

Air Merpati has three flights a week from Manado to Naha, the airfield 20 km from Tahuna, for 105,000 rp. Flights to Melangguane on Karakelong, in the Talaud group, cost another 66,500 rp.

Boat For ships to these islands ask at the shipping offices near the entrance to the harbour terminal in Manado – see under Manado earlier in this section for fare details. There are at least three dodgy companies servicing this route with small ferries, plus Pelni now sends the commodious *KM Tilongkabila* through here on its fortnightly runs. Also ask about ships to Beo and Lirung on Karakelong.

Maluku

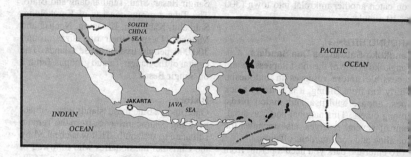

From Halmahera in the north to Wetar off the north-eastern end of Timor are the thousand islands of Maluku (previously called the Moluccas). Sprawled across a vast area of ocean, but making up only a tiny proportion of Indonesia's land area, what these islands lack in size they more than make up for in historical significance. These were the fabled 'Spice Islands' to which Indian, Chinese, Arab and later European traders came in search of the cloves, nutmeg and mace which grew there and nowhere else. It was these islands which bore the brunt of the first European attempts to wrest control of the Indonesian archipelago and the lucrative spice trade.

The island province contains four districts: North Maluku (the capital is Kota Ternate on Pulau Ternate); the oddly shaped and curiously conciliatory Central Halmahera (capital, Soa Siu on Pulau Tidore) Central Maluku (capital, Masohi on Pulau Seram), which does not include Kota Ambon and nearby villages because they are part of a separate municipality; and South-East Maluku (capital, Tual in the Kai Islands).

HISTORY

Before the arrival of Europeans, the sultanate of Ternate held tenuous sway over some of the islands and parts of neighbouring Sulawesi and Irian Jaya, but there was little

---

HIGHLIGHTS

- **A Tropical Paradise** – The scattered island groups of Maluku offer sun, sand and crystal clear water. Studded with buildings and forts dating from the colonial era, plus remnants from WWII, Maluku will take some time to explore fully (at least three weeks by plane or six weeks by boat).
- **Pulau Ambon** – This island's main city, Kota Ambon, is a modern city, and a good base from which to explore great beaches, hiking trails, diving spots and a superbly renovated fort. The nearby islands of Seram, which is undeveloped but offers wonderful scenery, tough trekking and traditional cultures, and Saparua, with its tempting beaches, friendly villages and fort, are perfect side trips.
- **The Bandas** – South of Pulau Ambon, The Bandas are the highlight of Maluku and have it all: magnificent forts; the awesome Gunung Api volcano to admire and climb; stunning diving and swimming; and plenty of islands to explore.
- **Other Islands** – To the north, Ternate has stunning volcanic scenery, black sand beaches and even more forts. Close by, Halmahera, including Morotai and Bacan islands, has unspoiled beaches, crumbling forts, trekking and diving opportunities, and plenty of WWII remnants. Further south, the Kai Islands have arguably the best beaches east of Bali.

political unity. When the Portuguese reached the Indonesian archipelago, Maluku was known to them as the 'land of many kings', or Jazirat-al-Muluk from which the name Maluku apparently originated. (Another explanation – promulgated by the Malukan government – is that Maluku is derived from the words *yasiratul jabal malik* meaning mountainous'.)

The spice trade goes back a lot further than the Portuguese and Dutch presence in this part of the world. The Roman encyclopaedist Pliny described trade in cinnamon and other spices from Indonesia to Madagascar and East Africa and from there to Rome. By the 1st century AD Indonesian trade was firmly established with other parts of Asia, including India and China, and spices also reached Europe through the caravan routes from India and the Persian Gulf.

Apart from Marco Polo and a few wandering missionaries, Portuguese sailors were the first Europeans to set foot on Indonesian soil. Their first small fleet and its 'white Bengalis' (as the local inhabitants called them) arrived in Melaka (Malaysia) in 1509; their prime objective was to reach the Spice Islands. A master plan was devised for the Portuguese to bring all the important Indian Ocean trading posts under Portuguese control. The capture of Melaka in 1511, then Goa (India), preceded the Portuguese attempt to wrest control of the Spice Islands: Ternate, Tidore, Ambon, Seram and The Bandas.

Ternate and Tidore, the tiny, rival clove-producing islands of northern Maluku, were the scene of the greatest Portuguese effort. They were ruled by sultans who controlled the cultivation of cloves and policed the region with fleets of war boats with sails and more than a hundred rowers each. But they had no trading boats of their own – cloves had to be shipped out, and food and other goods imported, on Malay and Javanese ships. Early in the 16th century Ternate granted the Portuguese a monopoly over its clove trade in return for help against Tidore. The Portuguese built their first fortress on Ternate the following year, but relations with the Muslim sultan were continually strained

and they began fighting each other. The Portuguese were finally thrown out in 1575 after their fort had been besieged for several years; undeterred, they ingratiated themselves with the Sultan of Tidore and built another fort on that island.

Meanwhile, Ternate continued to expand its influence under the fiercely Islamic and anti-Portuguese Sultan Baab Ullah and his son Sultan Said. The Portuguese never succeeded in monopolising the clove trade; they moved south to Ambon, Seram and The Bandas, where nutmeg and mace were produced. Again they failed to establish a monopoly – and even had they done so, they lacked the shipping and labour force to control trade in the Indian Ocean. By the end of the 16th century the Dutch arrived bringing better guns, bigger ships, larger financial backing, and an even more lethal combination of courage and brutality.

The first Dutch fleet to Indonesia reached Maluku in 1599 and returned to the Netherlands with enough spices to produce a massive profit. More ships followed and the various Dutch companies eventually merged in 1602 to form the Vereenigde Oost-Indische Compagnieinsert (VOC) whose ships sailed back to Maluku with some devastating consequences for the inhabitants of The Bandas, most of whom were exterminated.

By 1630 the Dutch were established on Ambon in the heart of the Spice Islands and had their headquarters at Batavia (Jakarta) in the west. Melaka fell to them in 1641, but a monopoly of the spice trade eluded them for many years; they first had to fight the Ternateans, and then the Ambonese with their Makassarese allies. It was not until around 1660 that the Dutch finally succeeded in wiping out all local opposition to their rule in Maluku, and not until 1663 that the Spanish, who had also established a small presence, evacuated their remaining posts in Ternate and Tidore. Inevitably, however, the importance of the islands as an international supplier of spices faded, as European competitors managed to set up their own plantations in other countries.

After a brief British occupation of the

MALUKU

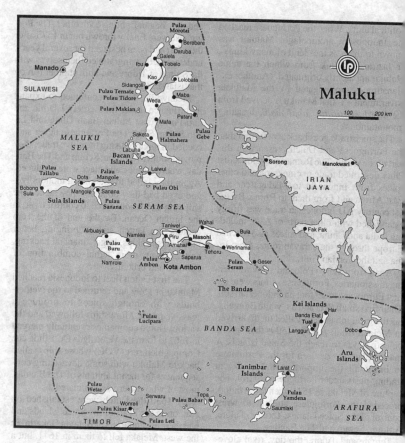

Maluku

0   100   200 km

SULAWESI

MALUKU
SEA

Manado

Pulau
Morotai
Berebere
Danuba
Galela
Ibu   Tobelo
Kao   Lolobata
Sidangoli
Pulau Ternate   Maba
Pulau Tidore
Weda
Pulau Makian   Patani
Mafa   Pulau Gebe
Saketa
Labuha   Pulau
Bacan   Halmahera
Islands
Laiwul
Pulau   Pulau
Tailabu   Mangole
Dofa
Bobong   Mangole   Sanana
Sula   Pulau Obi
Pulau Saumana
Sula Islands   Pulau
Sanana   SERAM SEA

IRIAN
JAYA

Sorong   Manokwari

Fak Fak

Wahai
Taniwel
Airbuaya   Piru   Masohi   Bula
Namlea   Amahai   Werinama
Pulau Buru   Saparua   Tehoru
Namrole   Pulau   Pulau   Geser
Ambon   Seram
Kota Ambon
The Bandas

BANDA SEA

Pulau
Lucipara

Kai Islands   Har
Banda Elat
Tual
Langgur   Dobo

Aru
Islands

Tanimbar
Islands   Larat

Pulau
Wetar   Serwaru   Tepa   Pulau
Wonreli   Pulau Babar   Yamdena
Pulau Kisar   Saumlaki   ARAFURA
Pulau Leti   SEA

TIMOR

MALUKU

Dutch East Indies during the Napoleonic Wars, the Dutch returned in 1814, but soon began to encounter rebellious activity. The first was led by Thomas Matulessy ('Patti-mura' to his friends) in 1817. The uprising lasted only a few months and ended with the capture and execution of Pattimura. He is regarded as one of Indonesia's national heroes – Ambon's university and airport are called Pattimura, as is one of the city's main streets. In the middle of Kota Ambon, a giant statue (built in 1972) depicts Pattimura as a warrior of superhuman proportions. He came from Saparua, a small island just east of

Ambon, was a professed Christian and had been a sergeant-major in the British militia when the British occupied Ambon during the Napoleonic Wars.

When the Dutch left Indonesia after WWII, Maluku was to become part of the State of East Indonesia. However, when it became apparent that (mainly Christian) Maluku was actually going to be part of a (Muslim) Jav-anese republic, an independent Republic of the South Moluccas (Republik Maluku Sela-tan; RMS) was proclaimed in Ambon in 1950. It was supported, it appears, by most of the 2000 or so Ambonese KNIL troops on he island. A large number of Ambonese at he time worked for the Dutch in the civil service, as missionaries or as soldiers of the Loyal Netherlands Indies Army (Koninkljke Nederlandse Indisch Leger; KNIL).

In July 1950 Indonesian government troops occupied Pulau Buru and parts of Pulau Seram and, at the end of September, the first landings on Ambon took place. By the middle of November, most resistance on Ambon had been put down and, in early December, the RMS government fled to the Seram jungles (where many RMS troops had already gone).

At this time there were still several camps of Ambonese KNIL soldiers and their families on Java. Initially the Dutch intended to demobilise them and send them back to Ambon, but it was feared that this would virtually be sending them to their deaths. Instead, the Dutch government moved them (about 12,000) to the Netherlands. It was hoped that once the RMS was suppressed, they could be sent back to Indonesia, but they and their descendants have been in the Netherlands ever since. On Pulau Seram, there continued to be pockets of RMS resistance until the mid-1960s. The impossible dream of an independent 'South Moluccas' still has its adherents among the Malukans in the Netherlands. There was a train hijack in the Netherlands in the mid-1970s; but there has been negligible activity since. These days, many Malukans from the Netherlands, and/or their children, have returned to Maluku to establish businesses or to retire.

Maluku is now politically stable and 'Indonesianised', although, with its slightly Polynesian feel, it remains different from other parts of Indonesia. Despite its location in Indonesia's remote outer provinces, Ambon has as cosmopolitan an air as anywhere east of Denpasar and its people maintain a sense of their own distinctness from other Indonesians.

GEOGRAPHY

Maluku has an area, including sea, of 850,000 sq km, with 90% water and the remaining 10% islands – 1027 of them at last count. The largest islands, Halmahera and Seram, are the most undeveloped and underpopulated, while the smallest, Ambon and The Bandas, are the most populated and developed, mainly because of the past spice trade.

The islands are usually forested and mountainous, with the exception of the swampy Tanimbar and Aru islands in the south-east. The highest mountain is Gunung Binaya (3027m), on Pulau Seram, while many islands, such as Ternate, are simply volcanoes (about 700m high), with villages perched precariously on the side. Over 70 serious eruptions from volcanoes in Maluku have been recorded in the past few hundred years; and earthquakes around the region are not uncommon.

Cloves and nutmeg are still cultivated around the islands, although the quantity and price is nowhere near that of a few centuries ago. Businesses – jointly owned by non-Malukan Indonesians – export cocoa, coffee and fruit, such as bananas, while fishing is a big industry around Halmahera and the southern islands. On Seram, ironwood is heavily logged (ebony and teak on Buru), and oil is also produced.

CLIMATE

Timing a visit to Maluku is a bit different from the rest of Indonesia. In central and southern Maluku, what is referred to as the 'dry monsoon season' (average maximum of 30°C) lasts from October to April; the 'wet monsoon season' (average maximum of 23°C) is from May to August; and the months in between are called the 'transition periods'. However, the northern islands, ie Halmahera and Ternate, have their 'wet monsoon' from December to March.

Maluku is not an area where you can rely on strictly defined wet or dry seasons. Try to avoid the 'wet monsoon season', when it may rain for days on end, but also be prepared for rain at any time, anywhere. To add to the confusion, there are slight variations between each island group and, even on the coasts of Ambon, Halmahera and Seram, it can be clear and dry while the mountainous interiors are cloudy and wet. If you're trekking

MALUKU

in the hinterlands of these islands, be prepared for a lot of rain.

FLORA & FAUNA

Maluku was recognised as a 'transition zone' between Asia and Australia/New Guinea by the famous British naturalist Alfred Wallace, whose exploration of the region inspired Charles Darwin's theory of evolution.

Vegetation is luxuriant and includes some Australian species, such as *kayu putih* (eucalypts) as well as the usual tropical Asiatic species. Maluku hardwoods, such as Amboina, are prized by timber companies. Ambon and Tanimbar islands are famous for their wild orchids, while Ternate has some of the most brilliantly coloured bougainvillea you'll ever see. And, of course, the nutmeg – that little tree that has caused so much strife in the past – is still cultivated on parts of Ambon and Saparua islands, as well as The Bandas.

Cengkeh and Pala

Cloves (*cengkeh*) are still grown on Ternate and Bacan islands, and among the beautiful Bandas, but have also been introduced successfully to Tanzania, Malaysia and Sri Lanka. Cloves are simply dried, unopened buds from the flower of the tree, picked by hand and then dried in the sun. Each year trees, which can grow up to 15m high, produce up to 30 kg of cloves which are used for cooking, and in the manufacture of chewing gum, perfumes and toothpaste.

Nutmeg (*pala*), which was indigenous to Maluku, but is now grown in other tropical places like Brazil as well as Java and Sumatra, thrives in elevated positions near the sea, such as Pulau Banda Besar where you can still visit a nutmeg plantation. The nutmeg tree stands about nine metres tall. It bears yellowish fruit which has three sections: the outer skin is sometimes used by locals, but discarded during official production; the inner bright, orangey-red part is dried for many weeks (usually just on a sheet in the sun – as you will see in The Bandas) and becomes mace; and the inner nut is processed to make the nutmeg spice. Nutmeg and mace, which is regarded as spicier than nutmeg, are used as additives in fruit cakes, seafood sauces and liqueurs. ■

Maluku's seas teem with life, including dugongs, turtles, *trepang* (sea cucumber) sharks, and all manner of tropical and shell fish. In the forests, cuscus and long-nosed bandicoots thrive, while in the more open spaces you may see wallabies, miniature tree kangaroos and Timor deer. Crocodiles and monitor lizards are found in the mangrove regions of the islands in South-East Maluku. All over the province, insect life abounds and the butterflies are particularly brilliant. Pulau Bacan, just off the coast of southern Halmahera, is famous for its unique species of tail-less monkeys.

The birdlife around Seram, particularly in Manusela National Park, is abundant; many species of the bright and noisy *nuri* parrot and the cockatoo are endemic to the island. And with some patience and guidance, you may encounter the shy bird of paradise (*cenderawasih*) in the Aru Islands.

POPULATION & PEOPLE

Maluku has a population of 1,946,000 people, which is only about 1% of Indonesia's total population. It is in the 'transition zone' between the Malays of Asia and the Papuans of Polynesia, resulting in a unique and interesting mixture of people. In Maluku, there is European ancestry, particularly Portuguese, among the Ambonese, Ternateans and around southern Halmaherans. Descendants of people from Polynesian islands as far as Hawaii live in northern Seram, while the Javanese, Buginese and Chinese have intermarried in many places around Maluku over the centuries.

When the Javanese first traded in the region, they often called the indigenous people Alifuro, a less than endearing term meaning 'uncivilised'. The word is now an accepted way to describe the traditional Papuan Alfuro people who inhabit the interiors of Halmahera, Seram and Buru islands. Traditional people still live in the hinterlands of these islands after being driven inland by Javanese, Buginese, Chinese and European settlers over the centuries. Some Alfuros are now re-locating to the less harsh coastal regions.

A high percentage (45%) of Malukans are Christian – they are mainly in the central and southern parts of Maluku. The rest are Muslims, who live primarily in the north, or are not indigenous Malukans.

BOOKS

The 19th century naturalist Alfred Wallace spent six years roaming the Indonesian archipelago, spending much of that time in Maluku. His record of the journey, *The Malay Archipelago*, still makes fascinating reading. Marika Hanbury-Tenison's *A Slice of Spice* details a visit to Ambon and the wilds of Seram in the early 1970s. Lawrence and Lorne Blair's exciting *Ring of Fire* has chapters on The Bandas and the Aru Islands.

For an accurate picture of the current tourist scene in The Bandas, read the relevant chapter of Annabel Sutton's *The Islands In Between*. Shirley Deane's *Ambon, Island of Spices* is a very enjoyable account of her time on Ambon and her travels around Maluku.

For a readable history of the province, try to pick up *Indonesian Banda* by Willard A Hanna and *Turbulent Times Past in Ternate and Tidore* by Hanna and Des Alwi. Both are only available in Bandaneira on Pulau Neira in The Bandas.

PUBLIC HOLIDAYS & SPECIAL EVENTS

With some planning, it shouldn't be hard to fit in a festival or ceremony while in Maluku. They are not the sort of traditional events you would see on Irian Jaya, but are nevertheless a lot of fun. The festivals are often not tourist oriented, so you will be made very welcome by the locals.

January-March

In a *ceremony* in Mamala and Morela (Pulau Ambon), men beat each other with sticks and test the curative powers of a coconut oil a week after the end of Ramadan.

A similar sort of *festival* is held in Pelauw (Pulau Haruku in the Lease Group) every three years; it's next in January 2000.

Hila (Pulau Ambon) celebrates the (Christian) New Year with feasting and singing throughout January.

April-June

On 25 April a *commemoration* for Anzac Day is held at the Commonwealth War Cemetery (Kota Ambon on Pulau Ambon).

In April (and October) *canoe races* are held between islands of The Bandas.

On *Pattimura Day* (14 and 15 May) a flame is run from village to village on Saparua and Ambon islands to celebrate the Ambonese hero.

July-September

The *Darwin to Ambon Yacht Race* finishes each July or August at Amahusu (Pulau Ambon) with a pageant, a 15 km walk from Kota Ambon to Namalatu and lots of drinking.

On 7 September the *Anniversary of Pulau Ambon* (founded in 1517) is celebrated with various traditional ceremonies and dances.

October-December

In October (and April) *canoe races* are held between islands of The Bandas.

On 28 October *canoe races* and a *food festival* are held in Tual (Kai Islands)

On 31 October the *Anniversary of Soa Siu* (Pulau Tidore) is held.

On 3 November the *Anniversary of Masohi* (Pulau Seram) has traditional performances and kite competitions.

On the second Friday of December a 'bizarre village purification *ceremony*' is held in Soya Atas (Pulau Ambon).

On 27 December Pasar Mardika in Kota Ambon is famous for its *Christmas celebrations*.

On 28 December *canoe races* are held in Nolloth (Pulau Saparua).

ACTIVITIES

Ninety per cent of Maluku is ocean, so it is no surprise that scuba and skin diving is spectacular, particulary around The Bandas, Ambon and the neighbouring islands of Seram, Saparua and Nusa Laut. However, with the exception of Ambon and, to a lesser degree, The Bandas, you will need to bring all your own gear, and arrange your own boat and guide. Certificate courses are available on Ambon and The Bandas.

Most of the other 10% of the province is mountainous interior, offering unlimited trekking opportunities. There is a recognised trek across Seram and some smaller trails all around Ambon, while areas of northern Halmahera, with its fantastic volcanoes, volcanic lakes and villages, are begging to be explored. Otherwise you will have to arrange everything yourself and be prepared for lots

MALUKU

of rain and mud. It is relatively easy to scramble to the top of volcanoes in The Bandas and Ternate for indescribable views.

Around Maluku, you can easily find some of the most beautiful beaches in Indonesia – many are all but deserted by foreigners and are usually devoid of locals too. Beaches around Ambon are easy to get to, around Ternate they often have black volcanic sand and around the Lease Group they are picturesque – but the prize goes to the Kai Islands, with its beaches of powder-white sand, lined by angled coconut palms, and turquoise waters.

GETTING THERE & AWAY
Air
The capital of Maluku, Kota Ambon on Pulau Ambon, is connected daily by air to all parts of Indonesia by Merpati and, to a lesser extent, Bouraq, Mandala and Sempati airlines. The main centres for flights to/from western Indonesia are Jakarta, Surabaya (Java) and Denpasar (Bali), often through Ujung Pandang (Sulawesi).

In fact, with the exception of Ternate and Mangole (Sula Islands), which are both connected to Manado (Sulawesi), all flights to Maluku come to Ambon first. (Refer to the Getting There & Away section in the Kota Ambon section and the Maluku Airfares map for more details on flights to Maluku.) The Manado-Ternate and Manado-Mangole flights make northern Maluku a useful alternative stopover between Sulawesi and Irian Jaya.

The weekly Merpati flight (currently every Friday) between Darwin, in northern Australia, and Ambon has made Maluku even more accessible. The short flight costs US$207 one way. In Darwin, you can also find good-value packages, including accommodation and tours, to Ambon for little more than the airfare.

International departure tax from Ambon is 13,000 rp.

Sea
Several Pelni liners connect Maluku reasonably well with the rest of Indonesia every two

weeks. The *Kerinci* links Ambon and Ternate with Bitung (northern Sulawesi) and Bau Bau (southern Sulawesi), and goes onto Java. The *Dobonsolo* connects Ambon with Sorong and other ports of Irian Jaya, Dili (East Timor) and Java. The *Rinjani* has a great route to/from Ambon to The Bandas, Tual in the Kai Islands, Fak Fak in Irian Jaya, and then on to Bau Bau and Java. The *Ciremai* goes from Ternate to Bitung and Sorong, as well as other ports in Irian Jaya, Sulawesi and Java. The four weekly *Tatamailau* links South-East Maluku with Nusa Tenggara and all major ports along both coasts of Irian Jaya.

A ferry sails from Ternate to Bitung several times a week. Other passenger boats connect Maluku with Sulawesi and Irian Jaya, such as the *Asmara*, *Nusa Teratai* and *Namlea Star*, but trips across the seas to Maluku on slow, wooden vessels are more for the adventurous and frugal – it is far better to wait for a Pelni liner to take you to Maluku.

GETTING AROUND

Air

Merpati and, to a lesser degree, Bouraq have an extensive network of flights around Maluku, all of which start and finish at the two transport hubs, Ambon and Ternate. Just about every developed and populated island in Maluku is connected by air to Ambon or Ternate, but sometimes only once a week, so it is often still quicker by boat. To more remote destinations, the small Merpati Twin-Otter flights are sometimes cancelled or delayed for no apparent reason. Merpati often has (but sometimes forgets to check) a 10 kg baggage limit on its Twin-Otters. To avoid an extra (nominal) charge for excess kg, 'cheat' a little by wearing your heaviest clothes and carrying weighty items in your cabin luggage (which isn't weighed). Refer to the individual sections in this book and the Maluku Airfares map for more details on flights around Maluku.

Boat

Pelni doesn't service the islands within Maluku particularly well. The *Kerinci* travels between Ambon and Ternate every two weeks; the *Rinjani* has a very handy two weekly return service between Ambon and The Bandas during the day; and the *Tat-mailau* joins a few more remote southern islands with each other.

If you want to go to more remote places, or can't wait for the Pelni boat, a plethora of other boats is available; they are slower and less comfortable, but invariably cheaper, than Pelni. Perintis is the next best shipping service. The *Nagura*, *Nuburi* and *Iweri* crawl between Ambon and most of the remote southern islands of Maluku every three weeks – often with useful connections to Nusa Tenggara.

Almost all of the other useful boats start and finish in Ambon: the *Karya Laguna* is handy for trips to Bacan and Ternate islands; boats such as the *Asmara* and *Lumba Lumba* ply an interesting route between Ambon and the south coast of Irian Jaya, often through The Bandas; the *Catherina* crawls around Pulau Seram and South-East Maluku; the

Cahaya Pasific does a useful trip to Buru, Sula and Ternate islands every week or so; and the *Cahaya Bahari* sails to the Sula and Ternate islands. These boats are still reasonably comfortable, but they're slow and truly awful in rough seas (as we can attest!)

Between neighbouring islands and among villages on islands with no roads, speedboats and longboats are often the only method of transport – this is especially true along the coasts of northern Seram, South-East Maluku and Halmahera. These boats often only travel when there are enough passengers and can usually be chartered. They always offer an exhilarating ride.

Road

Maluku boasts 79 seaports and 25 airports, but less than 400 km of paved roads. Most of these are on the populated island of Ambon and the longish, but sparsely populated, islands of Halmahera and Seram. Maluku is mountainous and relatively undeveloped, so the roads are almost all potholed and narrow – a 100 km bus trip can easily take over three hours.

Pulau Ambon

Barely a dot on a map of Indonesia, the island of Ambon is the economic and transport centre of Maluku, with a population of 410,000. Its landscape is dramatic and mountainous, with little flat land for cultivation or roads. There are a few good beaches, some old forts (one is superbly renovated) and pretty villages, as well as coral reefs and plenty of opportunities for hiking. To appreciate the island and its culture, you need to get out into the villages where there's a definite Polynesian feel.

The island is just 48 by 22 km, with an area of 770 sq km. The larger northern peninsula is known as Leihitu and the smaller arrow-head shaped southern peninsula is called Leitimur. Kota Ambon, the capital, lies on the Leitimur peninsula, on the southern side of Ambon Bay.

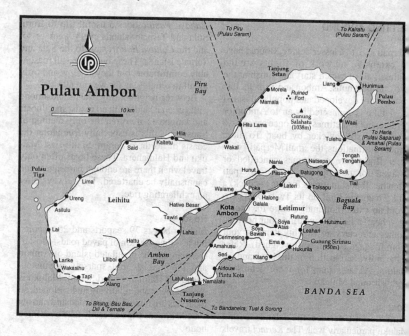

Pulau Ambon

0   5   10 km

To Piru (Pulau Seram)
To Kairatu (Pulau Seram)
To Haria (Pulau Saparua) & Amahai (Pulau Seram)
To Bitung, Bau Bau, Dili & Ternate
To Bandaneira, Tual & Sorong

Piru Bay
BANDA SEA
Baguala Bay
Ambon Bay

Tanjung Setan
Morela
Mamala
Ruined Fort
Liang
Hunimua
Pulau Pombo
Hitu Lama
Gunung Salahatu (1038m)
Waai
Tulehu
Tengah Tengah
Suli
Tial
Hila
Kaitetu
Said
Wakal
Nania
Natsepa
Batugong
Pulau Tiga
Lima
Hunut
Passo
Lateri
Tolsapu
Ureng
Leihitu
Waiame
Poka
Halong
Galala
Rutung
Leitimur
Hutumuri
Asilulu
Hative Besar
Kota Ambon
Soya Atas
Leahari
Tawiri
Cerimesing
Soya Bawah
Lai
Laha
Amahusu
Ema
Gunung Sirimau (950m)
Hattu
Seri
Kilang
Hukurila
Lilibol
Ambon Bay
Airlouw
Pintu Kota
Larike
Wakasihu
Latuhalat
Namalatu
Tapi
Alang
Tanjung Nusaniwe

History

Ambon had the misfortune to be almost at the dead centre of the Spice Islands. The original trade intermediary between central Maluku and western Indonesia was the Sultan of Ternate, who brought Islam to Ambon and seems to have had some influence in reducing the incidence of local head-hunting. The Javanese also showed some interest and established a base at Hitu Lama on the north coast of Ambon. At this time Ambon grew no spices, but was still an important stopover between Ternate and the nutmeg-producing Bandas.

The Ternatean rulers were displaced on Ambon by the Portuguese in 1512, who were then kicked out by the Dutch in 1599. When the Portuguese fort (in what is now Kota Ambon) was about to be attacked, the Portuguese appeared simply to have surrendered and sailed away. The Dutch occupied the fort, renamed it Victoria and made Ambon the base of their spice trade.

The British first settled on the island in 1615, although it was under Dutch control, and then captured the island completely in 1796. Ambon was then re-captured by the Dutch in 1802, taken over again by the British in 1810 during the Napoleonic Wars, but returned to the original 'owners' in 1814. The Dutch probably wished they hadn't bothered when, in 1817, rebellions by some Malukans started.

During WWII, Kota Ambon became a Japanese headquarters and prisoner of war camp. The city was subsequently bombed extensively by Allied planes, destroying most of its colonial and pre-colonial architecture and history. Ambon was the centre of the South Malukan independence movement in the 1950s, but this was extinguished by an invading Indonesian military force a few months later.

KOTA AMBON

Founded by the Dutch in 1517, Kota Ambon,

MALUKU

he capital of Maluku, was once a pleasant
olonial town before it was bombed in WWII
nd subsequently rebuilt. Sitting in the foot-
ills and overlooking a busy harbour, the city
now is not unlike many others in Indonesia,
elying its common moniker, *Ambon man-
se*, or 'beautiful Ambon'. The city doesn't
have a great number of attractions, but the
good facilities make it an ideal place to base
yourself while exploring the island and the
est of Maluku, or as a stopover between
Sulawesi and Irian Jaya.

Orientation

The main streets for shops, and a few restaurants and offices, are Jl Yos Sudarso, Jl Dr
Sam Ratulangi (between which the huge,
new Ambon Plaza shopping centre is
squeezed) and Jl AY Patty. At right angles to
these streets, Jl AM Sangaji, Jl Sultan Hairun
and Jl Raya Pattimura have many offices and
shops. Most of the hotels are in between all
of these streets. The main harbour is at the
junction of Jl Yos Sudarso and Jl AM Sangaji. Along Jl Sultan Babullah, past the
Al-Fatah mosque, the 'Muslim quarter' is a
noisy, vibrant place, with some cheap hotels
and restaurants.

Information

Tourist Office The Government of Maluku
Tourist Office (☎ 52471) is on the ground
floor of the Governor's Office (Kantor Gubernor) on Jl Raya Pattimura (enter from Jl
Sultan Hairun). It's open Monday to Thursday from 7.30 am to 4.30 pm; slightly earlier
on Friday. The helpful staff hand out brochures in English and Japanese, and
reasonable, free maps of Kota Ambon and
island. At the airport, an information booth
is officially open between 7 am and 4 pm
daily, but it may not be staffed.

Money Banks are generally open Monday to
Friday from 8.30 am to 2 pm, and Saturday
morning. One of the best is the Bank Exim
on Jl Raya Pattimura, which sometimes also
opens on public holiday mornings. Also
quick and efficient, Bank Central Asia on Jl
Sultan Hairun can also arrange cash advances

of up to two million rupiah on Visa and
MasterCard. The Bank Bumi Daya near the
Wisma Game on Jl Ahmad Yani is also
useful.

Often there is nowhere to change money
at the airport, which is a real nuisance if you
are arriving from overseas. As Ternate is the
only other place in Maluku where you can
change money, stock up with plenty of
rupiah in Kota Ambon.

Post & Communications The post office on
Jl Raya Pattimura is open Monday to Saturday from 8 am to 8 pm; until midday on
Sunday and public holidays. It has a haphazard, self-service poste restante system which
somehow works.

The modern Telkom office on Jl Dr JB
Sitanala, in the western part of the city, is
open 24 hours. You'll need to take a *becak*
(bicycle-rickshaw) or a LIN III yellow *bemo*.
More convenient *wartels* (for telephones and
faxes) can be found around the main roads,
such as Jl Diponegoro and Jl Anthony Rhebok.

Emergency The police headquarters (☎ 110)
is on the corner of Jl Rijali and Jl Raya
Pattimura. The general public hospitals are
Rumah Sakit Umum (☎ 43438), Jl Dr Kaya-
doe, and Rumah Sakit GPM (☎ 52373) on Jl
Anthony Rhebok. There's also an ambulance
service (☎ 118).

Markets

The bemo and bus terminals are based in and
around the Mardika and Batu Merah markets. While there are plenty of shops and
stalls, these concrete markets are constantly
noisy and dirty. The daily food market in the
village of Batu Merah, between the bus terminal and the main north-east road, is far
quieter and the closest 'village market' to the
city. Along Jl Yos Sudarso, towards the port,
masses of people sell masses of things, including fresh fish. New shopping centres like
the Ambon Plaza may eventually make some
of these markets obsolete.

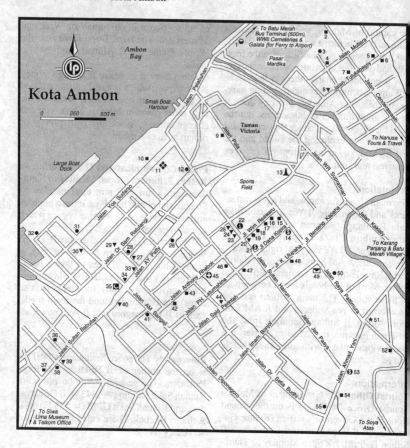

Kota Ambon

Ambon Bay

To Batu Merah
Bus Terminal (500m),
WWII Cemeteries &
Galala (for Ferry to Airport)

Pasar Mardika

Small Boat Harbour

Taman Victoria

Large Boat Dock

Sports Field

To Nanusa Tours & Travel

To Karang Panjang & Batu Merah Village

To Siwa Lima Museum & Telkom Office

To Soya Atas

Siwa Lima Museum

Well worth a visit, this museum (☎ 42841) contains a fascinating collection of Malukan, Indonesian and colonial artefacts, housing and clothing (with captions in English and Indonesian). There are also nice views from the museum, and the countryside nearby is great to hike around. Take the Amahusu or Taman Makmur bemo (300 rp). Ask the driver to let you off; the museum is a 10 minute walk at the top of a steep road. It's usually open daily, except Monday, from 8 am to 2 pm, but it's worth ringing first to make sure.

War Cemeteries

The **Doolan Memorial** is dedicated to an heroic Australian WWII serviceman, and generally to other unknown Australian WWII soldiers, but it's just a small, scrappy monument. Take the bemo to Kudamati and ask to be dropped off at the Tugu Doolan.

Far, far more interesting, the **Commonwealth War Cemetery**, in the suburb of Tantui, has stones and plaques for over 2000 Australian, Dutch, British and Indian servicemen killed in Sulawesi and Maluku during WWII. The gardens and layout are quite superb and it's worth a look around if

PLACES TO STAY		PLACES TO EAT		OTHER	
2	Hotel Mardika	52	Hotel Ramayana	1	Mardika Bemo Terminal
4	Wisata Hotel	54	Wisma Game	3	Boura Office
5	Hotel Cendrawasih			11	Matahari Department
6	Penginapan Simponi	**PLACES TO EAT**			Store & Ambon Plaza
7	Josiba Hotel	8	Citra Supermarket &	12	Amboina Theatre
9	Penginapan Sumber		Cafeteria	13	Pattimura Memorial
	Asia	20	Yang-Yang	14	Bank Exim
10	Hotel Maluku	23	Halim's Restaurant	21	Bank Central Asia
15	Hotel Mutiara	24	Tip Top Restaurant	22	Tourist Office
16	Hotel Transit Rezfanny	25	Restaurant Sakura	26	Mandala
17	Penginapan Beta	27	Andre's	28	PT Tujuh Jaya
18	Hotel Hero	29	CFC	31	Port Entrance
19	Baliwerti Hotel	30	Ratu Gurih	32	Pelni Office
36	Penginapan Wisma	33	Restoran Amboina	35	Al-Fatah Mosque
	Jaya	34	Sangranii	41	Sempat Office
37	Penginapan Nisma	39	Rumah Makan Ai	45	Rumah Sakit GPM
38	Hotel Abdulalie		Madur II		(Hospital)
42	Penginapan Gamalama	40	Rumah Makan Jawa	49	Post Office
43	Hotel Elenoor		Timur	50	Rinamakana
46	Limas Hotel	44	Rumah Makan Ujung	51	Police Headquarters
47	Hotel Carlo		Pandang	53	Bank Bumi Daya
48	Hotel Amboina			55	Merpati/Garuda Office

only for the peace and quiet. If the front gate is locked, use the side entrance. A ceremony is held here every ANZAC Day (25 April). A Tantui bemo takes you straight past the cemetery. To return, take the Tantui bemo which circles back to the terminal.

On the same road, closer to the city, the less-impressive **Taman Makam Pahlawan Indonesia** (Indonesian Heroes Cemetery) is dedicated to Indonesian servicemen killed fighting Malukan rebels during the 1950s and 1960s.

Other Attractions

The **Pattimura Memorial** stands at one end of the sports field. Pattimura – really called Thomas Matulessy – rallied against the Dutch in 1817, only to be betrayed by one of the village chiefs on Pulau Saparua who took him prisoner and delivered him to the Dutch on Ambon. The monument stands on the site where he and his followers were hanged.

Across from the monument, the few remains of the once-opulent Dutch fort **Benteng Victoria**, actually built in the late 16th century by the Portuguese, are now located in the army barracks and, therefore, off limits. Nearby, **Taman Victoria** (Victoria

Park) has been cleaned up and now offers some welcome space and greenery.

In the new suburb of Karang Panjang, the **Martha Christina Tiahahu Memorial** honours another Maluku freedom fighter. Tiahahu's father supported Pattimura against the Dutch and, after they were both captured, her father was executed on Pulau Nusa Laut and she was put on a ship to Java. Grieved by her father's execution, she starved herself to death and her remains were thrown into the sea. The memorial isn't that exciting, but the views of the city are captivating. Take the bemo marked KarPan.

Organised Tours

For organised tours around the city, Pulau Ambon and other nearby islands, Nanusa Tours & Travel (☎ 55334), Jl Rijali 53, is worth visiting. Some small agencies around the port are handy for buying Pelni tickets. For diving tours, refer to Diving in Around Pulau Ambon later in this section.

Places to Stay

While there is nothing really cheap in the city, discounts are always possible (especially if you are staying for a while) and reasonably good value can often be found. A

MALUKU

number of places to stay are also springing up around the island. They are generally quieter and better value than Kota Ambon, but still easily accessible to the city. Refer to the Around Pulau Ambon entry later in this section for details.

Places to Stay – bottom end

Central *Penginapan Gamalama* (☎ 53724), Jl Anthony Rhebok 27, is a decent place to stay. Singles/doubles are 13,200/19,250 rp with private mandi. Ask for quieter rooms upstairs, and get there early – it is often full. Next door, the *Hotel Eleonoor* (☎ 52834) has rooms with mandi for 26,400/38,400 rp; slightly more with air-con. The hotel, and landlady, have some charm which is unusual for Ambon.

The *Penginapan Beta* (☎ 53463), Jl Wim Reawaru 114, is deservedly popular and one of the best value places in town. Clean rooms with verandahs, mandi and fan are 14,000/21,000 rp. Next door, the *Hotel Transit Rezfanny* (☎ 42300) has rooms with shared mandi for 14,000 rp; more with air-con. Rooms overlook the inside (reasonable) bar and restaurant so it can be noisy.

The *Penginapan Sumber Asia* (☎ 56587), Jl Pala 34, is conveniently close to the small boat harbour and terminals. It's clean and well-run, with a range of rooms starting from 17,500 rp; 40,000 rp with air-con and TV. Also convenient – but it may double as a brothel – is the *Hotel Maluku* (☎ 51686) on Jl Yos Sudarso. Large, seedy rooms with mandi start from 15,000 rp.

Behind the police headquarters, on Jl Sirimau, a good option is the *Hotel Ramayana* (☎ 53369). The quiet rooms (some have no outside windows) are a reasonable 12,500 rp without fan or mandi; double that for air-con and mandi. Nearby, the *Wisma Game* (☎ 53525), Jl Ahmad Yani 12, not far from the Merpati office, continues to be a popular choice. Its rooms with fan, but outside mandi, cost 13,000/19,500 rp, or 17,500/30,000 rp with mandi.

The part of town known as the 'Muslim quarter', about 500m south-west of the main mosque, has several good cheap places,

although the area is a little inconvenient and noisy. On Jl Sultan Babullah, the *Hotel Abdulalie* (☎ 52057) has dorm-style beds for 12,500 rp; better rooms with fan, mandi and TV start from 17,000/20,000 rp. Opposite, the *Penginapan Nisma* (☎ 53942) has comfortable singles for 23,100 rp; a double with air-con and mandi is 44,000 rp.

The best in this area is the family-run and quieter *Penginapan Wisma Jaya* (☎ 41545) – look for the sign on Jl Sultan Babullah. Rooms, some sans outside windows, start at 16,500/22,000 rp with share mandi, or a fairly reasonable 27,000/32,000 rp for air-con and mandi.

Places to Stay – middle

Hotel Hero (☎ 42978) on Jl Wim Reawaru, next to the Beta, is good value in this range. All rooms, with TV, hot water and air-con, start at 40,000 rp – a discount is possible. Next door, the modern, comfortable and often empty *Baliwerti Hotel* (☎ 55996) has rooms with air-con and TV from 50,000 rp.

Around the Mardika bemo terminal and market are several convenient places if you can't be bothered lugging your pack into town, but otherwise they aren't great value. *Wisata Hotel* (☎ 53293) on Jl Mutiara is neat and comfortable. Rooms with hot water, TV, fridge and air-con start from 36,000 rp. Along Jl Tulukabessy, *Hotel Cendrawasih* (☎ 52487) and *Hotel Josiba* (☎ 42220) offer rooms with similar standards and service for 50,000/65,000 rp. Opposite, *Penginapan Simponi* (☎ 54305) is the cheapest in this area. Rooms with fan cost 22,000 rp, but this still isn't great value. The best in this area, the *Hotel Mardika*, on Jl Cenderawasih, is convenient and friendly, with rooms for 35,000 rp with air-con.

Quiet and clean rooms, centrally located just off Jl Anthony Rhebok, can be found at the *Hotel Carlo* (☎ 42220) on Jl Philip Latumahina 24A for 35,200 rp per room with fan, or 40,700 rp with air-con; and at the *Limas Hotel* (☎ 53269) on Jl Kamboja for 20,500/27,000 rp without mandi.

To avoid an early morning chartered taxi ride to the airport, or if you're just transiting

Kota Ambon, the *Hotel Maluku* (☎ 61415), five minutes by bemo or 25 minutes' walk east from the airport, saves you the long trip into town. If you ring, staff will pick you up (free) from the airport and will also take you there the next day. Negotiable, clean rooms cost from 30,000 rp.

Places to Stay – top end

The city has a surprising number of top range hotels. All have the modern conveniences you would expect for the high prices, but they are really nothing special. Singles/doubles start from around US$40/50, plus the obligatory 20% tax, and go up and up. The better hotels are the *Hotel Amboina* (☎ 41725) on Jl Kapitan Ulupaha and the *Hotel Mutiara* (☎ 53075) along Jl Raya Pattimura. In this range, the resorts around the island are better value – refer to the Around Pulau Ambon section for details.

Places to Eat

For genuine Ambonese food – such as colo colo, a type of sweet and sour sauce particularly delicious on baked fish, and kohu kohu, an odd sort of fish salad – you will probably have to go out into the villages around the island.

The cheapest places in the city naturally congregate around the bemo terminals, markets and along the waterfront, and also around the Penginapan Sumber Asia. During the evening, the footpath of Jl AM Sangaji is lined with women selling huge plates of nasi campur from around 1500 rp.

Ratu Gurih, near the port on Jl AM Sangaji, is popular with locals. Great baked fish is a speciality for 3000 to 7000 rp. One of the best places in the 'Muslim quarter', *Rumah Makan Ai Madura II*, on Jl Sultan Babullah, serves good, reasonably priced Javanese food.

On Jl Said Perintah, you can try Sulawesian food from around 2500 rp a dish at *Rumah Makan Ujung Pandang*, among a couple of others.

Halim's Restaurant on Jl Sultan Hairun is always popular, but often too busy. Good Chinese food costs around 7500 rp and the beer is always ice cold for the frequent Australian clientele. Next door, the *Tip Top Restaurant* (especially recommended for seafood at about 8500 rp a plate) and *Restaurant Sakura* are also good, and are generally cheaper and quieter than Halim's.

Restoran Amboina on Jl AY Patty has simple decor, but it's recommended for the quality and range of meals, ice creams and cakes. It's very popular with many Ambonese. *Andre's* on Jl Kopra, just off Jl AY Patty, has delicious assorted donuts (500 rp each), ice cream and pizza slices, but watch out for a bit of overcharging.

Conveniently along Jl Wim Reawaru, *Yang-Yang* has a nice open-air setting. Dishes, such as baked fish, cost from around 5000 rp, but a few other dishes are overpriced and cater for the tourist market.

The eatery on the 3rd floor of the *Matahari department store* in the Ambon Plaza is an air-conditioned relief. It has a range of good Asian meals (from 3000 to 5000 rp) and more expensive western food, such as spaghetti (9000 rp) and steak (12,000 rp). The cafeteria in the *Citra Supermarket* on Jl Tulukabessy, at the back of the Mardika terminal, has a tempting range of cheap dishes like nasi campur from 2000 rp.

The Colonel has now come to Ambon; *KFC* has a restaurant in the Ambon Plaza. The Indonesian equivalent, *CFC*, is also in the Plaza and along Jl Dr Sam Ratulangi.

For a splurge, the *Sangranii* on Jl AM Sangraji, opposite the mosque, has some of the best food in the city (dishes from 7000 to 10,000 rp) and excellent service. Also opposite the mosque, *Rumah Makan Jawa Timur* has a vast selection – the baked fish for 6000 rp is particularly good.

Entertainment

Kota Ambon doesn't offer much in the way of entertainment. The *Amboina Theatre*, on the corner of Jl Dr Sam Ratulangi and Jl Sultan Hairun, shows reasonably new films in English, French and Chinese languages (with Indonesian subtitles) for 2500 rp. The modern cinema at the top of the *Ambon Plaza* has better films in more comfort for

MALUKU

5000 rp. A number of particularly seedy bars, most with (the dreaded) karaoke machines, are located around the bemo and bus terminals; better and more convenient bars are along Jl Diponegoro. There are a few nightclubs for dancing and drinking along Jl AY Patty, and some tourist bars in nearby Amahusu and Halong.

Things to Buy

Jl AY Patty is lined with dozens of shops selling just about every conceivable tacky souvenir. Interesting, but a little smelly, are individual 'sculptures' made from cloves. These are priced from around 20,000 rp.

Exquisite, but often a little garish, are the portraits of birds, flowers and ships made from oyster shells on a black velvet background. As an example, a framed mid-sized portrait of two birds of paradise might set you back, after bargaining, about 75,000 rp. Oyster shell brooches are cheaper at around 2000 rp and a little easier to carry around. Some turtle-shell products are still for sale, but please don't encourage this by buying any.

It's worth a look around the small, hard-to-find Rinamakana shop, opposite the post

---

Oyster Shell Art

If you spend any time in Kota Ambon you can't help but notice, and admire, the portraits made from oyster shells (kulit mutiara). The art, which possibly dates back to the 15th century and seemed to flourish during the Japanese occupation in WWII, has recently resurfaced for the tourist industry. The oyster shells are carefully broken, painstakingly sliced into various shapes and then glued onto black velvet to make portraits, usually of the more saleable birds of paradise, Dutch galleons, horses and symbols from the Koran.

The village of Batu Merah, which is now part of Kota Ambon's sprawling mass, is still the centre for this ancient and complicated art. You can see the portraits being made, and buy one cheaper (with bargaining) than from the souvenir shops in the city, at several places around the Batu Merah mosque, along the main northeast road out of the city. ■

---

office on Jl Raya Pattimura. Here you ca pick up some authentic artefacts from a over Maluku, which is handy if you car make it out to places like the Kai Islands.

Getting There & Away

Air Kota Ambon is the centre for all fligh to and from Maluku, with the exception flights to/from Manado through Ternate ar Mangole (Sula Islands). Merpati is the maj carrier.

Locally, Merpati flies directly and reg larly to Bandaneira (92,900 rp), Terna (155,600 rp), Langgur (173,200 rp) in th Kai Islands and Saumlaki (183,100 rp) in th Tanimbars. To Irian Jaya, there are dai flights to the hubs of Biak (227,000 rp) ar Sorong (127,000 rp). Elsewhere in Indon sia, Merpati goes daily to Ujung Pandar (226,000 rp), with frequent connections other places such as Kupang, Denpasar ar Jakarta. For other destinations, check th Maluku Airfares map or the relevant individ ual sections.

The Merpati/Garuda office (☎ 52481) Jl Ahmad Yani 19 is open daily from 8 am t 7 pm; and from 10 am to 3 pm on Sunda and public holidays. The office cannot (c will not) confirm flights other than thos leaving Ambon, so it pays, if possible, t confirm your return ticket before flying to remote island with irregular flights.

Other airlines (with offices open daily service Kota Ambon for virtually the sam price as Merpati and each other. Mandal (☎ 42551), at Jl AY Patty 21, flies to Ujun Pandang, Surabaya (404,300 rp) and Jakart (464,700 rp) daily. Bouraq (☎ 51942), jus off Jl Mutiara, flies daily to Ternate and the onto Manado (236,100 rp) three times week, and regularly to Langgur. Sempat (☎ 51612), Jl AM Sangaji 46, flies daily t Surabaya, with connections to Jakarta an other places.

Boat Three large Pelni liners come to Am bon every two weeks. The *Kerinci* goes t Bitung (northern Sulawesi) for 33,000 126,000 rp in economy/1st class, Ternat (49,000/148,500 rp) and return, and Ba au, in southern Sulawesi (33,000/137,000). The *Rinjani* also sails to Bau Bau, has a seful return trip (both during the day) to andaneira (16,000/57,000 rp) and con- ures onto Tual (29,000/113,000 rp) in the ai Islands. The *Dobonsolo* travels to Dili, East Timor (37,500/124,000 rp) and to orong, Irian Jaya (29,000/112,500 rp).

The Pelni office (☎ 52049), in the main arbour complex on Jl Pelabuhan, is open om 8 am to 5 pm weekdays for informa- on; and from 9 am to midday daily for ticket ales when a boat is due to arrive or depart. or hassle-free tickets, try the numerous cket agencies (often open after hours) round the port area.

Other more basic boats going to lesser slands in Maluku usually leave from the arbour at the end of Jl Pala. A board at the arbour entrance shows what's going where nd when. Refer to the Maluku Getting here & Away and Getting Around sections, nd the individual chapters, for more details n boats run by Perintis and other shipping ines. Tickets for these boats are all available n offices around the city port area.

Ferries and speedboats between Ambon nd Saparua and Seram islands leave from he Hurnala port, just north of Tulehu, and rom Hunimua, near Liang – refer to the elevant sections for details.

Getting Around

The Airport Pattimura airport is 36 km from he city, on the other side of the bay – allow n hour for all forms of transport. Official irect taxis cost 20,000 rp, but will cost less f you bargain with the driver in the carpark.

The quickest, and most reliable, form of ransport is a combination of the regular PokaLaha bemo from the airport to the port of Poka (350 rp), the ferry across to Galala 200 rp) and then a bemo (250 rp) to the Mardika terminal. The daily Poka-Galala erry operates every few minutes from 6 am o midnight, so an early morning Merpati check-in (Bouraq and Sempati usually pro- vide free transport for early morning flights) may require a pre-arranged, expensive char- ered taxi – or avoid this by staying at the

Hotel Maluku (see the earlier Places to Stay section) near the airport the night before your departure.

Another good option, especially if you have some bulky luggage, is the comfortable DAMRI bus (3500 rp) which should be waiting in the airport carpark. It will take you directly to your hotel if it's centrally located.

Local Transport Getting around the city is fairly easy. Becaks (thousands of them with different colours on different days) cost about 1000 rp for a short trip, but foreigners are usually charged more and it's hard to bargain. Becaks will not go all the way into the bus or bemo terminals (you'll know why when you see the terminals!); instead they congregate around the nearby Wisata Hotel.

From the Mardika terminal, which is the most confusing mass of vehicles in eastern Indonesia, bemos go to all places in the city and southern peninsula. Bemos are well marked, and colour coded:

Yellow – all around the city and to Galala, Tantui, Amahusu, Takman Makmur, Karang Panjang (Kar-Pan) and Kudamati. Public transport around the city is cheap, crowded and their routes are usually confus- ing. Bemos stop only at designated places – you can't just flag one down from anywhere. In the city, each trip costs a standard 250 rp.
Red – to Hunut and Suli, and places towards the airport
Green – along the southern road to Namalatu and Latuhalat, and to Seri
Blue – to eastern villages, such as Leahari and Hutumuri, and up to Passo (for Natsepa) at the isthmus of the two peninsulas
Orange – to Soya Atas

From the Batu Merah terminal, a 10 minute walk further east of the Mardika terminal, buses (and even a few bemos, just to add to the confusion) with marked destinations, but of any colour, leave from specific lanes to everywhere else on the island: ie Liang (also for Hunimua, Tulehu and Waai); Hila; Hitu Lama, as far west as Asilulu and Liliboi; and many to Seram. Just keep walking along the front of the terminal until you find the lane with your bus.

AROUND PULAU AMBON

Pulau Ambon was once two separate islands but is now joined at Passo by a short isthmus between the northern peninsula (Leihitu) and the southern peninsula (Leitimur). There is plenty to see around the island, and it's easy enough to day trip from the city once you get the hang of the bemo and bus terminals (see the previous Getting Around section).

Public transport goes as far as Larike via the northern road on Leihitu, and as far as Liliboi on the southern road of the northern peninsula. To more remote places in the far west, such as Alang, boats leave daily from the small boat harbour in Kota Ambon. In the north-east, the main road and public transport finishes at Liang and Morela.

Around the Leitimur peninsula, roads and public transport connect the city with Latuhalat/Namalatu, Seri and Leahari. Along the south coast, between Leahari and Seri, the roads and public transport are often not reliable and sometimes non-existent.

Chartering a bemo for around 10,000 rp per hour is an excellent way of seeing the island, especially if you can get a group together. Ask, and bargain, at the terminal.

Diving

Pulau Ambon, and nearby islands, offer outstanding reefs and marine life for diving virtually year-round – the roughest time is from April to June. Popular dive sites include: Namalatu nearby; Pintu Kota and Leahari in the south; Tanjung Setan (Devil's Point) and Pulau Pombo in the north-east; Pulau Tiga in the south-west; and off the south-western cape of Pulau Seram. New sites are constantly being discovered and explored.

For information and equipment hire in Kota Ambon, you could try PT Tujuh Jaya (☎ 52342) on Jl Kopra, between Jl Dr Sam Ratulangi and Jl AY Patty. Better still, contact the Ambon Dive Centre (☎ 62101; fax 62104) opposite the entrance to the Namalatu beach, which is constantly recommended by users. The centre organises all day diving packages around Pulau Ambon, including two dives, transfers, gear, guide, boat and lunch from US$70; and five da all-inclusive certificate courses for US$350

Leihitu

Pantai Natsepa This is a lovely swimmin beach about 25 minutes (take the Passo o Suli bemo; 600 rp) from the city. On Sunda it's crowded, but certainly more entertain ing; normally the beach is empty. There's small entrance fee to the beach and to th **Taman Lunterse Boer** beach and park ju down the road.

Right on the beach, *Vaneysa Paradis* (☎ 61451) offers rooms with mandi, grea views and a quiet location for 30,000 rp, an 'bungalows' sleeping four people for 50,00 rp. (If you're staying there, enter from the to of the hill to avoid paying the entrance fee the beach.) The setting of its restaurant worth a trip out from the city. It serves del cious, cheap Indonesian food, but watch ov because the menu doesn't list prices. Ove

The beaches on Pulau Ambon and surroundin islands provide nesting sites for the Green Turtle The world's largest hard-shell sea turtle, it is an endangered species widely sought for its meat eggs, leather and carapace.

he road, the *Sea View Restaurant* is a little
more upmarket and serves cold beer.

On the main road, the *Miranda Beach
Hotel & Restaurant* (☎ 61244) is friendly,
but reasonably noisy and has no views.
Rooms cost 20,000 rp with fan; 30,000 rp
with air-con.

Waai Continuing north, Waai village has a
nice beach, but is more famous as the home
of the sacred eels in **Waiselaka Pool**. The
recalcitrant (over-fed?) eels are enticed out
from under the rocks by a villager with an
egg. The eel very quickly darts out and sucks
out the yolk from a hole in the shell. If you
see the eel (and you probably will), it's meant
to bring good luck. The pool is behind the
large church, which is on the main road and
opposite the port.

Liang & Hunimua The road continues as far
as Liang (via Hunimua), where there are
some lovely deserted beaches. From the city,
buses to Liang and Hunimua leave regularly
(1500 rp; one hour). Ferries depart Hunimua
daily for Waiprit on Pulau Seram.

Pulau Pombo This tiny, alluring island off
the north-east coast is now part of the Pombo
Island Marine Park. The combination of low
tides and clear water provide astounding
scuba and skin diving around the coral reefs.

You can stay in some huts on the island,
but you need to obtain permission first from
the relevant government office in Kota
Ambon (☎ 52602 or 43619) or ask at the
Kota Ambon tourist office. Bring your own
food and water.

The bad news is that you can only reliably
reach the island by chartered boat which will
be expensive (about 50,000 rp return) from
Tulehu, Waai or Liang. You may be lucky
and find a passenger boat from Waai, or take
an organised tour with a travel or diving
agency.

Hila & Kaitetu Hila's strategic position on
the north coast, overlooking Seram (once a
serious rival), has resulted in a long and
fascinating pre-colonial and colonial history.

The magnificently restored **Benteng Amsterdam** fort is grandly positioned along the
pretty coast. Originally built by the Portuguese in 1512, then taken over by the Dutch
VOC in the early 17th century, the fort is one
of the best in Maluku and is definitely worth
a visit. The fort is also famous as a former
residence of the respected, blind Ambonese
naturalist and author, GE Rumphius. Ask the
guard at the office, next to the small museum,
to show you inside the old spice warehouse.

Almost next door, the quaint Protestant
Immanuel Church is claimed as the oldest
church in Indonesia. Built in 1580 by the
Catholic Portuguese, but then taken over by
a Protestant Dutch governor 200 years later,
the church has been extensively restored
since. Ask the woman next door to let you in
(there's a helpful notice in English inside the
church which explains its history) or attend
a Sunday service. Hila celebrates the (Christian) New Year with feasting and singing
throughout January.

At the intersection where Christian Hila
and Muslim Kaitetu meet, only five minutes'
walk from the church, is the **Mesjid Wapaue**
mosque. Originally built in 1414 on nearby
Gunung Wawane, it was moved to the present site in 1664. According to some legends,
the mosque was moved by supernatural
powers. Direct buses (more regularly in the
morning) leave the city every hour or so
(1300 rp; 1½ hours).

Leitimur

Amahusu Along the road heading south-
west from the city, Amahusu is the finish
point and dock for the annual Darwin to
Ambon Yacht Race. There is really no beach
as such, but the coral around here is said to
be reasonable for snorkelling. The *Tirtha
Kencana Hotel* (☎ 42324) has comfortable
bungalow-style accommodation with air-
con, hot water and TV from 60,500 rp. The
hotel is a good place for a meal or drink while
watching the sun set. Bemos there cost 300
rp.

Namalatu & Latuhalat Along the south
coast, Namalatu ('King's Name') is the

MALUKU

pleasant public beach in the village of Lat-uhalat ('King of the West'). There's good scuba diving and snorkelling on coral reefs offshore and in nearby coves. Regular bemos cost 600 rp.

Two resorts offer comfortable bungalow-style rooms from around 60,000 to 75,000 rp with air-con and hot water: the *Santai Beach Resort* (☎ 56581), just off the main road; and the *Lelisa Beach Resort* (☎ 62106), on the main road. Their small artificial, sandy beaches, with restaurant and bar, are available to non-guests for about 500 rp.

On the main road in Latuhalat, the homey and new *Homestay Europa* (☎ 62105) is already popular. The prices are a little odd – 25,000 rp for a single with fan; 30,000 rp for a double with air-con – but the young, Dutch owners provide very good service.

Pintu Kota Not far from Namalatu, this small rocky beach (meaning 'city door') has some outstanding scuba diving (but beware of strong currents) and plenty of rocks to clamber around and admire the view. Costing 500 rp to enter, the beach is about a 30 minute walk from the village of **Airlouw** (600 rp by bemo from Kota Ambon), famous for its brick making. If you walk further north for a few km from Airlouw, you reach the traditional village of **Seri**, which is connected by bemo to the city.

Soya Atas & Gunung Sirimau Infrequent bemos (400 rp) go to the pretty village of Soya Atas, perched on the slope of Gunung Sirimau (950m) and famous for its bizarre 'village purification ceremony' on the second Friday of every December. The quaint church opposite the village square was built in the early 19th century.

A walk up the narrow, obvious path for half an hour takes you to the top of the hill for some stupendous views of the city and harbour. At the top, there is meant to be a sacred urn called *tempayang setan* (devil's urn) permanently filled with water. The urn may not be there, but if you see it magically fill with water you will be guaranteed instant good fortune.

From the top of the hill, gentle narrow trails (you'll need to ask for exact directions) lead past some WWII trenches to villages on the south coast, such as **Ema**, **Kilang** and **Hukurila**, (in)famous as the base for the distillation of Sopi liquor made from sugar palm leaves. A walk along Jl Sirimau, which starts behind the police headquarters in Kota Ambon, to the top of Sirimau shouldn't take more than a couple of hours; or take the bemo up to Soya Atas and walk down to the city.

The Lease Group

Formerly the Uliassers, this small group east of Ambon consists of Haruku, Saparua, Nusa Laut and Molana islands. Saparua, the most populated, developed and accessible island, is where the revered independence hero Pattimura, fought the Dutch but was later betrayed, handed over to the Dutch and hanged on Ambon. Nutmeg is still cultivated around the islands.

PULAU SAPARUA

Pulau Saparua is an alluring place, so quiet and relaxed compared to Ambon, only 70 km away. With its diving, stunning fort and captivating beaches, Saparua is an easy and enjoyable day trip from Ambon – but it's worth staying a few days. Kota Saparua is the only town of any size on the island; Haria is the port.

Benteng Duurstede

Only one block from the main road in Kota Saparua, this large Dutch fort was built in 1676 primarily to guard against Portuguese invasion. The well-restored fort sits majestically overlooking **Pantai Waisisil**, the site of the battles between Pattimura's troops and the Dutch. The museum opposite the fort has dramatic dioramas of this and other pertinent moments of Malukan history. All captions are in Indonesian, however; and while the effusive guide knows his history, he doesn't speak English well. The inevitable guest

ook must be signed and a small donation is
xpected.

Places to Stay & Eat
The only place in Kota Saparua is the *Penginapan Lease Indah* (☎ 21040), a few
minutes' walk from the bemo terminal along
l Muka Pasar. Comfortable rooms start from
l0,000 rp – up to 20,000 rp per person for
air-con – and an extra 10,000 rp per day if
you want meals. You can also hire full
snorkelling gear for 5000 rp per day.

Around the island, a couple of resorts,
such as the *Mahu Village Lodge* in Mahu,
cater for pre-arranged diving packages. They
cost around US$50 per person per day for
hotel and meals, which is not good value. If
you're interested, contact a travel or diving
agency on Ambon.

Besides one or two *rumah makans* around
the bemo terminal in Kota Saparua, there is
nowhere to eat on the island. Hotel food is
recommended.

Getting There & Away
The port of Haria is only ten minutes by
bemo (300 rp) from Kota Saparua. Two
ferries (4000 rp; 90 minutes) travel between
Hurnala port, just north of Tulehu on Pulau
Ambon, and Haria daily (one ferry on Sunday). They leave Hurnala at 9 am and 1 pm.
The views of Pulau Haruku on the way (sit
on the left-hand side) are worth the trip itself.

Boats between Hurnala and Amahai (the
port on Seram) sometimes go through Haria,
but don't count on it. Speedboats also travel

between Haria and Hurnala (5000 to 10,000
rp; one hour) when there's demand.

Getting Around
All bemos around the island start and finish
at the terminal in Kota Saparua. They are
marked: 'Hatawono' for the north-east road
to Nolloth via Mahu; 'Haria', the port for
boats to Seram and Ambon; and 'Tenggara'
for the south-east road to Sirisore and Ouw.
You may have to charter a bemo along the
less populated north-west road to Kulor. As
it often takes ages for a bemo to fill before it
leaves, chartering is worthwhile for around
3000 to 5000 rp for a short ride or about
10,000 rp an hour.

Around Pulau Saparua
The road to the small friendly village of **Ouw**
(bemos cost 500 rp) is dotted with pretty
beaches for snorkelling and swimming – just
choose one from the window of the bemo
and get off. Ouw is famous for its traditional
earthenware pottery called *kramik*. If you
look hard, or ask around, you can watch local
women make pottery at the back of their
homes. Of course, it's all for sale: tiny jugs
cost from 2000 to 5000 rp and very large urns
(not very handy for a backpack!) are 10,000
to 15,000 rp.

On the main road in Ouw, there's a small,
overgrown **fort** which locals, and historians,
seemed to have forgotten about. A walking
trail continues a little further on to **Tanjung
Ouw**, with more great diving sites.

Roads also go as far as **Nolloth** in the
north-east and **Kulor** in the north-west. Both
offer more sandy beaches and diving spots,
with plenty of coral and fish.

OTHER ISLANDS
The other main, populated islands in this
group are Pulau Haruku and Pulau Nusa
Laut. There's no accommodation and transport is limited, but both offer seclusion,
friendliness, and unspoiled scenery and
beaches.

Pulau Haruku
Haruku was once another Dutch stronghold

The Lease Group

Seram Strait

Nolloth
Kulor
Pelauw   Pulau
          Saparua
Hulaliu   Mahu
Kabau   Hulaliu   Kota Saparua
         Pulau   Sirisore
         Haruku   Haria
Haruku

Pulau   Ameth
Molana   Ouw
To Tulehu   Pulau
                       Nusa Laut
0   7.5   15 km   BANDA SEA

MALUKU

– the forts **Benteng New Zeland** and **Benteng Neuw Horn** are now decrepit, but still fascinating to wander around. The island, which boasts some beautiful, secluded beaches, such as **Pantai Hulaliu**, was also the site for some fierce fighting in WWII between Japanese and Australian troops. Every three years (the next is in January 2000), **Pelauw** village hosts the Sasi Lompa ceremony – a mock battle where real wounds are inflicted and then miraculously healed by special oils.

There are no losmen on Haruku, but staying on the island shouldn't be a problem if you ask the village head (*kepala desa*). The only way to the island is to charter a boat from Haria on Pulau Saparua or wait for a passenger boat on market days – Wednesday and Saturday.

Pulau Nusa Laut

Unimaginatively named 'Sea Island', Nusa Laut offers unspoiled beaches, an old ruine church at the village of **Ameth** and th decrepit Dutch **Benteng Beverwyk**.

The father of the famous Maluku freedor fighter, Martha Christina Tiahahu, was car tured on this island during the rebellion against the Dutch.

Again, there is nowhere official to sta but ask the kepala desa at Ameth. The onl public transport to the island is on marke days – Wednesday and Saturday. Alterna tively, you could charter a boat from Hari (Pulau Saparua) or visit as part of a divin package from Saparua or Ambon.

Pulau Seram

Maluku's second largest island (350 k long; 171,151 sq km), Seram is wild, mou tainous and heavily forested. The Malukan call it Nusa Ina ('Mother Island') as it believed that this is where the ancestors o central Maluku came from. Much of th centre is home to the indigenous Alfuro an Nuaula peoples, who are both of Papuar descent. The south and west coasts of Seran are populated by Malays, and there are trans migrants around the island from Java and Sulawesi. Both the Dutch and Indonesian governments resettled a number of the indig enous people on the coast. Pulau Seram' total population is 135,000.

A very tough four to seven day trek be tween the north and south coasts takes you through some of Manusela National Park home to many unique species of birds. The island is surrounded by coral reefs and there's plenty of *lumba lumba* (dolphins) also known as *ikan babi* ('pig fish'). Serar is a worthwhile and increasingly easy detou from Ambon and, with cheap, direct flight to Bandaneira, is a good way of heading t The Bandas. The capital, Masohi, is the onl town of any size.

Getting There & Away
Air Merpati flies between Ambon and Am ahai (55,000 rp), near Masohi, twice weekly

---

Sasi

A belief unique to most of Maluku is *sasi*, a warning created to protect property and safeguard against the theft of precious plants, fruit and animals. The disobedience of sasi could result in a spell against the perpetrator or, in modern Indonesia, a fine such as repaying (by a multiple of ten) the theft or damage. The installation of sasi and punishments are carried out by a villager called a *kewang*.

The difficulty is recognising the warning, which may be an intricate symbol of palm leaves hiding some potentially harmful bamboo sticks. These days, the kewang often simply attaches a sign, for example, to a coconut tree stating *sasi kelapa*, or coconut sasi, to stop people pinching the coconuts; a sign stating *sasi lompa* would attempt to stop locals pinching small fish from a pond because the fish may be still undersized, or few in number.

Sasi's origin is unknown, but it's taken seriously throughout most of Maluku. Visitors may encounter examples of sasi (and take heed!) in western Seram (especially along the trail leading to the waterfalls near Rumahkai), along the eastern and western roads in northern Halmahera, and around Pulau Saparua. ∎

MALUKU

an apparent anomaly in Merpati's price schedule (don't tell them!) makes the Amahai-Bandaneira flight (53,300 rp) considerably cheaper than Ambon-Bandaneira (92,900 rp) – another good reason for a detour to Seram. Every week, Merpati also flies directly, but less reliably, between Ambon and Wahai (101,700 rp) on the north coast of Seram. Bookings for flights to/from Seram should be made with the Merpati office in Kota Ambon.

Bus From Batu Merah terminal in Kota Ambon, buses leave every morning to Masohi (12,500 rp; six hours), Piru (in the far west), Taniwel (along the north-west coast) and Tehoru. For villages along the north coast, the bus marked 'Saleman' leaves from outside the Al-Fatah mosque in Kota Ambon. These buses go on the ferry between Hunimua (Pulau Ambon) and Kairatu (Pulau Seram), and are far easier than doing it in stages on your own (for about the same cost).

Boat Several ferries each day link Hunimua port, near Liang (Pulau Ambon), with Wairit, near Kairatu in the west of Seram. You can take the bus to Hunimua and catch the ferry yourself, but it is far easier, and just as cheap, to take the bus/ferry/bus packages from Kota Ambon (see the previous Bus section).

The *Superjet* (11,000 rp) speeds between Hurnala port, near Tulehu, on Pulau Ambon, and Amahai twice a day – it leaves Hurnala at 11 am and 5 pm. The slightly faster *Lai Lai Jet Foil* (14,000 rp; 1 hr 20 mins) also travels

between Amahai and Hurnala twice a day, leaving Hurnala at 8 am and 2 pm. When there's enough passengers, speedboats to villages in the west of Seram leave from Hila and Hitu Lama on the north coast of Pulau Ambon. You'll have to ask around the villages.

Every few days, slower, cheaper and crowded boats, such as the *Waisamar*, *Catherina* and *Wahai Star*, leave from Kota Ambon and crawl along the north coast of Seram to Taniwel, Wahai (30 to 35 hours from Kota Ambon), Kobi and Geser, and less often to Tehoru.

Getting Around

You will probably have to charter a bemo to/from the airport at Amahai (around 7000 rp) or hang around the terminal and wait for other passengers to share the cost.

Masohi is the centre for all bus travel around the island, while the main port and airport are in nearby Amahai. The bus terminal in Masohi is quite organised; buses are well marked and wait patiently until destination signs. They regularly go to Amahai (300 rp) and Kairatu, but to other places, services are far less regular.

To the north coast, about four buses marked 'Saleman' leave before 7 am from Masohi (7500 rp; 2½ rough hours). The bus actually takes you to the tiny port of Saka from where you must take public or chartered boats to other villages, including Sawai and Wahai. Speedboats are covered, faster and dearer than the slower, uncovered longboats, but you may not have much choice

---

Bird Tribes of Seram

Some villagers on the north coast of Pulau Seram believe their ancestors descend from a unique species of tiny birds called *lusiala* which live in a cave above the village. According to the legend, another area of Seram was originally inhabited by an aquatic tribe of humans which gradually dispensed with its marine features. A couple from this tribe continually prayed for a child, but eventually the female gave birth to two birds, similar to a bat, except they had human heads. Shocked, the couple left their village, rowed to a village on the north coast and cared for their 'children' in the cave. Many people along the north coast still fear the birds and regularly interpret their activities as omens.

The Bati, in the southern parts of Seram, claim they can fly. The 2000 or so Bati people are supposed to have piercing eyes and the power, during certain times of the year, to pick up a human and carry them around the sky. Many Ambonese and Seramese believe in the powers of the Bati. ■

---

anyway. There is a road, and daily bus, between Wahai and Kobi on the north-east coast.

MASOHI

Masohi is a quiet place with wide, empty streets. There is not a lot to do except admire the huge unfinished mosque and church along Jl Cengkeh, and respond to the inevitable shouts of 'HELLO MISTER!!!' and, more interestingly, 'I LOVE YOU!!!'.

Just about everything you will need is on the main street of Jl Abdullah Soulissa, which connects with Amahai, and is where the bus terminal is located. The helpful tourist office (☎ 21462) should now be in a new office on Jl Imam Bonjol (its exact location was unknown at the time of research). The office is open from 7.30 am to 4.30 pm weekdays. Head out there if you plan to do any trekking in the interior.

Places to Stay & Eat

All losmen are within walking distance of the bus terminal, although there are plenty of becaks around. Along Jl Abdullah Soulissa

(few places have street numbers), *Penginapan Nusantara* (☎ 21339) is central, b noisy and a little overpriced, with single doubles with mandi from 18,150/25,300 r more for air-con; the popular *Hotel S Lestari* (☎ 21178), with clean and comfor able rooms for 20,000/25,000 rp (the ext 15,000 rp for meals is not good value); ar the noisy but cheap family-run *Penginapa Beilohi Indah* (☎ 21251), with rooms f 13,750/16,500 rp.

You'll find the best value at the qui *Penginapan Nusa Ina* (☎ 21221) on th corner of Jl Cengkeh and Jl Pala, two bloc east of the market, with rooms for 13,750 per person.

On one side of the Sri Lestari, the *Vie Bar & Restoran* opens after 8 pm for u market meals and drinks. On the other sid *Rumah Makan Sate Surabaya* and, opposit *Rumah Makan Madura*, serve excellen cheap Indonesian food. Cheap *warungs* ar *teahouses* huddle around the busy and plea ant market.

AROUND PULAU SERAM
North Coast

The 'Saleman' bus goes to the tiny, busy po of Saka. From Saka, public longboats ar speedboats service the north coast, includin the villages of Sawai and Wahai. Boats leav when there is enough passengers, or you ca charter one easily enough – but bargain har To get a boat between Wahai and Sawai yc will probably have to head back to Saka.

Sawai After an exhilarating longboat ric from Saka (3000 to 5000 rp; half-hour), yc arrive at the friendly, pretty village of Sawa From the village, you can rent a boat, with driver/guide, for around 10,000 rp per hou and visit **Pulau Sawai** for swimming an **Pulau Raja** which has a colony of bats. It more fun to rent a canoe (which takes som time to get the hang of) for about 2500 rp pe day and explore some underwater cave complete with enormous turtles, or tin **Pantai Ora**, which is great for swimmin and snorkelling.

The one and only losmen, *Pondok Wisar*

isar, built literally on top of the clear water, is worth a trip here in itself. Simple rooms with stunning views cost 20,000 rp per person, including lots of complimentary tea and meals.

Wahai This is the main town on the north coast (8500 rp; 1½ hours by longboat from Saka). Two Portuguese cannons dated 1785 are in the main square indicating a colonial past which many historians seemed to have ignored. Wahai has plenty of shops if you need to stock up on food and water for the trek to Manusela National Park.

There are two good losmen. The *Penginapan Taman Baru* (☎ 222) is opposite the Telkom building (ask directions). It costs 11,000 rp per person without mandi; an extra 3000 rp for three meals. Along the main street, the *Penginapan Sinar Indah* (☎ 255) is far nicer than it looks from the outside – a good room without mandi, but with the most comfortable bed in Maluku, costs 15,000 rp; 20,000 rp with meals. Try not to strangle the screeching pet nuri bird just outside your room.

East Coast

Buses to the east of the island leave from Tamahai, so get a bemo there first from Masohi. Along the eastern road, the traditional village of **Bonara** is inhabited by the Nuaula people, recognisable by their bright red cloth hats. (You will probably see more Nuaulans along the road to Saka.) You may be disappointed if you visit Bonara because the villagers (understandably) resent being a tourist attraction; they actively discourage tourism by being unfriendly and insisting on about 25,000 rp for photos. The village has only a dozen traditional houses and many villagers are absent during the day anyway. Take the Sepa bemo (900 rp); it's a rough road but the scenery along the way is very pretty.

West Coast

Three hours by bus (9000 rp) along the rough, western road from Masohi are picturesque **waterfalls**, just outside the village of

Rumahkai. (Ask the bus driver to drop you off at the '*air tejun*'.) It's a lovely walk to the falls and the setting is superb, but it's a *long* day trip from Masohi – start early. If you take the bus and ferry between Kota Ambon and Masohi, through the port of Waiprit (at Kairatu), the bus goes past the entrance to the falls. You can get off the bus and leave your gear at the small rumah makan, where you pay a 300 rp entrance fee.

Another hour further west, the road passes the village of **Kairatu**; ferries to Hunimua on Pulau Ambon leave from Waiprit nearby. In Kairatu, there are one or two losmen, such as the *Penginapan Sudi Hampir*, about a two km walk towards Masohi on the main road.

Manusela National Park

A large part of Seram's centre is designated as Manusela National Park (Taman Nasional Manusela; 189,000 hectares). It is supposedly protected, but the park management has to contend with locals who want to use the area for purposes other than conservation.

The park hosts an abundance of birdlife, such as the bright nuri, cassowary and cockatoo, and the traditional Alfuro and Nuaula people in the main villages. There's no shortage of rugged scenery, including thundering waterfalls. You can trek (which is the only way into the park) between the north and south coasts, but this is a very, very tough, muddy and steep slog.

You may be able to stay in huts in the villages – check with the kepala desa first. There are some wooden shelters along the way and some caves to sleep in, or take your own tent.

Guides The office of the Indonesian National Park Service (Perlindungan Hutan dan Pelestrian Alam; PHPA), in Ambon may have a map of the park, but insists that you take a guide (which is definitely recommended). Guides should cost around 20,000 rp per day – enquire at the Masohi tourist office, or the PHPA offices in Mosso and Wahai. A porter (also recommended) costs around 10,000 rp per day, but they will only carry your stuff from one village to another because there's still a lot of animosity and distrust between villages. Generally, the best time to go is between July and September, but the weather will probably be miserable almost all the time. Bring all your own camping and cooking gear – and loads of wet weather stuff. You can buy food in Wahai and Hatumetan.

Permits You also need a permit from the PHPA. There may be a small 'administration fee', but the permits are actually free. These must be obtained from the following PHPA offices, listed in order of preference by the PHPA:

PHPA, Jl Kebun Cengkeh, Batu Merah Atas, near Kota Ambon (☎ 52602)
PHPA, Jl RA Kartini, Masohi (☎ 97577)
PHPA, at the home of the department head, Pak Eddy, on the main street, Wahai; or in Mosso, near Hatumetan (☎ 219)

Trekking Ironically, most of the recognised trail doesn't actually go through a lot of the park, but you wouldn't know – it is all jungle. From the south, the trail starts from Hatumetan, a boat trip from Tehoru. From the north, you can start from Wahai, or save two days hiking by chartering a boat from Wahai or Sawai to the logging centre of Opin. From Opin, you will have to wait for the daily truck to Roho. (This may not be a suitable starting point in the future if the centre for the logging industry moves from Opin – check the PHPA offices for current details.)

Theoretically, the trek between Roho and Hatumetan can be completed in four days, but you are strongly advised to allow about seven, and a few extra days to get to/from the start and finishing points.

Roho to Kanikeh – about seven hours
Kanikeh to Manusela village – about six hours
Manusela village to the place known as the 'rock shelter' – about seven hours. From the north, this is the most difficult section as you climb to about 2000m.
'Rock shelter' to Hatumetan – about six hours. From the south, this section is very steep.

The Bandas

South-east of Ambon lies the tiny cluster charming islands known as The Bandas. Th group consists of ten islands, with a total are of 55 sq km: the main three are Pulau Neir where the only town of any size, Bandaneir and the airport are located; the largish, cre cent-shaped Pulau Banda Besar (Big Banc Island); and the volcano, Gunung Api, loon ing menacingly from the sea. Although th total population is 25,000, the other seve islands are sparsely populated, if at all, ar are harder to reach.

The Bandas are littered with deserte forts, abandoned nutmeg plantations (som still functioning) and charming Dutch villa (some have been well restored). The island are surrounded by superb beaches and yc can easily snorkel around some of the mo stunning coral reefs you will ever see. If th isn't enough, there's even a volcano to clim The Bandas are understandably, and deser edly, becoming an increasingly popula place to visit and to stay a while.

History

The first Europeans to arrive in The Banda were the Portuguese who landed in 151. They had the islands to themselves until Dutch fleet arrived in Maluku in 1599 wit orders to seek out spices at their source an circumvent the Portuguese monopoly. Pa of the Dutch fleet came to The Banda loaded a cargo of spices, alarmed the Portu guese and sailed back to the Netherland Soon afterwards, the Dutch forced the Po tuguese out of the spice trade, but they sti had other rivals: in 1601 the British Ea India Company set up a fort on Pulau Run i The Bandas; and in 1606 the Spanish got int the act by taking Ternate and Tidore island in northern Maluku.

The turning point came in 1619, when Ja Pieterszoon Coen, the new governor genera of the VOC, envisaged a Dutch commerci empire in the east, the grandeur of whic would match the extent of his violent rutl ssness. He seized control of The Bandas, ot rid of the unhelpful Bandanese and arted producing nutmeg using imported aves and labourers, with Dutch overseers.

In early 1621 Coen attacked Pulau Lonor (now Pulau Banda Besar), the most nportant of the group, and almost totally iped out the indigenous Bandanese population. Coen then returned to Batavia (Jakarta) nd announced that the VOC would accept pplications for land grants in The Bandas if ne applicants settled permanently on the lands and produced spices exclusively for ne company, at fixed prices.

This was not broken until almost 200 ears later. The Bandas, like other Dutcheld parts of the archipelago, were occupied y the English during the Napoleonic Wars, t which time nutmeg seedlings were nipped off to Sri Lanka, Sumatra and Penang. By 1860 these areas were almost as nportant as The Bandas for producing utmeg and mace. The invention of refrigeration, however, which allowed meat to be ept without the heavy use of spices, saw the nd of the spice trade. (The Bandas still roduce nutmeg and mace for use in Indonesia, but these days more is actually grown in orthern Sulawesi.)

The islands continued to be ignored by the Dutch in the 19th and 20th centuries, and, nankfully, by the Japanese during WWII – ney saw no use for nutmeg or The Bandas. t really hasn't been until the last ten or so ears that The Bandas have once again been rediscovered' by foreigners – this time by ess destructive tourists.

Books

Indonesian Banda by Willard A Hanna is an engaging book which details the occupation of The Bandas by the various European powers. Co-written by Hanna and Banda supremo Des Alwi (owner of the Hotel Maulana in Bandaneira, among other things), *Turbulent Times Past in Ternate and Tidore* (35,000 rp) is only available in Bandaneira – not in Ambon or even Ternate! Both are smallish paperbacks and absurdly overpriced but, nevertheless, an interesting read. They are for sale at the shop opposite the Maulana, and at the Rumah Budaya museum in Bandaneira.

Diving

Some of Indonesia's most extraordinary scuba and skin diving can be found at nearly 50 dive sites around The Bandas. Some of the best places are: Pantai Wali and Belakang Selamon, both on Pulau Banda Besar; Sambayang and the lava around Gunung Api; anywhere around Pulau Karaka; and all around Syahrir, Run and Hatta islands (especially Skaro Reef) – but these places are more suitable for scuba diving. Malole, an hour's stroll from Bandaneira along a shady path, is a good local spot for swimming and snorkelling. The water surrounding Bandaneira provides excellent snorkelling; just off the jetty in front of the Governor's Residence is as good as anywhere. If you rent a boat, your driver will almost certainly know the best places to go.

The best season for all water activities is between October and March. The only place

MALUKU

The Bandas

0   2.5   5 km

Benteng Revenge

Pulau Neilaka

Pulau Ai

Pulau Run

Pulau Karaka

Pulau Gunung Api

Volcanic Crater

Sambayang

Benteng Hollandia

Pulau Batu Kapal

Pulau Neira

Airstrip

Bandaneira

Lonthoir

Pulau Syahrir

Selamon

Waling Besar

Waer

Benteng Concordia

Pulau Banda Besar

Pulau Hatta

BANDA SEA

to hire scuba equipment is the dive shop opposite the Hotel Maulana in Bandaneira. But beware, several divers have reported serious concerns about the poor maintenance of the equipment. The Maulana organises scuba diving packages for US$80 (two dives), including guide, gear and boat for half a day. All-inclusive full day trips to more remote islands cost US$90 – it will always be cheaper if you bring some or all of your own equipment. The shop also runs a four day PADI certificate course in English and Dutch for US$350.

If you can't scuba dive, don't despair, as you can easily see a lot of stunning coral and fish by snorkelling. In Bandaneira, some homestays, such as the Flamboyan and Matahari, and one or two shops around the port, rent full snorkelling gear for about 6000 rp per day. To nearby snorkelling sites, you can rent a one or two person canoe from the Matahari or fish market for about 10,000 rp per day, or with a guide/paddler for 15,000 rp. The Maulana can also organise boat trips at much higher prices.

Hiring a boat, with driver/guide, is the best way to visit other islands and diving sites, but it will be expensive without others sharing the cost. Nothing is organised on a regular basis, so ask guests and employees at the more popular places to stay if a boat is going out. Generally, a half-day snorkelling trip around Syahrir, Ai and Banda Besar islands, and Gunung Api, will cost a reasonable 6000 rp or so per person in a boat with 10 people – equipment, and a fresh coconut on the beach, are extra.

At the time of research, there were plans to use a glass-bottom boat for tours around the coral near Bandaneira. This should cost about 25,000 rp per person; enquire at Branta Penginapan.

BANDANEIRA

The main island in The Bandas is Pulau Neira. It has the only town, Bandaneira, most of the attractions, and is the location of the port and airport. In its heyday, Bandaneira was a town of spacious mansions and now, a few centuries later, is slowly being restored.

It is the only place to base yourself proper[l] although two other islands do have limite[d] accommodation (refer to the following Oth[er] Islands section for details).

Orientation & Information

Facilities in Bandaneira are more suited [to] the small town it is, and not (thankfully) the tourist trade. There is still no trav[el] agency or bank, nor anywhere to chang[e] money – so stock up on rupiah on Amb[on] and don't expect to use a credit card, exce[pt] at the expensive hotels. There is no hospit[al] a community health centre (puskesmas) near Pondok Wisata Rosmina. The poli[ce] station is in a lovely, restored villa along [Jl] Pantai.

There is no tourist office. A tourist count[er] at the airport hands out some brochure[s] though it's only open when planes arriv[e]. Don't be afraid to ask your hotel for info[r]mation. The comparatively large and mode[rn] Telkom office is a becak ride away in th[e] 'suburbs' on Jl Rajawali. It's open 24 hour[s]. In contrast, the quaint post office, near Be[n]teng Nassau, is often closed.

Museum

The **Rumah Budaya** (Culture House) on [Jl] Gereja Tua is an old Dutch villa with a sma[ll] but interesting collection of old cannon[s], muskets, helmets, coins, maps, jars an[d] china. On the walls, paintings graphical[ly] portray past wars and massacres, and i[n] another room a useful display neatly show[s] the layout of The Bandas. The museum als[o] sells the book Indonesian Banda, as well a[s] a few T-shirts and postcards. The museum [is] often closed; try around 9 am on weekday[s] or look out when you walk past.

Rooms behind the museum can be rente[d] for 20,000 rp; enquire at the side entrance[.] The owners do not promote the hotel at al[l] so you may have the place to yourself.

Benteng Nassau

The original stone foundations of this fo[rt] were built by the Portuguese around 152[?] when they sent troops from their base i[n] Ternate. The fort, however, wasn't com[pleted]

PLACES TO STAY
1 Hotel Maulana
6 Delfika Guest House
15 Matahari
18 Penginapan Gamalama
19 Pondok Wisata Bandaneira
20 Pondok Wisata Rosmina
23 Homestay Flamboyan
24 Branta Penginapan
27 Pondok Wisata Mawar

PLACES TO EAT
8 Rumah Makan Nusantara
9 Rumah Makan Teratai
10 Rumah Makan Namasawar

OTHER
2 Port
3 Pelni Office
4 Hatta Syahrir Mosque
5 Rumah Budaya
7 Syahrir's Residence
11 Captain Cole's Residence
12 Chinese Temple
13 Vegetable & Fish Market
14 Dock for Boats Around Island
16 Merpati Office
17 Dutch Church
21 Post Office
22 Hatta's Residence
25 VOC Governor's Residence
26 Police Station
28 Mangunkusumo's Residence

Benteng Belgica

To Likes (50m) & Hotel Laguna (80m)

To Top End of Airstrip & North of Island

To Pondok Wisata Florida (500m) & Telkom Office (2km)

Footpath

Jalan Pelabuhan

Jalan Gereja Tua

Jalan Hatta

Park

Jalan Syahrir

Benteng Nassau

Path

Jalan Kujali

Jalan Pantai

To Airport

Path

Bandaneira

0   50   100 m

leted and the foundations were abandoned. In 1608 a powerful Dutch fleet under Admiral Pieterszoon Verhoeven arrived with orders to annexe The Bandas. When negotiations stalled, Verhoeven simply confronted the Bandanese with a *fait accompli* by landing soldiers on Pulau Neira and building a fort on the old Portuguese foundations. Nassau was restored for use as a warehouse by the British in the early 19th century, but eventually lapsed into ruin.

Today the fort is really overgrown – only three walls and a gateway remain, and an old cannon lies on the ground. Still, it is pleasant enough for a clamber around and there are good views of Benteng Belgica. The best place to appreciate the size and shape of Nassau is from Belgica.

Benteng Belgica

The construction of Benteng Belgica began in 1611, at a staggering cost, under the direction of Pieter Both. He had been appointed governor general of the region, and assigned the task of creating a monopoly and kicking out the English. With the prospect of a Banda-English alliance, his men erected the imposing Benteng Belgica on the ridge overlooking Nassau. It was maintained as a military headquarters until 1860 and then lapsed into ruin until it was magnificently restored a few years ago.

With Gunung Api looming nearby, the fort's setting is quite stunning. It's a marvellous place to wander around and to imagine its former opulence. At the entrance, where you must report and pay a small donation, an information room has a limited display of artefacts, photos and diagrams. Captions are in Indonesian, but you still get an idea of the incredible effort that went into the restoration.

Exile Houses

In 1936 two nationalist leaders, Mohammad Hatta and Sutan Syahrir, who had both proved troublesome for the Dutch, were transferred from the horrors of the Boven Digul prison (in central Irian Jaya) to Bandaneira – showing what little respect The Bandas received at the time from the Dutch administration. The Dutch suddenly called them back to Java in 1942 in an effort to counter Japanese control of Indonesia. At the time of the proclamation of independence in 1945, Hatta became Indonesia's vice-president and, a little later, Syahrir was prime minister.

Appropriately situated along Jl Hatta, **Hatta's Residence** features some old typewriters, furniture and clothes left over from his stay in Bandaneira. Next to the Rumah Budaya, **Syahrir's Residence** has been nicely restored and contains some interesting furniture and memorabilia from that era. Another lesser-known nationalist leader was also exiled in Bandaneira between 1928 and 1940. **Dr Tjipto Mangunkusumo's Residence** on Jl Pantai has been nicely restored, but for some reason no one can find anything to put in it. Although the place is empty, the lovely old couple who live at the back are worth saying hello to.

Other Attractions

The quaint **Dutch church** on Jl Gereja Tua (Old Church Street) dates from 1680, although it has been extensively restored since.

A large number of people are buried benea the floor.

Now called Istana Mini, the **VOC go ernor's residence** was once the home of t infamous Jan Pieterszoon Coen, amor others. It's majestically located just bac from the waterfront, with a walkway juttin out to the sea. Although empty, it's wor wandering around, and have a look at t (unrestored) barracks at the back also.

Near Rumah Budaya, **Captain Cole Residence** has also been lovingly restore but is often closed. Cole was the command of the British Marines which captured Be teng Belgica in 1810 during the interlude the Napoleonic Wars. Not far from the Te kom office, a **Dutch graveyard** is full tombstones, some dating back to the 17 century – take a becak or ask directions.

Special Events

Every April and October, *kora-kora* (cano races are held around Pulau Neira. Gre examples of a kora-kora lie about 50m we of the governor's residence and right at t top of Jl Pelabuhan.

Places to Stay

In The Bandas, all accommodation is Bandaneira, with the exception of one lo men on Pulau Syahrir and three on Pulau (refer to the following Other Islands sectic for details). Prices of all places belo include all meals (unless otherwise stated which are invariably fish, vegetables ar rice, but are plentiful and delicious. If stayir a while at any place, it's worth negotiating better rate.

The cheapest places are the increasir number of losmen, called homestays or *po dok wisatas*, which are usually just a fe rooms at the back of a friendly, family hom Rooms, often with your own mandi, all co about 17,500 rp per person, which is goo value if you are travelling alone; if nc double rooms in other hotels are better valu

The convivial and helpful *Pondok Wisa Rosmina* (☎ 21145) on Jl Kujali has comfor able rooms and good meals.

ristine coastline south of Sebataibaru, Morotai, Maluku.

SIMON ROWE

SIMON ROWE

SIMON ROWE

Maluku
Top: View of a deserted fort, The Bandas.
Bottom Left: Superbly maintained colonial building, The Bandas.
Bottom Right: Birdlife is prolific on Pulau Seram, especially the exotic nuri parrot.

For views of the sea and Gunung Api, you cannot beat *Likes* (☎ 21089) between hotels Maulana and Laguna, and the *Matahari* (☎ 21050), just off Jl Pelabuhan. Likes costs little more than 17,500 rp with a mandi; Matahari has been renovated recently and isn't the value it was, with singles/doubles for 25,000/40,000 rp.

Also for 17,500 rp, the *Pondok Wisata Mawar* (☎ 21083) near the governor's residence is a real find – great location in a friendly atmosphere; and for antique furniture in huge old rooms and sparkling service, try the *Pondok Wisata Florida* (☎ 21086), two minutes' walk east of Hatta's Residence.

For slightly more, there are a number of recent places along Jl Gereja Tua: *Penginapan Gamalama* (☎ 21053) has very clean rooms and nice surroundings from 20,000/25,000 rp; opposite, *Pondok Wisata Banaeira* (☎ 21149) is about the same price and standard; and the *Delfika Guest House* (☎ 21027) is an old Dutch villa, with good rooms set around a garden for 50,000 rp with air-con – some rooms without air-con are cheaper.

Opposite each other on Jl Syahrir are two very popular places. The *Homestay Flamboyan* (☎ 21233) serves great food, has a lovely garden setting and organises boat trips; it also has rooms for 22,000/35,000 rp. In a renovated villa, the *Branta Penginapan* (☎ 21068) also has a lovely garden, and rooms cost 15,000/17,500 to 30,000/40,000 rp. The owners have good local information and can organise tours.

At the top end of the accommodation scale is the *Hotel Maulana* (☎ 21022) at the top end of Jl Pelabuhan. While you get good views and the rooms are comfortable, there is nothing else to justify its prices: from US$50/60 for a standard room and full meals for US$22 per day – all plus 20% tax. Over-priced boats and guides can be arranged, as well as visits to nutmeg plantations and deep-sea fishing. Part of the same group, but cheaper, the *Hotel Laguna* (☎ 21018) next door has rooms from a comparatively reasonable US$20/25 plus 20% tax.

Places to Eat

There is not a great choice of places to eat in Bandaneira, which is why most hotels and losmen offer meals (or is it the other way around?). It's cheaper to eat at your hotel, but if you want to try some local places negotiate a reduction in your room rate (maybe 5000 rp less in the losmen).

The following restaurants are next to each other along Jl Pelabuhan. *Rumah Makan Namasawar* has a nice outdoor setting, and sells reasonably good ice cream and pancakes for 2500 rp each. *Rumah Makan Teratai* offers the same sort of food, but the setting and service isn't quite as good. Try the *Ruman Makan Nusantara* for basic, but delicious, Indonesian food from 2500 rp. One or two other cheap places congregate around the port and opposite the Maulana.

Getting There & Away

Air Merpati flies from Ambon to Bandaneira (92,900 rp) and back six times a week; twice a week through Amahai, near Masohi on Pulau Seram. An apparent anomaly, the Amahai-Bandaneira flight (53,300 rp) is considerably cheaper, which is a good excuse for a detour to Seram first. Merpati in Ambon can contact its Bandaneira office to arrange return ticket (this is recommended), but you must *pay* for it in Bandaneira. Confirm and/or buy your ticket out of Bandaneira as soon as possible.

Currently, the pretty Bandaneira airport can only cater for planes seating about 15 people, so flights are often heavily booked. This also means a limit of 10 kg per person (you pay for extra kg), which is a real hassle if you're taking diving gear. This may all change when the airport is extended (currently underway) and larger planes can land.

The Merpati office (☎ 21040) on Jl Pelabuhan is open from about 9 am to 1 pm daily – except at flight times. The office can be a very frustrating place, and over-booked flights and misplaced luggage are not uncommon. Sit on the right-hand side of the plane from Ambon for the best views of these truly magnificent islands.

MALUKU

Boat The only Pelni liner to stop at Bandaneira, the *Rinjani*, has a very useful trip to/from Ambon and Bandaneira (16,000/57,000 rp economy/1st class) every two weeks – both trips are during the day. This boat also travels to/from the equally delightful Dutch colonial town of Fak Fak on the Irian Jayan coast (41,000/156,500 rp) and back, making Fak Fak an appealing side trip from Bandaneira. The *Rinjani* carries on to Tual in the Kai Islands (27,500/102,500 rp). Some travellers have unfortunately reported that the *Rinjani* has been the centre of some bag snatching in Kota Ambon – especially during chaotic disembarkations. Best beware. In Bandaneira, the Pelni office (no telephone) is just outside the port on Jl Pelabuhan.

The Perintis boat *Iweri* is the next best option. Every three weeks, it connects Bandaneira with Tual (7,900 rp); Saumlaki, in the Tanimbars (11,900 rp); Dili, East Timor (18,900 rp); and Ambon (6,400 rp). The *Omega* also has a four weekly return trip between Ambon, Banda and Fak Fak. Several other less-comfortable boats, such as the *Asmara* and *Lumba Lumba*, stop at Bandaneira along an interesting route between Ambon and Agats (the main town in Asmat Region on Irian Jaya) every few weeks. Ask at the harbour master's office, next to the Pelni office, for more details.

Getting Around

The Airport Public bemos (about 1000 rp) wait for all incoming flights and drop you off in the centre of the village from where you can walk to your hotel. You can also get a lift (usually free) on a bemo with one of the hotel touts. (Don't worry: their frantic hassling of visitors is not the least bit indicative of The Bandas.) If you ask directions, or know your way around, a walk between the airport and your hotel only takes about 20 minutes.

When departing, a free bemo organised by Merpati (tee it up earlier) picks up passengers outside their hotels just before the flight.

Local Transport Bandaneira and Pulau Neira are very small and are easy (and pleas-

ant) to walk around. Occasional bemos circl the island and becaks have now arrived. Th best way to get around is on a bicycle – lik the locals do. The Delfika may have one fo rent for around 10,000 rp per day. Hopefull more hotels will see the benefit of hiring ou bikes and will have some available soon.

Motorised boats are the only form of inter island transport (refer to the following Othe Islands section). A canoe with a paddler guide costs around 15,000 rp per day; 10,00 rp on your own. These canoes are ofte harder to steer than you think, but are useful for visiting nearby snorkelling sites aroun Pulau Neira, though only as far as Gunun Api and Pulau Karaka. Ask around at the fis market.

OTHER ISLANDS

Except for daily passenger boats betwee Bandaneira and Banda Besar and Ai island there is no regular public transport to othe islands. Boats holding up to 10 people ca be rented for a very negotiable price o around 10,000 to 12,000 rp per hour depend ing on tourist demand, distance (the mos important factor being petrol costs) an length of hire. All boats leave Bandaneir from around the fish market – the exac location varies considerably, so ask around

Gunung Api

Looming over Bandaneira, this volcano ha been a constant threat to Bandaneira and th villagers perched around its fertile slopes Gunung Api has erupted numerous time over the centuries, often when a fleet of ship planned to attack the town – which wa always regarded by the colonialists as a ba omen. As recently as 1988, two people wer killed; over 300 houses on its north and sout slopes and 120,000 coconut trees were als destroyed.

The 666m-high volcano can be climbed i about two hours. The first half is relativel easy with some wooden steps (often broken and resting places; the second half involve a tough scramble up steep, loose ground take good shoes and some gloves if you can This half is also particularly tricky on th

vay down. At the top, be careful of hot rocks
nd craters.

Start at about 5.30 am to ensure that you
each the top before the early morning cloud
overs the indescribable views for the rest of
he day, and so you can get down before it
ets too hot. Try to time your stay at the top
o you can watch the tiny Merpati Twin-
Otter plane circle the volcano before it lands
– an extraordinary sight.

Guides are available for about 10,000 rp,
ut are not really necessary unless you want
omeone to carry your gear – ask around at
our hotel or at the fish market. A short
addle from Bandaneira in a canoe to the
sland and back will cost about 4000 rp; the
river will know where you should start the
limb and he will somehow be there when
ou come down, or you can rent a motorboat
ll day for about 25,000 rp.

Pulau Karaka

Off the northern end of Gunung Api, Pulau
Karaka ('Old Woman's Island') has a small
each and some fine coral reefs in shallow
vater near the shore. It's close enough to
addle from Bandaneira in a canoe and takes
bout an hour.

Pulau Banda Besar

The largest island, Banda Besar, is worth a
rip or two from Bandaneira. From the top of
he obvious, steep steps in the main village
f **Lonthoir**, turn left and ask directions for
Benteng Hollandia. This fort was erected
fter Coen's capture of Banda Besar in 1621.
Placed high on the central ridge of the island,
vith great views of the surrounding islands
nd Lonthoir, the fort was once enormous,
ut an earthquake wrecked it in 1743. What
ittle that remains is derelict and overgrown
nd is a real disappointment after Benteng
Belgica. A local boy will ask you to sign the
visitors' book and you're obliged to pay a
mall donation.

A path heads along the east coast from
Lonthoir, initially over some rocks, and then
basses small swimming beaches, wild clove
rees and spotless villages such as **Bioyouw**.
f you continue, there's a **nutmeg planta-**
tion around Waling Besar village. This is
worth a visit if only to chat with Mr van den
Broek, one of the last plantation owners in
The Bandas.

At **Waer**, on the north-east coast, is the
decrepit **Benteng Concordia**. Close by,
Pantai Lanutu, behind Selamon village, is a
magical area for swimming and snorkelling.
If there are some boys hanging around the
beach, ask one to pick a fresh coconut from
a nearby palm and open it up for you for
around 500 rp. The only way to Waer is on
foot from Lonthoir (not really recommended
without a guide) or by chartering a boat from
Bandaneira.

To Lonthoir, the main village and dock on
the island, charter a boat (about 5000 rp one
way) or take the regular public boat (often
full of school kids) from the Bandaneira fish
market (500 rp; 25 minutes). Less regular
public boats also leave Bandaneira for
Waling Besar. There is no transport, or vehicles, on the whole island.

Pulau Syahrir

Also known as Pulau Pisang because of its
banana shape, Syahrir is about 50 minutes by
boat from Bandaneira. It has a good sandy
beach, and some stunning coral (with a big
drop-off) and colourful fish. You can wander
uphill to the small village behind the beach.

The friendly, secluded *Homestay Mailena*
has a few rooms right on the beach with three
meals for 30,000 rp per person (plus 5000 rp
boat fare). It's not great value compared to
Bandaneira and, especially, Pulau Ai, but the
place is comfortable and you get almost total
seclusion. The problem is finding the owner
of the homestay in Bandaneira (so ask
around) and arranging a boat out there – but
it's worth the effort. Otherwise, you will
have to charter a boat there for about 30,000
rp return.

Pulau Ai

This delightful island, not far from Bandaneira, is where the British attempted to gain
some ascendancy over The Bandas and the
spice trade in 1610. With its secluded
beaches, snorkelling sites, unhurried villages

and old fort, Ai is a popular alternative to the 'hustle and bustle' of Bandaneira.

From the boat ramp, head right for a few minutes to **Benteng Revenge**. Built by the British, then captured by the Dutch, the fort is decrepit, with only the walls remaining. More interesting is the former Dutch plantation house **Welvaren**, which is also mostly in ruins.

The island has three homestays. Normally they don't have private mandis; most have (and need) mosquito nets; and prices are per person, including three meals of (you guessed it) fish and rice. The *Homestay Welvaren* (ask directions) is the cheapest at 10,000 rp. The family is very nice, but the rooms are fairly stuffy. From the boat ramp, turn right along the main street for the *Homestay Revenge* – a popular, pleasant place with good meals for 15,000 rp. The best of the lot is *Homestay Weltevreden* at the top of the lane from the boat ramp. The rooms are also simple, costing 12,500 rp or 30,000 rp for better rooms with mandi, and the service is excellent. It also rents snorkelling gear.

Two or three passenger boats (2500 rp; one hour) leave from around the fish market in Bandaneira at around 1 pm for what is sometimes a rough trip (check the day before). Boats leave Ai for Bandaneira any time between 7 and 9 am (check with your homestay). Unfortunately, the timing prevents you from day tripping by public boat to Ai from Bandaneira, but you can always charter a boat for about 50,000 rp return.

Pulau Run

Run, once the centre of English activity in The Bandas, has very little to offer. It is mainly famous as one of the greatest swaps in history: after the Treaty of Breda in 1667, the British gave Run to the Dutch in exchange for another little island – Manhattan. There's an English fort on a spit of half-exposed coral rock on **Pulau Neilaka**, which lies just off Run. A large twin-engine boat chartered all day, with a stop at Pulau Ai, will cost about 110,000 rp.

South-East Maluku

The islands of South-East Maluku, whic make up the Maluku Tenggara district, ar dispersed across the sea between Timor an Irian Jaya. The three main groups are the Ka Aru and Tanimbar islands. West of the Tar imbars, two arcs of smaller islands stretc across to Timor: a southern, less fertile ar consisting of the Babar and Leti group Kisar and Wetar; and a northern arc of vo canic, wooded islands, including Seru Nila, Teun, Damar and Romang.

South-East Maluku was virtually ignore by Dutch colonialists and other Europea powers (because it didn't produce spice and by the Japanese during WWII, but n by missionaries who have successfully con verted a lot of the population. The centre fc transport to the islands is the provinci capital, Tual, in the Kais. The district remain undeveloped, with limited facilities, but does have some of the most magnificen beaches in Indonesia. You'll need a lot c time to really explore the region, and b prepared for some uncomfortable boat ride across potentially rough seas.

KAI ISLANDS

Also known as the 'Thousand Islands (although there are really only 287), the wor 'Kai' probably originates from the Portu guese word for 'stone'. The three mai islands are Pulau Kai Kecil (known locall as Nuhu Roa), Pulau Dullah, and the ver mountainous and sparsely populated Pula Kai Besar (also known as Nuhu Yut).

Information

The helpful tourist office (☎ 21466) ca provide useful information. It's badly sign posted, just off the lane at the end of J Pattimura in Tual. Neither bank in Langgu changes money. The police station (☎ 21110 is on Jl Dihir, near the port at Tual.

Pulau Kai Kecil

Known locally as Pantai Sar Nadan, **Pas**

Kai Islands

*ARAFURA
SEA*

0   20   40 km

...anjang is an isolated, unspoiled (so far) ...each with sparkling-blue water, powdery-...hite sand and thousands of coconut palms. ...is 17 km from Tual (500 rp by bemo) and ...the best and most accessible beach in the ...ais. Not far away, **Ohoideertawun** has an-...her fine beach, and the intriguing **Gua ...uwat** cave has some strange paintings.

...ulau Dullah

...he pretty village of Dullah (400 rp by be-...o) claims to have the **Belang Museum**, ...hich is nothing more than three decaying ...ngboats *(belang)*, also called kora-kora. ...n the way to Dullah, the **Taman Anggrek** Orchid Garden) has the small **Ngadi Lake** ...nd some pleasant picnic areas. The beach at ...amadan has some Japanese WWII wrecks. ...urther north, **Pantai Sorbat Indah** (1000 ...) by bemo) is another great beach with some ...iving opportunities.

...laces to Stay & Eat

...ost cheap places are in older, quieter Tual. ...he following have basic rooms with shared ...andi: the 'old' *Rosemgen I* (☎ 21045) on Jl ...arel Sadsustubun costs 10,000 rp per ...erson or 13,500 rp with simple meals, plus

lots of mozzies; the *Nini Gerhana* (☎ 21343) on Jl Raya Pattimura is noisy but friendly at 15,000 rp per room; and the *Mirah Inn* (☎ 21172) on Jl Mayor Abdullah costs 7700 rp per person. The popular, quiet but inconveniently located *Linda Mas Guest House* (☎ 21271) on Jl Antoni Rebok has comfortable rooms for around 15,000 rp, and more expensive ones with air-con and TV.

The only place to stay in Langgur is the quiet 'new' *Rosemgen II* (☎ 21477) near the bridge on Jl Merdeka Watdek. Rooms start at 24,000/36,000 rp with fan and mandi; ask for a room with a great water view.

The places to eat in Tual and Langgur are nothing to write home about. There are plenty of warungs around the markets in both Langgur and Tual, but the hotel food is probably your best bet. In Tual, *Rumah Makan Salero Anda* and *Prima Donna Restaurant* offer poor food and little variety. In Langgur, the *Angel Pub & Restaurant* at the 'new' Rosemgen II serves a good dinner, if you order earlier in the day, and cold beer with a great river view and live music. Along Jl Jenderal Sudirman are the Chinese *Dragon* and *Charlie* restaurants.

Getting There & Away

Air Langgur is the focal point for air travel to South-East Maluku. Merpati currently flies between Langgur and Ambon almost daily (173,200 rp), with ongoing connections to Dobo in the Arus (73,100 rp) twice a week. Bouraq also flies to Langgur most days for the same price as Merpati. The Merpati agency (☎ 21376) on Jl Pattimura is open Monday to Saturday from about 8 am to 4 pm.

Boat Tual is well connected to other islands in Maluku and nearby Irian Jaya. Every two weeks, the Pelni liner *Rinjani* goes to Fak Fak (Irian Jaya) for 15,300/99,300 rp (economy/1st class) and Ambon (48,300/165,300 rp) through The Bandas (38,300/129,300 rp). Every four weeks, the *Tatamailau* crawls to Tual on its way to Dobo (8300/32,300 rp) and Saumlaki (16,300/70,300 rp), and to

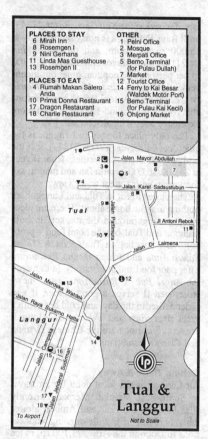

PLACES TO STAY
6 Mirah Inn
8 Rosemgen I
9 Nini Gerhana
11 Linda Mas Guesthouse
13 Rosemgen II

PLACES TO EAT
4 Rumah Makan Salero Anda
10 Prima Donna Restaurant
17 Dragon Restaurant
18 Charlie Restaurant

OTHER
1 Pelni Office
2 Mosque
3 Merpati Office
5 Bemo Terminal (for Pulau Dullah)
7 Market
12 Tourist Office
14 Ferry to Kai Besar (Watdek Motor Port)
15 Bemo Terminal (for Pulau Kai Kecil)
16 Ohijong Market

Tual & Langgur
Not to Scale

bemo (500 rp) from the main road or charte one from the terminal for about 5000 rp, b be wary of blatant overcharging.

Reasonable roads link the major villag throughout Kai Kecil and Dullah islands, b there is no regular public transport arour Kai Besar. Chartering a bemo (worth consid ering to avoid the crush, or waiting f irregular public transport to fill up) will co about 10,000 rp per hour.

The *Tanjung Burang* ferry goes to Band Elat on Kai Besar (2500/3500 rp) three tim a week from Tual's main port. At least or daily boat also goes to Banda Elat from th Pelabuhan Motor Watdek (Watdek Moto Port), near the bridge.

TANIMBAR ISLANDS

The 66 islands forming the Tanimbars we 'discovered' by the Dutch in 1629, but n settled because of a lack of fresh water fo nearly 300 years. The islands remain und veloped, and transport to and around th Tanimbars can be rough and irregular. The are renowned for their carvings, painting and other handcrafts, and for beautiful, wi orchids. The main town, **Saumlaki**, on Pula Yamdena, is little more than a 200m stretc of road called Jl Bhineka. The town is bus and friendly, but less pleasant when the hug tide is at its lowest.

Things to See & Do

At **Sangliat Dol**, on the east coast of Yam dena, a 30m-high stone staircase leads u from the beach to a large, boat-shaped carved stone platform 18m long. The ston structures are interesting enough and th people are friendly, but it's a long, uncom fortable ride (2500 rp; 90 minutes). You ca get off at Sangliat Dol, have a look aroun for an hour and catch the crowded bu (which goes further north to Arui) on its wa back. On the way to Sangliat Dol, the villag of **Inglei** also has a pretty swimming beach

Nearer Saumlaki, you can charter a bem to the lovely, tropical **Pantai Leluan** beach or take the bemo to Olilit Lama village an get dropped off there for the 20 minute walk

Kaimana and Timika, both on the coast of Irian Jaya.

Tual is also connected to Ambon, The Bandas and southern Maluku every three weeks by the Perintis boats *Iweri*, *Nuburi* and *Nagura*, and Tual is a slight detour on the six weekly run by the *Ilosangi* around Irian Jaya. For bookings for all boats, go to the Pelni office (☎ 21181) on Jl Fidnang Armau. All schedules and costs are helpfully displayed outside.

Getting Around

From Langgur's Dumatabun airport, take a

BANDA
SEA

Pulau
Molu

Pulau
Maru

Larat

Pulau
Larat
Lamdesar

Pulau
Wuliaru

Pulau
Yamdena

Watmuri

Arui

Pulau
Sera

Sangliat Dol

Amdasa

Ilngei

Wasletan

Saumlaki

Pulau Matkusa

Pulau
Astubun

Pulau
Nustabun

Pulau
Selaru

Tanimbar
Islands

0   25   50 km

The Pelni office, for all tickets and information, is near the port, which is just off the main street in Saumlaki.

Getting Around

From the tiny Olilit airport, you can charter a bemo for about 3000 rp, share a bemo with everyone else for about 300 rp or get a lift with the friendly Merpati guys.

The one main road on Pulau Yamdena goes up the east coast from Saumlaki as far as Arui. The road is rough and may be impassable in the wet season. All buses leave from the huge, incongruous Yamdena Plaza near the port in Saumlaki. Most buses are unmarked and leave irregularly, so a lot of asking and waiting is inevitable. Chartering at about 10,000 rp per hour will offset the waiting, but you will probably still stop for passengers along the way.

ARU ISLANDS

The closest islands to Irian Jaya, the Arus are little more than a collection of swampy islands in the 'transition zone' between Australia/New Guinea and Asia. A national reserve in the south is home to a diminishing number of birds of paradise, and crocodiles and deer are common. Pearl farming and fishing is being developed by foreign interests.

The Arus are difficult to get to and almost impossible to explore, so receive very, very few visitors. There is no official accommodation, but something will be arranged if you contact the district office at Dobo, the main town on the small, northern island of Wamar.

Merpati flights between Dobo and Ambon (231,500 rp) via Langgur leave (unreliably) twice a week. Dobo is a regular stop for boats between Ambon and the south coast of Irian Jaya. The Pelni ship *Tatamailau* connects Dobo with Timika and Tual during its four weekly run; and the Perintis boat *Nagura* links Dobo with Tual, Saumlaki and Ambon every three weeks. Smaller boats such as the *Katherina* also sail to the Arus and other nearby islands from Ambon.

Places to Stay & Eat

There are only three places to stay, all along Bhineka in Saumlaki. The *Penginapan Jatulel* (☎ 21014) is the cheapest at 15,000/20,000 rp for singles/doubles, plus an extra 2,500 rp for three meals. The best is *Penginapan Harapan Indah* (☎ 21019), which has small upstairs rooms for 24,000 rp with shared mandi – more for air-con and TV – including excellent meals.

Hotel food is definitely recommended, although it is nothing more than a variation of fish, rice and vegetables. There are a few warungs and Padang-style rumah makans around the market, but nothing else.

Getting There & Away

Merpati flies between Ambon and Saumlaki (183,100 rp) three times a week. The Merpati office (☎ 21017) at the Harapan Indah is officially open weekdays from 8 am to 2 pm.

The Pelni liner *Tatamailau* connects Saumlaki to Tual and Dili (East Timor) every four weeks. The next best choices are the Perintis boats *Iweri* to Tual, Bandaneira and Ambon; the *Nuburi* to Ambon; and the *Nagura* to Dobo, Tual and Ambon. The *Katherina* also passes by every four weeks.

MALUKU

Pulau Ternate & Pulau Tidore

The original 'Spice Islands', Ternate and Tidore were among the first places the Portuguese and, later, the Dutch, established themselves in Maluku. Once bitter rival sultanates, the two islands are littered with the ruins of European forts, surrounded by great beaches (usually with black sand), and full of beautiful volcanic and tropical scenery. With regular air and boat connections to Manado in northern Sulawesi, Ternate is an ideal place to stop over before heading down to Ambon or over to Irian Jaya.

History

Well before the Europeans came, the sultanate of Ternate was one of the most important in Maluku, with influence as far south as Ambon, west to Sulawesi and east to Irian Jaya. Ternate's prosperity came from its abundant production of cloves, which allowed it to become a powerful regional military force.

In 1511 the Portuguese were the first to settle in the region and establish a monopoly of the spice trade, but in 1575 they were expelled by the Ternateans. Five years later the British, under the command of Francis Drake, had a look around, but his visit didn't spark any British interest in the islands. The Dutch arrived in 1599 and re-established a local monopoly; the Spanish became the chief foreign power in Ternate and Tidore for much of the 17th century; during the Napoleonic Wars the British took control; and afterwards, the Dutch returned. Japanese occupation of the islands during WWII had little effect.

Books

If you can, pick up a copy of *Turbulent Times Past and Present in Ternate and Tidore* by Willard A Hanna and Des Alwi. It is an absorbing history of the conquests of the islands by the various European powers, but absurdly overpriced at 35,000 rp. Probably because Alwi is a supremo in The Banda; the book is only available in Bandaneira not in Ternate or Ambon.

KOTA TERNATE

The town of Ternate is, in contrast to Ko Ambon, a relaxed place, only occasional interrupted by rumblings from the huge still smoking Gunung Api Gamalama volcano which all towns on the island cling. Near th terminal, the market is one of the busiest an most colourful in Maluku and is certainl worth a look around. Some traders aroun the market may offer you some Dutch colo nial coins, but only an expert can tell if the are authentic.

Information

Tourist Office The reasonably useful touri office (☎ 22646) is on the ground floor of th Kantor Bupati complex on Jl Pahlawan Rev olusi. The friendly staff speak English, an have a few brochures and maps to give awa

Pulau Ternate & Pulau Tidore

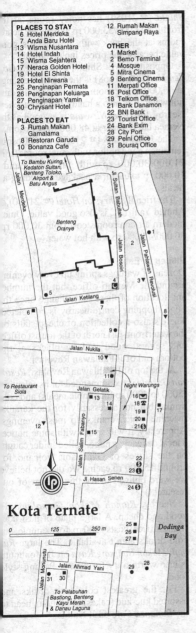

PLACES TO STAY
6 Hotel Merdeka
7 Anda Baru Hotel
13 Wisma Nusantara
14 Hotel Indah
15 Wisma Sejahtera
17 Neraca Golden Hotel
19 Hotel El Shinta
20 Hotel Nirwana
25 Penginapan Permata
26 Penginapan Keluarga
27 Penginapan Yamin
30 Chrysant Hotel

PLACES TO EAT
3 Rumah Makan
  Gamalama
8 Restoran Garuda
10 Bonanza Cafe

12 Rumah Makan
  Simpang Raya

OTHER
1 Market
2 Bemo Terminal
4 Mosque
5 Mitra Cinema
9 Benteng Cinema
11 Merpati Office
16 Post Office
18 Telkom Office
21 Bank Danamon
22 BNI Bank
23 Tourist Office
24 Bank Exim
28 City Port
29 Pelni Office
31 Bouraq Office

Kota Ternate

0   125   250 m

The office is open from 8.30 am to midday and 1.30 to 4 pm daily, except Sunday. You should visit the office for advice and current information before attempting to climb Gamalama (see Around Pulau Ternate for more details).

Money Ternate is the only place in Maluku (besides Kota Ambon) where you can change money. The best banks are BNI bank, Bank Exim and Bank Danamon, all along Jl Pahlawan Revolusi. They are all open weekdays from about 8 am to 2 pm.

Post & Communications Next to each other on Jl Pahlawan Revolusi, the post office is open from 8 am to 8 pm daily, with a useful poste restante; and the Telkom office is open 24 hours.

Kedaton Sultan
Built around 1250, Kedaton Sultan (Sultan's Palace) lies just back from Jl Sultan Babullah, the road leading to the airport. The palace is now a museum containing an absorbing collection of Portuguese cannons, Dutch helmets and armour, and memorabilia from the reigns of past sultans. The sultans' crown, which supposedly has magical powers (including the ability to stop Gamalama from erupting), is only displayed on special occasions.

The museum is officially open from 8 am to 4 pm weekdays but you're more likely to find it open in the mornings. This is regarded as a holy place, so shoes must be removed before entering the main rooms. A small donation is expected. The museum is an easy 15 minute walk north of the terminal, or take any bemo heading north for 250 rp.

Benteng Oranye
Opposite the bemo terminal, this fort was built by the Dutch in 1607 on top of an undated Malay fort, which explains its former name, Benteng Malayo. The fort was the headquarters of the entire VOC operation until about 1619 (when it was transferred to Jakarta) and was the residence of the Dutch governors in Ternate.

MALUKU

Inevitably, the fort has now been taken over by the Indonesian military and police, though you can still have a look around. It hasn't been restored, but a walk around gives you an idea of its former size and grandeur. A visitor's book will be produced and a small donation is expected.

Places to Stay – bottom end

Most of the cheap accommodation is around the noisy port area on Jl Pahlawan Revolusi. They offer very basic accommodation, mainly for Indonesians waiting for boats. The *Penginapan Permata*, just off Jl Pahlawan Revolusi (look for the sign), is good value at 5000 rp per person. The *Penginapan Keluarga* (☎ 22250) is another good option (also look for the sign off the main road) for 5000 rp per person, or 7500 rp for a room with a mandi. For around the same price, the *Penginapan Yamin* (☎ 21929) is also not too bad.

Near the 'second' ferry port at Bastiong (refer to the Getting There & Away section for details) one or two cheap places, such as the *Penginapan Mallioboro* and the *Wisata Inn*, have simple, noisy rooms for about 5000 rp per person.

A couple of family-run places on Jl Salim Fabanyo are not great value, but they are friendly and central. The *Wisma Sejahtera* (☎ 21139) can be noisy at times, and costs 15,000/20,000 rp for singles/doubles. The *Wisma Nusantara* (☎ 21086) costs 20,000 rp per room, but is often full.

One of the cheapest in this range, the *Anda Baru Hotel* (☎ 21262) on Jl Ketilang has good-value rooms for 13,250/22,000 rp, or 19,800/30,800 rp, including meals, but the mosque over the road can be deafening at times and the hotel owners are a little eccentric.

Places to Stay – middle & top end

The old *Hotel Merdeka* (☎ 21120) at Jl Merdeka 19 is one of the best. With rooms starting at 17,500 rp per person, the place has some charm, friendly staff and a pleasant outdoor seating area.

On Jl Pahlawan Revolusi, the *Hotel El Shinta* (☎ 21059) has noisy rooms at the front for 22,000/33,000 rp and better, dearer rooms at the back with air-con. It's good value because the prices include meals.

Opposite the El Shinta, the *Neraca Golden Hotel* (☎ 21668) is the top of the range at 66,000 rp per room with air-con, TV and hot water. It is also a handy Bouraq agency. Nearby, the *Hotel Nirwana* is as good as the Neraca but cheaper at 48,000 rp per room.

The *Hotel Indah* (☎ 21334) on Jl Bosoi remains a good option with quiet rooms from 21,000/30,000 rp with fan and mandi. 10,000 rp extra for a package including all meals.

The friendly *Chrysant Hotel* (☎ 21580), Jl Ahmad Yani 131, is also good value. Quiet modern air-con rooms cost from 30,000 rp, 40,000/45,000 rp with hot water.

Places to Eat

Dozens of warungs spring up every evening around the Merpati office, but the number and location of these may change once the huge shopping centre nearby is completed. There's also a collection of cheap stalls on the waterfront, just north of the tourist office, and several good Padang places at the bottom end of Jl Pahlawan Revolusi.

At the top of Jl Pahlawan Revolusi, *Restoran Garuda* is recommended for its selection (3000 to 4000 rp for simple meals) and cold drinks, but not necessarily for the karaoke machine which cranks up most evenings. Apparently, it will serve, with some notice, a local delicacy: a huge, boiled spider caught on the slopes of Gamalama volcano for around 15,000 rp each. (We did not believe we were obliged to try this as part of our research!)

Nearby, *Rumah Makan Gamalama* is good and cheap. A large plate of nasi ikan (fish and rice) costs 1300 rp, for example, but cold drinks aren't available. The large *Rumah Makan Simpang Raya* on Jl Monunutu is also worth a try for mainly Padang-style food.

For the greatest cold fruit drinks and assorted kue-kue (cakes) in Maluku, head to the *Bonanza Cafe* on Jl Nukila.

MALUKU

North of the market, *Bambu Kuring* on Jl ultan Babullah is worth a 10 minute stroll. he menu is vast with reasonable prices neals from around 5000 to 6000 rp), and the rivate tables are surrounded by rattan decor nd ponds.

ntertainment

everal times daily, two fairly good cinemas how English or Chinese-language films with Indonesian subtitles). The *Mitra* 'inema (2000 rp a ticket), opposite the Hotel Merdeka, has better sound and films than the *enteng Cinema* (1500 rp) on Jl Bosoiri. For araoke, late night drinking and dancing, the nly places to go are the *Restaurant Siola* on l Stadion, *Fujiyama* in the Hotel El Shinta nd *The Pub* in the Neraca Golden Hotel.

Getting There & Away

Air Ternate is the centre for all air transport n northern Maluku. Everything for Halma-era comes through Ternate and it's well onnected to Manado in northern Sulawesi.

Merpati flies to Manado (96,200 rp) daily, nd Ambon (157,000 rp) almost daily. Smal-er, less-popular flights to Galela (65,400 rp) nd Kao (43,400 rp) in northern Halmahera, nd to Pulau Gebe (105,000 rp) and Labuha 69,800 rp), on Pulau Bacan, have a habit of eing cancelled or delayed. The Merpati office (☎ 21651) on Jl Bosoiri is open daily rom 8.15 am to noon and 2.30 to 4.30 pm, nd Sunday and public holidays from 9.30 m to noon.

Bouraq has identical prices to Merpati, nd is often more popular because it is simp-y more reliable. It flies daily to Ambon and Manado. Bouraq's office (☎ 21288) at Jl Ahmad Yani 131, next to the Chrysant Hotel, s open from 8 am to 5 pm daily. There is also a Bouraq agent (☎ 21327) in the Neraca Golden Hotel.

Boat Ternate is also the major port for north-ern Maluku – but take note of the different ports.

Every two weeks, the *Kerinci* goes to/ from Ambon (35,500/134,500 rp economy/ 1st class), to Bitung in northern Sulawesi

(30,500/114,500 rp), and on to Ujung Pan-dang and Java. The *Ciremai* goes to Bitung, Sorong (42,500/162,500 rp) and other Irian Jayan ports, as well as Sulawesi and Java. These Pelni boats leave from the port in Kota Ternate, where the Pelni office (☎ 21434) is located.

There is a multitude of other boats. The Perintis boat *Pahala* goes up the north coast of Halmahera to Daruba, Tobelo and Pulau Gebe every week or so; and the *Cahaya Pasific* and *Cahaya Bahari* have a real milk run to Pulau Bacan, the Sula Islands, Pulau Buru and Ambon, among other places, every couple of weeks. Also, the *Nusa Teratai* goes to Manado (20,500 rp), Mangole (27,500 rp) in the Sulas and on to Ambon every week; the *Ternate Star* heads south to Obi and Bacan islands twice a week; and the *Ampera IV* sails to Bacan and Gebe islands and So-rong (Irian Jaya) twice a week. Overnight boats (which means you miss a lot of scen-ery), such as the *Garuda I* go to Tobelo (15,500 rp; 15 hours) via Daruba (12,500 rp; 12 hours) about every week. The boats to Tobelo and Daruba often also go to Manado (22,000 rp).

The three ports can be a little confusing, as two of the ports are only a few hundred metres apart at Bastiong, a few km south of the city (bemos to both ports cost 250 rp). The 'first' port as you arrive from the city has most slow and fast boats to Bacan and Obi islands and southern Halmahera; regular boats to Bitung (15,200 rp); and speedboats to Rum (1000 rp) on Pulau Tidore.

The 'second' port, a little further south of the 'first', is where speedboats leave for Sid-angoli, the nearest port on Halmahera, and where the ferry leaves every two hours daily to Soa Siu (800 rp), on Pulau Tidore, and Sidangoli (2700 rp). You can also buy bus tickets for the Sidangoli-Galela road on northern Halmahera here.

The larger port in the city, at the end of Jl Pahlawan Revolusi, caters for Pelni and Peri-ntis boats, most boats and speedboats to northern Halmahera, and boats to Sulawesi, the Sula Islands and Ambon. Noticeboards outside the shipping offices in the larger city

MALUKU

port, and along the entrances of the two Bastiong ports, tell you what is going where and when. Tickets for most boats (except speedboats and ferries) can, and should, be bought at least the day before departure. Refer to the Pulau Halmahera and Bacan Islands sections later in this chapter for more details on boats around this area.

Getting Around

The Babullah airport is just north of Kota Ternate. Charter a bemo to your hotel for about 5000 rp, or walk for less than one km from the airport terminal to the university and pick up a public bemo for about 300 rp to the bemo terminal. The city is small and you can easily walk to all places. Bemos around town cost 250 rp; and a horse and cart (bendi) usually costs from 500 to 1000 rp to any place in the central area.

AROUND PULAU TERNATE

It's easy to visit all the sights around the tiny island in one or two day trips from the city. Most of the circular, surfaced road is covered by public bemos. They go infrequently as far as Takome (550 rp) via the north and to Togafo (750 rp) via the south, but normally not between the two villages because the area is so sparsely populated – so you can't completely circle the island by public bemo. Chartering a bemo for about 8000 rp per hour is a very good option. If chartering, allow at least three hours to quickly see the sights; a couple of hours more if you really want to explore the lakes, climb forts and take a swim. It will take considerably longer by public bemo.

Benteng Toloko

Built by the Portuguese in 1512, and restored by the Dutch in 1610, this fort (also known as Benteng Holandia) is the best on the island. The setting by the sea and the views are superb and, although not restored, it's still fascinating. Ask the woman next door to let you in. She will produce the inevitable visitors' book, and a small donation is expected. The fort is just off the main road on the way to the airport. It's a pleasant three km walk from the bemo terminal, or take bemo heading that way for around 250 rp.

Batu Angus

Batu Angus (Burnt Rock) is a volcanic lava flow caused by the eruption of the Gama lama volcano in 1737. A huge area of black rocks heaped on top of each other as far as you can see, it is great for clambering around and admiring the views of nearby Pulau Hiri. It's on the main road, not far past the airport. A bemo there will cost 300 rp.

Sulamadaha

At the top of the island, Sulamadaha has black sandy beach which is looking a bit scruffy these days. It's empty, except for Sunday. Walk over the rocks and headland for 15 minutes to a tiny coral beach where the water is safe for swimming and snorkelling. From the Sulamadaha port, down a lane off the main road before the beach, public motorboats (500 rp) leave daily (but irregularly) to the tiny villages on **Pulau Hiri**; or you can charter a motorboat for an unreasonable 30,000 rp return.

Just before the Sulamadaha beach, the friendly *Hotel Pantai Indah* (☎ 21659), with clean rooms and mandi for 18,000 rp per person, including three meals, is a quiet alternative to the city. Bemos to Sulamadaha cost 550 rp.

Danau Tolire Besar

Ignore Danau Tolire Kecil, the smaller, dirtier lake next to a black sand beach in a small park, and head straight for Danau Tolire Besar. A 500m trail from the main road leads to this stunning, deep volcanic lake which contains crocodiles, fish and, apparently, even the wreckage of a WWII plane. The lake and foothills are a great area for hiking. Public bemos go as far as Takome (550 rp) from where you will have to walk a few km.

Afetaduma

This popular and clean black sand beach is especially crowded on Sunday, when you are far more likely to get a bemo there (750 rp).

MALUKU

Danau Laguna

This large volcanic, spring-fed lake near Ngade is covered with lotuses and is another great area for hiking. A whitewashed wall surrounds part of it. The main entrance is usually closed, so take the dirt track down to the lake from the start of the wall as you come from the city; or if that fails look for the guard to let you in.

Near the main entrance to the lake, **Taman Eva** (entry fee 500 rp) is a popular spot for Ternateans on Sunday. It has a pleasant garden area, a small cafe and splendid views across the bay to Tidore. You can scramble down to the rocks below and dive into the sea. The lake and park can be reached by bemo (500 rp) from the city.

Benteng Kayu Merah

One km south of Bastiong is 'Red Wood Fort', also known as Benteng Kalamata. Built in 1540 by the Portuguese and rebuilt by the Dutch in 1610, its location by the sea is spectacular, but it has been recently restored and, consequently, has lost a lot of its charm. Still, it is worth a look around. Take the bemo to Kalamata (300 rp).

Gunung Api Gamalama

This active volcano (1721m) is, in fact, the entire island of Ternate. It has erupted fiercely many times over the centuries, often resulting in mass evacuations and loss of life. In 1840 it destroyed almost every house on the island. The most recent eruptions were in 1980, 1983 and in October 1994, when hot ash sprayed 300m above the crater.

You can wait for an irregular public bemo (350 rp), or charter one, to **Marikurubu** village on the slopes of Gamalama. Although it is so close to the city, many people in the area still maintain their old customs and live in traditional housing. This is great hiking country, but beware: a white face will certainly cause a large gathering; you'll need a guide if you plan to do any walking in the area; and a few, big, black, hairy spiders set webs for unsuspecting tourists!

Ask to be dropped off on the way to the village of Torano (350 rp by public bemo),

and then walk a km or so (ask directions) to the enormous **clove tree** (cengkeh afo), on the slopes of the volcano. Claimed as the oldest clove tree in the world (nearly 400 years old), it still produces up to 500 or 600 kg of cloves each harvest.

Gamalama can be climbed in about four hours and is not difficult with some rests. Start at about 5 am to ensure that you see the breathtaking views before clouds cover the top of the volcano for the rest of the day and before it gets too hot. You should definitely talk to the tourist office in Kota Ternate before you plan anything. You will need a guide (ask at the tourist office, or try a hotel like the Merdeka) who will charge a fairly hefty 30,000 rp. The trek starts at Marikurubu or nearby Moya. Be careful, especially at the top, because some tourists – without guides – have disappeared while climbing the volcano.

PULAU TIDORE

Tidore was also once part of the pre-colonial spice trade and, like Ternate, a great Islamic sultanate which once claimed parts of Halmahera and areas as far away as Irian Jaya. Rivalry between the neighbouring sultanates resulted in frequent wars and it was only in 1814 that peace was finally established. To placate potentially troublesome modern Tidoreans, the oddly shaped Central Halmahera district was created by the Indonesian government. The capital of Tidore and the district, Soa Siu, is the only main town on the island.

The road which links the port of Rum to Soa Siu is virtually one long village; north of Soa Siu the island is far less populated and public transport is scarce. Ternate has far better facilities for visitors, but Tidore is an easy and very enjoyable day trip from Ternate.

Things to See & Do

Bemos regularly travel between Rum and the Soa Siu bemo terminal/market (1000 rp; 40 minutes). They are less frequent from Soa Siu to Maftutu in the north – and non-existent from Maftutu back to Rum – so you

MALUKU

cannot completely circle the island without chartering for about 10,000 rp per hour. Along the Rum-Soa Siu road you'll see plenty of pretty beaches, foundations of abandoned colonial houses and snorkelling spots – just get on and off the bemo as you like.

Rum, a busy, friendly village where nutmeg is still cultivated, is the port for ferries and speedboats to Ternate. From Rum, you can charter a sailboat, or take a public boat, to the gorgeous island of **Pulau Maitara**, which has clear, blue waters for snorkelling and swimming.

Just before you arrive in Soa Siu, ask to be dropped off at the **Sonyine Malige Sultan's Memorial Museum** which contains a small, but intriguing, collection of sultan memorabilia. If it isn't open, ask at the office at the side of the building. Only 50m from the museum, at the fork in the road, the ruins of the Spanish fort **Benteng Tohula** stand enticingly. Ask a local boy to show you how to climb up there.

Bemos (500 rp) leave irregularly from the Soa Siu market to the small, delightful village of **Gurabunga** perched on the side of **Gunung Api Keimatubu** (1730m). If you want to climb the volcano, go to the kepala desa for current information and to bargain for a guide. The climb can be tricky in parts and takes about five hours. The views from the village are superb; it's not a bad idea to take a bemo up there and walk back to the main road in less than an hour.

Places to Stay

There is no need to stay on Tidore but there are a few places anyway. Near the Soa Siu market, the *Johra Penginapan* is the cheapest at around 7500 rp per person. Also in Soa Siu, the friendly *Losmen Jangi* (☎ 21131), Jl Malawat 32, is the best place at around 15,000 rp per person. For both places, ask the bemo driver to drop you off, or take a becak from the market.

About five minutes by bemo from Rum, on the Rum-Soa Siu road, the *Penginapan Sejuk* is very inconvenient and of limited use.

Getting There & Away

The easiest way to Tidore is by speedboats (1000 rp; seven minutes) which travel every few minutes between the 'first' Bastion port, south of Kota Ternate, and Rum in northern Tidore. Older, slower wooden boats (500 rp), and a ferry (800 rp) between the 'second' Bastiong port and Rum, are also available, but are infrequent and slow.

Pulau Halmahera

The largest island in Maluku (17,780 sq km) Pulau Halmahera is strangely shaped with four peninsulas and dozens of islands off the western coast. Its population of 210,000 is mainly Muslim and, like the people of Ternate and Tidore, is a mix of Portuguese, Gujarati (from western India), Arab, Malay and Dutch – a result of the long contact with foreign traders who came to this area in search of spices.

Only the northern peninsula has any infrastructure, large villages or places to stay – the exception is Pulau Bacan just off the southern coast. Halmahera is an interesting and easy diversion from Ternate, which is linked regularly by air and boat with northern Sulawesi and the rest of Maluku. Halmahera and its nearby islands offer old forts, WWII remnants, beaches, diving, volcanoes and, if you have an adventurous streak, plenty of do-it-yourself trekking in the mountains among traditional people. The main town on Halmahera is Tobelo.

Getting There & Away

Air Frequent, and cheaper, buses and boats around Halmahera have severely affected the popularity, and therefore the reliability, of flights from Ternate – the centre for all flights to Halmahera. Officially, Merpati flies between Ternate and Galela (65,400 rp) three times a week, Kao and Ternate (43,400 rp) every week, and Galela and Pulau Morotai (30,000 rp) once a week. These flights are subject to change and cancellations, and shouldn't be relied upon.

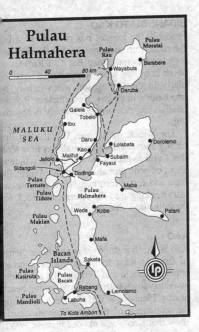

Pulau Halmahera

0   40   80 km

MALUKU SEA

Pulau Morotai
Pulau Rau
Wayabula
Berebere
Daruba
Galela
Tobelo
Ibu
Daru
Lolabata
Dorolemo
Kao
Malifut
Subaim
Jailolo
Fayaui
Sidangoli
Dodinga
Pulau Ternate
Maba
Pulau Tidore
Pulau Halmahera
Pulau Makian
Weda
Kobe
Patani
Pulau Kasiruta
Mafa
Bacan Islands
Saketa
Pulau Bacan
Babang
Lemolemo
Pulau Mandioli
Labuha
To Kota Ambon

Boat About once a week, boats such as the *Garuda* usually connect Tobelo with Manado (35,000 rp), in northern Sulawesi – otherwise all boats to northern Halmahera will start and finish in Ternate. Boats such as the *Karya Laguna* and *Cahaya Pasific* ply a common route between Ambon and Ternate (about 40 hours) stopping at Pulau Bacan and the nearby Obi and Sula islands.

Boats used to link Ternate with Tobelo and Daruba (Pulau Morotai) every couple of days, but there are fewer now because of the quicker bus services. About once a week, the *Garuda I* leaves Ternate for Daruba (12,500 rp) and Tobelo (15,500 rp), and often goes on to Manado.

Sidangoli is the closest port on Halmahera to Ternate. Speedboats (5000 rp; half-hour), which leave from the 'second' Bastiong port (refer to Getting There & Away in the earlier Kota Ternate section), are quick and frequent. The ferry between Bastiong and Sidangoli is cheaper (1700 to 3500 rp, de-

pending on the class of seat) than the speed-boat, but takes three times longer and leaves infrequently.

The *Hero Star* ferry (600 rp) and a speed-boat (3000 rp) travel daily directly between Jailolo and the harbour in Kota Ternate – you'll need to ask directions for the exact jetty in the latter harbour.

Getting Around

Bus A good road from Sidangoli heads up the west coast of the north-west peninsula through Jailolo as far as Ibu – from then on travel is by boat. Another rough road heads along the east coast of the north-west peninsula between Sidangoli and Galela via Kao and Tobelo.

From Ternate to Kao (12,500 rp; four hours) or Tobelo (15,000 rp; six to seven hours), it's far better to buy a Sidangoli-Kao/Tobelo bus ticket in Bastiong before you get on the ferry or boat to Sidangoli; this avoids the pandemonium of finding a seat on a bus at the Sidangoli terminal after the ferry arrives from Ternate. At Sidangoli, it's easier and safer to succumb to the becak driver's pleading and take a becak between the boat and bus terminals.

The comfort of buses along the Sidangoli-Galela road varies considerably and you just have to take pot luck – don't get too excited about promises of air-conditioning either. From Tobelo, Kao and Bastiong, you should book your ticket the day before you leave. Try sharing a Toyota taxi *(super kijang)* between Tobelo and Sidangoli, which costs about the same as a bus, but is quicker (and still crowded), if you can find one (not always easy). Unfortunately, all buses and taxis from Tobelo leave at 4 and 7 am to catch the Sidangoli-Bastiong ferry.

Boat The paucity of roads means that most travel around the island is by speedboat or longboat. To places on the north-east peninsula, boats go from Daru on the Sidangoli to Tobelo road to Fayaui, and a large, new ferry travels most days between Tobelo, Daruba and Subaim. Roads cover most of the north-west peninsula, but boats from Jailolo travel

MALUKU

to places further north such as Ibu and Pulau Morotai. For the southern peninsula, the hub for boat transport is Saketa, which is linked with Bacan and Ternate islands by regular boats.

Between Ternate and Bacan islands, boats such as the *Ternate Star* and *Garuda IV* (both around 10,500 rp) travel overnight (thereby missing the fantastic scenery) every two or three days; or there's a fast boat (see Bacan Islands later in this section for details).

SIDANGOLI

Sidangoli is little more than a terminal for boats to Ternate and buses to Tobelo, but it's pleasant enough to stay while you plan your assault on Halmahera or day trip to Jailolo.

The best place to stay is the *Penginapan Sidangoli Indah*, only about 50m from the bus terminal. It doubles as a brothel on occasions, but the place is nice – large rooms with mandi cost 25,000 rp, which is overpriced as it doesn't include meals. The only other place, the *Penginapan Ramayana* on the main road to the market, is far cheaper at 10,000 rp, but the rooms are nothing more than tiny cubicles. About the only place to eat is *Indah Fanny*, opposite the Ramayana, where you can order simple Indonesian food and cold beer (if the waitress can hear you over the booming karaoke machine).

JAILOLO

The town of Jailolo on the west coast of the north-west peninsula is not quite as grand as it was when it was one of four sultanates in the region. Very few white faces detour to this part of Halmahera, so crowds of on-lookers can be a little disconcerting. Ruins of the **Sultan's Palace** are meant to be near-by, but nobody in the village has ever heard of them.

Jailolo's one *penginapan* is unmarked and unnamed in the market area. Huge rooms with real antique furniture cost 20,000 rp, including meals. Jailolo is worth a day trip from Sidangoli or Ternate – the ride between Sidangoli and Jailolo (3500 rp; 40 minutes) by frequent bemo is delightful and smooth.

SIDANGOLI TO KAO

Probably the longest bus route in Maluku, the road from Sidangoli to Tobelo may not look too far on the map, but it's a hard six or seven hour slog along a rough road – particularly in the wet season when it may be impassable in places. Nevertheless, it is an exhilarating ride and the scenery is absorbing.

The wreck of a huge WWII ship lies mostly above water in a small bay near **Malifut** – you can see it from your bus window. The bus will probably stop in Malifut for food and rest. From here, or Kao, you can start trekking into the interior and look for the nomadic Tuhuru people.

KAO

Kao is worth a stopover if you have plenty of time or want to break up the journey between Tobelo and Ternate. It's a friendly and dusty town with a nice swimming beach nearby. Plenty of WWII remnants, including the shipwreck of the *Dai Nippon*, clearly show that Kao was a major Japanese WWII base (with up to 60,000 troops).

The *Penginapan Dirgahayu* has average rooms with mandi (and plenty of mosquitos) for 15,000 rp per person, including three good meals, or 12,500 rp without meals. Next door, the *Dua Puteri* is the only place to eat. It serves basic Indonesian food, but seems to cater more for frequent transiting bus passengers than the very occasional traveller staying at Kao.

TOBELO

Tobelo is the hub for buses and boats servicing northern Halmahera and Pulau Morotai, and is an ideal place to base yourself while exploring the area. Virtually everything you need in Tobelo is on Jl Kemakmuran, part of the main road south to Kao and north to Galela. The banks are reluctant to change money, so stock up in Ternate.

Tobelo is easy to walk around, although a becak (around 500 rp) is useful from the port to your hotel. The bus may drop you off at a new terminal out of town. If so, you have to ake another short bemo ride to your hotel for which you may be (over)charged 1500 rp.

Places to Stay & Eat

The simple *Penginapan Megaria* on Jl Baynkara (near the President Hotel) costs 0,000 rp per person with mandi, or 7500 rp with shared mandi – no meals are available. The *Hotel Karunia* (☎ 21202) on the main oad is basic and noisy, but better value for 0,000 rp per person. The best in this range s *Penginapan Alfa Mas* (☎ 21543), which as clean, quiet rooms with mandi from 5,000 rp. Look for its sign off the main road.

Hotel Pantai Indah (☎ 21064), just off the main road on Jl Iman Sideba, has good service but expensive beer. Singles/doubles with a fan cost 22,000/38,500 rp; almost double that for air-con. The price includes excellent meals. On the main road, the *President Hotel* (☎ 21231) has modern, clean ooms with good meals for 38,500/49,500 p, and there is a restaurant.

If you don't eat at your hotel, a few uninteresting places around the becak stop and market serve Padang food. The best place to eat is the *Rumah Makan Toboko*, just north of the President Hotel, for delicious, cheap baked fish and Indonesian food.

AROUND TOBELO

Along the road between Tobelo and Galela (1000 rp; 45 minutes), lined with swaying palms hugging the pretty coastal edge, there are a few places to stop off. **Pantai Luari**, a small, semi-developed tourist beach (for Indonesians), is nice enough for swimming and relaxing under the trees. From the bridge in **Mamuya** village, an 800m trail leads to the small *air panas* (hot water springs), which are definitely worth a soak. From Mamuya, you can organise five to six hour treks up the volcanoes **Gunung Api**, **Mamuya** and **Do** with the volcanology office in the village.

Closer to Galela, there's some great WWII wrecks at **Pune**. Fifty metres down a lane behind a church on the main road, sit two untouched and overgrown Japanese cannons (*meriam jepang*). To find other WWII remnants, you'll have to do some asking and exploring.

The road finishes at **Galela**, a sleepy Muslim village with nowhere to stay or eat. Nearby, there's a series of stunning volcanic lakes. The largest, **Danau Duma**, complete with small crocodiles (*buaya kecil*) is superb and definitely worth a look around. A good road around the lake starts only three km from Galela. If walking, ask for directions as the lake takes a few hours to walk around. Alternatively, charter a bemo (about 10,000 rp per hour) or take public bemos from Galela to villages on the lake, such as Igobul and Soa Konora.

From Danau Duma you can walk (ask directions; it's about five km), or take a bemo to Makete village from Galela, to the smaller, pretty **Danau Makete**. It's full of lotus flowers and very friendly women washing their clothes. This is another excellent hiking area.

PULAU MOROTAI

Morotai was an important Japanese base during WWII before it was captured by the Allies and used by General MacArthur to plan Allied offensives across the Pacific. Today the sparsely populated, 1600-sq km island offers unexplored tropical beaches, unused WWII airports and wrecks, and unlimited diving sites.

The major town and transport centre, **Daruba**, an unexciting and poor village where a westerner is a strange sight, has few facilities. The only main road on the island doesn't go too far out of Daruba, but there's plans for an extension as far as Berebere. The island is fairly flat, so it's a good place for hiking around the beaches, jungle and isolated villages.

The best and most accessible place to stay is the *Penginapan Panber*. An unsigned, light-yellow building along Jl Yasan, it has passable rooms for 20,000 rp per person, including meals. It isn't great value, but there is little other choice. Daruba has very few places to eat (but there are surprisingly good sugar donuts for sale at the market), so it's better to eat at the hotel.

MALUKU

A large, new ferry leaves Tobelo (3300 rp; three hours) almost daily at about 8 am for Daruba, often connecting to Subaim on the north-east peninsula of Halmahera. The ferry stops in Daruba for little more than an hour, so it's not much of a day trip from Tobelo, especially because the ferry ride itself isn't that exciting. The ferry's arrival in Tobelo is not timed to connect with the Tobelo to Sidangoli bus or taxi.

BACAN ISLANDS

The Bacan Islands refer to the group at the southern end of Halmahera, including Mandioli and Kasiruta islands. Almost all development, facilities and transport are based on Pulau Bacan, where Labuha is easily the largest town. Pulau Bacan's port, Babang, is about half an hour (1000 rp) from Labuha. Bacan is an easy trip (even a day trip) from Ternate, or a stopover between Ternate and Ambon.

Benteng Barnevald was originally built by the Portuguese to counter the expanding Spanish empire, but was soon captured by the Dutch (in 1609). Complete with a moat and several cannons, the fort is entirely overgrown, but still discernible and, in its own way, one of the most fascinating in Maluku. It's about 500m behind a Protestant church in Labuha – if in doubt ask directions. The **Sultan's Palace** is disappointing and not worth the effort – take a public bemo or charter one for about 15,000 rp per hour.

Air Belanda (Dutch Water), a pretty area with a stream and waterfall, is worth a three km stroll from the centre of Labuha (ask directions, or charter a bemo).

Places to Stay & Eat

Labuha has several good places to stay; the bemo or bus from Babang will drop you off at your losmen. *Pondok Indah* (☎ 21048), 50m from Labuha's centre, has clean, quiet rooms for 20,000 rp, including meals. Also close to the centre, the *Penginapan Borero* (☎ 21024) is worth paying a little extra – singles/doubles cost 25,000/30,000 rp, including meals.

If you don't eat at your hotel, the *Eka Ria*

Restaurant and *Sibela Cafetaria*, near the hotels, serve reasonable but not-so-cheap meals and, even here, they have karaoke machines.

Getting There & Away

Merpati has flights from Ternate to Labuha (69,800 rp) and on to Ambon (146,800 rp) via Sanana (96,200 rp) on the Sula Islands but these flights are often cancelled.

Several boats sail between Bacan and Ternate islands daily, but these travel at night which means you miss one of the most spectacular journeys of mountain, volcanic and island scenery in Indonesia. (Refer to the earlier Pulau Halmahera Getting Around section for details of some of these boats.)

The best, but most expensive, way to Bacan is the new 'super-fast' *Kie Raha Express* (20,000 rp; five hours). It travels to/from the 'first' Bastiong port (leaving at ? am) on Ternate and Babang daily, except Sunday. This even allows you time to day trip to Bacan from Ternate, but it's better to stay in Labuha for a day or two.

SULA ISLANDS

South-west of Pulau Halmahera – and far closer to central Sulawesi, but still part of the Northern Maluku district – are the Sula Islands. They are sparsely populated, densely forested and ignored by just about every traveller to Maluku. But if you want to *really* get away from the tourist trail and visit hitherto unexplored diving and hiking spots among traditional villages and rugged terrain, then the Sulas may be for you.

The best place to base yourself is **Sanana** on Pulau Sanana, though most transport goes to/from Mangole on Pulau Mangole. It's a very relaxed place, with a large decrepit Dutch fort near the port. Along the main road, the unmarked *Penginapan Sula Indah* (take a becak) costs from 15,000 rp per person without meals, or 10,000 rp extra for three meals. There is also another unmarked *penginapan* behind the fort. One of the few places to eat, the bizarrely named *Rumah Makan Elvis Raya* (*raya* means 'great').

MALUKU

opposite the port entrance, serves simple, cheap Indonesian food.

Roads are almost non-existent on the Sulas; boats are the major form of transport around, and between, each island. The islands are well linked to Ternate, Manado and Ambon by boats such as the *Nusa Teratai* to Mangole and Sanana; the *Cahaya Bahari* to Mangole, Dofa and Sanana; and the *Cahaya Pasific* to Sanana. The seas around the islands can be very rough (as we can attest!).

Merpati flies (unreliably) between Ambon and Mangole (146,800 rp) twice a week, and on to Manado (166,600 rp); and between Ambon and Sanana (123,700 rp), and on to Labuha on Pulau Bacan (96,200 rp). The Merpati offices are on Jl Pantai in Sanana (☎ 21078) and at PT Anugerah Jaya in Mangole (no telephone).

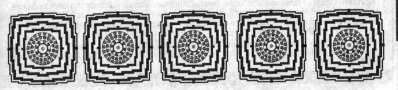

Irian Jaya

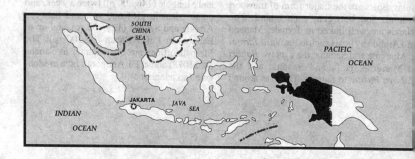

Irian Jaya, the western half of the island of New Guinea, was only acquired by the Indonesians from the Dutch in the 1960s. Over three times larger than Java and Bali combined, Irian Jaya's 421,981 sq km is mainly impenetrable jungle where traditional people still manage to survive the harsh conditions and modern intrusions. Almost all visitors head to the Baliem Valley (the only part of the interior generally accessible to tourism) with, perhaps, a side-trip to Biak and/or Jayapura. Irian Jaya has a lot more to offer, but it still suffers, and will for some time, from limited transport and excessive government travel regulations.

When the Portuguese sighted New Guinea as early as 1511 they called it Ilhas dos Papuas ('Island of the Fuzzy Hairs'), from the Malay word *papuwah*. Later Dutch explorers called it New Guinea because the black-skinned people reminded them of the people of Guinea in Africa. *Irian* is a word from the Biak language meaning 'hot land rising from the sea'. Under the Dutch, Irian Jaya was known as Dutch New Guinea and when sovereignty was transferred to Indonesia it was renamed Irian Barat (West Irian) then Irian Jaya (*jaya* means 'victorious'). Other names used by non-Indonesians include West Irian and West Papua.

HISTORY

In 1660 the Dutch recognised the sovereignty over New Guinea by the Sultan of Tidore (in northern Maluku) and, since the Dutch held power over Tidore, New Guinea

---

HIGHLIGHTS

- **Baliem Valley** – There is no doubt that the Baliem Valley is the major tourist attraction (and therefore becoming a little touristy) due to its unique culture and trekking among stunning scenery. The other accessible traditional area, the Asmat region, is difficult and expensive to explore properly, and is far, far less developed than the Baliem.

- **Northern Coast** – Manokwari and Nabire are pleasant towns with a few islands and lakes to explore. Biak is a popular stopover, and there's plenty of great diving spots, beaches and WWII remnants to explore around the island. Sentani, a better alternative to nearby Jayapura, is the place to explore the magnificent Danau Sentani.

- **Take Your Time!** – Don't underestimate the size of Irian Jaya and the amount of time and money it will take to really experience what it has to offer – at least four weeks by air and three times longer by boat.

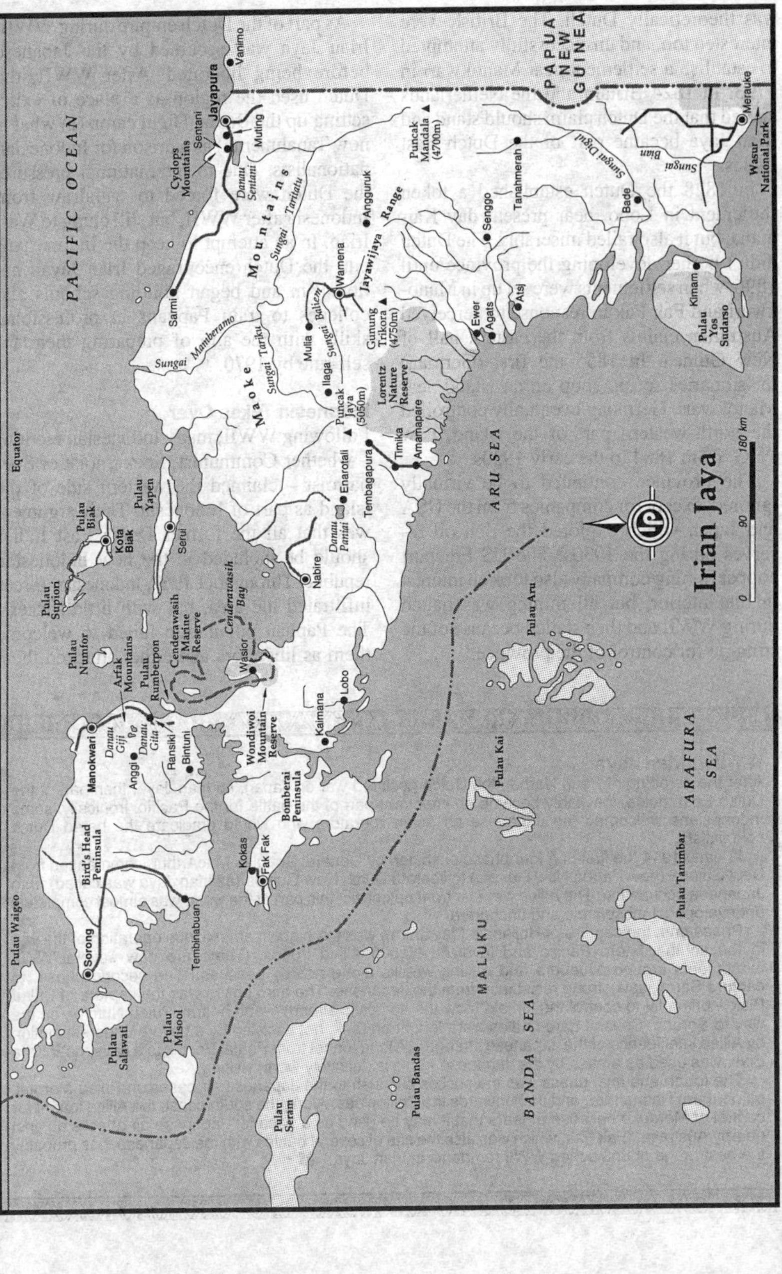

Irian Jaya

PACIFIC OCEAN

PAPUA NEW GUINEA

Vanimo
Jayapura
Moting
Sentani
Cyclops Mountains
Danau Sentani
Puncak Mandala (4700m)
Merauke
Sungai Digul
Sungai Buru
Wasur National Park
Bade
Tanahmerah
Sengo
Anggruk
Sungai Tariku
Maoke Mountains
Sarmi
Sungai Memberamo
Sungai Tariku
Wamena
Jayawijaya Range
Ewer
Agats
Atsj
Mulia
Ilaga
Sungai Balicm
Gunung Trikora (4750m)
Kimam
Pulau Yos Sudarso
Equator
Puncak Jaya (5065m)
Lorentz Nature Reserve
Timika
Amamapare
Enarotali
Tembagapura
Pulau Biak
Kota Biak
Pulau Yapen
Serui
Nabire
Danau Paniai
ARU SEA
Pulau Supiori
Pulau Numfor
Arfak Mountains
Pulau Rumberpon
Cenderawasih Bay
Cenderawasih Marine Reserve
Wasior
Manokwari
Danau Gita
Danau Gili
Ransiki
Bintuni
Wondiwoi Mountain Reserve
Bomberai Peninsula
Lobo
Kaimana
Bird's Head Peninsula
Kokas
Fak Fak
Tembrabuan
Pulau Aru
ARAFURA SEA
Sorong
Pulau Waigeo
Pulau Salawati
Pulau Misool
Pulau Kai
Pulau Tanimbar
MALUKU
Pulau Seram
Pulau Bandas
BANDA SEA

0   90   180 km

was theoretically Dutch. The British were interested too, and unsuccessfully attempted to establish a settlement near Manokwari in 1793. In 1824 Britain and the Netherlands agreed that the Dutch claim should stand and Irian Jaya became part of the Dutch East Indies.

In 1828 the Dutch established a token settlement in Lobo, near present day Kaimana, but it also failed miserably. The Dutch didn't bother developing the province until 1896, when settlements were set up in Manokwari and Fak Fak in response to perceived Australian claims from the eastern half of New Guinea. In 1855 the first (German) missionaries set up shop on an island near Manokwari. Germany eventually controlled the north-western part of the island, now PNG, from 1884 to the early 1930s.

The province continued to be virtually ignored, except for companies from the USA and Japan which explored the rich oil reserves during the 1930s. The US Freeport copper mining company also took an interest in the interior, but all mining was halted during WWII and then stalled because of the struggle for control of the province.

As part of the Dutch empire during WWII, Irian Jaya was occupied by the Japanese before being liberated. After WWII, the Dutch used the region as a place of exile, setting up the Boven Digul camp (in what is now Tanahmerah) as a prison for Indonesian nationalists. Due to international pressure, the Dutch were forced to withdraw from Indonesia after WWII, but still clung to West Irian. In an attempt to keep the Indonesians out, the Dutch encouraged Irian Jayan nationalism and began building schools and colleges to train Papuans in professional skills with the aim of preparing them for self-rule by 1970.

Indonesia Takes Over

Following WWII, many Indonesian factions – whether Communist, Soekarnoist or Soehartoist – claimed the western side of the island as part of Indonesia. Their argument was that all the former Dutch East Indies should be included in the new Indonesian republic. Throughout 1962, Indonesian forces infiltrated the area, but with little success. The Papuan population failed to welcome them as liberators and either attacked them

WWII In Irian Jaya

After the bombing of Pearl Harbor, the Dutch declared war on Japan, so Irian Jaya, then part of the Dutch East Indies, inevitably became an important part of the battle for the Pacific. Ironically, some Indonesians welcomed the Japanese as Asian liberators who would eradicate the hated Dutch colonialists.

In early 1944 the first of a four phase push, led by General Douglas MacArthur, commenced from New Guinea (now Papua New Guinea) to liberate Dutch New Guinea (as Irian Jaya was called) from Japanese occupation. The Allies were far from optimistic: this part of the world was almost completely undeveloped, inhospitable and uncharted.

Phase one, the capture of Hollandia (Jayapura), was the biggest amphibious operation of the war in the south-western Pacific and involved 80,000 Allied troops. (There are now several WWII monuments around Jayapura and rusting wrecks along nearby beaches.) The second phase, to capture Sarmi, saw strong resistance from the Japanese. The third phase was the capture of Pulau Biak – primarily to control the airfield (now the domestic airport) – and nearby Pulau Numfor, on the way to Sorong. Several hard battles were fought on Biak, not assisted by a severe underestimation by Allied intelligence of the Japanese strength. (A long tunnel from Pantai Bosnik to a cave, near Kota Biak, was used as a base by the Japanese.) This is definitely worth visiting.

The fourth and final phase was the successful push to the Japanese air bases on Pulau Morotai, off northern Halmahera, and then towards the Philippines. Along the south coast, the Allies fought for control of Merauke because of fears that it may be used as a base for Japanese air attacks against nearby Australia. (Fak Fak, which was also the site of several battles with the Japanese, has probably the best range of untouched WWII remnants in Irian Jaya.) ■

or handed them over to the Dutch. US pressure forced the Dutch to capitulate abruptly in August 1962.

A vaguely worded agreement in that year under United Nations' (UN) auspices essentially required that Indonesia allow the Papuans of West Irian to determine, by the end of 1969, whether they wanted independence or to remain within the Indonesian republic. This 'Act of Free Choice' was held in 1969, 'supervised' by the UN. The Indonesian government announced that it would use the procedure of *musyawarah*, under which a consensus of 'elders' would be reached. In July 1969, the Indonesian government announced that the assemblies in the Merauke, Jayawijaya and Paniai districts, in which the greater part of the population lived, had unanimously decided to become part of Indonesia. Irian Jaya is now Indonesia's 26th province, made up of nine districts, with capitals at Sorong, Manokwari, Kota (City) Biak, Serui, Nabire, Jayapura, Merauke, Wamena and Fak Fak.

Papuan Opposition

Even before the Act, the Indonesians faced violent opposition from the Papuans. In 1967 aircraft were used to bomb and strafe Arfak people threatening Manokwari. In 1969 rebellions broke out on Pulau Biak and at Enarotali in the highlands. Between 1977 and the mid-1980s, there was occasional conflict in the highlands around the Baliem Valley, Tembagapura (site of the US-run Freeport copper mine) and around the remote areas of the Paniai district.

After a lull of a few years, anti-Indonesian activity recommenced in the mid-1990s. In 1995, members and sympathisers of the major independence group, the Free Papua Movement (Organisasi Papua Merdeka; OPM), formed in 1965, stormed the Indonesian consulate in Vanimo (just over the border of Papua New Guinea) and rioted in Tembagapura and the nearby town of Timika. When the body of an indigenous academic and sympathiser, who died in captivity in Java, was flown back to Jayapura for burial in March 1996, up to 5000 Irianese rioted for

several days and burned the nearby Abepura market, resulting in several deaths. The most recent serious activity was the kidnap of some Europeans and Indonesians in a remote part of the Baliem Valley in January 1996. All Europeans were released unharmed four months later, but two Indonesian hostages were killed by the OPM.

The anti-Indonesian feeling by the Irianese is provoked by the use of their land for logging, mining and other commercial purposes without compensation or consultation; resentment about the unequal distribution of wealth from these enterprises; transmigration, which brings large numbers of western Indonesians to Irian Jaya; attempts to 'Indonesianise' the traditional people; and occasional brutal responses to political dissent.

Transmigration

The Indonesian policy of transmigration is one of the reasons for continuing unrest in Irian Jaya. According to unsubstantiated reports, possibly up to one-third of Irian Jaya's population originates from outside the province, mainly from Java, Bali and Sulawesi. Most of the transmigrants live in settlements near the main towns of Jayapura, Merauke, Manokwari, Nabire and Sorong.

As Irian Jaya represents about 22% of Indonesia's total territory, but only about 1% of its population, the Indonesian government continues to plan to move hundreds of thousands of people to Irian Jaya from other overcrowded islands. Poor locations and lack of planning for many existing settlements indicate that the main thrust of transmigration is less for the benefit of the transmigrants than to make the province truly Indonesian. Several highways in Irian Jaya will open in a few years, so further transmigration is inevitable.

GEOGRAPHY

A central mountain range, the 640 km-long Maoke Mountains, is the backbone of Irian Jaya. Incredibly, Puncak (Peak) Jaya (5050m) and other provincial peaks, such as Puncak Mandala (4700m), have permanent snowfields and small glaciers. Alpine grasslands, jagged bare peaks, montane forests, rainforests, ferocious rivers, gentle streams, stunning rock faces and gorges all add to the varying landscape of the highlands. The most cultivated areas of the highlands are the Danau (Lake) Paniai district and the Baliem Valley to the east.

Swamps with sago palms, and low-lying alluvial plains of fertile soil, dominate the south-eastern section around Merauke. The northern coastal plain is much narrower and less swampy, with larger-than-life tropical vegetation – real jungle. Coconut-palm-fringed, white sandy beaches along the north coast and on the islands of Biak, Numfor and Yapen make this part of Irian Jaya more like many travellers' expectations of the rest of Indonesia.

CLIMATE

Generally, the driest and best time to visit Irian Jaya is between May and October, although it can, and does, rain anywhere, anytime. (Rain falls in Kota Biak up to 25 days of every month.) Strong wind and rain is more common along the north coast from November to March. Along the south coast, however, it can be wild and woolly from April to October, but this is the dry season in Merauke – the only part of Irian Jaya with distinct seasons. The best time for the Baliem Valley is between March and August when the days are drier and cooler, but nights are usually cold year-around. Coastal towns are generally always hot and humid, while it's often cooler in the highlands.

FLORA & FAUNA

Seventy-five per cent of Irian Jaya is forest so it's no surprise that the flora is as varied as its geography. The usual luxurious collection of Asiatic species (some endemic to New Guinea island) lie in this transition zone between Asia and Australia. The south coast's vegetation includes mangroves and the vital sago palm (especially around the Asmat region), as well as eucalypts, paper barks and acacias in the drier south-eastern section. Highland vegetation ranges from alpine grasslands and heath to unique pine forests, bush and scrub. There are over 3000 orchid species in Irian Jaya.

Animals are largely confined to marsupials, such as bandicoots, ring-tailed possums, pygmy flying phalangers, big cuscuses, tree kangaroos and, in the south-east, wallabies. Reptiles include snakes (many poisonous) frill-necked and monitor lizards, and crocodiles. The spiny anteater is also found. Insect life is abundant – with many colourful butterflies around Manokwari – and Irian Jaya is host to about 800 species of spiders.

Despite large-scale plunder, Irian Jaya's exquisite bird life is still famous and an increasingly popular attraction for serious bird lovers. There are more than 600 species including the elusive bird of paradise (known as the *cenderawasih*) on the appropriately named Bird's Head Peninsula and Pulau

The saltwater crocodile is found along Irian Jaya's coastal fringes and estuaries. The male can reach seven metres in length and weigh as much as 1000 kg.

Yapen, bowerbirds, cockatoos, parrots, king-ishers, crowned pigeons and cassowaries around the southern coastal region.

With some effort you can visit two na-ional reserves on Pulau Biak; the Lorentz Nature Reserve (1500 sq km) near Agats; the Wasur National Park (4260 sq km) near Merauke; the Wondiwoi Mountain Reserve and a marine reserve (14,300 sq km) in the Cenderawasih Bay; and a reserve which cov-ers most of Pulau Yos Sudarso off the coast of Merauke.

POPULATION & PEOPLE

Approximately 1.9 million people inhabit Irian Jaya. Its interior is predominantly pop-ulated by pure Papuans, while along the coast there has been more intermarriage with Melanesians and Malays. The most popu-lated and interesting traditional areas have varying degrees of accessibility: the Paniai district is currently off limits; the Asmat region is difficult to get to; while the Baliem Valley is the easiest place to visit.

The Dani are the gentle people who in-habit the Baliem Valley. They often still use stone implements to farm their beloved sweet potato, they revere their precious pigs, and live in compounds of huts made from trees and mud.

After trekking for a day or two, you can visit other traditional people, such as the Manikom and Hatam near the Anggi lakes, and the Kanum and Marind near Merauke. With considerably more time and effort, you can visit the people known as the Asmat, who are renowned for their carvings and whose life is dictated by the swampy rivers of the southern coast. Further inland from the As-mat region, the Kombai and Korowai people live in truly extraordinary tree houses, some-times up to dozens of metres high, to avoid tides, animals and tribal invasion.

Christianity is the major religion of Irian Jaya. Churches of all denominations are dotted around the interior, although, despite what the missionaries may say, the indige-nous people enjoy a combination of traditional beliefs and Christianity. Centuries-old trade by Malays (and transmigration from western Indonesia) ensures that Islam is stronger in many coastal towns.

LANGUAGE

Estimates of the number of languages in Irian Jaya vary from 200 to over 700; nobody can really decide and there is very little study of the linguistics in the region. There is no doubt, however, that Irian Jaya and neighbour-ing Papua New Guinea, with a combined population of only a few million, speak an inordinately high percentage of the world's languages.

Since the takeover by Indonesia more than 30 years ago, and because of transmigration to the province, Bahasa Indonesia has spread quickly throughout Irian Jaya via schools, media and bureaucracy. Now everyone in Irian Jaya (except a few older, uneducated people in isolated areas) has at least a working knowledge of Bahasa.

VISAS & DOCUMENTS

Unfortunately, Garuda has now ceased stop-overs in Biak on its Los Angeles-Jakarta flight. If the stopovers resume, as Garuda reportedly plans, foreigners will be issued with a 60 day tourist visa on arrival in Biak. The other international airport is Jayapura, which has weekly flights to Vanimo just inside the PNG border. However, it is important to note that Jayapura is *not* a visa-free airport; you must obtain an Indonesian tourist visa (valid for four weeks, but often extendable) in Vanimo or Port Moresby.

Surat Jalan

For political and bureaucratic reasons, many places in Irian Jaya, particularly in the inte-rior, can only be visited with a travel permit known as a *surat jalan*. Currently, you can visit Jayapura, Sentani, Sorong and Pulau Biak without a surat jalan. You will need one for other areas, such as Merauke and vicinity, Agats and the Asmat region, Pulau Yapen, Timika, Manokwari and vicinity, and possi-bly Nabire, as well as Wamena and the Baliem Valley. Foreigners are currently not permitted to go anywhere near the PNG border, Gunung (Mt) Trikora, anywhere in the Paniai district, or around Sungai (River) Mamberamo and Ilaga in the central highlands. To go anywhere else, it is safe to assume that you will need a surat jalan.

A surat jalan lasts from one week to one month depending on what you ask for, the expiry date of your visa and the mood of the policemen. They are easy to obtain from major police stations; it's particularly straightforward in Kota Biak, Jayapura and Sentani (although in Sentani, the police may send you on to Jayapura). You will need two passport-size photos (B&W is OK) and you should list on the surat jalan everywhere you want to go, as well as everywhere you *may* go. The permit will take about an hour or so to process, and there is often an 'administration fee' of about 2000 rp.

Don't be concerned: the police are invariably helpful and friendly, and are as bored with the paperwork as you are. To save time and the hassle, your travel agent in Irian Jaya or hotel may be able to arrange the permit for an extra cost. Police stations may be reluctant to issue a permit allowing you to visit a more remote area of another district. If this is the case, you may have to apply at the particular district capital. One surat jalan will normally cover you for all of Irian Jaya, unless you are staying a long time or going to more remote regions.

Your hotel will advise whether you need to report personally to the police; the hotel will often report to the police for you. In remote areas, including the Baliem Valley (but not in Wamena), you will need to report to local authorities wherever you stay. Have a few photocopies of your surat jalan handy to give to regional police stations, or your hotel, when you report.

BOOKS

Peter Matthiessen's *Under the Mountain Wall*, based on his visit to the Baliem in 1961, chronicles his daily life among the Kurulu tribe. Robert Mitton's *The Lost World of Irian Jaya* was compiled from his letters, diaries, maps and photographs after his sudden death in 1976. The book bitterly criticises the reckless way in which the Irians

have been shoved into the modern world. The renowned travel writer Norman Lewis visited Irian Jaya to research his book *An Empire of the East*, in which he provides insights into the Baliem Valley and the Freeport copper mine.

Indonesia's Secret War: The Guerilla Struggle in Irian Jaya by Robin Osborne is a documented account of events up to 1984, and *West Papua: the Obliteration of a People* by Carmel Budiardjo and LS Liong, published by the TAPOL organisation, is also worth reading. George Monbiot's *Poisoned Arrows* details a remarkable journey to the wilds of Irian Jaya with the objective of uncovering the truth about transmigration and the true nature of OPM resistance.

The Asmat is a collection of photographs of the Asmat people and their art, taken by Michael Rockefeller in 1961. *Irian Jaya: The Timeless Domain* by Julie Campbell is an informative narrative, with good photos, mainly about the Baliem Valley and Asmat region. It is available in Irian Jaya, but expensive at about US$50.

Islands in the Clouds by Isabella Tree is part of Lonely Planet's new travel literature series, Journeys. The book deals mainly with visits to remote regions of the PNG highlands, but the author provides some entertaining and insightful chapters about Jayapura and the Baliem.

SPECIAL EVENTS

Festivals and ceremonies are an integral part of Irianese traditional culture, but very few are officially programmed; if you ask around when you arrive somewhere you may be lucky enough to witness something special.

Traditional ceremonies and cultures from all over Irian Jaya are on display during the Irian Jaya Tourism Week in mid-January each year at different district capitals. The Munara Festival in Biak takes place over three days around 20 August, and includes fire walking, traditional dancing and boat races. At the Asmat Art & Culture Festival in Agats and Merauke every October there are woodcarving exhibitions, canoe races and traditional dancing. From 15 to 17

November, the Celebration of the City of Fak Fak is celebrated with traditional dancing, *kora-kora* (canoe) races, ceremonies and sporting events.

As soon as you get to Wamena, ask your guide, or the tourist office, about any festivals or ceremonies in the Baliem Valley. Refer to the Baliem Valley section later in this chapter for details about the spectacular festival held there every August.

ACTIVITIES

Diving Not surprisingly, most activities centre around the mountains, traditional people and the coast. Biak and Yapen islands, and the specially designated Cenderawasih Marine Reserve, boast some astonishing coral and fish. The areas have the potential to rival northern Sulawesi, but the diving industry only exists in Biak and is still in its infancy. Diving near Jayapura is not as good, but is easier to organise. The best time for diving along the north coast is between April and September.

Trekking Trekking is the best way to really see the interior and traditional lifestyles, but if the harsh terrain and very limited transport doesn't put you off, then the Draconian government prohibitions may. Currently, the Baliem Valley is generally the only place in the interior where trekking is allowed, but this area does offer more than enough to satisfy most. To see the Dani people and the magnificent scenery, you can easily day trip from the main town of Wamena or nearby villages, trek for a few days to more remote areas and cultures, or organise serious expeditions as far south (with the aid of river transport) as the Asmat coast.

Limited trekking is also excellent – and allowed without special permission – around the Arfak mountains and the Anggi lakes, near Manokwari; the Cyclop Mountains and Danau Sentani, near Jayapura; and the floodplains and Wasur National Park, not far from Merauke. It may also be possible to trek, with a special permit, around the Wondiwoi Mountains (near Wasior) and the Bomberai peninsula (close to Fak Fak), but enticing

areas such as the Danau Paniai district, Sungai Mamberamo and Gunung Trikora are currently off limits.

Other Activities Organised bird-watching tours are increasingly popular around Manokwari and Sorong and, especially, on northern Pulau Yapen. You can see turtle colonies and other sea life in the Cenderawasih Marine Reserve if you have the time and money. Visiting WWII shipwrecks, tunnels and caves – as well as postwar monuments – on Pulau Biak, at Kokas (near Fak Fak) and near Jayapura, are popular with those who have an interest in the war. Rafting trips are now a possibility down Sungai Baliem between August and November.

GETTING THERE & AWAY

Almost all visitors to Irian Jaya head straight to Jayapura, through Biak or Ujung Pandang, for a connection to Wamena in the Baliem Valley, but several other routes offer a very satisfying look at some of Irian Jaya:

A flight to Port Moresby (the capital of PNG), then on to Vanimo, from where there are weekly flights to Jayapura, just across the border from PNG.

A boat stopping for a few hours at the delightful colonial town of Fak Fak, South-East Maluku and/or the Asmat capital of Agats, on the way to Timika or Merauke, from where there are daily flights to Jayapura.

A boat or plane to Fak Fak from Sorong, or a boat from Ambon (Maluku) through The Bandas to Fak Fak, from where there are regular flights to Nabire, then daily connections to Biak and Jayapura.

A combination of boat and plane along the northern coast stopping at Manokwari, Biak, Nabire and Yapen on the way to Jayapura.

If regulations allow, fly from Nabire to Mulia in the central highlands, where you will have to wait a day or two for a Merpati flight to Wamena.

Air

Unless you have a lot of time, flying is the best way to get to Irian Jaya. Merpati is the main carrier, but Garuda and Sempati airlines have a couple of flights to Jayapura, through Biak or Timika, from major places in the rest of Indonesia. The main regional centres for internal flights – Sorong, Biak and Jayapura – are connected daily with flights to major western Indonesian centres, such as Ambon, Ujung Pandang (Sulawesi), Denpasar and Jakarta. (Refer to the Irian Jaya Airfares map for details on flights to Irian Jaya.) Garuda hopes to reintroduce the stopover in Biak on its Los Angeles-Jakarta flight, but don't hold your breath. International departure tax from Jayapura is 14,500 rp.

PNG The only way to PNG is still by plane: there are no boats; and the border remains closed. Air Nuigini flies between Jayapura and Vanimo every Sunday for US$63. From Vanimo, there are connections to Port Moresby (US$359 from Jayapura). PNG visas are available in Jayapura within 24 hours (refer to the Jayapura & Sentani section later in this chapter for details). You must have an Indonesian (four week) tourist

visa before you arrive in Jayapura – they are available in Vanimo and Port Moresby.

Boat

The sheer size of Irian Jaya, and the increasing number of transmigrants from western Indonesia, means good Pelni connections with Maluku and the rest of Indonesia. The *Rinjani* has an interesting connection to Fak Fak from Ambon, through The Bandas and Tual (South-East Maluku), and onto Java and Sulawesi. The *Tatamailau* connects all major places along both coasts of Irian Jaya with South-East Maluku and Nusa Tenggara. The *Ciremai* links all of the north coast of Irian Jaya with Ternate (northern Maluku), and ports in Sulawesi and Java. The *Dobonsolo* sails along the Irian Jayan north coast and to Ambon, and ports in Nusa Tenggara and Java.

A few other less-comfortable boats regularly link the southern coast of Irian Jaya with South-East Maluku, but any other non-

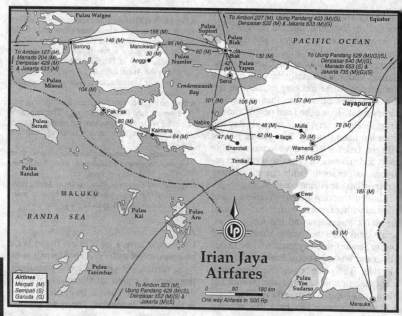

Irian Jaya Airfares

Pelni boat traversing the seas to Irian Jaya will be rough; it's better to wait for the Pelni liner or fly.

GETTING AROUND

Very few roads have successfully crossed the seemingly impenetrable jungles, mountains and rivers of Irian Jaya. Roads between Jayapura and Wamena, and Sorong and Manokwari, are due to be completed in the next few years, but, inevitably, construction problems continue to occur. Boats are slow, infrequent and can be uncomfortable, so flying is the popular option especially if you only have a two month visa.

Air

The centres for flights within Irian Jaya are Sorong for the north-west, Biak for the Cenderawasih Bay region, Jayapura for the Baliem Valley and Merauke for the south-east coast. Merpati still carries the bulk of all traffic. Except for the regular, popular Merauke-Jayapura-Biak-Sorong route and flights to Wamena, most Merpati planes are tiny Twin-Otters, which have a habit of being cancelled or delayed for any number of reasons. Merpati often has (but sometimes forgets to check) a 10 kg baggage limit on its Twin-Otters. To avoid an extra (nominal) charge for excess kg, 'cheat' a little by wearing your heaviest clothes and carrying weighty items in your cabin luggage (which isn't weighed). Refer to the Irian Jaya Airfares map for details about official flights around Irian Jaya.

In some places, particularly between Jayapura and Wamena, you can usually buy tickets on various cargo services, namely Airfast, SMAC and Trigana. Although they charge more than Merpati, they are usually more reliable. The Protestant-run Mission Aviation Fellowship (MAF) and the Catholic-run Associated Mission Aviation (AMA) fly to more obscure destinations and may accept passengers if they have room, but their primary concern is missionary business, and their prices are expensive. Book as far ahead as possible (at least a week in advance is recommended), though you might be lucky enough to get a flight sooner. You can also often charter their planes.

Boat

Travelling around Irian Jaya by boat will take some time and planning. Both coasts are well covered by three regular, comfortable Pelni liners. Every four weeks, the *Tatamailau* meanders along both coasts to/from Jayapura to Merauke, stopping off at every major town on the way. The *Dobonsolo* and *Ciremai* sail along the north coast between Jayapura and Sorong and back every two weeks, often hot on the heels of each other.

Boats run by Perintis are the next best option; they are usually still comfortable, but are certainly slower. The *Ilosangi* takes three weeks to travel between Jayapura and Merauke through Sorong, stopping at every major town, and minor village, along the way; and the *Embora* takes eight days to get from Jayapura to Manokwari. Many other more basic boats sail along certain, smaller sections of both coasts.

Cenderawasih Bay

Stretching from Manokwari on the Bird's Head Peninsula to the far east of Pulau Yapen, the region around Cenderawasih Bay (Teluk Cenderawasih) is one of the most underrated and undervisited parts of Irian Jaya. Despite outstanding diving and trekking, wildlife, deserted beaches, isolated islands, traditional cultures and easy-going towns, the region's potential is still hindered by limited transport and government prohibitions.

Activities

The two main towns, Manokwari and Nabire, have no diving centres so you must bring all your own gear, or arrange something from Biak – refer to the following Pulau Biak section for details. There are unorganised trekking possibilities around the Arfak mountains, near Manokwari (check with the tourist office in Manokwari for information on trails and guides); near Wasior; and around Pulau Yapen. It is important to check first to see if permits are required. Guides around these areas will cost about 20,000 rp per day, porters around 10,000 rp and simple accommodation in local houses from 2000 to 5000 rp per night. All supplies should be taken, including wet weather gear.

MANOKWARI

The first place in Irian Jaya to be settled by missionaries, Manokwari is a worthy alternative to Biak – it's easy to get around, has good facilities and is well connected. Translated as 'old village' in the Biak language, Manokwari, and the region, is famous for its unique species of butterflies.

Orientation & Information

Most of the town hugs the small Doreri Bay. The eastern side of the bay is the best place to base yourself because it's more convenient to most facilities.

The tourist office, near the port, is reasonably useful and worth visiting if you plan to trek in the Arfak mountains. It's open Monday to Saturday from 7.30 am to 3.30 pm. A surat jalan is needed for Manokwari and its immediate vicinity. You can get one at the police station (☎ 21365), on Jl Bayangkhara, or in Biak.

The only bank which changes money is Bank Exim on Jl Merdeka. It's open weekday mornings.

The main post office (open Monday to Saturday from 8 am to 2 pm) is near the port; a smaller one is next to Hotel Mulia. Telkom is near the Merpati office, and is open 24 hours.

Tugu Jepang & Taman Gunung Meja

A reasonably flat three km walk takes you through some lovely protected forest, known as Taman Gunung Meja (Table Mountain Park), with birds and Manokwari's famous butterflies – and, unfortunately, some mosquitos. The best way to start the walk is to take the local bemo (called a taksi) to Amban (a pleasant university town), but get off at the

sign to Tugu Jepang (Japanese Memorial) which is one km before the end of the well marked trail. The memorial is on the right. I isn't that exciting, but offers great views. Th trail ends not far from Hotel Arfak.

Goa Jepang

This cave is more a series of tunnels built b' the Japanese in WWII. The only entranc which you can look at, but not really explor very far, is on the lane leading up from th port to Hotel Arfak. The tunnel is a disap pointment; if you're going to Pulau Biak make sure you see the Japanese cave nea Bosnik.

Pulau Mansinam & Pulau Lemon

In the bay, with a dramatic backdrop of th Arfak mountains, a visit to these two island is a must. Two German missionaries settle on Mansinam in 1855 and became the firs in Irian Jaya to spread the 'Word'. Mansinam is a picturesque little island, with a smal village, some ruins of an old church, a memorial to the missionaries, a pleasan beach and loads of friendly people. It's bes to report to the village head (kepala desa before wandering around.

Pulau Lemon is nearby. It has some beaches, huts and WWII wrecks for snorkell ing, but isn't quite as enticing or accessible as Mansinam. A passenger boat from the jetty at Kwawi (only five minutes' walk past the Manokwari port, or take a taksi) goes to Mansinam three or four times daily. It's more fun to ask a local boy at Kwawi to take you out in his canoe, which should cost less than 5000 rp return to Mansinam, or about 8000 rp return to both islands.

Beaches

Pasir Sen Bebai and the adjacent Pasir Putih (White Sand) are pleasant beaches, but a little untidy. Take a taksi from the terminal for 400 rp. The other nearby beach, Pantai Amban, is a few km from Amban village, but transport there beach is limited and it reportedly has sea lice.

Places to Stay

One of the best-value places is the well-located *Hotel Pusaka Sederhana* (☎ 21263), Jl Bandung 154. Clean singles/doubles, with food service, cost from 10,000/15,000 rp; more for a private mandi and air-con. Opposite Merpati, on Jl Kota Baru, the friendly *Hotel Apose* (☎ 21369) is also a good option. Rooms are 15,000/20,000 rp with fan and outside mandi, while spotless, new air-con rooms go for 25,000/30,000 rp. At the top of Jl Sudirman, the inappropriately named *Hotel Maluku* has quiet rooms (but some are dark) for 15,000/20,000 rp with share mandi; more for air-con and TV.

Clean, friendly and quiet (except for the nearby mosque), the *Hotel Mulia* (☎ 21320) on Jl Yos Sudarso has rooms with mandi for 24,000/33,000 rp and air-con rooms for 36,000/51,000 rp. The old Dutch *Hotel Arfak* (☎ 21293), Jl Brawijaya 8, has some decaying, colonial charm and wonderful views, but isn't great value. A room with mandi and fan costs 30,000/36,000 rp; more for air-con.

In the top range, the *Mutiara Hotel* (☎ 21777) on Jl Yos Sudarso is good value – rooms start at 66,550/84,700 rp with air-con, TV and hot water.

Places to Eat

Manokwari doesn't really offer much to satisfy the tastebuds. All the cheap warungs congregate around the taksi terminal and market, and aren't that exciting. Around Bank Exim, on Jl Merdeka, one or two cheap places serve reasonable Padang and Sulawesian food from about 2000 rp a plate.

On the eastern side of the bay, the *Cafetaria Sederhana*, in Hotel Pusaka Sederhana, and the nearby *Warung Solo* are decent places for rice and noodle dishes from 2500 rp. Over the road, *Restaurant Evaria* no longer serves meals and is a dingy place for drinking small, warm beers (5500 rp).

At the top of Jl Sudirman, *Rumah Makan Kebon Sirih* has good service and decor, but offers little more than a baked fish meal, which is delicious but overpriced at 10,000 rp. Next door, *Rumah Makan Hawai* is better

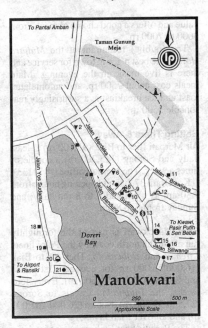

Manokwari

0   250   500 m

Approximate Scale

PLACES TO STAY
- 3 Hotel Maluku
- 4 Hotel Pusaka Sederhana & Cafetaria Sederhana
- 9 Hotel Apose
- 11 Hotel Arfak
- 18 Hotel Mulia
- 19 Mutiara Hotel

PLACES TO EAT
- 2 Rumah Makans Hawai & Kebun Sirih
- 5 Warung Solo
- 6 Restaurant Evaria

OTHER
- 1 Tugu Jepang
- 7 Merpati Office
- 8 Telkom Office
- 10 Intim Cinema
- 12 Goa Jepang
- 13 Bank Exim
- 14 Tourist Office
- 15 Main Post Office
- 16 Pelni Office
- 17 Port
- 20 Taksi Terminal
- 21 Market

IRIAN JAYA

value and offers a good choice of meals from 3000 to 7000 rp.

The (public) restaurant at the *Mutiara Hotel* is the best place in town for service and there is live music in the evenings. Main meals cost about 7500 rp, and an omelette, toast and tea breakfast is a surprisingly reasonable 3500 rp.

Getting There & Away

Air Merpati flies to Biak (95,100 rp) at least daily and Sorong (145,700 rp) a couple of times a week. The Merpati office (☎ 21133), Jl Kota Baru 37, has odd opening hours: from 7.30 am to 1 pm and 6 to 8 pm daily; and Sunday from 6 to 8 pm.

Boat Manokwari is part of the fortnightly run along the north coast by the Pelni liners *Ciremai* and *Dobonsolo*. They go to Biak (16,000/53,000 rp for economy/1st class) and Sorong (21,000/75,500 rp). Every four weeks, the *Tatamailau* travels to Sorong (27,500/99,500 rp), Nabire (26,000/101,000 rp) and all over Irian Jaya.

The Perintis boat *Embora* comes by about once a week, linking Manokwari with Pulau Serui and Wasior, as well as Jayapura and Biak; and the *Ilosangi* goes to Sorong and Biak once every three weeks during the long stretch between Jayapura and Merauke.

The Pelni office (☎ 21221), Jl Siliwangi 24, handles all bookings.

Getting Around

Rendani airport is only ten minutes' drive from most hotels. Taksi drivers may initially charge 10,000 rp, but will easily go down to 5000 rp. It's better to walk straight outside to the main road and catch a taksi for 300 rp to the taksi terminal from where you can, if necessary, take another to your hotel. The terminal is next to the market on the waterfront. Taksis leave regularly to the airport and beaches, less often to Ransiki and link both sides of the bay every few seconds.

ANGGI LAKES

Set 2030m high in the Arfak mountains, Danau Giji and Danau Gita, near Anggi,

offer exquisite scenery and wildlife, an excellent walking and swimming. You'll also see traditional lifestyles of the Manikor and Hatam people.

The two to three day trek to the lakes from Ransiki will involve some climbing and muddy trails. Ask at the district office in Ransiki (see the following Ransiki entry) for a guide (about 15,000 rp per day). You can sleep in local huts along the way for about 5000 rp per person; at Anggi, the district office can arrange somewhere to stay for about 10,000 rp. Take your own food, although you can buy some vegetables along the way.

Merpati flies to Anggi twice a week (30,200 rp; 25 minutes). The Mission Aviation Fellowship (MAF) service is more reliable than Merpati, but you will need to give at least a week's notice. MAF flies to Irai, a few km from Anggi, twice a week for 42,500 rp. The MAF office (☎ 21155) is in an unsigned hangar at the end of the Manokwari airport. Flights to/from Anggi are sometimes cancelled because of fog.

RANSIKI

Taksis leave every hour or so (more in the mornings) from Manokwari to the pleasant transmigration town of Ransiki (7000 rp; three hours). It's a rough, often crowded, ride – and is likely to be impassable in the wet season (November to March) – but the scenery through the jungle, along the coast and past transmigration villages, such as Oransbari, is superb. Even if you're not going to Anggi, it's still worth a day trip to Ransiki. Alternatively, a speedboat (known as a 'johnson') and a ferry leave Manokwari two or three times a week. Check with the local district office in the centre of Ransiki for somewhere to stay if you are going on to Anggi or Pulau Rumberpon (see the following section for details).

CENDERAWASIH MARINE RESERVE

This 14,300 sq km area, with 18 islands and over 500 km of coastline along the bay south of Ransiki, offers some of the best scuba diving, bird watching and trekking imaginable, but the possibilities are severely limited

PAUL GREENWAY

PAUL GREENWAY

PAUL GREENWAY

PAUL GREENWAY

PAUL GREENWAY

PAUL GREENWAY

Irian Jaya

Top four photographs: Annual Pulau Biak islanders' festival, representing all tribal cultures from Pulau Biak.

Bottom Left: Burning coal and wood for firewalking, Adoki, Pulau Biak.

Bottom Right: Firewalker, Adoki, Pulau Biak.

PAUL GREENWAY

PAUL GREENWAY

Irian Jaya

Top: Local children outside an authentic Dani house called a *honay*.

Bottom: Traditionally, Dani men wear no clothing except for a penis gourd and ornamentation such as bird of paradise feathers and cowry shell necklaces.

by available transport and government regulations. The larger inhabited islands are Rumberpon, Mioswaar, Roon and Angraneos. Rumberpon and the sub-district town of Wasior are the only places to really base yourself, although neither are strictly in the reserve.

Pulau Rumberpon

This island offers an exciting option: an 'ecotourism resort'. From the island, you can snorkel among superb fish and coral, hike in the jungle, and charter boats to other islands such as **Pulau Wairondi** with its untouched turtle population, and **Pulau Auri**. The resort has snorkelling gear for hire.

It shouldn't be a problem camping on the beach for a while with your own camping gear, or try to arrange to stay in a village hut. A single/double hut in the resort starts from US$30/40, plus meals and transport. Bookings must be made at PT Wamesa Alam Wisata (☎ 22731), Jl Sudirman 12, Manokwari, at least two weeks in advance.

If you want to travel there on your own, johnsons leave Ransiki for Rumberpon daily.

Wasior

Nestled along Wandammen Bay, Wasior is the other place where you can charter boats to nearby islands, or trek in the Wondiwoi Mountain Reserve (with a special permit), home to over a hundred species of birds. There is no official accommodation in Wasior, but finding somewhere to stay shouldn't be a problem – getting a surat jalan to cover this area may be.

Merpati flies to Wasior once a week. The ferry from Manokwari to Ransiki, which leaves two or three times a week, continues on to Wasior. The Perintis boats *Embora* and *Ilosangi* link Wasior with Manokwari, Nabire and Biak about once a week.

NABIRE

Capital of the Paniai district, Nabire is a forgotten part of Irian Jaya. A particularly pleasant town, with wide streets and nearby beaches and islands to explore, Nabire is a worthy stopover on the way to Biak, Jay-

apura and, possibly, Wamena. And for some reason, no-one (yet!) in Nabire has learnt how to yell 'HELLO MISTER!!!!'.

Orientation & Information

Along Jl Yos Sudarso, parallel to the waterfront, is the post office (open daily from 8 am to 2 pm, except Sunday), taksi terminal and most shops. Nearby, Jl Pepera has a few offices, including Bank Exim, which will change money (weekday mornings), and the 24 hour Telkom office. The airport is walking distance (ask directions) to the hotels listed in this section.

It's a good idea to have a surat jalan for Nabire; you will certainly need one for any trips into the interior. Get it at the police station (☎ 21110) on Jl Sisingamangaraja, or in Biak.

Things to See & Do

Like most of Irian Jaya, the accessibility of nearby attractions is limited by available transport and roads. You can charter a boat for an hour or two to islands such as **Pulau Moor** and **Pulau Papaya**. Boats to these and other islands usually leave from the MAF beach at the end of Jl Sisingamangaraja. A chartered taksi can take you to some **hot springs**, near the port; and by public taksi, **Pantai Whario** is not bad for snorkelling and swimming.

Places to Stay & Eat

The best of a limited choice is the *Hotel Nusantara* (☎ 21180) on Jl Pemuda. It has a range of rooms, good service, a nice setting and is handy to the next door Merpati office. Simple but clean rooms without mandi, including good meals, cost 26,400 rp; considerably more for air-con and TV (and meals). Next best, *Hotel Anggrek* (☎ 21066) on Jl Pepera has rooms starting at 17,500 rp without meals or mandi, and is set around a lovely garden.

Most of the restaurants congregate around the taksi terminal – the best are rumah makans *Sari* and *Kebun Sirih*. For some of the most mouthwatering baked fish you will ever taste, try the warungs (food stalls) on the waterfront, opposite the taksi terminal. The *Lucky Supermarket* on Jl Yos Sudarso is well stocked.

Getting There & Away

Air Nabire is a useful stopover on the way to Biak and/or Jayapura. Merpati flies daily to Biak (100,600 rp) and almost daily to Jayapura (156,700 rp). From Nabire, Twin-Otter flights leave nearly every day to Kaimana (84,100 rp), Fak Fak (160,000 rp) and Sorong (256,200 rp). Book as soon as you can, and be prepared for delays and frustrations.

The Merpati flight to Mulia (45,600 rp), from where you can get a connection a day or two later to Wamena, is an interesting alternative route into the Baliem Valley – if current government regulations allow.

The Merpati office (☎ 21360), next door to the Hotel Nusantara on Jl Pemuda, opens from 8 am weekdays and closes when it feels like it.

Boat The Pelni liner *Tatamailau* calls by every month between Serui and Manokwari. Twice a week, the *Teluk Cenderawasih* goes to Serui (16,500 rp; 12 hours), on Pulau Yapen, and onto Biak. Every three weeks the Perintis boat *Ilosangi* stops on its way between Wasior and Biak.

Nabire's port is about 20 km east of town; taksis are frequent when boats arrive and depart. The Pelni office (☎ 21350) is on Jl Sam Ratulangi behind the taksi terminal.

PULAU YAPEN

This elongated mountainous island south of Biak offers bird watching around its northern shores, and great scuba and skin diving at nearby Pulau Arumbai, but these activities are better arranged from Biak (refer to the following Pulau Biak section for details). Although Yapen is pleasant enough, it suffers from limited facilities and transport, and

---

Birds of Paradise

Over 40 different species of the bird of paradise, known as the *cenderawasih*, live in Papua New Guinea, small regional areas of northern Irian Jaya and southern Maluku. The first specimens were taken back to Europe after colonial explorations around the East Indies. Their feathers fetched remarkable prices for fashionable garments and the birds soon faced extinction. Because their legs and wings were often removed by traders to highlight the birds' beautiful plumage and several early colonial explorers only saw them in flight and never on land, it was originally thought the birds had no feet and always flew in the air.

The male bird is usually more brightly coloured than the female. The males display their magnificent plumage during mating, often hanging upside down from branches to show off their colours; they do this alone or in groups called leks. Cenderawasih mostly nest in open parts of a tree, feed on fruit and insects, usually have remarkable thin, curled 'tail-wires' up to 30 cm long with colourful tips, and often have loud calls.

The birds are scarce and very difficult to find, but with some patience, time and a good guide it may be possible. Locating the birds will involve chartering boats, organising guides and camping out on Waigeo, Misool, Batanta and Salawati islands, off the coast of Sorong; along sections of the aptly named Teluk Cenderawasih (Bird of Paradise Bay); the northern coast of Pulau Yapen; and in the remote Aru Islands of South-East Maluku. Organised tours can be arranged through travel agencies in Sorong and Kota Biak. The less adventurous can admire several of these creatures in aviaries at the Taman Burung dan Anggrek (Bird and Orchid Garden) near Bosnik, on Pulau Biak. ■

here is little to justify a detour. The only own of any size is Serui, the district capital.

A surat jalan, which is needed for a visit o Serui and anywhere on the island, can be easily obtained in Biak.

Places to Stay & Eat

Of the three places to stay in Serui the best is *Merpati Inn* (☎ 31154) on Jl Yos Sudarso. It's a bit noisy, but is good for information on boat trips and Merpati flights. Singles/doubles with fan cost 27,000/45,000 rp, including meals, and with air-con 40,000/50,000 rp.

Hotel food is recommended. A couple of *rumah makans* serving Padang food and some night *warungs* are along the port area.

Getting There & Away

Merpati only flies to Biak (41,500 rp) – and goes there daily.

The Pelni liner *Tatamailau* connects Serui with Jayapura and Nabire every four weeks. The overnight ferry *Teluk Cenderawasih I* sails to Nabire and Biak twice a week.

AROUND PULAU YAPEN

In the east and north of the island, the cenderawasih (bird of paradise) still manages to survive. If you can find someone willing to take you, a boat will cost about 50,000 rp per day (for about 10 people), plus 10,000 rp per hour for fuel. Departures will vary according to the tides. A guide (about 15,000 rp per day) will arrange for you to stay with villagers for around 10,000 rp per night. Bargain hard. There is also some sort of 'protection fee' of 50,000 rp levied on each group that wants to see a cenderawasih.

Pulau Arumbai offers great snorkelling (bring your own gear) among coral and dolphins. The island is also home to thousands of cockatoos and hornbills. Motorboats can be hired to Arumbai or other villages and islands around Yapen.

Infrequent buses go as far as Wooi in the west and Manawi in the east. Chartering for about 10,000 rp per hour is a quicker way of getting around. All roads on Yapen are rough and the terrain is mountainous.

Pulau Biak

Biak, an island in the top of the Cenderawasih Bay, was the location of horrific WWII battles between the Allies and Japanese. These days, the island is an important Indonesian naval base and a hub for sea and air travel along the north coast of Irian Jaya. The island has a great deal to offer and is a worthy stopover – you may have to stay on Biak anyway if waiting for a connection.

The island was hit by a massive earthquake in February 1996. (We were there at the time.) It destroyed the main mosque in Kota Biak and the tower at the airport, but the subsequent five metre tidal wave caused the most damage. Pretty seaside villages, such as Bosnik near Kota Biak and Wardo on the north-west coast, were all but devastated. Flimsy wooden huts and shops had no chance; approximately 150 people died, many more were missing and an estimated 10,000 became homeless. Within weeks, however, locals had started to resurrect their lives and most things will be back to normal eventually.

Diving

Pulau Biak and the general Cenderawasih Bay area have the potential to rival northern Sulawesi for diving, with the added attraction that it's cheaper and less overrun by tourists; however, the diving industry in Biak is currently frustratingly unorganised and undeveloped. The best time to dive is between April and September.

Currently, you *may* be able to rent a boat and guide, but there is little reliable equipment for hire and no instructors. PT Sentosa Tosiga rents equipment (the quality and maintenance may not be up to scratch), but doesn't organise trips; while the impressive outfit, Janggi Prima, runs trips from US$85 per person (minimum of two people), including two dives, lunch, boat and guide, but only basic equipment, if any, is available for hire. (Refer to the following Organised Tours section for details.)

At the time of research, Hotel Biak Beach,

Pulau Biak

near Bosnik (see Places to Stay in this section), planned to open a diving shop. If the prices of the rooms are any indication, rentals and tours will not be cheap, but this may be one of the few reliable options. In any event, it's a good idea to talk to the effusive staff at the tourist office to see what is currently available.

The following are the best places for scuba diving: around the Padaido Islands, especially Rurbas and Pakreki islands (refer to the Around Pulau Biak section); Tanjung Barari, the cape at the far east of the island, which is not connected by public transport; Pulau Meosindi, on the way to Pulau Yapen; Pulau Rani, off the west coast of Pulau Biak, accessible by boat from Kota Biak; and the very best, Pulau Mapia, far off the north-west coast of Pulau Supiori, which would take some real effort and money to reach.

Snorkelling is far less hassle and still great fun. Notables spots are: around Bosnik; the Padaido Islands, particularly Nusi and Mansurbabo islands; and around Korem. PT Sentosa Tosiga, and one or two places, like the Biak Art Shop (☎ 22913) in the market on Jl Selat Makassar, rent full snorkelling gear from 10,000 to 15,000 rp per day.

KOTA BIAK

The only town of any size on the island, Kota Biak is not particularly interesting, but is an ideal base for exploring the island's attractions and the Cenderawasih Bay region. There is no accommodation anywhere else on the island (except for a luxury hotel near Bosnik) and transport is limited in the north, but most places of interest can be visited on day trips from the city.

Only one degree south of the equator, Biak is always hot and humid, and rain often falls in sudden, short spells. It's a good idea to start your day early and hibernate like the rest of the locals between 1 and 4 pm.

Orientation

Kota Biak is a fairly compact town. A lot of what you'll need is along Jl Ahmad Yani (which joins Jl Prof M Yamin from the airport), Jl Sudirman (which goes past the port) and Jl Imam Bonjol – all of which meet at the Bank Exim building. The majority of hotels and restaurants are around this area, but a few offices, the terminal for taksis and buses, and the market, are a short taksi ride away.

IRIAN JAYA

Information

Tourist Office The helpful tourist office (☎ 21663) is inconveniently on Jl Prof M Yamin. Take a taksi there or get off on the way from the airport. It happily hands out free brochures about other places in Irian Jaya in English, Japanese and Dutch, but often runs out of ones about Biak. Its staff speaks little English. It is open Monday to Friday from 7.30 am to 3 pm.

Surat Jalan A surat jalan is not necessary for anywhere on Pulau Biak, but Biak is a very handy place to obtain one for the Baliem Valley or places elsewhere, such as Pulau Serui and Nabire. Just go to the friendly boys at the 'intel' section of the police headquarters on Jl Diponegoro. You'll need two photographs, there will be an 'administrative fee' of about 2000 rp and the permit can be ready in an hour or two.

Money Bank Exim, on the corner of Jl Ahmad Yani and Jl Imam Bonjol, and Bank Bumi Daya, on Jl Ahmad Yani, are the best places to change money. They are open Monday to Friday from 8 am to 1 pm. A bank at the domestic airport also changes money, but the rates aren't as good. It's open daily from 8 am to 1 pm.

Post & Communications The main post office is a taksi ride away on the way to the airport, opposite the tourist office, and has a useful poste restante service. It's open daily from 8 am to 6 pm. The modern Telkom office, open 24 hours daily, is on Jl Yos Sudarso, not far from the mosque.

Emergency The general hospital, Rumah Sakit Umum (☎ 21294), is on Jl Sri Wijaya, several km from town. The police headquarters (☎ 21810) is on Jl Diponegoro.

Cenderawasih Museum

Built in the traditional Biak architectural style, this museum has a small and mildly interesting assortment of Biak, Indonesian and colonial artefacts. There's a few Japanese WWII remnants, but the collection at the

Gua Jepang is far better (see the following Around Pulau Biak section). The gates of the grounds are always open; the hard part is finding someone to actually open the museum for you – just hope that the guy with the key hasn't gone swimming for the day. The museum is on Jl Sisingamangaraja, about 10 minutes' walk east of Hotel Maju.

Organised Tours

Biak is the place to organise diving (refer to the previous Diving section) and bird-watching tours anywhere between Sorong and Jayapura. For example, bird-watching tours of northern Pulau Yapen are far easier to organise from Biak than Serui, the capital of Yapen, which is only two hours by boat from Biak. Three places in Kota Biak are reliable:

PT Sentosa Tosiga, opposite the Hotel Mapia on Jl Ahmad Yani (☎ 21398). It's good for general tours and bird-watching packages; less reliable for diving.

Janggi Prima Tours & Travel, Jl Pramuka 5 (☎ 22-973). An impressive, new company which runs an interesting range of diving tours.

PT Biak Paradise Tours & Travel, in the Hotel Arumbai on Jl Selat Makassar (☎ 21835). The best agent for pricey local tours.

Places to Stay – bottom end

Biak is not endowed with many cheap places, but some reasonable basic rooms, without mandi, are available. The *Hotel Rahayu* (☎ 21196), behind the main mosque, is often full. Very simple rooms cost 10,000 rp per person. The huge, rambling *Hotel Sinar Kayu* (☎ 22137), Jl Sisingamangaraja, has tiny, quiet singles/doubles with outside mandi from 12,000/20,400 rp. The rooms with mandis are dark, unexciting and overpriced at 24,000/36,000 rp.

More central, the *Hotel Solo* (☎ 21397), Jl Monginisidi 4, has tiny rooms with paper-thin walls for 14,500/25,000 rp with shared mandi – it isn't great value. Simple, good meals for guests cost 2500 rp. The large *Hotel Mapia* (☎ 21383) on Jl Ahmad Yani is starting to look really rundown, but remains

IRIAN JAYA

popular. Very ordinary economy rooms start from 13,915/21,780 rp; better rooms with mandi and fan are 19,360/25,984 rp.

The *Hotel Maju* (☎ 21841), Jl Imam Bonjol 45, remains one of the better options in this range. Comfortable rooms with mandi, and good service, cost 19,400/30,250 rp. Good value triples (36,300 rp) are also available. Ask for the quieter rooms at the back.

Places to Stay – middle & top end

Two places either side of the airport are worth considering, especially if you're transiting overnight in Kota Biak. They are both comfortable, offer good service and are easily connected by taksi to town. The prices, including all meals, are about the same: 33,000/50,000 rp for singles/doubles with fan and mandi; more for rooms with hot water, TV and air-con. On the western side (towards town), the *Hotel Irian* (☎ 21939) is a charming, old place with a large seaside garden, bar and restaurant (which serves ordinary food). It's an appealing place to have a drink while waiting for a connecting flight. (Merpati will put you up there if/when your flight is cancelled.) To the east, the *Airport Beach Hotel* (☎ 21496) is modern and serves very good meals.

The *Basana Inn* (☎ 22281), Jl Imam Bonjol 46, is one of the best in the middle range. Quiet rooms with hot water, set around a delightful garden, cost 37,900/48,000 rp; more for rooms with TV.

The *Hotel Arumbai* (☎ 21835), Jl Sela Makassar 3, is the best in the top range. Luxury accommodation with air-con, hot water, swimming pool and airport transfer, costs from US$33/42; deluxe rooms will do considerably more damage to your wallet.

Overlooking the beach, in the village of Marao near Bosnik, the enormous (and usually empty) *Hotel Biak Beach* (☎ 81005) has all the luxury, views and service from US$108 for a standard room to a lazy US$605 for the presidential suite.

Places to Eat

To sample some traditional cooking by the *barapen* method you will have to be invited to a traditional party in a village. Barapen involves placing food under hot rocks, while some of the braver (and, possibly, more intoxicated) may attempt some impromptu fire walking.

PLACES TO STAY	PLACES TO EAT	OTHER
1 Hotel Sinar Kayu	6 Rumah Makan Nirwana	2 Taksi/Bus Terminal
9 Hotel Maju	12 Rumah Makan 99	3 Pasar Inpres
10 Basana Inn	13 Rumah Makan Rindu Alam	4 Port
16 Hotel Mapia	17 Cinta Rosa	5 Pelni Office
19 Hotel Arumbai	18 Rumah Makan Umum Jakarta	7 Market
26 Hotel Solo	20 Rumah Makan Megaria	8 Police Headquarters
30 Hotel Rahayu	23 Minang Jaya	11 Iriani Art Shop
	27 Restoran Cleopatra	14 Janggi Prima
		15 Cenderawasih Museum
		21 Garuda Office
		22 Bank Exim
		24 Bank Bumi Daya
		25 Bioskop Dewi
		28 PT Sentosa Tosiga
		29 Mosque

Kota Biak

Yapen Strait

To Adoki & the General Hospital (3km)

To Telkom (200m), Post Office & Tourist Office (1.5km), Hotel Irian, Airport, Airport Beach Hotel & Merpati (2.5km) & Post Office

To Gua Jepang & Bosnik

The city is surprisingly devoid of good, cheap warungs – try the markets at the taksi/bus terminal and on Jl Selat Makassar. Some places along Jl Sudirman, such as *Rumah Makan Megaria*, serve large plates of Indonesian food for about 4000 rp, but other dishes are not good value. The best spots for Padang food are *Rumah Makan Rindu Alam* on Jl Imam Bonjol and *Minang Jaya*, next to Bank Bumi Daya on Jl Ahmad Yani.

The pick of the bunch is the badly signed *Cinta Rosa*, near Hotel Mapia. Popular with locals, but only open in the evenings, it serves filling baked fish meals for 2700 rp and baked chicken for 3700 rp. On the other side of the road, *Restoran Cleopatra* has an impressive selection of meals starting from 3000 to 4000 rp, and an outdoor (but noisy) setting. For cold drinks and assorted kue-kue (cakes), head straight to *Rumah Makan Nirwana*, opposite the Pelni office.

Along Jl Imam Bonjol are the clean and modern *Rumah Makan 99* and *Rumah Makan Umum Jakarta*. Like several others, they have karaoke machines, but serve decent Indonesian food for 4000 to 5000 rp or 10,000 to 12,000 rp for seafood dishes. For western food, at western prices (steaks for 12,000 rp and full breakfasts for 11,000 rp), try the restaurant at *Hotel Arumbai*. There are several well-stocked supermarkets along Jl Imam Bonjol.

Entertainment

Biak isn't blessed with an enormous amount of things to do. There is no shortage of places offering beer and karaoke machines, and there's several billiard rooms around the streets, but no nightclubs to speak of. The *Bioskop Dewi*, opposite Hotel Mapia, is the only cinema in town. It shows mainly violent Chinese films (with Indonesian subtitles), but you may be lucky with something quieter and more comprehensible.

Things to Buy

There are two markets in town. Several shops in the market on Jl Selat Makassar sell locally made items, such as batik, carvings and souvenirs made from shells. They usually also sell Asmat and Baliem carvings which look OK, but aren't the real thing. The larger Pasar Inpres, next to the taksi/bus terminal (take a taksi there), is mainly for food and clothing, but is worth wandering around for some atmosphere.

The best place to look around is the Iriani Art Shop on Jl Imam Bonjol. It has a great selection of local and other Irianese art, carvings and jewellery at reasonable (often fixed) prices.

The kiosk at the domestic airport has a poor selection of souvenirs and high prices, but does sell day-old copies of the English-language newspaper, *Jakarta Post*.

Getting There & Away

Air Biak is the major centre for air travel throughout Irian Jaya. To western Indonesia, Merpati flies most days to Ambon (227,000 rp), and to Denpasar (521,900 rp) and Jakarta (662,700 rp) through Ujung Pandang (403,100 rp). Elsewhere in Irian Jaya, flights go daily to Jayapura (130,300 rp) and Manokwari (95,100 rp), and less frequently to Sorong (155,600 rp) and Timika (106,100 rp). There are local flights to Nabire (100,600 rp) and Serui (41,500 rp) virtually every day, and to Pulau Numfor (59,900 rp) twice a week.

The Merpati office (☎ 21386) is across the road from the domestic airport. It's officially open Monday to Friday from 7.30 am to 4.30 pm, and weekends from 9 am to 2 pm – and is closed for lunch daily from noon to 1 pm. This office is so perennially unhelpful and unreliable that it pays to make enquiries and bookings at one of the several authorised travel agencies around town.

Garuda hopes to reintroduce a stopover in Biak on its Los Angeles to Jakarta flight, but don't hold your breath. Garuda stops in Biak three times weekly on its Jayapura-Biak-Ujung Pandang-Jakarta route for the same price as Merpati. The Garuda office (☎ 21-416), Jl Sudirman 3, is open weekdays from 7.30 am to 4.45 pm, and in the morning only on weekends.

Boat Biak is a natural stop on the routes across the north coast of Irian Jaya. Pelni's

Dobonsolo and *Ciremai* sail from Biak to Jayapura (28,500/135,500 rp for economy/1st class) and Manokwari (15,000/69,500 rp) every two weeks, often hot on the heels of each other.

Every three weeks, the Perintis boat *Embora* stops at Biak and goes onto Kameri (on Pulau Numfor) and Serui as part of its crawl along the Cenderawasih Bay. The *Ilosangi* also links Biak with Serui and Nabire.

The Pelni office (☎ 21065), Jl Sudirman 37, handles bookings for all of these boats. It's open daily from 8 am to noon and 1 to 3 pm; longer when a boat is to due to arrive or depart. When a Pelni boat is in town, it's worth paying a little extra for a ticket from one of the agencies that spring up from nowhere rather than wait hours in line at the Pelni office. The port is about 200m west of the Pelni office.

The crowded, and occasionally unreliable, ferry *Teluk Cenderawasih I* connects Biak with Serui (14,500 rp; 12 hours) and goes onto Nabire twice a week. Tickets are available from an office in the port.

Getting Around

The Airport Regular taksis marked 'Ambroben' speed past the Frans Kaisiepo airport to any place in Kota Biak for 350 rp; simply walk outside the front door of the airport terminal. A private taxi from the airport to your hotel officially costs 8000 rp.

Local Transport The terminal for taksis, which services the entire island, is next to Pasar Inpres, a few blocks from most hotels. A few buses, waiting outside the terminal, go to more distant places and are slightly more comfortable, but less regular. Taksis can take some time to fill up, so chartering one for about 12,500 rp per hour is a good idea.

The taksis are well marked, but their destinations can be confusing if you don't know your way around. The following routes are available:

South-west coast – the 'Yendidori/Adoki' taksi goes to Adoki and Pantai Emfendi, and 'Urfu/Samber' continues as far as the road goes.

South-east coast – 'Ibdi/Bosnik' and 'Kajasi/Saba go to Bosnik; 'Kajasi/Marao' to Bosnik and Mar ao; 'Mokmer/Parai' for beaches close to the city and 'Anggaduber/Mnurah' to the end of the road

North-east coast – 'Maneru/Korem' goes to Korem and 'Wari/Moos' continues further on.

North-west coast – 'Yomdori/Wardo' goes to Wardo

Far north and Pulau Supiori – take the bus marke 'Kota Supiori Utara'.

AROUND PULAU BIAK

There are many exciting places to go on Pulau Biak, but you will be hindered by the availability of transport. Public buses and taksis traverse the rough roads as far south-west as Samber; Marao in the south-east Wardo in the north-west; the channel separating Pulau Supiori in the far north; and, less often, on Supiori. North of Wardo and on most of Supiori, a combination of trucks boats and foot is the only way to get around Remember that while towns on Biak may look biggish on a map, none are really more than a handful of village huts with no accommodation or food.

Adoki

Past the lovely beach at **Yendidori**, the village of Adoki is famous for its fire walking. While women dance around the fire, men take an hour to stoke it with coral and wood. About five men, aged between 12 and 70 years, walk across the fire and back again. It's all over in about three minutes. An exhibition of fire walking has to be prearranged days before and will cost about 200,000 rp. Ask around the market on Jl Selat Makassar in Kota Biak or in the village. You can reach Adoki by taksi for 750 rp from Kota Biak.

Next to Adoki, **Pantai Emfendi** has a white sand beach and great views. It's especially popular on Sunday.

Urfu & Samber

From Adoki, the road continues for another bumpy 20 minutes to the village of Urfu, surrounded by amazing **rock formations**. The road finishes near the pretty fishing village of **Samber** (1500 rp by taksi). Ask directions to the steps from the main road and wander around the friendly place. There's some remnants of a seemingly forgotten Dutch colonial past, and of the Japanese occupation in WWII.

Wardo

At the end of the bumpy north-west road is the small group of huts called Wardo ('deep water' in Biak) set in a picturesque bay. From Wardo you can charter a boat to the **Wapsdori waterfalls**. The falls *(air tejun)* are appealing and you can have a refreshing dip at the top (watch out for the very unstable ladder), but the ride along the peaceful, overgrown jungle river is the highlight.

The two hour return trip to the falls by motorboat will cost about 25,000 rp per boat (holding three or four people). Cheaper, slower and more fun is a trip by canoe. Bargain hard as the locals are getting used to tourists. Irregular taksis leave Kota Biak (2200 rp; 70 minutes) or you can charter one for about 15,000 rp one way.

Gua Jepang

This Japanese cave is known locally as Abyab Binsar ('binsar' means grandmother in the Biak language) because an old woman apparently lived there many decades ago. The cave (actually a tunnel) provides a chilling impression of the day in 1944 when 3000 to 5000 Japanese were killed by US bombs and fires. There are still many rusting remnants of the war around the place. The tunnel leads to Bosnik's beach several km away. Locals refuse to go in the dark cave; believe their warnings about snakes and bats!

From the road, a path leads down to the cave, which costs 1500 rp to enter. Ask one of the local boys to give you a tour (in reasonable English). A small **museum** over the road has a remarkable collection of Japanese WWII weapons and photos. If the museum is unattended, ask someone at the house next door to open it up.

A chartered taksi will cost about 5000 rp one way from Kota Biak. Or catch a frequent taksi from Kota Biak towards Bosnik, get off at the **Dennis Orchid Park** (which is nothing to write home about) and walk a few hundred metres up a small hill.

Taman Burung dan Anggrek

On the way to Bosnik, your taksi can drop you off at the Taman Burung dan Anggrek (Bird and Orchid Garden). The pleasant gardens contain 72 types of orchids and 48 species of birds in cages, such as the cenderawasih (bird of paradise; which is probably as close as you'll ever get to one) and, if you are really lucky, the Double Eyed Fig Parrot and Pink Spotted Fruit Dove. The entrance fee seems to vary according to who is working on the gates, but 2000 rp should be more than enough.

Bosnik

Bosnik (900 rp; half-hour), a former Dutch capital of the island and a landing site for the Allies, is the starting point for trips to the Padaido Islands (see below). Some **WWII relics** lie near the lovely white, sandy beach, and a small, busy **market** is held each Wednesday and Saturday.

The south-eastern road continues past a beach at **Opiaref** and then goes up the hill to the village of **Marao**, where the huge Hotel Biak Beach stands incongruously. Even if you can't afford to stay there (and who can?), it's worth a splurge on a meal or drink among the sheer luxury (refer to the Places to Stay section for details). A trail continues along the coast past more charming – and deserted – beaches until the village of **Anggaduber**.

Padaido Islands

From Bosnik, it's possible – but you will have to ask around and bargain hard – to charter a boat around this stunning cluster of 30, mostly uninhabited, islands. For swimming and snorkelling, concentrate on the Nusi and Mansurbabo islands; for scuba diving, Wundi, Rurbas, Pakreki and Owi islands are recommended (refer to Diving earlier in this section).

Owi and Auki islands are the closest to Bosnik. They are also the most populated, so you are more likely to be able to stay in a local hut and find a passenger boat from Bosnik. Public boats travel between Bosnik and some of the Padaido Islands on market days (Wednesday and Saturday).

Korem

A small village halfway along the north-east road, Korem was virtually destroyed by the tidal wave in 1996. There's a small, scrappy beach (which is sometimes good enough for surfing) and a busy market on Wednesday and Saturday, but Korem itself is probably not worth the effort – there are nicer beaches far closer to Kota Biak. Irregular taksis to Korem cost 1900 rp (one and a half hours); buses cost slightly less.

Pulau Supiori

Separated from Pulau Biak by a very narrow channel, most of Supiori is the **Pulau Supiori Reserve**, full of mangroves, montane forests, and endemic species of parrots and cockatoos. The north-east road from Biak goes past Korem and stops at the channel. The bridge is often broken (and was wiped out after the earthquake), so a pontoon with an ingenious system of pulleys takes passengers, even taksis, across the water.

The only road on Supiori continues as far as **Wapur** on the north coast, but transport is limited because the area is so sparsely populated. If you have the time, a day trip by public taksi from the city to the channel separating the two islands and back is certainly possible and worthwhile for the scenery.

PULAU NUMFOR

Part of the Biak-Numfor district, this irresistible, unspoilt and undeveloped island is between Biak and Manokwari. It has loads of beautiful beaches and friendly villages, although very limited facilities for tourists. There is no official accommodation, although you can easily arrange to stay with a local family if you contact the kepala desa in Kameri or Yemburwo, the two main villages, or tee up something with the tourist office in Kota Biak.

There are dozens of unexplored diving and swimming spots around the island. From Kameri, you can charter a boat (20 minutes) to the heavenly **Pulau Manem**, where there's no shortage of birdlife, sandy beaches and Japanese WWII wrecks.

Almost all planes and boats to Numfor leave from Biak. Merpati flies from Biak to Yemburwo (59,900 rp) twice a week. Boats occasionally travel to/from Manokwari, but don't count on it – it's far easier to organise a trip from Biak. From Kota Biak, johnsons leave on most days, depending on demand, for the rough 12 hour trip. The Perintis boat *Embora* connects Kameri with Biak every week or so.

Jayapura & Sentani

In Dutch times, Jayapura was known as Hollandia (then became Soekarnopura and Kota Baru) and was deliberately placed just a few km from the border with German New Guinea to emphasise the Dutch claim to the western half of the island. In April 1944 the Allies stormed ashore at Hamadi and captured the town after only token resistance from the Japanese. General MacArthur assembled his fleet for the invasion of the Philippines from near Jayapura.

As the capital of Irian Jaya, Jayapura is dominated by non-Irianese and looks little different from any other medium-sized Indonesian city, although it's pleasantly situated around Yos Sudarso Bay and is surrounded by steep hills. There's little reason to stay here unless you are arriving or leaving by sea. Sentani, a small town 36 km west of Jayapura, with the airport and the magnificent Danau Sentani nearby, is a far better place to stay – it's quieter, cooler and more convenient than Jayapura, and has most of the facilities you will need.

The area around Jayapura and Sentani has a lot to offer, so try to stay a few days on the way to/from Wamena. There is also accommodation at Hamadi and around Danau Sentani (refer to Around Jayapura & Sentani later in this section for details).

Surat Jalan

A surat jalan is not required if you visit only Jayapura or Sentani, but these are the final places to acquire one for the Baliem Valley and most places further south or west. The permit is easy to get at the police station in Jayapura or Sentani (although, sometimes, the police in Sentani may tell you to go to Jayapura). The process takes an hour or so and costs about 2000 rp – you will also need two photographs. If you are in a hurry or unsure of the process, some travel agencies and hotels in Sentani and Jayapura may be able to obtain a surat jalan, even at short notice, at an additional cost.

There is no shortage of places in the centres of Jayapura and Sentani which take passport photos. It is a good idea to take a few photocopies of your surat jalan to give to the police, including officials at the airport when you arrive in Wamena.

Organised Tours
Several reliable tour and travel agencies offer a range of tours around Jayapura and Sentani, to the Baliem Valley and as far as the Asmat region. They can also arrange diving (refer to Around Jayapura & Sentani later in this section); rafting down Sungai Baliem; and trekking and bird-watching trips around the Cyclop mountains and the forests near Nimbokrang, west of Genyem.

Three recommended agencies are:

Dani Sangrila Tours & Travel, Jl Pembangunan 19, Jayapura (☎ 31060; fax 31529). This agent is good for rafting, and tours to the Baliem Valley and Asmat region.

Best Tours & Travel, Jl Raya Sentani 84 (near the Hotel Carfin on the main road), Sentani (☎ 91-861; fax 91860). It's worthwhile for tours to the Baliem Valley and also has an agency in Wamena.

PT Kuwera Jaya, Jl Ahmad Yani 39, Jayapura (☎ 31583; fax 32236). This agent is especially good for diving tours and rental, and travel to PNG (refer to the relevant sections for details).

JAYAPURA
Orientation
Just about everything you will probably need – most hotels, shops, restaurants, airline offices and police station – is confined to the main parallel streets of Jl Ahmad Yani and Jl Percetakan. Along the waterfront, Jl Koti leads to Hamadi in the east, past the port; and

Jl Sam Ratulangi heads north towards Tanjung Ria, past some government buildings, such as the tourist office, in areas called Dok I to Dok V. A few other facilities, most government buildings and the taksi terminal are strung along the main road to Abepura.

Information
Tourist Office The tourist office (☎ 33381, ext 2441) three km north of town is a little hard to find, but is worth a trip out there by taksi. It can provide brochures about every district in Irian Jaya (which are often unavailable in the actual district tourist offices) in English, Dutch, German and Japanese. The office, on the ground floor (ask for the *dinas parawisata*) of the Governor's Office (Kantor Gubernor), Jl Soa Siu, Dok II, is open weekdays from 7 am to 3 pm.

PNG Consulate The address of the PNG consulate, and visa regulations for PNG, changes regularly. The consulate (☎ 31250), now at Jl Percetakan 28 next to the Hotel Dafonsoro (look for the PNG flag), is open weekdays from 8 am to 4 pm. Currently, a PNG visa for a maximum of one month can be issued in 24 hours. You will need one photograph, a ticket out of PNG and 20,000 rp.

Immigration This office (☎ 21647), Jl Percetakan 15, is open weekdays from 8 am to 4 pm.

Money Bank Exim and Bank Danamon, both on Jl Ahmad Yani, are quick and painless places to change money. They are open Monday to Friday from 8 am to 2 pm. It's not a bad idea to stock up on rupiah before heading out to the Baliem Valley (although there are a couple of banks in Wamena). A bank and moneychanger at the Sentani airport are open daily in the morning, except Sunday.

Post & Communications Along the waterfront on Jl Koti, the post office is open daily from 8 am to 9 pm. At the back of the building, a fairly chaotic poste restante functions reasonably well. Next door, the Telkom office is open 24 hours a day.

Bookshops The best bookshop in Irian Jaya, the Toko Buku Labor on Jl Sam Ratulangi 5, has a small selection of books in English about Irianese travel and culture. If you read Indonesian, Buku Labor sells *Deiyai*, a locally produced, bi-monthly booklet about Irianese culture and religion.

Emergency The public hospital, Rumah Sakit Umum Pusat (☎ 33616), is on Jl Kese-

hatan in the northern foothills. The police headquarters (☎ 31027) is on Jl Ahmad Yani

Museums

The **Museum Loka Budaya** is in the Cenderawasih University grounds (the closest building to Jayapura, on the western side of the road) in Abepura. The museum contains a fascinating range of Irianese artefacts including the best collection of Asmat carvings outside of Agats. The museum is open weekdays from 7.30 am to 4 pm, costs 500 rp to enter (3500 rp if you want to take photos; 5000 rp for a video camera) and is

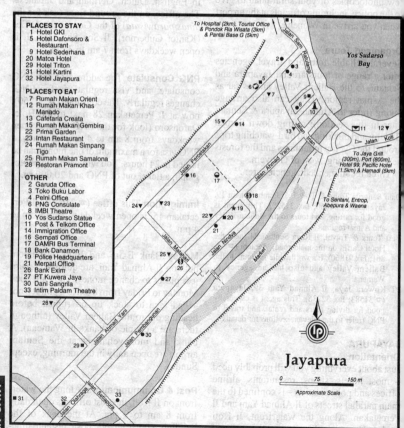

PLACES TO STAY
1 Hotel GKI
5 Hotel Dafonsoro & Restaurant
9 Hotel Sederhana
20 Matoa Hotel
29 Hotel Triton
31 Hotel Kartini
32 Hotel Jayapura

PLACES TO EAT
7 Rumah Makan Orient
12 Rumah Makan Khas Manado
13 Cafetaria Creata
15 Rumah Makan Gembira
22 Prima Garden
23 Intan Restaurant
24 Rumah Makan Simpang Tigo
25 Rumah Makan Samalona
28 Restoran Pramont

OTHER
2 Garuda Office
3 Toko Buku Labor
4 Pelni Office
6 PNG Consulate
8 IMBI Theatre
10 Yos Sudarso Statue
11 Post & Telkom Office
16 Immigration Office
17 DAMRI Bus Terminal
18 Bank Danamon
19 Police Headquarters
21 Merpati Office
26 Bank Exim
27 PT Kuwera Jaya
30 Dani Sangrila
33 Intim Paldam Theatre

To Hospital (2km), Tourist Office & Pondok Ria Wisata (3km) & Pantai Base G (5km)

Yos Sudarso Bay

Jalan Sam Ratulangi

Jalan Ahmad Yani

Jalan Koti

To Jaya Grill (300m), Port (800m), Hotel 99, Pacific Hotel (1.5km) & Hamadi (5km)

To Sentani, Entrop, Abepura & Waena

Jalan Percetakan

Jalan Irian

Jalan Matahari

Jalan Nindya

Market

Jalan Ahmad Yani

Jalan Pembangunan

Jalan Olahraga

Jalan Setiapura

Jayapura

0   75   150 m

Approximate Scale

on the Sentani-Abepura taksi route, almost as far as the Abepura terminal.

The **Museum Negeri** (State Museum) in Waena is also worth a visit. There is a small, but excellent, selection of carvings, clothing, boats, weaving and artefacts from all over Irian Jaya, as well as from the Dutch colonial past. Captions are in English. The museum is still being developed and will take several years to complete. A small shop inside sells souvenirs and books. Entrance costs 200 rp.

Next door, the **Taman Budaya** (Culture Park) is an assemblage of neglected traditional houses representing the nine districts of Irian Jaya. It looks a bit forlorn, but it is free to get in, so have a look around if you're going to the Museum Negeri.

The museum and park have the same opening hours – Tuesday to Saturday from 8 am to 4 pm; Sunday from 10 am to 4 pm. They are on the main road between Sentani and Abepura, and are easy to spot from the taksi (800 rp from Sentani).

Places to Stay

Most visitors stay in Sentani because it is nicer and more convenient, though there are a few cheap places in Jayapura.

Places to Stay – bottom end

The cheapest and most basic place is the grandly named, but badly sign posted, *Hotel Jayapura* (☎ 33216), Jl Olahraga 4. Noisy and very simple singles/doubles cost 12,000/16,800 rp with mandi, but there's little privacy. The central *Hotel Sederhana* (☎ 31-561) at Jl Halmahera 2 is good value for Jayapura. Clean doubles cost 25,300 rp without mandi, or 25,300/44,000 rp with air-con, TV and mandi. The *Hotel GKI* (☎ 33574) is a short walk along the waterfront on Jl Sam Ratulangi 12. It has a pleasant outdoor sitting area, but the rooms are a bit dingy and have no mandi. They cost 20,400/33,000 rp.

The best in this range is definitely the *Hotel Kartini*, Jl Perintis 2, but it's a little inconvenient – just over the bridge and to the right at the top end of Jl Ahmad Yani. Friendly service and rooms with fan and

outside mandi cost 17,600/26,400 rp, or 20,900/30,800 rp with mandi.

Places to Stay – middle & top end

One of the best in the mid-range is the busy, but helpful, *Hotel Dafonsoro* (☎ 31695), Jl Percetakan 20-24. Air-con rooms go for 60,500/72,600 rp. Rooms at the *Hotel Triton* (☎ 33218), Jl Ahmad Yani 52, are old, but have good facilities, and cost 43,560/72,600 rp with air-con, hot water and TV.

On the road to Hamadi, only a few minutes by taksi from Jayapura, two places have the potential for great views, but most rooms don't have any. The hotels have the added attraction of being secluded and away from the busy city. The *Hotel 99* (☎ 35689) has tiny rooms from 19,250/35,000 rp without mandi; better rooms cost 45,000/66,000 rp with air-con and mandi. Next door, the *Pacific Hotel* (☎ 35427) has a good range of rooms (many will have great views when the renovations are completed) starting from a reasonable 30,000 rp with air-con.

The flashiest place is the *Matoa Hotel* (☎ 31633), next to the Merpati office on Jl Ahmad Yani. Singles start at an exorbitant 132,000 rp and go much, much higher.

Places to Eat

Warungs serving gado gado and nasi campur huddle around the Pelni office, along Jl Ahmad Yani and around the waterfront. Plenty of stalls along Jl Nindya sell delicious, filling nasi campur and baked fish from about 2000 rp.

Along Jl Percetakan, the rumah makans *Gembira* and *Simpang Tigo* serve good, simple Indonesian food, and on Jl Ahmad Yani, *Rumah Makan Samalona* remains deservedly popular, with meals from 4000 rp. Opposite the IMBI Theatre, *Cafetaria Creata* on Jl Irian serves cheap Indonesian food and tasty fruit drinks; and on the same street, but upstairs, *Rumah Makan Orient* specialises in Chinese food.

The restaurant in the *Hotel Dafonsoro* is one of the best value places for range, price and setting. Scrumptious cakes and strong Irianese coffee can be enjoyed at the *Prima*

IRIAN JAYA

Garden, opposite the Merpati office, but unfortunately there is nowhere to sit. (A 250g packet of locally made coffee at the Prima Garden costs 5000 rp.)

For a splurge (seafood dishes from 15,000 rp or Indonesian food for about 4000 to 5000 rp) and great views across the harbour, try the *Jaya Grill* on Jl Koti towards the port, and *Pondok Ria Wisata* on the other side of the bay, opposite the tourist office. For the same views, but without the high prices, the cosy *Rumah Makan Khas Manado*, before the Jaya Grill, is recommended.

Entertainment

Karaoke machines are big business in Jayapura. You'll find them, as well as 'hostess girls', at bars like the *Restoran Pramont* and *Intan Restaurant*. The *IMBI Theatre*, near the waterfront, and the *Intim Paldam Theatre*, on Jl Setiapura, show newish films in English or Chinese (with Indonesian subtitles).

Getting There & Away

Air Merpati has flights daily directly to Biak (130,300 rp) and then on to Ujung Pandang (529,000 rp), Denpasar (639,600 rp) and Jakarta (734,700 rp). Flights go daily to Merauke (185,300 rp), and regularly to Nabire (156,700 rp) and Timika (134,700 rp). The Merpati office (☎ 33111), Jl Ahmad Yani 15, is open Monday to Saturday from 7.30 am to noon and 1 to 7 pm, and until 7.30 pm on Sunday.

For basically the same price as Merpati, Garuda flies three times a week to Jakarta, and also through Biak, Ujung Pandang and Denpasar. Its office (☎ 36217), Jl Percetakan 4-6, near the waterfront, is open daily from 8 am to 5 pm.

Sempati has daily flights to Jakarta via Ujung Pandang and Manado (653,300 rp), and to Timika for the same price as Merpati and Garuda. The Sempati office (☎ 31612), Jl Percetakan 17, is open daily from 8 am to 6 pm.

Wamena All flights to Wamena start and finish at Sentani airport (except for the possibility of flights between Nabire, Mulia and Wamena). Several, often heavily booked, Merpati flights go to Wamena (77,500 rp) daily.

Based in Sentani, the cargo services Airfast (☎ 21925), next to the police station, SMAC (☎ 91567), on the main road, and Trigana (☎ 91877), near the airport, leave two or three times a day. They are a useful alternative if Merpati is full or cancelled. They charge about 115,000 rp for a ticket from Sentani to Wamena, but only about 80,000 rp for Wamena to Sentani (when the planes are empty of cargo).

MAF (☎ 91109) and AMA (☎ 91009), both near the Sentani airport, offer some flights to more obscure places – destinations are listed outside their offices. Their overwhelming business is missionary work, so they are not interested in becoming an alternative passenger airline.

PNG There are no road or boat connections with PNG, so the only alternative is to fly between Jayapura and Vanimo, just over the border in PNG. Refer to the introductory Getting There & Away section of this chapter for details.

Boat Naturally, all boats head west from Jayapura; the first main stop is usually Serui or Biak. The Pelni liners *Ciremai* and *Dobonsolo* sail to Biak (29,000/135,000 rp for economy/1st class) every two weeks, and the *Tatamailau* goes to Serui (but not Biak) every four weeks on its way around the rest of Irian Jaya. The Pelni office (☎ 33270), opposite the waterfront on Jl Halmahera 1, sells tickets in the mornings from Monday to Saturday. To save lining up with the rest of Indonesia when a boat is in town, try buying a ticket at one of the authorised Pelni agencies (their addresses are listed on a noticeboard outside the Pelni office) for a small additional commission.

The Perintis boat *Embora* leaves Jayapura every two weeks and stops at Serui, Biak and Wasior, among other villages, on its way to

Manokwari. In Jayapura, the *Ilosangi* starts and finishes its extraordinary six-week run all the way to Merauke, also stopping at Serui and Biak on the way. Details and bookings for Perintis boats can be made at the Pelni office.

For information on other irregular boats along the north coast, enquire at the port, about 800m east of the Yos Sudarso statue. The taksi to Hamadi will take you there.

Getting Around

The Airport A private taxi from the Sentani airport to Jayapura will cost a whopping 25,000 rp. Try sharing with other equally stunned passengers or take a private taksi (see the following Local Transport entry).

Local Transport Travelling from Sentani to Jayapura involves an initially confusing combination of taksis. Catch one from Sentani towards the Abepura taksi terminal (800 rp); get off along the main road just before the terminal and wait for a taksi to the chaotic Entrop taksi terminal (400 rp); get off just before this terminal; and take another to central Jayapura (350 rp). It may sound complicated, but it works relatively easily (many

locals will be doing it, too) and takes about an hour. If in doubt, just tell the boy who takes your money in the taksi where you want to go. Taksis to all places nearby leave every second or two from stops along Jl Ahmad Yani and Jl Sam Ratulangi. Trips around the city cost about 300 rp.

Once or twice a day, a large DAMRI bus travels between Jayapura and the remote transmigration centres of Genyem and Demta, stopping off at Sentani on the way. These buses save the hassle of changing taksis, but travel times are infrequent and inflexible.

SENTANI
Orientation
Sentani is very compact and easy to walk around. Most shops, restaurants and offices are on the main road to Jayapura, Jl Kemiri Sentani Kota. The market and taksi terminal are a short taksi ride to the west.

Information
An information booth at the Sentani airport, open daily from 5 am to 5 pm, is useful for general enquiries.

The police station (☎ 91105) is at the entrance to the airport. You should be able to

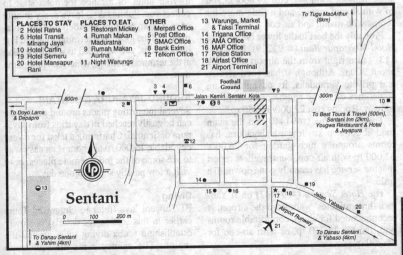

PLACES TO STAY	PLACES TO EAT	OTHER	13 Warungs, Market & Taksi Terminal
2 Hotel Ratna	3 Restoran Mickey	1 Merpati Office	14 Trigana Office
6 Hotel Transit Minang Jaya	4 Rumah Makan Maduratna	5 Post Office	15 AMA Office
10 Hotel Carfin	9 Rumah Makan Aurina	7 SMAC Office	16 MAF Office
19 Hotel Semeru	11 Night Warungs	8 Bank Exim	17 Police Station
20 Hotel Mansapur Rani		12 Telkom Office	18 Airfast Office
			21 Airport Terminal

Sentani

0   100   200 m

To Tugu MacArthur (6km)

To Doyo Lama & Depapre

Football Ground

Jalan Kemiri Sentani Kota

To Best Tours & Travel (500m), Sentani Inn (2km), Yougwa Restaurant & Hotel & Jayapura

To Danau Sentani & Yahim (4km)

Jalan Yabaso

Airport Runway

To Danau Sentani & Yabaso (4km)

800m

300m

get a surat jalan there, but regulations do change so staff may send you to Jayapura. Bank Exim, on the main road, changes money on weekday mornings.

The post office (with poste restante) is also on the main road. It's open Monday to Saturday from 8 am to 5.30 pm. The 24 hour Telkom office is one block behind it.

The Merpati office (☎ 91314), on the main road, can handle all bookings and confirmations, so there is no need to go to its office in Jayapura. It's open Monday to Saturday from 7.30 am to 8 pm, and Sunday from 5 to 9 pm.

Places to Stay

Many places in Sentani will give you a free lift to/from the airport if you pre-arrange it. In any case, most hotels are within 15 minutes' walk of the airport.

The *Hotel Ratna* (☎ 91435), on the main road, has been recently renovated. Air-con rooms, often without outside windows, go for 30,000/40,000 rp which isn't as good value as it once was. If you need a surat jalan in a hurry, staff here have 'connections'.

Over the road, the *Hotel Transit Minang Jaya* (☎ 91067) is better value, and offers friendly and helpful service. Small rooms, some without windows, cost 24,000/35,200 rp with shared mandi, and a little more for rooms with mandi and air-con.

Probably the best in the lower range is the *Hotel Mansapur Rani* (☎ 91219), Jl Yabaso 113 – turn right from the airport and walk about 300m. Although it has good service and private verandahs, its advantages are sometimes offset by engine noise from the runway. Rooms cost 22,000/30,250 rp.

The *Sentani Inn* (☎ 91440), on the main road about two km towards Jayapura, has rooms around a nice garden for 26,000/33,000 rp with air-con, but travellers report that the service has recently gone downhill a little.

The *Hotel Semeru* (☎ 91447) on Jl Yabaso, three minutes' walk from the airport, is recommended for clean, comfortable rooms with fan for 35,750 rp, or with air-con for 46,750 rp.

The *Hotel Carfin* (☎ 91478) is on the main road, about 800m east of the post office. Rooms with air-con and TV are modern, but dark, and aren't particularly good value for 66,000/78,000 rp.

Places to Eat

Warungs congregate around the market (a fair walk from the hotels) and opposite the football ground, just back from the main road. All the other places to eat are close to each other along the main road. *Restoran Mickey* remains the most popular place for travellers and expats. A good range of Indonesian food costs from about 3000 rp, while passable spaghetti is 6000 rp and hamburgers 3000 rp. It also has a reliable supply of cold beer.

Several places serve baked fish with rice and vegetables for around 3000 rp. The best is certainly *Rumah Makan Maduratna*. Also, a worthy alternative to Mickey's, *Rumah Makan Aurina* has tasty tuna steaks and baked fish meals from 5000 rp, and small bottles of cold beer for the same price.

Getting Around

A private taxi from the airport to Sentani costs 5000 rp. From the airport, you can walk to your hotel, or arrange for hotel staff to collect you. Public taksis leave every minute or two from Sentani to Abepura (for Jayapura) and the local taksi terminal/market. For other places, you will need to wait for a taksi at the terminal to fill up, which can take some time.

AROUND JAYAPURA & SENTANI

Several interesting places around the region can be easily reached in day trips from Jayapura or Sentani. Chartering a taksi for a very negotiable 15,000 rp per hour is an easy way to see some of the more remote places, or to visit a few nearby sights in one day.

Diving

PT Kuwera Jaya (refer to Organised Tours earlier in this section for details) is slowly establishing scuba diving tours around the region. The agency rents all scuba and norkelling equipment (the latter costs about JS$10 a day), boats, guides and so on. Scuba living trips start from about US$45 for a half-day or US$85 for a full day, including quipment and transport to/from your hotel n Jayapura or Sentani,. Two excellent spots or scuba diving and snorkelling among tunning coral and fish are around Tanjung Ria and Depapre (see below for details).

Pantai Base G

Another one of those places made famous by General MacArthur, Base G beach is known locally as Pantai Tanjung Ria. The beach is wide and desolate, except for Sunday when locals come in their hundreds for a picnic and walk. Taksis (400 rp) leave regularly from Jayapura for the pleasant ride to Tanjung Ria; ask to be dropped off at the beach which is a 10 minute walk down a hill.

Depapre

Set in front of the dramatic Cyclop mountains, the pretty village of Depapre is a very enjoyable and easy trip from Sentani. From the village jetty, you can charter boats around the sheltered Tanahmerah Bay for some scuba diving, or try to rent a canoe if you only want to paddle around the bay and/or go snorkelling. A five km track from the back of the village leads to the secluded **Pantai Amai**.

Taksis (1000 rp; one hour) leave every hour or so from the Sentani terminal. You can easily stop along the way and visit other pretty villages, such as **Maribua Tua**, and the hot springs at **Sabron Siri**.

Danau Sentani

The magnificent Danau Sentani is worth a trip to Jayapura/Sentani in itself. As you fly into Sentani you will see the enticing 9,630 hectares, 19 islands and fishing villages, such as Ayapo, full of wooden houses precariously raised on stilts above the water. Nobody runs any organised tours around the lake, so you will have to explore it yourself – but it's certainly worth the effort.

A boat trip is the best way to enjoy the lake and visit some of the islands. From Yahim, the Sentani boat harbour, a short ride south of the terminal, motorboats with room for five people can theoretically be rented for about 20,000 rp per hour, but you may have to spend some time looking for a boat. Canoes cost far less, but will limit your options.

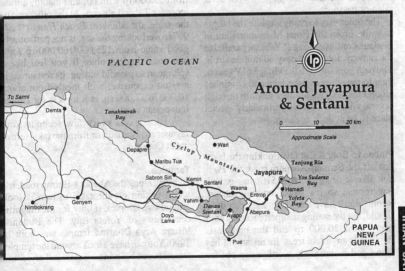

Around Jayapura & Sentani

The most expensive, but convenient, option, especially if you are in a group, is to charter a boat from the restaurant at the Pondok Wisata Yougwa (see Places to Stay & Eat in this section). A reliable motorboat, which can hold six or seven people as well as a knowledgeable guide, is not unreasonable at 40,000 rp per hour.

A boat can visit simple, friendly villages such as **Doyo Lama**, renowned for the manufacture of impressive, large woodcarvings and for strange, unexplained rock paintings nearby. Taksis also leave from Sentani two or three times a day (not Sunday) to Doyo Lama. Alternatively, take a more regular taksi to Kemiri along the main road to Depapre, and walk a few km to Doyo Lama.

For breathtaking views of Danau Sentani, visit the MacArthur monument on top of **Gunung Ifar**. Here, as the legend goes, Mac-Arthur sat and contemplated his WWII strategies. The road to the top is marked 'Tugu MacArthur' and is a very steep six km (don't try to walk). Irregular taksis (or charter one) go to the top; there are more on Sunday because the area is a popular picnic spot. Before the monument, you have to report to a local military office (which has taken over the area) and deposit your surat jalan or passport.

The other way to really explore the lake is to walk. From the Hotel Mansapur Rani in Sentani, continue along Jl Yabaso, parallel to the runway, for a very easy 40 minute stroll. The path goes through the village of **Yabaso**, then to the shores of the lake and continues around the lake for another few km through several villages. This is a particularly special place to be at dusk or dawn.

Places to Stay & Eat Overlooking the lake, just off the Sentani-Abepura road, the *Pondok Wisata Yougwa* (☎ 71570) has only a few rooms, so it's worth booking ahead. Rooms don't have the views they could, or should, but the setting is superb. Rooms with mandi cost 30,000 rp and the breakfasts (included) are a real treat. Its restaurant has views and is definitely worth a trip out for

lunch. Meals are reasonably priced, starting at 5000 rp for a very good nasi goreng.

Also on the main Sentani-Abepura road, near the lake, the *Hotel Surya* (☎ 71429) has rooms (also with no views) from 27,500 rp or 38,500 rp with air-con.

Hamadi

Hamadi's bustling, scruffy, daily market is fascinating to wander around; it is the most interesting market in the area. Plenty of stalls along the main road sell souvenirs, including tacky mass-produced Baliem and Asmat art – you will find better stuff in Wamena. From Hamadi, try to charter a boat to some of the smaller islands such as **Kayu Pulau** (curiously not called, as expected, Pulau Kayu).

Pantai Hamadi, the site of a US amphibious landing on 22 April 1944, is another two minutes' drive past the market. The beach is pleasant, if a little dirty, with some enticing islands close by, rusting WWII wrecks to explore and a WWII statue not far away. At the start of the trail to the beach, you will have to report and deposit your surat jalan with the military station.

On both sides of the noisy main road in Hamadi, the *Hotel Asia* (☎ 35478) has rooms from 25,000 rp with fan and mandi; a little more for TV and air-con. At the other end of the scale, the *Mahkota Beach Hotel* (☎ 32-997), overlooking the sea, is not particularly good value from 125,000/160,000 rp for a luxurious single/double. If you feel like a splurge in a splendid setting, its restaurant is not too expensive, with meals from about 10,000 to 12,000 rp, or a lot less for simple Indonesian food.

A taksi leaves every few seconds from Jayapura to Hamadi, or from the taksi terminal at Entrop.

Temples

Halfway along the Abepura-Entrop road, it's worth getting off the taksi to have a look around two temples, if only for the magnificent views of Yofeta Bay. The Buddhist **Vihara Arya Dharma** temple was built in 1990. You can have a look around the temple, which is not built in any classical style, but

s setting and views are worth climbing up
he steep, short trail.

About 300m further towards Jayapura, on
he other side of the road, the Hindu **Pura
Agung Surya Bhuvana** temple is pretty
standard, but its views and setting again are
more than enough reason to walk up there.

The Baliem Valley

The Baliem Valley, set in the central highlands, is easily the most popular destination
in Irian Jaya and the most accessible place in
the interior. While the Dani people who
inhabit most of the inner valley have adopted
some western conveniences, and the main
town, Wamena, has a few modern facilities,
the valley remains one of the few truly fas-
inating, traditional areas left in the world.

The first white men chanced upon the
Baliem Valley in 1938, a discovery which
came as one of the last and greatest surprises
o a world that had mapped, studied and
travelled the mystery out of its remotest
corners. WWII prevented further explora-
ion and it was not until 1945 that attention
was again drawn to the valley when a plane
crashed there and the survivors were rescued.

The first missionaries arrived in 1954, the
Dutch government established a post at Wa-
nena in 1956 and changes to the Baliem
ifestyle followed. Today Indonesia has
added its own brand of colonialism, bringing
schools, police, soldiers, transmigrants and
shops, but the local culture has, in many
ways, proved very resilient.

Geography
The Grand Valley of Sungai Baliem (known
as the Grand Valley) starts from points east
and west 120 km apart. The eastern arm rises
near the summit of Gunung Trikora (4750m),
south-west of Wamena, and flows west away
from Wamena. From the confluence of the
east and west arms, near Kuyawage, the river
travels east then turns south into what's
known as the Baliem Valley, 1554m above

sea level, and about 60 km long and 16 km
wide, with Wamena roughly at its centre. The
river then continues south through the massive Baliem Gorge – where it drops 1500m in
less than 50 km forming a spectacular series
of cataracts – and down to the Arafura Sea
on the southern coast.

Climate
The best time to visit the valley is between
about March and August. At this time, it rains
less (but be prepared for rain anytime of the
year), the days are fine (up to 26°C) and the
evenings are cool (about 12°C), but it is
always colder in higher parts, such as Danau
Habbema. The best season generally coin-
cides with the European summer which
means that the Baliem is often busy at this
time, especially in August. The wet season is
from about September to January, when trekking in some parts may be wet, muddy and
unpleasant.

The Dani
The tribes of the Baliem are usually grouped
together under the name 'Dani'; a rather
abusive name given by neighbouring tribes,
but one that has stuck. There are a number of
other highland groups, distinguished from
each other by language, physical appearance, dress and social customs. The Dani are
farmers, skilfully working their fertile land,
digging long ditches for irrigation and drainage, and leaving the land fallow between
crops. The clearing of the land and the tilling
of the soil for the first crop is traditionally
men's work; the planting, weeding and harvesting is women's.

Food The sweet potato (*erom*) is the staple
food of the highlands. The Dani recognise 70
different types – some varieties can only be
eaten by a particular group, such as pregnant
women or old men, and ancestor spirits get
the first potatoes from every field.

Houses Traditional Dani villages comprised
of several self-contained fenced compounds,
each with its own cooking house, men's
house, women's houses and pigsties. A

typical compound might be home to four men and their families, perhaps 20 people. A traditional Dani house (honay) is circular, topped by a thatched dome-shaped roof. You can see plenty of honays within a short stroll of Wamena.

Clothing Dani men wear penis sheaths, made of a cultivated gourd and known locally as a horim. The Indonesian government's campaign in the early 1970s to eradicate the penis gourds was mostly a failure. Many Dani (mainly in the more remote parts) wear pig fat in their hair, and cover their bodies in pig fat and soot for health and warmth. The fat makes their hair look like a cross between a Beatles' mop top and a Rastafarian's dreadlocks.

Naked except for their penis gourds, men (also in Wamena) stand with their arms folded across their chests to keep warm in the evenings. Traditionally, the men wear no other clothing apart from ornamentation such as string hair nets, bird of paradise feathers and cowry shell necklaces. If a woman wears a grass skirt it usually indicates that she is unmarried. A married woman traditionally wears a skirt of fibre oils or seeds strung together, hung just below the abdomen and covering the buttocks. Dani women (also in Wamena) carry string bags from their heads, usually heavily loaded with vegetables, and even babies and valuable pigs, on their way to or from the market.

Marriage Despite missionary pressure, many Dani have maintained their polygamous marriage system – a man may have as many wives as he can afford. Brides have to be paid for in pigs and the man must give four or five pigs (each worth about 250,000 rp today) to the family of the girl; a man's social status is measured by the number of pigs and wives he has. Dani men and women sleep apart. The men of a compound sleep tightly packed in one hut, and the women and children sleep in the other huts. After a birth, sex is taboo for the mother for two to five years, apparently to give the child exclusive use of her milk. As a result of this care, the average Dani life expectancy is 60 years. The taboo also contributes to both polygamy and a high divorce rate.

Customs One of the more unusual, but now prohibited, customs is for a woman to have one or two joints of her fingers amputated when a close relative dies; you'll see many of the older women with fingers missing right up to the second joint. Also, Dani women will often smother themselves with clay and mud at the time of a family death. Cremation was the traditional method of disposing of the body of the deceased, but sometimes the body would be kept and dried.

Fighting between villages or districts seems to have been partly a ritual matter to appease the ancestors and attract good luck, and partly a matter of revenge and settling scores. In formal combat, fighting was carried out in brief clashes throughout the day and was not designed to wreak carnage. After a few hours the opposing groups tended to turn to verbal insults instead. The Indonesian government, through sponsored mock battles each year, and the missionaries have done their best to stamp out Dani

warfare with a fair amount of success, although an outbreak between the Wollesi and Hitigima districts in 1988 led to about 15 deaths, and there were unsubstantiated reports of tribal fighting in the far north of the Grand Valley as recently as the early 1990s.

Language The northern and western Dani speak a dialect of Dani distinct from that in the Wamena area. Around Wamena, a man greeting a man says *nayak*; if greeting more than one man *nayak lak*. When greeting a woman, a man says *la'uk*; if greeting more than one woman *la'uk nya*. Women say *la'uk* if greeting one person; *la'uk nya* if greeting more than one person. *Wam* means pig; *nan* is to eat; *i-nan* is to drink; *an* is I; and *hano* is good. Most Dani speak Indonesian, but they appreciate a greeting in their own language.

The Dani are friendly, but some are shy and occasionally seem sullen. Long handshakes, giving each person time to really feel the other's hand, are common. Throughout the region, many locals request 100 to 200 rp, or a cigarette or two, if you want to take their photo, but sometimes 1000 rp is asked if they're dressed up in feathers or other ceremonial costume.

Surat Jalan

A surat jalan is absolutely essential if you want to stay more than one or two days in Wamena and travel around the Baliem Valley. You cannot get one in Wamena, but they are easy to obtain from police stations in Jayapura, Sentani and Biak. On the permit, list every major town and area you wish to visit, and take a few photocopies to give to regional police stations around the valley. (Refer to the Visas & Documents section earlier in this chapter for a further explanation about the surat jalan.)

Your surat jalan will be checked and stamped when you arrive and depart from the Wamena airport, so have a photocopy ready to give to the police. (If travelling by a cargo plane – ie not using the normal terminal – make sure you report to the police at the

Wamena airport anyway.) There are places with photocopy machines along Jl Trikora and in the market in Wamena.

You should report and show your permit to police stations or authorities if you stay in villages outside of Wamena, particularly in nearby district centres such as Jiwika, Kurima and Kimbim. Reporting to the police is often not necessary, or possible, if you're trekking to remote areas, but still report to local authorities as you go along. Some more remote areas in the region may be off limits to foreigners; the police in Wamena will fill you in on the current situation.

WAMENA

The main town of the Baliem Valley and the capital of the Jayawijaya district, Wamena is a neat, sprawling place. Although there's not much to do in the town itself, it's a good base from which to explore nearby villages and

---

Baliem Festival

To coincide with the busiest time for tourism (ie the European summer holidays), a festival is held in the Baliem Valley every August. Check with the tourist office in Wamena for current details, but the dates (normally between 9 and 14 August) and activities vary little from year to year.

With the encouragement of the Indonesian government and local missionaries, the highlight of the festival is the mock 'tribal fighting' (perang-perangan), where men from most villages dress up in full traditional regalia. The festival also features plenty of traditional dancing (tarian asli) by men and women, with Dani music. Pig feasts (karapan babi), using hot rocks (bakar batu), are also an integral part of the festival, while pig races are a lot of fun. Other lesser attractions include a festival of flowers, exhibitions of traditional archery, and foot and bicycle races.

The festival is held in Wamena, on the wider plains of Mulima (between Aikima and Jiwika), and along Sungai Yetni at Sugokmo (south of Wamena). Although it is tourist oriented and there is no shortage of foreigners watching the events, the festival is a magical (and very photogenic) occasion and the only chance to see some of the valley's attractions in a short space of time. ■

---

the countryside. Wamena is expensive compared to the rest of Indonesia, but this is understandable as *everything* has to be flown in from Jayapura, where most goods arrive from western Indonesia.

Orientation

Most of the hotels, places to eat and offices are along Jl Trikora, only one block from the airport. The rather scruffy, crowded Pasar Nayak market (which is due to move to HomHom, about three km north of its current location, after this book's publication) serves as the centre of town. While the market and taksi terminal areas are not particularly pleasant, just a few blocks to the west are some lovely, quiet streets, such as Jl Thamrin, worth wandering around. Take a torch (flashlight) at night as there are few street lights; many streets are badly sign posted, or not at all.

Information

Tourist Office The new tourist office (☎ 31 365) is worth a visit when you arrive to get current information on markets and ceremonies; it can also organise guides and even an all day dancing ceremony and pig feast for about 200,000 rp. Open daily from 8 am to 2 pm, except Sunday, the office is inconveniently located almost at the top of Jl Yos Sudarso, about three km from the Bank Rakyat building. A becak, or taksi towards Sinatma, will save a walk.

The policeman who stamps your surat jalan when you arrive doubles as an official tourist information officer. He can provide good, no-obligation advice about trekking, and arrange official guides. He is more likely to be in his small office at the airport when a plane is arriving.

Money Bank Exim, near the top of Jl Trikora, and the huge, incongruous Bank Rakyat, on the same street, will change money. They are both open weekdays between 8 am and 3 pm.

Post & Communications The post office on Jl Timor is open from Monday to Thursday and Saturday from 8 am to 2 pm, and on Friday until 11 am. The Telkom office on Jl Thamrin is open 24 hours daily. A more convenient *wartel* is near the market on Jl Trikora.

Emergency The Rumah Sakit Umum (Public Hospital; ☎ 31152) is at the southern end of Jl Trikora. Travellers have reported that the service and advice there is not too good. The police station (☎ 31072) is on Jl Safri Darwin. You don't have to report there, but the friendly officers are a good source of trekking information and will tell you of any places off limits.

Organised Tours

Several good – and not so good – travel and tour agencies are starting to spring up in Wamena, and in Jayapura and Sentani, catering for the popular organised trekking market. An agency can arrange (and prearrange with notice) completely packaged, all-inclusive trekking tours if you don't want the hassle of organising everything yourself, but they are usually (but not always) more expensive. Don't forget that the tourist office is more than willing to give impartial and free advice on treks, guides and so on.

The most reliable agencies, with the best range of treks around the Baliem Valley and the Asmat region, are listed below. (Refer to the previous Jayapura & Sentani section for details of branches there also.)

Best Tours & Travel, opposite the Hotel Trendy, Wamena (☎ 32101; fax 32102). It also has a branch in Sentani.

Dani Sangrila Tours & Travel has no branch in Wamena but has a contact telephone number (☎ 31952). Its main office is in Jayapura.

Chandra Nusantara Tours & Travel, Jl Trikora 17, Wamena (☎ 31293; fax 31299). This is the original agent, and still one of the best.

Places to Stay

Apart from Timika (which most travellers won't get to), Wamena is the most expensive place in Irian Jaya and, probably, Indonesia. Either accept that accommodation will cost more and choose somewhere nice in the

To Wamena Hotel (2km), Hom Hom (3km),
Honai Resort Hotel (5km) & Jiwika

To Pondok Wisata
Putri Dani (500m)

Jalan Irian

Jalan Thamrin

Jalan Safri Darwin

Jalan Pramuka

Jl Pramuka

Jl Angkasa

Jalan Trikora

Jl Ambon

Jalan Bhayangkara

Jalan Timor

Jalan Yos Sudarso

To Sinatma (4km), Mentari Restoran
& Tourist Office (3km) & Pyramid

Jalan Gato Subroto

Runway

Jalan Diponegoro

Jalan Jenderal A Yani

Jalan Panjaitan

To
Wesaput
(800m)

Airport

To Hospital (500m)
& Kurima

To Hitigima

Wamena

0   75   150 m

Approximate Scale

PLACES TO STAY	OTHER
1 Rannu Jaya Hotel	4 Best Tours & Travel
3 Baliem Palimo	8 Telkom Office
5 Hotel Trendy	9 Wijaya Theatre
7 Sri Kandi Hotel	10 Pasar Nayak
14 Hotel Anggrek	11 Bank Exim
19 Nayak Hotel	12 MAF Office
25 Baliem Cottages	15 Police Station
27 Hotel Syahrial	16 Bank Rakyat
Jaya	18 Post Office
	20 Airport Terminal
PLACES TO EAT	21 Airfast, SMAC &
2 Rumah Makan	Trigana Offices
Reski	22 Taksi Terminal
6 Rumah Makan Mas	23 Wamena Theatre
Budi	24 Silimo Pemuda
13 Kantin Bu Lies	26 Merpati Office
17 Restaurant	28 Chandra Nusantara
Pelangi	Tours & Travel

IRIAN JAYA

middle range, or go 'Dani' and stay in a cheap Dani-style hut near Wamena. Refer to the following Around the Baliem Valley section for details on places to stay in villages close to Wamena.

The cheapest place in Wamena is the *Hotel Syahrial Jaya* (☎ 31306) on Jl Gatot Subroto, a two minute walk south of the airport. Rooms now cost from 20,000 rp and are no longer the value they were. The *Hotel Anggrek* (☎ 31242) on Jl Ambon is central and comfortable. Singles/doubles cost 22,000/33,000 rp without mandi. Rooms with mandis cost 40,000 rp, but all guests have access to hot water.

The *Hotel Trendy* (☎ 31092) at the top of Jl Trikora has a terrible name, but good clean rooms (better ones at the front) for 27,000/33,000 rp, good-value triples for 46,000 rp and there is a nice lounge area.

The *Nayak Hotel* (☎ 31067) is opposite the airport. Its convenience is offset by the noise from the airport and taksi terminals nearby, and it isn't good value these days with rooms for 35,000/45,000 rp, including TV.

The *Sri Kandi Hotel* (☎ 31367) at Jl Irian 16 is a little inconvenient, but is quiet, friendly and worth a try. Rooms with enormous bathrooms cost from 30,000/35,000 rp. For some real peace and seclusion around a pretty garden, *Wamena Hotel* (☎ 31292) is worth considering for 30,000/40,000 rp. It is about two km north of Hotel Trendy; take a becak out there. It provides free transport to a restaurant of your choice in the evening.

There is very little value in Wamena's version of the middle to top range; air-conditioning isn't really necessary and most places don't even offer hot water, which is often very welcome after a hike. The best in this range (and one of the nicest in Irian Jaya) is the *Pondok Wisata Putri Dani* (☎ 31223), Jl Irian 40, about 500m west of the Sri Kandi. Spotless and very comfortable rooms cost 40,000 rp or 55,000 rp with mandi.

At the top of Jl Trikora, *Rannu Jaya Hotel* (☎ 31257) is recommended for 36,000/48,000 rp, while the *Baliem Palimo* (☎ 31-043) has large, modern rooms from 66,550

rp with TV and hot water. It also has a nice outdoor garden.

For something different, *Baliem Cottage* (☎ 31370) on Jl Thamrin has westernised comfortable and large (concrete) Dani 'huts' from 45,000 rp, depending on the size.

The top place is the absurdly overpriced *Honai Resort Hotel* (☎ 31515) in the village of Pikhe, about 10 minutes' north of Wamena by taksi. The rooms are, of course, very nice and include hot water, transport to/from the airport and dinner, but there is nothing else to justify the US$125/140 price tag.

Places to Eat

Other than a few cheap and ordinary Padang-style places around the market, most restaurants in Wamena serve the same sort of food for the same sort of price: rice or noodle-based Indonesian meals from 3000 to 5000 rp, while anything more exciting – such a locally caught prawns (udang), or baked goldfish (ikan mas), with one of three different sauces – will cost 9000 to 10,000 rp. Some places close on Sunday.

On one side of Hotel Trendy on Jl Trikora *Rumah Makan Mas Budi* remains deservedly popular and about the best place in Wamena, but (soft) drinks are reasonably expensive. *Rumah Makan Reski*, on the northern side of the Trendy, has good 'Chainese food'. *Kantin Bu Lies*, next to the airport, is also recommended for simple Indonesian food, but anything different, or not on the menu, may be pricey. *Restaurant Pelangi*, opposite Bank Rakyat, is OK for food, but is worth trying for fresh coffee and cakes. The delightful *Mentari Restoran*, Jl Yos Sudarso 47, is definitely worth a 20 minute walk or becak ride.

Wamena is designated a 'dry' area, so no alcohol should be brought into the capital by travellers. If you are desperate, however some of the more expensive hotels may be able to find you a bottle of something at an outrageous price.

Entertainment

Wamena isn't the most exciting place in Indonesia. Incredibly (but inevitably) most estaurants have karaoke machines, but thankfully (probably because no alcohol is available), they aren't really popular among patrons. The *Wijaya Theatre*, at the market, and the *Wamena Theatre*, on Jl Yos Sudarso, show films in English or Chinese (with Indonesian subtitles) nightly with varying quality of sound, picture and comfort.

Things to Buy

The Dani are fine craftspeople (traditionally the men are the creators), so it's no surprise that a wide selection of souvenirs is available. Usually it's cheaper to buy directly from the Dani in the villages, but they can strike a hard bargain so also check out prices in the shops and markets. Several reasonable souvenir shops have sprung up along Jl Trikora and impromptu stalls are often set up along Jl Gatot Subroto, near the airport. An increasing (and annoying) amount of traders will approach you on the streets of Wamena or hang around the doorways of popular hotels and restaurants. Bargaining is essential if you want a good price and bartering is acceptable in the villages.

The Silimo Pemuda on Jl Thamrin, next to Baliem Cottages, is a co-operative of Dani people making and selling carvings, weaving and pottery in stalls. The place is a good idea, but is looking forlorn and neglected these days and the stuff for sale in the shop is really tacky.

The cost of stone axe blades *(kapak)* depends on the size and amount of labour involved in making each one; blue stone is the hardest and considered the finest material, and thus more expensive – from at least 15,000 rp and up to 200,000 rp for something large and authentic. *Sekan* are thin, intricately hand-woven rattan bracelets which cost from 1000 rp. *Noken* are bark-string bags made from the inner bark of certain types of trees and shrubs, which are dried, shredded and then rolled into threads; the bags are coloured with vegetable dyes, with patterns varying according to their origin, resulting in a very strong smell. They cost 4000 to 10,000 rp.

Other handcrafts include: various head and arm necklaces *(mikak)* of cowry shells, feathers and bone; grass skirts *(jogal* and *thali)*; assorted head decorations *(suale)*, often complete with the horns of a wild pig and, gruesomely, an entire, squashed parrot, for up to 20,000 rp; woven baskets for around 5000 rp; carved spears and arrows for about 6000 rp each; and woven place mats for 2500 to 5000 rp. Asmat woodcarvings, shields and spears are also available in the souvenir shops, but be very wary of price and quality.

Of course, the most popular souvenir is the penis gourd (horim). The gourd is held upright by attaching a thread to the top and looping it around the waist. These are priced from 1000 to 20,000 rp depending on size (!) and quality of materials and craftmanship.

Getting There & Away

Air Merpati flies between Sentani (for Jayapura) and Wamena several times a day (77,500 rp). As flying is the only way in and out of the valley, flights are often heavily booked (especially around August), so confirm, and later reconfirm, your flight out of Wamena as soon as you can. The Merpati office (☎ 31488), Jl Trikora 41, is open daily from 7 am to 3 pm.

An interesting alternative way to/from Wamena – if current regulations allow – is the twice weekly Merpati flight to Mulia (29,100 rp) in the far west, from where there is a connection a day or two later to Nabire (46,000 rp) in the Cenderawasih Bay region.

On most days, cargo planes also fly between Sentani and Wamena. They are a useful alternative, especially if the Merpati flight is full or cancelled. Airfast (☎ 31053), Trigana (☎ 31611) and SMAC (☎ 31567), with offices around Wamena's airport, sell tickets to Sentani for around 80,000 rp, but the price from Sentani to Wamena (when the planes are jam-packed with cargo) is higher at about 115,000 rp.

Missionary services, MAF (☎ 31263) and AMA (☎ 31781), both near the airport, provide irregular flights to more obscure destinations, primarily for missionary work – they are not interested in becoming an

IRIAN JAYA

alternative passenger airline. Their schedules change weekly; it's better to check with their larger offices near the Sentani airport.

Getting Around

Almost all hotels in Wamena are within walking distance of the airport. For a rest, or a longer trip around town, take a becak. As a guide, the official becak price is about 500 rp per km, but you will be asked to pay far more than that; you need to bargain and always agree on a price. Becaks hang around the market and can often be hailed from around the streets, but they don't run at night and seem to disappear when it rains!

Opposite the prison, on the way to the Wamena Hotel, Baliem Valley Mountain Bikes plan to start operating at the time of this book's publication. They will charge 20,000 rp per day for a mountain bike, which is a great way of travelling along the nearby roads (but please don't use them on the trails).

AROUND THE BALIEM VALLEY

Trekking is certainly the best way to see particular scenery, witness special ceremonies and visit more remote people, but if you don't have the time, money (it may cost as much as 80,000 rp per person per day for a decent trek organised by yourself) or inclination to trek, don't be put off coming to the Baliem Valley. With the increasing number of places to stay in the valley and more transport along new, and improving, roads, visitors will be able to see most of the traditional people, villages and customs, mummies, markets, scenery, hanging bridges (*jembatan gantung*) and wild pigs they want during day trips from Wamena, Jiwika, Manda and Kurima – at a fraction of the cost of trekking.

Wandering around the valleys and hills brings you into close contact with the Dani, and makes even Wamena seem a distant metropolis! This is outstanding hiking country, but travel light (or hire a porter) because the trails are often muddy and slippery. You have to clamber over stiles, maybe cross rivers by dugout canoe or log raft, and traverse creeks or trenches on quaint footbridges or a single rough plank or slippery log. You can take all day or half-day trips from Wamena, Jiwika, Manda and Kurima or go for longer treks around the Baliem Valley staying in villages or camping as you go, depending on the remoteness of the area.

Mummies

Black, wizened mummies (*mumi*), most at least 300 years old, are found in several villages around the region. They are worth a look, but one is pretty much the same as another. You will have to pay from 2000 to 10,000 rp to see one, and the display by the villagers is often contrived and tourist-oriented. The most accessible mummy is at Sumpaima, just north of Jiwika, while the one at Aikima is a bit broken, as is the one at Musatafak. The mummy at Pummo is the best, but this involves a trek from Wosilimo to Meagaima and then taking a canoe to Pummo, or trekking from Kimbim. There are others at Araboda, near Kimbim, and near Angguruk, in the far east.

Markets

Attending a market in the countryside (don't be put off by the scruffy market in Wamena) is a great way of meeting locals, buying souvenirs and experiencing some Dani culture. Market dates are fairly rigid, but it's a good idea to check with the tourist office in Wamena before you take a long trip out to a particular village. Markets usually start early and may be over, or less interesting, by noon.

They are held in the following major villages: Jiwika (on Sunday); Kelila (Tuesday, Thursday and Saturday); Kimbim (Wednesday); Kurima (Tuesday and Friday); Manda (Monday and Thursday); Pyramid (Saturday); and Wosilimo (Monday).

Trekking

Guides A real cutthroat guide industry has emerged in Wamena. Guides will latch onto you as soon as you arrive off the plane and if you show any interest, they will never let you go. Before committing yourself to a guide, decide if you really want to go trek-

Tourism in the Baliem

It is really only in the last 10 years that tourism has started to make an impact on the valley. In 1988, 758 foreigners visited the valley; by 1994 over 5,500 came; and the Indonesian authorities hope to almost double that figure by the end of the decade. Seventy per cent come from Europe, often around the month of August. While the number of tourists may not seem large, the impact of tourism is still substantial. The main town of Wamena struggles to dispose of sewerage and rubbish, and pollution from public transport is bad. The Gua Wikuda caves, near Wosilimo, are being developed by (and with the benefits returning to) indigenous people, but generally the tourist and transport industries in the valley, with the exception of guides, are run by non-Irianese.

The following are ways to minimise the impact of tourism and improve the standard of living for the indigenous people: stay at places run by the Dani – usually just Dani-style huts at the moment; ensure that you take out everything you bring with you when trekking; urge guides and porters to look after local flora when building shelters and making tracks; underplay your comparative wealth by not flashing around loads of money and western goods; be sensitive when taking photos – ask first and don't begrudge them a few hundred rupiah, or a cigarette or two, because they get very little else out of the booming tourist industry; and don't exacerbate local inflation by overpaying guides and porters.

Several observers, however, can see some benefit to the Dani through tourism: interest in, and travel to, the valley ensures that the Indonesian government does not treat the indigenous people badly; interest in the traditional cultures encourages the customs and lifestyles to continue if only for the sake of tourist dollars; and some money does trickle back to help local community development.

One disturbing side effect was the kidnapping of several Indonesians and Europeans in early 1996 from a remote section of the valley by the Free Papua Movement (OPM). The incident received the publicity the OPM wanted. Although two Indonesians were killed, the remainder of the hostages were released unharmed four months later. The hostages were part of a research programme; there is currently no indication that the OPM are targeting tourists. ∎

ing (as opposed to taking day trips from Wamena and other villages), seek other travellers for advice or ask if they want to go in a group and share costs, visit the tourist office, and decide where you want to go and or how long.

If you are trekking, a guide is virtually essential. There are no decent maps of the area and a guide can help you decide where to go, facilitate communication with locals, and (or even create) places to stay and generally keep you informed about ceremonies, festivals etc. In addition, you'll get to know a local person. They should be licensed, which usually indicates some trekking experience; speak English (sometimes Dutch) and several local languages; and genuinely know the area you want to visit.

Prices for guides have increased with the amount of (often wealthy) tourists visiting the region. The 'official' price (according to the tourist office) is up to 20,000 rp per day, more for distant and difficult trekking. You may need two porters per person: one for your backpack, and another for camping and

cooking gear, food etc. They cost about 10,000 rp per day and are a very good idea.

You can organise a guide and a trek yourself (but bargain hard and long), or the tourist office and the tourist information counter at the airport can arrange licensed (and probably cheaper) guides and porters for you. Of course, the hassle can be avoided if you take an organised trek with a travel and tour agency (see Organised Tours in the Wamena section) and, depending on your skill at bargaining and knowledge of trekking in the valley, this may not be much dearer (if at all) than organising things yourself.

A tip at the end of a trip is expected. It's not a bad idea to test out a guide on a short walk before hiring one for a longer trip. Also ask other travellers for their recommendations.

What to Bring You can buy most things you need from Wamena's market and shops, such as food, bottled water and cooking gear, but there is nowhere to rent camping or cooking equipment. Things are naturally expensive in Wamena, so try stocking up in Sentani or Jayapura first, or bring your own equipment and food. Take a torch (flashlight) if you want to enter any of the caves in the area. The nights are always cold and usually wet, so bring warm clothes and waterproof gear. If you need a tent, bring your own or find a guide who's adept at constructing ad hoc forest shelters (many are). Please make an effort to take out everything you bring in, and encourage your guides and porters to do the same.

Accommodation There are simple, official tourist huts in a few places (see further in this section under destinations), and in many villages you can get a wooden bed in the house of a teacher or a leading family for 5000 to 10,000 rp per person – often food is available too. Ask at the village police station (if there is one) or kepala desa (there is always one of these), where you should report, or your guide will know where to stay. Sleeping on the floor of Dani huts is also quite possible, although make sure you've been invited before entering the compound or any particular hut. Missions can put you up in one or two places, but you're generally advised to try something else. Guides can make temporary shelters from trees and rocks, but please ask them to respect the native flora.

Food Some larger villages may have kiosks selling biscuits, canned drinks, noodles and rice. Heading north, the last reliable supplies are at Manda on the east side of the valley, Kimbim on the west and Kurima to the south. You can usually buy plenty of sweet potatoes along the way and maybe a few other vegetables and eggs at local markets, but you'll need to bring any other food yourself (which you can buy in Wamena).

Getting Around
Hopelessly overcrowded taksis go almost as far south as Kurima (1500 rp; 18 km); as far north on the western side of the valley as Pyramid (3000 rp; 35 km); and as far north on the eastern side as Manda (2500 rp; 29 km).

The destinations of taksis are marked (an often coded) but they can be a bit confusing

Baliem Valley (near Wamena; code DK) – th 'Sinatma' taksi will take you up Jl Yos Sudars (stopping at the Mentari Restoran and the touri office) to the taksi terminal at Sinatma villag and 'HomHom/Pikhe' goes to places just nor of Wamena, including the Wamena Hotel.

Baliem Valley (south; code SG) – 'Sugokmo Kurima' goes all the way to the end of the south ern road, a few km short of Kurima.

Baliem Valley (west; code KP) – 'Kimbim/Pyramic travels as far as this road goes; and 'Ibele' take you to Elagaima at the start of one trail to Dana Habbema.

Baliem Valley (east; code WL) – 'Wosilimo/Kurulu and 'Tanahmerah' stop at Wosilimo and Jiwika and 'Manda' goes as far as the public transpo does.

Chartering a taksi, from 10,000 to 15,000 r per hour (a lot more along remote an rougher roads), is worth considering to avoi these sardine-cans-on-wheels or to go t more remote places. Paying for empty seat will always hurry up your departure (an make you very popular with other impatien passengers).

Rafting
Rafting down Sungai Baliem is now possibl between August and November. All-inclu sive trips for five days from Manda t Kurima, staying in Dani homes along the way, cost from US$450 per person in a grou of five to eight. Enquire at Dani Sangril Tours & Travel in Jayapura (refer to th Jayapura & Sentani section for details). Nat urally, you should always be careful regardin the safety of rafting trips.

Baliem Valley – Near Wamena
Wesaput Almost a suburb of Wamena, Wes aput is just across the other side of the airport Take a path across the runway just befor Hotel Syahrial Jaya and head south, or a path from the small cemetery at the end of Jl Gato Subroto, then walk north. You will need t clamber over the airport fence and look fo the large orange clock marking the start o

...e path to Wesaput. Alternatively, a becak ...ill cost 3000 rp or you can charter a taksi ...r a lot more.

Halfway along the path to Wesaput, the ...digenously run *Wio Silimo Tradisional ...otel* is the best Dani-style place in the ...lley. The rooms are simple (but varied, so ...sk to see a selection) in a lovely, traditional ...etting and cost 20,000 rp. It provides free ...ansport in the evening to a restaurant of ...ur choice in Wamena.

At the end of the path, the traditionally ...uilt **Palimo Adat Museum** offers a small, ...teresting collection of Dani clothing, dec...rations and instruments; however, all ...aptions are in Indonesian and the guide ...peaks little else. Still, it is worth a look as ...ere is no other museum in the valley. A ...onation is expected (1000 rp should be ...nough), and it's open daily from 8 am to 4 ...m, except Sunday.

At the back of the museum, the nearest **anging bridge** to Wamena, strung across ...ungai Baliem, is about 50m long and unsta...le at times. A tiny, impromptu **market** run ...y the Dani is often set up just by the bridge.

...ugima A 50 minute walk from the bridge ...t Wesaput leads to Pugima which has a few ...ani compounds (past the huge church). ...lthough Pugima is not particularly inter...sting, the flat trail (with one small hill) ...rovides an easy and convenient glimpse of ...ani farms, villages and people, and of the ...agnificent scenery. Halfway along, behind ...small lake with fish, there's the eerie **Gua ...ugima** cave.

...inatma At the end of Jl Yos Sudarso is the ...uburb of Sinatma. It's a four km walk, or ...atch a taksi for 300 rp. The **Pasar Silimo** ...arket, opposite the taksi terminal, is con...rived and fairly dull. From the terminal, ...ead right as you face Wamena and some ...asy trails take you to the raging Sungai ...amena, some pretty Dani compounds and ...nse woodlands. Near the small hydroelec...ic power station further up the hill, you can ...ross the river on a treacherous **hanging**

bridge (broken at the time of research, but due for repair).

Baliem Valley – South

The area south of Wamena and hugging Sungai Baliem probably has the most dramatic mountain scenery in the whole valley.

Hitigima The road to Hitigima is a flat 13 km stroll past hills with neat chequerboards of cultivated fields enclosed by stone walls. From Wamena, walk down Jl Ahmad Yani, over the bridge and straight on. Hitigima is slightly above the road on the west side. The village has a school and a mission. A further 45 minutes or so on foot above Hitigima (you will have to ask directions) are some **saltwater wells** *(air garam)*.

Kurima Taksis can now go past **Sugokmo** (1500 rp; half-hour from Wamena), but stop three km short of Kurima. Kurima is the best place to base yourself for hiking trips around the southern valley. *Kuak Cottages*, near Kurima (ask directions), has reasonable rooms for about 15,000 rp; meals are available for guests at an extra cost.

A hanging bridge from Kurima leads to **Hitugi** about three hours on foot away. From Hitugi, two trails lead north to **Pugima**; one hugs the river while the other is more mountainous and difficult. You'll need at least two days to do a Wamena-Kurima-Hitugi-Pugima-Wamena circle on foot. It is about five hours from Kurima to **Tangma**. Nearby, the hanging bridge is *really* frightening, especially if the river is at full strength after some rain. Other popular trails are Kurima-Tangma-Wuserem-Senma-Sugokmo, which is not difficult if you allow about four days.

Baliem Valley – East

Aikima About eight km north of Wamena (longer by road), just to the east of the road to Jiwika, Aikima is a fairly nondescript village. It is famous for its 300-year-old **mummy**, but you will have to ask around, and pay, to see it – the mummy near Jiwika (see the Jiwika entry) is easier to arrange and just as good.

Suroba & Dugum Just off the main road, the villages of Suroba and Dugum are definitely worth exploring. Look for the sign to the Pondok Wisata Suroba Indah (see Places to Stay in this section). Walk along the path for 15 minutes through some of the nicest scenery you'll see around Wamena and over two of the more fascinating, and intricate, hanging bridges (one for locals; another for timid foreigners!). At a clearing nearby, traditional pig feasts and dancing can be pre-arranged at substantial cost. You can walk south along the foothills to Aikima or to Dugum, only a km or so north.

Jiwika This pleasant village and local administrative centre is an ideal place to base yourself while you explore the eastern valley, and/or a cheap, quiet alternative to Wamena. Jiwika (pronounced 'Yiwika') is 16 km by road from Wamena (1000 rp by taksi). Ask around and you may be able to arrange a mock 'fighting ceremony' between some villagers for about 45,000 rp.

An hour or so up a steep path (with some scrambling at the top) are some **saltwater wells**, similar to those at Hitigima. To extract the salt, banana stems are beaten dry of fluid and put in a pool to soak up the brine. The stem is then dried and burned, and the ashes are collected and used as salt. If a local boy in Jiwika doesn't offer his services as a guide, ask one to show you the way and ask him to make sure the women will be at the wells. Try to start the trek from Jiwika before 10 am. You may be asked to pay an entrance fee of about 2000 rp.

The nearby village of Sumpaima, a few hundred metres further north of Jiwika (look for the blue sign), has one of the better **mummies** near Wamena. The going price to view it is about 5000 rp.

The road between Jiwika and **Manda** (13 km) is flanked by rocky hills full of unexplored caves, with superb views of the valley. Although it can be a little steep at times, the road (and the nearby area) is great for hiking. Set at the back of an attractive Dani compound, before Waga Waga, the **Gua Kotilola** caves apparently contain the bones of victims

of a past tribal war. You have to pay a donation (1000 rp should be enough). Ask the taksi driver to drop you off outside the compound (it isn't marked) and yell for someone to open the gate.

Places to Stay Several Dani-style places along the road between Aikima and Jiwika offer simple, traditional accommodation often just a wooden bed (maybe with a mattress) and a floor full of straw. They cost 10,000 rp per person and include separate basic toilets. Simple meals cost extra. On the regular taksi route to Wamena and other attractions on this side of the valley, the following places offer a cheap alternative to Wamena:

Pondok Wisata Suroba Indah – just off the main road in Suroba, the setting is pretty, authentic and one of the best

Pondok Wisata Dani Homestay – on the main road in Wenabubuga, it has a nice setting with rooms rather than huts

Pondok Wisata Tumagunem Indah – on the main road in Mulima, it has a pretty setting

Niyuk Huts – on the main road, just south of Jiwika, these huts are authentic and some dancing can be arranged

Losmen La'uk in Jiwika has simple rooms without mandi for 11,000 rp per person and '1st class' single/doubles with mandi for 20,000/35,000 rp, though these are not good value. Meals (8000 rp) are available for guests if pre-ordered. This place is often full in August.

Wosilimo About 21 km by road from Wamena (1500 rp by taksi), Wosilimo (called 'Wosi') is a major village with a few shops. The **Gua Wikuda** caves, 500m along the trail to Pass Valley, are being well developed by indigenous people who can take you for a tour inside. A donation is expected. One hour on foot, along a small path behind the church and over a hanging bridge, **Danau Anegerak** is another great area for hiking. Locals can rent basic fishing equipment and arrange simple accommodation in a Dani-style hut (10,000 rp per person).

ass Valley Another popular trek is to Pass alley, 35 km east of Wosilimo, and on to **ombomi** and the **Apahapsili Falls**, where :nderawasih (birds of paradise) may be :en. For this trek, allow at least a week on ot from Wosilimo, or you can charter a .ksi as far as Pass Valley for the princely .m of 280,000 rp return.

anda From Wosilimo, it's less than a two our hike through wooded country to the tiny illage of **Meagaima** on a rise overlooking ungai Baliem. Another track from Wosi-mo leads to Sungai Baliem, which you can ross by canoe to **Pummo**, where there's nother mummy. It's about a four hour hike om Meagaima, through Manda, Munak nd across the Baliem, to Pyramid (see its ntry in the following Baliem Valley – West :ction).

Public transport stops at Manda, where ere is a shop, loads of very friendly people, nd some wonderful scenery to admire and ike around. Just back from the road, you can ay in a very authentic (ie muddy) Dani hut or 10,000 rp per person. A reasonable road ontinues as far as Kelila, but you will have) hitch, trek or charter to go any further than 1anda.

/olo Valley This is one of the most beautiful nd spectacular side valleys of Sungai Bal-:m. From Manda, the gently rising riverside rack to Wolo is about a three hour walk. Volo, inspired by a strong strain of Evangel-:al Protestantism, is a nonsmoking place .ith lovely flower gardens.

From Wolo, there are walks (about two ours each) to a **waterfall** in the hills to the orth, or up **Sungai Wolo** to where it nerges from another cave. The main track p the Wolo Valley leads to **Ilugua** (about ree hours). About two-thirds of the way to ugua, a side track to the right leads around huge sinkhole and down to **Gua Yogolok** ave and **Goundal**, a tiny *kampung* (village) n the floor of an awesome canyon. From Joundal, you can continue on to Ilugua – a ull day's walk from Wolo.

Baliem Valley – West
This side of the valley isn't as interesting for trekking or day trips by taksi, but it is probably still worth a look if you've already been to the south and east. The road between Pyramid and Wamena is fairly dull (about seven hours' walk). A trek along the lower, usually muddier, route via HomHom and Muai, along Sungai Baliem, is more interesting.

Kimbim Kimbim, 32 km from Wamena, is a local administrative centre. It's pleasant enough, with a few shops and a busy weekly market. You may be able to find somewhere to stay if you ask at the police station or district office. Not far from Kimbim (ask directions), the village of **Araboda** has a mummy called 'Alongga Hubi'.

Pyramid Three km from Kimbim, Pyramid is a graceful missionary village with churches, a theological college, an amazing airstrip carved out of the hill and a bustling weekly market. Taksis from Wamena go directly to Pyramid or you might have to change in Kimbim. The road to Makki, 25 km from Pyramid, is still being completed, so all public transport currently stops at Pyramid.

From Pyramid, a popular trek takes you to **Pietriver**, 45 km west. North of Pyramid, you can cross Sungai Baliem by bridge to Munak and walk up the other side of the valley to Manda.

North of the Baliem Valley
Directly north of the Baliem Valley, it's up-and-down trekking. From **Bolokme**, north of the bridge near Pyramid, it's about seven hours via Tagime to **Kelila**, which has some limited accommodation and a police station. From Kelila down to **Bokondini**, a missionary centre, is three to four hours. It will take about three days to cover the Mamit-Karubaga-Unin-Bokondini route, if you can get transport at either end, or three to four days to do the Kelila-Binime-Tagime-Pyramid trek. Kelila and **Karubaga** have some simple

accommodation, and there's weekly Merpati flights, and occasional missionary flights, to Karubaga, Kelila and Bokondini.

Lani Country (Western Dani)

West along Sungai Baliem, upstream from Pyramid, is the country of the Western Dani, who call themselves Lani. There are tracks to **Magi**, the first main village, from Kimbim, Pyramid and Bolokme. Between Sungai Pitt and Kuyawage, the Baliem disappears underground for two km. **Ilaga**, about 60 km west of Kuyawage, beyond the western Baliem watershed, is accessible by Merpati (from Nabire; 42,300 rp) and missionary flights (from Nabire or Wamena), but check local regulations first. It's often swampy west of Sungai Pitt.

Danau Habbema

At 3450m high, and not far from the 4750m Gunung Trikora, Danau Habbema offers wonderful hiking among unique flora (including orchids). You can walk around the lake and trek to nearby caves, such as **Gua Simalak** and near Gunung Trikora, depending on regulations (see later in this section).

There are two ways to the lake: a trekking trail (about 50 km) starts from Elagaima and goes through Ibele and Thalia; or a shorter, rough 42 km vehicle path starts from Sinatma, through Walaek (where you can stay at PT Agung Mulia) and Pabilolo. If trekking, you'll have to camp and bring everything you need. If you don't fancy this, a taksi there (less than two hours) and back will cost about 120,000 rp.

YALI COUNTRY

East and south of the Dani region are the people, who have rectangular houses and whose men wear 'skirts' of rattan hoops, their penis gourds protruding from underneath. Missionaries are at work here, but the Indonesian presence is thinner than in the Baliem Valley. Bordering the Yali on the east

are the Kim-Yal people, who practised cannibalism up until the 1970s.

Reaching Yali country on foot involves plenty of ups and downs along steep trails. **Pronggoli**, the nearest centre from Wamena as the crow flies, is a three day hard slog by the most direct route, with camping necessary along the way. Trekking from Pronggoli to **Angguruk** takes a day. Easier, but longer (about seven days) is a southern loop through Kurima-Tangma-Wet-Soba-Ninia, then north to Angguruk. Another popular trek includes Kosarek-Serkasi-Telambela-Membahan-Helariki-Angguruk (about six days). It's relatively easy trekking from Angguruk to nearby villages, such as Panggele, Psekm, Tulukima and Tenggil.

You can reduce the tough trek by trying to get on a missionary flight (more likely if you are part of an organised tour) to Kosarek or Angguruk. You can usually rely on a house belonging to a local family or a teacher's house for somewhere to stay in the region, but bring all your own food.

GUNUNG TRIKORA

At around 4750m, Trikora is just 300m short of Puncak Jaya (5050m), Irian Jaya's highest peak. Experience, good equipment and a guide are essential to climb it. A special permit is also required. This can only be obtained in Jakarta or with the assistance, given plenty of notice, of tour agencies in Jayapura or Wamena which can organise trips to the mountain. The mountain and surrounding area were off limits at the time of research, so check the situation in Jayapura or Wamena when you arrive.

FAR SOUTH

It's at least a two week trek from Wamena down to Dekai via Soba, Holuon and Sumo. From Dekai, it is possible to canoe down river as far as Senggo on the fringes of the Asmat region, and then take a motorboat to Agats on the south coast of Irian Jaya. You will probably need a special surat jalan and be on an organised (and expensive) tour.

South Coast

An underrated and undeveloped part of Irian Jaya is the extensive south coast stretching from Sorong to Merauke. A lot of the coast is swamp, many of the smaller towns have limited facilities and transportation is infrequent and often unreliable, but it's worth the effort if you have time and an adventurous streak.

SORONG

Sorong is a spectacularly uninteresting oil, logging and district administration centre. It is also a base for some increasingly popular bird-watching tours, but the only other reason to come here is to wait for a plane or boat connection along the north or south coast of Irian Jaya.

Information

Bank Bumi Daya on Jl Ahmad Yani will change money (open weekday mornings). The police station (☎ 23210) is on Jl Basuki Rahmat. No surat jalan is needed for Sorong, but one is required if you're travelling into the interior. Yellow bemos (called an *angkot*) travel frequently along the few main roads.

Things to See & Do

Pantai Casuari is a good beach for swimming and snorkelling, but you have to charter an angkot for about 8000 rp one way. The best outing is to **Pulau Jefman** by ferry (see Getting Around later in this section), where there's nice beaches and some walking trails.

Pulau Doom can be reached by public boat for 300 rp, or charter one for 3000 rp, from the dock near the Hotel Indah. An engaging walk around the island takes about 40 minutes (but beware: there are more 'hello misters' here per second than in most other places in Indonesia!)

Places to Stay & Eat

The best of the cheap places is the central *Losmen Mulia Indah* (☎ 22772) at Jl Sam Ratulangi 68, which costs from 15,000 rp for a tiny room.

Several reasonable hotels offer singles/doubles, with fan and mandi, from about 22,000/27,000 rp, such as the *Irian Beach Hotel* (☎ 23782), on Jl Yos Sudarso; the *Hotel Batanta* (☎ 21569), opposite the football ground; and the slightly cheaper *Hotel Indah* (☎ 21514), conveniently opposite the small boat dock.

Warungs are set up every evening along the waterfront. For spectacular sunsets and delectable baked fish try the restaurant in the *Irian Beach Hotel* or the *Rumah Makan Ruta Sayang* next door.

Getting There & Away

Air Merpati flies directly to Ambon (127,000 rp), Biak (155,600 rp) and Fak Fak (103,900 rp) daily; and weekly to Manado (204,000 rp) and Manokwari (145,700 rp). The Merpati office (☎ 21402), in the Hotel Grand Pacific on Jl Raja Ampat, is open Monday to Saturday from 8 am to 6 pm, and from 2 to 6 pm on Sunday.

Boat Sorong is the hub for sea travel along the south and north coasts. Every two weeks, the Pelni ship *Dobonsolo* goes to Ambon (39,500/149,000 rp for economy/1st class) and Manokwari (27,000/99,000 rp); and the *Ciremai* travels to Manokwari and Ternate (43,000/163,000 rp) in northern Maluku. Every four weeks, the *Tatamailau* sails to Fak Fak (25,000/91,000 rp) and Manokwari. The Perintis boat *Ilosangi* sails to Manokwari and Fak Fak every three weeks.

The Pelni office (☎ 21716), for all bookings, and the Pelni dock are on Jl Ahmad Yani, several km from Hotel Indah.

Getting Around

Jefman airport is spectacularly, but inconveniently, on Pulau Jefman. From the airport, speedboats cost 10,000 rp, and slower longboats 5000 rp. When going to the airport, check with the Merpati office about the infrequent ferry (4,000 rp). Twin-Otter flights to Fak Fak leave from the Minland airport, about five km from Sorong.

IRIAN JAYA

FAK FAK

The first successful Dutch settlement on Irian Jaya, Fak Fak (yes, it *is* pronounced *that* way) is a quaint, colonial town, nestled among the foothills and overlooking several sparkling bays. The main street along the waterfront is reminiscent of a small seaside European village – except for the mosque! Fak Fak is close and accessible to Ambon and The Bandas by sea, and to Sorong by air, so it's an easy and pleasant way to start or finish a visit to Irian Jaya.

Orientation & Information

Most facilities are either on, or close to, the main street, Jl Izaak Telussa, which hugs the coast. Along this street, Bank Exim changes money (weekday mornings); the Merpati office (☎ 22130) is open irregularly (you'll have to take pot luck); and *mikrolets* (bemos) to most places wait for passengers. The street leads to the tidy **Pasar Tamburani** market, which is worth a wander around, and to the mikrolet terminal behind it.

Some other places are in the steep suburbs: the tourist office (☎ 22828) is on Jl Nuri; the post office is on Jl Letjen Haryono; and the 24 hour Telkom office and hospital are on Jl Cenderawasih. The tourist office is open weekdays from 7.30 am to 3 pm and is worth a visit if you are staying a while. It may be able to arrange speedboats and traditional dancing.

You should report to the police (☎ 22200) on Jl Tamburani, opposite the Hotel Sulinah, after you arrive. You need a surat jalan for Fak Fak; preferably get one before you arrive (try Sorong).

Pulau Tulir Seram

The easiest and best trip from Fak Fak is out to the tiny, uninhabited Pulau Tulir Seram in the harbour. There's a short trail around the island, a huge monument with a museum underneath (tee it up with the tourist office to get a key for you) and some superb views. A two room *guesthouse* (organise it with the tourist office in Fak Fak and bring your own food) offers absolute seclusion. Ask around Danaweria village, a little east of Fak Fak,

for a longboat and driver, which should cost around 15,000 rp return, including waiting time.

Places to Stay & Eat

The best places are all along Jl Izaak Telussa. The central *Hotel Tembagapura* (☎ 22350) is quiet and often full. Singles/doubles with mandi cost from 19,250/30,250 rp; more for air-con. The *Hotel Marco Polo* (☎ 22228), on a lane opposite the mosque, is friendly. Dorm-style beds cost 18,000 rp per person and more for individual rooms. The *Hotel Sulinah* (☎ 22447) at the western end of the main street, opposite the police station, has very clean rooms, some with views, for 35,000 rp, including all meals.

Strung along Jl Kartini, just above Jl Izaak Telussa, several warungs serve mouthwatering baked fish meals from 2500 rp. *Rumah Makan Sahabat* along the main street is recommended for drinks and cakes, and the *Hotel Tembagapura* has a good public restaurant. The *Amanda*, at the bend on Jl Izaak Telussa, has good service and decor plus, of course, a (popular) karaoke machine. Excellent nasi goreng costs 5000 rp; seafood is 10,000 rp.

Getting There & Away

Fak Fak is definitely worth considering as a way into Irian Jaya. By air, it is linked to Sorong (103,900 rp) and Kaimana (80,000 rp) as part of the almost-daily Merpati Twin Otter route between Sorong and Nabire, from where there are daily flights to Biak and Jayapura.

By sea, the Pelni liner *Tatamailau* links Fak Fak with Kaimana (22,500/82,500 rp for economy/1st class) and Sorong (25,000/91,000 rp) every four weeks. The *Rinjani* has a very useful connection to/from Ambon (48,500/185,500 rp) via The Bandas (41,000/156,500 rp) every two weeks. The Perintis boat *Ilosangi* calls past every three weeks on its crawl along the south coast between Sorong and South-East Maluku; the *Omega* also connects Fak Fak to South-East Maluku and Ambon.

The port is centrally located at the eastern

nd of Jl Izaak Telussa, but the Pelni office
☎ 22335) is up in the steep suburbs on Jl
MA Negeri.

Getting Around
Torea airport was somehow carved out of the
illside and is frighteningly short. You will
probably have to take a shared (private) taxi
for 5000 rp or maybe you can get a public
mikrolet from Pasar Tamburani terminal for
'00 rp. The streets of Fak Fak are very, very
teep, so, unless you like mountain climbing
and enjoy aching knees, take a mikrolet.

Around Fak Fak
Travel to attractions near Fak Fak is often
hindered by limited local transport. Around
he village and beach at **Kokas**, on the north
coast of the peninsula, there is a plethora of
Japanese WWII cannons, tunnels and wrecks,
and an 1870 mosque. To inspect some
ancient rock paintings along the coast as far
as **Goras**, and to visit the **Ugar Islands** for
diving, you'll have to charter a boat.

With permission from the tourist office in
Fak Fak, you can stay in the *guesthouse* at
Kokas – but watch out for the huge coconut
crabs! Kokas is a four to six hour (often
rough) trip by chartered boat; or you can wait
a week or so for a passenger ship; or a year
or two for the 42 km road from Fak Fak to
be completed.

TIMIKA
About halfway down the south coast, Timika
exists almost entirely to service the Freeport
copper and gold mine in Tembagapura,
approximately 60 km north. Visiting the
mine is not possible unless you have been
'invited' by a Freeport employee living in
Tembagapura. You need a surat jalan to visit
Timika.

Timika is even more expensive than Wamena in the Baliem Valley. If you are staying
here, the overpriced *Hotel Surya* (☎ 21860),
opposite the market, has cubicles for 25,000
rp, while the *Losmen Amole Jaya* (☎ 21125)
on Jl Pelikan is comparatively good value for
38,500 rp a room.

Timika serves as a useful entry point to

The Freeport Mine and Traditional People
Not far from Puncak Jaya, in the southern highlands, the US-run PT Freeport Indonesia company
owns the second largest copper mine, and the largest gold deposits, in the world. Discovered in the
1930s, but not opened until the 1960s, Freeport has built a staggering complex of tunnels and private
roads carved through a mountain range, and the modern town of Tembagapura ('Copper Town'). Over
78,000 tonnes of ore is extracted per day and Freeport is actively exploring several million hectares
of Irian Jaya for further mining.

There are serious concerns: Freeport enjoys a special relationship with the Indonesian government,
so there was never any serious consultation with, or compensation for, the local Amungme and Komoro
people when the licenses were issued; Freeport employs about 17,000 people (easily the largest
private employer in Irian Jaya), but only about 10% are Irianese; copper tailings cause enormous
environmental damage and affect the health of villagers through contamination of sago palms and
drinking water; Freeport moves entire villages with thousands of indigenous people from their
homelands to undertake further mining; and the increased Indonesian military presence in the area
has resulted in several instances of human rights abuses.

Yet Jakarta is likely to remain unmoved. Freeport is Indonesia's largest foreign taxpayer (it has paid
an estimated US$760 million in taxes since 1989) and contributes about US$1 billion a year to the
Indonesian – but not necessarily the Irianese – economy.

Riots and sabotage in Tembagapura, and the nearby service town of Timika, intensified in 1996
and occasionally halted production from the mine – which makes a *profit* of well over US$1 million per
day. Local Irianese have demanded scholarships and other employment schemes for local youths,
1% of profits for local community projects, and changes to local Freeport and Indonesian security and
community-development personnel. To its credit, Freeport will spend over US$30 million in 1996 on
the local community, while Jakarta, which is happy to take its huge taxes, continues to allow Freeport
to act as a quasi-local government responsible for local development and welfare. ■

Irian Jaya. Sempati (☎ 21612) and/or Merpati (☎ 21006) fly directly and regularly to Ambon, Ujung Pandang and on to Denpasar and Jakarta; there are also daily connections from Timika to Biak and Jayapura. The Jayapura-Biak flight often detours through Timika (for no extra cost), allowing you a glimpse from the plane of the awesome Freeport mine and the snow-capped Puncak Jaya, Irian Jaya's highest mountain.

THE ASMAT REGION

The Asmat region, an inconceivably huge area of mangroves, pandanus and rivers with huge tides, remains undeveloped and one of the few truly unexplored regions left in the world. The Asmat people are justifiably famous for their woodcarvings, and less so for their past head-hunting exploits. They are semi-nomadic and their lives are dictated by rivers, which are a necessary source of transport and food.

To appreciate what the Asmat region has to offer will definitely take a *lot* of time and a *lot* of money. Individuals with a limited budget and no real interest in the particular regional culture may be very disappointed with how little they can see. Agats and the Asmat region is nowhere as developed or

accessible as Wamena and the Baliem Valley. Currently, limited air transport means the region is fairly inaccessible.

Agats

Facilities in the Asmat region are very limited and virtually nonexistent outside Agats, which has only two losmen, no daytime electricity, no telephones and limited fresh water. Due to the extraordinary tide and location, the 'streets' are simply raised wooden and broken walkways so, literally, watch your step. A surat jalan is a necessity for Agats and the Asmat region. On your arrival, report to the police station (well .. hut).

Pusat Asmat dan Pusat Pendidikan Asmat

The Asmat Centre and Asmat Education Centre are impressive buildings of interest for their architecture if nothing else (they are usually empty).

Museum Kebudayaan dan Kemajuan

The Museum of Culture and Progress offers some interesting, varied displays, but with little or no explanations in any language. It's only open from 8 to 10 am daily, except Sunday.

The Asmat People

The name Asmat either comes from the words *as akat* meaning 'right man' or *osamat* meaning 'man from tree'. The people refer to themselves as *asmat-ow*, or the 'real people'.

The tree features heavily in Asmat symbolism, which is not surprising given the immense jungles in the region. The Asmat believe that humans are the image of a tree: their feet are its roots; the torso, its trunk; the arms are the branches; and the fruit represents the head. Also an important element of their belief is that no person – except the very young or the very old – dies for any other reason than through tribal fighting or magic. So, each death of a family member must be 'avenged' if the spirit of the recently dead is to go to the spiritual world known as *safan*. Not so long ago, the 'avenging' was carried out through head-hunting raids and while it's now more ceremonial, it is still taken seriously.

The Asmat centre their beliefs around the figure of Fumeripitisj who first carved wooden figures, so 'creating' the Asmat people. Through their carvings, the Asmat remain in contact with their ancestors. Each village appoints a *wow ipits*, or woodcarver, based on their skills. Carvings are traditionally only made for ceremonial purposes and then left to rot in the jungle, but these days, inevitably, there is strong tourist demand for them.

A huge variety of carvings is important in funeral ceremonies, including decorated shields which represent and avenge the dead relative, the ancestor poles called *bis* and the ancestor figures *(kawe)*. Other ceremonial items include wooden masks, drums made from lizard skins, spears, paddles and horns, once used to herald the return of a head-hunting raid and to frighten enemies. ■

Agats

0   50   100 m
Approximate Scale
Pedestrian Streets Only

To Asmat Centre

Police Station ★

To Port

Mosque

To Dock for Boats to Airport

Asmat Inn

Post Office

Pasar Bhakti

Jalan Yos Sudarso

Jalan Kompsas Agats

Losmen Pada Elo

Warung Goyang Indah

Museum of Culture & Progress

Pelni ●

To Sjuru

Places to Stay & Eat

There are only two losmen. Singles/doubles at the *Asmat Inn* cost 15,000/30,000 rp, or 20,000/40,000 rp with mandi, plus tax. Good food (6000 rp per meal) and cold beer is available for guests, if ordered in advance. For the same price, the *Losmen Pada Elo* has friendly service, good local information and standard rooms. Guests can order food in advance for about 5000 rp a meal.

Getting There & Away

Merpati Twin-Otters normally fly between Merauke and the airport at nearby Ewer three times a week (63,000 rp); however, at the time of research, the damaged Ewer airport had been inoperable for eight months, with no signs of reopening in the immediate future.

The Pelni liner *Tatamailau* stops here on its way between Merauke and Timika every four weeks. The Perintis boat *Ilosangi* comes by during its three weekly crawl between

Merauke and Sorong. The port at Agats for large boats is a 10 minute walk north of town (and is a good place to watch the sunset).

Getting Around

If/when flights resume to Ewer, follow everyone else from the airport to the river and take a shared longboat (officially 5000 rp per person) for the exhilarating 20 minute trip to Agats.

Motorboats are the only form of local transport. Expect to pay at least 200,000 rp per day for a reputable boat, including driver. The boats take between 10 and 15 passengers, but Agats currently doesn't attract enough visitors to 'get a group together' to help share the cost. Cheaper prices are possible – maybe 150,000 rp a day – if you ask around the village of Sjuru, 10 minutes' walk from Agats.

Canoes are a far cheaper alternative, but they significantly limit where you can go. They cost about 5000 rp per hour, plus 5000 rp per hour for each rower. Ask at the nearby village of Sjuru or around the losmen – and bargain.

AROUND THE ASMAT REGION

To explore the region will take several days. In addition to the exorbitant boat hire, add about 30,000 rp for a guide and 15,000 rp for a cook per day, and take all your own supplies. There are no losmen outside Agats, but in the larger villages, such as **Senggo** and **Ayam**, you should be able to sleep at a mission or school house for about 10,000 rp per person, or take your own camping gear.

MERAUKE

Merauke is an interesting way to enter Irian Jaya and then to fly to Jayapura for the Baliem Valley. There is very little to do here, but the town is pleasant enough and laid-back. You can visit **Pantai Lampu Satu**, a five km walk (or take an irregular mikrolet) west of Bank Exim building, or bathe (if you don't mind an audience!) in the **hot springs** about 200m in front of the Hotel Asmat. If you have the time and money, try to arrange a trip into the interior.

Orientation & Information

Merauke has no town centre and virtually everything you will need is on the very long Jl Raya Mandala. Bank Exim at the bottom of Jl Raya Mandala is the only place to change money (open weekday mornings). A surat jalan is needed and will be inspected at the airport. The police station (☎ 21706), near Hotel Nirmala, will handle extra permits for the interior.

Places to Stay & Eat

The *Losmen Merauke* (no telephone) at Jl Raya Mandala 340 offers very, very basic singles/doubles with no mandi for 15,000/18,000 rp. The *Hotel Asmat* (☎ 21065), Jl Trikora 3, is the best place, with comfortable rooms with character for 21,500/29,200 rp; or slightly more with mandi.

Along Jl Raya Mandala, air-con rooms for about 40,000/50,000 rp can be found at the *Hotel Megaria* (☎ 21932) at No 166; the *Hotel Nirmala* (☎ 21849) at No 66; and the *Flora Hotel* (☎ 21879) at No 294.

Plenty of places around the port serve simple, cheap meals, and stalls in the Ampera market sell delicious nasi campur. Along Jl Raya Mandala, the *Beautiful Nusantara Restaurant*, near the Flora, is good, but watch for overcharging. The *Rumah Makan Sari Laut*, near the Megaria, serves delicious, cheap seafood for 3500 rp, but no beer.

Getting There & Away

Air Merpati flies to Jayapura (185,300 rp) and Ewer (63,000 rp) daily, if/when its airport reopens. The Merpati office (☎ 21242) is at Jl Raya Mandala 163. There continues to be speculation about sea and air links to nearby Darwin and/or Cairns in northern Australia, but, unfortunately, they are still only rumours.

Boat The Pelni ship *Tatamailau* sails to Timika and/or Agats every four weeks, and the Perintis boat *Ilosangi* starts its extraordinary run to Jayapura every six weeks. More basic boats, such as the *Enggang*, *Telu Sekar* and *Emprit*, make fortnightly runs up and down the south-east coast to Kimam (on Pulau Yos Sudarso), Bade, often Agats and, incredibly, as far inland as Tanahmerah.

The Pelni office (☎ 21591) at Jl Sabang 318 is often closed because there are so few departures.

Getting Around

Mopah airport is about five km from the Hotel Asmat. Take a private taxi for 7000 rp or, if you're lucky, a mikrolet outside the airport will take you down the main road for 500 rp. Hundreds of mikrolets go up and down the few roads for about 300 rp a trip.

AROUND MERAUKE
Wasur National Park

The national park is the joint project of the World Wide Fund for Nature (WWF) and the traditional people, mainly the Kanum and Marind, who contribute to, and benefit from the park and its management. The park's 4,260 sq km offers anthills, wetlands, traditional village life, birdlife (74 unique species) and wildlife, such as cuscus and even kangaroos. But with minimal transport and trails, these are very difficult to see and enjoy. The best (dry) season is from April to October, while the wet season, from November to March, severely restricts travel within the park.

The WWF asks that travellers report to its Merauke office first; it can arrange guides if necessary (about 15,000 rp per day) and transport, and take payment for accommodation. Its office (☎ & fax 21397; PO Box 284, Merauke) is on the corner of Jl Biak and Jl Missi, behind Hotel Flora.

The offices at the two entrances, Wasur and Ndalir, where you must register and pay 5000 rp, provide good local information. From **Yanggandur**, you can hire a horse (10,000 rp per day with guide) or go on foot to explore the wetlands which, apparently, have cenderawasih (birds of paradise).

There is no public transport to or around the park. A mikrolet for a day trip from Merauke will cost between 60,000 and

50,000 rp per day or you can take an organised tour from YAPSEL (see the following Sungai Bian & Muting entry).

Sungai Bian & Muting As an alternative to the comparatively overrun Baliem Valley, several areas near Merauke are worth visiting. The most accessible – and permissible – is an area 200 km north of Merauke (mainly around Muting and other villages strung along Sungai Bian), with rainforests, wildlife and traditional people. Getting there will involve some trekking (it's flat!) and canoe trips.

Foreigners are not permitted to visit this area independently. Tours can be easily arranged at the indigenously run YAPSEL agency (☎ 21489; fax 21610; PO Box 283, Merauke) on Jl Missi, a few hundred metres from the WWF office. For example, a ten day all-inclusive tour for a group of four will cost around 700,000 rp per person.

Glossary

abangan – nominal Muslim, whose beliefs owe much to older, pre-Islamic mysticism

adat – traditional laws and regulations

agung – high, noble

air – water

Airlangga – 11th century king of considerable historical and legendary importance on Bali

air panas – hot springs

air terjun – waterfall

aling aling – guard wall behind the entrance gate to a Balinese family compound; demons can only travel in straight lines so the aling aling prevents them from coming straight in through the front entrance

alun-alun – main public square of a town or village. They are usually found in front of the *bupati's* (governor's) residence and were traditionally meeting areas and the place to hold public ceremonies. Nowadays they tend to be deserted, open grassed areas.

anak – child

andong – horse-drawn passenger cart

angklung – musical instrument made of differing lengths and thicknesses of bamboo suspended in a frame

angkot or **angkota** – short for *angkutan kota* (city transport), these small minibuses cover city routes

angkudes – short for *angkutan pedesaan*, these minibuses run to nearby villages from the cities, or run between villages

anjing – dog

arak – colourless distilled palm-wine firewater

Arja – particularly refined form of Balinese theatre

Arjuna – hero of the *Mahabharata* epic and a popular temple gate guardian image

ayam – chicken

Ayodya – Rama's kingdom in the *Ramayana*

Babad – early chronicle of Balinese history

babi – pork

Bahasa Indonesia – Indonesia's national language

bajaj – motorised three wheeler taxi found in Jakarta

bakar – barbecued, roasted

bakmi – rice-flour noodles

bakso – meatball soup

balai – Dayak communal houses

bale – Balinese pavilion, house or shelter; a meeting place

Bali Aga – 'original' Balinese, who managed to resist the new ways brought in with *Majapahit* migration

balian – female shaman of the Tanjung Dayak people in Kalimantan

bandung – large cargo-cum-houseboats

banjar – local area of a Balinese village in which community activities are organised

banyan – see *waringin*

bapak – father; also a polite form of address to any older man

barat – west

baris – Balinese warrior dance

barong – mythical lion-dog creature; star of the Barong dance and a firm champion of good in the eternal struggle between good and evil

barong landung – enormous puppets known as the 'tall barong'; these can be seen at an annual festival in Serangan, Bali

barong tengkok – Lombok name for mobile form of *gamelan* used for wedding processions and circumcision ceremonies

batik – cloth made by coating part of the fabric with wax, then dyeing it and melting the wax out. The waxed part is not coloured and repeated waxings and dyeings builds up a pattern.

becak – trishaw (bicycle-rickshaw)

belauran – night markets (Kalimantan)

belian – spiritual healer

bemo – popular local transport. Traditionally a small pickup-truck with a bench seat down each side in the back, these have mostly disappeared in favour of small minibuses. Bemo (a contraction of *becak* and *motor)* is a dated term, now rarely used in

ndonesia, but still common on Bali and
ome other areas.

endi – two person *dokar* used in Sulawesi

ensin – petrol

erempah – traditional Sumbawan bare-
isted boxing

etang – communal house in Central Kali-
nantan

haga – miniature thatched-roof house ded-
cated to the ancestors of the Ngada people
f Flores

is – bus

is air – water bus

limbing – starfruit

ouraq – winged horse-like creature with
he head of a woman; also the name of the
lomestic airline which mostly services the
uter islands

Brahma – the creator; one of the trinity of
:hief Hindu gods, along with *Shiva* and
Vishnu

brem – fermented rice wine

bubur ayam – Indonesian porridge of rice
or beans with chicken

bukit – hill

bupati – government official in charge of a
kabupaten (regency)

camat – government official in charge of a
kecamatan (district)

candi – shrine, or temple, of originally Javanese design, also known as a *prasada*

candi bentar – split gateway entrance to a
Balinese temple

cap – metal stamp used to apply motifs to
batik

cap cai – fried vegetables, sometimes with
meat

catur yoga – ancient manuscript on religion
and cosmology

cidomo – horse-drawn cart (Nusa Tenggara)

cumi cumi – squid

dalang – storyteller of varied skills and
considerable endurance who operates the
puppets, tells the story and beats time in a
wayang kulit shadow puppet performance

danau – lake

dangdut – popular Indonesian music characterised by wailing vocals and a strong beat

delman – horse-drawn passenger cart

desa – village

Dewi Sri – rice goddess

dinas pariwisata – tourist office

dokar – horse cart, still a popular form of
local transport in many towns and larger
villages

dukun – faith healer and herbal doctor or
mystic

durian – fruit that 'smells like hell and tastes
like heaven'

dwipa mulia – moneychanger

fu yung hai – sweet and sour omelette

gado gado – traditional Indonesian dish of
steamed bean sprouts, vegetables and a spicy
peanut sauce

Gajah Mada – famous *Majapahit* prime
minister

Galungan – great Balinese festival, an annual event in the 210 day Balinese *wuku*
calendar

Gambuh – classical form of Balinese theatre

gamelan – traditional Javanese and Balinese
orchestra, usually almost solely percussion,
with large xylophones and gongs

Ganesh – *Shiva's* elephant-headed son

gang – alley or footpath

Garuda – mythical man-bird, the vehicle of
Vishnu and the modern symbol of Indonesia;
also the name of Indonesia's international
airline

gereja – church

gili – islet or atoll

gringsing – rare double *ikat* woven cloth in
Tenganan on Bali

gua – cave; the old spelling, *goa*, is also
common

gunung – mountain

haji, haja – Muslim who has made the pilgrimage to Mecca. Many Indonesians save
all their lives to make the pilgrimage, and a
haji (man) or *haja* (woman) commands great
respect in the village.

halus – 'refined', high standards of behaviour and art; characters in *wayang kulit*
performances are traditionally either *halus*
or *kasar*

harga biasa – usual price
harga touris – tourist price
homestay – small family-run *losmen*
huta – Batak village (Sumatra)
hutan – forest

ibu – mother; also polite form of address to any older woman
ikan – fish
ikat – cloth in which the pattern is produced by dyeing the individual threads before weaving; see also *gringsing*

Jaipongan – relatively modern, West Javanese dance incorporating elements of *pencak silat* and *Ketuktilu*
jalan – street or road; Jl is abbreviation
jalan jalan – to walk
jalan potong – short cut
jam karet – 'rubber time'
jamu – herbal medicine; most tonics go under this name and are supposed to cure everything from menstrual problems to baldness
jembatan – bridge
jeruk – citrus fruit
jidur – large cylindrical drums played widely throughout Lombok
jukung – see *prahu*

kabupaten – regency
kacang – peanuts
kain – cloth
kaja – towards the mountains (Balinese)
kamar kecil – toilet, usually the traditional hole in the ground with footrests either side
kampung – village, neighbourhood
kantor – office, as in *kantor imigrasi* (immigration office) or *kantor pos* (post office)
kasar – rough, coarse, crude; the opposite of *halus*
Kawi – classical Javanese, the language of poetry
kebaya – Chinese long-sleeved blouse with plunging front and embroidered edges
kebun – garden
kecapi – Sundanese (West Javanese) lute
kelapa – coconut
keliling – driving around (buses and bemos) to pick up passengers

kelod – towards the sea
kepala balai – Dayak village head (Sumatra)
kepala desa – village head
kepala stasiun – station master
kepeng – old Chinese coins with a hole in the centre which were the everyday money during the Dutch era and can still be obtained from shops and antique dealers for a few cents
kepiting – crab
ketoprak – popular Javanese folk theatre
Ketuktilu – traditional Sundanese (Java) dance in which professional female dancers (sometimes prostitutes) dance for male spectators
kijang – 4WD taxi
kina – quinine
klotok – canoe with water-pump motor used in Kalimantan
Konfrontasi – catchphrase of the early 1960s when Soekarno embarked on a confrontational campaign against western imperialism, and expansionist policies in the region, aimed at Malaysia
kopi – coffee
kora-kora – canoe (Irian Jaya)
KORPRI – Korp Pegawai Republik Indonesia, the Indonesian bureaucracy
kraton – walled city palace and traditionally the centre of Javanese culture. The two most famous and influential *kratons* are those of Yogyakarta and Solo.
kretek – Indonesian clove cigarette
kris – wavy-bladed traditional dagger, often held to have spiritual or magical powers
kueh – cakes
Kuningan – holy day celebrated throughout Bali 10 days after *Galungan*

ladang – non-irrigated field, often using slash-and-burn agriculture, for dry-land crops
lamin – communal house in East and West Kalimantan
langsam – crowded, peak-hour commuter train to the big cities
lesahan – traditional style of dining on straw mats

ongbot – high-speed motorised canoe used on the rivers of Kalimantan

ontar – type of palm tree. Traditional books were written on the dried leaves of the lontar palm

opo – beehive-shaped house found on Timor

osmen – basic accommodation, usually cheaper than hotels and often family-run

umpia – spring rolls

Mahabharata – great Hindu holy book, telling of the battle between the Pandavas and the Korawas

Majapahit – last great Hindu dynasty on Java, pushed out of Java into Bali by the rise of Islamic power

mandi – usual Indonesian form of bath, consisting of a large water tank from which you ladle water to pour over yourself like a shower

marapu – Balinese term for all spiritual forces, including gods, spirits and ancestors

martabak – pancake found at foodstalls everywhere; can be savoury, but is usually very sweet

menara – minaret, tower

Merpati – major domestic airline

meru – multi-roofed shrines in Balinese temples; they take their name from the Hindu holy mountain, Mahameru. The same roof style also can be seen in ancient Javanese mosques.

mesjid – mosque

mie goreng – fried noodles, usually with vegetables and sometimes meat

mikrolet – small taxi; a tiny *opelet*

moko – bronze drum from Alor (Nusa Tenggara)

muezzin – those who call the faithful to the mosque

muncak – 'barking deer' found on Java

naga – mythical snake-like creature

nanas – pineapple

nasi – cooked rice. Nasi goreng is the ubiquitous fried rice. Nasi campur is rice 'with the lot' – vegetables, meat or fish, peanuts and krupuk. Nasi gudeg is cooked jackfruit served with rice, chicken and spices. Nasi rames is rice with egg, vegetables, fish or meat. Nasi rawon is rice with a spicy hot beef soup.

ngadhu – parasol-like, thatched roof; ancestor totem of the Ngada people of Flores

nusa – island, as in Nusa Penida

Odalan – temple festival held every 210 days, the Balinese 'year'

ojek – (or ojeg) motorcycle that takes passengers

opelet – small intra-city minibus, usually with side benches in the back

opor ayam – chicken cooked in coconut milk

Padang – city and region of Sumatra which has exported its cuisine to all corners of Indonesia. Padang food consists of spicy curries and rice, and is traditionally eaten with the fingers of the right hand. In a Padang restaurant a number of dishes are laid out on the table, and only those that are eaten are paid for.

paduraksa – covered gateway to a Balinese temple

pak – shortened form of *bapak*

pandanus – palm plant used to make mats

pantai – beach

Pantun – ancient Malay poetical verse in rhyming couplets

parkir – a parking attendant. Anywhere a car is parked, these often self-appointed attendants will be on hand to find drivers a parking spot, look after their cars and stop traffic while they back out, all for a mere 300 rp or so tip. They may also do the job of traffic cops, blowing their whistles and directing traffic for small gratuities thrown by passing motorists.

pasanggrahan – lodge for government officials where travellers can usually stay

pasar – market

pasar malam – night market

pasar terapung – 'floating market' consisting of groups of boats to which buyers and sellers paddle in boats

patih – prime minister

patola – *ikat* motif of a hexagon framing a type of four pronged star

peci – black Muslim felt cap

pedanda – high priest

pelan pelan – slowly

Pelni – Pelayaran Nasional Indonesia, the national shipping line with major passenger ships operating throughout the archipelago

pemangku – temple priest

pencak silat – form of martial arts originally from Sumatra, but now popular throughout Indonesia

pendopo – large, open-sided pavilion in front of a Javanese palace that serves as an audience hall

penginapan – simple lodging house

perbekel – government official in charge of a *desa* (village) on Bali

peresehan – popular form of one-to-one physical combat peculiar to Lombok, in which two men fight armed with a small hide shield for protection and a long *rattan* stave as a weapon

Pertamina – huge state-owned oil company

pesanggrahan – see *pasanggrahan*

pinang – betel nut

pinisi – Makassar or Bugis schooner

pisang goreng – fried banana

pompa bensin – petrol station

pondok – guesthouse or lodge

prahu – traditional Indonesian outrigger boat

prasada – see *candi*

pulau – island

puputan – warrior's fight to the death; honourable, but suicidal, option when faced with an unbeatable enemy

pura – temple

pura dalem – Balinese temple of the dead

puri – palace

pusaka – sacred heirlooms of a royal family

rafflesia – gigantic flower found in Sumatra, with blooms spreading up to a metre

raja – lord, prince or king

Ramadan – Muslim month of fasting, when devout Muslims refrain from eating, drinking and smoking during daylight hours

Ramayana – one of the great Hindu holy books, stories from the *Ramayana* form the keystone of many Balinese and Javanese dances and tales

rangda – witch; evil black-magic spirit of Balinese tales and dances

rattan – see *rotan*

Ratu Adil – the Just Prince who, by Javanese prophecy, will return to liberate Indonesia from oppression

rebab – two stringed bowed lute

rijsttafel – Dutch for 'rice table'; a banquet of Dutch-style Indonesian food

rintek wuuk – spicy dog meat; a Minahasan (Sulawesi) delicacy

rotan (rattan) – hardy, pliable vine used for handcrafts, furniture and weapons, such as the staves in the spectacular trial of strength ceremony, *peresehan*, in Lombok

roti – bread; usually white and sweet

rudat – traditional *Sasak* dance overlaid with Islamic influence (Lombok)

rumah adat – traditional house

rumah makan – restaurant or *warung* (eating house)

rumah sakit – hospital

sambal – chilli sauce

Sanghyang – trance dance in which the dancers impersonate a local village god

Sanghyang Widi – Balinese supreme being, never actually worshipped as such; one of the 'three in one' or lesser gods stand-in

santri – orthodox, devout Muslim

saron – xylophone-like *gamelan* instrument, with bronze bars struck with a wooden mallet

sarong (sarung) – all-purpose cloth, often sewn into a tube, and worn by women, men and children

Sasak – native of Lombok

sate (satay) – classic Indonesian dish; small pieces of charcoal-grilled meat on a skewer served with spicy peanut sauce

sawah – an individual rice field, or the wet-rice method of cultivation

sayur – vegetable

selat – strait

selatan – south

selendang – shawl

selimut – blanket

Sempati – domestic airline which flies to Kalimantan, southern Sumatra and Java

Shiva – the destroyer; one of the trinity of

chief Hindu gods, along with *Brahma* and *Vishnu*

sirih – betel nut, chewed as a mild narcotic

sisemba – form of kick-boxing popular with the Torajan people of Sulawesi

situ – lake (Sundanese)

songket – silver or gold-threaded cloth, and woven using floating weft technique

sop, soto – soup

sudra – lowest or common caste to which most Balinese belong

suling – bamboo flute

stasiun – station

sungai – river

surat jalan – travel permit (Irian Jaya)

syahbandar – harbour master

tahu – soybean curd (tofu)

taman – 'garden with a pond'; ornamental garden

tari topeng – type of masked dance peculiar to the Cirebon area on Java

tarling – musical style of the Cirebon (Java) area, featuring guitar, *suling* and voice

tau tau – life-sized carved wooden effigies of the dead placed on balconies outside cave graves in Torajaland, Sulawesi

taxi sungai – cargo-carrying river ferry with bunks on the upper level

tedong-tedong – tiny structures over graves that look like houses (Sulawesi)

telaga – lake

teluk – bay

telur – egg

tempe – fermented soybean cake

timur – east

tomate – Torajan funeral ceremony

tongkonan – traditional Torajan house (Sulawesi)

topeng – wooden mask used in funerary dances

tuak – alcoholic drink fermented from palm sap or rice

uang – money

udang – prawn

ular – snake

utara – north

Vishnu – the 'pervader' or 'sustainer'; one of the trinity of chief Hindu gods, along with *Brahma* and *Shiva*

wali songo – 'nine holy men' who propagated Islam on Java

Wallace Line – imaginary line intersecting Bali and Lombok and Kalimantan and Sulawesi, which marks the end of Asian and the beginning of Australasian flora and fauna.

wantilan – open pavilion used to stage cockfights

waringin – banyan tree; a large and shady tree with drooping branches which root and can produce new trees. It was under a banyan *(bo)* tree that Buddha achieved enlightenment, and *waringin* are found at many temples on Bali.

wartel – private telephone office

warpostel or **warpapostel** – *wartel* that also handles postage

waruga – pre-Christian Minahasan (Sulawesi) tomb

warung – food stall; a sort of Indonesian equivalent to a combination of corner shop and snack bar

wayang kulit – shadow-puppet play

wayang orang – Javanese theatre or 'people wayang'; also known as wayang wong

wayang topeng – masked dance-drama

Wektu Telu – religion, peculiar to Lombok, which originated in Bayan and combines many tenets of Islam and aspects of other faiths

wisma – guesthouse or lodge

wuku – local Balinese calendar made up of 10 different weeks, between one and 10 days long, all running concurrently

Index

TEXT

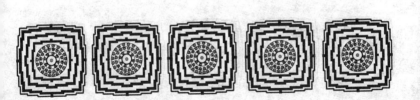

Thanks

Thanks to the many travellers who wrote in with helpful hints, useful advice and interesting and funny stories.

David W Allen, Lisa Allen, Moch Zakir Andjo, Lorrie Anshan, Caroline Apter, Nuke Ariyanie, John Armstrong, Greg Ashton, Brett Badenoch, Mat Bailey, David Bancovich, Mahmud Bangkaru, Chris & Tracy Bastian, Mrs J Bechinsale, Miss Gizela Bedford, Tim Birkett, Eric Birn, Johan Blok, Gavin Blue, Helen Bodycomb, Michael Bolger, Anna Bonomini, Anne Boxhall, David Boyall, Andrew Bray, Lester Brien, Gretchen Brown, Derrick Browne, Gwen Browning, Carina Buijs, Mat Burbury, Simon Burrows, Melissa Buttery, Greg Byrne

Rebecca Cairns, Kerry Calcraft, Simon Carr-Smith, R Cavicchioli, Budhi Tirto Chen, Michelle Chin, David Clarke, DK Clarke, Roland Cochard, Denise Collins, Grace Connolly, Keith Conroy, Andrew Cossen, David Cox, Steve Craddock, Christine Croxton, Lieve Daeren, Wendy Davies, Mrs M den Haan, Ann Dennehy, Tom Dobson, J Doupe, Keith Downham, A Drechsler, Meldrum Duncan, Colleen Duplock, Richard & Lyn Durham, Georgina Edwards, C Ekterhate, Bob Else, Steve Emmerman, Bea Erlina, Denise & Jos Eussen

Eric Findlay, Gerhard Flaig, Paul Fletcher, Michael Foster, Ariane Frey, Jane Fritz, Stacy Gall, May Goh, Miriam Goodwin, Eva Gotsis, Gigi Gabrielle Griffiths, Kimberly Guardino, Chester Gudowski, Chris Gymer, Robyn Haines, Brian Hancock, Rick Handley, David Hardacre, Veri Hardjono, Angela Harris, Joh Harrison, M E Hawkes, Barbara Healy, Dave Heckman, Kimberely Henden, Angela Hepi, W Hicks, Eddy Hill, Ben Hillman, W H Hooyer, Trevor Hopper, Graeme Ireland, Mark Jackson, Dorothy Jacobes, Richard James, Paul Jones, Greg Jones, Phillip & John Jongs

Tan Chee Keong, Angeline Khoo, T Kolesnikow, Peter Kuper, Jabar Lahadji, Christine Laurence, Peter Laws, Kirsty Leiigh, Manfred Lepp, David Lewin, Annette Low, Dennis Lowden, W Lown, Jan Maehl, Geoff Mathers, Bob McGuigan, RW McGuigan, David McKeown, Stuart McLay, RN McLean, Y Meder, David Miller, C Mills, Bernard Millward, Kathleen Mitchinson, Annestine Molin, Willie Monk, Andrew R Neale, MR Nijziel, Peter Nilhill, Jon Noble, M Nussbaum

H O'Brien, Lorna O'Connell, Barry O'Keeffe, Michael O'Neill, A & E Oldhoff, Peter Ottevaere, Olav Pelger, Alice Pennisi, R & J Perriber, Alexandra E Perry, Susan Pettifer, J Pickles, Alice Pitty, Rick & Gadis Pollard, Sybout Porte, Christophe Raguin, Geoff Ralph, Eliwar A Rasyid, Glen Real, Tony Richards, Penny Richards, Val Robbie, Andrew Robertson, Graham Robertson, Vanessa Robinson, Low Puay Hwa Roger, Mark Russell

Ary Sadar, Astrid Scheeve, George Scholz, Nigel Searle, Brendon Shaw, Martin Sherwood, Mr P Shuitemake, David Sebastian Shum, Jane Simon, Kartini Slamet, Tim Smith, A Sondang, Dennis Speakman, Claudia Spensberger, H Spierenburg, John Stevenson, Stuart Strong, Win Stroud, P & R Sullivan, Pieter Swart, Tibor Sztaricskai, Teck Tan, Nicole Teuwen, Dr David Thomas, Evian Ti, Paul Tolton, Jodie Tranter, Helen Trinca, Stephen Tuff, Andrew Tyson

Masato Uemori, Ketut Ur, Volker Vahrenkamp, Rob & Marianne van Klaveren, Simon Vardy, Suzanne Veletta, E Veno, Joe Verbiest, Henk Vermeulen, Nigel Vickers, Bronwyn Waddell, Jeff Wall, Sally Anne Watson, David Watts, Carla Weemaes, Nadine White, Mrs Betty Wilson, Ronald Wolff, Betty Wood, Chua Mok You, IP Zweip

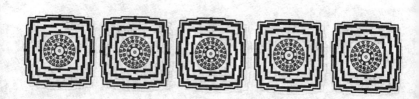

LONELY PLANET PHRASEBOOKS

Building bridges,
Breaking barriers,
Beyond babble-on

Nepali phrasebook

Ethiopian Amharic phrasebook

Latin American Spanish phrasebook

Ukrainian phrasebook

Greek phrasebook

Vietnamese phrasebook

Listen for the gems

Speak your own words

Ask your own questions

Master of your own image

- handy pocket-sized books
- easy to understand Pronunciation chapter
- clear and comprehensive Grammar chapter
- romanisation alongside script to allow ease of pronunciation
- script throughout so users can point to phrases
- extensive vocabulary sections, words and phrases for every situations
- full of cultural information and tips for the traveller

'...vital for a real DIY spirit and attitude in language learning' – Backpacker

'the phrasebooks have good cultural backgrounders and offer solid advice for challenging situations in remote locations' – San Francisco Examiner

'...they are unbeatable for their coverage of the world's more obscure languages' – The Geographical Magazine

---

Arabic (Egyptian)
Arabic (Moroccan)
Australia
  Australian English, Aboriginal and Torres Strait languages
Baltic States
  Estonian, Latvian, Lithuanian
Bengali
Burmese
Brazilian
Cantonese
Central Europe
  Czech, French, German, Hungarian, Italian and Slovak
Eastern Europe
  Bulgarian, Czech, Hungarian, Polish, Romanian and Slovak
Egyptian Arabic
Ethiopian (Amharic)
Fijian
Greek
Hindi/Urdu

Indonesian
Japanese
Korean
Lao
Latin American Spanish
Malay
Mandarin
Mediterranean Europe
  Albanian, Croatian, Greek, Italian, Macedonian, Maltese, Serbian, Slovene
Mongolian
Moroccan Arabic
Nepali
Papua New Guinea
Pilipino (Tagalog)
Quechua
Russian
Scandinavian Europe
  Danish, Finnish, Icelandic, Norwegian and Swedish

South-East Asia
  Burmese, Indonesian, Khmer, Lao, Malay, Tagalog (Pilipino), Thai and Vietnamese
Sri Lanka
Swahili
Thai
Thai Hill Tribes
Tibetan
Turkish
Ukrainian
USA
  US English, Vernacular Talk, Native American languages and Hawaiian
Vietnamese
Western Europe
  Basque, Catalan, Dutch, French, German, Irish, Italian, Portuguese, Scottish Gaelic, Spanish (Castilian) and Welsh

LONELY PLANET JOURNEYS

OURNEYS is a unique collection of travel writing – published by the company that understands travel better than anyone else. It is a series for anyone who has ever experienced – or dreamed of – the magical moment when they encountered a strange culture or saw a place for the first time. They are tales to read while you're planning a trip, while you're on the road or while you're in an armchair, in front of a fire.

OURNEYS books catch the spirit of a place, illuminate a culture, recount a crazy adventure, or introduce a fascinating way of life. They always entertain, and always enrich the experience of travel.

ISLANDS IN THE CLOUDS
Travels in the Highlands of New Guinea
Isabella Tree

Isabella Tree's remarkable journey takes us to the heart of the remote and beautiful Highlands of Papua New Guinea and Irian Jaya – one of the most extraordinary and dangerous regions on earth. Funny and tragic by turns, *Islands in the Clouds* is her moving story of the Highland people and the changes transforming their world.

Isabella Tree, who lives in England, has worked as a freelance journalist on a variety of newspapers and magazines, including a stint as senior travel correspondent for the *Evening Standard*. A fellow of the Royal Geographical Society, she has also written a biography of the Victorian ornithologist John Gould.

'One of the most accomplished travel writers to appear on the horizon for many years . . . the dialogue is brilliant' – Eric Newby

---

SEAN & DAVID'S LONG DRIVE
Sean Condon

Sean Condon is young, urban and a connoisseur of hair wax. He can't drive, and he doesn't really travel well. So when Sean and his friend David set out to explore Australia in a 1966 Ford Falcon, the result is a decidedly offbeat look at life on the road. Over 14,000 death-defying kilometres, our heroes check out the re-runs on tv, get fabulously drunk, listen to Neil Young cassettes and wonder why they ever left home.

Sean Condon lives in Melbourne. He played drums in several mediocre bands until he found his way into advertising and an above-average band called Boilersuit. *Sean & David's Long Drive* is his first book.

'Funny, pithy, kitsch and surreal . . . This book will do for Australia what Chernobyl did for Kiev, but hey you'll laugh as the stereotypes go boom'
– Time Out

LONELY PLANET TRAVEL ATLASES

Lonely Planet has long been famous for the number and quality of its guidebook maps. Now we've gone one step further and in conjunction with Steinhart Katzir Publishers produced a handy companion series: Lonely Planet travel atlases maps of a country produced in book form.

Unlike other maps, which look good but lead travellers astray, our travel atlases have been researched on the road by Lonely Planet's experienced team of writers. All details are carefully checked to ensure the atlas corresponds with the equivalent Lonely Planet guidebook.

The handy atlas format means no holes, wrinkles, torn sections or constant folding and unfolding. These atlases can survive long periods on the road, unlike cumbersome fold-out maps. The comprehensive index ensures easy reference.

- full-colour throughout
- maps researched and checked by Lonely Planet authors
- place names correspond with Lonely Planet guidebooks
  – no confusing spelling differences
- legend and travelling information in English, French, German,
  Japanese and Spanish
- size: 230 x 160 mm

Available now:
Chile & Easter Island • Egypt • India & Bangladesh • Israel & the Palestinian Territories •Jordan, Syria & Lebanon • Kenya • Laos • Portugal • South Africa, Lesotho & Swaziland • Thailand • Vietnam • Zimbabwe, Botswana & Namibia

---

LONELY PLANET TV SERIES & VIDEOS

Lonely Planet travel guides have been brought to life on television screens around the world. Like our guides, the programmes are based on the joy of independent travel, and look honestly at some of the most exciting, picturesque and frustrating places in the world. Each show is presented by one of three travellers from Australia, England or the USA and combines an innovative mixture of video, Super-8 film, atmospheric soundscapes and original music.

Videos of each episode – containing additional footage not shown on television – are available from good book and video shops, but the availability of individual videos varies with regional screening schedules.

Video destinations include: Alaska • American Rockies • Australia – The South-East • Baja California & the Copper Canyon • Brazil • Central Asia • Chile & Easter Island • Corsica, Sicily & Sardinia – The Mediterranean Islands • East Africa (Tanzania & Zanzibar) • Ecuador & the Galapagos Islands • Greenland & Iceland • Indonesia • Israel & the Sinai Desert • Jamaica • Japan • La Ruta Maya • Morocco • New York • North India • Pacific Islands (Fiji, Solomon Islands & Vanuatu) • South India • South West China • Turkey • Vietnam • West Africa • Zimbabwe, Botswana & Namibia

The Lonely Planet TV series is produced by:
Pilot Productions
The Old Studio
18 Middle Row
London W10 5AT UK

For video availability and ordering information contact your nearest Lonely Planet office.

Music from the TV series is available on CD & cassette.

PLANET TALK

Lonely Planet's FREE quarterly newsletter

'e love hearing from you and think you'd like to hear from us.

'hen...is the right time to see reindeer in Finland?
'here...can you hear the best palm-wine music in Ghana?
ow...do you get from Asunción to Areguá by steam train?
'hat...is the best way to see India?

or the answer to these and many other questions read PLANET TALK.

very issue is packed with up-to-date travel news and advice including:

- a letter from Lonely Planet co-founders Tony and Maureen Wheeler
- go behind the scenes on the road with a Lonely Planet author
- feature article on an important and topical travel issue
- a selection of recent letters from travellers
- details on forthcoming Lonely Planet promotions
- complete list of Lonely Planet products

o join our mailing list contact any Lonely Planet office.

lso available: Lonely Planet T-shirts. 100% heavyweight cotton.

LONELY PLANET ONLINE

Get the latest travel information before you leave or while you're on the road

'hether you've just begun planning your next trip, or you're chasing down pecific info on currency regulations or visa requirements, check out Lonely lanet Online for up-to-the-minute travel information.

s well as travel profiles of your favourite destinations (including maps and hotos), you'll find current reports from our researchers and other travellers, pdates on health and visas, travel advisories, and discussion of the cological and political issues you need to be aware of as you travel.

here's also an online travellers' forum where you can share your experience f life on the road, meet travel companions and ask other travellers for their ecommendations and advice. We also have plenty of links to other online ites useful to independent travellers.

nd of course we have a complete and up-to-date list of all Lonely Planet ravel products including guides, phrasebooks, atlases, Journeys and videos nd a simple online ordering facility if you can't find the book you want lsewhere.

www.lonelyplanet.com
or
AOL keyword: lp

LONELY PLANET PRODUCTS

Lonely Planet is known worldwide for publishing practical, reliable and no-nonsense trav information in our guides and on our web site. The Lonely Planet list covers just about eve accessible part of the world. Currently there are eight series: *travel guides, shoestring guid walking guides, city guides, phrasebooks, audio packs, travel atlases* and *Journeys* – a uniq collection of travel writing.

EUROPE

Amsterdam • Austria • Baltic States & Kaliningrad • Baltic States phrasebook • Britain • Central Europe on a shoestrin Central Europe phrasebook • Czech & Slovak Republics • Denmark • Dublin • Eastern Europe on a shoestring • East Europe phrasebook • Finland • France • Greece • Greek phrasebook • Hungary • Iceland, Greenland & the Faroe Islan • Ireland • Italy • Mediterranean Europe on a shoestring • Mediterranean Europe phrasebook • Paris • Poland • Portu • Portugal travel atlas • Prague • Russia, Ukraine & Belarus • Russian phrasebook • Scandinavian & Baltic Europe o shoestring • Scandinavian Europe phrasebook • Slovenia • Spain • St Petersburg • Switzerland • Trekking in Greec Trekking in Spain • Ukrainian phrasebook • Vienna • Walking in Britain • Walking in Switzerland • Western Europe o shoestring • Western Europe phrasebook

NORTH AMERICA

Alaska • Backpacking in Alaska • Baja California • California & Nevada • Canada • Florida • Hawaii • Honolulu • Los Angeles • Mexico • Miami • New England • New Orleans • New York, New Jersey & Pennsylvania • Pacific Northwest USA • Rocky Mountain States • San Francisco • Southwest USA • USA phrasebook • Washington, DC & the Capital Region

CENTRAL AMERICA & THE CARIBBEAN

Bermuda • Central America on a shoestring • Costa Rica • Cuba • Eastern Caribbean • Guatemala, Belize & Yucatán: La Ruta Maya • Jamaica

SOUTH AMERICA

Argentina, Uruguay & Paraguay • Bolivia • Brazil • Brazilian phrasebook • Buenos Aires • Chile & Easter Island • Chile & Easter Island travel atlas • Colombia • Ecuador & the Galápagos Islands • Latin American Spanish phrasebook • Peru • Quechua phrasebook • Rio de Janeiro • South America on a shoestring • Trekking in the Patagonian Andes • Venezuela

Travel Literature: Full Circle: A South American Journey

ANTARCTICA

Antarctica

ISLANDS OF THE INDIAN OCEAN

Madagascar & Comoros • Maldives & Islands of the East Indian Ocean • Mauritius, Réunion & Seychelles

AFRICA

Arabic (Moroccan) phrasebook • Africa on a shoestring Cape Town • Central Africa • East Africa • Egypt • Egy travel atlas • Ethiopian (Amharic) phrasebook • Kenya Kenya travel atlas • Morocco • North Africa • South Afric Lesotho & Swaziland • South Africa, Lesotho & Swazilan travel atlas • Swahili phrasebook • Trekking in East Afric • West Africa • Zimbabwe, Botswana & Namibia Zimbabwe, Botswana & Namibia travel atlas

Travel Literature: The Rainbird: A Central Africa Journey • Songs to an African Sunset: A Zimbabwea Story

MAIL ORDER

nely Planet products are distributed worldwide. They are also available by mail order from Lonely
anet, so if you have difficulty finding a title please write to us. North American and South American
sidents should write to Embarcadero West, 155 Filbert St, Suite 251, Oakland CA 94607, USA;
ropean and African residents should write to 10 Barley Mow Passage, Chiswick, London W4 4PH;
d residents of other countries to PO Box 617, Hawthorn, Victoria 3122, Australia.

RTH-EAST ASIA

ijing • Cantonese phrasebook • China • Hong Kong,
acau & Guangzhou • Hong Kong • Japan • Japanese
rasebook • Japanese audio pack • Korea • Korean
rasebook • Mandarin phrasebook • Mongolia • Mongo-
n phrasebook • North-East Asia on a shoestring • Seoul
aiwan • Tibet • Tibet phrasebook • Tokyo

avel Literature: Lost Japan

IDDLE EAST & CENTRAL ASIA

ab Gulf States • Arabic (Egyptian) phrasebook • Central
sia • Iran • Israel & the Palestinian Territories • Israel &
e Palestinian Territories travel atlas • Istanbul • Jerusa-
m • Jordan & Syria • Jordan, Syria & Lebanon travel atlas
Middle East • Turkey • Turkish phrasebook • Yemen

ravel Literature: The Gates of Damascus • Kingdom of
e Film Stars: Journey into Jordan

LSO AVAILABLE:

ravel with Children • Traveller's Tales

INDIAN SUBCONTINENT

Bangladesh • Bengali phrasebook • Delhi • Hindi/Urdu
phrasebook • India • India & Bangladesh travel atlas •
Indian Himalaya • Karakoram Highway • Nepal • Nepali
phrasebook • Pakistan • Rajasthan • Sri Lanka • Sri Lanka
phrasebook • Trekking in the Indian Himalaya • Trekking
in the Karakoram & Hindukush • Trekking in the Nepal
Himalaya

Travel Literature: In Rajasthan • Shopping for Buddhas

SOUTH-EAST ASIA

Bali & Lombok • Bangkok • Burmese phrasebook • Cambodia • Ho Chi Minh City • Indonesia • Indonesian
phrasebook • Indonesian audio pack • Jakarta • Java •
Laos • Lao phrasebook • Laos travel atlas • Malay
phrasebook • Malaysia, Singapore & Brunei • Myanmar
(Burma) • Philippines • Pilipino phrasebook • Singapore •
South-East Asia on a shoestring • South-East Asia
phrasebook • Thailand • Thailand travel atlas • Thai
phrasebook • Thai audio pack • Thai Hill Tribes
phrasebook • Vietnam • Vietnamese phrasebook •
Vietnam travel atlas

AUSTRALIA & THE PACIFIC

Australia • Australian phrasebook • Bushwalking in Aus-
tralia • Bushwalking in Papua New Guinea • Fiji • Fijian
phrasebook • Islands of Australia's Great Barrier Reef •
Melbourne • Micronesia • New Caledonia • New South
Wales & the ACT • New Zealand • Northern Territory •
Outback Australia • Papua New Guinea • Papua New
Guinea phrasebook • Queensland • Rarotonga & the Cook
Islands • Samoa • Solomon Islands • South Australia •
Sydney • Tahiti & French Polynesia • Tasmania • Tonga •
Tramping in New Zealand • Vanuatu • Victoria • Western
Australia

Travel Literature: Islands in the Clouds • Sean & David's
Long Drive

THE LONELY PLANET STORY

Lonely Planet published its first book in 1973 in response to the numerous 'How did you do it?' questions Maureen and Tony Wheeler were asked after driving, bussing, hitching, sailing and railing their way from England to Australia.

Written at a kitchen table and hand collated, trimmed and stapled, *Across Asia on the Cheap* became an instant local bestseller, inspiring thoughts of another book.

Eighteen months in South-East Asia resulted in their second guide, *South-East Asia on a shoestring*, which they put together in a backstreet Chinese hotel in Singapore in 1975. The 'yellow bible', as it quickly became known to backpackers around the world, soon became *the* guide to the region. It has sold well over half a million copies and is now in its 9th edition, still retaining its familiar yellow cover.

Today there are over 240 titles, including travel guides, walking guides, language kits & phrasebooks, travel atlases and travel literature. The company is the largest independent travel publisher in the world. Although Lonely Planet initially specialised in guides to Asia, today there are few corners of the globe that have not been covered.

The emphasis continues to be on travel for independent travellers. Tony and Maureen still travel for several months of each year and play an active part in the writing, updating and quality control of Lonely Planet's guides.

They have been joined by over 70 authors and 170 staff at our offices in Melbourne (Australia), Oakland (USA), London (UK) and Paris (France). Travellers themselves also make a valuable contribution to the guides through the feedback we receive in thousands of letters each year and on our web site.

The people at Lonely Planet strongly believe that travellers can make a positive contribution to the countries they visit, both through their appreciation of the countries' culture, wildlife and natural features, and through the money they spend. In addition, the company makes a direct contribution to the countries and regions it covers. Since 1986 a percentage of the income from each book has been donated to ventures such as famine relief in Africa; aid projects in India; agricultural projects in Central America; Greenpeace's efforts to halt French nuclear testing in the Pacific; and Amnesty International.

'I hope we send the people out with the right attitude about travel. You realise when you travel that there are so many different perspectives about the world, so we hope these books will make people more interested in what they see. These are guidebooks, but you can't really guide people. All you can do is point them in the right direction'.

– Tony Wheeler

LONELY PLANET PUBLICATIONS

Australia
PO Box 617, Hawthorn 3122, Victoria
tel: (03) 9819 1877 fax: (03) 9819 6459
e-mail: talk2us@lonelyplanet.com.au

USA
Embarcadero West, 155 Filbert St, Suite 251,
Oakland, CA 94607
tel: (510) 893 8555 TOLL FREE: 800 275-8555
fax: (510) 893 8563
e-mail: info@lonelyplanet.com

UK
10 Barley Mow Passage, Chiswick,
London W4 4PH
tel: (0181) 742 3161 fax: (0181) 742 2772
e-mail: 100413.3551@compuserve.com

France:
71 bis rue du Cardinal Lemoine, 75005 Paris
tel: 1 44 32 06 20 fax: 1 46 34 72 55
e-mail: 100560.415@compuserve.com

World Wide Web: http://www.lonelyplanet.com